History of the Theatre

HISTORY OF

FOUNDATION
EDITION

THE THEATRE

OSCAR G. BROCKETT
University of Texas at Austin

FRANKLIN J. HILDY
University of Maryland

Allyn and Bacon

BOSTON   NEW YORK   SAN FRANCISCO
MEXICO CITY   MONTREAL   TORONTO   LONDON   MADRID   MUNICH   PARIS
HONG KONG   SINGAPORE   TOKYO   CAPE TOWN   SYDNEY

Editor-in-Chief: Karon Bowers
Editorial Assistant: Suzanne Stradley
Marketing Manager: Suzan Czajkowski
Senior Production Administrator: Donna Simons
Composition Buyer: Linda Cox
Cover Administrator: Linda Knowles
Manufacturing Buyer: JoAnne Sweeney
Editorial Production Service: Nesbitt Graphics, Inc.
Electronic Composition: Nesbitt Graphics, Inc.
Cover Designer: Susan Paradise

For related titles and support materials, visit our online catalog at www.ablongman.com

Between the time website information is gathered and then published, it is not unusual for some sites to have closed. Also, the transcription of URLs can result in typographical errors. The publisher would appreciate notification where these errors occur so that they may be corrected in subsequent editions.

Cataloging-in-Publication Data is on file at the Library of Congress

ISBN 0-205-47360-1

Printed in the United States of America

10   9   8   7   6   5   CIN   10   09   08

Contents

Preface

Since its original publication in 1968, the text of *History of the Theatre* has constantly expanded as each edition has incorporated new information, outlined current debates, widened its coverage, and brought this history up to the present. This "foundation edition" is a carefully abridged version of the ninth edition of *History of the Theatre* intended to make the material more manageable for survey courses without losing the breadth of coverage or attention to detail for which this book has long been internationally known. The entire text has been revised, corrections have been made, and up-to-date information has been added. While the ninth edition ended its coverage with 2001, this text has brought the history up to 2005. All chapters are shorter, and several chapters from the ninth edition have been combined. Returning to the precedent of earlier editions of this book, the information on Asian theatres has been chronologically integrated back into the body of the text while the information on the theatre of Africa has been integrated for the first time. The theatre of Asia and Africa developed quite differently from theatre in the West, and each followed quite different time lines, making their integration into this scheme somewhat problematic; however, this arrangement does allow for increased cross-cultural comparisons. Because the theatre can often best be understood through visual materials, this foundation edition continues to be extensively illustrated, both to clarify the written text and to suggest the visual characteristics of the theatre in a given era.

Although the text has been significantly condensed, this foundation edition of *History of the Theatre* continues to examine the full complexity of theatre as an art form, from its function in a given culture to its many component parts including acting, audiences, theatrical space, texts (whether written or not), playwriting, production design, machinery, special effects, music, dancing, directing, management, criticism and more. All of these topics are addressed, although not every chapter addresses every topic and the space devoted to each topic varies from one chapter to another. The goal has been to survey the history of theatre as a cultural institution rather than to provide an exhaustive treatment of any one of its parts. It is possible to use this text to read the general histories of any one of these topics by selecting the relevant pages across several chapters and we leave it up to the readers to choose topical arrangements of this material if they so wish. Our concern has been the characteristic practices that give the theatre its flavor in each era, as well as those features that have contributed significantly to later eras.

As with all previous editions of *History of the Theatre,* this foundation edition outlines the current state of knowledge concerning theatre as it has existed as a distinctive form of performance. The distinctive nature of theatre is not always clear. Forms of performance that are called theatre by some artists and scholars are rejected as theatre by others, and the arguments on both sides can turn on very fine points of distinction. We do not attempt to engage those debates here, but we have given a sufficiently broad perspective on theatre for the reader to see the complexity of the issues involved.

With the inclusion of the theatre in Latin America, Canada, Australia, and New Zealand in the ninth edition, *History of the Theatre* covers theatre worldwide, from the earliest beginnings we can reliably document up to the present time. But Western theatre history is presented in significantly more detail than the theatres of non-Western cultures. While the coverage of theatre is broad and detailed, then, it is not all-inclusive, nor is it intended to be. Entire books have been written on topics that here can be given only a single sentence or even no comment at all. The allied arts of puppetry, opera, and narrative dance, along with the innumerable forms of performance that have both influenced and been influenced by the art of the theatre, each deserve their own history. In this history of the theatre, they are dealt with only insofar as is necessary to illuminate some aspect of our subject. Our goal is to provide a context for tracking the development of theatre through the ages. By development, we mean simply the patterns of change that can be seen as artist and artisans attempt to improve on the theatre they inherited from previous generations. While those who initiate changes in the theatre do so to "improve" it, such changes are not always seen as improvements, either at the time or by later generations. Change is inevitable in theatre, but that does not imply that theatre is always getting better (or worse)—only that it is always different.

The material in *History of the Theatre* is presented chronologically in units that are convenient to work with. No theatrical movement or trend, whether it is in acting, architecture, audience, drama, management, or criticism, starts and ends within such convenient blocks of time, however, so there is always a great deal of overlap. Chronological organization highlights the context for change as it makes clear what each generation inherited from the one before it, but this does not necessarily imply a cause-and-effect relationship. Artists and artisans in the theatre respond to the theatre as they find it, but their responses are complex and not often easily explainable. For this reason scholars have developed numerous theories that propose possible explanations as to why theatre has changed as it has and when it has. We encourage those who read this text and those who teach from it to explore any number of such theories. It is our hope that we have provided sufficient information to allow the reader to make informed decisions about each theory's ability to provide an explanation for the issue it set out to examine. We do not take any specific theoretical approach in this text, however, because to do so could limit the ways in which the materials can be synthesized by the reader.

The material in this book is also organized geographically, but this should not obscure the fact that theatre people have always borrowed ideas from other cultures and integrated those ideas into their own work. Neither the chronological nor the geographical arrangement needs to be rigidly followed by the reader as individual chapters and even units within chapters can be read out of order.

Historical accounts are a mixture of evidence and interpretation, and consequently scholars often differ markedly in the conclusions they reach even when they use the same pieces of evidence. The *History of the Theatre* editions have always alerted readers to significant differences in scholarly opinion. But this is not a history of historiography (the methods for writing history); it is a survey of the basic information those methods for written history have been applied to.

A book of this scope obviously depends heavily on the work of many scholars. It is impossible to acknowledge each debt within the text, since to do so would double its length. The chapter-by-chapter bibliographies provided with the *History of the Theatre* editions serve both as an acknowledgement of the principal sources used in writing the book and as a guide to reading in greater depth. For this foundation edition, those bibliographies have been moved to our website (www.ablongman.com/historyoftheatre).

The assistance of many other persons in the preparation of this edition is gratefully acknowledged. In addition to the scholars whose works are listed in the online bibliography, we are also indebted to countless students who have contributed to our knowledge in classes and seminars and to the many students and scholars who have contacted us through the website regarding needed corrections and suggested additions. Indebtedness to individuals, publishers, libraries, and collections for permission to reprint materials is acknowledged in the credits accompanying the illustrations and source materials.

We also wish to thank our editor, Karon Bowers, and our past editor, Molly Taylor, of Allyn and Bacon, who came up with the idea for this edition and have been enormously generous and patient as we moved the text through the editing process. We want to thank our editorial assistant, Suzanne Stradley, for her significant work in managing and converting our digitally edited files into a complete and clear manuscript. Our thanks too to Kathy Smith and the staff of Nesbitt Graphics for the care with which they have prepared this book for publication.

We gratefully acknowledge the contribution of the following reviewers: Darrell Anderson, University of Dayton; Deborah Currier, Western Washington University; David S. Escoffery, Southwest Missouri State University; Cynthia Gendrich, Wake Forest University; Melissa Gibson, Fresno State University; Woodrow Hood, Catawba College; Kristin Johnsen-Neshati, George Mason University; and John A. Rude, Victor Valley College.

History of the Theatre has been the major work in the field for over a generation and has been translated into many languages including Korean and Chinese. This foundation edition has been designed to continue, within an abridged format, the approaches that have made this book so useful.

1
The Origins of Theatre

Performative elements (including dramatic and theatrical) are present in every society, no matter how complex or how unsophisticated the culture may be. These elements are evident in our political campaigns, holiday celebrations, sports events, religious ceremonies, and children's make-believe, just as they are in the dances and rituals of primitive peoples. Nevertheless, most participants in these activities do not consider them to be primarily theatrical, even when spectacle, dialogue, and conflict play large roles. Consequently, it is usual to acknowledge a distinction between *theatre* (as a form of art and entertainment) and the presence of *theatrical* or *performative elements* in other activities. This distinction is crucial here, since it would be virtually impossible to write a coherent history of all the human activities that through the ages have made use of performative conventions. Therefore, this book is concerned primarily with the origin and subsequent development of the theatre as an autonomous activity.

THE THEORY OF RITUAL ORIGIN

But how did theatre originate?

In seeking to describe its origin, one must rely primarily on speculation, since there is little concrete evidence on which to draw. The most widely accepted of the early theories, championed by anthropologists in the late nineteenth and early twentieth centuries, envisions theatre as emerging out of myth and ritual. The process perceived by these anthropologists may be summarized briefly. During the early stage of its development, a society becomes aware of forces that appear to influence or control its food supply and well-being. Having little understanding of natural causes, its members attribute both desirable and undesirable occurrences to supernatural or magical forces, and they search for means to win the favor of these forces. Perceiving an apparent connection between certain actions performed by the group (or its shamans) and the results it desires, the group repeats, refines, and formalizes those actions into fixed ceremonies, or rituals. All rituals, then, reflect in some way the society's understanding of its relationship to the powers that govern its well-being and its own interrelationships. Ultimately, rituals also include elements that entertain and give pleasure through spectacle, the repetition of familiar patterns, and the skill of the participants.

Stories (myths), which explain, disguise, or idealize, may then grow up around a ritual. Frequently the myths include representatives of those supernatural forces that the rites celebrate or hope to influence. Performers may wear costumes and masks to represent the mythical characters or supernatural forces in the

FIG. 1.1

Bull dance of the Mandan Peoples of North America. Note the figures at center-front wearing buffalo headdresses and skins. George Catlin, *Bull Dance*, Mandan O-Kee-Pa Ceremony, 1832. National Museum of American Art, Washington, DC/Art Resource, NY.

rituals or in accompanying celebrations. As a people becomes more sophisticated, its conceptions of supernatural forces and causal relationships may change. As a result, it may abandon or modify some rites. But the myths that have grown up around the rites may continue as part of the group's oral tradition and may even come to be acted out under conditions divorced from ritualistic concerns. When this occurs, the first step has been taken toward theatre as an autonomous activity, and thereafter entertainment and esthetic values may gradually replace the former mystical and socially efficacious concerns. This, in brief summary, is the traditional view of how theatre developed out of ritual.

Many post–World War II anthropologists, however, tended to see almost all human transactions as basically performative—as enactments of relationships with specific purposes—involving a number of elements (which are also those found in ritual and

theatre). Thus, the earlier concern for the relationship between ritual and theatre was transformed. Both ritual and theatre came to be seen as merely different ways of organizing and using elements that are basic in almost all human activity. Therefore, theatre was not seen as necessarily originating in ritual; rather ritual and theatre were viewed as coexisting modes in which the same elements might be used for differing functions within the same society.

PERFORMATIVE ELEMENTS AND FUNCTIONS

Performative activities (which encompass most human transactions) make use of a number of common elements: time, place, participants (players/audience), scenario (agenda/goal/text/rules), clothing

FIG. 1.2
Costume and mask made of bark cloth and used for a jaguar dance. From the Amazon River region of Brazil. Courtesy Department of Library Services, American Museum of Natural History, New York.

(uniform/costume/mask/makeup), sound (speech/music), movement (gesture/pantomime/dance), and function or purpose. How each of these elements is treated, combined with others, and for what ultimate purpose distinguishes one kind of transaction from another.

Each element can vary widely and can be combined with others in many ways. It should also be clear that almost any event involving societal interaction can be viewed as manipulating the same basic set of performative elements. A business conference, for example, is scheduled for a particular time in a particular place; there is an agenda that sets forth the scope of the discussions; those asked to participate know what dress is appropriate, what type of behavior is acceptable, and what the hierarchy within the group is; and they know what the purpose of the conference is. Thus, the event is governed by a set of conventions that the participants understand and adhere to; failure to adhere to them usually results in some type of sanction. Ritual and theatre employ the same

basic elements as other human activities do but, having different purposes in mind, choose the particular form needed for each element and then organize these elements to achieve their purpose.

As should be evident, much that is found in ritual is also present in theatre. In ritual, beyond those elements already mentioned, there must be "actors"—those who enact the rites or stories—and those who exercise control over the performance ("directorial" functions often undertaken in rites by initiates, elders, or priests). Both theatre and ritual also use an "acting area" and an "auditorium," the shape, size, and organization of which may vary considerably from one society or period to another.

But, though theatre and ritual may use many of the same elements, the distinction between them ultimately depends on their functions. Perceptions about the function of an event may vary widely, depending on one's relationship to the event and familiarity with its conventions. As members of our own society, we may easily recognize the distinctions among church services, theatrical events, athletic games, and political rallies, but someone wholly unfamiliar with our cultural conventions might perceive all of these as essentially theatrical, just as we might those of some Asian,

FIG. 1.3
Horned god (or a man disguised as an animal). Drawing from a prehistoric cave in the Volp River region of France. The figure has been redrawn by the Abbé H. Breuil. From Henri Begouen and l'Abbé H. Breuil, *Les Cavernes du Volp* (1958). Courtesy Arts et Métiers Graphiques, Paris.

African or Native American group about whose cultural conventions we are entirely uninformed.

The recognition of specialized function, then, seems a necessary condition for the separation of theatre and ritual, but where the line between them is to be drawn is difficult to specify since it depends primarily on our perception of the function of an event or activity.

OTHER THEORIES OF ORIGIN

Although origin in ritual has long been the most popular, it is by no means the only theory about how the theatre came into being. Storytelling has been proposed as one alternative. Under this theory, relating and listening to stories are seen as fundamental human pleasures. Thus, the recalling of an event (a hunt, battle, or other feat) is elaborated through the narrator's pantomime and impersonation and eventually through each role being assumed by a different person.

Closely related theories see theatre as evolving out of imitations of animals or out of narrative forms of dances and songs. Admiration for the performers' skill, virtuosity, and grace is seen as motivation for elaborating the activities into fully realized theatrical performances.

In addition to exploring the possible antecedents of theatre, scholars have also theorized about the motives that led people to develop theatre. Why did theatre develop, and why was it valued? Most answers fall back on theories about the human mind and basic human needs. One, set forth by Aristotle in the fourth century B.C.E., sees humans as naturally imitative—as taking pleasure in imitating persons, things, and actions and in seeing such imitations. Another, advanced in the twentieth century, suggests that humans have a gift for fantasy, through which they seek to reshape reality into more satisfying forms than those encountered in daily life. Thus, fantasy or fiction (of which drama is one form) permits people to objectify their anxieties and fears, confront them, and fulfill their hopes in fiction if not in fact. The theatre, then, is one tool whereby people define and understand their world or escape from unpleasant realities.

But neither the human imitative instinct nor penchant for fantasy invariably leads to an autonomous theatre. Therefore, additional explanations are needed. One necessary condition, as with all arts, is the existence of a stable society in which some members are free to pursue things other than food gathering. The next seems to be a somewhat detached view that allows people to examine human problems rather than be seriously threatened by them. Other conditions include presence of people who can organize performative elements into theatrical experiences, and a society that acknowledges the value of theatre as an autonomous activity.

Western theories of the origin of theatre in ritual, narrative, human mimetic tendencies, and fantasy are also applied to the origins of Asian theatre. Joseph Campbell's analysis of the differences between Western and Eastern thought may throw some light, however, on why the forms developed so very differently. In Western myths, he argues, the dominant concern is the relationship between two types of beings—gods and humans—and the tension between the roles assigned to each.

These roles, which are not fixed, vary considerably from one period and group to another. Sometimes major emphasis has been placed on the supreme power of one or more gods, with humans relegated to a position of total dependence. This, in essence, is the religious view. At other times primary stress has been given to the ability of human beings to manage their own affairs—the humanistic view. The Greeks first enlarged the human role and established the dominant strain of Western thought, in which humans (sometimes as agents of the gods but often quite independently) are assigned a major share in action and control. After the Renaissance the humanistic view was increasingly accepted and the notion of divine interference steadily diminished. Thus, in Western thought the world came to be seen primarily from the human point of view—as a place of conflict, change, and progress—with humanity as the principal agent both for good and evil.

On the other hand, Campbell proposes, the dominant strain in Egyptian, Middle Eastern, and Far Eastern thought recognizes no basic dichotomy between god and human. In their myths, people seek to transcend temporal limitations and achieve oneness with the mystery of being, in which all divisions—including human and divine—disappear. Although on the surface everything may seem tempestuous and ever-changing, behind this apparent flux lies a harmony so complete as to defy all attempts to define it. The Eastern view encourages a conception of world order in which all duties, roles, and possibilities are fixed; it does not see reality as a series of constantly changing relationships (as does the West) but as a fixed state of being. Humanity cannot influence this being; it can only seek to become one with it. Consequently, to the traditional Eastern mind change and progress seem illusions, whereas to the Western mind they seem inevitable.

As electronic media have disseminated ideas throughout the world, the former differences between East and West have lessened. This book deals with the history of theatre throughout the world, but gives emphasis to the Western tradition. Before taking up that history, however, it should be helpful to look briefly at conditions in Egypt and the Near East, where civilization is thought to have begun.

NORTH AFRICA AND THE NEAR EAST

Between 3500 and 3000 B.C.E., cities grew up in both Mesopotamia and Egypt, and by 3000 Egypt had formed an effective central government. For the next 2500 years, Egypt, its southern neighbor, the Kush empire, and the Near East, were to be the major centers of civilization. Forms of writing were devised and elaborate monuments were erected. Although Egypt, Kush, and the Near East developed more or less simultaneously, in the brief overview that follows Egypt will be given primary emphasis, since the Kush empire has only recently begun to be excavated and numerous empires (Sumerian, Babylonian, Hittite, Assyrian, Chaldean, Canaanite, and Persian) flourished and declined during this period in the Near East.

Most of the information used in studies of ancient Egypt comes from the hieroglyphics, decorations, and artifacts preserved in the great pyramid tombs for the pharaohs and in the temples dedicated to the numerous Egyptian gods. More than fifty surviving "pyramid texts" date from 2800 to 2400 B.C.E., although certain passages may have been traditional by that time. Many of these hieroglyphic scenes depict the trials through which the spirit must pass before being admitted to an honorable place in afterlife. Some scholars have argued that these texts are dramas and were enacted by priests at regular intervals to ensure the well-being of the dead pharaoh. Their view is based principally on the presence of occasional passages of dialogue and indications of action. But there is no definitive evidence that they were ever acted or even that they were intended to be acted. Consequently, numerous other scholars have denied that these texts were performed, pointing out that such nondramatic works as epic poems and the Bible also contain passages in dialogue and indications of action.

Another similarly contested text tells of the death and resurrection of Osiris and the coronation of Horus. In Egyptian myth, Osiris, son of Geb (the earth) and Nut (the sky), succeeded his father as ruler and married his sister, Isis. His brother, Set, jealous of Osiris' power, killed Osiris and buried parts of the body at various spots in Egypt. Isis found the pieces and, with the aid of Anubis, later the jackal-god of embalming, revived Osiris. Unable to remain on earth, Osiris, after his body was buried at Abydos, went to dwell in the afterworld, where be became the judge of souls. Horus, son of Osiris, fought with Set

and won back his father's kingdom. This was the most revered of all Egyptian myths. A version of this story now preserved on the "Shabako Stone," carved while Egypt was under the rule of the Nubian Kush Empire (c. 747–633 B.C.E.), was found just south of Memphis. It is clearly a re-carving of a much earlier text, which some date to as early as 2500 B.C.E. Some historians interpret this particular hieroglyphic text as the libretto of a drama in which Horus, symbolizing the regenerated year spirit, was impersonated by the pharaoh, who performed it each year on the first day of spring. They have called it *The Memphite Drama*, although there are many experts who see no evidence of performance in the surviving text.

At Abydos, the most sacred spot in Egypt, scholars have claimed that some kind of performance relating to Osiris occurred annually from about 2500 until about 550 B.C.E. In spite of this long history, however, no part of the text remains. What we know of it is deduced from an account left by Ikhernofret, a participant sometime between 1887 and 1849 B.C.E., in which he tells what he did during

FIG. 1.4
Egyptian acrobatic dancers. Note how the hair is weighted and how the figures at left seem to be providing a clapping accompaniment. Relief sculpture from a tomb at Saqqara, Egypt.

FIG. 1.5
Ancient Egypt.

As this brief summary suggests, the difficulty in studying these early years lies not in establishing that numerous performances occurred but in determining the nature of the performances. Present-day religious services offer little help in envisioning rituals of those earlier times. In Egypt, Kush, and the Near East a temple was usually considered the private residence of the god, to which admission was granted to no one other than those (priests) appointed, usually by the ruler, to act as the god's servants. These priests dressed the god's image, served it food, and treated it as they might the king himself, who was often considered to be a god or a god's earthly manifestation. Through much of the year, then, the ordinary people participated in major religious rites only at second hand through the ruler and his priest-assistants. On a few occasions each year, the god's image was taken from the temple in a procession over some prescribed route

one of the celebrations. (The text is in the "Looking at Theatre History" section of this chapter.) On the basis of that report, they have called it *The Abydos Passion Play,* linking it clearly to the religious drama of the Middle Ages in Western Europe. Again, however, scholars disagree markedly in their interpretations of Ikhernofret's account. From this brief account, some have argued that the major events of Osiris' life were reenacted by priest/actors, with the people serving as the crowds. They propose that each section of the play, including battles, processions, and burial ceremonies, was performed at a different location, and perhaps over several weeks or months, making this one of the most elaborate dramatic spectacles ever staged. Others vigorously object. They argue that the basic premise of the event was that Osiris is dead and that consequently the event took on the characteristics of a royal funeral. Information sufficient to resolve this dispute is not presently available, although all apparently agree that some type of performative event took place.

In addition to Egyptian texts, others from the Near East—Sumerian, Babylonian, Hittite, Canaanite, and so on—dating from *c.* 2500 B.C.E. onward tell stories relating to an enormous array of gods, many showing an equal potential for dramatization. Theodor Gaster provides translations of a number of these in his book *Thespis,* in which he argues that they were full-fledged dramas. Even the Biblical Book of Job has come under scrutiny as a fifth-century play.

FIG. 1.6
The Ikhernofret stone (dated about 1868 B.C.E.), the primary evidence concerning the so-called Abydos Passion Play. At right, the events have been divided into acts by a modern scholar. From Schaefer, *Untersuchungen zur Geschichte und Altertumskunde Aegyptens,* IV (1904).

where at certain stations rites were performed in the presence of (and perhaps with limited participation by) the general populace. Thus, the majority of people were allowed only occasional glimpses of their earthly and heavenly rulers. It seems likely that the rites, both those performed within and without the temples, were elaborate, lavish, and precise, since nothing less would have been considered suitable. Such ceremonies both validated and reaffirmed the existing order. Their function was religious, social, and political but not necessarily theatrical.

Egypt, Kush, and the Near East had enormous cultural influence on Western culture as Western culture has had on them as well. Contacts among the civilizations of the eastern Mediterranean were constant, and the Greeks themselves acknowledged considerable indebtedness to the Egyptians, Phoenicians (from whom they borrowed the alphabet), Persians, and others. Images of black Africans turn up from pre-Greek, Minoan Art, through classical Greek art and beyond. In Greek myth, Andromeda, famously rescued from a sea monster by Perseus, is an "Ethiopian" Princess, a designation which meant black, rather than identifying a particular country. The Greek historian Herodotus (c. 484–425 B.C.E.), after visiting Egypt around 450, noted two performances there and commented that Dionysus, the god in whose honor plays were presented in Greece, was another version of Osiris. But although the intercultural influences were considerable, one important difference remains between their performance traditions. The Egyptians maintained an advanced civilization for some 3000 years (a period longer than the one that separates us from the beginnings of Greek drama) and never developed theatrically beyond ritualized performances, repeating the same ceremonies year after year for centuries. Theirs was a society that resisted changes that might have led to an autonomous theatre, whereas the Greeks went on to a theatre in which new plays were presented each year. Thus, despite the achievements of the Egyptians or the empires of the Middle East, it appears that Greece took the decisive step toward an autonomous theatre and that this step can be dated to 534 B.C.E. It happened in the city-state of Athens, in the region known as Attica.

LOOKING AT THEATRE HISTORY

Among the first problems faced by the historian is the amount of information that has survived (and is available) about the topic being studied. The more one is removed from an event in time, the more apt evidence is to be scarce. But it is not merely the ravages of time that cause information to be lacking. It may be difficult to find materials relating to certain conditions that existed as recently as 50 or 100 years ago because no one considered them sufficiently important to record. In most past eras, records were systematically maintained only about those things officially sanctioned by state and religious authority. Consequently, we tend to know much more about rulers, wars, political events, religious controversies, and similar matters than we do about the lives of ordinary people, the activities and contributions of women and ethnic minorities, or about popular culture (the entertainments of the common people as opposed to the "high" art favored by rulers or a cultural elite). The kinds of things a society thought important to record tell us much about its values but it hardly tells us the whole story of its culture. Similarly, the major monumental structures erected by a society also indicate priorities in its values—the pyramids of Egypt, the temples of Greece, the cathedrals of Medieval Europe, the palaces of the Renaissance, the government buildings of the nineteenth century, the office skyscrapers of the twentieth century—just as differences in types of monumental structures from one period to another help us see how priorities may vary, but these do not tell us how the average person lived.

Even if information has survived, it must be interpreted. Although historians have usually proclaimed their objectivity, they have inevitably brought to their work a set of beliefs and assumptions—that is, an ideology—that predisposes them to find some parts of the surviving evidence significant and other parts unimportant. Thus, they interpret events from a particular point of view, even when they try to avoid bias. Consequently, it can be revealing to ask about historical treatises what assumptions or ideological stances have shaped the authors' interpretations of the evidence they have used. To identify an author's stance does not necessarily invalidate an interpretation, but it does help us understand that this is only one among the possible interpretations that might emerge if the material were viewed from other perspectives.

Martin Bernal has argued extensively that the contributions of Egypt, black Africa, and the Near East to European culture were distorted during the nineteenth century by racial attitudes of that period. Here is one brief excerpt:

> The paradigm of 'races' that were intrinsically unequal in physical and mental endowment was applied to all human studies, but especially to history. . . . To be creative, a civilization needed to be 'racially pure.' Thus it became increasingly intolerable that Greece—which was seen by the Romantics not merely as the epitome of Europe but also of its pure childhood—could be the result of the mixture of native Europeans and colonizing Africans and Semitics.

Martin Bernal, *Black Athena: The Afroasiatic Roots of Classical Civilization,* vol. I (London: Free Association Books, 1987), 29.

One difficulty encountered by a present-day historian seeking to deal with Egyptian texts can be seen in this translation of Ikhernofret's account of his participation in the ceremonies at Abydos. It is upon this account that the concept of the *Abydos Passion* play as one of the most spectacular plays in history rests. [See Fig. 1.6. The dashes indicate gaps in the surviving Egyptian text.]:

> I celebrated the [feast of] "Going Forth" of Upwawet, when he proceeded to champion his father. I repelled the foe from the sacred barque. I overthrew the enemies of Osiris. I celebrated the "Great-Going-Forth," following the god at his going. I sailed the divine boat of Thoth upon _____. I equipped the barque (called) "Shining-in-Truth" of the lord of Abydos, with a chapel. [I] put on his regalia when he went forth to _____ Peker; I led

the way of the god to his tomb before Peker; I championed Wennofer at "That Day of the Great Conflict"; I slew all the enemies upon the flats of Nedyt. I conveyed him into the barque [called] "The Great," when it bore his beauty; I gladdened the heart of the eastern highlands; I ___ed the rejoicing in the western highlands. When they saw the beauty of the sacred barge, as it landed at Abydos, they brought [Osiris, First of the Westerners, lord] of Abydos to his palace, and I followed the god into his house, to attend to his _____, when he resumed his seat. I loosed the knot in the midst of his attendants, among his courtiers.

Translation from James Henry Breasted, *Ancient Records of Egypt,* vol. I (Chicago: University of Chicago Press, 1906), 300.

In recent years, theorists have sought to articulate a unifying theory that encompasses all types of performance:

> Performance is an inclusive term. Theater is only one node on a continuum that reaches from the ritualizations of animals (including humans) through performances in everyday life—greetings, displays of emotion, family scenes, professional roles, and so on— through to play, sports, theater, dance, ceremonies, rites, and performances of great magnitude [xiii]. . . . Whether one calls a specific performance "ritual" or "theater" depends mostly on context and function. A performance is called theater or ritual because of where it is performed, by whom, and under what circumstances. If the performance's purpose is to effect transformations—to be efficacious—the performance is a ritual. . . . No performance is pure efficacy or pure "entertainment." The matter is complicated because one can look at specific performances from several vantages; changing perspectives changes classification [120].

Richard Schechner, *Performance Theory,* rev. and expanded ed. (New York: Routledge, 1988.)

2
Theatre and Drama in Ancient Greece

While the civilizations of the Near East and Egypt were flourishing, others were maturing in neighboring areas. For our purposes, the most important were the Aegean forerunners of the Greeks. The Minoan culture flourished on Crete and the nearby islands from about 2500 to 1400 B.C.E. The Minoans had a highly advanced civilization and built three-story palaces decorated throughout with frescos and featuring such amenities as working sewers that would not be seen elsewhere in Europe for 1500 years. Excavations at the palaces of Knossos, Phaistos, Gournia, and Amnisos have revealed stone "theatral areas," but nothing is known about their function. The Mycenaeans, a Helladic culture on the Greek mainland, flourished from around 1600 to 1100 B.C.E. These were the Greeks who fought the famous war with Troy, a major city in Asia Minor near the entrance to the Hellespont, in the thirteenth century B.C.E. Shortly afterwards, Mycenaean civilization began to decline. These early Aegean civilizations had little to do directly with the development of the theatre, but their indirect influence was enormous, for their gods, heroes, and history supplied the material for Homer's (eighth century B.C.E.) *Iliad* and *Odyssey* and therefore for most Greek drama. Thus, these civilizations are in many ways the fountainhead of Western literature.

The Greek civilization that was to produce the first great era of the theatre took shape between the eighth and sixth centuries. The major political unit came to be the *polis* (or city-state, composed of a town and its surrounding countryside). The most important of these city-states were Attica (Athens), Sparta, Corinth, Thebes, Megara, and Argos, but there were others on the coast of Asia Minor and on the Aegean islands. In addition, after 750 B.C.E., numerous colonies were founded in places ranging from the Black Sea in Asia to the coasts of Africa, Spain, and France, although the most important were those in Sicily and southern Italy (Magna Graecia). All of these Greeks acknowledged their kinship, but they also insisted on differences among themselves based primarily on dialect. The primary divisions were Dorian (with Sparta and Corinth as the major cities) and Ionian (represented by Athens and the cities of Asia Minor). Most of these states depended on control of the seas (as the major avenue of trade) for their wealth, power, and well-being. Consequently, rivalries for dominance motivated them to form leagues or to wage war with each other or with non-Greek states.

For some time, the city-states were ruled by kings, but after 800 B.C.E. nobles were able to assume considerable power. The more ambitious nobles soon learned they could win support through promises of

FIG. 2.1

The Greek world during the classical period.

improved rights for tradesmen and farmers, who had few privileges. Through such means, a number of "tyrants" won control of states between 650 and 500 B.C.E. Many of these tyrants did much to improve social conditions and to promote the arts. For example, Peisistratus, who dominated Athens from 560 to 510, redistributed land, promoted farming and foreign trade, made Athens the leading center of the arts, and established or enlarged numerous festivals, including the City Dionysia, which was to be the major home of drama. But by the late sixth century Greeks were weary of tyrants and found means to prevent them from assuming power. Athens' solution was to found the world's first democracy (around 508 B.C.E.).

Although by 500 B.C.E. Athens was the artistic center of Greece, Sparta was the major power and the head of an alliance that encompassed most of the city-states, including Athens. War with Persia soon altered this arrangement. At the beginning of the fifth century, Persia, already the most extensive empire of the time, sought to expand into Europe. In 490 the Greeks defeated the Persians at Marathon, and in 480–479 the Athenians dealt the Persians a mor-

tal blow by destroying their fleet. Because of troubles at home, in 477 Sparta withdrew from further involvement in the conflict (which continued for many years as Greek cities in Asia Minor rebelled against Persia). Consequently, Athens rapidly became the major force in the Mediterranean, and in return for protecting others it exacted payments and gained other rights that brought it great wealth and power. In effect, Athens ruled an empire during the remainder of the fifth century. Under the leadership of Pericles (c. 495– 430 B.C.E.), Athens built numerous temples and public buildings (among them the Parthenon). Athens' political power was broken in 404 when it was defeated in the protracted war with Sparta known as the Peloponnesian War. But throughout the fifth century it enjoyed a privileged place both politically and artistically.

No doubt the Athenians' confidence in their strength and worth did much to motivate artistic expression during the fifth century. Equally important, however, was the Greek view of human beings and the gods, never a wholly coherent view since it was composed of diverse elements (some derived from the earlier Helladic civilization, some from more recent times, and others from Egypt and the Near East). For the most part, the Greeks conceived of their gods in human terms. Zeus presided over a number of other deities who were as unpredictable as their human counterparts. If wooed with prayers and sacrifices, the gods might help people, but they were just as apt to take offense and hold grudges. Furthermore, they often differed among themselves, and some assisted and others opposed the same people or undertakings.

Greek thought is characterized by a tension between belief in human rationality and acknowledgement of unpredictability. That the Greeks established democracy tells much about their faith in humanity, although even here they were not wholly consistent, for they did not hesitate to enslave others or severely restrict the role of women.

THE ORIGIN OF TRAGEDY

The Parian Marble, in the Ashmolean museum at Oxford, credits Thespis with the invention of tragedy, the first form of drama, in 534 B.C.E. It says he won a competition that year in the city-state of Athens and tradition has it that this was part of their Great Dionysia festival, now generally called the City Dionysia to distinguish it from the later festivals known as the Rural Dionysia which were done outside the city. Some ancient accounts, however, place Thespis as late as sixteenth in the line of tragic poets. The disparity is probably owing to impreciseness in the original meaning of *tragoidia* (literally, "goat song") from which we get the word tragedy. The earliest still-extant account of how Greek drama originated—for example, a chapter in Aristotle's *Poetics* (c. 335–323 B.C.E.)—states that tragedy emerged out of improvisations by the leaders of dithyrambs. A dithyramb was a hymn sung and danced in honor of Dionysus, the Greek god of wine and fertility, and it is said to have been given its first literary form by Arion of Corinth (c. 625–585 B.C.E.). Arion called his work *tragikon drama,* and those who performed them *tragoidoi.* For this reason Corinth (a Dorian Greek city-state), claimed to have invented drama well before Thespis performed at the Ionian Greek city-state of Athens. Unfortunately, none of the theories about how the term *tragedy* originated (and there are many) provides important clues as to how the dramatic form we call tragedy developed.

Almost nothing is known of Thespis except that he was from Icaria, near Athens. The Roman author Horace, writing some 500 years later, says that when Thespis invented tragedy, "a cart was the scene." Later Roman authors say he experimented

FIG. 2.2
Men dancing dressed in bird costumes. Note the flute player at the extreme left. A Greek vase of the late sixth or early fifth century B.C.E. Courtesy British Museum.

with different types of masks. The great innovation attributed to Thespis, however, was the creation of "dialogue," which we assume he exchanged with the leader of a dithyrambic chorus. This made him the first actor (and dramatist), or what the Greeks called *hypokrites,* meaning "interpreter" or "answerer."

In the nineteenth century scholars began to ignore Aristotle's association of tragedy with the dithyramb and started proposing various theories for how tragedy might have developed out of different kinds of rituals, thereby linking theatre more strongly to religion. Since the last half of the twentieth century, however, alternative theories have argued for drama emerging from experimentation with such performance forms as recited stories, sung poetry, and narrative dance. All such theories of origin are conjectural, since evidence to substantiate any of them definitively is lacking, but each theory asked us to look at the evidence in different ways. Whatever its origin, a major step toward drama was taken during the late sixth century when the first actor/dramatist appeared. The second major step occurred early in the next century when the actor/dramatist Aeschylus added a second actor, thereby permitting face-to-face conflict on stage.

TRAGEDY IN THE FIFTH CENTURY

Other than Thespis, only three actor/dramatists of the sixth century are known to us: Choerilus, who made unspecified innovations in costumes and masks; Pratinas, said to have invented the bawdy farce form known as "satyr plays"; and Phrynichus, who is credited with introducing female characters. But no play texts from that period have survived. Our knowledge of Greek tragedy, then, is based almost entirely on the work of three playwrights of the fifth century: Aeschylus, Sophocles, and Euripides. Historians usually assume that the surviving plays are representative, but it is perhaps well to remember that only thirty-one tragedies by three authors (possibly four) remain from the 1000 or more that must have been written by numerous playwrights between 534 and 400 B.C.E. This could change. In 2005, a new infrared system for reading ancient texts was developed that makes it possible to easily read texts that were previously unreadable, which make up as much as twenty percent of known classical literature. Previously unknown fragments of dramas and possibly entire plays could be among them.

By the time the surviving plays were written, each dramatist submitted a group of three tragedies (a trilogy) and one farcical satyr play for the competition at the City Dionysia festival. Only one trilogy has come down to us, so it is useful to keep in mind that when we read most Greek tragedies we are reading only one part of what the author considered to be a three- or four-part sequence. Still, there are a number of recurring structural features in the plays. Most of the tragedies begin with a *prologue* which provides information about events that have occurred prior to the opening of the play. Next comes the *parodos,* or entrance of the chorus; if there is no prologue, the *parodos* begins the play. The *parodoi* of extant plays vary in length from twenty to two hundred lines; they introduce the chorus, give exposition, and establish the proper mood. Following the *parodos,* a series of episodes, varying in number from three to six and separated by choral dance songs (or *stasima*), develop the main action. The *exodos,* or concluding scene, includes the departure of all the characters and the chorus.

The point of attack in the plays is late—that is, the story is usually taken up just prior to the climactic moment, and only the final part is dramatized. Thus, considerable exposition of earlier events is required. Most of the tragedies but not all (for example, Sophocles' *Ajax*) place scenes of death and physical violence offstage; this convention requires the frequent use of messengers to relate what has occurred elsewhere. In most of the plays, the time of the action is continuous and it occurs in a single location,

but there are notable exceptions, among them Aeschylus' *Eumenides.*

The oldest extant Greek tragedy, *The Persians,* is a history play, but all the others are based on myth. Each writer was free to alter the stories and to invent motivations (which are often not provided in myth) for characters and actions. Thus, though dramatists might begin with the same basic story, they ended with widely different interpretations of it.

Greek dramatists were very economical in the number of events and character traits they included, preferring a few broad strokes to multiplicity of detail. They paid little attention to the physical and sociological aspects of characterization, concentrating instead on the psychological and ethical attributes of their personages.

The oldest surviving Greek plays are by Aeschylus (c. 523–456), who began competing at the City Dionysia about 499 B.C.E. and is credited with thirteen victories. Although about eighty titles are known, the only ones to have survived are *The Persians* (472), *Seven Against Thebes* (467), the *Oresteia,* a trilogy of plays made up of *Agamemnon, Libation Bearers,* and *Eumenides* (458), *The Suppliants,* and *Prometheus Bound* (exact dates unknown but probably after 468). His authorship of the latter play, however, has been disputed by some modern scholars, who believe it may be the work of an unidentified author. The major innovation attributed to Aeschylus is the introduction of the second actor. It is usually assumed that this occurred early in his career, but no date can be fixed for it. After about 468, when Sophocles reputedly introduced the third actor, Aeschylus made use of this additional performer.

In the *Oresteia* (the only surviving Greek trilogy), Aeschylus uses all three plays to tell one story which is usually interpreted as showing the evolution of the concept of justice. In this story of "the curse on the house of Atreus," an endless chain of personal revenge is finally replaced with the rule of law. The action is resolved happily by reconciling conflicting claims for revenge in an all-encompassing principle of justice. This pattern (pitting one principle against another and then reconciling them through some larger principle) apparently characterized several of his works, and seems to indicate that Aeschylus was interested in philosophical issues quite different from those pursued by Sophocles and Euripides.

Sophocles (c. 496–406) is thought to have written more than 120 plays, but only seven have survived: *Ajax* (between 450 and 440), *Antigone* (c. 441), *Oedipus the King* (c. 430–425), *Electra* (c. 418–410), *Trachiniae* (c. 413), *Philoctetes* (409), and *Oedipus at Colonus* (406). A substantial portion of one satyr play, *The Trackers,* is also extant. Sophocles is said to have won twenty-four contests, the first in 468 when he defeated Aeschylus, and he never placed lower than second. He is credited with the introduction of the third actor, with fixing the size of the chorus at fifteen members, and with the first use of scene painting.

In comparison with Aeschylus, Sophocles placed increased emphasis on individual characters and reduced the role of the chorus. His personages are complex and psychologically well motivated. The protagonists, noble but not faultless, are usually subjected to a terrible crisis that leads to suffering and self-understanding, including the perception of a higher than human law behind events.

Sophocles is the most skillful of Greek dramatists in mastery of dramatic structure: his *Oedipus the King* is often called the most perfect of Greek tragedies (though it won only the second prize when it was first performed). In his plays, exposition is carefully motivated; scenes are built through suspense to a climax; the action is clear and logical throughout. His poetry has been universally admired for its beauty and clarity of expression. There are no elaborate visual effects; the impact derives almost entirely from the force of the dramatic action itself.

Euripides (*c.* 480–406) wrote about ninety plays, of which eighteen have survived: *Alcestis* (438), *Medea* (431), *Hippolytus* (428), *The Children of Heracles, Andromache, Hecuba, Heracles, The Suppliants, Ion* (dates unknown, but probably between 417 and 415), *The Trojan Women* (415), *Electra, Iphigenia in Tauris* (dates unknown, but probably between 417 and 408), *Helen* (412), *The Phoenician Women* (*c.* 409), *Orestes* (408), *The Bacchae, Iphigenia in Aulis* (produced after Euripides' death), and *Cyclops,* a satyr play (date unknown). The relatively large number of extant plays by Euripides is explained by his enormous popularity in later periods, although he was not highly appreciated during his lifetime, winning only four contests.

There are at least two reasons for the adverse judgment of Euripides by his contemporaries. First, he often introduced subjects thought unsuited to the stage and questioned traditional values. His use of Phaedra's love for her stepson, Medea's murder of her children, and Pasiphae's passion for a bull were denounced for their abnormality, and his realistic exploration of psychological motivations was sometimes thought too undignified for tragedy. Euripides' characters often questioned the gods' sense of justice, since they seemed sources of misery as often as of happiness. At times Euripides suggested that chance rules the world, and that human beings are more concerned with moral values than are the gods—at least as depicted in myths. Second, his dramatic method was not always clear. Because his basic themes are not always readily grasped, the significance of the dramatic action is sometimes obscure. His techniques, growing out of this thematic concern, often seem inadequate when compared with those of Sophocles. For example, many of his plays begin with a monologue-prologue baldly summarizing past events; the episodes are not always causally related and some may even appear superfluous; speeches often resemble forensic addresses; choral passages are at times only tenuously related to the dramatic action; and gods are frequently used to resolve conflicts and to foretell the future. Thus, Euripides was thought dangerous because of his ideas and artistically inferior because of his dramatic techniques. But, if Euripides' techniques call attention to themselves, they are counterbalanced by realistic strokes in characterization, dialogue, and costuming.

Euripides began many dramatic practices that were developed more fully in the fourth century. He often turned to minor myths for his subjects or severely altered the major ones. Such works as *Ion, Helen,* and *Iphigenia in Tauris,* which pass over into tragicomedy and melodrama, are often cited as signs that the late fifth-century Greek tragedy was already abandoning profundity for intrigue and startling reversals. As Euripides' popularity rose in succeeding centuries, it was the sentimental and melodramatic aspects of his work that were most often imitated.

THE SATYR PLAY

The tragic dramatist of the fifth century also had to master farce, since he was required to supply a satyr play each time he competed at the City Dionysia (though exceptions were apparently made as Euripides is said to have substituted *Alcestis* for a satyr play in 438). As with tragedy, little is known of the origin of the satyr play. Most of the evidence credits Pratinas with having invented this form sometime before 501 B.C.E.

Out of the hundreds of satyr plays written, the only complete example to survive is Euripides' *Cyclops.* It is based on an episode from the *Odyssey* in which Odysseus and his crew are captured by and escape from the Cyclops. In addition, a large part of Sophocles' *The Trackers* is extant. It tells of Apollo's attempt to find a herd of cattle stolen by Hermes, the god of thieves. Because of the limited evidence available to us, it is difficult to generalize about the form, although we may speculate about its typical features.

The satyr play takes its name from the chorus, which was made up of the half-beast, half-human companions of Dionysus. The leader of the chorus was Silenus, the father of the satyrs. Known titles suggest that the

FIG. 2.3

The so-called Pronomos vase from the late fifth century B.C.E. showing actors of a satyr play. Note the masks and various kinds of garments. From Baumeister, *Denkmaler des Klassischen Altertums* (1888).

story of a satyr play sometimes connected it in theme or subject with the tragedies it accompanied and other times was entirely independent. Essentially a burlesque treatment of mythology (often ridiculing gods or heroes and their adventures), the boisterous action occurred in a rural setting and included vigorous dancing, as well as indecent language and gestures. As with tragedy, the action was divided into a series of episodes separated by choral odes. Language and meter, however, were colloquial. Satyr plays served as afterpieces to the tragedies, providing comic relief from the serious plays that had gone before.

GREEK COMEDY IN THE FIFTH CENTURY

Comedy (*komoidia*) was accepted into the City Dionysia in 487–486 B.C.E., making it the last major dramatic form to receive official recognition in Athens. Aristotle says that comedy grew out of the improvisations by the leaders of phallic songs but because there were many phallic rites, none of which were dramatic, it is unclear which he had in mind. All of them provided opportunity for considerable byplay and mockery between participants and spectators but the process by which they achieved comic form is uncertain. Aristotle attributes the decisive step, however, to Epicharmus, who lived at Syracuse, a Dorian colony on the island of Sicily. Little is known about Epicharmus except that he was certainly writing plays between 485 and 467 B.C.E., and may have been writing as early as 500 B.C.E., in which case his work could have influenced the earliest comic writers in Athens. Another possible source of Dorian

influence on Athenian comedy is the "mime," short satirical treatments of everyday domestic situations which supposedly first appeared in Megara (a city some twenty-five miles from Athens) *c.* 581 B.C.E.

FIG. 2.4

Statuette representing an Old Comedy character. From Robert, *Die Masken der Neueren Attischen Komoedie* (1911).

The names of a few early comic dramatists in Athens have been recorded but all the extant comedies of the fifth century are by a single author, Aristophanes (c. 448–c. 380). He is thought to have written about forty plays, of which eleven survive. The first nine, *Acharnians* (425), *Knights* (424), *Clouds* (423), *Wasps* (422), *Peace* (421), *Birds* (414), *Lysistrata* (411), *Women at the Thesmophoria* (411), and *Frogs* (405), are known as "Old Comedies" and were all written while Athens was in a protracted war against its greatest rival, Sparta. The last two, *Assembly Women* (392/391), and *Plutus* (388), are known as "Middle Comedies" and were written over a decade after Athens lost that war. His plays are treated as typical of those two forms but we do not know how these plays compare with those of his predecessors or his contemporaries.

Probably the most noteworthy characteristic of Aristophanic comedy is its commentary on contemporary society, politics, theatre, and above all the war with Sparta known as the Peloponnesian War. The plays are organized around a ruling theme, embodied in a rather farfetched "happy idea" (such as a private peace with a warring power, or a sex strike to bring an end to war). Although the events of most Old Comedies could not occur in everyday life, parallels with real events are abundantly clear, the fantastic exaggerations serving to point up the absurdity of their real-life counterparts. In addition to fantasy, farcical situations are typical, and considerable emphasis is placed on the pleasures of eating, drinking, sex, wealth, and leisure. Coupled with the comic elements are some of the most beautiful lyrics and some of the most obscene passages in Greek literature.

Although there are many variants, the basic structural pattern of Aristophanic comedy is simple. A prologue establishes the mood and sets forth the "happy idea"; the chorus enters, and there follows a debate (or *agon*) over the merits of the idea and a decision is reached to try the scheme. A *parabasis* (or choral ode in which the audience is addressed directly) divides the play into two parts. In the *parabasis,* some social or political problem is often discussed and a line of action advocated. At times, however, the *parabasis* is used to praise the author of the play, to plead for the audience's favor, or for similar purposes. The second part of the play shows, in a series of loosely connected scenes, the results of adopting the happy idea. The final scene (or *komos*) usually concludes with the reconciliation of all the characters and their exit to a feast or revels. These features of comic structure are sometimes rearranged but are almost always present.

After Athens was defeated in the Peloponnesian War in 404, political and social satire gradually disappeared

FIG. 2.5
Old woman holding a child. Terracotta statuette of an actor from Old or Middle Comedy. Courtesy Metropolitan Museum of Art, Rogers Fund, 1913.

from comedy and new types, Middle and later New Comedy, evolved. The quality of tragedy declined after this time and satyr plays disappeared. Thus the world's first great age of dramatic writing was largely over by 400 B.C.E.

THE DRAMATIC FESTIVALS

The worship of Dionysus probably originated in the Near East and was only later imported into Greece. According to myth, Dionysus was the son of Zeus (the greatest of Greek gods) and Semele (a mortal). Reared by satyrs (who are often associated with him in dithyramb, drama, and art), he was killed, dismembered, and resurrected. As a god, he was associated with fertility, wine, and revelry, while the events of his life linked him with the year-spirit found in other early religions—that is, the cycle of the seasons and the recurring pattern of birth, maturity, death, and rebirth. Dionysian worshippers sought to promote human fertility and ample harvests and ward off evil from the community.

The Greeks honored each of their gods through one or more annual festivals. In the region of Attica, where Athens was the principal town, four annual festivals (Rural Dionysia, Lenaia, Anthesteria, and City Dionysia) were held in honor of Dionysus. Plays were presented only at the City Dionysia until 442 B.C.E. when a comedy competition was added to the Lenaia. By the late fifth century drama was added to the Rural Dionysia. There are no records of plays being done at the Anthesteria and drama was not part of the many other festivals held in honor of other gods in Athens.

The City Dionysia, which commemorated the coming of Dionysus to Athens, was held each year at the end of March or early April and extended over several days. Both a civic and religious festival, it was open to the whole Greek world and during the fifth century served as a showcase for Athenian wealth and culture. It was under the general supervision of the *archon eponymos,* the principal civil magistrate of Athens.

The first competition for tragedy was added to this festival in 534, presumably as an outgrowth of the dithyramb competition. At that time performances may have been done in the central market square (*agora*) or this may mark the move to the precinct of Dionysus Eleuthereus, a public park on the southeast slope of the acropolis. When Athenian democracy was created in 508 B.C.E., the inhabitants of Attica were divided into ten tribes and this led to an expansion of the dithyrambic competition to include one chorus of fifty men and one of fifty boys from each tribe, bringing 1000 performers into the festival. Around 501 the farcical "satyr plays" were added. In 499 some seating stands collapsed during the festival. If these were in the market square this event may have inspired the move to the precinct of Dionysus Eleuthereus; if the stands were already in that precinct, this may have triggered changes in design of the auditorium. The festival is known to have been in that precinct from that time on.

A few days before the festival began, each of three dramatists whose plays had been selected for performance, appeared at a *proagon* and announced the subject of his plays. After another preliminary event (the reenactment of Dionysus' coming to Athens), there was a procession, which included public officials who carried gifts or escorted sacrificial animals for the god. This procession wound through much of Athens and ended with the presentation of offerings and the sacrifice of a bull at the altar of Dionysus. The sacrificial animals, except for portions reserved for the god, were consumed at a public feast.

During the fifth century, five of the eight or more days of the festival were devoted to performances, though precisely what was presented on each day is a matter of some disagreement. On each of three days, one dramatist presented three tragedies and one satyr play. The other two days probably were devoted primarily to dithyrambic contests. After 487, each of five comic writers presented a single play (except during the Peloponnesian War, when the number was reduced to three). It is unclear whether all were performed on a single day or if one was added to the end of each performance day.

One of the high points of each festival was the awarding of prizes. Although not all of the details are clear, these are the probable procedures: at some time prior to the festival, a list of potential judges (one list for each of the ten tribes) was drawn up; all of the names from the same tribe were placed in a single urn; the ten urns were then sealed and placed under guard until the beginning of the contest, when they were brought into the theatre. The *archon* drew one name from each urn and these men then served as judges for the contest. After witnessing the plays, each judge placed his vote in an urn, from which the *archon* drew five. On the basis of these five votes, the winner was declared. In the case of a tie, additional votes could be counted until the tie was broken. Prizes were offered only for playwrights until 449, when a prize for actors was instituted. State records were kept of the winners and a victor's sponsor often erected a monument to commemorate the victory. Two days after the festival ended, an assembly was convened to consider the conduct of the officials in charge and to receive complaints about misconduct of individuals who attended.

The Lenaia was celebrated near the end of January under the supervision of the *archon basileus,* the principal religious official of Athens. The Lenaia was observed only in the city—no township (*deme*) of Attica celebrated both the Lenaia and Rural Dionysia. Dramatic activities were not officially recognized at the Lenaia until about 442, although plays may have been presented there on an informal basis before that date. Contests at the Lenaia were at first only for comic dramatists and actors and five comic writers competed each year. But in 432 competitions for tragic playwrights and actors were added. Only two tragic dramatists competed, each with two plays. Satyr plays and dithyrambs were not presented.

By the late fifth century the plays were being performed in the Theatre of Dionysus (Athens' major theatrical structure) but when they were first given there is unclear. Originally the Lenaia may have been held elsewhere, for Dionysus was worshipped under a number of guises, and each cult had its own sacred area, just as Christian sects do today. The City Dionysia was presented in honor of Dionysus Eleuthereus and the Theatre of Dionysus was erected within his precinct, but the Lenaia was held in honor of Dionysus Lenaios,

FIG. 2.6
The so-called Andromeda vase, dating from the late fifth century B.C.E. The figure at center and those in the upper corners are often cited as examples of tragic costuming, although there is little evidence to connect this vase with theatrical performance. Note also that some figures are nude. From Engelmann, *Archaeologische Studien zu den Tragikern* (1900).

whose sanctuary's location is unknown. It is possible that the Lenaia used a temporary theatre in the central market square until it moved to the Theatre of Dionysus when the comedies were officially recognized in 442 or when tragedies were added in 432.

The Rural Dionysia was celebrated in December, although not on the same day in all the townships of Attica. It was under the supervision of the *demarchos* (principal magistrate) of each township. The major feature of the festival was a procession in which a giant phallus was carried aloft on a pole, apparently with the purpose of reviving fertility at a time when the sun was at its weakest. It is unclear when dramatic performances became a part of this festival. It is unlikely that all of the more than 100 Attic townships included plays in their celebrations, but drama may have appeared in some of them before it was recognized at the Lenaia. It is certain that plays were being performed in a number of townships before the end of the fifth century, and the custom seems to have been widely adopted during the fourth century. Plato (*c.* 427–347 B.C.E.) wrote that in his time the Rural Dionysia was held on different days in different townships so that people might travel from one to the other to see plays presented by troupes of traveling actors.

By Plato's time actors were reviving works already produced elsewhere, but the source of plays presented in the fifth century is unknown. The Rural Dionysia may have served as an outlet for plays not accepted for the City Dionysia or Lenaia, or as a place where works already seen in the city were revived. While the Rural Dionysia probably had little effect on the development of Greek drama, its activities suggest how intense the interest in theatre was.

PLAY SELECTION AND FINANCING

Each author wishing to have his plays produced at a festival had to apply to the *archon* for a chorus. It is not known how this official chose the plays to be presented, but it has been suggested that each dramatist recited parts of his work before a committee. The choices of the next year's plays were made approximately one month after the end of each festival. Although this would have left about eleven months until performance, it is unknown how much of this time was actually used for rehearsals.

After about 501, a large share of the expense of play production was borne by the *choregoi* (singular is *choregos*), chosen by the *archon* from wealthy citizens who performed this duty in rotation as a part of their civic responsibilities. The *choregos* (one was appointed for each author and for each dithyrambic chorus) underwrote the training and costuming of the chorus, paid the musicians and supernumerary actors, and supplied properties. There were political advantages to having sponsored the winning production so the *choregoi* were generally quite generous. The responsibility of the state seems to have been restricted to the theatre building, prizes, and payments to actors and, possibly, to dramatists.

In Aeschylus' time, the author acted in his plays; trained the chorus, the second actor, and later the third; composed the music and dances; and supervised every aspect of production. Thus, the primary source of unity was the actor/playwright, whose task was as complex as that of any director today. The actor/playwright's key role is indicated by the term applied to him, *didaskalos* (teacher), for he was considered to be the instructor of both the performers (during the process of play production) and the audience (through the finished product). Comic playwrights, on the other hand, may have turned many of these tasks over to others.

ACTORS AND ACTING

Originally the actor and the dramatist were one. Separation of the two functions did not begin until early in the fifth century when Aeschylus introduced a second actor. Playwrights continued to act in their own plays, however, until Sophocles stopped acting in about 468 when he also added a third actor. It seems likely that when the contest for tragic actors was inaugurated (around 449) the separation of actor from playwright was complete. Nevertheless, in the fifth century actors were at best semiprofessionals, for there was as yet no demand for full-time performers and they must have supplemented their income through other activities.

After about 468, the number of actors available to each tragic playwright seems to have been fixed at three. Each actor had to impersonate a number of characters though supernumeraries could assume nonspeaking roles or even speak a very limited number of lines. All existing tragedies can be performed by three actors though the last play by Sophocles, *Oedipus at Colonus,* could only be performed by three actors if the same character was played by different actors in successive scenes.

In comedy too, most scenes could have been acted by three actors, but several require four and at least one would have required five. Here again the problem can be solved if a single role was sometimes divided among more than one actor.

Restrictions were probably established in order to make the contest fair, but the rules at the Lenaia may have differed from those at the City Dionysia, since other conditions differed at the two festivals.

Before about 449 (that is, up until the inauguration of contests for actors), each playwright probably selected his own cast, but after that time the leading actors were assigned by lot to the competing dramatists. This procedure was probably adopted to ensure that no writer had an unfair advantage over his rivals. The other two actors allotted to each dramatist were probably selected jointly by the playwright and his leading actor. Although all of the actors were paid by the state, only the leading actor could compete for the prize, which could be awarded for a performance in a non-prize-winning play.

It is now impossible to determine precisely the style of acting seen in fifth-century Greece. Both tragic and comic acting undoubtedly departed from the everyday—tragedy in the direction of idealization, comedy in the direction of burlesque—but they remained sufficiently recognizable to link the dramatic events to the spectator's own world. Several conventions are worth noting: all actors were men, all actors wore masks, all actors played more than one role—if not in a single play, over the course of the trilogy and satyr play—much of the dialogue was sung or delivered as recitative, and dance was part of many scenes. All of these make it clear that realism was not the goal. The Greeks seem to have placed considerable emphasis on the voice, for they judged actors above all by beauty of vocal tone and ability to adapt manner of speaking to mood and character. Actors did not attempt to reproduce the attributes of age or sex so much as to project the appropriate emotion. It is sometimes suggested that movement tended toward a set of conventionalized, stylized, or symbolic gestures like those used in mimetic dance or in the later Asian theatre forms. Facial expression was of no importance since the actors wore masks.

THE CHORUS

In the fifth century, the members of the chorus were amateurs. Nevertheless, they probably were not inexperienced, since choral dancing was so common in Greece and since there were at least 1000 participants each year in the dithyrambic contests at the City Dionysia. Although many types of choruses in Greece were performed by women, only men are mentioned in the choruses for tragedy, comedy, satyr plays, and dithyrambs.

In the extant plays by Aeschylus the chorus has as many as half of the lines. After Aeschylus, the role of the chorus diminished progressively. Choruses in the plays of Euripides are often only tenuously related to the dramatic action, though his inclusion of a second chorus in *Hippolytus* suggests that they continued to be an important part of the spectacle of performance.

The chorus serves several functions in Greek drama:

1. It adds dynamic energy to a play with its dances, songs, and visual spectacle.
2. It sets the overall mood of the play and of individual scenes.

3. It serves an important rhythmical function, creating intervals or slowing the action to allow the audience time to reflect or anticipate.
4. It can serve as a character, giving advice, expressing opinions, asking questions, and sometimes takes an active part in the action. In *The Suppliants,* it is the protagonist, while in *The Eumenides,* it is the antagonist.
5. It can establish the ethical or social framework of the events and sets up a standard against which the action may be judged.
6. It can serve as an ideal spectator, reacting to the events and characters as the dramatist might hope the audience would.

Historians disagree about the size of the tragic chorus. One view holds that the number was originally fifty (the same size as that of the dithyramb), but that it was reduced to twelve during the career of Aeschylus and was then raised to fifteen by Sophocles. There is no indisputable evidence to support any of these figures. The evidence for a chorus of fifteen, for example, is found in the commentaries of authors writing several centuries after Sophocles' lifetime. As a result, scholars generally site the size of the chorus as twelve to fifteen. In later times, the chorus diminished in size, sometimes having no more than three members.

The chorus of Old Comedy was most likely composed of twenty-four members. Sometimes it was divided into two semi-choruses, as in *Lysistrata* where the two are of opposite sexes.

Training and outfitting the chorus were the most important and expensive parts of the duties of a *choregos.* For tragedy, the chorus assigned to a playwright had to learn all the dances and songs for all three tragedies and the satyr play and they required a different set of costumes for each. In the *Oresteia,* they performed as old men in the first play, young slave women in the second, furies and townswomen in the third, and satyrs in the satyr play. They were judged on the artistry and skill with which they performed the wide variety of dances and songs associated with these very different roles. A comic chorus did only one play but was still held to very high standards of artistic skill.

In each dramatic form, the chorus normally made its entrance after the prologue and remained until the end of the play. In a few instances, however, it was present at the opening and occasionally it left and returned during the action. In tragedy the chorus may have entered with a stately march—later writers talk of them entering in rectangular formation—but occasionally members seem to come on singly or in small groups from various directions. In comedy it is thought they entered with an energetic dance. It

is assumed that most choral passages were danced and sung in unison, but at times the chorus was divided into two groups who performed in turn. Sometimes the chorus exchanged spoken dialogue with a character, and, in rare instances, individual members may have spoken single lines. All members must have responded appropriately to the situations in a play, but it is unknown how they were grouped or placed during episodes or how their formations changed during choral odes. Comedy seems to have enjoyed much more freedom than tragedy, and consequently the entrances, dances, and uses of the chorus were more varied. The texts of the plays suggest that the chorus was extremely active throughout the performance.

Most of the information that has survived about choral training concerns dithyrambs, but historians usually assume that the same practices were used with drama. This information suggests that training, like that of athletes, was long and arduous, involving diet, exercise, and disciplined practice under the watchful supervision of several persons. It also indicates that choruses were often pampered and given special treatment.

MUSIC AND DANCE

Music was an integral part of Greek drama. It accompanied the passages of recitative and was an inseparable part of the choral odes. Only rarely was it used apart from words, and then only for special effects. In the beginning, the musical accompaniment was probably subordinated to ensure that the words would be understood. By the time of Euripides, however, the accompaniment had become more elaborate, and lengthy trills prolonged some syllables. As a result, some passages may have become less intelligible. Critics have suggested that this may be one reason for the decline in importance of choral odes.

The musical accompaniment for drama was played on a "flute" (*aulos*) with tonal qualities resembling those of a modern oboe or clarinet. Other instruments, including the lyre, the trumpet, and various forms of percussion, were used occasionally for special effects. The flute player preceded the chorus into the orchestra, but his placement thereafter is uncertain. Some historians maintain that he wore a wooden shoe with which he marked the beat. Occasionally an actor used the lyre to accompany his own recitative or song.

It is unclear who composed the music. At first the playwright may have done so, but later this was probably the responsibility of the flute player. Flute players were considered so important to the success of a production that they were assigned to the *choregoi* by lot to insure fairness, a practice later adopted for assigning the lead actor to a playwright.

So little Greek music has survived that no comprehensive reconstruction of it is possible. The Greeks believed that music had ethical qualities. This suggests that they associated particular kinds of music with particular emotions or ideas, much as was later done in the theatre of India. They recognized a large number of *modes,* which differed from each other in tonality and in sequence of intervals. The tones of the various modes were not always equal in value, however, some of the intervals being as small as quarter-tones. In quality, Greek music probably resembled Middle Eastern more than modern Western music. The principal modes were the Dorian, Ionian, Phrygian, Aeolian, and Lydian, but there were many variations on these, such as Hypodorian or Myxolydian. Each had qualities which associated it with a particular range of feeling. Some modes were thought suitable to tragedy, others to comedy, and some unsuited to any form of drama.

Like music, dance was also considered to have ethical qualities. The Greeks defined dance as any expressive rhythmical movement; thus dance did not necessarily mean patterns created by footwork, since gestures or pantomime, if rhythmical, might qualify as dance. Most Greek dance was mimetic (expressive of a particular kind of character or situation). In theatrical performances, dance seems to have been closely related to the words through a set of moment-by-moment symbolic gestures (or *cheironomia*).

By the fourth century the dances of tragedy had come to be called *emmeleia* (a term that signifies harmony, grace, and dignity). This classification obviously was broad, for the choral passages range from religious processions to wedding dances, ecstatic frenzies, and many other types.

The dances of comedy (*Kordax*) were less dignified than those of tragedy. Many were intentionally ridiculous. Often at the end of plays the chorus exited dancing wildly. Comic choral dances were derived from many sources: animal movements, victory celebrations, and various other activities and rites. The individual actors performed dances that involved kicking the buttocks, slapping the chest or thighs, leaping, performing high kicks, spinning like a top, or beating other actors.

The basic dance of the satyr play (*sikinnis*), seem to have been burlesques of tragic dances and probably involved vigorous leaping, horseplay, and lewd pantomime.

COSTUMES AND MASKS

The overall visual style of a Greek theatrical production was greatly influenced by costumes and masks. Several historians have argued that the standard costume for all tragic actors was a sleeved, highly decorated tunic (*chiton*), usually full-length, although sometimes shorter. That the actor wore a standardized garment, however, is far from certain. Its presumed appearance is derived almost entirely from figures depicted on vase paintings. But this evidence is open to doubt for several reasons: (1) most of the vases are from a period later than the fifth century; (2) the relation of most paintings to actual theatrical practice is unclear; (3) other vase paintings, usually ignored by those who argue for a standardized garment, show figures in quite different costumes, and (4) even those vases showing the presumed standard often depict deviations from it, including complete nudity. Other evidence cited for a conventionalized garment is the statement of several ancient commentators (writing long after the fifth century) that robes designed by Aeschylus for his actors were later adopted by the priests at Eleusis. Aristophanes' *Frogs,* on the other hand, merely credits Aeschylus with clothing tragic actors in garments more dignified than those worn by ordinary persons. Thus, though the sleeved, decorated tunic apparently was used, there are many reasons for questioning whether it was standardized and worn by all actors.

It is possible that such characters as foreigners, gods, and other supernatural beings wore the sleeved, decorated tunic, for which there was no precedent in native Greek dress, while the more familiar personages

FIG. 2.7

Fragment of a vase from about 470 B.C.E. showing a mask, presumably an actor's. This is often cited as the oldest extant visual evidence concerning theatrical masks. Note the garment on the right (also supposedly theatrical) and the lack of foot covering. Courtesy the American School of Classical Studies at Athens.

wore some variation on Greek garments. In addition to the tunic, both actors and chorus might wear a short cloak (*chlamys*) or a long one (*himation*). The identity of both actors and chorus might be established in part by symbolic properties: the king by his scepter, the warrior by his spear, the suppliant by his branch, the herald by his wreath, and so on.

The plays surviving from this period contain few references to costume. Some indicate that the characters are in mourning, for which black was the usual color in Greek daily life. The protagonists of Sophocles' *Oedipus at Colonus* and *Philoctetes* refer to their torn clothing and Euripides was criticized by Aristophanes for dressing his tragic heroes in rags. In Aeschylus' *The Suppliants* the chorus is said to be wearing non-Greek garments, while in Sophocles' *Philoctetes* the opposite point is made. An oft-repeated (and very late) account of the first performance of Aeschylus' *Eumenides* states that the chorus of Furies was so frightening in appearance that several women

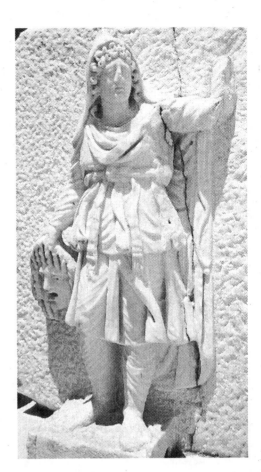

FIG. 2.9
Greek tragic actor of the mid fourth century. Photo by F. J. Hildy ©. Used by permission of the Aphrodisias, Turkey, Excavations, New York University.

in the audience miscarried. Other textual evidence suggests a wide variety of costumes for the chorus.

Footwear in tragedy varied. The usual foot covering seems to have been a soft shoe or boot, often reaching to the calf. In later times this was called a *kothornos* and was given a thick sole, but neither the name nor the elevation seems to have been used in the fifth century. In vase paintings, figures are shown in a wide variety of footwear, or even as barefoot.

Fortunately, there is more agreement among scholars about comic costuming, although the available evidence is no more reliable than that for tragedy. Most agree that costumes were adapted from those worn in everyday Greek life, especially for those characters who are being only mildly ridiculed in the play. For comic slaves and ridiculous old men the costuming was more grotesque with a tunic that was made too short and too tight so as to emphasize comic nudity. It was worn over flesh-colored tights, which were often padded and included an oversized *phallus*. Similarly, there is a wide range of female characters,

FIG. 2.8
Fragment of a vase from Tarentum showing a tragic actor holding a mask. Note the short fringed tunic and the tasseled boots. This fragment probably dates from the fourth century B.C.E. Courtesy Martin von Wagner Museum of the University of Würzburg.

whose sexual attributes were also exaggerated through costume. Since some comedies parodied scenes from well-known tragedies, it may be that tragic costume was sometimes adapted and ridiculed. Animal characters appear in several comic plays. In several plays by Aristophanes, *Wasps, Birds, Frogs,* the entire chorus is made up of animals and in *Knights,* half the chorus may have been horses. Another of his plays has a chorus of *Clouds.* Other comic choruses would have been presented in an appropriately exaggerated fashion.

Relatively little attention has been paid by historians to the costuming of satyr plays. The satyrs are thought to have worn goatskin loincloths, to which were attached the phallus in front and a horse-like tail in the rear; other parts of the body appeared to be nude, but in the theatre this probably meant some kind of flesh-colored garment though that is not necessarily the case. (See Fig. 2.3.) Silenus, the leader of the chorus, is usually depicted as wearing shaggy or fleecy tights under an animal-skin cloak. Since the characters in satyr plays are usually mythological personages, the costumes probably were the same ridiculous variations on tragic costumes found in some comedies.

All performers during the fifth century, with the possible exception of flute players, wore masks. According to ancient commentators, Thespis experimented with several types of disguise for the face—such as smearing it with wine dregs and dangling leaves in front of it—before adopting the mask. Tradition has it that Phrynichus was the first to introduce female masks and that Aeschylus was the first to use painted masks. No masks used by actors have survived, since they were made of perishable linen, cork, or lightweight wood. But masks depicted in art show that they covered the entire head and thus included the appropriate hairstyle, beard, ornaments, and other features. Although in later periods the masks seem to have been considerably larger than the face and to have had exaggerated features, in the fifth century neither the size nor the expression seems to have been unduly enlarged.

It is impossible to determine whether masks for tragedy were restricted to a few conventionalized types during the fifth century. Some historians have argued that they were, but others have suggested that experimentation was encouraged. The masks for the characters of a single play must have been sufficiently differentiated to make the frequent change of roles readily apparent. On the other hand, chorus members in tragedy were always identical in appearance.

The masks for comedy were extremely varied. The choruses often represented birds, animals, or insects, all of which were identified by appropriate, though not necessarily realistic, masks. The masks of human characters often exaggerated those attributes, such as baldness or ugliness, considered to be ridiculous. Although all of the members of some choruses wore identical masks, others were individualized (as in *The Birds*). When actors portrayed well-known Athenians, such as Socrates in *The Clouds,* "portrait masks" were used.

Members of the satyr chorus are usually depicted as snub-nosed, with dark, unkempt hair and beards, and pointed, horse-like ears. Sometimes they are shown as partially bald and at others they are given horns. Silenus is portrayed as having gray hair and beard. The actors probably wore masks similar to those used in tragedy.

The great importance of costumes and masks in the Greek theatre means that the costumer and mask maker were crucial. Nevertheless, virtually nothing is known about them or their working methods.

STAGES AND STAGING

In Greece, places of performance were constructed on public land, either in the parks associated with major temples or in the central marketplaces (the *agora*). The oldest known "theatral area" is at the Minoan palaces at Phaistos, which dates to about 2000 B.C.E. It has stone risers for a standing audience of about 500 arranged on two sides of a rectangular performance area approximately forty by thirty-five feet in size. The Minoan theatres are assumed to have been used for dances, ceremonies, and bull-leaping

FIG. 2.10

Plan of the theatre at Thorikos, at least part of which dates from the sixth century B.C.E. Note the modified rectangular shape. From Dörpfeld, *Griechische Theater* (1896).

FIG. 2.11
The Theatre of Dionysus as it may have looked in the late sixth century B.C.E. From Fiechter, *Antike Griechische Theaterbauten*. Courtesy Verlag W. Kohlhammer GmbH, Stuttgart and Dr. Charlotte Fiechter.

but no one really knows. The last of these theatres, the one at Knossos, would have disappeared by 1300 B.C.E., nearly 600 years before the emergence of theatres on mainland Greece. Early theatrical performance spaces on the Greek mainland, however, were also rectangular. The theatres at Thorikos (the oldest theatre in Greece), Trachones, and Isthmia in Attica along with the first theatre at Syracuse in Sicily, among others, still show this rectilinear origin. It is now thought possible that the circular orchestra traditionally associated with Greek theatres was not developed until the mid fourth century.

Although there were many theatres in Greece, major interest centers on the Theatre of Dionysus in Athens, for the surviving Greek plays were first presented there. The earliest feature of the Theatre of Dionysus (located in the precinct of Dionysus Eleuthereus on the southeast slope of the hill below the Acropolis) was the *orchestra* (or dancing place). Originally it was the only essential feature, since the audience sat or stood on the hillside to watch the choral performances which predated tragedy. Sometime during the sixth century a terrace was formed at the foot of the hill, and on it an *orchestra* was laid out. Since its excavation in 1886, scholars had accepted the view that this orchestra was circular, approximately sixty-six feet in diameter, and remained essentially unchanged until the Christian era. In recent years, however, archeologists have reexamined the ruins of this theatre and many have argued that the original orchestra was rectangular and remained so until the fourth century (that is, throughout the period during which the extant plays were written and performed). A table or altar (*thymele*) was located in the orchestra, but its location, whether in the center or off to one side, has been debated.

The scene building (*skene*) is of later origin than the orchestra. Since *skene* means "hut" or "tent," the scene house probably developed out of some temporary structure intended originally as a dressing room but later incorporated into the action by some imaginative playwright. Aeschylus' *Oresteia* (produced in 458 B.C.E.) is the first extant play to require a building as a background. Since virtually all parts of the early scene house have long since vanished, its appearance cannot be determined. Some of the many possible arrangements are shown in the accompanying illustrations (see Fig. 2.12).

Extensive changes were made in the Theatre of Dionysus when Pericles built the Odeion adjoining it, probably in the 440s. This was the first known *odeion* (plural *odea*) or roofed theatre. Odea were indoor theatres built as square or rectangular buildings and were primarily used for musical events and public meetings. Several opening events of the City Dionysia took place in the Odeion of Pericles. Ten grooves on the inner face of the orchestra terrace wall (facing the auditorium) in the Theatre of Dionysus are assumed to have held wooden posts used to support the *skene*, while a stone-surfaced area on the orchestra side of the wall is thought to have served as a foundation, either for theatrical machinery, a raised

FIG. 2.12
Three reconstructions showing possible appearances of the stage house of the Theatre of Dionysus in the fifth century B.C.E. From Fiechter, *Das Dionysostheater in Athen*. Courtesy Verlag W. Kohlhammr GmbH, Stuttgart and Dr. Charlotte Fiechter.

platform, or an entry portico. It was also long accepted that these sketchy physical remnants were all that remains of the fifth-century theatre but recent archeology suggests that even these belong to the fourth century. If so, there are no identifiable physical remains from the time of the great dramatists.

Historians usually assume that in the fifth century a temporary scene house was erected for each festival—at least from 458 onward. The features of the *skene* required by the extant plays are few: one or more doors (opening onto an acting area) and an upper level (either the roof or a platform on a second level) used primarily for the appearance of gods or to represent high places. A few historians have argued that one door is sufficient to accommodate the needs of all the extant plays; they have also suggested that there may have been one or more windows considerably above ground level, as the action of some comedies seem to demand them. Although scholars in the past argued that a stone scene building had been built by the late fifth century, most now date the permanent *skene* from the fourth century and thus after the era of great drama was over.

Questions relating to the *skene* are closely bound up with others about scenery. Was the background for all plays the conventional facade of the *skene,* or was some type of scenery used to suggest locale more specifically? Although these questions cannot be answered definitively, they can be illuminated.

It is important to distinguish between scenic practices before and after the scene building was introduced, for they probably changed when the *skene* became the background for the action. The challenges posed in the period before a *skene* was clearly available are well illustrated by the arguments over *Prometheus Bound,* when it was still thought to have been an early play. It is set in rugged mountainous locale which is engulfed in an earthquake during the final scene. Some commentators argued that for this play a set piece representing a mountain cliff was erected at the edge of the orchestra terrace and that during the earthquake it was tipped over the embankment wall, falling out of sight of the audience. Others argued that the whole performance was highly conventionalized and that the idea of an earthquake was conveyed entirely by lines, dance, and sound. Both are possible, but neither argument could be conclusive given the limited evidence. The scenic requirements of this play are, in fact, the primary reason why many scholars now believe it was written at a later date, in which case a fully developed stage house was already in use. This still does not solve the problem of how the earthquake was staged.

It is widely assumed that after 458 all plays used the *skene* as a background (an assumption that may be incorrect if the *skene* was a temporary structure). A *skene* could easily meet the demands of most plays since the majority are set before a temple, palace, or some other type of building. But what of those works set before caves (as are *Philoctetes* and numerous satyr plays), in groves of trees (*Oedipus at Colonus*), or in army camps (*Ajax*)? Answers to this question have varied. Some historians have argued that a few stock sets, designed to meet the range of possible locales, were used. Others have argued that a few symbolic properties (such as shields to identify an army camp, or shells and rocks to indicate a seashore, or a single tree to suggest a grove) were merely added to the otherwise undisguised scene house. Still others have suggested that the spoken lines provided the necessary indications of locale and that the facade of the *skene* served as a conventionalized background for all plays.

This controversy is closely allied with another concerning scene painting. Aristotle (writing in the late fourth century) credits Sophocles with introducing the decoration of the *skene,* while Vitruvius (first century B.C.E.) states that it originated in the time of Aeschylus. In seeking to reconcile these two statements, some historians have placed the beginnings of *skene* decoration (sometimes interpreted as scene painting) between 468 and 456, that is, during the years when the careers of Aeschylus and Sophocles overlapped. Vitruvius' description of the first painting on the *skene* suggests that it was an architectural design on a flat surface; this has been interpreted variously to mean that an attempt was made to create the illusion of real architectural details or, conversely, that a previously undecorated surface was now given some schematic but nonillusionistic pattern.

The issue of conventionalization versus illusionism is an important one, for, if illusion was attempted, then a single background could not have met the demands of all plays without changes of some kind. Consequently, those who have argued for a degree of representationalism have also had to suggest means whereby the appearance of the *skene* could have been altered. Two major devices have been proposed: *pinakes* (or painted panels similar to modern flats), and *periaktoi* (or triangular prisms with a different scene painted on each of their three sides). *Pinakes* supposedly could be attached to the scene building and changed as needed. But, though the use of *pinakes* in the fifth century is well documented, the practice of changing them for different plays is not. It is possible that *pinakes* were used only to create the visible exterior of a temporary *skene*. In later periods, a series of *periaktoi* were mounted on pivots and revolved to show the appropriate side, but the use of this device during the fifth century has not been established.

Most Greek tragedies occur in a single locale, but the successive plays offered on the same day were often set in different locations. Thus, if scene changes were attempted, they could have been made between plays in most instances. On the other hand, some tragedies (such as Aeschylus' *Eumenides* and Sophocles' *Ajax*) and numerous comedies change place during the action. How could these changes have been handled? *Pinakes* and *periaktoi* offer a representational solution to this problem, but several nonrepresentational solutions, like those found in many early forms of theatre in Asia, have been suggested as well. Individual doors or sections of the *skene* might have been understood to represent widely separated places. In some instances, the actors and chorus may have left the scene and then returned, thus indicating a change in the place of the action (as was later to be the practice in Shakespeare's theatre). A trip around the orchestra could accomplish the same result.

Enough has been said to demonstrate that the evidence concerning scenic practices in the fifth century is inconclusive. Nevertheless, it appears unlikely that illusionism was ever attempted to any marked degree. The use of a few symbolic properties or set pieces would not have been out of keeping with other Greek artistic conventions of the period, and the eventual erection of a permanent stone *skene* suggests that conventionalization predominated over illusionism.

Inconclusive evidence has also led to disagreement over whether the Theatre of Dionysus had a stage during the fifth century. Those who believe, as A. W. Pickard-Cambridge did, that there was not one, argue that: (1) during the fifth century there was no Greek word for stage (*logeion* was not adopted until later) and that there are no archaeological remains of a stage from this period; (2) the choral performances which preceded the invention of drama did not use a stage and thus would have provided no precedents for one; and (3) no extant plays require a stage but do require the free mingling of actors and chorus, which a raised stage would have prevented. On the other hand, those who follow Peter Arnott in arguing for a stage note that: (1) all ancient commentators, though they originally lived much later, unanimously believed that there was a raised stage in the fifth century, (2) a number of extant plays indicate that actors were on a higher level than the orchestra; and (3) the intermingling of actors and chorus was not often required so a low raised stage (four feet or less) with steps to the orchestra was quite workable. Pickard-Cambridge was concerned primarily with refuting the idea of an eight- to thirteen-

foot-high platform, and he admits that there may have been a stage one or two feet in height.

In the fifth century, a limited amount of machinery was available for special effects. The most important devices were the *ekkyklema* and the *mechane* or *machina*. The *ekkyklema* (a device for revealing tableaux, most often the bodies of characters killed offstage) was probably a platform that could be rolled out through the central doorway of the *skene*. On the other hand, some ancient accounts state that it was revolved or turned, while others associate it with the upper story of the scene house or with the side doors. The *mechane*, or crane, was used to show characters in flight or suspended above the earth. Occasionally characters are said to be in chariots or on the backs of birds, insects, or animals, while at other times actors seem to have been suspended by a harness. The crane was probably situated so that an actor could be attached to it out of sight of the audience (behind either the scene house or some part of an upper level) and then raised in the air and swung out over the acting area. The crane was most often used for the appearance of gods, but certain human characters in tragedy might require it (for example, Bellerophon on his flying horse). In comedy, it was often used to parody tragedy or to ridicule human pretensions. It is difficult to establish the use of the crane prior to about 430, but it may have been available much earlier. Its overuse in the last part of the century (especially by Euripides, who often employed gods to resolve his plots) led to the term *deus ex machina*, god from the machine, to describe any contrived ending.

Although stage properties were not numerous, they were essential elements of the productions. In several plays, characters sacrifice to a god or take refuge at an altar. Some scholars have argued that an altar in the center of the orchestra was used at these times; others have questioned the existence of such an altar and argued that if it did exist, it would have been dedicated to Dionysus so its use as a stage property would have been considered sacrilegious. Arnott suggests that there was a low structure in front of the central doorway that could be used either as altar or tomb. Other essential properties included chariots drawn by horses, biers for dead bodies, statues of various gods, and torches and lamps to indicate night scenes. Furniture was rarely required in tragedy and was restricted to couches for persons too ill or weak to stand. On the other hand, both furniture and other common domestic articles were numerous in comedy. In neither comedy nor tragedy were properties used to create the illusion of reality; they served instead to make some dramatic point.

AUDITORIUM AND AUDIENCE

Thus far, only those elements relating to the acting areas and performers have been considered. But the auditorium and audience were of great importance to a performance. The spectators, standing or seated on the slope of the Acropolis, commanded a view that included not only the performers but also a panoramic landscape that extended to the sea in the distance. The eye was not restricted to the interior of the theatre but rather was situated to see the theatre as part of that larger world whose drama was symbolically played out on the stage.

In Greek theatres, the auditorium and *skene* were always separate architectural units. Between the scene house and the auditorium lay the orchestra and the *parodoi* (or entrances into the orchestra at either side of the auditorium). The *parodoi* were used by spectators as auditorium entrances and exits (although not the only ones). They were also the primary entrances of the chorus, and actors might enter from there as well.

The first *theatron* (or "seeing place," as the auditorium was termed by the Greeks) of the Theatre of Dionysus was the hillside that sloped down from the southeast corner of the Acropolis. Originally, spectators probably stood to watch performances, but some wooden stadium-like seating may have been provided. Around 498 B.C.E., the hillside was apparently regraded to change the slope, and a series of terraces, on which rested wooden benches, were laid out. When the Odeion was built in the 440s, the slope was changed again. The seats seem to have remained temporary, for Aristophanes refers to them as *ikria,* a term normally reserved for wooden benches. Stone seats may have been introduced gradually, but the stone auditorium was not completed until some time between 338 and 326 B.C.E. (A plan of the first stone theatre is shown in Fig. 2.14.)

The completed stone auditorium seated 14,000 to 17,000 persons, so, only a small portion of the population could have attended the theatre at any one time. This may explain the introduction of tickets and an admission fee around the middle of the fifth century (although it is possible that admission was charged from the very beginning). To equalize the opportunity to attend, Pericles established a "theoric fund"

FIG. 2.14

Plan of the Theatre of Dionysus as it probably appeared when completed in the late fourth century B.C.E. The wall supposedly erected in the 440s is indicated by W-W. The square notches at the wall's front edge represent the slots allegedly used to hold the timbers of temporary stage houses. Below the wall is the hall, perhaps used for storage, and touching the wall at the left is the old temple of Dionysus; the new temple and the sacrificial altar are shown in the lower part of the plan. The *skene* and *paraskenia* are shown immediately above W-W. The upper crosswalk of the auditorium incorporated a public road. At the extreme top, a monument is set into the supporting walls of the Acropolis. O indicates the location of the Odeion, built in the 440s. From Dörpfeld, *Griechische Theater* (1896).

FIG. 2.13

Plan showing changes thought to have been made in the Theatre in Dionysus in the 440s. W = the new retaining wall with slots for timbers; OW = original retaining wall; T = stone terrace at orchestra level; H = the hall later built below the retaining wall. Drawing by Douglas Hubbell.

around 450 to provide tickets for the poor. He also may have specified the price to be charged, but there is no definite record of admission costs until the late fourth century, when all seats not reserved by the state were sold at a uniform charge (the nominal sum of two obols). This money seems to have gone for the upkeep of the theatre, which was leased to a manager.

Tickets admitted holders to a section of the theatre rather than to specific seats. Each tribe may have had its own section. The audience certainly included men and boys, but there is considerable scholarly debate as to whether it included women or slaves. Seats were reserved for certain state officials, visiting ambassadors, and persons the state wished to honor along with the priests of Dionysus, other priests, and perhaps for priestesses. Officials were responsible for keeping order and for checking tickets to see that their holders sat in the correct section. Violence in the theatre was punishable by death.

Performances probably lasted all day, since a number of plays were presented in sequence. If so, there must have been much coming and going and considerable eating and drinking in the theatre. The audience expressed its opinions noisily and at times hissed actors off the stage; tradition has it that Aeschylus once had to take refuge on the altar to escape the wrath of the spectators. Some ancient writers damned the audience as debased, but others praised it as discriminating. Probably the spectators represented a cross-section of tastes as well as of society.

Although there are many unresolved questions about the theatre in the fifth century, we can be reasonably sure that it was a vigorous institution, in high repute both with the general populace and with civil and religious authorities. Drama was the most prized form of literature and the theatre the most popular of the arts.

ATHENIAN THEATRE AFTER THE FIFTH CENTURY

Following the Peloponnesian War, economic prosperity returned and the old forms of government continued for a time, but loyalty to the *polis* had been severely undermined and internal dissensions greatly increased thereafter. Sparta's domination of Greece passed to Thebes in 371 and then in 338 to Macedonia, which made the Greek city-states dependencies. Nevertheless, the outward changes in Greek life were not extreme, and Athens actually gained in reputation as a cultural center. Thus, it is usual to consider the first three-quarters of the fourth century a

continuation of the classical age. Records indicate that in quantity artistic activity in the fourth century exceeded that in the fifth. Unfortunately, so few dramatic works have survived that we are unable to judge them fairly.

Theatre had never been confined to Attica, but Athens had always been the most important center. Before the end of the fifth century, plays by Athenian dramatists were in demand elsewhere (Aeschylus had twice visited Sicily and produced plays there, and Euripides had written plays while in Macedonia). After 400 B.C.E. tragic output continued unabated. Many writers who are no longer remembered, such as Theodectes, Astydamas, and Chaeremon, ranked at the forefront of dramatists in their day. But of fourth-century tragedies, only one—*Rhesus*, sometimes attributed to Euripides—has survived. Based on the tenth book of the *Iliad,* it is noteworthy primarily for its simulation of night, during which the entire action occurs.

During the fourth century, writers began to turn to the lesser myths, especially those of a slightly sensational nature, and to employ forensic elements and melodramatic devices with increasing frequency. Some of these changes may have come about because of Euripides' growing influence.

Little is known of the satyr play after the fifth century. It must have declined in popularity, however, for beginning around 341 B.C.E. only one satyr play was produced each year. On the other hand, comedy increased in popularity after the fifth century. Later commentators divided Greek comic writing into three periods: Old, dating from the beginning of the form until the end of the Peloponnesian War in 404; and Middle, from 404 until 336 (when Alexander the Great came to power); followed by the New Comedy of the Hellenistic period. Middle Comedy is essentially a transitional type, moving away from personal invective and political and social satire toward events based on contemporary life and manners or, alternatively, on mythological burlesque. Although we know the names of about fifty writers and have a number of fragments of Middle Comedy, the only complete plays that have survived are Aristophanes' *Assembly Women* (392–391) and *Plutus* (388). Both lack the political satire and the parabasis of Old Comedy, and the role of the chorus has been markedly reduced. Play fragments from this period show that many playwrights stopped writing choruses completely, simply inserting the equivalent of "a chorus goes here" into the play.

During the fourth century many changes were made in the dramatic festivals. At the City Dionysia, contests for the production of old plays were instituted in the last part of the century, a practice seemingly

FIG. 2.15

Scene from a misnamed *phlyax* vase of the fourth century B.C.E. possibly depicting a scene from middle comedy. Note the portico, steps, raised stage, and costumes. From Baumeister, *Denkmaler des Klassichen Altertums* (1889).

never permitted at the Lenaia. The increased popularity of comedy was reflected in the institution of a contest for comic actors at the City Dionysia.

By about 350, professional singer-dancers, who appeared in both comic and tragic choruses, were replacing amateurs used in earlier times, and they were being rehearsed by professional trainers. Acting also grew in importance and came to overshadow playwriting. Probably as a result, around 350 B.C.E. the rules governing tragic performers at the City Dionysia were changed to require each of the three leading actors to appear in one play by each of the competing dramatists. Many actors might rightfully be termed stars, for the fame of Polus, Theodorus, Thettalus, Neoptolemus, Athenodorus, Aristodemus, and others spread throughout the Greek world.

It is ironic that the Theatre of Dionysus was not given its permanent stone form until about 325 B.C.E., by which time the Athenian theatre was already losing its privileged position. This permanent structure is important, nevertheless, since its archeological remains have served as the primary basis for most conjectures about theatre architecture in the fifth century. It has usually been assumed that the

FIG. 2.16

The remains of the Hellenistic theatre at Epidaurus. This is the best preserved of all the ancient Greek theatres. The stage house at left is a temporary structure erected for performances at a modern festival. Courtesy Greek Embassy.

stone theatre was merely a more permanent version of earlier temporary structures, but this assumption is questioned by many archeologists. After 300 B.C.E., Athens was no longer in the forefront of developments, and its theatre building eventually came to seem outmoded.

LOOKING AT THEATRE HISTORY

One of the primary ways of approaching the Greek theatre is through archeology, the systematic study of material remains such as architecture, inscriptions, sculpture, vase painting, and other forms of decorative art. About the contributions of archeology to our knowledge of ancient civilizations, it has been said: "The recovery of these long-forgotten episodes in human history has been an astonishing performance—as remarkable . . . as . . . reaching the moon. As a result . . . our own generation is aware of more aspects of the distant past than were dreamed of by our great-grandfathers."

Serious on-site excavations began in Greece around 1870, but W. Dörpfeld did not begin the first extensive study of the Theatre of Dionysus until 1886. Since that time, more than 167 other Greek theatres have been identified and many of them have been excavated. These excavations have revealed much that was previously unknown, especially about the dimensions and layout of theatres. Nevertheless, they still do not permit us to describe the precise appearance of the *skene* (illustrations printed in books are conjectural reconstructions), since many pieces are irrevocably lost because the buildings in later periods became sources of stone for other projects and what remains is usually broken and scattered. That most of the buildings were remodeled many times has created great problems for those seeking to date the successive versions. Despite these drawbacks, archeology provides the most concrete evidence we have about the theatre structures of ancient Greece. But, if they have told us much, archeologists have not completed their work, and many sites have scarcely been touched.

The oldest surviving manuscripts of Greek plays date from around the tenth century, C.E., some 1500 years after they were first performed. Since printing did not exist during this time span, copies of plays had to be made by hand, and therefore the possibility of textual errors creeping in was magnified. Nevertheless, the scripts offer us our readiest access to the cultural and theatrical conditions out of which they came. But these scripts, like other kinds of evidence, are subject to varying interpretations. Certainly performances embodied a male perspective, for example, since the plays were written, selected, staged, and acted by men. Yet the existing plays feature numerous choruses of women and many feature strong female characters. Because these characters often seem victims of their own powerlessness and appear to be governed, especially in the comedies, by sexual desire, some critics have seen these plays as rationalizations by the male-dominated culture for keeping women segregated and cloistered. Other critics, however, have seen in these same plays an attempt by male authors to force their male audiences to examine and call into question this segregation and cloistering of Athenian women.

By far the majority of written references to Greek theatre date from several hundred years after the events they report. The writers seldom mention their sources of evidence, and thus we do not know what credence to give them. In the absence of material nearer in time to the events, however, historians have used the accounts and have been grateful to have them. Overall, historical treatment of the Greek theatre is something like assembling a jigsaw puzzle of which many pieces are missing: historians arrange what they have and imagine (with the aid of the remaining evidence and logic) what has been lost. As a result, although the broad outlines of Greek theatre history are reasonably clear, many of the details remain open to doubt.

One good example of the type of written evidence available to historians is *The Deipnosophists,* compiled by Athenaeus in Egypt around 200 C.E. In the following passage, he writes about events in Greece some 600 years earlier. Much of what he says is consistent with other reports, and his testimony has been repeated so often that it has been accorded the status of fact, but its reliability cannot be firmly established. It is amusing (and cautionary) to note, however, that his final statement is almost never quoted, although it is difficult to see why Chamaeleon should be considered an unreliable witness on this point if he is to be believed on others.

Aeschylus was not only the inventor of becoming and dignified dress, which the hierophants and torchbearers of the sacred festivals imitated; but he also invented many figures in dancing, and taught them to the dancers of the chorus. And Chamaeleon states that he first arranged the choruses, not using the ordinary dancing-masters, but himself arranging the figures of the dancers for the chorus; and altogether that he took the whole arrangement of his tragedies on himself. And he himself acted in his own plays very fairly. . . . But Aeschylus was often drunk when he wrote his tragedies, if we may trust Chamaeleon: and accordingly Sophocles reproached him, saying, that even when he did what was right he did not know that he was doing so.

Athenaeus, *The Deipnosophists, or Banquet of the Learned*, trans. C. D. Yonge, 3 vols. (London: H. G. Bohn, 1854), bk. I, ch. 39.

3
Hellenistic and Roman Theatre

During the Hellenistic period (336–*c.* 31 B.C.E.) Greek theatre was introduced to cultures throughout the eastern Mediterranean and as far east as India. During the later years of the Roman Republic (509–27 B.C.E.) and especially during the Roman Empire (27 B.C.E.–476 C.E.), theatre spread to the western Mediterranean and as far north as England.

THE HELLENISTIC THEATRE

Between 336 B.C.E. and his death in 323, Alexander the Great, ruler of mainland Greece, conquered the Persian Empire and extended his realm into present-day India and Egypt, creating the first great empire to be launched from Europe. Wherever he went he built new cities and promoted Greek culture and learning. As a result, the entire eastern Mediterranean was "Hellenized." (A Greek theatre still exists as far east as Ai Khanoum in central Afghanistan.) Athens continued to be a major cultural center, even after the loss of its democracy in 322 B.C.E., but its pre-eminence was challenged in the third century by Pergamum (in Asia Minor) and especially by Alexandria (in Egypt), which became the literary capital of the Greek world because of its library and institute for literary research.

Alexander's empire disintegrated after his death, but major parts were maintained by his followers. Mainland Greece regained a precarious independence, but it was so lacking in unity that it could put up no effective resistance to Rome and became a Roman province in 146 B.C.E. Egypt, which had been ruled by the descendants of Alexander's general, Ptolemy, since 305 B.C.E., fell to the Romans with the defeat of Cleopatra's forces in 31 B.C.E. bringing to an end the last of the Hellenistic states.

DRAMATIC THEORY

During the fourth century, Greek thought became increasingly secularized. Religious worship and festivals continued, but belief in their efficacy was seriously undermined by the intellectual scrutiny to which the gods and myths were subjected during this great age of Greek philosophy, epitomized above all by the work of Plato (*c.* 427–347) and Aristotle (384–322). During this time philosophers inquired into every aspect of Greek life, including the theatre. Plato argued for censorship and strict state control over drama, whose powerful influence he feared. Aristotle referred to the theatre in several of his works, but his major ideas are set forth in the *Poetics* (*c.* 335–323), the first systematic treatise on drama. In addition to its discussion of

31

tragedy, the *Poetics* contains in its early chapters the oldest surviving history of dramatic forms. While preparing this work, Aristotle is said to have compiled a record of the plays and winners at all the festivals, a major source of information for subsequent Greek and Roman historians; but only fragments of his list now survive.

Aristotle's influence has been especially great on critical theory, for his *Poetics* has been crucial in practically all discussions of tragedy since the sixteenth century, when it first became widely known. Because many of Aristotle's ideas are stated cryptically, however, the *Poetics* has been interpreted variously. It must be read with great care if it is to be helpful. Aristotle states in the *Poetics* that every drama has six parts: plot, character, thought, diction, music, and spectacle. He discusses unity of action, probability, the requirements of plot, characteristics of the tragic hero, problems of diction, and many other topics. His conclusions continue to be informative and controversial.

Three centuries later, the Roman poet, Horace (65–8 B.C.E.), wrote *The Art of Poetry* (*c.* 19 B.C.E.) in which he gave advice on subject matter, characterization, language, and style for drama. He insists that plays must be written in five acts and that their goal is to teach and to please. He especially encouraged writers to adhere to a purity of form and to revise and polish their works to ensure unity, grace, and decorum. In the Renaissance, his work was arguably even more influential than that of Aristotle.

NEW COMEDY

Hellenistic writers favored a form of domestic, middle-class comedy that is commonly identified as New Comedy. Unlike Old Comedy, New Comedy ignored political issues and favored a more generalized concern for love, financial worries, and familial or societal relationships. New Comedy eventually became repetitious both in terms of situation and dramatic devices (especially concealed identity, coincidence, and recognition). Many plays were essentially character studies, and others were based on myths. But a typical plot revolved around a young man who, against the strong opposition of his father, seeks to marry a girl, frequently a slave about to be forced into prostitution; after many comically unsuccessful attempts to circumvent the father's wrath, the son achieves his goal when it is discovered that the girl is the long-lost daughter of some wealthy Athenian. The entire action, then, rests on a misunderstanding, which, when cleared up, resolves the conflict. But in recent years some critics have come to view these plays as works that questioned

FIG. 3.1
Terracotta statuette of an old woman from New Comedy. Courtesy British Museum.

and then reaffirmed certain societal conventions during a period when values and mores were being challenged. Thus, they treat the plays as reflections of prevailing ideology rather than merely frivolous, diversionary entertainment.

Several plays of Euripides, most notably *Ion, Helen, Iphigenia at Tauris,* and *Alcestis* (staged in place of a satyr play in 438), are tragicomic and make use of such plot devices as long-lost children and scenes of recognition. These were very popular and may well have set the pattern for the structure of New Comedy, with a prologue followed by a series of episodes separated by choral passages that usually had little connection with the incidents. In many New Comedies the chorus appeared onstage only during the interludes between episodes. New Comedy was also mixed in tone, for in many plays pathetic and moral elements injected a serious note. Other plays, however, were primarily farcical. The language reflected everyday usage but was not extremely colloquial, for dialogue was still cast in verse.

Characters may have gradually become conventionalized into a restricted number of types. Pollux (a Greek lexicographer of the second century C.E.) lists the common characters in New Comedy as: nine types of old men, four of young men, seven of slaves, five of young women, and various soldiers, parasites, and others. Pollux differentiates each subtype within

FIG. 3.2
Statuette of a slave from New Comedy. From Robert, *Die Masken der Neueren Attischen Komoedie* (1911).

these broad groupings by some distinctive quality in both mask and costume.

Although the names of sixty-four writers of New Comedy are known and about 1400 plays of this type were probably produced, only one complete work—*Dyskolos* (*The Grouch*) by Menander—has survived, and it was not rediscovered until 1957. Menander (342–291 B.C.E.), who wrote more than one hundred plays after 321, is by far the most important author of New Comedy. In addition to *The Grouch,* a comedy of character about an irascible old man, Menander's works are now known from lengthy fragments of *The Arbitration, The Girl from Samos,* and *The Shorn Girl,* and lesser fragments of about eighty-five other plays. Fragments continue to be discovered. In Rome, where his plays were frequently adapted, Menander's reputation was higher than that of any Greek author except Homer.

After the third century B.C.E., comedy began to decline, just as tragedy had a century earlier. New Comedy was the last vital expression of Greek drama.

ACTORS AND ACTING

Alexander is said to have assembled more than 3000 performers from across the Greek world for a victory festival, and thereafter the occasions on which plays might be presented were numerous, especially since rulers began to encourage worship of themselves as gods and to establish festivals in their own honor or for primarily secular purposes. Consequently, plays were no longer performed exclusively at Dionysian festivals.

The rapid expansion in the number of festivals created a demand for qualified performers, and perhaps as a result the theatre of the Hellenistic period became almost totally professional. By 300 well-known actors were touring everywhere. Actors had also gained such ascendancy over dramatists that they changed texts to suit their talents. Acting competitions were no longer restricted to performances in plays but could involve the performance of scenes from plays or even just speeches from them. Actors were judged on the elaborate displays of vocal virtuosity and the ability to convey emotion.

During this period theatre professionals formed a guild, usually referred to as the Artists of Dionysus. Although the date of its formation is uncertain, it was clearly in existence by 277 B.C.E., for it was given official sanction in a decree of that year. During the first century C.E., the Roman emperor Claudius (reigned 41–54 C.E.) addressed a decree to the World Artists of Dionysus, and by the time of the emperor Hadrian (reigned 117–138 C.E.) the world headquarters was located in Rome.

The Artists of Dionysus included among its members poets (dramatic, epic, and lyric), actors, chorus members, trainers, musicians, and costumers—all the personnel needed to produce plays and to give recitations at festivals. Mime performers and other popular

FIG. 3.3
A bas-relief from Naples of a scene from New Comedy: two old men at the left, the flute player at center, and a youth and slave at the right. From Robert, *Die Masken der Neueren Attischen Komoedie* (1911).

entertainers were never admitted to this guild (although eventually they had their own).

As the name of the guild suggests, the performers retained their connection with Dionysus, even though they produced plays and acted at many non-Dionysian festivals. When planning a festival, a city apparently negotiated a contract with the nearest branch of the guild. The obligations of each party were clearly specified in the agreements. Because of the importance of the festivals and because following the death of Alexander the Hellenic world had broken up into a number of states, international agreements were reached under which the safety of the guild's members was guaranteed even in times of war.

COSTUMES

Tragic costumes and masks changed considerably after the fifth century. Although the progressive changes cannot be dated, it is reasonably clear that by the first century B.C.E. a tragic actor wore a padded costume, thick-soled boots (*kothornoi*), and a high headdress (*onkos*), all intended to increase the actor's apparent size. The facial features of the masks were also enlarged and exaggerated. In other words, tragic actors were now made larger than life and their overall appearance was distorted and conventionalized. In New

Comedy, costume, although somewhat conventionalized, was based on the dress of ordinary life. The character types of comedy apparently were considerably more extensive than those of tragedy. Most comic masks probably were realistic, but some, such as those for slaves and certain old men and ridiculous characters, were still caricatured. Hair color was also conventionalized. Most slaves, for example, had red hair, while courtesans usually had yellow.

THEATRE ARCHITECTURE

Theatre architecture also underwent considerable change in the Hellenistic period. Between the middle of the fourth century and the first century B.C.E., a theatre structure quite unlike that of the Theatre of Dionysus evolved. Important examples were built at Priene, Oropus, Ephesus, Delos, Epidaurus, Oeniadae, Sicyon, Pergamum, Corinth, and Alexandria. Of the 167 known Greek theatres, the vast majority are of the Hellenistic type.

Although the basic features of the Hellenistic theatre are reasonably well established, the date and place of origin are disputed. Some scholars argue that drastic deviations from the Athenian plan were made as early as the fourth century, but others date them from the second century B.C.E. The evidence is hopelessly confused, primarily because archeologists cannot

FIG. 3.4
Marble relief sculpture, often said to represent Menander with three masks: in his hand, the mask of a youth; on the table, masks of a young woman and a man. First–second century C.E. copy of a third century B.C.E. work. Courtesy the Art Museum, Princeton University.

FIG. 3.5
The Hellenistic theatre at Eretria. The upper view shows an early phase in the stage building's evolution, while the lower shows fully developed *thyromata*. From Fiechter, *Antike Griechische Theaterbauten*. Courtesy Verlag W. Kohlhammer GmbH, Stuttgart and Dr. Charlotte Fiechter.

agree on the dates when the original structures were built or when they underwent the various remodelings to which all were subjected. The details of this controversy are unimportant here; it is sufficient to note that the basic structural features of the Hellenistic theatre may have been present as early as 300 B.C.E. or may have taken shape over a period of 150 years. Almost all scholars agree that the Hellenistic theatre building was fully developed by 150 B.C.E.

Probably the most important Hellenistic innovation was the high raised stage. Varying from 8 to 13 feet in height, it was sometimes as long as 140 feet, although it was only from $6\frac{1}{2}$ to 14 feet deep. Since *paraskenia* (or side wings of the scene house) were eliminated, this long, narrow platform was open at both ends. In some theatres, ramps parallel to the *parodoi* led up to the stage; in others, steps to the orchestra were provided at the ends of the stage; in still others, the stage could be entered only from the scene house. The front edge of the stage was supported by the *proskenion* (or façade of the lower story), while the *episkenion* (or façade of the second story) rose at the back of the raised stage. In some theatres, the *proskenion* overlapped the outer rim of the orchestra circle by a few feet, although in others the full circle of the orchestra remained entirely

visible. The auditoriums underwent no significant changes, but they varied widely in seating capacity, ranging from 3000 at Oropus to 24,000 at Ephesus.

The alterations in the *skene* raise many questions about staging. Was the orchestra used by all performers when old plays requiring a large chorus were revived, and was the raised stage reserved for those newer plays in which the chorus was small or incidental? Did the actors use the stage and the chorus the orchestra? Was the upper stage at first used only for gods and special scenes and only later transformed into the usual acting area for all scenes? Was the orchestra used only for nondramatic performances (such as dithyrambic choruses)? Was the orchestra merely a vestigial structural feature that no longer served any necessary function? Each of these questions has received both affirmative and negative answers, none of which can be accepted with certainty. What is certain is that these buildings were multipurpose structures. They represented too large an investment to be used only for an occasional theatrical performance and served as general meeting places for many kinds of civic activities.

FIG. 3.6
Hellenistic Greece and the Near East.

Many problems also arise in relation to scenic practices. For example, in the early Hellenistic theatre the *proskenion* was composed of pillars spaced several feet apart; often these pillars were notched so as to hold *pinakes* (painted panels) inserted from the rear. In many theatres dating from later than the second century B.C.E., however, the pillars are no longer notched. On this basis, some historians have argued that as long as performances occurred in the orchestra a scenic background was provided; whereas later, when all action was transferred to the stage, the *proskenion* became merely an open colonnade, since *pinakes* were no longer needed at the orchestra level.

As time passed, the façade of the second story also underwent a number of changes. During the second century B.C.E., the *episkenion,* which originally had been fitted with from one to three doors, was converted into a series of sizable openings (or *thyromata*) varying in number from one to seven. These *thyromata,* averaging about 10 to 12 feet in width and extending upward as high as the roof would permit, were separated from each other by narrow upright supports. Thus, on the upper level there was now a long shallow forestage backed by a rear stage equally as deep or deeper.

Scholars have assumed that *thyromata* were created to permit greater scenic illusion, and have suggested that each opening served as a miniature proscenium arch behind which individual settings could be erected. But this theory (as well as all others about the *thyromata*) is entirely conjectural.

Vitruvius, writing in the first century B.C.E., describes the *episkenion* as providing spaces for *periaktoi*. Possibly *periaktoi* were set up in *thyromata*. Vitruvius also says that there were three kinds of backgrounds: one each for tragedy, comedy, and satyr plays. Though some historians have interpreted this passage to mean that illusionistic scenery was used, others have argued that it merely suggests some type of conventionalized painting on the *periaktoi*.

Although the Greek theatre continued until after 500 C.E., its vitality declined rapidly after the first century B.C.E. Beginning in the second century B.C.E., the Romans gradually gained power over all the eastern Mediterranean and, though Greek ideals persisted, Roman standards eventually altered them. After the first century C.E., most of the Greek theatres were remodeled to conform more nearly to the Roman ideal of theatre architecture. These remodeled structures are usually called Greco-Roman, since

FIG. 3.7

Reconstruction of the Hellenistic theatre at Ephesus. Note the *thyromata* treated as though each was a miniature proscenium stage. From Frickenhaus, *Die Altgriechische Bühne* (1917).

FIG. 3.8
The "golden courtesan" of New Comedy. From Robert, *Die Masken der Neueren Attischen Komoedie* (1911).

they have some features characteristic of each type. Many purely Roman theatres were also erected in Greek territories.

The theatre in Athens was not immune to these changes, although it long resisted them. The Theatre of Dionysus retained its classical form until sometime between the third and first centuries B.C.E., when it was remodeled along more fashionable Hellenistic lines. Other extensive changes were made in the first century C.E., when the stage was extended forward over part of the orchestra to make it conform more nearly to the Roman ideal. After this time, gladiatorial contests were sometimes staged in the orchestra (which was by then fenced in with a stone barricade); about the fourth century C.E. the orchestra was sealed so that water spectacles could be given in it.

It is not clear when the Athenian dramatic contests ceased. A decline in personal wealth among Athenians led (sometime between 317 and 307) to the discontinuance of the practice of appointing *choregoi*, a step that was also made practical by the declining use of choruses in plays. After this time an elected official, the *agonothetes*, was given a state appropriation out of which to finance all theatrical productions. The records of the City Dionysia continue until the first century C.E., while those of the Lenaia can be traced only until about 150 B.C.E. Nevertheless, the contests may have gone on for some time after the records stop. The Theatre of Dionysus was used for various kinds of spectacles until at least the fourth century C.E. and perhaps longer. It had a truly remarkable history of nearly 1000 years of continuous use.

GREEK MIMES

Greece had numerous forms of popular entertainment that, while they left fewer records, were certainly a significant part of the lives of the average person in the Hellenistic age.

Many of these were grouped under the heading of "mime," a term applied indiscriminately both to scripts and performers. Mime was a variety entertainment that could include short playlets, mimetic dance, imitations of animals and birds, singing, acrobatics, juggling, and more. Small troupes of mimes may have performed at banquets, at market fairs (on temporary stages), and on other occasions as early as the fifth century B.C.E. Thus, mimes were probably the first professional entertainers. As far as we can determine, mimes were the first theatrical performers to include women among their ranks and the first to perform regularly without masks, though some mime forms certainly did employ masks.

Short mime playlets seem to have originated in Megara in the sixth century B.C.E. The Greek colonies of southern Italy and Sicily favored mime during the fifth century, but not until Hellenistic times did it flourish throughout the eastern Mediterranean. Mime "plays" ranged from improvised skits, to sung dialogues, to danced stories. After 300 B.C.E., mime performers increasingly appeared at festivals, although they were never admitted to membership in the Artists of Dionysus.

In southern Italy, mimes were called *phlyakes*. Rhinthon, who lived at Tarentum in the first half of the third century B.C.E., is said to have formalized this type. Of the thirty-eight plays attributed to him, most are burlesques of tragedy, but only a few fragments survive. Although mimes were popular throughout the Hellenic world, *phlyakes* have received the most attention because a series of vases from southern Italy were once thought to depict scenes from this form. These vases have now been redated to 400–325 B.C.E., about a century before any known *phlyax* plays were written, but they are still generally called *phlyax* vases, even though most likely they depict scenes from Middle Comedy. The characters wear short tunics over padded tights and phallus. The subjects range from mythological burlesque (the adventures of Heracles is a favorite) to daily life. Lovemaking, gluttony, beatings, thievery, and trickery are popular motifs.

The vases show a raised platform varying in height and resting on posts or decorative columns, between which are draperies or painted panels. Steps, often being used by actors, lead up from the ground level to the stage. The façade at the back of the stage varies: sometimes it is composed of a portico and door; other times there are columns and decorative motifs; sometimes there is a window or gallery on an upper level. Trees, altars, thrones, chests, and tables appear among the properties. Some scholars have interpreted the paintings as evidence that performers used a temporary stage that could be erected as needed by traveling troupes; others have suggested that the vases show the stages of permanent theatres depicted in a simplified manner because of the limited space available to the painters. (See Fig. 2.17.)

Regardless of how the vases are interpreted, it is clear that the theatre flourished in southern Italy. It was there, in the third century B.C.E., that the Romans first encountered Greek culture. After this time historical interest shifts to Rome, where Greek forms and practices were adopted and transformed, though it should not be forgotten that the Greek theatre continued throughout the Roman era.

THE ROMAN THEATRE

According to tradition, Rome was founded in 753 B.C.E. (about the time the Greeks were colonizing southern Italy and Sicily). It remained an insignificant town under the domination of neighboring Etruria, the home of several of its early rulers, until it expelled its last Etruscan king and founded a republic in 509 B.C.E. (just as Athens was becoming a democracy). During the fourth century, Rome began to expand and by 265 controlled the entire Italian peninsula, including the Etruscan areas to the north and the Greek territories to the south. Next, following the first Punic War with Carthage (264–241), Rome acquired Sicily. As a result of its expansion between 270 and 240, Rome took over several Greek territories in which the theatre had long flourished. By 146 B.C.E., Rome had conquered Greece and thereafter it gradually absorbed the entire Hellenic world.

Rome was heavily influenced by Greek culture. From the third century onward, Greek tutors were in demand in Rome, and many Romans went to study in Greece. Much Roman art and literature was "borrowed" from Greek models. By 240 B.C.E., a sufficiently large number of Romans were familiar enough with Greek art and theatre that regular drama (either translations or imitations of Greek plays) could be introduced into Roman festivals. Consequently, the year 240 B.C.E. is often said to mark the beginning of Roman theatre. But while this date may establish when regular Roman drama began, it does not mark the beginning of Rome's theatrical activity, which can be traced back over a century earlier.

ETRUSCAN AND OSCAN ANTECEDENTS

The Roman historian Livy (59 B.C.E.–17 C.E.), dates the first theatrical performances in Rome to 364 B.C.E. when performers called *ister* were imported from Etruria in an effort to appease the gods while plague was ravishing the city. Rome derived its term for actors, *histriones,* from these *ister.* The Roman poet Horace (65–8 B.C.E.), meanwhile, says that Latin drama originated even earlier, in the improvised, abusive, and often obscene dialogues exchanged in verse between masked clowns at harvest festivals and wedding celebrations. These were the Fescennine Verses, thought to have originated in Fescennium, a town on the Etruscan border. Both may be right as Livy seems to equate drama with serious performance while Horace seems to be thinking of comedy.

FIG. 3.9

Etruscan musician playing the double flute. From the tomb of the Leopards, Tarquinii. From *Jahrbuch des Deutschen Archäologischen Instituts,* 31 (1916).

FIG. 3.10

Stands for audiences at an Etruscan entertainment. Wall painting from a tomb at Corneto. From *Jahrbuch des Deutschen Archäologischen Instituts,* 31 (1916).

Rome certainly inherited from the Etruscans many features of its festivals, which were the principal occasions on which theatrical performances were given. It was, in fact, an Etruscan ruler of Rome, the elder Tarquin (616–579 B.C.E.), who established the *ludi Romani,* Rome's most important festival and the one at which Greek drama was first introduced. The Etruscans belief that the religious portions of their festivals must be performed precisely and without error, was adopted by the Romans and often led them to repeat entire festivals when mistakes were made. But the Romans also adopted the Etruscan policy of holding festivals in conjunction with market fairs to which people came from faraway places, and they included acrobatics, juggling, and dancing (along with prizefighting, chariot racing, and other forms of competitive sports), practically all of which seems to have been accompanied by music, and all of which the Romans adopted.

In addition to Etruria, southern Italy contributed to Rome's early theatre. The primary influence came from the Atellan farce, which takes its name from the Oscan town of Atella, near what is now Naples. Atellan farce was probably imported to Rome during the first half of the third century, for by 275 B.C.E. the Romans had become undisputed masters of the Oscan region. Little is known of the early Atellan farce except that is seems to have featured stock characters, each with their own fixed costume and mask, doing short, improvised stories based on domestic situations or mythological burlesque. Many scholars argue that it was another form of Greek mime, much like the *phlyakes.*

If we are to understand Roman theatre, then, it is essential to recognize from the outset that drama in the Greek sense played only a small role in it, since it was always dominated by variety entertainment more closely related to the Greek mimes. Acrobats, trained animals, jugglers, dancers, actors doing dramatic skits and short farces, all kinds of musicians, and a variety of athletic events were all flourishing when regular drama based on Greek models was added to this entertainment mix.

THE ROMAN CONTEXT

As a people, the Romans are noted for adopting the ideas and practices of others. But they were neither indiscriminate nor unintelligent borrowers, for of all the people who came into contact with the Greeks,

FIG. 3.11

The Italian peninsula *c.* 500 B.C.E. before Rome began to expand.

the Romans embraced Greek artistic forms most fully. Nevertheless, Romans should not be viewed as mere extensions of the Greeks, for their own character made them reject much that was distinctively Greek.

The Romans had little of the philosophical bent so characteristic of the Greeks. A practical people, they were for the most part uninterested in theoretical questions. Though they were among the greatest engineers, military tacticians, and administrators the world has known, they speculated little about these subjects. They were content to discover how things worked without asking why. These traits also affected their art, which tended to be grandiose, sentimental, or diversionary rather than, as with the Greeks, a serious exploration of the human condition.

Rome's history can best be understood by dividing it into two phases: the republic (509–27 B.C.E.) and the empire (27 B.C.E.–c. 476 C.E.). It was the "republican virtues"—discipline, economy, endurance, military precision, and loyalty to family and state—that made it possible for Rome to become a world power. The Romans were noted for

their incorruptibility, their sense of duty to the republic, and their faith in law and order.

By the first century B.C.E., Rome ruled a vast territory that poured wealth into the capitol. Roman citizens were receiving grain free of charge, the army had become professionalized, and the government was bureaucratized. In 27 B.C.E., power passed from representative bodies to the emperor. Thereafter, the virtues that had built Rome lessened. The basic problem became how to maintain and administer Rome's farflung territories. That the empire endured so long is a testament to the Roman genius for organization.

Similar elements of change can be noted in the theatre. Under the republic, regular drama prospered for a time: tragedy's appeal probably lay in its echo of republican sentiments about virtue, honor, and loyalty, whereas comedy's was in the lighthearted treatment of domestic complications that were resolved happily. Neither form seems to have reflected any profound philosophical concerns or to have seriously questioned Roman values. Under the empire, regular drama was largely abandoned in favor of variety

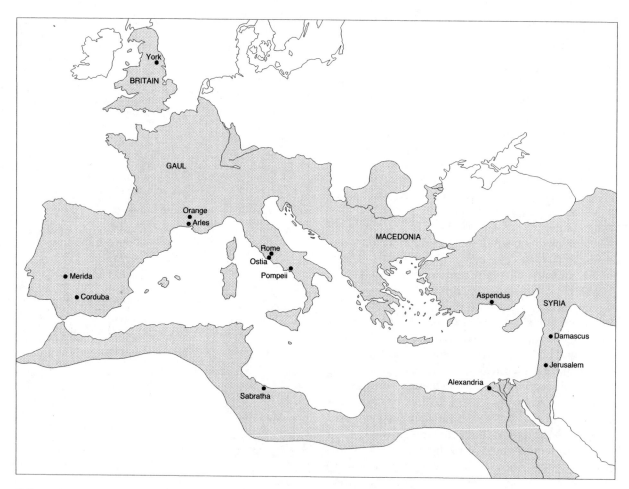

FIG. 3.12
The Roman Empire at its height.

entertainment; the theatre became increasingly diversionary, with novelties of all kinds demanded and offered—new types of entertainments, ever-increasing lavishness and elaborateness of spectacle, thrills of all sorts (nudity, sex, violence, and bloodshed among them).

Nevertheless, it should not be forgotten that the theatre in Rome almost always was associated with festivals, most of them religious, especially during the republic. Thus, theatrical offerings (regardless of content) were long thought to be pleasing to (or capable of propitiating) the gods. Not only were Roman counterparts of the Greek gods worshiped, but household spirits and animistic forces were venerated as well; as Rome expanded, new gods were continually added to the list. The Romans seem to have placed as much or more emphasis on the form as on the substance of religious ceremonies. Perhaps this explains why at the festivals honoring the gods the content of theatrical entertainments mattered less than the fact that the entertainments were offered.

Overall, it seems clear that Roman drama did not reach a level comparable to that of fifth-century Greece. But it is equally true that in Rome the theatre was far more highly developed, varied, and extensive than in any earlier culture.

ROMAN FESTIVALS

Most state-sponsored theatrical performances in republican Rome were given at official festivals or games called *ludi*. The oldest of the festivals was the *ludi Romani*, given each September. Established in the sixth century, it included various types of performance by 364 B.C.E., and regular comedy and tragedy beginning in 240. Eventually five additional festivals granted theatrical entertainments a major role: the *ludi Florales, ludi Megalenses,* and *ludi Ceriales,* all held in April/May; the *ludi Apollinares,* held in July; and the *ludi plebeii,* held in November. The spring festivals honored goddesses, the summer festival, Apollo, and the fall festivals, Jupiter; none of them honored Dionysus or Bacchus, his Roman counterpart. A number of other "extraordinary," "honorary," or "donated" festivals (*munera*) were given on special occasions (such as after major victories in war, at the dedication of public buildings or state funerals), and many of these included theatrical performances. In addition to the state and "donated" festivals, both under the republic and the empire, there probably were privately arranged indoor performances and even some public performances given for paying audiences by traveling troupes.

DRAMA UNDER THE ROMAN REPUBLIC

Of the more than 900 years over which the history of Roman theatre extends, only about 200 are of much importance for drama because it was during this time that most of the plays intended for performance were written.

Roman literature is usually said to have begun with Livius Andronicus (*fl.* 240–204 B.C.E.), for the comedies and tragedies that he wrote, translated, or adapted were the first important literary works in Latin. Little is known of Andronicus. Apparently he was from Tarentum (located in the Greek territories of southern Italy). The first native-born dramatist was Gnaeus Naevius (*c.* 270–*c.* 201 B.C.E.), who began writing about 235. He excelled at comedy, although like Andronicus, who was best at tragedy, he wrote both types. Naevius did much to naturalize the drama by introducing many Roman allusions into the Greek originals and by writing plays on Roman stories. By the time Andronicus and Naevius died, drama was well established in Rome. Since each of their successors tended to specialize in a single form, the development of tragedy and comedy followed separate paths thereafter. By this time also, a guild of writers (*collegium poetarum*) seems to have been established.

The names of many comic writers have come down to us. Two of these—Plautus and Terence—are of principal interest because they are the authors of the only surviving Roman comedies. Titus Maccius Plautus (*c.* 254–*c.* 184 B.C.E.) was the first important successor to Livius Andronicus and Naevius in comedy. His popularity was so great that after his death as many as 130 plays came to be attributed to him. In seeking to resolve the question of authorship, the Roman scholar Varro (116–27 B.C.E.) divided the plays into those certainly by Plautus, those possibly by Plautus, and those clearly not by Plautus. In the first group he placed twenty-one works, twenty of which have survived and are still credited to Plautus, among them: *The Comedy of Asses, The Merchant, The Braggart Warrior, The Casket, Pot of Gold, Amphitryon, The Menaechmi, The Haunted House,* and *The Rope.* The twenty-first play, *Vidularia,* survives only in fragments. (*Querolus* was once credited to Plautus but is now thought to be a fifth-century C.E. adaptation of *Pot of Gold.*) Few of these plays can be dated with certainty, although all were probably written between 205 and 184. Plautus was much admired for his Latin dialogue, his varied poetic meters, and his witty jokes. In his plays, about two-thirds of the lines were accompanied by music. Although his plays show a wide range of comic powers, he is best known for his farce.

FIG. 3.13
Wall painting from the Casa di Casca in Herculaneum showing a comic scene. At left a priestess and in the background an altar. First century C.E. From Baumeister, *Denkmaler des Klassischen Altertums* (1889).

All of Plautus' plays are thought to be adaptations of Greek plays, mostly those of Menander. It was long thought that he departed little from the structure of the originals, making only minor changes to Romanize the stories. A lengthy fragment of Menander's *The Double Deceiver,* on which Plautus based *The Two Bacchides,* has been discovered, however, permitting direct comparison between Plautus' source and his adaptation, and it is clear that Plautus' changes were significant. As a result, critics have come to acknowledge that Plautus was a creative adapter rather than merely a translator.

Publius Terentius Afer (195 or 185–159 B.C.E.) is said to have been born in Carthage, brought to Rome as a slave when a boy, educated, and freed. He wrote six plays, all of which have survived: *Andria* (166), *Mother-in-Law* (165), *Self-Tormentor* (163), *Eunuch* (161), *Phormio* (161), and *The Brothers* (160). Terence's plots are more complex than those of his predecessors, for he adapted and combined in a single play more than one Greek original, a practice for which he was denounced. Since he strove for consistency, he avoided inserting Roman allusions into the Greek plots upon which he drew. His language, that of everyday polite conversation, lacks the great metrical variety found in Plautus' plays but half the lines were still accompanied by music. As with the plays of Plautus, all of the action takes place in the street, with the result that scenes that logically would occur inside are placed out of doors. Eavesdropping is common and many complications turn on overheard conversations. His sympathetic treatment of characters moves his plays toward romantic or sentimental comedy.

Of the other comic writers, the most important was Caecilius Statius (c. 219–168 B.C.E.), the principal dramatist in the years between Plautus and Terence and considered by many Roman critics the greatest of all comic authors. Unfortunately, none of his plays survives. Sextus Turpilius (d. 103 B.C.E.) is the last known writer of comedy based on Greek originals. Comedy ceased to be a vital form before the advent of the Roman Empire. Though the plays were often revived, few new comedies were written. The works of Plautus and Terence survived beyond the fall of Rome because they were valued as models of spoken Latin. Since later critics turned to them as the foremost examples of comic drama, they exerted enormous influence on Renaissance comedy.

Although Roman tragedy is treated condescendingly today, it was highly regarded by critics and audiences of the time. Nevertheless, the names of only three tragic writers between 200 and 75 B.C.E. are known: Quintus Ennius (239–169 B.C.E.), Marcus Pacuvius (c. 220–c. 130 B.C.E.), and Lucius Accius (170–c. 86 B.C.E.). Judging from fragments, titles, and contemporary comments, however, the majority of

FIG. 3.14
A bas-relief allegedly showing a scene from a Roman comedy. From Dörpfeld, *Griechische Theater* (1896).

the plays were adapted from Greek originals. Although tragedy was regularly performed into the Christian era, the last tragedy clearly written with production in mind was *Thyestes* by Varius Rufus, presented in 29 B.C.E. Closet dramas, such as Ovid's (43 B.C.E.–*c.* 17 C.E.) *Medea,* were written, but apparently only for recitation at banquets.

DRAMA UNDER THE ROMAN EMPIRE

By the time Rome ceased to be a republic in 27 B.C.E., regular drama had already declined markedly and the minor forms had become dominant.

The only Roman tragedies, however, are from the early year of the Empire. Of these, all but one are by Lucius Annaeus Seneca (5 or 4 B.C.E.–65 C.E.). Born in Spain and educated in Rome, Seneca was famous for his works on rhetoric and philosophy and became one of the most influential men in Rome after his pupil Nero was named emperor in 54 C.E. Nero fancied himself a great actor and singer and actually competed for prizes. It is not known, however, if Seneca's plays were intended for his use. Seneca fell out of favor and committed suicide in 65 C.E.

Nine of Seneca's plays survive: *The Trojan Women, Medea, Oedipus, Phaedra, Thyestes, Hercules on Oeta, The Mad Hercules, The Phoenician Women,* and *Agamemnon.* All are adapted from Greek originals. *Octavia,* sometimes mistakenly attributed to Seneca, is the sole surviving example of *fabula praetexta,* or tragedy on Roman themes. It deals with the death of Nero's wife, and in it Seneca appears as a character, but the author is unknown.

Although it is not clear whether Seneca's plays were presented in Rome's public theatres, they were destined to become major influences in the Renaissance.

FIG. 3.15
Scene from a Roman tragedy. A wall painting in Pompeii of the first century C.E. or earlier. From Dieterich, *Pulcinella* (1897).

Since they helped shape tragedy in the age of Shakespeare, their characteristics are important.

1. The plays are divided into five episodes by choral interludes only loosely related to the action.
2. His plays are models for the use of technical devices, such as soliloquies, asides, and confidantes.
3. He makes extensive use of elaborate speeches, often resembling forensic addresses.
4. Seneca uses pithy, proverbial generalizations about the human condition (*sententiae*), to reinforce his moral points.
5. His plays show a preoccupation with magic, death, and the interpenetration of the human and superhuman worlds.
6. Seneca creates characters who are dominated by a single obsessive passion (such as revenge) that drives them to their doom.
7. He uses sensational deeds to illustrate the evils of unrestrained emotion (for example, in *Oedipus* Jocasta rips open her womb and in *Thyestes* the bodies of children are served at a banquet).

All of these elements were widely copied. Thus, even though his plays may not have been performed in Roman theatres, Seneca was to exert enormous influence in later times.

While Rome made the transition from republic to empire, Atellan farce (*fabula Atellana*) became very popular. Pomponius and Novius (writing between 100 and 75 B.C.E.) are credited with making the Atellan farce literary. At this time, Atellan farces seem to have been short, perhaps 300–400 lines, and to have served as *exodia,* or afterpieces, to regular drama. Atellan farce emphasized rural settings, characters, and speech, while its subject matter most often involved cheating, gluttony, fighting, or sexual exploits. Its rustic atmosphere and its use as an afterpiece led many Romans to associate it with the satyr play, and the two forms were often confused with one another.

Four stock characters appeared in Atellan farce. Bucco, a vivacious, boisterous braggart; Pappus, a comic old man; Maccus, a gluttonous fool; and Dossenus, a hunchback of frightening appearance. Standardized costumes were probably worn by these figures. Historians have noted the similarities between this form and the *commedia dell'arte* of sixteenth-century Italy but it is not known how they might be related. The peak of popularity for the Atellan farce was reached during the first century B.C.E. By the third century C.E. there are no more direct references to it.

The first clear reference to the mime, or *fabula riciniata,* is found in Rome in 211 B.C.E., although it probably had been performed there much earlier. Under the republic, mime was associated especially with the *ludi Florales,* which honored one of the fertility goddesses and was noted for female nudity and licentiousness. Under the empire, mime's popularity increased until it and pantomime virtually drove all other forms from the stage. The term *mime* seems to have been used to designate almost any kind of entertainment offered in the theatre. Basically, however, the mime was a dramatic form, usually short, but sometimes quite elaborate and complex in its use of spectacle and large casts. It might treat almost any subject and could be either serious or comic, but usually it dealt with some aspect of everyday life seen from a comic or satiric point of view. Premarital and extramarital sex were frequent subjects. Scholars have tended to discuss mimes almost wholly in terms of obscene and violent examples, but it is far from certain that these were typical. Mimes reflected the taste of the period, as can be seen from the numerous beatings, fights, and other forms of violence included in them. The mimes were especially disliked by the Christians, whose sacraments and beliefs they often ridiculed. Much of the testimony about the depravity and excesses of mime comes from Christian writers seeking to undermine the theatre's appeal. They had little of a positive nature to say about the form, but they preserved such examples as the order given by the teen-age emperor, Heliogabalus (ruled 218–222 C.E.), that sexual acts in mime be performed realistically on stage, though there is no evidence for it ever having been obeyed.

In addition to dramatic pieces, mime troupes also presented a wide range of incidental entertainment, including various feats performed on tightropes and trapezes, fire spitting, sword swallowing, juggling with balls, daggers, and other objects, stilt walking, trained animals (who sometimes performed in dramatic pieces), singing (sometimes approaching the operatic), dancing, and so on. In seeking to feed the audience's appetite for the novel and unusual, mime came to include an extremely wide range of offerings.

Under the empire, pantomime (or *fabula saltica*) was also popular. Roman pantomime was a forerunner of modern ballet for it was essentially a storytelling dance. The action of the storytelling dancer was accompanied by a chorus (who sang an explanatory text) and an orchestra of flutes, pipes, and cymbals. As a form it was known in Greece as early as the fifth century, although there it usually involved two or more dancers. In Rome, it was essentially a solo dance, though there was occasionally an assistant who was kept very much subordinate. This form of pantomime seems to have been introduced at Rome in 22 B.C.E. by Pylades and Bathyllus. Pantomimic plots were usually taken from mythology or history. Characteristically it was serious, but occasionally it was

FIG. 3.16

Greek and Roman dramatists and their surviving plays.

comic (a type in which Bathyllus excelled). Although the comic mode soon declined in popularity, the serious form of pantomime usurped the position formerly held by tragedy. Emperors and nobles often kept their own pantomime performers, and intense rivalries developed over the relative merits of dancers. Pantomime was also a favorite with the common people, although less so than mime, especially in late Rome.

FIG. 3.17

Dossenus of the Atellan farce, a mimic fool, or a grotesque actor of farce. Graeco-Roman bronze statuette found in southern Italy. It has been dated 300–100 B.C.E. Courtesy Metropolitan Museum of Art, Rogers Fund, 1912.

PRODUCTION ARRANGEMENTS

State festivals were under the jurisdiction of magistrates who received a grant to cover expenses. Days set aside for theatrical productions in a festival were called *ludi scaenici* and the magistrates contracted with managers (*domini*) of acting troupes (*greges,* singular *grex*) to produce them. Several companies were normally involved as each company had its own specialties, and actors of tragedy, comedy, or pantomime did not do mime or farce. Each company received a basic fee, but additional prizes or payments were made to companies, individual actors, and authors who especially pleased the audience. Occasional references are found to claques (people paid to respond positively or negatively to a play) and attempted bribery of audiences and officials in awarding favors. During the empire, rulers sometimes exerted considerable power over the plays, their content, and the awarding of prizes; they also often granted or withheld favors to actors. Ordinarily, however, it was the popular audience who most influenced theatrical performances. Play and pantomimes were given without intermissions. Even the intervals between plays were usually filled with incidental entertainment or short mimes so performances were continuous throughout the day.

Admission to state-supported performances was always free, and all classes attended. In his prologues, Plautus refers to women, magistrates, attendants, slaves, nurses with children, and prostitutes as being in the audience, and he indicates that there was considerable jostling for places. In some periods, special seats in the orchestra were reserved for the senators and designated rows of seats were held for the wealthy. Some tickets dating from the empire have survived, but it is not clear whether they were for the privileged few for whom seats were reserved, or whether they were required of everyone to prevent overcrowding in the theatre. The surviving tickets are quite precise in their indication of the entrance to be used and the section and level of the seat's location within the theatre.

The theatres seated thousands of persons. The capacity of the early temporary structures is unknown, but the first permanent theatre held approximately 17,500 persons. Obviously, only a fraction of Rome's population could be accommodated in the theatre at a given time, for Rome grew in size from about 215,000 persons in 200 B.C.E. to about 1,000,000 during the empire. Ordinarily, all of the plays for a festival were presented in the same theatre, but for one elaborate celebration in 17 B.C.E., three different theatres were used continuously for three consecutive days and nights.

Many spectators, though not necessarily all, were interested primarily in entertainment, and though special officials maintained order, the audience was free to come and go during a performance. Furthermore, other attractions competed for the audience's favor. The first two productions of Terence's *Mother-in-Law* were failures because at the first the audience left to see a rope dancer and at the second to watch gladiators. Spectators might also leave to buy food and drink, which were sold just outside the theatre. The audience seems to have been quick to express praise or condemnation, and since its response determined whether a troupe received additional payments, its favor was constantly sought.

ROMAN THEATRE ARCHITECTURE

The first permanent theatre building in Rome, the Theatre of Pompey, was not constructed until 55 B.C.E., almost 200 years after the introduction of regular drama, and over 100 years after the last surviving comedy was written. Consequently, as in Greece, the permanent structures date from a considerably later time than the period of significant dramatic writing.

In the third century B.C.E. there were several architectural precedents upon which the Romans could have drawn: (1) the Etruscan, (2) the Oscan, and (3) the Greek. Which of these, if any, they chose is unknown, but it seems likely that Livius Andronicus would have adapted the Greek structure for his plays, since he was most familiar with it. On the other hand, since a new temporary structure was apparently erected for each festival, considerable experimentation was possible.

The six festivals that included drama had an average of 150 years of experience with staging by 55 B.C.E., so as many as 900 temporary theatres could have been built by that time. Richard Beacham has

FIG. 3.18

Plan (made in late Roman times) of the Theatre of Pompey. Note the temple of Venus at top and the elaborate *scaena frons* at bottom. From Streit, *Das Theater* (1903).

argued that several surviving wall paintings from Pompeii and elsewhere depict the stages of temporary theatres, each of which is quite different in appearance, so their general characteristics are at best conjectural. Scholars who have attempted to reconstruct them have usually made them merely flimsier versions of the later stone theatres, disagreeing on the detail such as the elaborateness of the stage background, the size of the stage, and the extent to which seating was provided for the audiences.

The structures appear to have become progressively more elaborate and ornate by the end of the republic, however. In 99 B.C.E. Claudius Pulcher is said to have erected a theatre with such realistically painted details that birds tried to perch on them. Pliny the Elder (23–79 C.E.) states that Marcus Aemilius Scaurus built a theatre in 58 B.C.E. with a stage of three stories, the first of marble, the second of glass, and the third of gilded wood, the whole being decorated with 360 columns and 3000 bronze statues; the auditorium supposedly accommodated 80,000 people. Pliny also states that in 50 B.C.E., Gaius Scribonius Curio built two theatres, each on a central pivot; while the audience remained seated, the two parts were supposedly revolved to form an amphitheatre. Although modern historians seriously question their reliability, Pliny's accounts are indicative of structures sufficiently unusual and sumptuous to have become legendary by Pliny's time. There are many theories, none fully persuasive, as to why attempts to build permanent theatre in Rome in 179, 174, and 155 B.C.E. failed. Considering the growing elaborateness of temporary theatres, it is perhaps not surprising that Pompey was finally allowed to erect the first permanent theatre in Rome in 55 B.C.E. There was a temple dedicated to Venus at the top of the auditorium and legend has it that Pompey told the Senate he was simply building this temple, with a very large semicircular staircase in front of it. That "staircase"/auditorium had a diameter of 500 feet, seated approximately 17,500 and faced a stage 300 feet wide—the length of a football field.

Around 15 B.C.E., the Roman Architect Vitruvius, wrote ten books on all aspects of architecture and engineering, including theatres. He compares Roman theatres to those of the Greeks which he apparently had been able to study first hand. It is unclear, however, what he based his Roman theatres on beyond the theatre of Pompey. Before the end of the century, however, two other theatres were built in Rome: the theatre of Balbus (13 B.C.E.), seating approximately 8000, and the theatre of Marcellus (11 B.C.E.), seating approximately 14,000. A fourth theatre was built by the emperor Trajan (reigned 53–117 C.E.) but it was taken down by Hadrian (76–138 C.E.). No other permanent theatres were ever built in Rome, although temporary structures continued to be used there and elsewhere. The empire included approximately 1000 cities, over half of which had theatres, either permanent or temporary.

The permanent theatres of the empire are sufficiently similar in design to allow generalizations about their basic characteristics. Many were built on level ground, though those that are best preserved today were built at least partially on the slope of a hill as the Greek theatres were. Corridors and stairways around and beneath the auditorium allowed an efficient flow of traffic. When theatres utilized natural slopes, corridors were cut into the hillsides. Vertical aisles divided the auditorium (*cavea*) into sections, while at least one broad aisle about halfway up the auditorium and a covered portico along the top permitted horizontal movement from one side of the auditorium to another. The stage house (*scaena*) and the auditorium were joined to form a single architectural unit the same height all the way round. Thus, unlike in the Greek theatre, the spectator's view was confined within the structure. The entrance passages corresponding to the Greek *parodoi* were roofed over to provide corridors (*vomitoria*) into the orchestra and auditorium. Over each there was generally a box reserved for the emperor or the magistrates responsible for the festival. The orchestra, generally a half circle, was usually used for seating privileged groups, although at times it accommodated dancing, animal fights, gladiatorial contests, or water ballets.

The stage (*pulpitum*) was raised about five feet. Its front was placed on the diameter of the orchestra circle. The size of the stage was determined by that of the theatre, but most were very large by modern standards; from 100 to 300 feet in length and 20 to 30 feet deep. There were from three to five doors in the rear wall, and at least one door in the wings (or *versurae*) which enclosed the ends of the stage. The plays make frequent reference to a passageway behind the façade (*angiportum*), used to explain the offstage movement of characters.

The façade (*scaenae frons*) of the stage house stood three stories high and was decorated with columns, niches, porticos, and statues. It was often painted and gilded. The stage was covered by a roof, which improved acoustics and protected the elaborate *scaenae frons*. Most of the early permanent theatres probably had straight, painted façades; but after the second century C.E., curved niches, forming deep vestibules and alcoves, were usual. This later arrangement cut into the backstage space until little more than a corridor remained. Dressing rooms and other work spaces were then housed in the side wings. The Romans were concerned with the comfort of audiences. Under the empire they perfected a system of cooling based on air blowing over streams of water. To protect the audience from the sun, awnings (or *vela*) were introduced around 78 B.C.E. Attached to masts set in two rows of corbels (or supporting projections) around the top edge of the auditorium, the awnings were brightly colored and occasionally had a scene painted on the visible surfaces. (Nero, for example, had himself depicted on an awning as the Sun God driving a chariot.)

Like the Greeks, the Romans also built roofed theatres (*theatrum tectum*) generally called *odea* (singular *odeum*). The term literally means "place of odes," and has therefore most often been associated with music recitals, but there is growing evidence that they were also used for actor competitions and plays. An odeum was generally smaller and more ornate than a theatre and was fitted into a square or rectangular building. Illumination was provided by windows. Many Roman cities had both types of theatres. The oldest known odeum was built at Pompeii *c.* 80 B.C.E., so it predates the earliest permanent theatres in the capital. The odeum of Domitian was the first and only one to be built in the city of Rome (*c.* 90 C.E.).

FIG. 3.19
The theatre at Orange (at left front). Note the elaborate forecourt adjoining the stage house. Note also that the theatre is built into a hillside and takes advantage of it for some entrances. Beyond the theatre is the circus. From Caristie, *Monuments Antiques à Orange* (1856). Courtesy Boston Public Library.

A few purely Roman theatres were built in Greek areas of the empire, but the usual practice was to remodel existing Greek structures along Roman lines. In some of these Greco-Roman theatres the *thyromata* were replaced by a Roman *scaenae frons;* some retained the high stage, but in others it was reduced to the Roman level of just three to five feet. Since Hellenistic theatres had no side wings, an extra door was often placed at the extreme ends of the rear façade to give a total of five to seven entrance doors onto the stage. In some Greco-Roman theatres the old Greek stages and stage building were moved forward to reduce the size of the orchestra and sometimes to also increase the depth of a particularly narrow Hellenistic stage.

Roman theatres in what is now western France, lower Germany, and England were multipurpose structures intended to also serve as meeting halls and amphitheatres. These Gallo-Roman theatres were far less elaborate than the other imperial theatres and used larger amounts of wood in their construction. The orchestra areas were also generally much more than half a circle.

An archeological survey done in the early 1990s identified 790 known classical theatres. Of these, 167 are Greek; 123 were unclassified, but the majority are almost certainly Roman; 311 were definitely Roman; 62 were odea most of which are Roman; 16 were Greco-Roman, and 89 Gallo-Roman. These permanent theatres were built throughout Europe, North Africa, and Asia Minor.

FIG. 3.20
Reconstruction of the Roman theatre at Ostia, built between 30 and 12 B.C.E. and remodeled *c.* 200 C.E. From d'Espouy, *Fragments d'Architecture Antique,* 2 (1902).

SCENERY

The existing plays of Plautus and Terence predate the first stone theatres by over 100 years. In these plays the background is treated as a series of houses opening onto a city street. We do not know how much attempt there may have been to change the visual appearance of the stage from one play to another. The prologue of *The Menaechmi* says: "This city is Epidamnus during the performance of this play; when another play is performed it will become another city," which would suggest not much was needed. But the plays also contain many scenes involving eavesdropping or the failure of one character to see others who are also on stage. Scholars do not agree on how much this required actual three-dimensional structures for characters to hide behind, and how much it was simply a matter of convention.

The basic scenic background in the Roman theatre was the *scaenae frons*, with three to five doors leading on to the stage. There was also a door at each end of the stage. These doors are of considerable scenic importance, since in comedy each may represent a different house, and since they are referred to so frequently by the characters. In tragedy, all of the doors in the *scaenae frons* were probably treated as entrances to the same building; some ancient commentators state that the central doorway was reserved for the principal personage, while the side doors were used by the lesser characters. If so, staging must have been highly conventionalized. The doors leading into the wings (*versurae*) may also have had conventionalized uses, for several ancient writers say that one was understood to lead to the forum or city and the other to the harbor or country.

Vitruvius says: "The *scaena* itself displays the following scheme. In the center are double doors decorated like those of a royal palace. At the right and left are the doors of the guest chambers. Beyond are the spaces provided for the decoration—places that the Greeks call *periaktoi,* because in these places are triangular pieces of machinery which revolve, each having three decorated faces." As to what was painted on the *periaktoi,* Vitruvius adds: "There are three kinds of scenes, one called the tragic, second, the comic, third, the satyric. Their decorations are different and unlike each other in scheme. Tragic scenes are delineated with columns, pediments, statues, and other objects suited to kings; comic scenes exhibit private dwellings, with balconies and views representing rows of windows, after the manner of ordinary dwellings; satyric scenes are decorated with trees, caverns, mountains, and other rustic objects delineated in landscape style." The meaning of this passage has been the subject of endless debate. The most

sensible interpretation seems to be that the decoration for each type of play was conventionalized and painted on *periaktoi* placed near each end of the stage. In any case, the *periaktoi* could not have covered more than a very small portion of the vast *scaenae frons,* most of which would have remained visible. Other Roman commentators refer to sliding scenery (*scaenae ductilis*), apparently painted panels that could be moved to change the setting. It is not clear where these were mounted or how extensively they were used. It is perplexing that none of the excavated theatres, several of which are in very good condition, have provided any archaeological evidence for these devices.

Most discussions of the stage background concentrate on the requirements for regular drama, but the permanent theatres were built after the rise to prominence of the minor dramatic forms, some of which placed considerable emphasis on spectacle. Nevertheless, we know little of the scenic conventions of these lesser types. Perhaps some clues are offered by the uses made of two types of curtains: the front curtain (*auleum*) and the background curtain (*siparium*). The front curtain may have been introduced as early as 133 B.C.E. and was certainly in use by 56 B.C.E. Originally, it was lowered into a slot at the front of the stage by means of a series of telescoped poles. Extending the poles upward to their full height raised the curtain, while the reverse process lowered it. After the second century C.E., the curtain was suspended from overhead and raised by ropes. The front curtain was important to spectacle, for it permitted the sudden revelation of a scene or the rapid concealment of a striking tableau. Before its introduction, all characters had to be brought on and gotten offstage in full view of the audience. After its introduction, producers seem to have capitalized on the surprises and striking effects it made possible.

Background curtains probably came into the theatre with the mime. Originally a small curtain, it may have been hung at the rear of an improvised platform to serve both as background for the action and as masking for the offstage space. Entrances were probably made through slits cut in it. As the mime grew in importance, these background curtains increased in size and could be hung against the *scaenae frons* to provide places for hiding, mask changes of painted panels, or simply focus audience attention on a performance that might otherwise have been lost on these enormous stages. Overall, there appear to have been simultaneous and contradictory trends toward more elaborate curtains and more elaborate permanent façades.

Many spectacular effects were achieved through the use of large numbers of supernumeraries in dances, battles, and processions. This trend toward

FIG. 3.21

Scaenae frons and interior of the theatre at Orange; a reconstruction of what the theatre supposedly looked like in its original state. From Caristie, *Monuments Antique à Orange* (1856). Courtesy Boston Public Library.

mass effects had begun as early as the first century B.C.E., for Cicero states that at the dedication of the Theatre of Pompey in 52 B.C.E., 600 mules crossed the stage in one play and 3000 bowls were displayed in another. Special effects were widely available as well. The Greek engineer, Hero (or Heron) of Alexandria (10–70 C.E.), describes in his book on *Automata,* thunder machines, devices to magically open doors, and an "automatic theatre" which could roll itself before an audience, perform a short play in nine scenes, and roll away all on its own power. Under the empire, spectacle, sensationalism and novelty seem to have been among the primary goals of the theatre.

In addition to theatres, structures were erected in Rome and elsewhere to meet the demands of other types of entertainment. Mimes were often performed in these structures and some of the technology they developed may have found its way into the theatres. The Circus Maximus, designed for chariot races, was the oldest and largest of these. Laid out originally around 600 B.C.E., it was approximately 2000 feet long by 650 feet wide. Amphitheatres were later inventions, designed primarily to house gladiatorial contests and animal hunts (*venationes*), sea battles

(*naumachiae*) may also have been occasionally staged in them. Roman theatres were often modified to also serve some of the functions of the amphitheatres. Rome's first amphitheatre was built in 46 B.C.E., but this and its two successors were temporary structures. In 80 C.E., the Flavian amphitheatre (now called the Colosseum) was completed. Originally three stories high, it was increased to four in the third century C.E. It was then 157 feet tall, 620 feet long, and 513 feet wide and seated approximately 50,000 persons. The arena measured 287 by 180 feet and the space beneath it housed an extensive system of trap doors. A building was erected near the Colosseum to house scenic elements and properties, which could be transported as needed to the Colosseum's basement, some twenty-one feet beneath the arena, or to other sites of entertainments and a special ministry (the *summum choregium*) was created around 100 C.E. to manage this scenery. Martial (*c.* 40–*c.* 102 C.E.) speaks of intricate spectacles in the Colosseum, including "sliding cliffs and a miraculous and moving wood." On another occasion, the ground repeatedly opened and a magic wood with fountains appeared and was immediately filled with exotic animals from foreign places.

Sometimes plays or pantomimes were acted out in the arenas. In one instance, a criminal impersonating Orpheus appeared from below the arena level as if coming from Hades. He played music which enchanted rocks and trees so that they moved to greet him and animals crouched at his feet; then, at the end of this display, he was torn to pieces by a bear.

In the eastern part of the empire, where spectacles were less bloody, more emphasis was placed on Pyrrhic dances (or ballet-like performances). Apuleius (second century C.E.), in his novel *Metamorphoses,* describes such a performance in the amphitheatre at Corinth in Greece. The scenery seems to have been three-dimensional and practicable, for it represented a mountain on which were shrubs, trees, a stream, grazing goats, and a shepherd. An entertainment based on the story of Paris' judgment on the beauty of Hera, Athena, and Aphrodite was enacted on the mountain. At the end, a fountain of wine sprang out of the mountain's top and the entire structure sank out of sight. There are also references to devices (*pegmata*) for flying characters or objects, but it is not clear where these were located or operated.

Although these accounts concern amphitheatres, they make it clear that Roman engineers had developed scenic devices as complex as any that would be introduced into the theatre prior to modern times.

FIG. 3.22
Two Roman comic actors. Bronze figures on the cover of a third century B.C.E. box or chest found at Praeneste, near Rome. Courtesy British Museum.

ACTORS AND ACTING

The usual term for actors in Rome was *histriones,* although *cantores* (or declaimers) was also used. At first a clear distinction was made between the actors of regular dramas and the performer of mimes (the *mimus* or *saltator*), the latter being considered inferior. In late Rome, however, the term *histriones* came to be applied to all actors. The majority of performers were male, for only in mimes did women appear on stage.

Although there apparently were no restrictions on the number of actors that could be used on the Roman stage, the extant plays could have been performed by a company of five or six actors, if doubling was practiced and supernumeraries used occasionally. Troupes may have been much larger, however, for no information about their size during the republic has survived. In the first century B.C.E., as the regular drama declined, emphasis shifted to the "star" performer. Many stars amassed fortunes, and under the empire they had followings not unlike those of a modern movie star. In late Rome, many of the most popular performers were tightrope walkers, trapeze artists, jugglers, sword-swallowers, fire-eaters, and dancers.

Acting style probably varied according to the dramatic form. In comedy and tragedy, the actors were male, wore masks, and probably doubled in roles as the Greeks had done. In tragedy, delivery seems to have been slow, stately, and declamatory; in comedy, it was conversational. Most roles required proficiency in speaking, singing, and dancing. Contemporary writers also made it clear that expressive pantomimic gesture (perhaps heavily dependent on stock attitudes and poses) was a prominent ingredient in every performance. In tragedy, movement seems to have been slow and dignified, but in comedy it was more lively, for running, beatings, and farcical horseplay of all sorts were common. Since the theatres sometimes seated as many as 17,000 persons, the actors' gestures and movements probably were considerably enlarged. They were not greatly exaggerated, however, since Roman teachers of oratory suggested actors as suitable models for imitation by public speakers. Typical human movement, gesture, and intonation appear to have been reduced to their essentials, then enlarged and conventionalized for stage use. For the most part, actors specialized in one type of drama, although some famous actors did both comedy and tragedy.

FIG. 3.23

Female mime performer or dancer. In her hands she holds clappers and on her left foot she wears a footclapper. Bells are attached to her cap, skirt, and ankle. Bronze statuette, late second century c.e. Courtesy Art Museum, Princeton University.

In the mimes, masks usually were not worn and consequently facial expression was important. Through much of its history, mime was in part improvised, and therefore it required a talent for the invention of dialogue, business, and movement. Mime actors seem to have been selected either for their physical beauty or comic ugliness, for the plots most typically revolved around sexual desirability or some grotesquerie. In the second century B.C.E., the companies were probably very small, with perhaps no more than three or four members; but under the empire they included as many as sixty performers, although many of these were acrobats and variety entertainers. In the first century B.C.E., a school for mime actors was operating in Rome.

In pantomime, the emphasis was on the solo performer. Noted for their handsomeness and athletic qualities, these actors depended entirely upon gesture and movement to portray a series of characters and situations. Many were renowned for the subtlety and complexity of their portrayals at a time when tragic acting had become increasingly exaggerated.

The social status of the Roman actor has been much disputed. Mime actors appear always to have been considered infamous, and many of them certainly were slaves. There were also a number of private troupes and these too would have been slaves. Members of the actors guild, the Artists of Dionysus, however, are not likely to have been slaves. Roscius (131–63 B.C.E.), the most famous of Roman actors, was eventually raised to the nobility. His contemporary, Aesopus, was a member of the Optimates, a group that exercised considerable control over public affairs because of its wealth, influence, and ability. On the other hand, emperors occasionally forced noblemen to appear on stage as a form of punishment and degradation. Overall, it seems likely that, though the social status of actors could vary considerably, the majority always ranked low in public esteem.

MASKS AND COSTUMES

Greek comedy and tragedy, Atellan farce, and Etruscan dances all used masks and the Romans continued this tradition. The use of masks made the doubling of roles much easier and simplified the problem of casting characters of identical appearance, as in Plautus' *Menaechmi* and *Amphitryon*.

As in the Hellenistic theatre, masks were made of linen with an attached wig and formed a complete covering for the head. The masks for pantomime had

FIG. 3.24

Masks for Terence's *Andria*. From a ninth century c.e. manuscript now in the Vatican. Courtesy Biblioteca Vaticana.

FIG. 3.25
Ivory statuette showing a tragic actor, c. second century C.E. Note the distorted mask, high headdress, and thick-soled boots. Some scholars believe it represents a Greek actor of the Hellenistic period, but it is more likely Roman. From Baumeister, *Denkmaler des Klassischen Altertums* (1889).

which the Roman tunic covered by a cloak, or toga, was worn.

Tragedies on Greek themes (*fabula crepidata*) probably followed the conventions of the Hellenistic Greek theatre, although some scholars have suggested that it was Roman practice which led to the extreme stylization of dress in the late Hellenistic period. Regardless of the direction of influence, it seems likely that Greek and Roman tragic costumes were similar. For the tragedies on Roman subjects (*fabula praetexta*), the toga with a purple border (*toga praetexta*) was sufficiently typical that the dramatic form took its name from it.

It is usually assumed that each of the four stock characters of the Atellan farce had his own standardized mask and costume and that these remained the same from one play to another. Since most of the other characters were rustics, their costumes were probably exaggerated versions of country dress. Some of the known titles of Atellan farces refer to doctors, musicians, painters, fortune tellers, and fishermen, each of whom may have been indicated by costume.

The pantomime performer wore a long tunic and cloak that allowed freedom of movement. As a variation on tragedy, pantomime probably used a less exaggerated version of tragic dress. Nothing is known of the costume for comic pantomime, the popularity of which was short-lived.

Mime actors wore the tunic as a basic garment, but their most distinctive accessory was a hood (*ricinium*), frequently used for purposes of disguise. Some mime characters wore a patchwork jacket (probably *centunculus*) and had shaven heads. Others represented fashionable and sophisticated men and women who, like modern film stars, were dressed lavishly in the latest fashions.

closed mouths and according to Lucian (second century C.E.) were much more natural than those for tragedy, which were exaggerated, and comedy, which were grotesque. Quintilian, writing in the first century C.E., refers to masks with one cheerful and one serious side, apparently an attempt to indicate a change of emotion without a change of mask. Mime actors did not usually wear masks, and, as mime increased in popularity under the empire, the use of masks in the theatre declined.

Costumes varied with the type of play. Comedy based on Greek life (the *fabula palliata*) followed the costuming conventions of Greek New Comedy, for which everyday Athenian dress was adapted. Similar principles probably governed the costumes for comedies based on Roman life (the *fabula togata*), for

MUSIC

Although music was not highly valued by the Romans, it was used, perhaps because of Etruscan influence, more extensively in Latin than in Greek plays. Up to two-thirds of the lines of Plautus' plays were accompanied by music, and it figured only slightly less prominently in the works of other authors.

As with Greek music, we know little of the Roman modes. The accompaniment used in the theatre seems to have been composed by each troupe's own flute player, although probably he merely played suitable mood music. One reference from the first century B.C.E. suggests that the accompaniment was so conventionalized that the audience could tell what kind of character was to appear by listening to the music. Thus, it may have resembled the musical scores of

FIG. 3.26

Musicians shown on a mosaic in a villa in Pompeii. Some scholars interpret it as a choral interlude in Greek New Comedy but it is as likely an entertainment of another type. The musicians perform on double flute and percussion instruments. From Fiechter, *Die Baugeschichte des Antike Theaters* (1917).

our motion pictures. That the musicians were valued, however, is indicated by records which list their names immediately after that of the principal actor.

The music for plays was performed on a "flute" with two pipes, each about 20 inches long, that was bound to the performer's head to leave his hands free to work the stops. The flute player was on stage throughout performances and supposedly moved about to accompany first one character and then another.

The musical element in pantomime was more elaborate than that for regular drama, for it required an orchestra of flutes, pipes, cymbals, and other percussion instruments. It is also likely that the music for mimes became more extensive during the late empire as the performances became more spectacular and ornate.

THE DECLINE OF THE THEATRE IN ROME

In terms of numbers of performances, the Roman theatre reached its height during the fourth century C.E. Although it continued as a publicly supported institution for another two hundred years, it had already encountered difficulties that were eventually to overwhelm it.

One source of opposition was the rising Christian church. At first the new sect was very weak and, as it came to popular attention, met considerable opposition on political as well as religious grounds. Its

adherents refused to place allegiance to the state above the dictates of religious teachings, insisted that other gods were false despite the Roman tradition of accepting all gods out of a desire to offend none, and perhaps more importantly, refused to worship the emperor as a god. Romans, on the other hand, were willing to accept the Judeo-Christian god as another deity but were unwilling to abandon all others. The intractability of the Christians resulted in the decision of the emperor to stamp out the new religion as a subversive element in the state.

In spite of persecution, the power of Christianity gradually increased. Constantine (emperor, 324–337) made Christianity lawful in 313 and in 393 Theodosius I made the profession of any other religion illegal. After about 400 C.E., therefore, some of the excesses of the theatre abated and state festivals ceased to be given in honor of the pagan gods, but by that time the Roman populace considered theatrical entertainments one of its fundamental rights and thereby ensured their continuance. Gladiatorial contests were abolished in 404, however, and animal fights in 523 C.E.

The theatre was a favorite target of the Christians for at least three reasons. First, it was associated with the festivals of pagan gods. Second, the licentiousness of the mimes offended the moral sense of the church leaders. Third, the mimes often ridiculed such Christian practices as baptism and the sacrament of bread and wine. As a result, the break between church and theatre was inevitable. Tertullian (c. 150–c. 220 C.E.), the North African theologian, denounced the theatre in his *De Spectaculis*, arguing that Christians forswore the theatre when they were baptized. From about 300 C.E. on, church councils sought to dissuade Christians from attending performances, and in 398 the Council of Carthage decreed excommunication for any Christian who went to the theatre rather than to church on holy days. Actors were forbidden the sacraments of the church unless they forswore their profession, a decree not rescinded in many places until the eighteenth century.

But church opposition alone would not have succeeded in prohibiting performances. Two other forces were at work: the decay of the Roman Empire from within, and pressures from barbarian tribes from without. The sense of loyalty to the state was increasingly undermined after the second century C.E. as military and governmental bureaucracies took over all functions and made citizen concern irrelevant. Furthermore, the soldiers and bureaucrats were increasingly recruited from remote provinces that had little interest in the capital city. To simplify administering its vast territories, Diocletian divided the

285 Empire first divided East/West by Diocletian

307 Empire reunited under Constantine

331 Capital moved to Constantinople

395 East/West division becomes permanent after several attempts at reunification

FIG. 3.27
The division of the Roman Empire into East and West.

empire into two parts in 285. The Emperor Constantine reunited it for a time but moved the capital of the entire empire to a city he had built on the Bosporus, Constantinople, in 330. After 395 the division of the empire into East and West became permanent. The eastern empire was more stable and wealthier than the West, where internal weakness made it difficult to withstand invasions by barbarian tribes. In 476, the last Western emperor to hold Roman citizenship was deposed, and thereafter it was ruled by foreigners. Consequently, most historians use 476 to mark the end of the western empire, although the conquerors sought to continue it, for they were not so much interested in destroying as controlling it. Nevertheless, the Roman Empire rapidly disintegrated, and by the

sixth century C.E. its western half had lost all semblance of unity.

During the fifth and sixth centuries, however, the foreign rulers, like their predecessors, found it expedient to support the theatre, and after each upheaval theatrical performances were resumed. Theodoric (the Ostrogoth who ruled Italy from 493 to 526) even restored the Theatre of Pompey. But during the sixth century order crumbled. The last definite record of a performance in Rome is dated 549. The theatre may have persisted, but it does not seem to have survived the Lombard invasion of 568, after which state recognition and support of theatrical performances definitely ceased. Thereafter, the theatre in the western territories returned to the obscurity out of which it had emerged over 1100 years earlier.

LOOKING AT THEATRE HISTORY

Since the interests or unconscious assumptions of writers inevitably influence their view of events, students of history should learn to recognize the biases

of historical accounts. The theatre during the Roman era, more so than in most periods, has been especially subject to prejudicial views, partially because since the early nineteenth century there has been a tendency to praise the Greeks at the expense of the Romans. Thus, the Greeks are almost always treated reverently and seldom are their shortcomings acknowledged; on the other hand, the Romans are usually treated condescendingly and their strengths acknowledged only grudgingly. For example, Roman comic dramatists were long treated as mere adapters of Greek works (which were almost invariably pronounced superior to the Roman adaptations), although, since so few fragments of the Greek comedies adapted by Romans survive, it may well be that the Romans improved on the originals. Such prejudices are so deeply ingrained in modern thought that it is difficult to obtain a balanced view of Roman theatre from works written during the past two centuries. This problem is not confined to treatments of Greece and Rome, for there is a widespread tendency to take some aspect (often the sensational or what is so out of the ordinary as to stand out) and convert it into the typical. In this way, the best or most unusual or most shocking may be converted into the representative.

The following excerpts are from two accounts written about the Roman theatre in the second century C.E. In the first the author, seeking to persuade Christians to avoid the theatre, makes all that he dislikes typical. In the second, the author, concerned with showing the superiority of pantomime as a theatrical form, makes all that he likes typical. Both eventually acknowledge that there is another side, but each dismisses the deviations as insignificant or insidious.

> . . .[D]emons, . . . with the purpose of attracting man away from his Lord and binding him to their own service, achieved their purpose by granting him the artistic talents required by the shows.
> . . . Christians are forbidden the theatre . . . where . . . the best path to its god's favor is the vileness of the Atellan gestures or the buffoon in woman's clothing . . .
> in His law it is stated that the man is cursed who attires himself in female garments; what then must be his judgment on the pantomime, who is trained up to play the woman! . . . Granted you have in the theatre pleasant things both agreeable and innocent in themselves, even some excellent things, . . . , [for to accomplish his purposes] the devil puts into his deadly draught things most pleasant and acceptable stolen from God. . . .

From Tertullian, *On the Spectacles*, c. 200 C.E.

> Other entertainments of eye or ear are but manifestations of a single art. . . . The pantomime is all-embracing. . . . The performer's art is as much intellectual as physical: there is meaning in his movements; every gesture has its significance . . . he must be a critic of poetry and song, capable of discerning good music and rejecting bad. . . .So potent is his art that the licentious spectator is cured of his infirmity by seeing the evil effects of passion, and he who enters the theatre in sorrow leaves it serenely. . . . Pantomimes cannot all be artists; there are ignorant performers who badly bungle their work.

From *The Works of Lucian of Samosta*, c. 125–180 C.E.

One of the difficulties facing anyone seeking to envision a performance in a Roman or Greek theatre is that of scale. For the most part, we are used to relatively small theatres and tend to place considerable value on intimacy between actor and audience. But to get some sense of a Greek or Roman performance, we would do well to think of the performance space in terms of a football stadium or sports arena rather than the indoor theatres we know. Even a very large indoor theatre in our time usually holds no more than 3500 people, whereas a Greek or Roman theatre might be five times as large. This difference in scale is crucial, since it cannot help but affect conventions and performance modes.

4

Cross-Currents of Theatre History: Asian, Byzantine, and Early Western European Theatre

Asian theatre developed and changed at a pace quite different from that of the West, and it is worth remembering that it remained almost completely distinct from Western theatre until well into the twentieth century. According to the *Cambridge Guide to Asian Theatre*, the theatrical arts in Asia and the Western Pacific have taken on as many as 700 or 800 distinct forms or genres and are performed by perhaps as many as 25,000 theatre troupes. Only the best-known and most characteristic of Asian forms can be discussed in this history.

During the time of the pre-Greek, Minoan culture of the Mediterranean islands, the great Indus Valley or Harappan culture (*c.* 2500–1750 B.C.E.) dominated the northern Indian subcontinent. In the centuries between 1700 and 1500 B.C.E. it was replaced by Vedic (or Aryan) culture, which is roughly the same time period when the Mycenaean Greeks began to replace the Minoans. Also during this time, the earliest recorded dynasty in China, the Shang Dynasty, came to power. It is assumed that all these cultures had indigenous traditions of story telling, along with narrative dance and song and other forms of performance, but we know nothing definite about them. Current scholarship is finding evidence of exchange between these cultures, but there is not enough information to determine the extent to which they may have influenced one another and

scholars disagree on how to interpret the evidence. Debates have raged for some time, for example, over whether the Aryans who created Vedic culture were conquerors from the West, emigrants into a land that had been abandoned, or just a new development among local peoples.

After 700 B.C.E., the record gradually becomes clearer as the rise of the Persian Empire, which included both Greek and Indian peoples, made the interaction between East and West more feasible. Japanese culture, on the other hand, was almost completely isolated until the seventh century C.E. when Buddhism was introduced there.

In classical Greece and Rome, there are specific events associated with the establishment of theatre and therefore specific dates that can be pointed to. This is not true in Asian countries, where no single event has been agreed on for establishing that theatre then existed as a distinctive form of performance. How a scholar dates the beginning of theatre depends on what they believe theatre, as distinct from any other performance form, is. This accounts for the wide range of dates given for the establishment of theatre in these nations. The oldest existing dramas of India, for example, date to the second century C.E.; a few scholars, however, argue that Indian theatre actually started before Greek theatre, although most now seem to agree on a date closer to the end of the Vedic period, *c.* 200 B.C.E. The oldest surviving dramas in China date to the Sŏng Dynasty (960–1279 C.E.), but some scholars argue that Chinese theatre predates the theatre of both India and Greece. The earliest plays of Japan date to the late fourteenth or early fifteenth century C.E., but scholars generally agree that theatre was introduced there from China in the seventh century. The nature of Asian theatre is so different from the European tradition that narrative dance forms, which would not be classed as theatre in the West, are routinely discussed as theatre forms in the East. This makes it hard to use the term *theatre* the same way in both areas, which complicates attempts to integrate the histories of these two great cultures. We will see a similar complexity when the theatre of Africa is introduced. Still, when looking at theatre as a cultural phenomenon, it is valuable to look at it across cultures in any given time period.

The most accepted chronology has Indian theatre beginning 100 years or more after Alexander the Great invaded north India in 326 B.C. It has Chinese theatre beginning after it had been borrowing music and dance forms from India for over 400 years. And it has the theatre of Japan beginning after the reign of Prince Shotoku (573–621 C.E.), when cultural influences from China were actively sought. It is possible, therefore, to trace a chain of influence from the Greeks to India, into China, and on to Japan with exchanges going in more than one direction. But it is also true that each of these cultures had performance traditions of their own that were sufficiently developed to allow their theatre to have been created without reference to that of any other culture. No matter what the cultural influences might have been, each culture quickly made theatre something distinctly its own.

After the Roman period, Byzantium inherited the old territories of the Hellenistic Empire, which had always remained more Greek than Roman. It therefore found itself holding much of the remaining documents relating to classical Greek theatre, but the Roman theatre it inherited was in a serious state of decline. The Christian church kept Byzantium in constant contact with the remnants of the old Western Empire until it separated into Greek Orthodox and Roman Catholic in 1054. The crusades forced their continued interaction for the next 150 years, by which time Byzantium and Western Europe were important trading partners. Still, it remains unclear whether Byzantium influenced the reintroduction of theatre into Western Europe in the tenth century.

Because Indian theatre developed in parallel with the theatre of Imperial Rome, we will start with its examination and that of China and Japan, before returning to Byzantium and Western Europe.

ASIAN THEATRE: INDIA

It was during the Vedic period (1500–200 B.C.E.) that the features which were to be most significant in Indian life and art emerged. Perhaps the most important of these influences on drama were Hinduism, the caste system, and Sanskrit literary conventions.

Hinduism teaches that the essence of all things is spirit or soul and that the ultimate goal is to achieve union with the Supreme World-Soul, or Brahman, who is infinite, eternal, indescribable, and perfect. In all creation, only Brahman is unchanging, and since only what is permanent is real, Brahman is also the ultimate reality from which all else emanates and to which all else seeks to return. Although it emphasized oneness of spirit, Hinduism sanctioned the worship of hundreds of gods or spirits, since all are merely aspects of Brahman. Nevertheless, Hindus tended to honor three principal gods who personify different aspects of Brahman: Brahma, the creator; Siva, the destroyer; and Vishnu, the preserver. Hindus also believed it impossible to achieve spiritual perfection during one lifetime and posited the necessity of successive reincarnations.

Before the beginning of the Christian era, India had evolved a caste system based partly on social, economic, and racial concepts but also on notions of spiritual development. Although the number of castes eventually became numerous, there are four traditional ones: Brahmins, the priests and intellectuals; Kshatriyas, the warriors and rulers; Vaisyas, the artisans and farmers; and Sudras, the unskilled laborers. These castes were considered to be hereditary and binding, and each was assigned specific duties, rites, tasks, and diets. In addition, there were the Untouchables, who performed the most menial tasks and with whom any contact was considered to defile members of the other castes.

The language of Indian drama was primarily Sanskrit, part of the Indo-European language family that includes Greek and Latin. Originally, Sanskrit was the commonly spoken language, but by the early Christian era it was primarily a medium of written expression, and most people spoke one of the Prakrits, or dialects.

A Sanskrit literature began to emerge in India during the first part of the Vedic period (1500–800 B.C.E.). The *Rigveda,* a collection of prayers or hymns, is usually considered the oldest literary piece in any Indo-European language. It was followed by other religious works. But most important for drama

FIG. 4.1
Asia, showing theatrical centers.

are two great epics, the *Mahabharata* (*Great Battle of the Descendants of Bharata*) and the *Ramayana* (*Travels of Rama*). Both were inspired by events thought to have taken place between 1000 and 800 B.C.E. and were probably first written down in the third part of the Vedic period (500–200 B.C.E.). These two epics are to Sanskrit literature what the *Iliad* and *Odyssey* are to Greek and were to be the major sources of material for Sanskrit dramatists. As Hinduism spread throughout Southeast Asia, these epics inspired (and continue to inspire) numerous plays in those areas.

Both the *Mahabharata* and the *Ramayana* are compounds of history, legend, and myth. The *Mahabharata* tells of the struggle between various members of two ruling families, and the tales of love,

war, and adventure that revolved around them. The *Ramayana* tells of the expulsion of Prince Rama and his wife Sita from their kingdom because of the machinations of Rama's stepmother, their wandering during a period of fourteen years, Sita's abduction by a demon king, her rescue through the help of a monkey king, and their triumphant return to their kingdom. These epics, Hinduism, and the society summed up in the caste system, undergird most Indian drama.

A "golden age" of Indian culture began early in the second century and lasted until about 450 C.E. It reached its peak when the Gupta Empire (320–467 C.E.) of northern India was a major center of art, learning, and medicine. Beautiful cities arose there, universities were founded, and a great and graceful civilization flourished. Another high point came during the first half of the seventh century under the rule of King Harsa, who was also the major playwright of that time. During Harsa's reign, India's influence spread through Southeast Asia, laying the basis for future developments in drama in those areas.

SANSKRIT DRAMA

Our major source of information about theatre in India is the *Natyasastra* (*The Art of Theatre*), attributed to Bharata, although perhaps the cumulative work of many persons. The possible dates for its compositions are widely disputed but the text as we now have it seems to date to the second century C.E. It tells us that theatre began when the god Brahma taught the dramatic arts to the priest Bharata and his 100 sons. Brahma provided nymphs to do the dancing and had the heavenly architect Vishvakarma build a theatre. This tells us much about the importance of theatre in the culture and its recognition of the value of female participation, but it also illustrates the difficulties of dating events as Indian culture seems indifferent to chronology and record-keeping. Because the evidence is vague, modern scholars have assigned a wide range of dates to surviving dramas. Most agree, however, that the theatre of India could not have begun until after 200 B.C.E. (although shadow puppet plays may have begun earlier), and that the earliest existing fragments of Sanskrit drama date from after 100 C.E. About twenty-five plays have survived, some from perhaps as late as the ninth century, although the best come from the fourth and fifth centuries C.E. Sanskrit plays are not categorized according to such Western forms as tragedy, comedy, or mime; and, rather than action, character development, or philosophical issues, the central concern of Sanskrit drama is the appropriate *rasa* (variously translated as aesthetic delight, fundamental mood, or joyful consciousness). The *Natyasastra* states: "nothing has meaning in the drama except through *rasa*." There are eight *rasas* (erotic, comic, pathetic, furious, heroic, terrible, odious, and marvelous), and these in turn are related to the eight basic human emotions (*bhavas*) which can be portrayed on the stage (pleasure, mirth, sorrow, wrath, vigor, fear, disgust, and wonder) to make possible the realization of the appropriate *rasa*. There are also thirty-three transitory emotional states and eight types of character temperament. Basically, the *Natyasastra* is concerned with how emotional states (the *bhavas*) are to be presented on stage through words, actions, costume, and makeup in the manner

required to induce the appropriate *rasa*. Although a play may include elements related to more than one *bhava* and *rasa*, one *rasa* must dominate, for the final aim is to induce a sense of harmony and composure. For that reason, all plays end happily. Death and violence do not occur on stage, and right and wrong are clearly differentiated. During a play, joy and sorrow may be mingled, but at the conclusion all must be resolved into harmony with good triumphant over evil.

Because they intermingle so many elements, the plays are complex. The heroic and domestic, the exalted and commonplace exist side by side. The mixture is exemplified in the typical practice of making the hero's confidant a bald, dwarfish, gluttonous clown, who provides considerable comic relief in a basically serious story. The diversity may also be seen in the dialogue, a mixture of verse (used for heightened expression in scenes of intense emotion) and prose (used for more ordinary scenes) and of Sanskrit (the learned language, spoken by gods, kings, ministers, generals, and sages) and Prakrit (the everyday dialect, used for women, children, servants, peasants, and persons of low birth). Considerable variety is also achieved by grouping subsidiary plots, ranging from the farcical to the serious, around the main story.

Sanskrit plays vary in length from one to ten acts. According to the accepted rules, the events of a single act should be confined to a twenty-four-hour period, while no more than one year should elapse between successive acts. Events not represented on stage but necessary for understanding the plot are made known in interludes preceding acts. The place of the action may shift often and may range through both heaven and earth.

The *Natyasastra* describes ten major kinds of plays, of which the most important are the heroic and the social. The heroic is based on mythology or history and has an exemplary hero who defends a righteous cause; there is usually a love story in which the lovers are kept apart by some evil force until the end of the play. The social play resembles the heroic but its plot and hero are entirely imaginary, and a king is never the leading character. The surviving Sanskrit plays are mostly of these two types.

Among the oldest surviving Sanskrit plays are thirteen works by Bhasa (second or third century C.E.). The best known of these are *The Vision of Vasavadatta* and *Carudatta,* the latter based on the same story that King Sudraka (considered by many to be a wholly legendary person) was to use for *The Little Clay Cart* (*c.* fourth–eighth century), one of the most famous of all Sanskrit dramas. A social play, according to the traditional Hindu classifications,

The Little Clay Cart tells of the love of a Brahmin for a courtesan. Written in ten acts, it has a number of subplots which come together in the resolution in which the true prince, previously aided by the courtesan, recaptures his throne and unites the courtesan and Brahmin, who have narrowly escaped death at the hands of an evil prince.

Kalidasa's *Shakuntala* (late fourth–early fifth centuries), a heroic drama in seven acts, is generally considered the finest of all Sanskrit dramas. It tells of King Dushyanta's meeting with Shakuntala (the foster daughter of a hermit), their love and separation (prolonged by a curse pronounced by a holy man to whom Shakuntala has denied hospitality), and their eventual reunion. Renowned in part for its beautiful descriptive passages evoking the forest, stream, and other natural phenomena, it moves freely between heaven and earth, forest and court, from the serious and romantic to the comic. The lyrical and the fantastic mingle with the everyday as the play moves through a wide range of human experience.

Other Sanskrit dramatists include King Harsa (seventh century C.E.), with *The Pearl Necklace, The Lost Princess,* and *Delight of Snakes;* Bhavabhuti (late seventh century), with *The Story of the Great Hero, The Later Story of Rama,* and *The Stolen Marriage;* and Visakhadatta (seventh century?), with *The Signet Ring of Rakshasa.*

The *Natyasastra* also lists eighteen kinds of "lower" drama. What these were is not entirely clear. There is evidence that farce was being performed in the seventh century C.E., but lesser types of drama must have existed before that time.

Such forms as shadow plays, folk dramas, and incidental entertainments continued to flourish, but the great era of Indian drama was over. Nevertheless, between the second and seventh centuries, Sanskrit drama was more sophisticated and highly developed than anything being produced anywhere else in the world. Beginning in the late seventh century India was subjected to political upheaval, and the lack of stability probably contributed to the decline of Sanskrit drama. After the assumption of power by Muslims in the twelfth and thirteenth centuries, dramatic entertainments lost their position of honor, but a regional form, apparently (but not definitely) derived from this tradition, *kutiyattum,* continued to be given in the southwestern Indian state of Kerala by actors and musicians who were part of a hereditary temple-service caste. Their traditions can be traced back to at least the tenth century. The temple-theatres in which *kutiyattum* is performed vary in size, proportion being more important than dimensions, since each part of the whole is symbolic. There is a good deal of sculptural decoration, the most elaborate reserved for the stage. The square stage is equipped only with stools, a single bronze lamp, a removable curtain, and drums set between the two doors that lead to the dressing room back of the stage. The characters, who are representatives of the cosmic world, wear colorful costumes and makeup with strong visual patterns. *Kutiyattum* performances were given only at temple festivals. But after a Kalidasa festival was established in 1957, a series of public *kutiyattum* performances was arranged.

SANSKRIT PERFORMANCE

Performances seem to have been given on many occasions and for all types of audiences. Those most written about and praised were given at religious festivals, marriages, coronations, victory celebrations, or other special occasions. Each type of play was thought to be most appropriate to particular hours of the day or night, and consequently plays might be performed at almost any time.

Since Hindu drama was most concerned with the emotional and spiritual, rather than the external and material, it avoided realistic production practices. Its spiritual inspiration was always recognized in an elaborate preliminary ceremony preceding the play to acknowledge the gods and to prepare performers and spectators for the drama to come.

The *Natyasastra* describes three shapes of playhouses (square, rectangular, and triangular) and three sizes of each (large, medium, and small)—a total of nine theatres. The rectangular theatre of medium size is most fully described and idealized. It was 96 feet long by 48 feet wide and divided into two equal parts (auditorium and stage). The auditorium was shaped like a cave for acoustical purposes and had four pillars (white, red, yellow, and blue), probably intended to symbolize not only the four castes (and where each was to sit) but also geographical regions and compass points. The theatre in its totality symbolized the entire universe.

The half of the theatre devoted to the stage was further divided into two equal parts, one to be used as acting area, the other as backstage space. Two doors led from backstage to the acting area; between them was the place reserved for the vocal and instrumental musicians.

No scenery was used (but the stage was decorated with paintings or carvings as a decorative or symbolic background). At the beginning of the play, a preliminary section established the time, place, and situation. In each scene, descriptive passages and pantomime evoked place as needed. The actors used stylized movement and gestures to suggest such actions as climbing a hill, picking flowers, crossing a stream, riding a horse, or driving a chariot. A walk around the stage indicated a long journey; each part of the stage may have been associated with types of places or with different atmospheres or moods. Because no scenery was used, place could shift rapidly as one scene flowed into the next. Indoor and night performances were lighted with torches or lamps.

Neither of India's remaining ancient theatres follow the *Natyasastra* plan. The Sitābengā theatre at Ramgarh Hill in central India may date to as early as the second century B.C.E. It is a small theatre with seating reminiscent of a Greek odeum carved into the rock at the mouth of a cave facing an uncovered area just large enough for a small stage and a temporary scene building. The Rani Gumpa (Queen's Cave) theatre in northeast India probably dates to the first century B.C.E. This is a large two-story scene building, with an upper stage, cut into the living rock. The lower portion of the building looks much like the Greek *proskenion* while the upper part seems to contain openings much like the Greek *thyromata*. The seating area, however, was of wood, like the *ikria* of the Greeks. Both theatres lie well outside the area of India marched over by the armies of Alexander, so any similarities could simply be coincidental.

The primary emphasis in performance was on the actor, who was said to have four basic resources at his disposal: movement and gesture; speech and song; costume and makeup; and psychological insight. Movement and gesture, although based upon natural behavior, were codified into a system of prescribed signs as described in the *Natyasastra* and in other Hindu writings. Classified according to the parts of the body and inner feelings, gestures were codified (at least for some of the traditional performance forms) into thirteen movements of the head, six of the nose, six of the cheek, seven of the eyebrows, nine of the neck, seven of the chin, five of the chest, thirty-six of the eyes, thirty-two of the feet, and twenty-four of the single hand. Gait and stance also were prescribed. All these movements and gestures were combined (according to character type, emotion, and situation) to create a sign language as complex as speech.

There was a similar classification of verbal speech and music in which elaborate patterns of intonation, pitch, and tempo were mingled according to the emotion, character, and situation. Each play was accompanied by music, for which the instruments varied according to the type of play but might

A. *Patāka* hand   B. *Ardha-candra* hand

C. *Musti* hand   D. *Śikhara* hand

E. *Bhramara* hand   F. *Śukatuṇḍa* hand

FIG. 4.2

Some of the many hand positions used in Sanskrit drama and dance. From *The Mirror of Gesture* (1917).

include stringed instruments, flutes and woodwind instruments, cymbals and drums. There usually were also vocal musicians. The drum was considered most essential, for it followed the dialogue closely and enhanced rhythmic effects. The vocalists provided information about the situation or characters through entrance or exit songs; other songs indicated changes in mood or bridged gaps in the action.

Costume and makeup for each character were also strictly prescribed. Makeup indicated the character's caste, social position, and place of birth, as well as the historical period. Color was used symbolically: the Sun and Brahma were golden, lesser gods orange, high-caste characters red, and low-caste characters blue. Ornaments such as earrings, bracelets, belts, necklaces, and headgear differentiated characters within categories. Properties were used symbolically: as examples, the presence of an elephant was indicated by the use of a goad, a horse by a bit, and a chariot by a whip.

Characters were divided into clearly differentiated categories. There were four types of heroes, eight types of heroines, and numerous lesser types. Overall, each actor sought to weld conventionalized gestures and movements, speech and intonation, costume and makeup, emotion and character type into a performance capable of arousing the appropriate *rasa*. In sum, the Sanskrit theatre demanded a discipline and a knowledge of conventions probably equaled only in certain later forms in China and Japan.

There seem to have been many kinds of theatre companies. Each was headed by a director and each included the actors, musicians, and craftsmen required for the company's work. Some companies were entirely male, some entirely female, and some (the most admired) included both male and female performers. At times there were competitions among companies at which prizes were awarded by judges.

The production of Sanskrit plays ceased in the thirteenth century, but regional folk drama continued and by the seventeenth century several important forms, from the religious *Ankiya nat*, to the bawdy *Bhavai*, to the Christian *Cavittu natakam*, to the stately, all male, *Kathakali* had developed to a high level. By the twentieth century over 50 forms of folk dramas,

including puppet theatres and narrative dance forms, had been developed.

As with the Greek and Roman theatres, we can reconstruct a reasonably clear, though very general, overview of the Sanskrit theatre. Still, there is much that we do not (and probably will never) know about it. Obviously the Sanskrit theatre was highly developed, widespread, and sophisticated. Like its Greek and Roman counterparts, it too flourished for a time and then ceased to be vital. But before it declined, a great deal was shared with China.

CHINA

By 214 B.C.E. a large portion of China was united under a single ruler who ordered the building of the Great Wall to keep out invaders. This ushered in the Han Dynasty (206 B.C.E.–220 C.E.), the first great period of Chinese art and literature, during which China came to equal the Roman Empire in size. Han emperors were said to have kept thousands of entertainers at court. All sorts of entertainments flourished, so many that they came to be called the "hundred games," though none of them seem to have been dramas. Like the mimes of Rome, they included tight-rope walking, pole climbing, athletic displays, conjuring, juggling, sword and fire

FIG. 4.3
Purulia chhau dancer of northeastern India. Courtesy the Performing Arts Program of the Asia Society, New York.

swallowing, music and dance, and mime. Many of these entertainments were presented at fairs and markets as well as at court. The Han emperors actively encouraged the arts and in 104 B.C.E. established the Imperial Office of Music to organize entertainments and to promote music and dance.

The Han Dynasty was followed by some 400 years of conflict and unrest, but entertainments seem to have continued. We hear of marionettes between 265 and 420 C.E. and of impersonations of historical personages in the fourth century. After China was reunified under the Sui Dynasty (581–618 C.E.), the forms of entertainment were conglomerations of native traditions with elements imported from India and central Asia. The emperor Yang-Di became so interested in this new version of the "hundred games" that he set up a training school to encourage its development. Before his reign ended, he is said to have staged a festival involving 18,000 to 30,000 performers in an area extending over four miles.

During the succeeding Tang Dynasty (618–907) comic skits became popular, puppet shows flourished,

FIG. 4.4
Kathakali performers. Note the heavily stylized makeup and costume, especially on the figure at left. From Gargi, *The Theatre in India.* Courtesy Theatre Arts Books.

and great progress was made toward a distinctive theatrical form incorporating music, dance, dialogue, and acrobatics. In 714 Emperor Xuan Zong (reigned 713–756, also transliterated as Hsuan Tsung and sometimes called Ming-huang) established a school to train singers, dancers, and other court entertainers. It differed from earlier schools in its stress on popular and innovative (rather than traditional) forms and in its scope (at one time it included 11,409 students and entertainers). This school underwent several changes but it is usually known as "The Pear Garden." To the present day Chinese actors trace their descent from this school. "Student of the Pear Garden" has roughly the same meaning in China as "thespian" does in the West. Stories of considerable length that would become a fertile source for future dramatists also began to appear in abundance in this era.

The Tang Dynasty was followed by a period of unrest before the Sông Dynasty, which is broken up into the Northern Sông (960–1126) and the Southern Sông (1127–1279), brought China another of its great cultural eras. Short variety entertainments (*zaju*) were very popular and the first purpose-built theatres (*goulan*) were erected. The oldest extant Chinese drama, *The Doctor of Letters,* which includes a prologue summarizing the action, and a main story told through dialogue and songs, may date from this period. Just over 150 such texts survive. Not only did the arts flourish during this time, but its scientists produced such inventions as the magnetic compass, gunpowder, and movable type. Two of the most famous Chinese novels, *Romance of the Three Kingdoms* and *The Water's Edge,* both of which evolved over many centuries, took definite shape. These and other tales were narrated by professional storytellers at teahouses and were dramatized for puppet and shadow-play theatres, two of the most popular entertainments of the common people.

During the Sông Dynasty the best performers were recruited for the court, where elaborate celebrations were given on such occasions as the emperor's birthday. Other performers played wherever they could. They banded together into troupes of five to seven members and played in villages or cities, teahouses, or improvised theatres. In the cities, playhouses (*goulan*) were situated in special areas called "tile districts." According to contemporary accounts, these theatres were fenced enclosures, above which flags and banners flew; the stage was a roofed platform open on three sides; at ground level there was a large area where people might stand, and around this there might be raised stands or balconies. There are said to have been fifty or more theatres in Kaifeng, the northern Sông capital.

FIG. 4.5
Chinese shadow puppets made of skin. They are manipulated by rods attached to the back of the puppet. Courtesy the Performing Arts Program of the Asia Society, New York.

FIG. 4.6
A Chinese theatre used for a festival of the twelfth century C.E. at Kaifeng, the northern capital of the Sông dynasty. A silk scroll of the twelfth century, recopied in the eighteenth century. Courtesy John Hu and the Taipei Museum.

THE DEVELOPMENT OF CHINESE LITERARY DRAMA

Ironically, it was not until the Mongols conquered China in the thirteenth century that drama began to flourish. The Mongols, whose empire stretched across Asia into Europe, established the Yüan Dynasty, which was to rule China from 1279 until 1368. (It was during this time that Marco Polo visited China and alerted Europeans to the marvels of this rich and highly sophisticated country.)

Historians often say that advances in literature under the Yüan rulers are explained by the exclusion of native Chinese intellectuals from government posts, the traditional outlet for their talents. These intellectuals needed other employment and some began to practice and perfect native folk arts, including drama. Especially attracted to earlier forms of music-drama, these writers created works usually considered the foundation of the classical Chinese theatre. Thus, despite political and social repression, China enjoyed something of a golden age in drama.

Yüan dramatists drew their stories from history, legend, novels, epics, and contemporary events. The characters ranged through the entire spectrum of humanity, although the most important roles usually were those of emperors, scholars or students, government officials, generals, rebels, wives, daughters, or concubines. The plays advocated the virtues of loyalty to family and friends, honesty, and devotion to work and duty. They often showed a world out of joint, but one in which poetic justice usually prevailed, and even plays that ended unhappily for the protagonists often showed the villains being discovered and punished. In the final scenes, lovers or long-separated relatives were reunited or reconciled, deserving officials rewarded, and wealth or honor restored. Overall, the plays provided a wide and rich panorama of Chinese life, much of it based on the past but always made relevant to the contemporary scene.

Through most of the Yüan period the best dramatists lived in northern China, especially Beijing, where they developed a style usually labeled "northern" or *zaju*. Each play in this style usually (but not invariably) consisted of four acts with from ten to twenty songs or arias, all sung by the protagonist. The rest of the characters spoke or recited their lines. No scores for Yüan plays have survived. The writers were governed by strict rules which demanded that all songs in a single act use melodies from the same mode and that all lyrics make use of the same rhyme scheme; the mode and rhyme used for one act could not be used for any other act of the same play.

If the dramatic action could not be represented in four acts, one or more wedges (*chieh jie*) could be added as prologues or interludes. A wedge was short, with no more than two arias, which might be sung by a character other than the protagonist. At the end of the play a rhymed couplet or quatrain summed up the story. One of these final lines also served as the title for the piece.

The simple, unadorned accompaniment used a seven-tone scale and was usually played by an orchestra consisting of gong, drum, clapper, flute, and p'i p'a (a four-stringed plucked instrument similar to a lute). The action typically extended over months or years, only rarely was it confined to one place, and it occasionally ended unhappily, although poetic justice usually prevailed.

The many stage directions included in the texts, contemporary references, and a still-extant wall painting (dated 1324) indicate that many of the now-traditional staging practices of the Chinese theatre were already in use by the fourteenth century. The stage was essentially bare, with one door on either side at the rear for entrances and exits. Between the two doors hung an embroidered, purely decorative wall piece (the extant picture shows this in two pieces which meet at the center). In the painting the performers wear colorful costumes, some with long and extremely wide sleeves, makeup, and beards. Properties—such as

FIG. 4.7
A wall painting from northwestern China, 1324, showing that many features of the traditional Chinese theatre were already established by that date. Note the hangings at the rear of the stage, the character entering at rear left, and the costumes and accessories of the figures in the foreground. Courtesy Professor Wu-chi Liu.

fans, swords, and belts—are also in evidence. Both male and female performers were included in the companies, many of which were named for the leading actresses of the time.

It is unclear how many plays were written during the Yüan period, but about 700 titles are recorded; about 170 of these plays have survived. Some 550 dramatists are known to have written at this time, but little information about them (often not even life dates) has come down to us. One of the best of these authors was Guan Hanqing (or Kuan Han-ch'ing, *c.* 1245–*c.* 1322), often called the father of Chinese drama. He wrote sixty-seven plays, of which eighteen survive. Perhaps the best known of these plays is the domestic tragedy, *The Injustice*

FIG. 4.8
A scene from *Romance of the Western Chamber* showing a rendezvous between Ying Ying and Student Yang as the maid Hung Niang keeps watch. From an edition published during the Ming dynasty. Courtesy Professor Wu-chi Liu.

Done to Ngo Tou, based on a real-life murder and trial. It shows the suffering, courage, and virtue of a chaste widow wrongfully accused of murder by a wicked rejected suitor. After she has been executed, her spirit appears to her long-lost father, now a judge, who reopens the case and punishes the villain. The moral courage of Ngo Tou, who epitomizes the virtuous Chinese woman, is intended to provide a lesson for everyone.

The most popular of Yüan dramas is *Romance of the Western Chamber* by Wang Shifu. Unique among northern dramas, it is composed of twenty acts, although the traditional form is preserved by casting it into five parts, each with four acts. Based on a novel, it traces the trials and joys of a pair of ideal lovers, the beautiful Ying Ying and the talented Student Yang, and shows their reunion after long separation. It is noted especially for its characterizations and its poetic excellence, variety, and beauty.

Another well-known play of this period is *The Orphan of the House of Zhao,* probably by Qi Zhun

Xiang (or Chi Chün-hsiang), which concerns a child who is saved at great sacrifice to his rescuers so that he can grow up to avenge his family, who has been exterminated by a corrupt general. This was the first Chinese play widely known in the West, although only through Voltaire's adaptation of it as *The Orphan of China* (1755). An even more influential play in the West has been *The Story of the Chalk Circle* by Li Xingdao (or Li Hsing-tao). It tells of two women who both claim to be the mother of a young child and family heir; the judge places the child inside a chalk circle and orders the women to pull him out; he awards the child to the one who shows her love by refusing to hurt him. This drama was to serve as a basis for A. H. Klabund's *The Circle of Chalk* (1923) and Bertolt Brecht's *The Caucasian Chalk Circle* (1944). Other plays of this period deal with the religious and supernatural (as in Zhi Yüan's *Dream of the Yellow Millet*), bandit heroes (as in Gao Wenxiu's *The Black Whirlwind*), and many other topics.

Before the middle of the fourteenth century, another school of drama, the "southern," began to gain in popularity in the area around Hangzhou, where the northern style was little understood or appreciated. Of the Yüan dramas from this area, the best known is *Lute Song* (c. 1350) by Gao Ming. Its forty-two acts tell the story of Zhao Wu Niang (or Chao

FIG. 4.9
Ground plan of a traditional Chinese theatre. BS = backstage; EN = entrance to stage; ET = exit from stage; O = orchestra; E = main entrance to auditorium; R = raised side seats; C = tables and stools for audience. Drawing by Douglas Hubbell.

Wu-niang), a virtuous wife who stays at home when her scholar husband, Cai Bojie (or Ts'ai Po-chieh), sets off for the emperor's court. There he succumbs to the allure of fame and wealth and marries the daughter of a prime minister. After Cai Bojie's parents die, Zhao Wu Niang makes her way to the court, where she recalls her husband to his duty. They are reconciled, and he places her on an equal footing with his second wife. *Lute Song* is noted especially for its pathos, poetry, and songs of great beauty. The founder of the Ming dynasty (1368–1644), who ousted the Mongol rulers, admired *Lute Song* so much that he demanded to see it often. His patronage increased the prestige of the southern drama and helped to make it the dominant style.

During the Yüan period, several large cities had theatre districts, each with many theatres offering both standing room and stall seating for patrons. Surviving records from the period suggest that performers, both male and female, often served as both actors and prostitutes.

As early as the Tang Dynasty (618–907), when the "The Pear Garden" school for training entertainers was just underway and long before the building of theatres or the advent of a literary drama in China, Korean and Chinese artists found their way to Japan and Japanese artists found their way to the courts of these countries. This marks the traditional start of theatre in Japan.

JAPAN

The early history of Japan and its theatrical forms are shrouded in mystery, since the first written account, *Records of Ancient Things,* was not compiled until 712 C.E. Before that time, however, there were numerous rituals, many of them related to Shintoism, which began in nature and ancestor worship. All these rituals are now usually grouped together under the general label *kagura;* some have persisted to the present day. During this early period a form of rhythmic movement set to music—*sangaku,* "miscellaneous" or "scattered" music—was also being performed at court. In addition, jesters were common.

During the sixth century C.E. Japan began to undergo profound changes after Buddhism was introduced during the reign of Prince Shotoku

FIG. 4.10
A *Bugaku* Dance of the Left, "The Music of Great Peace," in which the dancers represent warriors who return to the capital in time to prevent a revolt. From Robert Garfias, *Music of a Thousand Autumns.* Courtesy Mr. Garfias and the University of California Press.

(573–621). During the following 200 years continental culture, especially from Korea, China, and India, was enthusiastically embraced. Writing and numerous forms of music were among the imports, as were masked dances that soon became regular features of Japanese festivals. Of these masked dances, one—*bugaku*—has survived to the present day and is still performed on important state occasions at the imperial court and at certain shrines and temples. *Bugaku* now designates any dance performed to classical court music (*gagaku*) by dancers whose art has been passed down through generations of families with hereditary rights. Some of the dances are Japanese in origin, but most were imported from continental Asia, especially from Korea, China, Tibet, and India. The dances are usually divided into two categories: "Dances of the Right," from Korea; and "Dances of the Left," from China or South Asia. Despite these labels, the dances are now almost wholly Japanese in character. *Bugaku* performers are also divided into two groups: "Dancers of the Music on the Right," who are dressed predominantly in green and perform to accompaniment played primarily on percussion instruments; and "Dancers of the Music on the Left," who are dressed predominantly in red and perform to accompaniment played primarily on woodwinds. The rhythms vary from the stately to the lively. *Bugaku* is a symbolic representation of one part, the most interesting, of a whole story, and is structured in terms of *jo-ha-kyu* ("beginning, breaking from, fast," indicating tempo, mood, emotional intensity, and vitality of performance). It probably exerted considerable influence on the early development of Noh drama.

In 1955 the Japanese government recognized *bugaku* and *gagaku* as national treasures. Since then they have gained a much wider audience (sometimes even being televised) and have become objects of international scholarly research. The future of these art forms seems to be assured.

EARLY PROFESSIONAL THEATRE IN JAPAN

Sarugaku-no probably originated when ritualistic elements, music, and dance from the continent were mingled with tumbling, dancing, and mimicry. The result was a kind of noisy merrymaking (*sarugaku* means "monkey music"). It was extremely varied, even circus-like. An early treatise, *New Notes on Sarugaku* (*c.* 1060), considers *sarugaku* to be an inclusive term for all kinds of comic entertainment. *Dengaku-no*, which may have been imported from Korea, came to be associated primarily with harvest rituals. It was both acrobatic and rural in character. The first reference to it as a dramatic performance (*c.* 1023) describes it as made up of rustic dances and songs.

Around the beginning of the twelfth century, *sarugaku-no* was adapted by Buddhists as a way of demonstrating their teachings. Thus, it was given a role similar to that of the medieval mystery and morality plays of Europe. At first the plays were acted by priests, but as performances came to attract large numbers of people to the temples, professional players began to imitate the temple performances at times other than festivals. As the skill of the professionals grew, some temples began to employ them to replace the actor-priests. *Dengaku-no* was developed in much the same way, but primarily at Shinto shrines.

After a time performers had so proliferated that controls were needed. As a result, guilds (*za*) were formed. *Dengaku* guilds can be traced back as far as 1150 and *sarugaku* guilds to about 1270. Most of these guilds were attached to some powerful shrine or temple which granted them a monopoly on performances in its area. In return, the players gave at least some free performances during ceremonies and festivals. By the beginning of the fourteenth century, then, there were numerous groups of well-organized players who mingled mimicry, song, and dance, although the results were probably not yet fully dramatic.

Sarugaku-no and *dengaku-no* paved the way for *Noh* drama, which reached its peak in the early 1400s while Western Europe was in the midst of the late Middle Ages and the great Corpus Christi cycle plays were beginning to proliferate. It is therefore necessary to return to Europe to examine development in Byzantium and Western Europe leading up to the late Middle Ages (1300–1500) and overlapping with the early Renaissance.

THE THEATRE OF BYZANTIUM

Although the Western Roman Empire had disintegrated by the sixth century C.E., the Eastern part remained and flourished. Thus, after the fall of Rome, the center of power shifted once more to the Hellenized areas of the eastern Mediterranean. In actuality, these areas had always been the most sophisticated parts of the empire, for though Rome was the center of power, the Hellenic territories were more advanced in terms of culture, manufacture, and trade, and Rome depended much on the East for its learning, luxuries, and crafts.

The East began to assume a dominant role politically in the early fourth century C.E. after Diocletian divided the empire into two parts to simplify its administration. In 330, the Emperor Constantine moved the capital of the entire empire to a city he had built on the Bosporus, Constantinople. After 395 the division of the empire into East and West became permanent. Consequently, the Byzantine Empire (as the eastern part came to be called) is considered by many historians to date from this time, though others prefer to identify its beginnings with the fall of the western half of the empire in 476. The Byzantine Empire was to continue, ever shrinking in size, until 1453.

The rulers of the Byzantine Empire considered their government a continuation of the Roman Empire. For centuries they viewed the territories in the West as temporarily lost to invaders or usurpers, and from time to time sought to regain them. Under Justinian (527–565) much of the West was retaken, but Byzantium became and remained primarily an eastern Mediterranean power. Justinian was also the last of the emperors to speak Latin, and thereafter the official language of the empire was Greek.

Between the time of Constantine and Justinian, the empire was converted into a Christian state. In Byzantium the emperor assumed leadership in religious as well as secular affairs and came to be considered God's regent on earth. He appointed all major church officials and took an active part in settling doctrinal differences, which were numerous and intense. This subordination of church to state (especially during times when the Byzantine Empire was ruled by empresses), along with disputes over the authority of the Bishop of Rome (the Pope), became a source of controversy so great that after 1054 the church permanently broke into two parts: Roman Catholic and Eastern Orthodox. The latter prevailed in most of Eastern Europe, Russia, and Asia Minor, and the former in the rest of Europe. To this schism can be attributed many of the differences in outlook and culture between Eastern and Western Europe down to the present time.

The Byzantines considered themselves the defenders of Christian territories from the encroachment of others. With Islam's rise and territorial expansion from the seventh century onward, the Byzantine Empire came under increasing pressure. Eventually Byzantium appealed to western Christians to aid in holding or recapturing the holy lands of the eastern Mediterranean. To meet this challenge, the West launched six "crusades" between 1096 and 1229. Unfortunately, the Westerners respected Byzantine Christians no more than they did Muslims, and in 1204 they took Constantinople itself and divided its territories. Although the empire was reestablished in 1261, it never regained its former strength, and in 1453 it fell to the Turks, who refashioned Constantinople into their own capital, the present-day Istanbul.

THE BYZANTINE THEATRE

Although it was self-consciously Christian, the Byzantine Empire was also proud of its Greek heritage, which it sought to preserve even as it denied the pagan gods and myths that had shaped it. The results were a paradoxical mixture of cultures, for thought Christianity was intertwined with almost every aspect of civic life, Byzantine popular entertainments resembled those of late Rome. In turn, Byzantine scholars scorned the popular theatre and devoted their attention to the drama of classical Greece. Thus, Byzantine theatre has three main aspects: popular, religious, and scholarly.

It is difficult to assess the extent and nature of Byzantine popular theatre because the surviving evidence is so slight and historians cannot agree on how the evidence should be interpreted.

Those charged with copying documents as they deteriorated in the Byzantine Empire, did not often give a high priority to documents which concerned contemporary theatre. Byzantium also experienced several *iconoclast,* movements in which any art relating to theatre is likely to have been a prime target, and such destruction was even more common in the parts of the empire conquered by Islamic forces. Existing records, however, suggest that at least for the first few centuries, the theatrical fare resembled that of late Rome: mime, pantomime, scenes or recitations from tragedies and comedies, dances, and variety entertainment of all sorts. And it seems that at least some of these continued, in modified forms, throughout the Byzantine period.

Theatrical performances were given at public festivals, fairs, private banquets, and many other occasions when entertainment was called for. Foreign visitors to Byzantium often reported their amazement and delight at the variety and skill of its entertainments, which exceeded anything then known in Western Europe. While the great Hippodrome was still in operation, these performances were an integral part of what went on between the all-important chariot races. Constantinople also had two theatres, and the Byzantine empire inherited nearly all of the Hellenistic and Greco-Roman theatres, but we really have little information concerning what went on in them and only scattered information as to when they went out of use. According to one account, the comedies of Menander were still being performed at Antioch (in Syria) as late as the fifth century but the performance of classical plays does not seem to have continued long after that.

The state denied actors many civil rights. According to ecclesiastical rules, both professional entertainers and anyone who married them were to be expelled from the church, although this had to be

FIG. 4.11
Eastern mimes of the eleventh century. Fresco in St. Sophia in Kiev (Ukraine). Redrawn and published in *Sapeski Emperatorskago Archaeologishago Obshchestva*, n.s. 3 (1903).

modified when the future emperor, Justinian, married the mime actress Theodora in 525. Churchmen continued to denounce actors, and in 692 the Trullan Synod sought to have all mimes and theatrical performances banned. Yet performances were still included in many religious festivals and the participants were generally blessed by the emperor or empress. After a time, the church seems to have ceased trying to abolish theatrical entertainments and contented itself with prohibiting them on Saturdays and Sundays, denying performers the church's sacraments, and threatening any member of the clergy who dared to attend.

Some have suggested that the theatrical impulse in Byzantium was satisfied by the numerous church ceremonies with their rich vestments, stately movements, and grand spectacle. Religious celebrations were especially elaborate during the Easter season,

FIG. 4.12
Ivory diptych *c.* 517 C.E. showing Byzantine entertainments. At left, trained horses (above) and mime scenes (below); at right, animal baiting. Courtesy Bibliothéque Nationale, Paris.

when the events of Christ's last days were recalled in processions that wound through the streets from one church to another to the accompaniment of responsive singing.

Where scholarly opinion divides, however, is on the question as to whether the Byzantines developed a liturgical drama. There are surviving homilies (or sermons) with dialogue sections (always involving episodes from the life of Christ or the Virgin Mary). Some scholars argue that some of these dialogues were so long (about thirty lines) that they must either have been acted or chanted responsively. Since they date from the period prior to the ninth century, these scholars think such homilies exerted direct influence on Western liturgical drama, which emerged in the tenth century. Such views remain theories, however, for there is no undisputed evidence to show that they were performed or that they influenced Western practices.

In the tenth century Liudprand of Cremona, a bishop sent by the German ruler Otto as an ambassador to Byzantium, describes a play he saw in which the prophet Elijah was flown up to heaven. It is not clear whether this was performed in a church, if it was a mime performance during a religious festival, or even if it was a religious play. The Byzantine play, *The Suffering Christ* (*Christos Paschon* or *Christus Patiens*), which begins: "Now in the manner of Euripides, I will the Passion tell which saved the world," and then goes on to paraphrase about one-third of its 2640 lines from tragedies by Euripides, was probably written in the eleventh century, but most scholars agree that it is a closet drama not intended for public performance. Another drama, a passion play in ten scenes or episodes, has also survived. Estimates of when it was written range from the tenth to the fourteenth century. There seems little doubt that it was staged, but the manuscript comes from Cyprus during the period when it was governed by Westerners, and therefore many scholars argue that it was imported from Europe, where religious drama was by then flourishing. On the basis of such evidence, it is impossible to know whether the Byzantines had a significant religious drama. It certainly does not appear that what they had could have been the inspiration for theatre in western Europe, and it may be that western Europe brought religious drama to them.

Regardless of what one concludes about Byzantine popular or religious performances, Constantinople is important in theatre history for another reason: its scholars preserved many classical Greek manuscripts and produced the massive encyclopedia, the *Suda* (tenth century), from which a good deal of our information on classical Greek theatre comes.

FIG. 4.13

Miniatures from the Byzantine *Homilies of the Monk John* depicting Mary and Joseph before the Sanhedrin. Courtesy Bibliothèque Nationale, Paris.

When Western powers ruled Constantinople from 1204 to 1261, they were able to send many important manuscripts to Europe. When Constantinople fell in 1453, many of the remaining scholars fled to the West taking with them the last of the manuscripts on which our texts of the existing Greek plays are based. Without the efforts of these scholars, many Greek plays would have been lost forever.

Though it seems clear that theatrical entertainments persisted throughout the 1000-year history of the Byzantine Empire, no indisputably Byzantine plays intended for performance have survived and our records concerning entertainments are so sparse that they render suspect any firm conclusions about the nature and extent of Byzantine theatre. Still, from what remains we gain glimpses that suggest a rich theatrical life and even more intriguing possibilities that Byzantine practices may have played a role in the revival of Western drama. That it would have been possible for Byzantium to influence Western Europe is clear, for communication and trade between the two never ceased. Without question, Byzantine art influenced Western church architecture and motifs in the early ninth century. The Crusades also increased contacts between East and West beginning in the eleventh century. But despite the obvious opportunities, it is impossible to prove

FIG. 4.14
Turkish shadow puppets. Courtesy Puppentheatersammlung, Munich Stadtmuseum.

direct influence on Western theatre. Nevertheless, Byzantium probably kept alive a theatrical tradition, and some parts of it may have affected later artists.

THE RISE OF ISLAM

The Byzantine Empire ultimately succumbed to the forces of Islam (the Muslims or Mohammedans). The Moslem world had expanded rapidly after the teachings of Mohammed (570–632 C.E.) began to be accepted around 622. In the century following his death, Mohammed's followers conquered all of North Africa and penetrated into Europe through Spain as far as southern France before they were finally halted in a battle at Tours in 732. They also spread eastward into Persia and northern India, and as far as present-day Indonesia and the Philippines.

The early Muslims had great respect for learning: they founded many universities; they preserved and transmitted much of the heritage from Greece, Persia, and Egypt to succeeding generations; and they made many contributions of their own to medicine, philosophy, mathematics, and geography. Because of their far-flung territories, they were the medium through which many Asian inventions—such as paper and the magnetic compass—reached the West. They created a brilliant and graceful civilization beside which Western Europe in the eighth and ninth centuries seemed barbarous and Byzantium backward.

In a history of theatre, however, Islam is largely a negative force. It forbade artists to make images of living things because Allah was said to be the only creator of life and to compete with him was considered a mortal sin. Thus, Islamic art remained primarily decorative rather than representational. The prohibitions extended to the theatre, and consequently in those areas where Islam became dominant, advanced theatrical forms were stifled. Storytelling survived almost everywhere, and in some places a crude folk drama persisted. In other areas, shadow puppetry, a minor form first developed in India, was allowed to flourish because it was seen as nonrepresentational. The puppets are two-dimensional cut-outs made of translucent leather and manipulated with sticks. Only their shadows—projected on a cloth by the light of lanterns or torches—are actually seen. In several countries shadow puppetry became a highly developed art and continues to be popular from Turkey to Indonesia. By the fifteenth century, shadow puppet plays revolving around Karagoz and his farcical adventures (which could be pointedly satirical and topical) became popular in Turkey. Eventually these entertainments came to be called *Karagoz*, and have survived as a distinctive form of shadow puppet theatre to this day. In other areas, means were also found to avoid direct representationalism and circumvent the prohibitions. So, the Moslems did not obliterate theatrical activities in their territories, but they did discourage them and in most instances succeeded in confining them to minor forms. Their presence significantly hampered future interactions between Byzantium and India, although trade with China actually expanded. Still, the Byzantine Empire's closest exchanges were with Western Europe.

WESTERN EUROPEAN THEATRE

Beginning in the fourth century C.E., general disorder increased in Western Europe, and gradually towns and industry decayed and long-distance trade diminished to a trickle. Wars, famine, and disease depopulated many areas and large tracts of tilled land returned to forest. As civil authority decreased, the church began to fill the gap with its own hierarchically organized bureaucracy. From the fourth century onward, the Bishop of Rome, claiming succession from St. Peter, asserted his precedence over all other church officials in the West, and gradually Rome's primacy was acknowledged both in church governance and in doctrinal matters outside of Byzantine territory. But during the sixth and seventh centuries even the church's power decayed considerably as education declined and as formerly pagan groups (who clung to many of their beliefs and rites) were incorporated into it. By this time, European society consisted primarily of three groups: a great mass of peasants who tilled the soil, and over them two kinds of lords, secular and ecclesiastical.

The arts held a precarious foothold in this insecure world. Building in stone almost ceased, and art objects were intentionally kept small so they might be transported easily in times of upheaval. Illuminated manuscripts, containers to hold the remains of saints or other sacred objects, articles used in church ceremonies, and various kinds of jewelry were the principal outlets for artistic expression. The writings of the period were primarily hymns, sermons, and similar theologically oriented works. Latin became merely a literary and ecclesiastical medium, whereas in everyday life local dialects, the forerunners of modern European languages, were the norm.

Monasteries became major preservers of learning. Christian monasticism had begun in Egypt in the fourth century and was adopted in the West both in Ireland and Italy in the sixth. These Celtic and Benedictine monasteries were oases in a turbulent world and became the primary repositories of manuscripts and learning. For several centuries the monastic schools were the only ones of consequence in Western Europe and their contribution to the reemergence of Western culture was enormous.

In the eighth century, Europe returned to greater stability under the Carolingian kings. The progenitor of this line, Charles Martel, defeated the Muslims at Tours in 732, primarily through his innovative use of armored horsemen as the principal military force (thus initiating what would develop into the tradition of knighthood). The most important ruler from this line was Charlemagne (reigned 768–814), who extended his realm eastward into Slavic territories (forcibly converting non-Christians on the way) and southward into Spain and Italy. In Rome on Christmas Day in 800, Charlemagne was crowned by the Pope, who pronounced him the legitimate successor to Constantine. This was the first attempt to establish what would later (from 962 to 1806) be called the Holy Roman Empire, ostensibly the continuation of the original Western Roman Empire. As the one who bestowed the crown, the Pope also asserted his precedence over all secular princes.

The arts revived under Charlemagne. He promoted learning and sought to increase literacy among the clergy. His palace school was the first major center of learning outside of the Benedictine monasteries. While in Italy, Charlemagne visited the Byzantine churches built by Justinian at Ravenna, and upon his return to Aachen (Aix-la-Chapelle) erected a chapel modeled on one of them. This was the first important stone structure built in Western Europe after the fall of Rome. It also opened a period of Byzantine influence on Western religious art.

Unfortunately, Charlemagne's empire rapidly disintegrated following his death in 814. Not only did his descendants fight among themselves, but they were also unable to withstand a new menace from the north: the still-pagan Vikings (later Normans). Just as the Muslims had come to control the Mediterranean, the Vikings controlled the northern seas, from which they launched devastating raids. Once more Europe broke into small units isolated from each other and the world at large. Gradually a system took shape that is usually called feudalism, the societal pattern that underlay early medieval culture.

Historians usually divide the Middle Ages into stages, early (c. 900–c. 1050), high (c. 1050–1300), and late (c. 1300–1500). In the early Middle Ages, life was still relatively simple, for towns and industry had not yet revived. During these years two patterns were established. Under manoralism, the basic unit was the *manor* (or large estate) whose owner assumed absolute authority over the serfs or peasants who worked his land collectively. Under feudalism, the lords of manors were the *vassals* (or subjects) of some greater lord, who was in turn the vassal of a king or ruler of a state. Vassals were bound to supply their lords a specified number of knights upon demand, and the lords in return were bound to protect their vassals. This arrangement was the origin of the various ranks and titles of nobility, many of which persist to the present day.

THE THEATRE, 500 TO 900 C.E.

The theatre also began to revive during the early Middle Ages. Following the disintegration of the

FIG. 4.15
Europe in 1096 C.E.

Roman Empire, organized theatrical activities had virtually disappeared in Western Europe as conditions returned to a state similar to the period that preceded the emergence of drama in the sixth century B.C.E. Nevertheless, theatrical elements survived in at least three different kinds of activities: the remnants of the Roman mimes; popular festivals and pagan rites; and Christian ceremonies. The theatre was to emerge again from these wellsprings during the early Middle Ages.

After the Western Roman Empire crumbled and the state ceased to finance performances, the mime troupes had broken up. Small nomadic bands seem to have traveled about thereafter, performing wherever they could find an audience. For the most part they became singers, storytellers, jesters, tumblers, jugglers, rope dancers, and exhibitors of trained animals. None of the surviving records indicate that they were giving dramatic pieces, although it is possible that they presented crude sketches. Such performers were most common in southern Europe, which had been most fully Romanized. From the beginning they were denounced by the church, which branded them infamous and sought to make them outcasts. In the ninth century they seem to have been especially active, for the number of church

FIG. 4.16

Miniature showing a trained horse. From *Li Romans d'Alixandre*, a manuscript from *c.* 1340. Courtesy the Curators of the Bodleian Library, Oxford.

edicts against *mimi, histriones,* and *ioculatores*—terms used interchangeably for all secular performers—are most numerous at the time; later they became identified under the generic term "minstrels."

There were numerous festivals throughout Western Europe featuring these itinerant, as well as local, entertainers. Most of these festivals were outgrowths of centuries-old pagan rites. Easter was tied to Passover and so was already linked to spring fertility festivals. But the church, in seeking to convert Western Europe to Christianity, usurped many others. Christ's birth, for example, was not fixed as December 25 until the fourth century, when it was intended to replace a Roman festival in honor of the birth of several minor deities from Dionysus to Osiris. Other existing festivals were also reoriented. Those honoring local deities were reassigned to a "patron saint" when the deity's temple was replaced by a Christian church. The few pagan rites that survived eventually lost their religious significance and became mere traditional entertainments.

As the church absorbed local festivals, its own rites became more elaborate, and liturgical drama was ultimately to emerge out of these elaborations. This final step, however, was merely a culmination of innovations that can be traced back into preceding centuries.

MONASTERY THEATRE—LITURGICAL DRAMA AND COMEDY

By the early Middle Ages (*c.* 900–1050), the church calendar provided an incentive toward dramatization because it commemorated particular biblical events on specific days of the year. By the tenth century a number of theatrical elements had been incorporated into these annual celebrations in an attempt to vivify them. Palm Sunday was observed with an elaborate procession in which a figure representing Christ riding on a donkey moved from outside the city to a church. On Good Friday, a cross was often wrapped in burial clothes and placed in a symbolic tomb, from which it was raised on Easter Sunday. Similar ceremonies commemorated other events of the Christian year.

Symbolic objects and actions—church vestments, altars, censers, and the pantomime of the priests—constantly recalled the events which Christian ritual celebrates. Certain emblems had also come to be associated with specific biblical characters (such as "the keys of the kingdom" with Saint Peter and the dove with the Virgin Mary), making it easy to identify these characters and also providing a basis for conventionalized costumes in plays. Thus, there were extensive sets of visual signs that could be used to communicate with an audience that was largely illiterate.

By the ninth century, the musical portion of church services in the Benedictine monasteries (other orders were not established until the 1200s) had become extremely complex and had motivated the introduction of tropes (or interpolations into an existing text). These first took the form of lengthened musical passages, originally of the final syllable of Alleluia. Eventually these extended melodies became so elaborate that words were added (in Latin), one syllable for each note, as an aid to memory.

Liturgical drama has traditionally been traced to such tropes. The oldest of these, found in the introductory portion of the Easter liturgy, is the *Whom do you Seek (Quem-Quaeritis)* Easter trope, dating from about 925. The translated Latin reads in its entirety:

> *Angels:*   *Whom seek ye in the tomb, O Christians?*
>
> *The three Marys:*   *Jesus of Nazareth, the crucified, O Heavenly Beings.*
>
> *Angels:*   *He is not here, he is risen as he foretold. Go and announce that he is risen from the tomb.*

FIG. 4.17

Figures wearing animal masks suggestive of rituals or entertainments of the early Middle Ages. Miniatures from *Li Romans d'Alixandre, c.* 1340. Courtesy the Curators of the Bodleian Library, Oxford.

This text was probably merely sung responsively by two groups and did not involve actors impersonating characters.

It is unclear just where liturgical "sung" drama first started to involve acting, but the earliest extant playlet, complete with directions for its performance, is found in the *Regularis Concordia* (or *Monastic Agreement*) compiled between 965 and 975 by Ethelwold, Bishop of Winchester (England). This may have been an attempt to stimulate and educate the monks and their young initiates who sometimes entered the monasteries as early as the age of seven. Although it is often assumed that Ethelwold was merely adopting practices already established on the continent, this is by no means certain. Regardless of where liturgical drama originated, it was widespread before the end of the tenth century.

In addition to liturgical dramas, a few nonliturgical plays have survived from this period. At about the time when liturgical drama was coming into being, Hrosvitha (c. 935–973), a canoness at the monastery of Gandersheim in northern Germany, wrote six plays modeled after Terence's comedies but using religious subjects. According to her own account, she was drawn to Terence because of his style, but fearing the adverse influence of these pagan works on her Latin students, she set out to provide a suitable alternative. There has been considerable disagreement over whether her plays—*Abraham, Callimachus, Dulcitius, Gallicanus, Paphnutius,* and *Sapientia*—were performed in her time. They were first published in 1501 and subsequently had considerable influence on religious and didactic plays of the sixteenth century. These plays have a special place in theatre history, however, for a number of reasons: (1) Hrosvitha is the first known female dramatist; (2) she is the first identifiable Western dramatist of the postclassical era; and (3) she provides us with the oldest extant feminist perspective in drama. She was followed by Hildegard of Bingen (*d.* 1179), a Benedictine abbess, who wrote a Latin musical drama, *Ordo Virtutum* (*c.* 1155), featuring a struggle between personified virtues and forces of evil. Nuns continued to contribute to theatre throughout the period (Katherine de Sutton, abbess of Barking, was producing theatre in England in the late fourteenth century), but most restricted themselves to more traditionally liturgical plays.

It was the emerging liturgical drama, nevertheless, that set the tone for what was to follow, although the full development of liturgical drama did not occur until the high Middle Ages (*c.* 1050– *c.* 1300).

FIG. 4.18
The three Marys encounter the angel at the tomb. From the *Benedictional* (*c.* 965–975) of Ethelwold, Bishop of Winchester, England. Courtesy Trustees of the British Museum.

THEATRE IN THE HIGH MIDDLE AGES, 1050–1300 C.E.

By the middle of the eleventh century the Vikings had been converted to Christianity and had ceased their plundering. Conditions had become sufficiently stable for town life to revive and industry and trade to flourish. This revival was rapid and felt throughout Europe. Sizable cities arose, many of them independently governed, and as they gained power manorial feudalism declined. Universities grew up in major cities, schools arose around cathedrals, and they soon displaced monasteries as the primary seats of learning. Contacts with the Byzantines and Arabs greatly increased because of trade and the six crusades that were launched between 1096 and 1229. These contacts greatly enlarged political, intellectual, and artistic horizons.

As confidence grew, monumentally scaled buildings increased in number. Earlier, fortified castles had begun to be built, and a few sizable churches had been erected. Large-scale buildings became common by the eleventh century. Romanesque-style churches, using the Roman arch as the primary unit, were built in increasingly larger sizes. Then, in 1144, the church of St. Denis, just outside Paris, introduced the Gothic style with its pointed arches, buttressed walls, and huge expanses of windows. By 1300 monumental Gothic churches, richly decorated with statuary, carvings, and stained glass, had been built throughout Western Europe. Liturgical dramas began to be performed in them, and thus they became more accessible to laymen than when they had been performed in monasteries.

Liturgical drama had spread as far east as Russia and from Scandinavia in the north to Italy in the south. The most prolific areas were France and Germany. In Spain the Muslim occupation prevented the spread of drama beyond those northern provinces conquered by Charlemagne. Because the number of surviving liturgical plays is so great, it is sometimes forgotten that a single church probably performed no more than one or two each year and that many never performed plays. Therefore, though a dramatic revival was underway, plays remained rarities almost everywhere.

The length and complexity of liturgical plays differed considerably from one area to another. Some of the simplest extant works date from the fifteenth century, while some of the most elaborate had been

FIG. 4.19
Hrosvitha's *Abraham and Maria*. From the first published edition of her plays (1501).

written by the eleventh century. Consequently, no clear pattern of development can be traced. Although several historians have argued that the plays grew in length and complexity through the gradual addition of new episodes, this is not necessarily true, for complex plays may have been written as soon as the desirability of dramatization was accepted, while simple plays may have satisfied the community needs at any time.

The oldest and most numerous of existing plays (more than 400) deal with the visit of the three Marys to the tomb of Christ. The most elaborate Easter dramas date from the thirteenth century. One of these, found at Klosterneuberg in Germany, includes the following episodes: after the burial of Christ, Jewish high priests ask Pilate to set a watch over the tomb; Pilate agrees and the priests lead Roman soldiers to the tomb and give them money; while the soldiers are keeping guard, an Angel appears and strikes them to the ground; the Marys stop at a perfume seller's stall to purchase ointments and then proceed to the tomb, where they discover that Christ has risen; the soldiers revive and report the news to the priests, who bribe them to declare that the body has been stolen; Mary Magdalene reports the news to Peter and John, who rush to the tomb; Mary Magdalene meets Christ disguised as a gardener; Christ is led by two Angels to the gates of Hell, which he forces open to free the imprisoned souls; the Marys and apostles proclaim the resurrection of Christ. Despite the number of events, there are only about 200 lines of dialogue in this play. It is long, nevertheless, in comparison with most liturgical dramas.

The crucifixion was rarely dramatized. Only a few plays on this subject have survived. The earliest comes from Montecassino (Italy) around 1150. It begins with Judas' betrayal of Christ and continues through the crucifixion. As it has survived, it includes twelve scenes (320 lines of dialogue), but apparently other scenes are now missing. Two other crucifixion plays are contained in the *Carmina Burana,* a thirteenth-century manuscript collection of plays and poems discovered at the monastery of Benediktbeuern in Germany. The longest treats several events in the life of Christ and ends following the crucifixion, the point at which most Easter plays begin.

Next to Easter, the Christmas season prompted the greatest number of dramas. Few, however, treat the nativity itself; those which do are simple. On the other hand, there are many plays about the Three Kings (performed on January 6), some of which include Herod's rage and his massacre of the children. A few separate plays dramatize this "slaughter of the Innocents," commemorated on December 28.

Another popular drama of the Christmas season was the Prophets play. Unlike other liturgical plays, it was derived from a nonbiblical source, a sermon of the fifth or sixth century (inaccurately attributed to St. Augustine throughout the Middle Ages) that sought to convict the Jews of error in their dealing with Christ by summoning their own prophets. The witnesses were called one by one, each speaking his prophecy concerning Christ. In the extant plays of this type, the number of characters vary from two to twenty-eight, and in some plays such pagan figures as Virgil and the Sybil appear. Most of these Christmas plays were short and most were associated with particular days of the church calendar. Only one surviving work, found in the *Carmina Burana,* unites all of the episodes of the Christmas story into a single drama.

Although Easter and Christmas plays are by far the most numerous, others dramatized a wide range of biblical materials: the Raising of Lazarus, the Conversion of St. Paul, the Wise and Foolish Virgins, Pentecost, Isaac and Rebecca, Joseph and his Brethren, Daniel in the Lion's Den, and various events in the life of the Virgin Mary. The most elaborate play of all is the *Antichrist,* dating from the twelfth century. Based upon the prediction that before the second coming of Christ a deceiver will appear and attempt to subvert Christ's mission, its scenes are set at places ranging over the known world, and its battles and other complex episodes are so numerous that some scholars have doubted that it was ever performed.

FIG. 4.20

Interior of St. Zeno's, a Romanesque church built in Verona (Italy) in the twelfth century. Note the raised apse and the crypt beneath it. This photograph was made around 1910. From *Romanesque Art in Italy* (1913).

THE STAGING OF LITURGICAL DRAMA

A number of staging conventions used in the church would remain standard throughout the Middle Ages. The playing area had two basic components: small scenic structures (variously called mansions, *sedes, loci,* or *domi*) and a generalized acting area (the *platea,* playne, or place). The mansions served to locate the scene and housed any properties required. But since the action could not be performed within the limited space provided by the typically small mansions, the actors appropriated as much of the adjacent floor area (the *platea*) as they needed. Mansions were arranged around or along this neutral floor space, and the performers moved from one mansion to another as the action demanded.

The earliest liturgical plays required only one mansion, but more complex plays used many mansions dispersed about the church. The individual mansions varied considerably in size and complexity. For example, a simple altar sometimes represented the tomb of Christ, but in some of the great cathedrals imitations of the "true sepulcher" in Jerusalem, large enough for several persons to enter at once, were used. A few mansions housed elaborate and numerous properties (especially those for the Last Supper, Nebuchadnezzar's fiery furnace, Daniel's lion den, and Isaac and Rebecca's kitchen), and some had curtains so that characters or objects might be revealed at the right moment or concealed at the end of an episode. The choir loft was sometimes used to represent high places or Heaven, while the crypt (usually located beneath the main floor) often served for low places or Hell. Flying machinery was also used at times to pull the star ahead of the Three Kings, to lower a dove for the Annunciation, or to create flames for Pentecost. That this machinery grew to be extremely elaborate in some churches is established by Bishop Abraham of Souzdal's account of liturgical plays he saw performed in Florence (Italy) in 1439. In one, showing Christ's Ascension into Heaven, the actor portraying Christ was raised upward by means of ropes and pulleys to be engulfed in simulated clouds and then united with God and the Angels in Heaven (a platform located some 50 feet above the church floor).

The costumes for these dramas were usually church vestments, to which were added realistic or symbolic accessories. Female characters usually wore dalmatics (a type of enveloping robe) with the hoods pulled up to cover their heads. Angels were signified by wings attached to the church vestments. The prophets and the Three Kings were sometimes given elaborate nonclerical garments, and symbolic properties were often used to identify personages.

In most cases, the actors were members of the clergy or choir boys, although in the thirteenth century some roles may have been taken by wandering scholars or schoolboys. Much of our knowledge about the staging of plays comes from the rather detailed prescriptions contained in the church manuals of the period. More space in these manuals is often taken up with stage directions, especially those concerning movement, pantomime, and tone of voice, than with lines of dialogue. As long as the plays were performed in the church, the majority of lines (all in Latin) were sung or chanted rather than spoken, and the acting in general was probably more schematic than realistic.

Liturgical drama continued to be performed in some churches until the sixteenth century, but by 1300 it had long ceased to play a significant role in the development of the theatre.

THE FEAST OF FOOLS

Although most of the performances in the church were serious and devotional, an element of buffoonery crept into some plays associated with Christmas. During this season a number of days were assigned to the minor clergy, who conducted the church services, staged processions through the town, and often collected gifts or exacted payments. St. Stephen's Day (December 26) was given over to the deacons; the Feast of the Holy Innocents (December 28) to the choir boys; and the Feast of the Circumcision (January 1 or alternatively January 6 or 13) to the subdeacons.

One of these festivals—the subdeacons' revelries, commonly called the Feast of Fools—was especially important in the development of comedy. The festival's appeal lay in the inversion of status that allowed the lesser clergy to ridicule their superiors and the routine of church life. Much of this is reminiscent of earlier pagan festivals, and many scholars have linked the Feast of Fools with pagan rites. Although such practices may not have been typical, at times during this feast the celebrants rang the church bells improperly, sang out of tune, wore strange garments and masks, and used puddings, sausages, and old shoes as censers. The Feast of Fools was presided over by a "bishop fool" who assumed ecclesiastical authority on festival days. It is not clear when this celebration began, but it was well established by the end of the twelfth century, and efforts to suppress it were not wholly successful until the sixteenth century. The festivities were accompanied by much revelry, some of which passed over into licentiousness. Sometimes plays were staged as a part of the occasion and a certain amount of burlesque and comedy probably crept into the liturgical plays in this manner. Although extensive development of comic episodes had to await the separation of drama from the liturgy, the Feast of Fools undoubtedly

FIG. 4.21

Major periods of drama, 2500 B.C.E.–1500 C.E.

influenced the development of comedy both in religious and secular plays.

By 1300 liturgical drama seemingly had developed as far as it could within the confines of the church, and consequently plays began to be given out-of-doors. Although liturgical plays would continue to be presented in some churches for another 300 years, they would undergo no significant change. However, innovations were to come in nonliturgical drama.

NONLITURGICAL DRAMA

Performances of religious plays outside the church seem to have begun during the twelfth century. Before the end of the fourteenth century, lengthy vernacular religious cycles (composed of many short plays or episodes) had come into being. We know little about the transition from drama tied to the Latin liturgy to vernacular religious drama done outside the church because so little evidence has survived. The long-accepted view was that vernacular drama came into existence through a gradual process in which individual short liturgical plays, having first been moved out of doors, were brought together to form long plays which were then translated into the vernacular tongues and performed by laymen.

Major support for this view is provided by *The Mystery of Adam* (*c.* 1150). Its detailed stage directions suggest that it was staged outdoors but adjacent to the church (although some historians argue strongly for indoor performance). The text has three main parts: the first section concerns Adam and Eve; the second Cain and Abel; and the third is a traditional Prophet's play, in which a number of figures from the Old Testament foretell the coming of Christ. In the first two sections, the dialogue is in French, but the stage directions and choral songs are in Latin; in the final section, the scriptural passages spoken by the Prophets are given first in Latin and then paraphrased in the vernacular. It is unclear whether the actors were clergy or laymen, or where and when the play was produced. This work seems to look both backward to liturgical drama and forward to the vernacular cycles and has been used to support the theory of gradual evolution. A few other plays and fragments using vernacular languages (among them *La Seinte Resurrection*, an Anglo-Norman play of the late twelfth century; the Spanish *The Play of the Magi Kings;* and the French *Sponsus* using Provençal) have survived, but they offer scant evidence on which to base an account of theatrical tradition over a 150-year period.

Many scholars argue that the vernacular plays developed quite independently of the liturgical drama, however, and that the similarity between the two types is attributable not to direct descent but to common sources—the Bible and other religious and devotional literature. We will look at this further when we examine the late Middle Ages (1300–1500), a period which overlaps extensively with the early Renaissance.

LOOKING AT THEATRE HISTORY

In studying the theatre of other cultures, it is important to become familiar with the context out of which it has emerged, for otherwise it will seem merely quaint rather than a vital expression. Obviously, it is difficult to enter fully into another culture, which is a compound of elements often quite unlike those we know. It is possible to gain insight into other ways of life, however, by reading social and cultural histories and by examining the arts these cultures have produced. This kind of approach is especially important if Westerners are to understand Eastern theatrical forms more than superficially.

The complexity of the "visual language" of Sanskrit drama can be appreciated if the following descriptions are read in relation to the drawings of hand gestures shown in Fig. 4.2. Note that each gesture has several possible meanings, the specific meaning at any given time depending on how it is related to other elements in the performance:

Pataka (flag): *the thumb bent to touch the fingers, and the fingers extended. Usage: beginning a dance, cloud, forest, forbidding things, bosom, night, river, world of the gods, horse, cutting, wind, reclining, walking, prowess, graciousness, moonlight, strong sunlight, knocking . . . entering a street, equality, . . . , taking an oath, silence, benediction . . . ,*

Ardha-candra (half-moon): *the thumb of the Pataka hand is stretched out. Usage: the moon on the eighth day of the dark fortnight, a hand seizing the throat, a spear, consecrating an image, origin, waist, anxiety, meditation, prayer, touching, greeting common people. . . .*

Musti (fist): *the four fingers are bent in to the palm, and the thumb is set on them. Usage: steadiness, grasping the hair, holding things, wrestling.*

Sikhara (spire): *in the same hand, the thumb is raised. Usage: the God of Love, bow, pillar, silence, husband, tooth, entering, questioning, the body, saying no, recollection, untying the girdle, lover, sound of a bell, pounding. . . .*

Bhramara (bee): *the second finger and thumb touching, the forefinger bent, the rest extended. Usage: bee, parrot, crane, cuckoo, union.*

Sukatundaka (parrot's beak): *the third finger of the Arala hand is also bent. Usage: shooting an arrow, throwing a spear, mystery, ferocity.*

From *The Mirror of Gesture*, trans. Ananda Coomaraswamy and Gopala Kristnayya Duggirala (Cambridge, Mass., 1917), 26–35.

The following brief passage points out the relationship between Chinese drama and the three great Chinese philosophies, Confucianism, Buddhism, and Taoism:

Whatever native ingredients and alien elements entered into the melting pot of Chinese civilization, its main component has been essentially Confucianism. . . . A practicable moral philosophy that teaches the rules of personal cultivation and virtues of human relationship, Confucianism has molded the Chinese national character and pervaded every aspect of Chinese society, the family, literature and the arts . . . but when the country was in disorder, Taoism and Buddhism took over [since] disappointments bred . . . a desire to wander astray in . . . otherworldliness. The majority of Chinese writers, however, have been conformists to the grand Confucian tradition. To them, literature has been a vehicle for the communication of the aim of Confucian doctrine: to teach and influence people to be good. . . . The three great Chinese doctrines merged in the common belief in retribution . . . [which] deterred the growth of anything like the Western concept of tragedy . . . From the Chinese point of view it would be a blemish in the literary work not to give its readers a sense of satisfaction in the ultimate vindication and triumph of the good and virtuous.

Wu-chi Liu, *An Introduction to Chinese Literature* (Bloomington: Indiana University Press, 1966), 4–5.

Students can learn a great deal about interpreting historical evidence by examining personally some of the primary sources on which certain interpretations have been based. When they do, they often find that some interpretations are very questionable. One good example of how sources can be used to extend conclusions beyond those supported by the evidence is found in interpretations of the following passage:

Also on the twentieth [of July] on which day the capricious Greeks celebrate the ascension of the Prophet Elijah with scenic plays, he [the emperor] ordered me to come to him . . .

From *Legatio Liudprandi ad Nicephorum Phocam*, trans. Barbara Spear. (The date referred to by Liudprand is 968 C.E.)

Some scholars have seen in this sentence a clear indication that dramas were staged inside Byzantine churches (even though the place of performance is not mentioned) and that elaborate machinery was used to fly Elijah up to the church's dome (even though neither the content of the plays nor their staging is described). The most that one can reasonably conclude, however, is that on Elijah's feast day plays were performed.

Stage directions are often one of the historian's most useful sources. Those included in some church manuals when dramatic episodes began to be performed in the churches of the West are very precise. In fact, they provide directions that permit many liturgical performances to be reconstructed more accurately than any earlier theatrical pieces can. The following is an excerpt from the oldest surviving instructions for presenting a liturgical play:

While the third lesson is being read, four brethren shall dress, one of whom, wearing an alb as if for some other reason, shall enter and go secretly to the site of the sepulchre, and holding a palm in his hand shall sit there quietly. And while the third respond is being pronounced, the remaining three shall follow, all wearing hoods and bearing censers with incense in hand, step by step as though looking for something, shall come to the sepulchre. These things are done in imitation of the angel sitting on the tomb, and of the women coming with perfumes to anoint the body of Jesus. When, therefore, the one seated shall see the three approach as if wandering and seeking something, he shall begin to sing in a sweet modulated voice Quem Quaeritis? *With this sung to its end, the three shall answer, with one voice.* Ihesum Nazarenum. *The former shall respond:* Non est hic. Surrexit sicut praedixerat. Ite, nuntiate quia surrexit a mortuis. *At this command the three shall turn to the choir saying,* Alleluia. Resurrexit Dominus. *With this sung, the one seated, as if calling the other back, shall say the antiphon* Venite et videte locum. *Then he shall rise and raise the veil and show them the place, empty of the cross but with the linen in which the cross was wrapped; at this sight they shall set down their censers in that same sepulchre, and shall take up the linen and hold it before the clergy and, as if showing that the Lord had risen and was no longer wrapped in it, they shall sing this antiphon:* Surrexit Dominus de sepulcro, *and shall then place the linen on the altar.*

From Ethelwold, Bishop of Winchester, *The Monastic Agreement of the Monks and Nuns of the English Nation,* trans. Barbara Spear.

The stage directions in *The Mystery of Adam* (*c.* 1150) provide evidence suggesting that plays were by that time being staged out-of-doors. Here is one of the crucial passages:

Then let God go to the church, and let Adam and Eve walk about, innocently delighting in the Garden of Eden. Meanwhile, let demons run back and forth through the square, making suitable gestures. . . .

5

European Theatre in the Late Middle Ages

Not until the late Middle Ages (c. 1300–1500) were performances of religious plays commonly given outside of churches. But once the innovation was made, many productions became extremely elaborate, often extending over several days and drawing on the resources of the entire community. As in Greece and Rome, the theatre became once more a cooperative effort of church, state, and citizens.

The flowering of drama in the late Middle Ages can be traced in part to economic and political changes that had occurred during the high Middle Ages (c. 1050–1300), especially the formation of guilds and the growth of towns. Guilds originated during the eleventh and twelfth centuries as protective organizations against local feudal lords and for merchants when traveling. By the thirteenth century, many craftsmen—bakers, brewers, goldsmiths, tailors, and so on—had formed organizations to regulate working conditions, wages, the quality of products, and other matters affecting their wellbeing. These guilds were organized hierarchically. Each was governed by a council of masters (those who owned their own shops and supervised the work of others); under each master were one or more journeymen (those skilled in the trade but who worked for wages); and below the journeymen were

apprentices (young men and boys who received room and board while learning a trade, usually over a period of seven years).

The rise of guilds was paralleled by the growth of towns. Originally towns were under the jurisdiction of local feudal lords, but as trade and manufacture grew the towns became sufficiently strong to win concessions, and eventually most of them became self-governing. Thereafter power resided primarily in the guilds, since they usually elected the mayor and the council from among their members.

The growth of guilds and towns brought a corresponding decline in feudalism. Kings and princes began to gain more control over subject lords, and as they did so the nations of modern Europe began to take shape. Princes were aided in this process by townsmen who contributed taxes in return for the ruler's protection and his maintenance of conditions favorable to manufacture and commerce.

As groups other than the church gained in prominence, it was probably inevitable that they should come to participate in and eventually to dominate theatrical production. Nevertheless, throughout the late Middle Ages drama continued to be primarily religious, and the major theatrical conventions were those that had been employed within the church.

FIG. 5.1
Europe during the late Middle Ages.

PERFORMANCES OUTSIDE THE CHURCH

In 1264, Pope Urban IV created a festival to honor the union of the human and divine in the person of Christ which was celebrated in the sacrament of the Eucharist. It was called Corpus Christi and was to be observed on the Thursday following Trinity Sunday. Since church holy days are set according to a lunar calendar, actual dates vary, so Corpus Christi can occur between May 21 and June 24 in any given year. It was made an official holy day of the Church in 1311, and was being celebrated almost everywhere by 1350. It was common for the plays at this festival to focus on Christ's passion, but since all biblical events could be related to the human and divine aspects of Christ, a cosmic drama grew up around Corpus Christi in a number of cities, which encompassed

events ranging from the creation to the destruction of the world. Such scope made demands far in excess of those found in the Latin liturgical dramas. But these outdoor plays were not bound by the restrictions of church architecture and church liturgy and were able to experiment. The result was great diversity in staging during the years after 1350.

The feast of Corpus Christi was partly motivated by the desire to make the church more relevant to the ordinary people and their lives. This became especially important at the beginning of the high Middle Ages as the papacy was forcefully moved to Avignon in southern France in 1305 (not to return to Rome until 1377), a great famine hit Europe from 1315 to 1317, and the Black Death destroyed as much as a third of Europe's population in the five years between 1347 and 1352. Secular groups (nobles, merchants, craftsmen), were, therefore, encouraged to take an active role in the Corpus Christi celebrations which in a number of cities came to include the most extensive productions of outdoor vernacular drama seen since the early Roman Empire. These Corpus Christi "cycle" plays became enormous sources of pride in many communities and a major generator of revenue as people came long distances to see them. This encouraged cities to want to avoid scheduling their event at the same time as a competitor, so "cycle" plays began to turn up at Easter, Whitsuntide (seven weeks after Easter), the feast day of a patron saint, and on special occasions to give thanks for deliverance from the plague, drought, or other disaster.

The abandonment of Latin in favor of the vernacular tongues in these plays was of major importance. It led to the substitution of spoken for chanted dialogue and facilitated the transition from clerical to nonclerical actors. But in adopting the local language, theatre took a major step toward nationalism and away from the international drama which Latin had made possible.

THE VERNACULAR RELIGIOUS DRAMA

Between 1375 and 1575 the medieval theatre reached its peak. Our knowledge of it is most extensive in the late fifteenth and especially the sixteenth century, for most of the surviving evidence dates from those years.

In the British Isles, plays were produced in 127 different towns at some time during the Middle Ages. Nevertheless, only a few texts survive. Most of the extant English works are parts of four cycles: York (48 plays), Chester (24), Wakefield (sometimes called the Towneley Plays; 32), and the N_____ town Plays (place unknown; 42). The last-named cycle is made up of three distinguishable groups of plays which could be staged as a single unit. It is often assumed that these four cycles typify English practice, but such cosmic dramas can be clearly established in only twelve English towns. Other towns did one play or small groups of plays.

The earliest English cycle dates from about 1375; others apparently date from the fifteenth century. All were performed until the mid sixteenth century. During the active life of the cycles, many individual plays were rewritten, some new ones were added, and others were dropped; consequently, the plays vary widely in dates of composition, as well as in quality. The surviving texts show the cycles as they existed at a specific time in their active production lives. In addition to these cycle plays, ten other religious dramas in English and three in Cornish have survived from the British Isles.

A much larger number of plays from France are extant. They range from short works to those requiring twenty-five or more days to perform. Rather than covering material from the Creation to the Last Judgment, as most of the English cycles did, the French plays are usually more restricted in time. Most end with the death and resurrection of Christ. In Germanic territories, major plays were staged at Frankfurt, Madgeburg, Tergensee, Lucerne, Alsfeld, Donaueschingen, Villengen, Bozen, and elsewhere. Spain was also very rich in vernacular religious plays which became known as *autos sacramentales* in the 1500s. In Italy, a type of devotional drama called *laudi* developed. Originally, *laudi* were essentially narrative. As they became more dramatic, they included choral portions, an element that distinguishes them from their successor, the *sacre rappresentazioni,* which resembled other European religious plays. While the vast majority of known religious dramas are from England, France, Germany, Italy, Spain, and Switzerland, there is scarcely any European country that did not have some religious drama.

The length and scope of the dramas varied widely, but they all dealt with the same basic subject matter: God's ordering of existence as revealed in the Bible, the Apocrypha, legends about biblical figures and saints, writings of the church fathers, and collections of sermons. These dramas are episodic, with little attempt to bridge the gaps between the short plays that make up long cycles. They are also filled with anachronisms, as biblical characters make reference to things that happened long after their own lives, and dress as if they were Medieval Europeans. But the stories were dramatized to make moral points, and the accurate representation of an historic event was not considered important. In spite of their essentially religious purpose, many plays contain extended comic scenes, usually involving devils, villains, or buffoons, which tend to reinforce rather than distract from the didactic purposes of these plays, while helping to keep the productions highly effective theatrical entertainments.

THE STAGES

The stages upon which the vernacular plays were performed might be long fixed structures (occasionally "U" shaped or even circular), or movable wagons. Fixed stages were most common, but in some parts of England, Spain, Italy, Belgium, the Netherlands, and a few other places, movable stages were used. Fixed stages used "simultaneous settings," that is, the scenic units needed to symbolically represent

FIG. 5.2
Reconstruction of a performance on a pageant wagon. From Sharp, *A Dissertation on the Pageants or Dramatic Mysteries . . . at Coventry . . .* (1825).

FIG. 5.3
A reconstruction of an English pageant wagon and a ground plan of the overall playing arrangement. From Wickham, *Early English Stages,* 1. Courtesy Columbia University Press and Routledge & Kegan Paul Ltd.

the locations used in the plays were present on stage from the start. Movable stages used "sequential settings," as each wagon had the set for one play only and the wagons were presented to the audience in sequence rather than all at once.

The sites of fixed stages varied considerably. Ancient Roman amphitheatres were sometimes used, as were the "Cornish rounds" of southwest England, and similar earthen rounds in Normandy. Purpose-built round structures may also have been built in France and Italy, though scholars disagree as to whether the artworks that show these were intended to indicate an actual stage or were just imagined performances. Sometimes stages were erected on land adjoining churches and sometimes the courtyards of monasteries or of private residences were used. Fixed stages were also set up in large public squares. These stages were usually long rectangular platforms about head height and set along a building or row of houses against which the scenic units were organized. Occasionally there was no platform, and the scenic units were placed directly on the ground. The size of the stages varied widely. At Autun (France) in 1516 the platform was about 200 feet long. At Lucerne, the playing space was irregularly shaped, being about 125 feet long.

In addition to outdoor fixed stages, indoor fixed stages in great halls were occasionally used. The

Brotherhood of the Passion (Confrérie de la Passion) in Paris, for example, played for more than one hundred years indoors at the Hôpital de la Trinité, where the stage could not have been more than 40 feet wide.

Movable stages were decorated wagons designed to handle the required scenic unit for one play. Because the York, Chester, and Wakefield cycles in England used movable stages, generally called "pageant wagons," movable staging is treated as typical in England although it may have actually been used in relatively few of the cities that staged vernacular religious plays. Wagons were used more extensively in Spain, where they were known as *carros,* and were an integral part of the *autos sacramentales.*

The appearance of an English pageant wagon is the subject of much controversy. There are no pictures and only one description, given by David Rogers in *A Breviarye, or Some Few Recollections of the City of Chester* (a manuscript of the late sixteenth or early seventeenth century). Rogers states that pageant wagons used for the Chester cycle had two rooms, a higher and a lower, mounted on six wheels. (A variant version of his account says four wheels.) In the lower room the actors dressed and in the higher room they performed. An inventory from Norwich done around 1565 lists: "A pageant, that is to say, a house of wainscot painted and built on a cart with four wheels. A square top to set over the said house," which would seem to confirm Rogers's account. But the Chester cycle's "Last Judgment" play depicts Heaven, Earth, and Hell, and includes more than twenty characters. It is hard to imagine that it could be staged on such a wagon. Glynne Wickham, therefore, argued that the pageant wagon was a one-leveled structure that held the scenic unit and a dressing room. A separate "stage"

FIG. 5.4

Denis van Alsloot's "The Triumph of Isabella," 1615. These wagons may have been similar to those used for English cycle plays. Courtesy of the Board of Trustees of the Victoria and Albert Museum.

wagon was parked at the places of performance and the pageant wagon merely pulled up beside it to give the actors space to perform. (But even that may not have been enough as stage directions indicate that characters sometimes moved down from the stage into the street to perform.) There is no indisputable evidence to support Wickham's theory but this arrangement was certainly used in Spain. There it is clear that at each site where an *autos sacramentales* was to be played, a stage platform was available, and the wagons, or *carros,* were drawn up to it for performance.

Pageant wagons were not necessarily uniform in size or design. Since a guild always performed the same play, its wagon could be built to meet its special requirements and used for years. In those rare instances when the same wagon was used by more than one guild, the scenic needs of the plays using that wagon were very similar.

SCENERY

As in the church, the playing space was composed of two basic elements, the scenic unit (mansion) and the acting area (*platea*). On fixed stages multiple mansions were visible at the same time but once the actors came out of one or started talking in front of one, that mansion represented the location of the scene no matter where the actors moved on the stage. Once they reentered the mansion or otherwise closed the scene, the stage became a neutral space until the next mansion was put in play.

Most pageant wagons carried only one mansion, though more than one was possible. To spectators, a fixed stage was undoubtedly more visually impressive than the movable ones, because all of the scenic units were visible simultaneously. In France, the plays making up a cycle were sometimes divided into groups (*journées*), which were performed together. Intermissions, varying in length from one hour to overnight, separated the groups; and during those intermissions scenic units could be changed so not all the scenic units needed for the cycle were necessarily visible at one time. It is difficult to know how many mansions were actually used to depict the places named in a cycle. In the play presented at Lucerne in 1583, about seventy different locales are indicated, but there seem to

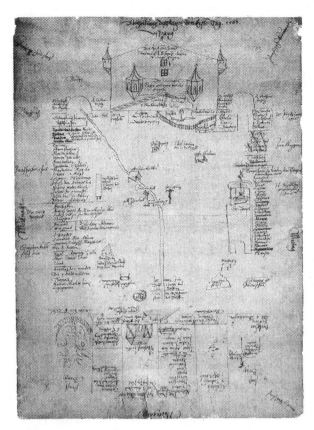

FIG. 5.5

Plan (above) and section (below) of a "round" at
Perranzabuloe in Cornwall (England). This structure,
which resembles those built by Vikings in Scandinavia,
may have been used for dramatic performances. Superim-
posed on it is a circular arrangement of the mansions
needed for staging one of the surviving Cornish plays.
From Albright, *The Shakespearian Stage* (1909).

FIG. 5.6

Renward Cysat's plan for the first day's performance of
the Lucerne Passion Play, 1583. At the top is the building
that served as Paradise, with, at its base, the Garden of
Eden. Down either side are mansions, each with a list of
the characters assigned to it; at lower left is the Hell
Mouth. Courtesy Bürgerbibliothek, Lucerne.

have been only thirty-two mansions. Some scenic
units may have been altered during performance
to represent a new location. The identity of some
locations may have been considered clear without
the use of a mansion.

The scenic complexity of a production could vary
daily. For a passion play at Arras (France) in the early
fifteenth century, the number of mansions required
by each of the four *journées* ranged from eight to
fifteen. Other plays might require twenty or more
mansions for a single *journée*. It was not taken for
granted that the identity of mansions would be clearly
evident. Therefore, the director usually appeared at
the beginning of each *journée* and indicated (among
other relevant information) what each structure
represented. At times, descriptive labels were suspended above mansions. But in all cases, one place
flowed into another.

The two places most often represented on the
fixed stages were Heaven and Hell. Characteristically,
Heaven was placed at one end of the platform and
Hell at the other. In arenas, Heaven was most likely

placed in the east and Hell in the west. The earthly
scenes were located between Heaven and Hell, which
symbolized people's dual nature and the choices
that faced them. Since Heaven and Hell were both
the most important and most permanent structures,
not being replaced each day, they were also the
most complex.

Heaven generally impressed audiences with its
splendor and magnificence, qualities not always evident in surviving illustrations. It was usually raised
above the level of the other mansions, supported
by an "earthly paradise" (the Garden of Eden), or
some other-worldly space at stage level. Sometimes
Heaven included a series of intricately contrived
turning spheres, and the whole was often gilded, then
illuminated by concealed torches to give the effect
that golden light was emanating from it even in daylight. In some instances, Heaven would open and
close, and often machinery permitted angels to "fly"

FIG. 5.7
Model showing Albert Koster's reconstruction of Renward Cysat's plan for the Lucerne Passion Play, 1583. Not shown, at bottom, is another section of bleacher seating. Courtesy Theatermuseum, Munich.

between Heaven and Earth, although stairs, either visible or concealed, were used in less elaborate productions. At Rouen (France) in 1474, God appeared in Heaven accompanied by Peace, Mercy, Justice, Truth, and nine orders of angels, indicating that the space was relatively large.

Conversely, Hell was made as terrifying as possible. The entrance to Hell was often represented by the head of a monster (the "Hell mouth") that seemed to swallow those who entered there. Fire, smoke, noise, and the cries of the damned issued from Hell. Devils with fireworks attached to their costumes sallied forth from it to seize sinners and thrust them into eternal damnation. Behind this entrance Hell might be treated as a fortified town, an especially effective device for the many "Harrowing of Hell" plays in which Christ forced open the gates of Hell to free the captive souls in Limbo, where unbaptized children and good people born before Christ's coming were languishing, awaiting his arrival.

The mansions representing earthly places were less elaborately depicted, although their complexity varied with dramatic need. Many were equipped with curtains that could be drawn to conceal or reveal interior scenes. Often they were furnished with beds, tables, benches, altars, or thrones. Sometimes they were lavishly outfitted with tapestries borrowed from wealthy families and churches. A curtain representing the sky (sometimes complete with sun, moon, and stars) might be hung at the rear of the stage. Painted cloths representing clouds frequently concealed the overhead flying equipment and other devices for special effects.

FIG. 5.8
The stage of the Valenciennes Passion Play, 1547. Note the Heaven mansion at the left and the Hell mansion (with Hell mouth) at right. The mansions between these two were changed each day as needed. Twenty-five days were required to perform the entire work. Courtesy Bibliothèque Nationale, Paris.

FIG. 5.9

Hell mouth and the interior of hell as conceived by a medieval artist. Redrawing of a fresco in the Chapel of the Holy Cross, Stratford-on-Avon (England). From Sharp, *A Dissertation on the Pageants or Dramatic Mysteries* (1825).

Although a number of persons were required to build and paint the settings, few records pertaining to them have survived. At Romans in 1509, the carpenters began work about four and a half months prior to the performance. At Lucerne, the director of the play supervised the labor of city-employed workmen, who built the mansions, and of skilled artists, who painted the mansions, curtains, and effigies. At Mons in 1501, master artists were imported to do this work. Many other persons were required to operate the scenic effects during performances.

SPECIAL EFFECTS AND MACHINERY

Most of the realistic touches in medieval productions involved special effects. These required enormous skill and ingenuity, so accomplished machinists were in great demand. At Mons in 1501, two directors of "secrets" (special effects) were imported from Chauny (France) and it took seventeen assistants to operate the special effects for the Hell scenes alone. Eight master machinists, aided by numerous assistants, were employed for one passion play at Vienna. During the sixteenth century the machinists were second only to the director in importance. They made detailed cue sheets and planned the operation of the effects as carefully as the director planned other parts of the production. The ultimate success of the plays depended much upon their skills, and the use of special effects grew in number and complexity as the machinists' abilities to contrive these seemingly miraculous events increased.

Many special effects involved "flying." The fixed stages often were set against buildings so that pulleys and windlasses could be installed on the roofs and concealed with painted clouds or sky cloths. Additional flying machinery was concealed within the Heaven mansion. Using such devices, angels passed between Heaven and Earth; Lucifer lifted Christ to the top of the temple (a distance of up to forty feet); the souls released from Limbo floated up to Heaven; and devils and fire-spitting monsters flew about the stage. In some instances, characters rose to or descended from the heavens on platforms disguised as clouds.

Other effects depended upon devices operated from beneath the stage. Trapdoors permitted sudden appearances, disappearances, and the skillful substitution of effigies for live actors. In such episodes as the feeding of the multitudes through the miracle of the loaves and fishes, the baskets could be replenished from beneath the stage. Concealed mechanisms allowed the fig tree cursed by Christ to wither, and fountains to spring up at a magical touch.

Water effects were important in many plays. At Mons, sufficient water was stored in wine barrels on the roofs of adjoining houses to produce a continuous rain of five minutes for Noah's flood. Other scenes included Christ walking on the sea and the apostles pulling in their nets filled with fish.

In the frequent scenes of torture and executions, effigies were substituted for live actors. In a production showing Barnabas burned at the stake, an effigy was filled with bones and animal entrails to give a properly realistic smell. In another, showing the decapitation of St. Paul, the severed head bounced three times, and at each spot a well flowed: one with milk, one with blood, and the third with water.

Many animals were required. While some could be live, others had to be impersonated by actors or by effigies. Lions kneeled to St. Denis and tigers to St. Andrew. In one play, tigers sprang up out of the earth, pursued the apostles, and eventually were turned into sheep. In other plays there were dragons, wolves, and wild or fanciful creatures.

Transformation scenes were popular. Moses' staff changed into a snake, Lot's wife into a pillar of salt, water into wine. Light also was treated as a special effect. As a nimbus or halo, it sometimes surrounded God, Christ, and saints. Normally this was achieved by reflecting the rays of concealed torches off of gilded or highly polished surfaces. Sometimes a change from light to darkness was indicated by substituting a painted cloth depicting the sun for another showing the moon and stars. In a few plays, buildings were burned. For these, wicker structures covered with cloth were actually set on fire.

AUDIENCES AND AUDITORIUMS

In most places, plays were not given every year. Even where the plays were well established, the interval between productions ranged from one to ten years. Some of the most elaborate performances were never repeated. In those years when plays were to be given, preparations extended over a period of months, and the days of playing were holidays.

Prior to performances, various devices acquainted the public with upcoming events. Invitations were usually sent to all the surrounding towns, posters were set up at the city gates, and a few days before the performance a procession, often with actors in costume, went about the town. On the days of performance a herald rode through the city sounding a trumpet and summoning people to the play. The audiences were drawn from all classes and from both local and neighboring areas. In some places, work was forbidden during the hours of performance, and special guards were sent to protect homes and businesses against robbery.

When a fixed stage was used, all spectators had to be accommodated in one place. Structures such as Roman amphitheatres or Cornish rounds provided ready-made seating; but in courtyards or city squares temporary auditoriums had to be improvised. In some instances, arrangements not unlike those that became typical in later professional theatres were used. For example, at Romans in 1509 standing room was available near the stage, and behind this there was scaffold seating which in turn was surmounted by a series of eighty-four boxes. At Vienna in 1560, private boxes could be rented for performances which extended over several days. At Lucerne, scaffold seating surrounded three sides of the playing area, and the owners of adjacent houses probably rented space to spectators in their windows and on their roofs. Windows and roofs were also rented when wagon stages were involved and a number of different performance locations were established. At York there

were twelve to fifteen stops where all the plays were performed, at Beverley there were six. In some of these spaces the majority of the audience simply stood to watch the plays, but in others, at least in York, wealthy citizens bought the right to control some of the stops, and it is thought that they erected scaffold seating and sold tickets for those wanting to watch the plays in greater comfort.

Entrance fees were not charged for many of the municipally sponsored productions. On the other hand, some productions were designed (in part) to make money. At Valenciennes in 1547, the members of the organization that produced the play divided the profits. Municipalities also sometimes charged fees in order to recover their outlay. Fees were certainly collected at Leicester in 1477 and a number of cities in eastern England seem to have adopted the practice. Except when fees were charged, it is difficult to estimate attendance. If the available figures are typical, attendance was large. At Reims in 1490, 5616 persons paid admissions; at Romans in 1509, 4780 attended the first day, 4420 the second, and 4947 the third.

The hours of performance varied. In most towns, performances lasted for several days. At Chester three days were required. York allotted only one day to present its nearly fifty-play cycle at twelve to fifteen locations, so performances began at 4:30 A.M. and ran until dark, around 10 P.M. Even in Europe spectators began to take their places as early as 4 A.M., because space was not reserved, except for officials, clergy, and important visitors. In some cases, plays began about 7 A.M. and ran until 11; after an hour's intermission, they continued until about 6 P.M. In others, plays were presented in a series of afternoon performances; in still others, a production might proceed uninterrupted for as long as twelve hours. Sometimes children, elderly persons, and pregnant women were forbidden entry. A barrier of some kind (a ditch, a fence, water, or guards) was used to prevent the audience from getting too near the stage. Guards were posted at night to protect the stage and its furnishings.

MUSIC

Music was prominent in most medieval productions. Frequently it was played until the actors were ready to begin. During the plays, a chorus of angels (composed of choir boys and usually visible in the Heaven mansion) sang hymns. Angels played fanfares on trumpets to introduce God's proclamations, and the transitions between scenes were bridged with instrumental or vocal music. Most plays included a number of songs ranging from popular secular tunes sung by individual actors to religious hymns sung by groups. The names and contents of songs, however, are seldom indicated in the scripts. Singing was usually done by choir boys or actors, whereas instrumental music was played by professional musicians. At least forty minstrels were hired at Chelmsford (England) in 1562, and 156 musicians were employed at Lucerne in 1571. The musicians also kept the populace amused during the intermissions and in the evenings after the performances had ended.

Some plays (or stage directions) indicate that dances sometimes played a prominent role, but little is known about them.

PRODUCTION ARRANGEMENTS

There were many kinds of producing organizations in the late Middle Ages. On the continent, religious guilds, or confraternities, were typical producers. The members of these groups, which began to appear about 1300, were mostly laymen who undertook charitable deeds and the production of plays was a way to raise funds to support that work. The best known of these was the Brotherhood of the Passion (*Confrérie de la Passion*) in Paris, which was organized in 1402 and dominated French theatre for over 250 years.

Religious guilds produced plays in many parts of Britain, but in some towns, trade or craft guilds assumed most of the responsibility. The trade guilds were primarily designed to protect the interests of craftsmen, so their participation in the production of religious drama may well have been at least partly motivated by their commercial interests in attracting potential shoppers to their community. But it was also an expression of religious belief and civic pride. Trade guilds generally banded together to stage something as complex as a cycle play, with each guild taking responsibility for one or more plays in the cycle. Small or poor guilds might join together to produce a play. Since each play was a distinct unit and since the individual plays were performed in sequence, the entire cycle could be coordinated without difficulty. When trade guilds were involved, the plays were sometimes assigned on the basis of appropriateness: the play of Noah to the shipwrights or watermen, the play of the Three Kings to the goldsmiths, Last Supper plays to the bakers, and so on. Each guild was then responsible for providing a pageant wagon, scenery, costumes, properties, special effects, actors, and supervisors.

Other arrangements for theatrical productions include those in which responsibility was assumed by a town or a group of neighboring towns, by the clergy or jointly by town and clergy, or by a temporary society formed for the express purpose of presenting a specific group of plays on a one-time basis. Several scholars have suggested that the 42 "N____ town Plays" were marketed around England and a producing group could buy all or just part of the cycle, possibly along with actors, costumes, and required scenic units.

THE DIRECTOR

It was common for those who produced a cycle to assign its day-to-day management to a small committee or even to hire a single individual to manage it. These complex productions required careful organization, sometimes including a cast of hundreds, multiple special effects, large component sets, and complex staging. Consequently, the "pageant master" (or stage manager, or director) was of considerable importance.

The pageant master's duties varied considerably from one locale to another. In the guilds of northern England, the wardens of each company were responsible to the town council for the proper staging of the plays, and they controlled finances and paid all bills. The wardens seldom did the actual work of play production, however, for normally each guild hired or appointed someone to do this job. Often this position was given to a member of the guild, but in some instances a pageant master was put under contract for a number of years at an annual salary. For example, at Coventry in 1454 the Smiths contracted for a period of twelve years with Thomas Colclow, who was to supply everything needed except the wagon and costumes. The pageant master secured actors, arranged rehearsals, and took charge of every phase of production. In addition, where processional staging was used, he supplied the men to move the pageant wagons from one location to another and to control crowds during the procession and the performance.

If one person directed an entire cycle on a fixed stage, he needed even more skills. Technically, a committee of supervisors (often with as many as twelve members) was usually in charge of the plays staged by confraternities, but it normally delegated its authority to one person or to a small group. At Lucerne in 1583 the committee turned over all details to the city clerk, Renward Cysat. At Mons (Belgium) in 1501, four actor-managers, each with one assistant, were employed to stage the plays. In Spain, Lope de Rueda, a professional actor-manager, was put under contract by the city of Valladolid in 1552 to serve as pageant master for its Corpus Christi festival.

FIG. 5.10

The Martyrdom of St. Apollonia. A miniature by Jean Fouquet, c. 1460. The figure at center right is often said to represent the director. Note the audience and raised mansions. Courtesy Musée Condé, Chantilly.

Jean Bouchet staged plays in a number of towns and was still in demand as late as 1532.

The pageant master's duties were outlined by Bouchet: he must oversee the erection of a stage and the placement of scenery and machines; he must find persons to build and paint scenery and to construct seating for the audience; he must ensure that all goods delivered are of the proper amount and quality; he must cast and rehearse the actors; he must discipline the actors and establish a scale of fines for those who infringe rules; he may act some roles himself; he must assign persons to take money at the entrances; he must address the audience at the beginning of the play and, after each intermission, give a resume of previous happenings and promise greater marvels in the portions yet to come. Although not all directors had to cope with so many problems, many did. Consequently, the men given such positions had to be versed in every aspect of theatrical production.

A few records kept by directors in the Middle Ages have survived. From a play staged at Frankfurt-am-Main around 1350 we have the director's scroll (some 14 feet long) giving all the actors' cues and complete stage directions. In addition, some detailed prompt books are extant. Those most readily available are from Mons (1501) and Lucerne (1583). Nothing in these books is left to chance; every detail has been prepared and recorded. They are the work of men who were stage directors in the modern sense.

It is clear that by the sixteenth century the producers of plays had learned to cope with many problems. They had achieved a high level of technical excellence, as well as considerable sophistication in organizing and producing plays of great scope.

ACTORS AND ACTING

The number of actors required for productions varied considerably. In the guild cycles of northern England, many of the individual plays include no more than five to ten characters, but with as many as forty-eight plays in a cycle, the total number of performers in the entire cycle was considerable. When plays were mounted on fixed stages under the supervision of a single organization, casting was more complicated. For *The Acts of the Apostles,* presented at Bourges in 1536, the 494 roles were distributed among 300 actors. Most plays of this scope date from the sixteenth century and seem to mark a considerable increase in numbers of roles over earlier works.

The majority of actors were drawn from the local population. Only in a few cases can we tell how they were selected. At York in 1476, the city council decreed that four of "the most cunning, discreet, and able players within this city" were to audition all persons who wished to act. No one was to appear in more than two plays. These provisions seem to indicate that guilds did not confine casting to their own members, and that actors might perform for two different guilds. At Seurre in 1496, the mayor, assisted by three other persons, cast the play. In 1540, heralds rode through the streets of Paris appealing for volunteers. At Lucerne in 1583, requests were made from the pulpit that all those interested in acting register with the city clerk, who then chose the cast with the aid of a committee. In those instances when plays were revived, an actor might play the same role many times over a period of years.

The majority of actors were chosen from the merchant or working classes, although members of the clergy and the nobility sometimes participated. Most were men or boys, but women and girls appeared occasionally. Doubling was a common practice. At

Valenciennes in 1547 the more than 100 roles were assigned to 72 actors, and at Mons in 1501 about 350 roles were cast with approximately 150 players. On the other hand, sometimes a single role required more than one actor, as when a character grew from childhood to adulthood. For scenes of violence, such as beheadings and burnings at the stake, realistic effigies were substituted for live actors.

The good faith and discipline of the actors were ensured by a number of devices. At Lucerne in 1583, actors were allowed fourteen days in which to decide if they wished to accept roles; once committed, they were bound by oath to continue. At Valenciennes in 1547 actors were required to take an oath before a notary, in which they agreed to appear on the days of performance. Other provisions of the Valenciennes agreement are also revealing: All actors were required to accept the roles assigned them and to attend rehearsals at the specified times; each agreed not to meddle in the affairs of the supervisory committee or to grumble against their decisions. There was also a schedule of fines for missing rehearsals or for other infringements of rules. Agreements from other towns indicate that jealousies, bickering, and resignations were common, and that producers had learned by the sixteenth century to guard against them.

The time devoted to rehearsals was not great by modern standards. For example, although the play given at Mons in 1501 required four full days to perform, there were only forty-eight rehearsals. Two to five rehearsals were considered sufficient for the individual plays in the English cycles.

Something of the overall process can be inferred from the detailed records preserved from Lucerne in 1583 for a play that required twenty-four hours to perform in its entirety. Prior to the first rehearsals, a general meeting of the entire cast was held; the script was divided into twelve units for rehearsal; in addition to the regularly scheduled sessions, actors were urged to arrange other opportunities for working together privately; when the action presented unusual problems, extra rehearsals were called; changes in dialogue, action, and properties were frequently made during the preparatory period. Although the performances were given out-of-doors, rehearsals were held in a large hall. About eighty days elapsed between the first rehearsal and the performance of the play, but the total number of rehearsals is unclear.

The sponsoring organization supplied the actors with food and drink at rehearsals. If participants had to miss work, someone was paid to replace them on the job. This expense usually fell to the actors, but if they were too poor the producing group absorbed the cost.

It is uncertain whether dress rehearsals were customary. Each episode was probably prepared separately; but some plays were so long (as for example the one at Bourges, France, in 1536 which required forty days to perform) that a dress rehearsal in the modern sense would have been impossible. On the other hand, at Romans (France) in 1509, after the dress rehearsal revealed that the playing time was much too long, extensive cuts were made. At Valenciennes in 1547, in a production taking up the afternoons of twenty-five days, the actors were required to report at 7 A.M. each morning for what was obviously a rehearsal of that day's episodes.

For the long plays given on fixed stages, actors assembled as a group and then went in procession to the site of the performance. Upon arrival, they marched around the playing area before taking their places inside or near the appropriate mansions. In many instances, the actors remained visible throughout, coming forward when needed and retiring to their places when no longer required. At Lucerne, elaborate plans were made so that the actors might slip away to change costumes and to eat during the two twelve-hour performances. At Valenciennes, the players agreed not to leave the stage during the performances without permission and to accept whatever food and drink might be passed to them there. At the end of the day's performance, the actors returned in procession to the place of assembly, where they were often served a banquet.

Undoubtedly the quality of acting varied considerably. Many contemporary accounts praise certain actors lavishly, but others condemn the performers. In acting, voice seems to have been valued above all else. The chanting that had been typical in liturgical drama was abandoned in the vernacular plays in favor of a delivery based on everyday speech but formalized by rhymed verse. Since characters in the extant plays are lacking in subtlety, they did not require highly versatile performers. Most characters are stereotyped with a few clear-cut actions and emotions (such as adoration, joy, anger, or grief). Serious characters are usually restrained, but the comic roles allow much scope for improvisation and pantomime.

Attempts to be realistic occasionally exposed performers to considerable danger. At Metz (France) in 1437, the actor playing Judas almost died while being hanged; at Seurre (France) in 1496, Satan's costume caught fire. Actors in Hell scenes were often injured by the cannons and other pyrotechnic devices used to create noise, fire, and smoke.

By the sixteenth century, a number of actors were sufficiently skilled to be employed as coaches, and a few were paid for performing. By the end of the Middle Ages, the professional actor was beginning to be in evidence.

COSTUMES

Most characters were dressed in garments resembling those worn by their counterparts in medieval life. Roman soldiers were attired in medieval armor, and Jewish high priests wore robes that recalled those of Catholic prelates. God was costumed as an emperor or pope, and angels wore church robes to which wings were attached. Supernatural characters also usually wore masks. If associated with Heaven, the masks were usually gilded. Devils were conceived most imaginatively, for they were made to resemble great birds of prey, monsters with animal heads, or creatures with scales, tails, horns, or claws. Any important character, human or divine, might carry an identifying emblem (the Archangel Michael, for instance, always wielded a flaming sword).

In most instances, actors had to supply their own costumes, unless these differed markedly from those available in daily life. Consequently, the records of producing organizations show payments only for such exceptional garments as those of devils and effigies or for accessories and emblems. Actors often incurred heavy expenses, especially when playing wealthy personages. Double casting increased the outlay, particularly in the sixteenth century when stage costumes, even for lower-class characters, were often made of rich fabrics. Occasionally, as at Chalons-sur-Marne (France) in 1507, nonparticipating wealthy citizens were required to buy costumes for actors unable to furnish their own. Other sources of supply included the clergy (who loaned or rented garments), other groups that regularly produced plays, and individuals (who occasionally contracted to outfit an entire production).

Because actors usually supplied their own costumes, supervision and coordination were needed. At Lucerne, the director gave performers detailed descriptions of the appropriate costumes for their roles. It seems likely that similar procedures were followed elsewhere. Many of these practices extended to hand properties as well. Unless an item was not readily available, it was supplied by the actor who used it. Unusual articles were made at the expense of the producers.

SECULAR DRAMATIC FORMS

Alongside the religious stage, a less elaborate secular theatre existed and grew steadily. It emerged from many sources: mimes and entertainers of all sorts, *jongleurs* with their stories and songs, and pagan rituals. Such antecedents seem to have existed throughout Europe, but a secular drama is not evident until the thirteenth century, at about the time that religious plays were first being performed outdoors.

Among the oldest extant medieval secular drama is *The Play of the Greenwood*, written by Adam de la Halle (1240–1288) of Arras (France) in 1276/77. It mingles satirical scenes about the residents of Arras with such folk material as fairies and supernatural occurrences. Folk materials are even more evident in Adam's other work, *The Play of Robin and Marion* (c. 1283), a pastoral tale of the wooing of a shepherdess by a knight, the objections of her shepherd lover, and the eventual resolution of the conflict, followed by dances and games. Other secular plays include the English *Dame Sirith* (c. 1275–1300) and *The Interlude of the Clerk and the Girl* (c. 1300), both of which show an old woman convincing a young girl to succumb to a would-be lover.

From the thirteenth century onward, the number of secular dramas grew steadily. But, as with religious plays, the majority of the works that have survived were written after 1400. The secular entertainments of the late Middle Ages were of many types: farces, moralities, plays of the Chambers of Rhetoric, and interludes, along with mummings, disguisings, tournaments, and royal entries.

FARCE

If the religious plays treat the triumph of virtue and the punishment of vice within an eternal order, the farces show imperfect humanity within the social order. Marital infidelity, quarreling, cheating, hypocrisy, and other human failings are the typical subjects. The clever man, even if a sinner, is usually the hero; the dupes deserve their fates because they are stupid or gullible. Sentiment is almost totally absent.

Farce can first be found in the thirteenth century. One of the oldest to survive, *The Boy and the Blind Man* (c. 1280), written in a Flemish dialect, shows how a rogue deceives a blind man through ventriloquism, then robs and beats him. The cynical tone typical of medieval farce is already fully developed in this work.

The majority of extant farces are from France and Germany. Most of them are similar in tone and form. Typically they are short (no longer than a few hundred lines), in verse, and emphasize sex and bodily excretions. The rapid and simple action uses few characters and no complicated exposition. Most of the extant French farces are mere dramatized anecdotes, but one—*Pierre Pathelin* (c. 1470)—is now

FIG. 5.11

Pierre Pathelin and his wife. Woodcut from the edition of the play published in 1490.

FIG. 5.12

Schembart revelers as depicted in a Schembart book of the sixteenth century. From Vogt and Koch, *Geschichte der Deutschen Literatur,* 1 (1887).

considered a minor masterpiece. It tells how a lawyer tricks a merchant out of a piece of cloth and is in turn cheated out of his fee by a supposedly stupid peasant, whom he has defended on a charge of stealing sheep. The play was so popular that it had gone through thirty editions by 1600.

Two variations on farce—*sotties* and *sermons joyeux*—also became popular in France. *Sotties* were only thinly disguised political, social, or religious satires; while the *sermon joyeuse* was a burlesque sermon, in which the characters wore variations on the fool's traditional parti-colored garments, including a hood with ass's ears or a cock's comb.

In Germany, farce seems to have grown out of folk festivals, especially the revels preceding Lent (thus early German farces are often called "Shrovetide" plays). Such plays can be found in southern Germany, Austria, Switzerland, and Holland. But most of the surviving farces are from Nuremberg. There plays came to be associated with the apprentices' revels (or *Schembartlaufen*) during the pre-Lenten carnival season. By around 1450 these revels centered around an elaborate and often riotous

procession and were an accepted part of Nuremberg life. As a part of the procession, the apprentices performed short plays that could be presented anywhere and repeated at various places along the way. By far the best known of the authors is Hans Sachs (1494–1576).

Sachs was a shoemaker but also a master singer, who traveled widely and learned much about the poetry and drama of other areas. He was the author of 198 dramatic works, of which he classified only sixty-four as Shrovetide plays. Nevertheless, his reputation now rests almost entirely upon his farces. Of these, one of the best is *The Wandering Scholar and Exorcist,* in which a student convinces a man that he can call up the Devil, whom he forces a priest to impersonate as a price for concealing the priest's illicit relationship with the man's wife; all bestow money on the student—the man to reward him for skill in exorcism, the priest and the wife to bribe him to remain silent about their adultery.

In England, *The Second Shepherd's Play* of the Wakefield cycle is the best known of the early farces. In it a trickster shepherd steals a sheep and, when he is tracked down, has his wife attempt to pass it off as their newborn child. That this farce could be inserted into the framework of a nativity play is an indicator of the amount of humor that could be absorbed into even the most serious religious dramas. As an independent form, however, farce did not emerge in England until the sixteenth century with the work of John Heywood (*c.* 1497–*c.* 1580), whose most famous play, *Johan, Johan* (1533), tells the story of a henpecked husband who, when ridiculed by his wife and her lover, a priest, drives them both from his house, only to worry about what they may be doing elsewhere.

In all countries, the conventions used in the staging of farces deviated in no important respect from those used for religious plays. Perhaps the most notable difference lay in the economy of means demanded by the farces, for rarely do they require more than two mansions or employ any complex special effects.

THE MORALITY PLAY

The immediate dramatic ancestors of the moralities are probably the Pater Noster which seem to have dramatized the continual struggle for the human soul between good, as represented by the seven cardinal virtues (prudence, justice, temperance, fortitude, faith, hope, and charity) and evil, represented by the seven deadly sins (pride, covetousness, lust, anger, gluttony, envy, and sloth). Many of the Pater Noster plays were presented by municipalities and trade guilds under the same general arrangements as those used for the religious cycles. At Beverley in 1469 there were eight pageant wagons, seven of which transported Pater Noster plays about the seven deadly sins. Unfortunately, no Pater Noster plays have survived, so their precise relationship to the moralities is uncertain.

As a distinct form, the morality play flourished between about 1400 and 1550. Although some examples have been found elsewhere, the morality was for the most part an English and French phenomenon. The oldest extant morality is a fragment of *The Pride of Life* (*c.* 1350), in which the King of Life displays an overweening pride, from which he cannot be dissuaded. No doubt the lost portions showed his humiliation and repentance.

In terms of staging, the most interesting morality is *The Castle of Perseverance* (*c.* 1400–1425), which depicts Mankind's progress from birth to death and shows the final judgment on his soul. The play is long (more than 3600 lines) and includes thirty-six characters. The manuscript provides some information about its performance. In a prologue, two heralds outline the action and declare that the play will be presented "on the green" beginning at 9 A.M. one week following the announcement. A diagram of the suggested playing arrangement is also included. It shows a circular area around the perimeter of which are placed five mansions; Mankind's castle is set in the center of the circle. Concerning the circle, a note declares: "This is the water about the place, if any ditch be made where it shall be played, or else let it be strongly barred all about."

Another play, *Mankind* (*c.* 1465), of which only part survives, may originally have been a completely serious work, but if so it was later altered to include comic interludes and a number of songs and dances.

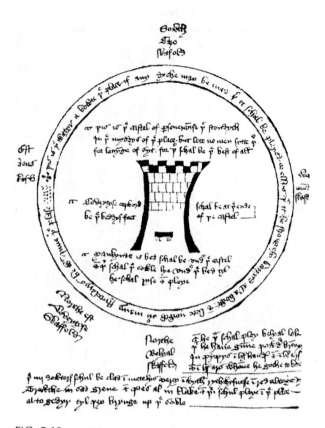

FIG. 5.13

Plan of the mansions and playing area for the *Castle of Perseverance*. In the middle is the tower of Mankind. The legend enclosed within the circles reads: "This is the water about the place, if any ditch be made where it shall be played, or else let it be strongly barred all about." The location of five mansions is indicated outside the circles.

In the version that has survived, the play's action is also interrupted to permit the actors to collect money from the audience. There are only seven roles and no scenery or complex properties. Thus *Mankind* demonstrates how the morality play was adapted to the needs of professional players and how the original didactic intention was altered to include various types of popular entertainment out of a desire to attract a paying audience.

Perhaps the best known of all moralities is *Everyman* (*c.* 1510), seemingly an English translation of the Dutch *Elkerlyc* (*c.* 1495) by Peter Dorlant. More restricted in its subject than most dramatic allegories of the time, in it Everyman receives Death's summons, struggles to escape, and finally resigns himself to necessity. Seeking companions to accompany him on his journey, Everyman is quickly deserted by such former associates as Kindred, Goods, and Fellowship. Eventually only Good Deeds goes with him into the grave.

In the sixteenth century the morality play underwent many changes. In some instances, it was used to

Here begynneth a treatyse how þ hye fader of heuen sendeth dethe to somon euery creature to come and gyue a counte of theyr lyues in this worlde/and is in maner of a morall playe.

FIG. 5.14

Everyman. Frontispiece to the edition published by John Sklot, *c.* 1530.

treat almost wholly secular subjects, as in John Skelton's *Magnificence* (c. 1520), which describes the lifestyle appropriate to a ruler, or in Nicolas de la Chesnaye's *Condemnation of the Banquet* (1507), which treats both mental and physical health and warns especially against the dangers of overeating. In other instances, the morality play was adapted as a weapon in the religious controversies that swept Europe during the sixteenth century. Perhaps the best of these plays is John Bale's (1495–1563) *King John* (1538), in which the English ruler holds out against the evil forces of the pope. Here historical personages and events are integrated with the allegorical figures and struggles typical of the original moralities. Bale's drama is often said to mark a major step toward the English chronicle play.

As religious controversy grew, doctrinal plays also began to be written in northern Europe. The first great stimulus to this movement came in 1501 with the publication of the previously unknown plays of

Hrosvitha, the tenth-century German canoness who had sought to write dramas in the manner of Terence but to tell stories about the "chastity of Christian virgins." Her works exerted considerable influence throughout the sixteenth century on a movement best summed up in the collective title used for Cornelius Schonaeus's plays, *Christian Terence,* or *Sacred Comedies* (1592).

Changes in the morality play can be attributed to the introduction of classical subjects when interest in Greece and Rome and in learning for its own sake revived. This resulted in plays that were primarily philosophical, informative, and educational, best exemplified in Henry Medwall's *Nature* (*c.* 1500) and John Rastell's *The Four Elements* (*c.* 1518).

By the early sixteenth century, then, the morality play had become extremely diversified, and all of the various strains were to be continued into Shakespeare's time. As the morality was increasingly secularized, the distinctions vanished between it and the type of play commonly labeled "interlude."

At first, morality plays were probably performed by amateurs, but gradually they were taken over by professionals. The basic conventions of the religious drama were followed in staging, although as professionalism increased, the number of actors and scenic elements declined. The costuming, especially of the allegorical figures, however, remained elaborate and imaginative. Consequently, they paved the way for the great secular plays of the succeeding period.

CHAMBERS OF RHETORIC

Closely related to the moralities are the plays performed by the Chambers of Rhetoric in the Low Countries. Originating in the fourteenth century, these societies were concerned with poetry, music, and drama. By 1500 there were about 160 societies spread throughout the Netherlands; Ghent had five. Competitions among societies were being held by 1413 and were especially popular in the period from 1493 to 1570. Typically a question was posed (such as "What is the greatest consolation to a person who is dying?"), to which the various Chambers composed and performed answers in the form of allegorical dramas. Prizes were given for those judged the best. These plays constituted the major (though not the sole) dramatic expression of the Low Countries.

Most plays were given outdoors on a stage which anticipated many features of the Elizabethan public theatre. At the back of a large platform, a fixed facade was erected. At the stage level there were normally three openings which could be closed with curtains or opened to reveal interior scenes. A second

FIG. 5.15
Rhetoric stage at Antwerp, 1561. This type of stage may
have influenced the layout of the Elizabethan public stage.
From Wilhelm Creizenach, *The English Drama in the Age
of Shakespeare* (1916).

level included similar openings while on the third
level there was a throne for the figure in whose honor
the festival was held (such as Wisdom, Lady
Rhetoric, or the Virgin). At the end of the contest,
this figure was often flown to stage level to distrib-
ute the prizes.

The productions became increasingly lavish. The
peak was reached in 1561 at a contest in Antwerp
which lasted for one month. The nine competing societies made elaborate processional entries into the city
using a total of twenty-three triumphal chariots and
197 pageant wagons. Plays were given over a period
of fifteen days. To finance this festival, the city spent
the enormous sum of 100,000 guilders, in addition
to the funds provided by the competing societies.

Until the sixteenth century, the Chamber plays
often sought to convey theological messages. But in
1516 Spain gained control of the Low Countries
and soon after the Protestant movement began to

gain force there. In an attempt to control the content of the plays presented by the Chambers of
Rhetoric, an edict was issued in 1539 forbidding
publication of the plays. Many groups insisted on
their right to express their views, but others turned
increasingly to less controversial subjects. After 1625
the Chambers declined rapidly and were eventually
replaced by professional companies.

INTERLUDES AND THE ADVENT
OF PROFESSIONAL ACTING

Interlude is an imprecise term, since it was at various times applied to almost every type of play presented in the Middle Ages. Today it is normally
used to designate the plays first presented indoors
as a part of the entertainments of rulers, nobles,
rich merchants, and schools. The label probably derives from the practice of presenting entertainment between the parts of some other event, such
as the courses of a banquet. The interlude might
be of any type: religious, moral, farcical, historical. Often there was singing and dancing as well.
Since they were often given in crowded banquet
halls, the interludes used little (often no) scenery
and few characters.

Like the morality play, the interlude was associated with the rise of the professional actor. From the
eleventh century onward, most professional entertainers were grouped under the general heading of
"minstrels," and various accounts speak of their popularity among the nobility and clergy throughout
Europe. During the fourteenth century, as wealthy
merchants began to emulate the nobility, demand for
the services of minstrels increased, and some took up
permanent residence in larger towns. By 1350 many
nobles were retaining their own companies of performers. Gradually some minstrels added acting to
their skills in entertaining and around 1425 the term
"interluders" starts to appear, indicating a troupe that
specializes in acting.

In England Richard III (reigned 1483–1485) and
Henry VII (reigned 1485–1509) each maintained a
small company. There were many similar troupes by
1500, and they proliferated rapidly during the sixteenth century as more and more nobles acquired
their own companies. Most troupes were permitted to tour under the names of their patrons when
their services were not required at home. When
they toured, the troupes presented their credentials
to the mayor of a town, gave a performance before
him and the aldermen, and, if approved, then gave
other performances for a paying public in the town

FIG. 5.16
Scene from a tournament. Miniature from a wedding chest. Painting by Domenico Morone (fifteenth century). Courtesy The National Gallery, London.

hall, an inn, or "on the green." In spite of their rising importance, however, professional players remained secondary to amateur performers until religious drama declined during the last half of the sixteenth century.

That professional actors were only beginning to appear in the late fifteenth century may explain why there are so few interludes prior to 1500. The oldest extant English play of this type, *Fulgens and Lucrece* by Henry Medwall, dates from 1497. A total of about seventy interludes survive, most from the sixteenth century.

The typical place for performing interludes was the "great hall" (or chief room) of a nobleman's residence, a university, a guild, or other organizations. These large rooms were constructed after a standard pattern: at one end was a raised platform reserved for the persons in authority and their favored associates or friends; at the opposite end was the "screen," a wall with two or three openings used as entryways for visitors and which provided access to the kitchen; above the screen there was sometimes a gallery for musicians. The great hall was used for official business and social activities. For banquets, tables were erected on the platform as well as on the floor of the room; the closer one was to the "high table," the higher one's status. Such an arrangement of tables would have been typical when performances were given at banquets. On other occasions, the tables might be replaced by scaffold seating or standing room for spectators.

In staging the interludes, elaborate mansions were sometimes built for court performances, but more typically no scenery was used. At times, the screen, each of whose openings could serve to represent a separate mansion or as an entrance, may have been used as scenic background. If there was a musicians' gallery, it might also have been incorporated into the action. But most plays seem to have been staged in the midst of the audience, where the acting space was small and, as the lines of several plays attest, the audience often encroached upon it and was asked to make room for the performers or to assist in some way.

Most interludes were written for small troupes. In England, the title page of Phillip's *Patient Grissell* states that it may be played by eight persons. The printed versions of Lewis Wager's *Mary Magdalene* and *Wealth and Health* are said to be suitable for a company of four, and the title page of Preston's *Cambises* shows how the thirty-eight roles may be distributed among eight actors.

TOURNAMENTS, MUMMINGS, AND DISGUISINGS

Alongside the interludes, other entertainments grew up around tournaments, mummings, and disguisings. Tournaments began in the tenth century as a means of training knights in warfare. During the thirteenth century, because a number of contestants had been killed, reforms were introduced that brought more dramatic elements into these events. Instead of merely seeking to unseat each other, knights were fighting to capture scenic units like the "Castle of Love" inhabited by suitably costumed ladies and attendants.

At the most elaborate of the tournaments (the *pas d'armes*), spectators were carefully segregated according to sex and rank in galleries that surrounded the field of combat. At various points around this field were placed the elaborate mansions that established the allegorical context of the tournament. Among the favorite emblematic devices were mountains, castles, woods, fountains, ships, and chapels. For the most part, tournaments used the same visual symbolism found in the religious plays but often gave it a secular turn.

Mummers' plays (derived from a French word meaning to play in dumb show, mask, or disguise) were performed during the Christmas season with Father Christmas as master of ceremonies or "presenter." Usually in these plays at least one character was killed in combat, after which a doctor arrived and brought the dead back to life through some grotesque device. Among the characters associated with these plays are a clown, a fool, a hobby horse, a man dressed as Maid Marian, St. George, and a dragon.

Throughout the Christmas season and into the carnival season preceding Lent, there were many types of "disguisings" in which costumed and masked revelers of various sorts took to the streets. Some went from house to house presenting plays, songs, and dances. Most took up collections, but some, wishing to show gratitude or respect to the king or other official, used this opportunity to offer gifts. Because such disguisings came to be used as a cover for criminal behavior, they were suppressed in England (except at court) in the fourteenth and fifteenth centuries. Elsewhere disguisings of various sorts continued among the common people; in many places they have persisted to the present day, especially in pre-Lenten carnival celebrations (such as those associated today with *mardi gras*). In theatre, however, the most important offshoots of mummings and disguisings were such courtly entertainments as English masques, Italian *intermezzi,* and French *ballets de cour.*

The disguisings given at court were largely pantomimic playlets intended as ingenious allegorical compliments to the persons being honored at banquets, weddings, birthdays, and other occasions. Characteristically, the entertainments concluded in a dance. In England, performers did not at first mingle with the audience, but beginning in 1513 the dancers chose partners from among the spectators. Since this practice was borrowed from the Italian courts, productions after this time were called "masques after the manner of Italy." In these masques, courtiers served as actors and dancers, and professional musicians provided music and song. Eventually they developed into complex spectacles with scenic units mounted on wheels that could be brought in and taken out much like a medieval pageant wagon. The first record of a courtly disguising with elaborate scenic structures dates from 1377. In England, they were very popular under Henry VII (reigned 1485–1509) and especially under Henry VIII (reigned 1509–1547), who had a House of Revels (1527) built for them and eventually created an Office of Revels (1545) just to manage them. Such court entertainments reached their peak in Italy, France, and England between the mid sixteenth and mid seventeenth centuries.

ROYAL ENTRIES AND STREET PAGEANTS

Theatrical productions also came to be incorporated into the street pageants given by municipalities in honor of coronations, royal weddings, military victories, or visiting rulers. These celebrations followed a basic pattern: Civic officials and representatives of the clergy and trade guilds met the person to be honored at a prearranged place outside the city; then they escorted the visitor along a carefully planned route through the town to the cathedral for a religious service, after which the visitor was taken to a place of residence. It was an occasion upon which the city could demonstrate its loyalty, respect, or gratitude.

Gradually small plays were added at strategic locations along the route to give emphasis to the honor. These may have appeared as early as 1236, but were definitely being used by 1298, when the city of London honored Edward I's victory over the

FIG. 5.17

Arch erected in Gracechurch Street for the entry of James I into London in 1604. Frontispiece to Vol. I of John Nichols, *The Progresses, Processions and Magnificent Festivities of James the First . . .* (1828).

Scots. In Paris, the first clear record of plays as features of royal entries is found in 1313, when Edward II of England visited France.

Most of these plays were pantomimic. Consequently, they are called *tableaux vivants* (or living pictures) in which an appropriate scene from the Bible, mythology, or history was shown, generally preceded or followed by a poem that explained its allegorical significance. Each play was mounted on its own separate stage, which could vary in size and complexity with the most elaborate being multistoried and employing the same equipment and conventions used for the most elaborate dramatic types of the period.

THE END OF MEDIEVAL DRAMA

During the sixteenth century the religious theatre that had been typical of the Middle Ages for nearly 600 years, almost completely disappeared despite its obvious popularity and broad-based support. The reasons for this change were numerous, but a few were of special importance.

Perhaps most significantly, the church had been weakened by internal conflicts. It had reached the peak of its power around 1200, when the pope's supremacy in both religious and secular matters was accepted throughout Europe. But as nations started to take shape, princes sought ways of gaining control over religious affairs within their own territories. It soon became evident that the most effective means of control lay in securing influence over the papacy. Between 1305 and 1377 the papacy was forcefully moved from Rome to Avignon in southern France and the pope became a virtual captive of the French. Between 1378 and 1417 there were rival popes: at one time three claimed the papacy. The devastation of the Black Death, which arrived in 1347, also caused people to question the church and its ability to protect them. As populations declined, standards of living increased, breaking down the old power structures of Feudalism. Learning had revived with the rise of universities and a new spirit of questioning had been fostered throughout Europe. By the fifteenth century, therefore, the church had been greatly weakened and many of its practices, perhaps most notoriously the selling of indulgences (or spiritual pardons), had led to demands for reform by figures like Martin Luther, which finally triggered the advent of Protestantism in 1517.

Obviously the theatre could not remain aloof from these events. In England, Henry VIII's break with the church of Rome in 1534 led to bitter controversies in which drama was used as a weapon to attack or defend particular dogmas. In an attempt to still the conflict, Elizabeth I forbade all religious plays in 1558 and by the 1580s, the great cycle plays had been silenced. Parallel events were underway in other countries. The Netherlands banned religious plays in 1539, the Papal States in 1547, and Paris in 1548. In some Germanic areas they continued into the seventeenth century, but in most of Europe the religious drama had been abandoned by 1600. Only in Spain, where the Inquisition had established its unquestioned control, did they continue (until 1765).

The abandonment of religious drama also destroyed the last remaining basis for an international theatre. Henceforth, each country developed its own characteristic style. On the other hand, the end of religious drama forced dramatists to turn to secular subjects. In doing so, they took advantage of the reviving interest in Greek and Roman works, and in the process gained a new appreciation of dramatic form. The resulting blend of classical and medieval heritages did much to create the great secular drama of the Renaissance.

In Greece, Rome, and Western Europe during the late Middle Ages, the theatre enjoyed the active support of governmental and religious bodies. Theatre was essentially a community offering used to celebrate special events considered significant to all. Beginning in the sixteenth century, however, it was deprived of its religious and civic functions and henceforth it had to wage a fight for recognition on purely commercial and artistic grounds. In the beginning, theatre was sustained by noblemen and rulers, who continued the system of private patronage that had grown up in medieval times. With this help, the professional theatre gradually established itself throughout Europe, although in some countries the process was not to be completed for another 200 years.

The same factors that were to bring an end to the Middle Ages were making room for the classical revival that we call the Renaissance. From 1300 to 1500 the two overlap, with the Renaissance manifesting itself more strongly in Italy than in the rest of Europe. In the sixteenth century Italian Renaissance thought opened the way for the creation of professional theatre throughout Western Europe. In England and Spain, however, the theatre still retained some important elements of its Medieval heritage, so we will look at those before going on to look at events in Italy and France.

LOOKING AT THEATRE HISTORY

Among the major sources for the historian of medieval theatre are the municipal records kept by towns that were directly involved in the production of plays. One of the most complete accounts can be deduced from the records of the city of Mons (Belgium), which sponsored a passion play in 1501. Here is an excerpt from which we learn how many rehearsals were held, where they were held, and how the actors were notified:

To Jehan Billet, for the 48 days of summoning he had carried out in having assembled the players at all the rehearsals held since the beginning of the said play at the City Hall, as agreed upon, 6.1.

Translation by Lenyth Brockett. All of the accounts of this production can be found (in French) in Gustave Cohen, *Le Livre de Conduite du Regisseur . . . pour le Mystère . . . à Mons en 1501* (Paris, 1925).

There appear to have been a variety of professional entertainers during the Middle Ages and an equally varied moral response to them. Here is one account written by the Bishop of Salisbury (England) in the first half of the fourteenth century:

There are three kinds of histriones. Some metamorphose and transform their bodies through unseemly leaps and foul gestures, either exposing themselves shamefully or donning fearful masks, but surely all are damned unless they abandon their employment. Likewise there are others who work at nothing, . . . but follow after assemblies of great men and tell of disgraces and scandals so as to please others. They are also surely damned, for the Apostle forbids us to take food with such men. There is also a third kind of histriones who have musical instruments for delighting men, and of these there are two kinds. Some frequent public drinking bouts and licentious societies, and there they sing various songs so that men are moved to wantonness; these are to be damned as are the others. But there are also others, who are called jesters, who sing the deeds of rulers and the lives of the saints, and provide solace for men whether in their sicknesses or in low spirits, and they do not invent countless infamies as do the dancers and dancing girls and the others who play in shameful representations and cause apparitions to be seen through enchantments or by another method. But these . . . bring comfort to men. . . .

Thomas de Cabham, *Penetential*, trans. Barbara Spear.

A major controversy has raged around David Rogers' account of the staging of the Chester cycle. Not only is his account important in discussions of the construction of the pageant wagons, but in the concern over whether the plays were actually performed on the wagons or whether they merely transported the actors who, during a procession, gave some brief indication of the longer play that was later seen at a fixed location:

They were divided into 24 pageants or parts, and every Company brought forth their pageant which was the carriage or place which they played in . . . they began at the Abbey gates and when the first pageant was played at the Abbey gates then it was wheeled from thence to the pentice at the high cross before the Mayor, and before that was done the second came, and the first went into the Watergate street and from thence unto the Bridge street and so all one after an other till all the pageants were played. . . . These pageants or carriage was a high place made like a house with two rooms being open on the top. [In] the lower room they apparelled and dressed themselves, and in the higher room they played, and they stood upon 6 wheels.

David Rogers, *A Breviarye, or Some Few Recollections of the City of Chester* (Harley Manuscript 1944, fol. 21–22). The spelling and punctuation have been modernized to facilitate reading.

6
English Theatre to 1642

Because of wars and internal strife, England was scarcely affected by the Renaissance until the late fifteenth century. Since the Norman Conquest in 1066, England's kings had controlled extensive territories in France and had intermarried with French ruling families. In 1337 England laid claim to the French throne, thereby precipitating a lengthy conflict (often called the Hundred Years' War) that continued until 1453. It was during this conflict that the Black Death ravaged Europe. For a time England seemed to be winning the struggle, especially after 1420 when Henry V (reigned 1413–1422) was named regent and heir to the French throne. But after his death and Joan of Arc's victory at Orleans in 1429, the English rapidly lost control. By 1453 England held only Calais in France. At about the same time a struggle for the throne of England (the War of the Roses) began between the rival houses of York and Lancaster. The conflict continued until 1485 when Richard III was defeated by the Earl of Richmond, who united the dissident factions. As Henry VII (reigned 1485–1509), he founded the Tudor line that ruled England until the death of Elizabeth I in 1603. The Tudors played a major role in the religious conflicts that were to dominate Europe in the sixteenth century, but they also brought a strong central government to England and despite continued internal and external conflicts made it a major international power.

Many forces eventually shaped the great English drama of the late sixteenth century. Among the most important of these were the religious and political controversies that led up to and followed Henry VIII's (reigned 1509–1547) break with the Roman Catholic church (1529–1536). While Henry's actions were arguably more political than religious, their effect was to make England the first nation to embrace the Protestant Reformation Luther had begun in 1517. Henry's policy of forced conversion caused deep divisions within the country. His dissolution of the monasteries (1536–1540) and distribution of the resulting wealth among his followers further polarized those on both sides. The early death of Henry's only son Edward VI (ruled 1547–1553) brought Henry's oldest daughter to the throne as Mary I (1553–1558), England's first ruling Queen in 400 years. She sought to return England to Catholicism, and married a Catholic, Philip II of Spain. When Mary died in 1558 Philip considered it a duty to remove Henry's second daughter, the Protestant Elizabeth I (reigned 1558–1603), from the throne. This religious animosity was compounded by England's challenging of Spain in the New World and aiding of the Netherlands in its attempts to throw off Spanish rule.

EARLY TUDOR DRAMA

Although medieval theatrical practices continued to be dominant, the spirit of the Renaissance began to be felt in England during the reign of Henry VII. Erasmus and other continental humanists came to England; Colet and other English humanists studied in Italy. These men taught at both Oxford and Cambridge, giving English scholars and writers an interest in ancient literature. The court saw the first influences of humanism on drama in 1497, with the performance of Medwall's *Fulgens and Lucrece,* and it saw this influence grow in the morality plays of Skelton, Rastell, and Bale (discussed in Chapter 5). The didactic nature of these works provided the models for the propaganda plays written during Henry VIII's break with the Catholic Church.

Oxford graduates were the early leaders in spreading the new approaches to learning into the schools. William Lily (1468–1522) studied the staging of Latin comedy with Pomponius Laetus in Rome before becoming first headmaster of St. Paul's grammar school. John Heywood (*c.* 1497–*c.* 1578) was a court musician and author of the first nondidactic interludes in England. Nicholas Udall (1505–1566) became headmaster of Eton (and later of Westminster) and wrote one of the best-known early Tudor comedies, *Ralph Roister Doister* (*c.* 1534–1541). Heavily indebted to Plautus' *Braggart Warrior,* Udall's play shows the foolish posturings of a boastful coward and his discomfiture in his courtship of a widow. Richard Edwards (1524–1566) worked with the children of the Chapel Royal and wrote *Damon and Pythias* (1564), the first English play with a complex plot.

Humanist performances were flourishing at Cambridge University by the 1520s where students performed plays, many in Latin but others in English, for members of the university community. In 1546 Queen's College mandated such performances and constructed a removable theatre structure for its main hall which was used until at least 1640 and may have influenced the design of the London playhouses. The best known of the plays in English was *Gammer Gurton's Needle,* written by "Mr. S." and acted at Christ's College sometime between 1552 and 1563. This play fuses subject matter and characters similar to those typical of medieval farce with techniques borrowed from Roman comedy. It develops a series of comic misunderstandings, most of them initiated by Diccon, the "bedlam" between two neighboring households over the loss of a needle.

The humanist influences seen in schools and universities were carried to London's Inns of Court: Gray's Inn, Lincoln's Inn, the Inner Temple, and the Middle Temple. Principally places of residence and training for lawyers, the Inns admitted young men, generally recent graduates of Oxford and Cambridge, for further legal education. These wealthy and aristocratic students were taught music, dancing, and other graces, which were practiced in part through the presentation of plays. Most performances came during the Christmas "revels," which extended over a period of four weeks. But the Inns also mounted many other elaborate entertainments to celebrate special occasions. The audiences were aristocratic, well educated, and interested in the latest fashions in drama, both at home and abroad.

In 1561, the Inner Temple presented the play now ranked as the first English tragedy, *Gorboduc* or *Ferrex and Porrex,* written by Thomas Sackville and Thomas Norton. The following year it was presented at Whitehall with Queen Elizabeth in attendance. The subject, chosen from the legendary history of England, was developed in a pseudo-Senecan manner in a five-act structure. It concerns the jealousy aroused between Ferrex and Porrex when their father, Gorboduc, decides to divide his kingdom between them. All the principal characters eventually are killed, and their fate is used to point a lesson for England about the dangers of leaving uncertain the order of succession to the throne. Although the play now seems weak, it made such a deep impression that it was printed five times by 1590. It established the fashion for modeling tragedies on the works of Seneca, and its use of blank verse, instead of the traditional rhymed verse, profoundly influenced subsequent playwriting. Gray's Inn presented George Gascoigne's (*c.* 1542–1578) *Supposes* in 1566. This adaptation of Ariosto's *I Suppositi* (*The Substitutes,* 1509) tells the story of a young nobleman who poses as a servant in the household of a well-to-do widower in order to win the love of the widower's daughter. Its success established prose as the medium for English comedy and set a fashion for Italian plots and settings.

Despite the humanist influence, medieval practices and conventions continued to dominate English theatre through most of the sixteenth century. Entertainers of all sorts traveled the country and local communities continued to produce mummings, farce comedies, and other kinds of amateur performances. Aiming to attract a wide audience, professional actors combined elements of popular entertainment with subjects drawn from many sources. Biblical stories were mingled with adaptations of foreign novels and chivalric tales, and classical myths with English historical and low-comedy figures. The entire popular tradition is probably best summed up in Thomas Preston's (1537–1598) *A Lamentable Tragedy Mixed Full of Pleasant Mirth, Containing the Life of Cambises, King of Persia, from the beginning of his Kingdom, Unto his Death,*

His One Good Deed of Execution, after that Many Wicked Deeds and Tyrannous Murders, Committed by and Through Him, and Last of All, His Odious Death by God's Justice Appointed (c. 1561). Although the play is set in Persia, many of the characters are mythological (Cupid and Venus), allegorical (Shame, Diligence, Trial, and Proof), or English (Hob, Lob, and Marian-May-Be-Good). It freely mingles the comic and the serious, ranges over a considerable period of time, and changes place with bewildering rapidity. The numerous bloody deeds, such as beheadings, flayings, and murders, are all shown on stage. And all of this, according to the printed version of c. 1569, could be performed by eight actors playing thirty-eight roles. As one of the most popular plays of the day, *Cambises* reveals much about the tastes of the audience that made a public theatre feasible. Its variety also illustrates the need for dramatists capable of unifying such diverse elements.

By the 1580s the ongoing religious and political intrigues had become focused around Mary, Queen of Scots. Mary (1542–1587) had been queen of Scotland from the time she was one week old and, as wife of Francis II (reigned 1559–1560), was briefly Queen of France. She was coerced by Protestant forces to abdicate the Scottish throne and fled to England in 1568. Many of Elizabeth's opponents, including Philip II, thought that the Catholic Mary, as grandniece to Henry VIII, was the true heir to the throne of England. Eventually Mary was implicated in a plot to overthrow Elizabeth and was executed in 1587. In 1588 Philip II sent an invasion fleet to England. The decisive victory of Elizabeth's navy over this seemingly invincible Spanish Armada established England as a major maritime power and left English Protestantism relatively secure. The resulting upsurge of England's national confidence seems to parallel a remarkable growth in its professional theatre. But problems continued at home and abroad. The war with Spain went on until 1604, rapid economic change led to serious food shortages, especially in London, the plague was an ever-present killer, and Protestant security was compromised by factionalism.

By 1600 the influence schools, universities, and Inns of Court had on professional theatre was waning. But they had performed a crucial role by familiarizing students with effective dramatic techniques. When classically educated writers began to work for the professional troupes, English drama entered an era of greatness.

THE UNIVERSITY WITS

During the 1580s all the strands of drama began to coalesce, primarily because of Thomas Kyd and a group of educated men, commonly called "the University Wits," who turned to writing for the public stage. The most important of these writers were John Lyly from Oxford and Robert Greene and Christopher Marlowe from Cambridge.

Thomas Kyd (1558–1594) is remembered primarily for *The Spanish Tragedy* (c. 1587), the most popular play of the sixteenth century. In telling his sensational story of murder and revenge, Kyd places all the important events on stage, lets the action range freely through time and place, and uses such Senecan devices as ghosts, a chorus (one person), soliloquies, confidants, and division into acts. Yet Kyd manages to construct a well-articulated plot with rapid, clear, and absorbing action. Although lacking in depth of characterization or thought, *The Spanish Tragedy* is a remarkable advance over preceding plays and established the vogue for "revenge" tragedy, of which *Hamlet* was to be the most lasting example.

John Lyly (c. 1554–1606) wrote primarily for boys' companies catering to aristocratic audiences. His most characteristic works are pastoral comedies that mingle classical mythology with English subjects. His is a fairy-tale world in which troubles vanish at the wave of a magic wand. All but one of Lyly's plays were written in the carefully balanced, refined, and somewhat artificial prose for which he was famous. Among his characteristic works are *Campaspe* (1584), *Endimion* (c. 1588), and *Love's Metamorphosis* (c. 1590). These delicate pastoral works established the tradition upon which Shakespeare built in *As You Like It*.

Robert Greene (1560–1592) also wrote pastoral and romantic comedies, but for the adult companies. In his *Friar Bacon and Friar Bungay* (c. 1589) and *James IV* (c. 1591), stories of love and pastoral adventures are mingled with historical materials. Greene is especially noted for his charming and resourceful heroines, who, after wandering in disguise

FIG. 6.1

Illustration from an edition of Marlowe's *Doctor Faustus* published about 1620.

through a series of temptations, are rewarded with the fulfillment of their fondest desires.

Christopher Marlowe (1564–1593) was by far the most influential of this group. Among the plays he wrote for the public theatre are *Tamburlaine*, Parts 1 and 2 (1587–1588), *Doctor Faustus* (c. 1588), *The Jew of Malta* (c. 1589), and *Edward II* (c. 1592). Marlowe's plays focus on the protagonist, whose complex motivations are illuminated by an episodic story. *Edward II* was especially important in the development of the chronicle play, for with it Marlowe demonstrated how to rearrange, telescope, and alter diverse historical events to create a sense of causal relationships and thus a coherent story, but *Doctor Faustus* has been his most influential work. When he was killed in 1593 he and Shakespeare had written about the same number of plays, but many critics believe that Marlowe had the better command of blank verse.

The University Wits bridged the gap between the learned and popular audiences. Their successful blending of classical and medieval devices with compelling stories drawn from many sources established the foundations upon which Shakespeare and his contemporaries built.

SHAKESPEARE AND HIS CONTEMPORARIES

William Shakespeare (1564–1616) is frequently said to be the greatest dramatist of all time. He entered the world of the London theatre as an actor sometime between 1585 and 1592. He is believed to have acted for Strange's Men, Pembroke's Men, and Sussex's Men before becoming a shareholder in the Chamberlain's Men in 1594. He remained with them for the rest of his career as an actor and resident playwright becoming a householder (part owner) in the Globe playhouse in 1598 and in the second Blackfriars playhouse in 1608. Shakespeare, then, was directly involved in more aspects of the theatre than any other writer of his day.

Shakespeare is generally thought to have taken up playwriting between 1589 and 1592. The exact chronology of his plays is often debated but *Henry VI*, Parts 1, 2, and 3 are thought to be his first plays, though other scholars argue for *Two Gentlemen of Verona* or *Taming of the Shrew*. He wrote the very popular tragedies *Titus Andronicus* and *Richard III* and an adaptation of a Roman comedy, *Comedy of Errors*, before joining the Chamberlain's Men. For the next ten years he wrote roughly one comedy and one tragedy per season, including many of his best-known plays: *Love's Labour's Lost* and *Romeo and Juliet* (1594–1595); *A Midsummer Night's Dream* and *Richard II* (1595–1596); *The Merchant of Venice* and *King John* (1596–1597); *Henry IV*, Parts 1 and 2 (1597–1598); *Much Ado About Nothing* and *Henry V* (1598–1599); *As You Like It* and *Julius Caesar* (1599–1600); *Twelfth Night* and *Hamlet* (1600–1601); *The Merry Wives of Windsor* and *Troilus and Cressida* (1601–1602); *All's Well That Ends Well* and *Measure for Measure* (1602–1603). His output declined over the last ten years of his career when he wrote only tragedies and tragicomedies, several in partnership with other playwrights. The plays of this period include: *Othello* (1604–1605); *King Lear* and *Macbeth*, the latter probably revised by Thomas Middleton (1605–1606); *Antony and Cleopatra* (1606–1607); *Coriolanus* and *Timon of Athens*, the latter possibly written with Thomas Middleton (1607–1608); *Pericles*, possibly written with George Wilkins (1608–1609), *Cymbeline* (1609–1610); *A Winter's Tale* (1610–1611); *The Tempest* (1611–1612); and *Henry VIII* and *Two Noble Kinsmen*, both written with John Fletcher (1612–1613). Along with these thirty-eight plays he wrote an early lost play *Love's Labour's Won* (though this may be an alternative title for *Taming of the Shrew*), and a late lost play *Cardenio* (1612–1614), written with John Fletcher. Some scholars believe he had a hand in several other plays including *Edward III* and *Thomas Moore*. Sixteen of his plays were published in quarto versions before his death, but the survival of his work can be credited in large part to the First Folio (1623), a collection of thirty-six of his plays edited by his fellow actors Henry Condell and John Heminges.

It is impossible to do justice to Shakespeare in a short space, for no playwright's work has been more fully studied. Only a few characteristics of his dramaturgy can be reviewed here. Shakespeare borrowed stories from many sources (history, mythology, legend, fiction, drama) but reworked them until they became distinctively his own. Typically, situations and characters are clearly established in the opening scenes, and the action develops logically out of this exposition. A number of plots are usually interwoven, at first proceeding somewhat independently of each other but eventually coming together as the denouement approaches, so that the resolution of one leads to that of the others; in this way apparent diversity is given unity. The action normally encompasses months or years and occurs in widely separated places. This broad canvas creates a sense of ongoing life behind the scenes.

Shakespeare's large casts are composed of well-rounded characters who run the gamut from the inept and ridiculous to the commanding and heroic, from the young and innocent to the old and corrupt. Despite the enormous range of his characters, Shakespeare entered into most of them sympathetically and made them appear to be living individuals rather than mere stage figures. His penetrating insights into human behavior have remained compelling.

No playwright uses language as effectively as Shakespeare. His poetic and figurative dialogue not only arouses specific emotions, moods, and ideas, it creates a network of complex associations and connotations that transcends the immediate dramatic situation.

Shakespeare was by far the most comprehensive, sensitive, and dramatically effective playwright of his time. He attempted almost all the popular dramatic types and subjects of his age, and in each instance gave them their most effective expression. In his own day, Shakespeare's critical reputation was lower than Jonson's or Fletcher's, but his fame began to grow in the late seventeenth century and reached its peak in the nineteenth century.

Ben Jonson (1572–1637) is usually considered the finest Elizabethan playwright after Shakespeare. An actor for a time, Jonson began writing plays in the mid-1590s and went to prison several times for his contributions to politically satiric comedies. More than any other English dramatist, Jonson turned attention to the classical precepts as a way of tempering the excesses of native playwrights, though he frequently deviated from those principles in his own works. Jonson gained the favor of James I, for whom he wrote more masques than any other dramatist and was granted a royal pension in 1616. When he published a carefully edited collection of his own plays that same year, he gave a new respectability to drama, which had long been seen as mere diversionary entertainment. His later public quarrel with the court designer Inigo Jones was a major contribution to the debate over the relative importance of language and spectacle in performance.

Of Jonson's twenty-eight plays, the comedies, especially *Every Man in His Humour* (1598), *Volpone* (1606), *Epicoene, or the Silent Woman* (1609), *The Alchemist* (1610), and *Bartholomew Fair* (1614), are now best known. Jonson was concerned primarily with reforming human behavior and concentrated upon the foibles of contemporary types. He popularized the "comedy of humours," based on a medical theory from classical times that posited four bodily "humours" (blood, phlegm, yellow bile, and black bile) that had to be kept in proper balance to sustain good health. By Jonson's day humours were seen as determinants of basic temperaments, and in his plays eccentricities of behavior are attributed to the imbalance of humours. He created a wide range of character types based upon this scheme. Because Jonson does not arouse sympathy for most of his

characters, the plays appear more harshly moralistic than do Shakespeare's. Jonson also wrote two tragedies, *Sejanus* (1603) and *Catiline* (1611), both of which were among the most respected plays of the century although they were not successful on stage.

Shakespeare and Jonson were surrounded by a host of less-celebrated figures. Chapman, Dekker, Marston, Heywood, and Middleton are among the most typical. George Chapman (c. 1560–1634) wrote twenty-one plays between 1595 and 1613, concentrating first on comedy in the vein of Jonson and then on tragedy in the manner of Marlowe. In such plays as *May Day* (c. 1600) and *Sir Giles Goosecap* (1603), he mingled satirical and romantic elements with "humours" psychology to produce a moral comedy less biting than Jonson's. His most famous tragedies, *Bussy D'Ambois* (c. 1604) and *The Revenge of Bussy D'Ambois* (c. 1610), center around strong men of action who seem doomed to failure.

Thomas Dekker (c. 1570–1632) wrote at least sixty-five plays, many in collaboration with other leading dramatists of the day. His most famous work, *The Shoemaker's Holiday* (1599), depicts the unsophisticated world of tradesmen and apprentices, emphasizing only its pleasant aspects, in the story of an industrious shoemaker who becomes Lord Mayor of London. Like many plays of the period, it appears to much better advantage on the stage than in print.

John Marston (1576–1634) wrote or collaborated on twelve plays between 1599 and 1608. He wrote for the boys' companies, which gives a perplexing context to his preoccupation with human imperfections as reflected in such comedies as *Histriomastix* (c. 1600) and *What You Will* (c. 1601), and such serious plays as *The Dutch Courtesan* (c. 1603–1605) and *The Malcontent* (1605). All his works lash out at a world in which people have substituted their own desires for the Christian virtues. Marston is noted for his violent and original imagery, which influenced many of his successors.

Thomas Heywood (c. 1574–1641) claimed to have had a hand in more than 220 plays. He was especially good at arousing the pathetic emotions, but he seldom rose to those of tragedy. Today he is remembered primarily for *A Woman Killed with Kindness* (1603). This domestic tragedy tells the story of a good wife caught in an adulterous affair with her husband's trusted friend. Rather than take revenge on the pair, the husband banishes his wife from home and children, after which she dies of grief for her transgression and he realizes too late the value of Christian forgiveness.

Thomas Middleton (1580–1627) wrote or collaborated on at least two dozen plays, covering a range of moods and subjects second in diversity only to Shakespeare's. Like Shakespeare, he could enter into all characters and situations, but unlike Shakespeare, Middleton seems lacking in strong feeling or original insight. In plays such as *Michaelmas Term* (1604–1606), *A Trick to Catch the Old One* (1604–1607), and *A Chaste Maid in Cheapside* (1611), he creates a vivid view of capitalist London and demonstrates a remarkable facility for inventiveness and verbal wit. His later work features more tragedy. With William Rowley (*c.* 1585–after 1625) he wrote *The Changeling* (1622) and *The Spanish Gypsy* (1623); his other works include the political satire *A Game at Chess* (1624) and the sinister *Women Beware Women* (1625). Middleton's serious plays tend to show the destruction of a potentially great person through gradual corruption, but the tragic effect is blunted because the characters do not progress significantly in self-knowledge. Scholars have become increasingly convinced that Middleton is also the author of *The Revenger's Tragedy* (*c.* 1606), one of the darkest dramas of the period. Traditionally, however, this play has been assigned to Cyril Tourneur (*c.* 1575–1626), who wrote the almost equally dark *The Atheist's Tragedy* (1611) and *The Nobleman* (1611–1612).

The plays of Shakespeare and his contemporaries display many technical similarities. Almost all use an early point of attack and follow a chronological organization with all important episodes shown on stage. In most plays, the short scene is the basic structural unit. Because they were written for a nonillusionistic stage, the plays are essentially placeless, although the locale is always specified in the dialogue when it is important to the action. The major concern is for developing action, in which time and place often shift rapidly. Tone also may vary frequently from serious to comic. Most of the plays are shaped in part by the belief in a moral order that allows us free will, but holds us responsible for the choices we make. Although less obviously than in medieval drama, the characters are still caught in a struggle between good and evil. Much of this moral tone is established through poetic imagery, soliloquies, and observations, although the lesser writers resort to straightforward statements of moral lessons.

JACOBEAN AND CAROLINE DRAMATISTS

Critics have traditionally identified a subtle change in English drama during the first decade of the reign of James I. Though some argue that this may not be as clear as it once seemed when the entire repertory is taken into account, plays during this period do appear to reflect increasing cynicism and doubt.

Tragicomedies, with their contrived happy endings for otherwise serious plays, were increasingly popular, encouraging the pathetic or sensational as substitutes for tragic emotions. Thrills and excitement took greater precedence over significant insights or complex characterization. Yet at the same time, technical skill increased. The playwrights handled exposition more adroitly, compressed the action into fewer episodes, built complications to startling climaxes, and alternated quiet with tumultuous scenes. As a result, the plays of this later period are more skillfully contrived than those written earlier, but they are often lacking in profundity. Much of this is evident in the plays of Tourneur and in the late collaborations of Middleton. Of the many other dramatists who worked between 1610 and 1642 the most important are Webster, Fletcher, Shirley, and Ford.

John Webster (*c.* 1580–1634) wrote about fourteen plays, some in collaboration with Dekker, Heywood, Middleton, Rowley, and others. He is remembered chiefly for *The White Devil* (1609–1612) and *The Duchess of Malfi* (1613/14), the Jacobean tragedies that rank closest to Shakespeare's in modern estimation. His plays are admired for their well-drawn characters and powerful dramatic poetry, but criticized for the obscurity of their action. His protagonists are surrounded by corruption, which inevitably destroys them, but they do not themselves achieve any deep new insights. Webster's plays lack that sense of affirmation found in Shakespeare's tragedies and manage only to raise important issues without illuminating them.

John Fletcher (1579–1625) was one of the most successful dramatists of his day and after collaborating with Shakespeare on several plays, probably replaced him as principal dramatist for the King's Men. His name is inextricably linked with that of Francis Beaumont (*c.* 1584–1616) who is best known today for *The Knight of the Burning Pestle* (*c.* 1607), a burlesque of middle-class taste in theatre, because a collection of about fifty plays published in 1647 and 1679 was attributed to their joint authorship. Actually they collaborated on only few of these works, among them *The Maid's Tragedy, Philaster,* and *A King and No King,* all written between 1608 and 1613. These works did much to establish the tone and technique of Jacobean drama. *A King and No King* is typical of the trend toward sensationalism in its depiction of a brother and sister caught up in an apparently incestuous love, only to have their moral problem resolved by the discovery that they are not related. Fletcher knew how to shape every element in terms of dramatic effectiveness, and his dialogue was especially admired by aristocratic theatregoers who saw in it the epitome of the way they would like to speak. During the Restoration, Fletcher's plays were more frequently performed than those of either Shakespeare or Jonson. His *The Scornful Lady* (1616), *The Chances* (1617), *The Spanish Curate* (1622), and *Rule a Wife and Have a Wife* (1624) were especially popular though he is now remembered more for *The Woman's Prize or the Tamer Tamed* (1610), his apology for the misogyny of Shakespeare's *Taming of the Shrew*. Philip Massinger (1583–1640) replaced Fletcher as the chief dramatist to the King's Men in 1625. He collaborated so often with Fletcher and later revised so many of Fletcher's plays that it is difficult to distinguish their individual contributions. Massinger's *A New Way to Pay Old Debts* (1621/22) is his best known play since the role of Sir Giles Overreach, whose villainy eventually leads him to madness and death, was a favorite with leading actors for over two hundred years.

James Shirley (1596–1666) succeeded Massinger as principal dramatist for the King's Men. He wrote about thirty-six plays and is known especially for his comedies, such as *Hyde Park* (1623) and *The Lady of Pleasure* (1635), which depict the manners and fashions of aristocratic London society. Shirley considered his best work to be *The Cardinal* (1641), a tragedy similar to *The Duchess of Malfi*.

The plays of John Ford (1586–c. 1639) are usually cited as exemplifying the decadence that characterized Caroline drama, since *'Tis Pity She's a Whore* (1629–1633) treats with apparent sympathy a love affair between brother and sister and ends with the destruction of nearly everyone in the play. Other significant plays among the seventeen attributed to Ford are *The Lover's Melancholy* (c. 1628) and *The Broken Heart* (c. 1627–1631). Scarcely noted in his own day, Ford is now admired for his ability to illuminate evil by associating it with ordinary human beings.

These are only a few of the 250 or more dramatists who were active between 1590 and 1642 when nearly 2000 plays were written. It is also well to remember that the precise authorship of most plays from this period is difficult to determine because collaboration was so common and plays were frequently revised by persons other than the original author. We can seldom establish the relationship of a surviving script to the playwright's original text.

GOVERNMENT REGULATION OF THE THEATRE

The development of playwriting as a profession was made possible by the emergence of a public theatre that constantly required new plays. In turn, the stability of the theatre was heavily dependent on government regulations. When she came to the throne, Elizabeth was faced with the challenge of gaining effective control over the numerous forces that made for divisiveness in England. During her reign she slowly consolidated her power to such an extent that her successors, James I and Charles I, were able to rule almost as absolute monarchs. The theatre was among those activities over which the crown gained control, and since the court was always more favorable to professional actors than local governments were, the growth of the theatre paralleled the central government's assumption of authority over professional performances.

When Elizabeth was crowned in 1558, any gentleman could sponsor a troupe of actors. Since any actor not employed by a member of the gentry or a local was classed as a vagabond and subject to severe penalties, some companies falsely claimed patronage they did not have. (There were as many as five troupes sponsored by cities, but we know little about them.) Troupes toured when not needed by their patron and were increasingly performing partisan plays that aggravated religious controversy. In 1559 Elizabeth's government banned plays on religious or political subjects, and made local officials responsible for licensing all public performances in their areas. Still, it took until 1581, when the Coventry Cycle was finally suppressed, to bring the religious cycle plays to an end. In 1572 the government attempted to reduce the number of companies by making it illegal for anyone below the rank of baron to maintain a troupe or to authorize one to tour. (Noble women were not excluded as the Duchess of Suffolk, the Countess of Essex, and the Countess of Pembroke, among others, maintained companies. The ability of cities to sponsor troupes was not affected.) In 1574 the first royal patent for a theatre company was granted to Leicester's Men, a company headed by James Burbage (1530–1597), one of the first builders of playhouses in England. The patent transferred the power to license this company's plays from local authorities to the Master of Revels, the official who, since 1545, had been responsible for the monarch's entertainment and who served under the manager of all royal household affairs, the Lord Chamberlain.

The rapid expansion of London's population brought troupes to London for longer periods of time. This probably explains the boom in theatre building, five being opened between 1575 and 1577. Critics of the theatre responded forcefully to this marked increase in professional theatre activity. The first major assault came in John Northbrooke's *A Treatise Against Dicing, Dancing, Plays, and Interludes* (1577). This was soon followed by former playwright Stephen Gosson's *The School of Abuse* (1579) and *Plays*

Confuted in Five Actions (1582). These works railed in the harshest terms against the theatre as an instrument used by the Devil to encourage vice and to take people away from honest work and other useful pursuits. The attacks were answered by Thomas Lodge in *A Defence of Poetry, Music, and Stage Plays* (1579), and especially by Sir Philip Sidney in *The Defence of Poesy* (*c.* 1580), which argued that literature is the most effective instrument for teaching morality and moving people to virtuous action. This was the first major statement of the neoclassical ideal in English and exerted a strong influence on the next generation of writers, especially Ben Jonson. Although they were not able to suppress the theatre, the critics voiced the ideas that dominated the governing councils of many English towns which opposed professional players.

The controversy encouraged the Queen's government to take further control of the professional theatre. In 1581 the Master of the Revels, Sir Edmund Tilney (served 1579–1610), was granted a special commission to license all plays (not just those for Leicester's Men), and this authority was expanded to include the licensing of playhouses in 1598. His successors Sir George Buck (served 1610–1622), was also granted the authority to license plays for publication, and Sir John Astley (served 1622–1623), received the additional authority of licensing acting companies. Fees paid for these licenses made the office a lucrative one, especially under Sir Henry Herbert (served 1623–1642 and 1660–1673). Many local officials, however, believed that the crown was usurping authority which should reside with them, since they were responsible for health, conduct, and morals in their communities. The Common Council of the City of London was especially adamant in asserting its own authority on these matters.

In 1583 the Crown attempted a compromise by establishing the Queen's Men, granting them a monopoly to perform in London and stipulating the Inns they could use for performance. This put crown support behind the city's attempt to limit the number of professional companies performing within the city of London, but the arrangement broke down as the Queen's Men declined. A new accommodation was made in 1594 when the Lord Chamberlain and the Lord Admiral replaced the monopoly held by the Queen's Men with dual monopolies held by their own troupes playing in the London suburbs. The first serious threat to this new arrangement came in 1597 when several members of the Admiral's Men illegally formed a third company at the Swan playhouse. This brought a surprisingly harsh order from the Queen's Privy Council that all playhouses around London were to be pulled down. For reasons that remain unclear

the order was not carried out, and the following year (1598) the monopoly status of the Admiral's and Chamberlain's companies was made official.

The Stuart monarchs, who succeeded the Tudor line in 1603, were strong believers in the divine right of kings and insisted on exerting authority more blatantly than Elizabeth had thought wise. During the reign of James I (1603–1625), only companies with a royal patent assigning them to members of the royal family were allowed to reside in the London area. Under Charles I (reigned 1625–1649), the patent for the King's Men continued, and one was issued for Prince Charles' Men in 1631, but other companies were licensed by the Master of the Revels. The two-patent system, complicated by the granting of licenses, was to influence the development of English theatre until it was finally abolished in 1843.

ACTING TROUPES

There were many acting troupes in England during the reigns of the early Tudor monarchs, but their activities are hard to trace before 1572, when they were required to have noble patrons. From 1572 to 1642 we know the names of well over 100 companies that toured England, though few have long histories. Many did nothing but tour, while others, especially after the 1580s, were London-based companies on occasional tours or offshoots of London companies using "exemplifications" (a duplicate copy of a license), while still others were illegal companies traveling with expired or forged licenses. A number of troupes also toured on the continent, and it is from those itinerant English companies that the professional theatre in Germany is descended.

Touring entailed many problems. The companies had to be able to adapt to a wide variety of performance conditions from the great rooms of manorhouses, to guild halls, to inn halls and yards, to market squares, to fairgrounds and even church yards, but they could carry very little with them because of the poor transportation system. Upon arrival in a city they had to present their licenses to the local authorities and were often expected to give a preview before the city council. Approval to perform allowed them to play throughout the city, or, if the city did not want them to play, could earn them a payment to move on. But companies could be denied permission to perform for a variety of reasons including fear of spreading plague, fear of public unrest, or the lack of suitable space which was especially a problem during holidays. Only three towns outside London are thought to have had playhouses at any time during this period, Bristol, Prescot, and York, though Great Yarmouth may also have had one. All, however, seem to have been intended primarily for local use.

From the 1570s on, acting companies sought to focus their activities in London, and the best companies eventually resided there. London-based companies could tour less often and were the beneficiaries of generous royal patronage. The number of such companies went from just one in 1583, to two in 1594, to three in 1602, to a high point of six in 1611, and four or five thereafter. Royal patronage of the companies provided the shareholders with a small annual stipend; allowances for food, light, and fuel; and occasionally sums for new costumes or to tide them over when the plague closed the playhouses. In return, these actors were called upon to perform on special state occasions.

There were two types of professional companies during this period: adult companies, which were organized on the sharing system, and boys' companies, which were led by an adult impresario. Of the many adult companies of the day, the Queen's Men, the Admiral's Men, and the Chamberlain's Men were the most influential. Of the boys' companies, Blackfriars Boys had the greatest influence.

The Queen's Men were established in 1583, when the Master of Revels was ordered to form an all-star company to perform for the Queen and to give that company a monopoly on playing within the city of London. With twelve shareholders this was the largest company in England; it started the vogue for large cast plays and pioneered the practice of dividing into two units by using a copy of its license. It raised the standards for acting in England until deaths and dissensions among its members caused it to go into decline after 1588.

The failure of the Queen's Men led to the formation, in 1594, of the two most famous companies of the age: the Admiral's Men, under the leadership of the actor Edward Alleyn and with the financial backing of the important theatre entrepreneur, Philip Henslowe; and the Chamberlain's Men, a cooperative venture of the Burbage family and a group of actors which included William Shakespeare. Like the Queen's Men, both companies were formed with players recruited from other troupes. The two companies vied for prominence in the London market for the next twenty years, and they were the first to acquire their own playhouses. When James I came to the throne in 1603, the Chamberlain's company was renamed the King's Men, a title it retained until the closing of the theatres in 1642 and which was renewed in 1660 for a company formed by Thomas Killigrew. The Lord Admiral's Men became Prince Henry's Men (1604–1613) and were the Elector Palatine's Men (the king's son-in-law) when they disbanded in 1625.

Like all the adult companies of the day, these companies were organized on the sharing plan. To become a shareholder, an actor had to put up a sizable sum of money and commit himself to the company for a minimum of three years. The companies bought back and resold the shares of those who left. Not all actors were shareholders, and not all owned equal shares. The number of shareholders in the London-based companies could be as high as twelve, while the touring companies generally had six or less. The shareholders formed a self-governing, democratic body that selected and produced plays. In addition to acting the major roles in the company's repertory, each shareholder generally had additional responsibilities such as business management, playwriting, the supervision of costumes and properties or the maintenance of an apprentice boy actor. After meeting all expenses, which included payments to authors, "hired men," and the fund out of which the "common stock" of costumes, properties, and other materials was purchased, the shareholders divided the company's portion of the house receipts. It is difficult to estimate their income, but as long as a season was not cut too short by the outbreak of plague, the sharing actors seem to have done quite well.

The nonsharing adult members of the company, the "hired men," worked under week-to-week contracts. They performed supporting roles, and served as prompters, wardrobe keepers, stage keepers, musicians, and janitors. Those who developed a good reputation as actors were eventually offered the opportunity to buy any available shares, and many borrowed money to do so.

Companies were further augmented by four to six boys apprenticed to a senior actor who was often, but not always, a shareholder. Apprenticeship could last from three to twelve years. Some boys may have begun as early as age ten but thirteen was the most common age and many remained apprentices into their early twenties. Boys played a variety of walk-ons and minor roles and nearly all of the female parts, although older women's roles, especially the comic ones, may have occasionally been played by men. Women did not act for professional companies during this period. All of the most famous female roles, from Juliet to Cleopatra to Lady Macbeth, were played by boys, generally in their late teens. The apprentices lived with their masters, who trained, fed, and clothed them. Some of the apprentices went on to become adult actors, but many followed other professions upon reaching maturity.

Each company had rules of conduct and fines for their infringement. In 1614 Lady Elizabeth's Men agreed to this schedule of fines, for example: one shilling (twelve pence) for lateness to rehearsals; three shillings for lateness to performance; ten shillings for being intoxicated during performance; one pound (twenty shillings) for missing a performance; and forty pounds (more than a year's income for many actors) for wearing a company costume outside the theatre or for taking company property.

The Blackfriars Boys was the most famous of the boys' companies. Originally boys' companies were formed in choir schools where the boys were given a good education and performed in plays to learn elocution and deportment. They were especially popular at court in the 1560s and 1570s, and some choir masters exploited their talents by staging plays to which they charged admission. After 1600 these companies became fully professional, but the boys were treated like hired men, not shareholders. The company managers paid expenses and received the profits. The Blackfriars Boys was the resident troupe for the first Blackfriars playhouse in 1576 and operated the second Blackfriars theatre from 1600 to 1608. This troupe was a special favorite of Queen Anne, who had it designated Children of the Queen's Revels in 1604 and exempted its plays from licensing by the Master of the Revels. Most of the greatest writers of the day wrote for this troupe. It was known for its "railing" comedies, which satirized just about everything. But in 1608 two of those satires so enraged the king that he ordered the company disbanded. It was allowed to reform in 1609 but was forced to move outside the city to the Whitefriars playhouse, where it continued until 1613. Its name and license was used by touring companies until at least 1635. This was the last of the great boys' companies, as the Caroline Young Company and Beeston's Boys of later decades were companies of young men.

THEATRICAL CONDITIONS

In a good year a season could run for over forty weeks, though the plague cut many seasons short. During a season, a company would perform from twenty-eight to thirty-five different plays, more than half of which would be new with the rest being revivals or continuations from the previous season. Bills were changed daily, though on a rare occasion a play might run for two days in a row. Middleton's *A Game as Chess,* for example, set an all-time record when it ran for nine consecutive days. Normally, after its first performance (for which ticket prices were doubled), a play would be performed several times over the next six to eight months. For those opening late in a season, this would carry them over into the next season. Some plays never made it past the first performance and it was rare for any play to be performed more than a dozen times without having new scenes, prologues, or epilogues added. Until about 1603 the average payment for a new play was six pounds, but by 1613 the price had risen to ten or twelve pounds. The demand for new plays made companies seek liaisons with dependable dramatists so that by 1635, Richard Brome (*c.* 1590–1653), who had trained as a dramatist under Ben Jonson, was being paid a weekly salary in addition to being given the receipts (minus the company's expenses) of the second performance for each play he supplied. This was the beginning of the benefit system that was to be especially important in the next century.

Once the playwright's fees had been paid the play belonged to the troupe who treated it as one of their most important assets. Legally, every play had to be submitted to the Master of Revels for licensing before performance. The principal result was the elimination of passages thought to be morally, religiously, or politically objectionable, though it is clear that those who worked for the Master of Revels were relatively liberal-minded about such things. The licensed script was the company's official copy of the play. Actors were merely supplied "sides," which included only their own lines and three-word cues.

On average, only three weeks transpired from the purchase of a play to its first performance. Since that included the time for licensing and copying out of the actors' sides, rehearsals could not have been extensive. As a rule, playwrights knew which troupe they were writing for, however, and could tailor their work to the size of the company and to the skills of individual actors. The prompter (sometimes called the bookholder or bookkeeper) was responsible for copying out the sides, posting the platt (an outline of the scenes with a list of the actors involved in each), making lists of the necessary properties, costumes, and music, and finally for running the performances.

We know the names of more than 1000 actors from this period, but we have cast lists for only 43 productions. Few performers achieved lasting renown. Richard Tarleton (?–1588) and Robert Wilson (?–1600) were both members of the Queen's Men. They were accomplished comic performers who also wrote plays and won wide followings. The first great tragic actor was Edward Alleyn (1566–1626), who created Marlowe's Faustus and Tamburlaine and Kyd's Hieronimo. He gave up acting in 1597 but returned to the stage when the Admiral's Men moved to the Fortune in 1600. He finally retired in 1604, but continued in management with his father-in-law, Philip Henslowe.

The members of the Chamberlain's (later King's) Men gained more lasting fame because Shakespeare was one of their fellow players. The leading performer was Richard Burbage (c. 1567–1619), who created such roles as Richard III, Hamlet, Lear, and Othello, and was generally acknowledged to be the greatest actor of his age. Other members of the company included William Kempe (?–c. 1603), noted for his low comedy acting and dances; Robert Armin (c. 1568–1615), who performed more refined comic roles; John Lowin (c. 1576–c. 1659), noted for his Falstaff and Henry VIII and replaced John Hemminges (1556–1630) as company manager; Joseph Taylor (c. 1585–1652), who replaced Burbage as the primary actor of heroic parts; and Nathan Field (1587–1620), considered by many second only to Burbage. Another company member, Christopher Beeston (c. 1580–1639), became the most successful theatrical impresario under the Stuarts.

The acting style of the Elizabethan performer can only be guessed at. Some scholars insist that double casting, the performance of female roles by male actors, the nonrealistic nature of the scripts, the conventionalized stage background, the large repertory which made detailed individualized characterizations difficult, and limited rehearsal time would have made the acting style "formal." Others argue for a relatively realistic style, based on Shakespeare's "advice to the players" in *Hamlet;* contemporary references to the convincing characterizations given by such actors as Burbage; the emphasis on contemporary life and manners in many comedies; the truthfulness of human psychology portrayed in the serious plays; and the proximity of spectators to actors during performances. Judging by contemporary accounts, many actors moved audiences with the power and "truth" of their playing, but this tells little about acceptable conventions, for what is considered "truth in acting" varies markedly from one period to another. The most that can be said is that the better actors represented well contemporary conceptions of artistic excellence.

THE PUBLIC THEATRES

By 1560 there were two well-established traditions in staging: the outdoor and the indoor. The religious cycles, street pageants, tournaments, and morality plays had been given out-of-doors. On the other hand, mummings, disguisings, interludes, academic

FIG. 6.2

Yard of the Tabard Inn, London. This sketch was made just before the inn was destroyed in the nineteenth century. Supposedly the yard had remained unchanged since the time of Elizabeth I. Although the Tabard was probably not used for plays, it illustrates the arrangement that made inns usable as theatres in Elizabethan times. From Thornbury, *Old and New London.*

plays, and special entertainments were normally given indoors. Consequently, there were many precedents upon which the Elizabethan troupes could draw when building permanent theatres. In London those permanent theatres were of two types. One was an open-air structure designed for a general public; the other was a smaller roofed structure which catered to a more aristocratic audience. It is customary to call structures of the first type "public" or "open-air" and those of the second type "private" or "roofed." Both types were in use by 1575.

Thirteen public open-air playhouses were built near London between 1567 and 1623. They were: The Red Lion (1567–?); The Theatre (1576–1598); The Playhouse at Newington Butts (*c.* 1576–1594); The Curtain (*c.* 1577–*c.* 1627); The Rose (1587–*c.* 1606, remodeled in 1592); The Swan (*c.* 1595–*c.* 1632); The Boar's Head, Whitechapel (1598–*c.* 1616); The Globe (1599–1613); The Fortune (1600–1621); The Red Bull (1605–1663, remodeled in 1625); The Second Globe (1614–?1644); The Hope (1614–1656), and The Second Fortune (1623–1662). Of these The Rose, the first Fortune, and the first and second Globe playhouses are the most important.

The Red Lion was built about a mile east of the City of London by John Brayne, the brother-in-law of James Burbage, the man who was heading Leicester's Men when it received its patent in 1572. We

FIG. 6.4

A Renaissance conception of the Roman theatre. Note the polygonal shape, the galleries, and the label "Theatrum." This illustration is from an edition of Terence's plays published in Lyon in 1493; it could have been an influence on Burbage's *The Theatre* (1576). From Bapst, *Essai sur l'Histoire du Théâtre* (1893).

FIG. 6.3

A portion of the Agas map of London (the sketches for which were made between 1569 and 1590 but not printed until 1631). Note that the bull- and bear-baiting rings appear more nearly corrals than three-tiered galleried structures.

do not know what became of The Red Lion but in 1576, with the financial backing of Brayne, Burbage built the far more famous playhouse called "The Theatre" and later acquired an interest in The Curtain. The inspiration for the design of these open-air public theatres has traditionally been traced from two sources: innyards and gaming arenas. Other possible sources, less frequently cited, are illustrations published in editions of Terence's works, some of which show circular, open-air structures with galleries labeled *"Theatrum."* Exactly how these sources influenced the building of the open-air public playhouses, however, is widely debated.

The stage area of these buildings is thought to have been derived from such diverse sources as the pageant wagons and fixed platforms of religious plays, the booth stages of traveling players, and the

FIG. 6.5

Map showing the location of London's playhouses. From Andrew Gurr, *The Shakespearean Stage, 1574–1642* (1970). The location of the Red Lion has been added. Courtesy Cambridge University Press.

hall stages of the universities. The façade erected at the rear of the stage has been compared to the Rhetoric stages used in the Netherlands, to the triumphal arches used in civic pageants, and to the "screens" found in manor halls where actors are known to have performed. But what links there may be between any of these elements and the building of the theatres in London remains unclear. The possible influences on the public theatres are therefore numerous, but direct connections are difficult to establish.

The Rose playhouse was built by the theatrical entrepreneur Philip Henslowe, whose careful records of his financial transactions, known as *Henslowe's Diary,* are the principal source of information about the operation of these theatres. The Rose was located just across the river Thames, to the south of the city. As the first home of the Admiral's Men, it was one of the most successful theatres of its day. In 1988–1989, archaeologists discovered the foundations of this playhouse, and their excavations of it have provided some of the most reliable information available (see Fig. 6.6). It shows that The Rose was originally a fourteen-sided polygon with an outside diameter of about

72 feet. The foundations supported galleries which were 11 feet deep, so the inner yard, where about one third of the audience stood for performances, must have measured roughly 49 feet across. A tapered stage 36 feet 9 inches wide where it intersected the galleries thrust out 16 feet 8 inches into the yard tapering to 26 feet 10 inches at the front (see Fig. 6.7). In 1592 the auditorium and stage were slightly enlarged.

The Rose was a smaller building than most scholars had expected for a public theatre of this period. The tapered stage was also something of a surprise, since other evidence had indicated that a rectangular shape was more likely. What was most unexpected, however, was the relatively small size of the stage, which is known to have supported some of the most spectacular large-cast plays of the period.

Henslowe and Alleyn had The Fortune theatre built north of the city for the Admiral's Men in 1600, just after The Globe opened across the street from The Rose. Before the recent archaeological discoveries, the builder's contract for the Fortune was the primary source of information about the open-air public theatres. From this contract we learn

Plan of the Rose Theatre Phase 1

Plan of the Rose Theatre Phase 2

FIG. 6.6
Ground plan of the first Rose theatre as revealed by excavations in 1989. Phase 1 shows the layout of the theatre when it was built in 1587; phase 2 shows the layout following alterations in 1592. Courtesy Museum of London.

that The Fortune was a timber-frame structure 80 feet square, not polygonal like The Rose. Its roofed galleries were three stories high, and this is our only source for the actual heights which are listed as 12 feet for the first, 11 feet for the second, and 9 feet for the third. It also states that the depth of the first gallery was 12 feet. Somewhere within these

FIG. 6.7
A reconstruction by C. Walter Hodges depicting a 1594 performance at The Rose theatre. Courtesy Mr. Hodges.

galleries were "gentlemen's rooms," "two penny rooms," and spaces for "quiet standing," but their exact locations are unknown. The stage was 5 feet high and 43 feet wide (leaving just 6 feet between it and the galleries on either side). It extended to the middle of the 55-foot yard so it has generally been assumed to be 27 feet 6 inches deep. Other evidence, however, suggests that the tiring house (that odd combination of back stage, dressing room, and green room spaces at the rear of the English Renaissance stages), may have taken up a significant part of that stage depth.

The first Globe playhouse has always received the greatest attention because of its association with Shakespeare, who owned at least a one-eighth share in the venture and saw most of his greatest plays performed there. Contemporary maps of London provide small and generally contradictory images of its exterior, but beyond that scholars have had little direct evidence to go on. The Chamberlain's (later King's) Men performed there and used it as a summer home even after they began performing in the private theatre at Blackfriars. When The Globe was destroyed by fire in 1613, it was immediately rebuilt, grander than before. That second Globe lasted until the Civil War closed it in 1642.

In 1989 archaeologists discovered a small part of The Globe's foundations (perhaps less than eight percent of the total) and these show that the first-level galleries were about the same depth as those at The Rose and Fortune, but this is all that can be said with confidence. Using a geometric analysis of the remains, John Orrell argued that The Globe was a twenty-sided structure (circular in appearance) and that the remains confirm his earlier conclusions, based on a meticulous examination of the 1644 Hollar map of London, that The Globe had an exterior diameter of approximately 99 feet. Others have concluded that the remains show an eighteen-sided structure with an outside diameter of 90 feet or even a sixteen-sided building with an outside diameter of 86 feet. Orrell's interpretation, however, has been the basis for the full-scale reconstruction called Shakespeare's Globe, which opened in London in 1997 (Fig. 6.11).

The Swan Playhouse, which was built west of The Rose, merits attention because of The Swan drawing (1596), often called the de Witt drawing. This is the only contemporary image we have of the interior of one of these open-air playhouses (see Fig. 6.8). The distorted scale makes it difficult to determine any dimensions but the drawing does provide our only record of a "tiring house" façade in a public playhouse. This façade has two doorways leading onto the rear of the stage with a balcony above. A letter attached to this drawing praised the ornateness of the decoration but the drawing does little to reflect this. What has proven even more troubling for scholars, however, is that what is shown in the drawing does not seem sufficient for staging the plays that were staged there. About 500 plays still survive from the 1056 Alfred Harbage has recorded as having been performed during this time. They occasionally provide stage directions and if we take only one of those plays, Middleton's *A Chaste Maid in Cheapside* (performed at The Swan between 1611 and 1613), we find that it calls for "a Shop being discovered," "a bed thrust out upon the Stage, Allwit's Wife in it," and "a sad song in the Music Room."

The music room is now generally thought to have been in one section of the tiring-house balcony, with the other sections being "Lords' Rooms," the most expensive seats in the theatres. But a certain number of plays require scenes to be performed at windows, balconies, battlements, or other high places, the balcony scene of *Romeo and Juliet* being the best-known example. It is not clear how those scenes could be staged in this space. Many present-day historians have argued that such scenes do not occur often, are not long, and generally involve few characters, so the actors could simply have used the music room for them. Earlier historians, most

FIG. 6.8

Interior of The Swan Theatre, 1596. The original drawing, made by a Dutch visitor, Johannes de Witt, has not survived; this is a copy made of it by Arend van Buchell. The drawing is accompanied by a descriptive passage which reads in part: "Of all the theatres, . . . the largest and most magnificent is . . . the Swan; for it accommodates . . . three thousand persons. . . . [It is] supported by wooden columns painted in such excellent imitation of marble that it is able to deceive even the most observant . . . its form resembles that of a Roman work . . . " Note the absence of a central discovery space and the human figures in the gallery above the stage. From Bapst, *Essai sur l'Histoire du Théâtre* (1893).

notably J. C. Adams, have offered far more complex solutions (see Fig. 6.9).

Either of the two doors shown at The Swan would provide enough space for a bed to be thrust out. But there seems to be no facility for a shop "being discovered," yet discoveries are called for in a number of plays. One possibility, proposed by Richard Southern, is that there was a large central opening in The Swan tiring house but it was covered by a curtain hanging from the balcony when de Witt made his drawing. References to curtains and hangings are sufficiently common to give this solution credence, and a central discovery space would also provide a third entrance onto the stage, something we know existed in the indoor theatres. Another possibility, proposed by C. Walter Hodges, is that theatres owned a "pavilion" that could be set up in front of the tiring house as needed (see Fig. 6.10), while a third, proposed by Richard Hosley, is that the discovery was made within one of the two doorways. All three theories

FIG. 6.9

J. C. Adams's reconstruction of The Globe theatre. Note the inner stages both on the first and second levels and the "musicians' gallery" on the third. Adams was a proponent of the "alternation theory" in which outdoor scenes on the open stage alternated with indoor scenes within the inner stages. Courtesy Folger Library and Mr. Adams.

FIG. 6.10

C. W. Hodges's reconstruction of the Elizabethan stage showing a pavilion at the rear. From Hodges, *The Globe Restored*. Courtesy Mr. Hodges.

and more are possible; none has been entirely persuasive.

Historians have paid relatively little attention to the backstage space and have little to say about dressing rooms or storage space for the wardrobe, furniture, properties, and other equipment. Some companies owned adjoining structures that may have been used for these purposes. When The Globe burned in 1613, there are no reports of major additional losses, but when The Fortune burned in 1621 the company was said to be undone by the loss of its wardrobe and playbooks. In general, however, little is known about the space used for preparing and maintaining productions.

These theatres were owned by "householders" who held shares in the building. Most were entrepreneurs like Philip Henslowe, a householder for The Rose, Fortune, and Hope, or Francis Langley, a householder for The Swan and Boar's Head. But others were actors such as James Burbage, Edward Alleyn, Richard Burbage, and William Shakespeare. Householders paid the expenses for maintaining these buildings and rented them out to the professional acting companies, amateur actors, fencers, tumblers, and miscellaneous entertainers.

Arrangements varied, but generally the householders received half the income from the galleries. They may also have received fees from the sale of food, drink, and other items, on their property.

THE PRIVATE THEATRES

Although historians have focused our attention on the public open-air theatres, it is likely that more performances were given indoors than outdoors in the years between 1558 and 1642. Many of these indoor productions were staged in manor houses, town halls, guild halls, inns, universities, or at court, but those at "private" theatres are of primary interest.

The term "private" is not used until 1600 in relation to theatres that were actually open to the public. It is then applied to indoor theatres being used by two boys' companies who had started performing in London in direct violation of the monopolies held by the Admiral's and Chamberlain's Men. It looks suspiciously as though the term was adopted as a ploy, since private performances were not covered by the laws which required companies to have their plays and buildings licensed. But whatever the

FIG. 6.11

Shakespeare's Globe, London. This highly ornate simulation of an Elizabethan public playhouse opened in 1997 and was adjusted in 1999. Photo by F. J. Hildy ©.

reason for the term's original use, it is now applied to the roofed theatres of the period. These theatres differ from the public theatres in that they were smaller (accommodating about one-fourth as many spectators), they charged considerably higher admission prices, they provided seats for all spectators, and they depended on candles (supplemented by windows) for illumination.

Eight "private" theatres and one roofed court theatre were built in and around London between 1575 and 1635: St. Paul's (*c.* 1575– 1590, 1599–*c.* 1608); First Blackfriars, at the Old Buttery (1576–1584); Second Blackfriars, at Parliament Hall (1596–1655); Whitefriars (?1580–1596 and *c.* 1606–1629); Porter's Hall (1615–1616); The Cockpit/Phoenix in Drury Lane (1616–*c.* 1667); Salisbury Court (1629–1658 and 1660–1666); and the French Theatre at Le Fevre's Riding Academy (1635–1636). England's only court theatre was the Cockpit-in-Court (1629–*c.* 1666). All these theatres (with the exception of Porter's Hall and possibly Salisbury Court) were conversions of existing buildings. Of the indoor theatres, the second Blackfriars was the most important.

The second Blackfriars was built in the City of London, within a "liberty," or property under the direct control of the Crown and therefore exempt from

FIG. 6.12

A reconstruction of the second Blackfriars Theatre, 1597. Note the curtained inner stages on both levels and the audience seated at the sides of the main platform. Drawing by J. H. Farrar. Courtesy the Architect of the Greater London Council.

city regulations. The Crown retained jurisdiction over this liberty until 1608. The second Blackfriars was built by James Burbage in 1596 as a replacement for The Theatre for which the land lease was about to expire. It was located in a large second-story hall in which Parliament had met on several occasions. Before it could open, the residents of the liberty secured an injunction against it. When Burbage died in 1597, he willed the Blackfriars to his sons, who were unable to use it and leased it to Henry Evans. Evans installed the Blackfriars Boys there in 1600 and

they soon became one of the most popular and successful troupes in London. When they were forced to disband in 1608, the lease reverted back to the Burbage brothers, who sold shares in it to several actors, including William Shakespeare. In 1609 it became the winter home for the King's Men. It was closed in 1642, sold in 1655, and finally destroyed in the great fire of 1666.

Because of its length of service and its association with Shakespeare, the second Blackfriars is by far the most important of the private theatres. It was created within a second-story room measuring approximately 46 feet wide by 66 feet long. It is not known whether the theatre had three levels of galleries or only two, but it did have private boxes and a pit with seats. Estimates for its audience capacity range from 500 to 1000. Since the King's Men moved plays freely from The Globe to The Blackfriars, it is assumed that both stages had the same basic characteristics, though the Blackfriars stage was almost certainly smaller, most likely measuring 30 feet wide by 23 feet deep. It would have been raised 3–4 feet above the hall floor. We assume three doors led onto the stage from the tiring house at the back and that there was a balcony above these, but this cannot be proven. There is no evidence of a proscenium arch. The King's Men played at Blackfriars from mid-October to mid-May and at The Globe for the remaining five months. The Blackfriars brought the company twice the income it got from The Globe and its success encouraged other troupes to acquire private playhouses of their own.

FIG. 6.14B
Façade and plan of the stage of the Cockpit in Court. An existing building converted to England's first court theatre for use by the professional troupes when playing at court. Drawing by John Webb. Courtesy Worcester College, Oxford.

FIG. 6.14A
Floor plan of the Cockpit in Court designed by Inigo Jones, c. 1629. The king's chair faces the stage. Drawing by John Webb, 1660–1661. Courtesy Worcester College, Oxford.

SCENERY, PROPERTIES, SPECIAL EFFECTS, AND MUSIC

Although historians usually assume that the stage façade provided the background for all plays in this period, scenic practices are by no means clear. The principal sources of information about scenery are the play scripts, the accounts of the Master of Revels, and *Henslowe's Diary*.

A number of scholars have analyzed the plays for scenic requirements, but their results conflict because they begin with different premises. One group assumes that the players relied primarily upon "spoken decor" (that is, they believe that places are mentioned only when dramatically relevant and because they were not scenically represented). Another group assumes that the audience would expect the things mentioned in the dialogue to be physically represented by some scenic piece. Probably neither of these views is correct. Reynolds's study of staging at The Red Bull concludes that the troupes were very inconsistent in their practices and varied them in accordance with available means rather than consistent theory.

A study made by T. J. King of all plays staged between 1599 and 1642 shows that the following items were used on stage: tables, chairs, and stools; beds; carpets and cushions; hangings, curtains, and traverses; thrones; tents and canopies; altars and pulpits; stocks, scaffolds, and gibbets; biers, coffins, dead bodies, and litters; barriers and lists; chariots and vaulting horses; banks and caves; and arbors, trees, bushes, boughs, and flowers. The Master of Revels' Office provides the items needed when professional companies appeared at court and the late sixteenth century records for that office list rocks, mountains, battlements, trees, and houses, among those items provided for the stage. Numerous hangings, cloths, and curtains are also mentioned, although the majority may have been used to decorate the hall. Nevertheless, all scholars agree that when scenic devices were used, they more nearly resembled medieval mansions than Italian perspective settings.

Elizabethan scenic practices too were adapted from medieval conventions. The main acting area was essentially a *platea,* the identity of which could be altered by several devices. As much as 80 percent of the scenes in Shakespeare's plays can be done on a bare stage, suggesting that the stage was most often treated as a neutral space. If it needed to be localized, this could be done either by the dialogue or by the use of set pieces such as arbors, tents, tombs, prison bars, beds, and thrones. It is possible that some scenic devices were so cumbersome that they could not be moved and remained throughout the performance, ignored except when relevant to the action. Other heavy pieces could be revealed in, or thrust out from, the doorways or central opening of the tiring house. Smaller articles were brought on and off stage as needed. The troupes probably suited their practice more to convenience than to principle and neither audiences nor actors were bothered by inconsistencies.

Emphasis on spectacle increased after 1603 as the influence of the court grew. The boys' companies introduced masque-like elements to their plays around 1605, and the adult troupes continued this trend when they took over the private theatres. Elaborate set pieces became more frequent during this period, and there is a marked increase in the use of flying effects, pyrotechnic displays, magic tricks, and displays of swordsmanship. Music, dance, the use of gorgeous costumes, and the appearance of characters from classical mythology also became more common. But still the professional theatres do not seem to have felt any need to adopt perspective settings.

Music played a very large part in English theatrical production from the beginning and was especially prominent in this period. Boys' companies, having originated as choirs, were famous for their music and offered concerts up to an hour in length before performances, a practice taken over by the adult troupes when they moved to the indoor playhouses. Most theatres seem to have had an orchestra composed of about six instrumentalists. In addition, there were trumpeters and drummers who provided flourishes before entrances or to introduce proclamations and provide sounds for battle scenes. Large numbers of incidental songs were written into the plays so most actors needed to be able to sing. Dance had a similar history. In the early days it was designed to appeal primarily to the popular audiences, but it became more sophisticated as the influence of aristocratic audiences increased. At the public theatres, performances generally ended with a "jig" or other displays of dancing skill and musical ability.

COSTUMES

Costume was the most important visual element in Elizabethan performance. Contemporary accounts mention the costliness and elegance of the players' costumes, and *Henslowe's Diary* records numerous loans for the purchase of costumes, such as seven pounds for "a doublet of white satin laid thick with gold lace" and nineteen pounds for a cloak. Henslowe often paid more for a costume in a play than he had paid for the play itself. It is little wonder that the most costly fine an actor could incur was the fine for wearing a company costume outside the playhouse. The sumptuousness of the costumes worn by English actors was often praised by foreigners and condemned by English conservatives.

The conventions that governed costuming between 1567 and 1642 differed little from those in effect during the Middle Ages. Most characters, regardless of the historical era in which they supposedly lived, were clothed in Elizabethan fashion. The deviations from contemporary dress may be divided into five categories: (1) "ancient," or out-of-style clothing, used to indicate unfashionableness, or occasionally, to suggest another period; (2) "antique," consisting of drapery or greaves added to contemporary garments, used for certain classical figures; (3) fanciful garments used for ghosts, witches, fairies, gods, and allegorical characters; (4) traditional costumes, associated with a few specific characters such as Robin Hood, Henry V, Tamburlaine, Falstaff, and Richard III; and (5) national or racial costumes, used

FIG. 6.15

A sketch, allegedly made in 1595, of a scene from Shakespeare's *Titus Andronicus*. Some scholars argue that this is a nineteenth-century forgery. Courtesy Marquess of Bath.

to set off Turks, Indians, Jews, and Spaniards. Although some of these costumes were conventionalized versions of garments from past periods, they were not historically accurate. With rare exceptions, even the "history plays" were costumed in Elizabethan dress.

Since the actors relied heavily upon costumes, the acquisition and maintenance of a sizable wardrobe was important. Actors were expected to own sufficient costumes to perform the basic roles assigned to them. The companies bought courtly costumes, women's dresses, and specialty items needed for specific plays. They probably also maintained a general wardrobe for use by the hired men. Sometimes noblemen gave them garments, and frequently servants who had been given parts of their masters' wardrobe sold these pieces to the actors. Actors were sometimes given the costumes they wore for performances before the nobility, and occasionally the royal family made grants to the troupes to replenish their wardrobes. It was also possible to rent costumes, either from the Revels Office or from enterprising businessmen. Once a costume was acquired, whether by an individual actor or by a company, it was used over and over again. A few records from the period refer to tiremen and tirewomen (wardrobe keepers), some of whom apparently had been trained as tailors, but there is little specific information about what they did for the companies.

AUDIENCES

The period from 1567 to 1642 was a time of great social, economic, intellectual, religious, and political change in England. London was the only city large enough to sustain a professional acting company for more than a few weeks of performances, and during this time its population increased considerably—from about 100,000 to over 400,000. Scholars estimate that only 10 to 20 percent of the greater London population could have been regular playgoers, so competition for audiences was intense.

Numerous devices were used to advertise plays. Posters appeared in London as early as 1563, and handbills were in use by the seventeenth century. Flags were flown above the roofs of London's theatres on the days when performances were to be given, and announcements of coming attractions were made from the stage. Occasionally a procession with drums and trumpets advertised performances, but this practice was largely restricted to touring outside London.

We do not know the capacity of the six or so London inns that were used for performance. Of the indoor theatres, St. Paul's may have seated as few as 100, while the second Blackfriars may have seated up to 1000. The capacity of the larger public theatres was perhaps as high as 3000. Several book-length studies have been done on the composition of these audiences. They agree that the cost of admission kept the poorer classes out of the private theatres. They disagree, however, on the composition of the audiences in the public theatres, some arguing for a predominantly working-class audience, while others see these audiences as predominantly upper middle class. It may even be true that different public playhouses attracted different sorts of audiences; audiences at The Red Bull, for example, were known for their rowdy behavior, while audiences at The Fortune appear to have been reserved. The very poor could not afford the theatre and the very rich did not attend, preferring to have performances brought to them. But regardless of the make up, audiences of the period seemed to have behaved in their playhouses more as we might at a sporting event than as we do in our theatres.

During Elizabeth's reign it was possible to see a play in London on any day of the week, except during Lent or when the companies were on tour. When the weekly deaths due to plague exceeded fifty the theatres were closed. This occurred on many occasions including for 18 months in 1582–1583, 11 months in 1593, 13 months in 1603–1604, and 17 months in 1636–1637. The crown had authorized daily playing in 1574, but the city always protested playing on Sunday, and James I made it illegal though this law does not seem always to have been obeyed.

A visit to a public playhouse involved going to a recreational district outside the city. As much as a third of the audience in these theatres stood in the yard, around three sides of the stage. It was possible to pay an additional penny to sit in the galleries, and a third penny for a cushioned seat in a box, or to spend six pennies for a seat in the Lords' Rooms. For a new play all the fees might be doubled. There were no restrictions on women in these theatres, but it does appear that it was detrimental to a woman's reputation to stand in the yard for a performance.

COURT PLAYS AND MASQUES

Professional actors performed regularly in the houses of the nobility and at court. Elizabeth I saw, on average, five professional productions each year. In Stuart times each member of the royal family produced plays, and an average of seventeen were seen in the court of James I and an average of twenty-five in the court of Charles I. Court performances were held at night and so rarely conflicted with public performances, and since the plays given at court were usually also played for the general public, they did not overburden the actors with additional preparation. The boys' companies were as likely to be seen at court as the adult troupes until 1610, when they fell out of favor.

Court performances apparently deviated little from those done in the indoor playhouses, though they might make use of extra scenery and costumes from the Master of Revels' stock when available. Though European troupes performed at the English court—Italian companies appeared occasionally after 1574, French troupes after 1602, and Spanish troupes after 1616—we have no evidence that the English troupes were encouraged to emulate them or their staging methods.

FIG. 6.16
Entertainment given for Queen Elizabeth by the Earl of Hertford in 1591 at Elvetham in Hampshire. This is the second day's entertainment for a four-day visit. A crescent-shaped lake was dug especially for the water pageant. Queen Elizabeth's chair is at upper left. From John Nichols's *The Progresses and Public Processions of Queen Elizabeth*, 2 (1788).

Amateur performances done by members of noble families, however, may have experimented with European staging methods; as they did when Queen Henrietta Maria and her ladies performed the French play *Artenice*, in 1626, on a proscenium arch stage designed by Inigo Jones. Jones built an entire free-standing proscenium arch theatre in a courtyard at Somerset House for the Queen's performance in *The Shepherd's Paradise* by Montagu in 1632, and adapted another hall for her proscenium arch production of the stage for *Florimène* in 1635. In all, Jones designed scenery for twelve such plays during the reign of Charles I. When Jones built the only permanent court theatre, however, the Cockpit-in-Court (1629–*c.* 1666), it had no proscenium arch and no mechanisms for scene changes, most likely because it was intended for visiting professional companies. Amateur performing offered women their first opportunities to be involved in theatre beyond the jobs as money takers, wardrobe keepers, and cleaners they held with professional companies, and may well have encouraged women, like Elizabeth Cary, Viscountess Falkland to write *The Tragedie of Mariam* (1602–1604), and Lady Mary Worth to write the comedy *Love's Victory* (*c.* 1620) to be read at family events. Since women acted only at court or in the houses of the nobility, William Prynne found himself charged with treason when he attacked women actors as *"notorious impudent, prostituted strumpets"* in *Histriomastix* (1633), his 1000-page attack on Catholicism. He was fined £5000, had both his law license and academic degrees revoked, had his ears cut off, and was sentenced to life imprisonment. In the aftermath of this incident, the Inns of Court felt compelled to demonstrate their loyalty by putting on the most expensive masque performance ever staged, *The Triumph of Peace*, written by James Shirley with scenery by Inigo Jones. It cost a staggering £21,000. One of the participants, Bulstrode Whitlocke, preserved an account of this production so complete that it could still be reconstructed in all important details.

Masques presented an allegorical story which suggested parallels between the person being honored or the occasion being celebrated and some mythological personage or event. The serious speaking and singing roles were assumed by professional musicians, while the comic or grotesque roles were played by professional actors. Narrative and dialogue (spoken or sung) were used sparingly as the story and its symbolism were conveyed primarily through visual means—scenery, costumes, properties, pantomime, and above all dance, which was performed by courtiers in allegorical costumes. Three "grand masquing dances" were usually embedded in a

FIG. 6.17

Jones's costume for a Fiery Spirit in *The Temple of Love,* 1635. Devonshire Collection, Chatsworth. Reproduced by permission of the Trustees of the Chatsworth Settlement.

masque's allegorical plot: an entry dance, sometimes accompanied by ornately decorated floats or wagons; a main dance, during which the performers usually went down into the hall to dance with selected spectators; and a "going out" dance. Many social dances of the period were incorporated into these productions, but the court dancing masters also invented elaborate symbolic choreography for them. The dancers in a masque were all of one sex, except for occasional double masques in which equally balanced groups of men and women were used. They were costumed as characters that might represent such figures as gods, goddesses, heroes, nymphs, "Signs of the Zodiac," "The Graces," or "Sons of Peace, Love, and Justice." Each dancer was usually accompanied by a "torchbearer" (that is, the carrier of a candelabrum who were generally young noblemen or children) who might be costumed as fiery spirits, Indians, Oceanae, "antique Britons," or other such figures. Often they performed a special dance of their own. In 1608, Ben Jonson introduced the "anti-masques" designed to provide a contrast with the main story by setting up a chaotic situation that the main masque would then bring into a state of order. Anti-masques

FIG. 6.18
Jones's setting for Act V of *Salmacida Spolia,* 1640. Note the "glory." Devonshire Collection, Chatsworth. Courtesy Trustees of the Chatsworth Settlement.

introduced humorous or grotesque characters and dances and provided ample opportunity for the scenic designer to contrive striking transformations from ugliness to beauty, from chaos to order. Obviously music played a major part in the masques. Unfortunately, no complete musical score for a masque has survived. We do have the music for about 50 songs and some 250 dances, but it is rarely possible to match them to specific masques.

The Inns of Court produced masques only occasionally, usually in honor of the royal family or an important visitor. At court, masques had been popular under Henry VIII (the term was first used *c.* 1512), but were infrequently given during the reign of Elizabeth, who contented herself with elaborate entertainments given by others. Under James I, however, masques were staged annually and under Charles I they were given twice a year, typically at Twelfth Night and Mardi Gras but also for special state occasions. Great sums of money were lavished on these productions which were rationalized as demonstrations of kingly virtue and magnanimity. In 1618, James I spent £4000 on a single production, considerably more than on all the performances of plays given by professional companies at court during his entire reign. Considering the rewards both in prestige and money, it is not surprising that many leading dramatists (among them Marston, Chapman, Beaumont, Middleton, Daniel, Milton, and Dav-

enant) wrote masques. The majority of the masques presented at the Stuart court, however, were written by Ben Jonson and designed by Inigo Jones. Eventually, Jonson objected to the dominant role given to spectacle and, after an open break with Jones in 1631, was replaced by other writers.

Great halls in the royal palaces were often adapted for the masques, but specially built banqueting halls were built for them in 1572, 1581, 1606, and 1619,

FIG. 6.19
Jones's floor plan of the setting for *Salmacida Spolia.* Note the use of nested wings and back shutters, all of which could be changed by sliding them in grooves. Possibly the first example of a completely changeable setting in England. Courtesy Trustees of The British Museum.

the last of which still exists at Whitehall in London. The physical arrangement was much the same for most of the masques. Tiers of seats were set up along the sides and across the back of a hall. The royal dais was well back in the auditorium to provide the best view of the stage and to leave room forward of it for the dancers. Steps connected the hall with the stage. Stages varied in size, but the average dimensions were about 40 feet wide by 27 feet deep and the platform was raised 5–6 feet above the hall floor, sloped upward toward the rear. It was used primarily for scenic effect, because most of the action and dancing took place at the front of the stage or on the floor of the hall.

THE ITALIAN IDEAL IN ENGLAND

The scenery, costumes, and special effects for most of the masques were by Inigo Jones (1573–1652), the first important English scene designer. Born in London, Jones went to Italy about 1600 to study, after which he worked for a time at the court of Denmark before returning to England around 1604. He designed his first masque for James I in 1605. He may have visited Italy again in 1607–1608, and certainly did in 1613–1615. In 1615 he was appointed Surveyor of His Majesty's Works, a post which he held until 1643.

Jones was thoroughly familiar with Italian artistic movements. At the court of Florence he obviously studied the work of Giulio Parigi, for almost all of his designs after 1630 are copied directly from Parigi's *intermezzi*. His surviving copy of Palladio's treatise on architecture contains notes comparing Palladio's ideas with those of Serlio, Scamozzi, Vignola, and others. As the court architect and designer, Jones was the most influential English artist of his day. At his death, he willed his papers to his pupil and assistant, John Webb, who was to be a leading architect and scene designer of the Restoration. Since William Davenant, one of the principal theatre managers of the Restoration, had written several of the last masques designed by Jones, and since Webb worked closely with Davenant after 1656, Jones exerted considerable indirect influence on Restoration scene design. To Jones, more than to any other artist, can be attributed the naturalization of the Italian ideal in England.

Jones's innovations were not all evident in his early designs; some of the most important did not appear until 1640, so it is useful to examine the evolution of his techniques. The nature of his contributions can be seen by comparing his designs with those used for the masques before he began his work at the Stuart court. The earlier masques had been staged with "dispersed decor" (that is, with mansion-like structures

FIG. 6.20
Sectional plan for *Salmacida Spolia*. Courtesy Trustees of The British Museum.

scattered around the hall). Jones ushered in a new era in 1605 when, for Jonson's *The Masque of Blackness*, he erected a stage at one end of the hall and placed all the scenery on it. Furthermore, instead of mansions, he employed a perspective setting composed of angled wings and a backscene, all concealed until the beginning of the masque and then revealed suddenly by dropping a front curtain.

Between 1605 and 1610 Jones made other innovations. In 1606, for *The Masque of Hymen*, the principle of the *periaktoi* was used to create a globe with no visible axle, which revolved to reveal eight dancers seated inside a "mine of several metals." In the same production, Jones suspended eight dancers in a cloud machine that moved from upstage to downstage. In 1608, for *The Hue and Cry After Cupid*, Jones made his first known use of the proscenium arch and of scenery that parted in the middle to reveal another scene behind it. In the *Masque of Oberon* (1610) two sets of shutters were worked in grooves to reveal three successive scenes. After 1610 Jones tended to repeat the devices he had already perfected.

In the 1630s, however, he began to experiment once more. Perhaps because of Parigi's influence, Jones's use of flying machinery increased considerably. But the most important change was the abandonment of angled for flat wings. This innovation may have been made as early as 1634, but clearly was used in 1635 when Jones designed settings for Davenant's *The Temple of Love*. Jones's experiments reached their culmination in 1640 with Davenant's *Salmacida Spolia*, the last of the pre-Commonwealth masques. He put four sets of flat wings and several back shutters in grooves so that the settings could be changed rapidly. By 1640, then, Jones had introduced into England all the features then characteristic of the Italianate stage. When the English theatres reopened in 1660, Jones's practices were to triumph over those that had characterized the pre-Commonwealth theatre.

In addition to designing the masques, Jones staged them. At least some of these plays were performed at the Cockpit-in-Court.

Like his father, Charles I believed in absolute monarchy and this often put him in conflict with Parliament. From 1629 until 1640 he ruled without them. When financial difficulties forced him to call Parliament back into session, it refused to authorize any new taxes until the king agreed to have limits set on his power. Charles refused, and in 1642 civil war broke out. Eventually Charles was defeated and in 1649 was beheaded.

The war rekindled religious opposition to the theatre. The antipathy was intensified because of the close association between the theatre and members of the royal family. In September 1642 Parliament used the disturbed state of the country as an excuse for closing the theatres for five years. When that time expired, the Puritans were in control of the government, and they declared the closure to be permanent. Thus ended one of the most brilliant and productive periods the theatre has known.

LOOKING AT THEATRE HISTORY

One of the most revealing approaches to theatre history in any period can be made through reconstructions of its theatre buildings, either in drawings, scale models, or full-size structures. Such an approach requires that decisions be made about the size, shape, and principal features. It also reveals what we do not know, for in seeking to convert the available evidence into concrete visual detail, we quickly learn that much information about the overall appearance, decorative detail, dimensions, and even the precise location of machinery and workspace is often mere conjecture. Still, unless we can visualize the space in which plays were performed, it is difficult to understand the theatrical practices of an age. In many ways, then, the attempt to reconstruct theatre buildings epitomizes the problem of the historian: how to create a defensible whole out of the fragmentary remains of the past.

Because of the great interest in Shakespeare's plays historians have been especially interested in reconstructing the theatre buildings of the era 1567–1642. Three examples of these efforts can be seen in Figs. 6.7, 6.9, and 6.11. In 1997 a structure simulating the first Globe Playhouse was built near the original location south of the Thames River in London (Fig. 6.11). It is a 20-sided polygon 100 feet in diameter with a yard 73 feet 9 inches across. The stage is 44 feet wide by 24 feet 9 inches deep, and the stage posts are set 27 feet 6 inches apart. A private theatre based on the drawings shown in Figs. 6.13A and 6.13B is planned for the same location. Much of the surviving visual evidence relating to English theatres prior to 1642 is reproduced in Figs. 6.6, 6.8, 6.13, and 6.14. In addition, short building contracts for The Fortune (1600) and The Hope (1614) have survived. Here is an excerpt from The Fortune contract describing the stage:

> *With a Stage and Tyring house to be made, erected & set up within the said frame, with a shadow or cover over the Stage, which Stage shall be placed & set, as also the stair cases of the said frame, in such sort as is prefigured in a plot there of drawn, and which Stage shall contain in length Forty and Three foot of lawful assize and in breadth to extend to the middle of the yard of the said house.*

These excerpts from The Hope contract describe the multipurpose nature of that structure:

> *[The builder shall] set up one other Game place or Playhouse fit and convenient in all things, both for*

players to play in, and for the game of Bears and Bulls to be baited in the same, and also a fit and convenient tyre house and a stage to be carried or taken away, and to stand upon trestles good substantial and sufficient for the carrying and bearing of such a stage . . . [He] shall also build the Heavens all over the said stage to be borne or carried without any posts or supporters to be fixed or set upon the said stage.

Shakespeare is considered one of the world's greatest dramatists, but we know little about his life or his approach to writing. His fellow playwright Ben Jonson gives us one of the few contemporary glimpses into Shakespeare's qualities as writer and man:

I remember that the players have often mentioned it as an honor to Shakespeare, that in his writing, whatsoever he penned, he never blotted out a line. . . . He was . . . honest, and of an open and free nature; had an excellent fancy, brave notions, and gentle expressions, wherein he flowed with that facility that sometime it was necessary he should be stopped. . . Many times he fell into those things could not escape laughter. . . But he redeemed his vices with his virtues. There was ever more in him to be praised than to be pardoned.

Ben Jonson, *Timber; or Discoveries Made Upon Men and Matter* (1620–1635?).

Because it was so controversial, the theatre motivated numerous decrees, proclamations, petitions, and other documents during the reign of Elizabeth I. These public documents are among our important sources of information about the theatre of that age. Many of the documents are reprinted in Glynne Wickham, Herbert Berry, and William Ingram, *English Professional Theatre 1530–1660*, (Cambridge, 2000).

On May 16, 1559, Elizabeth issued a proclamation that effectively outlawed religious and political subject matter. In part it read:

her majestie doth likewise charge every [official] . . . that they permit [no interludes] to be played wherein either matters of religion or of the governance of the estate of the common weale shall be handled or treated . . .

Foreign visitors often provide important information about the theatre, especially when what they see differs markedly from what they are used to in their own country. One particularly helpful description is provided by Thomas Platter, a Swiss who visited London in 1599:

Thus daily at two in the afternoons, London has two, sometimes three plays running in different places. . . . The playhouses are so constructed that they play on a raised platform, so that everyone has a good view. There are different galleries and places, however, where the seating is better and more comfortable and therefore more expensive. For whoever cares to stand below only pays one English penny, but if he wishes to sit he enters by another door, and pays another penny, while if he desires to sit in the most comfortable seats, which are cushioned . . . then he pays another English penny at another door. And during the performance food and drink are carried round the audience . . . . The actors are most expensively and elaborately costumed; for it is the English usage for eminent lords or knights at their decease to bequeath and leave almost the best of their clothes to their serving men, which it is unseemly for the latter to wear, so they offer them for sale for a small sum to the actors. . . .

Thomas Platter, *Travels to England* (1599).

Salmacida Spolia (performed at Whitehall in January 1640), the last of the great Stuart Masques, illustrates well the characteristic masque form. The subject was allegorical, as this summary by the author, William Davenant, indicates:

Discord, a malicious fury, appears in a storm, and by the invocation of malignant spirits, . . . endeavors to disturb these parts [England], envying the blessings and tranquility we have long enjoyed. These incantations are expressed by those spirits in an Antimasque: who on a sudden are surprised, and stopt in their motion by a secret power [Wisdom]. . . . This secret Wisdom, in the person of the King and attended by his nobles, and under the name of Philogenes or Lover of his people, hath his appearance prepared by a Chorus. . . . Then the Queen personating the chief heroine, with her martial ladies, is sent down from Heaven by Pallas as a reward of his prudence, for reducing the threatening storm into the following calm.

The final scene is depicted in Fig. 6.18. D'Avenant describes it thus:

. . . The scene was changed into magnificent buildings composed of several selected pieces of architecture: in the furthest part was a bridge over a river, where many people, coaches, horses, and such like were seen to pass to and fro: beyond this, on the shore were buildings in prospective, which . . . showed as the suburbs of a great city. From the highest part of the heavens came forth a cloud far in the scene, in which were eight persons richly attired representing the spheres; this,

joining with two other clouds which appeared at that instant full of music, covered all the upper part of the scene, and, at that instant beyond all these, a heaven opened full of deities, which celestial prospect with the

Chorus below filled all the whole scene with apparitions and harmony.

The Dramatic Works of Sir William D'Avenant, 2 (London, 1872).

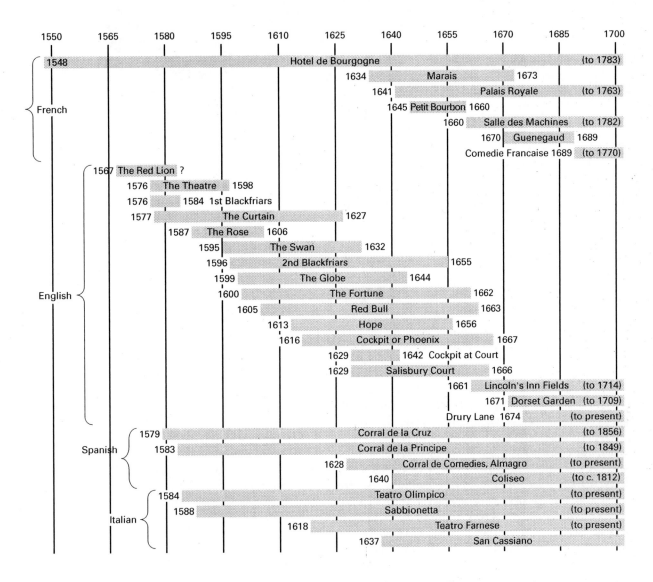

FIG. 6.21
Major permanent theatres of Europe, 1548–1700.

7

The Theatre of Spain and New Spain to 1700

As in England, the theatre in Spain flourished during the sixteenth and seventeenth centuries. The period of 1580–1680 was so productive it is called the Golden Age (*Siglo de Oro*) of Spanish drama. But the influences on Spanish and English drama differed markedly. In Spain, many of the influences were related to the Moorish culture that had supplanted the Visigoths on the Iberian Peninsula by 711. For nearly 500 years the Muslims ruled all of Spain except for a small northern portion. Moorish Spain was the most prosperous region in the Mediterranean and far more advanced culturally than feudal Europe. Its philosophers and scholars exerted strong influence on medieval universities and its craftsmen were the envy of Europe. Around 1200 the Christian kingdoms of northern Spain united against the Moors, and by 1276 had driven them from all but the southeastern portion. Spain was not to become a major power, however, until after 1479, when Aragon and Castile united under Ferdinand and Isabella. By 1492, these rulers had conquered all of the peninsula except for Portugal and united it into a single nation. To insure Christian purity in the new kingdom, the Inquisition was established in 1480 to hunt down and punish heretics. Moors and Jews who would not convert were expelled from the country. The Inquisition ensured

that Spain would not experience the challenges to Roman Catholicism that were to spread over the rest of Europe.

Another important influence on drama was Spain's sense of its own position as a world power. Following Columbus's first voyage in 1492, Spain rapidly became the dominant force in the New World, and in 1519 its king, Charles I, became the Holy Roman Emperor. Under Philip II (reigned 1556–1598), Portugal, Sicily, the Kingdom of Naples, Milan, the Netherlands, and parts of northern Africa were all brought under Spanish control, making it the most powerful nation in the Western world. By 1640 the decline of Spain's empire had already begun, but this was not fully evident until the end of the seventeenth century.

THE RELIGIOUS DRAMA

Because of the Islamic disapproval of theatre, only the Christian portions of Spain developed medieval drama. As the Christian forces conquered Moorish territory, religious plays similar to those performed throughout medieval Europe were introduced. But after 1500 the Spanish developed a distinctive form of morality play,

FIG. 7.1

The Spanish peninsula *c.* 1700.

the *autos sacramentales,* that they retained until religious performances were banned in 1765.

The *autos sacramentales* (acts of the sacrament), were associated exclusively with the feast of Corpus Christi, which, in its celebration of Christ's human and divine nature, was focused on the sacrament of the Eucharist. The highly ornate two-storied wagons (*carros*) that were used to perform the *autos*—pulled by bullocks with gilded horns—along with the spectacularly costumed actors who performed them, were an integral part of the procession that carried the sacred "host" (representing the body of Christ) through the streets at the start of the festival, after which the plays were performed. In some towns the first official performance was given inside the cathedral but this practice had largely been discontinued by the seventeenth century. The first performances were then sometime given just outside a church or in the courtyard of an important public building, but most performances occurred in town squares.

Like other forms of morality plays, *autos* told allegorical stories with characters representing such things as the virtues, the vices, the elements, hope, sin, beauty, death, and humanity. Some *autos* had no human characters in them. Several of the earliest *autos* were merely nativity plays in which the waiting shepherds were greeted not by an angel announcing Christ's birth, but by a figure like "Faith" explaining

FIG. 7.2

Reconstruction by Richard Southern of an *auto sacramental* performed in the Plaza Mayor, Madrid. It is based on a ground plan of 1644. Note the two *carros* alongside a platform and the boxlike seating provided for the City Council and the Council of Castile. From *Le Lieu Théâtrale à là Renaissance.* Courtesy Centre National de la Recherche Scientifique, Paris.

the meaning of the Eucharist. Later plays were far more philosophical, poetically intricate, and visually complex, and were as likely to include classical stories as biblical ones.

Although production arrangements varied from one area to another, those in the capital city of Valladolid, and afterwards, Madrid (the new capital after 1561), were sufficiently typical to stand for all. Until 1550 trade guilds were responsible for staging the plays, but at some time between 1551 and 1558 the City Council assumed control. Professional troupes were then employed to produce the plays, which were written by Spain's finest dramatists, making the connection between the public and religious stages a close one.

The plays were mounted on *carros,* or wagons, supplied by the city, which also furnished everything needed for the productions except the costumes and hand properties. Until the end of the sixteenth century, three *autos,* sometimes new, sometimes old, were presented by a single company each year. Each of the three autos had two *carros* to provide its scenery and at each playing location there was a portable stage (in the form of another wagon) the two *carros* for a given play could pull up to. In 1592, two companies started to be hired in Madrid to stage two *autos* each. Then in 1647, Calderón was hired to write the *autos* for the city of Madrid, which he continued to do until his death in 1681. Two companies were then hired to do one Calderón *auto* each, but they continued to use four *carros,* thereby doubling the scenic spectacle for each play. It was now necessary to have a fixed stage at each performance location large enough for four *carros* to pull up to, two across the side opposite the audience and one on each end. There is little information about the size of the *carros* until the mid-1630s, but by then they were about 20 feet long by 10 feet wide so the stage they attached to had to be quite large. When, in 1692, the awkwardness of taking away the four *carros* used for one *auto* and bringing in four others for the next, led to arranging all eight wagons around the platform throughout the performance, that stage would have had to have been no less that 40 feet wide by 20 feet deep.

The *carros* served as scenic pieces, entrances to the stage, and as dressing rooms for the actors. They were very ornate, two-storied structures made of wooden frames covered with painted canvas and equipped according to instructions supplied by the dramatists. The façade of the upper story was often hinged so that it might open to reveal something within. Scenic devices might also rise out of the lower story, and many of the wagons included machinery for flying actors or objects and for pivoting scenes out onto the stage.

Troupes were chosen during Lent. In addition to being paid a sizable fee, these companies were awarded exclusive rights to give public performances of other plays in Madrid from Easter until Corpus Christi. Between eight and twenty days before Corpus Christi, however, they had to give a preview performance of the *autos* for the City Council. After Corpus Christi, the actors toured the *autos* to neighboring towns and performed them in the public theatres of Madrid as well. Thus, there were many incentives for the actors to participate in the festivals.

After 1600, the first performance in Madrid was usually given before the king in a palace courtyard. The plays were then presented in the square before the city hall, on one day for the Council of Castile (the most powerful of governmental groups), and on the next for the City Council. Several other state councils were also entitled to special showings, and at least two performances were given for the general public before the plays went on tour.

In addition to the *autos,* the actors performed short farcical interludes and dances. Other performers were employed by the city to carry large carnival figures of giants and dragons about the streets and to perform the traditional dances. When the *autos* were finally forbidden in 1765, the reasons given were the predominance of the carnival spirit, the objectionable content of the farces and dances, and the undesirability of having religious plays performed by actors of questionable morality. All these complaints had been voiced since the sixteenth century, however, and other reasons must have been equally important. Certainly interest had declined since the death of Calderón in 1681, after which the *autos* became merely imitative of older works. The general loss of interest is probably also indicated by the abandonment of processional staging in 1705, after which the *autos* were performed only in the public theatres. Regardless of the reason for their decline and prohibition, *autos* were an important supplement to the professional stage for more than 200 years.

SECULAR DRAMA

From about 1470 the connections between Spain and Italy were close, and the awakening interest in classical learning found its way into Spanish intellectual circles. Printing was introduced to Spain in 1473, and over the next century many Latin and Greek works were translated into Spanish and widely disseminated. In 1508 a university was founded at Alcala de Henares to encourage the study of Latin, Greek, and Hebrew, and this study soon led to an interest in classical drama. The performance of plays by Plautus and Terence was mandated at Salamanca University in 1538, and Jesuit schools, which spread rapidly throughout Spain in the 1540s, used drama as an important component of their teaching system.

It was during this period that a Spanish secular drama began to emerge. Perhaps the most important early work is *The Comedy of Calisto and Melibea* (attributed to Fernando de Rojas, c 1465–c. 1541), a novel in dialogue rather than a true play. It was so widely read that it influenced later writers through its depictions of conflict between idealized and realistic behavior. Especially famous were the low-life scenes portraying La Celestina, who served as go-between for the lovers, Calisto and Melibea.

Juan del Encina (1469–1529) is often called the founder of Spanish drama. After studying with the great Spanish humanist, Nebrija, Encina turned to writing and acting in "eclogues" in the manner of the Italian pastoral drama. But it was not until he went to live in Rome that he turned to more purely secular works, such as *The Eclogue of Placida and Victoriano* (1513). His relatively simple plays were the first Spanish secular dramas to be performed. Bartolomé de Torres Naharro (*c.* 1485–*c.* 1520) at first imitated Encina's work but went on to write much more sophisticated farces and comedies. Like Encina, he lived for a time in Italy, where his plays were performed before being published in 1517. His preface to this collection provides one of the first contributions to dramatic theory in Europe, and his most famous play, *Comedia Himenea* (*c.* 1516), established the honor-vengeance theme that was to be a major influence on later dramatists. Gil Vicente (*c.* 1453–*c.* 1537) wrote primarily for the Portuguese court,

but many of his plays were in Spanish. He is generally considered superior to his contemporaries because of his considerable lyrical gift, great range, comic sense, and spontaneity. In addition to these native works, Italian plays were being performed at the Spanish court by 1548.

All the early secular drama in Spain was aimed at an aristocratic audience, and its influence on the professional theatre was negligible. Nevertheless, these plays established a foundation which later Spanish dramatists recognized as the source of their own practice.

EARLY PROFESSIONAL THEATRE

As in other countries, the early history of professional playing in Spain is obscure. Records show that by 1454, actors were being paid to perform at Corpus Christi, and that in 1539 six men were employed to perform farces at the Cathedral in Toledo. But it is not until the 1540s that notices concerning professional actors become common. Although most of these relate to Corpus Christi festivities, they show that by 1550 a number of troupes were in existence. In 1548, the first important Italian company appeared at Valladolid, and for the next fifty-five years Italian troupes provided a significant source of competition and influence for the Spanish companies (though scholars do not agree on the extent of that influence).

The first important figure of the Spanish professional theatre is Lope de Rueda (*c.* 1510–*c.* 1565). He received payment for his performance in several religious plays at Seville in 1542. By 1551 he was sufficiently well known to be summoned to Valladolid, then the capital of Spain, to perform for the king. From 1552 until 1558, Rueda was employed there at a considerable annual salary to supervise the Corpus Christi festivities. Rueda petitioned to build a theatre at Valladolid in 1558, but there is no evidence of its having actually been built.

In addition, he performed frequently at court and toured widely. Rueda was also the first successful writer of plays for popular audiences. A number of his full-length works have survived, including *The Frauds, Medora, Armelina,* and *Eufemia*. But he is best known for his farce sketches (*pasos*), of which *The Mask* and *The Olives* are probably the most famous. The plots serve primarily as an excuse for the earthy humor and picturesque dialogue. Fools and simpletons (roles played by Rueda) are the most fully developed characters. Like his English and Italian counterparts, he had to adapt to many conditions, acting in city squares, courtyards, and great halls at court or in houses of the nobility. Although Rueda

FIG. 7.3
Frontispiece to an edition of *Calisto and Melibea* published in Toledo in 1538.

is now almost universally considered the founder of the Spanish professional theatre, in actuality he was merely the most successful actor-manager of his day.

Between 1565 and 1590 plays were contrived primarily by the actor-managers of theatrical companies, a fact which led to the continuing designation of managers as *autores de comedias* (authors of plays). In the last quarter of the sixteenth century, two authors—Cueva and Cervantes—achieved a measure of fame as dramatists. Juan de la Cueva (1550–1610), working in Seville, wrote fourteen plays. He was one of the first dramatists to draw on Spanish history in plays such as *The Seven Children of Lara*. He also wrote on contemporary and classical subjects but is best known for popularizing polymetry, using different meters to fit the needs of different characters and situations within a single play. Miguel de Cervantes (1547–1616), remembered principally for his novel *Don Quixote* (1605–1615), also wrote about thirty plays, of which ten comedias and eight *entermeses* survive. The best of these are *The Siege of Numancia,* about a Roman attack on a Spanish town in 134 B.C.E.; *The Traffic of Argel,* a semi-autobiographical drama of his own years of slavery after being captured by Algerian pirates; and *The Fortunate Ruffian,* a play of contemporary Spanish life. Like the University Wits in England, Cueva, Cervantes, and other educated dramatists of the 1580s provided the link between academic drama and the professional stage.

The term *Comedia* was used to describe any full-length play, whether serious or comic. Most were divided into three acts (the five-act form being used only occasionally). There were many types of *comedia,* among them "cape and sword plays," named for the dress of gentlemen of minor ranks about whom these plays revolve; comedies of manners; saints plays; mythological plays; pastoral plays; and machine plays that required special effects technology to create the desired effects. The most common subjects were honor, love, patriotism, and religion.

Until about 1615, every performance began with a *loa* (compliment), or prologue, either a monologue or a dialogue. It was designed to gain the good will of the audience, and was usually preceded by singing and dancing. *Entremeses* ("interludes"), or short topical sketches, were performed in the intervals between the acts of plays. Some *entremeses* were sung, others were spoken, and still others mingled speech and song. The play ended with a dance. Professional companies also performed short farces known as *pasos* or just *entremeses* until the mid-seventeenth century, when they became known as *sainete.* Most Spanish dramatists wrote all these forms.

LOPE DE VEGA AND HIS CONTEMPORARIES

By far the most prolific Spanish playwright was Lope Félix de Vega Carpio (1562–1635), whose personal life was as flamboyant as the plays he wrote. He sailed with the Spanish Armada in 1588, was secretary to a nobleman and participant in many business and love affairs, and, after 1614, became a priest. In spite of his many activities, he declared in 1609 that he had written 483 *comedias.* Estimates of his total output run as high as 1800 plays, although 800 is probably more nearly accurate. Of these, 331 have survived, with another 200 surviving plays being attributed to him. He also found time to write on dramatic criticism in *The New Art of Writing Plays for Our Time* (1609) in which he rejects the neoclassical theories then being promoted in Italy and France. He was the first Spanish dramatist to make his living as a playwright, and no other dramatist has so dominated the professional theatre of any period.

It is difficult to assess the quality of Lope's work because of its quantity, but some broad generalizations are possible. Above all, his plays are notable for clearly defined actions which arouse and maintain suspense. Many revolve around the conflicting claims of love and honor, a theme which Lope popularized and bequeathed to virtually all succeeding Spanish drama. Since he disliked unhappy endings, Lope usually found means for resolving conflicts on an optimistic note. His characters include representatives of practically every rank and condition, into all of whom Lope entered sympathetically. The female roles are among his best. He also extended the scope of the *gracioso,* or simpleton, a standard character in the plays of the day. Lope's dialogue is natural, lively, and appropriate; it ranges through many verse forms, for Spanish dramatists never developed an equivalent to English blank verse.

Lope was by far the most popular writer of his age. To modern audiences, his most appealing work is perhaps *The Sheep Well (Fuente Ovejuna, c.* 1614), in which a tyrannous feudal lord is killed by villagers, who refuse to confess even under torture and are saved by the intervention of the king. Many critics have seen revolutionary sentiments in the play, but it is more likely that Lope was praising the king for abolishing the feudal system. Recently his *The Dog in the Manger (El pero del hortelano,* 1613–1615) has been popular. Others among his best-known plays are *The Foolish Lady* (1613), *Finding Truth through Doubt* (1620–1624), and *Punishment without Revenge* (1631).

Although Lope is now acknowledged as perhaps the greatest of all Spanish playwrights, he was surrounded by a host of other writers. The most important of these were Guillén de Castro, Tirso de Molina, and Juan Ruiz de Alarcón. Guillén de Castro (1569–1631), a friend and follower of Lope, wrote forty-three plays but is now remembered almost entirely for his *The Youthful Adventures of the Cid* (*Las Mocedades del Cid*, 1612–1618), which was to serve as the basis for the French playwright Corneille's controversial *Le Cid* in 1637. Tirso de Molina (*c.* 1584–1648) wrote a wide variety of *comedias,* including tragedies based on biblical stories and comedies dealing with contemporary political issues. The latter got him into trouble with the Council of Castile in 1625, and he was exiled from Madrid, after which his dramatic output decreased significantly. He is said to have written about 400 plays, of which eighty survive. He is known for creating intelligent, determined, and daring heroines, though by far the most famous of his plays today is *The Trickster of Sevill* (*El Burlador de Sevilla,* 1616–1630), the first dramatic treatment of the Don Juan story. Juan Ruiz de Alarcón (*c.* 1581–1639), born in Mexico and educated in Spain, where he worked for the government, wrote about twenty-five plays, the best of which center around court life in Madrid. The finest is *The Suspicious Truth* (1619), which explores the consequences arising from the inability of a young man to tell the truth. In his plays, Alarcón makes characterization and subtle moral sentiments the bases of dramatic action.

CALDERÓN AND HIS CONTEMPORARIES

Before Lope de Vega died, his preeminence had been challenged by another writer, Calderón, who was to be ranked above Lope by many critics. Unlike Lope and his contemporaries, who were associated principally with the public theatres, Calderón and the best dramatists of his time wrote primarily for the court theatre. In this shift, many historians have seen a major cause of the decline of Spanish drama.

Pedro Calderón de la Barca (1600–1681), the son of a court official, received a university education and then entered the service of a nobleman. In 1651, after a series of personal disasters, Calderón became a priest, although he continued to write *autos* for the city of Madrid and occasional plays for the court. Of his approximately 200 plays, about 100 have survived. Eighty of these are *autos.*

Calderón wrote practically all of his best secular plays between 1622 and 1640. These fall into two major categories: "cape and sword" such as *The Phantom Lady* (1629), which depend on numerous misunderstandings in love intrigues that are ultimately happily resolved; and honor plays, like *The Physician to His Own Honor* (1635) in which a man, suspecting that his wife is unfaithful, kills her in a manner that will avoid scandal. Although the play on the surface seems to treat the man's action sympathetically, some critics insist that it is intended to make audiences aware of a practice of which Calderón disapproved.

Calderón's most famous secular play, *Life Is a Dream* (*c.* 1636), is a philosophical allegory about the human situation and the mystery of life. The main character, Segismundo, a prince by birth, is reared in anonymity, taken to court while unconscious, and returned to his former state after being found unworthy; when he awakens, he believes that the interlude at court was a dream. Eventually, after he comes to understand that life is a dream from which only death awakens us, he takes the throne in a civil war and becomes a wise ruler.

In the chaotic years following 1640, when Catalonia and Portugal revolted against Spain, Calderón wrote only one outstanding *comedia, The Mayor of Zalamea* (*c.* 1642), the story of a peasant who exacts revenge for the violation of his daughter by an army officer. After 1652, all of Calderón's secular plays were written on demand for the court. They are short and light, often based on classical myths or pastoral subjects, with choral passages and much of the dialogue set to music. Because so many of them were performed at the royal hunting lodge, La Zarzuela, this type of musical play, which later was to be (and still remains) one of the most popular of Spanish dramatic forms, came to be called the *zarzuela.*

Above all, Calderón is noted for his *autos,* for he perfected the form. In his *autos,* Calderón effectively embodied Catholic dogma in symbolic stories told in lyrical dialogue of great beauty. Although he had written *autos* from the beginning of his career, he turned to them especially after 1647, writing two each year for the city of Madrid until his death. Nevertheless, his finest *autos, The Constant Prince* (1629) and *Devotion to the Cross* (1633), were written before he became a priest.

The output of the Golden Age was phenomenal. Estimates of the total number of plays written prior to 1700 range from 10,000 to 30,000. In quantity, the drama of Spain greatly exceeded that of England between 1590 and 1642. Its preoccupation with a narrow code of honor and failure to probe deeply into human destiny are limitations which make it less universal than the best English work. Nevertheless, many of the plays were widely known and imitated outside of Spain, and at home they established a lasting standard.

ACTING COMPANIES

It is difficult to estimate the number of acting companies in Spain between 1550 and 1600, for many lasted only a single season and mergers or separations were frequent. In addition to the Spanish troupes, Italian *commedia dell'arte* companies frequently visited during this time. The Italian troupe led by Alberto Naselli (1574–1584), who used the stage name Ganassa, seems to have been influential in the early creation of the theatres (*corrales*) in Madrid. Among the many other Italian troupes those led by Estefanelo Botarga, Maximiliano Milanino, and Tristano Martinelli were especially popular. The number of Spanish troupes increased rapidly after permanent theatres were built in the 1570s and 1580s, so in 1603 the government sought to regulate them by severely restricting the Italian companies and reducing the number of Spanish troupes to eight licensed companies. In 1615 the number of licenses was raised to twelve.

There were two kinds of licensed companies: sharing troupes (*compañías de parte*) and salaried actors working for a manager under one- or two-year contracts. Companies licensed by the Royal Council could be contracted to do the *auto sacramentales* for a city, for which the companies received relatively high fees. Licensed companies could also be contracted to perform in the *corrales*. Generally only one licensed company at a time would perform in a city, but in Seville and Madrid there could be as many as four. Payments to companies varied widely. Usually a troupe was given a fixed sum for each performance, and a percentage of the receipts was sometimes added. Occasionally companies were paid entirely through a fixed percentage of receipts. If a company had to travel a long distance to keep an engagement, it might receive additional payments since traveling from one engagement to the next was time-consuming and costly. In 1586, for example, it took one company thirteen days to travel the 270 miles between Madrid and Seville. The mode of transportation, depending upon the company's finances, ranged from walking to using carts, pack animals, and coaches. Contracts often specified allowances for travel, as well as the type of lodging and food to be provided on the road.

Between 1610 and 1640, the period of the theatre's greatest popularity, the average licensed company consisted of sixteen to twenty actors and included men, women, and apprentices performing a repertory of up to sixty plays. In addition, companies generally had their own prompter, wardrobe keepers, stage hands, and money collectors.

Each play in a company's repertory had to be licensed separately. After 1600 all plays were subject to censorship, and dramatists could be excommunicated if they did not comply with recommendations. Before 1590, many playwrights were attached to troupes as actors. After 1590, such close connections were unusual, though company managers generally commissioned new plays so the playwrights still wrote with a specific company in mind. At the height of his career Lope de Vega received about 500 reals for each play, at a time when an actor's average annual salary was about 6000 reals. This disparity in income may explain why dramatists were so prolific. By the 1650s the payment had increased somewhat—to about 800 reals—for works by the best writers. Plays commissioned for the court paid two to three times that amount.

Actors not contracted to licensed companies often joined "companies of the road" (*compañías de la legua*) which performed anywhere they could outside of the cities reserved for the licensed companies, and shared the takings for each performance. Since there were no copyright laws, a play could be performed by any company that could obtain a copy and its license, and it was common practice for the licensed companies to lease licensed plays to these unlicensed troupes (which were not above stealing such plays when necessary). The size of these companies varied considerably. Augustín de Rojas Villandrando's fictional *Entertaining Journey* (1604) describes troupes ranging in size from the single performer, who recited monologues or scenes from plays, to those with sixteen members. During the long closure of the theatres from 1646 to 1651 the "companies of the road" seem to have continued in operation (even though they had been made illegal in 1644), while the licensed companies disbanded. When the theatres reopened, only eight companies were licensed and their energies were focused increasingly on the court.

ACTORS AND ACTING

The position of the professional performer in Spain was ambiguous. Since Roman times actors had been forbidden the sacraments of the church, and Alfonso X (1221–1284) declared that all actors were to be branded infamous. These strictures were not officially removed in Spain until the twentieth century. During the Golden Age the usual attitude was one of tolerance, however, so long as actors did not perform plays that contradicted church teachings; certainly many actors, especially those in licensed troupes, were married and buried in the church. They were employed by city officials to produce the *autos* at Corpus Christi and their work was essential to the funding of many charities. Nevertheless, many churchmen were opposed to the theatre, especially to the use of professional actors in religious plays. They often petitioned the king to ban professional theatre, and while such petitions were rarely granted, they did result in a very close supervision of the theatre by government officials.

A major concern of those opposed to theatre was the presence of professional actresses. Professional female performers in Spain can be traced back as far as the fifteenth century, and by the mid-sixteenth century, they were included in several acting troupes. Nevertheless, most women's roles were played by boys or men until 1587, when women were first licensed to appear on the stage. Churchmen secured a royal decree banning actresses in 1596, but it seems never to have been enforced. After a bitter controversy in 1598 and 1599, the royal council declared that no actresses were to perform unless their husbands or fathers were in the company, and that neither sex might appear in the dress of the other. This decree too, however, especially the later portion of it, seems not to have been enforced. Further attempts to still criticism probably lay behind the decree of 1608, which stated that only actors were to go backstage, forbade friars to attend the theatre, and banned the presentation of secular plays in churches or religious houses. At this time strict censorship was established over plays, and in 1615 it was extended to dancing, about which there had been many complaints.

In his *Entertaining Journey,* Rojas Villandrando describes the actor's life around 1600: Performers, he says, must rise early and study their roles from 2 until 9 A.M., and then attend rehearsals until noon; after eating, they go to the theatre to perform, completing their work about 7 P.M.; if they are summoned by officials or nobles to perform, they may work well into the night. Under Philip IV (reigned 1621–1665), the actors were much in demand at court, and Philip's practice of sending for companies on such short notice that they had to cancel public performances is sometimes cited as a reason for the decline of public interest in theatre, though the long closure of the theatre from 1646–1651 is undoubtedly a larger factor in this.

In 1631 the actors were allowed to form a guild similar to those of other recognized trades. Called the Cofradía de la Novena, it still exists and is open to all theatrical personnel. It did much to raise the social status of the actor.

The Biographical Dictionary of Actors in Spanish Classical Theater database now being developed by the University of Valencia contains the names of over 6500 professional actors who worked in the theatre prior to 1700. Most performers were recruited from the common people, although occasionally members of the minor aristocracy went on the stage. The best known of these actors include Damien Arias de Penafiel (*fl.* 1617–1643), who, with his "pure, clear voice, vivacious manner, and excellent memory," was universally regarded as the finest actor of his time. Other outstanding performers included Cosme Perez (*c.* 1585–1673), the most famous comic actor of the age, and Jusepa Vaca (*fl.* 1602–1634), the most celebrated actress.

In sharing companies, the receipts were divided after all expenses were subtracted. Salaried actors were paid by the day, and since the number of performances might vary widely from one year and troupe to another, it is difficult to calculate the average income. One historian has estimated it at about 6000 reals per year, a rather liberal sum for the time. Most salaries were supplemented by a daily maintenance allowance, and additional payments might be made for traveling expenses and costumes. Thus, though actors did not rank high in the social scale, they were in many ways better off than their French contemporaries, who were denied religious rights, or English actors, who were always at odds with the civic authorities.

COSTUMES

The costume practices of the Spanish stage were similar to those of England during the same period. Expensive contemporary clothing served in most cases, although historical and legendary figures were sometimes differentiated by outmoded or fanciful dress. Moors, toward whom the Spaniards felt a special antipathy, were always clearly distinguished from other characters.

Contracts for the *autos* specified costumes of silk and velvet. Often the actors petitioned civic officials for additional funds to pay for unexpectedly expensive garments, and their requests were frequently granted. In addition, towns voted special prizes to companies or actors who had distinguished themselves in the *autos* either through acting or costuming. These costumes were then reused by the companies in their performances at the *corrales.*

Although a sharing company usually maintained a wardrobe that was available to all its members, many actors supplied their own costumes. Actors' contracts often specified allowances for costumes. The manager was responsible for the wardrobes of apprentices.

In most cases, actors seem to have dressed as lavishly as finances permitted. In 1653 actresses were forbidden to wear strange headdresses, decolleté

FIG. 7.4

The *corral* theatre of Almagro (near Ciudad Real), Spain. Built in 1628, it was restored in 1953–1954. The stage is 28 feet wide and 13 feet deep to the row of posts at the rear, where a curtain would have hung from the gallery. It is another 2 feet 8 inches from the posts to the doors in the rear wall. Photo by F. J. Hildy.

FIG. 7.5

Plan by J. J. Allen and Carlos Dorremochea of the second level of the Corral del Príncipe, c. 1697. The letters at the sides indicate boxes. The stage *(escenario)* and side stages *(tablado lateral)* are shown at top. Benches *(taburetes)* for seating in the *patio* are forward of the stage. Courtesy the University Presses of Florida and Mr. Allen.

necklines, wide hooped skirts, or dresses not reaching the floor. In addition, they were restricted to one costume for each play unless the scripts clearly demanded a change. Records of extravagance are numerous. In 1589 an actor paid 1100 reals and in 1619 another paid 2400 reals for a single costume, sums equivalent to about one-fifth to one-half of a typical actor's annual income. No doubt the minor performers were less richly dressed. A good wardrobe was considered one of the actor's greatest assets, for it helped secure employment and could be pawned in bad times.

THE CORRALES

Early acting companies performed in the courtyards *(corrales)* that are a distinctive feature of Spanish urban architecture. City blocks are organized around a series of such courtyards. The term *corral,* therefore, came to be used for theatre. The first public theatre structure in Spain was built by the Italian architect Juan (Giovanni) Marin Modeñin Bellini in Seville in 1574. The last one was built at Almagro in 1628 for Don Leonardo de Oviedo, a priest who had it purposely built within the courtyard of his inn, The Bull. (This is the only Golden Age theatre that still exists.) Between these two dates, *corral* theatres (and often more than one) were built in at least eighteen other cities in Spain and four in the Americas, and probably many more besides. Most

of what we know about *corral* theatres concerns Madrid, however, and the account that follows is primarily about that city, although it is unclear to what extent Madrid's practices were typical. In Madrid, the *corrales* were at first under the direct control of three charitable "confraternities" like those which had presented religious plays throughout Europe during the Middle Ages. The Cofradía de la Pasión y Sangre de Jesucristo, founded in 1565 to feed and clothe the poor and support a hospital, was the first to be granted the privilege of operating a theatre as a means of raising money. By 1568 it was using a rented courtyard in the Calle de Sol for performances and soon added two others. In 1574 the Confradía de la Soledad de Nuestra Señora, founded in 1567, petitioned to have one of the existing courtyards placed under its control, a move which led to a sharing of revenues and expenses by the two *cofradías*. In 1583 the General Hospital of Madrid was also given a share in the revenues. These three organizations controlled the public theatres of Madrid until 1615. This made the theatre a means of raising money for charity, which helped to isolate it from public criticism.

A new phase in the career of the theatres began in 1615 when the City of Madrid was ordered to pay the hospitals an annual subsidy. After this time, the *cofradías* gave up direct control over theatrical management and leased the theatres to entrepreneurs, normally for four-year periods. In 1638 control of the *corrales* passed to the city, and two commissioners were appointed to oversee them, although the theatres continued to be leased. Despite some alterations in the system during the eighteenth century, the theatres were used to finance charities until the mid-nineteenth century. At no time during the Golden Age did the actors control the *corrales,* which were occupied by them merely for short-term engagements under contracts with the theatres' lessees.

At first the *corrales* were temporary, at least five different ones being used in Madrid during the 1570s. The desirability of permanent theatres became evident after one was built in Seville in 1574, however, and in 1579 the Corral de la Cruz, the first permanent theatre in the capital, was opened in Madrid. It was followed by the Corral del Príncipe in 1583. After

1585 these were to be the only public theatres for drama in Madrid until the mid-eighteenth century.

Madrid's *corrales* were built around a square or rectangular courtyard (unroofed until the eighteenth century). Adjustable awnings were used to shade the audience and provide some lighting effects, an innovation introduced by the Italian Ganassa company in 1574. A stage (*encenario*) with a tiring house (*vestuario*) behind it, occupied one end of the courtyard. The Madrid *corrales* had discovery spaces in the *vestuario* and side stages that could be used for medieval style mansions or for extra audience seating. These features were shared by some, but not all, of the *corrales* outside the capital.

The large central courtyard (*patio*) was occupied primarily by standing spectators, although by the mid-seventeenth century a row of benches (*taburetes*) had been set up immediately in front of the stage. Along each side of the *patio* was bleacher-style seating (*gradas*), divided from the *patio* by a railing and protected from the weather by an overhanging roof. The *gradas* extended up to the second-story level of

FIG. 7.6

Interior of the Corral del Príncipe, *c.* 1697. At center left is the main stage, and to the right of it one of the side stages (occupied by spectators). At bottom left is the *patio,* and at bottom right the *gradas* backed by the grated windows of the first level of boxes; at top right are the *desvánes* and below them a row of open boxes. Drawing by Carlos Dorremochea. From John J. Allen, *The Reconstruction of a Spanish Golden Age Playhouse* (1983). Courtesy the University Presses of Florida and Mr. Allen.

the four-story houses that surrounded the *patio*. Each window in a house served as a theatre box (*aposento*), and those on the second floor were fitted with grilles to prevent climbing into the theatre. The fourth-floor boxes were often called *desvanes* (attics) because of their location and cramped space.

At the rear of the *patio* was a refreshment booth (*alojería*), above which was the gallery for unaccompanied women (the *cazuela*). Strict segregation of men and women was enforced by an *alcalde* (Justice of the Peace). Women were forbidden the *patio* and men the *cazuela*. Women could, however, sit in boxes if accompanied by an adult male member of their own family.

Above the *cazuela* were two other galleries, the first divided into boxes (two of which were assigned to the City of Madrid and the Council of Castile), and the other used at different stages of the theatre's development as a seating area for clergymen and intellectuals (*tertulia*) or as an upper *cazuela*.

Some of the theatres outside of Madrid deviated from this typical pattern. Some were roofed from the beginning. Some were purposely built as theatres and did not have to contend with surrounding houses. Many were only three-story rather than four. In most of these, the *aposentos* were replaced by open galleries divided into compartments like those later used in the Italian public opera houses; others had one row of *aposentos*, above which there were open galleries. Nevertheless, the basic arrangement—an enclosed courtyard—was the same everywhere.

Madrid's two theatres had several entrances; at each entrance there were two money takers, since two entrance fees were paid, one to the lessee and one to a representative of the charities. About three-fifths of the combined total income went to the lessee and the actors. The entrance fee admitted women to the *cazuela* and men to the *patio*. Additional fees were collected from the men if they wished to sit on the *gradas*, *taburetes*, or side stages. The theatre controlled all the boxes facing the stage, but the arrangement with the boxes located in the side houses varied. Some homeowners collected entrance fees for their boxes on certain days and the theatre lessee collected the fees on other days; some owners had sole rights to their boxes in return for allowing passageways through their property to other boxes; and some owners paid the theatre an annual fee for the right to watch the plays. (The problems created by such arrangements was a primary motivation for tearing down the *corrales* in the mid-eighteenth century and building self-contained theatres on the same sites.)

Until the 1580s performances were confined to Sundays and feast days. But in 1579 the Italian Ganassa

FIG. 7.7

A rough plan of the Corral del Príncipe made about 1730. The stage is shown at the bottom, and the refreshment booth, *cazuela,* and *tertulia* at the top; the side walls, showing the boxes, are drawn as though the various levels were side by side. From a plan published in 1881.

troupe was permitted to play on a weekday, and this privilege was soon extended to Spanish companies. By the seventeenth century performances were allowed daily except on Saturdays. The theatrical season ran from September to Lent and from just after Easter until July. About 198 days each year were devoted to performances, but the theatres were often closed for periods of official mourning, plagues, and wars.

The Madrid *corrales* probably had a capacity of about 1000 when they opened, but this had increased to about 2000 by the 1630s, when Madrid's population stood at about 150,000. It has been estimated that roughly 350 places were reserved for unaccompanied women in the *cazuela,* but it is not known how many more may have been in the boxes at any one time. Performances began at 2 P.M. in the fall and winter season and at 3 to 4 P.M. during the spring; they were required to end at least one hour before nightfall. The daily bill began with music, singing, and dancing; next came the *loa*, or prologue, which was followed by another dance; then came the *comedia*, the acts of which were separated by *entremeses;* a dance concluded the performance.

Spectators, especially those in the *patio* and *cazuela,* were often noisy. The *mosqueteros* in the courtyard were usually the most unruly, but the women sometimes threw fruit at the actors, and both men and women carried such noisemakers as whistles, rattles, and bunches of keys. They were equally voluble in approval, which they demonstrated by applauding and shouting "Victor!" Refreshments, such as fruit, wafers, and drinks, were sold throughout performances. On any occasion when a full house was expected, the *alcalde* was seated on one side of the stage as a visual reminder that order would be enforced. He had a number of attendants (*alguaciles*) to assist him in case disturbances broke out.

THE STAGE AND SCENERY

Like the costuming and the theatres themselves, the stage and scenery of the Spanish public theatre were in many ways similar to those of England. The stage was a raised platform without a proscenium arch and was bounded at the back by a permanent façade. Since side-stage seating and *aposentos* extended up to that façade, the action was viewed from three sides, though the majority of spectators sat or stood in front of the stage.

Although the dimensions of the Corral de la Cruz are uncertain, its stage was probably about 26 feet wide by 16 feet deep. At each side of the stage were lateral platforms that could serve as additional seating for *capa y espada* plays and as space for scenic units, such as the commonly referred to "mountain" in *comedias de fábrica.* The stage at the Corral del Príncipe was about 28 feet wide by $14\frac{1}{2}$ feet deep. (A semicircular extension about 5 feet deep was added to the front in the eighteenth century.) It too had lateral platforms for additional seating or special scenic pieces. At both theaters, the stage was raised about 5 to 6 feet above the *patio.* All *corrales* for which we have information on stage size roughly share these measurements (the smallest is 20 feet by $11\frac{1}{2}$ feet). This open platform was backed

FIG. 7.8

Setting for *Los Celos hacen estrellas* by Juan Velez de Guevara at the court in 1672. Courtesy Bildarchiv, Osterreichische Nationalbibliothek, Vienna.

by a facade of two or three levels. The lower level had three openings, those at the sides serving as entrances and the larger central space primarily as a place for "discoveries." The discovery space was about 13 feet deep at the Corral de la Cruz and about $8\frac{1}{2}$ feet deep at the Príncipe. The upper levels, essentially galleries, could be used in a variety of ways, but normally represented towers, city walls, or hills. At times, discoveries were also made there by drawing curtains. It was sometimes necessary to go from the stage to an upper level in full view of the audience, and to meet this need portable stairs were brought on and then removed when no longer required.

For the most part, the simple staging conventions resembled those of the Elizabethan theatre. An exit and reentry was sufficient to mark a change of place. In addition, three different kinds of scenic background might be used. First, the facade often served as the sole background for the action. Second, curtains were drawn aside to reveal properties or scenic pieces set up in the discovery space when localization of the action was required. Third, medieval-like mansions were sometimes set up on the lateral platforms at the sides of the stage. Surviving scripts clearly show that scenic pieces were used at times to represent gardens, fountains, mountains, rocks, trees, forts, and castles. Sometimes they are specified when not strictly required by the action, while in other instances the spectators are requested to imagine some place not shown. It seems likely that practice was inconsistent and was guided more by the availability of scenic pieces than by any conscious theory of stage decoration. On the other hand, as spectacle increased after 1650, painted flats and practicable windows and doors began to be set into the facade in lieu of curtains. Except in rare instances, however, there was no attempt to use perspective painting. The stage was equipped with several trapdoors, while the roof over the stage housed machinery for flying, which was increasingly popular after 1650. Essentially, however, scenic practices changed little during the course of the Golden Age.

THEATRE IN THE AMERICAS

Once the voyages of Columbus brought the Americas into European consciousness, the Spanish set about to conquer this territory just as they had done the Iberian Peninsula. By 1519 they had conquered the Bahamas, the Caribbean islands, and Cuba; by 1522 the Aztec empire of Mexico and Central America; by 1533 the Inca Empire of western South America. Florida came under their control by 1565. In 1581 Spain gained control of Portugal and along with it came Brazil (until 1668). Southeastern South America was added about the same time.

Among the hundreds of cultures they conquered, there were certainly traditions of storytelling, narrative dance, epic songs, rituals, ceremonies, and popular entertainment that would be of great interest to the study of theatre. Unfortunately the conquistadors had little interest in such things. By the time the Dominican and Franciscan friars recorded their observations of these cultures in the mid to late sixteenth century, much had already changed. As early as 1512 Europeans began to insert Christian elements into native performance traditions. By 1523 the Spanish were introducing large numbers of African slaves into the region, and their performance traditions soon merged with those of the native peoples. The Maya were already a fading culture before the Spanish arrived, and they, along with the other major cultures of the Americas, were soon experiencing near total collapse as European disease and constant warfare (with both Europeans and other indigenous peoples) are thought to have destroyed over 90 percent of the native populations within just thirty years of colonization. Smaller cultures simply vanished. With the exception of the Maya and Aztecs (whose records were systematically destroyed), the cultures of the Americas were nonliterate and had not recorded their own traditions. It is therefore difficult to assess the remaining evidence for pre-Columbian performance traditions.

The Spanish recorded a type of farce called *baldzamil* among the Maya and described stages with staircases used for these performances. There is also a Mayan dramatic text from Guatemala for the epic dance-drama, *The Rabinal Warrior (Rabinal Achí)* or the *Dance of the Tun*. It was not recorded until 1855 (from the memory of a performer who had appeared in the work several times before 1820), but some scholars believe that it reflects performance traditions that go back to the thirteenth century. The play tells the story of an unnamed Quiché warrior who is captured by the Rabinal Warrior and taken before the Rabinal ruler named Five Rains. It ends with the ritual slaying of the captured warrior by a group of twelve eagles and twelve jaguars. Though as many as a hundred performers were involved in the production, there are only three speaking roles. In Nicaragua sometime in the sixteenth or seventeenth centuries, a comedy called *The Old Man (El Güegüence)* was composed incorporating what are thought to be pre-Columbian traditions of a comic buffoon character, but this play was not transcribed until 1883. A similar "buffoon" tradition was noted in conjunction with the ceremonial *kachina* dances of the Pueblo peoples when the Spanish encountered them in what is now the Southwestern United States around 1540. The Spanish observed, as well, a thriving performance tradition of social satire among communities subjugated by the Incas in Peru. In the 1780s Antonio Valdés produced *Ollantay,* an epic drama he claimed was of pre-Columbian origin, which he had transcribed from the oral tradition of these people, but its authenticity is questioned by many scholars.

The earliest known performance of a European play in the Americas took place at a seminary in Puerto Rico in 1510. But the Dominican and Franciscan friars who set out to Christianize the Americas were soon adapting local performance traditions to Christian purposes just as had been done in Europe in the Middle Ages. They wrote numerous *autos,* generally in the local language, to be performed by those they were converting. Native dance, music, and costuming were incorporated into many of these. By 1539 the *autos* of New Spain (Mexico) had gained political overtones with *The Conquest of Rhodes* and *The Conquest of Jerusalem* being performed by rival groups in two different cities. Over 1000 Indians were used as musicians and extras in these plays. In 1544 the archbishop of New Spain ordered an end to this kind of activity. But the evangelical use of theatre simply moved on to Peru in 1546 and Brazil by the 1570s, and it never really stopped even in New Spain.

México (Mexico City) established a prize for the best play at Corpus Christi in 1565. But the real turning point for theatre in the Americas came in 1574. At the consecration of the new archbishop, the first Spanish-language play to be written by a native-born dramatist was performed: *Spiritual Contract between the Shepard Peter and the Mexican Church* by Juan Pérez Ramires (1545–?). The first plays of the first major dramatist of the New World, Spanish-born dramatist Fernán Gonzáles de Eslava (1534–c. 1601), were also performed for this event, which in addition is celebrated for the appearance of the first professional actor of the Americas.

In 1586 *autor* Alonso de Buenrostro brought his acting troupe from Spain, and by 1601 there were three acting companies based in Mexico City. In 1597 Francisco de León built the first *corral* theatre there. A second was built sometime before 1602, and others were built at Lima (Peru) and New Veracruz. Throughout the seventeenth century theatre was performed in many parts of the Spanish territories, but New Spain, and especially Mexico City, continued to be the focal point.

Three volumes of religious *comedias* attributed to Juan Bautista were published in New Spain in 1599. The Mexican nun Sor Juana Inés de la Cruz (*c.* 1648–1695), a towering intellect of the period and one of the most admired women of her day, wrote her first play, *The Second Celestina,* in 1676. She also wrote *The Trials of a Noble House* (1683), which was thought to have achieved a lyric beauty matched only by Calderón. In the 1680s Juan del Valle y Caviedas (1652–1694) become the first playwright in Peru. His fame was quickly eclipsed, however, by Pedro de Peralta Barnuevo (1664–1743), who wrote full-length plays on French and Greek themes. These New World dramatists and the many others who surrounded them wrote fairly typical Spanish Golden Age plays of all types, but the local color and native characters they included made their works distinctive.

COURT ENTERTAINMENTS

Although court entertainments like those found elsewhere in Europe had been seen in Spain since the thirteenth century, it was not until the reign of Philip III (1598–1621) that theatrical performances were given regularly at court.

But the court theatre reached its height during the reign of Philip IV (1621–1665), who between 1623 and 1653 saw about 300 different plays there. Although Italianate scenery had been used occasionally since the sixteenth century, it did not become common until Cosme Lotti (?–1643), a student of the great Italian designer, Alfonso Parigi, was brought from Florence in 1626. Until the 1630s most of the court entertainments were staged in a large hall at the Alcázar or in the gardens at Aranjuez; after 1633 the new palace in Madrid, the Buen Retiro, became the center of court entertainments.

Many lavish outdoor productions were staged on the palace grounds. One of the most famous of these was Calderón's *The Greatest Enchantment Is Love* (1635), which treated Ulysses' encounter with the enchantress Circe. For this production Lotti built a floating stage on a lake. The special effects included a shipwreck, a triumphal chariot drawn across the water by dolphins, and the destruction of Circe's palace. The whole was lit by 3000 lanterns, and the king and his retinue watched from gondolas. In 1636 the three acts of Calderón's *The Three Great Prodigies* were given on three separate stages, each act being performed by a different professional troupe. In addition, there were many lavish masquerades, tournaments, and machine plays. For a carnival in 1637,

FIG. 7.9

An opera at court, *c.* 1680. The suspended figures on stage indicate that the theatre was equipped with Italianate machinery. From *Histoire de France.* Courtesy Bibliothèque Nationale, Paris.

FIG. 7.10

A play at the court of Carlos II, *c.* 1680. The king is seated on a dais at lower right. Note the proscenium arch and the perspective scenery. From *Histoire de France,* published at Antwerp by Philibert Buttats the Younger. Courtesy Bibliothèque Nationale, Paris.

Lotti designed huge wheeled structures measuring 22 feet in width, 32 feet in length, and 46 feet in height.

In 1640 a permanent theatre, the Coliseo, was constructed by Lotti in the Buen Retiro. This theatre seems to have resembled the public *corrales,* for it had a *patio,* three levels of *aposentos,* and a *cazuela.* The royal box was situated above the *cazuela.* It differed from the *corrales* in being roofed and probably in having a proscenium arch, often said to be the first in Spain. The Coliseo was frequently open to the public, who paid the same entrance fees as at the public *corrales.* Furthermore, the same percentage of the receipts was given to charities. The plays were performed by troupes that normally appeared in the *corrales,* and the scenic demands for most of the plays were similar to those written for the public theatres. Other plays, however, were machine plays; spectacular pieces that required Italianate scenery and special effects. Sometimes private performances for the court preceded those open to the public. More intimate entertainments were given in other rooms or in one of the courtyards in the palace.

The 1640s saw a marked decline in theatrical activities, both at court and in the public theatres. The Catalan and Portuguese rebellions of 1640 ushered in a period of uncertainty, and, following the deaths of Lotti in 1643 and of the queen in 1644, court theatricals virtually came to an end.

Between 1646 and 1651 the public theatres were closed.

By 1650 Philip had remarried and had settled many of his political problems; consequently, the Coliseo was reopened to the public in 1651, the same year in which the public theatres were permitted to resume performances. Another Italian designer, Baccio del Bianco (?–1657), was imported in 1652, and the use of spectacular scenery increased markedly. Court performances were frequent until Philip's death in 1665. They were resumed about 1670, and the old practices were continued. In these years José Caudi became the first native scene designer at court. After the death of Carlos II in 1700, the court theatre declined rapidly.

By the late seventeenth century, the financial resources of Spain were virtually exhausted, and Spain's political power was rapidly declining. The great dramatic impulse was also over, for after the death of Calderón in 1681 new writers sought primarily to recapture a past glory instead of exploring new paths. As a consequence, the most vital and productive period of Spanish theatre had ended by 1700.

LOOKING AT THEATRE HISTORY

Public archives often contain some of the most valuable information concerning the theatre. This is especially true for a study of *autos sacramentales:* The Municipal Archives in Madrid contain numerous documents relating to the preparation and performance of Corpus Christi celebrations there. Many of the pertinent documents have been published by N. D. Shergold and J. E. Varey in an ongoing series of volumes under the collective title *Fuentes para la Historia del Teatro en España*.

Other major sources of information are accounts written by visitors from other countries. Often they provide more graphic details of theatrical conditions than native writers who are so familiar with local situations that they consider it unnecessary to record them. One of the best descriptions of the Corpus Christi festivals in Madrid is found in an account written by the Dutchman Francis van Aerssen, who visited Spain in 1654–1655. His account was published in French in 1666 and in English in 1670.

> . . . they begin by a procession, whose first ranks include several [musicians]; a great many habited in parti-colored clothes, skip and frolic as extravagantly as in a Morris dance. The king . . . after Mass, returns with a torch in his hand, following a silver Tabernacle, in which is the Holy wafer, attended by the Grandees of Spain and his several Councils. . . .Before these . . . move Machines, representing Giants; these are Statues of Pasteboard carried by men concealed under them. . . . The Tarasca is a Serpent of enormous greatness in form of a Woman, moving on wheels, the body covered with scales, a vast belly, long tail, short feet, sharp talons, fiery eyes, gaping mouth, out of which extend three tongues, and long tusks. This Bulbeggar stalks up and down . . . and sometimes lays hold on Country fellows, whose fright moves laughter amongst the people. . . . The Procession having filed to the Piazza, returns by the . . . Calle Mayor, adorned by many tapestries waving on the balconies filled with men and women of all conditions. . . . In the afternoon about five o'clock, Autos are represented. . . . The two companies of Players that belong to Madrid at this time, shut their theatres, and for a month represent these Holy Poems: this they do every evening in public on scaffolds erected to that purpose in the streets before the houses of the

> Presidents of several Councils. They begin at Court the day of the Solemnity. . . . The stage is at the foot of these Scaffolds, and little painted booths are rolled to it, . . . and serve as tiring houses.

> *A Journey into Spain* (London, 1670), 118–124.

In his account of a visit to Spain in 1659, François Bertaut describes the theatres:

> . . . there are troupes of players in nearly all the towns, and they are better, in comparison, than our own [the French], but there are none in the pay of the King. They perform in a courtyard, where a number of private houses join together, so that the windows of the rooms . . . do not belong to the players but to the owners of the houses. They perform by day and without torches, and their theatres . . . have not such fine decorations as ours. . . There are two places . . . in Madrid, which they call Corrales, and which are always filled with merchants and artisans, who leave their shops and repair thither. . . . Some of the spectators have seats close to the stage. . . . The women all sit together in a gallery at one end, which the men are not allowed to enter.

> *Relation de l'Estat et Gouvernement d'Espagne* (Cologne, 1666), 59–60.

In 1679 the Comtesse D'Aulnoy wrote a number of letters recording her impressions of her travels in Spain. In one she describes her visit to an opera (*Alcina*) at the court theatre located in the Buen Retiro palace:

> I never saw such wretched machinery. The gods descended on horseback upon a beam which extended from one end of the stage to the other; the sun was lighted up by means of a dozen lanterns of oiled paper in each of which was a lamp. When Alcina practiced her enchantments and evoked the demons, the latter arose leisurely out of hell upon ladders. . . . The building is certainly very beautiful and handsomely painted and gilded; the boxes are furnished with blinds . . . [which] reach from top to bottom, so that they seem to form a kind of room.

> *Relation du Voyage d'Espagne* (The Hague, 1693), 10th letter.

Considerable information about the sharing companies of the seventeenth century can be gleaned from the contractual agreements made when the companies were formed. One contract dated June 1614 sets forth the agreement between Andrés de Claramonte and eleven other actors. Some of the provisions are these:

Andrés de Claramonte binds himself to furnish . . . as many as forty comedias and such others as the said company may require, besides the necessary entreméses, letras, *and* bailes.

Item: . . . the various roles in the comedias shall be assigned amongst the members . . . in such manner as shall seem most suitable to each in the opinion of the said company.

Item: . . . members . . . are bound to attend with care and punctuality the rehearsals of all the comedias to be represented each day, at nine o'clock, at the house of . . . Andrés de Claramonte, where rehearsals are ordinarily to take place, and shall not fail to be present at any of the said rehearsals, under penalty of two reals. . . .

Item: . . . if, during the said time, any member of . . . the company shall absent himself from it, he shall lose all that would have fallen to his share. . . .

Hugo A. Rennert, *The Spanish Stage in the Time of Lope de Vega* (New York, 1909), 147–149.

Although the neoclassical mode never made a marked impact in Spain, its precepts were not unknown there. Lope de Vega, writing in 1609, made it clear that he was familiar with the neoclassical rules. After setting forth these rules, Lope goes on to explain the precepts he has followed in writing his plays and then concludes with these reflections:

These things you may regard as aphorisms which you get not from the ancient art. . . . Nobody can I call more barbarous than myself, since in defiance of art I dare to lay down precepts, and I allow myself to be borne along in the vulgar current, wherefore Italy and France call me ignorant. But what can I do if I have written 483 plays . . . ? For all of these, except six, gravely sin against art. Yet, in fine, I defend what I have written, and I know that, though they might have been better in another manner, they would not have had the vogue which they have had; for sometimes that which is contrary to what is just, for that very reason, pleases the taste.

Lope de Vega, *The New Art of Writing Plays in This Age* (1609), trans. William T. Brewster.

8
Italian Theatre to 1700

The late Middle Ages and the early Renaissance coexisted, for historians usually date both from about 1300, although they recognize that medieval elements remained dominant until well into the 1500s in many places. In addition, the same forces that undermined medieval culture were crucial in creating the culture of the Renaissance, for both the waning of the Middle Ages and the emergence of the Renaissance can be attributed in part to the decline of feudalism, the growth of cities, the increased power of princes, and challenges to church dominance over learning and life.

Perhaps most of all, the Renaissance is associated with a revived interest in the humanist ideals of the classical world. Humanism, as the name implies, marked a return to concern for the worth of humanity and earthly life, not merely as preparation for eternity but as valuable in themselves. Nevertheless, the humanists were not irreligious, for they championed human virtues and ideals grounded in Christian as well as classical teachings: justice, courtesy, magnanimity, integrity, loyalty, courage, and duty to self and others, including developing one's potentials to the fullest. They established as ideals those qualities they thought humans at their best capable of; these ideals were to dominate Western thought into the twentieth century. Yet, the humanists were not ascetics. They acknowledged the

pleasures of the flesh and the proneness of humans to temptation and error, but they also, explicitly or implicitly, judged all behavior by the standards of the humanist ideal. As the first champions of humanism, the classical world of Greece and Rome provided inspiration for Western Europe as its own interest in humanism revived.

As these new concerns grew, so did curiosity and the spirit of adventure. The Renaissance was an era of expansion, through geographical exploration, scientific experimentation, philosophical inquiry, and artistic creativity. In education the goal became the development of the universal human being skilled in many fields: science, politics, sports, and art.

There are many reasons why the Renaissance emerged first in Italy, causing its theatre to develop quite differently from that of England and Spain. Everywhere in Italy, the ruins of the old Roman Empire were an everyday reminder of past glories that could be recaptured. As the major terminus of trade routes to Asia and Africa, Italy was more strategically placed than the rest of Europe to absorb ideas from Byzantium, Islam, and other cultures. Trade with the eastern Mediterranean also produced the wealth needed by Italy to support the arts and learning. Additionally, Italy, as the seat of the Roman Catholic Church, was strongly affected by the controversies that afflicted the papacy beginning in the late thirteenth

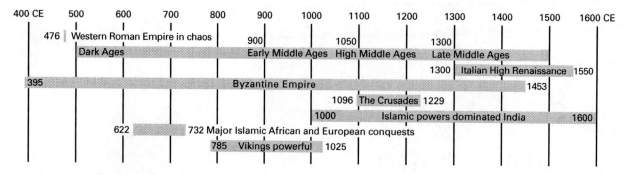

FIG. 8.1

From late Rome to the Renaissance, 400–1600 C.E.

century. The years of papal exile to Avignon in France (1305–1377), gave the rulers of the numerous Italian city-states an excuse to vie with each other for power and prestige and one way to secure them was through the support of artists, writers, and scholars. As patronage increased, the Renaissance flourished.

As appreciation for individual potential grew, the anonymous craftsmen and writers of the Middle Ages gave way to artists whose personal accomplishments were honored. In this new art, Biblical and theological subjects were often supplanted by classical myths, history, and invented stories. Renaissance art began in Italy around 1300 with Dante (1265–1321) who—though he treated a theological subject—took the Roman poet Virgil for his guide in *The Divine Comedy,* the first major literary work written in a modern vernacular language. In painting, Giotto (1266–1337) explored new paths after breaking with the stiff decorative style of medieval art. The Renaissance spirit was still more evident in the writings of Petrarch (1304–1374), who collected ancient manuscripts, urged scholars to study ancient Greece, modeled his style after Cicero and Seneca, and championed human over theological subjects. Boccaccio (1313–1375) too urged the study of the classics, compiled information about classical myths, wrote a spirited defense of secular authors, and celebrated the human lust for life in his collection of bawdy tales, *The Decameron.* But it was Manuel Chrysoloras (c. 1350–1415), a Byzantine diplomat who taught the Greek language in Florence in the late 1390s, who made it possible for a significant number of European humanists to finally read Greek texts.

RENAISSANCE DRAMA

In drama, the first sign of change was a new awareness of dramatic form that came from the study of Roman plays. The study of Latin plays had never been completely out of favor, but Seneca's tragedies had been read principally as illustrations of moral lessons or rhetorical display and the comedies of Terence and Plautus as models of oral style. During the fourteenth century a few persons began to appreciate the plays for their dramatic values and to compose imitations of them. The earliest tragedy, Albertino Mussato's *Eccerinus* (c. 1315), used a modified Senecan form but drew its subject matter from Christian doctrine. Beginning with *Achilles* (c. 1390) by Antonio Laschi, however, classical form and subject were united. Therefore, *Achilles* is frequently called the first Renaissance tragedy. Comedy in the classical mold also began to appear at this time. The oldest known example is Pier Paolo Vergerio's *Paulus* (1390), a satire on contemporary student life.

All of these early comedies and tragedies were written in Latin, and were probably not performed. Drama written in the vernacular did not appear until the early sixteenth century. By that time, other events had accelerated classical influence: In 1429, twelve of Plautus' lost plays were rediscovered; in 1453, the fall of Constantinople brought many scholars, along with manuscripts of Greek plays, to Italy; in 1465, the introduction of the printing press into Italy made the wide dissemination of classical texts possible, and between 1472 and 1518 all of the then-known Greek and Roman plays were published. Consequently, interest in classical drama, which had been confined principally to scholars, spread to the courts of the many small states into which Italy was then divided. Around 1485, Italian rulers began to finance productions of Roman plays. The desire to make the plays more accessible to courtly readers and spectators was probably the major motivation for translating the Roman plays into Italian and eventually for writing new plays in the vernacular.

New vernacular drama had been launched by 1508 with a production at the court of Ferrara of *The Casket (La Cassaria)* by Lodovico Ariosto (1474–1533). In this comedy, a favorite Roman plot (in which lovers are united following the discovery that the girl is the long-lost child of a rich father) is given a contemporary Italian setting. The development of vernacular comedy was also encouraged by Cardinal Bernardo Dovizi da Bibbiena's (1470–1529) *La Calandria* (1513), a successful blending of Roman and contemporary elements. Based in part upon Plautus's *Menaechmi*, Bibbiena's play uses twins of different sexes and reunites them only after subjecting them to a complicated intrigue based on disguises and illicit love affairs. This combination of traditional and contemporary materials served as a model for those who came after.

Another significant strain of comedy is exemplified by Niccolò Machiavelli's (1469–1527) *The Mandrake* (c. 1518), in which the subject matter is invented but the form borrowed from Roman comedy. Showing how a clever lover overcomes the hesitations of a virtuous young wife and cuckolds her overcredulous husband, the play is similar in tone to medieval farce. By 1540 a native comedy was well established and the numerous Italian dramatists of the time were the first in Renaissance Europe to master the techniques of Latin comedy and to adapt them to contemporary taste.

FIG. 8.2
The Italian states, showing places that figured prominently in theatrical development during the Renaissance.

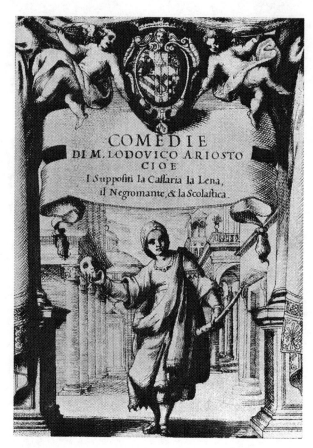

FIG. 8.3

Frontispiece to an edition of Ariosto's plays published in Rome, 1535.

The first important vernacular tragedy was *Sofonisba* (1515) by Giangiorgio Trissino (1478–1550). Following the example of the Greek tragedians, Trissino used a chorus of fifteen and avoided the division into acts. Trissino, with his deliberate attempt to counteract the pervasive influence of Seneca, launched a controversy that was to last for many years over the relative merits of Greek and Roman drama as suitable models for Italian authors. That this struggle was eventually won by the partisans of Rome was due in large part to the popularity of one author—Giambattista Giraldi Cinthio (1504–1574), whose *Orbecche* (1541), a tale of revenge in the Senecan manner, was the first tragedy written in Italian to be produced. After writing two other tragedies, *Dido* and *Cleopatra,* Cinthio turned to serious plays with happy endings because he found that audiences preferred this kind of plot. As a result, his late plays are essentially melodramas. Nevertheless, Cinthio influenced almost all of his successors, even those who avoided happy resolutions. No other serious dramatist rivaled Cinthio in

popularity, but several were admired both at home and abroad (Shakespeare's *Othello* is based on a novella by Cinthio) and did much to reestablish the tragic mode which had languished since Roman times. After 1550 Italian plays were read and translated with increasing frequency in France, Spain, and England, and consequently they exerted considerable influence on the emerging drama of those countries.

In addition to comedy and tragedy, pastoral drama also thrived in Renaissance Italy. This form perhaps developed out of the interest in the satyr plays of antiquity, although in the Renaissance the boisterous and licentious world of Greek satyrs gave way to an idyllic society of shepherds and nymphs. The principal subject was love, which usually triumphed over the many obstacles placed in its path. The first pastoral appeared in 1471, and the form reached a peak of popularity in the late sixteenth century with Torquato Tasso's *Aminta* (1573) and Giambattista Guarini's *The Faithful Shepherd* (1590), both of which were admired and imitated throughout Europe.

During the 200-year period, then, between the late fourteenth and the late sixteenth centuries, Renaissance drama developed in Italy. Today these Italian plays are considered artistically inferior and are seldom read or performed. They are valued primarily because they marked the first clear break with medieval practices and because they served as models for dramatists in other countries (especially England and France) where drama of more lasting value would be written. But it should be remembered that these plays were only parts, often very minor parts, of a larger artistic and political context. A dramatic performance was only one among many events offered at festivals and celebrations mounted to mark some special occasion.

MANNERISM AND THE BEGINNINGS OF THE BAROQUE

The challenges posed by Protestantism brought a new sense of purpose for the Roman Catholic Church, which convened the Council of Trent (1545–1563) to find the means to reassert its authority, discourage dissident opinion, and ensure orthodoxy. The immediate result was a curtailment of freedom at a time when Italy was already being forced to reassess its economic position as the fall of Constantinople had closed many of the traditional trade routes (shifting trade to the Atlantic coast nations of Portugal, Spain, and Holland). This lead to a sense of anxiety in Italy that was reflected in the visual arts by a self-conscious, static, and artificial visual style referred to as *mannerist.*

In theatre, it is reflected in the development of what many have come to view as an equally self-conscious and overly rigid approach known as Neoclassicism. But as the Catholic Church became reinvigorated by the changes it had made, and Italy found a new place for itself through banking, mannerism soon gave way to a new period, the *baroque*. This was a period of unprecedented self-confidence reflected by grandeur, richness, and monumentality in the visual arts, in which energy and movement were conveyed through the prolific use of elaboration, decoration, and the S-curved line. The baroque style dominated the visual arts of Europe in the seventeenth century and gradually influenced the design of stage sets and theatre buildings. Baroque thinking emphasized unity among the arts which brought new enthusiasm for the theatre, where so many of the arts naturally came together. It also sought to engage the viewer both physically and emotionally. The exact nature of that engagement in the theatre would be hotly debated by the neoclassicists and would become a major concern for the sentimentalists and Romantics of the eighteenth century.

THE NEOCLASSICAL IDEAL

In drama, the new concern for authority was first felt through the formulation of the neoclassical ideal. This had been given full expression in Italy by 1570, and thereafter it spread to the rest of Europe where it was to dominate criticism from the mid-seventeenth until the late eighteenth century.

Prior to 1550, interest in dramatic theory developed slowly and was concerned above all with two classical treatises: Horace's *Art of Poetry* and Aristotle's *Poetics*. Horace's work had never been lost and was often discussed, but Aristotle's was little known prior to 1498, when it was published in a Latin translation. The Council of Trent put new focus on *Poetics* when it adopted the teachings of St. Thomas Aquinas (1225–1274), who had drawn heavily on Aristotle's works, as the expression of the official position of the Church. In 1548 the first commentary on the *Poetics* was published (by Robortello), and in 1549 it was translated into Italian. Of the many treatises written on drama after 1550, almost all make use of Horace, but accept Aristotle as the primary authority. This approach is exemplified in the work of the three men—Antonio Minturno (?–1574), Julius Caesar Scaliger (1494–1558), and Lodovico Castelvetro (1501–1571)—who laid the foundation for what we now call the neoclassical ideal.

Neoclassicism follows Aristotle in reducing all "regular" drama to two basic forms, comedy and tragedy, each having their own normative patterns. Tragedy was said to draw its characters from the ruling classes (though Aristotle had suggested people of significance, without reference to class), to base its stories on history or mythology, to have unhappy endings, and to employ a lofty and poetic style. Comedy was said to draw its characters from the middle or lower classes, to base its stories on domestic and private affairs, to have happy endings, and to imitate the style of everyday speech. Other forms were considered inferior because they were "mixed." Consequently, "purity of dramatic form"—that is, no intermingling of comic and serious elements—was demanded.

Neoclassicism followed Horace in insisting that plays be divided into five acts and in stating that their main function was "to teach and to please." Comedy was said to teach by ridiculing behavior that should be avoided, tragedy by showing the horrifying results of mistakes and misdeeds. Because the neoclassicists wished to depict drama as a useful tool, they tended to emphasize the instructional over the pleasurable potentials of drama.

The fundamental demand of neoclassicism, however, was for verisimilitude, or the appearance of truth. A complex concept, verisimilitude may be divided into three subsidiary goals: reality, morality, and universality.

Reality tended to be discussed in terms of believability. Fantasy and supernatural events were to be avoided because they were not part of human experience, but if they were integral parts of some received story from myth, history, or the Bible, they would be believable to the audience and could be used. Soliloquies were discouraged on the grounds that it is unnatural for characters to speak aloud while alone or to discuss private matters in the presence of a large group like a chorus. A *confidant* (trusted companion), on the other hand, was someone to whom the principal characters could believably reveal their inmost secrets. Battles, crowd scenes, violence, and deaths were to be kept offstage on the premise that it was too difficult to represent such occurrences convincingly onstage.

The "three unities" of time, place, and action were in some ways offshoots of this concern with reality or believability. The unity of time was first advocated around 1543 on the basis that since an audience knows it has been in the theatre for only a few hours, it cannot be convinced that long periods of time have elapsed and therefore a play should take no longer to occur than the actual events would take in real life. But Aristotle had said the best tragedies covered the events of one day, which at first was taken to mean daylight hours but eventually was extended to a twenty-four–hour period. The unity of place was proposed in 1570 on the same basis, that the audience knows it has been in only one place, so it cannot accept any change of locale. Later this was modified to say that locations that could logically be reached within a twenty-four–hour period could be believably included. The unity of action was the only one of the three advocated by Aristotle, who considered it essential to the absolute focus a drama should have, and eventually all three unities were seen to be advantageous to the building of dramatic intensity.

The neoclassical concept of reality was considerably modified by another demand—that drama teach moral lessons. A dramatist was not merely to copy life, but to reveal its ideal moral patterns, that is, to show the world over which God reigns as a reflection of His power and justice. Wickedness was to be punished and good rewarded. Aberrations in the workings of justice were recognized as part of life, but were thought unsuitable subjects for dramatic art, which should only be concerned with ultimate truth.

Both reality and morality were further modified by still another demand—for universality. No moral purpose could be served by a detailed representation of reality because truth was to be found only in common characteristics, not in a welter of surface details. Those characteristics that vary from one example to another were accidental and therefore not essential parts of truth. It was in the universals, the typical and normative traits that are discoverable through the rational and systematic examination of phenomena, that truth was to be found. Since these norms were considered to embody truth in its most essential form—one that remains unchanged regardless of historical period or geographical location—they were declared the foundation upon which all drama creation and criticism should rest.

This concept of norms was extended to characterization, since the dramatist was expected to write about the permanent aspects of human nature rather than those peculiar to one time and place. In establishing norms (or the proper *decorum* for characters), all humanity was categorized according to age, rank, sex, profession, and predispositions, and the attributes of each were described. As a result, neoclassical drama tended to depict types, who prosper if they observe the appropriate decorum and who are punished when they deviate from it.

The concept of norms also extended to costume and scenic practices. No purpose could be served by attempting to bring individuality to a costume or specificity to a setting. Costumes illustrated character types; scenery represented types of locations.

Both could be used over and over in many different plays.

Although many of the neoclassical principles now seem arbitrary and restrictive, they were an attempt to define the world that playwrights should seek to mirror in their works and as such were widely accepted as reasonable and desirable among critics and scholars from about 1570 until after 1750. Neoclassical principles were rarely championed by theatre professionals, yet when they did write about their work in this period, it was generally to take credit for the ways in which they adhered to neoclassicism or to justify their deviations from it.

During the sixteenth century the neoclassical rules were little known outside of educated circles (or outside of Italy), however, and the plays written in accordance with them did not reach large audiences. Tragedy met a mixed reception even with educated groups, and comedy, which was produced primarily at court, was popular in part because of the *intermezzi* inserted between the acts.

INTERMEZZI AND OPERA

Intermezzi were descended from the *mascherata* of carnival time and the entertainments given at court on special occasions. (For a discussion of their early history, see Chapter 5.) They were first coupled with comedies in the late fifteenth century. The principal appeal of *intermezzi* lay in their scenery, costumes, lights, special effects, music, and dance: Dialogue was used only when the allegorical plots had to be explained. Since entertainments were given at court almost solely on such special occasions as betrothals, weddings, births, and state visits, *intermezzi* were often used to pay elaborate compliments to those being honored by drawing parallels between mythological figures and contemporary persons. Thus, not only were they stunning as spectacle, they were instruments of power, politics, and diplomacy.

Intermezzi were typically presented in groups of six, a prologue, four to fill the intervals between the five acts of a regular drama, and one as an afterpiece. At first this interruption of a dramatic action with allegorical spectacle met considerable opposition, but the *intermezzi* soon become more popular than the plays they accompanied. Originally, the various *intermezzi* seen on a single occasion had no connection with each other or with the play being performed. Gradually, however, they were often related both to each other and to the theme of the main drama. Critics became fond of likening *intermezzi* to the choral interludes of Greek drama.

FIG. 8.4

Costume designs by Bernardo Buontalenti for an *intermezzo* at the Uffizi palace, Florence, 1589. Courtesy Theatre Museum, Victoria and Albert Museum.

Since the *intermezzi* depended upon spectacle, they motivated many experiments with scenery. Furthermore, the need to change settings rapidly for the alternating segments of plays and *intermezzi* encouraged the development of new devices for shifting scenery. In the seventeenth century, the *intermezzi* were gradually absorbed into opera, although for a time they were performed between the acts of this new form as they had been with comedy. By 1650, they had virtually disappeared.

Opera grew out of attempts by the Camerata of Florence to recreate Greek tragedies in the late sixteenth century. Their first full-length work, and the first "opera," was *Dafne* (1594). The dialogue and choral passages were recited or chanted to a musical accompaniment, which served merely to enhance the dramatic effectiveness of the dialogue. From this simple beginning, opera grew into one of the major art forms of the baroque era and in Italy, displaced interest in spoken drama.

Until 1637, however, opera remained principally an entertainment of the nobility. In that year, however, an opera house was opened in Venice to make the form available to the general public. So successful was this venture that between 1640 and 1700 four opera houses operated regularly in Venice, a city of about 140,000 people. From Venice, opera spread throughout Italy and then to the rest of Europe. All of the scenic wonders of the court

intermezzi were incorporated and elaborated in opera. Consequently, when opera was imported into other countries, so were Italian scenic practices.

THE DEVELOPMENT OF NEW SCENIC PRACTICES

Although interest in classical drama revived in the fourteenth century, no ancient play was performed until 1486, when the Roman Academy (an association of wealthy individuals who shared common interests), began its experiments with Roman comedy. In that year Vitruvius's *De Architectura* (*c.* 15 B.C.E.) was finally published. This was the primary source of information on Greek and Roman theatre buildings and staging practices. It had been studied since its rediscovery in 1414 but it contained no illustrations for its sometimes cryptic descriptions. By 1521 it would be translated into Italian and there would be numerous commentaries and critical editions, but in 1486 the Roman Academy, under the leadership of Pomponius Laetus (1424–1498), was doing pioneering work in seeking to attempt the first reconstruction of a Roman stage based on this text.

Young men from all over Europe studied in Rome at this time and some certainly saw these early experiments by Laetus, which were later copied in Ferrara (where twenty-two plays by Plautus and Terence were performed by 1505), and Urbino. One of these men, Jodius Bodius Ascensius (1462–1535), was involved in the performances at Ferrara and later supervised the illustrations for an edition of Terence's plays printed by Johannes Treschel at Lyon, France, in 1493. This was the first edition to show a reconstruction of a Roman stage, and if it does not directly reflect the work of Laetus, it at least reflects the general thinking of the time. In these illustrations, a stage area is backed by a continuous façade, either straight or angled and divided into a series of curtained openings, each representing the house of a different character. These illustrations were imitated in a Venetian edition of Terence's comedies in 1497 and thereafter were used throughout Europe. Some scholars have argued that during the sixteenth century this "Terence stage" was in use almost everywhere, especially in schools, but others argue that there is insufficient evidence to prove this. If stages of this type were widely used, they must also have been regularly modified to allow for the addition of perspective, which was soon to have a greater influence on the stage than even Vitruvius.

FIG. 8.5
The "Terence Stage." Note the several doors, with the names of characters above them, an arrangement characteristic of this type of stage. From the edition of Terence's plays published at Lyon (France) in 1493.

Although perspective developed over a long period, its systemization is usually credited to the architect, Filippo Brunelleschi (1377–1446) and the painter Masaccio (1401–1428) around 1425. But it was Leon Battista Alberti's *Della Pittura* (1435), the first treatise on the subject, that disseminated practical directions for making perspective drawings. Alberti's understanding of perspective was limited, however, for with his method all objects had to be drawn as if parallel to the picture plane. It was not until the time of Leonardo da Vinci (1452–1519) that space was perceived as spherical, curving away from the viewer in all directions. But it would take almost a century to learn how to transfer that kind of perspective onto the various flat surfaces of a stage setting.

It is difficult now to appreciate the fascination that perspective drawing, with its seemingly magical ability to manipulate illusion, exerted on the Renaissance mind. But perspective settings may have been used in theatre as early as the 1480s, although the first documented use dates to 1508 when Pellegrino da San Daniele used perspective for the backdrop of Ariosto's *The Casket*, done at Ferrara. Around 1513, a single set of wings was added to such backdrops and shortly thereafter additional wings were being included. So by the 1540s the arrangement of wings and backdrops had taken the form it would follow, with only minor elaborations, for the next 250 years.

Originally, artists used perspective as a way of capturing Vitruvius's description of classical theatrical settings:

Tragic scenes are delineated with columns, pediments, statues, and other objects suited to kings; comic scenes exhibit private dwellings with balconies and views representing rows of windows after the manner of ordinary dwellings; satyric scenes are decorated with trees, caverns, mountains, and other rustic objects delineated in landscape style.

But Vitruvius's overall purpose had been to provide a guide for laying out the ideal Roman city. Renaissance artists were fascinated by the "ideal city" concept and sought in their stage settings to embody various aspects of it by depicting in the tragic scene, the royal and ceremonial sections of a town, and in the comic scene those neighborhoods occupied by ordinary citizens.

FIG. 8.6
The ancient theatre according to fifteenth-century humanists. Frontispiece to an edition of Plautus's plays published in Venice, 1511.

FIG. 8.7
Serlio's comic scene. From Serlio's *Architettura*, book 2, 1569 edition. Courtesy Fine Arts Library, Indiana University.

FIG. 8.8
Serlio's tragic scene. From Serlio's *Architettura*, book 2, 1569 edition. Courtesy Fine Arts Library, Indiana University.

The practices of the early sixteenth century are recorded in Sebastiano Serlio's (1475–1554) *Architettura* (1545) This was the first Renaissance work on architecture to devote a section to the theatre and it included illustrations of the tragic, comic, and satyric scenes, described by Vitruvius—illustrations that would later be reprinted in editions of Vitruvius's *De Architectura,* thereby encouraged readers to transpose Vitruvius's descriptions into perspective settings. Serlio was heavily indebted to other artists, especially Baldassare Peruzzi (1481–1537), a major early designer of perspective settings, with whom he had studied, so the practices he describes are probably typical of his time. Since Serlio's work was circulated throughout Europe, it was a prime disseminator of Italian ideas abroad.

Serlio took for granted that theatres would be set up in already existing rooms, for that was the standard practice at the time. Vitruvius's description of the semicircular auditorium in Roman theatres was therefore fitted into a rectangular space by constructing stadium-like seating around an orchestra (used almost exclusively to seat the ruler and his attendants). There was nothing Vitruvian about his stage, however, as it was designed primarily for the display of perspective scenery. A narrow front portion of the stage floor was level, since it was intended for use by the actors, but back of this the floor sloped upward at a sharp angle so as to increase the illusion of distance. All scenery

was placed on this raked portion. Since the perspective scenery was designed so that the ideal view of it was seen from the chair in the center of the orchestra, the height of the stage was determined by the eye level of the spectator sitting there.

FIG. 8.9
Serlio's pastoral scene. From Serlio's *Architettura*, book 2, 1569 edition. Courtesy Fine Arts Library, Indiana University.

FIG. 8.10
Cross-section of Serlio's hall stage.

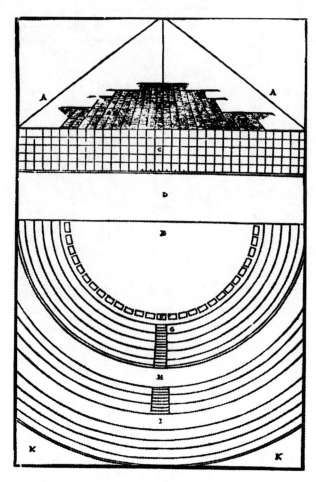

FIG. 8.11
Ground plan of Serlio's hall stage.

Serlio considered his perspective renderings of Vitruvius's three sets adequate to meet the needs of all plays. Each one required four sets of wings, the first three angled, and the fourth flat, as well as a backdrop. The wings closest to the audience were given many three-dimensional details and some even had open arcades and galleries. Although Serlio mentioned no framing device for his stage pictures, the downstage wings probably extended to the walls of the hall, and a valance probably limited the overhead view to preserve the illusion. By 1560 a temporary proscenium arch provided this framing device, and by 1586 that arch was made permanent.

Serlio's settings were conceived in architectural terms and the changeover from one to another was a substantial undertaking. When *intermezzi* were performed, pageant wagons were drawn into the space just forward of the stage, or portable set pieces were carried onto the platform, but his set remained fixed. Shortly after Serlio's treatise was published, however, interest in spectacle increased sufficiently to create a demand for settings that could change during performances. Vitruvius had described the use of *periaktoi* to facilitate such changes. These were prism-shaped units that rotated on a central axis showing a different picture on each of its three faces. So Renaissance artists, like Aristotile de San Gallo (1481–1551) attempted to recreate *periaktoi*, as he did at Castro in 1543. They were in use at Florence by 1569, and in 1583 Giacomo Barozzi da Vignola (1507–1573) recommended structures with from two to six sides, as a means of changing sets, in his book, *The Two Rules of Perspective Practice*.

When Nicola Sabbattini (1574–1654) published his *Manual for Constructing Theatrical Scenes and Machines* (1638), he was able to describe two additional methods for changing a set. In the first, new wings were maneuvered around those already in place. In the second, new painted canvas coverings were pulled quickly around the wings to conceal the previously visible scene. In addition, Sabbattini explained how to change the backdrop using several flat wings mounted in such a way that they could be turned like pages in a book or by sliding flat wings in grooves.

The ultimate solution to scene shifting required that all angled wings be replaced with flat wings, but this change had to await new developments in perspective drawing. Throughout the sixteenth century,

FIG. 8.12
Joseph Furttenbach's plan and section of a stage showing the use of *periaktoi,* bow-shaped borders, and a rear pit for special effects. From *Die Theater Weins* (1899).

the angled wings had been painted in position: The vanishing point was established on the back wall of the stage and a cord was anchored there; this cord was then stretched downstage and used to determine the relative height and size of all the details to be painted on the angled wings. Drawing was, therefore, relatively simple, for the two faces of each wing were treated as different sides of a single structure, one parallel and the other at an angle to the picture plane. On flat wings, however, all details had to be depicted on a series of surfaces set parallel to the picture plane. The problems of transferring a perspective picture to a series of flat wings were not adequately solved until 1600, when Guido Ubaldus's *Six Books of Perspective* was published. The first application of Ubaldus's principles to stage settings composed entirely of flat wings has been attributed to Giovan Battista Aleotti (1546–1636) at Ferrara in 1606, but flat-wing settings were probably in use elsewhere prior to this time. By 1650 angled wings were considered to be outmoded.

Using flat wings, any number of settings could be easily shifted. At each wing position as many flats as there were settings could be set up, one immediately behind the other. Changes were accomplished simply by withdrawing the set of visible wings to reveal another set behind them. To support the flats and to permit their easy movement on and off stage, grooves were installed on the stage floor and overhead. The back scene was normally painted on two flats (or shutters) which met at the center of the stage, although backdrops that could be rolled up would eventually be used.

Until about 1650, most scenes, following classical practice, showed exteriors. Consequently, overhead masking was usually painted to represent the sky or clouds. Sometimes an unbroken canvas was mounted to curve over the entire setting, but as flying machinery of various sorts became common, a bow-shaped border was hung above each set of wings. When interior settings were introduced, the borders were painted to represent ceilings, beams, domes, or other appropriate details.

By the early seventeenth century, then, the three basic elements of Italian settings were the side wings, back shutters, and overhead borders, and all could be changed simultaneously. At first, many stagehands were utilized to make quick changes, but the results were not entirely satisfactory, since it was difficult to synchronize the movements of so many persons precisely.

The next significant step was the chariot-and-pole system of scene changing, usually credited to Giacomo Torelli (1608–1678), who perfected it at the Teatro Novissimo in Venice between 1641 and 1645 (see Fig. 8.13). Torelli cut slots through the

FIG. 8.13

Diagram of chariot-and-pole shifting mechanism. A = the tracks in which the chariots ride; B and C = chariots; D = the stage walls; E = the stage floor; F, G, H, and I = the lines, pulleys, and levers that operate the system. From Rees, *Cyclopedia,* 20 (1803).

stage floor so that upright supports (poles or ladders) could pass through. These poles, on which flats were mounted above the floor level, were attached beneath the stage to "chariots" that ran in tracks parallel to the front of the stage. As the chariots rolled toward the center of the stage they carried flats into view, while the opposite movement took them out of sight. By means of an elaborate system of ropes and pulleys, every part of a setting could be attached to a single winch which, when turned, changed all of the elements simultaneously. This innovation, which at first seemed magical in its ability to produce transformations, was soon adopted almost universally in Europe, where it was to be the standard method of shifting scenery until the late nineteenth century. The older and simpler groove system would persist principally in England, Holland, and America.

The advent of the flat wing coincided with and probably facilitated the development of the baroque visual style that began to take shape in theatre around 1600. As long as angled wings had predominated, each wing usually represented a separate building, a tradition that persisted for a time with flat wings. But this convention did not lend itself to effects of grandeur and, as the taste for monumentality grew during the seventeenth century, the former series of buildings gave way to a sequence of columns, porticos, or other architectural features that were treated as parts of a single structure. This change increased both the unity and the apparent size of stage settings. These trends

FIG. 8.14
Torelli's setting for Act III of Strozzi's opera, *La Finta Pazza*, the work that launched Torelli's career in Venice in the early 1640s. Courtesy Theatersammlung, Osterreichische Nationalbibliothek, Vienna.

foreshadowed and probably helped create the visual style that was to become so elaborate during the baroque era. His finest work was done in 1589 in connection with the festivities honoring the marriage of the Grand Duke Ferdinand I, when three weeks were devoted to masquerades, animal hunts, water shows, comedies with *intermezzi,* and numerous other events. Buontalenti's fertile genius enriched the court spectacles with highly imaginative costumes, scenery, machinery, and special effects. He was succeeded by his pupil Giulio Parigi (*c.* 1570–1635), who designed major festivals in 1606, 1608, and 1616, of which many engravings have survived. It was from Parigi that Inigo Jones learned much that he applied in staging English masques between 1605 and 1640, and Cosmi Lotti learned what he took to the court of Spain from 1626 to 1643. It was also from Parigi that Joseph Furttenbach (1591–1667) absorbed many of the ideas that he was to take back to Germany and

toward monumentality were not completed until the eighteenth century, when the baroque style in scene design reached its fullest expression.

By the late seventeenth century, the box setting (enclosed on three sides and with a ceiling) seems already to have been developed in Italy. In *Construction of Theatres and Theatrical Machinery* (1668), Fabrizio Carini Motta (1627–1699), director of theatrical activities in Mantua for almost thirty years, describes how box settings are to be created by mounting two-part flats on each chariot, one part attached to the pole, the other hinged so it can be folded out to fill in the space between the wings.

Since scenic design was long an adjunct of architecture or painting, many of Italy's finest artists designed scenery in the years between 1490 and 1650. Because designers moved about frequently, essentially the same scenic conventions were current throughout Italy. The prestige to be gained through lavish productions encouraged many rulers, notably those of Ferrara, Florence, Mantua, Urbino, Milan, and Rome, to patronize the theatre. Scenic grandeur was especially highly developed under the Medicis at Florence, and reached its peak there in the work of Bernardo Buontalenti (1536–1608), who served as architect and supervisor of entertainments at the Medici court for nearly sixty years. Buontalenti's work

FIG. 8.15
First *intermezzo* of an evening's entertainment entitled *The Liberation of Tyrrhenus,* performed in Florence at the Medici court at carnival time, 1616. The setting is by Guilio Parigi. Etching by Jacques Callot.

disseminate through his books, *Civil Architecture* (1628), *Recreational Architecture* (1640), and *The Noble Mirror of Art* (1663).

With the opening of the Venetian public opera houses beginning in 1637, scenic splendor was made available to the general public. From opera it spread to the other dramatic forms and to the public playhouses. By the end of the seventeenth century, Italian scenic practices had been adopted almost everywhere in Europe. By that time also, scene design had become more nearly the province of the painter than of the architect.

DEVELOPMENT OF THEATRE ARCHITECTURE

In spite of the great interest in theatrical production, plays were presented by courts and academies only on special occasions. Therefore, the need for permanent theatres was slow in arising. Many early productions were given out-of-doors in courtyards or gardens, but during the sixteenth century banqueting halls or other large rooms became the typical sites. These temporary theatres were usually arranged in the manner described by Serlio.

Some permanent theatres were built during the sixteenth century. Allegedly a theatre at Ferrara burned in 1532, and an elaborate theatre was created within Florence's Uffizi palace in 1586. The oldest surviving Renaissance theatre, however, is the Teatro Olimpico, built between 1580 and 1584 by the Olympic Academy of Vicenza. Founded in 1555 to study Greek tragedy, this academy at first used temporary stages for its occasional productions.

FIG. 8.16
Interior of the Teatro Olimpico as it appears today.

FIG. 8.17
Ground plan of the Teatro Olimpico. From Streit, *Das Theater* (1903).

When the members decided to build a permanent theatre, Andrea Palladio (1518–1580), eminent architect, student of Vitruvius and of Roman ruins, and a member of the academy, undertook to reproduce a classical theatre inside a preexisting building. In the Teatro Olimpico, semi-elliptical seating curves around a small orchestra. The rectangular stage, 82 feet wide by 25 feet deep, is enclosed at the back and ends by a façade decorated with pillars, niches, statues, and bas-reliefs. Five openings pierce the façade, one at either end and three at the back. The overall effect is that of a miniature Roman odeon. Palladio died before the theatre was completed, and his work was finished by Vincenzo Scamozzi (1552–1616), who added (as Palladio seems to have intended) street scenes built in perspective behind each of the stage openings to create the impression that the stage is a city square into which a number of streets lead. Each spectator has a view down at least one of the streets. These vistas still remain as permanent parts of the stage. The theatre opened in 1585 with a production of *Oedipus Rex,* about which so much information has been preserved that it could be recreated today with considerable accuracy.

The Teatro Olimpico was designed for the performance of tragedy, and it served as the inspiration for a smaller theatre built by Scamozzi at Sabbioneta in 1588 for the performance of comedy. As the only two surviving sixteenth-century theatres, they are of considerable importance in showing the evolution of theatre architecture. Both, however, were used for only a very short time and neither was in the main line of development in theatre architecture.

FIG. 8.18
Ground plan of the Teatro Farnese, Parma. From Streit, *Das Theater* (1903).

The prototype of the modern stage is usually considered to be that of the Teatro Farnese at Parma (designed by Giovan Battista Aleotti, completed in 1618 and first used in 1628), since it is the oldest surviving structure with a permanent proscenium arch. But that stage was certainly not the first to use a proscenium arch. The oldest extant depiction of a proscenium arch is found in a drawing made around 1560 by Bartolomeo Neroni (*c.* 1500–1571), but that arch was probably temporary. The theatre built by Buontalenti in the Uffizi palace in Florence in 1586, however, certainly had a structurally permanent proscenium arch (see Figure 8.15), perhaps Europe's first. The destruction of the Uffizi theatre in the eighteenth century left the Teatro Farnese our oldest surviving example of the picture-frame stage, although it is in part a reconstruction, having been heavily damaged during World War II.

FIG. 8.19
Auditorium of the Teatro Farnese. The floor is left free for dancing, water ballets, and other uses. The ducal box is located above the entrance at center left. From Streit, *Das Theater* (1903).

FIG. 8.20
Proscenium wall of the Teatro Farnese, 1618. From Streit, *Das Theater* (1903).

The proscenium came into use only gradually. In early sixteenth-century settings, the first pair of wings and an overhead valance provided sufficient masking. But as the desire to change settings increased, so did the need for downstage masking to conceal the changes. For a time, the first set of angle wings was neutralized to blend with the various settings; in some temporary theatres, an appropriate proscenium arch was erected for each new production. But in permanent theatres the desirability of a permanent framing device was clear, especially after the flat wing was adopted. Consequently, during the seventeenth century the architectural proscenium arch became standard.

The usefulness of an arch was not restricted to the front of the stage; the Teatro Farnese (as well as many later theatres) had two additional frames further back on the stage. This feature encouraged the use of settings of varying depths, since the openings made it easy to increase or restrict the visible stage space. The concept of internal arches increased in importance as the desire for grandeur and monumentality grew during the baroque era. The opening between the last set of wings came to serve as a second frame behind which a deep perspective vista was placed.

Although the stage of the Teatro Farnese may serve as the prototype of virtually all those that were to follow during the next 300 years, its auditorium was still that of a conventional court theatre. In it, U-shaped, stadium-like seating surrounded a large open space that could be used for dancing or for other forms of spectacle. (During the initial production, this space was even flooded for a water spectacle.) The prototype of the later auditorium is found in the public theatres.

The professional public theatre began to emerge in Italy during the second half of the sixteenth century. The first record of an Italian public theatre building is found in 1565 at Venice. By the early seventeenth century there were a number of public theatre buildings, although none was elaborate. Major architectural innovations did not come until the San Cassiano opera house was built in Venice in 1637. But the only extant seventeenth-century plan of a Venetian opera house is that for the SS. Giovanni e Paolo, built in 1639. It shows five balconies, each with twenty-nine boxes. The first two levels, the most expensive, were patronized by the wealthier classes; the upper three were used by persons of lesser rank and wealth; the open area on the ground floor (the pit or *parterre*) attracted those to whom propriety was unimportant. The arrangement of tiers, one above the other, permitted large numbers of persons to be accommodated in a restricted space, and the division of the tiers into boxes permitted small groups or families to attend the theatre without mingling with the general public.

Although the Venetian opera houses established one prototype of the "pit, box, and gallery" auditorium, they were not without precedents, for many of the theatres erected for the religious plays of the Middle Ages had employed variations on this arrangement, and less elaborate versions of it were used for the public theatres of Paris, London, and Madrid before opera houses were opened in Venice. Nevertheless, the prestige of opera gave approval to the pattern that was to dominate auditorium design until the end of the nineteenth century. Furthermore, since the Venetian opera houses also incorporated the proscenium arch, elaborate machines, and perspective scenery, they were the first public theatres to include all of the features that were to be most characteristic of the picture-frame stage.

MACHINERY AND SPECIAL EFFECTS

Much of the wonder inspired by the productions at courts and academies resulted from special effects. Continuing and elaborating on medieval practice, the Renaissance machinists arranged seemingly magical transformations, and made gods, monsters, and mythological creatures appear on the sea, in the air, in Heaven, or in Hades. Just as playwrights turned to classical subjects, the machinists found justification for their work in Pollux's list of machines and Aristotle's inclusion of spectacle as one of the six basic parts of drama. Even in plays that observed unity of

FIG. 8.21

A public theatre of the early seventeenth century, thought to be in Centro (Italy). Drawing by G. F. B. Guercino. Courtesy British Museum.

place, spectacle was often introduced to reduce the austerity imposed by a single setting. Typically, however, elaborate special effects were reserved for *intermezzi* or operas.

Much of the spectacle depended upon machinery for "flying." Gods appeared frequently to resolve the dramatic action, and these and other mythological characters were suspended above the stage in chariots, on clouds, or on the backs of animals or birds. From one to fifty figures might be shown in "the glory" of a brightly lighted paradise formed of clouds. To achieve these effects, appropriately shaped figures, such as chariots, horses, or clouds, were made of wood and canvas and then painted. Since the overhead space was limited in theatres of this period, beams with tracks for casters overhead, in combination with fulcrums, ropes, and pulleys at the sides of the stage, allowed objects or characters to be flown into and out of view. Some structures were hinged to fold up in the overhead space and to unfold as they descended. Ingenious riggings were devised for moving objects up and down stage while they were suspended in the air. In many productions transformations were masked by clouds that engulfed the stage (as painted cloths or flats were lowered from above or moved on from the sides); the transformed scene was then revealed as the clouds dissipated.

FIG. 8.22
Design by Bernardo Buontalenti for the *Harmony of the Spheres,* an *intermezzo* given at the Uffizi palace in Florence, 1589. The design also illustrates the use of "glories." Courtesy Theatre Museum, Victoria and Albert Museum, London.

Other effects depended on trapdoors in the stage floor. Since the temporary theatres used platforms only about four to six feet high, the working space beneath the stage was restricted. Nevertheless, the effects were elaborate: mountains, rocks, trees, and other objects rose and sank. Most of these objects were painted on cloths or were hinged so they might collapse into the limited below-stage space. To create the effect of a ghost rising through the floor, for example, a figure was painted on cloth, attached to a pole, and elevated through a slot in the floor. Through traps characters appeared or disappeared, and objects and persons were transformed through substitutions from beneath the stage.

Fire and smoke were common. Sabbattini describes a device for making flames seem to rise out of the earth, and an arrangement of fire in front and in back of actors to make it appear that they are dancing in flames.

The popularity of sea scenes motivated the invention of several devices for simulating waves. In one,

a large sheet of painted cloth was moved up and down rhythmically by means of cords attached to its underside; in another, a series of two-dimensional pieces shaped like waves as seen from the front were moved in such a way that as one line of waves rose, another lowered to simulate the movement of the sea; in a third, a series of long, spiral cylinders was rotated one behind the other to create the sense of waves swelling and falling. Sometimes a sufficient number of units were utilized so that changes from calm to storm, from darkness to light, and various other conditions at sea could be simulated.

Ships, whales, and dolphins moved through the waves. To create the proper illusion, miniatures were usually mounted on poles and operated from beneath the stage. When ships had to accommodate a number of people, they were mounted on casters and pulled across the stage by means of concealed ropes. One of the *intermezzi* designed by Buontalenti at Florence in 1589 showed Amphitrite moving through the waves on a shell accompanied by dolphins and

Tritons; then a ship bearing twenty men sailed into view as a watchman in the crow's nest sang a song and a dolphin danced in the waves below.

Sometimes spectacles demanded that walls, fortified castles, or other buildings collapse. In these instances, the scenery was constructed in sections (like building blocks) and held together by concealed bars; when the bars were removed, the structures fell.

Sound was also important. Thunder was created by rolling cannon balls or stones down a rough channel; wind was simulated by whirling thin-layered strips of wood through the air rapidly.

The front curtain might also be considered a special effect, since it was used to conceal the scenic wonders and to increase amazement when they were suddenly revealed. It was used only to begin performances and never to divide them into acts. At first, the curtain was dropped; but, since this created too many hazards, the roll curtain (which wound the curtain into the space above the proscenium), or the divided curtain (that could be pulled to the side), was eventually adopted.

MUSIC AND DANCE

Music and dance were integral parts of Italian ceremonies, festivals, and theatrical presentations. They are referred to so often in accounts of performances that both obviously were used liberally. Music often continued throughout a procession, pageant, ceremony, or other theatrical event. It might be vocal or instrumental, solo or in various combinations. Before 1600, it figured most prominently in the *intermezzi*, in which it accompanied the numerous songs and dances and much of the primarily pantomimic action. It was also played during scene shifts to bridge scenes and to disguise unwanted noise.

With the coming of opera, music played an even more prominent role. A considerable amount of music has survived from this period, but unfortunately we can associate very few of these pieces with particular performances. Even with opera, few libretti can be assigned to specific musical scores. Thus, our understanding of the musical element in theatrical entertainments of this period is more general than precise.

This conclusion is even more applicable to dance, since for dance there was no equivalent of a musical score or dramatic text to record it. What remains are some pictorial illustrations and verbal descriptions. Nevertheless, we know that dance contributed much to theatrical entertainments and that in this period the foundations of ballet were laid (to be more fully exploited in the *ballet de cour*, the French variation on the *intermezzi*).

FIG. 8.23
An outdoor carnival pageant, *The War of Love*, at the Medici court, 1615. The procession includes pageant wagons representing Africa and Asia. Etching by Jacques Callot.

THE FESTIVAL CONTEXT

Much of the information we have about Italian theatrical performances in the sixteenth and seventeenth centuries has survived because the performances were included in festivals, which were then memorialized in engravings and descriptions. All the elements that made up a festival were treated as parts of an overall design and all were related to some theme, usually one that suggested parallels between the occasion being celebrated and some significant story drawn from classical mythology.

For these festivals, the Italian courts revived many of the spectacles of the Roman Empire and continued others from the Middle Ages. Roman triumphal entries were transformed into *trionfi*: elaborately choreographed processions with pageant wagons and costumed classical or allegorical figures. One of the most elaborate of these processions was mounted in Florence in 1566 as *A Masque of the Genealogy of the Gods* with twenty-one pageant wagons and 392 costumed mythological figures, all designed by Giorgio Vasari (1511–1574), many of whose drawings for this pageant still survive. Water spectacles (*naumachiae*) were also revived. Usually they were presented on rivers, but at times flooded courtyards and other structures were used. Perhaps the most elaborate *naumachia* was *The Battle of the Argonauts*, given on the Arno River in Florence in 1608 as one event among others for a court festival. After 1600, the kind of spectacle developed earlier in *intermezzi* began to be staged quite apart from plays.

STAGE LIGHTING

Although some of the medieval courtly entertainments had been performed indoors, it was not until the sixteenth century that indoor productions were common. At that time, techniques for lighting the auditorium and the stage had to be devised.

The illuminants available were candles and oil lamps. Candles were preferred for the auditorium because they smoked less and had a more pleasant odor than oil. Usually the auditorium was lighted by chandeliers hung just in front of the stage, illuminating both the auditorium and a portion of the platform.

The downstage acting area was also lighted by footlights, often mounted behind a parapet placed a short distance in front of the stage. Sabbattini states that the smoke from footlights and chandeliers often created a haze, and other writers comment upon the heat and fumes. The lights mounted on stage were concealed behind overhead or side masking pieces. Several oil lamps were placed in evenly spaced rings attached to vertical poles set up behind the proscenium and each

of the wing positions. Other lamps were mounted on horizontal battens in back of the front valance and each of the borders. To increase efficiency, reflectors made from tinsel, mica, or polished basins were placed behind the lamps.

At least three methods of darkening the stage were used: Lamps were extinguished (although this was awkward if the lights had to brighten again); open cylinders were suspended above the lamps and lowered over them to darken the stage or raised to brighten it; or all lamps might be mounted on rotating poles that could be turned either toward or away from the visible portions of the stage. When exceptionally bright light was required, some scenic device such as a cloud, shell, or grotto was equipped with a downstage rim inside which lamps could be concealed and directed toward persons or objects inside the structure.

Sometimes the sun, moon, or lightning was shown. At Florence in 1539, San Gallo filled a crystal sphere with water and lighted it from behind with candles to form a sun that rose at the beginning of the play, moved across the sky, and set as the action closed. The moon was often represented in similar fashion. Bolts of lightning were made from jagged pieces of wood covered with tinsel and shot across the stage on wires. Occasionally attempts were made to color the light by placing containers filled with tinted liquids between the lamps and the stage. Since this reduced intensity markedly, it was normally reserved for such decorative devices as jeweled windows or festive lights mounted on top of buildings.

Since the intensity of lamps and candles was so limited, providing an adequate level of illumination took precedence over the other functions of stage lighting. Nevertheless, Renaissance theorists formulated several artistic principles similar to those advocated in modern times. Leone di Somi argued that tragedy benefits from a lower level of illumination than that needed for comedy, and both he and Ingegneri stated that the stage will appear brighter if it can be contrasted with a darkened auditorium. For the most part, however, Renaissance artists had to depend upon general illumination, for they had only limited control over color, distribution, and intensity. Nevertheless, they mastered most of the techniques that were to be typical until the late eighteenth century.

FIG. 8.24
Device for dimming candles. The hollow pipes could be lowered to obscure the light or raised to brighten it. From Sabbattini, *Manual for Constructing Theatrical Scenes and Machines* (1638).

COMMEDIA DELL'ARTE

Productions at courts and academies were given for aristocratic audiences on special occasions. The plays were usually written by court poets and the scenery and costumes designed by court architects and painters. Acting was done by courtiers and music was supplied by court musicians, and productions usually received only one performance. Thus, in spite of the high visual quality of the productions and their influence on later theatrical practice, they were essentially coterie performances. The development of a public, professional theatre in Italy was to come primarily from another source—*commedia dell'arte.*

Commedia dell'arte (comedy of professional players), *commedia all'improviso* (improvised comedy), and *commedia a soggetto* (comedy developed from a plot, theme, or subject) are terms used to distinguish the plays performed by professional troupes from those (*commedia erudita* or learned comedy) presented by the amateur actors at courts, academies, and in residences of prosperous citizens. Historians do not know when the *commedia dell'arte* came into being. A contract dated 1545 appears to be that for a *commedia* troupe, but the first clear reference to a *commedia* performance is found in 1568.

Several theories have been advanced to explain the origin of *commedia*. One school seeks to trace it from the Atellan farce of Rome as preserved by wandering mimes during the Middle Ages or by Byzantine mimes who came west when Constantinople fell in 1453. The principal evidence for this view is the similarity of stock characters in the two forms.

FIG. 8.25
Scene from an Italian comedy of the early seventeenth century. From Rasi, *I Comici Italiana* (1895–1905).

A second school traced it to the Italian farce of the early sixteenth century. Written farce reached its height in the work of Angelo Beolco (c. 1495–1542), who, disliking the formality of *commedia erudita,* turned for inspiration to the everyday life and natural speech of northern Italy. His plays often center around the peasant Ruzzante, a role he played, who is cited as a forerunner of the *commedia's* use of stock characters. Others argue that it was invented by young scholars who had worked on the early productions of Plautus and Terence. None of the theories can be confirmed or refuted. Many influences probably contributed to its development.

Regardless of its source, before 1600 it had spread throughout Europe, where it was a typical and popular form of entertainment into the eighteenth century.

The two fundamental characteristics of *commedia dell'arte* were improvisation and stock characters: the actors worked from a plot outline, on the basis of which they improvised dialogue and action, and each performer always played the same character with its fixed attributes and costume.

Historians have disagreed over the extent to which improvisation was used in performances. Certainly, several factors worked to reduce it. Each actor usually played the same character throughout his career, which must have encouraged the repetition of lines or stage business that had been well received. Many comic bits (*lazzi,* singular *lazzo*) were sufficiently standardized to be indicated in plot outlines as *lazzo* of fear, hat *lazzo,* and so on. The rhymed couplets used to close scenes were probably memorized, and the actors playing the fashionable young lovers were encouraged to keep notebooks in which to record appropriate sentiments of poetry and popular literature. Consequently, most of the actors probably stored up lines and action which they repeated frequently. On the other hand, no actor could be sure what the others would say or do and thus had to concentrate upon the unfolding action. As a result, performances must have created the impression of spontaneity.

The scenarios were refined over a period of time and passed down from one troupe to another. More than 1000 have been preserved; the oldest fifty were published by Flaminio Scala (*fl.* 1600–1621) in 1611. Most scripts were comic, although a few were serious and many were melodramatic. The *commedia* actors also performed occasionally in written plays and at court; consequently, they may have been influenced by the *erudita.*

Every troupe had its own stock characters, each with a name and traits that set that character off from similar characters in other companies. Nevertheless,

FIG. 8.26
Two *commedia* figures. From Jacques Callot's *Balli di Sfessania,* a series of twenty-four etchings made *c.* 1621–1622. The figures are considerably exaggerated.

the same character types tended to be repeated from one troupe to another. Consequently, although variations were numerous, the basic outlines remained relatively constant.

The character types in *commedia* can be divided into two general categories: the unmasked and the masked. The unmasked roles were those of the young lovers, who usually served as a norm against which the peculiarities of other characters were seen. Typically they were depicted as witty, handsome, well-educated young men and women, but they might also be characterized as naive, even not-too-bright. They dressed in the fashionable garments of the day. Each company had one or two pairs of lovers. The young man, the *innamorato* or *amoroso,* was often opposed in his love affairs by an older man, sometimes even his father. The young woman, or *innamorata,* was usually a young lady courted by both young and old. When there were two pairs of lovers, the contrasts between them were usually emphasized.

The masked roles can be divided into masters and servants. Of the masters, three recurred most fre-

quently: the Capitano, Pantalone, and Dottore. Originally the Capitano was one of the lovers and unexaggerated in manners and dress. Eventually, however, he was transformed into a braggart and coward who boasted of his great prowess in love and battle, only to be completely discredited in both. The sword, cape, and feathered headdress were standard features of his costume, though the degree of exaggeration varied considerably. He was often given such fanciful names as Spavento da Vall'Inferno, Coccodrillo, or Rinocorente. He frequently figured in the action as an unwelcome suitor to one of the young women, and his discomfiture was often a high point of the comedy.

Pantalone was always a middle-aged or elderly merchant. He spoke in a Venetian dialect, was fond of proverbs, and, in spite of his age, often posed as a young man and courted one of the young women. Typically, his costume included a tight-fitting red vest, red breeches and stockings, soft slippers, a black, ankle-length coat, a soft brimless cap with trailing wisps of hair, a brown mask with a large hooked nose, and a scraggly gray beard.

FIG. 8.27
The lover of *commedia dell'arte.* Etching by Jacques Callot.

own love affairs with the male servants. Occasionally, they were older and might be the hostess of an inn, wife to a servant, or the object of an old man's affection.

Of the *zanni,* Arlecchino (Harlequin) was by far the most popular after the mid-seventeenth century, although he did not figure prominently in the early scripts. He was a mixture of cunning and stupidity and was an accomplished acrobat and dancer. He was usually at the center of any intrigue. His costume underwent many changes. Originally, it was a suit with many irregularly placed patches, but these were gradually formalized into the diamond-shaped red, blue, and green pattern now associated with Harlequin. On his shaven head Harlequin wore a rakish hat above a black mask, and at his side he carried a wooden sword, or "slapstick," that figured prominently in the many fights and beatings of the *commedia.* Other related characters are Truffaldino and Trivellino.

Harlequin's most frequent companion was a libidinous, cynically witty servant who went by a

Dottore was usually Pantalone's friend or rival and, like Pantalone, held an established place in society. He was a pedant, usually a doctor of law or medicine, who spoke in a Bolognese dialect interlarded with Latin words and phrases. He loved to show off his spurious learning, but was often tricked by others because of his extreme credulousness. His dress was the academic cap and gown. He was a jealous husband, but was often cuckolded.

The most varied of all the *commedia* types were the servants, or *zanni.* Most scripts required at least two of these characters, one clever and the other stupid, but the number might vary from one to four. They usually figured prominently in the intrigues, and their machinations kept the plots moving as they sought to help or thwart their masters. Most of the servants were male, but there might be one or more maids, or *fantesca,* who served the *innamorata.* Typically young, coarsely witty, and always ready for an intrigue, they carried on their

FIG. 8.28
The Capitano of the *commedia dell'arte.* From Sand, *Masques et Bouffons* (1859).

variety of names. He was often called Brighella in the eighteenth century, when his mask had a hooked nose and mustache, and his trousers and jacket were ornamented with green braid. Other variations on this character included Buffetto, Flautino, Scapino, and Mezzetino. Scaramuccia, another popular character, varied considerably in his attributes, sometimes resembling Harlequin, at others Brighella or the Capitano.

Pulcinello was always a Neapolitan, but his function in the plays varied. Sometimes he was a servant, or he could be the host of an inn or a merchant. He was a mixture of foolishness and shrewdness, villainy and love, wit and dullness. He had an enormous hooked nose, a humpback, and wore a long pointed cap. He was the ancestor of the English puppet character, Punch. In addition to these common types, many other servants and incidental characters are listed

FIG. 8.30

In the foreground, characters of *commedia dell'arte* and in the background members of the French royal family. Seen at right are Pantalone and Harlequin. Painting attributed to Paul and Frans Porbus, 1572. Courtesy Bayeux Museum.

in the scripts, since each troupe tended to develop its own variations on the traditional character types.

In size, the troupes averaged ten to twelve members: seven or eight men and three or four women. A typical troupe included two sets of lovers, a servant girl, a Capitano, two *zanni*, and two old men (Pantalone and Dottore), but this pattern might be augmented or reduced according to the financial state of the group.

Productions were supervised by the leader or most respected member of a troupe. It was the leader's responsibility to explain the character relationships, clarify the action, enumerate the *lazzi*, and acquire the properties needed. Although it is not clear whether the plays were actually rehearsed, pains were taken to see that each actor understood what was expected.

Most companies were organized on a sharing plan (under which the members assumed the financial risk and divided the profits), although some of the younger actors may have been salaried until they were granted full membership. The troupes traveled frequently, and at each new town they had to petition for the right to perform, a favor not always granted. Usually they hired large rooms in which to play, but they were equally at home on improvised outdoor stages and on indoor court stages. When perspective settings and elaborate effects were available, they were used, but the actors could perform just as easily with no scenery. Adaptability was one key to their success.

FIG. 8.29

Zanni, or Scapino. Etching by Jacques Callot, 1618–1619. Note the audience and performers in the background.

FIG. 8.31
Scene from a *commedia* play, *The Fairies, or the Tales of Mother Goose,* first performed at the Hôtel de Bourgogne, Paris, 1697. Harlequin is depicted at center. From Gherardi, *Le Théâtre Italien,* 6 (1741).

The *commedia* was most vigorous between 1570 and 1650, though it continued until about 1775. It was always most popular in Italy, but France was its second home, and troupes often traveled in Spain, Germany, Austria, England, and elsewhere in Europe. Wherever they went, they influenced native actors and writers.

THE DECLINE OF THEATRE IN THE ITALIAN STATES

In the century following the Council of Trent the spirit of the counter-Reformation motivated a final burst of creativity in church architecture and painting that produced the great baroque churches of Italy, including St. Peter's in Rome. In the theatre, the greatest of baroque creations was opera, which permitted Italy to remain a strong force in Europe's artistic life even after its drama had ceased to be significant. By 1650 the Italian states had developed the dramatic types, critical principles, and theatrical practices that were to dominate the European theatre for the next 150 years. The neoclassical ideal, classically inspired comedy and tragedy, opera, *commedia dell'arte,* theatre architecture, perspective scenery, indoor lighting techniques, complex special effects and stage machinery—all of these were to find their way to other countries, where they would be mingled with native practices and adapted to local needs.

Despite these achievements, by 1650 Italy had lost its privileged position in Europe. This decline was not immediately evident, since Italy long remained a major banking center of Europe but by about 1700 the Italian states had been reduced to secondary status.

LOOKING AT THEATRE HISTORY

One hazard in historical study is the necessity of dividing the whole into segments, since not everything can be examined simultaneously. Common ways of dividing history are by period, country, topic, artistic or political movement, or theme. Each of these can be justified, but all have their shortcomings. When divisions are made according to country, the interconnections among events occurring in two or more countries may go unnoticed or remain unexplored. Division into time periods may interrupt or obscure ongoing developments, or may give undue emphasis to some event or type of activity (especially war or politics) as crucial in marking the end or beginning of a period or movement. Therefore, students should be aware that in theatre history what is selected for inclusion and how it is interpreted are influenced in part by the system of segmentation being used, and that another way of dividing the whole would likely yield a somewhat different view of the same historical events or processes. In this book, for example, the division into Medieval and Renaissance periods separates many simultaneous and interconnected developments; through the choice of what is included (and excluded) in each of the chapters, lines of development and directions of change are made to seem clearer than they might were all of the material treated together. Nevertheless, each historian must choose some scheme of division, even though each scheme encourages some form of over-simplification. No historical work can ever convey the "whole" truth.

In theatre history, the context in which we place events is crucial to our vision of their significance. This is well illustrated in Roy Strong's study of Renaissance courtly theatrical activities and festivals as reflections of royal power.

Through [festivals] the prince was able to manifest himself at his most magnificent in the sight of his subjects. By means of myth and allegory, sign and symbol, gesture and movement, festival found a means to exalt the glory of the wearer of the Crown. In such a way the truths of sacred monarchy could be propagated to the court and a tamed nobility take its place in the round of ritual. [21]

For the modern reader the central thought tenet that motivated Renaissance court fetes is the least interesting one. We can see them in retrospect for what they were: extravagant assertions of a mirage of power. They retain their fascination 350 years later only because through this alliance of art and power arose our modern opera and ballet and the theatre of illusion. In this century festivals have been studied seriously mostly as a curious ancestor of theatre, but they are in reality much more a branch of political history and thought. [247–248]

Roy Strong, *Splendor at Court: Renaissance Spectacle and Illusion* (Boston: Houghton Mifflin, 1973).

In 1571 Castelvetro reduced to strict rules many of the tenets that were to dominate critical thought for the next 200 years. Here are a few key excerpts from his lengthy treatise:

Dramas do not show on the stage murders and other things that are difficult to represent with dignity, . . . such deeds should be done off stage and then narrated by a messenger. . . . A drama spends as many hours in performing things as was taken by the actions themselves . . . therefore tragedy and comedy . . . cannot last longer than the time permitted by the convenience of the audience, nor include more things than can occur in the space of time that the comedies and tragedies require in performance. . . . It is not possible to make the audience believe that several days and nights have passed when they have the evidence of their senses that only a few hours have gone by.

Lodovico Castelvetro, *The Poetics of Aristotle Translated and Annotated* (1571), sections 57 and 109.

One of the major sources of information about the *commedia dell'arte* is Perrucci's description of all aspects of the form. Here are some excerpts from his account of rehearsal practices:

The scenario is no more than the fabric of scenes woven from a plot, with brief hints of the action, divided into acts and scenes, which are to be acted extemporaneously by the performers. In the margins are indications as to where each character is to enter and . . . exit.

The manager or more experienced actor rehearses the scenario before it is acted, so the actors know the contents of the play, where the dialogue should end, and where new lazzi can be inserted . . . he will plant the lazzi, . . . giving attention to the things needed in the play, such as letters, purses, daggers, and other properties. . . .

After the actors have been told what they must do . . . , they will be able to go through the scenes and rehearse new lazzi or material of their own invention. It is wise, however, not to depart from the plot so far that . . . the audience will lose the thread of the plot. . . . [Then] the actors ought to think about bringing in something . . . they have memorized for use in any play.

Andrea Perrucci, *Dell'arte rappresentativa, premeditata, ed all' improvviso* (1699).

9
French Theatre
to 1700

Medieval influences in France continued throughout the sixteenth century. Some of the most elaborate outdoor religious dramas were staged there between 1500 and 1550, and farces and *sotties* were among the most popular of dramatic types. From 1494 on France maintained close relationships with the Italian states and in the early sixteenth century controlled several of them. Francis I (reigned 1515–1547) was especially interested in the new artistic and literary movements of the Italian Renaissance and invited several Italian scholars and artists, including Leonardo da Vinci, and Serlio, to his court. Renaissance influence accelerated after Henri II (reigned 1547–1559), who had married Catherine de' Medici (1519–1589), succeeded to the throne. When Henri II met his death in a tournament in 1559, Catherine de' Medici came into a position of power that lasted throughout the lives of her three sons: Francis II (reigned 1559–1560), husband of Mary of Scotland, Charles IX (reigned 1560–1574), and Henri III (reigned 1574–1589).

During this time France became the center of the religious wars as it was embroiled in the growing struggle between Catholics and the Huguenots (Protestants). Persecution of Huguenots had begun about 1540 but did not assume major proportions until 1572, when thousands of Protestants were murdered in the St. Bartholomew's Day Massacre. Subsequently, as the

Catholics gained strength under the leadership of the Duke of Guise, Henri III began to fear them and had the Duke assassinated in 1588. Henri III was, in turn, assassinated the following year, and since he left no heir, Henri of Navarre, a Protestant who had married Henri III's sister, succeeded to the throne as Henri IV (reigned 1589–1610). Open civil war followed and Henri IV was not able to enter Paris until 1594 when he agreed to convert to Catholicism. Peace was still not fully restored until the Edict of Nantes, granting almost complete autonomy to Protestants, was issued in 1598. Under Henri IV, order was finally restored, but he too was assassinated in 1610, bringing to the throne Louis XIII (reigned 1610–1643), then only nine years old. His mother, Marie de' Medici (1573–1642) and her ministers followed policies that stirred up trouble, and the Huguenot question resurfaced because Protestant towns had become so independent as to constitute a nation within the nation. Beginning in the 1620s, the real power behind the throne was Cardinal Richelieu (1586–1642), who, following new civil wars, was able to wrest power from the Protestants and the nobles and concentrate it in the Crown. Richelieu died in 1642 and Louis XIII in 1643. When Louis XIV (reigned 1643–1715) succeeded to the throne he was only five years old and his mother, Ann of Austria (1601–1668) was named regent, although the major force was Cardinal Mazarin

(1602–1661), her chief minister. Mazarin was unpopular not only because he used his position to enrich himself but also because he was Italian. The nobility, sensing a chance to regain its old rights, joined together in a movement called La Fronde ("the sling") which developed into open rebellion in 1648. By 1652 the resistance of the nobility had been completely broken, and thereafter those of the highest rank were forced to live at court where they could be watched. As a result, all authority was concentrated in the Crown, where it was to remain until the Revolution of 1789. In 1660 Louis XIV married Marie Thérèse of Spain, and in 1661 Mazarin died. These two events mark the coming of age of Louis, who thereafter assumed complete control over governmental affairs. By this time, the crown's power was so firmly established that Louis could convincingly declare, "I am the State." During the years that followed, French artists developed their own distinctive version of the baroque visual style, appropriately called Louis Quatorze. In 1682 Louis moved the seat of government to Versailles, and forced all of France's leading noblemen to live there so he might keep an eye on them. By this time the nobility had become relatively powerless, though it had been deprived of none of its major privileges. Forced to live at court, the nobles lost touch with lesser ranks, especially those in the provinces. Versailles not only became the symbol of the king's absolute power, but also of the conditions that led to the French Revolution a century later.

THEATRE AT COURT AND IN SCHOOLS PRIOR TO 1600

Before the end of Francis I's reign, Renaissance drama had made an impact both on schools and at court. Around 1540, classical plays and critical treatises began to be translated into French. Plays by Sophocles, Euripides, Aristophanes, Seneca, Plautus, and Terence and critical works by Aristotle and Horace were printed before 1550. Recent Italian plays also were translated, as were Italian commentaries on Aristotle's *Poetics*.

By 1550 a group of seven French writers, led by Pierre de Ronsard and known as the Pléiade, had come to the fore. Seeking to develop French as the medium for a literature modeled on classical works, they formulated rules of grammar and prosody, enriched the language by inventing new words, and illustrated their ideals in their own literary works. Of necessity, the Pléiade addressed itself primarily to the educated classes.

The first plays in French modeled on classical forms were written by Etienne Jodelle (1523–1573),

who wrote the comedy *Eugène* (1552), and the first tragedy in French, *Cléopâtre Captive* (1553). This tragedy was presented at court, before the king. The setting was described as "antique," but it is not clear whether this was a "Terence stage" or a perspective set; either was possible as the "Terence stage" was first published in France and perspective scenery had been used in Lyon in 1548. Most of the spectacles at court, however, used a version of simultaneous staging known as "dispersed decors," in which medieval-like scenic elements were scattered around a hall rather than concentrated in a single area.

Other playwrights soon followed Jodelle in using classical models. Their tragedies emphasize the suffering of the characters who are the victims of fate and who describe their suffering in a series of set rhetorical speeches of great dignity but little dramatic tension. Their comedies, though classical in form, resemble medieval farces in their subjects. Pierre de Larivey (c. 1540–1619) moved comedy away from medieval farce later in the century. He modeled his works on Italian *commedia erudita* but adapted them to French locales and manners. His comedies were the most popular of the French plays that have come down to us from the period prior to 1630.

By 1572, when Jean de la Taille published a work advocating the three unities, the neoclassical ideal had been fully set forth in France. French playwrights adhered to its rules only sporadically, however, perhaps because, as in England and Spain, medieval influence was still potent and because playwrights considered it more important to please audiences than to adhere to the rules. Whatever the reasons, the works of this period display considerable variety of form and style.

Among the most characteristic entertainments of this period were the court festivals. Catherine dé Medici was especially fond of royal entries and festivals which she could use to illustrate France's power and to encourage alliances or reconciliations.

Through such spectacles, the *ballet de cour* (the French variation on Italian *intermezzi* and English masques) evolved. Their creators sought to unite dramatic plot, song, dance, and spectacle in the "antique manner." These experiments culminated in 1581 in the *Ballet Comique de la Reyne* with text by LaChesnaye, music by the Sieur de Beaulieu, scenery by Jacques Patin, and the whole planned and directed by Baltasar de Beaujoyeulx. It was based on the myth of Circe, who lures men into a life of vice and transforms them into beasts. The action was treated as a moral struggle between virtue and vice, with the King depicted as the deliverer. This story was developed through a series of *entrées* by various allegorical and mythological figures and ended with the

FIG. 9.1

Catherine de' Medici's water fête given during the Festival at Bayonne, 1565. Drawing by Antoine Caron, who also probably designed the fête. Courtesy Pierpont Morgan Library, New York.

FIG. 9.2

Ballet Comique de la Reyne as given at the Petit Bourbon in 1581. Note the dispersed decor and the placement of spectators. The king and his retinue are in the foreground. Courtesy Bibliothèque Nationale, Paris.

triumph of reason and virtue and with praise for the wisdom of the kings of France. It was staged in the Salle du Petit Bourbon (located in the palace adjacent to the Louvre), which was to be one of the important court theatres of the seventeenth century. It measured about 49 feet wide by 177 feet long, with an apse extending another 44 feet. The king and courtiers sat at one end, while other spectators occupied two balconies extending around the side walls. The *Ballet Comique de la Reyne* is often said to be the first full expression of the *ballet de cour,* which was to be revived and extended in the seventeenth century.

THE PUBLIC THEATRE IN PARIS BEFORE 1597

While court spectacles and neoclassical plays were gaining in strength, the French public stage was at a low ebb. This was due, at least in part, to the Confrérie de la Passion (Brotherhood of the Passion), which had a monopoly on theatrical production in Paris. Organized in 1402 to produce religious drama, the Confrérie (Brotherhood) performed in a large hall at the Hôpital de la Trinité for many years. In 1548, after a series of relocations, the Confrérie began constructing a new building, probably the first permanent public theatre to be built in Europe since Roman times. Because it was located on land formerly owned by the Dukes of Burgundy, the theatre was called the Hôtel de Bourgogne. But before the theatre was completed, religious plays were banned, though the Confrérie was allowed to keep its monopoly. The Confrérie attempted to do farce and other secular dramas, but without much success. By the 1570s they were deriving more of their income from renting out their theatre and their monopoly powers to visiting companies from the provinces, but the religious wars kept this activity sporadic. In 1597 they gave up producing completely, though they retained their monopoly until 1629. The Confrérie de la Passion was dissolved in 1677.

THE PUBLIC THEATRE, 1597–1629

Numerous professional companies had developed outside of Paris by the mid sixteenth century, possibly as offshoots of the confraternities formed to produce religious plays there. Many toured, but only those few licensed by the Confrérie could perform in Paris. The civil war that followed the assassination of Henry III in 1588 shut down performances in Paris until Henri IV entered Paris in 1594. Public performances resumed at the fairs of St. Germain and St. Laurent the following year, and when the Confrérie gave up active participation in production, in 1597, skilled companies and playwrights began to appear in Paris. The usual popular fare was farce, much of which was improvised under the influence of the *commedia dell'arte* troupes, which had played sporadically in Paris between 1571 and 1588 and were to return frequently after 1599. The most famous of these, the Gelosi troupe, included the great Italian actress, Isabella Andreini (born Canali 1562-1604), and it is argued that her presence did much to encourage the acceptance of actresses in Paris.

Around 1597, Alexandre Hardy (*c.* 1572–1632), France's first professional dramatist, also began his career. Hardy was inspired by the Spanish dramatists and, like them, wrote an exceptional number of plays. He claimed to have written over 500, but only thirty-four have survived. Working for a popular audience, Hardy adapted his plays to its tastes. So while he used such neoclassical devices as the five-act form, poetic dialogue, messengers, and the chorus, he did not permit reverence for antiquity to interfere with his primary aim of telling an interesting story. He seldom observed the unities of time and place, and he put all important episodes, no matter how violent, on stage. At first he wrote tragedies, but since these did not please, he turned to tragicomedy and pastoral. Because he worked under contract to acting companies who retained ownership of the plays he wrote for

them, Hardy was unable to publish any of his work until 1624. Five volumes were in print by 1628, but scholars debate the extent to which these plays were changed for publication and how much they actually reflect the original texts used by the actors.

Hardy's early work was done primarily for Valleran LeConte (*fl.* 1592–1613, sometimes Valeran Lecomte), the first important French actor manager. By 1598, when Valleran's company first appeared in Paris, it had been performing in major provincial cities for six years and was already being called The King's Players (*Les Comédiens du Roi*), probably because it had at some time performed before Henri IV. The title, however, carried with it no special privileges or subsidy. When Valleran's troupe left Paris in 1612, company member Robert Guérin (*c.* 1554–*c.* 1634), who used the name LaFleur in serious roles and played the famous farce character, Gros-Guillaume (a character with a flour-whitened face and obese body, emphasized by a belt above and below his enormous stomach), formed his own company. He was joined by another company member, Hugues Guéru (*c.* 1573–1633), who played as Fleschelles in serious drama but was best known as Gaultier-Garguille (a tall, thin, bowlegged creature who could contort his body like a marionette.) Two years later they were joined by Henri LeGrand (*c.* 1587–*c.* 1637), who used the name Belleville in serious roles, but was known for his Turlupin (a rascally servant similar to Brighella of the *commedia dell'arte*). These were the most popular actors in Paris for the next fifteen years and eventually gained the title of The Royal Company and a subsidy from Louis XIII. When not on tour, they rented the Hôtel de Bourgogne and their success was key to the building of an audience for professional theatre in the Paris.

Throughout the seventeenth century, there were large numbers of French companies outside of Paris. We can identify about 400 between 1590 and 1710, although we know little about them. No company, however, was allowed to settle in Paris permanently until 1629.

In the early seventeenth century, acting companies were bound together by two- or three-year contracts. All were organized on the sharing plan, under which profits were divided after each performance. The manager normally received two shares, while lesser actors might be allotted less than a full share. Companies ranged in size from eight to twelve members, sometimes supplemented by "hired men" and apprentices. Women had acted occasionally in provincial companies since 1545 when Marie Fairet (or Ferré) was contracted to act with l'Esperonniere, "player of histories," at Bourges. But few actresses are mentioned before the 1590s and they do not act in

Paris until 1607, and even then some comic roles continued to be played by men. Marie Vernier (*fl.* 1590–1619) is one of the few actresses known to us from this period. But if acting gained steadily in popularity between 1597 and 1629, the social and religious stigma attached to it led most performers to assume stage names when they went into the theatre.

Until 1629 the Hôtel de Bourgogne was the only permanent theatre in Paris. Even though it was used from 1548 to 1783, we know little about it. The most reliable estimate indicates that it was about 40 feet wide and 105 feet long. The first floor was taken up entirely by the pit, or *parterre*, in which there were no permanent seats (with the possible exception of a bench running along each of the side walls). Around the auditorium ran two or three galleries, portions of which were divided into boxes, or *loges*. That part of the first gallery facing the stage was left undivided so as to form the *amphitheatre*. The total capacity of the auditorium may have been about 1600. The stage was raised about 6 feet above the pit. Although there was no proscenium arch, the side galleries, which extended to the stage, created a frame. The stage occupied the full width of the building, but the visible space was probably no wider than 25 feet. The depth of the stage is unknown, but estimates range from 17 to 35 feet.

Although the Confrérie probably had used medieval mansions on this stage, the little that is known of scenic practices before 1629 can be summarized briefly: the Confrérie may have owned scenery which it rented with the theatre; Valleran's records show that he sometimes paid painters for scenic pieces; Hardy's extant plays require from three to seven locations, each probably represented by a separate mansion and all arranged around the periphery of the stage; the few extant illustrations of farces show a stage with a compartment on either side, and either a cloth or doors at the back (see Fig. 9.3). Since all of the troupes were itinerant, none probably attempted elaborate settings.

For those who did not play at the Bourgogne, the usual choice was a tennis court. Since the Middle Ages, tennis (or *jeu de paume*) had been a favorite European game, and by the sixteenth century many courts were enclosed and roofed. Estimates of the number of courts in Paris in the seventeenth century range from 250 to 1,800. By 1600, the measurements of tennis courts were standardized at about 30 by 90 feet. Thus, they did not differ markedly in size from the Hôtel de Bourgogne. A number of features recommended the use of tennis courts as theatres: the presence of a gallery for spectators along one side; the large open floor space; and the row of windows just below the roof which provided ample light. To convert a tennis

FIG. 9.3

Farce actors at the Hôtel de Bourgogne, *c.* 1630. On stage are Turlupin, Gaultier-Garguille, and Gros-Guillaume. Engraving by Abraham Bosse. Courtesy Bibliothèque Nationale, Paris.

court into a theatre, therefore, required primarily the addition of a platform, an operation so simple that it was often done for a single performance. For more permanent conversions, the galleries were extended around the other walls and divided into boxes. Throughout Europe, the tennis court became the first choice of actors seeking buildings to convert into theatres.

In Paris, performances were given two or three times a week during the early seventeenth century. By 1600, posters were being used to advertise productions, and announcements of coming attractions were made from the stage. The starting times varied, but official regulations required that performances end sufficiently early that spectators might reach home before dark. Because the starting time was indefinite and spectators came early to secure good places, each company employed a "prologuist" to entertain the audience until the performance began. The daily bill might include a long play followed by a farce, although an entire program might be made up of short plays and variety entertainment. Music was a part of all performances.

The audience was drawn from all classes. Many spectators wore swords or daggers, and fights in the pit were common. Probably there was much jostling and moving about by the up to 1000 persons who might be standing in the pit. The confusion was increased by the sale during performances of food, drink, and other articles.

In 1629 for the first time a company was permitted to settle permanently in Paris. Up to this time, the French theatre fared poorly when compared with the theatres of England, Spain, or Italy, but soon it was to undergo changes that would elevate it above all others in the critical estimate of the time.

THE TRIUMPH OF THE NEOCLASSICAL IDEAL

With the return of stability in the 1620s came a resurgence of interest in literature and theatrical performance at court. This renewal had begun somewhat tentatively in the early years of Louis XIII's reign, when in 1610 the *ballet de cour* was revived with *Alcine*, performed in an Italianate perspective setting. During the next ten years, largely due to the importation of such designers as Tomaso Francini (1571–1648), most of the Italian scenic innovations were seen at the French court. At first, sets were composed of painted cloths which could be dropped to reveal others. But in 1617 angled side wings and back shutters were introduced for *The Deliverance of Renaud*. By 1620, perspective scenery, unified settings, the raked stage, and scene shifting were in use at court.

During the 1620s, rekindled interest in neoclassical principles began to affect playwriting. Of the dramatists who began their careers in the late 1620s, four were to be of special importance: Mairet, du Ryer, Rotrou, and Corneille. Jean de Mairet (1604–1686) came to Paris in 1625, the year in which his first play, *Chryséide and Arimand*, a tragicomedy, was performed. In 1626 he turned to writing pastorals, which he helped to popularize through such works as *Sylvie* (1628) and *La Sylvanire* (1631). Soon recognized as the leading dramatist of his day, he confirmed his reputation with *Sophonisba* (1634), the first tragedy of the new age to observe the neoclassical rules. It did much to revive interest in tragedy, which had been dormant since the first years of the century. By the time he retired in 1640, he had probably done more than any other writer of his day to set drama on its new path.

Pierre du Ryer (*c.* 1600–1658), a well-educated government official, wrote prolifically. His early works were either irregular tragicomedies, such as *Clitophon* (*c.* 1629) and *Argenis and Poliarque* (1631), or farce vehicles for Gros-Guillaume. After coming under Mairet's influence about 1634, however, he turned to tragedy in the neoclassical mode. Of these later works, the best is *Scévole* (1644), which remained in the repertory for more than a century. Along with Mairet and Corneille, du Ryer established tragedy as a popular form.

FIG. 9.4

A tennis court of the type used for remodeling into theatres. Redrawing by Michael Heil from a sixteenth-century French engraving.

Jean de Rotrou (1609–1650) began writing plays in 1628, and eventually succeeded Hardy as principal dramatist to the Hôtel de Bourgogne. Through Rotrou's adaptations of Spanish drama, the theme of love versus honor became a staple of the French stage. Interested primarily in rapid and absorbing actions, Rotrou failed to create characters of depth.

Despite the accomplishments of his contemporaries, Pierre Corneille (1606–1684) is the dramatist most often linked to the triumph of the neoclassical mode in France. Born in Rouen and educated for the law, he began to write plays after seeing the Montdory-LeNoir troupe perform in his hometown. The result was *Mélite* (1629), a comedy unlike either farce or pastoral, the major comic forms of the time. Consequently, *Mélite* is often said to have set French comedy on a new path, one in which the intrigues and misunderstandings of lovers replaced the earlier emphasis on comic servants or sentimental love affairs. Until 1636, most of Corneille's plays were comedies and, though much admired, they served only to establish his reputation as a promising writer.

Le Cid (1636–1637) marked the turning point in Corneille's career and in French drama, for it precipitated a battle destined to clarify the conflict between the old and new ideals. Based upon Guillén de Castro's *The Youthful Adventures of the Cid,* a play in six acts treating events occurring over eleven years and in many places, Corneille's play compresses the events into five acts, twenty-four hours, and four locations in a single town. Revolving around the theme of love versus honor, the action forces both the hero, Roderigue, and the heroine, Chimène, to choose between their love for each other and their duty to family and state.

Although an enormously popular success, it was publicly attacked by several critics for its violations of neoclassical principles.

While the unity of time had been observed, they noted, verisimilitude had been strained by crowding numerous and complex incidents (including a war) into one day. Furthermore, Chimène's apparent agreement to marry Roderigue, who has killed her father less than twenty-four hours earlier, violated the neoclassical notion of decorum. The play did not fit any recognized dramatic type: It resembled tragicomedy in the number and variety of incidents, in the perils overcome by the hero, and in the happy ending; it resembled pastoral in the love story; and it resembled tragedy in its narrative and lyrical passages. The bitterness of the controversy prompted Cardinal Richelieu to request a verdict on the play from the newly formed French Academy. The results were destined to focus public attention on the neoclassical ideal.

After his rise to power in the 1620s, Richelieu had used his position to encourage the development of French literature and the arts so that France might become the cultural leader of Europe. He favored Italian ideals of writing and staging and provided financial support and other incentives to those authors who sought to implement the neoclassical ideal. He also promoted the formation of the French Academy as an arbiter of literary taste.

The French Academy originated in 1629 when a small group of men began meeting to discuss literature. Hearing of their work, Richelieu urged them to form an organization modeled after the Italian academies. In 1636 they reluctantly did so, and in 1637 the French Academy received the state charter under which it still operates. Membership in the Academy was (and continues to be) restricted to forty, presumably the most eminent literary figures of the age. Upon its formation, the Academy took as its primary task the study and codification of French language and style.

FIG. 9.5
The second scene, "Garden of Delights," from *The Deliverance of Renaud,* produced at the French court in 1617. This seems to have been the first production in France to use angled side wings and back shutters. Courtesy Bibliothèque Nationale, Paris.

It was to this newly formed group that Richelieu referred the controversy over *Le Cid.* The verdict, written principally by the group's leader, Jean Chapelain (1595–1674), was contained in *The Judgment of the Academy on Le Cid* (1638). In it, Chapelain praised *Le Cid* insofar as it adhered to neoclassical doctrine and censured it for all deviations. He also restated the neoclassical ideal and urged its universal adoption.

After *Le Cid,* Corneille wrote the works now considered most characteristic of his style: *Horace* (1640), *Cinna* (1640), *Polyeucte* (1642–1643), and *The Death of Pompey* (1643). Each centers around a hero of indomitable will who chooses death rather than dishonor. Since Corneille's protagonists are never in doubt about their goals, they often appear one-sided; never divided within themselves, they are revealed in a series of episodes showing their reactions to external obstacles. Consequently, Corneille's characters are simple, but his plots complex. Beginning with *Rodogune* (1644), Corneille's stories often became so involved that they were difficult to follow. This trend toward complexity was not unique to Corneille's plays, for most dramatists of the time followed the same path until the 1660s when Racine's simplicity began a reaction against it.

Corneille set the standard in comedy as well. His *The Liar* (1643), adapted from Alarcón's *The Suspicious Truth,* is considered the finest French comedy before Molière. Only one other comic writer, Paul Scarron (1610–1660), challenged Corneille's supremacy. Scarron paved the way for Molière by combining the comedy of intrigue, in which Corneille excelled, with farce, most notably in *Jodelet, or The Servant The Master* (1643) and *Jodelet Insulted* (1645), both written for the farceur Jodelet. In *The Scholar of Salamanca* (1654) Scarron introduced the character Crispin, who became so popular that other dramatists incorporated him into their plays. Scarron's novel, *A Comical Tale* (1651), is also noteworthy for its depiction of the life of touring actors.

The vigor of the 1640s was followed by another civil war. Tragedy lost its appeal and, after the failure of his *Pertharite* in 1652, Corneille gave up writing for many years. (He wrote his last play, *Suréa,* in 1674.)

ACTING COMPANIES, 1629–1660

When the Confrérie lost its monopoly on theatre in 1629, The Royal Company, with its famous trio of farce characters, Gros-Guillaume, Gaultier-Garguille, and Turlupin, took up permanent residence in the Hôtel de Bourgogne. The actor who played Gaultier-Garguille died in 1633, and was replaced by Bertrand Hardouin de St. Jacques (1600–1648), who acted under the name Guillot-Gorju; he was famous for his witty repartee. Gros-Guillaume died the following year and was replaced by Jodelet (Julien Bedeau, *c.* 1600–1660), who performed in a flour-whitened face in the manner of Gros-Guillaume and was especially noted as the comic valet, a role which he raised to great popularity (though his greatest successes would come after he left the Bourgogne in the 1640s). But by this time another former member of Valleran's old company, Pierre le Messier (*c.* 1592–1670), who used the stage name Bellerose, was the company's rising star. He was a fine actor in both comedy and tragedy and brought dignity to the theatre just as the new drama was achieving greater subtlety and the taste for farce was declining. In 1634 he became the company's actor-manager.

That same year, a second company obtained permission to settle in Paris. The rival troupe was headed by Guillaume des Gilleberts (1594–1654), known as Montdory. Montdory began his career about 1612 in Valleran's company, joined the Prince of Orange's Players in 1613, and finally formed a company with Charles LeNoir (*fl.* 1610–1637), an actor-manager who had performed in Paris intermittently since 1610. They returned to Paris in 1629, bringing with them Corneille's first play, *Mélite.* Because of his preference for the new drama, Montdory soon won the favor of Cardinal Richelieu, who awarded him a subsidy and established the company in the newly converted tennis court, the Théâtre du Marais, in 1634. This was the first serious rival to the Hôtel de Bourgogne.

Sometimes called the first great French actor, Montdory was at his best in the roles of tragic heroes. *Le Cid* and many of the other outstanding plays of the 1630s were first played by the Montdory's company at the Théâtre du Marais. Under Montdory's leadership, the Marais became the leading theatre of Paris, a position it was to hold until 1647.

Montdory suffered a partial paralysis in 1637 and was forced to retire. He was replaced by Floridor (Josias de Soulas, 1608–1672), an aristocrat who had played in a touring company for many years. When the Théâtre du Marais burned in 1644 he quickly got it rebuilt. But when Floridor went to the Hôtel de Bourgogne to replace Bellerose in 1647, the Marais company was never able to fully recover. It closed in 1673.

At the Bourgogne, Floridor continued as the leading serious actor of Paris until his retirement in 1671. He shared tragic roles with Montfleury (Zacharie Jacob, 1600–1667), who had joined the Bourgogne company in 1639 and rose rapidly to a position second only to Bellerose and Florida.

In 1641 Louis XIII sought to remove the stigma attached to acting by issuing a decree stating his desire that "the actors' profession . . . not be considered worthy of blame nor prejudicial to their reputation in society." But though it abolished certain legal restrictions, this decree did not alter the church's decrees, under which actors were supposed to be denied the sacraments—including baptism, marriage, and death rites. But whether these decrees were enforced depended much on actors' moral reputations in their own parishes and the judgment of the parish priest.

THE PUBLIC THEATRES, 1629–1660

The major public theatres of Paris between 1629 and 1660 were the Hôtel de Bourgogne and the Théâtre du Marais, though the two court theatres, the Palais Royal and the Petit Bourbon, were occasionally open for public performances. Presumably the physical attributes of the Bourgogne (already described) remained relatively unchanged from 1548 until 1647, when it was remodeled by order of the King's Council.

Almost nothing is known of the first Théâtre du Marais (1634), except that it was converted from a tennis court. When it burned in 1644, it was replaced immediately with a more elaborate structure that remained in use until 1673. The second Marais apparently measured 38 feet wide by 115 feet long and was 52 feet high. Three levels of galleries surrounded the standing area (parterre) in front of the stage, the first two divided into boxes, the third given over to an undivided space or *paradis*. The capacity of the auditorium was probably about 1500 persons.

The stage, raised roughly 6 feet above the *parterre*, sloped upward toward the back. It occupied the full width of the building and had a proscenium opening 25 feet wide. Documents show that the Marais had a *théâtre supérieure,* or second stage, perhaps thirteen feet above the first, but scholars disagree about its size, its placement, and even how it was used. Some argue that it was essential to almost every play, while others state it was rarely employed. Although its precise use cannot be established, the *théâtre supérieure* was unquestionably available at both the Marais and the Bourgogne (where it may have been removable).

It was probably the need to compete more effectively with the new Marais that led to the remodeling of the Bourgogne in 1647. The imprecise contract for the changes still exists. It specifies that the stage is to be some 45 feet deep and "as wide as the building" (about 40 feet). The floor was raked upward toward the back and beams were installed at the front, probably to accommodate a curtain and to form a proscenium arch, neither of which apparently was used earlier. The stage opening was about 25 feet wide. In the auditorium, the galleries were curved into a U shape to eliminate the former sharp angles at the rear corners. In spite of the remodeling, the Hôtel de Bourgogne remained the Parisian theatre least concerned with spectacle. Additional changes were made in 1656 to allow for increased spectacle and special effects.

SCENIC PRACTICES IN THE PUBLIC THEATRES, 1629–1660

The scenic practices of the early 1630s are well documented in *Le Mémoire de Mahelot, Laurent, et d'Autres Décorateurs,* . . . one of the most valuable theatrical records of the seventeenth century. This document is divided into three parts, each relating to widely separated years. The first part ends in 1635. Some

FIG. 9.6
Setting for du Ryer's *Lisandre and Caliste* (c. 1635). Note the various locales represented simultaneously. From *Le Mémoire de Mahelot.* . . . Courtesy Bibliothèque Nationale, Paris.

scholars assume that it summarizes only the season of 1634–1635, while others argue that it records usage from about 1622 to 1635. It consists of seventy-one notices (that is, summaries of the scenic requirements) and forty-seven designs for plays in the repertory of the Hôtel de Bourgogne. Most scholars believe that the designs are by the compiler, Laurent Mahelot, although others have suggested that Mahelot was merely the theatre's machinist and that the designs are by George Buffequin, the major scenic designer of the period.

Mahelot's compilation demonstrates clearly that in 1635 scenic practices in the public theatres were still essentially medieval. Since the unity of place was not yet common, most plays required a number of locales, each of which was represented by a mansion. All mansions were present simultaneously, arranged along the sides and across the back of the stage to leave the center free for the actors. The back scene usually represented a single place, but typically there were two mansions on each side. Many of the mansions were of such a general nature—a house, a wood, a palace, a grotto, a cave, a tomb, a prison, a tent, a seacoast— that they reappeared in a number of different plays. When a play required more mansions than could be accommodated on stage at once, units were converted by removing painted canvas coverings or by opening curtains to reveal an interior.

A few visual characteristics relate these simultaneous settings to Italian perspective scenery: Some of the backcloths are painted in perspective; balanced pairs of mansions sometimes resemble Serlio's arrangement of angled wings; in some settings decorative details are repeated from one mansion to another to give greater unity to the whole. In spite of these superficial similarities, however, the effect is clearly more medieval than Italianate.

FIG. 9.7

Setting for Act V of *Le Martyre de Sainte Catherine* by Jean Puget de la Serre, produced at the Hôtel de Bourgogne, 1643. In this production the basic structure remained fixed, while the view behind the central doorway and on the upper level changed with each act. The scene on the upper level apparently made use of the *théâtre supérieure*. From the original edition of the play. Courtesy Bibliothèque Nationale, Paris.

A few machines and special effects are mentioned by Mahelot: Gods and other supernatural characters appear above the stage; boats with passengers move from one side of the stage to the other; clouds, fire, smoke, and sound effects are specified. Properties, such as human heads and sponges filled with blood, are noted. Furniture seems to have been restricted to an occasional throne or stool.

ITALIAN SCENIC CONVENTIONS AT THE FRENCH COURT: ITALIAN OPERA, MACHINE PLAYS, AND BALLET

Although Italianate scenery had been introduced to France in 1548 and was seen increasingly at court by 1625, its use did not become a matter of artistic principle until after 1640. Perhaps to provide a model, Cardinal Richelieu had the architect

FIG. 9.8

Theatre built by Cardinal Richelieu in his palace in 1641. Seen in the foreground (right to left) are Richelieu, Louis XIII, and the Queen. After Richelieu's death, this theatre was called the Palais Royal.

LeMercier construct in his palace the first theatre in France with a permanent proscenium arch and a stage designed to use flat wings. This theatre, called the Palais Cardinal, had a stage 59 feet wide by 46 feet deep and an auditorium 59 feet wide by 65 feet deep with two levels of undivided galleries around three sides. Most of the ground floor was taken up by an amphitheatre that rose in broad steps from a small pit. Since the theatre was intended only for invited guests, the auditorium did not follow the arrangement used in the public theatres. It opened in January 1641 but its capabilities were not fully displayed until later that year when the *Ballet de la Prospérité des Armes de la France,* with nine settings, was produced. The theatre came under the control of the crown when Richelieu died in 1642 and became known as the Palais Royal thereafter.

Italy's most accomplished designer, Giacomo Torelli (1606–1678) was brought to Paris and began working on operas for Richelieu's successor, Cardinal Mazarin. For his first opera in Paris, in 1645, Torelli chose *The Conterfit Madwoman (La Finta Pazza),* the work that had made him famous at the Teatro Novissimo in Venice. To house this opera, Torelli converted the Petit Bourbon in the Tuileries Palace, into an Italianate theatre. He erected a platform 6 feet high to make a stage about 49 feet wide by 48 feet deep, somewhat larger than the one he had used in Venice. He also installed his famous chariot-and-pole system of scene shifting, probably his only major improvement over Richelieu's theatre. Most historians date the full triumph of the Italian ideal in France from this production.

FIG. 9.9

La Prospérité des Armes de la France as performed at Cardinal Richelieu's new theatre in 1641. Note the figures atop the walls and the chariot in the sky. Courtesy Theatre Museum, Drottningholm.

In 1646 Torelli remodeled the Palais Royal to accommodate the chariot-and-pole method of shifting, and in 1647 *Orphée* was staged there at a tremendous cost, which Mazarin paid for out of state funds. The presence of so many Italians, the hostility which the French nobles felt against Mazarin, and the use of state money to finance operas aroused considerable resentment. Mazarin, seeking works more compatible with French taste, then commissioned Corneille to write *Androméde,* for public presentation at the Petit Bourbon in 1650. *Androméde* was called a "play with machines" since,

like regular drama, its story progressed through spoken episodes, but as in opera, each act contained pantomimic episodes accompanied by music that provided an excuse to introduce elaborate machinery and special effects. The Marais attempted to adopt "machine plays" with productions like *The Golden Fleece, The Loves of Venus and Adonis,* and *The Marriage of Bacchus and Ariadne,* but ended up bankrupted by the sums required to mount these spectacles.

In the late 1640s ballet began to recapture the popularity it had enjoyed at court before 1620. It was especially prominent between 1651 and 1660, when Louis XIV appeared in many of the productions. Called *ballets d'entrées,* these entertainments did not require the proficiency in dance technique needed for modern ballet. They were allegorical stories, explained by a spoken libretto and pantomimed by performers in elaborate choreographic patterns based upon ballroom dances of the time. One of the most characteristic works, *The Ballet of the Night* (1653), was divided into forty-three "entries," featuring such groups as hunters, bandits, shepherds, gypsies, astrologers, the Four Elements, Venus, and Aurora, each related to a different phase of the night. Finally, the Sun, danced by Louis XIV, appeared to disperse the darkness. This piece of transparent flattery was one of many works that helped to create the image of Louis XIV as the "Sun King" (around which everything revolves), a symbol promoted assiduously throughout his reign.

In 1654 Mazarin, seeking once more to adapt opera to French taste, commissioned Isaac Bensérade (1613–1691), who had composed the librettos for the majority of the court ballets, to write an opera

FIG. 9.10

Giacomo Torelli's setting for Act II of Pierre Corneille's *Andromède* at the Petit Bourbon, 1650. Engraving by François Chauveau. Courtesy Bibliothèque Nationale, Paris.

with ballets interspersed between the acts. For this production, *The Marriage of Peleus and Thetis,* Torelli designed seven sets and a number of spectacular special effects. Louis XIV appeared in six roles. Thus, opera and ballet were joined in a relationship that would continue thereafter. After Louis gave up performing around 1661, he established the Royal Academy of Dance so ballet could be turned over to professionals.

FRENCH COURT THEATRE: THE SALLE DE MACHINES, COMEDY BALLET, AND FRENCH OPERA, 1660–1700

The innovations in scenic practice that had been introduced by Torelli were strengthened by the preparations made for the marriage of Louis XIV. In 1659 Mazarin sent to Italy for Gaspare Vigarani (1586–1663), famous at this time as a scenic designer and builder of theatres. The Petit Bourbon was torn down, and a new wing was added to the Tuileries Palace. Within this wing Vigarani constructed the largest theatre in Europe, the Salle des Machines. Although only 52 feet wide, the new theatre was 232 feet long; of this length, only 92 feet were occupied by the auditorium, leaving 140 feet of depth for a stage which had a proscenium arch only 32 feet wide. This enormous depth is symptomatic of the trend then underway toward settings of ever-increasing size. Completed in 1660, the Salle des Machines was inaugurated in 1662 with the opera *Hercules in Love,* a transparent compliment to the king. Interlayered with ballets, the opera featured Vigarani's scenery and machines, on one of which, 60 feet deep by 45 feet wide, the entire royal family and their attendants were flown. This machine was used again in *Psyché* (1671) to display 300 deities surrounded by clouds. Despite this auspicious beginning, the Salle des Machines was seldom used after the 1660s because of its size and poor acoustics.

Gaspare Vigarani replaced Torelli as court designer when Mazarin died in 1661. Having established the Italian ideal in France, Torelli returned to his native Fano, where he later built a theatre and staged his last production in 1677, the year before he died. When Vigarani died in 1663, the post of court designer was given to his son, Carlo (1623–1713), who retained it until 1680. Carlo Vigarani's principal work was done at the opera in Paris and at the court at Versailles.

After 1660 Louis XIV's attention turned increasingly to the palace he was building at Versailles twelve miles outside of Paris. Eventually this palace would be more than a half mile long with several wings

FIG. 9.11
Plan of the Salle des Machines designed by Gaspare Vigarani and first used in 1662. From L. P. de la Guepière, *Théâtre et Machine* (1888).

and hundreds of rooms. While it was being built, Louis staged several festivals there, using temporary theatres set up at various spots in the palace grounds. One of the most spectacular of the celebrations was that of 1664, called "The Pleasures of the Enchanted Island," which extended over three days, and included processions, tournaments, ballets, and plays.

Throughout the 1660s, "comedy ballets," in which scenes in dialogue alternate with ballet entries, were a favorite with Louis. Many of these were written by Molière and Jean-Baptiste Lully (1632–1687), destined to become the founder of French opera. Lully was born in Italy, but came to France when only twelve years old. Appointed a court musician in 1653, by 1661 he was superintendent of all court music. In this capacity, he worked closely with Molière and others on court entertainment, and his experience with ballets, machine plays, and other forms familiarized him with French musical taste. In 1672 he obtained a monopoly on musical performances in Paris from Louis XIV, and in 1673 after Molière's death, he wrested control of the Palais Royal from Molière's widow to use as the home of his Royal Academy of Music and Dance (created in 1672 by the amalgamation of the Royal Academy of Dance and the Royal Academy of Music), more commonly called simply the Opéra. Although the terms of Lully's monopoly were vague, he interpreted them to cover any performance that required more than six instruments, two trained singers, or elaborate spectacle. The latter provision is indicative of the period's association of spectacle with opera, for, as the neoclassical ideal triumphed in drama, staging had become increasingly simple. Lully's monopoly put an end to the "machine plays" at the Marais and thus further

weakened that company, which had steadily declined since 1647.

Between 1672 and 1687 Lully created a series of works considered to mark the beginnings of French opera. His principal collaborator was Phillippe Quinault (1635–1688), author of fourteen librettos, of which the most famous are *Atys* (1676) and *Armide* (1686). Until 1680, when he returned to Italy, Vigarani designed the scenery for these operas.

Carlo Vigarani was succeeded by Jean Berain *père* (1637–1711). Educated entirely in France, Berain is credited with the first complete realization of the visual style associated with the reign of Louis XIV. Employed at court in 1671 to design embroidery, tapestry, woodcarving, and furniture, he succeeded Henri Gissey as "Designer of the Cabinet of the King" in 1674. Since Gissey had customarily designed costumes for the opera, Berain also assumed this job. After 1680, Berain was principal designer for the court and the opera until his death, when he was succeeded by his son, Jean Berain *fils* (1678–1726), who held the posts until 1721. To the Berains goes the credit for

FIG. 9.12
Design by Vigarani, *c.* 1660. Courtesy National Museum, Stockholm.

FIG. 9.13
One of the entertainments from the first day of "Pleasures of the Enchanted Island," given by Louis XIV at Versailles in 1664. The stage in the middle of a lake represents the palace of Alcine; after an elaborate ballet was performed there, the palace was destroyed by fire. A contemporary engraving by Israel Silvestre.

establishing a distinctively French style of design emphasizing heavy line, reverse curves, and encrusted ornamentation. Most of the operas designed by Berain required only one set but many machines and special effects for each act. This combination of static scenery and dynamic machinery was to remain typical of French operatic design through the eighteenth century.

By the time the court moved to Versailles in 1682, the Italian ideals of staging had been completely naturalized, and France had replaced Italy as the cultural center of Europe. Court taste had been decisive in this process but once the courtiers no longer made up a significant part of the audience, the influence of the court on the Parisian stage declined.

FRENCH DRAMA, 1660–1700

Following its decline during the Fronde rebellion, drama began to recover in the late 1650s. Tragedy returned to favor with *Timocrate* (1656) by Thomas Corneille (1625–1709), younger brother of Pierre Corneille. Author of more than forty plays, the best of which are *Ariane* (1672), *The Statue's Banquet* (1673), and *The Count of Essex* (1678), Thomas Corneille was one of the most successful dramatists of his time, although his reputation has suffered by comparison with that of his brother.

Pierre Corneille returned to writing in 1659 with *Oedipe*. Although many of his late works are of unquestioned merit, they are overshadowed by Jean Racine's (1639–1699) plays, with which French tragedy reached its peak. Racine received an excellent education which instilled in him a lasting admiration of the Greek dramatists, whose example he

sought to follow. His first tragedy, *La Thébaide,* was produced in 1664 by Molière, who, in spite of the financial failure of the play, also produced Racine's second work, *Alexander the Great* (1665). Dissatisfied with the production, Racine permitted the Hôtel de Bourgogne to present the same play two

FIG. 9.14
Berain's costume design for an Indian in *The Triumph of Love,* 1681. From Adolphe Jullien, *Histoire du Costume au Théâtre* (1880).

FIG. 9.15
Jean Berain's design for Lully's opera, *Armide* (1686). Courtesy National Museum, Stockholm.

weeks later, an unprecedented breach of contract, and induced Mlle DuParc, Molière's principal tragic actress, to join the Hôtel de Bourgogne. This double treachery led to a permanent rupture between the two men.

Racine's reputation, established by *Andromaque* in 1667, grew steadily during the next ten years with *Britannicus* (1669), *Bérénice* (1670), *Bajazet* (1672), *Mithridate* (1673), *Iphigénie* (1674), and *Phèdre* (1677). In addition to his tragedies, Racine wrote one comedy, *The Litigants* (1668), based in part on Aristophanes' *The Wasps*. After *Phèdre,* Racine was appointed historiographer to Louis XIV and abandoned his literary life. Some years later he wrote *Esther* (1689) and *Athalie* (1691) for a school for girls favored by Mme de Maintenon (Louis XIV's second wife).

Racine's reputation is based on the tragedies written between 1667 and 1677, of which *Phèdre* (whose uncontrollable passion for her stepson Hippolyte brings disaster) is the acknowledged masterpiece. Racine's greatness stems from his ability to develop compelling dramatic actions out of the internal conflicts of his protagonists. In contrast with Corneille's use of simple characters and complex plots, Racine constructed simple plots and complex characters. Because Racine's protagonists vacillate between two courses of action, torn between their sense of duty and their uncontrollable desires, dramatic interest is centered on the inner struggle rather than on the external events. The plays usually begin some time after the protagonists have become aware of a dilemma. In a state of high emotion, they usually lay their souls bare to *confidants* during the opening scene. The protagonist's psychological struggle makes up the dramatic action. Therefore, Racine was able to express

his tragic vision adequately within the confines of the neoclassical ideal. Upon Racine's retirement, tragedy began a long decline, although this was not immediately apparent, since at the time other writers seemed worthy successors.

Like tragedy, comedy reached its peak in the 1660s and 1670s. As Racine represents the summit in tragic writing, so Molière epitomizes comic dramaturgy. With his work, comedy was raised to a level equaling tragedy.

FIG. 9.16
Scene from Racine's *Bérénice,* first performed in 1670 at the Hôtel de Bourgogne with Mlle Champmeslé in the title role. Engraving from the edition of Racine's plays published in 1676.

Molière (Jean-Baptiste Poquelin, 1622–1673), the son of a prosperous upholsterer and furniture maker, was given an excellent education and was destined for a court position until he joined with nine other young people to form the Théâtre Illustre in 1643. Having failed in Paris, the troupe set off on a tour of the provinces in 1646, which lasted until 1658. By 1651, Molière was head of the troupe. He then turned to writing plays, his first important work being *The Blunderer* (1655). The turning point in the troupe's fortunes came in 1658 when it was invited to court by the king's brother, who had seen it perform in the provinces. The company was sufficiently well received to be granted permission to use the Petit Bourbon for public performances.

The company was not very successful with the public, however, until it presented Molière's *The Affected Ladies (Les Précieuses Ridicules,* 1659), a satire on contemporary affectations. After this production, its fortunes were assured. When the Petit Bourbon was torn down, Molière was allowed to use the Palais Royal, built by Richelieu and remodeled by Torelli. Here the company played from 1660 until 1673, enjoying a position of preeminence in comedy similar to that attained by the Bourgogne in tragedy. In 1665 they were granted an annual subsidy and the title "The King's Troupe." The reputation of the Palais Royal troupe derived primarily from Molière's plays, the core of its repertory. Now remembered principally for his comedies of character, Molière wrote other kinds of plays as well. Many of his works are farces in the manner of the *commedia dell'arte,* by which he was much influenced. Some of the most popular of these were *Sganarelle,* or *The Imaginary Cuckold* (1660), *The Doctor in Spite of Himself* (1666), and *The Tricks of Scapin* (1671). Other works were written especially for court festivities, although most were later performed for the general public. A large number of these were "comedy ballets," such as *The Bores* (1661), *The Forced Marriage* (1664), *The Princess of Elide* (1664), and *Monsieur de Pourceaugnac* (1669). Others, such as *Amphitryon* (1668) and *Psyché* (1671) were "machine plays" with much spectacle. On most of the court plays, Molière collaborated with Lully, who provided the music. Molière attempted serious drama, as in *Don Garcie de Navarre* (1661), but with little success.

Molière's great achievements are his comedies of character and manners, such as *The School for Husbands* (1661), *The School for Wives* (1662), *Tartuffe* (1664, 1667, 1669), *The Misanthrope* (1666), *The Miser* (1668), *The Learned Ladies* (1672), and *The Imaginary Invalid* (1673). His observations on contemporary manners and character types in these works embroiled him in much controversy. The first important battle was precipitated by *The School for Wives* (1662), which treated the upbringing appropriate to young girls who are to be faithful wives. Although enormously popular, the play was attacked on both artistic and moral grounds. Molière answered in two plays: *The Critique of The School for Wives* (1663) and *The Rehearsal at Versailles* (1663). By far the bitterest controversy centered around *Tartuffe,* a play in which the title character is exposed as a religious hypocrite. Many saw this as a condemnation of all religion when it was performed at court in 1664, and Molière had to rewrite it twice (in 1667 and 1669) before it was authorized for performance. The 1669 production ran for thirty-three performances, a record for the time.

These quarrels clearly indicate that Molière had made comedy a vital reflection of contemporary life and manners. In his long plays, Molière usually conforms to the neoclassical ideal of five acts and the unities. Some of the plays are written in verse, others in prose. Although his language is varied, it is rarely witty for its own sake; aptness to character and situation is the secret of his dialogue. Many of his plays are set in drawing rooms, a clear departure from previous comedy, which had usually been placed out of doors in the manner of Roman comedy. With Molière, the settings are a reflection of the manners and characters depicted, and his example did much to popularize the interior setting for comedy. Molière wrote for his own company and knew who would play each character. Furthermore, he directed his

FIG. 9.17

Plan of the Palais Royal. This theatre was built by Richelieu and remodeled by Torelli. It served as the home of Molière's company from 1660 until 1673, and was used by the Opéra from 1673 until 1763, when it was destroyed by fire. Note the seatless pit (marked O at left). From Blondel, *Architecture Française* (1754).

FIG. 9.18
Scene from Molière's *The Learned Ladies,* first performed at the Palais Royal in 1672 with Molière in the role of Chrysale (at left). From the edition of Molière's plays published in 1682.

own plays and often played the leading role himself. Hence, details were probably added during rehearsals that are not explicitly stated in the scripts.

ACTING COMPANIES, 1660–1700

When Molière died in 1673, Paris had five professional troupes: Molière's, Lully's opera company, a *commedia dell'arte* troupe, and the companies at the Hôtel de Bourgogne and at the Marais. All received some financial assistance from the crown. By 1700, only two would remain.

At Molière's death, many doubted his company's ability to continue. To allay anxieties, the troupe resumed performances after one week. Soon, however, a number of actors seceded, and Lully was able to evict the troupe from the Palais Royal. The company sought control of the theatre in the rue Guénégaud, which had housed Lully's troupe, but the Marais

company also was vying for it. Louis XIV intervened by ordering the closing of the Marais and the amalgamation of the two companies. The combined groups opened at the Guénégaud in July 1673.

This situation continued until 1679, when Mlle Champmeslé, the Bourgogne's principal tragic actress, left that company to join the troupe at the Guénégaud and the Bourgogne's leading tragic actor, LaThorillière, died. This crisis was also resolved by a crown order joining the two companies. Thus came into existence the Comédie Française, the world's first national theatre. The new company gave its first performance on August 25, 1680, at the theatre in the rue Guénégaud.

Upon its formation, the Comédie Française was given a monopoly on the performance of all spoken drama in French that the Confrérie had given up

FIG. 9.19
Angelo Constantini receiving Arlequin's mask and baton from Columbine. In the background are seen the figure and tomb of Domenico Biancolelli, the Arlequin who has died. This is the *commedia dell'arte* company that played in France from 1661 until 1697. Watercolor by Lichery, 1688. Courtesy Bibliothèque Nationale, Paris.

when it dissolved in 1677. Almost immediately, however, an exception to this monopoly was granted the *commedia dell'arte* troupe headed by Tiberio Fiorillo (1608–1694) that had made Paris its permanent home since 1661 and had begun to perform in French. They were installed at the Bourgogne, which they refurbished, adding a third level of *loges*, remodeling the stage, and installing machinery that permitted the use of complex spectacle. This troupe became increasingly popular with the middle classes, but the audacity of its plays, like *The False Prude*, a supposed satire of the second wife of Louis XIV, lost it the support of the court and it was finally expelled in 1697. There were to be no more Italian troupes in Paris until 1716. Thus, in 1697 the Parisian companies were reduced to two: the Comédie Française and the Opéra.

THE ORGANIZATION OF FRENCH ACTING COMPANIES

All of the French acting companies of the seventeenth century were organized on the sharing plan, under which all regular members participated in the management and divided the profits. The number of members varied with the company's prosperity. Before 1650, there were usually eight to twelve; when Molière returned to Paris in 1658, his troupe included ten members, but was increased to twelve (seven men and five women) in 1659. When the Comédie Française was formed in 1680, 21 shares were divided among twenty-seven members (17 full shares, 7 one-half shares, and 3 one-quarter shares). Thus, an actor's share varied according to his or her importance in the company.

Since the number of shares in the Comédie Française was fixed by the First Gentlemen of the Chamber (the court officials who superintended the troupe), not all the actors were sharing members (or *sociétaires*). No new member could be admitted as a sharer until an actor resigned, retired, or died. When a vacancy occurred, the *sociétaires* elected a new member, usually from among the *pensionnaires* (the actors who worked for the troupe on salary). To obtain a position with the Comédie Française, actors were required to play a series of roles in regular public performances; if the troupe wished to retain them, they placed them on salary until a vacancy in membership occurred, although many *pensionnaires* never became *sociétaires*. When they became *sociétaires*, actors bound themselves to the company for twenty years and made themselves liable to a heavy fine if they quit. The *sociétaires* had a voice in all matters of policy, including the acceptance of new plays. The actor with the longest service acted as head (or *doyen*) of the troupe. The Comédie Française also continued the pension system that had evolved among the earlier troupes. Under it, actors could retire after twenty years of service with an annual pension. The government also continued to provide the troupe with an annual subsidy.

A member of the Comédie Française had considerable security, but an assured position as a *sociétaire* sometimes led to complacency and arrogance. The opportunities for employment had also been considerably restricted, since after 1680 the Comédie Française was the only troupe employing French actors in Paris.

Of the actors who achieved fame in the years between 1660 and 1700, several were associated with Molière. Madeleine Béjart (1618–1672) was already an established provincial actress when Molière met her. She is credited with inducing him to become an actor and was intimately involved in his work until her death. In the early years she often played tragic heroines, but later she was best as the saucy maids of Molière's comedies. Geneviève Béjart (c. 1622–1675) and Joseph Béjart (c. 1620–1659), who played young lovers; and Louis Béjart (1625–1678), who played comic valets, were also members of the troupe. Armande Béjart (1642–1700), who became Molière's wife in 1662, made her debut in 1663 and thereafter played the heroines in his plays. A versatile actress, she did much to hold the company together after her husband's death.

Along with Molière's wife, LaGrange (Charles Varlet, c. 1639–1692) was responsible for the continuation of Molière's company. Employed in 1659 to replace Joseph Béjart, he played a variety of roles (including young lovers) and also kept the company's records until 1685. His *Registre,* which records receipts, performances, and all deliberations, is the principal source of information about Molière's troupe and the early years of the Comédie Française. LaGrange also wrote the only contemporary biography of Molière, published in 1682 in the first edition of Molière's works.

Of tragic performers, the most important were Mlle DuParc, Mlle Champmeslé, and Michel Baron. Mlle DuParc (1633–1668) joined Molière's troupe in the provinces and remained with him until 1666, when Racine is said to have lured her to the Bourgogne, where she became the leading tragic actress. Mlle Champmeslé (1642–1698) came to the Marais in 1669, also after a career in the provinces. Within six months she was considered the finest tragic actress in Paris and had moved to the Bourgogne. Her eventual desertion of the Bourgogne may have motivated the formation of the Comédie Française.

Michel Baron (1653–1729) had been a child actor even before Molière took him into his home in 1666 and trained him further. His adult career began in 1670 as Domitien in Corneille's *Titus and Bérénice.* By the time of Molière's death, Baron was noted as a fine actor of the natural school. He joined the Bourgogne in 1673 and was soon recognized as the leading tragic actor of the day and continued to be so regarded until he retired in 1691. (His return to the stage in 1720 will be considered later.) To many, Baron was the epitome of great acting and the finest serious actor of the seventeenth century.

Actors were not as yet employed to play a specified range of character types, as they were to be in the eighteenth century, although type casting seems often to have been used. A new play was cast by the author, and actors were forbidden to refuse a role. Old plays were cast by the company in consultation. Rehearsals, perfunctory by modern standards, were held in the late morning. Although authors allegedly staged their own plays, they probably relied heavily upon the advice of a leading actor. Once a play had been performed, the actors were considered ready to present it at any time thereafter. There were usually about seventy plays in the active repertory, and these plays were rotated in a daily change of bill.

The expenses of a company were subtracted before the sharing actors were paid. The troupe did not supply costumes. Although most characters were dressed in contemporary garments, others, especially classical, Near Eastern, and Native American figures, were usually played in elaborate and costly costumes quite unlike those worn in daily life. The typical dress of classical heroes, the *habit à la romaine,* an adaptation of Roman armor, tunic, and boots, accompanied by a full-bottomed wig and plumed headdress, cost about 2000 livres, a sum roughly equivalent to one-third of the actor's annual income. This financial burden was somewhat relieved by the royal practice of paying actors 400 livres for each costume they provided in plays mounted especially for court. In spite of the expenses, the sharing actor in the Comédie Française was well paid by the standards of the time.

Until 1680, the troupes played only three or four days each week, the preferred days being Tuesday, Friday, and Sunday. After 1680, the troupes began to play daily; in the 1682–1683 season the Comédie Française gave 352 performances. After 1680, the usual starting time was about 5 P.M. Although the population of Paris was about 500,000, the average attendance at the Comédie Française between 1680 and 1700 was only about 450 persons in theatres designed to hold 1500 to 2000. Spectators still stood in the pit and moved about freely. Others sat on the stage, a practice which some scholars date from the first production of *Le Cid* in 1636. By the late seventeenth century, there were occasionally as many as 150 spectators on the stage during a performance, a condition that undoubtedly affected acting style and the sense of illusion.

THEATRE ARCHITECTURE AND SCENIC PRACTICES, 1660–1700

The Marais was abandoned in 1673, and the Palais Royal was refurbished for the Opéra. Little is known of the theatre in the rue Guénégaud, occupied by the Marais-Molière troupe from 1673 to 1680 and

FIG. 9.20
Theatre in the rue Guénégaud, built in 1670, and used by the Opéra, the Molière-Marais company, and the Comédie Française successively. Note the chandeliers over the stage and the spectators on the stage and in the boxes. Courtesy Bibliothèque Nationale, Paris.

by the Comédie Française from 1680 until 1689. Built in 1670 by the Marquis de Sourdéac, it housed Lully's operatic productions from 1671 until 1673, when he gained control of the Palais Royal.

The Comédie Française was ordered to leave the rue Guénégaud in 1687, when the Sorbonne decided to build a new college nearby. Not until 1689 was it able to acquire a new home, the Etoile tennis court in the rue Neuve-des-Fossés in the St. Germain-des-Prés quarter of Paris. Remodeled by the architect François d'Orbay at a cost of 200,000 livres, it put the company in debt for many years. It was to be the home of the Comédie Française until 1770.

D'Orbay ignored the exterior walls of the tennis court and constructed inside them a U-shaped auditorium. On the ground floor, a standing pit was backed by an amphitheatre raised about 6 feet above it. Along the walls, two levels of nineteen boxes were surmounted by an undivided gallery. The total capacity of the auditorium was about 2000.

The stage was about 41 feet deep by 54 feet wide, but the available acting area was considerably restricted by spectators on the stage. A few benches were placed in the orchestra pit, which was not used

by the musicians because of objections raised by the Opéra. When musicians were needed, they were placed in a box at the rear of the auditorium. The stage was equipped for flat wings and shutters, but since changes of scene were seldom required, the machinery was minimal.

This stage reflects the changes which had occurred in scenic practices since the 1630s. *Le Mémoire de Mahelot, Laurent, et d'Autres Décorateurs,* the last part of which was compiled between 1678 and 1686, contains notices of fifty-four plays performed at the Hôtel de Bourgogne between 1678 and 1680, and sixty-nine notices of plays staged at the rue Guénégaud between 1680 and 1686. Most of these notices were written by Michel Laurent.

The principal change indicated by Laurent's notices of 1678 to 1686, in comparison with those by Mahelot in 1634 and 1635, is the trend toward simplicity. By Laurent's time, most settings represented a single place and were composed of flat wings. The rear shutters may have been pierced by doors, since entrances from the sides were impeded by onstage spectators.

The typical, though not invariable, background for tragedies was the *palais à volonté,* a neutral set-

FIG. 9.21

Plan of the theatre used by the Comédie Française from 1689 until 1770. It opened 18 April 1689 with *Phèdre* and *The Doctor in Spite of Himself.* The benches for spectators on stage were added in the eighteenth century. From Adolphe Jullien, *Les Spectateurs sur le Théâtre* (1875).

ting suited to the action but without particularizing details. Consequently, it could serve as a background for all scenes in the same town without any changes, for it was usually so anonymous that it might represent a street, a square, a vestibule, or a palace. A variation showed tents near a battlefield, often with a sea or city in the background. For comedy, the *chambre à quartre portes* (a room with four doors) was typical. It differed in no important way from the *palais à volonté*, except that it depicted domestic architecture, usually an interior, whereas the *palais à volonté* was more formal. The unity of place was never completely adopted, however, for in some plays the settings changed with each act. In others, a shutter or curtain was opened to reveal another place behind the one previously shown. By the end of the seventeenth century, the typical setting at the Comédie Française supplied a suitable, though neutral, background which placed little emphasis upon illusion and concentrated attention upon the actor.

THE CLOSE OF THE SEVENTEENTH CENTURY

By 1700, then, two Parisian troupes with monopolistic privileges divided the whole range of drama between them. The vigor of earlier years had been replaced by a spirit of conservatism. Rather than searching for new horizons, dramatists looked to the past for standards. The prevailing mood can be seen in the "Battle of the Ancients and Moderns" which raged in the French Academy and elsewhere after 1688 over the relative merits of classical and seventeenth-century French writers. The battle, which continued into the eighteenth century, was decided in favor of French authors, which meant that Corneille and Racine replaced the Greek tragedians as standards for tragedy and that Molière replaced Plautus and Terence as models for comedy. Although French drama long continued to set the standard for Europe, its period of greatest vitality, like the Golden Age of Spanish Theatre, was over by 1700.

LOOKING AT THEATRE HISTORY

One of the earliest nonfictional attempts to describe how a company functioned was written by a playwright, Samuel Chappuzeau (1625–1701). It treats almost all aspects of theatrical production in the 1670s. Here is his summary of rehearsal practices:

The roles being duly distributed, each actor goes off to memorize his part, and if time is pressing and a special effort is made, a full length play can be memorized in a week. . . . When they feel themselves secure in their parts, they gather for the first rehearsal, which serves only to give a rough sketch of the whole, and it is not until the second or third rehearsal that it is possible to judge what success the play may have. They do not risk producing a play until it has been perfectly memorized and well staged, and the final rehearsal ought to be exactly like a regular performance. Ordinarily the author attends these rehearsals and instructs the actor if he falls into some error, if he fails to grasp the sense, if he fails to be natural in voice and gesture, if he expresses more or less emotion than the action demands. Intelligent actors are allowed to give their opinions in these

rehearsals, without offending their comrades, since it is a question of the common good.

Le Théâtre Français (Paris, 1674), book II, ch. 17.

During the seventeenth century French scenic conventions underwent a complete transformation. The scenic practices of the Hôtel de Bourgogne are well documented in *Le Mémoire de Mahelot, Laurent, et d'Autres Décorateurs,* . . . the first part of which ends in 1635. Here is Mahelot's summary of the requirements for du Ryer's *Lisandre and Caliste.* (The sketch of this simultaneous setting is reproduced in Fig. 9.6.)

It requires at the center of the stage the little castle of Saint Jacques and a street where the butchers are located, and in one of the butcher's houses a window which is directly across from the grilled window of the prison, from which Lisandre can speak to Caliste. This must be hidden during the first act, and it should be made to appear during the second act and to close again during the same act; in closed position it serves as the palace. At one side of the stage a hermitage on a mountain and a cavern below from which a hermit enters. On the other side of the stage, there should be a room into which one enters from behind, raised by two or three steps. Some helmets, bucklers, shields, trumpets, and an unsheathed sword. It is also necessary in one scene for it to be night.

By the mid-century the Italian scenic ideal had triumphed, largely because of Torelli's work after 1645. Torelli's settings for Corneille's *Andromède* (presented at the Petit Bourbon in 1650) are described in the playwright's script and are depicted in a series of contemporary engravings. Here are the descriptive passages for Act II. The engraving of this setting is shown in Fig. 9.10.

The public square vanishes in an instant to give way to a delightful garden; and the great palaces are changed into so many white marble vases, which alternately bear statues from which jets of water spring, others blossoming with jasmine, and other plants of that nature. On each side stands a line of orange trees in similar vases, which form an admirable bower in the middle of the stage, and separates it into three paths,

which the ingenious art of perspective makes appear more than a thousand feet deep. . . .

Here thunder commences to sound with so great a noise with lightning redoubled so quickly that it arouses astonishment with its naturalness. Meantime one sees Eolus descend with eight winds, of which four are at either side. . . . Two [winds] . . . descend, seize Andromède by the arms and lift her into the clouds.

Oeuvres de Pierre Corneille, vol. VI (Paris, 1821).

When Molière died without having renounced his profession as actor, he was denied a Christian burial in part, no doubt, because of the enemies he had made during the controversy over *Tartuffe*. Louis XIV intervened, but even then the Archbishop of Paris authorized only the minimal service:

We authorize the vicar of St. Eustache to give ecclesiastical burial to the body of the deceased Molière in the cemetery of the parish on condition that there shall be no ceremony, with two priests only, after nightfall, and that there shall be no solemn service for him either in the parish of St. Eustache or elsewhere, in any church of the regular clergy.

10
Asian Theatre to 1800

In the sixteenth, seventeenth, and eighteenth centuries, India, China, and Japan experienced the same kind of expansion, and to some degree the same kind of transition towards professionalism in their theatre, that occurred in Western Europe during the Renaissance. The forms developed in this period remained characteristic of their theatres until the twentieth century.

INDIA

By 1192 large portions of India had come under the domination of what later became known as the Delhi Sultanate (1210–1526), and by the early fourteenth century Muslim rule extended over all the regions of the subcontinent. But several of the southernmost states began regaining their independence as early as 1350, setting off the gradual decline that led to the Delhi Sultanate being replaced by the Mogul or Mughal empire (1526–1857), which represents the high point of Islamic culture in India.

The Portuguese arrived on the southwest coast of India in 1498 at what is now the Kerala state, and by 1510 had colonized Goa, north of Kerala; Goa remained Portuguese until 1961. The British, Danish, Dutch, and French arrived in the seventeenth century, setting up trading centers in the northwest around Bombay, in the northeast around Calcutta, and along the southeastern and southwestern costs. From 1746 to 1763, India, like North America, became part of the battleground in the war between England and France with the result that from 1757 on, India was being absorbed into the British Empire.

Because of Muslim opposition to theatre, those forms that had come out of the Golden Age of the fourth and fifth centuries were steadily driven east and south as Islamic territories expanded. By the early fourteenth century they had almost ceased to exist, though *Kutiyattum,* the offshoot of Sanskrit theatre, survived—possibly because it was both limited to performance in certain temples and because the Kerala region in which it was preserved had spent the shortest time under Muslim control.

As other regions gained their independence from Muslim overlords, traditions of folk theatre were revived, and in those areas exposed to European colonialism, theatre was encouraged, often as a tool for teaching Christianity. In extreme northern India, and in the area around the Taj Mahal, rare forms of Muslim theatre were even developed; largely farcical, satiric, and topical, they allowed these ruling communities to make fun of themselves.

Changes in the Hindu sect of Vaisnavism, which were fully underway by the sixteenth century, were of the greatest importance to the spread of theatre among the growing number of non-Muslim states in this period. This new Vaisnavism put renewed focus on Krishna and Rama as reincarnations of the great god Vishnu. Furthermore, the depiction of the stories of Krishna or Rama became devotional acts in themselves, both for those who performed and for those who watched. As a result, there was a rapid evolution of theatrical forms across India. This expansion of theatre was especially prevalent in the Orissa region on the northeast coast (just south of Calcutta), in the center-east region of Andhra Pradesh (just south of Orissa), and in the Kerala region on the extreme southwest coast.

One of the most elaborate forms to be inspired by the new Vaisnavism of the sixteenth century was *Ramlila*, a devotional theatre form that tells stories from the Ramayana staged along a processional route that gradually came to feature elephants, floats, chariots, earthen stages raised four feet high, and gigantic effigies of the ten-headed demon, Ravenna, and his five demon brothers, all of whom are consumed by fire in the final scene. This is a major celebration of north central India and in modern times it includes people from every major religion and every class, though it is not likely to have been nearly so elaborate or inclusive in its early years. Another form inspired by Vaisnavism comes from the northeastern region of Assam, and is known as *Ankiya nat*. The invention of this form is attributed to Sankaradeva (*c.* 1449–1568) who wrote one-act dramas featuring traditional tales of the Lord Krishna. They are performed by companies of fifteen, usually monks, but sometimes village artists, in which case women are often included in the cast. Elaborate masks are used in these productions along with large effigies that take several actors to operate. These plays also feature a stage manager who stays with the actors on stage, holding a text to ensure the accuracy of their lines. Like many such forms in India, there is a long festive buildup to the performance, during which major characters are introduced and high levels of energy are created. Other characteristics of this form that are common to many dramatic forms in India are:

1. The acting is stylized, but uses conventions that are fully understood by the local audience.
2. Music accompanies the entire performance and is coordinated with the performers.
3. Scenery is not used.
4. Stage hands and stage managers appear on stage in full view of the audience but are ignored by them.
5. Performances start late and continue all night in the light of flickering torches.

Tamasha, one of the most popular comic forms of theatre today in west-central India, seems also to have started in the sixteenth century but not under the influence of Vaisnavism. It seems more likely to have originated in the satiric sketches done for the troops fighting the Mogul armies.

The variety of dramatic forms found in the Kerala region is representative of the range to be found across the country, so its forms are a convenient focus for any discussion of Indian theatre between the middle ages and the eighteenth century. First there are the shadow puppets (*Pavaikuthu*) and the glove puppets (*Pavai kathakali*). Under different names, both forms of puppets, as well as certain kinds of doll puppets, are common throughout India, but little has been done to establish a date of origin for any of them. Then there are the narrative dance forms done by solo female dancers; the *Mohiniyattam* is the most famous in Kerala, while *Bharata natyam* would be an equivalent form in the north, and *Odissi*, the oldest such form, in the northeast. (Odissi had to be completely reconstructed from temple paintings and statuary in the twentieth century.) *Kathak* is another such form, but it is performed by solo dancers of either sex.

After that come the dance forms performed by companies, like *Kathakali,* which is done by highly skilled, all-male companies of actors in Kerala. They rely entirely upon dance, mime, costume, and makeup, while musicians tell the story through song and instrumental accompaniment. Its subject matter is taken primarily from the Hindu epics. Perhaps because it is pantomimic, Kathakali has exaggerated many of the features found in Sanskrit drama and has brought violence and death onto the stage. Its stories center around the passions and furies of gods and demons, or the loves and hates of superhuman characters; the forces of good and evil clash in desperate struggles, but good always wins. The gestural language includes more than 500 separate signs. Characters fall into about seven basic types, each with its own elaborate and layered costume and symbolic makeup, which takes hours to apply. Kathakali uses boys or men to perform female roles. The Kathakali dancer must begin his training as a child and is not considered mature until he has performed a role for about twenty years. Kathakali traditionally has been presented in a family or temple courtyard or other open space, upon a stage about 20 feet square covered with a flower-decked canopy and lighted by torches, but in recent times it has frequently been seen on proscenium stages. Performances last all night.

The *Bhagavata mela* performed in west-central India also dates from the sixteenth century and is also performed by all-male companies of dancers, but its actors speak some dialogue. *Yakshagana,* from that same region, also resembles *Kathakali* in the way the story is sung while the actors pantomime the action, but in *Yakshagana,* not only is there some dialogue, it is improvised. The sung portions of this form make up the oldest non-Sanskrit texts we have for Indian folk drama.

Finally come the forms that use dialogue. Kerala's *Cavittu natakam* was inspired by the Portuguese and must originally have resembled the Spanish auto sacramentales. They focused on stories of St. George and St. Steven as they had the most interesting correspondences to heroes of Hindu epic. In later years the most successful play of this form was "The play of Charlemagne" and still later, a version of Ariosto's *Orlando Furioso* was popular. Where much of the dance drama of India stresses graceful, beautiful movements, the *Cavittu natakam,* like a number of other forms, uses martial arts training as its basis for dance movements.

Each of these types found in Kerala has parallels in other regions of India, but the regional differences are generally more significant than the similarities. While Sanskrit drama, like the Catholic dramas of medieval Europe, had easily crossed state boundaries, the folk dramas that came out of sixteenth and seventeenth century India were distinctive to each region and the variations are extremely numerous. In some locales they assume operatic form and feature legendary heroes or themes of love and chivalry; in others they are light farces, dance-dramas, or devotional plays. While all of the forms named here, and many more, are still performed in India today, all have changed considerably since their origins in the sixteenth and seventeenth centuries and many had to be recreated in the nineteenth century. Many others have been lost to us.

The great exploring expedition of the Chinese Ming Dynasty admiral, Zheng He (1371–1435, also Cheng Ho), arrived in Kerala in 1406. It is not known what information he may have brought with him concerning Chinese theatre, or what he took back concerning the theatre of India, but at the time Chinese theatre, too, was about to undergo a major expansion.

CHINA

In China the north/south divide in theatrical style that had started in the Sông dynasty (960–1279) continued through the Yüan dynasty (1279–1368), when the "northern" or *zaju* style became the most influential. But in the mid-sixteenth century, during the Ming dynasty (1368–1644), Wei Lianfu introduced changes to the southern style (*nanxi*) that introduced a new musical form, *Kunshan-qiang* (later known as *Kunqu*), which was a radical departure from tradi-

tional music. The playwright Laing Chenyu (1520–1580) incorporated this new music into his play, *Wishing Silk* (1579) and it became so successful that this new southern style came to dominate Chinese theatre for the next 200 years.

A southern play may have as many as fifty or more acts, each with its own title. In the opening act, usually called the argument or prologue, a secondary character sets forth the author's purpose and explains the story. Succeeding acts introduce many plot strands, all of which are happily resolved by the final scene. Any of the characters may sing, and there are solos, duets, and even choruses. The music is composed from a five-tone scale (except for those tunes borrowed from northern drama). The melodies are usually soft and slow (four or five times as slow as in northern drama). The basic accompaniment is played on a horizontal bamboo flute (*di ci* or *ti tzu*), noted for its lingering and emotionally evocative effects. The orchestra also includes other (especially percussion) instruments.

For the most part this later southern drama followed the traditions established by Kao Ming in *The Lute* (1367). The main changes lay in greater harmony between words and melody, more elaborate and standardized musical scores, and the exclusive use of the Suzhou dialect (noted for its sweet, liquid sounds) in the dramatic songs. This dramatic form was known as *chuanqui*, and it became the dominant drama for elite audiences. Although northern dramas continued to be written after 1600, they were mainly poetic exercises, and the earlier northern dramas ceased to be performed.

The best of the Ming dramatists was probably Tang Xianzu (or Hsientsu, 1550–1616) whose four plays, collectively called the "Four Dreams," all develop the theme that life is but an illusion. *The Peony Pavilion* is the most admired of the four. In fifty-five acts it tells a complex story of a girl who pines her life away for a lover she has seen only in a dream; later, when he actually appears at her grave she is resurrected. Her father, believing that a deception is being practiced on him, has the lover arrested and beaten before harmony is restored. The play has great variety—a trial in Hades, combats, farcical episodes, suspense, and rescues—but it is most renowned for its love scenes and poetry. (This play became the focus of an international incident in 1998 when New York's Lincoln Center commissioned a production for its annual festival. Mounted in Shanghai with Chinese actors, the production was forbidden by cultural censors, but was remounted in the United States in 1999. This was the first time the work, in fifty-five scenes taking nineteen hours to perform, had ever been mounted in its entirety.) Tang Xianzu's greatest rival was Shen Jing (1553–1610), an expert in prosody whose most lasting contribution was a treatise on the musical patterns of southern drama, long the standard work on the subject.

Although in the beginning southern drama was a vital theatrical form, it too gradually became mere closet drama. The scripts often became too long to be produced in their totality; the language became too formal and filled with allusions to be understood by anyone other than scholars; and the writers came to follow prescribed rules of prosody so slavishly that spontaneity suffered. Nevertheless, the southern style continued to dominate literary output until well after the Manchu invaders from the north established the Qing (also Ch'ing) or Manchu dynasty (1644–1912). The most important dramatists of the Qing period are Kong Shang Ven (1648–1718), whose *Peach Blossom Fan* shows a series of tragic episodes during the closing years of the Ming dynasty, and Hong Sheng (*c.* 1646–1704), whose *The Palace of Long Life* deals with the love of a Tang emperor for his concubine.

Alongside these literary works there were others intended primarily for theatrical performance. The best of the popular writers was Li Yu (1611–*c.* 1680), noted especially for his intricate comedies of situation, such as *Ordained in Heaven* and *Be Circumspect in Conjugal Relations*. He was a master craftsman who invented his own plots based on the ludicrous situations of everyday life. Although extremely effective, these works were largely ignored by literary people of the time. It is ironic, therefore, that Li Yu, through his *A Temporary Lodge for My Leisure Thoughts* (1671), came to be known as China's first dramatic critic.

Unfortunately neither Li Yu nor his more literarily inclined contemporaries could stem the decline of southern drama, although it continued to be the principal type until 1853, when Suzhou, its primary home, was destroyed during a rebellion. Still, southern drama must be admired for the resiliency that permitted it to survive for some 500 years. Even after 1853, its theatrical traditions and texts were to influence its principal successor, the Beijing Opera.

BEIJING OPERA

In 1790, to celebrate the eightieth birthday of Emperor Qian Long (*r.* 1735–1795, also Ch'ien-lung), the best performers from various regions of China were brought to Peking (now Beijing). Many of these performers remained in the capital where they combined features of their regional forms into a new form called *Jingxi* (capital drama). When Westerners encountered *Jingxi* they called it Peking Opera, but it has also been known as Beijing Opera since China

changed the way its words are transliterated into the Western alphabet late in the twentieth century. Though Beijing Opera is a late eighteenth century invention, it is taken up here because it was an amalgamation of several regional forms, of which there were more than 300, distinguished from each other by musical mode, dialect, and performance traditions. Beijing Opera is primarily a theatrical rather than a literary form; its emphasis is upon rigidly controlled conventions of acting, dancing, and singing rather than upon the text. Instead of a single work, an evening's program in Beijing Opera is usually made up of a series of selections, many of them acts or portions of longer works intermingled with acrobatic displays. There are no intermissions and usually the scenes are arranged to ensure that the best actors are saved for the final episodes.

The plays of Beijing Opera are generally classified under two headings: civil plays (dealing with social and domestic themes) and military plays (involving the adventures of warriors or brigands), although the two are often mingled. The dramas are derived from earlier literary plays, novels, history, legend, mythology, folklore, and romance. All end happily. The text of a work is seldom strictly followed, for all great actors make changes at certain points, and each troupe has its own version of standard works. The dramatic action is often obscure because the selections are chosen to emphasize the high points of a story. A text, however, is merely an outline for a performance, and the audience goes to see a production rather than to hear a play so it is not thought necessary to list the names of the dramatists on the programs.

FIG. 10.1

The orchestra of Beijing Opera. Note the variety of stringed and percussion instruments. From *Peking Opera* by Rewi Alley (Beijing, 1957).

The actor is the heart of the Beijing Opera. On a bare stage furnished only with a few properties and served by drably clothed stage attendants and musicians, the lavishly and colorfully dressed actors speak, sing, and move according to rigid conventions. Acting roles are divided into four main types: male, female, painted face, and comic. The male roles (*sheng*) are subdivided into old men (*lao sheng*), young men (*xiao sheng*), and warrior types (*wu sheng*). Actors playing these roles wear simple makeup and, except for young heroes, beards. The female roles (*dan*) are subdivided into the quiet and gentle (*qing yi*), the vivacious or dissolute (*hua dan*), warrior maidens (*wu dan*), and old women (*lao dan*). Originally all *dan* roles were played by women, but from the late eighteenth century until the twentieth century actresses were forbidden. Perhaps as a result, the *dan* roles were always considered secondary until Mei Lan-fang (1894–1961), the most famous of Chinese actors, raised them to prominence. After 1911, actresses returned to the stage and now have largely supplanted the male *dan* actors. The painted face (*jing*) roles are so called because of the brilliant and elaborate patterns painted on the actors' faces. They may be rough but frank and open-minded or crafty and treacherous characters. They include warriors, bandits, courtiers, officials, gods, and supernatural beings, but the basic attributes of all are their swagger and exaggerated strength. They are also subdivided according to whether they are principal or minor characters, civilians or warriors, and whether they emphasize fighting and gymnastics or singing and acting.

The comic actor or clown (*chou*) speaks in an everyday dialect, is free to improvise, tells many jokes, and is the most realistic of the characters. He may be a servant, businessman, jailer, watchman, soldier, shrewish mother-in-law, or matchmaker. He combines the skills of the mime and the acrobat.

Upon first entrance, each important character describes his or her basic nature and appearance in a half-spoken, half-chanted passage. This is often followed by other lines in which actors explain the story, tell their names and family background, and give other essential information. Such speeches clarify situation and character quickly and leave time to develop fully the moments of high interest.

The actor's delivery of lines is rigidly controlled by conventions. Each role has its prescribed vocal timbre and pitch, and syllables are often drawn out without regard for conversational usage in order to maintain the appropriate rhythm. Even spoken passages are governed by strict rhythms and tempos. Chanted and sung passages are freely inserted into spoken monologues or dialogues. Thus, the lines are rendered in an extremely stylized manner.

FIG. 10.2

The contemporary Chinese actress Hu Hongyan in a *dan* role from Beijing Opera. Courtesy Performing Arts Program of the Asia Society.

All stage movement is related to dance, since it is rhythmical, mimetic, and symbolic. Furthermore, each word is accompanied by movement intended to enhance or explain its meaning. Such stage gesture has been fully codified. There are seven basic hand movements, many special arm movements, more than twenty different pointing gestures, more than twelve special leg movements, and a whole repertory of sleeve and beard movements. Methods of walking or running vary with each role. The prescribed gestures and movements are combined according to character, mood, situation, or other conditions.

Costumes, most of which are heavily patterned and gaudy in color, are also extremely important in the Chinese theatre. Each of the more than 300 standard items is designed to describe its wearer's character type, age, and social status through color, design, ornament, and accessories. Color is always used symbolically: red for loyalty and high position, yellow for royalty, dark crimson for barbarians or military advisors, and so on. The designs also have symbolic significance: the dragon is the emblem of the emperor; the tiger stands for power and masculine strength; the plum blossom indicates long life and feminine charm. Headgear is almost as varied as the

FIG. 10.3

A *wu sheng* (military role) character, noted for acrobatics and excellent physical coordination. From Alley, *Peking Opera* (Beijing, 1957).

FIG. 10.4

A bearded *lao sheng* (old man) role in Beijing Opera. The headdress, beard, and costume are those of a civil courtier. From Alley, *Peking Opera* (Beijing, 1957).

garments, but the approximately one hundred variations are all used symbolically. Most costumes are made of rich materials regardless of the wearer's rank, but occasionally linen or cotton is used for very poor characters or clowns.

The visual appearance is completed by makeup. Bearded *sheng* actors and old women wear very little makeup. For other female roles, the face is painted white and the eyes surrounded by a deep red, shading into pink. A similar makeup, although with less marked contrasts, is used for the unbearded *sheng* roles. The clown's distinguishing feature is the white patch around the eyes; the various types of clowns are differentiated by distinctive black markings. By far the most complex makeup is that of the *jing* roles, the entire face being painted in bold patterns symbolic of the particular character.

Such a complex and formalized system of performance requires long and rigorous training. Would-be actors enter a school between the ages of seven and twelve, where they undergo a period of strict discipline for six to twelve years. At first their training is generalized, but as a student shows suitability for a particular type of role, training

becomes specialized. If actors are to achieve fame, they must remain within the prescribed conventions of their roles but somehow endow them with their own personalities.

Above all, Beijing Opera is characterized by conventions inherited from earlier periods and developed into a strict system. Since they differ so markedly from Western practices, these conventions need to be described in some detail. Many are related to the architectural features of the playhouse.

The stage of the traditional Chinese theatre was an open platform, generally square, covered by a roof supported by lacquered columns. It was raised only a few feet above the ground, covered by a carpet, and surrounded by a wooden railing about two feet high. There were two doors in the rear wall, the one on stage right for all entrances, the one on stage left for all exits, and in between hung a large embroidered curtain. The only permanent properties were a wooden table and a few chairs, which were used symbolically to represent anything from a bed, to a banquet hall, to a law court, based on a prescribed formula of presentation. The significance of the table and chairs was further extended through their combination with other simple properties: an incense tripod on the table indicated a palace; paper and an official seal indicated an office; an embroidered, divided curtain hung from a bamboo pole signified a general's tent, an emperor's chamber, a drawing room, or a bride's bedroom, depending upon the other properties with which it was combined. The dialogue provides any further clarification needed to establish location.

Other properties served to clarify setting and action. A wall painted upon a blue flag represented a fort, city gate, or mountain pass; a whip indicated that an actor was riding a horse; two yellow flags with wheels painted on them signified a chariot or wagon. Circling the stage with one of these devices indicated a lengthy journey from one location to another. Four pieces of cloth carried by an actor running across the stage represented the wind; a banner with a fish design indicated water; a stylized paddle was used to mime rowing. A rolled water banner on a tray became a fish, while a corpse was represented by a paddle wrapped in a garment. Weapons, although modeled after real ones, were made of bamboo, wood, or rattan and were decorated. Thus, the audience's imagination was stimulated, but much was left to be filled in.

The overall conventionalization is well illustrated by the presence on stage throughout the performance of assistants who helped the actors with their costumes and brought on, removed, or rearranged properties as needed. No attempt was made to disguise their presence; in contrast with the gaudily attired actors, they wore ordinary street clothes, often of an extremely informal type.

Traditionally, the musicians also remained in full view throughout the performance and were dressed in the same style as the stage assistants. They came and went freely and were never considered part of the stage picture. (In contemporary China, where the traditional stage has largely been supplanted by the proscenium stage, musicians are usually seated in the wings rather than onstage.) Music was and remains an integral part of every performance. It provides an atmospheric background, accompanies the many sung passages, controls the timing of movements, and welds the performance into a rhythmical whole. Since Chinese musical notation is very imprecise, theatre musicians learn their parts by rote. Most music used in Beijing Opera has been worked out collaboratively between actors and musicians; most is borrowed from existing sources and recombined according to the requirements of a par-

FIG. 10.5
Scene from a Beijing Opera, *The Wild Boar Forest*, showing the hero (center) and his companion (right) buying a sword. From Alley, *Peking Opera* (Beijing, 1957).

ticular play. Although they may be classified as string, wind, and percussion, the instruments of the Chinese orchestra have no counterparts in the West. The leader of the orchestra plays a drum, which establishes the time and accentuates the rhythm. Gongs, cymbals, brass cups, flutes, stringed instruments, and more exotic items complete the orchestra. Songs are accompanied only by flute and strings, but entrances and exits are signaled by deafening percussion passages. Much of the onstage action is performed to music.

The peculiar flavor of the Chinese theatre also owes much to the audience. In the seventeenth century actors began to perform in teahouses where customers sat at tables. Permanent theatres retained this arrangement, and the ground floor was fitted out with tables and stools at which spectators were served tea while watching the play. The permanent theatres also included a raised balcony around the sides and back of the auditorium where poorer spectators sat on benches. A balcony, divided into sections much like the boxes of a Western theatre, was also added. In some periods the balcony was occupied by the wealthy class, but in others it was reserved entirely for women. After the Chinese Republic was formed

FIG. 10.6
Examples of face painting in Beijing Opera. From top left, clockwise: a heroic face; an unstable character; a dragon character; a fierce but stupid general. From *Peking Opera* by Alley (Beijing, 1957).

in 1912, the traditional arrangement of the auditorium began to change and most urban theatres eventually were furnished with Western-style chair seating. Until recently, audiences felt free to carry on conversations, to eat and drink, and to come and go during performances. They were usually familiar with the plays, having favorite passages to which they attended carefully while ignoring others.

Many of the same influences that are blended in Beijing Opera had found their way into Japanese theatre centuries before. In this same period, Japanese theatre was developing traditional theatre forms that have also become world famous.

JAPAN

During the fourteenth and fifteenth centuries Japanese theatre underwent what was probably its most crucial change, a development that can best be understood within the sociopolitical context of the time. In 1192 the emperor ceded his secular powers to a *shogun* (military dictator), a post that became hereditary, although new families won possession of the title from time to time in civil wars. Under the shogunate, Japan developed a strict feudal system that lasted until the late nineteenth century. Within this rigidly organized society, the highest rank was accorded the *samurai* (warriors), with the *shogun* at their head. Beneath the *shogun* were *daimyo* (feudal chiefs), directly responsible to him; below the *daimyo* were the *hatamoto* (or lesser warriors), many with their own fiefs but all receiving an annual allowance of rice according to their ranks. The distinctive badge of the *samurai* was the right to wear two swords. A *samurai* followed a strict code of behavior which demanded that he always be ready to face death, fulfill his filial duty, and be absolutely loyal to his lord and his class. If a *samurai* lost his position because of disgrace or poverty, he and his followers became *ronin* (men adrift), common figures in Japanese drama. Below the *samurai* were the other ranks: *shonin* (merchants), *shokunin* (artists and craftsmen), and *hyakusho* (farmers and peasants)—all with numerous subdivisions. These lesser ranks were usually denied access to the pleasures of the *samurai,* a situation that was to have considerable effect on Japanese theatre.

In 1338 the Ashikaga family assumed the shogunate and held it until the late sixteenth century. It was during the Ashikaga shogunate that Japan, after centuries of domination by imported culture, rediscovered its own heritage. The result was an era of great creative energy during which foreign and native elements were mingled in new and distinctive ways. During this time, the shoguns patronized the arts and the *daimyo,* perhaps in emulation, sought to demonstrate their cultural sophistication.

It was within this context that the first great Japanese theatrical form, Noh, emerged in the late fourteenth century.

NOH (OR NO) DRAMA AND KYOGEN

In 1374 Kan'ami Kiyotsugu (1333–1384), a major performer of *sarugaku-no,* appeared before the *shogun* Yoshimitsu Ashikaga (1358–1408), who was so impressed that he took Kan'ami and his son Zeami Motokiyo (1363–1444) under his patronage and granted them privileges that placed them among the highest officials of the court. Within this rather refined atmosphere, Noh drama assumed its characteristic form.

Kan'ami (sometimes Kwanami) was the great innovator, for he seems to have amalgamated elements of *sarugaku kuse* (a narrative song which he brought into Noh and set to dance), and Zen Buddhist ideals to create a form suited to the tastes of the *shogun* and his followers. It remained for Zeami to perfect the form. Its triumph was rapid. *Dengaku-no* quickly declined in popularity and eventually disappeared, and *sarugaku-no* came to be called merely *no* (Noh).

Zeami (sometimes Seami) is considered the greatest of all Noh dramatists. He wrote more than 100 of the approximately 240 plays that make up the active Noh repertory today. Furthermore, it was Zeami who summed up Noh's aesthetic goals and described its practices in some twenty-six theoretical treatises. Consequently, Noh is above all a product of the fourteenth and fifteenth centuries; no play written during the past 400 years holds a permanent place in the Noh repertory.

The major influence on Noh's vision is Zen Buddhism, with its belief that ultimate peace comes through union with all being, through acceptance that individual desire must be abandoned and that nothing in earthly life is permanent. The most typical Noh plays have as protagonists ghosts, demons, or obsessed human beings whose souls cannot find rest because in life they had been too much devoted to worldly honor, love, or some other goal that keeps drawing the spirit back to the physical world. Although Noh plays are extremely varied, all draw on these Buddhist views.

Noh dramas are classified into five types: *kamimono,* or plays praising the gods; *shuramono,* plays about warriors; *kazuramono,* plays about women; *zatsu,* miscellaneous plays, most often about deranged persons (usually women who have suffered grievous loss of a child or husband) or spirits but sometimes about unmasked "living persons"; and *kirimono,* plays about demons, devils, or other supernatural beings. Traditionally, a program is made up of one play of each type performed in the order listed above, making up a pattern which shows, first, the innocence and peace of the world of the gods; then human

FIG. 10.7

Scene from a Noh play. Note the audience seated at the front and side of the main platform. At upper center left is the *hashigakari* (bridge). The orchestra may be seen at the rear of the main stage; an actor stands by the *shitebashira* (upstage-right pillar). From Haar, *Japanese Theatre in Highlight.* Courtesy Charles E. Tuttle Co., Tokyo.

FIG. 10.8

The Noh stage and auditorium today. Note the Western-style seating. The bridge is at left.

error, repentance, and possibility of redemption; and, finally, the glory of defeating those forces that stand in the way of peace and harmony. Since World War II, programs of five plays have been considered too lengthy, and now they are usually made up of two or three plays, although still chosen to provide some sense of the older scheme.

Zeami taught that beauty lies in suggestion, simplicity, subtlety, and restraint. Virtually all of his premises are summed up in the complex term *yugen,* which essentially means gentle gracefulness, the mysterious beauty of impermanence in which elegance is always accompanied with awareness of its fragility. It is the qualities summed up in *yugen* that Noh seeks to capture.

Because it relies on indirectness, suggestion, simplicity, and restraint, Noh makes great demands on its audience, for it is not easy to comprehend fully or to enter the realm it embodies. It is not present-time enactment so much as recollection and reenactment through retrospection of some past event which evokes an emotional state or mood. A musical dance-drama, the written script of a Noh play (typically shorter than the average one-act drama of the West) provides a framework for telling a story through choreography. All Noh plays culminate in a dance, and the dialogue and song that precede it serve primarily to outline the circumstances that motivate it. A chorus (*ji*) of six to ten narrates many of the events during the play, sings all lines required while a character is dancing, and may sing some of the actor's lines at other times. Those sections in verse are sung in a rhythmic fashion to instrumental musical accompaniment, while sections in prose are intoned without musical accompaniment. Ordinary speech is used only when a player comes on stage between the parts of a two-act piece to summarize what has happened during the first act.

Acting in Noh is sometimes referred to as "the art of walking" as a great deal of focus is given to the way in which a character enters, moves around stage, and exits. All movement, including the main dance, is restrained and seems to be almost in slow motion.

The main actor (*shite*) can be masked or unmasked. Masks are of painted wood, many of which have been handed down for generations. These masks fall into five basic types—aged, male, female, deities, and monsters—but each has many variations. In addition, special masks are sometimes used. An actor will often change masks during a play and when a female mask is worn, no attempt is made to feminize the voice. The secondary actors (*waki*) are generally not masked. All Noh performers traditionally have been male, but many female amateurs learn Noh and perform in recitals. Professional Noh actors derive a substantial income from teaching amateurs.

Costumes, rich in color and design, are based on the official dress of Kan'ami and Zeami's time. Most are made of silk decorated with elaborate embroidery, but they are never as gaudy as those used in the Chinese theatre. The garments may be divided into four categories: the outer garments; garments worn indoors or without an overdress; lower garments, such as divided skirts; and headdresses and wigs. Each category has many variations, but the same garments may be combined (or layered) for use in different roles. Thus, costumes are less rigidly conventionalized in color and design than in the Chinese theatre. The chorus and orchestra wear a simple black kimono and divided overskirt.

Hand properties are few and conventionalized. The fan is by far the most important, for it can be used to suggest the blowing of the wind, the ripple of water, a rising moon, falling rain, and many subtle emotional responses. The meaning of the fan is determined by the actor's movement and the music. Occasionally the actor may use a sword or spear. Stage properties are simple. A miniature wooden or bamboo structure may represent a palace, mountain, bedchamber, or other place; a bamboo frame represents a boat. Usually no more than one or two stage properties are present at once. There is no machinery or scenery.

A stage attendant is always present to assist the main actor in changing or adjusting costumes or masks, to set stage properties or remove them when no longer needed, to prompt if it should be needed, and in an emergency to assume the main role if the actor cannot continue. Thus, the attendant is usually a senior actor. He is never considered to be a part of the action or the stage picture.

The Noh stage has been standardized since about 1615. Traditionally, these stages were outdoors in garden spaces but are now generally built indoors in large halls. Its two principal areas, the stage proper (*butai*) and the bridge (*hashigakari*) at stage right are both roofed like the shrines from which they are descended, even when the stages are built indoors. The stage roof is supported by four columns, each with its own name and significance. At the upstage right pillar, *shitebashira* (principal character's pillar), the *shite* pauses when he enters to announce his name and where he comes from. While reciting this speech, he faces the pillar at the downstage right corner, the *metsukebashira* (the gazing pillar). The pillar at the downstage left corner is called *wakibashira* because of its association with the secondary character. The upstage left pillar, *fuebashira* (flute pillar), indicates the flute player's position on stage.

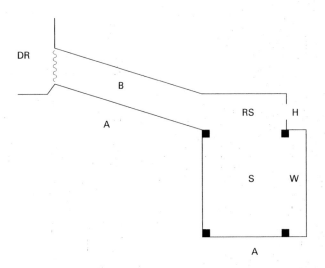

FIG. 10.9
Ground plan of a Noh stage: A = audience; B = bridge; DR = dressing room; H = hurry door; RS = rear stage; S = main stage; W = chorus area. Drawing by Douglas Hubbell.

The stage is divided into three principal areas, although none is marked off architecturally except by the pillars. The largest area, the main stage, is enclosed within the four pillars and is about 18 feet square. The floor of this area is specially constructed of polished cypress, and sounding jars are placed beneath it to make the rhythmic and emphatic stamping of feet, a distinctive feature of Noh, more effective. Back of the upstage pillars is the rear stage (*atoza*), occupied by the orchestra which is composed of a flute and two or occasionally three drums. The musicians are seated so they may see both the main stage and the bridge, since they must always adapt what they do to the principal actor's performance. To stage left of the main stage is the *waki-za*, occupied by the chorus throughout the performance. The chorus sits in two rows, with the chorus leader in the center of the second row.

There are two entrances to the stage. The principal one, the bridge (*hashigakari*), is a railed gangway about 6 feet wide and from 33 to 52 feet long leading from the dressing room. In front of this bridge are three small pine trees symbolizing heaven, earth, and man. The bridge is used as an entrance for the musicians and for all important characters. The other entrance, the "hurry door," upstage left and only about 3 feet high, is used by the chorus, stage assistants, and for the exit of dead characters. The rear walls of the stage and bridge are made of wood. On the wall back of the orchestra is painted a pine tree (usually said to symbolize the Yogo pine tree, through which the god descended to sanctify the first

Noh performance) and on the stage-left side-wall bamboo, perhaps as a reminder of the natural scenery which formed the background of the earliest performances. The audience views the stage from two sides: from in front of the main stage and from the side in front of the bridge. Contemporary Noh theatres usually seat 300 to 500 persons.

There is usually only one rehearsal for a Noh performance. The performers have been trained in the same tradition and know the plays thoroughly. Any combination of actors and musicians occurs only once. In performance all the elements come together in a very dynamic way, for each participant must be able to adjust to the nuances created during that particular performance. Perfection comes not from the mere mastery of conventions and traditions but from the fusion of elements in a collective collaboration.

Noh is intimately bound up with *kyogen* (wild words), short farcical pieces used as interludes between Noh plays. Kyogen, like Noh, is descended from *sarugaku,* but unlike Noh it maintains the comic tone that characterized the earlier form. Again, like Noh, kyogen's conventions were probably set in Zeami's time.

By the sixteenth century there were three main schools of kyogen performers: Okura, Sagi, and Izumi. None of the plays was written down until 1638–1642, when Toraaki Okura (?–1662) recorded 203 of them. These have remained important in the kyogen repertory. In 1660 Okura also published the first treatise devoted wholly to kyogen.

Kyogen covers a wide range of comic subjects that place more emphasis on situation than character. It shows the unexpected dilemmas in which the drunkard, cowardly *samurai,* ignorant lord, sly servant, greedy monk, shrewish woman, and others find themselves. Sometimes the plays parody Noh; occasionally subjects are taken from folklore with animals, gods, or devils as characters. Two- and three-character plays are most common. Prose dialogue comprises the bulk of most kyogen texts. In many plays short songs and dances occur in climactic scenes, occasionally accompanied by the drums and flute of Noh. But though kyogen depends on humorous dialogue and pantomime, it is performed according to strict conventions. Its performers also appear in Noh plays as villagers, peasants, or commoners, thereby adding an earthy and occasionally humorous touch to otherwise stately plays.

Although during the Middle Ages Noh and kyogen were from time to time given publicly for "subscription" audiences, they were essentially aristocratic entertainments. The *shoguns* took Noh under their protection, accorded the performers *samurai* status,

and granted them a stipend raised through a system of national requisitions. Five schools, or branches, of Noh were recognized and the headship of each made hereditary. These schools still exist.

When the shogunate fell in 1868 Noh lost its privileged position and survived through the difficult period immediately following primarily because of the patronage of societies organized for that purpose. Since World War II it has been recognized as a national treasure and has drawn devoted audiences. Furthermore, its prestige has been greatly enhanced by tours abroad and the growing interest of international scholars. Each of the five Noh schools owns its own theatres. At the National Noh Theatre opened in Tokyo in 1983, performances by all the schools can be seen. The actors of both Noh and kyogen have also established a strong economic base by teaching amateurs.

KABUKI

While Noh was assuming its role as a major aristocratic art form, other entertainments were being addressed to more plebeian audiences. At the beginning of the Tokugawa shogunate (1603–1867), major popular forms began to emerge. As with Noh, the new forms can best be understood within the sociopolitical context of the time. Through most of the Tokugawa era, Japan was at peace. As a result, the *samurai* declined in importance while the lesser ranks improved their economic position. Beginning in the early seventeenth century, the shoguns also expelled all foreigners and deliberately isolated Japan from outside influences. The resulting emphasis on native social and artistic forms encouraged the elaboration of ceremonies and entertainments of all kinds just when the increased wealth of the lesser classes permitted them to patronize the arts. This conjunction of events helps to explain why during the course of the seventeenth century there evolved two of Japan's most distinctive theatrical types—the puppet (or doll) theatre, to be discussed later under *bunraku,* and *kabuki.*

Kabuki is usually traced back to 1603 when Okuni, a female dancer from the Izumo Grand Shrine, began to give public performances on an improvised stage set up in the riverbed at Kyoto. Her programs were composed of playlets interspersed with dances. Kabuki was a genuinely new expression of an optimistic, hedonistic urban society. Most of the performers were women, although they sometimes dressed as men, and they were obviously erotic. The programs caught on rapidly, and by 1616 there were seven licensed theatres. They came to be associated with prostitution, however, and in 1629 local authorities forbade women to appear on the stage. Women's Kabuki was succeeded by Young Men's Kabuki, which was suppressed in 1652, for the boys proved to be as seductive as the women. Next, came Men's Kabuki, destined to be the permanent form, although the men were required to shave their foreheads and to avoid any emphasis upon physical charms.

Kabuki developed rapidly, and between 1675 and 1750 evolved most of its characteristic techniques. New methods of acting were introduced, fully developed plays replaced the former improvised entertainments, and artistry increased personal appeal. In mature Kabuki of the eighteenth century the repertory consisted in more or less equal measures of three general categories of plays: "pure" Kabuki plays written especially for the Kabuki stage; adaptations of major Bunraku dramas; and dance dramas. Many purists consider that true Kabuki ended in 1868, when the emperor resumed his authority from the shogunate and Western influence began. Since World War II ticket prices have made Kabuki something of a luxury, while the patronage of tourists has brought alleged debasements of the traditional practices. Nevertheless, Kabuki remains the most popular of Japanese theatrical forms, and its future now seems assured since the Japanese National Theatre was opened in 1966.

Kabuki drama has undergone many changes. It began as sketches about life of the urban commoner and dance scenes often improvised by the main actors, and gradually expanded to multiscene plays written by professional playwrights. The first multi-act play dates from 1664. In the 1670s the major playwright Chikamatsu Monzaemon began to write for a major Kyoto actor and troupe manager, Sakata Tojuro. Over a period of some twenty-seven years he wrote scores of plays both for the Kabuki stage and for the puppet theatre. Many of the domestic plays which he first wrote for the Kabuki stage in the late seventeenth century became models for the domestic lovers' suicide plays that he wrote for the puppet theatre in the early eighteenth century, and which Kabuki actors later readapted for their performances.

As drama increased in importance, the staff of each troupe came to include a playwright and a number of assistants who prepared each of the six annual productions of the season. After the 1860s playwrights were usually novelists, journalists, or literary figures who worked outside the professional system of the preceding era. Among the writers of the nineteenth century, two of the most famous are Kawatake Mokuami (1816–1893), famous for his domestic plays, especially those about thieves and other low-life characters, such as *Benten Kozo and His Gang of Thieves* (1862) and *Gorozo the Dandy* (1864); and Tsuruya Namboku (1755–1829), whose *The Ghost of Yotsuya* (1825) is still often revived.

Kabuki writers never thought in terms of Western dramatic forms, and no clear line was drawn between comic and serious works. Most Kabuki plays are made up of loosely connected episodes that bring together three or four separate dramatic worlds.

Kabuki programs have traditionally been lengthy. From around 1650 until after 1850 they usually lasted about twelve hours. In this period it was customary to arrange programs according to a four-part division: first came a historical play (*jidaimono*) that glorified the traditions and values of the *samurai*; a dance (either with or without a story but with a strong emotional flavor) either came next or was included within the *jidaimono;* then a domestic drama (*sewamono*) set in the milieu of merchants, traders, or artisans was presented; and the performance concluded with a striking one-act dance drama, often humorous. All parts of the performance were related thematically whenever possible. In 1868 the maximum length of performances was reduced to eight hours a day. (Night performances were not given until 1878, when gas lighting was introduced.) Since World War II, the length of performances has been reduced and complete full-length plays are seldom performed, but the four-part arrangement, with as many as ten acts from a variety of plays, is usually followed. At commercial theatres today, it is customary to give two programs a day. Plays are performed every day from the second to the twenty-sixth day of the month.

Many critics consider dance to be the basis of Kabuki, although dance must be understood to include rhythmical movement, studied posture, and conventionalized gesture. Originally only the female roles were danced, but by the late eighteenth century dance was such an essential part of all performances that a professional choreographer was added to each company. Since then dance has grown more complex and new forms have been created. The choreographers founded hereditary schools. Many of the present schools date back to the eighteenth century. These choreographers also teach amateurs outside the Kabuki world.

Dance in Kabuki is always expected to reflect the verbal text. It seeks to distill the essence of real emotions and deeds into stylized gesture, movement, and posture. Thus, weeping becomes a rhythmical movement of the head accompanied by precise hand gestures. Kabuki dance is accompanied by narrative and descriptive music that helps to establish its character but always remains subordinate.

FIG. 10.10
A Kabuki theatre in the eighteenth century. Note that the stage still retains some features of the Noh, although they have been modified, and that the *hanamichi* has been added. An eighteenth-century print. Courtesy British Museum.

Three types of music are heard in Kabuki, each identifiable by sound quality, theatrical function, and the placement of the musicians on stage. First, Kabuki's basic music is in Nagauta style (*samisen*, drums, flute, and singers). Because in Naguata the musicians are placed offstage, the music is known as *geza* ("lower seat"). This style of music may be augmented by special drums, gongs, bells, and cymbals. It underscores entrances, exits, dialogue, and fighting scenes. *Geza* musicians draw on a repertory of several hundred known melodies and rhythmic patterns; in each production the music is chosen for its appropriateness to season, location, and the emotional quality of individual scenes. Second, for dance plays, dance music of several kinds is played and sung; in addition to Naguata, several styles have developed within Kabuki specifically to accompany dances. Third, puppet-style music accompanies plays adapted from puppet theatre and some dance plays. The dance-play and puppet-play musical ensembles are placed on stage (at the rear or at stage left, depending on the type of play); for these plays the score is "through composed" and unique to each puppet or dance play as in a Western opera or ballet. Onstage musicians wear the ceremonial dress of the *samurai* (divided skirt, kimono, and stiff horizontal shoulder pieces). When not performing, they sit upright and motionless.

FIG. 10.11
Ichikawa Danjuro V in the role of Kagemasa Gongoro in the Kabuki play *Shibaraku* (1697). Depicted is one of the characteristic features of Kabuki acting, the pose struck and held *(mie)*. In this play the character exits along the *hanamichi* through a series of these poses. The popularity of the play and this exit were such as to motivate woodcuts of the type shown here. Woodcut by Katsu Shunsho (1770). Courtesy Rietberg Museum, Zurich.

Song and narration are important in Kabuki, especially in dance plays or those taken from the puppet theatre. The actors never sing. In dance plays, the chorus sings lyrics which describe the scene or narrate the story; the chorus may also sing lines supposedly said or thought by the dancers. In puppet-derived plays, the narrator chants or sings the third-person descriptive and narrative passages, but the actors speak their own dialogue. Even the actor's spoken lines follow conventionalized intonational patterns.

Kabuki acting is a combination of speaking and dancing. Because it follows established rules, it requires long and diligent study. The actor begins his training at the age of six or seven, first studying dance and then proceeding to diction, intonation, and the wearing of costumes. Since there are many children's roles, the student is usually on stage from the beginning of his career and learns his profession at first hand. Most of the leading performers come from a few families for whom acting is a hereditary profession. Each family has an elaborate system of stage names, some of which are so honored that they are awarded only to those considered undisputed masters of their art. An actor is almost never judged mature until after he has reached middle age.

The roles in Kabuki are divided into a few basic types: *tachiyaku,* loyal, good, and courageous men; *katakiyaku,* villainous men; *dokekata,* comic roles, including comic villains; *koyaku,* children's roles; and *onnagata,* women's roles of various kinds, all played by men. These basic types are subdivided into a score of subtypes.

Kabuki actors do not wear masks, but some roles require boldly patterned makeup to exaggerate the muscular conformation of the face. Red and black patterns are normally painted upon a white base, although demons and evil characters may use blue or brown. The *onnagata* draws in false eyebrows and adds rouging at the corner of the eye and to the mouth but otherwise leaves the face completely white. Married women blacken their teeth and obliterate their eyebrows. For some of the more athletic male roles, the musculature of arms and legs is outlined in a conventional pattern. The makeup of each role is symbolic of the character.

Every role also has its traditional costume. Most are based upon historical garments which have been altered for dramatic purposes. Dress from different periods is often seen in a single play, for historical accuracy is of no importance in Kabuki. Some costumes weigh as much as fifty pounds, and stage attendants assist the actors in keeping them properly arranged while on stage.

In visual style Kabuki lies somewhere between the conventionalism of Noh and the illusionism of Western theatre. This combination can be seen most clearly in the properties, stage, and scenery. Properties range from the symbolic to the relatively realistic. Especially in dance plays, the fan, as in Noh, can indicate riding a horse, shooting a bow and arrow, the

FIG. 10.12
The Nakamura-za in 1859 during a Kabuki performance. Note the two *hanamichi* and the arrangement of the auditorium. A contemporary engraving.

FIG. 10.13

A Kabuki stage of the nineteenth century showing the revolving stage (first used in 1758) and a small elevator trap (first used in 1736). At center left is the *hanamichi*. Note also the screens at either side of the stage, the one at right raised like a venetian blind. A woodcut published in *Scribner's Magazine 7* (1890).

rising of the moon, or opening a door. A scarf serves a multitude of similar purposes. On the other hand, many properties are representational although none is intended to be convincingly real. The Kabuki horse probably best exemplifies the degree of illusionism: a wooden framework shaped like a horse, covered with velvet, and ridden by an actor is supported by two actors, whose human legs clearly show. Many other properties—armor, swords, human heads, tigers, elephants, monkeys, household goods—are represented through similar conventions.

The stage also is a melding of convention and illusion. The earliest Kabuki performances were on temporary stages modeled after the Noh stage. When multi-act plays evolved in the 1660s, a curtain was added to conceal the stage; the bridge was also widened to provide more acting space. Mats suspended over the audience provided shade until 1724, when government regulations for the first time allowed theatres to be permanently roofed. After that time machinery began to be used for special effects. A small elevator trap was installed in 1736, and soon more elaborate devices were exploited. In 1753 Namiki Shozo invented the large elevator stage and in 1758 he introduced the revolving stage (first used at the Kado-za in Osaka). After 1827 the revolving stage was sometimes constructed in two sections, one revolving inside the other, and worked independently. A forestage had become a permanent feature of the Kabuki theatre by 1736 and was the principal acting area after 1745. Some scenic pieces began to appear in the late seventeenth century and grew ever more complex thereafter.

Some time between 1724 and 1736 one of the Kabuki's most distinctive features, the *hanamichi*, was introduced. A raised gangway which connects the stage with a small room at the rear of the auditorium, the *hanamichi* is used for all major entrances and exits, as well as for many important scenes. The *hanamichi* was so popular that a second had been introduced by the 1770s. By 1830, the Kabuki stage had achieved its characteristic form. The Noh roof had been abandoned, and the stage now occupied the full width of the auditorium and was equipped with revolving stage and elevator traps. The area between the two *hanamichi* was divided into numerous square enclosures, or floor boxes, in which spectators sat on mats. Two levels of boxes (*sajiki*) ran along each side of the auditorium.

After 1868 several changes were made as a result of Western influence. The proscenium arch was introduced in 1908 and became standard after 1923, as did Western-style seating. The second *hanamichi* was eliminated, although it is still installed temporarily when required for a particular play. Except for the introduction of flying machinery, electric lighting, and the proscenium arch, however, the stage has remained relatively unchanged. The proscenium arch of the present Kabuki-za in Tokyo is 93 feet wide but only about 20 feet high, and the auditorium is only 60 feet deep. Thus, the spatial relationship between stage and audience differs considerably from that of the typical Western theatre.

Unlike Noh, Kabuki uses a great deal of scenery, both for decorative and functional purposes. Every locale in a Kabuki play is suggested scenically. When there is no intermission between scenes, settings are changed in full view of the audience by means of the revolving stage, elevator traps, grooves, or by visible stage attendants. More often, scenery is changed during intermissions behind the stage's striped front curtain. Kabuki emphasizes lateral composition; sets are never pie-shaped, and almost all scenery is placed parallel to the front of the stage. Painting is usually flat and is not intended to appear three-dimensional. Typically the stage is enclosed at the rear by flats painted with a distant view, but illusionism is avoided by letting the cracks between individual flats show and by using a black curtain to cut off the top of the scene.

Sometimes relatively realistic Japanese buildings are erected on stage, but the entry gates to houses are often removed by stage assistants when they are no longer needed, and other theatrical conventions constantly remind the audience of the contrivance. Many scenic pieces are used symbolically. White mats represent snow, blue mats water, gray mats the ground; different kinds of trees indicate changes of locales. This mingling of the familiar with the conventional makes Kabuki, among all the traditional Asian forms, most accessible to Westerners.

Like other traditional forms, Kabuki has gained considerable international fame through tours abroad and the interest of scholars. Kabuki has also been influenced by Western conventions and many productions have introduced innovations into Kabuki plays, acting, and scenery. But traditional practices still dominate.

BUNRAKU

Although Kabuki and Bunraku developed during the same period, and the two forms often influenced one another as the best playwrights of the day wrote for both, Bunraku reached the form it now takes slightly later than Kabuki did.

The puppet theatre (*ningyo shibai*) first came to prominence during the seventeenth century as an amalgamation of numerous earlier influences, although some types of puppet performances can be traced back to the Heian era (781–1185), during which Oe Tadafusa published his *Book of Puppeteers* (1100); thereafter some type of puppet theatre was always practiced by wandering entertainers.

FIG. 10.14
Scene from a Kabuki play at the present-day Kabuki-za in Tokyo. Note the mingling of representational and conventionalized elements. From *Décor de Théâtre dans le Monde depuis 1935*.

FIG. 10.15
Japanese puppets and their handlers. From Haar, *Japanese Theatre in Highlight*. Courtesy Charles E. Tuttle, Tokyo.

FIG. 10.16
Scene from a Japanese doll theatre performance. The principal puppeteer is seen at left and two others can be glimpsed at right. Courtesy Performing Arts Program of the Asia Society.

Even before this puppet theatre came to the fore, there was another entertainment in which stories or legends were recited or chanted to the accompaniment of a stringed instrument, the *biwa.* After 1560 this form underwent a major change when another stringed instrument with quite different qualities, the *samisen,* was introduced from the Ryukyu Islands. By far the most popular work in this altered genre treated the love story of Joruri, the daughter of a wealthy family. It became so dominant that the form itself came to be called *joruri.*

The first major step toward a mature puppet theatre was taken sometime between 1596 and 1614 when puppet performances were combined with *joruri* narration. This combination became increasingly popular, especially after 1648 when Toraya Gendayu established a company in Tokyo. The perfection of the form, however, had to await Takemoto Gidayu (1650–1714), who founded a company in Osaka in 1685. His style was to dominate the doll theatre thereafter. Takemoto's popularity owed much to the plays of Chikamatsu Monzaemon (1653–1724), Japan's greatest playwright, who began writing specifically for Takemoto in 1686.

Chikamatsu wrote many kinds of works but was noted especially for his five-act history plays and his three-act plays on contemporary life. Modern critics especially admire the sensitive characterizations and the beautiful language of his dramas about the double suicides of lovers. Among his best-known plays are *The Double Suicide at Sonezaki* (1703), *Drumming of the Waves at Horikawa* (1707), *Battle of Coxinga* (1715), and *The Love Suicide at Amijima* (1721).

Another important Bunraku dramatist is Takeda Izumo II (1691–1756), who worked with Chikamatsu and succeeded him as principal writer for the Osaka doll theatre. His masterpiece is *Chushingura* (1748), written with the assistance of Namiki Sosuke and Miyake Shoraku. Based upon an actual event, it tells of forty-seven faithful *samurai* who avenge the wrongs done to their master. (This story was so popular that between 1748 and 1900 more than 100 full-length puppet and Kabuki plays were based on it.)

The puppets used in these performances underwent many changes, becoming ever more complex. Originally the puppeteers used a head only, but later hands and feet were added, and by 1678 rather complete figures were in use. In 1730 a mechanism was introduced that allowed the dolls to move their eyes; in 1733 jointed and movable fingers were added; later, the puppets were fitted with movable eyebrows. As the figures grew in complexity, the number of operators increased. Originally one handler, hidden from view, was sufficient, but after 1734 each doll was operated by three men, all visible to the audience. One person manipulated the head and right arm, a second the left arm, and a third the feet. In 1736 the figures were doubled in size to their present height of 3 to 4 feet.

The stage also grew in complexity. The use of movable stage settings after 1715 soon led to the invention of stage machinery which has since been adopted throughout the world. In 1727 elevator traps were introduced to raise scenery through the floor, and after 1757 they were used to create different stage floor levels.

The puppet theatre reached the height of its popularity in the eighteenth century. Its most successful playwrights at that time were Takeda Izumo (1691–1756) and Chikamatsu Hanji (1725–1783). Most of the conventions were also fixed at this time. Around 1780 the puppet theatre began to decline as it was overshadowed by Kabuki. Some of its vitality was restored after Uemura Bunrakuken (1737–1810) came to Osaka sometime between 1789 and 1800. The name Bunraku, used by the only present-day puppet theatre, was derived from him. Despite Bunrakuken's work, the puppet theatre was to lead a precarious existence throughout the nineteenth and twentieth centuries. Its future now seems secure, however, for in 1963 the Bunraku Association was formed to manage all phases of the art, and in 1984

the luxuriously equipped National Bunraku Theatre was opened in Osaka. The Bunraku troupe performs six to eight months a year, divided among their home theatre in Osaka, a small theatre in the National Theatre in Tokyo, and on tour both in Japan and abroad.

Like Noh, Bunraku has its own conventions. Its stage is about 36 feet wide by 25 feet deep and is divided into three levels from front to rear, each indicated by low partitions between which the handlers work. All locales are represented scenically and changed as required by the story. Numerous properties are used. At the right side of the auditorium just forward of the stage is a platform for the narrator and *samisen* player. This platform is equipped with a turntable which is revolved to bring the narrator and *samisen*

FIG. 10.18
Shadow puppet from Malaysia representing Seri Rama (the hero). From the private collection of Molly and Walter Meserve.

FIG. 10.17
The masked dance-drama of Pongsan, Korea. In the background are the musicians. Courtesy Performing Arts Program of the Asia Society.

FIG. 10.19
Shadow puppet from Malaysia representing Hanuman (the monkey king). From the private collection of Molly and Walter Meserve.

these are suggested by the way the kimono is handled. Minor puppets do not have movable mouths, eyes, and eyebrows. The handlers seek to become one with their puppets and to absorb themselves in the drama. They undergo long and arduous training before appearing on stage, first learning to operate the feet (usually about ten years is spent mastering this operation), then progressing to the left hand (requiring another ten years), and then to the head and right arm. Their artistry has exerted considerable influence upon Kabuki.

OTHER ASIAN COUNTRIES

Each Asian country has its own dramatic traditions, often quite diverse and highly developed. The theatre of Southeast Asia is allied to that of India, perhaps because the people of that area share the heritage of Hinduism, the Hindu epics, and Buddhism. Dance-drama, especially, is highly developed in Indonesia, Thailand, Cambodia, Laos, and Burma. But there are

FIG. 10.20
Performer in the *wayang topeng* masked dance theatre of Bali. Courtesy Performing Arts program of the Asia Society.

player into position. At the end of each act a new team replaces the earlier one.

A puppet performance begins with the appearance of an announcer, clad in black and wearing a hood (this costume is worn by all the stage assistants except the principal handlers, the musicians, and the narrator), who proclaims the title of the play and the names of the *samisen* player and the narrator, both of whom command greater prestige than the puppet handlers. The *samisen,* a three-stringed instrument related to the lute, has a skin-covered base and is played with a heavy ivory plectrum. Extremely varied in sound, it can follow the rise and fall of the voice, give special emphasis, and provide punctuations to the narration and action. Its accompaniment is considered essential in the puppet theatre. The narrator tells the story (the handlers do not speak) and expresses the feelings of each puppet. He smiles, weeps, starts with fear and astonishment.

The handlers and the puppets occupy center stage. The puppets vary somewhat in size and complexity according to their importance in the play. The female figures ordinarily do not have feet, although

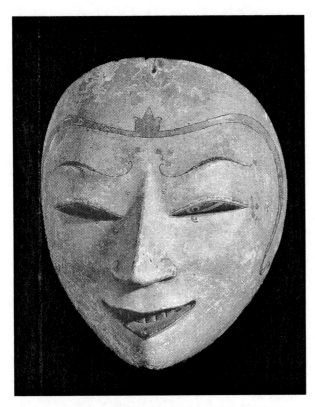

FIG. 10.21
Wayang topeng mask of wood for the role of Pandji, Prince of Djenggala. From Java, eighteenth century. Courtesy Rietberg Museum, Zurich.

many other theatrical forms in Southeast Asia as well—folk drama, operetta, spoken drama, pantomime, improvised plays, shadow puppet plays, doll puppet plays, and Western-style drama, though space does not allow for a review of them here.

The Western world for the most part remained ignorant of the Asian theatre until the late eighteenth century. The Sanskrit plays were the first to be translated and read, but Asian theatrical conventions were unappreciated until Eastern companies began to appear in the West. A Chinese troupe played in Paris in 1895; a Japanese group appeared in London in 1900; and individual performers toured with some frequency thereafter. Nevertheless, it was not until such Western producers as Yeats, Meyerhold, Vakhtangov, Brecht, and Artaud began to advocate them as alternatives to the Western emphasis on illusionism that Asian conventions began to affect Western practices. At first viewed as perverse or exotic, the innovations have been increasingly accepted since World War II, largely because of the influence of Brecht and Artaud. In recent years, Ariane Mnouchkine, through her highly acclaimed productions of Shakespearean and Greek plays in which she drew heavily on Sanskrit, Kathakali, and Kabuki conventions, Peter Brook, with his adaptation of the *Mahabarata*, and Julie Taymor with her Asian-influenced design style, have intensified interest in Asian theatre. Although it is doubtful that many Westerners have fully mastered Asian theatre conventions, many have drawn inspiration from them, especially when seeking alternatives to the realism that has so long dominated Western theatre. Increased research and study of Asian theatre in Western universities has also contributed to greater familiarity.

LOOKING AT THEATRE HISTORY

In his study of Kabuki, A. C. Scott points out the influence of Buddhism, Shintoism, and Confucianism on Japanese life and theatre. He also discusses domestic architecture, dress, food, social relationships, etiquette, and other aspects of daily life that have contributed to theatrical subjects and conventions:

Formerly, everything and everybody in Japan was bound by a strict code of etiquette. There were correct ways of

eating, drinking, wearing clothes and moving about according to time and place. . . . This fact, coupled with their characteristic manner of living, such as for instance sitting, dining and sleeping on the tatami [reed mats] created gestures and movements which were individual in style, and these translated into terms of stage technique have developed a very special visual effect, both in the case of the single actor or group composition. . . . The legends, customs, habits, religion, loves and hates of the Japanese people are drawn upon freely and woven into the pattern of construction of this colorful drama.

The Kabuki Theatre of Japan (London: George Allen and Unwin, Ltd., 1955), 32–33.

Even with a knowledge of the intellectual and cultural context, a Western observer often has difficulty, at least in the beginning, with many conventions of the Asian theatre. Among these are the color symbolism and face painting of Beijing Opera. (For some examples, see Fig. 10.6.)

The more admirable characters are usually painted in relatively simple colors. Enemy leaders or very special people have more complicated designs on their faces— toughs, bandits, hardened soldiers, rebels. A lot of red indicates courage, loyalty, straightforwardness; more black denotes impulsiveness, while a blue face is a cruel one. A crook who is completely untrustworthy is given a white, often twisted face.

Musical modes are also apt to seem strange. To the Westerner the Chinese orchestra has "a superabundance of gongs, cymbals, and drums."

The accompaniment for the voice is played on the "chinghu"—the two-stringed fiddle. . . . Flutes are also used, the bamboo kind, held parallel to the face when played. The "sheng" or reed flute is really a small organ and has chords. Then there are the moon guitars and three-stringed guitars, a kind of Chinese clarinet . . .; big and small drums, a bell, cymbals and the "pan" or wooden time-beater which does for the orchestra what the conductor does for his musicians in a Western performance. . . . Entrances and exits have a musical accompaniment. An actor, before breaking into song, will speak his last words in a certain way so that the orchestra knows the song is about to begin.

Rewi Alley, *Peking Opera* (Beijing, 1957).

In the advice he gave to Noh actors in his *Works,* Zeami emphasizes restraint, which is to be accomplished in part through the reconciliation of opposites:

In representing anger the actor should yet retain some gentleness in his mood, else he will portray not anger but violence.

When the body is in violent action, the hands and feet must move as though by stealth. When the feet are in lively motion, the body must be held in quietness.

Translated by Arthur Waley in his *The No Plays of Japan* (New York: Alfred A. Knopf, 1922), 26.

A number of works that give advice to actors or preserve anecdotes about acting in Kabuki have survived from the late seventeenth and early eighteenth centuries. In "The Words of Ayame" this passage appears about the *onnagata* (female) role, at that time always played by men:

The onnagata role has its basis in charm, and even one who has innate beauty, if he seeks to make a fine show in a fighting scene, will lose the femininity of his performance . . . if he does not live his normal life as if he was a woman, it will not be possible for him to be called a skillful onnagata.

From "A Sequel to 'Dust in the Ears'" comes this account of playwriting for Kabuki prior to the late seventeenth century:

The normal way of working was that after the discussion of a new play and a decision upon it, the construction of each scene was worked out. Then the actors in a scene were called together, placed in a circle, and taught the speeches orally. They stood there until they made their exit, and then either rehearsed it again . . . or the authors worked out the speeches for the next section, and got them fixed by repetition.

The Actors' Analects, ed., trans., and with an introduction and notes by Charles J. Dunn and Bunzo Torigoe (New York: Columbia University Press, 1969), 53, 118.

11
English Theatre to 1800

Because of the civil war between the Royalists (Cavaliers) and Parliamentarians (Roundheads or Puritans), life in England was very unsettled during the 1640s. England did not return to peace until Charles I had been captured, tried, and beheaded by the Puritans in 1649. For a time England was governed by a committee appointed by Parliament, but after 1653 Oliver Cromwell was a virtual dictator. When he died in 1658, his son was chosen as his successor, but he could not maintain control. In 1660 the Stuarts were restored to the throne.

THEATRICAL ACTIVITY, 1642–1660

During the eighteen years between 1642 and 1660, the Puritans sought to stop all theatrical activity. As a result, few records relating to performance have survived, although playing certainly continued intermittently. At first the actors complied with the law passed in 1642 suspending performances for a period of five years. The King's Men sold its wardrobe, and its Globe Theatre was torn down. Actors soon began to perform surreptitiously, however, and performances were given at the Fortune, Phoenix/Cockpit, and Salisbury Court theatres. Although Parliament ordered officials to halt the violations, suppression was sporadic and ineffectual.

When the law prohibiting performances expired in 1647, open playing was immediately resumed. But in 1649, Parliament passed a new law ordering that all actors be apprehended as rogues and that the interiors of the Fortune, Phoenix/Cockpit, and Salisbury Court be dismantled. The actors continued to perform, nevertheless, using The Red Bull, which had escaped demolition, or, when that appeared too dangerous, private houses, tennis courts, or inns. Often officials were bribed to ignore violations. In these years, the usual form of entertainment seems to have been the "droll," a short play condensed from a longer work.

Apparently, the actors believed that the theatre would eventually be legalized. Around 1650, William Beeston (c. 1606–1682) acquired The Salisbury Court, and John Rhodes bought The Phoenix/Cockpit. Perhaps most significantly, William Davenant, who in the 1630s had succeeded Jonson as the principal writer of court masques and received a theatre patent in 1639, began openly to stage what have been called England's first operatic productions. His initial offering, *The First Day's Entertainment at Rutland House*, was presented in May 1656.

The production of *The Siege of Rhodes*, also in 1656, is a far more important event, however, for it marks the first clear use in England of Italianate scenery for a public performance. Designed by John

FIG. 11.1

The proscenium and side wings for *The Siege of Rhodes* as designed by John Webb and presented by William Davenant at Rutland House in 1656. The wings, representing cliffs, remained fixed throughout, and scenic units were changed behind them. This perspective setting with movable units is the first known use of Italianate scenery on a public stage in England. Devonshire Collection, Chatsworth. Reproduced by permission of the Trustees of the Chatsworth Settlement.

Webb (1611–1672), pupil of Inigo Jones, the settings were mounted on a stage measuring only 22 feet in width, 18 feet in depth, and 11 feet in height. Behind the proscenium, a series of fixed wings, painted to represent rocky cliffs, terminated in movable shutters which, in combination with set pieces, depicted the various locales required by the action.

These first entertainments were given in Rutland House, Davenant's residence, but in 1658 and 1659 Davenant presented at least three others at The Phoenix/Cockpit, in which a proscenium arch was erected. Although some opposition was expressed, by this time the restoration of the monarchy was imminent and no action was taken. On the other hand, Davenant was not violating any law, for his pieces were "musical entertainments," which had not been forbidden.

THE REESTABLISHMENT OF THE THEATRE

The restoration of the monarchy occurred in 1660 when Charles II (reigned 1660–1685) was restored to the throne. The period we call Restoration theatre extends to 1700 because about that time a significant change in the drama can be identified. Under Charles, England rejected the strict Puritanism of the Commonwealth, so much so that the Restoration became noted for its permissiveness, even libertinism. Charles maintained an uneasy political truce

FIG. 11.2

A composite drawing of the stages used during the Commonwealth for "drolls." Note that characters from several plays are included. Note also the chandeliers and footlights. From Kirkman, *The Wits,* a collection of drolls, published in 1672.

with Parliament, since neither wished to give up any rights or engage in another open conflict. Charles's belief in his rights as a monarch are nowhere more evident than in his relation to the theatre, which he treated as a royal property to dispose of as he saw fit.

As soon as it became evident that the monarchy would be restored, the reopening of the theatres began. John Rhodes opened The Phoenix/Cockpit under license from General Monk. Michael Mohun reformed what was left of the prewar King's Men and began to play at The Red Bull. Sir Henry Herbert resumed the position of Master of Revels, which he had held since 1623, and licensed a company under William Beeston at The Salisbury Court. Upon his return to England, Charles II issued a warrant giving exclusive rights to open theatres, hire actors, and perform plays in London to Killigrew and Davenant, who soon set to work closing down their competitors. The issue was not resolved until 1662/63, however, when the

FIG. 11.3
The first background for *The Siege of Rhodes,* a distant view of Rhodes and the harbor. The drawing is divided into squares to facilitate transfer to the shutters. Devonshire Collection, Chatsworth. Reproduced by permission of the Trustees of the Chatsworth Settlement.

king reissued the two patents that had existed before the war. The one that had belonged to the King's Men went to Thomas Killigrew (1612–1683), who had grown up in the English court, had been a successful playwright before 1642, and had been with the royal family throughout its exile. The second pre-civil war patent was granted to Davenant for a company to be sponsored by the king's brother James, Duke of York.

Henry Herbert was deprived of the right to license theatres and companies in London, but his authority to license companies outside of London and to collect fees for licensing plays was confirmed. (When Herbert died in 1673, Killigrew became Master of the Revels, followed by his son, Charles, who held the post until 1725.) The actors from the rival companies soon signed contracts with the new patent holders.

Meanwhile, in late 1660, George Jolly (*fl.* 1648–1673) was granted a license by the king to perform in London. During the Commonwealth years, Jolly had headed a touring company in northern Europe which had performed for the future Charles II in 1655 when Jolly was given some kind of commitment from Charles about the future.

In 1662, Davenant and Killigrew leased Jolly's license while he went on a tour. During his absence, the two managers convinced the king to revoke it. When Jolly attempted to return to London after the long plague closure in 1665 (during which London lost one-fifth of its population) and the great fire of

1666, Davenant and Killigrew were able to prevent his company from performing, but, to avoid legal challenges, Jolly was hired to manage a Nursery company to train young actors. After 1673 no more is heard of him.

Thus, Davenant and Killigrew established complete control over theatrical performances in London. The patents issued to them by Charles II were to remain in effect until 1843, seriously hampering the growth of the British theatre.

ACTING COMPANIES, 1600–1700

Killigrew, as manager of the King's Company, recruited older actors, many of whom had been professionals before the civil war, while Davenant's Duke's Company was left with younger performers. Although Killigrew began with the advantage of experienced actors, his company did not prosper. He devoted little attention to the theatre, delegating authority to three of his actors. Perhaps as a result, the company was wracked by constant dissension. Davenant, on the other hand, supervised his theatre closely until his death in 1668, after which the actors Thomas Betterton and Henry Harris (the latter succeeded by William Smith in 1677) assumed artistic direction under the control of the Davenant family. By 1682 Killigrew's company was in such serious financial difficulties that the two troupes were merged.

The arrangement reached in 1682 lasted until 1695, when several actors seceded to form another troupe after a series of events had placed them in an untenable position. Alexander Davenant, who had controlling interest in the Davenant patent, fled England to escape his creditors in 1693. His financial support had come from Christopher Rich and Sir Thomas Skipworth; Rich, a lawyer without any theatrical experience, seized control of the company. He proved himself so unpleasant, by withholding salaries and favoring those actors who catered to his whims, that the major performers, under Betterton's leadership, secured a license from William III to form a second troupe. This separation was to last from 1695 until 1708.

In addition to the London companies, a number of troupes were licensed to perform in the provinces. The most important provincial center was Dublin, perhaps because it had its own Master of Revels. In 1637 John Ogilby (1600–1676) had been given a license to open a theatre in Dublin and was named Master of Revels for Ireland. Ogilby's patent, dormant after 1641, was renewed in 1661, and in 1662 he opened the Smock Alley, the first theatre built in

Great Britain after the Restoration. Upon Ogilby's death, the patent passed to Joseph Ashbury, who maintained the finest company outside of London for the next forty-five years.

ENGLISH DRAMA, 1660–1700

One of the problems facing managers in 1660 was a suitable repertory. At first they depended on pre-Commonwealth plays, which the Master of Revels divided between the companies. Of these, the works of Beaumont and Fletcher were the most popular; Jonson's, though much admired, were seldom produced. Several of Shakespeare's plays were revised to bring them into line with contemporary tastes. Many of the older works soon proved too outmoded, and they were dropped from the repertory as soon as new ones were available. Others, however, remained favorites.

Several types of serious plays were written between 1660 and 1700. Until 1680 the dominant mode was "heroic" tragedy, which, heavily indebted to Spanish and French authors and set in exotic locales, emphasized stories centering around the rival claims of love and honor. This type first reached popularity through the works of John Dryden (1631–1700) with *The Indian Queen* (1664), *The Indian Emperor* (1665), *The Conquest of Granada*, parts 1 and 2 (1669–1670), and *Aureng-Zebe* (1675) and through the works of Roger Boyle, Earl of Orrery (1621–1679), especially *The Tragedy of Mustapha* (1665), *The Black Prince* (1667), and *Tryphon* (1668). Other popular writers of this genre were Elkanah Settle (1648–1724), author of *Cambyses, King of Persia* (1671), and *The Empress of Morocco* (1673); and Nathaniel Lee (1653–1692), author of *The Rival Queens* (1677).

In these works, typically an idealistic hero and a beautiful heroine are faced with a situation in which the fulfillment of their mutual love will precipitate other events apt to bring ruin or dishonor to themselves, their families, or country. Often the background is martial, and frequently a happy ending is contrived. Filled with ranting speeches in rhymed couplets, the plays now seem hopelessly stilted. The genre was dealt a heavy blow in 1671 by *The Rehearsal*, written by George Villiers, second Duke of Buckingham (1628–1687), which burlesqued the typical themes, plot devices, and staging conventions of heroic tragedy. Buckingham's play outlived its target, remaining in the repertory until the late eighteenth century.

As the heroic mode declined, it was replaced by tragedy written in blank verse and according to the neoclassical rules. Using relatively simple plots and observing the three unities, the form first gained popularity through Dryden's *All for Love* (1677), a "regularized" reworking of Shakespeare's *Antony and Cleopatra*. It was to remain the dominant mode through the remainder of the century. English neoclassicism was always more liberal than the version that prevailed on the continent. Unity of action was interpreted to permit a number of related subplots, and the unity of place was thought to have been adequately observed if the characters could move easily between the various locales without violating the 24-hour time limit.

The combined influence of neoclassicism and of Shakespeare is evident in the work of the best serious playwright of the age, Thomas Otway (1652–1685), whose *The Orphan* (1680) and *Venice Preserv'd* (1682) remained in the repertory until the late nineteenth century. The first of these plays focuses on a woman who is loved by two brothers, one of whom she marries secretly, upon which the other brother, suspecting an illicit relationship, brings ruin to them all. *Venice Preserv'd* deals with a conspiracy to overthrow the government of Venice and ends in death for the three principal characters, Pierre, Jaffier, and Belvidera.

Building upon Davenant's Commonwealth "entertainments," opera also flourished during the Restoration. It differed from heroic tragedy primarily in the addition of music, song, and spectacle, and it departed from the conventions of Italian opera by substituting spoken passages for recitative. Not only were Shakespeare's *Macbeth, The Tempest,* and *A Midsummer Night's Dream* adapted to the operatic mode, but such original works as Dryden's *Albion and Albianus* (1685) and *King Arthur* (1692) also achieved considerable popularity. This English strain of opera was to decline rapidly after the vogue for Italian opera began in England around 1705.

But the Restoration is noted above all for its diverse comic drama: comedies of "humours," comedies of intrigue, farces, and comedies of manners. Because of Jonson's reputation, "humours" were much exploited during the Restoration. Of the major authors, Thomas Shadwell (1642–1692) was the most successful writer of humours comedy with *The Sullen Lovers* (1668), *The Humourists* (1670), *The Squire of Alsatia* (1688), and *Bury Fair* (1689). Each of these plays introduces a series of eccentric characters in a story of contemporary life, told with frank and outspoken dialogue.

Perhaps because of the influence of Corneille and the Spanish dramatists, the comedy of intrigue was also popular in these years. The best exemplar of this genre was Aphra Behn (1640–1689), the first woman

FIG. 11.4

Congreve's *The Way of the World.* At center is Lady Wishfort and her nephew from the country. From an edition of Congreve's plays published in 1753.

known to have made her living as a playwright. She wrote at least seventeen plays along with a comic opera and a novel, and is best known for *The Rover,* parts 1 and 2 (1677–1680). Farce reached its height in the works of Edward Ravenscroft (*fl.* 1671–1697), whose *London Cuckolds* (1681) and *The Anatomist* (1697) were played throughout the eighteenth century.

Above all, however, the Restoration is noted for its sprightly comedy of manners. John Dryden, the most versatile dramatist of the age, contributed to its formation with such works as *Sir Martin Mar-All* (1667), *The Mock Astrologer* (1668), and *Marriage à la Mode* (1672), each of which includes a pair of care-free, witty lovers. The fully developed comedy of manners, however, is usually traced to the plays of Sir George Etherege (*c.* 1634–1691), who, after a somewhat erratic beginning in *Love in a Tub* (1664), set the pattern for later writers with *She Would If She Could* (1668) and *The Man of Mode* (1676). Here for the first time we find the elements that were to be typical of the type: characters drawn from the upper classes and preoccupation with seduction, arranged marriages, the latest fashions, and witty repartee.

Of the later writers in this vein, Wycherley and Congreve were of special importance. William Wycherley (1640–1715) began writing for the stage in 1671 with *Love in a Wood,* and continued with *The Gentleman Dancing Master* (1672), *The Country Wife* (1675), and *The Plain Dealer* (1676). Although these plays are well constructed and present subtly depicted characters, their moral tone has offended many critics. *The Country Wife,* in which the hero circulates the rumor that he is sexually impotent in order to facilitate his seductions, is often cited as evidence of the moral laxity of Restoration comedy. The comedy of manners reached its peak in the plays of William Congreve (1670–1729), whose *Love for Love* (1695) and *The Way of the World* (1700) are still considered masterpieces because of their brilliant scenes, sparkling dialogue, and clear-cut characterizations. *The Way of the World,* in which the witty lovers Millamant and Mirabell reach their own unique marital agreement based on their knowledge of the ways of their world, inhabited primarily by intriguers, fops, and fools, is usually thought to be one of the best of all English comedies.

By 1700 changes in English life and drama were becoming evident. When Charles II died, he was succeeded by his brother James II (reigned 1685–1688), who was suspected of plotting to reestablish Catholicism. He was tolerated until his son was born, raising the threat that his policies would be perpetuated. A group of leading politicians then invited James's Protestant daughter Mary and her husband William of Orange, ruler of the Netherlands, to assume the throne. William invaded England; James fled; and Parliament declared Mary II (reigned 1689–1694) and William III (reigned 1689–1702) co-rulers of England. Parliament passed and the new rulers accepted a bill requiring Parliament's consent on all important matters and giving it the right to determine the succession to the throne, which went to Mary's sister, Anne (reigned 1702–1714). The new rulers were sympathetic to the mercantile class, which was rapidly becoming the major source of England's wealth and power, as its fleet of merchant ships and overseas enterprises steadily increased. In effect, the legislation that brought William and Mary to the throne put an end to absolute monarchy in England, thereby resolving the major cause of the dissension that had plagued England throughout the century. But in overthrowing James II and denying the succession to his son, it set in motion the Jacobite rebellions that would plague the country for the next half century.

FIG. 11.5

Scene from Farquhar's *The Beaux' Stratagem*. From an edition of the play published in 1733.

Still, it is not surprising that the middle class should begin to make its tastes felt in the theatre or, since it was morally conservative, that, when it did, Puritan sentiment would surface again. This reawakened conservatism was expressed through several attacks on the theatre during the 1690s, but none was truly effective until Jeremy Collier's *A Short View of the Immorality and Profaneness of the English Stage* (1698) appeared. Collier succeeded where others had failed because he began with the accepted neoclassical doctrine that the purpose of drama is to teach and to please and went on to show the disparity between theory and practice. Most dramatists found it impossible to answer Collier effectively, since they too had accepted moral teaching as the basic aim of drama. A few playwrights, among them Dryden, made public recantations; Congreve at first protested and then gave up playwriting altogether. Even as the controversy raged, English drama began to move in new directions.

ENGLISH DRAMA, 1700–1750

The transition toward a new approach is best seen in the plays of Cibber and Farquhar, in which the characteristics of the established comic types are modified considerably by a more conservative moral outlook and by greater sentimentality. In Colley Cibber's (1671–1757) *Love's Last Shift* (1696), *The Careless Husband* (1704), *The Double Gallant* (1707), and *The Lady's Stake* (1707), profligate characters pursue their fashionable follies until the fifth act, when they undergo rapid and sentimentalized conversions. George Farquhar (1678–1707) preserved much of Congreve's wit, but set his plays in the country and resolved them in a manner that removed moral obstacles. His best plays are *The Constant Couple* (1699), which introduced Sir Harry Wildair, one of the most popular characters of the eighteenth century, *The Recruiting Officer* (1706), and *The Beaux' Stratagem* (1707), the latter two still perennial favorites.

This transition period is also significant for its large number of female playwrights (more than at any time until the present). Between 1695 and 1715, thirty-seven new plays by women were produced on London's stages. These writers, including Mary Pix (1666–1706), Delariviere Manley (*c.* 1672–1724), Catharine Trotter (1679–1749), and Susanna Centlivre (*c.* 1670–1723), who wrote such plays as *The Busy Body* (1709) and *The Wonder* (1714), were among the most successful dramatists of their time.

The trend in comedy toward sentimentality and toward protagonists drawn from the middle class first reached full expression in *The Conscious Lovers* (1722) by Sir Richard Steele (1672–1729). Based on Terence's *Andria,* Steele's play transfers the action to eighteenth-century London. The play's penniless heroine, Indiana, after withstanding many trials of her virtue, is discovered to be the daughter of a rich merchant, thus making a suitable marriage possible. In Steele's play the purpose of comedy has been seriously altered: Rather than seeking to arouse laughter or ridicule, it sought to arouse noble sentiments through the depiction of trials bravely borne by sympathetic characters who are rescued from their sufferings and handsomely rewarded. As Steele put it, he wished to arouse "a pleasure too exquisite for laughter."

Today much of the drama of the eighteenth century is called "sentimental" because so many of the characters appear unnaturally good and their problems seem too easily overcome. These plays were accepted in the eighteenth century, nevertheless, as truthful representations of human nature. The disparity in attitude is explained by our changed view. Eighteenth-century philosophers conceived of humanity as good by nature, a state which individuals could retain by following their instincts, but from which bad examples might divert them. Consequently, it was thought possible to reclaim people from vice by appealing to those virtuous human feelings that had been glossed over by thoughtless or callous behavior. For this reason, characters could be reformed quickly if their "hearts" could be touched. Pathetic situations were also considered to be useful devices because they demonstrated the goodness of the characters who withstood all trials and because they provided spectators with an occasion for displaying their own goodness, since to be moved by the sight of virtue in distress was a sign of a properly sensitive and moral nature.

Although Richard Steele was to have no important successors in comedy until after 1750, this new vein in drama was exploited effectively in tragedy. In the early eighteenth century, Nicholas Rowe (1674–1718) had written a number of tragedies, featuring pathetic heroines, as in *The Ambitious Step-Mother* (1701), *Tamerlane* (1701), *The Fair Penitent* (1703), and *The Tragedy of Jane Shore* (1714), which were to hold the stage until the nineteenth century. A significant new direction was taken in 1731 when George Lillo (1693–1739) wrote *The London Merchant,* in which the hero-apprentice, George Barnwell, is led astray by a prostitute, kills his kind uncle, and ends on the gallows in spite of his abject repentance. Lillo chose his subject from everyday life because he believed that the lessons of traditional tragedy, with characters drawn from the nobility, were not sufficiently applicable to the ordinary person. It is clear that he was considered successful, for until well into the nineteenth century the apprentices of London were sent each year during the Christmas season to see this play as a warning against going astray.

Although during the eighteenth century neoclassicism remained the dominant mode, a number of minor dramatic types (pantomime, ballad opera, comic opera, and burlesque) undermined its authority. Pantomime combined elements from *commedia dell'arte* and farce with topical satire and stories drawn from classical mythology. *Commedia dell'arte* troupes had appeared occasionally in England since the sixteenth century, and *commedia* types had been incorporated into the dances and entr'acte entertainments of English performers since the late seventeenth century. In 1702 John Weaver became the first to organize the dances into a connected story, but it remained for John Rich (1692–1761), son of Christopher Rich and manager of Lincoln's Inn Fields and Covent Garden theatres, to establish the accepted pattern of English pantomime with such works as *Harlequin Executed* (produced during the season of 1716–1717) and

Amadis, or the Loves of Harlequin and Columbine (1718). In Rich's pantomimes, serious scenes based on classical mythology alternated with comic episodes featuring *commedia* characters. The comic scenes were mute, but the serious plot used dialogue and song. Music accompanied much of the action. But the dominant feature was spectacle, motivated by Harlequin's acquisition of a magic wand that could transform places or characters. Unlike most pantomimes, Rich's were long-lived. In forty-five years he created only about twenty, thirteen of which were first performed between 1717 and 1732. Under the name Lun, Rich was also the most famous and the most accomplished English pantomimist of the eighteenth century.

By 1723, pantomime was the most popular form of theatrical entertainment. Although pantomimes served only as afterpieces, many were more popular than the plays they accompanied. Prices were always raised for new pantomimes, several of which had initial runs of forty to fifty performances. Rich trained a number of other pantomime players.

Rich is also associated with the rise of ballad opera, since he produced the first one, *The Beggar's Opera* (1728) by John Gay (1685–1732), after it had been refused by Drury Lane. Ballad opera emerged in part out of the vogue for Italian opera, which began around 1705 and accelerated in 1710 with the arrival in England of George Frideric Handel (1685–1759). In 1719 the Royal Academy of Music was founded as the home of opera. Although always in financial difficulties after 1730, the opera continued to enjoy great prestige with the aristocracy through the remainder of the century. Gay's ballad opera drew upon many operatic conventions (even as it satirized them) but it departed from them by alternating spoken dialogue with lyrics set to popular tunes. Gay's work was more than popularized opera, however, for its story of London low-life commented satirically on the political situation of the time and set the tone for much of the minor drama of the next ten years. No subsequent ballad opera, however, achieved the popularity of the first one.

The satirical burlesque, which differed from ballad opera principally in the absence of sung portions, appeared in the 1730s. The finest writer of this form was Henry Fielding (1707–1754), who began his dramatic career with adaptations of Molière and then turned to topical satire in his burlesque of contemporary tragedy, *Tom Thumb, or the Tragedy of Tragedies* (1730). His later plays, such as *Pasquin* (1736), *Tumble-Down Dick* (1736), and *The Historical Register of 1736* (1737), burlesqued the major figures and events of the day. Like ballad opera, burlesque waned after the passage of the Licensing Act in 1737.

FIG. 11.6

A pantomine at the Haymarket Theatre in the late eighteenth century. Note also the theatre's architecture: proscenium doors, wide apron, stage box, and backless benches in the pit. From Wilkinson, *Londina Illustrata* (1825).

FIG. 11.7

Gay's *The Beggar's Opera*. Polly and Lucy are pleading for Macheath's life. Note the spectators on the stage. An engraving by William Blake after William Hogarth's painting of 1729. Courtesy Harvard Theatre Collection.

GOVERNMENTAL REGULATION OF THE THEATRE

The Licensing Act of 1737 was an outgrowth of both political and theatrical conditions. During the reign of Queen Anne, political parties became more important as the role of Parliament increased. Her successor, George I (reigned 1714–1727), was a German prince who spoke no English and permitted his chief minister, Sir Robert Walpole (usually said to be Britain's first prime minister), to run the government. George I's practice was continued by his son, George II (reigned 1727–1760). Thus, after 1714 political factions and government officials and policies provided fertile ground for satire. Dramatists did not fail to capitalize on this opportunity, especially during the 1720s and 1730s.

By this time, the legal status of the patents issued by Charles II was also being debated and questions concerning the patents led several men to defy them and open unlicensed theatres. England's first Prime Minister, Walpole, was highly sensitive to the political satires being offered at these unlicensed theatres.

Following a particularly scurrilous attack on him in a play by Fielding, a bill was hastily rushed through Parliament, the Licensing Act of 1737. Its provisions were simple: (1) it prohibited the acting for "gain, hire, or reward" of any play not previously licensed by the Lord Chamberlain, and (2) it restricted authorized theatres to the City of Westminster (the official seat of government). The Drury Lane and Covent Garden thus were confirmed as the only legitimate theatres in England, for no provisions were made for troupes in any other city.

At first the law was obeyed, but in 1740 Henry Giffard, who had managed the best of the unlicensed troupes between 1731 and 1737, reopened the Goodman's Fields Theatre. By charging admission only for concerts, to which plays were added free, Giffard sought to evade the Licensing Act by interpreting literally the prohibition against unauthorized acting for "gain, hire, or reward." The attention drawn to this theatre by David Garrick's debut there in 1741 soon brought its closure. Others were to use similar ruses; Samuel Foote, for example, offered his "free" entertainments to those who paid for a "Dish of Chocolate" or to attend an "Auction of Pictures." Such ventures were tolerated for a time, but most were eventually forbidden.

Other public entertainments did not require licensing until 1752, when abuses led to the passage of a new licensing bill. Under the licensing bill of 1752, all places of entertainment within a twenty-mile radius of London were required to secure licenses from local magistrates. Although regular drama was expressly forbidden to them, the permissible kinds of entertainment were left undefined and this opened many new opportunities for skirting the law.

The Licensing Act of 1737 had technically made provincial theatres illegal and the licensing bill of 1752 did nothing to remedy that. Nevertheless, the provincial theatre had continued to operate (either by ignoring the law or by using various ruses to circumvent it), and a number of regular circuits had grown up. By the 1760s, the larger towns were objecting to being denied lawful theatres. As a result, Parliament began to authorize theatres in specific towns: in Bath and Norwich in 1768, in York and Hull in 1769, in Liverpool in 1771, and in Chester in 1777. The licensing bill of 1788 finally permitted magistrates outside the twenty-mile radius of London to license theatres for legitimate drama. As a result, the theatre was once again legitimized throughout the British Isles.

In London no exception to the monopoly held by Drury Lane and Covent Garden was made until 1766, when, in recompense for having been crippled

FIG. 11.8
Strolling players dressing in a barn. Note the many stage props, bits of scenery, costumes, and the preparations for performance. An engraving by William Hogarth. Courtesy Indiana University Libraries.

by a prank instigated by the Duke of York, Samuel Foote was granted a license to present plays at the Haymarket Theatre between May 15 and September 15, a period during which the patent houses normally closed. Although Foote's license was granted only for his lifetime, he sold it to George Colman in 1777 and it was renewed thereafter until 1843. Thus, the Haymarket became a third legitimate theatre.

ENGLISH DRAMA, 1750–1800

Drama was seriously affected by the Licensing Act of 1737, since thereafter it had to pass the scrutiny of a censor. The minor forms suffered most, for topical and political satire were strongly discouraged. Consequently, both ballad opera and burlesque declined rapidly. Ballad opera was replaced by a new musical type, comic opera, that had sentimental plots and original music. The most famous writer of the new type was Isaac Bickerstaffe (1735–1812), with such works as *The Maid of the Mill* (1765) and *Lionel and Clarissa* (1768). Other works in this vein include Richard Brinsley Sheridan's (1751–1816) *The Duenna* (1775), John O'Keeffe's (1747–1833) *The Poor Soldier* (1783), and George Colman the Younger's (1762–1836) *Inkle and Yarico* (1787).

FIG. 11.9

Isaac Bickerstaffe's *The Maid of the Mill*. The setting is by Inigo Richards, one of the major scene designers of the late eighteenth century. From *The Magazine of Art* (1895).

Few burlesques were written in the last half of the eighteenth century, and in those few the targets were literary and dramatic works rather than politics. By far the best of the burlesques was Sheridan's *The Critic* (1781), a satire on tragedy, critics, authors, and the vogue of spectacle. It replaced Buckingham's *The Rehearsal* and was regularly performed until the end of the nineteenth century.

Pantomime was little affected by the Licensing Act, but no devisor of this form stands out in the last half of the century. The major change is seen after 1760 in the waning popularity of Harlequin and the rise of the more sentimentalized clown. Still, pantomime continued to be the most popular of all theatrical entertainments.

After 1750 domestic tragedy declined in favor. The only work of this type to win continuing fame was Edward Moore's (1712–1757) *The Gamester* (1753), which depicted the downward career of a gambler. As domestic tragedy declined in popularity, sentimental comedy flourished, perhaps because audiences preferred to see characters rescued from misfortune rather than punished for mistakes. The most important later writers were Hugh Kelly (1739–1777), whose *False Delicacy* (1768) treats the disentanglement of three pairs of unsuited lovers; Richard Cumberland (1732–1811), whose *The West Indian* (1771) tells the story of a young rake who, after being reformed by marriage, is rewarded by the discovery that his wife is an heiress; and Thomas

Holcroft (1745–1809), whose *The Road to Ruin* (1792) shows a gambler so touched by his father's shame that he is restored to virtue. Such sentimental drama, with its emphasis upon moral teaching through poetic justice, was to develop into melodrama in the nineteenth century.

Robust comedy did not altogether die out. Between 1720 and 1760, however, "laughing" comedy was restricted primarily to farce, usually short plays performed as afterpieces. Samuel Foote (1720–1777) did much to keep the comic spirit alive through such works as *The Knights* (1749), *The Orators* (1762), *The Minor* (1760), and *The Maid of Bath* (1771), for all combine farcical wit and situations with satire on such contemporary targets as the rising Methodist religion.

After 1760 a few writers began to oppose sentimentalism. George Colman the Elder (1732–1794) approached the spirit of Restoration comedy in *The Jealous Wife* (1761) and other plays, but it was Goldsmith and Sheridan who are universally seen as having brought "laughing comedy" back to the British stage. Oliver Goldsmith's (1730?–1774) *She Stoops to Conquer* (1773) is a comic masterpiece. Subtitled *The Mistakes of a Night,* it shows how two young men are duped into mistaking the home of a country gentleman for an inn, their consequent ill-mannered treatment of their host, and the misunderstandings, intrigues, and discoveries that eventually lead to the satisfactory conclusion of the love affairs of the principal characters.

Richard Brinsley Sheridan (1751–1816) is noted primarily for *The Rivals* (1775) and *The School for Scandal* (1777), which recall Congreve's comedies of manners with their sparkling and witty dialogue and their vivid pictures of the fashionable society of the day. But Sheridan's morality is more conventional than was Congreve's, for he always made true virtue triumphant. In *The School for Scandal,* for example, though he permitted his scandalmongers to murder reputations through witty gossip and comic intrigue and to promote the sentiment-spouting but hypocritical Joseph Surface at the expense of his rakish but open-hearted brother Charles, eventually Joseph is exposed, Charles is united with the virtuous Maria, and the strong-willed but naive Lady Teazle is recalled to her duty to her elderly and comically crotchety husband, Sir Peter.

Goldsmith and Sheridan did much to recapture the brilliance of English drama, and, with the exception of Shakespeare's, their plays have held the stage more consistently than have those by any other English dramatists. Unfortunately, Goldsmith and Sheridan had no successful emulators, and after 1780 English drama moved steadily toward melodrama.

FIG. 11.10
The "screen scene" from Sheridan's *The School for Scandal* at Drury Lane in 1777. A contemporary print.

The eighteenth-century theatre was by no means restricted to production of contemporary plays. The pattern followed throughout the eighteenth century had been set during the Restoration, when a company's repertory of thirty-five to forty plays was divided about equally between pre-Commonwealth plays and new plays or successes from recent seasons. By the early eighteenth century, the repertory had increased to forty to seventy-five plays, and by the last quarter of the century had increased to about ninety works. After 1750, about one-third of the repertory was drawn from Shakespearean and other pre-Commonwealth plays, another third was made up of Restoration or early eighteenth-century works, and the remaining third was composed of recent successes or new plays. Consequently, new plays constituted the smallest portion of the repertory.

THE PLAYWRIGHT

After 1680, dramatists were paid by the "benefit" system, under which they received the proceeds (less house expenses) of the third night of the initial run. After 1690, they might also be given a benefit on the sixth night, if the play ran so long, and in the eighteenth century on every third night of the original run. Few plays ran beyond the third night,

however, and some did not run that long. Once a play's initial run was over, the playwright received no further payments from the company, even though the play might be placed in the repertory and remain there for many years. Throughout the eighteenth century dramatists depended primarily upon benefit performances for their income and only a few plays brought their authors significant financial rewards.

FINANCIAL POLICIES

Since the building of the Theatre in 1576, playhouses in England were erected on leased land with money obtained by the sale of shares in the buildings. In return for their investment, shareholders were paid a fixed sum for each day the theatre was used for performances. This policy was continued after the Restoration but the number of investors steadily increased, and fewer and fewer of them had any interest in the operations of the theatre beyond its ability to generate a profit for them.

For a time after 1660, the old system under which actors shared in the company's risks and profits was revived, but as the theatre declined in prosperity London actors came to prefer a fixed salary. Consequently, by 1690 the old sharing arrangement had been abandoned in London, though it was revived for a time by Betterton's troupe (1695–1708), and provincial theatres maintained it until well into the nineteenth century. Under the new system in London, company managers assumed all the financial risks and reaped all the financial rewards, but in hard times they had to borrow money by mortgaging their patents, scenery, and costumes. When the mortgages were not redeemed, partial ownership of the companies also passed to persons who had little or no interest in the theatre except as a commercial investment. The danger of this system first became evident in 1693 when Christopher Rich, ostensibly to protect the investors, assumed control of the United Companies, even though he had had no theatrical experience of any kind. He was merely the first of many similar persons who were to gain control over theatres in London and elsewhere.

Out of the many failures of those managers who knew too little about the theatre came the actor-manager system. Betterton and Garrick had lead the way, but it did not become common until near the end of the century, after which it dominated British theatre until the First World War and still continues in rare instances to this day. The trend between 1660 and 1800 was toward larger companies and more carefully mounted productions, both of which demanded greater financial resources. (Whereas the typical company of the Restoration had included 35 to 40 persons, the troupe of 1800 had about 80 actors and as many as 120 other employees.)

Expenses were calculated in terms of a single playing day. This was necessary in part because by the eighteenth century benefits were an important feature of theatrical life and a manager had to state the amount to be deducted from the receipts as the theatre's expenses on these occasions. In the early eighteenth century the average daily expenses were about £40; by 1735 they had risen to £50, and by 1790 to £105.

Since managers depended primarily upon ticket sales for income, only two paths were open to them as expenses increased: to raise the price of tickets or to increase attendance. Although at times they did both, they were cautious about raising prices. Consequently, the scale of entrance fees did not change markedly.

Beginning in the 1690s spectators were allowed to enter at the end of the third act at "half price," except when a new pantomime or other attraction was to be given as an afterpiece. On the other hand, if prices were raised because of the afterpiece, the spectator who left at the end of the main piece was refunded the additional charge. Besides tickets, the managers realized some income from the lease of concessions to those who hawked food, drink, playbooks, and playbills in the theatre.

Steadily increasing expense, however, forced most managers to enlarge their theatres to accommodate additional spectators. Most of the changes in theatre auditoriums were motivated by this need, whereas alterations of the stage resulted from changing fashions in spectacle.

THEATRE ARCHITECTURE

In 1660 the old Salisbury Court, Phoenix/Cockpit, and Red Bull theatres were used for a short time, but none was thought sufficiently suited to the Italianate scenery which was then coming into vogue. Killigrew used Gibbon's Tennis Court until his Theatre Royal in Bridges Street was ready for occupancy in 1663 and when it burned in 1672 he built the first Drury Lane Theatre on the same lot.

Davenant converted Lisle's Tennis Court into the Lincoln's Inn Fields Theatre in 1661 and he replaced it with the Dorset Garden Theatre, designed by Christopher Wren, in 1671. These theatres varied in size and detail, but they shared common features that established the pattern for English playhouses until the nineteenth century.

In those theatres the auditorium was divided into pit, boxes, and galleries. Unlike its French equivalent, the English pit was raked to improve sightlines

FIG. 11.11

Sectional plan of a theatre, believed to be Drury Lane, as designed by Christopher Wren in 1674. The auditorium is at left. Note the backless benches in the raked pit; the deep apron with two proscenium doors; and the relatively shallow stage behind the proscenium. Copyright the Warden and Fellows of All Souls College, Oxford.

and equipped with eight to ten rows of backless benches for all spectators. There were two or three galleries. The first was partitioned into boxes; the uppermost was undivided and equipped with benches; the middle gallery, when present, might be partially devoted to boxes and the remainder to benches. The early theatres were small. At the Drury Lane, for example, the distance from the front of the stage to the back of the auditorium was only about 36 feet, so seating capacity was limited to only about 650 persons; Lincoln's Inn Fields held even fewer. But the size of auditoriums increased throughout the eighteenth century, although the trend toward largeness did not accelerate until after 1760. When the Covent Garden theatre was built in 1732 to replace Lincoln's Inn Fields, for example, it seated nearly 1400, but in 1784 it was enlarged to hold 2500 and in 1792 it was rebuilt to accommodate 3000. By this time, Drury Lane was being rebuilt to hold 3600. In spite of the increase in size, however, the basic arrangement remained constant.

When the Drury Lane theatre opened in 1674, it had a stage about 34 feet deep, divided into two roughly equal parts by the proscenium arch, the forestage and the stage house. The forestage was where the acting took place and it thrust the action into the auditorium, rather than confining it behind the picture frame. Actors entered the forestage through doors on either end. The stage house, behind the proscenium, was for stage sets.

The floor of the stage sloped upward from the front of the forestage to the back wall of the stagehouse. Behind the proscenium, grooves were installed to accommodate wings and shutters, while trapdoors and flying machinery provided for special effects.

FIG. 11.12
Stage of the Dorset Garden Theatre. The proscenium doors can be glimpsed at the extreme sides. The scene is from Settle's *The Empress of Morocco*, produced in 1673. From Wilkinson, *Londina Illustrata* (1825).

FIG. 11.13
The auditorium of the Drury Lane Theatre after it was remodeled and redecorated in 1775. Engraving by R. and J. Adams. Courtesy Theatre Museum, Victoria and Albert Museum, London.

With minor changes, these basic characteristics were to continue through the eighteenth century.

As the auditorium grew in size, so did the stage. Around 1700 the stage behind the proscenium at Drury Lane was increased to about 30 feet, and by 1790 some theatres had stages more than 50 feet deep. At the same time, the forestage dwindled. Around 1700 Rich removed one set of proscenium doors and shortened the forestage to make room for more seats in the pit. Consequently, throughout the eighteenth century there was usually only one proscenium door on either side of the stage. The forestage, now reduced to about 12 feet in depth, remained the primary playing area, however, though after about 1765, some of the action might also occur within the stage house, behind the proscenium.

The work areas needed for production were also enlarged during the eighteenth century by remodeling the existing structure or by acquiring or constructing smaller buildings adjoining it. These spaces included dressing rooms, greenrooms, storage of various kinds, areas used in the construction of scenery and for costumes and properties. In spite of all additions and alterations, by 1790 most of the theatres were considered inadequate, and soon after they were to be replaced by larger, more elaborate buildings.

SCENIC PRACTICES

After 1661 the scenic practices of the English stage differed little from those then in use in Italy and France. Wings, borders, and shutters were the standard units, although after 1690 roll drops were sometimes used in the place of shutters. Sets were shifted by means of grooves installed on the stage floor and overhead. Stagehands made the necessary changes upon a whistled signal from the prompter. (For reasons that are unclear, the chariot-and-pole system, the standard method of shifting scenery in continental theatres, was seldom used in England, except at the opera house.) Since the front curtain was raised after the prologue was spoken and not lowered until the end of the performance, all changes were made in full view of the audience. Even entr'acte entertainments were given in front of a full stage setting until about 1750, after which an "act drop" was used as a background. Heavy properties or furniture could be set up and removed behind the shutters or the act drop. Occasionally they were brought on by servants in full view of the audience.

Between 1660 and 1800 each theatre accumulated a stock of scenery that was reused often. When a new theatre was built, settings were commissioned even before the repertory was fixed. This practice was made possible by the neoclassical attitude that specific times and places are irrelevant in drama, and that attempts to particularize only diminish universality. The aim was to capture the essence of a type of place rather than to re-create the features of a particular place. Thus, settings were so anonymous that they could be used in many different plays. One author, writing about 1750, lists the necessary scenes as: (1) temples, (2) tombs, (3) city walls and gates, (4) palace exteriors, (5) palace interiors, (6) streets, (7) chambers, (8) prisons, (9) gardens, and (10) rural prospects. He adds that other settings are needed only occasionally. During the Restoration, a few comedies depicted well-known places in London, but this type of particularity diminished markedly during the eighteenth century, except in those minor dramatic types, such as pantomime, in which spectacle played a major role. Even in these instances, however, the scenery created for them was reused extensively in other plays.

The development of spectacle was retarded by the presence of spectators on the stage. Although well established before 1642, this practice was not revived until about 1690, and was not usual until about 1700. It continued until 1762, when Garrick banished the audience from the stage. Between 1700 and 1762, rows of benches extended upstage from the proscenium, and at benefits additional amphitheatrical seating often was erected across the back of the stage. On the other hand, the audience was sometimes forbidden to sit on the stage if a production depended heavily on spectacle.

Because most plays were performed in stock scenery, ticket prices were raised when new sets were introduced. The additional revenue that this provided may be one reason why spectacle increased, for Rich's successful exploitation of spectacle in pantomimes led him to experiment with it in regular drama. In the 1730s he added a procession and coronation scene to *Henry VIII,* in 1750 a funeral procession to *Romeo and Juliet,* and in 1761 the coronation of George III to several of Shakespeare's history plays. Elaborate spectacle was ordinarily reserved for the minor genres, however, until about 1765, when Garrick returned from the continent with new ideas of staging. Through the remainder of the century, scenery was to become more particularized and new settings more common. Of the thirty-seven new plays presented at Drury Lane between 1765 and 1776, nineteen were given entirely new scenery.

During the Restoration John Webb (1611–1672) worked with Davenant, and Samuel Towers (*fl.* 1676–1682), Robert Robinson (*c.* 1653–1706), and

Robert Streeter (1624–1680) painted settings for Killigrew. Complex designs could cost up to £800 at a time when a leading actor was paid about £2½ per week. By the early eighteenth century, however, payments were considerably less and scenery was commissioned only sporadically. Covent Garden spent only £253 on scenery for the 1746–1747 season, and until after 1750 only about one-tenth of any company's budget was spent on settings.

From occasional references we know the names of many scene painters of the first half of the eighteenth century. Some of the more important are James Thornhill (1675–1734), who flourished in the early years of the century; John DeVoto (*fl.* 1708–1752), who worked between 1719 and 1744; George Lambert (*c.* 1699–1765), a landscape painter who did settings for Rich at Lincoln's Inn Fields and Covent Garden and some of whose settings remained in use until 1808; and Francis Hayman (1708–1776), who painted settings for Drury Lane in the 1730s and 1740s.

The situation began to change in 1749, when Rich imported designers from the continent. The most significant of these was Jean-Nicolas Servandoni (1695–1766), famous for his work at the Paris Opéra. Others included Nicholas Thomas Dall (?–1776), a Dane who settled in England around 1750, and Giovanni Battista Cipriani (1727–1785), a Florentine painter who came to London in 1755. John Inigo Richards (*c.* 1729–1810), a distinguished English painter noted especially for his picturesque landscapes, was also a major designer of the period.

The most important designer of the late eighteenth century, however, was Philippe Jacques de Loutherbourg (1740–1812), a French artist who was hired by the great actor-manager, David Garrick, to design for Drury Lane in 1772. De Loutherbourg was the first designer in England to achieve unity of design by overseeing all the visual elements of the productions assigned to him. At this time the normal practice was for a designer to produce one new set for a play while the rest were pulled from stock, or to be part of a team of designers, each of which did the set for a single act of a play. De Loutherbourg did all the sets, and took an interest in props, costumes, and lighting as well. To increase illusion, de Loutherbourg broke up the stage picture with ground rows and set pieces to gain a greater sense of depth and to avoid the symmetrical composition imposed by parallel wings and shutters. He used miniature figures at the rear of the stage to depict battles, marching armies, and sailing vessels; and added sound effects, such as waves, rain, hail, and distant guns, to increase the illusion. His work also reflects the growing interest in

FIG. 11.14
Setting for Act 1, scene 1 of *Arsinoe*. Design by James Thornhill. Courtesy Theatre Museum, Victoria and Albert Museum, London.

both local color and history, which was gradually replacing the neoclassical preoccupation with generalized, universalized settings. Most of his innovations would not be copied by others, however, until the next century.

Little is known of lighting practices during the Restoration. Performances were given in the afternoon, and windows probably provided some illumination. Since most of the action occurred on the forestage, both auditorium and stage were illuminated throughout the performances. Chandeliers hung above the forestage and behind the proscenium. Pepys, in his *Diary*, often complains of headaches caused by looking into those candles. Footlights were certainly in use by 1672. (See Fig. 11.2.)

By 1744, lights were apparently being mounted on vertical "ladders" behind each wing and dimmed by "scene blinds," which were shields that could be manipulated to intervene between the light source and the stage. Footlights were mounted on pivots which allowed them to be lowered below the stage level. Oil lamps were used in some positions, since reflectors made candles wilt.

Starting in 1765, Garrick seems to have had all visible light sources removed from the stage and to have

increased brightness, perhaps with improved lamps and reflectors. He also popularized the continental system of making the light ladders rotate so that they

FIG. 11.15
A sketch by de Loutherbourg for the battle scenes in Shakespeare's *Richard III*. Note the tent at left and others in the background. From *The Magazine of Art* (1895).

FIG. 11.16

A riot at Covent Garden in 1763. Dressed for Arne's *Artaxerxes,* the actors wear Near Eastern dress while the actresses wear fashionable English clothing. Note also the chandeliers hanging over the stage. Courtesy Theatre Museum, Victoria and Albert Museum, London.

FIG. 11.17

Whitehead's *The Roman Father* at Drury Lane in 1750. At center is Garrick. Note the *habit à la romaine* worn by the men and the few exotic touches at the shoulder and waist of the women's dresses. Courtesy the Folger Shakespeare Library, Washington, D.C.

could be made to reflect light toward or away from the stage. During the 1770s de Loutherbourg experimented with silk screens to reflect light, and perhaps transparent silk filters, to gain control over color for the first time. The increased concern for lighting significantly increased its costs. In 1745 theatres were spending about £350 a year on lighting, while during the 1770s expenses rose to nearly £2000.

Lighting further improved after the introduction in 1785 of the Argand, or "patent," lamp. Using a cylindrical wick and glass chimney to control the relative proportions of oxygen and oil, this lamp produced a much brighter and steadier light than earlier instruments had. After this time, oil largely superseded candles for stage lighting. Since the chimneys could be colored, experimentation with color effects also increased.

Improvements in lighting and increased emphasis upon illusion encouraged managers to place more of the action behind the proscenium arch. This trend was not fully completed during the eighteenth century, however, and the auditorium continued to be lighted as a part of the total picture.

COSTUME PRACTICES

The principles governing costume between 1660 and 1800 differed little from those of pre-Commonwealth times or from those of seventeenth-century France. Since time and place were considered unimportant, most characters wore contemporary garments and most actors dressed their characters as sumptuously

as possible. The exceptions to contemporary dress were classical heroes who wore the *habit à la romaine,* and ethnic costumes like Near Eastern characters who were identified by turbans, baggy trousers, fur-trimmed robes, and feathered headdresses.

FIG. 11.18

The play-within-the-play from *Hamlet* as shown in a painting by Francis Hayman, who also painted scenery for the Drury Lane Theatre in the 1730s. At center, Claudius is rising from his seat; Hamlet is seated on the floor in the lower right corner. Note the costumes. Courtesy the Folger Shakespeare Library, Washington, D.C.

Each company maintained a "common stock" of costumes, which was preserved and added to regularly. By the late 1760s the Covent Garden wardrobe had grown so large that it had to be moved to an adjoining house. But actors with sufficient means always supplied most of their own costumes. Some demanded and received a special allowance from the manager for this purpose. The actors' desire to dress as sumptuously as possible led to intense rivalries, and costumes often reflected the actor's purse rather than the appropriate dress for the character's position.

ACTORS AND ACTING, 1660–1800

A major innovation of the Restoration was the introduction of women into acting companies. By 1661 both Davenant and Killigrew had a full complement of actresses, and within a short time men appeared only in such female roles as witches and comic old women, a practice that persisted through the eighteenth century.

Between 1660 and 1800 beginning actors usually entered a company on a probationary status and learned by observing established performers.

The beginners, or "utility," actors played an enormous number of small roles each season and eventually discovered the types for which they were best suited. After a few years, they advanced into a "line of business" (a limited range of character types) in which they usually remained for the rest of their careers. It is impossible to determine when lines of business were first recognized, for they may extend back to pre-Commonwealth times. By the late eighteenth century four clearly distinguishable ranks existed: (1) players of leading roles, (2) players of secondary roles, (3) players of third-line parts (often called "walking ladies" or "walking gentlemen"), and (4) general utility performers. The first rank was usually restricted to players of heroes and heroines of tragedy and light comedy. The lesser ranks included specialists in such lines as "singing chambermaids," elderly men, and eccentrics.

The extent to which actors specialized depended upon both their versatility and the size of the company in which they performed. A small, provincial company required its actors to play a wider range of parts than did the large London troupes. Most actors had a serious and a comic line, although they were seldom equally good in both. Lines of business led to the "possession of parts," since once actors were cast in roles they continued to play them as long as they remained in the company (though those who started with young lover roles generally moved into more mature parts). Under the repertory system, actors were assigned a large number of roles, each of which, once learned, they were supposedly able to perform on 24-hour notice. Mrs. Oldfield had an average of about twenty-six, Barton Booth about thirty-five, and Garrick, ninety-six.

The lesser actors in a company were employed by the season, but leading actors were usually put under contract for a longer period, although almost never exceeding five years. On the other hand, after 1743 Macklin usually performed only under short-term engagements, a practice which foreshadowed the "starring" arrangements which dominated the nineteenth-century theatre. The concept of starring engagements also received considerable impetus from those eighteenth-century performers who made brief appearances with provincial troupes during the summer months when the major theatres in London were closed.

The income of actors varied considerably. Salaries, though quoted by the week, were paid only for those days upon which the theatres were open; and closure brought a proportionate deduction from the actors' pay.

This salary was usually augmented, however, by at least one benefit annually. Benefit performances for groups of actors were instituted in the 1660s and were first accorded to individuals in the late 1680s. After 1695 Betterton began offering benefits as inducements to actors to remain with his company, and this custom was gradually extended until it included every employee of the playhouse. Major performers had separate benefits, but lesser actors and most of the nonperforming personnel usually shared benefits. Typically the beneficiaries received all the receipts in excess of house expenses, although there were many variations on this arrangement. At first the benefits were scattered throughout the season, but after 1712 they were normally concentrated in the period between March and the summer closing.

A well-attended benefit might bring a performer more income in a single evening than was made throughout the rest of the year, especially since spectators often voluntarily paid higher admission fees and presented gifts of money or jewelry to popular performers. On the other hand, the receipts sometimes did not meet the house expenses and the actor lost money. The lure of a profitable benefit, however, probably permitted managers to pay actors considerably less than might otherwise have been demanded.

Usually an experienced actor was appointed to stage the plays (and was given the title "acting manager") when the theatre manager was not qualified for this task. Betterton was acting manager of the companies in which he worked for most of the years between 1668 and 1709; at Drury Lane between 1710 and 1732, the triumvirate of actor-managers divided the rehearsal duties; John Rich staged pantomimes and spectacles, but employed such actors as James Quin, Lacy Ryan, and James Lacy to rehearse the regular drama; Charles Macklin was acting manager at Drury Lane from 1734 to 1743, and Garrick was in charge of the repertory and staging at that theatre from 1747 until 1776.

The first three rehearsals of a new play fell to the dramatist, who presumably helped the actors with interpretation. The acting manager was responsible for revivals. Rehearsals were few by modern standards; they were held from about 10 A.M. until 1 P.M. and seldom extended beyond two weeks. Little time was spent on blocking or movement patterns. Actors learned by experience how to move about the stage and when to give the dominant positions to the major performers. Most scenes were played on the forestage and lines were addressed to the audience as much as to the other characters. Since furniture was seldom used, actors usually stood throughout and gave little thought to creating realistic stage pictures. During rehearsals the players seldom attempted to give full portrayals. Consequently, innovations conceived by an actor were usually not revealed until the first performance, when they surprised fellow actors as much as the audience. The typical brief rehearsals usually meant that on opening night actors were often still uncertain of their lines and depended much on improvisation. Furthermore, their relatively secure positions seem to have made many actors neglectful. As a result, managers sought to impose discipline through an elaborate system of fines for such faults as tardiness at rehearsals, failure to learn lines, refusal of roles, and a variety of other lapses.

The orderly operation of a company depended much upon the prompter, whose duties included securing licenses for the plays, copying out the actors' "sides," holding rehearsals when requested to do so, and assessing fines. During performances the prompter gave cues for scene shifts and music, dispatched call boys for actors, and prompted as necessary.

Acting was a mixture of tradition and innovation. Roles were passed down from one generation to the next, and with them went the traditional interpretation. When one actor succeeded another, he or she was expected to learn the business used in that company, since the repertory could not be restaged to suit one actor. Because so much of playing became traditional, new conceptions of characters, or even new line readings, often produced sensations. Thus,

Charles Macklin greatly altered the conception of Shylock in 1741 by departing from the traditional low-comedy interpretation.

The style of acting varied from formal to realistic. Until about 1750, the dominant approach was oratorical, as epitomized in the playing of Betterton, Booth, and Quin. Then Macklin and Garrick urged the adoption of a style based upon direct observation of life, although they too probably idealized reality. The two styles came into direct conflict in the 1740s when Quin and Garrick were the leading performers of London. Garrick's ultimate victory parallels the changes evident in the other theatre arts, since it marks a movement away from the idealized generality of neoclassicism, which Quin favored, to a more specific and individualized characterization. But even among Garrick's troupe, two rather distinct modes were often seen in the same production.

Despite changes many conventions remained relatively constant, and clearly distinguish the "realism" of the eighteenth century from that of today. First, whenever possible, actors played at the front of the stage and as one reporter put it, "They never turn their backs on the public, and seldom show their faces in profile." They seem also to have exchanged stage positions after each speech; as one observer noted, "An actor passes invariably to the right as his interlocutor passes to the left, and vice versa." Other conventions included "affected prolongation of certain cries and exclamations, the sort of 'organ-point' by which all of the oh's and ah's are emphasized; the frequent transports in which the actors feel compelled to precipitate themselves full length to the floor, and the frightful noise of these oft-repeated plunges."

During the early part of the century, actors seem to have observed the meter of verse in a long intoned chant, but from Garrick's time onward they attempted to disguise the verse so as to make it sound as "natural" as possible. Throughout the century actors seem in speaking to have distinguished between less important passages and high points by delivering the former in a manner called "level speaking" and the latter with great vehemence. Actors sought and expected to receive applause as they made "points" throughout the play.

By far the most important actor of the Restoration was Thomas Betterton (c. 1635–1710). On the stage from 1660 to 1709, he excelled in heroic and tragic parts and was universally considered the greatest actor of his day. Betterton performed a wide range of roles, both comic and serious, although he was probably best in such parts as Hamlet, Othello, Hotspur, and Brutus. He remained completely in character throughout a performance and commanded attention with his restrained but powerful

FIG. 11.19

Charles Macklin as Shylock and Mrs. Pope as Portia in the trial scene of *The Merchant of Venice*. Macklin's manner of playing and dressing the part created a sensation because it departed so markedly from earlier treatments. Note the contemporary garments worn by the other characters. Courtesy the Folger Shakespeare Library, Washington, D.C.

action and speech. His somewhat formal and elocutionary style established the model for others. Three of the outstanding actresses were Nell Gwynn, Mrs. Barry, and Mrs. Bracegirdle. Nell Gwynn's (1650–1687) acting career was brief, 1665 to 1669, but sufficient to establish her fame as a comedian (especially in roles requiring male attire), dancer, and speaker of witty prologues and epilogues. Elizabeth Barry (1658–1713) played leading tragic roles opposite Betterton. Ann Bracegirdle (c. 1663–1748), trained by Betterton, excelled in comedies of manners from 1680 until 1707, when she retired at the height of her career.

Of the leading actors of the first half of the eighteenth century, Colley Cibber and Anne Oldfield were English while Robert Wilks, Thomas Doggett, Barton Booth, James Quin, and Charles Macklin came from Ireland. Colley Cibber, Robert Wilks, and Thomas Doggett (replaced after 1713 by Barton Booth) made up the "triumvirate" of actor-managers that made Drury Lane the most successful company in London from 1710–1733.

Colley Cibber (1671–1757) began his acting career in 1690. Remaining with Rich when the more experienced actors seceded in 1695, he was soon playing leading roles and writing popular plays. As one of the three managers of Drury Lane he was especially known for his performances of foppish characters. In 1740 he published his autobiography, which is now a principal source of information about the English theatre of the time. Anne Oldfield (1683–1730) went on the stage in 1700 and achieved her first success about 1704. After the retirement of Mrs. Bracegirdle, she was considered the finest actress of her time. She played both comic and serious roles, but was especially admired in high comedy. Her burial in Westminster Abbey is an indication of the respect in which she was held.

Robert Wilks (c. 1665–1732) began his acting career in Ireland in 1691. He was at Drury Lane by 1698, playing leading roles, and became one of the managers in 1710. Though he was successful in tragedy, he was especially admired as the dashing young hero of comedy. Thomas Doggett (c. 1670–1721) was considered the finest low comedian of his day. He began his career in Dublin and worked in several provincial companies before coming to London in 1691 and joining the management of Drury Lane in 1710. Barton Booth (1681–1733) started his career in Dublin about 1698 and came to London in 1700. He played only secondary roles until 1713, when he made a great sensation in Addison's *Cato*. From that point on he became part of the management team at Drury Lane and was considered the finest tragic actor of London.

James Quin (1693–1766) began his career in Dublin in 1712, came to Drury Lane in 1714, and in 1718 joined John Rich at Lincoln's Inn Fields, where he also worked as the acting manager. He returned to Drury Lane in 1734 and retired at the height of his popularity in 1751. Charles Macklin (1699–1797) began acting in Ireland about 1719 and first came to London around 1725. His acting style was considered too prosaic, however, and he returned to the provinces until 1730. He served as acting manager at Drury Lane with Quin from 1734 until 1743, when he and other actors, including Garrick, tried to form their own theatre. Refused a license, they capitulated, but the manager would not employ Macklin again. For a time he ran an acting school, and thereafter for the most part played short engagements in London and elsewhere. Macklin's reputation was based primarily upon a few roles, especially Shylock and the protagonists of his own comedies, such as *Love à la Mode* (1759) and *The Man of the World* (1781). Although he was more devoted to naturalistic acting than Garrick was, Macklin's limited

FIG. 11.20

The closet scene from *Hamlet* as performed in the early eighteenth century. Note the contemporary dress worn by Hamlet and the Queen. From Rowe's edition of Shakespeare's plays, 5 (1709).

range as an actor and his quarrelsome nature restricted his success.

From the 1740s until 1776 David Garrick (1717–1779) dominated the English stage. After making his London debut at Goodman's Fields Theatre in 1741, he alternated between Drury Lane and Covent Garden until 1747, when he became joint manager with John Lacy of Drury Lane, a position which he held until his retirement in 1776. Garrick influenced the theatre through his managerial policies as much as through his acting, for in addition to being a careful and devoted director, he was responsible for several significant innovations in staging. As an actor, he had an extremely wide range, playing almost every kind of character, although he

was considered best as Lear, Macbeth, and Hamlet. He had a mobile face, piercing eyes, and expressive body, all of which he used to great effect in the pantomimic byplay for which he was famous. His agreeable and well-controlled voice was somewhat lacking in fullness. Through intense concentration upon the immediate situation, Garrick made whatever he did seem compellingly real. Above all, he seemed to grasp the complexities of each role, and he gave them fuller expression than did any of his contemporaries.

Among the outstanding actresses of the period were Peg Woffington (*c.* 1714–1760), noted especially for her portrayal of spirited heroines of comedy and for "breeches" parts (roles played in male attire); Kitty Clive (1711–1785), who began her career in 1728 and remained a favorite with audiences in farce and spirited comedy; and Frances Abington (1737–1815), noted for high comedy roles. Equally important was Mrs. Hannah Pritchard (1711–1768) who was universally considered the finest tragic actress of her time. So thoroughly did she make Lady Macbeth her own that Garrick never appeared in the play after she died.

Garrick's greatest rival was Spranger Barry (1719–1777), who began his career in Ireland in 1743 and came to London in 1746. From 1750 to 1758 he played at Covent Garden in competition with Garrick. Although Garrick outshone him in most roles, Barry was considered superior as the romantic lover. From 1766 until his death, he often appeared with Garrick at Drury Lane.

By the 1790s the leadership in acting was passing to the Kemble family, who were to dominate the next generation.

AUDIENCES AND PERFORMANCES

The theatrical season ran from September or October to May or June. The number of performances during the regular season varied, but the average was between 170 and 200.

Performances were advertised in various ways: posters set up around the city; handbills distributed at coffee houses, private homes, and elsewhere; advertisements in newspapers, after these began to appear in the early eighteenth century; and announcements made from the stage each evening. The performance time was gradually moved from midafternoon to early evening.

During the early Restoration, the beginning time was 3 or 3:30 P.M. but by the last quarter of the eighteenth century it had shifted to 6:15 or 6:30. The doors of the theatres were usually opened long before

FIG. 11.21
David Garrick as Macbeth and Mrs. Pritchard as Lady Macbeth just prior to the murder of Duncan. Note that Macbeth is costumed as a British army officer, while Lady Macbeth wears eighteenth-century fashionable garments. Courtesy Theatre Museum, Victoria and Albert Museum, London.

performances began and, since seats were not reserved, many persons came early or sent servants to hold seats. By the 1730s tickets for boxes could be bought in advance, but specific seats were not reserved. Each part of the house—boxes, pit, and galleries—had its own entrance, ticket sellers, and ticket takers. Since seats were unnumbered, squabbles over places often occurred.

The evening's bill was complex. In the Restoration, it consisted of a full-length play, with singing and dancing between the acts. Around 1700, Christopher Rich added acrobats, trained animals, and other circus-like performers in an attempt to compete more effectively with Betterton's troupe; this kind of entertainment was never completely absent from the theatre thereafter. Around 1715 the afterpiece was introduced and soon became standard. Thus, by 1720, a typical evening's bill lasted from three to five hours.

The relationship between audience and performers was close. Actors often took their grievances to the spectators, who sometimes refused to let performances proceed until explanations from alleged offenders were forthcoming. Riots, precipitated by changes in casting, in the evening's bill, or well-established customs,

were not uncommon. Thus, spectators believed firmly in their rights and did not hesitate to exert their power to correct any grievance, actual or supposed.

Throughout the eighteenth century the theatre gained steadily in popularity as commercial prosperity enlarged the potential playgoing public. Consequently, by the 1790s the theatre buildings had grown too small to accommodate all those who wished to attend. Also by this time new values had undermined neoclassicism. England was on the threshold of new developments in both its theatre and drama.

THE PROVINCIAL THEATRE

During the eighteenth century, theatre in the British Isles was not confined to London. Dublin was especially important as a theatrical center; it not only supported thriving companies but also supplied London with many of its most prominent playwrights and actors. The theatre in Dublin prospered in part because Ireland was exempted from the provisions of the Licensing Act of 1737, and consequently until the 1760s it maintained the only legitimate theatres in the British Isles outside of London.

Nevertheless, though they lacked legal sanction, companies continued to perform throughout England and Scotland after 1737. They evaded the law by advertising their programs as medleys of songs, dances, and dramatic scenes. Provincial officials ignored the infringements of the law, except on those rare occasions when citizens instituted legal proceedings against the actors. After the 1760s, when Parliament began to authorize provincial troupes, the theatre outside of London prospered. The best companies were those of Edinburgh, Bath, York, Norwich, Liverpool, Manchester, Bristol, Newcastle, and Brighton. They were the training ground for most of Britain's actors, and they offered a steady supply of new talent to London's companies. But no city outside London was able to fully support a professional company, so touring circuits were developed, with companies spending from a few days to a few weeks in each of the several towns that made up their circuit. Together, the provincial troupes provided entertainment for virtually the whole of the British Isles.

THEATRE OF COLONIAL NORTH AMERICA

British attempts to establish a colony at Roanoke (1585) failed, so it was not until the founding of Jamestown (1607) that any permanent British colonies were established in North America. As colonization spread, the British came into contact with a great diversity of distinctive American peoples from the Iroquois Confederacy and the Algonquian-speaking peoples in the northeast and mid-Atlantic region to the Cherokee, Creek, Choctaw, and Chickasaw nations of the southeast. But these cultures were already under stress from the devastation of epidemics introduced and reintroduced by Europeans since 1514. As native groups fought Europeans and each other, their cultures declined further. We know little, therefore, about the pre-Columbian performance traditions of these preliterate peoples. Many certainly had a sophisticated tradition of narrative dance. Others had complex ceremonies and rituals that were theatrical in nature. But if they had the kinds of epic dance drama found in the Spanish occupied territories, few records remain of it. Early Jesuits saw dramatic elements in the masked "False Face" dances of some of the Iroquois peoples. Paul Radin transcribed the text for a ritual drama of the Winnebago people, *The Road of Life and Death,* but this is unlikely to represent traditions from earlier than the eighteenth century (the transcription did not occur until 1908). Europeans would not be exposed to native theatre on the scale found in New Spain until they encountered the highly elaborate *potlatch* ceremonies of the peoples of the Pacific Northwest.

The first play written and performed in North America was Marc Lescarbot's *The Theatre of Neptune in New France* in 1606, in the French colony of Nova Scotia. A number of other plays were presented by amateurs there before a controversy over *Tartuffe* brought a prohibition in 1694. But by this time England was already winning its competition with other European countries for control of North America, and by 1763, when Canada came into its possession, England was the dominant power (until it lost the American Revolution of 1775–1783).

The earliest record of a performance in British held territories is not found until 1665, when three men in Virginia were hauled into court for performing a playlet, *The Bear and the Cub.* No other instances are noted until the end of the century, when students presented plays in the colleges at Harvard and William and Mary. In New York sometime between 1699 and 1702, Richard Hunter obtained permission to give theatrical entertainments, but it is not certain that he did so. In 1703 Anthony Aston (?1682–1753), the first professional actor to arrive in North America, gave a few performances in Charleston and New York to earn money for his return passage to England. *Androboros* (or "Maneater")

by Robert Hunter, governor of New York, became the first extant American play when it was published in 1714. A rather crude satire, it ridiculed Hunter's political opponents.

Between 1715 and 1735, however, theatrical activities increased. In 1716 William Levingston of Williamsburg, Virginia, built the first theatre in what was to become the United States, and here until about 1732 Charles and Mary Stagg arranged entertainments, the precise nature of which is uncertain. The theatre operated until 1745 and was torn down by 1770. In Philadelphia strolling players performed in 1723 and 1724; in Lancaster performances were given irregularly between 1730 and 1742; and in New York amateur players staged plays and fitted out a theatre between 1730 and 1733. In Charleston, South Carolina, amateurs gave a season of three plays in 1735 and built a theatre for performances in 1736 and 1737. This flurry of activity came to an end in the late 1730s, however, probably because of the religious fervor that accompanied the appearances of George Whitefield and John Wesley in the colonies.

A significant new beginning was made in 1749, when a company under the leadership of Walter Murray and Thomas Kean made its initial appearance in Philadelphia. Almost nothing is known about the origin or qualifications of the actors in this company. Most of the players probably were amateurs. This troupe played in a converted warehouse on Water Street in Philadelphia until 1750, when it toured New York and various towns in Virginia and Maryland. Nothing is heard of it after 1752. Regardless of its artistic stature, the Murray-Kean company was the first to present seasons of some length in several towns. It established a precedent that was to be followed by its more important successor, the Hallam troupe.

Before turning to the Hallams, however, it is necessary to glance briefly at Jamaica, which had been seized from Spain by the English in 1655. Theatrical performances had been given sporadically there since about 1680 and a playhouse was built in 1682. The arrival in 1745 of John Moody (?–1812), an Irish actor, marked a significant change. After playing with an amateur group, he returned to England to recruit professional actors, among them David Douglass (?–1786), who became head of the company after Moody left Jamaica permanently in 1749. It may have been Moody who alerted English actors to opportunities in the colonies at a time when the Licensing Act had seriously curtailed the theatre in England. His news came at an especially crucial moment in the career of the Hallams.

William Hallam (?–c. 1758), one of a large family of actors, had opened the New Wells Theatre in Goodman's Fields, London, in 1740. At first he presented only minor entertainments, but in 1744 turned to more ambitious works in spite of the Licensing Act. Although he prospered for several years, in 1751 his theatre was closed. It was at this time that Hallam conceived the idea of sending a troupe to America. The new company was headed by his brother, Lewis Hallam (1714–1755), an actor of secondary roles, with Mrs. Lewis Hallam (?–1773) as the leading actress. It consisted of twelve adults and Hallam's three children. Upon arrival in America, they fitted out a theatre at Williamsburg and opened in September, 1752. From this date can be traced the effective beginning of the professional theatre in America.

In addition to Williamsburg, the Hallams played in New York, Philadelphia, and Charleston before sailing to Jamaica in 1755. When they arrived, David Douglass was preparing to leave for England to recruit new actors, and the amalgamation of the troupes solved difficulties for both companies. Lewis Hallam died in 1755, and in 1758 Mrs. Hallam married Douglass, who remained head of the troupe until the Revolution. From 1758 to 1764 Douglass' company played in the mainland colonies. During these years Mrs. Douglass continued as the leading actress, while Lewis Hallam, Jr. (c. 1740–1808) was now the leading man. Between 1759 and 1761, the troupe performed in New York, Philadelphia, Annapolis, Williamsburg, and elsewhere, and in 1761–1762 in Rhode Island, where his company gave the first professional performances in New England.

After another interval in Jamaica, Douglass returned to the mainland from 1766 to 1775. By now, he had developed considerable optimism about the future and began to build substantial permanent playhouses. The first, the Southwark Theatre in Philadelphia, was opened in 1766. In 1767 he built the John Street Theatre in New York, and thereafter erected theatres in major towns between New York and Charleston. During these years Douglass also performed the first American play to be given a professional production, Thomas Godfrey's (1736–1763) *The Prince of Parthia*. A neoclassical tragedy with echoes of many Shakespearean works, it was given

in Philadelphia in 1767. At the outbreak of the Revolution in 1774, the Continental Congress called for the cessation of theatrical entertainment. In 1775 Douglass sailed for Jamaica. Although many members of his company were to return after the war, Douglass' theatrical career soon ended.

In Canada, performances by soldiers were common, and these garrison companies revived the tradition of having female roles played by men, though many eventually used local women in their casts. A professional company with the borrowed title of the "American Company of Comedians," led by Mr. Mills (with Henry Giffard as the leading man), came from Brunswick, North Carolina to perform in Halifax, Nova Scotia, in 1768. The garrison began regular performances by 1773, and in 1774 they produced *Acadius, or Love in a Calm,* a romantic comedy with an antislavery slant set in Boston. The author is unknown, but the play is generally considered to be the first English-language play written in Canada. The Halifax garrison built Canada's first purpose-built theatre in 1789, the 500-seat Grand. Charles Stuart Powell arrived with a company, recruited from Boston's Federal Street Theatre, in 1795 and ran a professional theatre in Halifax for twelve years.

The garrison at Montreal was also quite active, producing several seasons of plays between 1774 and 1790 (in both English and French). The first professional company of English actors played there in 1786. William Moore, Edward Allen, and John Bentley had left the John Street Theatre in New York to form this company, which also toured to Québec City where the restrictions on theatre established by the French during the *Tartuffe* incident of 1694 were gradually being relaxed.

When the peace treaty that made the United States fully independent was ratified in 1783, the British territories in North America were permanently divided, although relations between the theatres of the United States and Canada remained close. Theatrical activity in the United States began to revive in the early 1780s. Thereafter, it would grow steadily and spread widely as new territories were opened up. But, it would be many years before North American theatre would deviate significantly from English patterns.

LOOKING AT THEATRE HISTORY

The versions of plays performed in the theatre are not necessarily those now commonly available for reading. This is especially true in dealing with Shakespeare's plays. Restoration and eighteenth-century audiences found many of Shakespeare's scripts unacceptable and preferred adaptations of them. Thus, when eighteenth-century actors appeared in *King Lear* (to name only one conspicuous example), they did not perform the text we know. The student can gain considerable insight into eighteenth-century taste from reading the *King Lear* that held the stage through that century. Written by Nahum Tate and first performed in 1681, it has Cordelia and Edgar in love with each other, and omits the Fool altogether. At the end, Lear is restored to the throne, Goneril and Regan die of poison, and Cordelia and Edgar are united in marriage. Thus, the neoclassical demand for poetic justice was upheld.

Neoclassicism also motivated the use of generalized scenery, as this passage makes clear:

> The stage should be furnished with a competent Number of painted scenes sufficient to answer the Purposes of all the Plays in the Stock, in which there is no great variety, being easily reduced to the following classes. 1st. Temples 2ndly. Tombs 3rdly. City Walls and Gates 4thly. Outsides of Palaces 5thly. Insides of Palaces 6thly. Streets 7thly. Chambers 8thly. Prisons 9thly. Gardens and 10thly. Rural prospects of Groves, Forests, Desarts, &c. All these should be done by a Master, if such can be found: otherwise they should be as simple and unaffected as possible to avoid offending a judicious eye. If for some particular purpose, any other Scene is necessary, it can be got up occasionally.

The Case of the Stage in Ireland (Dublin, 1758).

During the course of the eighteenth century, pantomime did much to cultivate a taste for more spectacular scenery as can be seen from this stage direction in *Harlequin a Sorcerer* (one of John Rich's pantomimes, first presented in 1725 and revived often thereafter):

> The Curtain rises, and discovers dark rocky Caverns, by the Side of a Wood, illumin'd by the Moon: Birds of Omen promiscuously flying, Flashes of Lightning faintly striking.

Under his stage name of Lun, Rich also perfected pantomimic acting. Here is a description of his portrayal of the scene in *Harlequin a Sorcerer* in which Harlequin is hatched from an egg:

> This certainly was a masterpiece in dumb show. From the first chipping of the egg, his receiving motion, his feeling the ground, his standing upright, to his quick Harlequin trip around the empty Shell, through the whole progression every limb had its tongue, and every motion a voice, which "spoke with most miraculous organ" to the understandings and sensations of the observers.

John Jackson, *The History of the Scottish Stage* (Edinburgh, 1793), 367–368.

Probably the most important first-hand account of the English theatre between 1690 and 1740 is that written by Colley Cibber. He covers almost all important topics, and is especially helpful in describing the qualities of the principal actors of the period. Here is a passage about Thomas Betterton:

> Betterton had so just a sense of what was true or false applause, that I have heard him say he never thought any kind of it equal to an attentive silence; that there were many ways of deceiving an audience into a loud one; but to keep them hushed and quiet was an applause which only truth and merit could arrive at: of which art, there never was an equal master to himself . . . . In all his soliloquies of moment, the strong intelligence of his attitude and aspect, drew you into such an impatient gaze, and eager expectation, that you almost imbibed the sentiment with your eye, before the ear could reach it.

Colley Cibber, *Apology for His Life* (London, 1740).

By the mid-eighteenth century, ideas about acting and costuming began to change. Here is a description of a performance in which both Quin (the major exponent of the older school) and Garrick (the major exponent of the newer school) appeared:

> Quin presented himself . . . in a green velvet coat embroidered down the seams, an enormous full bottomed periwig, rolled stockings and high-heeled square-toed shoes, with very little variation in cadence, and in a deep full tone, accompanied by a sawing kind of action, which

had more of the senate than of the stage in it, he rolled out his heroics with an air of dignified indifference. . . . Garrick, then young and light and alive in every muscle and in every feature, came bounding on the stage . . . it seemed as if a whole century had been stept over in the transition of a single scene; old things were done away, and a new order at once brought forward, bright and luminous, and clearly destined to dispel the barbarisms and bigotry of a tasteless age, . . . superstitiously devoted to the illusions of imposing declamation. Yet in general [the audience] seemed to love darkness better than light, and . . . bestowed far the greater show of hands upon the master of the old school than upon the founder of the new.

Richard Cumberland, *Memoirs* (London, 1806), 59–60.

Before the end of the century, dissatisfaction with anachronistic costuming was becoming more intense. Here is one complaint about the mixture of modes in *Richard III*:

King Richard's troops appear in the present uniform of the soldiers in St. James's park, with short jackets and cocked-up hats. King Richard wears indeed the habiliments of his time, but Richmond is dressed à la vraie moderne; . . . The Lord Mayor . . . figures in his own character, but the other attendants in the play not so. . . . How is it possible to reconcile Macbeth or Hamlet dressed in our fashionable short coats, with the idea of habits of ages so far anterior?

Gentleman's Magazine (May, 1789).

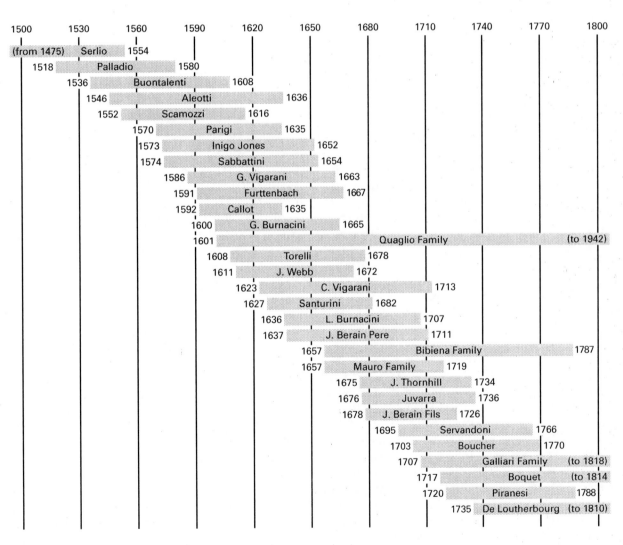

FIG. 11.22
Major scene designers of Europe, 1500–1800.

12
Continental European Theatre to 1800

By 1700, Italy was of little consequence in European politics. Many of its northern states were included within the Holy Roman Empire, which from 1559 until 1806 was always headed by a member of the Hapsburg family that ruled Austria. In effect, then, much of northern Italy was a dependency of Austria while the Kingdom of Naples remained in the hands of the Spanish.

Throughout the eighteenth century, France remained a major power, but its former position of dominance was considerably weakened by a series of wars and by disastrous economic policies. The War of Spanish Succession, which broke out when Louis XIV tried to put his grandson on the Spanish throne, pitted France against most of the rest of Europe between 1701 and 1713. France suffered a number of humiliating defeats by England and Austria, who thereafter kept France in check. After 1750 France also lost its major territories in the New World and India to England. It retaliated by investing heavily in the war for American independence in the 1770s and 1780s, which humiliated the English but brought France little gain. These wars put a heavy strain on France's economy, with the burden falling on the middle and lower classes, since the nobility and clergy were exempted from taxation. Such conditions created increasing unhappiness, which eventually erupted in the French Revolution of 1789.

Although by 1700 the professional theatre was firmly established in England, France, Italy, and Spain, it had scarcely begun in Northern or Eastern Europe. The slowness of Northern Europe to develop a professional theatre can be attributed in large part to unsettled religious and political conditions dating back to the early sixteenth century. The conflict between Protestants and Catholics had led to the Treaty of Augsburg in 1555, but the results were never wholly satisfactory, and in 1618 open warfare broke out again with the Thirty Years War, which lasted until 1648. By 1635 it had become more political than religious, as France, under Cardinal Richelieu's guidance, actively aided the Protestant faction out of a desire to curb the power of Austria. By the time of the peace of Westphalia (1648), the population and resources of Germanic territories had been so seriously depleted that it would take almost 150 years for full recovery. In the eighteenth century, the Seven Years War (1756–1763), pitted Austria against Prussia with Prussia emerging as the leader of the German states. In addition, the area was divided into more than 300 independent units, some large but others only a few square miles in size, making "Germany" the designation of a region, not a reference to a nation-state. Under these political, economic, and religious conditions, an adequate professional theatre could come into existence only gradually. In this struggle for survival, professional troupes received little encouragement, since the policies of both court and church discouraged rather than assisted native spoken drama.

Russia had had extensive dealings with the Byzantine Empire since adopting Greek Orthodox Christianity in the tenth century. After Constantinople fell in 1453, the Russian ruler Ivan III (1462–1505) declared his nation to be the new Byzantium, or the "third Rome," as he called it, and undertook a building campaign to make Moscow into the second Constantinople. But it was not until the time of Peter the Great (reigned 1682–1725) that Russia began to focus its attention on Western Europe, and it would not be until the time of the Empress Catherine II (reigned 1762–1796), called Catherine the Great, that theatre was able to gain a place of any real significance to Russian culture.

THE EVOLUTION OF ITALIAN SCENIC DESIGN

By 1700 Italian scenic practices had been adopted throughout most of Western Europe. Proscenium arches, perspective settings (composed of flat wings and borders), and rapid shifts of scenery had become common almost everywhere. Most theatres continued to use the basic sets favored by neoclassicism but in opera, spectacular special effects and elaborate settings were pushing the limits of Italianate stage technology.

Through the seventeenth century, the visual conventions had tended to follow those popularized by Torelli and Vigarani; symmetrically arranged perspective alleys depicting a series of buildings terminating in a view of a distant prospect. But the styles had become increasingly more baroque as the restlessness, monumentality, grandeur, and richness that had been finding its way into art and architecture since the late sixteenth century, became increasingly more prevalent in stage design for Italian opera. Through a careful juxtaposition of mass and space, the manipulation of foreshortening and forced perspective, and the liberal use of swirling details, opera designers were giving a sense of activity and movement to their sets. Fortunately, such effects could be achieved with a limited color palette, because throughout the eighteenth century, the colors available in the quantities needed to cover large surfaces were limited to sepia or pastel shades of green, yellow, and lavender.

In the eighteenth century, baroque set design reached its fullest expression in the work of the Bibiena family, perhaps the most influential designers of the age. Of the many Bibienas, the most important were Ferdinando (1657–1743), Francesco (1659–1739), Giuseppe (1696–1757), Antonio (1700–1774), and Carlo (1728–1787). The family's reputation was first established widely through Ferdinando's work at Bologna and Parma.

By 1711 Ferdinando was sufficiently famous to be appointed "court architect" at Vienna, where he succeeded Ludovico Ottavio Burnacini (1636–1707), who, together with his father, Giovanni Burnacini (1600–1665), had staged some of the most lavish productions seen in the seventeenth century. Thereafter the Bibienas were in demand everywhere in Europe.

Before the Bibienas, the stage had generally been treated as an extension of the auditorium, and the scenery had been proportioned accordingly. In Torelli's settings the tops of the buildings were always visible along the central perspective alley that was laid out based on the center line of the auditorium and stage. The Bibienas, on the other hand, treated the wings near the front of the stage as though they were merely the lower portion of a building too vast to be contained in the narrow confines of the proscenium. They also minimized the importance of the central vista by employing a multi-point, or angled perspective (*scena per angolo*). Angle perspective carried the viewer's eye off into side alleys where the vistas were not fully shown, thus implying greater space beyond the audience's vision, which reinforced the sense of vastness.

To achieve these effects, the Bibienas divided the stage into a forward section composed of the usual wings mounted as dictated by the chariot-and-pole machinery, and a background section where numerous flats were placed wherever needed to create the receding planes demanded by the angled perspective. It was in the manipulation of this background section that the Bibienas demonstrated their greatest scenic innovations.

Surviving engravings of Bibiena sets often show stairs and multiple levels, sometimes with human figures on them. These details were painted onto the actual set to add to the grandeur of the image, and the presence of painted human figures on background scenery became an accepted convention of the period.

The baroque sets of Filippo Juvarra (1678–1737), who was resident designer in the great opera center of Turin, offered an important alternative to the approach popularized by the Bibienas. Juvarra used curvilinear perspective that always led the eye of the observer in a circular motion back to the foreground rather than off to the sides, as was the case with angled perspective. But because it did not imply space just outside the audience's view, his sets seem less monumental than those of the Bibienas. Juvarra was one of the first designers to work from floor plans, which are often included at the bottom of his drawings.

Juvarra was succeeded by the Galliari brothers at Turin, Bernardino (1707–1794) and Fabrizio (1709–1790), the progenitors of a family of designers who were active until 1823. There were many such families of designers in this period, the most long-lasting of which has to be the Quaglio family. Beginning with Giulio (1601–1658), six generations of this family were designers, ending with Eugen (1857–1942). From 1778 until 1917 they maintained a headquarters at Monaco, where the museum now preserves many of their designs.

The visual style established for opera between 1700 and 1750 underwent many changes in the late eighteenth century as new interests emerged. As comic opera (*opera buffa*) grew in popularity, domestic and rustic settings became common and a few designers began experimenting with the use of box sets to better represent them. The rediscovery of Herculaneum in 1709, and of Pompeii in 1748, set off a vogue for engravings of classical ruins. Soon aristocrats were having fake ruins constructed in their gardens and designers were depicting them on stage. This had profound effects on the stage designers, primarily in opera but gradually in the theatre as well: (1) It got designers thinking about "mood" in design, for it was not the clean lines of architectural detail that gave these images their appeal, but the deterioration seen in broken shapes partly hidden in

FIG. 12.2

Design by Filippo Juvarra. At the bottom are two variants on the setting, probably indicating that this is a permanent setting with changeable back scenes. Courtesy Theatre Museum, Victoria and Albert Museum, London.

shrubs and vines. The widely disseminated grey-scale engravings of such ruins often added atmospheric qualities like moonlight or a dramatic shaft of sunlight streaming into dark interiors, and scenic artists were inspired to imitate such qualities in their own work. (2) The stark natural simplicity of these ruins helped to stimulate a rebellion against the baroque style with all its ornamentation and its nonfunctional, unnatural details. (3) It got designers outside Italy thinking about the heroic past of their own nations, for which Gothic architecture was a stronger symbol than the ruins of Roman buildings.

In spite of the trend toward greater visual variety, the types of places represented in late eighteenth-century operas can be reduced to about twelve and those for theatre to even less. Because each locale was idealized, settings could be reused for a number of

FIG. 12.3
Design dating from about 1780 by Giuseppino Galliari.
Note the classical forms in a state of picturesque ruin.
Courtesy Museo Civico, Turin.

different works. The basic compositional techniques
also remained unchanged, as the *scena per angolo* continued to dominate. The many innovations after
1750, especially in the increased concern for mood,
are indicative of the widespread dissatisfaction with
the strictures of neoclassicism, and are also the har-
bingers of romanticism, which soon was to become
the dominant mode.

ITALIAN DRAMA OF THE EIGHTEENTH CENTURY

If Italy's designers dominated the theatre of Europe,
the same cannot be said for its dramatists. Italy's most
famous tragic writer of the period, Vittorio Alfieri
(1749–1803), did not start writing until 1775. In a
series of plays, including his acknowledged masterpiece, *Saul* (1782), Alfieri sought to recapture the
style of Racine, in which the most powerful emotions are expressed in the most tightly focused dramatic form. In his plays everything not essential is
pared away. Most of Alfieri's works are marked by his
strong political interest in independence for Italy,
which sometimes led him to place too great an emphasis upon doctrinal messages.

Until 1750, the comic impulse was largely channeled into the *commedia dell'arte.* Unfortunately, since
1700 this form had been losing its vitality. Minor
characters, music, and spectacle were added to in-

FIG. 12.4
Goldoni's *The Servant of Two Masters*, Act 1, scene 7.
From Carlo Goldoni, *Commedie* 14 (1824).

crease its variety, but, as sentimentalism in other
forms grew, *commedia* came to seem crude and un-
feeling. In the 1740s, Carlo Goldoni (1707–1793),
who began his career writing scenarios for *commedia*
troupes in Venice in 1734, began to write plays and
pamphlets that championed the new sentimental
comedies of England and France and proposed
changes that would bring *commedia* more in line with
the new style. This set off a public debate with the
dramatist Carlo Gozzi (1720–1806), that was to make
Venice the most vibrant theatre center in Italy.

Goldoni began his program for reforming the
commedia by writing out the principal role in *Man of
the World* (1738). By the time he wrote his most successful *commedia* play, *The Servant of Two Masters*
(1743), only the part of the comic servant hero, Truffaldino, was left to be improvised as it was played by
Italy's greatest comic actor, Antonio Sacchi
(1708–1788). When the play was published in 1753,
however, even this role was fully scripted. In the
meantime Goldoni had written *The Comic Theatre*

FIG. 12.5

Performance in the Roman ampitheatre in Verona. In his
Memoirs, Goldoni writes: "Spectacles of all kinds are
given [in the amphitheatre]: courses, jousts, bull-fights;
and in summer, plays are even represented. . . . For this
purpose . . . there is erected, on very strong supports, a
theatre in boards, which is taken down every winter and
refitted again in the fine season." Painted by Marco
Marcola, Italian (Veronese), c. 1740–1793, *An Italian
Comedy in Verona,* oil on canvas, 1772, 115.3 × 84.2 cm
(oval). Gift of Emily Crane Chadbourne, 1922. 4790.
Photograph © 1993, The Art Institute of Chicago.
All rights reserved.

(1750), in which he argued that the methods of the
commedia were antiquated. He called for abandoning
masks (because they prevented subtle facial expression), adopting better stage speech (he used the
Venetian dialect because it was closer to the audience's experience), and substituting subjects based on
real life for the conventionalized situations of
commedia. Since he had already abolished improvisation, he was calling for the elimination of virtually
all of *commedia's* essential characteristics. These innovations won him an invitation to go to Paris in
1762 to write for the Comédie Italienne. He remained there until his death.

Goldoni was a prolific dramatist who wrote in a
variety of forms, including tragedy, and is credited
with making *opera buffa* acceptable to the major opera
companies. Although he depicted almost every profession and class, he idealized the middle and lower
classes, and often characterized the nobility as decadent and useless. Above all he idealized his female
characters, as his most famous play *The Mistress of
the Inn* (1753) illustrates. In this play, Mirandolina is
wooed by three nobles, each representing an aspect
of that class that Goldoni found repugnant. In the
end she chooses her honest, resourceful servant
Fabrizio. There is a sentimental strain in this play that
is found throughout Goldoni's work, but there is sufficient wit, charm, and vivacity to avoid the cloying
sentimentality that afflicts most plays of the era.

Goldoni did a great deal to banish fantasy, vul-
garity, and nonrealistic devices from the *commedia.*
He had also humanized and softened the stock characters, making the ridiculous, miserly, and lecherous
old Pantalone of the traditional scenarios, for example, into an honest merchant, good father, and solid
citizen. But in making these changes, he also removed the distinctions between *commedia* and regular comedy.

Carlo Gozzi strongly objected to Goldoni's reforms of the *commedia,* to the sentimentalism of his
plays, and to his denigration of the upper classes. In
The Love for Three Oranges (1761), *King Stag* (1762),
Turandot (1762), and *The Magic Bird* (1765), Gozzi
emphasized the elements that Goldoni sought most
to suppress: fantasy, enchantment, masked characters and improvisation. He called these plays *fiabe* and
chose his subjects from fairy tales or legends (which
provided many opportunities for spectacular effects).
Gozzi satirized the sentimental trends Goldoni championed, and this topicality, along with a dependence
on improvisation, makes the plays difficult to comprehend fully today, though they are often revived.

FRENCH DRAMA OF THE
EIGHTEENTH CENTURY

Paris continued to be the major cultural center of
Europe throughout the eighteenth century, and its
drama was the standard against which all others were
judged. Most eighteenth-century tragic writers
sought to follow in Racine's footsteps, but seem to
have given plot devices priority over the development of the internal conflicts within the main characters for which Racine was so justly famous.

Voltaire (François-Marie Arouet, 1694–1778)
dominated tragedy in eighteenth century Paris, as he
did virtually all French literature and thought. Beginning with *Oedipe* (1718), he wrote fifty-three
plays, more than half of them tragedies. Although superior in many respects, Voltaire's tragedies continue

the existing trend toward complex plots, involved character relationships, and sudden reversals based upon last minute recognitions.

After living in England from 1726 to 1729, Voltaire came to consider the French neoclassical ideal overly restrictive and sought thereafter to liberalize it. His reforms, however, were confined to introducing ghosts and a limited amount of violence onto the stage, to widening the range of permissible subjects, and to increasing spectacle. But Voltaire's attempts to use spectacle more effectively were frustrated by the presence of spectators on the stage, and it was largely due to his influence that the practice was abolished in 1759. This innovation, coming at just the time when public interest in history and local color was growing, encouraged the exploitation of spectacle in the regular drama.

Comedy, perhaps because of its less-privileged position, underwent more changes than did tragedy. Alain-René LeSage (1668–1747), after adapting plays by Lope de Vega and Calderón, launched a remorseless attack upon contemporary tax collectors in *Turcaret* (1709). Often called the first great French comedy of manners, it depicts a world of clever rascals who prey upon each other. Under the surface lurked a thinly disguised criticism of Louis XIV's economic policies, which permitted the privileged and unscrupulous to thrive at the expense of lesser and more honest citizens. Other dramatists took aim at the pretensions of the rising middle class. But just as had happened in England, a trend toward sentimentalism began around 1720, in a form called *comédie larmoyante*.

French sentimentalism is most clearly evident in the works of Pierre Carlet de Chamblain de Marivaux (1688–1763) who came to prominence with *Arlequin Refined by Love* (1720). Unlike earlier comedies, in which lovers are kept apart by some external force (usually parents or guardians), the obstacles in Marivaux's plays arise from the inner conflicts of the characters. In *The Game of Love and Chance* (1730), for example, two friends arrange a marriage between their children, but only on the condition that the boy and girl are willing to accept each other; the young couple, who have never met, are skeptical about the match and each hits upon the idea of changing places with a servant to observe the other; then, each irresistibly and unwillingly falls in love with a supposed servant. Here, as in most of Marivaux's plays, interest is focused on subtle changes in feelings within characters rather than upon external intrigue. He is also noted for his distinctive prose style, often labeled *marivaudage*.

Most of his thirty-five plays were written for the Comédie Italienne, the same company Goldoni would later join. With his emphasis on feeling, Marivaux contributed significantly to the development of sentimentalism, but his charm and wit raise him far above his contemporaries. Because of his interest in inner psychological conflicts, his critical stature has grown steadily since the late nineteenth century.

After 1750, *comédie larmoyante* was absorbed into other types as writers like Denis Diderot (1713–1784) advocated an expansion of the dramatic genres allowed by neoclassicism. At this time virtually all traditional concepts, including those about drama, were being reevaluated by a group of advanced thinkers (the *philosophes*) through controversial essays in the *Encyclopédie,* edited by Diderot and published in twenty-eight volumes between 1748 and 1772. Diderot's own ideas about drama are expressed primarily in a few dialogues and in two plays, *The Illegitimate Son* (1757) and *The Father of a Family* (1758). In these works, Diderot argued that neoclassicism was too narrow in restricting the acceptable dramatic types to traditional comedy and tragedy, and that additional "middle" genres—the *drame* (or domestic tragedy) and a comedy concerned with virtue—should be added. Since the Comédie Française did not encourage it, the *drame* had little chance to develop, except in the minor theatres, where it was to mingle with pantomime and music and emerge in the nineteenth century as melodrama.

Diderot also suggested many innovations in staging, for he believed that drama would move an audience profoundly only if it created an illusion of reality. Consequently, he advocated subject matter chosen from everyday life and presented in settings that duplicated real rooms. He urged the use of prose dialogue, detailed pantomime, and the "fourth wall" convention in acting. Diderot's ideas on staging foreshadowed some aspects of late-nineteenth-century realism. His theories on acting as expressed in such works as *Observations on Garrick* (1770) and *The Paradox of the Actor* (published 1830) were more immediately influential.

The late eighteenth century produced only one major French dramatist, Beaumarchais (Pierre-Augustin Caron, 1732–1799). Now remembered chiefly for his comedies, Beaumarchais also wrote a number of *drames,* such as *Eugénie* (1767) and *The Two Friends* (1770). But his assured fame rests on *The Barber of Seville* (1775) and *The Marriage of Figaro* (1783). The former, a comedy of intrigue in which an elderly guardian's plans to marry his young ward are thwarted, introduces Figaro, the culmination of all the comic servants of French drama. Although *The Marriage of Figaro* includes many of the characters found in the earlier play, its tone is quite different, for intrigue is now subordinated to commentary

FIG. 12.7
Final act of Beaumarchais's *The Marriage of Figaro*. From the 1785 edition of the play. Courtesy Lilly Library, Indiana University.

FIG. 12.6
Scene from Regnard's *The Universal Heir* at the Comédie Française, 1708. From the original edition of the play.

upon society and class relationships. It is a far more complex play than *The Barber of Seville*. Although the setting ostensibly is Spain, *The Marriage of Figaro* clearly reflects contemporary France, for by this time the nobility had become superfluous and Louis XVI's (reigned 1774–1793) attempts to curb its privileges had proven wholly ineffectual, much to the chagrin of the middle and lower classes who bore the burden of taxation, even though they enjoyed few civil rights. Beaumarchais recaptured the spirit of "laughing" comedy, much as Goldsmith and Sheridan had done in England, but he added to it a sense of political and sociological concern that made his plays quite controversial.

By 1785, then, French drama had taken a few tentative steps away from neoclassicism. Nevertheless, though the typical subject matter and treatment often differed considerably from those of 1700, no startling innovations had been made before the Revolution inaugurated a new era in France.

PARISIAN ACTING TROUPES

In 1700 there were only two legitimate troupes in Paris, the Opéra and the Comédie Française, each with monopolistic privileges. The Comédie Française maintained control on tragedy and "regular" comedy (defined primarily by its five acts). Consequently, there was a very limited demand for new works. By the late eighteenth century the Comédie Française had to be required to produce at least one new play or revival each month just to generate some demand. The Opéra retained control of all works that use music, dance, or elaborate spectacle. It enjoyed the greatest prestige but was also often in financial trouble and had to generate revenue by licensing other theatres to perform certain kinds of musical performances. After 1762 the Comédie Italienne paid the Opéra from 20,000 to 54,000 francs yearly for the right to present musical plays, and after 1784 all troupes not officially designated as state troupes were made subsidiaries of the Opéra. These two

FIG. 12.8
Scene from a fair-theatre play, *The Quarrel of the Theatres,* satirizing the Comédie Française (represented by the figure on the right) and the Comédie Italienne (represented by the figure on the left) for plundering the fair theatres of their stock in trade. From *Le Théâtre de la Foire, ou l'Opéra Comique* by LeSage and D'Orneval 3 (1723).

he sought to diversify his offerings. Thus, when the company's initial popularity in Paris slackened, he began to perform Italian translations of French tragedies and tragicomedies. In 1718 he added a few works in French, and in 1719 he began to present parodies. By 1721, Riccoboni had added four French actors to his company and had induced important authors like Marivaux to write plays for him. The turning point in the company's fortunes, however, came in 1723, when it was made a state theatre with the official title Comédiens Ordinaires du Roi; more commonly known as the Comédie Italienne.

A constant challenge to the state theatres was posed by the illegitimate companies at the fairs, especially those of St. Germain, which ran February to Easter, and St. Laurent, which ran July through October. While Italian companies were banned from France (1697–1716), the fairs seized the opportunity to enlarge their theatrical activities though the legitimate companies strove continuously to suppress them and did succeed in getting them closed from 1718 to 1723. In their attempts to circumvent the monopolies, the fair companies experimented continuously with dramatic forms. The popularity of the new forms they created did much to undermine the neoclassical ideal and to usher in the new theatre of the nineteenth century.

The first significant minor form to emerge was comic opera. Forbidden to use dialogue, the fair troupes condensed the necessary exposition and speech into couplets, which were printed on placards held by small boys dressed as cupids and suspended above the stage. The couplets, set to popular tunes, were then sung by confederates planted in the audience. In 1714 the Opéra licensed the fair troupes to do *opéras comique,* a form perfected by LeSage after he gave up on the comedy of manners. It featured *commedia* characters, in which spoken dialogue alternated with verses set to popular tunes much as in English ballad opera. These short pieces parodied tragedies and operas and satirized current events and fashions. By the 1740s, *opéra comique* began to drop its farcical and satirical subject matter in favor of more sentimental stories, which became so popular that the Opéra tried to suspend the license that allowed the fair troupe to perform them. This led to such a violent controversy that the crown issued an injunction against all performances of *opéra comique.* While that injunction was in effect (1745–1751), English pantomime was introduced to fill the void. It was received so enthusiastically that it remained a staple of the Parisian minor theatres for the rest of the century.

Two significant innovations were made in *opéra comique* after its revival in 1751. First, ordinary

companies were to remain the major ones until monopolies were abolished in 1791, although they were to encounter considerable competition.

Their most significant competition came in 1716 when a *commedia dell'arte* troupe was invited back to Paris, following an absence of almost twenty years, and installed in the Hôtel de Bourgogne. The Italians were led by Luigi Riccoboni (*c.* 1676–1753), who in 1713 had attempted unsuccessfully to establish a state theatre in Italy. By 1716 Riccoboni had already recognized that *commedia* was declining, and

FIG. 12.9

Booth theatres at the Fair of St. Ovid (one of the lesser Parisian fairs). On the right, Nicolet's booth. Note the balconies on which *parades* (brief skits used to entice customers inside) were performed. From Pougin, *Dictionnaire du Théâtre* (1885).

characters began to replace the *commedia* figures. As a part of this shift, local color, in the form of picturesque characters, places, and customs, came into the minor theatres long before they were seen in the major houses. Second, following the great success in Paris of Pergolesi's *The Servant the Mistress* (1752), original music began to replace the popular tunes which had characterized the form.

After 1760 the fair troupes began to relocate on the Boulevard du Temple, a fashionable recreational spot, and became year-round companies. From that point on, all Parisian companies catering to popular audiences became known as "boulevard theatres." Of the troupes that moved to the Boulevard, four were especially important: Audinot's, Nicolet's, the Théâtre des Associés, and the Variétés Amusantes.

The boulevard theatres lost their right to do *opéra comique* when the Comédie Italienne was awarded a monopoly on the form in 1762, the same year Goldoni joined the company. But the success of Goldoni and of *opéra comique* allowed the Comédie Italienne to drop all French plays from its repertory in 1769. This opened up an entire range of *drames* and irregular comedies for the boulevard theatres to perform since playwrights now had no other market if their works were refused by the Comédie Française. The boulevard theatres also returned to the original form of comic opera, which they now called *comedies-en-vaudevilles,* and made changes to the imported English pantomimes, adding mood music to underscore emotional scenes which were increasingly about persecuted innocents being rescued from villainy. Soon, dialogue was being introduced into this previously silent form, giving many of the fundamental characteristics of what would later be known as melodrama.

Unfortunately, after Goldoni's retirement in 1773, the fortunes of the Comédie Italienne began to decline. In 1780 they decided to abandon their Italian actors and their Italian repertory, thus severing the last connections with Italy. They now needed to return irregular French comedies and *drames* to their repertory so the boulevard theatres were forced to give them up. In 1784 the Opéra petitioned for, and was granted, authority over these minor companies. This situation continued up to the time of the Revolution. Then, in 1791 the National Assembly abolished all monopolies, thus freeing the theatres from former restraints. Although other restrictions were soon to be imposed, the act of 1791 marks the end of an era.

The evening's bill at a theatre in Paris was simpler than in a London theatre. The Comédie Française normally presented a long play and an afterpiece. After 1757 ballets were given as entr'actes. The Comédie Italienne often gave programs made up of several short pieces, and its bills were organized to reserve certain days of the week for each of the genres it was permitted to perform. In the 1740s it added a dance troupe, and after 1750 pantomimes and displays of fireworks became typical offerings. The Opéra normally presented one major work along with incidental ballets. After the 1770s, when Jean-Georges Noverre (1727–1810) became ballet master, ballet increased in importance at the Opéra. Noverre's book, *Letters on the Dance and Ballet* (1760), was instrumental in transforming ornamental and spectacular dances into storytelling works that have made him known as the father of modern ballets. At the fair theatres, variety was always the key, for there the carnival atmosphere predominated. Thus, the Parisian theatre included as wide a range of entertainment as the English, but the restrictions on the French companies led to more specialization by each troupe.

During the second half of the eighteenth century, theatre also flourished in the provinces, where at least twenty-three cities built new theatres between 1750 and 1773. These companies offered little that was new, emulating instead Parisian trends in repertory and staging, but they are an indicator of the strength of theatre across the culture.

ACTORS AND ACTING

The eighteenth century also brought the first successful attempt to establish an orderly system for training actors. Until the 1780s, most French actors received their training while playing utility roles in a provincial troupe. A few beginners were accepted into the Parisian companies after being coached by leading actors (who were paid 500 francs for each pupil taken into the company). These methods were eventually judged insufficient, however, and in 1786 the Royal Dramatic School, forerunner of the present Conservatoire, was founded as an adjunct to the Comédie Française.

Gaining admission to the Comédie Française was difficult. Applicants had first to be approved by a committee of actors; they then played at least three roles in public performances; if deemed successful, they were accepted as *pensionnaires* until a vacancy occurred among the *sociétaires*. By the late eighteenth century, a *pensionnaire* had to be either admitted as a *sociétaire* or released by the end of the second year with the troupe. This rule often led to reassignments of shares or forced retirements in order to make room among the *sociétaires* for desirable performers.

A young actor often began as understudy, or *double,* to a major performer. As in England, most casting was governed by "lines of business." The major lines in tragedy were kings, tyrants, lovers, princesses, mothers, and female lovers, while the major lines in comedy were old men, lovers, valets, peasants, old women, coquettes, and soubrettes. In addition, there were a number of secondary lines, and the bottom rank was made up of general utility players. Certain tragic and comic lines were usually filled by the same actors. For example, the *jeune premier* (or leading male performer) played the lover in both comedy and tragedy, while the actress who played princesses in tragedy normally assumed the roles of coquettes in comedy. As a rule, actors remained in the same line of business throughout their careers.

The eighteenth century produced many distinguished performers, most of them members of the Comédie Française. Around 1720 the performance style became more realistic, partially because of Michel Baron's return to the stage from 1720 to 1729.

But the most famous players of the eighteenth century were Mlle Dumesnil, Mlle Clairon, and Lekain. Mlle Dumesnil (Marie-Françoise Marchand, 1713–1803) began her acting career in the provinces around 1733. Accepted as an understudy at the Comédie Française in 1737, she became a *sociétaire* in 1738 and was soon the leading performer of such strong tragic roles as Clytemnestra and Medea. In his *Paradox of the Actor,* Diderot depicts her as an erratic performer dependent on inspiration and thus sometimes magnificent and at others mediocre. She

FIG. 12.10

Painting by Antoine Watteau, probably showing actors of the Comédie Française, *c.* 1720. Note the *habit à la romaine* worn by the actor in the foreground. At right rear, a figure dressed as one of Molière's characters, some of whom continued to be costumed in seventeenth-century dress. Courtesy Metropolitan Museum of Art, Jules S. Bache Collection, 1949.

retired in 1776. Mlle Clairon (Claire-Josèphe-Hippolyte Léris de la Tude, 1723–1803) began her career in 1736 at the Comédie Italienne and, after performing in the provinces and at the Opéra, was admitted to the Comédie Française in 1743 as understudy to Dumesnil. Diderot idealizes her as an artist conscious of every detail in performance. Voltaire and Garrick also considered her superior to Dumesnil. At first declamatory in style, Clairon was persuaded by the critic Marmontel in 1753 to assume a more conversational tone. This change made her question the old traditions of costuming, and in 1755 she began to adopt more realistic and historically accurate stage dress. She retired in 1766 at the height of her career. Mlle Clairon's reforms were supported by Henri-Louis Lekain (1729–1778), who was admitted to the Comédie Française in 1750 largely because of Voltaire's influence. He worked hard to overcome his vocal and physical shortcomings, but was not awarded a full share in the company until 1758 and did not become an important figure there until after 1768. Thereafter, Lekain was considered the greatest tragic actor of his age. Together he and Mlle Clairon did much to bring greater realism to the acting of the time.

The most potent influences on acting during the eighteenth century were tradition, learning by observation and imitation, and an orderly system of passing along lines of business and roles.

FIG. 12.11
Crowning a bust of Voltaire during a performance of his *Irène* at the Comédie Française, 1778. At this time the Comédie was performing in the Théâtre des Tuileries. From Pougin, *Dictionnaire du Théâtre* (1885).

With the coming of the Revolution, French actors achieved full civil and religious rights. The National Assembly forbade discrimination against players and, though this act did not make performers entirely socially acceptable, it removed the legal grounds that had encouraged prejudice in the past.

COSTUME PRACTICES

Costume practices in France differed little from those of England. Most characters were dressed in contemporary garments and as sumptuously as the performers could afford. Ordinarily, fashionable garments were used in both comedy and tragedy until 1727, when Adrienne Lecouvreur adopted the much more elaborate and formal court dress for tragedy. Her practice soon became standard for all tragic heroines. The actors also adopted court dress for tragedy except in classical roles, for which the *habit à la romaine* was retained, although it, too, grew more elaborate and conventionalized; the plumed helmet was often replaced by a three-cornered hat and the skirt of the tunic was frequently hooped.

By 1730 the major actors were engaging in bitter competition to outdo each other in the lavishness of their stage dress. When Adrienne Lecouvreur died, her wardrobe was sold for 40,000 francs, and Mlle Raucourt was given a wardrobe valued at 20,000 francs when she made her debut in 1772. This ideal of lavishness began to be challenged in the 1750s, however, when Marie-Justine Favart (1727–1772), perhaps the most famous performer of the Comédie Italienne, wore an authentic peasant dress as the heroine of *The Loves of Bastien and Bastienne* in 1753. In

FIG. 12.12
Mme Favart in the costume she supposedly imported from Istanbul to ensure authenticity of dress in *The Three Sultans*, 1761. From *Costumes et Annales des Grand Théâtres de Paris* (1786–1789).

1761 she supposedly sent to Constantinople for an authentic dress to wear in *The Three Sultans*. At the Comédie Française, Voltaire asked the artist Joseph Vernet to design clothing based on Chinese dress for *The Orphan of China* (1755). The results were more nearly Turkish than Chinese in appearance, but the innovation was favorably received, nevertheless, and thereafter Clairon and Lekain sought to dress each role appropriately. In 1756 Lekain outraged audiences by appearing in *Sémiramis* with bare arms, disarrayed hair, and bloody hands. Even Voltaire disapproved of this much realism, calling it "too English." Voltaire's *Tancrède* (1760) introduced medieval costumes, and thereafter other periods and locales were occasionally represented in costumes. The increased concern for costume is seen at its peak perhaps with Beaumarchais, who described in detail the dress for each of his characters, even when the plays had contemporary settings.

None of these reforms had far-reaching effects. Nevertheless, the seeds of change had been planted.

FIG. 12.13
Lekain and Dumesnil in Voltaire's *Sémiramis,* 1756. Although the play is set in ancient Assyria, Mlle Dumesnil wears an elaborate court dress of the eighteenth century and Lekain a formalized costume similar to that used for classical heroes. An English print of 1772.

FIG. 12.14
Plan of the theatre built for the Comédie Française in 1782. It later became the Odéon. Note the horseshoe-shaped auditorium; also the seated pit, an innovation in France. Note too that the stage is deeper than the auditorium. From Donnet and Kaufmann, *Architectonographie des Théâtres* (1836–1857).

The conflict between the old outlook, in which art was expected to idealize, and the new, in which art was expected to copy life, had begun. As yet, neoclassicism still reigned, but its foundations had been undermined.

THEATRE ARCHITECTURE

The major theatre buildings of Paris remained virtually unchanged until after 1750, when interest in theatre architecture increased. Articles appeared in Diderot's *Encyclopédie,* and Dumont's *Comparison of the Most Beautiful Theatres of Italy and France* (1763) contrasted the outmoded French structures with their newer Italian counterparts. Perhaps as a result, the new buildings followed the Italian trends toward the ovoid auditorium and the enlarged stage.

The first major change in the Parisian theatres came in 1763 when the Palais Royal (home of the Opéra) burned. From 1763 until 1769, the opera company performed in the Théâtre des Tuileries, converted from the stage (an area 52 by 140 feet) of the disused Salle des Machines. With its three tiers of boxes, it recreated the principal features of the Palais Royal. The Opéra's new theatre opened in 1769 and burned in 1781. The troupe then moved to the new Porte-Saint-Martin Theatre, where it remained until 1794.

The Comédie Française continued to use its converted tennis court until 1770. Alterations to it were minor. Around 1716, five benches, holding about 140 persons, were permanently installed on either side of the stage. In 1759, when spectators were ban-

ished from the stage, these benches were removed, but seating for about 180 persons was provided at the front of the pit. At the same time, in order not to diminish the space allotted to standing spectators, the amphitheatre was reduced in size. In 1770 the troupe moved to the Théâtre des Tuileries, recently vacated by the Opéra, until its new theatre, on the site of the present-day Odéon, was opened in 1782. The new building provided seats for all spectators and wholly abolished the standing pit for the first time in a Parisian theatre devoted to nonoperatic performances. The auditorium was ovoid in shape, and the stage much better equipped than that of its predecessor.

The Comédie Italienne played in the Hôtel de Bourgogne from 1716 until 1783, when this theatre, built in 1548, was abandoned. Changes in the Bourgogne during the eighteenth century paralleled those made at the Comédie Française. A number of large boxes were subdivided in 1760, and in 1765 benches were installed at the front of the pit to accommodate the spectators who were banished from the stage at that time. Perhaps out of a desire to compete with the Comédie Française, the Comédie Italienne moved into a new building in 1783. It, too, incorporated the latest Italian features, but it retained a "standing pit" sufficiently large to hold 650 spectators. In 1788 the attempt to furnish this area with benches was met with such opposition that the plan was abandoned. Not until the early nineteenth century was seating in the pit fully accepted in Paris.

The boulevard theatres also began to acquire elaborate buildings in the late eighteenth century. The Variétés Amusantes, designed by Victor Louis and

FIG. 12.15
The Hôtel de Bourgogne in 1769 when the repertory of the Comédie Italienne was restricted to *opéra-comique* and Italian comedies. On stage is a scene from an *opéra-comique*. Note the footlights, prompter's box at front-center of the stage, and the orchestra. Note also that most of the action is placed on the platform forward of the proscenium. There are a few benches at the front of the auditorium but the remainder of the spectators in the pit are standing. Drawing by P. A. Wille the Younger. Courtesy Bibliothèque Nationale, Paris.

FIG. 12.16
Theatre designed by Victor Louis in 1785 for the Opéra, but never used by that company. When this engraving was made *c.* 1790 it was the home of the Variétés Amusantes. Note the emphasis on spectacle with the practicable suspended bridge. This theatre was to be the home of the Comédie Française after 1799. Courtesy Bibliothèque Nationale, Paris.

originally intended for the Opéra, opened in 1785. It was modeled on an earlier structure designed by Louis, the Grand Theatre in Bordeaux, built between 1773 and 1780, one of the most influential theatre buildings of its time. When the Variétés Amusantes opened, it was the finest theatre in Paris and after 1799 was to be the home of the Comédie Française.

By the time the Revolution began, all the major theatres of Paris had been modernized. The changes appear to have been motivated by the desire to provide better facilities for spectacle, to increase seating capacity, and to improve sightlines.

SCENIC PRACTICES

Until about 1760 the *palais à volonté* and the *chambre à quatre portes* continued to be the usual settings for nonoperatic productions. The removal of spectators from the stage was motivated primarily by the desire to use more elaborate settings. An important turning point had already occurred at the Comédie Française when Voltaire's *The Orphan of China* (1755)

was billed as having new and accurate Oriental costumes and settings. In 1760 Voltaire's *Tancrède* directed attention to the Middle Ages, and soon other plays were being set in such locales as Norway, Russia, Spain, America, and the Near East and in many different historic periods. Diderot's plea (made in the 1750s) for greater fidelity to everyday life was also met in a few plays, such as Voltaire's *The Scots Girl* (1760), set in the common room of an inn, and Beaumarchais's *Eugénie* (1767), which sought to reproduce a domestic background in all its details. In spite of these innovations, however, the majority of plays continued to be presented in stock scenery.

At the Opéra considerable emphasis was placed on spectacle throughout the century. After the retirement of Jean Bérain in 1721, the most important designer was Jean-Nicolas Servandoni (1695–1766), a Florentine who worked for the Opéra from about 1728 to 1746. His principal contributions to French design were the *scena per angolo* and monumentality in the manner of the Bibienas. Servandoni is also noted for his "mute spectacles," mounted in the Salle des Machines between 1738 and 1742 and again from 1754 to 1758. In these, he recreated faithfully a number of well-known places, and the naturalism of these actorless spectacles probably did much to motivate the other theatres of Paris to improve their settings. Servandoni's successors at the Opéra changed so rapidly that none was able to establish a dominant style. Scenic design in France seldom rose to the level

FIG. 12.17
The auditorium of the Comédie Française, 1726. Note the audience on stage peering through and around the curtain. Note also the standing pit. From Adolphe Jullien, *Les Spectateurs sur le Théâtre* (1875).

FIG. 12.18
Stage setting by Jean-Nicolas Servandoni, who popularized the *scena per angolo* in France. From Bapst, *Essai sur l'Histoire du Théâtre* (1893).

achieved by the Italian designers of the period. The frequent changes in management and the constant financial difficulties at the Opéra, the continued adherence to the neoclassical ideal, and the reticence of the actors to authorize large expenditures for scenery at the Comédie Française did much to keep scenic practices in old paths. Although new directions had been suggested before the Revolution, they had not yet been fully exploited.

THE END OF EIGHTEENTH CENTURY THEATRE IN FRANCE

In 1789 the country was in such financial distress that Louis XVI was forced to call a meeting of the States-General (the French national assembly) for the first time since 1614. When one group within the assembly demanded a constitution and basic social reforms, Louis attempted to disband the States-General, thereby precipitating a reaction that led to the fall of the Bastille, which initiated the French Revolution. At stake was the class system that had existed since the Middle Ages. The new doctrine of equality and of government as a social contract had been forcefully stated by the American Declaration of Independence in 1776, but its impact was to be far more radical in France, which was still governed as an absolute monarchy. But the true revolution lay not so much in the violent events of the 1790s as in the ideas about social organization and human rights, for they gave the common people a new vision of themselves and their worth, the effects of which are still being felt today.

THE COURT THEATRES OF THE GERMAN STATES

France's decisive role in negotiating an end to the Thirty Years War in 1648 gave it considerable prestige throughout the German states, where soon rulers were seeking to create their own versions of the French court. As a result, opera, ballet, and theatrical spectacles of all sorts became a regular part of court life. The more affluent rulers imported Italian or French designers, musicians, and performers, but the less prosperous had to rely on native Germans to copy the foreign models.

Austria set the pattern when in 1652 the emperor imported Ludovico Burnacini from Venice to stage court entertainments. At Vienna an elaborate court theatre was opened in 1668. To serve it, the most famous composers and librettists of the age were brought from Italy. As a result, Vienna was to be the most important center for operatic production in Europe from about 1660 to 1740. It was in Vienna that the Bibienas mounted some of their most sumptuous productions.

Other German rulers followed the Austrian example. At Munich, a court theatre opened in 1654 and there Francesco Santurini, one of Italy's most outstanding designers, mounted numerous lavish spectacles. An opera house was built in Dresden sometime between 1664 and 1667 and another in Gotha about 1683. By the end of the seventeenth century, opera and Italianate scenery were to be seen at numerous courts in Germany, but little attention was paid to spoken drama or to German troupes.

FIG. 12.19

Northern and Eastern Europe during the eighteenth century. The Holy Roman Empire was divided into many small states, the borders of which are not shown here.

It is not surprising then that opera also became the most admired form with the prosperous middle class and retained its position of dominance until well after 1750. Spoken drama only gradually won support.

THE JESUIT THEATRE

In the seventeenth century numerous German schools, both Protestant and Catholic, presented plays, since drama was thought effective not only for teaching doctrine but also for training students in speaking and deportment. Many plays were presented in Latin, others in the vernacular. The school drama reached its peak in the Catholic schools run by the Jesuits.

The Society of Jesus, an outgrowth of the Counter-Reformation, was founded in 1534. By 1600 it had established 200 schools, universities, and seminaries, and by 1706 the number had increased to 769. The first recorded Jesuit production occurred in 1551, but soon almost every Jesuit school was performing at least one play a year.

During the seventeenth century many of the Jesuit schools were using well-equipped proscenium theatres, complete with perspective scenery, machinery, and elaborate special effects.

By 1700, Jesuit theatre could be found wherever the order established schools, but it was especially highly developed in Austria and southern Germany, where it gave the most elaborate productions to be seen outside the courts. Out of these schools came many of the most important works on theatrical practice published in the seventeenth and eighteenth centuries, among them Dubreuil's *Treatise on*

FIG. 12.20

The court theatre at Vienna designed by Ludovico Burnacini and opened in 1668. On stage is seen part of *The Golden Apple,* the opera which opened the theatre. On the dais are the Emperor Leopold I and his retinue. Engraving by Franz Geffels, 1668. Courtesy Bildarchiv, Osterreichische Nationalbibliothek, Vienna.

Perspective (1649), Pozzo's *Pictorial and Architectural Perspective* (1693–1700), and Lang's *Dissertation on Stage Acting* (1727). As the eighteenth century progressed,

FIG. 12.21

Scene from Nikolaus of Avancini's *Pietas Victrix,* a Jesuit play performed before the emperor in Vienna in 1659. The setting is by Giovanni Burnacini. From *Die Theater Wiens* (1899).

the order had begun to make powerful enemies because of its political intrigues and attempts to gain a monopoly on education. As a result, in 1773 it was suppressed. Although it was later revived, it never regained its former power and its period of contribution to the art of theatre was over.

Despite their theatrical sophistication, the Jesuits did not encourage the professional theatre, which, in their view, did not serve an educational or moral purpose. By setting high standards in production and by demanding a high moral tone, they may even have made the early German professional troupes look bad by comparison. But they stimulated a taste for theatre among the middle classes and produced many of the books that would help professionals improve their art.

THE EARLY PUBLIC THEATRE IN THE GERMAN STATES

Prior to the Thirty Years War, professional acting companies in the Germanic states were English in origin, and consequently the German professional theatre can be said to descend from those Elizabethan actors who began to tour widely on the continent around 1586. In seeking to increase their appeal, English actors developed such stock comic fools as Johan Posset, Stockfish, and Pickelherring. They added German phrases, speeches, and entire scenes to their productions and by 1626 had begun to include German actors in their troupes. These troupes enjoyed considerable reputations and the designation of a company as "English" became synonymous with high quality. The last important English troupe was headed by George Jolly, who performed in Germany during the 1650s when the English theatres were closed by Parliament. By 1660 English actors had virtually disappeared from the continent.

The first German troupe of note was that managed by Carl Andreas Paulsen from 1650 to 1687. More significant was that of Johannes Velten (1640–1695), a well-educated man who sought to raise the level of the German theatre by rejecting the English models and adapting the plays of Corneille and Molière for his company. But there were no cities large enough to support a professional theatre so troupes were forced to travel constantly. There were also no permanent theatres so they had to set up stages wherever they could find space. They had to change their bills daily and replenish their repertories often in order to attract the small potential audience. Velten's troupe usually had eighty-five to ninety plays in its repertory. At the end of the seventeenth century, a program was made up of a long play and an afterpiece, both of which might include such incidental entertainment as songs, dances, and acrobatic feats. The main offering, called the *Hauptaktion* (chief play) or *Haupt-und-Staatsaktion* (chief and state play), might be either serious or comic. The afterpiece, or *Nachspiel,* was usually a farce.

The first permanent public theatre in the Germanic states was the Karntnertor, built by the town council of Vienna in 1708 to support the work of Joseph Anton Stranitzky (1676–1726). Stranitzky had become famous for creating the character Hanswurst, a jolly, beer-drinking peasant with a Bavarian accent who was an amalgamation of all the various farce characters that had come before. Eventually this character would become the mainstay of companies throughout Germany.

In the early eighteenth century, then, several factors contributed to the theatre's low state: a repertory designed to attract an unsophisticated audience; the uneducated actors, who were little better than sideshow performers; and conditions which made it impossible to rehearse and mount plays with care.

FIG. 12.22
Stranitzky (foreground) as Hanswurst. From *Die Theater Wiens* (1899).

Under the circumstances, it is not surprising that aristocrats and churchmen held the professional theatre in contempt.

THE REFORMS OF GOTTSCHED AND NEUBER

The first significant steps toward reform were taken in the 1720s by Johann Christoph Gottsched (1700–1766), who, after being educated at the University of Könisgberg, rapidly became the intellectual leader of Germany. The development of German as a medium for literary expression ranked high among his many interests, for Latin was still the language of the universities (the first lecture in the vernacular had not been given until 1687), while French was favored by the aristocracy. Above all, Gottsched was interested in raising the moral level and refining the artistic taste of Germans, not only of the educated and aristocratic but also of the common people. The theatre attracted him because he saw in it a means of reaching the masses who could not read, so he actively sought liaisons with theatre professionals. His

FIG. 12.23

A company believed to be that of Caroline Neuber in Nuremberg, *c.* 1730. Note the heroic figures at center flanked on either side by clownish figures. Courtesy Theatermuseum, Munich.

overtures were unsuccessful until 1727, when he met the Neubers.

Caroline Neuber (1697–1760) had run away from home in 1717 with Johann Neuber, whom she married in 1718. They formed their own company in 1727 and acquired the title "Royal Polish and Electoral Saxon Court Comedians," which brought with it the right to play during the annual fair at Leipzig, then the intellectual capital of Germany and Gottsched's home.

The Neubers and Gottsched found common interest in the reform of the German theatre. Gottsched offered to provide the Neubers with a new repertory that would imitate the refined tastes of French neoclassicism and allow them to abandon the old plays, improvisation, burlesque afterpieces, and Hanswurst farces. Caroline Neuber, for her part, agreed to develop the Neuber company into one that could do justice to the new repertory by undertaking careful rehearsals, abandoning improvisation, and encouraging a greater sense of discipline and ensemble by assigning each actor additional duties, such as painting scenery, making handbills, or sewing costumes. In order to overcome public prejudices against actors, she also proposed to police the private lives of her company members.

Although the effort attracted some powerful supporters, notably the ruler of Schleswig-Holstein, and the educated classes of Leipzig and Hamburg, ultimately it did not succeed as they had hoped. An audience for the new drama could not be built fast enough to support the company, so it was constantly necessary to revert to the use of popular favorites like the Hanswurst plays. Touring and the daily change of bill also had to continue so there was little time to spend on rehearsals and the other changes needed

for the company to perform at the level required to make the new plays successful. Neuber sometimes rebuked audiences publicly for their lack of taste while Gottsched grew impatient at the seeming lack of progress. In 1739 Neuber broke with Gottsched. Thereafter, her career declined. In 1740 she was invited to St. Petersburg, but the death of the Empress Anna six months after her arrival cut that venture short. Returning to Leipzig in 1741, she found one of her former actors established in her theatre. There followed a pitched battle, in the course of which Neuber satirized Gottsched and his ideas. Although her attack signaled the end of Gottsched's leadership, it did not aid her. She remained in Leipzig for a few years, then moved on to Vienna and elsewhere until her death in 1760.

Although Gottsched and Neuber were sometimes ridiculed by later theatre professionals, their pioneering efforts made the future gains for German theatre possible. By the 1740s regular drama was in the repertory of all German companies, much of it from the six volumes of plays published by Gottsched between 1740 and 1745 under the title, *The German Stage*. Furthermore, Neuber's production ideals were adopted by other troupes, two of the most important of which were established by actors from her company, Schönemann and Koch, and others by actors who were trained by these two men.

ACTING COMPANIES AND THE STATE THEATRES

Johann Friederich Schönemann (1704–1782) entered the Neuber company in 1730. Originally a clown, Schönemann played comic valets in the new drama. When Neuber left Leipzig in 1740, he formed his own troupe, borrowing both her repertory and her methods. The vitality and refinement of his young and relatively well-educated actors attracted much support in the towns of north and east Germany. Three of his performers—Konrad Ackermann, Konrad Ekhof, and Sophia Carlotta Schröder—were to become among the most famous actors of the age. Ackermann left to form his own company after just a few years with Schönemann, taking Mrs. Schröder and several other company members with him. But Ekhof (1720–1778) stayed, gradually becoming the company's leading man and perhaps the first important theorist of the German stage. When Schönemann retired in 1757, Konrad Ekhof asked another former member of the Neuber troupe, Heinrich Koch, to take over the Schönemann company.

Heinrich Koch (1703–1775) had entered Neuber's company in 1728 and remained with her until she left Leipzig in 1740. Obtaining her former license, he toured in that area until he assumed control of the Schönemann troupe in 1758. Between 1758 and 1763, at the height of the Seven Years War, Koch and Ekhof succeeded in playing most of each year in one city, Hamburg, a feat not yet accomplished by any other troupe. When Ekhof left the company in 1764, Koch returned to Leipzig, where he built that city's first permanent theatre in 1766. (In spite of the city's importance as the cultural center of Germany, all previous public theatres had been temporary.) Koch later played at the court theatre in Weimar (1768–1771) after which he performed in Berlin until his death in 1775. He was probably the first German manager fully to achieve Neuber's ideals.

Ekhof had left Koch in 1764 to join the Ackermann family company, founded by Konrad Ackermann (1712–1771), and featuring his wife, Sophia Carlotta Schröder (1714–1793), and his stepson, Friedrich Ludwig Schröder (1744–1816), destined to become one of the greatest of German actors. All except Friedrich had been introduced to the ideas of Neuber while working with Schönemann's company in the 1740s, and Ekhof had received additional insights into Neuber's methods from Koch. The Ackermann company had built a permanent theatre in Königsberg (in East Prussia, now Kaliningrad in Russia), perhaps the first in Germany intended for sole use by a dramatic company. Unfortunately, in 1756 the Seven Years War forced the Ackermann troupe to flee west, where they played in Switzerland, Alsace, and elsewhere before coming to Hamburg in 1764 where Ekhof joined them. In 1765 Ackermann built Hamburg's first permanent theatre. The following year he turned over the theatre and some of the best members of his company to his son-in-law, Johann Friedrich Löwen (1729–1771), for an important project known as the Hamburg National Theatre.

Löwen was the author of the first history of German theatre (published in 1766) and had concluded that theatre's low repute was due to the prevalence of uncultivated managers and actors, the shortage of German dramatists, the profit motive, the necessity of touring, and the lack of state support. To remedy the situation, he proposed the establishment of a permanent, subsidized, nonprofit theatre, run by a salaried manager. He advocated establishing an academy to train actors, high salaries and a pension system to attract the best performers, along with prizes to encourage dramatists. Löwen persuaded twelve businessmen to back his venture and secured the services of G. E. Lessing, by this time considered the finest German playwright, to be its *dramaturg* (literary and artistic advisor, reader of plays, recommender of repertory, and in-house critic), a position now considered essential in most major European companies. The venture came to an inglorious end in 1769. Its most lasting achievement was Lessing's theatrical journal, *Hamburg Dramaturgy,* now considered one of the major critical works of the eighteenth century. But the Hamburg National Theatre remains a landmark as the first German attempt to establish a theatre on noncommercial lines. It popularized the notion that the German states needed such theatres and paved the way for those that were soon to appear.

The first state theatre was established at Gotha in 1775 from the remnants of the Hamburg National Theatre troupe including its business manager, Abel Seyler (1730–1801), his wife, the highly regarded actress, Sophie Hensel (1738–1789), and its star performer, Konrad Ekhof. The company had toured, then taken up residency at the Weimar theatre (1772–1775), but when that theatre burned down, they moved to Gotha where the first state theatre was being organized. Seyler soon left Gotha with part of the company but Ekhof and the better actors remained.

The Gotha Court Theatre was a nonprofit organization, in which each member was a state employee with pension rights. Ekhof, who was responsible for staging the plays, was at this time the most respected actor in Germany. He brought to Gotha a number of talented young people, including August Iffland, who received fine training and later became the leading actors of Germany after Ekhof's death. Ekhof was very conservative in his tastes, however, and did nothing to forward the new drama. In 1779, upon Ekhof's death, the Gotha theatre was closed. The remaining actors rejoined Seyler's company for another state theatre project, the Court and National Theater at Mannheim, which from 1784 to 1795 was considered one of the finest theatres in Germany.

Before the Gotha venture ended, a far more important state theatre was founded in Vienna. Although it had always been the most powerful Germanic city, Vienna had lagged behind the others in the development of a public theatre. The court had spent lavishly on opera, but it had almost completely ignored German drama. The general public had been served by the Karntnertor theatre since 1708, but because of the traditions established by Stranitzky and his successors, improvised drama had been the usual fare. Written drama began to gain a foothold after Koch appeared in Vienna in 1748, but it was not until the 1760s, when Josef von Sonnenfels (1733–1817) waged a campaign in its favor, that regular drama was widely accepted and performed at the Karntnertor. In 1776, these developments culminated in the Emperor Joseph II's establishment of the Imperial and National Theater, called "the Burgtheater" after the building in which it performed. Its organization and procedures were modeled after those of the Comédie Française. By 1825 it was considered the best of all the German-language troupes.

After 1780 state theatres were established throughout German-speaking areas. Among the best were those at Cologne, Mainz, Salzburg, Weimar, and Passau, but the theatre founded in Berlin in 1786 was destined to become the most important. As in other states, drama had been given little encouragement in Prussia during the early eighteenth century, although Frederick the Great (reigned 1740-1786), who was devoted to French culture, had engaged a French troupe for his private theatre and had supported lavish operatic productions. Neither Schönemann nor Koch received any recognition from the court when their companies played in Berlin. A new era did not begin until 1786 when Frederick William II (reigned 1786-1797) established a subsidized state troupe. Prussia's position of leadership in Germany made its theatre especially influential after 1800.

The establishment of state theatres was paralleled in the same period by the building of permanent theatre buildings in a number of towns that were not the seats of state governments. By the 1790s there were more than seventy Germanic companies, over half of them permanently located. Touring was now restricted to minor troupes.

In contrast with the period between 1725 and 1740, when troupes were virtually ignored by the aristocracy, by 1780 rulers vied with each other in establishing theatres, much as they had formerly competed in supporting opera.

LESSING AND THE STORM-AND-STRESS MOVEMENT

By the 1740s Gottsched and his circle had laid the foundations for a new repertory but had provided no plays of lasting value. As their influence waned, a new group of dramatists appeared. The finest among these was Gotthold Ephraim Lessing (1729–1781), the first truly significant German dramatist.

Lessing began his career in 1748 with *The Young Scholar,* performed by Neuber's troupe. He won his first widespread fame in 1755 with *Miss Sara Sampson,* a domestic tragedy that swept Germany and won a resounding triumph for sentimental drama. In writing this play, Lessing drew upon the Medea myth but set it in contemporary England. He also changed the focus of the story by making the victim of Medea's wrath the central figure. His play tells the story of a naïve and loving young girl who is persuaded by a rakish young man to run away with him; when the young man's mistress learns that she has been deserted, she contrives to poison Sara, and to escape across the English Channel. First performed by Ackermann's troupe, *Miss Sara Sampson* was soon the most popular play in the German states and the most widely imitated. Gradually, Lessing came to believe that English drama was the most suitable model for German writers, and in both his plays and in the *Hamburg Dramaturgy* journal, he sought to discredit Gottsched and the French neoclassicists.

Lessing's second influential play, *Minna von Barnhelm* (1767), is often called Germany's first national comedy. Treating events immediately following the Seven Years War, the play presents lovers drawn from opposing sides who symbolize problems and divisions within Germany. The union of the lovers at the end of the play therefore had a significance beyond the literal. In spite of its topical subject, it is one of the most durable of eighteenth-century comedies, for, though the play is sentimental, Minna's resourcefulness and humor give it freshness.

Lessing's last important work, *Nathan the Wise* (1779), a dramatic poem not intended for the stage, is considered by many the greatest philosophical drama of the eighteenth century. In it, he depicts characters representing Judaism, Islam, and Christianity to demonstrate that universal love is the only fruitful doctrine. It is the first major German work to be written in blank verse rather than the Alexandrine or prose, and it paved the way for the experiments with verse drama that would later be undertaken by Goethe at Weimar, after which blank verse became standard in German tragedy. *Nathan the Wise* was soon performed and has continued to be one of the most frequently produced German works.

Lessing demonstrated that a native playwright could attract a wide following. His plays established a new standard while remaining firmly within the mainstream of eighteenth-century rationalism, which viewed the universe as ruled by a benevolent god, saw man as essentially good, and believed the human mind was capable of solving all important problems through the exercise of reason. His criticism,

FIG. 12.24

Klinger's *The Twins,* a Storm-and-Stress play. Engraving by Albrecht. Courtesy Österreichische Nationalbibliothek, Vienna.

however, had served to undermine the hold of the neoclassicism that had been championed by Gottsched. Consequently, before Lessing died a new and more radical group of dramatists had appeared.

Storm-and-Stress (*Sturm und Drang*) was a frankly experimental movement of young men in revolt against eighteenth-century rationalism. Traditionally dated 1767–1787, the movement reached its peak in the 1770s. Storm-and-Stress plays have often been described as completely formless rebellions against neoclassicism, primarily because of Goethe's *Goetz von Berlichingen* (1773), with its fifty-four scenes and tangle of plots, and Friedrich Maximilian Klinger's (1752–1831) *Storm and Stress* (1776), with its rhapsodic emotionalism. These have been taken as typical of the movement but in actuality, most Storm-and-Stress plays are written in five acts, and as many observe the unities of time and place as violate them. Since the dramatists in this movement had no agreed upon philosophy beyond rebellion, the plays show wide variations both in thought and

expression. The very diversity of the plays was bewildering to audiences, for the young authors seemed to be challenging all artistic and social values. The subject matter was often shocking. Jacob M. R. Lenz's (1751–1792) *The Soldiers* (1776) proposes a state-sponsored system of prostitution to protect respectable young women from seduction, while in Heinrich Leopold Wagner's (1747–1779) *The Child Murderess* (1776), a rape occurs just off stage and a baby is killed on stage by having a hatpin thrust into its brain.

Few Storm-and-Stress plays were produced, and even fewer were well received. The major exceptions were *Goetz von Berlichingen* and Friedrich Schiller's early plays starting with *The Robbers* (1782). Nevertheless, Storm-and-Stress plays were widely read and discussed. Consequently, they helped to break down old barriers and to pave the way for other writers who adapted many of the new ideas and techniques to popular tastes. They also probably aided in gaining acceptance for Shakespeare's plays, then being introduced on the German stage, since to many critics they seemed similar in structure and outlook. Out of these beginnings, a more mature drama was to come between 1785 and 1805.

EVOLUTION OF STAGING IN THE EIGHTEENTH CENTURY

So long as there were no permanent theatres, spectacle was not extensively developed. Furthermore, during the early years the necessity of touring forced companies to rely upon a few settings which might be adapted for almost any play. Before 1725, three sets were considered sufficient: a wood for all exterior scenes, a great hall for palaces, and a cottage room for domestic interiors. After 1750 the typical stock settings were somewhat more numerous: a Prachtsaal (or *palais à volonté*), a street, a village, several middle-class rooms, a prison, and a scene depicting several hills and shrubs. The 1770s brought significant innovations in spectacle. Permanent theatres introduced the chariot-and-pole system of scene shifting just when new esthetics were creating a demand for more appropriate, varied, and detailed settings.

By the 1790s dramatists were writing plays that demanded the use of practical bridges, walls, and other complex set pieces. Doors and windows began to be set up between wings, thus marking the first steps in Germany toward the box set. As elsewhere, however, the trends toward greater representationalism and accuracy of detail were not to be fully exploited until the nineteenth century.

FIG. 12.25
Cross section of the Residenztheater, Munich, 1771, designed by François de Cuvillié *père.*
The forward part of the stage and space beneath it are at the left. The pit floor could be raised so that
it was level with the stage for balls and similar events. The machinery used to lower and raise the
floor is seen at bottom center. The ruler's box is at center right. Engraving by Valerian Funck.
Courtesy Theatermuseum, Munich.

Costumes followed the same general trends. Before about 1725, extreme simplicity was the rule. Each actor was expected to own a pair of black breeches, while the manager supplied a coat and waistcoat. The basic costume, used in numerous roles, was altered by the addition of simple accessories; a king carried a scepter and wore a feathered headdress; a classical hero draped a scarf diagonally across his chest and wore a helmet. Actresses wore the most fashionable garments they could afford. Lace was often made from cut paper.

As the influence of French drama increased, the costuming conventions of the Parisian troupes were adopted. Most tragic heroes and heroines were played in French court dress, while classical heroes wore the *habit à la romaine,* and Near Eastern characters adopted baggy trousers and turbans. Performers sought to accumulate their own wardrobes, and managers to increase the common stock.

The success of Lessing's *Minna von Barnhelm* (1767) and the subsequent vogue for plays with war backgrounds encouraged managers to seek the cooperation of local army garrisons, borrowing soldiers in full uniform to use as supernumeraries, thereby introducing authentic costumes to the stage. Soon, even the authors of domestic plays began to prescribe the costumes to be worn by their characters. This attention to authenticity was then carried into historical costumes.

Beginning with Gottsched, intermittent attempts were made to introduce a measure of historical accuracy. Gottsched recommended the use of Roman togas in classical plays and, after their break, Neuber revenged herself on him by following his prescriptions for costuming *The Dying Cato,* much to the amusement of audiences who were reduced to uncontrollable laughter. In 1766 Koch created a considerable stir when he opened his new theatre in Leipzig. For

FIG. 12.26

The Margrave's Opera House, Bayreuth, designed by Guiseppe and Carlo Galli Bibiena, 1748. This theatre captures baroque splendor at its height. Gouache by Gustave Bauernfeind, 1879. Courtesy Theatermuseum, Munich.

FIG. 12.27

A German theatre in the second half of the eighteenth century. Note the pit, boxes, footlights, prompter's box, and wings of the interior setting. Note also that upstage a door has been set between the wing and backshutter, a practice that prefigured the fully developed box set. Courtesy Theatermuseum, Munich.

his production of *Goetz von Berlichingen* in 1774, the great actor-manager F. L. Schröder dressed the knights in armor, the monks and bishops in appropriate ecclesiastical garments, and the courtiers, citizens, and gypsies in allegedly accurate clothing. Thereafter, some attempt at historical costuming was considered necessary for any play set in the past.

F. L. SCHRÖDER AND THE HAMBURG SCHOOL

Probably the most influential troupe in the years between 1770 and 1800 was that of Friedrich Ludwig Schröder (1744–1816). The son of Sophia Carlotta Schröder, he was on the stage from the time he was three years old. Separated from the Ackermann troupe at the time of the Seven Years War (1756–1763), he learned to fend for himself by joining with itinerant performers who taught him acrobatics and dancing. Later he rejoined his parents and came into contact with Ekhof, who first made him realize what great acting might be. When the Hamburg National Theatre was formed in 1767, Schröder left the company and performed for a time with Kurz-Bernadon, from whom he learned improvisational playing. Schröder returned to Ackermann's Hamburg troupe in 1769 and became artistic director of the company when

FIG. 12.28
Schröder as Falstaff. From *Literatur und Theaterzeitung* (1780).

his stepfather died in 1771. Except for a six-year hiatus (1780–1786) during which he did starring engagements at Mannheim and Vienna, he ran the Hamburg company until he retired in 1798.

The challenge of management seems to have transformed Schröder. Previously a careless performer who could scarcely be induced to rehearse, he became a firm disciplinarian who insisted upon perfection in every detail. His company became one of the most truly integrated ensembles in Germany, performing a distinguished repertory of plays including Lessing, Storm-and-Stress dramas, and Shakespeare.

In addition to his managerial duties, Schröder performed about thirty-nine new roles each year, and between 1771 and 1780 he translated, adapted, or wrote twenty-eight plays. During the 1780s he was generally recognized as Germany's greatest actor.

In his lifetime Schröder played more than 700 roles. Historically, he is perhaps most important for creating what came to be called the "Hamburg school" of acting and production. This was not an actual school, but a style of acting (and staging) in which character, emotion, and setting were carefully delineated and differentiated.

IFFLAND AND THE MANNHEIM SCHOOL

August Wilhelm Iffland (1759–1814) began his acting career in the Gotha company under Ekhof and joined the newly created Mannheim state theatre in 1779. During Iffland's tenure, the Mannheim theatre was one of the most vital in Germany. Schröder played there in 1780, introducing the company to Shakespeare, and for a time in the early 1780s, Friedrich Schiller was the resident dramatist. Iffland rapidly came to the fore, both as actor and dramatist. From 1784, when his *Crimes of Ambition* established his fame as a writer, until 1796, when he left the troupe, Iffland was the most influential member of the Mannheim company. Thirty-seven of his plays were first performed by this theatre. As Iffland's plays became widely known, he began to be in great demand for starring engagements in his own plays, and thereafter he traveled extensively. From 1796 until 1814 he was head of the Berlin state theatre, which he molded into one of the finest ensembles of its time.

Iffland's own plays provided him with his best acting vehicles. Offering idealized portraits of ordinary men and women, their touching situations tended to romanticize the simple life, as in *The Huntsmen* (1785), which contrasts virtuous middle-class persons with oppressive aristocrats. Although some aspects of his work seemed to anticipate romanticism, Iffland

FIG. 12.29
Iffland and Mme Bethmann in a scene from Iffland's *The Family Friend*. Contemporary engraving.

to St. Petersburg to serve as director of the German theatre there.

From 1789, when he won his first major success with *Misanthropy and Repentance* until his political assassination in Mannheim, he was the most popular playwright in the world. One-fourth of all the performances done in Vienna's Burgtheatre between 1789 and 1867, were of Kotzebue's plays; at other theatres the proportion was often higher. Thirty-six of his plays were translated into English, and several remained starring vehicles throughout the nineteenth century. Kotzebue's more than 200 plays range through domestic drama, historical spectacle, verse plays, and farces but he is most identified as the first writer to develop sentimental comedy into a form that came to be called melodrama. Kotzebue's success can probably be explained by his ability to adapt new trends to public tastes. Thus, while he used

FIG. 12.30
Kotzebue's *Misanthropy and Repentance* (or *The Stranger*). The final scene of reunion as shown in the edition of the play published in 1790. Courtesy Osterreichische Nationalbibliothek, Vienna.

opposed the new movement and sought to keep the romantic drama out of the repertory at Berlin.

Iffland was considered by many Schröder's equal or superior in acting. As a performer, he depended especially upon his expressive body and face, for his voice was weak. His major appeal lay in his ability to humanize all roles, making his characters seem naturally noble but average human beings. His "Mannheim school" of acting is often said to form a bridge between Schröder's romantic-realistic mode and the Weimar classical mode.

KOTZEBUE AND THE BEGINNINGS OF MELODRAMA

August Friedrich von Kotzebue (1761–1819) was born in Weimar but entered the Russian diplomatic service in St. Petersburg in 1783. During the years from 1797 to 1799, Kotzebue worked as a resident dramatist in Vienna and Weimar, before returning many of the themes and devices introduced by Storm-and-Stress dramatists, he was successful where they had failed. Both his plays, and his many novels, were read widely.

GOETHE, SCHILLER, AND WEIMAR CLASSICISM

If Iffland and Kotzebue raised German drama to the peak of its popularity, Goethe and Schiller were considered its greatest literary dramatists. In their joint work at Weimar, they also created a distinctive style of production known as Weimar Classicism, that was to influence the German theatre throughout much of the nineteenth century.

Johann Wolfgang von Goethe (1749–1832) is usually considered the greatest literary figure Germany has known. A "universal genius," Goethe's interests ranged through almost every field, and to most he made significant contributions. He began his literary career at a very early age, but it was his play *Goetz von Berlichingen* (1773) and his novel *The Sorrows of Young Werther* (1774) that made him the most famous young writer of his time and the center of the Storm-and-Stress school. In 1775, at the request of the young ruler, Duke Karl August, Goethe settled in Weimar, which he helped to make one of the cultural centers of Germany.

Goethe's visit to Italy (1786–1788) marks a turning point to his outlook. His new appreciation of the classical past made him reject his former Storm-and-Stress period in favor of the classical mode. His *Iphigenia in Tauris* (1787) is often considered one of his greatest achievements.

In 1791 the Duke of Weimar appointed Goethe as managing director of The Weimar Court Theatre. Goethe took little interest in the theatre, leaving it in the hands of its actor/manager Franz Fischer, until Iffland performed there in 1796 and gave him a vision of what the troupe might become if given sufficient guidance. This interest was deepened by the dramatist Schiller, who stimulated Goethe to take a more active part in the company's work.

Friedrich Schiller (1759–1805) was the son of an army officer and had been forced by the Duke of Wüttemberg to enter military school. Following the success of his first play, *The Robbers* (1782), Schiller was forbidden to write, so he fled to Mannheim where he was appointed resident dramatist to the state theatre. He wrote *Fiesko* (1783) and *Intrigue and Love* (1784) for them, with Iffland playing the leading roles. Like Goethe, Schiller underwent a significant change in the late 1780s. He wrote no plays between 1787 and 1798, devoting himself instead to

FIG. 12.31
Schiller's *Fiesko* as performed at Weimar in 1805. Aquatint by J. C. E. Müller after a painting by G. E. Opitz. Courtesy Theatermuseum, Munich.

historical studies, becoming professor of history at the University of Jena, only twelve miles from Weimar. In 1794, Goethe and Schiller established a close friendship and Schiller moved to Weimar (1799) where the two began their reforms of the Weimar theatre.

Goethe and Schiller sought to counter the major artistic trends of their day. They argued that drama should transform ordinary experience rather than create an illusion of real life. For them, the formal conventions of Greek tragedy served as useful devices to "distance" the spectators from the play's events so they might perceive the ideal patterns behind everyday reality. Consequently, they adopted blank verse, conventionalized structural patterns, simple but harmonious settings and costumes, and precise rhythmic speech in an attempt to lead spectators beyond their normal perceptions into the realm of ideal truth. Out of these views came "Weimar classicism."

Schiller expressed these ideas in his late plays. They are extremely complex works in which philosophical, historical, and individual conflicts are interwoven. For most, Schiller chose subjects that represent turning points in history. *Wallenstein's Camp* (1798), *The Piccolomini* (1799), and *Wallenstein's Death* (1799) form a trilogy on the Thirty Years War conceived on a vaster scale than any dramas between Schiller's and Shakespeare's. *Mary Stuart* (1800), *The Maid of Orleans* (1801), and *William Tell* (1804) treat decisive events in English, French, and Swiss history.

Meanwhile, Goethe turned his attention to transforming the second-rate Weimar troupe into a true ensemble. At Weimar, the number of rehearsals for a play did not differ markedly from typical practice elsewhere—usually no more than six to ten. Unlike other managers, however, Goethe worked with individual actors, sometimes over several months, on the interpretation of their roles prior to the first company rehearsal. Group preparations began with a series of reading rehearsals during which Goethe corrected line readings and interpretation, with special attention to the proper speaking of verse and to rhythmic patterns. At the same time, Goethe sought to make his actors so comfortable with these patterns that on stage they would seem natural rather than artificial. The number of onstage rehearsals were few and did not begin until the actors knew their lines.

Rather than seeking to create the illusion of reality, Goethe attempted to achieve a harmonious and graceful picture which, combined with intelligent and euphonious line readings, would attune the spectator to an ideal beauty. He drew on his knowledge of painting to create the most pleasing pictorial composition on stage. To aid in the creation of movement patterns (blocking), he introduced the system of dividing the stage into squares and specified the actors' movements in relation to them. By requiring strict adherence to his directions, Goethe achieved the most integrated ensemble of his day. Because of his working methods, he is now considered one of the first modern "directors."

Despite Goethe's ideals, the repertory was not confined to plays of the type that he and Schiller admired. Since the court subsidy covered only about one-third of the company's expenses, Goethe had to arrange the repertory so as to ensure popular support. Consequently, of the three weekly performances, one was usually devoted to musical plays or opera, one to popular drama (especially by Kotzebue or Iffland), and the third to plays that Goethe admired. The actors complained, probably with good cause, that Goethe devoted two-thirds of the preparation time to plays of the last type. Goethe often experimented with

FIG. 12.32
Interior view of the theatre at Drottningholm near Stockholm, Sweden (1766). This theatre was unused for over 200 years when it was rediscovered in 1922. It contains the most complete set of chariot-and-pole machinery in existence and numerous sets of eighteenth century wing and border sets. On stage is a *palais à volonté* setting designed by Carlo Bibiena in 1774. Note the wave machine in the background. Courtesy Drottningholm Theatermuseum, Stockholm.

unusual production devices or plays. He used half-masks in Terence's *The Brothers,* revived several *commedia dell'arte* scripts, and presented plays by Shakespeare, Calderón, and others. With this repertory, Goethe sought to enlarge the experience of both his actors and his audience, and he did not hesitate to reprimand the audience in the theatre if they responded in ways he considered inappropriate.

The combined fame of Goethe and Schiller attracted many visitors, and soon "Weimar classicism" was famous throughout Germany. Its actors were in great demand, and disseminated the Weimar approach wherever they went. Their admirers praised the Weimar style extravagantly, but others found the performers so uniform that they might exchange roles without any noticeable effect. After Schiller died in 1805, Goethe's interest in the theatre was sporadic and the troupe was handed over to Caroline Jagemann (1777–1848), an accomplished actress and the duke's mistress. Goethe resigned his post in 1817.

Of Goethe's later dramatic works, the most famous is *Faust,* the first part of which was published in 1808 and the second in 1831. Not intended for the stage, this dramatic poem seeks to depict the human search for fulfillment, and it suggests that people find salvation through such striving. Its episodic structure and philosophical viewpoint are similar in all important respects to the work of the romantic playwrights. Thus, while Goethe stands as the culmination of German classicism, he also contributed much to romanticism, which came to the fore after 1798.

THEATRE IN RUSSIA TO 1800

The eighteenth century also saw the establishment of theatre and drama in Russia. As in other parts of Europe, folk and ritual drama in Russia can be found from the earliest times and wandering entertainers can be traced back as far as the tenth century. In the seventeenth century drama was introduced into the Jesuit schools of the Ukraine, and until the eighteenth century students from these schools toured plays as far east as Siberia.

The first clear record of theatre in Moscow is found in 1672 during the reign of Alexis (1645–1676), who persuaded Johann Gottfried Gregory, a Lutheran minister and schoolteacher in the resident German colony, to produce plays for the theatre that Alexis had built. Upon Alexis's death in 1676, this theatre was abandoned.

Russian theatre then lay fallow until Peter the Great (reigned 1682–1725) decided to use it in his campaign to westernize Russia. In 1702 he imported Johann Kunst's company from Gdansk and installed it in a theatre on what is now Red Square. But Peter was too preoccupied with wars and building his new capital city, St. Petersburg, to devote much attention to the theatre, and consequently it did not prosper.

Between 1725 and 1750 theatrical activities were largely confined to the court. For the coronation of the Empress Anna (reigned 1730–1740), the Polish king sent a *commedia dell'arte* troupe. Their success led to the demand for other Western forms, and consequently Francesco Araia, a Neapolitan opera composer, was imported in 1735 and in 1738, Jean-Baptiste Landet, a French dancing master was brought to court, later becoming the founder of Russian ballet. In 1740 the Neuber troupe was invited to St. Petersburg, but their engagement was cut short by the death of the Empress Anna.

Under the Empress Elizabeth (reigned 1741–1762), a French troupe was employed to perform plays twice a week while an Italian company was retained to perform operas. It was left to the amateur cadets of the Academy of the Nobility to perform the first play in Russian in 1749. The play, *Khorev* (1747), launched the career of Russia's first important playwright, Alexander Sumarokov (1717–1777), who went on to write neoclassical tragedies and satirical comedies.

Another group of amateurs were to establish Russia's first native professional company in the provincial capital of Yaroslavl. Around 1750, a merchant's son who had seen theatrical performances by foreign companies in St. Petersburg, decided to present plays in his hometown of Yaroslavl. Assembling a troupe from among his family and friends, Volkov fitted up a barn as a theatre. Enthusiasm was so great that he had moved into more adequate quarters before being summoned to play for the empress in 1752. Impressed by their work, the empress sent some of the actors to the Academy of the Nobility for further education and permitted them to perform for the general public. Thus, Volkov is usually considered the founder of the Russian professional theatre.

The next significant development came in 1756, when the Empress Elizabeth established a state theatre for Russian plays. The troupe, made up primarily of Volkov's actors, was placed under the direction of Sumarokov, although ultimate authority resided in a court official. The relatively slight value placed on this Russian company, however, is indicated by its subsidy of 5,000 rubles as compared with the 20,000 given the French actors. The Russian plays, treated condescendingly by the court, were attended primarily by the middle class.

FIG. 12.33
Interior of the Bolshoi Theatre, St. Petersburg, in the late eighteenth century. A contemporary engraving.

Under Catherine II (reigned 1762–1796) the theatre spread to many parts of Russia. Playwrights increased, although few won lasting fame.

The majority of the plays in the repertory were translations, and, after the 1760s, as the works of Diderot, Lillo, Lessing, Beaumarchais, and Kotzebue were imported, domestic tragedy and sentimental comedy were the most popular types. Musical plays in the manner of ballad opera or *opéra comique* also gained an enormous following.

All plays were subject to strict censorship, and the subsidized theatres operated under regulations established by the crown. Although opera continued to be the favored form with the aristocracy, the dramatic troupes achieved increased security. In 1776 a pension system was inaugurated, and after 1789 the companies were allowed four annual benefit performances, the proceeds of which were divided among all the actors. In general, acting companies followed "lines of business" similar to those current in France. A state document of 1766 lists the lines as follows: first, second, and third comic and tragic lovers, noble fathers, comic fathers, first and second domestics, moralizers, clerks, confidants, first and second tragic and comic female lovers, first and second chambermaids, old women, and confidantes.

By the end of the eighteenth century, itinerant companies were touring to the principal cities of Russia. Many privately owned theatres also had appeared; some gave public performances, while others were maintained by nobles for private entertainments. Few of those giving public performances were successful. In Moscow, for example, the public theatre was open only sporadically. When one venture failed, after lasting only from 1759 to 1761, there was no professional troupe until 1786, when M. E. Medox's company opened and struggled along until 1796. Moscow was not to be given a state-supported theatre until the nineteenth century.

By far the majority of the privately owned theatres were maintained by the great landowners. With the encouragement of Catherine II, the aristocracy patronized the arts as a sign of their enlightenment, and many nobles established small courts of their own. Many maintained theatrical troupes composed of their serfs.

Unlike the rest of Europe, where it had largely disappeared during the Renaissance, in Russia serfdom was not established until the late sixteenth century, when a series of decrees bound the peasants to the land. Thereafter, serfdom became the principal basis of the Russian economy, and a landowner's wealth was measured primarily in terms of the number of serfs bound to his estate. During the late eighteenth century many nobles began to select serfs and train them as performers. In 1797 in Moscow alone there were fifteen serf theatres, many of which rivaled in quality the court and state theatres of St. Petersburg. The most important serf companies operated between 1790 and 1810, but some continued to operate until serfdom was abolished in 1861.

By 1800, then, Russian theatre and drama had gained a relatively firm foothold. Few important dramatists had appeared and the theatre was still largely imitative of French and Italian practices, but the basis for future developments was clearly evident. The Russian situation also shows that by 1800 the professional theatre had spread throughout Europe. It remained for the nineteenth century to bring it to full flower.

LOOKING AT THEATRE HISTORY

As a branch of theatre, opera is especially important in the study of scenic design and theatre architecture. In fact, the majority of extant pictorial evidence about scenery between the Renaissance and the nineteenth century is from opera, and thus studies of scenic design emphasize musical more than nonmusical production. This is especially true of the eighteenth century, during which the Bibiena family dominated operatic design. In 1785 Stefano Arteaga wrote of Ferdinando Bibiena's contributions:

The art of making tiny space seem vast, the ease and speed of changing sets in a twinkling of an eye, . . . and above all buildings seen at an angle brought the science of illusion to the highest possible pitch . . . the change from perspectives that limit sight and imagination by running to a central vanishing point was like opening a new world to busy the imagination . . . and could represent and ennoble the real things of this world . . .

From A. Hyatt Mayor, *The Bibiena Family* (New York: H. Bittner and Co., 1945), 24.

Italy was the traditional home of opera and *commedia dell'arte*. But before the middle of the eighteenth century the *commedia* was beginning to be out of tune with the sentimental tastes of the age. In his *Memoirs*, Goldoni tells of his attempts to reform it:

The mask must always be very prejudicial to the action of the performer . . . and however he may gesticulate and vary the tone, he can never convey by the countenance . . . the different passions. . . . [For this and other reasons, I attempted] the reform of the Italian Theatre, and to supply the place of farces with comedies. . . . I undertook to produce a few pieces merely sketched, without ceasing to give comedies of character. I employed the masks [in some] and I displayed a more noble and interesting comic humor in the others. . . . with time and patience I brought about a reconciliation [of the two]; and I had the satisfaction, at length, to see . . . my own taste [become] in a few years the most general and prevailing in Italy.

Carlo Goldoni, *Memoirs*, trans. John Black (London, 1814), II, 56–57.

Diderot did not find the two forms of drama sanctioned by neoclassicism sufficient, and he proposed two "middle genres" to enlarge the range to four types:

Laughing comedy, whose purpose is to ridicule vice; serious comedy, whose function is to depict virtue and duty; the kind of tragedy that is concerned with domestic troubles; and finally, the kind of tragedy that deals with public catastrophes and the misfortunes of the mighty.

In addition, Diderot wished to reform theatrical production to make it as illusionistic as possible. He became the first to propose the "fourth wall" conception of the stage:

Regardless of whether you are writing or acting, think no more about the audience than if it did not exist. Imagine a wall across the front of the stage, dividing you from the audience, and act precisely as if the curtain had not risen.

Denis Diderot, *On Dramatic Poetry* (1758).

In France in the 1750s reforms began to be made in acting and costume to achieve greater naturalness. Here is a brief comment by Marmontel on one of the first attempts:

I went to see [Mlle Clairon] in her dressing room, and, for the first time, I found her dressed in the habit of a sultana; without hoop, her arms half-naked, and in the truth of Oriental costume. . . . The event surpassed her expectation and mine. It was no longer the actress, it was Roxanne herself. . . . The astonishment, the illusion, the enchantment, was extreme. . . . [The audience] had heard nothing like it. I saw her after the play. . . . "Don't you see that it ruins me? In all my characters, the costume must now be observed; the truth of declamation requires that of dress; all my rich stage-wardrobe is from this moment rejected. . . ."

Jean François Marmontel, *Memoirs* (London, 1805), 44–45.

In the early eighteenth century, when Germanic rulers disdained the native drama, the theatre was at a low ebb, as this account by Konrad Ekhof testifies:

Travelling troupes of mountebanks, going from one fair to another all over Germany, amused the mob with low farces. . . . The performance of the plays was just as ridiculous as their plots. One very frequently presented everywhere was entitled Adam and Eve, *or the Fall of the First Men. . . . I remember seeing it acted at Strasbourg. You saw a fat Eve, in tights made of coarse flesh-colored linen, to which a narrow girdle of figleaves was attached. The costume of Adam was equally ridiculous, while God the Father appeared in an old dressing gown. . . . The comic element was provided by the devils . . . the old German plays . . . were not written out in full. The actors usually had just a scenario and played everything extempore. Hanswurst above all found abundant scope for his sallies. . . . A miserable wooden hut served as playhouse; the scenery was lamentable. . . . In a word, the theatre was an amusement for the mob.*

Quoted in F. J. von Reden-Esbeck, *Caroline Neuber und ihre Zeitgenossen* (Leipzig, 1881), 37.

Lessing, the first major German critic and playwright, more than any one else was responsible for turning German taste away from the French neoclassical ideal championed by Gottsched and his circle. In the final numbers of his *Hamburg Dramaturgy* (1767–1769), he sums up his fundamental views:

I set myself the task of judging . . . some of the most celebrated models of the French stage. For this stage is said to be formed quite in accordance with the rules of Aristotle, and it has been particularly attempted to persuade us Germans that only by these rules have the French attained to the degree of perfection from which they can look down on all the stages of modern peoples. We have long so firmly believed this, that with our poets, to imitate the French was regarded as much as to work according to the rules of the ancients.

Nevertheless this prejudice could not eternally stand against our feelings. These were fortunately roused from their slumbers by some English plays, and we at last experienced that tragedy was capable of another quite different effect from that accorded by Corneille and Racine. . . . No nation has more misapprehended the rules of ancient drama than the French.

Gotthold Ephraim Lessing, *Hamburg Dramaturgy*, trans. Helen Zimmern (New York: Bohn's Standard Library, 1890).

By the end of the eighteenth century Weimar's theatre was one of the best known in Germany because of Goethe and Schiller. In one of his many conversations with J. P. Eckermann, Goethe describes some of his methods for achieving what came to be called Weimar classicism:

I did not look to magnificent scenery and a brilliant wardrobe, but . . . to good pieces. . . . By means of good pieces I educated the actors. . . . I was, also, constantly in personal contact with the actors. I attended the readings of the plays, and explained to every one his part; I was present at the chief rehearsals, and talked with the actors as to any improvement that might be made; I was never absent from a performance, and pointed out the next day anything which did not appear to me to be right.

Conversations of Goethe with Eckermann and Soret, trans. John Oxenford (London, 1874), conversation of 22 March 1825.

Two actors who were coached by Goethe, Pius Alexander Wolff and Karl Franz Grüner, set down precepts they learned from their teacher. These were later arranged by Eckermann and published as Goethe's "rules for actors." Here are a few of the ninety-one rules:

35. . . . the actor must understand that he not only should imitate nature but present it ideally . . . uniting the true with the beautiful.

36. . . . the actor must gain complete control over every part of his body so that he may use each part freely, harmoniously and gracefully as expression demands.

39. The actors should not out of a mistaken idea of naturalness play to each other as if no third person were present. They should never play in profile or turn their backs to the audience. . . .

91. These rules are to be observed primarily when noble and worthy characters are to be represented.

Johann Wolfgang von Goethe, *Werke*, 40

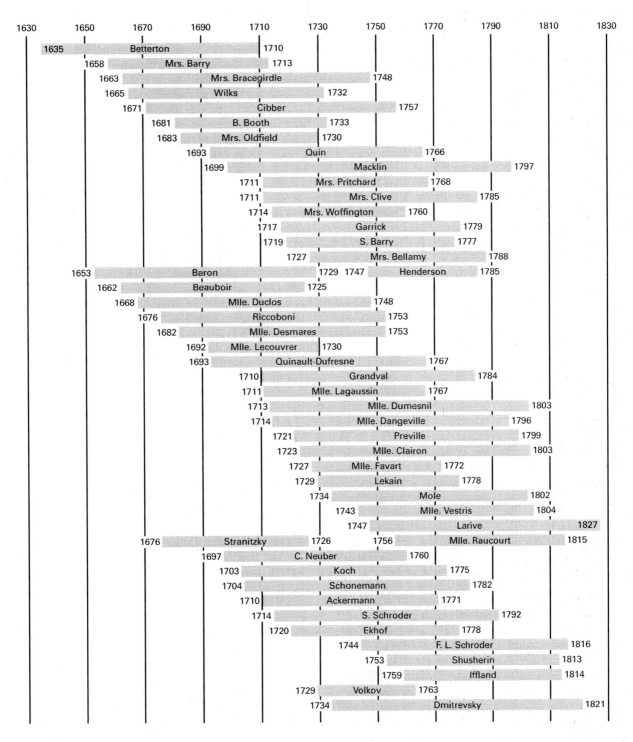

FIG. 12.34
Major European actors, 1700–1800.

13
Continental European Theatre in the Early Nineteenth Century

The nineteenth century was to bring the most radical social and political changes since the Renaissance. Most of the period from 1790 to 1850 was taken up with a struggle between those seeking to maintain the *status quo* and those working for a more equitable society. France played the key role in this struggle since the French Revolution was the principal motivating force.

What had begun in France in 1789 as a relatively modest demand for a constitutional monarchy soon became more radical, especially after other countries, worried that the Revolution might spread, declared war on France, and its royal family was accused of aiding the enemy. By 1792 France had been declared a republic, and in 1793 Louis XVI was guillotined. There followed the "reign of terror" during which thousands of persons were executed, many on mere suspicion of treason or lack of sympathy with the Revolution. This bloodbath finally ended in 1795, but by then most of the Revolution's major leaders had themselves been executed. Thereafter revolutionary fervor abated, but France's affairs, both internal and external, continued in disarray until Napoleon (1769–1821) came to power in 1799 and brought order out of chaos. In 1804 Napoleon named himself emperor, and between 1805 and 1812 gradually became master of practically all of Europe, placing members of his family or army on the thrones of Spain, Holland, and many German and Italian states. Thus, he assembled the most extensive European empire since Roman times. Within this empire he made many reforms. He abolished the Holy Roman Empire in 1806, reduced the number of German states to less than forty, and put an end to serfdom in parts of Eastern Europe.

In 1812 the tide began to turn against Napoleon. He was deposed in 1814 and after a brief comeback was defeated at the Battle of Waterloo and permanently exiled. The aftermath was a blow to liberal sentiments, for the Congress of Vienna (1814–1815) sought above all to restore the sociopolitical conditions that had existed before 1789, although it did not hesitate to alter national boundaries or to award territory to its major participants. As a result, after 1815 repressive regimes returned to power throughout Europe. For Spain, however, it was already too late. Wars of independence broke out among its North, Central, and South American colonies in 1810, and by 1828 it had lost all of them, retaining only its Caribbean holdings. Portugal lost Brazil in 1822.

The period after 1815 was one of great economic hardship. The Napoleonic wars had severely depleted Europe's resources, and the wars of independence in Latin America were followed by territorial conflicts among the new nations. Industrialization (which had been spurred on by the military needs created by war) accelerated as such inventions as the power loom, the steamship, and the locomotive promoted the factory system over individual craftsmen. Factories forced people to move into towns in order to be near their work. With urbanization came wretched living conditions that cried out for social legislation at a time when conservative governments viewed any request for reform as a prelude to revolution. Therefore, it is not surprising that around 1830 frustrations boiled over into a series of uprisings throughout Europe. Most were unsuccessful, and in many instances even more intense repression resulted. Not until after another series of revolutions in 1848 and 1849 did significant change begin. Industrialization, which led to competition among nations for raw materials and markets, fueled the desire to acquire additional overseas territories, bringing with it increased nationalism and imperialism.

It is within this context that the theatre operated during the first half of the nineteenth century. A new dramatic form, melodrama, with its action-packed stories, strong emotional appeals, and unambiguous moral tone became the most popular form of theatre in the Western world. At the same time, the movement called romanticism spread across the arts, bringing into the theatre exotic settings, the glorification of rugged individualism, a yearning for an idealized past, and an appeal to the concept of a higher truth.

THE THEATRE UNDER NAPOLEON—MELODRAMA AND ROMANTICISM

Theatre monopolies were abolished in Paris in 1791, leading to the proliferation of many new companies and the rapid decline of the old royally subsidized troupes. Actors sympathetic to the Revolution left the Comédie Française in 1792 to form the Théâtre de la République and this new company was soon considered the finest in Paris. The Comédie Italienne, renamed the Théâtre Favart, was dangerously weakened by its fierce competition with the Théâtre Feydeau, and the Opéra survived only because it was taken over by the city of Paris. Theatres vied with each other to appeal to the increasingly radical politics of the Parisian public. When Napoleon came to power in 1799, however, he immediately made clear his opposition to partisan drama by suppressing several plays favorable to his own cause. His government ordered the reuniting of the Comédie Française troupe, declared its theatre to be state property, and reinstated its pensions and subsidies. It ordered the Théâtre Feydeau and Théâtre Favart troupes to unite under the new name, Théâtre National de l'Opéra-Comique and gave it a subsidy. The Opéra

too was brought back under state control and granted a subsidy. In 1807 a new set of monopolies were established with the Comédie Française once again assigned exclusive rights to do regular comedy and tragedy, the Opéra given grand opera and serious ballet, the Opéra-Comique light opera and comic ballet, and the newly created subsidized theatre, the Théâtre de l'Impératrice, usually called the Odéon, assigned the lesser drama. The unsubsidized Théâtre de la Gâité and the Ambigu-Comique were allowed to do melodramas and pantomimes while the Théâtre des Variétés and the Vaudeville were allowed to perform short plays, parodies, and *comédies-en-vaudevilles*. All other theatres were closed, though the Porte-Saint-Martin and the Cirque Olympique were eventually allowed to reopen, performing minor genres. These strictures continued under the restored monarchy in 1815 until the uprising of 1830 brought another reorganization.

Napoleon sought to pattern his empire after Rome, so he favored neoclassical drama. It was not neoclassical plays, however, but melodramas that attracted the audiences. Although melodramatic works, most often in the guise of tragicomedy or pastoral, can be traced back to classical Greece, the term *mélodrame* does not appear until 1766 and did not come into widespread use until after 1800. August von Kotzebue's play, *Misanthropy and Repentance* (1789) is often cited as the first true melodrama. In translation it was possibly the most performed play in Paris in the early 1790s. But the characteristic elements of melodrama had long been present in many of the boulevard theatres. It was left to René Charles Guilbert de Pixérécourt (1773–1844), with *Victor, or The Child of the Forest* (1798), *Coelina* (1800), and numerous others of his 120 plays, to give melodrama its most distinctive form. The remarkable success of the plays of Kotzebue and Pixérécourt established melodrama as the dominant dramatic type of the nineteenth century.

Melodramas were complex and varied but their basic characteristics can be summarized briefly:

1. A focus on emotional appeal. The manipulation of emotion was given priority over plausibility of the story or depth of the characterization.
2. Musical underscoring of emotion. Music was played throughout, generally as a background to the action but also as songs or dances within the plot. This distinctive use of music was incorporated into the film industry when it began at the end of the century.
3. Vocal and physical underscoring of emotion. The texts were written for a style of acting that emphasized powerful vocal delivery and emphatic gesturing.

4. Virtue under siege. A virtuous hero (or heroine) is relentlessly hounded by a villain and will undergo a seemingly insurmountable series of threats to life, reputation, or happiness.

5. Strict poetic justice. The plays end in a way that satisfied the moral beliefs of the audience. Generally the villain is defeated and may even be reformed. The virtuous are saved and rewarded though in some melodramas, like those dealing with the evils of gambling, alcoholism, or slavery, the moral point being made may require that some of the virtuous find their reward after death.

6. Comic relief. There is generally a comic sidekick to one of the principal characters whose statements and actions counterpoint the emotional seriousness of the story.

7. Fast-paced, episodic, and sensational action. After a short expository scene, the story progresses quickly, with all important events occurring on stage, often with elaborate spectacle (battles, floods, or earthquakes) and local color (festivals, dances, or picturesque working conditions).

8. Extensive use of typical plot devices. The plays incorporated numerous instances of fortunate coincidence, concealed identity, startling discoveries, reversals, and other devices. Each act ends with a strong climax or "curtain line."

Melodrama was written in a three-act structure. It could be understood and enjoyed by the least sophisticated of theatregoers at a time when people were moving to cities in unprecedented numbers. Consequently, it attracted larger audiences than had been seen in the theatre before or since. Melodramas also made full use of all the technical capabilities of nineteenth-century theatre buildings. The texts and the acting style worked together to create compelling performances that could hold audiences spellbound. Unfortunately, the text of melodrama, like film scripts in the twentieth century, do not lend themselves to literary study. Their prolific use of plot devices and dependency on a forceful acting style also made them easy to ridicule, even in their own day. Later generations, therefore, tended to dismiss the form in spite of its enormous appeal on the nineteenth-century stage and in twentieth-century cinema.

The vitality of the theatre in the Germanic states was curtailed by the French occupation (1805–1815), during which many state troupes lost their subsidies. Nevertheless, these theatres championed the trend towards historic accuracy in costumes and settings, revolutionized theatre architecture, and introduced the dramatic form we call romanticism, the most significant challenge to the theories of neoclassicism in over 200 years. The companies in two cities, Berlin and Vienna, stood out above all the others during this period. At the National Theater in Berlin, Iffland mounted the most sumptuous productions to be seen in the German theatre. His production of Schiller's *The Maid of Orleans* (1801), designed by Bartolomeo Verona, for example, featured a coronation procession with over 200 extras in period dress, before a Gothic cathedral setting.

Even greater emphasis on historic accuracy in costumes and sets was undertaken by Count Karl Brühl (1772–1837), who ran the theatre from 1814 to 1828. His principal designer, Karl Friedrich Schinkel (1781–1841), also designed a new theatre for the company in 1820. The classical revival style of this building, along with its half-circle auditorium and its extensive work space, influenced almost all subsequent theatre architecture in Germany for the rest of the century.

In 1810 Vienna's state theatre, the Burgtheater, became the first theatre in the Germanic states to restrict its repertory to spoken drama. Under the leadership of Josef Schreyvogel (1768–1832), who ran the theatre from 1814 to 1832, it popularized the idea that a theatre's repertory should reflect the nation's culture. The Burgtheater developed an outstanding acting company with an ensemble style that was compared to that of Iffland's Mannheim school in the way it melded the restrained, classical style of the Weimar school with the more vigorous, naturalistic style developed by Friedrich Schröder and known as the Hamburg school. Schreyvogel emphasized beauty and grace in acting and in pictorial composition and he prided himself on the historic accuracy of the designs provided by Philip von Stubenrauch, who worked at the Burgtheater from 1810 to 1848.

A change in the German consciousness became prominent under Napoleonic dominance. Influenced by trends in philosophy and the visual arts, German writers were developing an increasing sense of nationalism and a fascination with their Teutonic past, which they idealized as a time when people lived in a natural state, free from the shackles of despotic rulers. The closet dramas of the *Storm-and-Stress* playwrights, along with the regularly produced plays of Lessing, Goethe, Schiller, and Shakespeare, inspired a growing faith in feeling and instinct as guides to moral behavior. These trends contributed to shaping a new view of human nature, political theory, and literary forms, which around 1800 became known as romanticism.

The Romantics borrowed liberally from the writings of Immanuel Kant (1742–1804) and other idealist philosophers in formulating the theoretical basis of a "romantic" art. The philosophical foundations of Romanticism are complex, but the fundamental tenets can be outlined:

FIG. 13.1
Werner's *The Twenty-Fourth of February*, Act V. From *Le Monde Dramatique*.

1. Beyond earthly existence there is a higher truth. All that exists has been created by an absolute being (variously called God, Spirit, Idea, Ego) and all things are therefore part of the whole and of each other. Since all creation has a common origin, a thorough and careful observation of any part may give insights into the whole. Truth, then, can be viewed in relation to infinite variety rather than to observable norms as the neoclassicist had held.

2. The less a thing deviates from its natural state, the more likely it is to embody some fundamental truth. In drama this often translated into a preference for topics involving people in rebellion against the unnatural restraints of a highly structured and bureaucratic society—the kind of society neoclassicists had thought was necessary.

3. Human beings, held back by their physical limitations, can never grasp truth in its totality. Humanity longs for some ideal existence but is kept from achieving it. We must live in the physical world but our spirits constantly strive to transcend this limitation.

4. Through the glimpses of ultimate truth provided by art, people become more fully aware of their potential—artistically, socially, and politically.

5. Only an exceptional imagination can perceive the final unity behind the apparently endless diversity of existence, and only the artist-genius and the philosopher has this. The artist is a truly superior being capable of providing guidance for others willing to listen.

FIG. 13.2
Grillparzer's *The Dream of Life*, Act IV. Engraving by Andreas Geiger. Courtesy Bildarchiv, Osterreichische Nationalbibliothek, Vienna.

In the romantic scheme, art is of enormous significance since it gives eternal truth a concrete, material form that can be apprehended by the limited human sensory apparatus. Romantic theory implies, however, that complete happiness and truth are to be found only in the spiritual realm. Therefore, the romantic playwrights were faced with an impossible task, for not only was the highest truth always just beyond their grasp, but the physical limitations of the stage made it nearly impossible to realize their great artistic visions. Many of the romantic dramatists, therefore, refused to write with the realities of staging in mind, preferring instead the freedom of "closet" drama for a reading public. This made the number of romantic plays actually seen on stage relatively small, but the movement still had enormous influence in stimulating a rethinking of the nature of the arts. Its interest in variety rather than neoclassical norms and its concern with an idealized past helped to feed the trend towards historic accuracy in costume and setting. Its concept of the artist-genius encouraged first the star system, then the advent of the director in theatre. Romanticism followed the *Storm-and-Stress* school, in its all-out rejection of neoclassicism, yet it recognized the value of the five-act structure and use of poetic language in drama—two characteristics of the form that separate it from melodrama.

Romanticism first reached ordinary theatregoers through productions of "fate tragedy," which were in great vogue between 1810 and 1820. Fate tragedy was initiated by Zacharias Werner's (1768–1823) *The Twenty-Fourth of February* (1809), which tells of a series of widely separated tragic events, all stemming from a curse and all occurring on the 24th of February. Among those who actually called themselves

FIG. 13.3

Nestroy's *The Ground Floor and the First Floor*, showing the use of two settings simultaneously, one above the other. Engraving from *Theaterzeitung*. Courtesy Bildarchiv, Osterreichische Nationalbibliothek, Vienna.

romantics, Schlegel and Tieck were the most deeply concerned with theatre.

August Wilhelm Schlegel (1767–1845) formulated and disseminated romantic theory in Germany and elsewhere through his lectures and essays. Schlegel was the first critic to use classicism and romanticism as polar terms, and it was largely through his influence that they passed into currency almost everywhere. In his criticism Schlegel paid little attention to dramatic form, preferring to discuss tragic and comic "moods" as states of perception out of which differing types of drama come. Mood, emotion, and character were for him the main ingredients of drama, while plot was treated as a contrivance used by lesser playwrights to keep a story moving. This conception of dramatic elements dominated much critical thought after Schlegel's time and shifted attention from structure to vision. Schlegel considered Shakespeare to be the greatest of all dramatists and translated seventeen of Shakespeare's plays.

Ludwig Tieck (1773–1853) was the most involved in the application of romantic ideals on the stage and did more even than Schlegel to familiarize Germans with the works of Shakespeare. *Kaiser Octavianus* (1802) is the best known of Tieck's romantic dramas. Set in the Middle Ages, its subject is the development of Christianity and the union of all humanity in a universal church. Its extremely episodic plot is held together by the allegorical figure, Romance. The prologue became famous for its evocation of twilight as that time when the logic of daylight meets the mystery and magic of night. Tieck's contemporaries considered this passage so characteristic of the romantics that they dubbed them the "twilight men."

The most successful of his dramatic works, however, were "fantastic comedies" based on such fairy tales as "Little Red Riding Hood" and "Puss in Boots" which serving as springboards for his satirical comments on eighteenth-century rationalism. These comedies are surprisingly modern in tone, breaking dramatic illusion frequently, and calling attention to the theatrical medium and to contemporary artistic taste.

The ideas of the German romantics were eventually disseminated throughout Europe and the Americas (where they encouraged the idealization of lost native cultures), although seldom were they articulated so completely or consciously as they had been in Germany. It is ironic, then, that the German dramatist of this period who is now most highly regarded was not a romantic. Heinrich von Kleist (1777–1811) was more interested in the sensual than the spiritual. Though overlooked in his own day, many of his plays still figure prominently in the German repertory and his *The Prince of Homburg* (1811) is universally regarded as a masterpiece. In it, a young army officer is sentenced to die even though his disobedience of an order led to a military victory. Following a scene in which he comes to recognize that his action was motivated by ambition, he is pardoned. Kleist here seems to be concerned with the conflict between selfishness and selflessness.

GERMAN-LANGUAGE DRAMA AFTER NAPOLEON

The melodramatic/romantic plays of Kotzebue, along with the plays of Iffland, Goethe, Schiller, and Shakespeare remained popular for some time after 1815. Still, Austria produced a number of influential actor/playwrights who wrote the kind of folk and peasant play that had dominated the repertories since Stranitzky created Hanswurst around 1707. This long tradition culminated in the plays of Ferdinand Raimund (1790–1836) and Johann Nepomuk Nestroy (1801–1862). Both writers incorporated traditional regional dialects, folklore, allegory, farce, and fantasy into their works, but they also increasingly used scenes of realistic peasant life. Nestroy's use of four apartments shown simultaneously on stage, two above and two below, in *The House of Temperaments* (1837), was an innovation in simultaneous staging that inspired the imagination of later authors. His play, *Out for a Lark* (1842) was not only a great success in its own day but also served as the basis for Thornton Wilder's famous play, *The Matchmaker* (1954), and later for Tom Stoppard's *On the Razzle* (1981). Franz Grillparzer (1791–1872) was Austria's first major serious dramatist and the first to express the general sense of disillusionment that followed the

Congress of Vienna. He began his career in 1817 with *The Ancestress* (a melodramatic work likened by critics to the fate tragedy then in vogue) and wrote regularly for the stage until 1838. His plays range through classical subjects, as in the trilogy *The Golden Fleece* (1821); history, as in *The Jewess of Toledo* (1837); and philosophical fantasy, as in *The Dream of Life* (1834) inspired by Calderón's *Life is a Dream*. In his plays, the protagonists usually are rootless or alienated from their society. Motivated by some high ideal, they strive for reconciliation with others or with themselves but usually end in disaster.

Of those writing serious plays in the rest of the Germanic states, Grabbe, Büchner, and Hebbel stand out. Christian Dietrich Grabbe (1801–1836), like Kleist before him, was ignored during his lifetime but is now recognized as a precursor of expressionism, epic theatre, and absurdism. Grabbe used a chaotic structure in plays like *Comedy, Satire, Irony, and Deeper Meaning* (1822) to depict his views

FIG. 13.5

The coronation procession from Schiller's *The Maid of Orleans* as staged by Iffland at the Berlin National Theater in 1801. This production was one of the first anywhere to emphasize historical accuracy in costumes and scenery, although many elements were more nearly sixteenth than fifteenth century, the time of the action. From Weddigen, *Geschichte der Theater Deutschlands* (1904).

FIG. 13.4

Hebbel's *Agnes Bernauer* at the Burgtheater, Vienna, 1868. The performers are Friedrich Krastel as Albrecht and Friederike Bognar as Agnes. Courtesy Osterreichische Nationalbibliothek, Vienna.

of society as a tangle of selfish interests, outworn clichés, and static conventions. In the final scene Grabbe himself appears as a character. Most of his plays are difficult to stage even today, however. *Napoleon, or the One Hundred Days* (1831), for example, demands the European continent as a stage and has the populace as protagonist.

Georg Büchner (1813–1837) was also ignored in his own day but inspired later movements. He wrote only three plays but they seem the precursors of expressionism in their structure and of naturalism in their subject matter. His play, *Danton's Death* (1835), is an episodic drama set during the "reign of terror" following the French Revolution. Its central character is an idealist who, seeing his highest aims wrecked by pettiness, comes to suspect that his ideals were merely a disguise for sensual appetites.

FIG. 13.6
Ludwig Tieck's production of *A Midsummer Night's Dream* in Berlin, 1843. Note the tapestries downstage on either side; note also the steps that curve up to form an inner stage between them. A contemporary lithograph.

His superior sensitivity causes him to question the meaning of existence but will permit no resolution of his doubts, leaving him to end in despair and death. Büchner's unfinished play, *Woyzeck* (1836), is the first to treat a lower-class protagonist sympathetically. It shows the gradual degradation of a man trapped by his heredity and environment, a topic that would be taken up by the naturalists around mid-century.

Friedrich Hebbel (1813–1863) began his play-writing career in 1840 with *Judith*. Among his most important works are *Maria Magdalena* (1844), *Agnes Bernauer* (1853), and the trilogy *The Niebelung* (1855–1862). Like many of his contemporaries, Hebbel embraced the romantic outlook but later underwent a serious crisis in belief. He came to view society as a reflection of the Absolute Spirit which lies behind human existence and works out its own perfection through humanity, a concept he borrowed from the philosopher Hegel. In Hebbel's view, the most significant human problems arise because values tend to harden into conventional patterns rather than remaining flexible to meet changing situations. Consequently, advances in morality are accomplished only after a violent conflict has destroyed worthwhile human beings seeking a better way of life because only their deaths will raise enough doubts about the old patterns to make way for new ones. Since the new values will rigidify in their turn, the process must be repeated. Most of the protagonists in Hebbel's plays are women and their stories reflect his preoccupation with this moral evolution. His most famous play, *Maria Magdalena,* is now usually studied as a forerunner of realism because its characters are drawn from ordinary life, its dialogue is in prose, and its story ends in the suicide of the heroine, a victim of society's narrow-mindedness.

Following the abortive revolutions of 1830 a new movement—Young Germany—came to the fore and provided some of the most controversial plays of the 1830s and 1840s. In many ways quite diverse, its members were united by their scorn for the abstraction and idealism of romanticism. They championed social awareness and the relevance of ideas to contemporary affairs. Consequently, the writers were often in trouble with the censors and only after the revolution of 1848 were their works widely produced. Though their plays were too firmly tied to contemporary situations to remain in the repertory for very long, they did inspire later movements that insisted that theatre should be used as a tool for political or social change.

THEATRICAL CONDITIONS IN GERMAN-LANGUAGE THEATRES

While the downfall of Napoleon brought the reinstatement of financial aid, it also brought greater political control. In many states censorship became quite severe. Government officials, many with no theatrical experience, were appointed as superintendents of state theatres and too often favored routine efficiency over artistic excellence. Still the theatre in general prospered. Actors were relatively secure because they were civil servants with pension rights. Companies were provided with buildings that had good facilities and deficits were made up by the state. By 1842 the German states had sixty-five permanent theatres employing about 5000 actors, singers, and musicians. By 1850 both state and municipal governments took it for granted that they should support the theatre, and because of this attitude each sizable city had a troupe of reasonably good quality.

Throughout this period the contrast between actors who trained in the romantic style first championed by Schröder in Hamburg, and those who favored the more stately classical style promoted by Goethe at Weimar, was seen in theatres throughout the Germanic states—often within the same company. The ensemble performance attained by Schröder and Goethe, however, was in decline as emphasis shifted to starring performers (perhaps because of the romantic glorification of individual genius). Since stars did minimal rehearsals with the local companies and often insisted that other roles be curtailed so as not to detract from their own, ensemble performance became increasingly difficult. Such starring engagements grew in number during the nineteenth century, especially after the opening of the first railroad in 1835, thereby accelerating the decline in ensembles. This growth also brought stars into conflict with another trend of the period, the move towards putting every aspect of a production under the control of a single master artist or director.

A trend toward the use of historical accuracy for the creation of spectacle was evident in virtually all of the German theatres at this time. In costuming, however, five generalized periods were considered sufficient for all plays set in past eras: classical, medieval, sixteenth century, seventeenth century, and mid-eighteenth century. More precise treatment was not to come until after 1850, when additional information became readily available in Jakob Weiss's authoritative histories of costume (published between 1856 and 1872). Historic accuracy in setting could be more precise but it was still achieved through painting on the traditional wing, drop and border units which continued to be changed by use of a chariot-and-pole system or by the less expensive groove system. Box sets were occasionally created for interiors by filling in the spaces between the wings with door or window flats. Gradually, other units were added, until the acting area was completely enclosed to create a more realistic effect. The first fully developed box set in Berlin was used in 1826 but the box set did not become common until about 1875.

Ludwig Tieck, whose interests in theatre extended far beyond his work as a playwright, provided the most influential alternatives to the growing spectacle of the German stage. He was a Shakespeare scholar who was among the first to investigate the way plays were staged in Shakespeare's day. In 1836 he persuaded the great German architect, Gottfried Semper (1803–1879), to study the existing contract for London's Fortune playhouse of 1600 and make drawings for a possible reconstruction, the first such attempt of its kind. In his novel, *The Young Master Cabinetmaker* (1837), he described what he thought a performance of *Twelfth Night* would have been like on an Elizabethan public stage. Through this work he came to believe that true illusion results from convincing acting, which is destroyed by scenic spectacle, and he began to advocate a return to the stages that existed before the advent of the proscenium arch.

Tieck served as literary advisor (or *Dramaturg*) to the Dresden state theatre from 1824 until 1842. He had considerable influence on the quality of its repertory but his ideas on staging were considered impractical. Only Karl Immermann (1796–1840), director of the Düsseldorf Municipal Theatre, attempted to apply Tieck's ideas by using a fixed façade around three sides of an open space for a private performance of *Twelfth Night* given in 1840. In 1841, however, William IV of Prussia decided to devote his court theatre at Potsdam to experimental productions. He summoned Tieck to stage Sophocles' *Antigone,* and gave him complete authority over the production. Tieck extended the apron over the orchestra pit in a semicircle and constructed a Greek *skene,* which served as the only background for the action. After its success at Potsdam, the production was moved to the state theatre in Berlin and was soon adapted by companies at Dresden, Leipzig, Mannheim, Munich, and Karlsruhe. But Tieck's most famous production was of Shakespeare's *A Midsummer Night's Dream,* presented in 1843 with incidental music by Felix Mendelssohn. For it, Tieck adapted Elizabethan conventions to the proscenium stage. Letting the forward part of the stage form a large open space, he constructed a unit at the rear, with curving stairs leading to an acting area eight feet above the main stage with another beneath it at stage level. The sides of the stage were masked by tapestries hung at right angles to the proscenium. This production was repeated forty times at the Berlin theatre during the first season and was imitated by numerous troupes throughout Germany. Tieck's experiments with the pre-proscenium Greek and Shake-

FIG. 13.7
Immermann's stage for Shakespeare's *Twelfth Night*, 1840. The forestage and façade remained unchanged but some scenic pieces were changed within or behind the openings at rear. Courtesy Theatermuseum, Munich.

spearean stages would not be widely copied until the Munich Art Theatre took them up again in 1889.

Throughout the first half of the nineteenth century the German-language theatre enjoyed considerable popularity. In general it was prosperous, and the number of companies steadily increased. Not only were theatres opened in cities previously without them, but in such major centers as Vienna and Berlin several theatres were in operation simultaneously. They would continue to grow in number during the second half of the century.

FRENCH DRAMA AFTER NAPOLEON

The romantic movement was slow in getting underway in France because of political conditions. Its first important impetus came with the publication of Mme de Staël's *Of Germany,* which described the beginnings of the movement in Germany. A bitter enemy of Napoleon, she spent the years of his reign in the Germanic states where Schlegel was, for a time, tutor to her children. *Of Germany* was published in France in 1810 but was immediately suppressed. Following Napoleon's downfall in 1815, it was quickly reissued. The notoriety of Mme de Staël's feud with Napoleon brought the book much publicity and thereafter the debate over the relative merits of neoclassicism and romanticism raged in earnest. Stendhal (Marie-Henri Beyle, 1783–1842) contributed to the controversy with *Racine and Shakespeare* (1823–1825), in which he declared Shakespeare's plays to be more suitable as models for dramatists than those of Racine. But the major French statement of romantic doctrine came in Hugo's preface to his play *Cromwell* (1827). Victor Hugo (1802–1885) called for the abandonment of the unities of time and place, denounced the strict separation of genres, and advocated placing dramatic actions within specific historical milieus. Perhaps most important, he insisted that art should go beyond the neoclassicist's "idealized nature" to one that included both the sublime and the grotesque. Since for Hugo the sublime was related to spiritual qualities and the grotesque to animal nature, he argued that a truthful depiction of humanity requires that both be represented.

Several events accelerated the trend toward romanticism in France: Charles Kemble's troupe of English actors had performed Shakespeare's plays to admiring Parisian audiences in 1827; W. C. Macready had appeared in Paris in English romantic plays in 1828; Sir Walter Scott's novels were attracting a wide reading public; and Shakespeare's plays were being read and produced with increasing frequency. Furthermore, French romantic plays were making their way into the repertory with plays like Alexandre Dumas *père's Henri*

III and His Court and Alfred de Vigny's adaptation of *Othello* as *The Moor of Venice* being produced in 1829. The culmination of the debate came in 1830 with the production of Hugo's *Hernani* at the Comédie Française. A pitched battle between the romantics and traditionalists, during which the actors were scarcely heard, raged for several nights. The bitterness of the contest is probably explained by the feeling on both sides that principles involving the future course of the theatre were at stake.

Hernani tells the story of the noble outlaw, Hernani, and his attempt to wed Dona Sol over the opposition of the king and her guardian, both of whom also love her. Eventually he succeeds, and a happy future seems to lie ahead when he is reminded of a pledge made to the guardian earlier in a moment of crisis—that Hernani would give his life if the guardian ever demanded it. When the vindictive guardian asks that the pledge be redeemed, the couple chooses suicide above a dishonored oath. In *Hernani,* Hugo deliberately violated many of the rules that the advocates of neoclassicism sought to retain.

1. He made innovations in the alexandrine, the standard verse form for neoclassical tragedy.
2. He used many words considered beneath the dignity of tragedy.
3. He shifted the mood of his scenes frequently and mixed humor with seriousness.
4. He showed deaths and violence on stage.
5. He broke the unities of time and place.

It is usual to date French romanticism from the triumph of *Hernani.* But the upsurge in the production of romantic plays is probably also explained by the lifting of censorship (later reimposed) and the easing of genre restrictions following the Revolution of 1830. In addition to Hugo, whose popularity continued to increase with such plays as *Marion Delorme* (1831), *The King Amuses Himself* (1832—made into the opera *Rigoletto* by Giuseppe Verdi), and *Ruy Blas* (1838), other important dramatists include Dumas *père,* Musset, and Sand.

The ninety or so plays of Alexandre Dumas *père* (1802–1870) are of two types: historical spectacles, such as his dramatization of his novel *The Three Musketeers* (1844); and domestic dramas, such as *Antony* (1831). Although Dumas had a surer sense of dramatic situation than did Hugo, he lacked Hugo's poetic gift and ability to express profound emotion or significant thought.

Alfred de Musset's (1810–1857) plays are primarily concerned with the inner feelings of his characters, especially their inability to resist love's compelling force. Musset's characters are essentially selfish, however, and seek desperately to protect their egos by

FIG. 13.8
The expansion of France under Napoleon.

FIG. 13.9
Pixérécourt's *The Marseilles Plague*, Act III, at the Théâtre de la Gâité, Paris, 1828. Setting by Gué. Note the various levels and numerous entrances and places of concealment. Courtesy Bibliothèque de l'Arsenal, Paris.

forcing others to reveal their feelings first. But since the others also are hesitant to lay themselves open to hurt or rejection, the participants indulge in a series of ploys and counterploys. His *Lorenzaccio* (1834), the story of a Hamlet-like character who seeks to right the Florentine state, is one of the finest historical dramas of the nineteenth century.

George Sand (Aurore Dupin Dudevant, 1804–1876) was one of the few women who made an impact as a dramatist in this period, although she was better known as a novelist. Some twenty-five of her plays were performed in Paris between 1840 and 1872. Her first produced play, *Cosima* (1840), concerns a married woman who enters into a love affair largely out of boredom. *Francois le Champi* (1849), a realistic folk play, was a great success and was revived often.

Following the easing of genre restrictions, romantic drama found a ready home in the boulevard theatres. There it mingled with melodrama and absorbed still more melodramatic traits even as it helped to elevate that genre. But by the mid 1840s the enthusiasm for romantic drama had waned. The failure of Hugo's *Les Burgraves* in 1843 is usually considered to mark the end of the brief romantic era in France. Romanticism was succeeded by the

FIG. 13.10
The battle over *Hernani,* 1830. Onstage is the final
scene. From Grand Carteret, *XIXe Siècle* (1892).

"Theatre of Common Sense," which sought a middle ground between neoclassicism and romanticism. But, as with most compromises, it also soon lost its appeal. By the 1850s it was giving way to still another movement—realism.

THEATRICAL CONDITIONS IN FRANCE TO THE 1850s

The number of theatres in Paris grew steadily during the first half of the nineteenth century. Although the government retained firm control over licensing, the eight companies authorized by Napoleon in 1807 had grown to twenty-eight by 1855. Of these, the four state-supported troupes commanded the greatest prestige and the Opéra remained the most favored. Not only was its subsidy often four times as great as that of the Comédie Française, but between 1811 and 1831 it was allotted up to one-twentieth of the receipts of all private theatres. After genre restrictions were eased in 1831, the Odéon and Opéra-Comique often rivaled the Opéra and the Comédie Française in the quality of works presented and in the mounting of their productions. The boulevard theatres remained the most innovative, often championing new playwrights or methods of production long before they were accepted by the state troupes.

Of the secondary theatres, the most influential were the Vaudeville, Gymnase, Porte-Saint-Martin, Gâité, and Ambigu-Comique.

Parisian theatres (with a few minor exceptions) were run by managers who hired actors on contract. State theatres were let (under renewable contracts) to managers who had full control over the performers and the repertory, although their work was subject to close governmental scrutiny. The Comédie Française, however, continued to be a sharing company. Ostensibly the actors were responsible for all policy decisions, but as the century progressed, the government-appointed supervisor assumed considerable authority.

All the Parisian theatres retained the repertory system although the long runs began to alter the old patterns. In the early years of the century, the bill was changed every day and only unusually popular plays were performed for several consecutive nights. But as early as 1835 a run of one hundred nights had been achieved and this trend continued, though runs of this length were not common until the 1870s.

Spectators at Parisian theatres had to present their tickets to three persons: the theatre's official ticket taker; the government employee, who made a record of the poor tax; and a representative of the Society of Dramatic Authors, who calculated royalties. The Society of Dramatic Authors, which succeeded the Bureau Dramatique in 1829, was a "closed shop" that boycotted any theatre refusing to accept its authority over contracts. The standard contract specified the maximum permissible delay between the acceptance and production of a play, required that each play be performed at least three times, and allowed a cessation of rehearsals for ten days so that authors might revise their work. Dramatists received from 10 to 15 percent of each performance's receipts. The society also established a pension fund for playwrights who had been members for more than twenty years and who had had more than a minimum number of plays produced. French playwrights were the first in the world to collect a royalty for each performance of their works and to achieve the financial security of a pension fund.

Every theatre had a *claque,* a well-organized and well-trained group of audience members who were paid to respond in certain ways to the plays. Claques were first employed by dramatists wanting to ensure the success of their plays, especially if the first night did not go as well as expected. Gradually star actors began to specify in their contracts the amount of applause they were to receive at their first entrance in each play, and the claque provided this. As a result of this prearranged approval, other spectators often restricted overt response to show only their disapproval.

But outside claques could also be hired by those who wanted to undermine a production with negative responses, and this could lead to a competition between claques with one responding positively while another responded negatively to the same moment in a performance.

DIRECTING AND ACTING IN FRANCE TO THE 1850s

In France melodrama initiated a concern for "directing," for much of its effect depended upon the precise manipulation of coincidence and spectacle. Plots often evolved around overheard conversations, fortunate entrances, and spectacular feats of physical courage. The resolutions often saw the villain foiled by an earthquake, a volcanic eruption, or some other fortuitous cataclysm. The effectiveness of many melodramas, therefore, depended upon the precise coordination of many elements. It was for this reason that Pixérécourt insisted upon absolute control over the staging of his works. He later declared that his preeminence as a dramatist was due to his care in production.

Pixérécourt's example was followed by several of the romantics, and above all by Hugo. But, whereas Pixérécourt had been concerned primarily with the coordination of special effects, Hugo was additionally concerned with the actor's stage positions and the overall composition. Prior to 1830, French actors tended to form a straight line or semicircle at the front of the stage near the prompter's box, for though the amount of stage furniture had begun to increase by the 1820s, it was seldom used by the actors and was treated primarily as decoration. Movement involved following the established traditions of giving and taking focus. Contrary to earlier practices, Hugo utilized the entire stage space, replaced the usual long diagonal movements with short curved movements, and even occasionally had an actor play a scene with his back to the audience. By 1835 critics were noting that in the boulevard theatres actors sometimes sat on the arms of chairs, leaned on tables, or remained seated while speaking. Still, most directors were more concerned with picturesque local color, historical accuracy, or precision of stage business than with creating an illusion of real life. Those who did move toward greater lifelikeness met considerable opposition from critics, who argued that art should idealize rather than copy life.

Throughout the first half of the nineteenth century French actors continued to be employed according to lines of business. But, as elsewhere, there was a trend toward stars. Even at the Comédie Française leading actors were listed on the bills after 1805 as a means of stimulating audience interest. Among those who were the greatest draws were Talma, Mlle Mars, Mlle George, and Rachel.

François-Joseph Talma (1763–1826), often called the greatest of all French actors, spent much of his youth in England, but returned to France in 1785 and was one of the first students at the École Royale Dramatique when it opened in 1786. Entering the Comédie Française in 1787, he was a constant source of friction because of his dissatisfaction with the troupe's acting style, costuming practices, and politics. However, after the troupe was reunited in 1799, Talma became and remained its acknowledged leader until his death. He was a favorite of Napoleon, who summoned him to play before the rulers of Europe. Talma was devoted to authenticity in costume (at least for classical roles) and to detailed study of every role. To this care, he joined intense feeling and vigor. It is sometimes said that he was by temperament a romantic but by circumstance doomed to perform in neoclassical plays.

Mlle Mars (1779–1847), on the stage from childhood, joined the Comédie Française in 1799 and

FIG. 13.11

Talma as Titus in Voltaire's *Brutus* in 1791. From Adolphe Jullien, *Histoire du Costume au Théâtre* (1880).

after 1805 was the idol of Paris. She created Dona Sol in *Hernani* and all critics spoke of her in glowing terms. When the Comédie Française began to go into debt in the 1830s, she resigned as a *sociétaire* so that she might demand an exorbitant salary as a *pensionnaire,* thus setting a precedent that was to plague the troupe through much of the century. She continued to play young heroines until her retirement at the age of 62.

Mlle George (1787–1867), daughter of a provincial manager, made her debut at the Comédie Française in 1802 at the age of fifteen. Her rivalry with Mlle Duchenois (*c.* 1777–1835), who was Talma's usual companion in tragedy, was intensified when Napoleon took her as his mistress and the Empress Josephine retaliated by taking Mlle Duchenois

under her protection. In 1808 Mlle George left Paris to play in St. Petersburg, Stockholm, and elsewhere before returning in 1813. After Napoleon's downfall, she fled France once more. She returned in 1822 and when Romantic dramas came into vogue in the 1830s, her performances did much to popularize the new form.

Rachel (1821–1858) made her professional debut in 1837 at the Gymnase. In 1838 she was engaged at the Comédie Française, where she soon became its major attraction. Like Mlle Mars before her, she insisted on an enormous salary (sometimes equaling that of France's prime minister). Her performances revived the popularity of the classical repertory, which had declined markedly after romanticism came to the fore, but while she filled the Comédie

FIG. 13.12
Rachel's farewell appearance during a highly successful engagement at Her Majesty's Theatre in London, 1841. Courtesy Theatre Museum, Victoria and Albert Museum, London.

Française on the nights when she played, she impoverished the company by taking most of the receipts. Largely because of this experience, the Comédie has refused to give any performer star billing to this day and lists all actors according to seniority. Rachel's repertory was not large, and only one of her major roles, Scribe's Adrienne Lecouvreur, was from a contemporary play, but her death throes in that role aroused both admiration and horror for their lifelikeness. By 1841 she was touring throughout Europe and even appeared in America in 1855. Her intensity and power established a standard remembered through the rest of the century.

The success of melodrama, romantic plays, and other "minor" forms brought many boulevard actors to the fore. Of these, the most influential were Deburau and Lemaître. Jean-Baptiste Deburau (1796–1846) was born into a family of touring acrobats. In 1811 he settled in Paris, where he was associated principally with the Théâtre des Funambules. His fame came after 1825 as he developed the character Pierrot, a pale, lovesick, ever-hopeful seeker after happiness. In this role he became one of the most popular performers in Paris and the Pierrot character he created was often copied. Frédérick Lemaître (1800–1876) was the most renowned romantic actor in France. He entered the Conservatoire at the age of fifteen and performed at the circus in pantomime and melodrama while still undergoing this rigorous classical training. In 1823 he achieved renown by turning the villain of a melodrama into a comic caricature. Thereafter he took considerable liberties with his roles until he was employed by the Odéon and Porte-Saint-Martin, where he became a dedicated performer. Lemaître was the most versatile actor of his day, for he refused to be bound by the usual lines of business. He delighted in astonishing audiences by novel interpretations and passionate outbursts. The peak of his popularity was reached between 1830 and 1850, but he went on acting until his death.

SCENERY, COSTUME, AND LIGHTING IN FRANCE TO THE 1850s

Although local color and historically accurate motifs had been introduced before the Revolution, they were not exploited fully until the nineteenth century. During the 1790s many managers sought to re-create actual places and real events, but a consistent emphasis upon spectacle first became evident in the boulevard theatres between 1800 and 1830. Here it served at least two major functions: as a plot device in dramatic action and as a novelty designed to attract audiences. Both promoted the increased use of detailed settings and special effects.

Early nineteenth-century melodramas often depended upon natural disasters to forward the plot. Pixérécourt's *The Exile's Daughter,* for example, shows a flood uprooting trees, inundating the stage, and carrying the heroine away on a plank. Similarly, his *Death's Head* uses a volcanic eruption to engulf the stage and foil the villain. The Cirque Olympique, under the direction of Laurent Franconi, re-created famous battles, using more than one hundred persons and thirty horses, in which a troupe of cavalry not uncommonly arrived at the crucial moment. Thus, many of the boulevard plays depended heavily upon spectacle to keep plots moving or to resolve them.

Emphasis was also placed on the novelty of the spectacle. Playwrights sought to include new places or examples of local color never before represented on the stage. Consequently, a variety of historical periods, exotic locales, and fantastic settings was introduced. Spectacle was so highly developed by 1828 that the new Ambigu-Comique opened with a play in which the "Muse of the Mise-en-Scène" demanded admission to Mount Parnassus. As evidence of her worth, she displayed all the scenic marvels of the theatre and so impressed the other Muses that she was granted admission to their ranks. Nevertheless, spectacle did little to enrich characterization, for usually it merely gave variety to an otherwise routine story.

FIG. 13.13
Setting by Daguerre for the third act of *Elodie* as produced at the Théâtre de l'Ambigu Comique, Paris. Courtesy Bibliothèque Nationale, Paris.

During this period two designers, Ciceri and Daguerre, laid the foundations for many later developments. Pierre-Luc-Charles Ciceri (1782–1868) was the most admired designer of the period, probably because of his ability to depict the favorite visual themes of the time: quaint local color, nostalgic ruins, and picturesque historical milieus. From about 1810, Ciceri was the Opéra's principal designer, but he also worked for the Opéra-Comique, Comédie Française, Porte-Saint-Martin, Panorama-Dramatique, and other theatres. After 1822, he was in such demand that he opened one of the first scenic studios in Paris, where he eventually employed specialists (one for architectural details, another for landscapes, and so on), a practice which was to prolong the use of different designers for a single production. From Ciceri's time, the independent scenic studio began to replace those maintained by individual theatres. Ciceri's students were to dominate stage design in France for the rest of the century.

Louis-Jacques Daguerre (1787–1851) is best known today for his 1839 invention of the first effective form of photography, the daguerreotype. But he began his career as a scene painter under Ciceri at the Opéra before becoming the principal designer at the Ambigu-Comique, where he worked from 1816 to 1822, when it was known for the quality of its scenic spectacles. He is especially noted for his work with the *panorama* and *diorama*, which brought stage illusion ever closer to reality. The *panorama* was invented in

FIG. 13.14

Design by Ciceri for Meyerbeer's *Robert le Diable* at the Paris Opera in 1831. Seen here is a cloister in which was danced the ballet of dead nuns. Courtesy Bibliothèque Nationale, Paris.

1787 and first shown in Paris in 1800, after which they became very popular and were displayed throughout the Western world. Panoramas were shown in circular buildings in which the audience, occupying a central platform, was completely surrounded by a continuous painting giving them a commanding view in every direction. In Paris their theatrical uses were first fully exploited at the Panorama-Dramatique where, between 1821 and 1823, panoramic spectacles with only two characters made up the entire repertory. In the theatre, flats representing architectural units or natural objects were erected near the front of the stage to form an arch through which was seen a distant view painted on a panorama curving across the back and down the sides of the stage. Not only did this eliminate sky borders, but an entire scene, with the exception of the downstage masking pieces, could be painted on a continuous surface. This practice would eventually lead to the development of the neutral cyclorama to surround the acting area. Daguerre experimented with variations on the panorama and in 1822 he quit the theatre to display his *diorama*. Here the spectator was not surrounded by a painting, but sat on a platform which revolved every 15 minutes to reveal one of two different paintings, each about 71 feet wide by 45 feet high, on proscenium-like stages. By controlling light, he was able to depict the gradual change from fair weather to storm, from day to night, and other conditions. He soon perfected the *diorama à double effet,* the forerunner of our modern scrim. Parts of scenes were painted on the front and some on the back of a translucent cloth. Through changes of light, Daguerre could make details visible or invisible. One of his most famous dioramas, *Midnight Mass at St. Etienne-du-Mont,* showed the church empty by day, then gradually filling with people for midnight Mass, and finally returning to emptiness. The complex lighting controls needed to create diorama effects were hard to achieve in theatres, even with the advent of gas light in Paris in 1822. This may have motivated other designers to develop the "moving panorama" in which a continuous scene was painted on a cloth of enormous length which was suspended from an overhead curtain track. Upright rollers, or "spools" were on each end and most of the scene would be rolled up when the play started. When the spools were turned, the cloth would move across the stage as it was taken up by the opposite roller and the landscape painted on it would appear to be moving behind whatever objects—ships, carriages, characters on horseback—were on stage in front of it. This made the objects appear to be moving across the landscape. (An alternative arrangement had the spools above and below the stage so that the cloth would move to mimic a waterfall.) On-stage panoramas did not surround the audience so they resembled Daguerre's dioramas in the way they appeared within a proscenium arch. Perhaps for this reason, the terms *panorama* and *diorama* were often used interchangeably. Daguerre's *diorama à double effet* proved very effective for creating volcanic eruptions or distant battle scenes but it was not until the advent of electric light that it became practical on most stages. Both his diorama and his daguerreotype are considered important developments in the creation of motion pictures.

Interest in spectacle accelerated after 1820. The new Opéra, opened in 1822, incorporated all of the latest developments, including gas lighting and a water system for creating realistic fountains and waterfalls. After 1825, when Baron Taylor was appointed its supervisor, even the Comédie Française began to follow the new trends. Taylor, previously director of the Panorama-Dramatique, employed Ciceri in 1826 to provide historically accurate settings for a number of plays, among them *Hernani*.

After 1828 the increased interest in spectacle led to the publication of *livrets scéniques*, or promptbooks, describing in detail the scenery and special effects used in the Parisian theatres, with suggestions for simplifying spectacle in less well equipped theatres. Concern for historical accuracy also increased since romantic playwrights were scornful of the inconsistencies often seen in productions of melodramas. Hugo consulted the Commission on Historical Monuments and other sources before making the sketches that he provided for productions of his plays. Dumas *père* often publicly castigated those producers who failed to provide

FIG. 13.16
Costumes for Dumas's *Don Juan de Marana*, 1836. From *Revue du Théâtre* (1836).

sufficiently accurate spectacle for his works. From 1847 to 1850 he headed his own Théâtre Historique where he staged productions so lavish they almost bankrupted him.

By 1840 dramatic critics were writing detailed accounts of scenery, costumes, and lighting and often even criticized fairy-tale pantomimes for alleged inaccuracies. The classical repertory, for which the *palais à volonté* had continued in use, largely escaped the trend toward historical accuracy until 1842, when the revival of *Le Cid* with six settings established a new pattern.

Although local color and historical accuracy were the most popular forms of scenic illusionism, realism of daily life also made headway. Under its impact, the box set, complete with ceiling, gradually came into use for interior scenes. It is impossible to say when the box set was first used in France, but by the 1820s it was no longer unusual. Only gradually, however, was it furnished with complete realism, for until 1850 most of the properties and furniture were mere painted cut-outs. In 1846 *Pierre Fevrier* created a sensation with its real furnishings and its decorated floor cloth, simulating black-and-white marble squares, the first seen in Paris.

As with scenery, costumes between 1790 and 1850 became increasingly realistic. In the early years Talma did much to popularize historical accuracy in tragic costuming. As early as 1787 he startled audiences by appearing in a toga and with bare arms and legs, the first attempt in France to achieve true authenticity in classical dress. Although a consistent approach was long in developing, progress was steady, especially in serious plays. Comedy continued to be performed in contemporary dress until 1815. Then, seventeenth-century garments began to be adopted for Molière's plays, although Mlle Mars refused to accept the changes and continued to wear the latest fashions. Baron Taylor, who became superintendent of the Comédie Française in 1825, placed considerable

FIG. 13.15
Opening performance at Alexandre Dumas *père*'s Théâtre Historique, Paris, 1847. From *The Illustrated London News* (1847).

emphasis on accuracy of spectacle, a view which the romantic dramatists strongly favored. Consequently, by 1840 critics were almost universally scornful of anachronisms in dress.

In lighting, eighteenth-century practices were continued until 1822, when the Opéra introduced gas. The flexibility and greater intensity of gaslight soon led other theatres to adopt it, although the Comédie Française did not install it until 1843. Even then, the Comédie retained its oil footlights because the actresses considered gas light too harsh. Allowing greater control over intensity and direction, gas encouraged more realistic lighting effects. Since spotlights had not yet been invented, however, stage lighting still consisted primarily of general illumination, and the auditorium was generally lit as brightly as the stage throughout the performances.

RUSSIAN DRAMA AND THEATRE TO THE 1850s

Russia was one of France's major foes during the Napoleonic era, and it was during his Russian campaign of 1812 that Napoleon suffered his first major defeat. As in other countries of Europe, the end of the Napoleonic era in Russia brought new repressions. Alexander I (ruled 1801–1825) talked of freeing the serfs and making other reforms, but when it became evident that nothing would be done, revolutionary groups began to organize. After Nicholas I (ruled 1825–1855) came to the throne in 1825 this dissatisfaction boiled over into open rebellion. The revolt was quickly put down, and to prevent recurrences the czar established a secret police force and the most stringent censorship in Europe. Although his reign was one of great creativity, the best plays were almost always severely mutilated before they were licensed for production.

The most accomplished playwrights of the period were Griboyedov, Pushkin, and Polevoy. Alexander Griboyedov (1795–1829) is remembered primarily for *Woe from Wit* (1822–1825), one of the masterpieces of Russian drama and sometimes said to be the only significant Russian play in the neoclassical style. As in Molière's *The Misanthrope*, the disillusioned hero of *Woe from Wit* seeks to make others aware of the shortcomings of a materialistic and hypocritical society. To demonstrate his point, Griboyedov brings together a gallery of character types representative of Moscow life. Unfortunately, it was completed just as censorship was tightened following the revolt of 1825. As a result, it was long kept from the stage. The complete version was not seen until 1869; since then, it has never been absent from the Russian repertory.

Alexander Pushkin (1799–1837) is considered to be Russia's greatest romantic poet and novelist. He was an admirer of the English romantics, especially Sir Walter Scott and Lord Byron, and like Byron, he wrote plays. His *Boris Godunov* (1825), with its variety, magnitude, poetic strength, and historical subject, marks the first victory in Russia of romanticism over neoclassicism. Sometimes called the first Russian play on a political theme, it deals with the relationship of a ruler to his subjects. Censorship kept the play out of print until 1831 and off the stage until 1870. Mussorgsky's operatic version, presented in 1873, has largely supplanted the original text in the theatre.

Nikolai Polevoy (1796–1846) achieved his greatest success with melodrama, which had become popular in Russia following the production in 1829 of Ducange's *Thirty Years*. Polevoy's greatest contribution, however, was the introduction of Shakespeare to the Russian stage through his translation of *Hamlet* in 1837. Thereafter, the works of Shakespeare became increasingly prominent.

As elsewhere, the repertory in Russia was dominated by melodrama and musical plays. A large number were translations, especially of French works, but native writers cultivated the genre. The *comédie-en-vaudevilles,* a one-act comedy with couplets sung to familiar tunes, was especially popular. A more realistic drama began to appear in the 1830s with the work of Nikolai Gogol (1809–1852). As a playwright Gogol is now remembered primarily for *The Inspector General* (1836), the story of a young man mistaken for an official from St. Petersburg. Satirizing the corruption and boorishness of provincial officials, the play was original for its time, since it included neither a

FIG. 13.17

Griboyedov's *Woe from Wit*. At center, Mikhail Shchepkin as Famusov. From Komissarzhevsky, *Moscow Theatres* (1959).

love story nor sympathetic characters. Its production, allegedly after the personal approval of the czar, encouraged other authors to turn to more realistic portraiture and it has remained a popular play into the twenty-first century.

During the nineteenth century the Russian theatre expanded constantly, but always under close government supervision. Prince Alexander Shakhovskoy (1777–1846), Director of Repertory in the Imperial Theatres from 1801 to 1826, initiated several important changes. In 1805 a state theatre was opened in Moscow, for which the crown purchased a company of seventy-four serf actors. In 1809 a training school was added; gradually, the Moscow troupes grew in theatrical importance, although the companies in the Russian capital, St. Petersburg, continued to receive favored treatment and higher subsidies. Shakhovskoy, after visiting Paris and other Western theatrical centers, also attempted to raise the level of production, and worked out regulations for governing the troupes which were to remain in effect from 1825 until 1917.

Throughout this period the imperial theatres had a total monopoly on theatrical production in St. Petersburg and Moscow. St. Petersburg had three theatres: the Bolshoi for ballet and opera; the Maly for drama (replaced by the Alexandrinsky in 1832 which is still in use); and the Mikhailovsky for foreign works. Moscow had two theatres, one for opera and ballet and the other for drama. Both Moscow companies were originally housed in temporary buildings, but in 1824 a permanent home for spoken drama, the Maly, was opened; it remains in use. In 1825 the Bolshoi was inaugurated for opera and ballet; after it burned in 1853, it was replaced in 1856 with the present building. Because of their prestige, the state troupes set the standard for all Russia, which for the most part depended upon touring companies of poor quality.

FIG. 13.18
Interior of the Bolshoi Theatre, Moscow. From Barkhin, *Architektura Teatra* (Moscow, 1947).

Between 1800 and 1850, actors in the state troupes were still hired according to lines of business adopted from French usage. State-approved rules governed rehearsals, the behavior of actors, and every aspect of their lives. In 1839 they were placed under civil service and divided into three ranks according to length of service.

The actors in the St. Petersburg troupes were long considered superior to those in Moscow. After 1825, however, the lead gradually passed to Moscow. Among the early performers there the most important were Mochalov and Shchepkin. Pavel Mochalov (1800–1848) was on the stage from the age of seventeen. An uneven, emotional actor, he swept audiences away when he was at his best. He was especially admired in melodrama and in such roles as Richard III and Hamlet. According to Stanislavsky, Mikhail Shchepkin (1788–1863) was the first great Russian actor. Shchepkin spent his early career in a serf troupe but began to travel with a professional company in 1808, obtaining his freedom in 1821. By 1823 he was a member of the Maly troupe in Moscow, with which he remained the rest of his life. After 1832 he taught at the dramatic school and toured frequently throughout Russia. Shchepkin was a painstaking technician who strove for naturalness in acting. Because of his influence, ensemble effects were achieved at the Maly long before they were usual elsewhere in Russia. He initiated the practice of reading the play to the company before the roles were cast and guided other actors in their characterizations. He excelled in Gogol's comedy, and his natural style is said to have encouraged playwrights to draw more realistic characters.

In general the Russian theatre was very conservative in its scenic practices, and for the most part it continued to depend on a limited range of stock settings made up of wings and drops. The box set was introduced in the 1830s but it found little favor until much later in the century.

Opera, which had been primarily an aristocratic entertainment, began to win a wider following in the 1830s, when Mikhail Glinka (1804–1857) initiated the Russian school of composers. Nevertheless, foreign influence remained dominant throughout the century. Ballet was also under foreign influence. Between 1801 and 1829, Charles Didelot, a Frenchman, introduced Noverre's reforms of ballet into Russia. He emphasized vertical movement, replaced the soft shoe with one permitting difficult turns, introduced leotards, and shortened skirts. Foreign stars, such as Marie Taglioni (1804–1884), the most celebrated ballerina of her day, were imported beginning in the 1830s and gave further emphasis to technical excellence. Not until the late nineteenth century, however, was Russian ballet to be given its distinctive form.

LOOKING AT THEATRE HISTORY

Melodrama, like pantomime before it, brought to drama the kind of spectacular effects that since the Renaissance had been associated primarily with opera. Pixérécourt, the "father of melodrama," was a master of spectacle. The second act of his *Daughter of the Exile*, for example, includes a flood in which the heroine escapes by floating away on a plank. Here is a contemporary review of the production:

The scenery of the second act must be considered a marvel of perspective and mechanics. The progressive heightening of the waves, the falling of snow and of rocks, the uprooting of trees, the balancing of the plank on the surface of the waters, all is a striking and realistic imitation.

Journal des Debats, March 16, 1810.

Spectacle became even more realistic with the introduction of moving panoramas and dioramas. Daguerre's dioramas *à double effet*, especially, created a great sensation, since on a single canvas, through the manipulation of painting and lighting, more than one picture could be made to appear and to change before one's eyes. These dioramas marked one step toward the development of the motion picture. Daguerre has left a detailed description of the process he used in creating these dioramas, of which only a few excerpts are given here. Other passages tell precisely how both painting and lighting were controlled:

One indispensable essential is to employ [cloth] which is exceedingly transparent . . . it is necessary to prime it, on both sides, with at least two coats of parchment size. The first effect, which ought to be the clearer of the two, is executed on the right side of the canvas. . . . The second effect is painted on the wrong side of the canvas. . . . The first effect . . . is lighted . . . only by a light which comes from the front, while the second effect . . . receives its light . . . from behind only. . . . We may employ both lights at once, in order to modify certain portions of the picture.

L. J. M. Daguerre, *An Historical and Descriptive Account of the Various Processes of the Daguerreotype and the Diorama* (London, 1839), 81–86.

This was also an era of great actors, many of whom developed international followings much like those of movie stars today. One of the most famous was

the French actress, Rachel. Here is a review of her performance in Racine's *Phaedra*:

Her entrance as she appeared, wasting away with the fire that consumed her, standing on the verge of the grave, her face pallid, her eyes hot, her arms and hands emaciated, filled us with a ghastly horror. . . . In the second act, where she declares her passion, Rachel was transcendent. There was a subtle indication of the diseased passion, of its fiery but unhealthy—irresistible and yet odious—character, in the febrile energy with which she portrayed it. It was terrible in its vehemence and abandonment . . . when she left the scene our nerves were quivering with excitement almost unsupportable.

J. Foster and G. H. Lewes, *Dramatic Essays* (London, 1896), 84–85.

The fame of such actors created a desire to see them in person, and extensive tours were arranged for them. Soon lesser actors were emulating them, much to the detriment of resident companies, which began to disintegrate. Here are the American manager William Wood's comments on this situation:

When the performance of great leading parts were claimed by Cooke or Kean as stars, the regulars [in the resident company] never, in my experience, showed dissatisfaction. . . . But when we had cast upon us, as stars . . . actors of all grades, the case became widely different. The companies here found, night after night, some new person they had never before heard of, announced in big letters—all their own plans deranged, themselves forced into extraordinary and severe study, and their whole time absorbed . . . merely that they might act as subsidiaries . . . to some foreign adventurer, who possessed no merit half so great as their own; while he took away in one night twice as much as they could earn as their whole weekly wages. . . . Accordingly men who, up to this time, had been perfectly contented with their wages, and with their home reputation of clever stock actors . . . now abandoned that safe position for the attractive honors of the star.

William B. Wood, *Personal Recollections of the Stage* (Philadelphia, 1855), 446–447.

14
English-Language Theatre in the Early Nineteenth Century

George III (reigned 1760–1820) had overseen perhaps the most remarkable period in British history. Under his rule the British consolidated their control of India (since 1757), and added Canada (1763), Australia (1788), South Africa (1814), and many smaller territories to their overseas empire. George III also saw the American Revolution, the French Revolution, the Napoleonic Wars, and a host of revolutions that would lead, during the reign of George IV (1820–1830), to the independence of all Spanish colonies on the American continents.

In the years between 1790 and 1815, England, more than any other country, opposed France. (Its attempt to interrupt all shipping to France precipitated the War of 1812 with the United States.) The Industrial Revolution, which began in the late eighteenth century, had made England the leading manufacturing and trading nation of the world by the early nineteenth century. But the Napoleonic Wars severely strained English resources and thereby emphasized the long-standing need for social and political reforms. In England, as elsewhere, the post-Napoleonic era was one of governmental conservatism that led to financial stress and social upheaval during the 1820s and 1830s. Fortunately, Britain was more flexible than other European countries, and made significant parliamentary and labor reforms.

Nevertheless, from the 1790s until about 1840 England was almost always in a state of unrest because of war, economic instability, urbanization, and social displacements.

Under William IV (reigned 1830–1837) the rapid construction of railroads and steamships, combined with improvements in road construction and the advent of the first working telegraph (1833), led to improvements in transportation and communication that were to have far-reaching effects on theatre. But it was under Victoria (reigned 1837–1901) that Britain developed the most extensive modern empire in the world.

The United States continued to be the destination for large numbers of English-speaking immigrants, and it experienced its greatest period of territorial expansion during this time. The Louisiana Purchase was made in 1803; Florida and the Oregon Territories were acquired from Spain in 1818, the Republic of Texas in 1845, and California, New Mexico, and Arizona in 1848. Except for a small portion of Arizona and New Mexico, all the contiguous territory it now possesses had been acquired by 1850, more than tripling the nation's size. Politically, the country struggled to define the exact nature of republicanism, however, and the issue of slavery was the constant focal point in that struggle.

FIG. 14.1

One of the many theatres built in London between 1810 and 1840, the Royal Coburg, as it looked when it opened in May 1818. Later called the Old Vic, it is still in use. From Wilkinson, *Londina Illustrata* (1825).

TRENDS IN ENGLISH THEATRE, 1800–1843

By 1800 London was the world's largest city, and by 1843 its population had doubled, to two million. During these years the working classes began to attend the theatre in large numbers for the first time and to exert important influences on it. The results were several:

1. The patent theatres were enlarged. The seating capacity of Covent Garden was increased in 1792 to about 3000, and in 1794 Drury Lane was rebuilt to accommodate more than 3600.
2. Minor theatres were opened. Starting in 1807, the laws were interpreted as authorizing minor theatres within the City of Westminster, so long as they did not infringe upon the rights of the patent houses. By 1843 there were twenty-one theatres in the London area, as compared to six in 1800.
3. The evening's bill was expanded. In seeking to cater to all tastes, a bill composed of two full-length plays, an afterpiece, and numerous variety acts was common between 1820 and 1843. An evening at the theatre could last five or six hours.
4. The repertory expanded. Only the major houses (Covent Garden, Drury Lane, and the Haymarket) were authorized to perform regular drama; other theatres were restricted to lesser forms and incidental entertainment. In an attempt to retain audiences despite growing competition, the patent theatres increased their offerings of minor drama which forced the minor theatres to seek loopholes to allow them to compete more effectively with the major theatres.

Two dramatic types, burletta and melodrama, provided the loopholes the minor theatres needed. Burletta, imported into England in the mid-eighteenth century as a type of comic opera, had become such an ambiguous label by 1800 that the Lord Chamberlain allowed any work in three acts with at least five songs per acts, to be licensed as a burletta. This was first exploited by Robert Elliston, manager of the Surrey Theatre. One of the finest actors of his day, Elliston was not content to perform in the usual fare of the minor theatres so in 1809 he transformed Farquhar's *The Beaux' Stratagem* into a burletta and followed it with *Macbeth* presented as a "ballet of action." Thereafter, almost any work might be altered to meet the licensing requirements.

Melodrama, which most minor theatres were allowed to perform, offered a similar loophole. Characteristically it was written in three acts and was accompanied by a musical score. Thus, regular plays could be billed as melodramas by being converted to that format. This ruse became so perfunctory that *Othello* is said to have been performed as a melodrama with the mere addition of a chord struck on the piano every five minutes.

Although minor theatres were occasionally penalized for such evasions, the distinctions between patent and minor theatres became increasingly blurred. The demand for reform became so insistent that action was at last taken by Parliament. In 1843 the Theatre Regulation Act abolished the monopoly privileges of the patent houses. Thereafter any licensed theatre could perform licensed works of any type. Licensing allowed the government to censor performance texts until that too was abolished in 1968.

ENGLISH DRAMA TO THE 1850s

Most of the great English Romantic poets wrote plays, but only Shelley and Byron produced works of significance. Percy Bysshe Shelley (1792–1822) was probably the best poetic dramatist of the time, but his plays *The Cenci* and *Prometheus Unbound* were not acted until much later in the century. *The Cenci* (1819), which tells of Beatrice Cenci's revenge upon her father for his inhuman behavior, comes closer to Jacobean drama than does any play of its period.

George Gordon, Lord Byron (1788–1824), was the most successful of the romantic poets in the theatre. Not only did he write more plays, but more were suited to the stage. As a member of the governing committee of Drury Lane, Byron probably had more knowledge and interest in production than did his contemporaries. Nevertheless, only *Marino Faliero* (1821) was acted during his lifetime (and that over his objections). But all of his plays were eventually performed. *Sardanapalus* (1821) offered such later producers as Charles Kean irresistible opportunities for historical spectacle, while *Werner* (acted 1830), the

story of a man destroyed by his obsession with revenge, became one of Macready's vehicles.

Although Sir Walter Scott (1771–1832) had an abiding interest in the theatre and wrote several plays, his influence came primarily through his romantic novels, most of which were adapted by others for performance. With their emphasis on local color and history, they helped to establish the vogue for the historical romance.

If romantic drama did not fare well, melodrama certainly did. Thirty-six of Kotzebue's plays were translated into English, and several remained in the repertory throughout the nineteenth century. In 1802 Thomas Holcroft (1745–1809) wrote *A Tale of Mystery* (an adaptation of Pixérécourt's *Coelina*), the first play in English to be labeled a melodrama. Soon this new form was attracting large audiences and thereafter they were a mainstay of the minor theatres. Astley's and the Royal Circus featured melodramas which incorporated daring feats of horsemanship. Dog dramas, featuring trained canines performing heroic acts, were also popular (though they did not reach their peak until mid-century at the Bower Saloon). The Sadler's Wells Theatre had a water tank installed in 1804 so that it might perform "aquatic" plays featuring sea battles and rescues from drowning. Finally Pierce Egan's *Tom and Jerry, or Life in London* (1821) began a trend toward melodramas of contemporary life and local color. Egan's work featured a number of well-known places in London and told a story based on contemporary events.

The trend toward contemporary stories in melodrama was further developed by Jerrold, Fitzball, and Buckstone. Douglas William Jerrold (1803–1857) began his playwriting career in 1821 and gained his greatest success with a series of "nautical" melodramas; *Black-Eyed Susan* (1829) was to become one of the most popular plays of the century. Edward Fitzball (1792–1873) had dramatized a number of Scott's novels before turning to original compositions; soon his nautical melodramas rivaled those of Jerrold. One of the most prolific playwrights of the century, he is now remembered for initiating the vogue for melodramas based on actual crimes. His *Jonathan Bradford or the Murder at the Roadside Inn* (1833) had an initial run of 160 nights, a record not surpassed until 1860. John Baldwin Buckstone (1802–1879), a popular actor-manager, wrote or adapted more than 200 plays between the 1820s and the 1870s. His early work, especially *Luke the Laborer* (1826), helped to popularize "domestic" melodrama. Although the older exotic melodrama continued, domestic themes began to dominate after 1830.

Actor-dramatist James Sheridan Knowles (1784–1862) first gained renown with *Virginius* (1820), soon

FIG. 14.2
An aquatic spectacle at Sadler's Wells Theatre where the stage was equipped with a water tank. From *Microcosm of London,* 3 (1902).

a standard play in theatres throughout England and North America. Knowles consolidated his fame with *William Tell* (1825), *The Wife* (1833), and *The Hunchback* (1832). His success stemmed from a skillful blending of melodramatic stories with a pseudo-Shakespearean form. For many years he enjoyed a considerable critical and popular following. His successor

FIG. 14.3
An equestrian melodrama at Astley's Amphitheatre. Both the ring and the stage could be used for dramatic performances. From Wilkinson, *Londina Illustrata* (1825).

was Edward George Bulwer-Lytton (1803–1873), who established "gentlemanly" melodrama as a recognizable form. Already noted for his novels, Bulwer-Lytton was persuaded by Macready to turn to playwriting. Three of his works, *The Lady of Lyons* (1838), *Richelieu* (1839), and *Money* (1840), which owe much to Macready's suggestions, held the stage throughout the nineteenth century. With "gentlemanly" melodrama, the theatre began to regain its former prestige with the upper classes.

ENGLISH THEATRICAL CONDITIONS, 1800–1843

Between 1800 and 1817, the English theatre maintained its stability largely because of the work of John Philip Kemble (1757–1823). When Kemble became acting manager of Drury Lane in 1788, it had fallen considerably from the height to which Garrick had lifted it. Richard Brinsley Sheridan, the manager, had devoted himself increasingly to politics but had failed to delegate sufficient authority to Thomas King, who ran the theatre in his absence. Although Kemble did much to reestablish the reputation of the Drury Lane, he tired of coping with crises induced by Sheridan's frequent financial difficulties, and in 1803 he moved to Covent Garden, where he remained until his retirement in 1817. During his tenure, Covent Garden became the leading theatre of the English-speaking world. Kemble's greatest trial as a manager came in 1809 at the opening of the newly completed Covent Garden (rebuilt at great expense after its destruction by fire in 1808). Kemble's attempt to recover costs by raising entrance fees precipitated the "Old Price" riots that continued for sixty-one nights, despite the attempt of police and soldiers to intervene. The riots ended only after Kemble capitulated to the audience's demands.

By the time Kemble retired, England, as a result of the Napoleonic Wars, was in a financial crisis that was to last until 1840. Scarcely a theatrical management escaped bankruptcy between 1817 and 1843 as revenues declined but rents paid for theatres remained high. In addition, greater financial outlays were being required by the increasingly elaborate spectacle. It is sometimes suggested that the enormous auditoriums made subtlety in acting impossible and shifted emphasis to visual effects. Covent Garden was destroyed by fire in 1808 and Drury Lane in 1809. In the new Covent Garden (1809) the distance from the stage to the back of the upper gallery was 104 feet, and at the new Drury Lane (1812) it was 101 feet. Such size, coupled with the growing interest in melodrama, local color, and history, undoubtedly encouraged greater emphasis upon the visual elements.

FIG. 14.4
Interior of Drury Lane as it appeared before it was destroyed by fire in 1809. From *Microcosm of London, 1* (1902).

FIG. 14.5
Setting by William Capon for J. P. Kemble's Shakespearean revivals at Covent Garden after 1809. From *The Magazine of Art* (1895).

The major designer of the Kemble era was William Capon (1757–1827), who came to the fore when the Drury Lane was reconstructed in 1794. This theatre had a stage 85 feet wide and 92 feet deep, with a proscenium opening 43 feet wide by 38 feet high. One of Capon's sets in 1799 showed the nave, choir, and side aisles of a fourteenth-century cathedral; it measured 36 feet in width, 52 feet in depth, and 37 feet in height. Another, for Sheridan's *Pizarro* (1799), required a gorge spanned by a bridge, which could be cut loose so that the hero might escape from his would-be killers. Capon continued as principal designer at Drury Lane until it burned in 1809, after which he rejoined Kemble at Covent Garden. He was one of the first important advocates in England of historical accuracy in scenery, which reflected the important transition from the "generality" favored by the neoclassicists to the "individuality" advocated by the romantics. Nevertheless, consistency had not yet been attained, for often several different designers, each working independently, provided settings for a single play, and frequently one act was newly mounted while the others were performed in stock scenery. Theatrical effectiveness was also always put above archaeological accuracy. But by the time Kemble and Capon retired, it was accepted that all drama should be "illustrated" as completely as possible.

Charles Kemble (1775–1854), brother of John Philip Kemble, managed Covent Garden from 1817 to 1832. In a major step toward antiquarianism, James Robinson Planché (1796–1880) persuaded him to use historically accurate costumes for every role in his 1823 production of Shakespeare's *King John*. Planché continued to be a leader in the movement toward antiquarianism by producing the meticulously illustrated book, *History of British Costume* (1834), long the standard English work in the field. Authenticity was consistently used as a design element in London only after Macready accepted the concept when he took over management of Covent Garden in 1837.

By the 1830s it was assumed that each theatre would prepare a number of handsomely mounted productions each season. The increased financial outlay meant, however, that longer runs were required to justify the investment. Consequently, from this time the trend toward long runs accelerated, although it was not to be widely exploited until after 1850.

Between 1800 and 1843 several important actors appeared on the English stage. Until 1815 it was dominated by the Kemble family. Almost all of the twelve children of Roger Kemble (1721–1802), a provincial actor-manager, became actors, but it was John Philip and Sarah Kemble Siddons (1755–1831) who achieved the greatest fame. John Philip Kemble was on the stage from 1776. He came to London in 1783 and from 1790 until his retirement he was considered the leading actor of the English-speaking world. Mrs. Siddons was on the stage from childhood. From her reappearance in London in 1782 until her retirement in 1812, she was recognized as the greatest tragic actress of her day.

Kemble and Mrs. Siddons established a style usually called "classical" because of its emphasis upon stateliness, dignity, and grace. (In its major outlines, it resembled Weimar classicism.) Their characterizations

FIG. 14.6

Costume design by J. R. Planché for Henry IV in Charles Kemble's production of 1824. From J. R. Planché, *Costume of Shakespeare's King Henry IV, Parts 1 and 2* (1824). Courtesy Lilly Library, Indiana University.

were always worked out studiously and sustained with care. As a result, John Philip was sometimes accused of self-consciousness. Mrs. Siddons, while attaining a comparable dignity, rose far above her brother because of her greater emotional intensity.

Other members of the Kemble family included Stephen (1758–1822), who acted primarily in the provinces but became famous in London for his Falstaff; Eliza Kemble Whitlock (1761–1836), who, after performing in the provinces, migrated to the United States in 1794 to become one of its most noted actresses; and Charles, who excelled as the young heroes of John Philip Kemble's productions before taking over the management of Covent Garden. Much of Charles Kemble's later fame was linked to his daughter Frances Anne (Fanny) Kemble (1809–1893), a popular leading lady from her debut in 1829 until her retirement in 1834. Charles Kemble retired in 1836 and later served as Examiner of Plays for the Lord Chamberlain.

The classical approach was challenged after 1814 by the romantic school. Although Edmund Kean was the greatest exponent of the new style, he was preceded by George Frederick Cooke (1756–1812). At his best in villainous roles such as Richard III and Iago, he cared little for grace or nobility but was unequaled in portraying hypocrisy and evil. His alcoholism made him unreliable, but when in full possession of his powers, no one could so captivate an audience. He was the first major English actor to undertake a starring tour of the United States (1810–1812), which established a precedent that was to have far-reaching consequences.

Edmund Kean (1787–1833) began his career as the child prodigy Master Carey. He did not appear in London until he was twenty-seven, but from his debut there in 1814 he was considered a major star and, after Kemble's retirement, the foremost actor of his day. Like Cooke, he excelled in somewhat villainous roles, such as Richard III, Shylock, Sir Giles Overreach (in *A New Way to Pay Old Debts*), and Barabas (in *The Jew of Malta*); he seldom appeared in comedy. He worked out every movement and intonation with care. Once set, a role was much the same at every performance, although Kean sometimes revised a characterization, and his intentions were often subverted by his alcoholism. In later years, he was inclined to save his strength for great moments and to slight the remainder of a role. Unlike Kemble, Kean did not value grace and dignity; he was willing to cringe or crawl on the floor if he thought it necessary to convey the proper effect. Thus, he tended to emphasize powerful emotion, whereas Kemble had sought to convey an ideal nobility. Kean was never a regular member of an acting company after the early 1820s. Instead, he worked exclusively as a star performer. His demonstration that a star could command a high salary with a limited repertory established a precedent followed by many of his successors.

Although no comic actors achieved the lasting fame enjoyed by Kemble, Siddons, and Kean, many won popular acclaim and for the first time were able to command salaries equaling or exceeding those of the major serious actors. The leading actors of melodrama too were in great demand and attracted substantial followings. Child prodigies were especially popular, the most famous of which was William Henry West Betty (1791–1874), often called the Young Roscius. When Master Betty came to London in 1804 after winning fame in the provinces, his following became so great that Kemble and Mrs. Siddons gave up playing for a time. On one occasion, Parliament was adjourned so that its members might see him perform. Betty's fame soon passed, and after 1811 he sank into obscurity.

Except during starring engagements, actors were still employed by the season at a weekly salary and a yearly benefit. Although "lines of business" continued to be the norm, specialization increased. After 1809, Kemble employed the equivalent of three troupes, one for serious drama, one for comedy, and one for music and dance. Thereafter, the trend in large

FIG. 14.7
Edmund Kean as Richard III. A contemporary engraving.

companies was to hire actors who were outstanding in a limited range, though diversity was still achieved because each troupe included so many specialized performers.

Rehearsals remain perfunctory. Although Kemble aimed at ensemble effects, he did little beyond holding line rehearsals, probably because by this time conventional groupings and movement served in most instances. It was customary for actors to space themselves an arm's length apart so as not to inhibit gestures. Because the footlights had a large cluster at center stage ("the rose"), actors moved to this bright spot each time they had an important speech. After delivering the speech, they then moved three steps to the left or right to make way for the next speaker. This continuous shifting of places was typical of acting through most of the early nineteenth century.

MACREADY AND VESTRIS

In the 1830s two English managers, Macready and Vestris, began to bring order out of the near-chaos that had reigned since about 1815 and to lay the foundations for the recovery of the theatre.

William Charles Macready (1793–1873) had no intention of going on the stage until a financial crisis

FIG. 14.8
A poorly attended benefit performance in an English provincial theatre. Note the many architectural and staging features of the early nineteenth century theatre. From Pierce Egan, *The Life of an Actor* (1825).

FIG. 14.9

Macready's production of *King Lear*, 1838. Macready at center as Lear; to his left Priscilla Horton as the Fool (often played by women in the nineteenth century). From George Scharf, *Recollections of the Scenic Effects of Covent Garden Theatre, 1838–1839 (1839).*

in his father's theatre at Birmingham forced him to leave school in 1810. By 1816 he was playing in London, where he was soon considered a serious rival to Kean, although it was not until Kean's death that he was acclaimed England's foremost actor. As a performer, Macready combined much of Kemble's dignity and studiousness with Kean's fire. Unlike Kemble, however, he sought to give an illusion of everyday life and included many domestic and familiar details in his stage business. He was famous for his lengthy pauses, during which he seemed to reflect and compose his responses.

Macready's profound dissatisfaction with theatrical conditions eventually led him into management as the only effective means of reforming them. He managed both Covent Garden (1837–1839) and Drury Lane (1841–1843) each with more artistic than financial success.

Macready first sought to improve the repertory. He placed considerable emphasis upon Shakespeare's plays and claimed much credit for restoring the original texts, although he was not always scrupulous in this matter. He persuaded some of the foremost literary figures of his time to write for the stage and from these efforts came "gentlemanly" melodrama. Macready also considered it important to perform no work more than three times a week, regardless of its popularity. (From this policy stemmed many of his financial difficulties.) Next Macready maintained a company of high quality. His company included Helen Faucit (1817–1898), an actress of the Kemble school who made her London debut in 1836, and was generally considered the finest actress of the day;

Mrs. Mary Warner (1804–1854) who was recognized as the leading performer of such mature roles as Lady Macbeth; and Samuel Phelps, second only to Macready in the company who eventually became one of the most famous actor-managers in London. Finally, Macready paid attention to every detail of his productions. He was the first actor-manager in England who consistently sought historical accuracy in both costumes and scenery. His usual designer was Charles Marshall (1806–1880), one of the finest landscape artists of the day, but he also employed many other noted designers. For *Henry V*, Clarkson Stanfield designed a moving diorama to illustrate the sea voyage from Southampton to Harfleur, and Col. Hamilton Smith (1776–1859), a noted antiquarian, was often consulted on costumes.

As a manager Macready did not allow actors to choose their own stage positions, but sought instead to prescribe positions for them. He insisted upon acting during rehearsals rather than letting actors "save themselves" for performances, the usual practice of the day. While he did not convert all of his company, his superior success as a performer won many converts and he is generally recognized as one of the first directors, in the modern sense, in England. Macready gave up management in 1843 and thereafter was a touring star. His last appearance in the United States in 1849 was marred by the Astor Place Riot, stemming from his rivalry with Edwin Forrest, during which twenty-two people were killed. He retired in 1851.

Vestris's most significant work was done with minor forms. Born Lucia Elizabetta Bartolozzi (1797–1856), she married in 1813 and went on the stage in 1815. She achieved her first outstanding success in a "breeches role" in *Giovanni in London* (1820), a burlesque of Mozart's *Don Giovanni*. She remained one of the most popular performers of light comedy and burlesque until her retirement in 1854.

Vestris's importance, however, stems from her work as a manager, notably at the Olympic Theatre from 1831 to 1839. Here she had the assistance of J. R. Planché, who wrote many of the plays in her repertory, which was restricted to burlesques, extravaganzas, and similar minor types. Planché, one of the most prolific writers of these forms, turned out about 175. With their whimsy and wordplay, Planché's works were to be a major influence on the comic operas of Gilbert and Sullivan.

As a manager, Vestris is important for several reasons. First, she paid close attention to all elements of production and coordinated them into an integrated whole. Second, she gave special consideration to spectacle and is the first actor-manager to

FIG. 14.10

Mme Vestris and Charles Mathews the Younger (both at left) in W. B. Bernard's *The Conquering Game* at the Olympic Theatre, 1832. The set is considered to be one of the first box sets on the English stage. Drawing from the title page of the acting edition, *Duncombe's British Theatre*, 35 (c. 1865).

use the box set with some consistency. As in other countries, there is much dispute over the date when the box set was introduced at the Olympic, but 1832 seems most likely. By 1834 it had been seen at Drury Lane and by 1837 was in use at Covent Garden. Nevertheless, the box set remained something of a novelty and was not widely adopted until after 1870. Not only did Vestris use box sets, she equipped them like rooms in real life. This care also extended to costumes where she replaced the ridiculously exaggerated costumes that had been typical in burlesque with garments like those worn in real life. Finally, Vestris was instrumental in simplifying the evening's bill. She curtailed her offerings so that the program ended no later than 11 P.M., a drastic measure since programs at this time usually lasted until 1 or 2 A.M. The popularity of the innovation began the trend that eventually led to the one-play bill.

In 1838 Vestris gave up the Olympic Theatre and married Charles Mathews the Younger (1803–1878), a performer of light comedy roles in her company. Together they managed Covent Garden (1839–1842) where she staged a number of influential Shakespearean

productions using virtually uncut texts. From 1847 to 1856, she and her husband managed the Lyceum. Both managerial ventures ended in bankruptcy, but nevertheless, Vestris's reforms inspired many others.

THEATRE IN NORTH AMERICA, 1781–1815

In the United States, the first professional performances were given in 1781 (the year hostilities ceased) at Annapolis and Baltimore by Thomas Wall, a former member of Douglass's troupe. Irish actors Dennis Ryan and his wife joined Wall's company in 1782. By 1783 (the year the war officially ended), Ryan had assumed control of the "American Company of Comedians," which played between New York and Charleston until 1785.

In that year, two former members of Douglass's pre-war company, John Henry (1738–1794) and Lewis Hallam, Jr. (1740–1808), formed the "Old American Company" and built the John Street Theatre in New York. From 1785 to 1794 they were the new country's major troupe and the nucleus of a permanent theatre in that city.

Philadelphia became the dominant theatrical center between 1794 and 1815. It rescinded its 1774 ban on acting in 1789 and within two years, Thomas Wignell (1753–1803), who had worked as the principal low comedian in the Old American Company, and Alexander Reinagle, a musician, established a theatre company there. They erected the Chestnut Street Theatre, the largest in the country, which seated about 1200 and had a stage 71 feet deep with a proscenium opening about 36 feet wide. While it was being built Wignell sailed for England, where he engaged the best company yet seen in America, including Eliza Kemble Whitlock, sister of John Philip Kemble and Mrs. Siddons. By 1796 the company was further strengthened by other outstanding British actors who had been unable to find suitable engagements in London. The most important of these were William Warren (1767–1832), an actor of old men's roles who became one of the co-managers of the theatre (1806–1827), and Thomas Abthorpe Cooper (1776–1849), one of England's most promising young actors, who by 1800 was considered the leading actor in North America. He popularized the Kemble style in the United States and became an important actor-manager in New York. With this superior company Wignell and Reinagle were able to set the highest standards for North American theatre, standards their successors, William Warren and William Wood (1779–1861), joint managers of the company from 1810 to 1826, strove to maintain.

FIG. 14.11
Chestnut Street Theatre, Philadelphia, 1794. A plate published in *New York Magazine,* 1794. Courtesy Hoblitzelle Theatre Arts Collection, University of Texas at Austin.

The secondary position of the New York theatre between 1794 and 1815 is explained in part by dissensions within its company. In 1792 John Hodgkinson (*c.* 1765–1805), a versatile and ambitious English provincial actor, joined the troupe, and by 1794 he had replaced Henry in the management. He and Hallam did not get along, however, and William Dunlap (1766–1839), the leading American playwright of the period, had to be induced to take over the management of the John Street Theatre and oversee the building of its replacement, the Park Theatre, in 1798. Factions within the troupe, however, still made it difficult to maintain discipline or achieve high artistic standards even though it now included performers like Mrs. Charlotte Melmoth (1749–1823), an actress who had won considerable fame at Covent Garden and Drury Lane; and Joseph Jefferson I (1774–1832), a popular comic actor who was to found an important acting dynasty in America. In spite of a popular repertory that featured Dunlap's adaptations of Kotzebue's plays, the theatre went bankrupt in 1805.

In 1807 Thomas A. Cooper left the Chestnut Street Theatre to become the actor-manager of New York's Park theatre. The following year he brought in Stephen Price (1783–1840), a lawyer, as the business manager and together they made the Park the premier theatre in America. Cooper and Price brought George Frederick Cooke from London for the 1810–1812 tour that then created a demand for stars of the first magnitude. They served as Cooke's agents in the United States and arranged engagements in Boston, Philadelphia, and Baltimore. This tour was so profitable that others were inevitable, although the War of 1812 (the American portion of the Napoleonic conflicts then underway in Europe) prevented immediate successors.

The 1790s also saw the introduction of professional theatre in Boston. Performances there seem to have begun in 1792, even though its long-standing prohibition against acting was not actually lifted until 1793. In that year the Federal Street Theatre was erected for an undistinguished company of English actors headed by Charles Stuart Powell (1748–1811). This theatre did not reach a position of prominence until John Bernard, one of the leading actors at the Chestnut Street Theatre, came to share the management in 1806.

Charleston emerged as the fourth important theatrical center of the 1790s. While the Ryan-Wall troupe had played in Charleston as early as 1782, no continuing company settled there until 1795, when John Joseph Sollee assumed control of the City Theatre. Much of the vitality of the Charleston theatre came from the influx of French refugees, both at the time of the French Revolution and following the slave uprising in Santo Domingo in 1793. In the 1790s many plays were performed in French, and many outstanding actors were of French origin. Perhaps the most important French artist was Alexandre Placide (*c.* 1750–1812), a dancer, acrobat, and pantomimist from the Parisian fair and boulevard theatres, who appeared with all of the major troupes in America before becoming manager of the Charleston theatre from 1798 until 1812.

By the 1790s, then, the theatre was firmly established along the Atlantic seaboard, where most of the nation's four million inhabitants were concentrated. Four main circuits were established: the Charleston troupe controlled all of the towns northward to Richmond; the Philadelphia troupe controlled Baltimore, Annapolis, and later Washington; the New York company toured in the adjacent area, but after 1800 tended to remain fixed; and the Boston troupe dominated New England. While there were other lesser ones, these were the principal companies until 1815.

After 1790, the major troupes abandoned the sharing arrangement in favor of salaries and a yearly benefit, although lesser groups continued the older tradition through much of the nineteenth century. Performances were still given only three times a week, and the length of seasons in each town was variable, since most troupes toured and yellow fever

FIG. 14.12

Final scene of Tyler's *The Contrast* (1787). The Yankee character Jonathan is seen at center. From the first edition of the play (1790). Courtesy Humanities Research Center, University of Texas at Austin.

and the discomfort of winter cold and summer heat often required the suspension of playing.

For the most part the repertory was English. Nevertheless, American playwrights, notably Tyler, Dunlap, and Payne, laid the foundations for a native drama. Royall Tyler (1757–1826) is remembered now primarily for *The Contrast* (1787), the first American comedy to be professionally produced. It owed much to Sheridan's plays, but was saved from being mere imitation by the Yankee servant, Jonathan, whose frank and naive responses to New York social life illuminate the manners of the period.

Tyler's success may have inspired William Dunlap to turn to playwriting. Dunlap had spent the years between 1784 and 1787 in England and had seen most of the important performers and plays of the time. After the success of *The Father* (1789), he went on to write some sixty plays, at least thirteen of which were adapted from works by Kotzebue. His most famous original drama, *André* (1798), is based on a true incident involving a British spy during the

Revolutionary War. The majority of Dunlap's plays were written before 1812, after which he devoted his time primarily to painting. Dunlap is also important for his *History of the American Theatre* (1832) and the first history of American art (1834).

John Howard Payne (1791–1852) came to public attention when only fourteen years old as the publisher of *The Thespian Mirror*, a critical journal. In the following year, his first play, *Julia* (1806), was acted at the Park Theatre, and in 1809 he made his acting debut, billed as a child prodigy. In 1813 he went to England, where he spent the next twenty years as dramatist and critic. Payne wrote or adapted between fifty and sixty plays. His best-known plays were *Brutus* (played by Edmund Kean in 1818), *Charles II* (performed by Charles Kemble in 1824), and *Clari* (1823), famous for the song, "Home, Sweet Home." Payne was America's first internationally successful dramatist. After 1832, he ceased writing for the stage.

THE EXPANDING AMERICAN THEATRE, 1815–1850

Following the War of 1812 the westward movement of American settlement accelerated. As the United States acquired the territories that would soon link it to the Pacific Ocean, settlers began to move into this new territory and the theatre followed. The first theatres were community theatres with performances by local amateurs. But the French had established a significant professional theatre in New Orleans by 1791. In 1810 the James Douglass company came to Lexington, Kentucky, from Montreal, and the William Turner troupe split off from this organization to establish a theatre in Cincinnati, Ohio, shortly thereafter.

But the first major step toward establishing a lasting professional theatre in the "West" came in 1815 when Samuel Drake (1769–1854) took a company overland from Albany to Pittsburgh and down the Ohio River to Kentucky. Here Drake established a circuit, including Lexington, Louisville, and Frankfort, although he ventured at times into Ohio, Indiana, Tennessee, and Missouri. His scenery was designed to meet all situations. An adjustable cut-drop served as a proscenium that could be erected in any large room; a roll drop served as a front curtain; three sets of wings (one for exteriors, one for fancy interiors, and a third for plain interiors) and six roll drops (garden, street, wood, palace, parlor, and kitchen) served all scenic demands. Plays were altered so that they could be performed by his company of ten actors, who also doubled in backstage capacities.

Drake's work is typical of all the pioneers who came after him, for like the Hallams he improvised to meet whatever situation he encountered and remained in each town as long as attendance permitted. Typically, troupes began by touring over a large area and, as the population increased, confined themselves to an ever smaller territory until touring could be given up altogether.

Drake soon had competitors. The most important was James H. Caldwell (1793–1863), an English light comedian who came to America in 1816. Appearing first in Charleston and Richmond, he moved to New Orleans in 1820. Between 1825 and 1835, Caldwell dominated the theatre in the Mississippi Valley, for he controlled theatres in Natchez, St. Louis, Nashville, and elsewhere. Thus, Caldwell could offer attractive contracts to touring stars as they came to include the West in their tours around 1830. After suffering serious financial losses during the depression of 1837, he gave up his theatrical interests in 1843.

Caldwell was succeeded by Ludlow and Smith. Noah Ludlow (1795–1886) came west with Drake, and in 1817 set off to tour through Tennessee, Alabama, and elsewhere, giving the first theatrical performances ever seen in many areas. He alternated between management and acting engagements until 1835, when he formed a partnership with Solomon Smith (1801–1869), who had begun his acting career in 1823 and had played for a number of managers in the West before joining Ludlow. Between 1835 and 1853 they dominated the St. Louis theatre, controlled the Mobile theatre until 1840, and from 1843 to 1853 succeeded to Caldwell's position of preeminence in New Orleans. Thus, during the 1840s they were the most powerful managers in the West. Ludlow and Smith are also important for having written accounts of their experiences which are now major sources of information about the "frontier" theatre.

This westward expansion was facilitated by improvements in transportation. During the early nineteenth century canals and toll roads were constructed; in 1830 the first railroad began operation, and others soon followed. But during this period the most common mode of travel was by water. The steamboat was invented in 1807, and by 1846 some 1200 steamboats were in operation on the Mississippi and its tributaries alone.

Most theatres in the West were situated on rivers easily reached by boat. Few were located north of the Ohio River. Chicago did not see a professional production until 1833 and had no permanent theatre until 1847. Small itinerant companies were to be found almost anywhere, however, for just as the new

FIG. 14.13

Advertisement for a showboat circus in 1853. From Hulbert, *The Ohio River* (1906).

territory provided a buffer against financial crises and overpopulation in the East, so too it offered a chance to actors who had been unsuccessful in the major theatrical centers.

Most itinerant companies set up temporary theatres in each town they visited. In the 1830s, however, a new answer, the showboat, was conceived. While actors had long traveled by water, no one seems to have thought of fitting out a boat as a theatre until 1831, when William Chapman (1764–1839), an English actor who had come to the United States in 1827, converted a flatboat and gave performances on it while floating downstream from Pittsburgh to New Orleans. Unfortunately, flatboats had to be abandoned when they reached the end of the trip, and it was not until 1836 that a steamboat, which could return up-river, was used to tow showboats both up and down stream. Showboats were eminently practical, for they allowed traveling companies to take well-equipped theatres wherever there was a navigable river. Interrupted by the Civil War, showboating resumed immediately afterward. The most lavish "floating palaces" were in service between 1875 and 1900, when A. B. French, E. A. Price, and E. E. Eisenbarth dominated the river. Showboats continued in regular use until about 1925, after which they became quaint relics.

While the frontier was being settled, the eastern cities continued to grow. The population of New York increased from 60,000 in 1800 to 312,710 in 1840, and Philadelphia grew from 41,000 in 1800 to 93,665 in 1840. Much of this growth can be attributed to the rapid industrialization of the eastern United States after 1820.

The demand for theatrical entertainment resulting from this growth was met in several ways. Existing theatres were enlarged. In Philadelphia the Chestnut Street Theatre, which originally seated 1200, was remodeled in 1805 to hold 2000, and the Park Theatre in New York was enlarged in 1807 to accommodate 2372. After both theatres burned in 1820, they were rebuilt for audiences of between 2000 and 2500. In New York the Bowery Theatre, built in 1826, seated 3000. The number of weekly performances was also increased. In 1820 the Park Theatre began to play six times a week, a move which was adopted in 1823 by the Chestnut Street Theatre. Others soon accepted the new trend.

New companies were also established. By 1825 there were about twenty resident troupes in the United States, and by 1850 about thirty-five. In addition, there were countless temporary or itinerant groups. In the major cities of the East, expansion followed a typical pattern. Usually a second theatre began as an amphitheatre or circus, which occasionally added a theatrical production to its offering, and then progressed to a full season of plays. New York gained its second theatre in 1812, when a circus was converted into the Olympic Theatre (later called the Anthony Street and then Pavilion Theatre). By the 1830s New York had four theatres, and the number increased steadily thereafter. In spite of competition, the Park Theatre retained its preeminence. By 1815

FIG. 14.14

Auditorium of a showboat, the Dixiana, c. 1920 at the end of the showboating era. From the Robert Downing Collection, Hoblitzelle Theatre Arts Collection, University of Texas at Austin.

the management had passed to Stephen Price and Edmund Simpson (1784–1848), an English actor who came to New York in 1809. After 1840 Simpson was sole manager until 1848, the year in which the Park Theatre burned, thus ending its dominance of New York theatrical life. One of the most ambitious of the Park's competitors was the Bowery Theatre, the largest in the country when it opened in 1826. It soon turned to melodramas so gory that it came to be called the "slaughter house." When it was rebuilt in 1845 it could seat 4000 persons.

A similar pattern can be seen in Philadelphia. In 1812 a former circus began to offer occasional dramatic entertainments and later became the Walnut Street Theatre. When the Arch Street Theatre opened in 1828, a three-way struggle for supremacy left all of the companies weakened. William Wood, who had left the Chestnut Street Theatre in 1826, headed the Arch Street Theatre, but both he and Warren, who had continued to manage the Chestnut Street, were bankrupt before the season of 1828–1829 ended. Both then retired. Nevertheless, after 1828 Philadelphia usually had at least three theatres in operation. The Chestnut Street's preeminence passed to the Arch Street during the 1830s, and after 1850 the Walnut Street came to the fore. The Chestnut Street was closed in 1855.

In Boston the Federal Street Theatre encountered its first competition in 1827 when the Tremont Street Theatre was opened. The two companies were amalgamated in 1829, but new competition appeared in 1832 with the opening of the National Theatre. Thereafter, Boston always had more than one troupe. The most important company was to be that of the Boston Museum. Opened in 1841 as a collection of sideshow exhibits, the Museum included a music salon in which short entertainments were given. By 1843 regular plays were being offered, and in 1846, following the enormous popularity of *The Drunkard* (1844), a melodrama written by the company's stage manager, William H. Smith (1806–1872), a regular theatre was erected. This was to house one of North America's leading companies until 1893.

In New Orleans, English-language companies usually performed at the Orleans Theatre, home of the French troupe, and alternated performance nights with that company until 1824, when the American (or Camp Street) Theatre opened. This new theatre, which was equipped with gas lighting two years earlier than any theatre in New York, was to have a major rival after 1835, when the St. Charles Theatre was completed. Perhaps the most magnificent theatre in America at that time, the St. Charles certainly had the largest stage (90 by 95 feet). After 1835 the rivalry between companies in New Orleans was intense.

FIG. 14.15

The Park Theatre, New York, 1822. On stage are Charles Mathews the Elder and Ellen Johnson in *Monsieur Tonson.* Courtesy of the New York Historical Society, New York.

During this period the theatre in Canada slowly built on the success of the garrison theatres of the late eighteenth century. A company headed by the Scottish actor known only as Mr. Ormsby built the first theatre in Montreal in 1804. In 1807 the 600-seat New Theatre was built there by an English actor, Mr. Prigmore. In 1810 many of the best actors in the city were recruited for a company headed by English actor James Douglass to start a theatre in Lexington, Kentucky, apparently the first professional company west of the Alleghenies. This troupe included William Turner, who soon formed a second troupe in Cincinnati. Royal circuses were built in both Montreal and Quebec in 1824 for the exhibition of trick riding and hot-air ballooning, but both were often used as theatres in the evenings, and the first professional French company to tour these cities (headed by Scévola Vistor) played these circuses in 1827. Toronto (called York until 1834) recorded its first theatrical performances in 1809. But it was not until the Erie Canal opened in 1825, providing a direct link to New York, that touring companies and star performers from England, France, and the United States began to include regular stops in Canada. The

Theatre Royal, Montreal, with an audience capacity of over 1000, marked the coming of age for Canadian theatre when it opened in 1825. It had an American company (supplemented by local talent) under the management of Fredrick Brown (*c.* 1794–1838). Edmund Kean played there in 1826, Charles Kean and Edwin Forest in 1831, Charles and Fanny Kemble in 1833, and William Charles Macready in 1844. This theatre was replaced by a new Theatre Royal in 1847 with seating for 2400 and a stage that was 76 feet wide by 110 feet deep. But this theatre proved too large for the needs of drama and was used primarily for opera and musical extravaganzas. The Royal Circus in Quebec was converted to the Theatre Royal in 1832. Toronto built its first important theatre in 1834 and added the Royal Lyceum in 1848. To a great extent, however, professional theatre in Canada was treated as an extension of theatre in the United States. It was not until the construction of a substantial railway system in the 1850s that Canada began to develop its own theatre identity.

THEATRICAL CONDITIONS IN THE UNITED STATES AND CANADA

The rapid expansion of the theatre during a period of financial crisis brought many bankruptcies and frequent changes of management. The battle for audiences was reflected in many ways, but perhaps most importantly in the increased use of visiting stars. George Frederick Cooke's tour (1810–1812) was followed by Edmund Kean's tour (1820–1821) after which it was easy to persuade other major actors to cross the Atlantic. After 1820 Price spent much of his time in London recruiting performers for American tours. Stars came with ever-increasing frequency: Charles Mathews the Elder in 1822 and 1833–1835; Macready in 1826–1827, 1843–1845, and 1849; Charles Kean in 1830, 1839, and 1845–1847; Charles and Fanny Kemble in 1832–1834; Mme Vestris and Charles Mathews the Younger in 1838. At first, tours were restricted to the Atlantic Coast and Canada, but as transportation improved, stars ventured to New Orleans and up the Mississippi River.

In the beginning, visits from major actors elevated the quality of local companies, but after 1830, as starring engagements came to be a mark of distinction, lesser actors began to tour. Consequently, few good actors were content to remain within the confines of a local troupe. The quality of performances also began to suffer, for stars usually arrived too late for adequate rehearsals, performed only in vehicles adapted to their talents, and relegated local leading actors to secondary roles. Often stars demanded enormous salaries and one or more benefits, leaving the managers with little profit from their visits. Nevertheless, managers were soon trapped by the system for audiences were loathe to attend unless some novelty was offered.

The struggle for survival was also reflected in the repertory. Entr'acte entertainments increased in number and variety, novelties (such as child actors, animals, and specialty performers) abounded, and melodrama and minor forms composed an ever-larger part of the repertory. While this pattern did not differ markedly from that current in England, it was complicated by the American ambivalence toward foreign plays and performers. As Americans developed a national consciousness, especially after the War of 1812, the mass audience tended to be suspicious of anything foreign, while the better-educated and more sophisticated groups looked to Europe for their standards and gave only condescending attention to native talent. Consequently, after 1815 American dramatists and performers gained recognition only gradually and were usually accepted by the mass audience before winning critical approval. Acceptance was won more easily after 1830 as "Jacksonian democracy" encouraged faith in the tastes of the common man and native institutions.

Until around 1830 the majority of actors, both major and minor, were English-born and English-trained. The dominant performer up to 1825 was Cooper, but his "classical" style was less admired as Kean's approach triumphed. Of the new school, perhaps the most important was Junius Brutus Booth (1796–1852). On the stage from 1813, Booth came to the United States in 1821 and remained for the rest of his life. Although he managed theatres for brief intervals, he was essentially a touring star, one of the first to appear in the Mississippi Valley and the first major actor to play in California. It is sometimes said that Booth did more than any other performer to create America's taste for tragic acting. His erratic behavior made him undependable, however, and lessened his potential influence in the major theatrical centers. Another English actor who contributed significantly to the American stage in this period was Mary Ann Duff (1794–1857). When Mrs. Duff came to the United States in 1810, she had had little experience or training, and did not emerge as a leading player until 1818. The major actors of the day thought her the greatest tragic actress in America, and Edmond Kean declared her superior to any actress on the English stage.

Although there had been many native-born actors before his time, Edwin Forrest (1806–1872) was the first American performer to win an international reputation. On the stage from the age of fourteen, Forrest gained much of his early experience in frontier theatres. He made his New York debut in 1826 and by 1828 was the major attraction at the Bowery Theatre. A man of powerful physique and great vocal strength, he disliked the repressed acting of the Kemble and Macready schools. Forrest established an "American" school of acting (sometimes called the "physical" or "heroic" school) characterized by its focus on athletic and uninhibited performance. Thereafter, he was considered America's leading actor. Forrest began offering prizes for plays by American authors in 1828 and two of the prize winners proved very important to Forrest's career. Robert Montgomery Bird (1806–1854) began his playwriting career in 1827 with *The City Looking Glass,* one of the first American plays of local color and low-life. He subsequently supplied Forrest with some of his most lasting vehicles, *The Gladiator* (1831), *Oralloosa* (1832), and *The Broker of Bogota* (1834). John Augustus Stone (1801–1834) is remembered primarily for *Metamora* (1829), a play about a noble Native American chief in which Forrest performed throughout his career. Following the Astor Place Riot of 1849 and his sensational divorce, Forrest's popularity diminished somewhat and after 1852 he appeared infrequently. He retired in 1872.

The first native-born actress to win international fame was Charlotte Cushman (1816–1876). Originally

FIG. 14.16
Edwin Forrest in the role of Virginius. Courtesy Hoblitzelle Theatre Arts Collection, University of Texas at Austin.

an opera singer, she turned to drama when her singing voice failed. After serving as a utility actress at the Park Theatre (1837–1840), she played leading roles in Philadelphia and New York. Appearing with Macready in 1843, she was much affected by his methods. In 1845 she went to London, where she won immediate and lasting fame, soon being considered the finest tragic actress of the English-speaking world. After 1852 she appeared only sporadically and confined herself to a restricted repertory, notably Lady Macbeth, Queen Katherine in *Henry VIII,* and Meg Merrilies in *Guy Mannering.* In some ways, Cushman's acting style was not unlike Forrest's, for it depended upon energy and constant motion, but her intelligent line readings and emotional control won her a much wider following among sophisticated audiences.

American plays of the early nineteenth century popularized two important native types: the Native American and the Yankee. The Native American was presented sympathetically, following the romantic tradition of the "noble savage," and provided strong roles for serious performers. The Native American had been introduced in American drama as early as 1766 in Robert Rogers's *Ponteach,* but James

FIG. 14.17
Charlotte Cushman as Meg Merrilies in an adaptation of Sir Walter Scott's *Guy Mannering.* This was one of Miss Cushman's most popular roles. Courtesy Hoblitzelle Theatre Arts Collection, University of Texas at Austin.

Nelson Barker's (1784–1858) *The Indian Princess* (1809) sketched the outline that was to be followed by others. The vogue for Native American dramas was given its major impetus by George Washington Parke Custis's (1781–1857) *The Indian Prophecy* (1827) and *Pocahontas* (1830). Between 1825 and 1860, more than fifty plays about Native Americans were seen in the United States, many performed by Forrest. The type was dealt a serious blow by John Brougham's burlesque, *Po-ca-hon-tas* (1855), but not until after 1870 was the "noble savage" tradition abandoned.

The Yankee character was the province of the comic actor or "specialty" performer. Although the Yankee had appeared in many plays after his introduction in *The Contrast* (1787), the idea of making him the central character seems to have stemmed from Charles Mathews's *A Trip to America* (1824), a work satirizing various American types. (With his "At Homes," Mathews also did much to popularize the "specialty" performer in America.) After 1825, the Yankee became a favorite character, and a number of "specialists" appeared. The Yankee was the symbol of the American common man, simple and naive on the surface, but upholding democratic principles and despising pretense and sham. The first important American actor of Yankee roles was James H. Hackett (1800–1871), who conceived the character Solomon Swap in *Jonathan in England* (1828), the first important Yankee play. Hackett gave up Yankee roles in 1836, but continued his distinguished career as manager and actor, being especially noted for his portrayal of Falstaff. Hackett was succeeded by George Handel Hill (1809–1849), by 1832 considered the best of the Yankee specialists. In addition to monologues and skits, Hill performed full-length plays, such as J. S. Jones's *The Green Mountain Boy* (1833) and *The People's Lawyer* (1839). With Hill, the Yankee became more sympathetic and sentimental.

A variation on the Yankee was the backwoodsman or frontiersman, the most famous example of which is found in *Davy Crockett* (1872) by Frank H. Murdoch (1843–1872). Ultimately, the vogue for the Yankee, which reached its height between 1830 and 1850, is perhaps most important for its role in establishing a native American comedy.

The African American, another important native type, also fell to specialists. The African American is present in American drama from the beginning as a faithful servant or comic caricature, but the popularity of the type dates from about 1828 when Thomas D. Rice (1808–1860) introduced his "Jim Crow" song and dance. (The popularity of this song gave rise to the practice of using the label "Jim Crow" for any law or regulation designed to keep

African Americans segregated.) Soon a major star, Rice spawned a host of imitators. In an effort to enlarge his repertory, Rice began to offer "Ethiopian Operas" around 1833. Building upon these, Dan Emmett (1815–1904) put together a full-length entertainment, "Virginia Minstrels," in 1843, and in 1846 the Minstrel Show was given its distinctive form by E. P. Christy (1815–1862).

The Minstrel Show was divided into two parts. In the first, the performers (all white actors in blackface) were arranged in a semicircle, the tambourine player at one end and the "pair of bones" player at the other. These "end" men came to be called Tambo and Bones. The "middle" man, or Interlocutor, served as master of ceremonies and exchanged jokes with the end men between musical numbers. The second part, or "olio," consisted of specialty acts and songs. In the Minstrel Show, whites acknowledged and appropriated the potential of African American music and dance, even as they exploited racial stereotypes. Beginning in 1865 with a company headed by Charles Hicks, there were also Minstrel troupes made up entirely of African Americans, who "blacked up" in the manner of the white companies. The Minstrel Show reached the peak of its popularity between 1850 and 1870. After 1870, companies began to increase in size, some including more than one hundred performers. The popularity of the form declined, nevertheless, and by 1896 only ten companies remained. By 1919 there were only three, and soon the Minstrel Show was a mere curiosity.

Such appropriations of African American performance did not keep African Americans from making their mark in other ways. In 1821 the first known company of African American actors in the United States was assembled in New York by William Henry Brown, who presented occasional theatrical performances at the African Grove, an outdoor tea garden, and later at an indoor theatre. The repertory included *Richard III, Othello,* and other plays, and starred James Hewlett, a native of the West Indies. It also included the first known American play written by an African American author, Brown's own *King Shotaway,* which dealt with an insurrection on the island of St. Vincent. Unfortunately, the company was plagued by white thugs, and perhaps because of these difficulties it fades from surviving records after 1823.

The African Company left one important legacy, however, for it seems to have provided Ira Aldridge (1807–1867) with his first acting experience. Unable to pursue a theatrical career in America, Aldridge went to London, where he made his debut in 1825; within a few years he was known throughout England as "the celebrated African Roscius." In 1852 he undertook his first European tour and aroused such an enthusiastic

FIG. 14.18
George Handel Hill, a leading Yankee specialist, in *The Yankee Pedlar.* An aquatint published in 1838.

response that he spent much of his time thereafter on the continent. Noted for his performances of Othello, Shylock, Macbeth, and Lear, he was decorated by the rulers of Prussia, Russia, and Saxe-Meiningen. He died while performing in Poland. By all indications, Aldridge was one of the great actors of his age, but racial barriers prevented him from ever exercising his mature power in the land of his birth.

Another native type, the city boy, came into prominence in the 1840s, perhaps to give the increasing urban population its own folk hero. City low-life had appeared on the stage occasionally since Pierce Egan's *Tom and Jerry, or Life in London* was adapted in the 1820s as *Life in Philadelphia, Life in New York,* and so on. The city boy was not popular, however, until Benjamin Baker's *A Glance at New York* (1848) introduced the volunteer fireman and good-natured roughneck, Mose the Bowery Boy. The phenomenal success of this play led to many sequels in which Mose visits various countries and becomes embroiled in new situations. Frank S. Chanfrau (1824–1884) spent much of his career acting this role. The Bowery Boy faded in popularity after the 1860s, but was assimilated into other plays about city life.

Between 1800 and 1850 the percentage of American plays in the repertory increased from about 2 percent to about 15 percent. As elsewhere, melodrama was the most important dramatic type. Its emphasis on

FIG. 14.19
Thomas D. Rice as Jim Crow. Courtesy the Albert Davis Collection, Hoblitzelle Theatre Arts Collection, University of Texas at Austin.

FIG. 14.20
Frank Chanfrau as Mose the Bowery Boy and volunteer fireman. Courtesy Hoblitzelle Theatre Arts Collection, University of Texas at Austin.

suspenseful plots, theatrical effects, and moral preaching made it especially appealing to the audiences that flocked increasingly to the theatre. It was also a medium into which commentary about current concerns (such as slavery, the rights of workers, and slum life) could be inserted. So, despite its oversimplifications, it served to reflect contemporary conditions, while its happy endings reassured audiences that their faith in justice and democracy was justified.

By the 1840s American writers and actors were no longer novelties. Anna Cora Mowatt (1819–1870) won immediate and widespread acceptance with *Fashion* (1845), a comedy of manners about New York social life. Of a well-to-do family, Mrs. Mowatt turned to writing when her husband lost both his fortune and his health. Since playwriting paid little, Mrs. Mowatt went on the stage in 1845. With no previous experience, she was a star from the first. In such roles as Juliet and Rosalind, she won fame in both the United States and England before retiring in 1854.

Between 1815 and 1850 spectacle began to be given greater emphasis. For the most part, plays continued to be staged in stock settings, but occasionally an effort was made to provide more specific and elaborate backgrounds. Interest in historical accuracy is first found in John J. Holland's Gothic settings at the Park Theatre in 1809. Archeological detail did not make a deep impression, however, until 1845–1846, when Charles Kean staged *Richard III* and *King John* at the Park Theatre. Thereafter, accuracy was gradually accepted as an ideal.

Panoramas and dioramas were introduced in an attempt to gain greater realism. Nontheatrical panoramas had been seen in New York since the 1790s, and in the 1820s Daguerre's dioramas were regularly shown there. Perhaps as a result, Dunlap was commissioned by the Bowery Theatre in 1827 to write *A Trip to Niagara,* which depicted a journey by steamboat up the Hudson River. During her tour in 1838, Vestris allegedly attracted attention to more detailed settings and properties, and it is possible that she introduced the box set into the United States at that time.

In 1816 the Chestnut Street Theatre in Philadelphia became the first theatre in the world to light its stage with gas. This new medium had been demonstrated in England by William Murdoch in the late eighteenth century but it had not then been sufficiently perfected as an illuminant. It was adopted for exterior lighting at Covent Garden in 1815 and may have been installed in the auditorium of the Lyceum in the same year. It was first used for lighting the stages of Covent Garden and Drury Lane in 1817. By the early 1820s, gas was being used experimentally in most countries of the Western world.

Gas did not win immediate acceptance, however, for it presented many problems. Since there were as yet no gas mains, each theatre had to install and maintain its own plant, an expensive undertaking. Furthermore, gas gave off unpleasant fumes and oppressive heat; the danger of fire was always great. It was not until the 1840s, when a dependable, centralized supply became available in many cities, that gas was widely adopted.

Gas eventually triumphed because of its advantages over candles and oil. For the first time, the stage could be lighted as brightly as desired. Since the burners did not have to be trimmed, as did the wicks of candles and lamps, they could be distributed more advantageously. As a result, border lights were used more extensively. Furthermore, complete control over intensity was now possible. At first each gas line was controlled separately, but in the 1840s the "gas table," comparable to the modern control board, made it possible for an operator to control all lights from one position. After 1850 many of the objections to gas were eliminated by the "fishtail" burner, which increased efficiency and reduced fumes by controlling the relationship of the fuel to oxygen. In the 1880s an incandescent mantle made gas even safer, but by this time electricity had begun to replace it.

The limelight (or calcium or Drummond light) was to be of special importance during the nineteenth century. Invented by Thomas Drummond in 1816, it required, in addition to gas, one cylinder of compressed hydrogen and one of oxygen, all of which were directed against a column of lime so as to heat it to incandescence. Placed inside a hood and fitted with a lens, the limelight was the prototype of the spotlight. Macready was the first to recognize its potential for the stage, but after using it for a time in 1837 he gave it up as too expensive. Nevertheless, by the 1850s it had been adopted widely and played a prominent role in productions thereafter. Its mellow and brilliant rays were first used for creating such atmospheric effects as sunlight or moonlight; only gradually was its potentiality for lighting the acting area developed. Eventually it came to be used primarily as a "follow" spot to emphasize starring performers. The major disadvantage of the limelight was its need for constant supervision: since the lime had to be kept in proper alignment with the gases and flame, it required a separate operator for each instrument.

These innovations—gas, gas table, limelight, and the various refinements on each—revolutionized stage lighting in Europe and North America between 1815 and 1880, although the artistic principles needed to guide usage were yet to be formulated.

Between 1800 and 1850, then, the theatre underwent many changes. During this time the last vestiges of neoclassicism almost wholly disappeared under the onslaught of romanticism. In England, the United States, and Canada the melodramatic and pseudo-Shakespearean mode in playwriting, local color, historical accuracy in settings and costumes, and emotional and psychological realism in acting had made themselves felt and had combined to create a theatre in 1850 quite unlike that of the late eighteenth century. But by 1850 the romantic outlook itself had come to pall, and new forces, destined to lead to realism, were already coming to the fore.

LOOKING AT THEATRE HISTORY

In theatre history there is a tendency to judge an era by the excellence of its drama. In most instances the best plays come to be treated as typical, while lesser works and other types of performance are swept aside as unimportant. This approach results in considerable distortion, for it suggests that "popular culture" is insignificant. As Lawrence W. Levine writes in *Highbrow/Lowbrow*, an impression is given that "culture is something created by the few for the few, threatened by the many, and imperiled by democracy; the conviction that culture cannot come from the young, the inexperienced, the untutored, the marginal." Yet the entertainments of the masses are more apt to represent the norm of the age than is the elitist art of "high culture." As Leo Lowenthal says in *Literature, Popular Culture and Society*, "By studying . . . the mass media, we learn about typical forms of behavior, attitudes, commonly held beliefs, prejudices, and aspirations of large numbers of people." In recent times, as Susan Sontag has noted in *Against Interpretation*, "the distinction between 'high' and 'low' culture seems less and less meaningful. . . . It is important to understand that [this] is not a new philistinism . . . or a species of anti-intellectualism or some kind of abdication from culture. . . . It reflects a new, more open way of looking at the world. . . . The new sensibility is defiantly pluralistic."

Concern for "popular culture" is especially pertinent in studying nineteenth-century theatre history, since the repertory was dominated by melodrama and minor forms usually scorned until recently by literary critics. Thus, nineteenth-century drama and theatre have often been treated condescendingly or passed over lightly as unworthy of serious attention. David Grimsted has sought to counter the typical approach by demonstrating how melodrama can be a key to understanding aspects of nineteenth-century culture:

> *The aesthetically poor quality of its plays has encouraged stage historians to view the period's theatrical history as a strange interlude either preparatory to twentieth-century improvements or simply full of quaint plays, practices, and anecdotes. Seen as a product of particular intellectual and social preconceptions . . . the melodrama becomes less an inexplicable monstrosity and more an emotionally valid attempt to dramatize an era's faith. [x]*

At the end of his study, Grimsted concludes:

> *[Melodrama's] conventions were false, its language stilted and commonplace, its characters stereotypes, and its morality and theology gross simplifications. Yet its appeal was great and understandable. It took the lives of common people seriously and paid much respect to their superior purity and wisdom. . . . And its moral parable struggled to reconcile social fears and life's awesomeness with the period's confidence in absolute moral standards, man's upward progress, and a benevolent providence that insured the triumph of the pure. [248]*

David Grimsted, *Melodrama Unveiled: American Theatre and Culture, 1800–1850* (Chicago: University of Chicago Press, 1968).

The introduction of gas, with its brilliance and ease of control, gave stage lighting previously unknown potential. Here is an account of the inauguration of gas lighting at Drury Lane in London in 1817:

> *Gas lights . . . are introduced not only in front of the stage, but at the various compartments on each side: Their effect, as they appear suddenly from the gloom, is like the striking of daylight; and indeed it is in its resemblance to day that this splendid light surpasses all others. It is as mild as it is splendid—white, regular, and pervading. . . . If it is managed as well as we saw it on Friday [it] will enable the spectator to see every part of the stage with equal clearness. If the front light could be thrown, as daylight is, from above instead of below (and we should like to hear the reasons why it cannot) the effect would be perfect.*

Review by Leigh Hunt in *The Examiner*, September 7, 1817.

15
English-Language Theatre in the Late Nineteenth Century

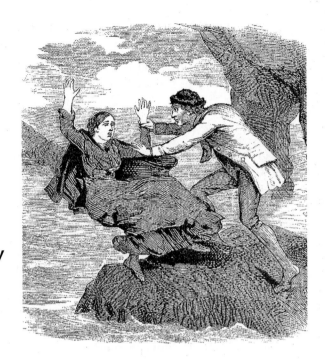

The last half of the nineteenth century brought many changes to Western Europe. When the revolutions of 1848 demonstrated the working classes' overwhelming desire for political, social, and economic reform, governments initially were frightened into promising change, but after the violence abated most declined to implement their pledges. The republic established in France in 1848 gave way to another empire under Napoleon III from 1852 until 1871, and throughout Europe it was not until late in the century that the demands made in 1848 began to be met. England was probably the most compliant: in 1867 it greatly extended the franchise; in 1872 it introduced the secret ballot; and in 1884 it finally extended the vote to all adult males; in 1870 Parliament also made government appointments dependent on examination rather than patronage. But all such reforms were bitterly opposed by those who championed a benevolent despotism of the privileged over the working classes, and none of these reforms extended to women.

During the late nineteenth century the United States was involved in the same movements then underway in Europe. It too was extending its territories and consolidating its power, although most of its energies were expended on preserving the nation and filling up the continent over which it had won control. The most important event of the half-century was the American Civil War, which brought an end to slavery and the influence of the rural South; it ensured the preservation of the union, but at great human and financial sacrifice. The empty reaches of western land, however, always held out the lure of wealth and security; consequently, adventurers and settlers streamed westward in search of mining strikes and free homesteads, displacing the Native Americans as they went.

This westward movement and the needs of commerce and industry motivated the development of networks of railroads, which by the end of the century extended throughout the land. The first transcontinental railroad was completed in 1869, and by the 1880s there were others. This expansion of the transportation system was paralleled by a race to gain control over and to exploit the country's resources. During this era the United States was looked upon by many Europeans as a brawling giant lacking in refinement and culture, but to commoners everywhere it was the "land of opportunity," and immigrants streamed in, contributing to the labor force and slum population, but also bringing diversity and talent. As in Europe, the United States government was not prepared to deal with such complex developments, and consequently the rapacious made enormous fortunes at the expense of others. But the cry for reform grew—in labor conditions, women's

315

rights, education, civil rights, and protection against exploitation by "robber barons"—although it was not to be answered effectively until the twentieth century.

THEATRE IN THE UNITED STATES, 1850–1870

During this period the theatre continued to expand. In the cities, companies often resembled their European counterparts, but elsewhere they retained their pioneering quality as actors who could not find steady employment in urban centers tried their luck in frontier towns and mining camps. As the westward movement accelerated, especially after the discovery of gold in California in 1848, the theatre kept pace.

The Eagle Theatre opened in Sacramento in 1849 and by 1850 a theatre was opened in San Francisco, which soon became the theatrical center of the newly established state. From 1853 to 1856, Catherine Sinclair (1817–1891), Edwin Forrest's divorced wife, ran San Francisco's Metropolitan Theatre and made it into the finest theatre in the region. When the California Theatre opened there in 1869, it was considered among the best in the country.

New mining strikes led to still further expansion of the western theatre. Nevada's Comstock Lode, discovered in 1859, had by the mid-1860s spawned five

FIG. 15.1

An unpopular actor pelted with fruit and vegetables at Baldwin's Theatre, San Francisco, c. 1870. From the Albert Davis Collection, Hoblitzelle Theatre Arts Collection, University of Texas at Austin.

legitimate theatres and six variety houses in Nevada City. Soon mining towns were attracting actors to Idaho, Montana, and Colorado. In the late 1850s touring groups began to appear in Oregon, where a theatre was established at Willamette in 1861. The Washington territory saw its first professional troupe in 1862, but no permanent theatre was established there until 1879.

In Utah the Mormons began to produce plays as early as 1850, and in 1862 they erected the Salt Lake Theatre, the first major structure built in Salt Lake City. Performances were at first given by amateurs, but in 1863 professional actors began to be added and a permanent company was maintained after 1865. The theatre in all these western areas was considerably strengthened with the opening of the transcontinental railroads beginning in 1869.

Despite tedious journeys overland or by sea, stars began to visit the new territory almost immediately. Among the first were Junius Brutus Booth, Frank Chanfrau, and J. W. Wallack, Jr. The first national star to come out of the western theatres, however, was Lotta Crabtree (1847–1924). On the stage from the age of eight, she embarked on her first eastern tour by the age of seventeen. In vehicles written especially for her, she usually played several characters to demonstrate her versatility and display her talents for singing, dancing, and playing the banjo. In many of the plays she portrayed a ragged waif who regenerates drunken miners.

Between 1850 and 1870 the number of resident companies increased throughout America. The thirty-five of 1850 had grown to about fifty in 1860, and remained constant until after 1870. Among these the most important were Burton's and Wallack's, and Keene's.

William E. Burton (1804–1860) had been a low comedian in the English theatre before coming to the United States in 1834 to begin a successful career as an actor-manager in Philadelphia. He opened Burton's Chambers Street Theatre in New York in 1848 and for the next eight years maintained the most respected company in America. With his excellent company and broad-ranging repertory Burton demonstrated at the Chambers Street Theatre that success did not require stars. He also gained much prestige with his productions of Shakespeare's plays in historically accurate settings and costumes. Because his theatre seated only 800, in 1856 Burton moved to the Metropolitan Theatre, one of the largest in the world. But success did not follow him. He gave up management in 1858 and retired in 1859.

Before Burton retired, his preeminence had already been seriously challenged by James W. Wallack (1791–1864), who in 1853 had taken over the

FIG. 15.2
Burton's Chambers Street Theatre, New York, in the late 1850s. Burton is on stage. Note the numerous posts used to support the balcony, since cantilevering had not yet been perfected. Courtesy Hoblitzelle Theatre Arts Collection, University of Texas at Austin.

Lyceum Theatre and renamed it Wallack's Lyceum. Wallack's theatre presented a repertory primarily of standard works presented with the highest standards of acting and production. His son, James W. Wallack, Jr. (1818–1873), was a leading actor of tragic roles for the company, while his other son, Lester Wallack (1820–1888), was a fine leading actor of romantic roles who succeeded his father as manager and continued his father's policies until 1887.

Another outstanding company was assembled by Laura Keene (c. 1820–1873), an English actress who had worked for Vestris. Following her American debut in 1852, she played for Wallack before going on tour. Between 1855 and 1863, she ran her own theatre in New York. After 1863 she toured and was playing at Ford's Theatre in Washington on the night of President Lincoln's assassination.

Not all of the major troupes were located in New York. The Boston Museum, one of the finest in the country, owed much of its prestige to William Warren, Jr. (1812–1888), who performed there from 1847 until 1883. Because of his wide range, Warren is considered by many critics the finest comic actor of his age. Philadelphia's Arch Street Theatre, under the direction of Mrs. John Drew (1820–1897), became famous throughout the United States for its fine company and the training it gave young actors. Born Louisa Lane, Mrs. Drew was on stage as a child, came to the United States in 1827, and in 1850 married John Drew (1827–1862), an actor of Irish roles.

In Chicago, James H. McVicker (1822–1896), who had worked for Ludlow and Smith and starred in Yankee roles, formed his own company in 1857. Until his death, his Chicago theatres were among the finest outside of New York.

While the resident stock company continued to be the standard theatrical organization between 1850 and 1870, it was gradually undermined by several innovations. One of the most damaging was the introduction of the long run. The increase in the length of runs brought a decrease in the size of the repertory. In 1851–1852 the Boston Museum, for example, gave 140 plays (68 full-length and 72 afterpieces), but by 1875 the number had declined to 75 and by 1893 to 15. With the extended run came the elimination of the afterpiece and greater emphasis upon new plays. Adaptations of recent novels, burlesques, extravaganzas, and melodramas were prominent.

Probably the most popular play of the period was *Uncle Tom's Cabin,* based on Harriet Beecher Stowe's novel. Although it was adapted many times, the most popular version was George L. Aiken's, first played in Troy, New York, in 1852 as two separate plays and then combined into a single six-act work. It was written for the Howard family (George C. Howard as St. Clare, Mrs. Howard as Topsy, and their daughter, Cordelia, as Little Eva), who played it until 1887. Although the craze for *Uncle Tom's Cabin* died down before 1860, it revived in the 1870s, when about fifty traveling companies were performing it. In 1927 there were still twelve touring companies who performed only this play. At the same time, *The Escape* (1858), the oldest extant play by an African American author, William Wells Brown (c. 1816–1884), never reached the stage. Brown, an historian and former slave, had to content himself with reading his work about the dilemma of the slaves Glen and his wife Melinda to literary societies and abolitionist meetings.

As in England between 1850 and 1870, burlesque-extravaganza was one of the most popular dramatic types. Parodying well-known plays, performers, or topical events, and featuring songs and dances, it appealed to the taste for broad comedy and spectacle. Probably the most successful writer of burlesque was John Brougham (1810–1880), an Irishman who had worked for Vestris before coming to the United States in 1842. Of all his plays, perhaps the most famous was *Po-ca-hon-tas,* or *The Gentle Savage* (1855), a burlesque of the "noble savage" tradition, popular especially after the 1820s. Many others also wrote and performed in burlesques.

Of the serious dramatists of this period, the best perhaps was George Henry Boker (1823–1890). Son of wealthy parents, he began to write plays about

FIG. 15.3

Uncle Tom's Cabin as produced by William Brady in 1901. Eliza is about to cross the frozen river. The use of horses and dogs had become usual by this time. Note the cut wings used to represent trees. Courtesy Harvard Theatre Collection.

FIG. 15.4

A ballet-extravaganza at Niblo's Theatre, 1855. Courtesy Hoblitzelle Theatre Arts Collection, University of Texas at Austin.

1848. His first work, *Calaynos,* was produced in London by Phelps in 1849. His *Francesca da Rimini* (1855) is considered by many the finest poetic tragedy of the nineteenth century.

THEATRE IN THE UNITED STATES, 1870–1895

The years between 1870 and 1895 brought enormous changes to the American theatre as the resident company was further undermined by the rise of the "combination" company, that is, one that travels with stars, a full company, and all the costumes, properties, and sets needed for a single show or a small repertory. Sending out a complete production was merely a logical extension of touring by stars who, by the 1840s, were already taking along a small group of lesser players to ensure themselves of adequate support in secondary roles.

There is much disagreement about the origin of the combination company. Boucicault claims to have initiated it around 1860 when he sent out a troupe with *Colleen Bawn,* but this was in England and a book published in the United States in 1859 speaks of combination companies as already established. The practice may have begun with the Howard-Aiken company's production of *Uncle Tom's Cabin* in 1852. Further development of the combination company was interrupted by the Civil War, but it accelerated in the 1870s, as the rapid expansion of the railway system made transporting full productions increasingly feasible. By 1876 there were nearly 100 combination companies on tour, and by 1886 there were 282 of them. Foreign combination companies usually played a small repertory; American combination companies most frequently performed a single play. Major foreign stars like Henry Irving, Salvini, Coquelin, and Sarah Bernhardt toured America with combination companies on a regular basis.

During the early years of the combination system, local managers maintained resident companies to perform between traveling productions. Often the local company toured small towns in the vicinity while the visitors occupied its theatre. In some areas a more modest form of the resident company began to present a winter season of varied plays for short runs to neighborhood audiences at ticket prices less than half those charged for touring attractions. About 40 of these companies were formed during the 1890s, and by World War I there were about 120. Little known outside their immediate areas, they posed no threat to large touring attractions. But, as local support was withdrawn from the resident troupes and given to touring productions, many managers dismissed their actors and became mere landlords.

Most of the significant contributions of the years between 1870 and 1895 came from those managers who maintained permanent troupes in major cities. Of these, the most important were Edwin Booth, Augustin Daly, and Steele MacKaye.

As a young man, Edwin Booth (1833–1893) accompanied his father, Junius Brutus Booth, on his tours and made his own acting debut in 1849 in Boston. From 1852 to 1856 he played with various companies and toured in California, Australia, and the southern United States before appearing at Burton's Theatre in New York. From 1856 until his death, he was one of the country's major stars. In 1863, he leased the Winter Garden Theatre in New York and gave a number of Shakespearean productions which surpassed in quality any yet seen in America. His *Hamlet* ran for 100 nights, a record for that play not broken in the United States until the twentieth century. When his brother killed President Lincoln, Booth retired for a time but he opened his own theatre in New York and returned to the stage in 1869.

FIG. 15.5

Boucicault's *Colleen Bawn.* From an acting edition of the play, *c.* 1865.

FIG. 15.6

Backstage at Booth's Theatre, 1870. Note the use of traps (hydraulic lifts) to raise and lower heavy props and pieces of scenery. This was perhaps the first stage to have a level floor and to dispense with grooves. Note the stage braces used to support scenery now that grooves were no longer available for that purpose. From *Appleton's Journal* 3 (May 28, 1870).

FIG. 15.7

The "ghost scene" from Act 1 of *Hamlet* in Edwin Booth's production at Booth's Theatre. Sketch by Thomas B. Glessing, *c.* 1870. Courtesy the Walter Hampden-Edwin Booth Theatre Collection and Library, New York.

At Booth's Theatre, which had been built to his specifications, several important innovations were introduced: the stage floor was level and had no grooves. Several hydraulic elevators were used to raise set pieces from the 50 feet of working space below the stage, and flying machinery raised other pieces into the 76 feet of overhead space. This "free plantation" of scenery would be adopted by Irving some years later in England. Booth's Theatre also had no apron, and box settings were used extensively to increase the illusion of reality. Unfortunately, Booth produced on such a lavish scale that by 1874 he was bankrupt. From then until his retirement in 1891, he played starring engagements in the United States and abroad.

Augustin Daly (1836–1899) was a critic before winning fame with *Leah the Forsaken* (1862), adapted from a German play, Mosenthal's *Deborah*. His first original work, *Under the Gaslight* (1867), also saw his debut as a producer. In 1869 he leased the Fifth Avenue Theatre and formed his own company. From that time until his death he was one of the most influential figures in the American theatre. In 1879 he opened Daly's Theatre in New York and opened a second one in London in 1893.

Daly helped to establish the director as the major force in the theatre. He retained absolute control over every element of his production. In many ways, he was comparable to Saxe-Meiningen in Germany, and to Irving and the Bancrofts in England. Daly assumed the right to coach his actors in interpretation, stage business, and blocking, and he abandoned the traditional practice of casting according to lines of business. Because of his working methods, Daly usually attracted young performers, many of whom he raised to stardom. Consequently, he was one of the earliest "star makers." Daly's mainstays after 1879 were "the big four": Ada Rehan (1860–1916) and John Drew II (1853–1927), players of leading roles; James Lewis (1840–1896) and Mrs. G. H. Gilbert (1822–1904), chief comic actors. Between 1879 and 1892 they helped Daly create the finest ensemble in America. Both Drew and Rehan had been trained by Mrs. Drew and continued to perform together until 1892, when Drew left Daly's company. For Daly, Rehan played more than 200 roles, of which her best was Katherine in *Taming of the Shrew.* Her personal magnetism and beautiful voice made her one of the most popular actresses of her day. Unable to adapt to other working conditions after Daly's death, she retired in 1905.

Steele MacKaye (1842–1894), actor, playwright, director, inventor, designer, and teacher, was more versatile than Daly but probably less influential, because few of his enterprises were sustained long enough to establish their worth. As an actor and teacher, he is remembered primarily for introducing

FIG. 15.8

Daly's Fifth Avenue Theatre, New York. Note that all but a few boxes have been replaced by open balconies. Note also the chair seating in the orchestra and the center aisle. The apron has virtually disappeared. Courtesy Albert Davis Collection, Hoblitzelle Theatre Arts Collection, University of Texas at Austin.

the Delsarte method into the United States. After studying with Delsarte in France, MacKaye came to believe that Delsarte's system could reform the stage, and he promoted it through a series of acting schools. In 1872–1873 he created a short-lived training program, probably the first in North America, at his St. James's Theatre in New York. His greatest contribution, however, came in 1884, when at his Lyceum Theatre he began another training program which was to become the American Academy of Dramatic Art. Two of MacKaye's students founded other schools, both in Boston: Samuel S. Curry created the Curry School of Expression, and Charles W. Emerson the Emerson School of Oratory. As the most important of the early acting schools in the United States these three spread MacKaye's and Delsarte's system.

MacKaye also wrote or adapted nineteen plays, three of which were especially successful: *Won at Last* (1877), *Hazel Kirke* (1878–1880), and *Paul Kauvar* (1887). After achieving an initial run of 486 performances in New York, *Hazel Kirke* was taken on the road by fourteen different companies in 1884.

MacKaye was one of the most fertile inventors of the late nineteenth century. His Madison Square Theatre, opened in 1879, had two elevator stages, each 22 feet wide by 31 feet deep, which permitted complete scene changes in forty seconds. His Lyceum Theatre in 1885 was one of the first to use electric lighting and to emphasize safety devices. At Madison Square Garden, in a play on the westward movement written and staged for "Buffalo Bill" Cody, MacKaye created a realistic cyclone and stampede. Few American producers have been so inventive, and few have been dogged by so many misfortunes.

FIG. 15.10

Sectional drawing of the Madison Square Theatre, opened in 1879. Note the two stages, one above the other, mounted on elevators and operated by counterweights. From *The Scientific American* (April 5, 1884).

FIG. 15.9

Daly's production of Shakespeare's *The Merchant of Venice* (Act I). Note the attempt to reproduce actual places in Venice. At left is the Grand Canal, with boats. Courtesy Harvard Theatre Collection.

As the emphasis shifted to new works, playwriting emerged as a full-time profession in the United States. Bronson Howard (1842–1908), America's first professional dramatist, began his playwriting career in 1864, but did not attract wide attention until his *Saratoga* (1870) ran for 101 nights. Of his eighteen plays, *The Banker's Daughter* (1878), *Young Mrs. Winthrop* (1882), and *Shenandoah* (1888) are the best known. Howard was one of the first dramatists to receive regular royalty payments, and in 1891 he founded the Society of American Dramatists and Composers, the forerunner of the present-day Dramatists' Guild.

Much of the drama of this period illustrates the trend toward realism, which was developed most extensively in the plays of Gillette and Herne. William Gillette (1855–1937), on the stage after 1875, wrote his first play, *The Professor*, in 1881. Of his twenty works, the most important are *Held by the Enemy* (1886), the first major play on a Civil War theme, and *Sherlock Holmes* (1899). Gillette's most realistic drama, *Secret Service*, also has a Civil War background. Built around minutiae, the play's stage directions take up more space in print than does the dialogue. One act requires an authentic telegraph office, complete with a working telegraph key. Although Gillette's plays are essentially melodramas, they create the illusion of real life through the accumulation of external details. Gillette was also one of the finest actors of his day. By concentrating on the moment-by-moment development of the action, he sought to create the "illusion of the first time" regardless of how often he had performed a role.

James A. Herne (1839–1901) began his career in 1859 as an actor. During the 1870s while serving as a stage manager in San Francisco, he adapted several plays, some in collaboration with David Belasco. He first attracted favorable critical attention with *Drifting Apart* (1888), a work about the evil effects of drink on a Massachusetts fishing village. Encouraged by William Dean Howells and other realists, Herne thereafter consciously sought fidelity to life in writing, staging, and acting. His most important play, *Margaret Fleming* (1890), is usually considered the most realistic American drama of the nineteenth century. It tells the story of a woman who, upon learning of her husband's infidelity, takes his illegitimate child to rear with her own. While it includes much realistic visual detail, its major emphasis is upon psychological conflicts. Its subject matter made it unacceptable to commercial managers, and Herne had to present it in halls and out-of-the-way theatres. After suffering heavy financial losses, he recovered his fortunes with *Shore Acres* (1892), a play about a quiet, lovable, New England character. Although in the realistic mode, it did not offend moral sensibilities and was soon a popular favorite. Not a great playwright, Herne nevertheless did more than any other American dramatist of his day to establish the realistic mode.

Despite the trend toward realism, the majority of theatres continued to emphasize more popular fare. After 1870, minor dramatic forms were combined with variety acts to create new conceptions of burlesque and vaudeville. Burlesque began to change in 1866 when a troupe of ballet dancers stranded in New York were incorporated into *The Black Crook*. The resulting combination of spectacular scenery, lightly clad girls, music, dance, and song was so popular that it ran for sixteen months and spawned many imitations. This vogue was given further impetus in 1869 by the appearance of Lydia Thompson and her "British Blondes" in burlesques that emphasized feminine charms more than parody, the previous domain of burlesque. Soon burlesque had assumed its modern form: a collection of variety acts mingled with musical numbers featuring beautiful women. With its sexual overtones it came to appeal primar-

FIG. 15.11

Miss Whitlock, who played the leading role in the original production of *The Black Crook* at Niblo's Garden, 1866. This costume, modest enough by today's standards, was considered shocking in the 1860s. From the Albert Davis Collection, Hoblitzelle Theatre Arts Collection, University of Texas at Austin.

ily to male audiences. Burlesque reached the height of its popularity just prior to World War I, but it was not until around 1929 that the "striptease" became a feature that placed burlesque on the fringes of legality.

Modern vaudeville grew out of the same movement. In the 1880s Tony Pastor (1837–1908) reshaped the burlesque to make it suitable for the family audience. From about 1890 until 1930, vaudeville was one of the most popular of theatrical entertainments. Essentially a collection of variety acts, it also featured sketches and short plays in which leading actors often performed.

By 1895 the actor's position in the theatre had changed radically. Benefits had been abandoned in the 1870s in favor of straight salary payments. With the triumph of the traveling company, most actors had to go to New York to seek employment. Furthermore, they were hired for the run of a play rather than by the season, and since there was as yet no union to protect their rights, they received no salary during rehearsal periods and were often stranded

FIG. 15.12
Joseph Jefferson III as Rip van Winkle, a role he played
for some forty years. Courtesy the Albert Davis
Collection, Hoblitzelle Theatre Arts Collection, University
of Texas at Austin.

when productions closed on the road. From the position of dominance they had held for some 200 years, actors were now subordinate to both the director and the producer.

THEATRE IN CANADA

Canada had experienced the same large-scale emigration from English-speaking countries that the United States had experienced in the first half of the century, but its expansion into the western territories was slower. Since 1791 Canada had been divided into the largely French Catholic Lower Canada (now Quebec province) and the British loyalist Upper Canada (now Ontario). Attempts by the United States to annex Upper Canada in the War of 1812, and later conflict over borders in Oregon, had given emphasis to the need for a political system that would better provide for its defense. Reorganization into East and West Canada in 1841 did not provide the political authority needed to manage the expansion into the western territories, however, so in 1867 the Federation of Canada, which included Ontario, Nova Scotia, New Brunswick, and Quebec, was established. By 1949 all the territories we now know as Canada had entered that federation, and it became a fully sovereign country in 1982.

During the second half of the nineteenth century Canada developed its first resident repertory companies (each with its own local touring circuit) and a chain of theatres in cities from the Atlantic to the Pacific coast. The companies played a season of thirty weeks, with the bill changing weekly. Actors were generally recruited from New York, but the star performers were often English. Still, the companies had close connections with the cities they resided in, and as local apprentice actors moved up in the companies more and more of the actors were Canadian. Thus, the potential for a national drama was there, but it failed to be realized primarily because of the rapid and unexpected success of the combination companies. Since touring shows had to be successful in the larger cities of the United States, economics did not allow for the development of a distinctly Canadian theatre. As the resident repertory system was abandoned, Canadian theatres became more dependent on tours booked out of New York, ensuring the dominance of American shows and leaving plays by local talent to receive only occasional regional presentation.

For this reason the vast majority of plays written by Canadian authors during the late nineteenth century were published but not performed. Charles Heavysege's poetic drama *Saul* (1857), for example, was highly regarded but did not receive more than a public reading. The French comedies of Pierre Petitclair (1813–1860) were produced by amateur societies, but generally not for a decade or more after they were published. Political satires were quite popular but were generally by anonymous authors and were intended for a reading public. The first exception to this was Graves Sinco Lee's (1828–1912) *Fiddle, Faddle, and Foozel* (1853), which was a great success at the Royal Lyceum, Toronto. Two Gilbert and Sullivan-inspired pieces, *HMS Parliament* (1880), a biting satire on Canadian government by W. H. Fuller, and *Bunthorne Abroad* (1883), J. W. Bengough's caricature of his fellow Canadians, were also notable stage successes and rare examples of Canadian touring shows. Winnipeg author Charles W. Handscomb's (1867–1906) *The Big Boom* (1886) was another play on a Canadian subject to be produced, but other Canadian authors saw their plays performed only when they wrote dramas with no particular connection to Canada.

When Canadian actors like William Burke Wood (1779–1861) and Julia Arthur (1876–1958) became famous, it was for their work in U.S. or British markets, not for their work in Canada. One of the most noted exceptions to this was Charlotte Morrison (1832–1910), who became a star in Toronto, toured Canada as a star performer, and became the first manager of the Grand Opera House, Toronto, which she ran from 1874 to 1878.

By the mid-nineteenth century Halifax had become the summer home for companies from Boston and New York City. The Academy of Music was built there in 1877 but Halifax generally stayed outside the main Canadian touring circuits. Montreal, on the other hand, had become the largest city in Canada and was at the center of theatrical activities. It acquired its first resident repertory company, the Theatre Royal Stock Company, under John Willington Buckland (1815–1872) in 1852. By the 1870s Montreal was the home for companies that toured throughout Canada. The Academy of Music opened there in 1875, the Crystal Palace and the Victoria in 1884, and five additional theatres by 1900. The Roman Catholic Church took an increasingly strong stand against theatre starting in 1859, and this had a chilling effect on French-language theatre both there and in Quebec City. Visiting French companies tended to restrict themselves to noncontroversial operettas. It was not until Sarah Bernhardt's visits in 1880, 1891, 1896, and several more times in the next decades that French dramas were able to attract a substantial audience.

Toronto acquired its first resident company at the Royal Lyceum in 1853 under the management of John Nickinson (1808–1864). Nickinson had started in garrison theatre but bought out his military commission to go into professional acting. The Grand Opera house, Toronto (1874; capacity 1323), quickly took over from the Lyceum as the home of standard drama, and when it burned down in 1879 it was immediately rebuilt with an increased capacity (1751). The Royal Opera house produced melodrama and the Queen's Theatre specialized in variety. Both burned in 1883 but the Toronto Opera House (with a capacity of 1900) soon replaced them. The Princess Theatre was added in 1896 with a capacity of 1815.

Resident companies and theatre buildings appeared in cities all over Quebec and Ontario, most notably at Ottawa where three theatres were built; one in the governor general's residence in Rideau Hall in 1873, the Grand Theatre in 1875, and the Russel Theatre in 1897. As the population moved west, theatre moved with it. Winnipeg was in many ways typical of what happened in towns throughout the West. The Red River Hall, on the second floor of a saloon, was built as a theatre there in 1866. The Theatre Royal replaced it in 1870. A professional minstrel company made its way to Winnipeg in 1877, and when the rail link was made with Minneapolis in 1879, Winnipeg became a thriving city and a regular stop on the touring circuits. By 1883 the Princess Theatre was built with a capacity of 1300. On the Pacific coast the

garrison at Victoria performed plays on warships in the harbor until the gold rush of 1858. George Chapman's Pioneer Dramatic Company arrived the following year and built the 360-seat Colonial Theatre (1860). Three theatres were built in Vancouver by 1900, and dozens of tiny mining communities built "opera houses" for the use of touring companies.

THEATRE IN AUSTRALIA AND NEW ZEALAND

The first colony on the continent of Australia was the British penal colony at Port Jackson, now Sydney, founded in 1788. By 1829 England had laid claim to the entire continent, dividing it into the colonies of New South Wales, Victoria, Queensland, South Australia, Western Australia, and Tasmania. These colonies were formed into a federation under a unified constitution in 1901.

The aboriginal peoples of Australia and New Zealand encountered by the Europeans had developed sophisticated narrative dances telling stories of the history and myths of their cultures. Some stories were told as part of initiation rites while others served religious purposes and still others were primarily for entertainment. Each of the over 200 different aboriginal groups had its own distinctive form of dance narratives, but body painting and decoration with plants and feathers were common characteristics. Protestant missionaries, unlike the Catholic missionaries of Latin America and French Canada, did not use theatre as a tool for teaching religious doctrine, so there was less interaction between these native traditions and the techniques of Western theatre than was found in colonies elsewhere.

The first European play to be performed in Australia was a production of Farquhar's *The Recruiting Officer* staged with a few yards of stained paper and a dozen candles in a convict's hut in 1789. (The first continental European play, Kotzebue's *The Stranger,* was not performed there until 1833.) Robert Sidaway (1757–1809) opened a theatre in Sydney Town in 1796, but little is known of it beyond its unusual policy of accepting goods in place of money for entry. It was "dismantled" by order of the governor in 1798 but seems to have been in operation again from 1799 to between 1804 and 1808, when the government began to enforce the order that all theatrical activity should cease. Nonetheless, a convict theatre was started at Emu Plains, west of Sydney, in 1825 and managed to operate successfully for five years before it too was ordered closed.

Such government restrictions on the theatre meant that the first play written on an Australian topic, *The Bushrangers* (1828) by David Burn (1799–1857), had to be performed in Burn's hometown of Edinburgh. The play featured an outlaw hero based on a real person and a tyrannical British lieutenant-governor. It also featured savage aboriginals who, when they were not out to murder "honest" settlers, were dancing the *corraboree,* a supposedly authentic aboriginal dance. Burn returned to Australia and to playwriting with *Our First Lieutenant* (1844) and *The Queen's Love* (1845), which were performed in both Sydney and Melbourne. Meanwhile, a system for licensing plays had been established by 1832. Plays on local topics were discouraged but Henry Melville (1800–1873) still managed to get his own version of *The Bushrangers* (1834) performed, making it the first play on a local theme to be performed and published in Australia. In Melville's version, the outlaws are not heroic and the main aboriginal character, Murrahawa, helps to rescue a settler family. But the first play on a local topic to get a license under the 1832 law was *The Currency Lass* (1844) by Edward Geoghegan (1813–?). In the 1840s, Charles Nagel (*fl.* 1837–1846) became Australia's first successful comic playwright with the burletta *The Mock Catalani* (1842) and the burlesque *Shakespiriconglommorofunnidogammonae* (1844), neither of which dealt with local themes.

The licensing law of 1832 allowed local Sydney businessman, music hall operator, and self-proclaimed father of the Australian stage Barnett Levey (1798–1837) to start a professional theatre. The new company performed in his hotel in December and opened the Theatre Royal, George Street, in the fall of 1833. His license stipulated that he could produce only plays already staged by the licensed theatres in London. He produced the first professional productions of Shakespeare's plays there, but was best known for short London farces adapted with a good deal of local color and called "at homes." Levey's theatre was supplanted by the Royal Victoria Theatre and its professional company, managed by Joseph Wyatt, in 1838. This company produced a large number of actor-playwrights including Conrad Knowles (*c.* 1810–1844) with *Salathiel* (1842), Francis Nesbitt McCron (1809–1853) with *Ravenswood* (1843), and Joseph Simmons (1810–1893) with *The Duellist* (1844). Their plays were, however, adaptations of novels and pirated translations of French melodramas that were common in this half of the nineteenth century. Two other theatres were built in Sydney in the 1840s, but the Royal Victoria dominated the market until 1880. Many of the Sydney-trained actors became actor-managers and stars in Australia, but only Eliza Winstanley (1818–1882) went on to become a success in London. She was followed by Nellie (Eleanor) Stewart (1858–1931), who started acting at five and went on to have a successful career in Australia, England, and the United States.

During the 1830s and 1840s theatre followed the colonization of other parts of the continent, which was often motivated by the discovery of gold and a subsequent gold rush. A Theatre Royal was built at Hobart in Tasmania in 1837 (which still stands, much altered, today). The free colony at Adelaide (founded 1836) opened its first theatre in 1838 and added two more before the Queen's Theatre opened in 1841. The Queen's became the Royal Victoria when English actor-manager George Selth Coppin (1819–1906) took it over in 1843. By 1850 he owned another theatre in Port Adelaide and four theatres in the free colony of Melbourne (founded 1835), including the prefabricated Olympic Theatre (1855, called the "Iron Pot") sent by ship from Manchester. Melbourne had an active theatre scene before Coppin arrived, however. The Pavilion Theatre (later renamed the Royal Victoria) had been built there in 1841 and the Theatre Royal in 1845, both managed by former members of Wyatt's company in Sydney.

Coppin introduced Australia to the star system and brought most of the important stars to tour there over the next twenty years. Among the British stars were Barry Sullivan (toured 1862–1866), Charles Kean and Ellen Tree (toured 1863), and Charles Mathews the younger (toured 1870–1871). Among the American stars were Edwin Booth (toured with Laura Keene, 1854) and Joseph Jefferson (toured 1861–1865). By the 1870s Australia was part of the international touring circuit and the American James Cassius Williamson had replaced Coppin as the foremost producer in the country. Williamson formed a "triumvirate" with Arthur Garner and George Musgrove and their firm, in various manifestations, dominated the Australian market for the next hundred years (until 1976). The Italian tragic actress Adelaide Ristori toured in 1875, Dion Boucicault in 1885 (his son stayed to found an important company in Melbourne), and Sarah Bernhardt in 1891. Janet Achurch brought the highly controversial *A Doll's House* to Australia in 1889, just after its London staging. Unfortunately Williamson had no interest in indigenous Australian drama and his control of the theatres stultified its development. A few playwrights did find success with Australian plays in spite of this, however; these included George Darrell (1841–1921) with *The Sunny South* (1882), the highly regarded actor Alfred Damper (*c.* 1847–1908) who wrote plays like *Robbery Under Arms* (1890 with Garnet Walch), and Charles Reade, who wrote, among other plays, *It's Never Too Late To Mend* (1893), which included "forty Queensland Aboriginals."

Australia's most successful actor-manager of this period was the Englishman Bland Holt (1851–1942). Holt had secured what amounted to a monopoly on the most recent successes from Drury Lane and the Adelphi Theatre in London and mounted them with meticulous attention to spectacle and detail. He was able to operate without assistance from the Williamson organization. In 1899 he began to "localize" English and American melodramas into Australian settings, scoring one of his greatest successes with *The Breaking of the Drought* (1902).

New Zealand was governed from New South Wales until it became a separate colony in 1840. In 1907 it became completely self-governing, and in 1947 it became fully independent. Theatre there followed the pattern seen in Canada and Australia of garrison companies, followed by amateur companies, then by professionals, both resident and touring. New Zealand's touring companies were extensions of Williamson's Australian circuit. The most distinctive feature of theatre in New Zealand was that, because it was established so late, its railway system only started to facilitate theatrical touring about the time moving pictures arrived to undermine it. George Darrel's *Transported for Life* (1876) and George Leitch's (1842–1907) *Land of Moa* (1895) were the most successful plays on the New Zealand circuit.

ENGLISH DRAMA, 1850–1890

In England, as elsewhere, melodramas, light comedies, burlesques, pantomimes, and musical dramas kept large audiences coming to the theatre. Perhaps the most successful dramatist of the age was the comic actor Dion Boucicault (1822–1890). Born Dionysius Lardner Boursiquot in Dublin, he took up acting as Lee Morton before beginning his writing career as Dion Boucicault in 1841 with *London Assurance,* a sprightly comedy of manners. From 1844 to 1848 he lived in France, where he mastered the techniques of French romantic drama and melodrama. He spent the years between 1853 and 1860 in the United States where he wrote and produced plays, acted, and managed theatres. Thereafter he divided his time between the United States and England, traveling to Australia in 1885. During the 1850s Boucicault perfected the basic ingredients of his melodramas—sentimentality, wit, sensationalism, and local color. His *The Corsican Brothers* (1852), brought the special "ghost glide" trap into common use. *The Poor of New York* (1857), was re-titled and rewritten with local references in each major city it played. *The Octoroon* (1859), was a powerful indictment against slavery that had two alternate endings, one of which

FIG. 15.13

Tom Taylor's *The Ticket-of-Leave Man* as produced at the Olympic Theatre, London, 1863. At center, Horace Wigan as Hawkshaw, perhaps the first stage detective. Courtesy Theatre Museum, Victoria and Albert Museum, London.

had the main character die. His other important plays, *The Colleen Bawn* (1860), *Arrah-na-Pogue* (1864), and *The Shaughraun* (1874), all tell suspenseful and melodramatic stories set in picturesque locales, and most are resolved through sensational spectacle, such as fires, explosions, snowstorms, or avalanches. Boucicault was one of the most prolific and skillful playwrights of his age and his penchant for making the latest scientific inventions important elements in his plots exerted considerable influence on theatrical production.

Not until the 1860s did a dramatist interested in the realistic mode appear. Thomas William Robertson (1829–1871), son of a provincial actor, was originally a performer and for a time Vestris's stage manager. He began writing in 1851 but had little success until 1864 when *David Garrick* was produced. The plays upon which his reputation rests—*Society* (1865), *Ours* (1866), *Caste* (1867), *Play* (1868), and *School* (1869)—all tell stories of contemporary life and take place in highly particularized locales, every detail of which is meticulously described in the scripts. Furthermore, many important points are made primarily through pantomime and stage business which re-create everyday domestic events, such as making, serving, and drinking tea. As produced by the Bancrofts, these plays also popularized several innovations in performance.

In terms of popular appeal, the most favored forms between 1850 and 1900 were pantomime, burlesque-extravaganza, and musical entertainments. During these years pantomime underwent significant change as the traditional short form was enlarged into full-length entertainments. This transformation owed most perhaps to the playwright E. L. Blanchard

(1820–1889) and to the Vokes family of performers at Drury Lane between 1869 and 1879. Then, during the 1880s Augustus Harris (1851–1896) made still other changes when he began to import music hall performers to Drury Lane to play the "principal boy" (a breeches role) and the "dame" (played by a man) and to present numerous specialty acts as a part of the pantomime.

At mid-century the most popular of all dramatic types was burlesque-extravaganza. Almost all theatres performed it, and a few built their repertory around it. By this time Planché's light touch and delicate irreverence had given way to broad travesties of popular plays, operas, myths, and fairy tales, all filled with topical allusions, low comedy business, and anachronisms. Puns appeared in almost every line of the doggerel verse in which they were written. Numerous songs set to already existing music and elaborate spectacle, including a magical transformation scene, completed the appeals. By the 1870s burlesque-extravaganza began to decline in popularity. As it declined, its place was taken by comic opera, especially that of Gilbert and Sullivan. William S. Gilbert (1836–1911), encouraged by Robertson to take up dramatic writing, was the author of some forty plays, mostly comedies, quite independent of Sullivan's music. Several of these—most notably *Pygmalion and Galatea* (1871), *Sweethearts* (1874), *Broken Hearts* (1875), and *Engaged* (1877)—enjoyed considerable success. But Gilbert is now remembered primarily for the comic operas he wrote with Arthur Sullivan (1842–1900). Their first important work, *Trial by Jury* (1875), also brought an alliance with Richard D'Oyly Carte (1844–1901), who in 1881 built the Savoy Theatre to house their plays. Among their many collaborations, some of the best are *H. M. S. Pinafore* (1878), *The Pirates of Penzance* (1879), *The Mikado* (1885), and *The Gondoliers* (1889). Eventually a quarrel between Gilbert and Sullivan disrupted their partnership, but their comic operas have continued to hold the stage.

The success of Gilbert and Sullivan prompted still other developments in musical drama, most notably in the work of George Edwardes (1852–1915). Business manager of the Savoy Theatre, in 1885 Edwardes became manager of the Gaiety Theatre. There, beginning with *In Town* (1892) and *The Shop Girl* (1894), Edwardes established a type of musical comedy in which a sketchy plot provided an excuse for songs, elaborate production numbers performed by beautiful chorus girls, and specialty acts. In this form, musical comedy was to flourish without significant change until the First World War.

The music hall also prospered in the late nineteenth century as regular drama was separated from the incidental entertainment that had accompanied

FIG. 15.14

Puss in Boots, a pantomine at Drury Lane Theatre in 1887. Script by E. L. Blanchard, setting by Wilhelm. From *The Graphic* (7 January 1888).

it since around 1700. Music halls developed out of the "music rooms" attached to taverns, but it was not until about 1850 that Charles Morton (1819–1904) took the significant step of erecting a separate adjacent building to house entertainment. Other tavern owners followed his example, but it was many years before the link with taverns was broken. This form of variety entertainment remained a favorite with the British public until after World War I, when the motion picture began to replace it.

FIG. 15.15

Slave auction scene in Boucicault's *The Octoroon*, first performed in 1859. A contemporary engraving.

ENGLISH THEATRICAL CONDITIONS, 1843–1860

When the Theatre Regulation Act was passed in 1843, the London stage seemed at a low ebb. Many persons assumed that the new law would bring rapid change and that many new theatres would be built. However, the period between 1843 and 1860 was to be one of reassessment and gradual recovery. Unlike the years between 1810 and 1843, when many new buildings were erected, no new theatre was built in London until after 1860. Yet in retrospect, 1843–1860 was a period of unprecedented prosperity and prestige.

After 1843, Drury Lane and Covent Garden rapidly lost their positions of dominance. Covent Garden soon became the home of opera, while Drury Lane turned increasingly to spectacle and musical drama; both have continued these specialties to the present. The Haymarket and the Adelphi took over as the homes for regular drama. Major new developments came with the rise of the Sadler's Wells and Princess's theatres.

In 1844 Sadler's Wells was a remote house noted for its bloodthirsty melodramas. Since about 1730 it had been producing plays and had been the principal target of the bill of 1752, which required the licensing of all places of entertainment. In the early nineteenth century it gained renown for its aquatic melodramas and later as the summer home of Joseph Grimaldi (1778–1837), the most famous clown of pantomime. It is unclear why Samuel Phelps (1804–1878), an actor since 1826 and Macready's principal support since 1837, chose this out-of-the-way, rundown theatre for his experiment in management, but it is probably explained by the low rent. Contrary to expectations, not only was Phelps financially successful but also he made Sadler's Wells the principal home of poetic drama in London between 1844 and 1862. Phelps's significance lies in his demonstration—at a time when it was almost universally believed that only popular entertainment could attract a large audience—that fine drama could bring success. Except for six of the minor works, Phelps produced all of Shakespeare's plays in versions more complete than any since Shakespeare's time.

If Phelps revived poetic drama, Charles Kean (1811–1868) perfected pictorial realism and brought the fashionable audience back to the theatre. The son of Edmund Kean, he went on the stage in 1827 but, lacking his father's powers, gained little initial

FIG. 15.16

The Haymarket Theatre that in 1821 replaced the older structure, torn down in 1820. It is still in use. The ground plan is seen at bottom. From Wilkinson, *Londina Illustrata* (1825).

FIG. 15.17

Samuel Phelps as Macbeth, Act II, scene 1, just before the murder of Duncan. Courtesy Hoblitzelle Theatre Arts Collection, University of Texas at Austin.

FIG. 15.18
Lord Byron's *Manfred* at Drury Lane, 1863. Shown here is the Steinbach Waterfall, haunt of the Witch of the Alps. Samuel Phelps appeared in this production after leaving Sadler's Wells. From *The Illustrated London News* (1863).

FIG. 15.19
One of the witches scenes from Charles Kean's production of *Macbeth* in 1853 at the Princess's Theatre, London. Courtesy Hoblitzelle Theatre Arts Collection, University of Texas at Austin.

recognition. During his third tour of America (1845–1847), he produced *King John* and *Richard III* following Macready's prompt books. These were the most detailed productions yet seen in North America and their success encouraged Kean to try his hand at management by leasing the Princess's Theatre in London in 1850. There he would become known as the "illustrator" of Shakespeare by replacing many of the finest descriptive passages in Shakespeare's plays with historically accurate spectacle and pantomime. He was quite willing to rearrange the texts to allow for the desired scenery, which took antiquarianism farther than any English producer had ever done. Beginning with *Macbeth* in 1853, he provided the audience with a printed list of the authorities he had consulted in his search for authenticity.

His greatest successes, however, came not with Shakespeare but with such "gentlemanly" melodramas as Boucicault's *The Corsican Brothers* and *Louis XI*, both adapted from French works blending melodrama with romantic drama. With plays like these, and with the help of Queen Victoria, Kean brought fashionable audiences back to the theatre. The Queen had appointed him to the position of Master of the Revels when that office was revived in 1848, and she showed her favor for his work by inviting Kean's company to play at Windsor Castle and even attended performances at the Princess's Theatre. The combination of her prestige and the respectable tone of Kean's management soon made his theatre a fashionable resort. In spite of his success with audiences, his lavish productions cost more than his theatre could support and he was forced to retire from management in 1859.

FIG. 15.20
Boucicault's *The Corsican Brothers*, Princess's Theatre, London, 1852. Charles Kean is seen at left as the dying Louis dei Franchi. Kean also played Louis's twin brother, Fabien, who avenges his brother's death. Courtesy Theatre Museum, Victoria and Albert Museum, London.

ENGLISH THEATRICAL CONDITIONS, 1860–1880

After 1860 new theatres once again began to be built, and by 1870 the twenty-one theatres of 1860 had increased to thirty. The population of London also grew from 3,316,932 in 1864 to 4,766,661 in 1881. This growth brought a number of changes in theatrical production, as can be seen in the work of Boucicault and the Bancrofts.

After Dion Boucicault returned to England in 1860, he helped to gain acceptance for several innovations. He introduced the concept of the combination company to England with his touring production of *Colleen Bawn* in 1860 and popularized the "out-of-town tryout" when *Arrah-na-Pogue* was played in the provinces before opening in London in 1865. He seems also to have grasped the implications of a long run and became one of the first major producers to employ actors for the run of the play rather than on a season's contract. As a playwright, Boucicault was the first to demand a percentage of the receipts for every performance as a condition for allowing others to produce his plays. This established the basis for the royalty system that would ultimately make playwriting a potentially lucrative profession, though royalties were not generally paid to dramatists until after the adoption of the International Copyright Agreement of 1886.

The Bancrofts combined earlier trends with their own innovations at the Prince of Wales's Theatre to create a theatre quite unlike any other of the period. Mrs. Bancroft, born Marie Wilton (1839–1921), was on the stage as a child, appearing with both Macready and Charles Kean. Her success as an adult actress began in burlesque-extravaganza in 1856. When she decided to manage her own company in 1865, she induced the popular burlesque dramatist H. J. Byron to join her as co-manager of the Prince of Wales's theatre and two years later replaced him with the realist playwright, William Robertson. In the same year, 1867, she married Squire Bancroft (1841–1926), her leading man. The distinctive Robertson-Bancroft style these three developed—a form of domestic realism—first appeared with *Caste* (1867). While several earlier producers had emphasized realistic visual detail, they had used spectacle primarily as embellishment. In this production, as in all of Robertson's plays, character and stage business were inseparable, for the attitude and emotions of the characters were revealed primarily through the minutiae of everyday life. Without spectacle Robertson's plays scarcely exist, and the printed versions require lengthy and detailed stage directions to be comprehensible. They marked the advent of a new kind of realism in England.

Robertson worked with the actors of the Bancroft troupe on every detail; he substituted understatement

FIG. 15.21
Robertson's *Caste* as produced by the Bancrofts at the Prince of Wales's Theatre, 1879.
Courtesy Enthoven Collection, Victoria and Albert Museum, London.

for bravura acting and emphasized ensemble effects. Lines of business, still dominant in other companies, were ignored. The company had no stars, and even the Bancrofts often played small roles. The Bancrofts ensured that the acting would be firmly anchored behind the proscenium arch by eliminating the traditional forestage. The retreat from the forestage had begun in the eighteenth century, but despite several attempts to abandon the proscenium doors, they were not removed at Drury Lane until 1822 and at Covent Garden until 1823. In 1831 the Olympic became the first minor house to dispense with them. The apron persisted, however, and actors continued to use it. But after 1867, the "fourth wall" was always respected at the Prince of Wales's Theatre. When the Bancrofts moved to the Haymarket in 1880, they extended the gilded proscenium arch across the bottom of the stage to emphasize the picture frame. By 1900 the use of the apron had been seriously curtailed in virtually all of London's theatres. The Bancrofts also won acceptance for the box set and because of their example, most theatres devoted as much care to accuracy in modern plays by 1875 as they had dedicated to period plays before then.

The Bancrofts helped to establish the single-play bill in London by dropping the curtain-raiser and afterpiece, but more importantly they aided in establishing matinee performances. Used occasionally since the 1850s, matinees became usual with the Bancrofts during their production of Sardou's *Diplomacy* in 1878. Matinees were adopted for Gilbert and Sullivan's comic operas in the 1880s and were standard in most theatres by 1900.

What made all this possible was their embracing of the long run. They produced only thirty full-length plays in their twenty years of management, half of which were by Robertson. This encouraged them to follow Boucicault in employing actors on a "run-of-the-play" contract. But it also allowed them to abandon benefits for actors, then still prevalent in most theatres, and raised salaries markedly. When other managers were paying actors £5 to £10 weekly, the Bancrofts were offering £60 to £100. Like Boucicault, the Bancrofts created combination companies to take their more successful productions on the road, which allowed them to extend actors' contracts and make even more returns from their investment in the original production.

The Bancrofts were also instrumental in establishing the orchestra level as the favored seating area. In 1800 the pit still consisted only of backless benches. The King's Theatre, which was used for opera, converted some benches into seats with backs in the 1820s, and in 1822 the Drury Lane added a few of these "stalls." Gradually other theatres accepted the change, although the stalls were restricted to a few rows at the front, and the pit continued to occupy the remainder of the ground floor. In 1863 the Haymarket replaced its stalls with upholstered chairs, and the last pit benches were removed when the Bancrofts took over in 1880. Other theatres eventually followed this example. With the introduction of chair-style seating came the numbering and reservation of places. In turn, the ability to reserve seats reinforced the long run, since popular plays encouraged the booking of seats in advance, and advance sales encouraged the extension of runs.

These changes are representative of many others in auditorium design. Since the Restoration, the pit had been surrounded by boxes only slightly raised above it. Around 1820, however, the Adelphi Theatre established a new trend when the boxes were raised sufficiently to permit the extension of the pit to the outside walls. Other changes came after 1860. Probably most important was the movement away from large houses. The Criterion, opened in 1874, held only 660, and the Prince of Wales's seated only 600. Few theatres built after 1875 held more than 1500. This reduction in size meant fewer galleries, while the growing prestige of stall seating motivated the replacement of boxes with open balconies, usually called the Dress Circle, Upper Circle, and Gallery. Furthermore, the balconies were foreshortened on the sides so that they no longer extended to the proscenium wall. As a result, the proscenium arch could be lowered. The cantilevering of balconies, made possible in the late nineteenth century by the introduction of structural steel and concrete, permitted the removal of visible supporting posts in the auditorium. All these changes did much to improve sight lines and comfort. Many of these innovations were made by C. J. Phipps (1835–1897), architect of about forty theatres in England.

ENGLISH THEATRICAL CONDITIONS, 1880–1900

Between 1880 and 1900 the English theatre was dominated by the actor-manager Henry Irving (1838–1905). Born John Henry Brodribb, Irving played in the provinces from 1856 to 1866 and then in London with several leading actors before going to the Lyceum Theatre in 1871 as leading man and stage manager. At that time, the Lyceum was under the management of H. L. Bateman (1812–1875), an American who had leased the theatre to star his daughters, Kate (1843–1917), Virginia (1853–1940), and Isabel (1854–1934). Kate and her sister Ellen (1844–1936) had achieved acclaim in the United

States as child prodigies in such roles as Richard III, Macbeth, and Shylock. Ellen had retired at the age of sixteen, but Kate had won considerable fame as an adult performer before the family came to London. After Bateman died in 1875, his wife continued as manager until 1878, when the Lyceum passed to Irving. Under Irving's management from 1878 to 1898, the Lyceum became the foremost theatre of London. Irving also played throughout England and made eight tours of the United States. He retired in 1902.

In 1874 his *Hamlet* ran for 200 nights, a new record for a Shakespearean play. By the time he became a manager in 1878, he was considered the finest serious actor in London. He was a master of byplay, which clarified every reaction and thought. His roles were boldly conceived and carefully portrayed. Like Charles Kean, Irving was at his best in melodrama; though now remembered chiefly as a Shakespearean actor, the only Shakespearean role in which he was consistently successful was Shylock. Irving promoted no new playwrights and never appeared in the new realistic drama.

Irving's fame is bound up with that of his leading lady, Ellen Terry (1847–1928), who came from a large family of actors, which, two generations later, included John Gielgud, one of the greatest actors of the twentieth century. As an adult, Ellen Terry had played in the provinces, had worked for the Bancrofts, and performed at the Court Theatre before joining Irving in 1878. She remained Irving's leading lady until he retired. She then managed the Imperial Theatre for a time, where she allowed her son, Gordon Craig, to try out many of his ideas. After 1907 she performed only occasionally, although she did not retire fully until 1925. At her best in such

FIG. 15.22
Henry Irving (foreground) as Mathias in *The Bells* seeing a vision of the Polish Jew he has murdered. Irving played this role for more than thirty years. A contemporary engraving.

roles as Beatrice in *Much Ado About Nothing,* Olivia in *Twelfth Night,* and Portia in *The Merchant of Venice,* Terry had an excellent sense of timing and a masterful command of movement and speech. To all of her roles she brought freshness and vitality.

Despite the personal fame of Irving and Ellen Terry, the reputation of the Lyceum rested upon the total effect of its productions. Building upon the tradition of Macready and Charles Kean and stimulated by the London appearance of the Meiningen Players from Germany in 1881, Irving's work climaxed the trend in England toward pictorial realism. Although never the stickler for accuracy that Kean had been, Irving often employed archeologists to aid him. At other times he commissioned designs from such famous painters as Edward Burne-Jones (1833–1898). In addition, he had on his staff the finest scenic artists of the day, Hawes Craven (1837–1910) and Joseph Harker (1855–1927). Craven had worked in London since 1857 and to him probably should go much of the credit usually given Irving. Craven was later to open a scenic studio which supplied many theatres with settings. Harker began his career as an assistant to Craven and later took major responsibility for many of Irving's productions. After leaving Irving, he became Herbert Beerbohm Tree's principal designer. Continuing to work into the 1920s, Harker was one of the major links between Victorian and modern scenic practices. But if Irving employed the finest artists available, he had no consistent policy. Sometimes a single artist designed the scenery and costumes for a production, but more frequently the tasks were divided among a number of designers.

Many of the innovations at the Lyceum resulted from changes in the method used to shift scenery. In 1881 Irving decided to copy the revolutionary steps taken at Booth's theatre in New York in 1869. He abandoned the grooves that had been the standard method of shifting scenery in England for more than 200 years. By adopting "free plantation," Irving could place scenery wherever he desired and achieve complete flexibility. Irving's solution was the culmination of many earlier trends. Since the beginning of the century, heavy set pieces had proliferated and many of them had been shifted by means of large elevator traps located upstage. Thus, while a "short scene" occupied the forward part of the stage, a "set scene" could be arranged behind a drop and revealed when needed. In this way, heavy pieces could be shifted without the necessity of closing the front curtain. Other complex changes were often made while the "act drop" was serving as a background for the entr'acte entertainment. Irving was the first English producer consistently to use the front curtain to mask major changes of scenery, although he too continued the alternation of shallow and deep scenes to avoid breaks in the action.

During the nineteenth century, as the requirements of spectacle increased, the layout of the stage floor grew ever more complex. Thus, after 1850 the stage was usually constructed in the following manner. The supporting joists, which ran parallel to the footlights, were arranged in groups of three or four set about 1 to 2 inches apart. The spaces between the joists could be covered with narrow strips of wood or left open to form "cuts," through which pieces of scenery, such as ground rows, might be raised or lowered. Occasionally, a vertical moving panorama ran from overhead through a cut to aid the illusion, for example, of climbing a cliff or falling from a height. The groups of joists were spaced about four feet apart. Between them were laid floorboards, some of which could be removed for the insertion of traps or all to form "bridges" the width of the proscenium through which large set pieces could be raised or special effects manipulated.

Many traps were required by nineteenth-century plays. The "vampire" trap, named for Planché's *The Vampire* (1820), consisted of two spring-leaves that parted under pressure and immediately reclosed. It could be set into the floor to permit an actor seemingly to sink into the earth or set into a flat to permit the illusion of walking through a solid wall. The "Corsican" trap (so-called because of its use in *The Corsican Brothers*) or "ghost glide" was more complex. For it, a "bridge" was removed the full width of the stage. The flooring removed to create the bridge was replaced by a covering like that of a roll-top desk. Beneath the bridge an inclined track was installed. As a wheeled platform moved up this track, the actor standing on it was forced up through a "bristle" trap (an opening covered with bristles colored to match the floor). The roll-top covering over the bridge was geared to move with the platform so that no opening in the floor was ever seen by the audience. Thus, figures appeared to rise from or sink into the earth while gliding through space.

A number of nineteenth-century innovations were brought together around 1890 to create some of the most spectacular productions ever seen on an indoor stage. Treadmills were installed in the stage bridges and coupled with moving panoramas to create such scenes as the chariot race in Ben Hur, for which the stadium was painted on the panorama and moved past the galloping horses, which were kept on stage by the treadmills, whose speeds were controlled by recently developed electric motors.

As the desire for complete illusion grew, so did the use of three-dimensional scenic elements. Charles Kean had still depended primarily on two-dimensional painted pieces, and it was not until the 1870s that

FIG. 15.23
Section drawing showing the operation of a star trap. The flexible parts of the trap opening, here displaced by the actor's body, conceal the opening when it is not in use. From Georges Moynet, *La Machinerie Théâtrale* (1893).

steps, platforms, and similar three-dimensional units were common. It was probably Irving's desire to make more effective use of three-dimensional pieces that motivated his removal of the grooves, which were suited only to flat wings. Since he then had to depend primarily upon manual shifting, Irving employed about 135 persons to "arrange and conduct the scenes," and he rehearsed them as thoroughly as he did his actors.

Irving also paid careful attention to costumes, but his chief improvement over his predecessors lay in the care given to minor characters. Even Kean had dressed the supernumeraries in armor made of zinc and tinfoil and had substituted glazed cotton for satin. Irving reputedly applied the same standard to all costumes and consequently achieved a more unified effect.

Irving was probably the first English producer to make an art of stage lighting, for while the many

FIG. 15.24

An English stage of the late nineteenth century. Note how the stage floor is divided; note also the sinking trap, the overhead grooves, and the strong beam of light (either a limelight or carbon arc). Footlights are visible in the extreme lower right corner, as is a row of vertical lights immediately back of the proscenium arch. From *The Magazine of Art* (1889).

technical advances (such as the introduction of gas, the gas table, and limelight) had created new potential for stage lighting, few directors had explored the artistic applications. Irving's improvements were gained through care for details. He broke up the footlights and borders into short sections, each of which was equipped with different colors and controls. He experimented with transparent lacquered glass to achieve varied hues and with several means of distributing light more effectively. Critics almost always commented on his lighting, although many termed it arbitrary and distracting because each moment had obviously been contrived for beauty and effectiveness. Irving also introduced black masking pieces at the front of the stage to prevent "light spill" and was the first English producer consistently to darken the auditorium during performances. It required thirty "gas men" to mount and operate the lights at the Lyceum.

Until the end of his career, Irving used gas, even though by that time he was in the minority. In 1879 Edison's invention of the incandescent lamp had made it possible to light the entire stage electrically, and almost immediately the changeover began, in part because several disastrous theatre fires made managers anxious to adopt the first illuminant yet developed that did not require an open flame. In 1881 the Savoy Theatre became the first in London to be lighted throughout with electricity, and by 1900 almost all English theatres had followed its example. Because early incandescent lamps could be made only in very low wattages, limelight continued to be an important supplement. To this was added the carbon arc, which served much the same purpose.

The carbon arc was first demonstrated in 1808 by Sir Humphrey Davy, but the lack of a satisfactory source of power left its theatrical uses unexplored until the 1840s. By 1860 it had been placed in a housing and equipped with a lens to create a spotlight. It was not widely used, however, until after 1880, when electricity began to replace gas. To create a carbon arc, each electrical pole was attached to a stick of carbon; when the carbons were brought into close juxtaposition, the current leaped between them, creating an incandescence. Giving off a rather harsh light, the carbon arc also tended to be noisy and to flicker. Many of the drawbacks were eliminated with the invention in 1876 of the Jablochkoff Candle, which kept the carbon in proper alignment without the aid of an operator.

Beginning in 1905, significant improvements in the filaments of lamps made higher wattages possible and, as the potential intensity of lamps increased thereafter, the carbon arc and limelight were used less frequently. The limelight went out of use around World War I, but the carbon arc continued in use until late in the twentieth century, although primarily as a follow spot.

Irving's care with each element of production was crowned by even greater care for coordinating them into an integrated whole. It was for this reason that Irving's work was superior to that of his English contemporaries. His practices as a director pointed the way toward the future, even if his emphasis on pictorial realism was merely the culmination of the nineteenth-century tradition.

In 1895 Irving became the first performer in English history to be knighted, an indication that actors had at last achieved social acceptance and that Irving was considered preeminent in his profession. In 1897 Squire Bancroft was knighted, and by 1914 such performers as John Hare, Johnston Forbes-Robertson, and Herbert Beerbohm Tree had been similarly honored. Comparable awards were not given to women until 1925, when Ellen Terry was named Dame Commander of the British Empire.

FIG. 15.25

A horserace on stage, using a moving panorama and treadmills run by electric motors, the speed of which was controlled by the man at upper right. Union Square Theatre, New York, 1889–1890. From Georges Moynet, *La Machinerie Théâtrale* (1893).

LOOKING AT THEATRE HISTORY

One way of studying theatre history is through an examination of the technology available for creating the effects desired by playwrights, directors, and designers. All ages, from the Greek to the present, have used technological devices, and an understanding of the available means and how they were used can do much to clarify the stylistic and visual qualities of theatrical art in any era. Few periods have been as self-conscious as the late nineteenth century about the application of scientific knowledge to stage production. Perhaps the most obvious results were in stage machinery, but in all areas of production a major goal was to create illusion so true to nature that it could withstand the scrutiny of the most demanding observer. Stage technology became a frequent subject in periodicals,

perhaps most notably in *The Scientific American*. Albert A. Hopkins, for many years editor of that magazine, drew heavily on articles first published there for his *Magic: Stage Illusions and Scientific Diversions* (1897), a section of which is devoted to "Science in the Theatre." It is a valuable source of information about the theatre technology of that time.

Among the devices described in *Magic* is the elevator stage installed in MacKaye's Madison Square Theatre (see Fig. 15.10):

The shaft through which the huge elevator moves up and down measures one hundred and fourteen feet from the roof to the bottom. . . . The whole construction is fifty-five feet high and twenty-two feet wide and thirty-one feet deep, and weighs about forty-eight tons. . . . Only about forty seconds are required to raise or lower the stage in position, and the entire structure is moved by four men at the winch. The movement is effected without sound, jar or vibration, owing to the balancing of the stage and its weight with counterweights. . . . The borders and border lights are supplied to each of the movable stages, and each stage has its own trap floor. . . . [271]

Hopkins also describes MacKaye's Spectatorium, Lautenschläger's revolving stage, the horse race illustrated in Fig. 15.25, and various other devices, including many required by Wagner's operas (such as floating the Rhine Maidens in *The Rhinegold* and making and operating the dragon in *Siegfried*). One technological milestone of the period was the development of electricity as a motive force for stage machinery and lighting. Here is a report concerning the Savoy Theatre, built to house Gilbert and Sullivan's comic operas:

An attempt will be made here for the first time in London to light a theatre entirely by electricity. The system used is that of the "incandescent lamp." . . . About 1,200 lights are used, and the power to generate a sufficient current for these is obtained from large steam engines, giving about 120 horse power, placed on some open land near the theatre. The new light is used not only in the audience part of the theatre, but on the stage for footlights, side and top lights, etc. . . . What is being done is an experiment, and may succeed or fail.

The Times, 3 October 1881.

The nineteenth century also sought to apply scientific (that is, precise) knowledge to the design of scenery and costumes so as to ensure their authenticity. Charles Kean sometimes even supplied his audiences with an account of the sources he had consulted and the reasoning that had led to his decisions. Such an account (some parts of which follow) were first used by Kean for his production of *Macbeth* in 1853:

The very uncertain information . . . which we possess respecting the dress worn by the inhabitants of Scotland in the eleventh century, renders any attempt to present this tragedy attired in the costume of the period a task of very great difficulty. . . . In the absence of any positive information I have borrowed materials from those nations to whom Scotland was constantly opposed in war. . . . I have introduced the tunic, mantle, cross gartering, and ringed byrne of the Danes and Anglo-Saxons. . . . The coats of mail appear to have been composed of iron rings or bosses, sewn upon cloth or leather, like that of the Anglo-Saxons. . . . The . . . architecture previous to the Norman conquest has been adopted throughout the play. . . . On this subject I have availed myself of the valuable knowledge of George Godwin, Esq., F. R. S. of the Royal Institute of Architects, to whose suggestions I take this opportunity of acknowledging my obligation.

Shakespeare's Tragedy of Macbeth, . . . Arranged for Representation at the Princess's Theatre, with Historical and Explanatory Notes by Charles Kean (London, 1853), v–ix.

16
Continental European and Latin American Theatre in the Late Nineteenth Century

While the early nineteenth century was marked by a loss of colonial power and the rise of nationalism in the Americas, the late nineteenth century was the heyday of nationalism and imperialism in Europe. On the continent the number of independent states declined markedly as they were brought into the German empire, the kingdom of Italy, the Austro-Hungarian empire, and the Russian empire. This trend toward centralization at home was paralleled by overseas expansion, motivated in part by the need for raw materials and markets to support rapid industrialization. Much of Africa and Asia came under the direct control of European nations. Britain acquired the largest empire, but it was followed closely by France and Germany.

Industry and trade encouraged technological advances, and each new invention increased faith in science and engineering to solve human problems. Nevertheless, benefits were not evenly distributed, and the working classes had to fight for every increase in their rights.

For the most part, the theatre during the late nineteenth century was merely a logical outgrowth of what had gone before. But increasingly, acting styles, production techniques, and even entire productions were being praised for their "realism." This all-purpose term could include any production dealing with contemporary life, even melodramas, or any play that used historically accurate clothing, properties, and settings, even those in which the characters were speaking in verse. Gradually "realism" came to be applied to a form of drama which sought to represent scientifically observed actions in physical spaces that demonstrated the interdependence of character and environment. Realism as a dramatic form will be dealt with in the next chapter as it spans the period between the 1870s and the outbreak of World War I in 1914.

RUSSIAN THEATRE TO 1900

During the late nineteenth century Russia wavered between reform and harshness. Alexander II (ruled 1855–1881) initiated a series of changes, including loosening censorship, freeing the serfs (in 1861), and extending the educational system. But after an attempt on his life in 1866, he lost his zeal for reform, and his assassination in 1881 led Alexander III (ruled 1881–1894) to reinstitute strict censorship and to strengthen the power of the aristocracy.

It is surprising, therefore, to find that realism appeared in Russian drama earlier than it did in the rest of Europe and that it was more uncompromising. It was first fully realized by Ivan Turgenev (1818–1883). Most of his plays were written between 1843 and 1852, but their influence on other dramas came

FIG. 16.1

Setting by Andreas Roller for a ballet. From Syrkina, *Russkoe Teatralne Dekoratsione Iskusstvo.*

much later since his finest work, *A Month in the Country* (1850), was not produced until 1872. Turgenev's major concern in this play is the inner life of the characters. He renders the daily routine of a country estate faithfully, but he does so only as a means of showing the permanent psychological changes wrought in several characters by the presence of a young tutor. Turgenev's contribution to realism comes from his use of domestic detail to reveal inner turmoil. Chekhov was to build upon his work. After 1863 Turgenev lived abroad, where he became the best known of all Russian authors.

Before Turgenev's plays appeared on the stage, realism had already been popularized through the work of Alexander Ostrovsky (1823–1886), Russia's first professional playwright and the first Russian writer to confine himself exclusively to drama. Ostrovsky wrote his first play in 1847, and from 1853 until his death completed at least one new drama each year. Working primarily from observation, Ostrovsky is often credited with creating a peculiarly Russian drama free from Western influence. Although he wrote in a variety of forms and used a wide range of subjects, his major works draw on the life he knew best, that of the middle class. He sought to eliminate Gogol's penchant for caricature and to avoid stage tricks and irrelevant spectacle by concentrating upon characters and their relationships to each other and to a particular milieu. Ostrovsky is perhaps best known for *Enough Stupidity in Every Wise Man* (1868, sometimes called *The Diary of a Scoundrel*) and

The Thunderstorm (1859). The former is the comic chronicle of a man's rise through his manipulation of other people's vanities, while *The Thunderstorm,* which shows the tragic outcome of parental tyranny, is noteworthy for its use of the storm as a symbol of turmoil in human affairs. In his use of symbolism, Ostrovsky anticipates Chekhov.

Ostrovsky was instrumental in founding the Russian Society of Dramatic Authors and Composers in 1866. Until this time, the dramatist usually received no pay for work beyond a set fee from the state troupes; provincial companies did not pay at all. After 1866, playwrights gradually won full copyright protection.

Of Ostrovsky's contemporaries, the most important were Pisemsky, Sukhovo-Kobylin, and Saltikov-Shchedrin. A. F. Pisemsky (1820–1881) wrote many kinds of plays but is now remembered primarily for one of the most naturalistic works of the nineteenth century, *A Bitter Fate* (1859), which antedates by many years the naturalist movement in France. The story is simple: A peasant learns that his wife has been seduced by a wealthy landowner; he kills the child born to her and turns himself over to the authorities. A masterfully written work, it more nearly realizes the aims of the French naturalists than does any of their own dramas. Alexander Sukhovo-Kobylin (1817–1903) is noted primarily for a trilogy of plays treating the Russian legal and bureaucratic systems, with which he was personally entangled. *Krechinsky's Wedding* (1854) is relatively lighthearted, but *The Case* (1861) and *Tarelkin's Death* (not produced until 1917) seem intended to arouse shudders rather than laughter. The work of Mikhail Saltikov-Shchedrin (1826–1889) is related to that of Sukhovo-Kobylin, for he too gives a satirical picture of corruption in his *The Death of Pazukhin* (1857, banned until 1900).

Near the end of the nineteenth century Leo Tolstoy (1828–1910), already famous as a novelist, turned to playwriting. Of his dramas, the most important is *The Power of Darkness* (1886, first performed in Russia in 1895), a story of greed and murder among Russian peasants. Like *A Bitter Fate,* it is one of the most effective of naturalistic plays.

Although the major Russian plays of the late nineteenth century fall into the realistic school, they were by no means the standard fare of the public theatres, which continued to favor melodrama, farce, musical drama, and romantic spectacles. Of the writers outside the realistic trend, probably the most important was Alexey K. Tolstoy (1817–1875), whose plays idealized the Russian past and emphasized the clash of strong personalities against picturesque historical backgrounds. His trilogy, *The Death of Ivan the Terrible, Tsar Fyodor Ivanovich,* and *Tsar Boris* (written between 1865 and 1870) are among the finest of their genre.

Thus, during the late nineteenth century Russia produced a number of outstanding playwrights, many of them still little known in the West. It is difficult to avoid speculating about the heights that might have been reached had censorship been less strenuous and theatrical conditions more favorable.

Perhaps because it did not arouse official displeasure, Russian ballet reached a peak of perfection during the last half of the century under the influence of Marius Petipa (1822–1910). Born in France, Petipa came to Russia in 1847 and was appointed ballet master of the Imperial Schools in 1862. After 1870 he was the virtual dictator of ballet in Russia. He choreographed seventy-four long works (among them *Swan Lake, Sleeping Beauty,* and *The Nutcracker,* with music by Tchaikovsky), in which considerable emphasis was placed on sets and costumes as well as upon storytelling dance. By the time he retired in 1903, Russian ballet had assumed the characteristics for which it is still noted.

THEATRICAL CONDITIONS IN RUSSIA TO 1900

Russian theatrical conditions changed little until after 1882, when the monopolies on performances in Moscow and St. Petersburg, held by the state theatres, were abolished. In actuality these monopolies had been violated for many years by performances disguised as private entertainments. The Nobility Assembly, the Painters Club, the Merchants Club, and others had regularly scheduled "dramatic evenings" and "family reunions" which often featured theatrical entertainment. By 1875 about twenty-five such groups offered performances regularly in Moscow and St. Petersburg.

After the monopolies were rescinded, the public theatre expanded rapidly, although the state troupes continued to command the greatest prestige. The quality of the provincial theatres also improved. Prior to the 1880s, even the best of them had to tour and felt it necessary to import stars to increase their appeal. Costumes and scenery were meager, and amateurs were often employed as stagehands. By the 1870s permanent buildings had been built in eight provincial cities, but not until about 1890 were any companies able to cease touring. In 1897 the first All-Russian Convention of Theatrical Workers was held to discuss common problems.

The trend toward accuracy in settings and costumes, which in Western Europe had preceded the development of realism in character and situation, was slow to develop in Russia. In 1853 one of Ostrovsky's plays is said to have startled audiences with its simple and accurate spectacle when the heroine appeared in a cotton dress and with natural hair rather than the usual fashionable garments and coiffure. Thereafter, realism of detail increased, especially at the Maly, upon which Ostrovsky exerted considerable influence. It was not until the 1880s that managers began to be much concerned about accurate settings. Until then, most theatres used conventionalized settings devoid of national or period flavor. Such decor had been popularized by Andreas Roller (1805–1891), a German designer who dominated Russian scenic practices, since he and his pupils or disciples held the major posts in the state theatres. Nevertheless, archeologically correct settings began to appear sporadically after the 1860s. In 1865 the Alexandrinsky Theatre employed an archeologist to assist with historically accurate settings and costumes for Tolstoy's *The Death of Ivan the Terrible,* and after 1870 such major Russian painters as Mikhail Bocharov and M. A. Shishkov organized a special class in theatrical design at the Art Academy. By the 1890s a number of prominent painters were working for the private theatres. Nevertheless, Ostrovsky's response to the Meiningen Players (then universally admired for realism) when they played in Moscow in 1885 tells much about Russian attitudes of the time: He labeled them a talented group of amateurs who placed far too much emphasis upon spectacle except in the admirable crowd scenes. On the other hand, Stanislavsky was deeply impressed by the Meiningen troupe's attention to pictorial values, which contrasted so sharply with the typical Russian approach. Stanislavsky states that in Russia around 1890 costumes from three periods were considered sufficient for all plays, and that, since these were used repeatedly, they were usually old and dirty. He adds that leading actresses still insisted upon wearing stylish (often inappropriate) clothing and that the secondary characters could always be identified by their drabness.

In acting, the troupe at Moscow's Maly continued to be superior to those in St. Petersburg. Shchepkin's major successor at the Maly was Prov Sadovsky (1818–1872), who was so effective in Ostrovsky's plays that the theatre came to be called "the House of Ostrovsky." Discovered in the provinces by Shchepkin, in 1839 Sadovsky came to the Maly, where he played minor roles until Ostrovsky's plays offered him parts suited to his style of performance. While Shchepkin had excelled at external detail, Sadovsky's ability to project both internal and external realism created more fully rounded characterizations than any previously seen in Moscow.

FIG. 16.2

Setting by M. A. Shishkov for Griboyedov's *Woe from Wit*. From Syrkina, *Russkoe Teatralne Dekoratsione Iskusstvo*.

Until the 1860s, actors were trained either in service or at the state dramatic schools, which combined the course of study for actors, dancers, and singers. After the private Russian Musical Society opened a conservatory in St. Petersburg in 1862 and another in Moscow in 1866, the state schools reevaluated their approach. Training for opera and ballet were separated from acting, and graduates were no longer automatically eligible for employment in the imperial theatres. In 1882 lines of business were abandoned as the basis of employment in the state troupes. Although typecasting continued, greater flexibility became possible.

But true ensemble effects of the type exemplified by Saxe-Meiningen's company in Germany were not to be achieved in Russia until after 1898, when the Moscow Art Theatre was founded. Prior to this time, however, a few Russian companies had pointed the way. Especially important was the troupe founded in Moscow in 1882 by F. A. Korsh (1852–1921). Korsh maintained a high standard of production, introduced many significant plays from Western Europe, established matinee performances in Russia, and trained a number of actors later to be famous. The company continued until 1932, many years after Korsh's death. In Korsh's theatre the early productions achieved a consistent style and all roles were cast and prepared with care. By the 1890s, this meticulousness had begun to fade. Nevertheless, by 1898 the conditions and possibilities of a new theatre had been created. It remained for Stanislavsky and Nemirovich-Danchenko to consolidate the gains and to inaugurate a new era in the Russian theatre with the Moscow Art Theatre.

GERMAN AND AUSTRIAN THEATRE TO 1900

Germany produced few dramatists of note in the second half of the nineteenth century. The major playwrights of the 1850s were Otto Ludwig (1813–1865) and Gustav Freytag (1816–1895). Ludwig sought a middle ground between idealism and realism. He opposed the political and social stance of Young Germany and sought to substitute a realism lacking in tendentiousness. His best plays are *The Hereditary Forester* (1850), a middle-class tragedy which reflects Othello in its treatment of a misunderstanding between friends, and *The Maccabees* (1854), which treats the revolt of Judas Maccabeus against Antioch. Freytag is remembered primarily for *The Journalists* (1853), a good-humored view of politics in a small town. In addition, his *The Technique of Drama* (1863) was long considered to be a major treatise on playwriting.

Following the death of Hebbel in 1863, German-language drama entered a state of decline from which it did not recover until the 1890s. The general level of serious drama in this period is indicated by the works of Ernst von Wildenbruch (1845–1909), an ardent admirer of the Hohenzollern rulers and of the Teutonic heritage. His plays gained wide popularity following the unification of Germany in 1871. Wildenbruch had a considerable gift for writing crowd scenes and for depicting picturesque working-class life, but much of his drama, such as his two-part *Heinrich and Heinrich's Dynasty* (1896), now seems merely derivative.

In Austria, the peasant play was kept alive by Ludwig Anzengruber (1839–1889), who gave it a serious turn by using it to present a faithful picture of rural life. *The Priest of Kirschfeld* (1870) reflects the controversy over the recently promulgated doctrine of papal infallibility, while his *The Double Suicide* (1875) is reminiscent of *Romeo and Juliet*. But Anzengruber was not always serious; *He Who Signed With a Cross* (1872), for example, is a variation on *Lysistrata*. Because of his realism, Anzengruber was little appreciated until the end of his life, when the rise of naturalism called attention to his depiction of characters rooted in particular environments. His fame aroused new interest in peasant drama, as a result of which a theatre was founded in Bavaria in 1891 especially to produce and tour folk plays.

During the late nineteenth century, variety theatres, cabarets, summer theatres, and pleasure gardens flourished. Operetta also became increasingly popular, especially in Vienna. The vogue began around 1858 with the importation of Offenbach's works. The first important native composer was Franz von Suppé (1820–1895) with such pieces as *Fatinitza*

(1872) and *The Devil on Earth* (1878), but he was soon surpassed by Johann Strauss (1825–1899) with *Die Fledermaus* (1874), *A Night in Venice* (1883), *The Gypsy Baron* (1885), and many others. Operetta was long to be one of Vienna's major attractions.

The lack of significant new dramatists was not keenly felt, since the plays of Shakespeare, Lessing, Goethe, and Schiller were prominent in the repertory and those of Kleist began to assume the status of classics. Following Grillparzer's death in 1872, directors vied in giving his works lavish productions. After 1850, foreign plays, especially those of Scribe, Sardou, Augier, and Dumas *fils,* also made up an increasingly large part of the German and Austrian repertory and helped to compensate for the lack of good new native plays. The period of stagnation was ultimately broken around 1890 with the emergence of the "modern" school.

In contrast to changes then underway elsewhere, in Germany resident companies did not decline markedly in number or prestige during the last half of the nineteenth century, probably because the major troupes were supported by state or municipal governments. By 1871 there were about 200 theatres in Germany with about 5000 artistic employees. By 1896, the number of such employees had tripled. Until German unification (1871), classics could only be performed by state theatres, but after that time any licensed theatre could perform any work passed by the censor.

During the late nineteenth century the major German-language theatre was Vienna's Burgtheater, in large part because of Laube and Dingelstedt.

FIG. 16.4

Franz Dingelstedt's production at Weimar in 1861 of Hebbel's *The Niebelungen.* Seen here is the final scene in the second play of the trilogy. From *Leipziger Illustrierte Zeitung* (1861).

Heinrich Laube (1806–1884) was a well-known playwright of the Young Germany school before he was appointed director of Vienna's Burgtheater, a post he held from 1849 until 1867. Laube placed primary emphasis on the text and especially on diction and characterization. Under his direction, the Burgtheater regained the preeminence it had enjoyed under Schreyvogel. Its ensemble was the finest of any German-language company, including among its members Bogumil Dawison; Adolf Sonnenthal (1834–1909), who portrayed a wide range of serious and comic roles but was especially admired for his elegance and seeming normality in drawing room comedy; and Charlotte Wolter (1833–1897), one of the great international stars of the age and an exponent of "naturalistic" acting. Laube was opposed to elaborate historical settings because he thought them distracting and "operatic." On the other hand, he was the first German producer consistently to use the box set, which he adopted because it increased the sense of immediacy and intimacy. Nevertheless, he never permitted more furniture on stage than was demanded by the action. His was a rather austere realism aimed at riveting attention on the actor rather than on the spectacle. In the history of German directing, Laube holds a position comparable to Montigny's in France.

Laube was followed at the Burgtheater between 1870 and 1881 by Franz Dingelstedt (1814–1881), who, unlike his predecessor, emphasized lavish and historically accurate decor. Dingelstedt had become well known throughout Germany because of his work in Munich between 1851 and 1857 and in Weimar

FIG. 16.3

Interior of the Burgtheater, Vienna, in the late nineteenth century. From *Die Theater Wiens* (1899).

between 1857 and 1867. In Munich in 1851 he staged Sophocles' *Antigone* with the assistance of some of the most respected scholars, artists, and musicians of his day. The high point of his work in Munich probably came in 1854 with a festival (held in conjunction with the Munich Industrial Exposition) during which outstanding German actors presented plays by Goethe, Schiller, Lessing, and others. This venture aroused such enthusiasm that thereafter festivals began to appear elsewhere. At Weimar, Dingelstedt restored the reputation of the company, which had been in decline. He was especially noted for his staging there of Schiller's *Wallenstein* trilogy in 1859, Hebbel's *Niebelungen* trilogy in 1862, and almost all of Shakespeare's plays during a single week in 1864 (which motivated the formation of the German Shakespeare Society). In 1870 he became director of the Burgtheater, where, with his costume designer Franz Gaul (1837–1906) and scene designer Herman Burghart (1834–1901) he presented some of the most lavish productions of the age. Perhaps his major achievement came in 1875 with the presentation of Shakespeare's history plays as a connected cycle.

Another major director of the period was Friedrich Haase (1825–1911), especially at Coburg-Gotha's theatre from 1866 to 1868 and at the Leipzig Municipal Theatre from 1870 to 1876. Through his work at these theatres and elsewhere he came to be especially noted for his staging of such Shakespearean plays as *Hamlet* and *The Merchant of Venice* in the manner of Charles Kean, whose influence he freely acknowledged. As a major star, Haase extended his own influence through engagements with other companies.

By 1875 historical accuracy was accepted as an ideal by almost all German-language troupes. Nevertheless, the same settings were still reused for different plays of the same historical period, and inconsistencies abounded. Perhaps the greatest needs were for ensemble playing and for a controlling artistic consciousness. It was to these problems, above all, that the two major innovators of the period—Wagner and Saxe-Meiningen—addressed themselves so effectively that they would lay the foundations for the modern movement.

FRENCH DRAMA TO 1900

It was in France that dramatists first consciously sought to implement the realists' program. Among these pioneering playwrights, the most important were Dumas *fils* and Augier. But they owed much to their predecessors and perhaps most to Eugène Scribe (1791–1861), for he had popularized the structural pattern they were to appropriate. Between 1811 and 1861, Scribe contributed over 300 pieces to Parisian theatres, twenty-three of them to the Comédie Française. He ranged through *comédies-envaudevilles*, opera libretti, comedies, and serious drama. Perhaps the best of his works were *Marriage for Money* (1827), *A Glass of Water* (1840), and *Adrienne Lecouvreur* (1849). Today, Scribe is remembered primarily as the popularizer of the "well-made play" formula. Often used as a term of derision, "well-made play" can perhaps best be understood as a combination and perfection of dramatic devices common since the time of Aeschylus: careful exposition and preparation, cause-to-effect arrangement of incidents, building scenes to a climax, and the skillful manipulation of withheld information, startling reversals, and suspense. Because they sacrifice depth of characterization and thought to intrigue, Scribe's plays now seem shallow. To theatregoers of the nineteenth century, however, they appeared more substantial, probably because they manipulate so effectively the attitudes and prejudices of the time. Although Scribe was not associated with the realistic movement, his well-made play formula, emphasizing as it did the seemingly logical development from cause to effect, supplied Dumas *fils* and Augier with a suitable form for their ideas.

Alexandre Dumas *fils* (1824–1895) came to public attention with a dramatization of his own novel, *The Lady of the Camellias* (now usually referred to as *Camille*). Although today *Camille* (performed 1852) seems merely an idealized treatment of the

FIG. 16.5
Friedrich Haase as Hamlet in his own production at Leipzig. The play-within-the-play scene. Woodcut by Knut Ekwall, 1871. Courtesy Theatermuseum, Munich.

FIG. 16.6
Scribe's *A Glass of Water,* Act V, scene 7, first performed at the Comédie Française, 1840. From *Oeuvres Complètes de M. Eugène Scribe* 5 (1847).

"prostitute with a heart of gold," it was forbidden production for three years because of its realism. Set in Paris in the 1840s, the play used prose dialogue and depicted a protagonist based upon a well-known courtesan of the time.

Dumas soon underwent a change of attitude and in *The Demi-Monde* (1855) treated unsympathetically the same kind of characters that were presented sentimentally in *Camille.* He now set out to show that "women with a past" must be prevented from marrying into good families. After this time, Dumas wrote "thesis plays" about current social problems, utilizing Scribe's well-made play formula to create suspenseful and entertaining stories. His works are marred by didacticism, for in most a message is clearly stated by an articulate *raisonneur,* or author's mouthpiece. In spite of this lack of objectivity, Dumas considered himself a realist and his duty the betterment of society. In an open letter to the critic Francisque Sarcey, he wrote: ". . . if I can exercise some influence over society . . . if I can find some means to force

people to discuss the problem, and the lawmaker to revise the law, I shall have done more than my duty as a writer, I shall have done my duty as a man."

Emile Augier (1820–1889) was a more versatile writer than Dumas *fils.* He began his career in 1844 as an adherent of the "theatre of common sense" but, after seven verse plays, adopted the realistic style. One of his first prose works, *Olympe's Marriage* (1855), was intended as a direct reply to Dumas' *Camille,* for it shows the disastrous results of a courtesan's marrying into an aristocratic family. It is Augier's most didactic play. His more characteristic works are comedies of manners, such as *M. Poirier's Son-in-Law* (1854) in which Augier depicts the struggle for supremacy between the impoverished but proud nobility and the well-to-do and ambitious middle class. Others of his plays treat the power of money, the influence of the church on politics, and numerous additional problems.

Although they occasionally shocked audiences, Dumas and Augier were viewed not as extremists but as sane citizens seeking to raise the moral tone of their times. Their plays treated subjects of concern to the middle-class citizenry of Napoleon III's materialistic and conservative Third Empire. Thus, Dumas and Augier were rapidly assimilated into the mainstream of drama not only in France but throughout Europe. It would be left to their more uncompromising successors to bring hitherto unacceptable topics onto the stage. Furthermore, perhaps because they used Scribean techniques, Dumas and Augier did not seem at the time to differ markedly, except in tone, from their less serious contemporaries, such as Sardou and Labiche.

FIG. 16.7
Final scene from *The Lady of the Camellias* by Alexandre Dumas *fils,* first performed in 1852. From *Le Théâtre Contemporain Illustré* (1867).

Victorien Sardou (1831–1908), Scribe's true heir, was one of the world's most popular playwrights between 1860 and 1900. Like Scribe, Sardou used the well-made play formula and adapted it to almost every dramatic type. His early successes included comedies, such as *A Scrap of Paper* (1860) and *Our Intimates* (1861), and satires on contemporary life, such as *The Family Benoîton* (1865). He later wrote a number of plays for Sarah Bernhardt, including *Fedora* (1882) and *Tosca* (1887), and some of the most lavish historical spectacles of the nineteenth century, such as *Fatherland!* (1868) and *Theodora* (1884). The latter works elicited praise even from the naturalists for their faithful recreation of particular milieus. To George Bernard Shaw, however, Sardou's shallow dramas seemed to epitomize the decadence and mindlessness into which the late nineteenth-century theatre had descended, a state he labeled "Sardoodledom."

Eugène Labiche (1815–1888) was one of the finest writers of farce in the nineteenth century. Uninterested in theories, Labiche wrote for the popular audience and only reluctantly agreed to the publication of his plays. Most of his works, of which *The Italian Straw Hat* (1851) is representative, appear delightfully irresponsible, but others, such as *M. Perrichon's Journey* (1860) and *Dust in the Eyes* (1861), make penetrating observations on human nature. Many of his plays have worn better than those of his more self-consciously serious contemporaries.

Of the minor forms, the most popular in France during the late nineteenth century was operetta,

FIG. 16.9

Sardou's historical spectacle, *Fatherland!*, directed by Sardou at the Théâtre de la Porte Saint-Martin in 1868. Setting by Cambon. Courtesy Bibliothèque de l'Arsenal, Paris.

which as a distinct form emerged around 1848. A mixture of song and speech, fantasy, buffoonery, and irreverent subject matter, operetta made its mark above all through the work of Jacques Offenbach (1819–1880), especially *Orpheus in the Underworld* (1858) and *La Belle Hélène* (1865).

THEATRICAL CONDITIONS IN FRANCE TO 1900

The playwrights discussed here are only a few of those who sought to fill Parisian theatres, which sometimes numbered as many as fifty during the last half of the century. Until that time most of the stable minor houses specialized in one of five genres: melodrama, comedy, vaudeville, spectacle drama, or operetta, and therefore assembled companies best at performing one kind of play and sought authors who wrote that type. In 1864, a new law removed all remaining strictures on genre (except censorship of plays) and eased most other controls (among them one that since 1814 had forbidden women to manage theatres). These changes coincided with many others. Among the most important was the increase in the length of runs. By 1880 no play was considered successful unless it was given at least 100 performances; many were given 300 or more times. In turn, length of run as a standard of success led managers to search for works likely to attract large audiences; it also led them to replace the resident company with performers hired only for the run of a play to which their talents were especially fitted. The long run meant as well that each theatre needed to produce only a few works each year to fill out its

FIG. 16.8

Augier's *Giboyer's Son*, Act IV, scene 6, at the Comédie Française, 1862. Courtesy Bibliothèque de l'Arsenal, Paris.

season. Furthermore, the provincial theatre was so undermined by touring companies that by 1900 Paris was the only important theatrical center in France. Near the end of the century, one writer complained that about twenty-five authors had come to monopolize the market, since the demand for new plays had been so much reduced and since managers favored works by proven authors. Censorship (which was not done away with until 1905) encouraged conservatism in the choice of plays.

The theatre also had a formidable rival in the *café-concert,* a form somewhat analogous to the British music hall and American vaudeville. By 1894 there were as many *café-concerts* as there were theatres in Paris. The *café-concert* had originated in the eighteenth century with cafes that offered musical entertainment. In the late nineteenth century it still retained its table seating and did not charge admission, but it did demand that spectators order drinks and food. The entertainments became increasingly varied; in addition to music, song, and dance, there were stand-up comedians, well-known actors performing scenes from famous plays, and other diversions.

Overall, the theatre in Paris during the last half of the century was prosperous. After 1875 matinee performances were added, and by 1900 ticket agencies had appeared and were being accused of buying up seats to popular plays so they might resell them at inflated prices.

During this period, then, the French theatre was characterized by conservatism motivated in part by material prosperity but also by taste. It was this conservatism that would stimulate concern for reform and eventually give rise to the "modern" era in French theatre.

Throughout the last half of the century, two demands—for increased realism (and a consequent need for greater control over production) and for virtuosity (which tended to encourage defiance of control)—were evident and often in conflict. Of the two, the trend toward realism is perhaps most apparent, for it can be seen clearly in every aspect of production. It was certainly one of the decisive elements in the development of directing.

Both Sardou and Dumas *fils* credit Adolphe Montigny (1805–1880), director of the Gymnase, with first treating directing as an art in France. According to Dumas, Montigny, beginning around 1853, placed a table downstage center in order to prevent the actors from taking up the semicircular formation then common. Next, he put chairs around the table, seated the actors, and made them speak to each other rather than to the audience, as had been typical in the past. Finally, he furnished his settings like real rooms and placed properties, such as cigar boxes,

handkerchiefs, or letters, about the stage to motivate movement from one place to another. In this way, he gradually arrived at an illusion of real life. According to Sardou, Montigny's success encouraged others to adopt his innovations.

Most of Montigny's work was done with contemporary plays written in the realistic mode. Thus, it was left to Sardou, who supervised the production of his own plays, to perfect historical spectacle, which he insisted be absolutely faithful to fact. By the end of the century practically all companies employed a director and two or three assistants to oversee the various aspects of staging and performance.

The movement toward realism was also evident in scenery and costuming. In terms of archeological accuracy, it reached its peak in Sardou's spectacles. For *Hatred* (1874), set in medieval Siena, unprecedented sums were spent on armor, costumes, and scenery. *Theodora* (1884), laid in Byzantium, was given an even more elaborate mounting; in their reviews of this piece, some critics spoke of almost nothing except the scenic marvels.

Realistic details from daily life also proliferated. For example, *My Friend Fritz,* produced at the Comédie Française in 1876, featured a farmyard in which real water flowed from a pump and real cherries were picked from trees; in another scene, real food and drink were served and consumed on stage.

The visual style and favored motifs differed little from those of earlier years, because the major designers were those who had begun their careers before 1850 or their students: A. A. Rubé, Philippe Chaperon, C. A. Cambon, J. B. Lavastre, Edouard Despléchin, Jean Daran, and Eugène Lacoste.

By the end of the nineteenth century, methods of obtaining scenery had become standardized. The

FIG. 16.10

Setting by Philippe Chaperon for *Oedipus Rex.* From *Revue des Arts Decoratifs* (1881–1882).

director, after consultation with the playwright, gave a summary of requirements to the scenic designers, who then made cardboard models of the sets. When these were approved, scale drawings were made to guide the theatre's carpenters, who built the settings. After completion, the scenery was sent to one of Paris's five or six scenic studios for painting. Each theatre hired a relatively small number of stagehands, for since French plays almost never changed place within acts, shifting was usually confined to intermissions when haste was not of major concern.

For costumes, theatres began after 1850 to employ special designers for historical plays and to increase their staffs of tailors and seamstresses to construct and maintain garments. Special supply houses were founded to meet the growing demand for armor and other articles too difficult to be made by the theatres. Professional wig makers supplied wigs, and several hairdressers were hired to assist the actors. By the late nineteenth century, Racinet's *Le Costume Historique* (completed 1888) had become the standard guide for the design of historical costumes.

In acting, realistic touches also increased. Actresses began to knit, actors to smoke or perform other familiar business on stage. One performer at the Comédie Française in the 1870s consulted toxicologists in order to make a death scene more convincing (it was judged one of the most realistic ever seen on the French stage); in 1890 a seemingly authentic blood transfusion was performed on stage. Such instances could be extended almost indefinitely.

There was also at least one important attempt to revolutionize training so that acting might become a more precise mode of communication. At this time most French actors still received their training while in service, although study at the Conservatoire became increasingly important as the repertory system began to decline. But even at the Conservatoire students learned primarily by imitating their teachers, and thus they perpetuated earlier acting techniques and styles. Given the temper of the nineteenth century, it was probably inevitable that someone would try to approach acting analytically and "scientifically." François Delsarte (1811–1871) took on this task when he set out to demonstrate that the laws of stage expression are discoverable and that these laws can be formulated as precisely as mathematical principles.

Delsarte sought to analyze emotions and ideas and to determine how they are outwardly expressed. He divided human experience and behavior into the physical, mental, and spiritual, and he related these to each action, thought, and emotion. He also divided and subdivided the body into parts and related each to the physical, mental, and spiritual. Eventually he arrived at an elaborate scheme whereby he

FIG. 16.11
Backstage at a theatre in the late nineteenth century. Note the division of the floor and the poles supporting the wings. From Pougin, *Dictionnaire du Théâtre* (1884).

sought to describe how the feet, legs, arms, torso, head, and every other part of the body can be used in communicating particular emotions, attitudes, or ideas.

Although Delsarte's system as applied by others eventually came to seem overly mechanistic, it remains important as the first significant attempt to reduce every aspect of the actor's training to method. By the end of the nineteenth century it was being taught nearly all over the world and, though it is now usually treated derisively, it has contributed to most subsequent attempts to formulate training programs for actors.

If many forces encouraged realism in late nineteenth-century French theatrical production, perhaps an equal number worked against it. In scenery, for example, the same settings were still being used for several different plays. Thus, while a company might have many more settings than in the eighteenth century, it usually did not have specially designed scenery for each play. Furthermore, since the various settings for a single production were often designed by different artists, unity was lacking. Similarly, in

FIG. 16.12
Constant-Benoît Coquelin as Cyrano de Bergerac, a role written for him by Edmond Rostand. The original production in 1898. From *Le Théâtre* (1898).

costume many actors continued to supply their own wardrobes, and actresses were often outfitted by couturiers. Even when a manager employed a costume designer, the leading actors felt free to supply their own dress and were often praised by critics for their novel touches. Although consistency was most nearly achieved in historical spectacles, even here it was seldom complete. As with scenery, the same costumes were used for many different plays.

But earlier practices were probably most evident in acting. Until near the end of the nineteenth century, actors were employed according to lines of business, and thus they tended to build up a repertory of tricks and business which they drew on in every role. Contrarily, supernumeraries were almost always recruited amateurs, and they rarely rehearsed with the company before performing. Most theatres employed someone to secure and rehearse the supernumeraries and to provide leadership on stage during performances. The composition of the group might differ each night.

But most significant, the late nineteenth century glorified starring performers. Consequently, most productions were built around them. If the stars had strong artistic consciences, this practice could lead to excellent results, but all too often it brought the subordination of everything to their whims. Even the Comédie Française did not escape this trend, and bickerings and jealousies there did much to undermine that company's ensemble.

Stars were legion during the late nineteenth century, but among the most important were Got, Coquelin, Mounet-Sully, and Réjane. Edmond Got (1822–1901), who performed at the Comédie Française after 1844, was noted for his excellent characterizations in classical and, especially, contemporary comedy. Constant-Benoît Coquelin (1841–1909) performed at the Comédie Française from 1860 to 1886, after which he toured throughout the world before returning to Paris. In the early 1890s Coquelin created a major scandal when he defied the rule that forbade any actor who left the Comédie Française to perform elsewhere in Paris. (Bernhardt had also defied this rule, but she had been such a troublemaker at the Comédie that no one wished her to remain in the company.) Coquelin's example tended to undermine the Comédie's discipline by making it easy for any disgruntled actor to leave its ranks. In 1897 Coquelin became manager of the Porte-Saint-Martin, where he created the role of Cyrano de Bergerac, written especially for him. At his best in Molière's comic roles or in flamboyant romantic parts, Coquelin was noted for his technical proficiency, about which he wrote extensively in such works as *The Art of the Actor* (1880). Mounet-Sully (1841–1916) had been trained at the Conservatoire and had played at the Odéon before he entered the Comédie Française in 1872. He was soon acknowledged as the finest tragic actor of his time. With his striking physique, beautiful voice, and fiery temperament, he brought considerable originality to all the great tragic roles in both the classical and romantic repertory. Gabrielle Réjane (1857–1920) made her first appearance in 1875 and soon was considered the finest player of comedy of her age. She seldom ventured outside light contemporary drama, but in that she was unsurpassed. She appeared with considerable success in London, New York, and elsewhere before she retired in 1915.

But the most famous French star of the late nineteenth century was Sarah Bernhardt (1844–1923). She made her debut in 1862 and, after performing in several minor theatres and at the Odéon was engaged at the Comédie Française in 1872, where she soon became a great attraction and a source of

FIG. 16.13
Sarah Bernhardt (at center) in Sardou's *Theodora* in a 1902 revival in Paris. From *Le Théâtre* (1902).

controversy. After considerable unpleasantness, she left the company in 1880. The rest of her career was devoted to starring tours throughout the world and to the management of a series of Parisian theatres. Noted for her slim figure, dark eyes, "golden" voice, and portrayals of seductiveness, pain, tearful rage, and death, she achieved her greatest success as Camille, Tosca, Adrienne Lecouvreur, Phaedra, Dona Sol in *Hernani,* and the title role in Rostand's *The Eaglet.* Her technical skill and her magnetic personality combined to create the image of the "grand actress." Many still consider her the greatest actress of her age.

The tension between tradition and change, so evident in every area of production, was also reflected in theatre architecture. During the 1860s, many new theatres were built as Napoleon III's scheme for an elaborate network of "grand boulevards" took shape. In this process, the Boulevard du Temple, the original home of the boulevard theatres, was obliterated. The new theatres that replaced the old ones retained many traditional features but included some innovations. In the au-

ditorium, the area immediately forward of the stage was fitted out with comfortable armchairs (a practice begun at the Opéra-Comique in the 1840s) but behind this area there continued to be, as in the past, a section (the pit or *parterre*) equipped only with benches. This ground level was surrounded by a row of boxes (or *baignoires*), above which rose two or three additional galleries. The first contained two or three rows of chairs and behind these a row of boxes; the second gallery was usually devoted entirely to boxes, and the third entirely to benches. The more fashionable theatres had a number of lavish *loges á salon,* fitted up like sitting rooms complete with bell cords so that the occupants could ring for service during the performances. The seating capacity of the theatres averaged from 1200 to 2000. Not until near the end of the century was there much concern for safety. The aisles were narrow and often filled with folding chairs; fire exits were inadequate and ventilation poor. After 400 persons perished in the fire that destroyed the Opéra-Comique in 1887, attention was at last turned to achieving greater safety.

FIG. 16.14

Sectional plan of the Paris Opéra, opened in 1874. The stage house is at right. Note the many levels below the stage. Note also the great amount of space given over to lobbies and other audience uses. From *Monde Illustré* (6 February 1875).

The proscenium arch was usually very high in order to provide adequate sight lines for spectators in the galleries, which not only rose to the ceiling but extended along the sides of the auditorium to the proscenium. The proscenium arch was also usually very thick, for in most theatres a box was set into it on the level of each gallery. This thickness created a wide apron that was much used by the actors, especially before realism was fully established. The prompter was housed in a compartment at the front of the apron. The floor of the stage raked upward toward the rear. The chariot-and-pole system remained the usual method of scene shifting, although it was supplemented by flying and the movement of set pieces by hand. During the nineteenth century, space above and below the stage was greatly enlarged to permit more effective handling of the increasingly detailed settings; in several theatres elevator traps were installed.

Perhaps no theatre summed up earlier tradition so thoroughly as did the Paris Opéra, completed in 1874. Designed by Charles Garnier and begun in 1862, the Opéra cost about 40 million francs. Enormous foyers and stairways led to the auditorium with its four levels of galleries and seating capacity of 2,100 persons. A proscenium arch 55 feet wide framed a stage 175 feet wide by 85 feet deep. The depth could be increased to about 150 feet by including the dance salon immediately behind the stage. The stage floor was raked upward two inches in every 40 inches. Above the stage there was 119 feet of space, and below it 50 feet. The stage floor was divided from front to back into ten sections, or *plans*, each of which was subdivided into (1) several slots about 1½ inches wide, (2) narrow traps about 18 inches wide, and (3) larger traps about 40 inches wide. An entire plan could be opened the width of the proscenium arch. This flexibility permitted the operation of almost any effect from beneath the stage. Scenery was shifted by chariots, each about 10 feet long and equipped with four upright poles upon which flats could be mounted. In addition, scenery could be flown or moved through the stage traps. When it was built, this was the most elaborate theatre in the world. Ironically, this enshrinement of past practices was completed just as Wagner's Festspielhaus at Bayreuth, which initiated a new ideal, was being built.

In France, then, the late nineteenth century brought increased attention to every aspect of theatrical endeavor. At the same time, an uneasy tension between innovation and tradition was evident. Still lacking was a theory of theatrical production capable of welding the diverse elements into a unified whole. During the last years of the century this need would begin to be met.

THE THEATRE IN ITALY AND SPAIN TO 1900

During the late nineteenth century, Italy made its greatest impact internationally through touring stars, especially Ristori, Salvini, and Rossi. Adelaide Ristori (1822–1906) was on the stage from the age of twelve and at fourteen was already playing leading roles in the company of Giuseppe Moncalvo (1781–1859). In 1838 she joined the Royal Theatre at Turin, where she received formal training in classical poetic drama. By 1850 she was famous throughout Italy for her studious and regal performances. In 1853 she took her company to Paris, and from that time until 1885, when she retired, she toured internationally. She made four visits to America and in 1874 went around the world. Although she made no striking innovations, she raised the received tradition to new heights.

Tommaso Salvini (1829–1915) began his career at the age of fourteen in the troupe of Gustavo Modena (1803–1861) at Padua. By 1848 he was in Adelaide Ristori's company in Rome, where he won his

first fame as Alfieri's Orestes. Around 1860 he began a series of international tours. Salvini excelled as Macbeth, Lear, Alfieri's heroes, and, above all, as Othello. An actor of great passion and energy, he is said to have terrified his leading ladies. Throughout the world, Salvini's name became synonymous with fiery tragic acting. He retired in 1890.

Ernesto Rossi (1829–1896) entered the theatre in 1846, replacing Salvini in Modena's company. He later performed with Ristori, and in 1857 took his own troupe to Vienna. After that time, he toured all over the world in plays by Alfieri and Shakespeare. A polished performer, he was considered by many too studied, a reaction which probably explains his failure to rival the fame of Ristori and Salvini.

Italy's contribution to theatre and drama in the late nineteenth century, then, was minor, since for the most part, it merely followed traditions already established elsewhere.

In the Spanish theatre, conditions were by 1849 so chaotic that a state council was created to establish guidelines for its regulation. This council was to accomplish the first significant reforms since the seventeenth century. At this time, the Teatro del Príncipe was renamed the Teatro Espagñol and made the Spanish national theatre, a position which it still holds. Its building was remodeled, gas lighting was installed, and its production methods modernized. (The Teatro de la Cruz was abandoned in 1856.) The use of theatres to support charities was discontinued so that the revenue might be used to raise the quality of production. All theatres were classified into three ranks, and each was restricted to particular dramatic genres.

Although the latter provision was never fully enforced, it encouraged the growth of minor dramatic types. In 1870 only eight of Madrid's thirty-two theatres were devoted to regular drama. Furthermore, the major theatres found it difficult to compete with the minor houses, which soon established the custom of offering an evening's bill composed of four distinct entertainments, thereby allowing considerable flexibility in the time when one could be admitted and greatly increasing the popularity of the minor houses. This custom handicapped theatres wishing to present full-length plays and consequently seriously affected playwriting.

During the nineteenth century, then, the theatre of Spain burgeoned, growing from a few companies in 1800 to more than fifty by 1875. From an antiquated institution, it had been brought more nearly into line with current practices in other European countries. Nevertheless, it retained much of its insularity, participating in major international movements only at a distance.

FIG. 16.15
Interior of a Spanish theatre, c. 1855. A contemporary print.

THEATRE IN LATIN AMERICAN TO 1900

Throughout the eighteenth century the Spanish colonies of the Caribbean and of North, Central, and South America had followed the theatrical traditions of Spain. Just over 500 Golden Age play scripts were sent to the Americas in 1713 for the use of the professional theatres. While most companies still maintained an extensive repertory, some producing over 140 plays in a season, these Golden Age plays, supplemented by translations of French neoclassical dramas, were able to meet the theatrical needs of the colonies for over a century, with only a few new plays added to the repertories from year to year. With little demand for new plays, local dramatists generally came from the ranks of successful poets, novelists, or government employees who wrote plays as a sideline.

Mexico City was the capital of New Spain, an area that extended from what is now the southwestern United States down to Panama. From the sixteenth through the eighteenth centuries it was home to the most extensive theatre operations in the colonies. Eusebio Vela (1688–1737) was the most noted actor-manager of the eighteenth century, and of his three surviving plays, the most interesting for a modern audience is *Apostleship in the Indies and the Martyrdom of a Chief,* because of its focus on Mexican history and its sympathetic treatment of native peoples.

The Corral of the Royal Hospital of the Indians, which had been built around 1602, was destroyed by fire in 1722. It was replaced in 1725 by the Coliseo de México, which was in turn replaced by the Coliseo Nuevo in 1752. The Coliseo Nuevo was probably the first stone theatre in the New World. Its patio had standing room for 350 with benches for 75. Surrounding the patio were three levels of galleries with eighteen boxes per level. There was a *cazuela* for the unaccompanied women and a city box above. Renamed the Teatro Principal in 1826, it was Mexico City's most influential theatre for most of the nineteenth century. The Principal was renovated in 1880, 1893, and 1895, but by the time it was destroyed by fire in 1931 it had become the home of musical entertainments.

The attempts by Spain to assert crown control over religion by banning religious drama in 1765 and expelling the Jesuits in 1767 generated considerable resentment throughout Latin America. When Napoleon conquered Spain in 1808, animosities grew until open rebellion broke out in New Spain in 1810. After eleven years of warfare the independent Empire of Mexico was finally declared in 1821. But the empire did not last; it lost its Central American holdings in 1823, Texas in 1836, California in 1845, and New Mexico and Arizona in 1848. The War of Reform (1858–1861) and the occupation by the French under Maximilian (1864–1867), followed by revolts in 1876 and 1880, left Mexico with few opportunities to develop its professional theatre in the nineteenth century. But this did not stop Luciano Corés from opening the Corral del Palenque de los Gallos in 1823. In 1841 this theatre was roofed and renamed the Teatro Provisional, which lasted until 1884.

Despite the political upheavals, theatrical activities expanded rapidly in the 1840s and 1850s. In response, three major theatres were built: the Teatro Nuevo México (1841), the Teatro de la Unión (1843, also called the Puente Quebrado), and El Grand Teatro de Santa Anna (1844, later called the National or the Imperial). El Grand Teatro was designed by Lorenzo Hidalga and was considered to be the finest theatre in Latin America. Even this was not enough to meet the growing demand, however, and five more theatres were added in the next decade, including the Teatro del la Esmeralda (1858, later called the Fama and then the Hidalgo). But musical and variety entertainments were becoming so popular that by the end of the century only the Hidalgo was still staging legitimate drama.

Important authors continued to write for the stage. José Joaquín Fernández de Lizardi (1776–1827), Mexico's first novelist, wrote several plays during the 1820s concerning events (some of them quite recent) in Mexican history. Manuel Eduardo de Gorostiza (1789–1851) wrote a number of neoclassical plays including *Bread and Onion with Thee* (1833), satirizing the exaggerations of romanticism. Ignacio Rodriquez Galván (1816–1842) wrote *Muñoz, Inspector General of Mexico* (1838), a history play modeled on the plays of the French romantics. And Fernando Calderón (1809–1845), who was known primarily for romantic dramas set in the Middle Ages, wrote *None of the Three* (1839), a light comedy that was immensely popular. In mid-century, Juan A. Mateos (1831–1913), first in collaboration with Vicente Riva Palacio (1832–1896) and then on his own, was the dominant playwright, producing a long string of successful melodramas and comedies. But for the most part the rapid expansion of theatre in the 1840s and 1850s did not lead to an equivalent growth in local playwriting. That was not to come until the last quarter of the century when Alfredo Chavero (1841–1906), José Peón y Contreras (1843–1907), Manuel José Othón (1848–1906), and José Rosas Moreno (1838–1883) all wrote highly successful plays, several of which foreshadowed the realism that would enter Latin American theatre in

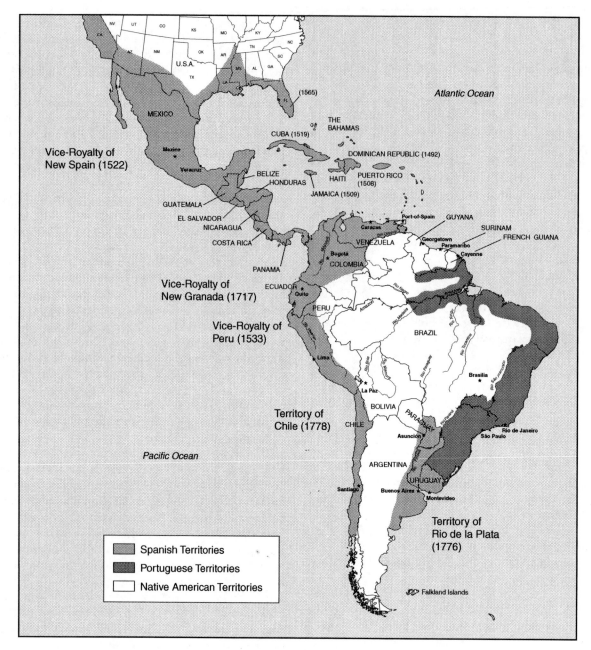

FIG. 16.16

Map of Mexico and Central and South America

the next century. *Zarzuela* and other forms of musical and variety entertainments still dominated the stages of Mexico.

All of Spanish South America was under the viceroyalty of Peru until its northern territories became New Granada in 1717, its southeastern territories became Rio de la Plata in 1776, and Chile was separated off in 1778. These territories all became independent of Spain by 1824, but it would be a number of years before the territories subdivided themselves into the countries we know today. The War of the Triple Alliance (1864–1870), which pitted the Argentine Confederation, the Republic of Uruguay, and the Brazilian Empire against the Republic of Paraguay, was the most devastating ever to be fought in Latin America.

Lima was the capital of Peru and the center for its limited theatrical activities well into the nineteenth century. Pedro de Peralta Barnuevo (1664–1743) encouraged the adoption of neoclassical techniques there with his adaptations of Corneille and Molière in the early eighteenth century, while Fray Francisco del Castillo (1716–1770) became the most popular writer of *entermeses* (short comic interludes) at mid-century. Peru's first important play after independence was *The Fruits of Education* (1830) by Felipe Pardo y Aliaga (1806–1868), whose conservative views reflect the lack of enthusiasm Lima's citizens had for the independence that had been thrust on them. A neoclassical comedy about a matchmaker in Lima, *Missy Catita* (1856) by Manuel Ascensio Segura, is the best-known Peruvian play of the period. By the second half of the nineteenth century, Peruvian plays were done in a satiric, *costumbrismo* style (one that depends on regional customs, dialects, and local color for its effects). As a consequence, the plays are difficult to appreciate today. Outside of Lima the Chilean dramatist Daniel Barros Grez (1834–1904) was highly regarded for his critiques of the social-climbing middle-class in plays like *As in Santiago* (1875) and *The Almost Wedding* (1881).

Buenos Aires, Argentina, was the capital of the Rio de la Plata viceroyalty. A theatre for *zarzuela* was built there in 1757 and the Teatro de la Rancheria in 1783. *The Love of the Ranch Girl* (probably written between 1787 and 1792 by Juan Bautista Maciel but possibly of a later date by an unknown author) established the pattern for later "*gaucho* melodramas," but more serious plays continued to be influenced by French neoclassicism. Argentina produced few dramatists of note but it did produce a number of actors, most notably the actor-manager Luis Ambrosio Morante (1775–1837), who were among the most successful touring actors of the age. Of the ten theatres built in Argentina in the nineteenth century, the Teatro Colón (1857–1944) was the most significant.

Bogotá, Colombia, the capital of New Granada, did produce a large number of local dramatists including Luis Vargas Tejada (1802–1829), José Fernández Madrid (1789–1830), José Caicedo Rojas (1816–1897), Santiago Pérez (1830–1900), José María Samper (1828–1888), Constancio Franco (1842–1917), and Adolfo León Gómez (1858–1927). The Corral de Ramírez, later rebuilt as the Coliseo de Ramírez, was erected there in 1791; in 1892 it became the Teatro Colón. But for the most part, theatre in Colombia was provided by local amateurs and touring companies from Argentina, Mexico, and Spain.

Brazil was a Portuguese colony, and in 1807 the king of Portugal fled Napoleon's troops and established Rio de Janeiro as the capital of the Portuguese Empire. When the king returned to Lisbon in 1821, he entrusted Brazil to his son, who promptly declared it an independent nation in 1822. Throughout the nineteenth century theatrical activities in this vast country were concentrated in São Paulo and Rio de Janeiro.

Gonçalves de Magalhães's (1811–1882) tragedy *Antonio José, or the Poet and the Inquisition* (1838) is said to be the first Brazilian play on a national theme, though its subject was a Portuguese playwright of the previous century. Magalhães was a romantic poet and, while this play was neoclassical, its theme and his poetry proved to be an inspiration for Latin America romanticism. The nineteen domestic comedies of Luís Carlos Martins Pena (1815–1848), especially *The Frontier Justice of the Peace* (1838) and *The Novice* (1845), became extremely popular after his death and are especially noteworthy for their depiction of contemporary life in Brazil. Later writers like Joaquim Manuel de Macedo (1820–1882) with *The White Phantom* (1850) and the important novelist José de Alencar (1829–1877) with *The Family Demon* (1858) exploited Pena's comic style. Pena's five serious plays were written under the influence of romanticism, which had come to dominate by the 1840s. His *Nero in Spain* (1841), along with Gonçalves Dias's (1823–1864) historic drama *Leonor de Mendonça* (1847), the strangely nightmarish *Macário* (1852) by Alvaress de Azevedo (1831–1852), and novelist Castro Alves' (1847–1871) antislavery masterpiece *Gonzaga, or the Minas Revolution* (1867), are the notable examples of Brazilian romanticism. The serious plays of Mecedo and Alencar, on the other hand, were thesis plays in the style of Alexander Dumas *fils*. Puerto Rico playwrights Alejandro Tapia y Rivera (1826–1882) and Salvador Brau (1842–1912) wrote similar kinds of social problem plays, concerned with racism and the unequal treatment of women. Such plays had been promoted by Joaquim Heliodoro Gomes, who created the Ginásio Dramático in 1855 to popularize the "theatre of common sense" and French realism in Brazil. The remarkable success of Artur Azevedo (1855–1908), however, undercut this movement. Azevedo wrote highly successful musical comedies that dominated the stage, the best known of which is probably *The Second-Rate Traveling Theatre* (1896).

Of the Caribbean colonies, Cuba had the most extensive theatrical activity. The first Cuban play in Spanish was *The Presumed Gardener Prince Cloridano* (1730), by Santiago Pita y Borroto (?–1755). But Francisco Covarrubias (1755–1850) is considered the father of Cuban theatre. As an actor-manager and author of over twenty plays, he developed the *negrito* (c. 1812), a farcical blackface character reminiscent of those to be seen later in the minstrel shows of the United States which toured Cuba in 1860–1865. Versions of this character became a mainstay of Cuban comedy, and late in the century José Martí (1853–1895) wrote independence plays that made the *negrito* character into a dramatic hero. The first

Cuban romanticist was actually an exile from Santo Domingo, Francisco Javier Foxá (1816–1865), best known for *Don Pedro de Castillo* (1838). His lead was followed by such noted writers as Bartolomé José Crespo y Borbón (1811–1871), who also wrote comedies in an Afro-Cuban dialect, José Jacinto Milanés (1814–1863), and Gertrudis Gómez de Avellaneda (1814–1873), one of the most successful woman authors of the age. Joaquín Lorenzo Luaces (1826–1867) was the most nationalistic of the Cuban writers. His plays are critical of colonialism and ridicule foreign fashions. They probably helped inspire *bufos habaneros* (Havana bufo), which were burlesques of both Spanish melodrama and *zarzuelas*. The *bufos* became popular about 1866 but were quickly suppressed in the unsuccessful rebellion (1868–1878) against Spain. They were revived and performed extensively from 1879 until Spain lost Cuba to the United States in 1898.

A Coliseo was built in Havana in 1775. Remodeled in 1792 and called the Teatro Principal after 1803, it was finally abandoned in 1846. It had already been replaced by the Gran Teatro Tacón (1838). With a capacity of 2287 and standing room for 700, it was the largest theatre in Latin America when it opened. Havana also acquired a Teatro Mecânico in 1794. Like de Loutherbourg's "Eidophusikon" in London, this was a small-scale theatre designed to create moving pictures with special effects, but this teatro made one major improvement: it included "automated dolls." A diorama was built in Havana in 1829 and saw use as a theatre on an occasional basis.

Few cities in Latin America were able to support full-time acting companies in the nineteenth century. Professional theatre was largely provided by touring companies from Spain, Italy, and France. Troupes from Mexico, Argentina, and Cuba also traveled widely, but they generally featured European actors and performed a European repertory. Many local companies were, therefore, amateur, and many of the plays by local dramatists were written for these companies. But it was from the work of these groups that Native American, African, and European folk traditions found their way into theatrical performances. It was not until World War I prevented the steady flow of touring companies from Europe that Latin American theatre was able to establish its own identity, and when it did, those folk traditions would play a major role.

LOOKING AT THEATRE HISTORY

The psychological realism being developed in European theatres in the last half of the century depended on the audience giving its full attention to the subtleties of events depicted on stage. Scholars have noted, therefore, that there is a close interrelationship between the success of this kind of realism and the change from a tradition of keeping the auditorium well lighted during performance to one of darkening the auditorium, which began in the mid-1870s. F. W. J. Hemmings notes a possible economic impetus for this change. Here he quotes from a French complaint of the 1870s that when the curtain was down,

> . . . for the sake of not wasting gas, the house is plunged into a sort of artificial night. The contrary would be more logical—to maintain a half-light in the auditorium when the curtain is up and when the stage, well lit, [is] drawing everyone's attention.

Hippolyte Hostein, *Historiettes et souvenirs d'un homme de théâtre*, Paris, 1879, p. 279, quoted in F. W. J. Hemmings, *The Theatre Industry in Nineteenth-Century France*, Cambridge, 1993, p. 45.

Like so many things in the nineteenth century, acting was subjected to "scientific" examination. François Delsarte sought to reduce acting to a set of laws that would permit it to be taught with precision:

> I had learned how vain is advice dictated by the caprice of a master without a system. . . . I knew that certain laws existed. . . . I had the nucleus of the science . . . and I did not despair of formulating it.

One of his disciples sums up the basic assumptions on which the system rested:

> There is no science without principles which give a reason for its facts. Hence to teach and to learn [this subject] it is necessary: 1. to understand the general law which controls the movement of the organs; 2. to apply this general law to the movements of each particular

organ; 3. *to understand the meaning of the form of each of these movements; 4. to adapt this meaning to the various states of the soul.*

The Delsarte System . . . with the Literary Remains of
François Delsarte (New York, 1887).

The study of postcolonial theatre has been an important focus in theatre history. The romantics had wanted to find evidence of an idyllic pure culture in the native peoples they encountered, but modern scholars have been much more concerned with the ways in which the imposition of Western forms of self-expression and identity were resisted by indigenous populations. In "Transculturating Transculturation," Dianna Taylor observes:

The deceptive familiarity of Latin American theatre, then, has led to errors in criticism. As no indigenous theatre survived intact after the century following the conquest, it goes without saying that all the dramatic forms currently used in Latin America are derived in some degree from Western drama. While certain dramatic forms were forcefully imposed during the colonial period, since then Latin American dramatists have tended to "borrow" models. . . . Nonetheless, they do not borrow indiscriminately. . . . What they did adopt were forms that could help change their positions with regards to their socio-political exploitation and marginalization [97].

Performing Arts Journal (May 1991), 90–104.

In considering performance traditions of Native Americans on the northern continent, Linda Walsh Jenkins warns of the difficulties in getting past the limits of our Western worldview.

Where the European aesthetic draws large distinctions between secular theatricality (the production of a Shakespeare play) and sacred theatricality (a church service), indigenous peoples, who see everything as sacred, might distinguish the two as public and private, both of spiritual and aesthetic importance to the tribe, and both incorporating performers, spectators and a predetermined oral text [400].

The World Encyclopedia of Contemporary Theatre, The Americas, edited by Don Rubin and Carlos Solórzano. London, 1996.

17
The Beginnings of Modern Realism

In the 1870s the map of Europe was largely redrawn by the unification of Italy, the formation of Germany, the Franco-Prussian War (1870–1871), and the Russo-Turkish War (1877–1878). Economic depression encouraged European powers to seek additional colonies in Africa and Southeast Asia, leading to even greater competition in the building of navies and military forces. An increasingly wealthy upper class, meanwhile, sought diligently to protect those privileges to which it had come to feel entitled. The working classes turned to unionization and strikes as the principal weapons for assuring that their worth and dignity be recognized and respected. In this context, the relative merits of communism, capitalism, democracy, socialism, and other forms of social order were passionately and publicly debated. A wide variety of utopian communities were set up and many nations experienced religious revivals. At the same time anarchists became a powerful and often violent political force. Most reformers, however, were in search of pragmatic solutions to social ills, and it was out of this pragmatism that a new artistic movement—realism—emerged.

Several writers and directors made a marked break with the past, though in the beginning the changes were essentially intensifications of trends already underway. The German nobleman, Georg II, Duke of Saxe-Meiningen, demonstrated the value of the all-powerful director who can weld all the elements of production into a unified whole. The Norwegian dramatist Henrik Ibsen made the public aware of "realism" as a dramatic form with a series of plays that explored the relationship between environmental forces and the internal psychological motivations of characters. The French writer, Zola, meanwhile, provided the theoretical framework that was to take realism to its most extreme form in "naturalism."

THE BEGINNINGS OF REALISM

Realism owed much to the "positivism" of Auguste Comte (1798–1857), author of *Positive Philosophy* (1830–1842) and *Positive Polity* (1851–1854). Comte classified the sciences according to their relative simplicity, placing sociology at the apex as the most complex and important of the sciences. Since to him the ultimate aim of all knowledge was the betterment of society, Comte argued that all the sciences must contribute to sociology, which, when it rigorously applied scientific methodology, would be able to discover the causes of social problems and the remedies needed to bring about desirable change. Above all, Comte demanded that metaphysical explanations of events and behavior be abandoned in favor of material explanations based in observation and analysis. Comte's arguments fell on willing ears, not only among scientists and philosophers, but also among many artists, who sought to make art "scientific" and "realistic."

The realistic mode in art had been attempted sporadically since the time of the Greeks. From the Italian Renaissance on, pictorial illusion dominated the theatre; melodrama and romanticism had accelerated the demand for a realism of appearances. Almost all the approaches before 1850, however, had emphasized "beautiful" nature, norms, picturesque local color, or pleasing contrasts. Even Hugo, who had demanded the inclusion of the grotesque in art, avoided the sordid in his own practice. Around 1850, however, some critics began to advocate a close and objective observation of life, no matter how squalid or elevated. Out of these demands came a movement called realism. As a conscious movement, realism is first discernible around 1853 in France. By 1863 the theoretical foundations had been fully expressed there in such periodicals as *L'Artiste, Le Figaro, Réalisme* (first published in 1856), and *Le Présent*. The main tenets of the new movement were: Art must depict truthfully the real, physical world, and, since only the contemporary world can be observed directly, truth can be attained most fully through impersonal, objective observation and representation of the world around us.

SAXE-MEININGEN

Perhaps the most important of the new forces, the Meiningen Players, came to the fore in the 1870s and demonstrated the value of unity to the growing tendency toward realism in the theatre. Although plays had been performed in the Duchy of Meiningen since the late eighteenth century, a permanent court theatre was not opened until 1831, and the productions there remained commonplace until Georg II (1826–1914) succeeded to the throne in 1866. Georg II, Duke of Saxe-Meiningen, had received extensive art training, had been at the Prussian court in Berlin when Tieck worked there, and had seen Charles Kean's Shakespearean productions in London, Friedrick Haase's in Coburg-Gotha, and the superior ensemble of the Burgtheater. Thus, his intense interest in the theatre was well developed before a Prussian invasion of Meiningen forced his father to abdicate in his favor.

Upon succeeding to the throne in 1866, Georg II immediately began to change the repertory of the court theatre and took a personal interest in its affairs. In managing the troupe, the duke at first depended heavily on Friedrich von Bodenstedt (1819–1892), and after 1871 on Ludwig Chronegk (1837–1891). Trained as a singing comedian, Chronegk had been employed at Meiningen in 1866 as a comic actor. His appointment as director came as a surprise to the company, for there seemed little in his background to justify it. Nevertheless, the fame of the troupe probably owes as much to Chronegk as to Saxe-Meiningen, since not only was he an indefatigable worker, but he also conceived and arranged the tours, which made the company famous. A third major influence was Ellen Franz (1839–1923), an actress who in 1873 became the duke's third wife. After this time she assumed responsibility for proposing the repertory, adapting the texts, and supervising stage speech. Thus, it is difficult to assign credit for the company's accomplishments, although it is now typical to allot it solely to the duke.

From 1866 until 1874 the company played entirely in Meiningen, and when it appeared in Berlin in 1874 it took the astonished spectators completely by surprise. After its initial success, the company began a long series of tours. Between 1874 and 1890, it played in thirty-eight cities in nine countries, including Russia, Sweden, Austria, Denmark, Belgium, Holland, and England, giving about 2600 performances of forty-one plays. By 1890, when it gave up touring, the Meiningen commanded the greatest respect of any company in the world.

The repertory of the Meiningen Players, composed primarily of works by Shakespeare, Schiller, Grillparzer, and nineteenth-century romantic playwrights, was not unlike that of other companies except in its inclusion of more plays of high merit. Ibsen's *Ghosts* was presented for a few performances, but the other contemporary plays in the repertory were mostly poetic, romantic works.

Although the duke's productions are often considered the most historically accurate of the nineteenth century, historical accuracy was not for him an end in itself. His primary goal was to do full justice to the scripts he chose. It was his perception of what this goal demanded that led him to pursue a pictorial illusionism which excelled all previous standards because of its great accuracy. The duke divided each century into thirds and further distinguished among national differences within each time period. As a result, his productions attained unprecedented authenticity. Accuracy was further ensured by the duke's refusal to permit actors to tamper with their costumes. In most theatres of the times, the stars either supplied their own garments or altered as they saw fit those provided by the theatre. Actresses often wore crinoline petticoats under dresses of all periods. Furthermore, the duke insisted upon authentic materials in place of the usual cheap substitutes. He used heavy upholstery fabrics, many imported from France and Italy and some made to his specifications; he introduced genuine chain mail, armor, swords, axes, halberds, and other instruments. Authentic period furniture was always used. The success of the Meiningen Players led to the establishment of theatrical supply houses which manufactured furniture, properties, costume materials, and armor to meet the new demand from other troupes.

Saxe-Meiningen designed all of the costumes, scenery, and properties used by his troupe. The settings were usually painted by the Brückner brothers of Coburg, who also designed Wagner's and Haase's settings. Strong colors were used in scenery for the first time, reversing the former practice of having actors play against pastel scenery. This innovation probably accounts for the adverse comments by critics on the "garishness" of the Meiningen settings. The duke was opposed to sky borders and used foliage, beams, banners, or other devices as overhead masking. He avoided symmetrical balance, for he thought this unnatural, and was careful to keep each detail in correct proportion and to blend painted and three-dimensional elements convincingly. He was also one of the first artists consistently to treat the stage floor as part of the design, breaking it up with fallen trees, rocks, hillocks, steps, and platforms.

While its use of scenery and costumes was probably superior to that of other troupes, the company's principal sources of power were totality of effect and, especially, ensemble acting. The duke maintained as complete authority over his actors as over the scenic investiture. Because he could not afford major performers, his company was composed either of beginners or of older actors who had not attained outstanding success. Guest actors sometimes performed with the troupe, but they had to conform to the company's rules against stars. Perhaps to discourage any tendency toward the "star complex," Saxe-Meiningen required all actors not cast in leading roles to appear as supernumeraries. This, in turn, made possible the effective crowd scenes for which

FIG. 17.1
Saxe-Meiningen's sketch for Act II of Julius Winding's *Pope Sixtus V.* Courtesy Theatermuseum, Munich.

the company was noted. Saxe-Meiningen used no supernumeraries who were not permanent members of the troupe. While this limited the number of persons available for crowd scenes, the effect of large masses was achieved by settings kept sufficiently small to force many of the actors into the wings (thus suggesting that great numbers were out of sight offstage) and by diagonal and contrasting movements to create effects of confusion and agitation. In rehearsing crowd scenes, the duke divided his actors into small groups, each under the charge of an experienced performer who aided in training those under him. Furthermore, each member of a mob was given individualizing characteristics and specific lines; then all were carefully coordinated. The results obtained in this manner, contrasting sharply with the usual mob scenes, were considered revolutionary.

Fortunately, the duke could depend upon long rehearsal periods. Since Meiningen had a population of only 8000, the theatre was open only twice a week for six months of the year. This schedule and the duke's authority made it possible to rehearse in a way quite different from the usual practice elsewhere. Each work was rehearsed from the first with full settings, furniture, and properties. Costumes were not always available from the beginning, but were always used for some time prior to the premiere. Actors were required to "act" from the first day rather than merely "walk through" the part as was typical in many theatres. Rehearsals, held in the evening after the duke's state duties were completed and often lasting five or six hours, continued until the play was judged ready for performance, even if this required several months. Because he did not work against a deadline, the duke conceived many details as he went along, and rehearsals were frequently delayed while furniture was rearranged or new plans made.

The impact of the Meiningen Players came from the complete illusion attained in every aspect of the production. Thus, the company stands as the culmination of trends that had begun in the Renaissance. More important, it stands at the beginning of the new movement toward unified production, in which each element is carefully selected because of its contribution to the total effect. The actor had given way to the director as the dominant artist in the theatre. Saxe-Meiningen's example influenced such men as Antoine and Stanislavsky, who were to figure significantly in the formation of the modern theatre. By the time the Meiningen Players discontinued touring in 1890, the theatre was already entering the new era which they had helped to inaugurate. By that time the public had also become aware of a new direction in playwriting, primarily through the work of Ibsen.

IBSEN

Henrik Ibsen (1828–1906), after publishing his first play in 1850, was appointed resident dramatist and stage manager at the newly created Norwegian National Theatre in Bergen in 1851. By 1857 he had assisted in staging 145 plays, and had written seven of his own. Between 1857 and 1862, he worked at the Norwegian Theatre in Christiania (now Oslo), and after 1864 he lived abroad until 1891.

Ibsen wrote twenty-five plays. Most of the early works are verse-dramas about the Scandinavian past. These include *Lady Inger of Ostraat* (1855), *The Vikings at Helgeland* (1858), and *The Pretenders* (1864). The most important early works, however, are *Brand* (1866) and *Peer Gynt* (1867). *Brand*, a dramatic poem, depicts an uncompromising idealist who sacrifices everything, including his family, to his vision. It established Ibsen's reputation, and the financial security which it brought made it possible for him to work as he pleased. *Peer Gynt* contrasts sharply with *Brand,* for its protagonist is a man who avoids issues by skirting them. A skillful blending of fantasy and reality, *Peer Gynt* was interpreted by many as a satire on the Norwegian character.

In the 1870s Ibsen made a sharp break with his past when he announced his intention of abandoning verse because it was unsuited to creating an illusion of reality. The future direction of his work first became apparent with *Pillars of Society* (1877), but it was with *A Doll's House* (1879), *Ghosts* (1881), and *An Enemy of the People* (1882) that Ibsen established his reputation as a radical thinker. Above all, it was *A Doll's House* and *Ghosts* that shocked conservative readers and served as a rallying point for supporters of a drama of ideas. Unlike Dumas *fils* and Augier, who also wrote about controversial subjects, Ibsen did not resolve his plays in ways that confirmed received ideology. Rather, he made ideology the cause of problems and suggested the need to change it.

In *A Doll's House,* Nora, upon realizing that, as a woman, she has always been kept ignorant of the practical world and treated as a plaything, chooses to leave her husband and children in order to learn about the world so she can make decisions for herself. Contrarily, in *Ghosts,* Mrs. Alving, conforming to traditional morality, has remained with a depraved husband only to have her only son go mad, presumably from inherited syphilis. Thus, both plays were greeted as attacks on family and home, the

FIG. 17.2

Ibsen's *Rosmersholm* at the Norwegian National Theatre, Oslo, 1906. Eleanora Duse is seen at left. From *Bühne und Welt* (1906).

bedrocks of civilized society, while the allusions to venereal disease and sexual misconduct in *Ghosts* were considered so offensive to standards of public decency that the play was a forbidden production in most countries.

Ibsen soon turned in new directions. In *The Wild Duck* (1884), *Rosmersholm* (1886), *The Master Builder* (1892), *John Gabriel Borkman* (1896), and *When We Dead Awaken* (1899) he made increasing use of symbolism and of subjects more concerned with personal relationships than with social problems. In actuality, the basic theme of Ibsen's plays remained relatively constant: the struggle for integrity, the conflict between duty to oneself and duty to others. Mrs. Alving of *Ghosts* discovers too late that she has destroyed her life by overvaluing duty to others, whereas in many of the late plays the protagonists, while pursuing some private vision, destroy the happiness of others and finally their own.

Much of Ibsen's work contributed to the development of realism. In the prose dramas he refined Scribe's "well-made play" formula and made it more fitting to the realistic style. Ibsen discarded asides, soliloquies, and other nonrealistic devices, and was careful to motivate all exposition. Most often characters who have just returned after a long absence elicit information in a manner that appears completely natural by asking questions about happenings while they were away. All scenes are causally related and lead logically to the denouement. Dialogue, settings, costumes, and business are selected for their ability to reveal character and milieu, and are clearly described in stage directions. Each character is conceived as a personality whose behavior is attributable to hereditary or environmental forces. Internal psychological motivations are given even greater emphasis than external visual detail. In these ways, Ibsen provided a model for writers of the realistic school.

Ibsen's late plays were to influence nonrealistic drama as extensively as the earlier prose plays did realistic works. In them, ordinary objects (such as the duck in *The Wild Duck*) are imbued with significance beyond their literal meaning and enlarge the implications of the dramatic action. Furthermore, many of the works border on fantasy. In *Rosmersholm* a phantom white horse is significant, and in *When We Dead Awaken* the mountain heights exert an irresistible pull. This sense of mysterious forces at work in human destiny was to be a major theme of symbolist drama.

Whether realistic or nonrealistic, almost all drama after Ibsen was influenced by his conviction that art should be a source of insights, a creator of discussion, a conveyor of ideas, something more than mere entertainment. He gave playwrights a new vision of their role. Almost everywhere Ibsen's plays came to epitomize the break with the past and to be a rallying point for producers seeking new paths.

ZOLA AND THE FRENCH NATURALISTS

Even as Ibsen was writing his prose plays, the French naturalists, working quite independently, were also demanding a new drama. The naturalists considered heredity and environment to be the major determinants of human fate. This doctrine was grounded (at least in part) in Charles Darwin's *The Origin of Species* (1859). Darwin set forth two main theses: (1) All forms of life have developed gradually from a common ancestry; and (2) the evolution of species is explained by the "survival of the fittest." These theories had several important implications. First, they implied that heredity and environment are the primary causal factors. Second, human behavior, when viewed (as it soon was) as a product of hereditary and environmental forces, came to seem determined by factors largely beyond any individual's control; thus, at least partial responsibility for undesirable behavior had to be accepted by the society that has allowed adverse hereditary and environmental factors to exist. Third, Darwin's theories strengthened the idea of progress since, if human beings had evolved from an atom of being to the complex creatures they now were, increasing complexity and improvement appeared to be inevitable. Nevertheless, it was argued, progress could be hastened by the consistent application of scientific method and new technology. Fourth, human beings were absorbed into nature. Prior to the nineteenth century humans had been set apart from the rest of nature as superior to it. Now they lost their privileged status and, like animals or plants, were often considered subjects to be studied and controlled like the members of any other biological species.

Naturalism also attracted many adherents because of contemporary political and economic conditions. The Franco-Prussian War (1870–1871) was a severe blow to French pride, for not only was France defeated, but it lost Alsace and Lorraine to Germany and brought an end to Napoleon III's empire. In Paris a commune was established, but this was soon overthrown and France once more became a republic. The war and its aftermath served to emphasize that the working man enjoyed few privileges, and during the last quarter of the nineteenth century socialism began to gain support throughout Europe as many came to believe that only this form of social organization could ensure equality for all. Such pressures motivated several European governments to adopt constitutions at last; by 1900 every major country in Europe except Russia had some degree of constitutional government. This interest in the lot of the working classes and the rights of the common people was to provide a major focus for naturalism. As means of dealing with contemporary problems, science and technology were considered the major tools, and the naturalists argued that all social problems could be solved if only the scientific method were applied to them systematically.

Naturalism as a conscious movement first appeared in France in the 1870s. Its primary spokesman was Emile Zola (1840–1902), an admirer of Comte and an advocate of the scientific method as the key to all truth and progress. Believing that literature must either become scientific or perish, Zola argued that drama should illustrate the "inevitable laws of heredity and environment" or record "case studies." He wished the dramatist, in his search for truth, to observe, record, and "experiment" with the same detachment as the scientist. Zola compared the writer with the pathologist, who seeks the causes of a disease so it may be cured, not glossing over infection but bringing it out into the open where it can be examined. Similarly, the dramatist should depict social ills so they may be corrected. In addition, Zola argued that on stage the events should be reproduced with sufficient exactness to demonstrate the relationship between cause and effect.

Zola's first major statement of the naturalist doctrine came in 1873 in the preface to his dramatization of his novel *Thérèse Raquin*; he expanded his views in *Naturalism in the Theatre* (1881) and *The Experimental Novel* (1881). Some of Zola's followers were even more radical than he in their demands for theatrical reform, arguing that a play should merely be a "slice of life" transferred to the stage. Thus, in their zeal to approximate scientific truth, they often obliterated virtually all distinctions between art and life.

Naturalism, like many movements before it, was handicapped by a lack of good plays embodying its principles. Although a few plays, such as *Henriette Maréchal* (1863) by Edmond and Jules Goncourt and *L'Arlesienne* (1872) by Alphonse Daudet, were produced, they made little impact. Even *Thérèse Raquin* failed to live up to Zola's critical precepts except in the setting, for rather than a slice of life it was more nearly a melodrama about murder and retribution.

Ironically, it was Henri Becque (1837–1899) who most nearly captured the naturalist ideal in France, even though he and Zola were equally contemptuous of each other. Becque's *The Vultures* (1882) shows the fleecing of a family by their supposed friends following the death of the father; there are no sympathetic characters, the ending is pessimistic and ironical, and there are no obvious climaxes, merely a slow progression toward the cynical outcome. *La Parisienne* (1885) depicts a wife who considers her infidelity an asset to her husband's advancement in business. In these plays Becque raised French naturalism to its highest point.

That *The Vultures* was presented by the Comédie Française, a bastion of conservatism, would on the surface suggest that by the 1880s naturalism had been fully accepted in Paris. But Becque's play was ineffectually produced because he refused to comply with the company's request for revisions that would have brought the work more nearly into conformity with contemporary tastes. Because virtually all naturalist dramas that received a hearing were inadequately staged, the prevailing attitudes of both the public and theatrical workers remained unchallenged. Something more was needed if significant change was to come. This new element was to be added by Antoine at the Théâtre Libre, where after 1887 naturalistic staging and writing were united for the first time.

FIG. 17.3

Zola's *The Earth* as dramatized by Ménessier and directed by Antoine at the Théâtre Antoine, 1902. Note the many naturalistic details, including the chickens in the foreground. From *Le Théâtre* (1902).

ANTOINE AND THE THÉÂTRE LIBRE

André Antoine (1858–1943) seemed a most unpromising source of revolution in 1887, for he was merely a clerk in a gas company, and his theatrical experience was limited to supernumerary acting with Parisian professional companies and occasional appearances with an amateur group (of which there were many in Paris). When Antoine sought to produce a program of new plays, including a dramatization of Zola's *Jacques Damour,* his amateur circle refused its sanction and Antoine set off on his own. In search of a name for his company, he adopted Théâtre Libre (or "Free Theatre"). The success of his first program won him the endorsement of Zola and other influential figures. His second program was attended by major theatrical critics, who wrote lengthy reviews. Before the end of 1887, Antoine had given up his clerk's job and thereafter until 1914 devoted himself to theatrical production.

Organized on a subscription basis, the Théâtre Libre was open only to members and therefore was exempt from censorship. As a result, many of the plays available to Antoine were those that had been refused licenses, and most were naturalistic. Much of the notoriety of the Théâtre Libre stemmed from its *comédies rosses* (plays in which the usual principles of morality are reversed), many so extreme that they repelled even Antoine's tolerant audience. It was

largely because of these works that naturalism gained a reputation for depravity, but the publicity they attracted also gradually paved the way for greater freedom in established and conservative theatres.

In 1888 Antoine also began to produce one foreign work each year. After Tolstoy's *The Power of Darkness,* he went on to Ibsen's *Ghosts* and *The Wild Duck.* In this way, controversial foreign as well as domestic plays were given their first Parisian performances.

In addition to serving as a showcase for new dramas, the Théâtre Libre became the proving ground for production techniques. Although Antoine had used a realistic approach from the beginning, he intensified his search for authenticity after witnessing the Meiningen Players and Irving's company in 1888. He then sought to reproduce environment in every detail. In *The Butchers* (1888), for example, he hung real carcasses of beef on the stage. The "fourth wall" was observed consistently; in designing settings, he arranged rooms as in real life and only later decided

FIG. 17.4

Antoine's production of Iben's *The Wild Duck* at the Théâtre Libre. The final scene. From a contemporary lithograph.

which wall should be removed. Often furniture was placed along the curtain line, and actors were directed to behave as though there were no audience. Through his belief in the importance of environment, Antoine helped to establish the principle that each play requires its own setting quite distinct from that of any other work. After witnessing the Meiningen company, Antoine also gave special attention to ensemble acting. Although most of his performers were amateurs, he coached them carefully and autocratically. He discouraged conventionalized movement and declamatory speech, seeking natural behavior instead.

Antoine's success worked against him, for as soon as playwrights or actors established their worth, they were employed by a major company. Furthermore, Antoine's high standards of production kept him constantly in debt. Even at the height of its popularity, the Théâtre Libre gave no production for more than three performances. By 1893, the company began to weaken and in 1894 Antoine left it. By then he had presented sixty-two programs composed of 184 plays. In addition to playing in Paris, he had toured in Belgium, Holland, Germany, Italy, and England. The example he had set was to be followed in several other countries.

Antoine did not stay away from the Parisian theatre long. In 1897 he opened his Théâtre Antoine, run as a fully professional theatre, and in 1906 he was appointed director of the state-subsidized Odéon, which he completely modernized. Although he practiced it less assiduously, realism still dominated his work. Probably his most famous productions of this era were of French classical dramas, for which he attempted to re-create the theatrical conventions of the seventeenth century. Costumed actors served as onstage audience, chandeliers were hung over the stage, and candle footlights were conspicuous. Through this approach, he helped to establish a realism based upon past theatrical conventions rather than upon architecture and dress, as had been usual with other producers. Antoine also directed several outstanding productions of Shakespeare's plays. Near the end of his tenure at the Odéon, he staged a few works in which stylization (based on visual sources) was clearly evident, but he resigned his post before this new trend was fully explored. By 1914 he had presented a total of 364 works. No one else had influenced the French theatre of the period so profoundly as had Antoine.

After 1890, most of the major new French dramatists were realists and many of these were given their first hearing by Antoine. Among these the most important were Porto-Riche, Curel, and Brieux. Georges Porto-Riche (1849–1930) was noted for subtle characterizations which emphasized internal conflicts. Probably his best play is *Infatuated* (1891) in which a husband tries to rid himself of his wife by arousing her interest in another man, only to discover that he cannot give her up. François de Curel (1854–1928) had his first play produced by Antoine in 1892. He made few concessions to popular taste, and his disregard for ordinary principles of dramatic construction often obscured his intentions. His concern for internal psychological conflicts, however, did much to forward realistic subject matter. Among his best works are *The Fossils* (1892), depicting a decaying aristocracy, and *The Lion's Feast* (1897), in which the protagonist attempts to improve the lives of workers. Eugène Brieux (1858–1932) was said by George Bernard Shaw to be the most important dramatist in Europe after the death of Ibsen. Given his first production by Antoine in 1892, Brieux went on to write *The Red Robe* (1900), showing the difficulty of obtaining justice from judges concerned primarily with promotion, *Damaged Goods* (1902), concerning syphilis and its transmission to a child, and *Maternity* (1903), in which a blistering attack is launched on a society that does not permit legal birth control. Controversy over *Damaged Goods* led to the abolishment of censorship in 1905. Thus, a subject that had been unacceptable to censors when Ibsen wrote *Ghosts* in 1881 was allowed in French commercial theatres by 1905.

THE FREIE BÜHNE AND GERMAN REALISM

The pattern that emerged in France was repeated in Germany. The first step toward theatrical reform came in 1883, when the Deutsches Theater was opened in Berlin by Adolf L'Arronge (1838–1908) and Ludwig Barnay (1842–1924), with a company headed by Josef Kainz (1858–1910), the major exponent of the new realism, and Agnes Sorma (1865–1927), later to be Germany's leading actress. Here a repertory of old and new plays was produced in the manner of the Meiningen Players. In 1888 Barnay left the Deutsches Theater to found the Berliner Theater, and in the same year Oskar Blumenthal (1852–1917) founded the Lessing Theater. Thus, by 1890 Berlin had several private companies of excellent quality. Nevertheless, their choice of plays was severely restricted by censorship.

Meanwhile, a group calling itself "Youngest Germany" had begun to advocate a new art based upon an objective observation of reality, while another calling itself *Durch* (or "Through") went even further than Zola in its demands for a naturalistic drama. Both groups found inspiration in Ibsen's plays, sixteen of which had been translated into German by 1890.

As in France however, the new movement lacked focus until an "independent" theatre was formed. Taking its inspiration from the Théâtre Libre, the Freie Bühne (or "Free Stage") was organized in Berlin in 1889. Unlike Antoine's company, however, the German group was a democratic organization with officers and a governing council. Otto Brahm (1856–1912), a dramatic critic, was elected president and became its guiding spirit. In order to secure the services of professional actors, the Freie Bühne gave its performances on Sunday afternoons since its actors and most of its personnel were regularly employed by established theatres, especially the Deutsches, Berliner, and Lessing. Each production usually involved different actors, over whom Brahm had little control. Thus, the Freie Bühne exerted little influence on theatrical production. Its major contribution was made by giving a hearing to plays forbidden by the censor. The opening production of *Ghosts* was followed with plays by the Goncourts, Zola, Becque, Tolstoy, Anzengruber, and Strindberg. After the season of 1890–1891, regular performances were discontinued, although occasionally programs were arranged when a worthy play was forbidden a license. The Freie Bühne came to an end in 1894, when Brahm was named director of the Deutsches Theater.

At the Deutsches Theater between 1894 and 1904 and at the Lessing Theater from 1904 until 1912, Brahm perfected the realistic mode. He had little success with the classics and increasingly concentrated on developing an ensemble of actors and designers attuned to the demands of contemporary drama, especially that of Ibsen, Hauptmann, Schnitzler, and Sudermann, in the presentation of which the company was unexcelled.

The only truly important German dramatist introduced by the Freie Bühne was Gerhart Hauptmann (1862–1946). The furor that greeted his *Before Sunrise* (1889), the story of a Silesian family that sinks into viciousness after the discovery of coal on their land, established Hauptmann as a major new playwright. During the next fifty years he wrote about thirty plays. Of the early works, the best is *The Weavers* (1892), remarkable for its group-protagonist of desperate workers driven to revolt. Like Ibsen, Hauptmann went on to write plays in a more symbolic vein, notably *The Assumption of Hannele* (1893) and *The Sunken Bell* (1896). After 1912, his plays became increasingly nonrealistic. Before his death, Hauptmann lost much of his prestige because of his passive acceptance of Hitler's regime. All of Hauptmann's work shows great compassion for human suffering, but his protagonists, who are victims of circumstances beyond their control, are more pitiable than heroic.

The Freie Bühne stimulated the formation of several other stage societies in Germany. Although none achieved the fame of the original group, they helped to pave the way for a new drama. Perhaps of equal importance, a "people's" theatre was organized by socialist groups (the ban on which was lifted in 1890) interested in raising the cultural standards of the working classes. Using the Freie Bühne as a model, the Freie Volksbühne was organized in Berlin in 1890 to produce plays at Sunday matinees, for which season tickets were distributed by lot at a nominal price. Beginning with 1150 members, the organization included 12,000 by 1908. In 1892 the Neue Freie Volksbühne, founded by the former director of the original group, began a similar program. By 1905, it was offering its subscribers a choice among productions at several major theatres. Before World War I the two groups had amalgamated, and with a combined membership of 70,000 it was sufficiently stable that it could build one of the most modern theatres in Germany and employ its own permanent company. The workers' theatre movement flourished throughout Germany and Austria. To it must go considerable credit for creating a broad-based theatre-going public in those countries.

Before 1900, the new realistic drama was being accepted almost everywhere. At the Burgtheater in Vienna a wide selection of recent works was presented between 1890 and 1898, when Max Burckhardt (1854–1912) was director of the theatre. His successor, Paul Schlenther (1854–1916), a friend and admirer of Hauptmann and a founding member of the Freie Bühne, continued his policies between 1898 and 1910. A somewhat similar pattern was followed elsewhere, for as public interest in the new plays grew the repertory expanded to include them.

In addition to Hauptmann, other important new dramatists include Sudermann and Schnitzler. Hermann Sudermann (1857–1928) was even more instrumental than Hauptmann in making realism acceptable to the public, for he tended to retain the well-made play techniques and to conform more nearly to accepted morality while writing about "provocative" subjects. His most popular play, *Magda* (1893), concerning a singer whose bohemian life brings her into conflict with her father, became a favorite vehicle of such actresses as Bernhardt and Duse. Sudermann continued to write until well into the twentieth century. The most important Austrian dramatist of this period was Arthur Schnitzler (1862–1931), a recorder of the melancholic world-weariness that characterized the turn of the century, and of the shallow sexual attitudes that accompanied it. The most famous of his works is *Anatol* (1893), a series of short plays, each of which records a different love intrigue. Even in the midst of happiness, Anatol knows that his momentary pleasure will dissolve into jealousy and boredom. A similar work is *Reigen,* variously translated as *Hands Around, La Ronde,* and *Round Dance* (1900, but not performed in Germany until 1920), with its ten characters engaged in a series of sexual encounters. Schnitzler, a friend of Sigmund Freud, was much concerned with the centrality of sexual behavior, but was also convinced that love cannot be built upon pure ego satisfaction. While he seldom strayed from this theme, Schnitzler wrote on other subjects, as in *Professor Bernhardi* (1912), a play about anti-Semitism.

THE INDEPENDENT THEATRE AND REALISM IN ENGLAND

After the death of Robertson in 1871, the English theatre was given over largely to works in the tradition of Boucicault and Sardou or to lavish productions of the classics. A new direction was not evident until the 1890s, with Jones and Pinero. These writers hold a place in English drama comparable to that of Dumas *fils* and Augier in French theatre, for both were sufficiently provocative to be slightly scandalizing, yet both were conventional enough to be acceptable to the censor and the theatre-going public.

Henry Arthur Jones (1851–1929) began his playwriting career with a successful melodrama, *The Silver King* (1882), and did not turn to more serious drama until after 1890 with *The Dancing Girl* (1891), *The Liars* (1897), and *Mrs. Dane's Defence* (1900). His most unusual play, *Michael and His Lost Angel* (1896), treats a love affair between a minister and one of his parishioners. Although Jones had high ideals for drama, he was not an original thinker. He aroused suspense and titillation without giving any significant new insights.

Arthur Wing Pinero (1855–1934) began his career in 1874 as an actor and turned to writing in 1877. His first major success came with a farce, *The Magistrate* (1885), a form in which he excelled. Although Pinero never professed interest in a "drama of ideas," it was his *The Second Mrs. Tanqueray* (1893), the story of a "woman with a past," that brought the first change in public attitudes, for when it proved a popular hit, producers began to look more favor-

ably upon "Ibsen-esque" drama. Pinero continued to write for another thirty years, turning out such successful plays as *The Notorious Mrs. Ebbsmith* (1895), *Iris* (1901), and *Mid-Channel* (1909), but his popularity declined steadily after 1910.

While Jones and Pinero paved the way for public acceptance, the development of a more significant drama owes most to Ibsen. By 1880, William Archer and others had begun to translate Ibsen's plays and by 1890 all those then written were available in English. In 1889, two actresses, Janet Achurch (1864–1916) and Elizabeth Robins (1862–1952), both began to appear in Ibsen's plays. Achurch made a strong impression in *A Doll's House,* the first unadapted version of a play by Ibsen seen in England. Robins first produced *Pillars of Society,* and subsequently appeared in seven of the plays. These early productions, by reminding the English how far behind the continent their own drama had fallen, supplied one motivation for founding the Independent Theatre.

Modeled on the Théâtre Libre and the Freie Bühne, the Independent Theatre was headed by J. T. Grein (1862–1935), a Dutch-born critic who had lived in London for many years. Like its predecessors on the continent, the Independent Theatre was organized on a subscription basis to avoid censorship, and like the Freie Bühne, it gave its productions on Sundays in order to gain the cooperation of theatre managers and actors. The opening play in 1891, *Ghosts,* prompted more than 500 articles, most of them vituperative. The second program, Zola's *Thérèse Raquin,* created almost as great a storm. This publicity began to make the general public aware of the new drama for the first time.

Between 1891 and 1897, the Independent Theatre presented twenty-six plays, mostly translations. It did little in the way of mounting the plays. Thus, like the Freie Bühne, it served primarily as a rejuvenator of drama rather than as an influence on production. Grein had hoped to produce new English plays, for he was convinced that the low state of English drama was attributable to the conservatism of producers. He soon found, however, that no significant plays were available. His disappointment prompted George Bernard Shaw to complete *Widower's Houses,* the production of which in 1892 launched Shaw's career as a dramatist.

George Bernard Shaw (1856–1950), previously a novelist and critic, wrote regularly for the theatre from 1892 until his death. Unlike most of the new writers, who tended to be gloomy and intensely serious as a reaction against the shallowness of their predecessors, Shaw wrote primarily in the comic form. This choice may be explained in part by Shaw's

FIG. 17.5

Pinero's *The Second Mrs. Tanqueray*. Act I of the original production with Mrs. Patrick Campbell and George Alexander. From *The Graphic* (1893).

belief in the perfectibility of human beings and his interest in persuasion, which was best served by having characters arrive at perceptions that remove the barriers to a happy resolution. Shaw also delighted in using paradoxes to make both characters and audiences reassess their values. Thus, *Arms and the Man* (1894) punctures romantic notions about love and war, while *Major Barbara* (1905) upholds a munitions manufacturer as a greater humanitarian than an officer in the Salvation Army, because the Salvation Army prolongs an inequitable system by caring for victims whereas the manufacturer provides his workers with the means whereby to help themselves. Many of Shaw's plays, notably *The Doctor's Dilemma* (1906) and *Getting Married* (1908), are essentially extended discussions of specific problems. Other works, such as *Man and Superman* (1901) and *Back to Methuselah* (1919–1921), show Shaw's interest in "creative evolution" and the "life force," which he believed were striving to create a "superman" by working through superior individuals. In still other plays, like *Caesar and Cleopatra* (1899) and *Saint Joan* (1923), Shaw sought to question popular misconceptions of historical figures and events. Perhaps his least characteristic work is *Heartbreak House* (1914–1919), a parable about the failures of Europe at the time of World War I.

Although Shaw is related to the realistic movement through his concern for ideas and social problems, he differs markedly from most of the writers of this school. While acknowledging the importance of heredity and environment, Shaw always implies that human beings have freedom of choice. Furthermore, although his characters often speak in dialect, they are always articulate and seldom follow closely the patterns of everyday speech. Shaw was not objective, for he chose his characters and invented his stories to illustrate a point of view. His comic method eventually won a wide audience for the drama of ideas.

Shaw was not immediately successful, however, for at first his unconventional ideas and paradoxical situations only puzzled or irritated audiences. His reputation was built slowly through the efforts of organizations that succeeded the Independent Theatre. The first of these was the Incorporated Stage Society, founded in 1899 to present modern plays. At first its programs were given on Sunday afternoons but, as its membership grew from the original 300 to 1500 by 1914, it added Monday matinees as well. By the time the group disbanded in 1939 it had presented about 200 works, many of which would otherwise not have been seen. It served as an experimental theatre which kept the English theatrical world abreast of the latest movements both at home and abroad.

Among the most significant companies in this period was the Royal Court Theatre, where between 1904 and 1907 Harley Granville Barker (1877–1946) and John Vedrenne (1863–1930) gave the new drama its first full hearing in an English public theatre. Barker had begun his career as an actor in 1891, had worked with several organizations, including the Incorporated Stage Society, and had established himself as a dramatist before being invited to assist Vedrenne with a production of *Two Gentlemen of Verona*. This beginning soon developed into a permanent arrangement, under which one play was offered each evening for several weeks while another little-known or seldom-performed work was given at matinees. If the matinees engendered enough enthusiasm, the play was moved to evening performances. Even successes, however, were not played consecutively for more than a few weeks. Between 1904 and 1907, the Court presented thirty-two plays by seventeen different authors, including Euripides, Hauptmann, Ibsen, Galsworthy, and Yeats. The mainstay of the theatre, however, was Shaw, eleven of whose plays were presented in productions directed by Shaw himself. These productions established Shaw's popularity with the British public.

FIG. 17.6

Shaw's *Caesar and Cleopatra* at the Savoy Theatre, London, 1907. Forbes-Robertson as Caesar, Gertrude Elliott as Cleopatra. From *Play Pictorial*, 10 (1907).

The Court made other important contributions. It was noted for ensemble acting by a company that included some of the best actors of the period: Lillah McCarthy, Edith Wynne Matthison, Louis Calvert, Lewis Casson, and Godfrey Tearle. There were no stars. Since Barker believed that it is the director's primary task to give a thoughtful interpretation of the playwright's script, he sought to find in each work the style suited to it. Nevertheless, the dominant style was a subtle realism which avoided bravura. Simplicity and suggestion were the keynotes of both the acting and scenery. In 1907 Barker and Vedrenne moved to the much larger Savoy Theatre, but closed after one season because of lack of attendance and trouble with the censor. When Charles Frohman established a repertory company at the Duke of York's Theatre in 1910, he employed Barker to head it. After presenting seventeen plays in seventeen weeks and incurring a sizable deficit, Barker resigned.

In spite of these failures, the Barker-Vedrenne experiments engendered several imitators, especially in the provinces, where repertory companies began to be opened once more. The first important company was established by Miss A. E. F. Horniman (1860–1937) in 1907 at the Gaiety Theatre in Manchester. Until it was discontinued in 1917, this was to be one of the best companies in England, offering a wide variety of English and continental plays. Its encouragement of local writers gave rise to the "Manchester School," of which Stanley Houghton (1881–1913), author of *Hindle Wakes* (1912), and Harold Brighouse (1883–1958), author of *Hobson's Choice* (1916), were the most important. Other vigorous repertory companies were founded at Liverpool in 1911 and at Birmingham in 1913. The Birmingham Repertory Company, under the direction of Barry Jackson (1879–1961), was to be especially influential after the First World War.

In addition to Shaw, a number of other dramatists in the realistic vein appeared after 1900. John Galsworthy (1867–1933), already one of England's most successful novelists, turned to playwriting in 1906 with *The Silver Box*, in which the justice meted out to a poor and a rich man for the same crime is contrasted. His later plays, *Strife* (1909), *Justice* (1910), and *Loyalties* (1922), were in the same vein. All are objective treatments of social problems and demonstrate Galsworthy's considerable gift for creating dramatic dialogue and clear-cut conflicts. Harley Granville Barker won fame as a dramatist with such plays as *The Marrying of Ann Leete* (1902), *The Voysey Inheritance* (1905), *Waste* (1907), and *Madras House* (1910). Similar to Shaw in his interests, Barker lacked Shaw's sense of the comic. After being ignored for many years, Barker's plays began to be performed again in the 1980s.

FIG. 17.7

Shaw's *Mrs. Warren's Profession* in its original English production, a private performance by the Incorporated Stage Society in 1902. Granville Barker is at left. Courtesy Enthoven Collection, Victoria and Albert Museum, London.

THE CONTINUING TRADITION IN ENGLAND TO 1914

Despite these "modern" trends, pictorial realism continued to be the principal goal in England until World War I. Furthermore, most of the major figures of the London stage between 1900 and 1914 had been trained in the Bancroft-Irving tradition, and they made few innovations. Of the actor-managers, the most important were Forbes-Robertson, Martin-Harvey, and Tree.

Johnston Forbes-Robertson (1853–1937) differed from most of the major actors of his day in being an excellent speaker of verse, an art which he had learned from Samuel Phelps. On the stage from 1874, Forbes-Robertson acted with Phelps, the Bancrofts, and Irving. He also served as leading man to Helena Modjeska (1844–1909), the Polish actress who appeared with great success in England and the United States between 1877 and 1905, and to Mary Anderson (1859–1940), an American actress who won fame in England between 1883 and 1889 for her Shakespearean performances. Occasionally Forbes-Robertson undertook management, but

FIG. 17.8
Beerbohm Tree's production of Shakespeare's *A Midsummer Night's Dream* at Her Majesty's Theatre, London, 1900. Oberon stands in front of the tree center; Titania is at left surrounded by fairies. Courtesy Enthoven Collection, Victoria and Albert Museum, London.

his reputation rested primarily upon his acting. Some critics (including Shaw, who wrote *Caesar and Cleopatra* for him) consider him the finest Hamlet of all time. He was knighted in 1913, the year in which he retired.

John Martin-Harvey (1863–1944) made his debut in 1881 and after 1882 played for Irving, whom he succeeded as manager of the Lyceum Theatre. In his first independent production, an adaptation of Dickens's *A Tale of Two Cities,* he won such popularity that he was condemned to play the role of Sidney Carton through most of his remaining career. He gained new fame in 1912 for his performance in Max Reinhardt's London production of *Oedipus Rex.* Until about 1910, Martin-Harvey continued Irving's practices, but gradually accepted modern trends and after World War I abandoned pictorial realism altogether. More than any other producer, he successfully bridged the Victorian and the modern stage.

The most famous actor-manager between 1900 and 1914 was Herbert Beerbohm Tree (1853–1917). On the stage from 1878, he assumed the management of the Haymarket in 1887. From the profits made there on melodramas and light contemporary plays he built Her Majesty's Theatre in 1897. Although he had had little previous experience with Shakespearean drama, Tree's new theatre was to be the principal home of Shakespeare in London between 1900 and 1914. Tree continued, and even extended, the trend toward actualistic detail. His *A Midsummer Night's Dream* in 1900 featured live rabbits and a carpet of grass with flowers that could be plucked; although the scene changes added 45 minutes to the playing time, the production's literal realism attracted more than 220,000 spectators, perhaps the largest number to witness any Shakespearean play in London up to that time. Beginning in 1905, Tree annually held a festival of Shakespeare's plays in which many other companies took part.

Although not a very good actor, Tree often starred in his own productions. On the other hand, he surrounded himself with the best performers available, and he worked on every production with unbounded enthusiasm. As the repertory system declined, Tree became concerned about the lack of effective training for young actors, and in 1904 he established the acting school which was to become the Royal Academy of Dramatic Art, still the most prestigious in England.

Following the outbreak of the war in 1914, Tree gave up his theatre. Before the hostilities ended, he was dead. With him died much of English tradition, for after the war the actor-manager system, the dominant type of organization since the sixteenth century, was largely abandoned, and pictorial realism, long the standard of perfection, had come to seem old-fashioned.

THE MOSCOW ART THEATRE AND REALISM IN RUSSIA

Russia also had to await the "independent theatre" movement before needed reforms were to come. Although such Russian dramatists as Turgenev, Ostrovsky, and Pisemsky had already inaugurated a realistic school of writing, theatrical production still preserved conventions inherited from the eighteenth century, and the visit of the Meiningen Players in 1885 and 1890 had revealed to many Russian producers how far behind they were. Little significant progress was made, however, until the formation of the Moscow Art Theatre by Konstantin Stanislavsky (1863–1938) and Vladimir Nemirovich-Danchenko (1858–1943) in 1898.

The Moscow Art Theatre (MAT) differed from the other independent theatres in being a fully professional organization from the beginning and in emphasizing theatrical production rather than neglected plays. Its first program, Alexei Tolstoy's *Tsar Feodor Ivanovich,* created a sensation because of its painstaking re-creation of the Russia of 1600, its ensemble acting, and its absence of stars. Public interest waned, however, until the production of Chekhov's *The Sea Gull* established the originality of both the author and the company.

Anton Chekhov (1860–1904) began his dramatic career with vaudeville sketches and short plays in the comic-pathetic vein and then went on to long plays. When *The Sea Gull* (1896) was performed at the Alexandrinsky Theatre in St. Petersburg, it was a failure because the actors did not understand their roles and had not learned their lines. As a result, Chekhov was determined to give up playwriting. After reluctantly permitting the Moscow Art Theatre to revive *The Sea Gull,* he went on to provide it with three other plays: *Uncle Vanya* (1899), *The Three Sisters* (1901), and *The Cherry Orchard* (1904). Chekhov's reputation rests primarily upon these four plays.

Each of Chekhov's four major plays is set in rural Russia and depicts the monotonous and frustrating life of the landowning class. All of the characters aspire to a better life, but do not know how, or have the initiative, to achieve their goals. The plays are composed of infinite detail, the connections among which are not always obvious. Yet gradually a unifying mood, clearly delineated characters, and a complete and simple action emerge.

FIG. 17.9

Chekhov's *The Sea Gull* (Act I) at the Moscow Art Theatre, 1898. Setting by V. A. Simov. From *Moscow Art Theatre, 1898–1917* (Moscow, 1955).

The methods of the MAT were well adapted to the demands of Chekhov's plays. Stanislavsky always undertook a long study of each play before rehearsals began. He insisted upon careful attention to detail from each actor, and he sought to recreate the milieu only after visiting the site of the play's action, or after extensive research.

Despite its success with *The Sea Gull,* the MAT ended its first season in debt and was saved only by the generosity of patrons. With the new support, it was able in 1902 to build its own theatre, with workshops and such up-to-date equipment as a revolving stage, and increase its acting company from 39 to 100 members. Thereafter, it staged from three to five new plays each year, while keeping successful works in the repertory. The influence of the MAT was soon felt throughout Russia, and by 1906 it was sufficiently well known abroad to undertake a foreign tour.

Stanislavsky is now remembered above all for his attempts to perfect an approach to acting. He became fully aware of the need in 1906 and made the first outline of his ideas in 1909. In 1911 he founded the First Studio to train students and work out problems as they arose. Stanislavsky did not begin to publish his ideas until *My Life in Art* (1924) and *An Actor Prepares* (1936). The overall plan was not revealed extensively outside of Russia until the appearance of *Building a Character* (1949) and *Creating a Role* (1961). It is now acknowledged that neither the

English-language nor the Russian-language version of Stanislavsky's writings were reliable. Since the USSR did not subscribe to the International Copyright Agreement when Stanislavsky's works were published in the West, they were copyrighted under the name of the American translator, Elizabeth Reynolds Hapgood. Thus, she, and subsequently her estate, controlled the international rights. Unfortunately, her versions considerably distorted Stanislavsky both through many mistranslations and through considerable cutting and rearrangement. Similarly, the Soviet versions altered the texts to make them conform to official ideology. Only recently, through the cooperation of the Hapgood estate and Soviet authorities, have new and apparently accurate translations of Stanislavsky's writings appeared.

Still, no summary of Stanislavsky's system can claim to be entirely accurate or hope to please all of Stanislavsky's admirers and critics. Nevertheless, the main outlines can be sketched.

1. The actor's body and voice should be thoroughly trained so they may respond efficiently to all demands.
2. Actors should be schooled in stage techniques so they can project characterization to an audience without any sense of contrivance.
3. Actors should be skilled observers of reality as a basis for building a role.
4. Actors should seek inner justification for everything done on stage using "the magic 'if,'" that is, "If I were this person faced with this situation, I would . . ." and "emotion memory," relating the unfamiliar to some analogous emotional situation in the actor's own life—though Stanislavsky eventually rejected this part of the approach.
5. Actors must make a thorough analysis of the script and work within the "given circumstances" found there to avoid merely playing themselves.
6. Actors must define the character's primary "objective" or the "through line" of the role, by understanding the character's motivations in each scene.
7. Actors must focus attention upon the action as it unfolds moment by moment on stage, giving the "illusion of the first time."
8. Actors must continually strive to perfect understanding and proficiency, subordinating their own egos to the artistic demands of the production.

Various aspects of this method have been emphasized by different interpreters. Taken as a whole, it is an attempt to analyze each phase of the actor's work and to make it as efficient as possible. Stanislavsky was never fully satisfied with his system and continued to refine it up to the time of his death. He also cautioned others against adopting it without making changes required by different artistic needs and cultural backgrounds.

In addition to Chekhov, the MAT also encouraged Maxim Gorky (1868–1936), already famous as a writer of realistic stories. *The Lower Depths* (1902), set in a flophouse and featuring a collection of characters defeated by life, became one of the troupe's greatest successes. Other plays by Gorky include *Summer Folk* (1904) and *Enemies* (1907). Gorky was much involved in the political struggles of the day, including the Revolution of 1905, which though largely unsuccessful won a small measure of representative government. Gorky's activities caused him to be exiled, but his reputation as a champion of the proletariat would eventually make him head of the Soviet writers' union and the MAT would become known as the House of Gorky.

THE THEATRE IN ITALY AND SPAIN TO 1914

Italy's major creative energies continued to be poured into opera. In drama, realism arrived first in the works of Paolo Ferrari (1822–1889), a writer in the vein of Dumas *fils*, and then through the "Verist" (or naturalistic) school. Neoromanticism found its major exponent in Gabriele D'Annunzio (1863–1938), who, under the influence of Maeterlinck, wrote such plays as *The Dead City* (1898), *La Giaconda* (1898), and *Francesca da Rimini* (1902).

The strong Italian acting tradition was continued by Eleanora Duse (1859–1924). On the stage from the age of four, she became Rossi's leading lady in 1879. After touring South America in 1885, she formed her own company and played throughout the world. She retired in 1909, but returned to the stage in 1921 and died in Pittsburgh while on tour. Duse played an extremely wide range of roles, many of them favorites of Bernhardt, with whose flamboyance her quiet style contrasted sharply. Noted for subtlety, she used simple means to convey complex conceptions. She scorned makeup and prided herself on her ability to make the physical adjustments required by each role unaided by external means. To many discerning critics, she was the greatest of modern actresses.

In Spain, the realistic drama found its first important exponent in José Echegaray (1848–1927), notably in *The Son of Don Juan* (1892), patterned on Ibsen's *Ghosts*, and *The Great Galeoto* (1881), a play about the power of gossip to ruin lives. After the

THEATRE IN THE UNITED STATES TO 1917

By 1895, the touring company had become the usual source of theatrical entertainment in the United States. In New York, the principal theatrical center, the long-run hit was the goal. For managers outside of New York, booking productions became a major problem, since they usually had to go to New York to arrange a season of attractions. If they wished to schedule a forty-week season, they often had to deal with forty different producers, each of whom was negotiating with many other local managers. Furthermore, producers often defaulted on their agreements, leaving local theatres to deal with sudden cancellations. To remedy these ills, new procedures evolved. Theatres in a restricted area joined together to form circuits, and booking agents began to serve as middlemen between managers and producers.

In this confusion, a small group of men saw the possibility of gaining control of the American theatre. In 1896 Sam Nixon and Fred Zimmerman of Philadelphia, and Charles Frohman, Al Hayman, Marc Klaw, and Abraham Erlanger of New York formed what came to be called "The Syndicate." The new organization began by offering a full season of stellar attractions on the condition that local managers book exclusively through it. This arrangement was welcomed by many managers, for it permitted them to deal with a single agent and to obtain outstanding productions. Managers who refused to deal with the Syndicate were systematically eliminated through simple, if ruthless, maneuvers. The Syndicate did not seek to gain direct control over all theatres in the country; rather, it concentrated on key routes between large cities, for unless productions could play along the way, touring was not financially feasible. Where it could not gain control over key theatres, the Syndicate encouraged the building of rival houses and booked into them the finest productions at reduced prices until the competing theatres were bankrupt. New York producers who refused to cooperate were denied bookings, and many actors were "blackballed," since the Syndicate would not send on tour any production in which they appeared. By 1900, the Syndicate was in effective control of the American theatre. Now in a position to influence the choice of plays, it refused to accept works not likely to appeal to a mass audience and favored productions that featured stars with large personal followings. As a result, between 1900 and 1917, the American theatre remained a conservative, largely commercial venture.

Of the Syndicate members, Charles Frohman (1854–1915) was by far the most important, since

FIG. 17.10
Eleanora Duse in the title role of D'Annunzio's *Francesca da Rimini* at the Teatro Constanzi, Rome, 1902. From *Le Théâtre* (1902).

war of 1898 with the United States had stripped Spain of her last shreds of glory, a new movement, "the Generation of '98," sought to revitalize literature. The most famous of the new writers was Jacinto Benavente (1866–1954), a versatile dramatist who composed nearly 300 works ranging through many styles and forms. Of his realistic plays, the best is probably *The Passion Flower* (1913), the story of a man's love for his stepdaughter, while of the nonrealistic works *The Bonds of Interest* (1907), a philosophical work using *commedia dell'arte* conventions, is the best known.

The modern movement in Spain was helped considerably by the Teatro Intim, an independent theatre founded by Adria Gual (1872–1932) in 1898 at Barcelona. Here a cross section of drama from Aeschylus to the present was offered for some thirty years. Through his experiments in production styles, Gual brought many of the new trends to Spain.

he was the only one directly involved in theatrical production. Working his way up from program seller to business manager and agent, Frohman entered management in 1889, and in 1893 opened the Empire Theatre in New York, where he maintained a fine stock company for many years. In 1896, he extended his interest to London and later controlled five theatres there. As an entrepreneur, Frohman was guided by two convictions: public taste is infallible, and stars are necessary to attract audiences. After Frohman was killed when the Lusitania was torpedoed in World War I, the Syndicate found it difficult to continue and disbanded in 1917.

Despite the Syndicate's strength, it did not go unopposed. James O'Neill (1847–1920) is now remembered as the father of Eugene O'Neill, but he was one of America's most popular actors from the 1880s until World War I. Despite great early promise, he became identified with the leading role in *The Count of Monte Cristo,* which he first played in 1883 and appeared in continuously thereafter. For some time the popularity of his touring production made him immune to the pressures of the Syndicate and they were forced to come to terms with him.

The Fiskes too were able to resist the Syndicate. Minnie Maddern (1864?–1932) who was on the stage from the age of three, married Harrison Grey Fiske (1861–1942), a dramatist and editor of the most influential theatrical newspaper of the day, *The New York Dramatic Mirror* in 1889. After she returned to the stage in 1893, she championed the new realistic drama and was the first American to give Ibsen an extensive hearing through her productions of *A Doll's House, Hedda Gabler, Rosmersholm, Pillars of Society,* and *Ghosts.* When the Syndicate closed its theatres to her, she and her husband leased the Manhattan Theatre, where from 1901 to 1907 they produced many outstanding plays in which they sought to subordinate stars to ensemble effect. As a performer, Mrs. Fiske relied upon direct observation of life and a close study of psychology and she probably did more than any other American performer to pave the way for the modern theatre.

But the most significant opposition to the Syndicate came from David Belasco (c. 1854–1931), a producer and dramatist who shared many of Frohman's ideals. Born in San Francisco, he was on the stage as a child and by the time he left California in 1882 had written or adapted over 100 works and had staged some 300. In New York he served as manager of the Madison Square Theatre and later was MacKaye's stage manager at the Lyceum. He also continued to build his reputation as a dramatist with

FIG. 17.11
Mrs. Fiske and Holbrook Blinn in Edward Sheldon's *Salvation Nell,* 1908. Courtesy Hoblitzelle Theatre Arts Collection, University of Texas at Austin.

such hits as *The Heart of Maryland* (1895), *Madame Butterfly* (1900), and *Girl of the Golden West* (1905). In 1902 he acquired his own theatre and in 1907 opened the Stuyvesant (renamed the Belasco in 1910), with all the most modern technology, which he ran until 1928. He always worked on the single-play principle.

Belasco never maintained a stock company but became known as a "star maker" by tailoring plays for certain individuals and coaching them carefully. Like Daly and MacKaye, he insisted on controlling every aspect of his productions, and with him, naturalistic detail reached its peak on the America stage. For *The Governor's Lady* (1912), for example, a Childs Restaurant was reproduced on stage and the Childs chain stocked it daily with the food consumed during each performance. For Eugene Walter's *The Easiest Way* (1909), Belasco bought the contents of a boarding-house room, including the wallpaper, and had it transferred to his stage. His crowd scenes were famous for their authenticity and power. In collaboration with Louis Hartman, Belasco experimented extensively with stage lighting and in *Madame Butterfly* was able to show the passage of night in a twelve-minute sequence that moved from sunset to night to dawn. Around 1915, Belasco replaced footlights with spotlights mounted in the auditorium and developed new color media.

Belasco first came into conflict with the Syndicate when he sought to take a production on the road in 1902. Further difficulties led to a court battle in

1906. By 1909 Belasco's productions were in such demand that the Syndicate agreed to Belasco's terms, even though he refused to book exclusively through it. Its concessions to him marked the first important break in the Syndicate's power.

The willingness of the Syndicate to make concessions had been hastened by the rise of the Shuberts. Three brothers, Sam (1876–1905), Lee (1875–1954), and Jacob J. (1880–1963), after beginning in Syracuse, New York, leased a theatre in New York City in 1900. When the Syndicate closed its theatres to their productions in 1905, the Shuberts began to establish a rival chain. Unlike the Syndicate, which was always merely a cooperative arrangement among independent businessmen, the Shuberts created a corporation (a new organizational form at that time) and used its financial base to buy or build its own theatres throughout the country. By this time, the high-handed methods of the Syndicate had created much dissatisfaction, and the Shuberts were welcomed by many local managers as allies. The struggle between the Shuberts and the Syndicate reached its peak in 1913, after which the Syndicate's grip was broken. Unfortunately, the Shuberts became as dictatorial and monopolistic as the Syndicate had been. As producers, they were noted for lavish musicals with little substance. They continued to control "the road" until 1956, when an antitrust ruling forced them to sell many of their theatres. Despite this divestiture, the Shubert organization remains a powerful force in the American theatre.

Probably the most successful dramatist of this period was Clyde Fitch (1865–1909), who, after being commissioned by Richard Mansfield to create *Beau Brummel* (1890), wrote about sixty plays, of which the most important were *Captain Jinks of the Horse Marines* (1901), *The Girl with the Green Eyes* (1902), and *The Truth* (1907). During the season of 1900–1901, ten of Fitch's works were being played in New York or on the road. A careful observer, Fitch reflected the life of his times and was known for the quiet, intense scenes, he brought to his plays. As the first American playwright to publish his works regularly, he established a pattern continued until the present.

During the first decade of the century William Vaughan Moody (1869–1910) seemed the dramatist with greatest promise. Moody was a professor at the University of Chicago and a poet of stature when he began writing closet dramas about 1900. His first produced work, *The Great Divide* (1906), was considered a landmark because it combined considerable literary merit with an exciting action which dramatized the "great divide" between the effete and self-

FIG. 17.12
David Belasco's production of *The Governor's Lady*, 1912, showing the replica of Childs Restaurant. From *Le Théâtre* (1912).

conscious East and the rough and open-hearted West. Moody's early death blighted the hopes of those who saw in his work the potential for a truly significant American drama.

During the early twentieth century, American female playwrights began to make their presence felt, although today most have long been ignored. Perhaps the most important of these was Martha Morton

FIG. 17.13
William Vaughan Moody's *The Great Divide*, Princess's Theatre, New York, 1906, with Henry Miller and Margaret Anglin. Act I. Courtesy Hoblitzelle Theatre Arts Collection, University of Texas at Austin.

(1865–1925), author of some thirty-five plays and sometimes called America's first female professional playwright. Among her plays are *The Merchant* (1891), *Her Lord and Master* (1903), and *The Movers* (1907). She is also significant for founding the Society of Dramatic Authors in 1907 when female writers were denied admission to the American Dramatists Club (the forerunner of today's Dramatists Guild). Josephine Preston Peabody (1874–1922) won international fame with her *The Piper* (1910), a poetic drama based on the story of the Pied Piper of Hamelin. It won the Shakespeare Memorial Prize in worldwide competition with more than 300 other writers, and was translated and performed in several languages.

By 1917 the professional theatre was beginning to decline in popularity. While increased ticket prices were partially responsible, effective competition, most notably from spectator sports and motion pictures, was also appearing. Soon after Thomas A. Edison demonstrated the "kinetoscope" in 1894, "penny arcades" began to show short motion pictures. Only one person at a time could be served, however, until George Eastman's flexible film and Thomas Armat's projector made it possible to show movies to an assembled audience.

In 1905 the first movie theatre was opened, and by 1909 there were 8000. The early theatres seated only about 100 and offered only short films. Then in 1914, the Strand Theatre in New York, with its 3300 seats, began the trend toward large houses. But it was not until D. W. Griffith's *The Birth of a Nation* (1915) surpassed Belasco's realism and melodramatic power that films became a serious competitor to the theatre. With their superior ability to capture spectacle and their markedly lower admission costs, motion pictures began to draw away that audience that had sought illusionism and thrills in the theatre. The competition from films did not bring an overnight revolution. In 1915 there were still about 1500 professional theatres outside of New York and the number of theatrical productions on Broadway continued to increase until the season of 1927–1928. The invention of sound motion picture in 1927 and the depression of 1929 dealt serious blows, however, and by 1930 only 500 professional theatres remained outside of New York. Thereafter, the number steadily declined.

Although these new directions were not readily apparent in 1917, it was already clear to many that the old production methods were outmoded and that commercialization had gradually reduced the repertory to works calculated to appeal to the mass audience. Reassessment, new methods, and changing ideals were in the offing.

MAJOR TECHNICAL INNOVATIONS, 1875–1914

Between 1875 and 1914 several important technical innovations were introduced, which aided the cause of scenic realism. One of the most important of the new devices was the elevator stage, first installed in the Budapest Opera House in 1884. The entire stage was divided into sections, each of which could be lowered, raised, or tilted to create a variety of acting levels or to raise or lower scenic elements. The revolving stage, first used in the Kabuki theatres of Japan, was introduced to Europe by Karl Lautenschläger (1843–1906) at the Residenz Theatre, Munich, in 1896. Its ability to accommodate several settings and to change them merely by revolving a turntable, led to its wide adoption. Another innovation was the rolling platform stage, introduced by Fritz Brandt (1846–1927) at the Royal Opera House in Berlin around 1900. With it, settings could be mounted on a large platform offstage and then moved on stage by means of rollers set in tracks. By 1914, a complex arrangement of elevators and sliding platforms was installed in the Dresden State Theater by Adolf Linnebach (1876–1963), setting a new standard for technology in the theatre. Many German theatres of this period also installed a plaster dome (or *kuppelhorizont*) which curved around and above the stage to give the effect of infinite space and eliminated the need for many overhead and side masking pieces. To fulfill the same function, other theatres used a cloth cyclorama hung from a pipe which curved around the stage.

After 1907, improvements in the filaments of incandescent lamps made it possible to increase wattage and to create the first spotlights (other than the limelight and carbon arc). By 1913, 1000-watt lamps were available in Europe, and color media and spotlights were beginning to be common. Consequently, footlights were gradually replaced by spotlights mounted in the auditorium. One of the most ambitious lighting systems of the period was devised by Mariano Fortuny (1871–1949), who directed strong light against colored silk panels, which reflected the light onto a *kuppelhorizont* and then onto the stage to create realistic ambient light. With elaborate machinery for changing the panels and controlling the light, the system gave the most subtle variations of any then known, but its complexity and cost prevented its widespread adoption. Nevertheless, it is indicative of the growing interest in lighting as an important element of design.

Auditoriums also underwent considerable change, largely under the influence of Wagner's theatre at Bayreuth. Boxes tended to disappear, the number of balconies to decrease (sometimes there were none),

FIG. 17.14

The first revolving stage in Europe, installed in the Residenz Theater, Munich. At right, the floor plan for two settings for Mozart's *Don Giovanni:* the Commandant's Garden and a street in Seville. At left, the design for the Commandant's Garden. Courtesy Theatermuseum, Munich.

and center aisles to be eliminated, thereby improving sight lines. As the interest in breaking down the barriers between performers and audience grew, the apron stage returned to favor and in a few instances the proscenium arch was eliminated. Thus, the Italianate theatre, dominant since the seventeenth century, was challenged for the first time.

By 1914 the standards of production that had been accepted almost universally in 1875 had begun to seem outmoded. Although pictorial realism still dominated the popular theatre, it had been undermined by a host of experiments. A common theme ran through all of the experiments: the need for unified production, a strong director, and artistic integrity, so that the theatre might once more assume the role it had played in ancient Greece as a source of insight and place of communion. Although the war interrupted developments, it also provoked reassessments, out of which new conventions and renewed vigor came in the postwar years.

LOOKING AT THEATRE HISTORY

A study of critical responses to plays and production styles can be very helpful. For example, such responses suggest that in the late nineteenth century Saxe-Meiningen's approach was readily accepted because it was essentially an intensification of trends with which the audience was already familiar and of which it approved. When the company appeared in London in 1881, reviewers were not impressed by all aspects of the productions, since they thought that in some areas the English did as well or better, but they especially admired the crowd scenes. Here are portions of a review of *Julius Caesar.*

> It may . . . be maintained that no spectacular play of Shakespeare, such as "Julius Caesar" may claim to be considered, has ever been put upon our stage in a

fashion equally effective . . . the principal gain is in the manner in which those who are little or nothing more than supernumeraries wear the costumes of a bygone age, and take intelligent part in actions and movements of which they can have had no experience in real life. . . . The openly manifested desire to obtain an ascendancy over his fellows, which has been the disgrace of the English actor, is kept out of sight. . . .

In the case of "Julius Caesar" the most noteworthy features consisted of the arrangement of the tableaux and the disposition of the supernumeraries when as in the case of the oration of Antony over the body of Caesar, strong and growing emotion has to be expressed. From the picturesque standpoint these things were perfect.

The Athenaeum, June 11, 1881, 796.

A study of critical responses can also help us understand the great uproar caused by scripts or productions that now seem uncontroversial. As a playwright, Ibsen was a special focus for contention. Here are some of the responses of Clement Scott, one of London's foremost theatre critics, to *Ghosts* when it was first produced in London:

If people like the discussion of such nasty subjects on the stage . . . if it is desirable to drive decent-minded women out of the playhouse, and to use the auditorium as a hospital-ward or dissecting-room, let it be so. . . . But in our hurry to dramatize the Contagious Diseases Act let us first set about writing a good play. Who in their sense can say that Ghosts is a good play? . . . If, by the examples we have seen, Ibsen is a dramatist, then the art of the dramatist is dead indeed. . . .

The Illustrated London News, 21 March 1891.

During this period, Stanislavsky began to evolve his system of acting. *In My Life in Art,* he tells how his system took shape over many years, beginning in 1906 when he became concerned over his inability to remain fresh in his roles:

How was I to save my roles from bad rebirths, from spiritual petrifaction, from the autocracy of evil habit and lack of truth? There was the necessity not only of a physical make-up but of a spiritual make-up before every performance. [460–461]

As he experimented with a system capable of meeting the actor's problems, his ideas began to attract others:

For the young people who came to seek my help I founded a Studio [in 1911] . . . here we gathered all who wanted to study the so-called Stanislavsky System. . . . I began to give a full course of study in the shape in which I had at that time formed it. Its aim was to give practical and conscious methods for the awakening of superconscious creativeness. [531]

About his system, Stanislavsky warned:

My system cannot be explained in an hour or in a day even. It must be systematically and practically studied for years. It does good only when it becomes the second nature of the actor, when he stops thinking of it consciously, when it begins to appear naturally, as of itself. [529]

Constantin Stanislavsky, *My Life in Art,* trans. J. J. Robbins (New York: Theatre Arts Books, 1948).

18
Modern Alternatives to Realism

The nationalist movements, colonialist expansion, and growing militarism of the late nineteenth century culminated in a series of localized wars around the globe from the Spanish American War (1898) in Cuba and the Philippines, to the Boxer Uprising (1898–1900) that made China subject to European, American, and Japanese power, to the Boer War (1899–1902) in South African, and the Russo-Japanese War (1904–1905) that led to the destabilization of the Russian Empire—all of which now seem merely a prelude to World War I. But many saw these as just the most visible results of the long-developing inequalities created by rapid industrialization and seriously questioned whether scientific methods could provide the answers to the political, social, and moral dilemmas facing their cultures. In the art world, these concerns intermingled with aesthetic issues, such as how painting was to respond to photography, and generated a remarkable range of responses that sought alternatives to realism.

Although the "modern theatre" is often said to begin with Saxe-Meiningen, Ibsen, and Zola, "modernism" is now usually thought to have begun with the symbolists. In the late nineteenth century, both realists and nonrealists questioned the views that had dominated Western thought and art since the Renaissance and that were summed up in the "humanist ideal" (which posited a set of universal, unchanging values as the very basis of civilization). The belief that truth should be depicted representationally—that there should be a direct relationship between reality as normatively perceived and its artistic representation—had dominated artistic theory and practice since the time of the neoclassicists. The realist/naturalist attempt to reduce truth to what is scientifically knowable revealed just how much human values are based on the scientifically unknowable. Modernists, abandoning both the scientific and the humanist ideal, substituted their own subjective visions and esthetic modes (often abstract and usually departing drastically from objective appearance) for the traditional approach that had allowed the audience to compare the subject with its artistic rendering. The rejection of this long-accepted relationship between perception and representation, beginning with the symbolists, is often considered the true beginning of modernism.

WAGNER AND THE NONREALISTIC THEATRE

Richard Wagner (1813–1883) may be thought of as one of the significant forerunners of modernism. He was brought up in a theatrical family (his stepfather and four of his brothers and sisters were employed in the theatre). His first opera, *Die Feen,* was written in 1831, but he did not achieve critical success until 1842 with *Rienzi,* which also brought him an appointment as conductor at the Dresden opera house. Banished for his part in the revolution of 1848, he spent twelve years in exile, during which he formulated those theories that were to influence the course of the modern theatre.

Wagner rejected the contemporary trend toward realism, arguing that rather than a recorder of domestic affairs the dramatist should be a myth-maker—that he should portray an ideal world through the expression of the inner impulses and aspirations of a people as embodied in its racial myths and so unite them as a "folk." (This idea would later endear Wagner to the Nazis.) To him, true drama was concerned with the ideal world, which is left behind as soon as spoken dialogue is admitted. He suggested that drama should be "dipped in the magic fountain of music" to combine the greatness of Shakespeare and Beethoven. He also argued that music, through melody and tempo, permits greater control over performance than is possible in spoken drama, in which interpretation is subject to performers' personal whims. Thus, for Wagner the effectiveness of music-drama depended upon performance as well as upon composition, and he argued that the author-composer should supervise every aspect of production to unify all the elements into a *Gesamtkunstwerk,* or "master art work." These ideas undergird much of modern theory about the need for a strong director and unified production.

In addition to his theories, Wagner's practice also exerted considerable influence, especially on theatre architecture, since to house his idealized music-drama, Wagner demanded a new type of theatre structure. Begun in 1872 and opened in 1876, the Festival Theatre, originally planned for Munich but built in Bayreuth, was soon famous throughout the world and was to inspire many reforms in architectural design. Since Wagner wished to create a "class-less" theatre, he abandoned the box, pit, and gallery arrangement. The main part of the auditorium had thirty stepped rows of seats; there were no side boxes or center aisle, and each row led directly to a side exit. At the rear of the auditorium was a single large box surmounted by a small gallery. The total seating capacity was 1745. To ensure good sight lines, the auditorium was shaped like a fan, measuring 50 feet across at the proscenium and 115 feet at the rear of the auditorium. Since all seats were said to be equally good, a uniform price was charged. The orchestra pit was hidden from view, much of it extending

FIG. 18.1

Plan of Wagner's Festival Theatre at Bayreuth. From Sachs, *Modern Opera Houses and Theatres* (1896–1898).

underneath the apron of the stage. This feature helped to create a "mystic chasm" between the "real" world of the auditorium and the "ideal" world of the stage, an effect reinforced by darkening the auditorium during performances and by framing the stage with a double proscenium arch.

The arrangement of the auditorium was the theatre's greatest innovation, since the stage was essentially conservative in design. The stage floor was raked upward toward the back, and the chariot-and-pole system of scene shifting was retained. The principal innovation was a system of steam vents to create realistic effects of fog and mist and a "steam curtain" to mask scene changes. The proscenium opening, about 40 feet wide, gave onto a stage 80 feet deep by 93 feet wide. About 100 feet of overhead space and 32 feet of below-stage space were provided. The building also included ample workshops, storage, dressing rooms, and rehearsal space.

Although Wagner's theories later inspired several nonillusionistic approaches, his own productions aimed at complete illusion. He forbade the musicians to tune their instruments in the orchestra pit and allowed no applause during performances or curtain calls at the end. He sought precise historical accuracy in scenery and costumes and employed such devices as moving panoramas. His taste for minute detail may be seen in *Siegried,* for example, in which he used a dragon with realistic scales and movable eyes and mouth. To Wagner, the ideal was to be reached through total illusion. Thus, Wagner's theatrical practice was grounded solidly in the nineteenth-century tradition. Nevertheless, his conceptions of the master artwork, unified production, and theatre architecture were to inspire many pioneers of the "modern" theatre.

NONREALISTIC THEATRE IN FRANCE

The realistic and naturalistic outlook that dominated the late nineteenth century did not go unchallenged. Although the intellectual climate between 1850 and 1900 was largely anti-idealistic, the sweeping claims made for science at this time brought several protests. The most significant of these came from the symbolists, who launched their counterattack in 1885 in a "manifesto." Taking its inspiration from the works of Edgar Allan Poe, Charles-Pierre Baudelaire's poems and criticism, Fyodor Dostoevsky's novels, and Richard Wagner's music and theory, symbolism

FIG. 18.2
Auditorium and stage of the Bayreuth Festival Theatre. On stage is a setting for *Parsifal* designed by Max Brückner. From *Le Théâtre* (1899).

attracted representatives from all the arts. The unknowable and relative were the bedrocks of anti-realism (and for many critics "modernism"). Artists, no longer shackled to the natural world, could now be valued for novelty and experimentation with form rather than for accurate renditions of recognizable subjects. To the symbolists, subjectivity, spirituality, and mysterious internal and external forces were the sources of a truth more profound than that derived from the mere observation of outward appearance. This truth, they argued, cannot be represented directly but can only be evoked through symbols, legends, myths, and moods.

The principal spokesman for the movement was Stephane Mallarmé (1842–1898), whose views of drama—as an evocation of the mystery of existence through poetic and allusive language, performed with only the most essential and atmospherically appropriate theatrical aids, for the purpose of creating a quasi-religious experience—set the tone for the antirealistic works of the 1890s.

As with naturalism, symbolism made no marked impression in the theatre until an "independent" group, modeled on the Théâtre Libre, appeared. In 1890, Paul Fort (1872–1962), a seventeen-year-old poet, founded the Théâtre d'Art, where by 1892 he had presented works by 46 authors, ranging from readings of poems and adaptations of portions of the *Iliad* and the Bible to new plays. Most of the programs were given only one performance, and the actors, primarily amateurs, were often inadequate. Unlike Antoine, Fort received predominantly hostile critical notices, perhaps because his productions seemed incomprehensible to those accustomed to illusionism.

When Fort left the theatre in 1892, his work was carried on by the Théâtre de l'Oeuvre, headed by Aurélien-Marie Lugné-Poë (1869–1940). An actor and stage manager at the Théâtre Libre for a time, Lugné-Poë was converted to the idealist outlook after seeing and appearing in some of the productions at the Théâtre d'Art and while sharing an apartment with the symbolist painters Edouard Vuillard, Maurice Denis, and Pierre Bonnard. The Théâtre de l'Oeuvre gave its first performance in 1893. From that time until 1897 Lugné-Poë used a similar style for virtually all of his productions. Guided by the motto "the word creates the decor," he reduced scenery to simple compositions of lines and color painted on backdrops. Using settings by Toulouse-Lautrec, Denis, Vuillard, Bonnard, Odilon Redon, and others, Lugné-Poë sought to create a unity of style and mood rather than of milieu.

The opening production, Maeterlinck's *Pelléas and Mélisande,* was typical. Few properties and little

FIG. 18.3

Hamlet at the Théâtre de l'Oeuvre, 1913. Directed by Lugné-Poë and Gémier. The structure in the foreground remained throughout and set pieces were changed behind the central opening. From *Le Théâtre* (1913).

furniture were used; the stage was lighted from overhead and most of the action passed in semidarkness; a gauze curtain, hung between the actors and the audience, gave the impression that mist enveloped the stage; backdrops, painted in grayed tones, emphasized the air of mystery; costumes were vaguely medieval, although the intention was to create draperies of no particular period. The actors spoke in a staccato chant like priests and, according to some critics, behaved like sleepwalkers; their gestures were strongly stylized. Given this radically new approach, it is not surprising that many spectators were mystified.

Lugné-Poë's repertory was made up primarily of French plays mingled with some works by Ibsen, Hauptmann, Sanskrit dramatists, and others. Of the French dramas, those by Maeterlinck were the best. Maurice Maeterlinck (1862–1949), after coming to Paris from Belgium, turned to playwriting in 1889 and by 1896 had written *The Intruder* (1890), *The Blind* (1890), and *The Death of Tintagiles* (1894). Of his early work, the best known is *Pelléas and Mélisande* (1892), in which a young woman, after marrying a prince who has found her in a forest, falls in love with his brother and dies of grief after her husband kills his brother. The interest does not reside in the triangular relationship, however, but in the mood of mystery which envelops it and which is evoked through symbols, such as a wedding ring dropped

into a fountain, doves that fly away from a tower, subterranean pools and grottoes, enveloping shadows, and blood stains that cannot be washed away. In the early 1890s Maeterlinck argued that the most dramatic moments are those silent ones during which the mystery of existence, ordinarily obscured by bustling activity, makes itself felt. After 1896, Maeterlinck revised his view and modified his style to include more straightforward action. The most famous of his later plays is *The Blue Bird* (1908), an allegory about childrens' search for happiness, eventually found in their own backyard.

In 1896 Lugné-Poë presented Alfred Jarry's (1873–1907) *Ubu Roi*, sometimes called the first absurdist drama. Jarry's play is related to symbolist works in being antirealistic but its moral topsy-turvydom more nearly resembles that of the naturalists' *comédies rosses*, although it completely avoids their scientific bias and realistic techniques. *Ubu Roi* shows in all its grotesqueness a world without human decency. Its central figure, Ubu, violent and totally devoid of moral scruple, is the epitome of all that Jarry found inane and ugly in bourgeois society and of all that is monstrous and irrational in human beings. The action of the play shows how Ubu usurps the throne of Poland and keeps his power by killing and torturing all those who oppose him; eventually he is driven from the country but he promises to continue his exploits elsewhere. Jarry wrote two other plays about Ubu, *Ubu Bound* (1900) and *Ubu the Cuckold* (published 1944), but these were not produced during his lifetime. At first Jarry's influence was negligible, but in the 1920s he attracted a following among the surrealists and after World War II his grotesque vision of man won him a place of honor as a major prophet of the absurdist movement.

The first major phase of the antirealistic movement came to an end in 1897 when Lugné-Poë broke with the symbolists after concluding that most of their plays were immature and that his commitment to a single style of production was too limiting. His decision was influenced by his admiration for Ibsen, whose plays he found unadaptable to the extreme stylization favored by the symbolists.

The Théâtre de l'Oeuvre closed in 1899, but Lugné-Poë was to revive it in 1912 and again after World War I until 1929. Nevertheless, it is his symbolist productions of the 1890s that constitute his most significant contribution to the theatre. Through tours with his company and articles written about his work, Lugné-Poë influenced almost every departure from realism between 1893 and 1914.

FIG. 18.4

Jarry's *Ubu Roi* at the Théâtre Antoine, 1908. Gémier directed the play and appeared as Père Ubu. From *Figaro* (16 February 1908).

THE REVIVAL OF IDEALISM IN FRANCE

After the closing of the Théâtre de l'Oeuvre in 1899, Paris settled once more into its complacent conviction that it was the artistic capital of Europe. Antoine's productions became the standard, and nonrealistic experiments were few and sporadic. Thus, the appearance of the Ballets Russes in 1909 came almost as a revelation. A new wave of experimentation was given further impetus by the publication in 1910 of *Modern Theatre Art* by Jacques Rouché (1862–1957). After describing the work of Fuchs and Reinhardt in Germany, of Meyerhold, Stanislavsky, and Kommissarzhevskaya in Russia, and the theories of Appia and Craig, Rouché called for similar experiments in France. Not only was his book widely read and discussed, Rouché himself set out to implement his ideas at the Théâtre des Arts between 1910 and 1913. Rouché did not aim at extreme stylization, but sought a simplicity in which color and line characterize a milieu and mood without calling attention to themselves. Working with his designer Maxime Dethomas (1867–1929), Rouché was the first French producer to be truly eclectic. He went on to become director of the Opéra, where between 1914 and 1936 he renovated the repertory and brought to it a new generation of designers.

Rouché's work had important consequences. Lugné-Poë revived the Théâtre de l'Oeuvre, where he presented a series of plays with designs by Jean Variot. More important, Rouché inspired Jacques Copeau (1879–1949) to open his own theatre. A dramatic critic, Copeau gained his first practical experience at the Théâtre des Arts when his adaptation of *The Brothers Karamazov* was produced there in 1911. Copeau was convinced that Rouché's suggested reforms put too much emphasis on visual elements and that no significant progress could come except through the drama itself.

In 1913 Copeau published a manifesto for a new theatre. In it, he adopted a position almost opposite to that of Meyerhold, for he argued that the director's primary task is the faithful translation of the dramatist's script into a "poetry of the theatre." Furthermore, he stated that the actor, as the "living presence" of the author, is the only essential element of theatrical production, and that a rejuvenation of the drama depends upon a return to the bare platform stage.

Copeau assembled a company of ten actors, including Louis Jouvet and Charles Dullin, both of whom were to be significant in the postwar theatre, and retired to the country to perfect his first productions. Meanwhile, with the assistance of Francis Jourdain, Copeau converted a small hall into the Théâtre du Vieux Colombier, seating only 400. It had a forestage forward of the proscenium, but no machinery except for a set of curtains and asbestos hangings which could be moved on rods to effect

FIG. 18.5

Copeau's adaptation of Dostoyevsky's *The Brothers Karamazov* at Rouché's Théâtre des Arts, 1911. At center Charles Dullin as Smerdiakov. Setting by Maxime Dethomas. From *Le Théâtre* (1911).

rapid changes of locale. To these curtains were added only the most essential furniture and set pieces. In 1913–1914, before the war forced him to stop, Copeau presented fifteen plays, including works by Shakespeare, Molière, Heywood, Claudel, and others. In 1917 Copeau was asked to revive the troupe and take it to New York. There, between 1917 and 1919, he presented plays for American audiences before returning to Paris to reopen his theatre. It is impossible to overrate the importance of the Théâtre du Vieux Colombier, for with its formation the leadership of the French theatre passed from Antoine to Copeau, who was to dominate the interwar years in France.

APPIA AND CRAIG

At about the time Lugné-Poë was closing the Théâtre de l'Oeuvre in 1899, two other men, Appia and Craig, working independently of each other, were beginning to lay the theoretical foundations of modern nonillusionistic theatrical practice. Adolphe Appia (1862–1928), born in Switzerland, first came into contact with the theatre through his musical studies. Deeply impressed by Wagner's music-dramas and theoretical writings, Appia recognized that the usual mounting (including Wagner's) of the operas did not properly embody Wagner's theories. After years of thought, he published *The Staging of Wagner's Musical Dramas* (1895), *Music and Stage Setting* (1899), and *The Work of Living Art* (1921). In these, he set forth ideas about theatrical production that were eventually accepted almost everywhere.

Beginning with the assumption that artistic unity is the fundamental goal of theatrical production, Appia sought to analyze failures to achieve it. He concluded that stage presentation involves three conflicting visual elements: the moving three-dimensional actor; the perpendicular scenery; and the horizontal floor. He considered painted two-dimensional settings to be one of the major causes of disunity and recommended that they be replaced with three-dimensional units (steps, ramps, platforms) that enhance the actor's movement and provide a transition from the horizontal floor to the upright scenery. Above all, however, Appia emphasized the role of light in fusing all of the visual elements into a unified whole. Since to him light was the visual counterpart of music, which changes from moment to moment in response to shifting moods, emotions, and action, Appia wished to orchestrate and manipulate light as carefully as a musical score. Attempts to implement this theory, which require control over the distribution, brightness, and color of light, have

FIG. 18.6
Adolphe Appia's design for the sacred forest in Wagner's *Parsifal.*

led to much of modern stage-lighting practice. Appia also argued that artistic unity requires that one person control all of the elements of production. Thus, his ideas strengthened the role of the director.

In 1906 Appia met Emile Jacques Dalcroze (1865–1950), who, next to Wagner, was to be the greatest influence on Appia's work. Dalcroze was the deviser of "eurythmics," a system under which students were led to experience music kinesthetically by responding physically to the rhythms of musical compositions. Under Dalcroze's influence, Appia came to believe that the rhythm embedded in a text provides the key to every gesture and movement to be used on the stage and that the proper mastery of rhythm will unify all the spatial and temporal elements of a production into a satisfying and harmonious whole. In 1910 Appia designed the first theatre of modern times to be built without a proscenium arch and with a completely open stage, for Dalcroze's school at Hellerau, where he also designed a series of productions for the 1912 and 1913 seasons.

In the 1920s Appia began to win his long-delayed recognition. In 1923 he staged Wagner's *Tristan and Isolde* in Milan and in 1924–1925 two parts of the *Ring* cycle in Basel. Nevertheless, it was not through

FIG. 18.7
Craig's set for *Hamlet* at the Moscow Art theatre, 1912. The screens were supposed to be sufficiently mobile to change configurations quickly and without closing the front curtain, but they never functioned as envisioned. From *Moscow Art Theatre, 1898–1917* (Moscow, 1955).

practice but through theory that Appia was to exert lasting influence on the modern theatre.

Gordon Craig (1872–1966), son of Ellen Terry and Edward Godwin, began his career as an actor in Irving's company. His first important practical experience as a designer was gained in his mother's company at the Imperial Theatre in London in 1903. An exhibit of his work in 1902 and the publication of his book, *The Art of the Theatre* (1905), created such controversy that within a few years he was well known throughout Europe. In 1904 he designed a play for Brahm in Berlin, in 1906 one for Eleanora Duse in Florence, and in 1912 one for the Moscow Art Theatre. Everywhere controversy followed him. He continued to set forth his provocative and original ideas in *On the Art of the Theatre* (1911), *Towards a New Theatre* (1913), *The Theatre Advancing* (1919), and *The Mask,* a periodical issued sporadically between 1908 and 1929. In 1908 he settled in Florence, where he ran a school for a time. Although Appia had voiced many of the same ideas, it was Craig who publicized them. To many conservative producers, Craig seemed as dangerous as Ibsen had in the 1880s.

Craig thought of the theatre as an independent art and argued that the true theatre artist welds action, words, line, color, and rhythm into a product as pure as that of the painter, sculptor, or composer. He acknowledged the kind of theatre in which a craftsman-director, beginning with a literary text, coordinates the work of several other craftsmen, but he sought a higher form in which the master-artist, without the medium of a literary text, would create every part of a wholly autonomous art.

Craig's influence was felt most heavily in design, perhaps because he conceived of the theatre primarily in visual terms. He argued that the public goes to see rather than to hear a play. His own drawings show a marked predilection for right angles and an obsession with parallelism. Their most notable feature, however, is height and the resulting sense of grandeur. Perhaps Craig's favorite project was the mobile setting. Throughout most of his life he experimented with screens, out of which he hoped to create a setting that by invisible means, could move in ways analogous to the actor and to light.

Craig always refused to assign a hierarchy to the theatrical elements and blamed many faults of the past on the dominance of one or another part. Thus, he often denounced the dramatist, upon whom he

FIG. 18.8
Craig's design for *Electra,* 1905. From City of Manchester Art Gallery, *Exhibition of Drawings and Models by Edward Gordon Craig* (1912).

blamed the overemphasis on the spoken word. Similarly, he often blamed starring actors for the low state of the theatre, since they sought to aggrandize themselves and to interject their own conceptions between those of the director and the public. Consequently, he once suggested that ideally the master-artist should use an *Ubermarionette,* a superpuppet without any ego but capable of carrying out all demands. No idea voiced by Craig aroused a greater storm.

Although Appia and Craig arrived at many of the same ideas, they also differed on important issues. Appia's artist was to be primarily an interpreter of the composer-dramatist's work; Craig's was a full-fledged artist in his own right. Appia assigned a hierarchy to the theatrical elements; Craig refused to do so. Appia thought in terms of successive settings (a different setting for each locale); Craig sought a single setting capable of expressing the spirit of the entire work or of reflecting changes through mobility.

Appia and Craig were often denounced as impractical men who knew little of the workaday theatre and whose ideas were useless in practice. But they championed ideals and goals that practical men of the period could not provide. Together they forced their contemporaries to reconsider the nature of the theatre as an art, its function in society, and its elements (both separately and in combination). They influenced the trend toward simplified decor, three-dimensional settings, plasticity, and directional lighting—toward evocation rather than literal representation. At first highly controversial, their theories were to prevail after World War I.

STRINDBERG AND FREUD

The first decade of the twentieth century also brought works of another type that were to be a major influence on modern drama: the nonrealistic plays of the Swedish dramatist, August Strindberg (1849–1912). Strindberg had already established his reputation as a realistic dramatist with *The Father* (1887) and *Miss Julie* (1888), both of which demonstrate his preoccupation with what he considered to be the elemental and inevitable conflict between men and women. *Miss Julie* especially won high praise for its emphasis upon heredity and environment, its unusual setting (a triangular view of one corner of a kitchen), and its use of pantomimes to replace intermissions. Many critics considered it an excellent exemplar of naturalistic principles.

Powerful as these plays are, they were not to be as influential as those Strindberg wrote after undergoing a bout with insanity during the 1890s. Partially because of his recent experiences and partially under Maeterlinck's influence, Strindberg now began to write "dream plays," of which he said: "The author has tried to imitate the disconnected but seemingly logical form of the dream. Anything may happen; everything is possible and probable. Time and space do not exist. On an insignificant background of reality, imagination designs and embroiders novel patterns, free fancies, absurdities and improvisations. The characters split, double, multiply, vanish, solidify, blur, clarify. But one consciousness reigns above them all—that of the dreamer; and before it there are no secrets, no incongruities, no scruples, no laws." In such plays as *To Damascus* (a trilogy, 1898–1901) and *The Dream Play* (1902) Strindberg reshaped reality according to his own subjective vision. Time and place shift frequently and without regard for logical sequence, the real and the imaginary merge, and the seemingly commonplace is invested with a sense of significance. In these late works Strindberg treats with great compassion alienated human beings, lost and rootless, seeking meaning in an incomprehensible universe, trying to reconcile disparate elements: lust and love, body and spirit, filth and beauty.

From 1907 to 1910 Strindberg was associated with August Falck (1882–1938), an actor and producer, at the Intimate Theater in Stockholm. Seating only 161, this theatre was intended as a home for Strindberg's plays, and for it he wrote five "chamber plays," of which the best known is *The Ghost Sonata* (1907), a work which echoes many of the ideas found in *The Dream Play.*

By the time Strindberg died in 1912 he was one of the most famous writers in the world. Although his plays have never been widely popular, they have never ceased to be a source of controversy and inspiration. His vision of human beings as tortured and alienated was to attract many later writers, and his dramatic devices were to show others how psychological states and spiritual intuitions might be externalized. As the first dramatist to make extensive use of the unconscious, he was to be a major influence on subsequent playwrights.

Strindberg's acceptance was probably aided by widespread interest in the psychoanalytic theories of Sigmund Freud (1856–1939), who in such books as *The Interpretation of Dreams* (1900) and *Three Contributions to the Theory of Sex* (1905) sought to analyze the structure of the mind, to describe its functionings, and to suggest means for dealing with abnormal behavior. Freud's explanation of human behavior, with its revolutionary emphasis on the unconscious, dreams as a key to understanding suppressed desires, and the human propensity for telescoping experience, gave strong authority to Strindberg's dramaturgy. Unlike Comte, Zola, and others who had placed primary emphasis on external environment as a determinant of human behavior, Freud emphasized internal, unconscious, psychological causality. His interest in aggression and sexuality as basic human instincts also did much to break down taboos against using these subjects in drama. Additionally, the idea that culturally unacceptable instincts, feelings, and behavior are sublimated and buried in the subconscious opened infinite possibilities for disparities between surface appearance and suppressed realities. Truth became extremely complex, perhaps unknowable, since not only is it difficult to penetrate the masks of others but our own as well. The unspoken and unacknowledged (the subtext) became as important as the stated and conscious (the text). Freud's conception of reality, intermingling as it did the rational and irrational, the conscious and unconscious, the objective and subjective, the real and the fantastic, was to become a means of bridging many of the divisions that had previously existed between realistic and nonrealistic drama.

NONREALISTIC THEATRE AND DRAMA IN GERMANY

In Germany, a number of dramatists, most notably Hauptmann and Sudermann, eventually were to write alternately in realistic and nonrealistic styles. But others, among them Hofmannsthal and Wedekind, fall more clearly into the antirealist camp. Hugo von Hofmannsthal (1874–1929) is usually considered an exponent of neoromanticism, a movement which in Germany roughly parallels symbolism in France. His early plays are mostly short, as in *The Fool and Death* (1893) and *The Adventurer and the Singing Girl* (1899), and written in a verse that led many critics to praise him as the finest poet since Goethe. Around 1900 he underwent a crisis during which he came to believe that words are meaningless. Although he moved beyond this belief, he thereafter reworked existing materials, as in *Elektra* (1903), *Everyman* (1912), and *The Great World Theatre* (1922), and wrote opera librettos, such as *Der Rosenkavalier* (1911) and *Ariadne on Naxos* (1912), in collaboration with Richard Strauss. Some of his plays continue to be mainstays of the Salzburg Festival.

Benjamin Franklin Wedekind (1864–1918) is more nearly related to Strindberg than to the French symbolists. After working as a journalist, publicist, and actor, Wedekind toured Germany in a repertory of his own plays, which were never widely appreciated during his lifetime. Wedekind's first important play, *Spring's Awakening* (1891), is the story of adolescent struggle with sexual awareness. One

dies from a botched abortion, another commits suicide, and still another is saved from a similar fate only by the mysterious "Man with the Mask." The play is interesting in part because of its intermingling of naturalism and symbolism, of brutal frankness and lyrical expression. Wedekind's interest in sexual themes continued in *Earth Spirit* (1895) and *Pandora's Box* (1895), both treating the same protagonist, Lulu, the eternal temptress. In the first play, a series of admirers seek to impose their own vision on Lulu and die when they fail. In the second, Lulu descends into prostitution and ultimately is murdered by Jack the Ripper. In these plays, Wedekind suggests a relationship between commercialized art (seen as a form of prostitution which caters to the public's taste for disguised sexuality) and commercialized sex (prostitution). Many of Wedekind's later plays also reveal his preoccupation with sexual themes, but in such late works as *Samson* (1914) and *Herakles* (1917) the treatment sometimes borders on lunacy. Wedekind's plays are of such uneven quality that it is difficult to judge them fairly. But after 1900 his reputation grew steadily and he exerted considerable influence on the expressionists, who were attracted both by his rebellion against conventional values and by his experiments with stylistic elements.

After 1900 German producers also came to be increasingly interested in nonrealistic staging. Some of the most important innovations were made at the Munich Art Theatre, founded in 1907 and headed by George Fuchs (1868–1949), a critic and theorist, with Fritz Erler (1868–1940) as designer. In two

FIG. 18.9
Munich Art Theatre production of Shakespeare's *Twelfth Night,* 1908. Design by Julius Diez, directed by Albert Heine. Courtesy Theatermuseum, Munich.

FIG. 18.10

Reinhardt's production of Wedekind's *Spring's Awakening* at the Kammerspiele, Berlin, 1906. Act III, scene 6. Design by K. Walser. Courtesy the Max Reinhardt Archive, State University of New York, Binghamton.

books, *The Theatre of the Future* (1905) and *Revolution in the Theatre* (1909), Fuchs expressed the need for a theatre to meet the needs of modern humanity and declared pictorial illusionism outmoded. Under the slogan "retheatricalize the theatre," he sought to unite all the arts in a new kind of expression.

For the project, Max Littmann (1862–1931) designed a theatre with an auditorium and sunken orchestra pit similar to those at Bayreuth. The stage, however, differed markedly from that at Bayreuth. The acting area could be extended into the auditorium by covering over the orchestra pit, while an adjustable inner proscenium, containing a door at stage level and a balcony above, made it possible to adjust the size of the stage opening. The stage floor was broken into sections, each of which was mounted on an elevator, permitting the floor to be arranged into levels. The stage was backed by four cycloramas, each of a different color, which could be changed electrically. The most controversial aspect of the productions was the acting, which typically was confined

to the plane outlined by the inner proscenium, while the area back of this plane was reserved for scenery or for crowd scenes. The aim was to keep performers close to the audience so as to establish a sense of community and to emphasize the actors' plasticity by framing them against a simplified background. Erler sometimes used the adjustable proscenium as the principal scenic element; sometimes in combination with other pieces, but often employed merely as a frame for the area behind it. His effects were achieved primarily with simple forms, painted drops, and the play of colored light.

Like Appia and Craig, Fuchs believed that rhythm fuses all the elements of production. Unlike them, however, he placed the actor in front of the setting rather than within it and so tended to mute the three-dimensionality they so avidly sought. Still, as the work of the Munich Art Theatre became widely known, Fuchs's theories reinforced those of Appia and Craig and helped to establish the trend toward stylization in all theatrical elements.

Ultimately, virtually all of the ideas and innovations introduced between 1875 and 1900—whether realistic or nonrealistic—came together in the work of Max Reinhardt (1873–1943). On stage as an actor from the age of nineteen, Reinhardt was brought to the Deutsches Theater by Otto Brahm in 1894. While acting with Brahm's troupe, Reinhardt experimented with staging at a cabaret and developed a strong appreciation for its intimate atmosphere. His first experience as a producer was gained between 1902 and 1905 at the Kleines Theater, where he presented nearly fifty plays drawn from many countries and styles. His major work began in 1905, when he succeeded Brahm as director of the Deutsches Theater. In 1906 he opened the Kammerspiele, a small theatre, in conjunction with the larger house. The flexibility in programing and style of production which this arrangement permitted was to influence almost all state theatres in Germany and eventually America and elsewhere.

Reinhardt's major contribution was his recognition that no single approach is appropriate to the staging of all plays. Until the twentieth century, directors in each era staged all plays in much the same style. Despite widespread experimentation in the late nineteenth century, each director had adopted a distinctive approach and applied it to all plays. With Reinhardt, each new production became a problem to be solved, not through the employment of proven formulas but through clues found within the work itself. Unlike his predecessors, he could embrace antirealism without denying realism. He developed eclecticism into an artistic creed. His was to become the most common approach to directing in the twentieth century.

Reinhardt's conception of theatrical style included the physical arrangement of the theatre and the spatial relationship of the audience to the performers. In his view, some plays required intimate surroundings, others large spaces; similarly, some needed a proscenium, others an open platform. For example, he staged *Oedipus Rex* in a circus building, because, of all modern structures, the physical configuration of the circus seemed most like that of ancient Greek theatres. He was to extend such experiments with production and theatre architecture after World War I.

Reinhardt believed that the director must control every element of production. For each play he prepared a *Regiebuch* (or prompt book) in which he recorded each detail of movement, setting, properties, sound, lighting, and costume. Some critics charge that Reinhardt's actors were mere puppets that he manipulated, while others maintain that Reinhardt was so sensitive that he knew exactly how to help each performer. In any case, Reinhardt worked closely with his actors to achieve performances that became world-famous for their stylistic excellence. Among his actors, the best known were Alexander Moissi (1880–1935), noted especially for his Shakespearean and Greek roles; Max Pallenberg (1859–1934), a versatile comic actor; Albert Bassermann (1867–1952), famous for his performances in Ibsen's plays and later as an actor in U.S. films; Werner Krauss (1884–1959); and Emil Jannings (1887–1950).

Reinhardt also worked closely with his scene designers, notably Ernst Stern (1876–1954), Alfred Roller (1864–1935), Oscar Strnad (1879–1935), and Emil Orlik (1879–1932). Often his productions centered around a motif, a ruling idea, or the staging conventions of a past period; overall, they ranged through many styles. Reinhardt has been accused of debasing the ideas of others, but more so than anyone else he made new movements and techniques acceptable to the general public through his eclectic approach.

NONREALISTIC THEATRE IN ENGLAND

In England, few playwrights departed markedly from the realistic mode. Oscar Wilde (1854–1900), a member of the "Art-for-Art's Sake" or "Aesthetic" movement that paralleled French symbolism, rejected the idea that drama should be utilitarian or that the popular audience is a suitable judge of merit. He suggested that we should seek to turn life into a work of art rather than to make art imitate life. Nevertheless, of Wilde's plays only *Salomé* (1893) resembles French symbolist drama. His phenomenally popular comedy, *The Importance of Being Earnest* (1895), illustrates his best-known work through its parody of the stock devices of comedy and its epigrams that puncture the conventional sentiments of his time. Others of his plays, among them *Lady Winderemere's Fan* (1892), *A Woman of No Importance* (1893), and *An Ideal Husband* (1895), resemble Pinero's social dramas.

J. M. Barrie (1860–1937), after beginning as a journalist and novelist, turned to drama in 1892 and wrote regularly for the stage until 1936. Through all of his work shines an optimistic, whimsical view of life in which humor is infused with sentiment. His most popular play, *Peter Pan* (1904), is a sentimental fantasy which romanticizes childhood and the child's view of reality. Other popular works by Barrie include *The Admirable Crichton* (1902), *What Every Woman Knows* (1908), and *Dear Brutus* (1917).

Although few English plays departed from the realistic mode, several innovations in staging were to depart from illusionism. Many of these stemmed

FIG. 18.11

Reinhardt's production of Friedrich Freska's pantomime, *Sumurun,* at the Kammerspiele, Berlin, 1910. Design by Ernst Stern. Courtesy Harvard Theatre Collection.

from interest in staging Shakespeare's works. An early step toward more simplified staging was taken by Frank Benson (1858–1939), who, after acting with Irving, founded his own troupe in 1883 and continued to tour the provinces in a Shakespearean repertory until 1933. Benson produced almost all of the plays seen at the annual festival at Stratford-on-Avon (instituted in 1879) between 1886 and 1913, and after 1900 gave a few performances in London each year. Benson began by producing plays in the style of Irving, but by 1900 he had reduced the scenic background to a few stock settings and was placing primary emphasis upon the actors. Although his solution was at best a compromise, Benson helped to make simplified staging acceptable to the public, as well as providing a training ground for a whole generation of Shakespearean actors.

A more drastic reform was sought by William Poel (1852–1934). After his debut as an actor in 1876, Poel worked for Benson and others before undertaking those experiments with staging Shakespeare's plays for which he is now remembered. In this work, Poel had, between 1894 and 1905, the support of the Elizabethan Stage Society, of which he was the guiding spirit. In staging Elizabethan drama, Poel did not always use the same solution, but he is now consid-

ered noteworthy almost entirely because of his attempts to reconstruct the Elizabethan public stage. He also popularized several conventions: dressing the actors in Elizabethan garments to reflect Shakespeare's own day rather than the historical epoch of the dramatic action; using costumed pages to draw the curtains of an "inner stage" and to arrange properties and furniture; and employing an on-stage audience to emphasize the audience-actor relationships of the Elizabethan era. But, above all, Poel desired continuity of action, integrity of text, and lively pace. Although his productions were not always successful, they demonstrated the advantages of unbroken playing and of concentrating attention upon text and performers. Poel's approach represents another form of antiquarianism, one that sought to substitute the theatrical conditions of a past era for historical accuracy in performance.

Poel's work is representative of similar approaches then being tried in several countries. At the Royal Court Theatre in Munich in 1889, Karl von Perfall and Jocza Savits had attempted to approximate the Elizabethan plan on a picture-frame stage by using a deep apron behind which a playing space was

FIG. 18.12

Reinhardt's production of Sophocles' *Oedipus Rex* at Covent Garden, London, 1912. John Martin-Harvey as Oedipus. Courtesy the Max Reinhardt Archive, State University of New York, Binghamton.

FIG. 18.13
Barrie's *Peter Pan*. The original production at the Duke of York's Theatre, London, 1904. The pirate's ship. Courtesy Theatre Museum, Victoria and Albert Museum, London.

enclosed by an architectural facade with several doors and, at center back, a curtained inner stage where furniture and realistic scenic pieces could be set up and revealed as needed. This and a similar attempt made in Munich in 1909–1910 by Julius Klein and Eugene Kilian differed little from the solution used

FIG. 18.14
Poel's production of Shakespeare's *Measure for Measure* in 1893. Act II, scene 2. Note the Elizabethan public stage (complete with costumed spectators) erected on a picture-frame stage. Courtesy Theatre Museum, Victoria and Albert Museum, London.

in 1840 by Immermann. In a somewhat similar vein, Antoine staged a number of seventeenth-century French plays at the Odéon between 1907 and 1910 for which he sought to reproduce the playing conditions and conventions used in the original productions. In Russia, Nikolai Evreinov undertook similar "historically authentic" productions of plays of the Middle Ages and the Spanish Golden Age between 1907 and 1912.

Many of the earlier experiments in staging Shakespeare's plays were synthesized by Granville Barker in productions at the Savoy Theatre in London between 1912 and 1914. Barker, who had worked for Poel before going to the Royal Court Theatre, amalgamated Poel's continuous staging with the visual simplicity advocated by Craig and others. He remodeled the Savoy Theatre by adding an apron and doors forward of the proscenium. Back of the proscenium the stage was divided into a main acting area and a modified inner stage, raised a few steps and equipped with curtains. This division of the stage into three parts allowed a continuous flow of action and eliminated the extensive cutting and rearrangement of the scripts usual in illusionistic staging. Barker employed such artists as Norman Wilkinson (1882–1934) and Albert Rutherston (1884–1953) to design scenery and costumes. Settings were composed primarily of painted, draped curtains, while the costumes were of no certain period. Such colors as magenta, scarlet, and lemon replaced the somber tones usual in Shakespearean productions. The forest of *A Midsummer Night's Dream* (presented in 1914) contained no three-dimensional trees; rather, it was suggested by foliage painted on drapes that hung in folds. Similarly, Titania's bower was made of gauze suspended from a crown of flowers. The fairies were gilded and directed to move like marionettes in order to set them off from the mortals. Although many conservative critics were deeply offended by Barker's productions, his approach pointed the way toward the future.

THE IRISH RENAISSANCE

Around 1900 Ireland began to assert its artistic independence from England. Since the sixteenth century, England had ruled Ireland, although it had never been able to suppress Roman Catholicism or to command the full loyalty of the people. As elsewhere in Europe, in Ireland nationalistic sentiment became especially strong during the nineteenth century, and the increased interest among the Irish in their Gaelic and Celtic heritage inevitably found its way into the theatre.

FIG. 18.15

Harley Granville Barker's production of *A Midsummer Night's Dream* at the Savoy Theatre, London, 1914. The forest is represented by trees painted on draperies, and Titania's bower is formed of gauze hanging from a wreath. Courtesy Theatre Museum, Victoria and Albert Museum, London.

Although Dublin had been one of the major British theatrical centers since the seventeenth century, it saw no significant attempt to create an indigenous Irish drama until 1898, when the Irish Literary Society was established. Between 1899 and 1902, this group produced seven short plays and demonstrated the possibility of creating an Irish theatre. The leaders of the Society were William Butler Yeats (1865–1939), Lady Augusta Gregory (1863–1935), George Moore (1853–1933), and Edward Martyn (1859–1923).

Meantime, another organization, the Ormond Dramatic Society, headed by W. G. Fay (1872–1947) and Frank Fay (1870–1931), was also presenting plays with an Irish flavor, and soon the two united to form the Irish National Theatre Society. An appearance by this new group in London in 1903 won the support of Miss A. E. F. Horniman, who acquired a building for the company and remodelled it into the Abbey Theatre, which opened in 1904. Until 1910 Miss Horniman also provided the troupe with a subsidy. Originally the group gave only three performances a month, but after it obtained a permanent home it began to present a different play each week.

Not until 1908, however, was it able to pay royalties or actors' salaries. Nevertheless, its finest achievements came before 1910, after which many of its best authors and actors began to defect.

Of the Abbey's playwrights, three—Yeats, Lady Gregory, and Synge—were most important. Yeats wrote about thirty plays between 1892 and 1938. Much of his early work resembled that of the French symbolists, many of whom he had known in Paris. Of these early plays, the best known is probably *Cathleen ni Houlihan* (1902), in which the spirit of Ireland, incredibly old but forever lovely, is embodied in the figure of an old woman who is transformed into a young girl. Around 1910 Yeats ceased to write specifically for the Abbey and soon afterwards came under the influence of Japanese Noh drama. Thereafter he made increasing use of masks, dance, music, and chant. Among the late works, one of the best is *At the Hawk's Well* (1917), in which a chorus describes the action as two characters await the appearance of waters that will confer immortality. Yeats disliked realistic drama and sought to arouse a community of feeling and ideals among spectators through poetic plays based on Celtic myth or legend.

From the first there were two conflicting styles at the Abbey: the poetic-mythic (best represented by Yeats) and the realistic-domestic (best represented by Lady Gregory). Most of Lady Gregory's dramatic writing was done between 1902 and 1912, although she did not cease altogether until 1926. She was most at home in one-act peasant comedies, such as *The Spreading of the News* (1904), which shows how the account of an event is distorted as it passes from one person to another. But she also virtually invented the Irish folk-history play based primarily on oral tradition, as in *Kincora* (1905), which centers around a legendary Irish king. Only rarely did she venture into the fully serious realm, as in *The Gaol Gate* (1906). Though she does not rank in critical stature with Yeats, she was far more successful than he with audiences, perhaps because she wrote about familiar subjects and in a familiar style.

It remained for John Millington Synge (1871–1909) to fuse the two styles represented by Yeats and Lady Gregory, for he made the mythic seem familiar and the familiar mythic; he also created his own distinctive language, a lilting, poetic prose. Synge was also the most controversial of the Abbey's writers. *In the Shadow of the Glen* (1903) was denounced as a slander on Irish womanhood because it showed a wife happily leaving home to go away with a tramp after her husband has ordered her from the house. Here as in others of his plays Synge is concerned with the conflict between a repressive life and

FIG. 18.16
William Bulter Yeat's *The Hour Glass*. Design by Gordon Craig. From Yeats, *Plays for an Irish Theatre* (1911).

the urge toward joy and freedom. *The Playboy of the Western World* (1907) aroused even greater wrath, for its story, in which a young man becomes a village hero after boasting of killing his father, was considered an insult to the national character. Wherever it played, riots occurred. Not all of Synge's plays were controversial. Many critics consider *Riders to the Sea* (1904) to be the finest short play in the English language. In it, Maurya loses the last of her six sons to the sea, but achieves a new peace, since fate can do no more to her. Although Synge is now considered the finest Irish dramatist of his day, at the time his plays did much to create dissension in the company and motivated many actors and playwrights to desert the Abbey. Consequently, although in the 1920s the Abbey was to recapture some of its former glory with the plays of Sean O'Casey, its major contribution had been made by 1915.

ITALY AND THE FUTURISTS

Many major Italian artists during the interwar years were adherents of futurism, a movement launched in Italy in 1909 by Filippo Tommaso Marinetti (1876–1944). Like the expressionists, the futurists rejected the past and wished to transform humanity. But, whereas the expressionists associated the past with soul-destroying materialism and industrialism,

the futurists deplored the veneration of the past as a barrier to progress. Consequently, they glorified the energy and speed of the machine age and sought to embody them in artistic forms. From 1910 onward they gave performances during which they read their manifestoes, gave concerts, read poems, performed plays, and exhibited works of visual art—at times several of these simultaneously. Sometimes they moved about among the spectators, using various parts of a room sequentially or concurrently. They especially outraged audiences with their demand that libraries and museums be destroyed as the first step toward creating a more dynamic future.

Among the art forms championed by the futurists were "picture poems" (or concrete poetry), kinetic sculptures, collages, and *bruitisme* (or "dynamic music," based on the sounds of everyday life). As for theatre, they denounced past practices and declared music halls, nightclubs, and circuses to be better models on which to base future forms. They found earlier drama too lengthy, analytic, and static and proposed instead a "synthetic drama" which would compress into a moment or two the essence of a dramatic situation. In 1915–1916 they published seventy-six of these short plays. Later futurists experimented with the stage as a multidimensional space in which spiritual forces (represented by light and abstract forms) would play out a drama of semireligious significance in which human actors were replaced by luminous forms.

Though futurism never became a major theatrical movement, it pioneered innovations that would be revived and extended in the 1960s, including:

1. Direct confrontation and intermingling of performers and audiences,
2. The exploitation of modern technology to create multimedia performances,
3. The use of simultaneity and multiple focus,
4. An anti-literary and alogical bias, and
5. The breaking down of barriers between arts.

During World War I futurism lost many followers because it glorified war as the supreme example of energy.

RUSSIAN MODERNISM

In Russia, the antirealistic impulse at first centered around *The World of Art,* a periodical begun in 1898 by Sergei Diaghilev (1872–1929). In addition to keeping Russians abreast of events in the artistic centers of Europe, the magazine sought to encourage Russian artists and composers. Diaghilev's major contribution, however, was to involve ballet. After Petipa retired, Prince Sergei Volkonsky, Director of the Imperial Theatres, and Mikhail Fokine (1880–1942), choreographer at the Mariinsky Theatre, introduced several innovations. Fokine disliked the long narrative works that Petipa had favored, and sought more limited subjects that offered greater opportunity for novel choreographic design. Using music by such composers as Igor Stravinsky, he emphasized complex rhythms and an overall harmony of mood.

Meanwhile, Diaghilev had been arranging exchanges of art with other countries, and in 1909 he took a ballet company to Paris for a six-week season. The ecstatic response led Diaghilev to form his Ballets Russes, which then toured throughout Europe. Everywhere it was praised both for its dancing and for its scenic design. When the Revolution came, the company elected to remain in the West.

The scenic style of the Ballets Russes did not depend upon any new technical devices, for it relied on painted wings and drops. Nevertheless, it departed markedly from illusionism, since line, color, and decorative motifs were considerably stylized to reflect moods and themes rather than specific periods or places. Costumes also emphasized exaggerated line, color, and mass. Thus, although the artists drew on familiar forms and decorative motifs, they created a sense of exoticism and fantasy through stylization. The influence upon European scenic art of the Ballets Russes' designers—among them Leon Bakst, Alexandre Benois, Alexander Golovin, Mstislav

FIG. 18.17
Leon Bakst's design for the Ballet Russes' *Tamar,* 1912. From the souvenir program.

Dobuzhinsky, and Natalie Gontcharova—was incalculable. Bakst and Benois later settled in Paris and continued to work there.

During the 1890s the symbolist ideal began to be championed in Russia and after 1900 became a major literary movement. Stanislavsky, after presenting a bill of Maeterlinck's short plays in 1904–1905, decided that his company needed to supplement its realistic approach, and in 1905 he established a studio to experiment with nonrealistic styles. To supervise the work, Stanislavsky employed Vsevelod Meyerhold (1874–1940), a founding member of the Moscow Art Theatre who had left in 1902 to form his own troupe. A number of productions were planned for the new studio, but Meyerhold's subordination of the actors to his directorial concepts displeased Stanislavsky so much that he discontinued the experiment.

Nevertheless, the Moscow Art Theatre went on to produce other nonrealistic works, including Maeterlinck's *The Blue Bird* in 1908 and *Hamlet* in 1912, the latter with scenery by Gordon Craig. It also encouraged Leonid Andreyev (1871–1919), Russia's foremost symbolist dramatist. After beginning in the realistic mode, Andreyev was converted to symbolism in 1907, the year in which he wrote his most famous play, *The Life of Man,* an allegory which dramatizes the major stages in human existence. Stanislavsky staged it against black curtains, on which windows, doors, and walls were outlined in white rope. Although the production was popular, Stanislavsky withdrew it because he felt the acting was too abstract. In 1911 the Moscow Art Theatre established the First Studio, under the direction of

Leopold Sullerzhitsky (1872–1916), primarily to give training in the Stanislavsky system but also to encourage nonrealistic approaches. Here a number of future leaders, notably Richard Boleslavsky, Mikhail Chekhov, and Yevgeny Vakhtangov, received their training. But, if Stanislavsky experimented with nonrealistic approaches, any marked departure from realism was ultimately unacceptable to him since all tended to "dematerialize" the actor.

The most important early experiments with nonrealistic staging in Russia were undertaken in the company maintained by Vera Kommissarzhevskaya (1864–1910). On the stage from 1891, she attracted an enormous following and opened her own theatre in St. Petersburg in 1904. Interested in new approaches, she employed Meyerhold when he left Stanislavsky. For his production of Ibsen's *Hedda Gabler* for her theatre, Meyerhold ignored Ibsen's stage directions and realistic detail. Each character wore a distinctively colored costume devoid of realistic detail. Furthermore, each character was restricted to a limited number of sculpturesque gestures and always returned to the same pose. The setting and furniture were greenish-blue and white; Hedda, seated on a white, fur-covered throne at center stage, dominated the action. For Wedekind's *Spring's Awakening,* Meyerhold placed everything to be used in the production on stage at once and spotlighted each area as needed. His favorite work, which he would direct several times, was Alexander Blok's (1880–1921) *The Fairground Booth* (1906), a combination of *commedia dell'arte* and the grotesque, which dispensed with the proscenium arch and exposed all the mechanisms of the theatre.

When audiences did not respond favorably to these and other experiments, perhaps because Kommissarzhevskaya's considerable talents were not adequately exploited, Meyerhold was asked to leave. Immediately afterward he was employed as a director in the Imperial theatres where he continued his experiments. When he staged Molière's *Don Juan* at the Alexandrinsky Theatre in 1910, he removed the front curtain and footlights, extended the forestage into the auditorium, kept the house lights on throughout the performance, used visible stagehands to change properties and scenery, and set the actors' movements to Lully's music. After the enormous success of this production, he went on to stage several operas, among them Wagner's *Tristan and Isolde.*

Between 1910 and 1914 Meyerhold also established studios where he experimented with circus and *commedia dell'arte* techniques. In one studio the entire auditorium was treated as a performance space which intermingled actors and spectators. Actors evolved their own scripts and experimented with geo-metrically patterned movement, improvisation, and rhythm. Meyerhold also began to turn the scenic background into a mere apparatus for acting—a collection of steps and levels. Meyerhold was the first important director to believe that the director is the major creative force in the theatre and that a script is simply material to be molded and reworked as the director wishes. His was the most persistent exploration of the possibilities and limitations of the theatre as a medium of expression to be found anywhere at that time. He would continue his experiments after the Revolution.

At Kommissarzhevskaya's theatre, Meyerhold was succeeded by Nikolai Evreinov (1879–1953). Although equally opposed to realism, Evreinov sought to enlarge the actor's place in the theatre by emphasizing theatricality and the grotesque. Evreinov is probably most famous for his "monodramas," the basic principle of which was first set forth in his "Apology for Theatricality" in 1908. He suggested that an inborn theatrical instinct leads humans into "role playing" and makes them seek to transform reality into something better. Consequently, he argued, the theatre should not imitate life, but life should seek to become like theatre at its best. In his "monodramas," he aimed to help the audience achieve its desires by making it the alter-ego of the protagonist. Through identification, the audience was led to participate in the theatrical experience through which it came to perceive an existence more satisfying than that of ordinary life. The most famous of the monodramas was *The Theatre of the Soul* (1912). Evreinov was also a director and, considering illusionism mistaken, he sought to provide alternatives, some of which he demonstrated in seasons of works from the past, one devoted to works from the Middle Ages and another to plays of the Spanish Golden Age. Additionally, he conducted experiments with *commedia dell'arte,* and ran two of the most noted cabaret theatres of the time.

Theodore Kommissarzhevsky (1874–1954) worked with his sister, Evreinov, and others before opening his own theatre in 1910. Probably the most balanced Russian producer of his day, he adopted an eclectic approach out of his desire to remain faithful to each playwright's intention. His eclecticism extended farther than Reinhardt's, however, for he adopted what might be called "internal eclecticism," in which, rather than choosing a historical period or single style for a play and then staying consistently within it, he sought for each character and action a meaningful visual metaphor that would evoke the appropriate associations within the mind of the spectator. Thus, his productions often combined elements from many periods and styles (thereby anticipating postmodernist

FIG. 18.18

Tairov's production of Wilde's *Salomé* at the Kamerny Theatre, 1917. Costumes and settings by Alexandra Ekster. Each costume combined materials of varying color and texture to create the effect of figures from stained glass windows.

techniques). Kommissarzhevsky was associated with numerous theatres between 1910 and 1919 (when he emigrated to the West); at one time he was head of four theatres and a training school. He later was to continue his work in France, England, and America.

Alexander Tairov (1885–1950) worked for a number of producers before opening his own theatre, the Kamerny (or Chamber) Theatre in Moscow in 1914. Tairov argued that there is no relationship between art and life and that the theatre must be viewed as analogous to the sacred dances of an ancient temple. Like Meyerhold, he viewed the text as an excuse for creativity, although he objected to Meyerhold's suppression of the actor, who, according to Tairov, is the basic creative force in the theatre. Because he was concerned with rhythmical movement, Tairov's settings were essentially architectural, being composed primarily of sculptural elements, steps, and levels. Productions were approached as if they were musical compositions; speech was a compromise between declamation and song, and movement always tended toward dance. The effect was nearer to ritual than to the usual dramatic performance. By the time of the Revolution, Tairov had staged fourteen plays drawn from a wide variety of countries and dramatic types. Most productions featured his wife, Alice Koonen (1899–1974), his ideal interpreter. Tairov was to continue his work after the Revolution.

By 1917, Russian directors had experimented with techniques far removed from those employed by Stanislavsky in 1898. Some methods were as determinedly nonrealistic as any ever devised. One of the least advanced countries of Europe at the end of the nineteenth century, Russia had by the Revolution witnessed some of the most daring theatrical experiments of the time, although, with the exceptions of the Ballets Russes and the Moscow Art Theatre, the work had made little impact outside its borders.

LOOKING AT THEATRE HISTORY

One of the most persistent features of the period between 1875 and 1915 was the attempt to redefine the "art of the theatre." In this effort, the leaders were Appia and Craig. Here are some excerpts from one of Appia's essays. After pointing out the weaknesses of the nineteenth-century theatre (which he blames on the disparity between the static, two-dimensional painted scenery, the flat stage floor, and the three-dimensional, moving actor), he goes on to ask:

What would happen if we begin with . . . the plastic, moving human body? . . . An object is three-dimensional to our eyes only because of the light that strikes it . . . [Furthermore] human movement . . . requires obstacles if it is to be fully expressive. Therefore, *the actor's mobility cannot be used to artistic advantage except when it is integrally related to objects and the floor. Thus the two basic conditions required for the artistic use of the human body on the stage are: light that reveals its plasticity, and its harmonization with the setting so as to enhance its attitudes and movements . . .*

The effects of lighting are limitless . . . [When it is used properly] the actor no longer walks about in front of painted light and shade; he is enfolded in an atmosphere destined for him . . . Scenic illusion may be defined as the living presence of the actor . . . [If we are to create the appropriate scenic illusion] we must greatly simplify [the setting] . . . completely rearrange the stage floor, and above all make adequate provisions for lighting . . .

"Comment Reformer Notre Mise en Scène," *La Revue*, 50 (June 1, 1904), 342–349.

Craig saw theatre as an autonomous art created by a master artist, rather than as an assemblage of other arts put together by craftsmen:

The Art of the Theatre is neither acting nor the play, it is not scene nor dance, but it consists of all the elements of which these things are composed: action, which is the very spirit of acting; words, which are the body of the play; line and colour, which are the very heart of the scene; rhythm, which is the very essence of dance . . .

When [the director] interprets the plays of the dramatist by means of his actors, his scene-painters, and his other craftsmen, then he is a craftsman—a master craftsman; when he will have mastered the uses of actions, words, line, colour, and rhythm, then he may become an artist. Then we shall no longer need the assistance of the playwright—for our art will then be self-reliant.

On the Art of the Theatre (Chicago: Browne's Bookstore, 1911), 138, 148.

When Granville Barker attempted to do away with illusionistic scenery in his Shakespearean productions, he met considerable derision. Here are portions of a review of *A Midsummer Night's Dream* written in 1915 (for an illustration of one setting, see Fig. 18.15):

Let it be said that it represented the last cry in the new stage decoration. . . . The . . . changes of scene were indicated by curtains that waved, to the loss of all illusion. . . . No human being . . . can be expected to be anything but worried and annoyed by pink silk curtains that are supposed to be the roofs of houses, or green silk curtains that are supposed to be forest trees . . . I hope this is not indicative of what will happen when stage setting ceases to be scenery and becomes only decoration.

Review by G. C. D. Odell, reprinted in his *Shakespeare from Betterton to Irving*, 2 (New York, 1920), 467–468.

Probably the most extreme departure from the realistic mode, and a clear example of "modernism," was seen at Paris' Théâtre de l'Oeuvre, where more startling than the abandonment of illusionistic scenery was the highly stylized acting:

The most simple and sensible things take on a different appearance in passing through the mouths and gestures of the l'Oeuvre's actors under the direction of Lugné-Poë. They have a continual ecstatic air of perpetually being visionaries. As if hallucinatory, they stare before them, far, very far, vaguely, very vaguely. Their voices are cavernous, their diction choppy. They seem to be attempting to give the air that they are fools.

Moniteur Universel, 5 March 1894.

Sets of binary relationships are often used to help distinguish key aspects of premodernist and modernist approaches: rules/freedom; nature/artificiality; tradition/novelty; convention/innovation. Modernist approaches rapidly gained adherents and came to dominate much of twentieth-century art. Eventually it would be challenged, if not replaced, by "postmoderinism."

19

Twentieth Century Theatre Between the Wars

World War I (1914–1918) utilized not only the largest armies ever assembled up to that time, but new and improved instruments of destruction—tanks and other mechanized vehicles, airplanes and bombs, submarines and torpedoes. Before it ended in 1918, some 8,300,000 people had died and more than $337 billion were spent. To many, the war seemed an exercise in madness.

Nevertheless, some saw reasons for optimism as republics replaced monarchies, as small ethnic groups were allowed to form their own nations, and as a League of Nations and a World Court were established to arbitrate national disputes. But optimism soon declined because of the great economic problems created by human and material destruction and because of the vindictive treatment of the losing nations. As the scope of the influenza epidemic (1918–1919), which killed between 25 and 37 million people worldwide, became fully realized, life seemed even more uncertain. Rampant inflation in the 1920s was followed by severe economic depression in the 1930s. In several countries conditions became so chaotic that dictators were able to gain complete control: Mussolini of Italy in 1922, Stalin of the USSR around 1928, Vargas of Brazil in 1930, Hitler of Germany in 1933, and Franco of Spain in 1939. During the 1930s,

conflicts—over ideology, territorial claims, trade, and imperialistic designs—increased steadily. When the League of Nations proved ineffective, the great powers set about rearming. In 1939 the tensions erupted into World War II (1939–1945), which was to be even more destructive than the first.

World War I seems to have had a catalytic effect, however, in many realms, perhaps most notably those involving moral standards, codes of dress and behavior, women's and worker's rights, and artistic experimentation.

ENGLISH THEATRE AND DRAMA, 1914–1939

World War I brought many changes to the English theatre. The actor-manager system all but disappeared, to be replaced by the commercial producer and the long run. Tree's theatre, for example, the home of Shakespeare since 1900, was by 1916 given over to *Chu Chin Chow,* a musical version of *Ali Baba and the Forty Thieves,* which ran for 2238 performances. After World War I, the United States began to establish itself as an international power. It also began to produce playwrights and other theatre personnel who won widespread respect in Europe for the first time. The theatres of Canada, Australia, and New Zealand, on the other hand, continued the search for their own identities.

Probably the most significant occurrence of the war years was the emergence of the "Old Vic" as the principal producer of English classics. Built in 1818 as the Royal Coburg and later renamed the Royal Victoria, the Old Vic was taken over in 1880 by Emma Cons, a social reformer who converted it into a "temperance music hall." Miss Cons' niece, Lilian Baylis (1874–1937) came to assist her aunt in 1897, taking over the theatre when Cons died in 1912. Under Ms. Baylis's management the Old Vic ran both an opera company and an acting company and her theatre became the new home for Shakespeare. In 1931 she acquired the Sadler's Wells Theatre, and formed a ballet company under the direction of Ninette de Valois (Edris Stannis, 1898–2001), who had been trained in the Diaghilev company and later established her own school. Between 1931 and 1935, the opera, ballet, and dramatic companies alternated between the Old Vic, in a poor suburb of southwest London, and Sadler's Wells, in a poor suburb of northeast London. When this arrangement became too cumbersome, drama was confined to the Old Vic, and opera and ballet to Sadler's Wells. The Sadler's Wells Ballet Company became the finest in England and was rechristened the Royal Ballet after World War II, and its opera troupe developed into the present-day English National Opera.

When Baylis died in 1937, Tyrone Guthrie (1900–1971) was appointed administrator and operated it with distinction until 1945. Guthrie had made his debut as an actor in 1924, but soon turned to directing. His first London production came in 1931, but his finest prewar work was done with the Old Vic. As a director, Guthrie was noted for his novel interpretations of standard works (sometimes considered merely bizarre by critics), and for the restless but vital quality of stage movement in his productions. By 1939 the Old Vic was the most respected troupe in England. With its own theatre, a permanent company, and a policy of producing the finest plays at reasonable prices, it set a standard for the entire country.

Other notable theatres of the period included The Lyric Theatre, Hammersmith, which was leased by Nigel Playfair (1874–1934) in 1918. Although Playfair presented many kinds of plays, his reputation rests upon his productions of Restoration and eighteenth-century works, most notably *The Beggar's Opera* (which opened in 1920 for a run of 1,463 performances), *The Way of the World* (1924), *The Rivals* (1925), *The Beaux' Stratagem* (1927), and *Love in a*

Village (1928). Most of his productions were decorative, stylized caricatures, but in the late 1920s, the Lyric was the most fashionable theatre in London. The Gate Theatre was opened in 1925 by Peter Godfrey (1899–1971), a former circus clown and Shakespearean actor. Unable to secure a license for the only hall he could afford, Godfrey ran his theatre as a private club. In nine years, he produced over 350 plays. His most characteristic productions were of expressionist plays or those with a psychoanalytic bias. Using set pieces against black drapes, unusual lighting effects, and stylized acting techniques, Godfrey was the principal exponent of expressionism in London.

Of the several important groups outside of London, perhaps the best was the Birmingham Repertory Company, which, under Barry Jackson's (1879–1961) direction between 1913 and 1935, produced about 400 plays ranging through the entire history of drama. Jackson also presented 42 plays in London, many remarkably successful despite their departure from commercial formulas. Through his productions of *Hamlet* (1925), *Macbeth* (1928), and *Taming of the Shrew* (1928), Jackson began the vogue for playing Shakespeare in modern dress. When Jackson transferred ownership of his theatre to the City of Birmingham in 1935, it became England's first civic theatre. Jackson also founded the Malvern Festival in 1929, thereby giving considerable impetus to the summer festival movement.

FIG. 19.1
The Norwich Players in *As You Like It* (1921), the inaugural production at The Maddermarket Theatre, Norwich, England. Walter Nugent Monck director.

FIG. 19.2

The Old Vic's production of *The Tempest,* 1934. At rear, Charles Laughton as Prospero; front left, Elsa Lanchester as Ariel. Courtesy Debenham Collection, British Theatre Museum, London.

The Cambridge Festival Theatre was established by Terence Gray in 1926 with the avowed purpose of undermining realistic acting and production, a policy that was followed consistently. Gray took a standard box, pit, and gallery theatre, removed the proscenium arch, and let the stage carry out into the auditorium. Scenery normally consisted of ramps or other constructions set against a cyclorama, upon which patterns of light were projected. The actors' movement was often described as "choreographic" and was always highly stylized. Gray thought the text an excuse for a director's improvisations. He performed *Romeo and Juliet* in flamenco costumes; put some characters in *Twelfth Night* on roller skates; and had the Judge in *Merchant of Venice* play with a yo-yo. Gray's productions generated much controversy but had little immediate influence. The theatre closed in 1933.

The Oxford Repertory Company, headed by J. B. Fagan (1873–1933) from 1923 to 1929, presented twenty-one plays a year drawn from many countries and periods. The schedule meant that productions were often rough, but all had vitality and clear interpretations. Little scenery was used, for the theatre had only a small stage fronted by a large apron, upon which most of the action transpired. The importance of this company rests in part on the many young actors, most notably Tyrone Guthrie, John Gielgud, Raymond Massey, Flora Robson, and Glen Byam Shaw, who received their first major experience under Fagan.

FIG. 19.3

Gate Theatre production of Kaiser's *From Morn to Midnight,* 1928. Directed by Peter Godfrey. Courtesy Enthoven Collection, Victoria and Albert Museum, London.

The Shakespeare Memorial Theatre at Stratford-upon-Avon gained in prestige after they resumed in 1919 under the direction of W. Bridges-Adams (1889–1965). After the old theatre burned in 1926, the company played in a motion picture house until a new building was completed in 1932. Although

FIG. 19.4

Cambridge Festival Theatre production of *Henry VIII,* 1931. Directed by Terence Gray. Note the abstract setting and the playing-card costumes.

the new auditorium was largely satisfactory, the stage was a conventional picture-frame structure; its sliding platform stages could not move entirely out of sight and the elevator stages only sank 8 feet. Such blunders required several remodelings. Bridges-Adams resigned in 1934 and was succeeded by B. Iden Payne (1881–1976), whose most characteristic productions were in the style of Poel—using a reconstructed Shakespeare stage and Elizabethan costumes. London critics largely ignored the Stratford company, which did not achieve high critical stature until after World War II.

The Norwich Players (founded 1910) were perhaps the most influential of the many amateur experimental groups that developed during these years (known as "little theatres" in the United States). They were led by Walter Nugent Monck (1878–1958), a professional director who had trained with William Poel and had worked for W. B. Yeats at the Abbey Theatre in Dublin, from 1911 through 1913. In 1921 Monck built the Maddermarket Theatre in Norwich, the first theatre to be modeled on an Elizabethan indoor playhouse. By 1929, when the Norwich Players presented *Everyman* at the first Canterbury Festival, they were internationally famous. Hugh Hunt (1911–1993) directed the Norwich Players for the 1933 and 1934 seasons before going to the Abbey Theatre in 1935, the Bristol Old Vic in 1946, and Old Vic in 1949. (In 1955 Hunt became the first director of the Elizabethan Theatre Trust in Sydney, Australia.) By the start of World War II, however, the period of greatest influence for such amateur groups was over.

During this period there were many performers of high merit. Of the actresses, the best were probably Sybil Thorndike (1882–1976) and Edith Evans (1888–1976). Thorndike began her career in Ben Greet's company and after 1914 acted often with the Old Vic troupe. She was especially noted in the 1920s for her portrayal of Shaw's *Saint Joan*, although her performances ranged from Greek tragedy to modern comedy. Evans began her career with Poel and gained fame as Millamant in the Lyric Theatre's production of *The Way of the World*. She also appeared frequently with the Old Vic, at the Malvern Festival, and in many London commercial theatres. Other outstanding actresses included Lilian Braithwaite (1873–1948), Marie Tempest (1864–1942), Flora Robson (1902–1984), Gertrude Lawrence (1898–1952), and Peggy Ashcroft (1907–1991).

Of the actors, the most important was John Gielgud (1904–2000), who made his debut in 1921 and won major acclaim with Hamlet in 1934. He soon became one of England's major directors as well. In 1937–1938 he leased the Queen's Theatre, assembled

FIG. 19.5
Laurence Olivier as Romeo, Edith Evans as the Nurse, and John Gielgud as Mercutio in Gielgud's production of *Romeo and Juliet,* 1935. From *Theatre Arts* (1936).

a company that included Peggy Ashcroft, Michael Redgrave, and Alec Guinness, and produced a repertory of classics. By the time the war began, Gielgud was accepted as England's finest actor and director. Other outstanding performers included Cedric Hardwicke (1893–1964), who worked closely with Barry Jackson after 1922, Donald Wolfit (1902–1968), who played at the Old Vic, Stratford, and with his own touring company, and Maurice Evans (1901–1986), who played for Terence Gray and the Old Vic before emigrating to the United States in 1935. A number of young men, who would be of greater importance after the war, also established their promise in this period including: Laurence Olivier (1907–1989), who played with the Birmingham Repertory Company, Gielgud, and the Old Vic; Michael Redgrave (1908–1985), on the stage after 1934; Ralph Richardson (1902–1983); Alec Guinness (1914–2000), who made his debut in 1934; Anthony Quayle (1913–1989), on the stage after 1931; and Glen Byam Shaw (1904–1986), who played with the Oxford Repertory Company and Gielgud.

Few major dramatists emerged between the wars, although a number of older ones, such as Shaw, Barrie, Galsworthy, and Pinero, continued to write. During the 1920s three authors—Maugham, Lonsdale, and Coward—excelled in sophisticated comedy. Somerset Maugham (1874–1965) wrote his first play in 1904 and until 1933 was one of England's most prolific playwrights. His major achievement came with his comedies of manners, *Our Betters* (1917), *The Circle* (1921), *The Constant Wife* (1927), and *The Breadwinner* (1930), in which sardonic humor and unusual personal outlooks avoided trite happy endings. Often compared with Maugham, Frederick Lonsdale (1881–1954) drew a wide following with his amusing situations and effective dialogue in *The Last of Mrs. Cheyney* (1925), *On Approval* (1927), and *The High Road* (1929). Noel Coward (1899–1973) captured the spirit of the postwar era with such works as *Fallen Angels* (1925), *Hay Fever* (1925), *Bittersweet* (1929), *Private Lives* (1930), and *Design for Living* (1932), in which unconventional behavior was combined with sophisticated wit.

Of the serious writers, J. B. Priestley (1894–1984) gained the greatest prestige. He began his dramatic career in 1932 with *Dangerous Corner* and went on to *Time and the Conways* (1937) and *An Inspector Calls* (1946). Although he wrote many kinds of plays, Priestley is most noted for his compression or distortion of time to illuminate characters and ideas. Of the sentimental and melodramatic school, Emlyn Williams (1905–1987) was perhaps the most successful. After writing two sensational plays, *A Murder Has Been Arranged* (1930) and *Night Must Fall* (1935), he presented *The Corn Is Green* (1938), a sentimental story about a Welsh teacher and her star pupil.

This period also brought several attempts to revive poetic drama. Gordon Bottomley (1874–1948) wrote *King Lear's Wife* (1915), *Britain's Daughters* (1922), and *Laodice and Danae* (1930), and W. H. Auden (1907–1973) and Christopher Isherwood (1904–1986) collaborated on *The Dog Beneath the Skin* (1935) and *The Ascent of F6* (1936). The most lasting achievement, however, was that of T. S. Eliot (1888–1965) with *Murder in the Cathedral* (1935), the story of Thomas à Becket's martyrdom. Eliot went on to write *The Family Reunion* (1939) and, after the war, several other verse plays. In general, however, the attempt to revive poetic drama was ineffective, primarily because of shortcomings in the plays rather than because of opposition to poetry.

England's deep involvement in World War I offered Ireland the chance to throw off British rule. In 1916 it began a rebellion which was put down after much bloodshed. But the demand for independence grew, and in 1919 Ireland declared itself a republic. Three years of armed conflict ensued before a treaty was signed in 1923 which granted independence to all but six northern counties.

This struggle provides the context for the early plays of Sean O'Casey (1884–1964), Ireland's most important postwar playwright. O'Casey turned attention away from folk and legendary subject matter to the urban life of his time. The plays that established his fame—*The Shadow of a Gunman* (1923), *Juno and the Paycock* (1924), and *The Plough and the Stars* (1926)—were realistic in tone and dealt with the effects of the rebellion on the lives of ordinary people. After this time O'Casey adopted expressionistic techniques in such works as *The Silver Tassie* (1928), *Within the Gates* (1934), *Red Roses for Me* (1943), and *Purple Dust* (1945). His change of style precipitated a break with the Abbey Theatre in 1928, after which O'Casey lived in England. Many of O'Casey's works have been more widely read than produced, largely because, in spite of many powerful scenes, the dramatic action is sometimes obscure. Nevertheless, his characterizations, vivid use of language, and human compassion make him one of the finest writers of modern times.

THEATRE AND DRAMA IN THE UNITED STATES, 1917–1941

The United States was finally drawn into World War I in 1917. Not only was it decisive in the outcome of the war, it was a leader in founding the League of Nations and in establishing independent states for the ethnic and language groups of Europe. Following the war, however, the United States entered another period of isolationism, during which it sought to divorce itself from foreign affairs and imposed tariffs to reduce imports. The economic results were disastrous for farmers and workers and ultimately were instrumental in bringing on the Great Depression of the 1930s. It was during the interwar years that women won the right to vote and that mass production and new developments in transportation and communication revolutionized American life.

During the 1930s the energies of the nation were devoted to overcoming economic problems. For the first time, the government assumed a key role in social planning and began such programs as social security and public works. By 1940, U.S. life was vastly different from what it had been in 1917. The United States had become one of the world's great powers and an industrial giant. It had also won a measure of respect in artistic and cultural affairs for the first time.

Around 1912 several "little theatres" were established in the United States emulating the independent theatres of Europe. Among the most important of these were the Toy Theatre, Boston (1912), the Chicago Little Theatre (1912), the Provincetown Players (Massachusetts, 1915), the Neighborhood

Playhouse (1915), the Washington Square Players in New York (1915), and the Detroit Arts and Crafts Theatre (1916). By 1917 there were at least 50 of these groups. Generally these theatres had full-time directors but used amateur actors, designers, and staff. This was both an economic and an esthetic choice. Because these theatres were building new audiences they could not afford professional actors. But many also believed that professionals were too dependent on the melodramatic tricks they learned in the commercial theatre to stage a more challenging repertory effectively, and they argued that amateurs were more open to new approaches. Little theatres produced a series of plays for a subscription audience each year, using techniques already widely accepted in Europe. The little theatre movement made its greatest contributions between 1912 and 1920 by preparing audiences to accept new drama and production methods.

After 1920, the little theatres began to be indistinguishable from community theatres. Originating like its European counterpart in attempts to revive the spirit of ancient Greece, the community drama movement had begun in the United States around 1905. Its most ardent supporter was Percy MacKaye (1875–1956), whose *The Civic Theatre* (1912) and *Community Drama* (1917) outlined a program and whose outdoor pageants provided texts designed to involve several thousand participants. Interest in mass spectacles soon declined, however, and after 1920 most local groups turned to the performance of recent Broadway hits. By 1925, nearly 2000 community or little theatre companies were registered with the Drama League of America, an organization which encouraged local interest in drama.

The primary competition for these community theatres came from the traveling tent theatres. From the first traveling tent theatre introduced by Fayette Lodawick "Yankee" Robinson (1818–1884) in 1857 at Rock Island, Illinois, the movement reached its peak in the 1920s when over 400 companies were on tour to over 16,000 cities, generating more productions and greater attendance than all the legitimate theatres in the country combined. While the repertory of these companies was little different from that of the community theatres, they employed large numbers of professional theatre artists and contributed greatly to building audiences. Few of these companies survived the combination of the Depression followed by World War II, after which fixed summer stock companies, which had existed in small numbers since the founding of Elitch's Garden Theatre of Denver in 1890, became dominant.

Drama programs also began to be introduced into colleges and universities during the interwar years.

Although plays had been produced by students since the seventeenth century, no courses in theatre were offered until about 1900. The first important change came in 1903 when George Pierce Baker (1866–1935) began to teach playwriting at Radcliffe College. Later opened to Harvard University students, the course was enlarged in 1913 to include a workshop for the production of plays. Baker attracted many of America's most talented young people, including Eugene O'Neill, S. N. Behrman, Hallie Flanagan, and Robert Edmond Jones, instilled in them high standards, and helped them to acquire skills. In 1925 Baker moved to Yale University where he established a drama school which provided professional training for many later theatre workers across America and Mexico. There he hired Stanley McCandless (1897–1967) to teach the first courses in stage lighting design. McCandless' book *A Method for Lighting the Stage* (1932) was the most influential work in the field until the advent of computerized lighting controls. Thomas Wood Stevens (1880–1942) instituted the country's first degree-granting program in theatre, at the Carnegie Institute of Technology, in 1914, where many of the outstanding leaders of university theatres across the country were trained. In 1918 Frederick Koch (1877–1944) founded the influential Carolina Playmakers. Many other programs soon followed and by 1940 theatre education was an accepted part of many U.S. universities.

In the years following 1910, the "new stagecraft," as the European trends were called in America, began to find its way into the commercial theatre. Winthrop Ames (1871–1937), who had gone to Europe in

FIG. 19.6
Robert Edmond Jones's design for *The Man Who Married a Dumb Wife,* 1915; directed by Harley Granville Barker. This setting is usually said to be the first important native example of the "new stagecraft" in the United States. From *The Theatre* (1915).

1907 to study new developments there, was employed in 1909 to manage the New Theatre in New York, an ambitious nonprofit repertory company. The large theatre soon proved both financially and artistically unsatisfactory, however, and Ames then built the Little Theatre, seating only 300, where in the years preceding World War I he presented a number of plays in the new style. In 1912 he imported Reinhardt's production of *Sumurun,* which also aroused much interest in European ideas.

In 1912 the Boston Opera Company hired Joseph Urban (1872–1933), a well-established Viennese designer of the new school, to mount its productions. Urban later worked in New York (most notably for Florenz Ziegfeld), where he was famous for the fresh coloring and simplicity of his settings. In 1915 the New York Stage Society invited Harley Granville Barker to direct a series of plays for its members. For Barker's production of *The Man Who Married a Dumb Wife,* Robert Edmond Jones (1887–1954) provided settings usually considered the first native expression of the "new stagecraft." Jones was one of several young men, including Lee Simonson and Sam Hume, who had studied in Europe between 1912 and 1915 and had been impressed by the changing theatrical trends. In 1914 Hume arranged an exhibit of continental scene design which was shown in New York, Detroit, Chicago, and Cleveland. Hume later joined the Detroit Arts and Crafts Theatre; there his associate, Sheldon Cheney, launched *Theatre Arts Magazine* in 1916, which until 1948 was to be the principal disseminator of new ideas in the United States. Visits by the Abbey Theatre (1911–1913), the Ballets Russes (1916), and Copeau's troupe (1917–1919) also helped to stimulate interest in foreign movements. Nevertheless, when the war ended in 1918 the U.S. theatre was only beginning to be aware of European practices.

The triumph of the new ideal owes most to the Provincetown Players, the Theatre Guild, and Arthur Hopkins. After presenting a few programs on Cape Cod, the Provincetown Players moved to New York in 1916. In its early years the company concentrated upon plays by U.S. playwrights and by 1925 had presented ninety-three plays by forty-seven authors. After 1923, the group split into two branches. One continued the older practices, while the other, under Eugene O'Neill, Robert Edmond Jones, and Kenneth Macgowan, performed foreign and period plays along with the noncommercial works of O'Neill and others. Although it succumbed to financial pressures in 1929, the Provincetown Players had served an important role as an experimental theatre both for new plays and for new production techniques.

The Theatre Guild was opened in 1919 by former members of the Washington Square Players. It was fully professional, with the avowed purpose of presenting plays of merit not likely to interest commercial managers. Under its principal director, Philip Moeller (1880–1958), and its principal designer, Lee Simonson (1888–1967), it soon became the United States' most respected theatre, presenting plays each year to an audience of subscribers. In 1928 it also began a subscription series in six other cities. During the 1930s the company gradually curtailed its activities and by World War II was merely another commercial producer investing in long-run hits.

In 1918 Arthur Hopkins (1878–1950) began a series of productions that were to mark him as the most adventurous of New York's commercial producers. Working with Robert Edmond Jones, Hopkins presented plays by Tolstoy, Ibsen, Gorky, Shakespeare, O'Neill, and others. In 1921 his production of *Macbeth* created a sensation with its expressionistic use of tilted arches, and in 1922 *Hamlet,* starring John Barrymore (1882–1942), was declared one of the best productions of the century. After Hopkins and the Guild demonstrated the commercial viability of the "new stagecraft," it was adopted by others, and by 1930 had become the standard approach.

The "new stagecraft" was primarily a visual movement, but the total effect of most productions might best be described as "simplified realism." In addition to Jones and Simonson, the major influence on scene design was Norman Bel Geddes (1893–1958), a visionary not unlike Appia. Geddes' plan (published in 1921) for staging Dante's *The Divine Comedy* on a series of terraces is still considered one of the most brilliant conceptions by a U.S. designer. His penchant for steps, platforms, and imaginative lighting was also seen in his productions of *Hamlet* (1931) and Werfel's *The Eternal Road* (1936), in which the platforms soared to a height of 50 feet. Other important designers included Cleon Throckmorton (1897–1965), Mordecai Gorelik (1899–1990), Boris Aronson (1900–1980), Aline Bernstein (1882–1955), Howard Bay (1912–1986), Donald Oenslager (1902–1975), and especially Jo Mielziner (1901–1976), who was to be the United States' most prolific and respected designer after 1945. While all did not follow the same style, they shared a respect for simplicity and a desire to capture the spirit of a text.

Continental influence continued to be felt in the 1920s through a series of visitors: the Moscow Art Theatre toured the United States in 1923–1924; Reinhardt presented *The Miracle* (with designs by Geddes) in 1924 and staged a season of plays in 1927–1928; and Copeau directed *The Brothers Karamazov* for the Theatre Guild in 1927. Two of

FIG. 19.7
Robert Edmond Jones's setting for the banquet scene, *Macbeth,* 1921. Directed by Arthur Hopkins. Note the expressionistic elements, including the masks above the stage. From *Theatre Arts Magazine* (1924).

Stanislavsky's actors, Richard Boleslavsky (1889–1937) and Maria Ouspenskaya (1881–1949), were induced to head the American Laboratory Theatre between 1923 and 1930. Here the Stanislavsky system was taught in a version later popularized by Boleslavsky's book *Acting, the First Six Lessons* (1933).

Among the more than 500 students who studied at the American Laboratory Theatre were Stella Adler (1904–1992), Lee Strasberg (1901–1982), and Harold Clurman (1901–1980), who with Cheryl Crawford (1902–1986) established the Group Theatre in 1931, America's most distinguished troupe of the 1930s. With a company including Morris Carnovsky (1898–1992) and Elia Kazan (1909–2003), the Group Theatre was modeled after the Moscow Art Theatre, whose methods and ensemble approach it emulated. For ten years it produced an exceptional repertory and became especially well known for its productions of plays by Clifford Odets. Though it foundered in 1941 due to policy disagreements, many of its former members became the major figures in theatre in the United States after World War II.

The Great Depression, which began in the United States with the stock market crash of 1929, motivated the creation of a unique experiment in American theatre, the Federal Theatre Project (1935–1939). This was a unit of the government-funded Works Progress Administration (WPA) which was established to combat unemployment. Headed by Hallie Flanagan Davis (1890–1969), at its peak it employed 10,000 persons in 40 states. About 1000 productions of all types were mounted, 65 percent of them free. In spite of its diversity, it is now remembered primarily for developing the "Living Newspaper," a cinematic form which integrated factual data with dramatic vignettes. Each script centered around a problem: *Triple-A Plowed Under* (1936) dealt with agriculture, *Power* (1937) with rural electrification, and *One-Third of a Nation* (1938) with slum housing. Most of the plays had as a central character the "little man" who, upon raising questions about a current problem, was led through its background, human consequences, and possible solutions. Much of the dialogue was taken from speeches, newspaper stories, or other documents. Many of the techniques

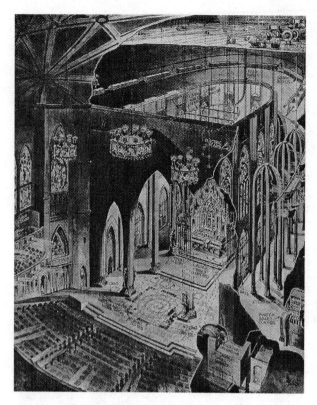

FIG. 19.8

Norman Bel Geddes's setting for *The Miracle* as staged by Max Reinhardt at the Century Theatre, New York, 1924. This sectional plan shows the arrangement of the scenery and machinery in this theatre after it was converted to look like a medieval cathedral. From *The Scientific American* (1924).

Citizen Kane (1941), one of the most admired of the century.

The Federal Theatre also promoted African American theatre by establishing African American units in several cities. These units presented over seventy-five plays in four years, building on the early foundations of African American theatre going back to the nineteenth century. In the years between 1890 and 1917, several musicals had been written for African American casts. In 1903 George Walker (1873–1911) and Bert Williams (1875–1922) had become major Broadway stars, and from 1910 to 1922 Williams was one of the highest paid performers in New York.

An important early step for African American theatre had been taken in 1915 when Anita Bush (*c.* 1883–1974) organized a stock company, which soon became the Lafayette Players, to perform a weekly repertory in Harlem. The company took most of its plays from Broadway, but it gave African American actors their longest continuous employment in regular drama to that time. By 1928 the company had a theatre in Chicago and two touring units, but it could not survive the depression and closed in 1932.

A few dramatists also began to write sympathetically about African Americans. The first serious plays for African American actors to be seen on Broadway were Ridgely Torrence's *Three Plays for a Negro Theatre* (1917), which not only marked a turning away from the stereotyped treatment of African Americans but also the first time that African Americans were welcomed into Broadway audiences.

were borrowed from Epic Theatre. The political tone of many works eventually alienated Congress, which in 1939 refused to appropriate funds for its continuance.

When the Federal Theatre withdrew its support for Marc Blitzstein's anti-capitalist musical, *The Cradle Will Rock,* in 1937, Orson Welles (1915–1985) and John Houseman (1902–1988) formed the Mercury Theatre company to present it. Welles had already established a reputation as an actor with his portrayal of Doctor Faustus and as an imaginative producer with *Macbeth,* which he set in Haiti and performed with an African American cast. Between 1937 and 1939 the Mercury Theatre presented works by Büchner, Dekker, Shaw, and Shakespeare both on stage and for the radio. Its greatest success came with *Julius Caesar,* played as a comment upon fascism, then rampant in Europe, but its most notorious production was the radio broadcast of *War of the Worlds,* which caused a national panic in 1938. After leaving the Mercury Theatre, Welles produced the film

FIG. 19.9

A "living newspaper," *One Third of a Nation,* staged by the Federal Theatre Project in 1938. Tenement house setting by Howard Bay. From *Theatre Arts* (1939).

There followed such works as O'Neill's *The Emperor Jones* (in which the African American actor, Charles Gilpin, played the leading role in a serious American play on Broadway for the first time), DuBose and Dorothy Heyward's *Porgy*, Marc Connelly's *The Green Pastures*, and Paul Green's *In Abraham's Bosom*, all by white authors.

There were several African American authors as well, although they were given relatively little encouragement. Among the best of the plays were Willis Richardson's (1889–1977) *The Chipwoman's Fortune*, Frank Wilson's *Sugar Cane*, Hall Johnson's *Run Little Chillun*, Langston Hughes' (1902–1967) *Mulatto*, Georgia Douglas Johnson's (1880–1966) *Plumes* and *A Sunday Morning in the South*, and Zora Neale Hurston's (1891–1960) *Mule Bone* (written with Langston Hughes). There were also musical plays, among the most successful of which were Noble Sissle (1889–1975) and Eubie Blake's (1883–1983) *Shuffle Along*, *Chocolate Dandies*, and *Runnin' Wild*. All of these plays helped such African American performers as Richard Harrison (1864–1935), Frank Wilson, Rose McClendon, and Abbie Mitchell to demonstrate that they could compete with the best actors of the period. Of all African American actors of this time, however, Paul Robeson (1898–1976) is probably the best known, both in America and abroad. Among the plays in which he appeared were O'Neill's *Emperor Jones* and *All God's Chillun Got Wings*, the groundbreaking musicals *Porgy and Bess* and *Showboat*, and *Othello* (in which he played the title role in three productions).

By World War II many plays about African American life had found their way onto the stage. Perhaps the most disturbing of these was *Native Son*, Paul Green and Richard Wright's adaptation of Wright's novel, which showed the terrible effects of social evils on the life of the protagonist. But, if there was still a long way to go, there had been much improvement since 1915. The African American theatre artists had made their presence felt, even if they had not yet been permitted to demonstrate their full potential.

The Depression also gave impetus to the "worker's theatre" movement, which had begun in 1926 with the Worker's Drama League. In 1932, a national organization was formed, later called the New Theatre League. Most of the member groups were amateur, but in 1933 a fully professional organization, the Theatre Union, was formed in New York and provided leadership for the entire movement. After the failure of the Theatre Union in 1937, the League declined and by 1942 had virtually ceased to exist. For the most part, the worker's theatres presented socialist propaganda plays designed to arouse protest.

These dissident groups had little effect upon the basic pattern of the commercial theatre. The length of runs steadily increased, reaching a peak with *Tobacco Road* (1933), which played for seven years. The number of new productions also grew each season until 1927–1928, when about 300 plays were mounted, but rapidly declined after 1930, having fallen to eighty by 1939–1940. Theatrical production was complicated in these years by the emergence of powerful labor unions. The stagehand's union, the National Alliance of Theatrical Stage Employees, had achieved full recognition during the season of 1910–1911, and in 1918 the United Scenic Artists was formed. Actors Equity Association, founded in 1912, was recognized in 1919; it became a "closed shop" in 1924 and was able to establish a minimum-wage scale in 1933. The Dramatists' Guild, formed in 1912, became the bargaining agent for all playwrights in 1926. As each group bettered working conditions, it also demanded considerably higher pay for its members and thereby added to the economic problems of the theatre.

Between 1915 and 1940, American dramatists began to command international respect for the first time. Few were members of any particular movement, but most shared a dislike for romantic melodrama with realistic trappings. Only one American dramatist—O'Neill—achieved genuine stature. Eugene O'Neill (1888–1953), son of James O'Neill, turned to playwriting around 1912, attended Baker's playwriting classes at Harvard for a time, and in 1915 had his first works presented by the Provincetown Players. The group continued to encourage him through the 1920s by performing those works rejected by commercial producers. His first full-length play, *Beyond the Horizon*, brought him to Broadway in 1920. After 1934, although he continued to write, no new works were performed until 1946.

O'Neill wrote about 25 full-length plays of uneven quality. Many were seriously flawed, and even the best often suggest that more was intended than achieved. But despite all shortcomings, the plays, with their compelling characters in search of meaning and fulfillment in human existence, achieve a stature surpassed by few modern dramatists. O'Neill also experimented with many novel theatrical devices and dramatic techniques. In *The Great God Brown* (1926), *Lazarus Laughed* (1926), and *Days Without End* (1934) he made use of masks; in *Strange Interlude* (1928) he employed lengthy "interior monologues" to express the characters' inner thoughts; in *Mourning Becomes Electra* (1931) he gained scope by adopting the trilogy form. O'Neill also ranged through many styles. The devices of expressionism were adopted for *The Hairy Ape* (1922) and *The Great God Brown;* those of symbolism for *The Fountain* (1922) and to a lesser extent for almost all the plays; those of realism for *Beyond the Horizon, Anna Christie* (1921), and *Desire Under the Elms* (1924), as well as in those plays that would be produced following World War II.

Probably O'Neill's greatest rival was Maxwell Anderson (1888–1959), who after achieving renown for his antiromantic war play, *What Price Glory?* (1924), turned to blank verse drama in *Elizabeth the Queen* (1930), *Mary of Scotland* (1933), *Winterset* (1935), and other plays. Although dramatically effective, Anderson's plays offered few new insights, being merely skillful retellings of familiar stories. Other serious playwrights included Elmer Rice (1892–1967) with *The Adding Machine* (1923), an expressionistic drama about the dehumanization of modern life, and *Street Scene* (1929), a naturalistic play set in the New York slums; Sidney Howard (1891–1939), with *They Knew What They Wanted* (1924), an antiromantic comedy about three people who get their wishes by accepting compromises, *The Silver Cord* (1926), about a mother's attempt to retain her control over her newly married son, and *Yellow Jack* (1934), a semi-documentary play about the fight to control yellow fever; and Paul Green (1894–1981), with his tragedies, *In Abraham's Bosom* (1926) and *The House of Connolly* (1931), and the expressionistic antiwar play, *Johnny Johnson* (1936).

The comedy of manners was well represented by Phillip Barry (1896–1949) with *Paris Bound* (1927) and *The Philadelphia Story* (1939), both treating divorce among the upper classes; and S. N. Berhman (1893–1973), with *Biography* (1932), *Rain from Heaven* (1934), and *End of Summer* (1936), all of which contrast tolerance with inhumanity. Among the writers of farce, the best was George S. Kaufman (1889–1961), who worked with a number of collaborators, most successfully with Moss Hart (1904–1961), on *You Can't Take It With You* (1936) and *The Man Who Came to Dinner* (1940). William Saroyan (1908–1981) glorified the simple life in such plays as *My Heart's in the Highlands* (1939), *The Time of Your Life* (1939), and *The Beautiful People* (1941), all of which depict eccentric characters who find beauty and redemption while living on the fringes of society.

The drama of social consciousness was most persistently practiced by John Howard Lawson (1895–1977), whose *Roger Bloomer* (1923), *Processional* (1925), and *Internationale* (1928) were experimental in form and militantly propagandistic in theme. Clifford Odets (1906–1963) called for group action in his early plays, *Waiting for Lefty* (1935) and *Awake and Sing* (1935), while his later works, *Paradise Lost* (1935) and *Golden Boy* (1937), took a more complex view of social conditions. Odets was essentially a chronicler of family relationships; his strength lay in his ability to create believable characters struggling to achieve more than life will give them.

Two of the finest dramatists of the 1930s were Sherwood and Wilder. Robert E. Sherwood (1896–1955) in *The Petrified Forest* (1935) created an allegorical cross-section of U.S. life, in *Idiot's Delight* (1936) depicted through melodramatic farce the horrors of war and the spiritual bankruptcy which gives rise to it, and in *Abe Lincoln in Illinois* (1938) sought to remind Americans of the high ideals upon which their country had been founded. Thornton Wilder's (1897–1975) reputation was created primarily by three plays, *Our Town* (1938), which stresses the archetypal patterns of human experience which undergird seeming change, *The Skin of Our Teeth* (1943), a testimonial to humanity's ability to survive all disasters, and *The Merchant of Yonkers* (1938), later rewritten as *The Matchmaker* (1954), and then adapted into the musical *Hello, Dolly* (1963). Wilder's frank theatricality and simplicity won him a wide following both at home and abroad.

America also produced an unusually large number of female playwrights during this period, among them Rachel Crothers (1876–1958), author of *He and She* (1920), *When Ladies Meet* (1932), and *Susan and God* (1937); Zona Gale (1874–1938), whose *Miss Lulu Bett* (1920) was the first play by a woman to win the Pulitzer Prize; Susan Glaspell (1876–1948), whose *Alison's House* (1931), also won a Pulitzer Prize; Zoe Akins (1886–1958), whose *Declassée* (1919) was a major vehicle for Ethel Barrymore and whose *The Old Maid* (1934) won the Pulitzer Prize; Lulu Vollmer (1898–1955), whose *Sun-Up* (1923) began a vogue for folk plays; Edna Ferber (1885–1968) who adapted her own novel into the musical *Showboat* (1927) and wrote several successful plays with George S. Kaufman, including *Royal Family* (1927) and *Stage Door* (1936); and Sophie Treadwell (c. 1885–1970), whose expressionistic *Machinal* (1928) depicts a woman eventually driven to murder by her machine-like world. Despite the accomplishments of these women during the interwar years, they were, unlike their male contemporaries, subsequently relegated to oblivion. Only recently, under the influence of the women's movement, has interest in them revived. The only female playwright to escape this amnesia was Lillian Hellman (1905–1984), author of *The Children's Hour* (1934) concerning teachers whose lives are ruined by a student who maliciously accuses them of being lesbians, and *Little Foxes* (1939), a story of rapacious greed among the rising industrialists of the new South around 1900.

Much popular entertainment between the wars took the form of musical comedy and revues. Every year between 1907 and 1931, Florenz Ziegfeld (1869–1932) mounted a new edition of *Ziegfeld Follies*, each more lavish than the last. Musical comedy, long merely the excuse for presenting beautiful chorus girls, began to move in a new direction after 1928, when Jerome Kern and Oscar Hammerstein II shifted major emphasis to coherent story in *Showboat*. This new direction reached its culmination in Richard Rodgers's and Oscar Hammerstein's *Oklahoma* (1943), in which music, story, dance, and setting were fully integrated to tell a semi-serious story. With the triumph of the new approach, the old type of musical largely disappeared.

Of the United States' many outstanding performers, only a few can be mentioned: Jane Cowl (1884–1950), on the stage from 1903 and most famous for her portrayals of Juliet, Cleopatra, and the heroines of Sherwood; Pauline Lord (1890–1950), especially remembered for her performances in *Anna Christie* and *They Knew What They Wanted;* Laurette Taylor (1884–1946), one of the most versatile actresses of her day, whose last major appearance was as Amanda in Tennessee William's *The Glass Menagerie;* Ina Claire (1895–1985), who appeared in many *Ziegfeld Follies* before playing the heroines of Behrman's comedies; Helen Hayes (1900–1993), noted especially for her appearances in Barrie's plays, Anderson's *Mary of Scotland,* and Housman's *Victoria Regina;* Katherine Cornell (1898–1974), who gave outstanding portrayals in *Candida, The Three Sisters, The Barretts of Wimpole Street,* and many other plays; Lynn Fontanne (1887?–1983), an English actress, who came to the United States in 1910 and whose later career was tied up with that of her husband, Alfred Lunt (1893–1977), with whom she appeared in *The Guardsman, Reunion in Vienna, Amphitryon 38,* and many other works.

THEATRE IN CANADA TO 1940

From 1902 to 1910 Harold Nelson Shaw (1865–1937) ran the only successful "all Canadian" touring company. Except for A. J. Small's Great Lakes Circuit, the Canadian market for touring shows was dominated by New York's Theatrical Syndicate. To combat this, the British-Canadian Theatrical Organization was formed in 1912 to import British touring companies and stars. This organization was able to show some success, especially after the demise of the Syndicate in 1917, but growing competition from film made that success short-lived. With the advent of radio drama in the 1920s and the Great Depression of the 1930s, Canadian touring would be abandoned by both British and U.S. companies. Canadian theatre was finally left to develop on its own.

The foundation for a distinctively Canadian theatre was being laid during this period by its own "little theatre" movement. Toronto's Arts and Letters Club of 1908 was the first of these organizations, but it was not until its founding director, Roy Mitchell (1884–1944), took over the Hart House Theatre in 1919 that the production of Canadian plays became a goal. Of the dramatists Hart House encouraged, Merrill Denison (1893–1975) was the first to be successful. An anthology of his Hart House plays was published in 1923 under the title *The Unheroic North,* but he is best known for *Contract* (1929). The most famous actor to have started a career with Hart House was Raymond Massey (1896–1983), brother of the theatre's main financial supporter, Vincent Massey. But the actress Elizabeth Sterling Haynes (1897–1957) was the more important Hart House actor for the future of Canadian theatre as she went on to establish several theatres in Alberta.

A large number of Canadian playwrights appeared in the years between the wars, especially after Canada was given autonomy from England in 1931. Some were cultivated by theatre groups like the women's collective Playwrights Studio Group (founded 1932) and the experimental Play Workshop (founded 1934). Others were inspired by the competitions set up by the Dominion Drama Festival (founded 1932) and the Barry Jackson Trophy (1934). Of these many dramatists, Herman Voaden (1903–1991), John Coulter (1888–1980), Gwen Pharis Ringwood (1910–1984), and Robertson Davis (1913–1995) are still considered important today, and the latter three did most of their best work after World War II. Plays were also developed collectively in this period, the most famous example of which was the Toronto Worker's Theatre production of *Eight Men Speak* (1933), a highly controversial drama in support of the Communist party. Working for little theatres did not pay well, so when the Canadian Broadcasting Company was established in 1936 much of the best writing and acting talent of Canadian theatre began working in radio drama, an art form that had been growing in importance since 1925.

From 1890 to 1914, the theatre in French-speaking Montreal experienced its greatest period of growth. The number of theatres increased from three to ten, and the number of professional resident companies grew from one to eight, three of which did

English-language drama. In 1902 the city's first independent theatre, the Société Anonyme des Théâtre, opened at the Théâtre des Nouveautés. Like its European counterparts, it was dedicated to modern production methods and a repertory of plays that went beyond the standard commercial fare of melodrama and musical reviews. But it showed little interest in Canadian authors and closed in 1908. French-Canadian playwrights from Julien Daoust (dates unknown) to Yvette Mercier-Gouin (1895–1984) would make their careers writing unchallenging drama for the commercial stage. The Community Players, founded in 1921, was the city's first little theatre. When it disbanded in 1925 one of its founders, Martha Allan, joined the Pasadena Playhouse before returning to establish the Montreal Repertory Theatre in 1929. But as early as the start of World War I, the French-Canadian theatre was entering a decline from which it would take three decades to recover.

THEATRE AND DRAMA IN AUSTRALIA AND NEW ZEALAND, 1915–1940

The movement towards realism manifested itself in "bush drama" at the turn of the century. These plays were not concerned with the colonial past but rather focused on the virtues and ingenuity of Australians as they faced the hardships of their difficult environment with good-natured humor and fortitude. Independent women were often the central characters; Australian English rather than British English was used; and upper-class characters tended to be villains, not heroes. *On Our Selection* (1907–1910) was by far the most successful representative of this type. It was the most popular play of its day and seems to have been in performance somewhere in the country constantly from 1912 to 1929. The play was a series of individual sketches focused on Dad, Mum, Dave, Joe, and Sarah Rudd, based on a collection of short stories by Steele Rudd (who was one of the several adapters). It became the model for a number of other plays including *Possum Paddock* (1919) by Kate Howard, which held the stage for twenty years. There were also more serious versions of this type, like Jo Smith's *The Bushwoman* (1909) and *The Girl of the Never Never* (1910). In the 1920s detective dramas, starting with *The Flaw* (1923), by Emelie Polini and Frank Harvey, came into vogue. In the 1930s historic dramas, like Allan Wilkie's *Governor Bligh* (1930), were most popular. But in general the commercial repertory was dominated by productions of comedies, reviews, melodramas, and lightweight realism imported from the United States and Great Britain.

As the Theatrical Syndicate dominated the theatre of the United States and Canada in the first years of the twentieth century, JCW, the management firm founded by American actor James Cassius Williamson (1844–1913), dominated the market in Australia and New Zealand. The theatrical boom that had started in Australia in 1870 continued right up to World War I, but the theatre remained conservative. To counterbalance the standard commercial fare, Leon Brodsky (1883–1973) established The Australian Theatre Society at Melbourne in 1904. It was modeled after the Independent Theatre in London but its members soon lost interest in experimental work and chose to become a play-reading group. It was followed, however, by the Melbourne Repertory Theatre Company, founded in 1911 by Gregan McMahon (1874–1941), which proved to be a "little theatre" of outstanding quality. The Adelaide Literary Theatre (1908), founded by Bryceson Treharne (1879–1948), was even more successful. It exposed its audiences to the works of many of the more controversial European playwrights of the time as well as to the works of New Zealand dramatist Arthur H. Adams (1872–1936). This group became the Adelaide Repertory Theatre in 1911, perhaps the most influential little theatre of the era. The clearest indication of the success of these companies came when J. and N. Tait Ltd. (the equivalent of the Shubert brothers in the United States) hired McMahon to establish the Sydney Repertory Theatre Society in 1918 in a unique marriage of the independent theatre spirit with a dominant commercial operation of the time. (This operation became even more dominant when it bought JCW in 1920.) Mutual suspicion brought an end to this project in 1928, but McMahon continued to direct and influenced many of the best theatre artists of the next generation.

Large numbers of little theatres sprang up all over Australia between the wars, and several even appeared in New Zealand, but few outlasted the energy of their original founders. This energy could last a long time, as it did with Doris Fitton (1897–1985), one of McMahon's former students who started the Independent Theatre in Sydney in 1930 and ran it for forty-seven years. But the Ab Intra Studio Theatre in Adelaide, founded in 1931 by Alan Harkness (1908–1952) and Kester Baruch (1903–1992), was more typical. It produced some of the most experimental and visually spectacular productions ever seen in Australia, but when its founders left for England in 1935, the theatre closed. The New Theatre Sydney, founded in 1932, and the New Theatre Melbourne, founded in 1935, are exceptional in having continued to the present day. Of the numerous other little theatres, Melbourne's Dolia Ribush Players, named for the Russian immigrant who founded it in 1932, deserves special mention. Through this theatre, Ribush (1896–1947) popularized the Stanislavsky system in Australia and was probably second only to McMahon in his influence on young directors. In 1937, the Australian Drama League was established to provide mutual assistance and communication among the many diverse groups that made up the little theatre movement.

Despite the rapid expansion of little theatres, the commercial theatre in Australia and New Zealand was collapsing under the onslaught of film, the Depression, and radio drama. Governments imposed taxes on "entertainment," making it even harder for commercial theatre to be competitive. In 1929, the tax records report 2,460,000 tickets sold at theatres in Australia; five years later that number was down to 166,000. Of the ten theatres used for live performances in Sydney in 1929, only two were still used for that purpose in 1935, and one of those was used only for musical reviews. The strength of the little theatre movement was a testimony to people's interest in the art of the theatre, but they were no longer in a position to support it commercially.

The Second World War, like the first, interrupted the theatre's normal patterns. The war also raised serious doubts about a world that had created such horrors as the Nazi extermination camps and such destructive weapons as the atomic bomb. Out of the questioning would come many innovations in theatre and drama.

THEATRICAL CONDITIONS IN THE SOVIET UNION, 1917–1940

The most drastic changes brought by World War I were felt in Russia, where the czar's policies had been unpopular for many years. The economic hardships created by the conflict fed the unrest, which in early 1917 broke into open rebellion, ending both Russian participation in the war and more than 300 years of rule by the Romanovs. Moderate socialists controlled the government at first, but in late 1917 the Communists seized power. Civil war continued until the early 1920s, by which time more than twenty million people had died and Russia's economic resources were severely depleted. For several years thereafter the government was so preoccupied with rebuilding the nation that the theatre was left relatively free to experiment with new forms.

The Communists viewed the theatre as a national treasure to be made available to the proletariat. Also considered a major tool of instruction, it was placed under the authority of the Commissariat of Education. The Commissariat divided theatres into two groups: the well-established theatres, which the government subsidized and allowed relative autonomy; and the unproven theatres, which were permitted to exist but given little encouragement. Thus, the government favored pre-Revolutionary groups. By 1923, only 33 percent of the theatres were subsidized. By 1926, the percentage had increased to 63, but the process was not completed until 1936. Not only was attendance at professional productions encouraged, amateur groups were organized among peasants, workers, and soldiers. By 1926, there were about 20,000 dramatic clubs among the peasants alone.

In 1920 Meyerhold was appointed head of the theatre section in the Commissariat of Education, a position that made him nominal head of the theatre in Russia. At the same time, he continued his own work as a director, staging *The Dawns* (written in 1898 by the Belgian symbolist, Emile Verhaeren) as a Soviet propaganda piece, in which real news bulletins were read from the stage and a public meeting was held with the audience taking part. This production was denounced by the Central Committee of the Communist Party as foreign to the needs of the proletariat, and Meyerhold resigned his government post, but he was quickly appointed head of the state's workshop for directors, and in 1922 was given his own theatre. In his theatre Meyerhold perfected the techniques he called *biomechanics* and *constructivism*.

FIG. 19.10

Meyerhold's adaptation of Gogol's *The Inspector General*, 1926. Shown here is the "bribery" scene. The set opened at the back to allow wagons to move in and out.

FIG. 19.11
Constructivist setting by Lyubov Popova for Meyerhold's production of Crommelynck's *The Magnanimous Cuckold*, 1922. The action occurs in and around a mill, suggested by various wheels, all of which turned at speeds that varied according to the rhythmical and emotional demands of the action.

Biomechanics referred primarily to Meyerhold's approach to acting, intended to create a style appropriate to the machine age. His performers were trained in gymnastics, circus movement, and ballet in order to make them as efficient as machines in carrying out "an assignment received from the outside." This was an attempt to apply the James-Lange theory (1884) that particular patterns of muscular activity elicit particular emotions. Consequently, actors, to arouse within themselves or the audience a desired emotional response, need only to enact the appropriate kinetic patterns. Thus, Meyerhold sought to replace Stanislavsky's emphasis on internal motivation with one based on physical and emotional reflexes. To create a feeling of exuberant joy in both performer and audience, for example, Meyerhold thought it more efficient for actors to plummet down a slide, swing on a trapeze, or turn a somersault than to restrict themselves to behavior considered appropriate by traditional social standards.

Constructivism was a term taken over from the visual arts, where it had first been applied about 1912 to sculpture composed of intersecting planes and masses without representational content. Meyerhold applied it to his "machine for acting," in which nonrepresentational platforms, ramps, turning wheels, trapezes, and other objects replaced the normal representational decor.

Meyerhold's most famous production using these techniques was Gogol's *The Inspector General*, presented in 1926. He transferred the locale from a remote village to a large city, reshaped all of the characters and invented several new ones. Costumes, scenery, and properties were based on stylized nineteenth-century

motifs, and the action was accompanied by period music. The most striking scene was one in which Meyerhold arranged fifteen doors around the stage, and an official emerged simultaneously from each door to offer the inspector a bribe. From this time on, he continually modified these techniques to make them more subtle.

Another important innovator in these early years was Yevgeny Vakhtangov (1883–1922), who had become the artistic leader of the First Studio of the Moscow Art Theatre in 1916. Vakhtangov's reputation rests primarily upon four productions: Maeterlinck's *The Miracle of Saint Anthony*, Strindberg's *Erik XIV* (both staged in 1921), Ansky's *The Dybbuk,* and Gozzi's *Turandot* (both staged in 1922).

In these productions he managed an effective blending of the Moscow Art Theatre's realistic approach with Meyerhold's theatricalism. From Stanislavsky he preserved the emphasis upon concentration, each character's biography, and exploration of hidden meanings; to this he added a heightened and stylized use of movement and design not unlike that of the German expressionists. Vakhtangov's greatest achievement came with *Turandot,* throughout which the actors seemed to be improvising effortlessly. This production was retained in the repertory as a memorial to Vakhtangov, who died shortly after it opened. Because he worked with several student groups and trained so many actors, Vakhtangov's influence was considerable. His approach was continued by such associates and students as Yuri Zavadsky (1894–1977), Boris Shchukin (1894–1939), Reuben Simonov (1899–1968), Boris Zakhava (1896–1976), Nikolai Akimov (1901–1968), and Alexander Popov (1892–1961) all of whom became important leaders in Soviet theatre.

In 1924 the First Studio became an independent organization, the Second Moscow Art Theatre, headed by Mikhail Chekhov (1891–1955), a nephew of Anton Chekhov. After entering the Moscow Art Theatre in 1910, Chekhov soon found the Stanislavsky method inadequate in the way it restricted the actor to copying nature. After playing the part of Erik XIV for Vakhtangov, Checkhov began to stress inspiration above analysis as the actor's primary tool. His conceptions were always somewhat mystical, however, and in 1927 seventeen of his associates resigned and published a denunciation. Chekhov then left Russia and ultimately settled in the United States where he ran an acting school for many years and published *To the Actor.* The Second Moscow Art Theatre was dissolved in 1936.

Although the innovators of the 1920s attracted most attention, the conservative groups, notably the Maly Theatre in Moscow and the Alexandrinsky

FIG. 19.12
Vakhtangov's production of Gozzi's *Turandot*, 1922.
Setting by I. Nivinsky.

Theatre in Leningrad, were favored by political leaders and most of the public. Meyerhold disliked the Maly Theatre's realistic productions so much that in 1921 he recommended that the troupe be liquidated. In response, Alexander Yuzhin, the Maly's director, launched an attack on "formalism" that began a struggle not to be resolved until the 1930s.

Next to Meyerhold, the most influential Russian director of the 1920s was Tairov, who continued the methods he had introduced before the war. Working at the Kamerny Theatre, Tairov took little notice of the Revolution, producing a predominantly Western repertory and touring Western Europe with his troupe in 1923, 1928, and 1929. But the political atmosphere was changing and it became increasingly necessary for him to stage more Soviet plays. He won considerable praise for his staging of Vishnevsky's *The Optimistic Tragedy* in 1933, but by 1937 he was so out of favor that his company was merged with that of the Realistic Theatre. The Kamerny Theatre was allowed to reopen in 1939, but the company was sent to perform in Siberia during the war years.

Between 1917 and 1925, the Moscow Art Theatre played a minor role in Russian theatrical life. It mounted only two new productions and its troupe was decimated in 1919 by the defection of several actors to the West. In 1922 it was granted permission to tour abroad, and in 1923–1924 the troupe performed in the United States to universal praise. When the company returned to Russia in 1924, it was at its lowest ebb. Its studios were alienated, and the company was so depleted that Stanislavsky had to add eighty-seven new members. In 1926 it achieved its first postwar success with Ostrovsky's *The Burning Heart*, and in 1927 presented Vsevelod

Ivanov's *Armored Train 14–69*, its first important Soviet play. From that time, the company's fortunes steadily improved.

Around 1927 the Soviet attitude toward the theatre began to change. After Lenin died in 1924, Stalin gradually gathered power into his hands and in 1928 began his campaign to industrialize Russia and collectivize farming. Concessions formerly granted dissident elements were withdrawn and the central government extended its power over all aspects of Soviet life. In 1927 a training program to equip party members to manage theatres was initiated and "artistic councils" within each theatre were given considerable power over repertory, style, and policy. Nevertheless, attacks on nonconformists in the theatre came primarily from the Russian Association of Proletarian Writers (RAPP), a radical group that sought to abolish everything not deriving directly from the proletariat. Its violence sufficiently alienated party leaders that it was disbanded in 1932 and replaced by the Union of Soviet Writers, headed by Gorky. At first, greater freedom seemed to be in store, but in 1934 "socialist realism" (realistic in form, socialistic in content) was declared the proper style for all art, and pressure began to be exerted to discourage "formalism" (any type of nonrealism). In 1936 all theatres were placed under the Central Direction of Theatres, and after 1938 the "stabilization" of companies made it almost impossible for workers to change jobs without specific government approval.

The new policies meant the gradual suppression of the *avant-garde* troupes and greater prestige for the Maly, Alexandrinsky (now renamed the Pushkin Theatre), and the Moscow Art Theatre, which after 1932 was called "the House of Gorky." The nonrealistic groups attempted to adapt to the new demands. Meyerhold adopted a style usually called "impressionistic," exemplified in his productions of Dumas' *Camille* in 1934 and Tchaikovsky's *Queen of Spades* in 1935. He did not alter the text or use biomechanics in either production. Both were given lavish, if stylized, decor and both were popular successes. Nevertheless, Meyerhold's completely apolitical interpretations displeased officials even more than his formalism, and in 1938 his theatre was closed. In 1939 he made his last official appearance; in a speech to the First All Union Congress of Directors he is reported to have admitted errors, but to have added: "The pitiful and wretched thing called socialist realism has nothing in common with art. . . . Where once there were the best theatres in the world . . . in hunting formalism, you have eliminated art." Meyerhold was arrested shortly thereafter and executed for subversion in early 1940. Despite these

FIG. 19.13
Okhlopkov's Realistic Theatre, Moscow, 1932. Note the two levels of action and the placement of the audience for this production of *The Beginning,* adapted from a novel.

repressions, stylization received official approval when it was used to convey acceptable political messages.

The most significant experiments of the 1930s were those of Nikolai Okhlopkov (1900–1966) at the Realistic Theatre. Originating as the Fourth Studio of the Moscow Art Theatre in 1921, the Realistic Theatre attained independent status in 1927. Okhlopkov, who had worked with both Meyerhold and Tairov, was appointed its director in 1932. He eliminated the platform stage and placed all action in the auditorium. Although he often used a central playing area, Okhlopkov also staged scenes around the periphery of the auditorium or on a bridge overhead. Realistic set pieces might be placed almost anywhere, and sound effects from many directions made the audience feel at the center of events. Okhlopkov preferred to work with dramatizations of novels, and his productions were "cinematic" in their rapid cutting from one scene to another. But while his selection of plays was acceptable, his production approach was considered too anarchic. For a time his theatre was merged with Tairov's. In 1943 he was named head of the Theatre of the Revolution, where he was to be one of the most important directors of the postwar period.

DRAMA IN THE SOVIET UNION, 1917–1940

Gorky was the only pre-Revolutionary author who played an important role under the Communists. In 1932 he was named head of the Union of Soviet Writers as his early works came to be seen as models for socialist realism. But he wrote only two new plays, *Yegor Bulichev and Others* (1932) and *Dostigayev and Others* (1933), and even these concern life before the revolution.

In the relatively unfettered years before 1927 the futurist playwright Vladimir Mayakovsky (1894–1930) scored a great success with *Mystery-Bouffe* (1918) which parodied the Bible and ended with the proletariat entering the promised land in a production done by his close friend, Meyerhold. But his later works, *The Bedbug* (1929) and *The Bath-house* (1930) satirized Soviet bureaucracy and were so adversely criticized that Mayakovsky committed suicide. Similarly, the great melodrama writer Mikhail Bulgakov (1891–1940) scored a surprising success with *The Days of the Turbins* (1925), which sympathetically depicted the counterrevolutionary White Army faction against which the Communist Red Army had struggled for many years. Among the most popular of Soviet plays, it made Bulgakov suspect by the government, and thereafter his plays were often withdrawn from production. His *A Cabal of Hypocrites* (1929), about Molière and the censorship of *Tartuffe,* eventually led to a ban on all his plays. Other significant dramatists avoided these pitfalls by writing plays that praise life under Communism, and glorify Lenin and Stalin.

By the beginning of World War II, the Russian theatre had been subjugated to political pressures. Nevertheless, no country in the world took its theatre more seriously as a medium of ideas and as an integral part of society.

FIG. 19.14
Mayakovsky's *The Bedbug* as produced by Meyerhold in 1929.

FIG. 19.15
Trenyov's *Lyubov Yarovaya* at the Maly Theatre, Moscow, 1926.

GERMAN THEATRE AND DRAMA, 1918–1939

During World War I the German theatre continued without interruption and, unlike its English, French, and American counterparts, did not turn primarily to popular entertainment. When Germany became a republic and brought the war to an end in 1918, the former "royal" theatres were rechristened "state" theatres, but with few changes in organization or policy, and they continued to offer seasons composed of varied plays performed by permanent companies. After 1920, as economic conditions worsened and inflation skyrocketed, nonsubsidized groups found it necessary to abandon the repertory system in favor of new works tailored to popular tastes. Eventually most of the private theatres were taken over by municipalities.

Of the prewar producers, Max Reinhardt remained the most important. In 1918 he joined Hugo von Hofmannsthal and Richard Strauss in founding the Salzburg Festival in Austria were he annually produced von Hofmannsthal's *Everyman* (beginning in 1920) and *The Great Theatre of the World* (beginning in 1922). In Berlin he continued his management of the Deutsches and the Kammerspiele theatres while he also remodeled the Circus Schumann into the Grosses Schauspielhaus (seating more than 3500), where between 1919 and 1922 he presented a series of monumental productions, most notably the *Oresteia*, *Julius Caesar*, and Romain Rolland's *Danton*

(1900). The venture ultimately failed, perhaps because the theatre's great size discouraged subtlety and because the compromises demanded by the combined open and picture-frame stages were never entirely satisfactory.

In 1922 Reinhardt became director of Vienna's Theater in dem Redoutensaal, converted from an imperial ballroom of the 1740s, where against a background of screens he presented plays and operas of the eighteenth century. The intimacy of this theatre contrasted markedly with the immensity of the Grosses Schauspielhaus. Reinhardt continued his manifold activities until Hitler's rise to power forced him to give up his German theatres in 1933. Between 1905 and 1933 Reinhardt had personally directed 136 plays and through his experiments with production styles and theatre architecture had exerted a pervasive influence on the German stage. In the United States in the final years of his life, Reinhardt directed a few plays and films, but he never fully adjusted to his new situation.

Reinhardt's postwar activities were essentially continuations of practices he had begun before 1914. But other directors championed a new mode—expressionism—which for a few years dominated the German stage. The term *expressionism* first gained currency in France around 1901 as a label used to distinguish the kind of painting done by Van Gogh and Gauguin from that of the impressionists. Impressionism had sought to capture the appearance of objects as seen under a certain light at a particular moment, whereas expressionism was thought to project strong feelings into objects and to portray them

FIG. 19.16
Plan of Reinhardt's Grosses Schauspielhaus, remodeled from a circus building. At left, note the full proscenium stage with its revolving stage. Forward of the proscenium are a platform and arena. The theatre seated about 3500. From Barkhin, *Architectura Teatra* (Moscow, 1947).

FIG. 19.17
Europe, c. 1925.

as modified and distorted by the painter's own vision. Unfortunately, almost any departure from realism soon came to be labeled "expressionism" but its basic premises can still be outlined.

1. Expressionists shared the romanticist's view that truth is to be found in humanity's spiritual qualities.
2. Expressionists went beyond the romanticists in arguing that external reality is alterable and should be changed until it is brought into harmony with humanity's spiritual nature.
3. Expressionists had an anthropomorphic view of existence which led them to project human emotions and attitudes onto inanimate objects.

Drawing on these premises, expressionists opposed realism and naturalism on the grounds that those movements focused attention on surface details and implied that observable phenomena of contempo-

rary materialistic and mechanistic society represent fundamental truth. Since the expressionists' "truth" existed primarily within the subjective realm, it had to be expressed through new artistic means. Distorted line, exaggerated shape, abnormal coloring, mechanical movement, and telegraphic speech were devices commonly used to lead audiences beyond surface appearances. Often everything was shown through the eyes of the protagonist, whose view might alter emphases and impose drastic interpretations upon the events. Most expressionist plays were structurally episodic, deriving their unity from a central idea or argument, often holding out the promise of a future Utopia.

The Beggar (1912) by Reinhard Johannes Sorge (1892–1916) is often considered to be the first true expressionist play. It shows the struggle between established conventions and new values, between the older and younger generations, and the attempt of a visionary poet to achieve fulfillment in a materialistic

FIG. 19.18
Reinhardt's Redoutensaal Theater, Vienna, 1922, created within the ballroom of an eighteenth-century palace. The stage was erected without harming the walls of the ballroom. There was no proscenium arch or front curtain. From *Le Théâtre* (1922).

and insensitive society. Much the same idea is found in Walter Hasenclever's (1890–1940) *The Son* (1914), in which the protagonist threatens to kill his father because his freedom to experience life in all its glory is restricted by his puritanical and hypocritical parents; it was probably intended as a symbolic treatment of the need to rid the world of those old values and social forms standing in the way of the "new man."

With the coming of World War I, expressionism began to change as its emphasis moved from personal concerns to warnings of impending universal catastrophe or pleas for the reformation of humanity and society. Hasenclever's antiwar play *Antigone* (1916), for example, suggests that love is the only path to happiness but that it cannot be followed until unjust and autocratic rulers are overthrown. Similarly, Fritz von Unruh's (1885–1970) *One Race* (1918) shows how mistaken values and deeds (especially war) have dehumanized people, and it ends with a plea to storm "the barracks of violence" as a prelude to a better world.

By 1919 there were forty-four German-language expressionist periodicals, and German theaters began to take expressionist plays into their repertories. But the optimism that accompanied the end of the war (and that seemed to promise the possibility of achieving the expressionists' ideals) soon gave way to disappointment and disillusionment. By 1924 expressionism was virtually dead. This shift from optimism to pessimism is especially evident in the work of the two major expressionist playwrights—Kaiser and Toller.

Georg Kaiser (1878–1945) began his playwriting career in 1911 but his first important work in the ex-

pressionist vein was *From Morn to Midnight* (1916), in which a machine-age Everyman searches for the meaning of life only to become a martyr to callousness and greed. But, though the world is not yet ready for transformation, Kaiser seems to believe that his protagonist has pointed the way. Kaiser's trilogy of plays—*Coral* (1917), *Gas I* (1918), and *Gas II* (1920)—show the movement toward despair. In the first, the protagonist gradually comes to recognize the primacy of the soul, and in the second his son sets out to regenerate society. Though in neither play is the protagonist successful, both works are essentially optimistic about the future. But in *Gas II* Kaiser seems to have despaired of humanity, and when the play ends, the world is undergoing a cataclysmic destruction. After this time Kaiser abandoned the expressionist mode, though he continued to write until his death.

Ernst Toller (1893–1939) wrote his first play, *Transfiguration* (1918), while serving a prison term for antiwar activities. It shows the gradual evolution of its hero from a naive patriotic soldier to ardent antiwar revolutionary seeking to help fight oppressors. Toller's most influential work was to be *Man and the Masses* (1921), the story of a woman's struggle to aid workers, and her defeat by those who place ideological above humanitarian principles. By the time Toller wrote *Hurrah, We Live!* (1927) his disillusionment was complete. This play shows former idealists, now settled into comfortable lives, repeating the mistakes they once rebelled against. In protest against such madness, the protagonist commits suicide.

Between 1919 and 1924 expressionism also became a major style of production, especially as

FIG. 19.19
Jessner's production of Shakespeare's *Richard III* at the Berlin State Theater in 1919. Setting by Emil Pirchan. Courtesy Theatermuseum, Munich.

applied by Jessner and Fehling. Leopold Jessner (1878–1945) had worked in Hamburg and Königsberg before becoming director of the Berlin State Theatre from 1919 until 1933. Here he won international fame for his imaginative use of flights of steps (*Jessnertreppen*) and platforms as the major compositional elements in his productions. His principal designers, Emil Pirchan and Cesar Klein, discarded representational scenery for stylized pieces which, along with costumes and lighting, were selected primarily for their emotional and symbolic qualities. Jessner's production of *Richard III* is typical of his approach; the blood-red costumes and light used at the peak of Richard's power dissolved into white costumes and light as Richmond's forces came to the fore. Despite his fame as an expressionist director, Jessner worked primarily with the classics. In 1933 he emigrated to the United States.

Unlike Jessner, Jürgen Fehling (1890–1968) made his reputation with expressionist drama, beginning with Toller's *Man and the Masses* at Berlin's Volksbühne in 1921. Fehling sought to arouse intense emotional response in spectators. In his production, bankers fox-trotted to the sound of jingling coins while workers did a wild dance set to the tune of a concertina and accompanied by constantly shifting colored lights. Fehling was more eclectic than Jessner, both in the kinds of plays he directed and in the devices he used. He remained in Germany under the Nazis, serving as director of the Berlin State Theatre.

As expressionism declined, a more militant approach, eventually to be called "Epic Theatre," arose. Its first major practitioner was Erwin Piscator (1893–1966). Piscator served as director of Berlin's Volksbühne theatre (1924–1927), where he sought to create a "proletarian drama," as opposed to merely producing standard plays for a working-class audience. His ideological reshaping of texts, however, aroused such controversy that he resigned in 1927 to found the Piscator Theater. There he perfected many of the techniques later associated with Epic Theatre and pioneered the use of filmed sequences, cartoons, treadmills, segmented settings, and other devices to draw strong parallels between the dramatic events of the plays he produced and recent European history, thus arguing the need for social and political reforms. Like Reinhardt and Jessner, Piscator left Germany in 1933 and in 1939 went to the United States, where until 1951 he taught at the New School for Social Research and staged a number of plays in New York and elsewhere.

Despite Piscator's pioneering work, Epic Theatre is now associated primarily with Bertolt Brecht

FIG. 19.20
Piscator's setting for Toller's *Hurrah, We Live!* From *Theatre Arts* (1932).

(1891–1956), the movement's major theoretician and dramatist. Brecht entered the theatre as a director in Munich and later worked as a *dramaturg* for Reinhardt in Berlin. As a playwright, he experimented with dada and expressionism in such early plays as *Baal* (1918) and *Drums in the Night* (1922) before arriving at his more characteristic style with *Man is Man* (1926). His first major success came with a play he cowrote with Elizabeth Hauptmann, *The Three-Penny Opera* (1928). With music by Kurt Weill (1900–1950) and settings by Caspar Neher (1897–1962), it ran for 400 performances. In 1933 Brecht went into exile, during which he wrote most of his major works: *Mother Courage and Her Children* (1938–1939), emphasizing both the endurance and the callousness of a woman during the Thirty Years' War; *Galileo* (1937–1939); *The Good Woman of Setzuan* (1938–1940); and *The Caucasian Chalk Circle* (1944–1945), Brecht's last major play. Because of his exile, Brecht's works were little produced until he returned to Germany in 1947, but subsequently they became increasingly important throughout the world. Noted Brecht scholar John Fuegi has argued that while Brecht was a remarkable director, most of the dramatic writing for which he took credit was actually done by Elizabeth Hauptmann, Margarete Steffin, Ruth Berlau, or Martin Pohl, but this is an accusation that is still being debated.

Regardless of the outcome of the debate over the authorship of these highly regarded plays, Brecht's theory of theatre has been enormously influential in its own right. Brecht called his approach "epic" in order to indicate its broad sweep and its mixture of narrative and dramatic techniques. He wished to assign audiences an active role in the theatre by making them watch critically rather than passively. Consequently, he arrived at the concept of "alienation" *(verfremdungseffekt)*, or making stage events sufficiently strange that the spectator will ask questions about them. To create this thoughtful contemplation and to prevent the spectator from confusing stage events with real-life events, Brecht wanted theatrical means (such as lighting instruments, musicians, scene changes) to be visible and as simple as possible. He also deliberately separated episodes by inserting songs, captions, or narrative passages between them. Brecht hoped to lead the audience to relate what they saw on the stage to socioeconomic conditions outside the theatre; ultimately, he wished the audience to apply its new perceptions by working for change in their own world.

Unlike Appia and Craig, Brecht did not believe that a unified effect should be sought from all the theatrical elements. Calling such unity redundant, he argued that each element should make a different comment on the action. He also rejected Stanislavsky's approach to acting and advised performers to think of their roles "in the third person" and through their acting comment on the characters'

FIG. 19.21

Brecht's *Threepenny Opera*, first production, at the Theater am Schiffbauerdamm. Berlin, 1928. Directed by Erich Engel, setting by Caspar Neher. Courtesy Theatermuseum, Munich.

motivations and actions. Brecht's theory and practice have profoundly influenced directors throughout the world.

Still another experiment of the 1920s—the Bauhaus—was to have considerable international impact. In 1919, Walter Gropius (1883–1969) established a School of Fine Arts and of Arts and Crafts at the Staatliches Bauhaus in Weimar. Its goals were to unite architecture, painting, sculpture, and other arts into a communal expression and to make it a part of daily life free from the elitist status which had confined it primarily to museums or the homes of the wealthy. Ultimately the Bauhaus wished to shape daily surroundings into a "master art work" in which everything from the landscaping to the house, its furnishings, decorations, and even its kitchen utensils are conceived as parts of a total design for living. It sought to make the functional artistic and the artistic functional.

From 1923 until 1929 the Bauhaus's stage workshop was under the direction of Oskar Schlemmer (1888–1943), who was concerned primarily with three-dimensional figures in space. Rather than trying to adjust stage space to the natural human form, he sought to unify the human body with the abstract stage space, and consequently he altered the human shape through three-dimensional costumes that transformed actors into "ambulant architecture" and controlled their movement with mathematical precision. Schlemmer ignored the verbal element, but he systematically analyzed each visual element (empty space, the human figure, movement, light, and color) both in isolation and in various combinations. Like much of the Bauhaus's work, Schlemmer's can probably best be viewed as a form of basic research, the results of which might be applied in various ways to practical problems. Beginning in the 1920s his experiments were especially influential on dance. A painter, Schlemmer also designed scenery for a number of German directors.

In theatre architecture, the Bauhaus's most important work was done by Gropius, who in 1927 designed a "total theatre" for Piscator. Although never built, its design has continued to influence thinking about theatre architecture. According to Gropius, there are only three basic stage forms—arena, thrust, and proscenium—and in his total theatre he sought to accommodate all. He mounted a segment of seats and an acting area on a large revolvable circle forward of the proscenium. When this acting area was moved to a position contiguous with the proscenium, it formed a thrust stage, and when rotated 180 degrees it became an arena. From the wings of the proscenium stage ran an open platform which continued completely around the outer edge of the auditorium,

FIG. 19.22

Gropius's "total theatre." Note the gray circle which joins the mainstage to form a thrust stage. This circle, along with the seating shown on the larger circle, could be revolved to place the acting area in the middle of the auditorium to create an arena stage. Note the ramp surrounding the auditorium which also could be used for acting. The triangles represent the beams of projectors which made it possible to surround the audience with projected settings or moving pictures. From Barkhin, *Architectura Teatra* (Moscow, 1947).

and could be used as an acting area or for scenery shifted on it by means of wagons. A wide stage house also permitted rolling platforms to move horizontally. Spaced around the perimeter of the auditorium were twelve columns between which projection screens could be mounted. A translucent cyclorama at the rear of the proscenium stage also provided a surface for projections, and other screens were mounted in the auditorium above the heads of the spectators. Gropius declared that he wished to place the audience in the midst of the action and "to force them to participate in experiencing the play."

The Bauhaus was always controversial, and when the Nazis came to power it was forced to close. Its members dispersed throughout the world, but their influence upon design and architecture (especially furniture, interior decor, and the steel and glass build-

ings of our cities) became so pervasive that its source is now often unrecognized.

With the advent of Hitler in 1933, many important theatre artists left Germany. Many of those who remained underwent what has been called an "inner emigration"—writing or staging historical works or deliberately distancing their work from the contemporary scene. The Nazis encouraged plays about the Teutonic past, enormous outdoor spectacles, and a production style calculated to evoke a grandiose, larger-than-life picture of an all-powerful Nordic world. Theatrical personnel were seldom overtly required to comply with Nazi ideology, and several were able to retain relative independence. For the most part, however, the German theatre between 1933 and 1945 was subordinated to political demands.

THEATRE AND DRAMA IN FRANCE, 1914–1939

World War I severely curtailed theatrical activities in France. Practically all able-bodied actors were inducted and others spent much of their time performing for the armed forces. The Parisian companies were so depleted that even the Comédie Française had to fill out casts with students from the Conservatoire. The wartime mood turned the theatre toward popular entertainment, a direction which continued to dominate the "boulevard theatres" after the war. Of the boulevard producers, the most successful was Sacha Guitry (1885–1957), author of about 150 plays, most of which he produced, directed, and starred in.

At the opposite extreme, a series of revolts against tradition—fauvism, cubism, futurism, constructivism, dada, and surrealism—helped to break the hold of realism and to turn attention to new forms. During the war many artists and political dissenters sought refuge in Switzerland, where dada, the most extreme of the revolts, was launched in 1916. The principal spokesman for dada was Tristan Tzara (1896–1963), who published seven manifestoes between 1916 and 1920. Dada was grounded in a thoroughgoing skepticism about a world that could produce a global war. Since insanity seemed the world's true state, the dadaists sought in their actions to replace logic and reason with calculated madness, and in their art to substitute discord and chaos for unity, structure, and harmony. They presented a number of programs composed of recitations, "chance" (words arranged in chance order) or "sound" (wordless) poems, dances, visual art, and short plays. Often several things were going on simultaneously. As the war drew to a close, the dadaists dispersed. For a time, the movement thrived in Germany, but it received its greatest support in Paris. Much of what it stood for was to resurface in the 1960s under other names.

In France, dada was absorbed into surrealism, which drew much of its inspiration from the works of Jarry and Apollinaire. Guillaume Apollinaire (1880–1918), friend to almost all *avant-garde* writers and painters after 1900 and the principal spokesman for cubism, influenced surrealism largely through his play, *The Breasts of Tiresias* (1903, revised and produced in 1917), subtitled a "drame surréaliste." Purporting to be a plea for the repopulation of France, the play concerns Thérèse, who after releasing her breasts (balloons, which float away) is transformed into Tiresias. Her husband, now forced to take over her functions, eventually discovers the means of creating children (sheer willpower) and becomes the parent of more than forty thousand offspring. This work exemplifies many of Apollinaire's theories in which he rejected everyday logic and suggested that comedy, tragedy, burlesque, fantasy, acrobatics, and declamation should be mingled with music, dance, color, and light to create a form of expression free from everyday logic.

André Breton (1896–1966) was the acknowledged leader of the surrealists and issued the movement's first "manifesto" in 1924. Freud's considerable influence upon Breton is evident in his definition of surrealism as "pure psychic automatism, by which is intended to express, verbally, in writing, or by other means, the real process of thought. Thought's dictation, in the absence of all control exercised by the reason and outside all esthetic or moral preoccupation." Thus, the subconscious mind in a dreamlike state represented for Breton the source of artistic truth. After his conversion to communism in 1926, Breton sought to make surrealism more militant, and his second manifesto (1929) denounced many of the movement's former members. Thereafter, surrealism declined, although its crowning achievement did not come until 1938, when an international exhibition of painting demonstrated the movement's considerable accomplishments.

Surrealism's impact on the theatre was essentially indirect. The most effective uses of its techniques were made by Jean Cocteau (1892–1963), who began his theatrical work with *Parade* (1917), a ballet staged by the Ballets Russes, and *The Ox on the Roof* (1920), a pantomime performed by the Fratellini family of circus clowns. His finest plays, *Antigone* (1922), *Orpheus* (1926), and *The Infernal Machine* (1934), based on the Oedipus legend, are reworkings of myths. Cocteau's power came in part from his ability to make the mythic seem familiar and the familiar seem mythic. For example, in *Orpheus* the Orpheus and Eurydice of Greek mythology are depicted as a modern married couple, but this commonplace situation soon takes on an air of mystery when a glazier remains suspended in mid-air when a chair on which he has been standing is removed and when a horse speaks oracular messages. Associational patterns create relationships which illuminate both ancient myth and modern values.

Many of the new movements in the visual arts came into the theatre through the Ballets Russes, which after 1915 replaced its Russian designers with such major painters as Picasso, Matisse, Juan Gris, Marie Laurencin, and Braque. The Ballets Suédois, which performed in Paris between 1920 and 1925 under the direction of Rolf de Maré (1888–1964), also commissioned settings from Léger, de Chirico, and Picabia. This company extended the traditional conceptions of ballet as well through such works as Cocteau's *The Marriage Party on the Eiffel Tower* (1921), in which dance was accompanied by dialogue and narrative spoken by actors costumed as phonographs.

Of all the *avant-garde* figures between the wars, Antonin Artaud (1896–1948), originally a surrealist, was to be the most important. Associated with the theatre from 1921, Artaud had worked with Lugné-Poë, Dullin, and Pitoëff before founding the Théâtre Alfred Jarry in 1926 in association with Roger Vitrac, a surrealist playwright. Devoted entirely to nonrealistic drama, this theatre lasted only two seasons. Artaud's most significant contributions were to be made after 1931, when the stimulation of a Balinese dance troupe motivated him to

FIG. 19.23
Cocteau's surrealistic version of *Antigone,* as produced by Charles Dullin at the Atelier, Paris, 1922. From *Le Théâtre* (1923).

formulate his theory of the theatre, published in 1938 as *The Theatre and Its Double.*

According to Artaud, the theatre in the Western world has been devoted to a very narrow range of human experience, primarily the psychological problems of individuals or the social problems of groups. But to Artaud, the more important aspects of existence are those submerged in the unconscious, those things that cause divisions within people and between people and lead to hatred, violence, and disaster. He believed that if given the proper theatrical experiences, people can be freed from ferocity and can then express the joy that civilization has forced them to repress, for the theatre can evacuate those feelings that are usually expressed in more destructive ways. Or, as Artaud put it, "the theatre has been created to drain abscesses collectively."

Artaud was certain that his goals could not be reached through appeals to the rational mind. Rather, it would be necessary to operate directly upon the senses and break down the audience's defenses. Artaud sometimes referred to his as a "theatre of cruelty," since in order to achieve its ends it sought to force the audience to confront itself. Thus, the cruelty he advocated is not primarily physical but moral or psychological.

Artaud's intention to operate directly on the nervous system led him to suggest many innovations in theatrical practice. Among these was the substitution of new myths for outworn dramatic "masterpieces," replacement of the traditional theatre building with remodeled barns, factories, or airplane hangars. He wished to place the audience in the center of the action by locating acting areas in corners, on overhead catwalks, and along the walls. In lighting, he called for a "vibrating, shredded" effect, and in sound he favored shrillness, abrupt changes in volume, and the use of the human voice to create harmonies and dissonances. Thus, Artaud wanted to assault the audience, to break down its resistance, to purge it morally and spiritually, and he sought to do this through devices "addressed first of all to the senses rather than to the mind," for "the public thinks first of all with its senses."

Like Appia and Craig, Artaud was a visionary rather than a wholly practical man, and like them he was at first little appreciated. But Artaud differed drastically from Appia and Craig in his conception of the theatre's ultimate purpose. Appia and Craig tended to value art for its own sake, whereas Artaud saw in it the salvation of mankind. Theirs is a world of idealized beauty, his a region of cruel torment. Consequently, as the post-World War II view of humanity darkened, the influence of Appia and Craig declined as that of Artaud increased.

Somewhere between the commercial and *avant-garde* figures of France were Gémier, Hébertot, and Copeau. Firmin Gémier (1869–1933) began his acting career with Antoine in 1892 and later worked with groups ranging from the Théâtre de l'Oeuvre to melodrama troupes. Perhaps for this reason, Gémier followed an eclectic approach not unlike that of Reinhardt. From 1906 until 1922 he served as director of the Théâtre Antoine, and from 1922 until 1930 as director of the Odéon. Under Gémier, the Odéon became almost an *avant-garde* theatre, in part because his designer, René Fuerst, drew upon practically all of the recent movements. Despite Gémier's fine work as a director, his major contribution probably was his ongoing attempt to bring the theatre to all the people.

The desire to make cultural activities available to the common people had led in the 1890s to the Volksbühnen of Germany and the less ambitious "people's theatres" of France. In 1903 Romain Rolland's *The Theatre of the People* outlined a program under which local groups would write and perform plays for their fellow citizens as in Greek times. Attracted by this movement, Gémier sought to make the best professional productions available to provincial audiences through his Théâtre Ambulant, which between 1911 and 1913 toured France with a tent theatre. In 1920 Gémier persuaded the government to create the Théâtre National Populaire (TNP). Given only a token subsidy, Gémier relied on other companies to contribute occasional productions to the TNP. Although never a significant force during Gémier's lifetime, the TNP was to become one of France's finest theatres after World War II. Gémier's interests in a popular theatre also led him into other experiments. In 1919 he took over the Cirque d'Hiver, where he staged *Oedipus, King of Thebes* by Bouhélier and *The Great Pastoral,* a Provençal nativity play. In this and other ways, Gémier's work in France paralleled that of Reinhardt in Germany.

Jacques Hébertot (1886–1971) exerted his primary influence as an entrepreneur. In his three contiguous theatres, the Théâtre des Champs-Elysées, the Comédie des Champs-Elysées, and the Studio des Champs-Elysées, between 1920 and 1925, he employed the most imaginative directors of his age. Furthermore, he imported such companies as the Moscow Art Theatre, the Kamerny, and others. Thus, Hébertot made the best of both domestic and foreign theatre available to the Parisian public.

The most pervasive influence on the theatre between the wars was exerted by Jacques Copeau, who reopened the Vieux Colombier in 1919 and rededicated himself to the ideals he had set forth before the war. Unlike Gémier, Copeau thought it impossible to maintain high standards while appealing to the masses. Consequently, he was often accused of snobbery and of treating the theatre as a religion. Eventually, Copeau found it difficult to reconcile his high standards with a full schedule of public performances, and in 1924 he left Paris to open a school in Burgundy, where he hoped to perfect his ideas.

Although Copeau's company performed for only five years after the war, its ideals were to be continued by four other producers—Jouvet, Dullin, Pitoëff, and Baty—who dominated the Parisian theatre until World War II. In 1927 they formed an alliance, commonly called the *Cartel des Quatre,* under which they agreed to counsel each other, to share publicity, and to negotiate jointly with theatrical unions.

Louis Jouvet (1887–1951) began his career in Rouché's Théâtre des Arts where he met Copeau, for whom he acted minor roles in 1913–1914. Jouvet formed his own company in 1924, taking into it many members of Copeau's recently disbanded troupe. Jouvet's greatest success came after he began his collaboration with playwright Jean Giraudoux in 1928. In 1934 he moved his company to the Théâtre de l'Athenée, a boulevard house, where he remained until 1941, after which he went into voluntary exile until the end of the war. Jouvet, like Copeau, put primary emphasis on the text. Above all, he respected language and its nuances. He demanded lucid analysis and careful attention to detail from his actors. In the early years he designed his own scenery, which was always tasteful without being innovative. At the Athenée, he usually worked with Christian Bérard (1902–1949), one of the finest designers of the period.

FIG. 19.24
Stage of the Vieux Colombier as adapted for Shakespeare's *Twelfth Night*. From *Theatre Arts Magazine* (1924).

Charles Dullin (1885–1949) had played at many minor theatres before joining Rouché and then Copeau. After returning to Paris in 1919, he worked for Gémier before establishing his own theatre, l'Atelier, in 1922. He remained in this small, out-of-the-way theatre until 1939. Dullin was extremely eclectic, presenting works ranging from the Greeks to the present and from tragedy to farce. Through painstaking analysis of the text, he sought to let each play dictate the proper approach to it. His aim was to capture the "inner poetry" through honesty and unity. He refused to do any play that he thought depended upon machinery or upon a director's tricks. Nevertheless, he put considerable emphasis on visual design and music, dance, and mime figured prominently in practically all of his productions. Dullin's perennial hope of attracting a wider audience led him in 1941 to become director of the Théâtre Sarah Bernhardt, a very large house, where he struggled along until 1947. His last years were spent in Geneva as director of the theatre section of the Maison des Arts. Ultimately, Dullin's impact on the theatre was to come in large part through his school, in which such significant later figures as Barrault and Vilar received their early training.

Georges Pitoëff (1884–1939) had performed widely in his native Russia before emigrating to Switzerland in 1914. He and his wife, Ludmilla (1896–1951), came to Paris in 1922 and formed their own company in 1925. Pitoëff was noted for his knowledge of foreign drama, of which he was the principal producer in France. As a director, Pitoëff placed primary emphasis upon the text. For him, the most powerful element was perhaps rhythm, which he sought to find and project for each character and scene. He designed his own scenery, which ranged stylistically from the abstract to the realistically pictorial. Characteristically, however, he used a few indispensable set pieces which he invested with symbolic significance. Of all the members of the Cartel, Pitoëff was probably the most versatile and experimental.

Gaston Baty (1882–1951) was the only member of the Cartel who was not an actor and who did not place primary emphasis on the text. He began his career under Gémier in 1919, managed the Studio des Champs-Elysées from 1924 to 1928, and then settled in the Théâtre Montparnasse in 1930. After 1935, Baty became extremely interested in marionettes, as a result of which his productions became increasingly stylized. To Baty, the director was the major theatrical artist. In his productions, a mysterious and poetic world, created by the skillful manipulation of mood, seemed to lurk behind a realistic surface. His emphasis on costumes, scenery, properties, music, and lighting was sometimes criticized, but he was also known as the "magician of the *mise-en-scène.*"

In 1930 students from Copeau's school formed the Compagnie des Quinze under the direction of Michel Saint-Denis (1897–1971), Copeau's nephew, and from 1931 to 1933 they played at the Vieux Colombier. After the company disbanded, Saint-Denis opened the Theatre Studio in London, which, in combination with his directing work at the Old Vic and elsewhere, served to carry Copeau's influence into the British theatre. Copeau returned to a more active role in the theatre during the 1930s. In addition to directing both in Paris and abroad, he was associated with the Comédie Française after 1936 and served as its director in 1939–1940 until dismissed by the Vichy government.

Under Emile Fabré's direction between 1915 and 1936, the Comédie Française had steadily declined, in large part because of low subsidy and political interference. After 1936, the new director, Edouard Bourdet (1887–1945), was able to make many improvements. Not only was the subsidy doubled, Bourdet imported Copeau, Dullin, Jouvet, and Baty to direct several revivals. For the first time in its history, the Comédie Française began to list each play's director on its programs. By the time the war began, the prestige of the company was fully revived.

Although France produced few truly outstanding playwrights between the wars, a number achieved

FIG. 19.25

Pitoëff's production of *Romeo and Juliet.* Note the strong emphasis on triangular shapes and converging lines, giving an expressionistic effect. From *Theatre Arts* (1935).

considerable renown. Henri-René Lenormand (1882–1951) was one of the first French writers to emphasize the subconscious mind and the relativity of time and space through such works as *Time Is a Dream* (1919) and *The Eater of Dreams* (1922). Henri Ghéon (1875–1944) sought to revive religious drama and for many years toured with his Compagnons de Notre-Dame. Of the satirical writers, the best were Jules Romains (1885–1972), whose *Doctor Knock, or the Triumph of Medicine* (1923) shows the exploitation of people's anxieties about their health, and Marcel Pagnol (1895–1974), whose *The Merchants of Glory* (1925) satirizes the business schemes built around the war dead. Surrealistic farce was exploited by Fernand Crommelynck (1888–1970), whose *The Magnificent Cuckold* (1921) tells of a man who, upon becoming suspicious of his wife's fidelity, insists on testing it endlessly.

The plays of the Belgian dramatist Michel de Ghelderode (1898–1962) resemble those of Jarry, the surrealists, and the expressionists, and his theories recall those of Artaud. Throughout his more than thirty plays runs his vision of humans as creatures whose flesh overpowers spirit. Corruption, death, and cruelty are always near the surface, although behind them lurks an implied criticism of degradation and materialism and a call to repentance. Like Artaud, Ghelderode downgrades language in favor of spectacle. Place is apt to shift rapidly and unexpectedly; characters are usually exaggerated and many are descended from the clowns of music hall, circus, and fair. His scorn for traditional dramaturgy is shown by the labels he applied to his work: "tragic farce," "burlesque mystery," "tragedy for the music hall," and so on. After 1949, when he came to the attention of the absurdists, Ghelderode's reputation rose considerably.

Probably the most important French dramatist between the wars was Jean Giraudoux (1882–1944), a novelist and member of the Foreign Service, who in 1928 began his theatrical career with a dramatization of his novel *Siegfried.* In Jouvet, Giraudoux found his ideal interpreter and he wrote most of his important works for him: *Amphitryon 38* (1929), *Judith* (1931), *The Trojan War Shall Not Take Place* (1935), and *Ondine* (1939). Giraudoux often took his subjects from familiar sources but gave them novel interpretations, for he delighted in pointing out the simple in the complex and the surprising in the familiar. His dramas take place at the moment when people are faced with a choice between two contradictory positions; he explores the contradictions and usually suggests means whereby they can be reconciled, often through some novel perception. Language, which he considered the highest expression

FIG. 19.26

André Barsacq's setting for Dullin's production of *Volpone*, 1929. From *Décor de Théâtre dans le Monde depuis* 1935.

of human reason, is Giraudoux's primary means. Writing at a time when the playwright had been subordinated to the director, Giraudoux sought to reaffirm the literary worth of drama. He wrote in a euphonious and highly expressive prose, with a marked disposition for fantasy, irony, and humor. Throughout all his work runs a deep faith in humanity.

Giraudoux's position of preeminence was to be challenged after the war by Jean Anouilh (1910–1987), who began as Jouvet's secretary and turned to writing in 1932 under Giraudoux's inspiration. His first success came in 1937 with *Traveller Without Baggage,* presented by Pitoëff. Most of Anouilh's later works, such as *Carnival of Thieves* (1938) and *Antigone* (1943), were produced by Barsacq. Anouilh divided his plays into the serious, or "black" pieces, and the comic, or "red" pieces. In the former, typically young, idealistic, and uncompromising protagonists are able to maintain their integrity only by choosing death. *Antigone* is perhaps the best-known example. In the "red" plays, although the characters are in many ways similar, a fairy-tale atmosphere permits a happier resolution. Anouilh was to be one of France's most prolific writers after World War II.

With the coming of war in 1939 and the surrender of Paris to the Nazis, theatrical activities were at first seriously curtailed. Some major figures went into exile and those who remained were subject to close surveillance. For the most part, the theatre was reduced to politically inoffensive plays or popular entertainments, but a few productions were to attain true eminence despite all strictures.

ITALIAN THEATRE AND DRAMA, 1914–1939

During World War I a new school of writing, usually called "the theatre of the grotesque," appeared in Italy. Its name was derived from *The Mask and the Face* (1916), "a grotesque in three acts," by Luigi Chiarelli (1880–1947). Turning upon the contrast between public and private role-playing, this comedy tells the story of a man who, after confessing to the murder of his wife because he thought her unfaithful, is tried and acquitted, although in actuality she is merely locked up at home.

Luigi Pirandello (1867–1936) was by far the greatest Italian playwright of the period. After winning fame with his novels and short stories, Pirandello turned to playwriting in 1910 and after 1915 devoted himself increasingly to the theatre. From 1924 to 1928 he headed the Art Theatre of Rome, where he presented many significant Italian and foreign plays.

Pirandello's plays, of which the best are *Right You Are—If You Think You Are* (1916), *Six Characters in Search of an Author* (1921), *Henry IV* (1922), *Each in His Own Way* (1924), and *Tonight We Improvise* (1930), usually turn upon a question of fact that cannot be resolved because each character has his own version of the truth. Thus, Pirandello raises doubts about the validity of the scientific approach to truth—the direct observation of reality. He seems to suggest that "truth" is necessarily personal and subjective. Since for him even the most realistic play could only give a travesty of truth, he thought the only remedy lay in writing philosophical plays that show reality as ever changing. Pirandello made a profound impression on his age. Perhaps no other writer did so much to popularize the philosophical view that was to be espoused by dramatists of the post-World War II period.

For the most part the Italian theatre between the wars was made up of touring companies playing the latest hits. A step toward improvement was taken in 1936 with the formation of the Academy of Dramatic Art in Rome under the direction of Silvio D'Amico (1887–1955). Here the principles of Stanislavsky, Copeau, and Reinhardt were taught. The coming of the war interrupted the academy's work, however, and its impact was not to be felt until after 1945.

THEATRE AND DRAMA IN SPAIN, 1914–1939

The most significant Spanish drama of the immediate postwar years was written by Miguel de Unamuno (1864–1936), one of Spain's most respected philosophers. He first expressed his theory of drama in *The Tragic Sense of Life* (1913). His declaration that tragedy stems from a conflict between the human desire for immortality and skepticism about its possibility was to contribute much to existentialist drama following World War II.

A new spirit began to enter Spanish literature with the "Generation of '27," a group which blossomed especially after censorship was eased under the second Republic (1931). Of the new dramatists, the most significant was Federico García Lorca (1899–1936) who wrote his first play, *The Butterfly's Crime*, in 1920. After its failure, he cultivated his interests in symbolism, surrealism, music, painting, and Spanish folklore, and wrote a number of puppet plays. Lorca's major plays were written only after he had worked closely with La Barraca, a troupe composed of university students and subsidized by the government under its program to bring cultural events to the people. Formed in 1932, La Barraca played Golden Age dramas to rural audiences, and it was the enthusiastic response of these unsophisticated spectators that influenced Lorca to turn to similar themes of love and honor. The results are seen in *Blood Wedding* (1933), *Yerma* (1934), and *The House of Bernarda Alba* (1935). Blending poetic imagery with primitive passions, these plays are usually considered the finest Spanish works since the Golden Age. Lorca, however, was executed during the Civil War of 1936.

During the war, the theatre served primarily as an instrument of propaganda for both sides of the conflict. Following the victory of Franco's forces in 1939, it suffered from severe censorship. The plays of Lorca, Casona, and Unamuno were forbidden, and the Spanish theatre entered another period of isolation.

THEATRE AND DRAMA IN LATIN AMERICA

Throughout Latin America, commercial theatres in the early twentieth century continued to be dominated by late nineteenth-century Spanish and French traditions of light comedy, musicals, and melodrama. They were also dependent on tours by European acting companies. World War I brought these tours to an end and opened the way for an independent theatre movement much like that seen in Europe a generation before. It was mid-century, however, before most countries in Latin America could claim the beginnings of a distinctive national theatre of their own.

Argentina was one of the first to lay the foundations for an identifiable national theatre. Over 200 shows by local writers, ranging from short farce comedies to serious full-length plays, were produced in its "glorious decade" of 1904–1914. But the period was best know for the triumph of *género chico* and naturalism. *Género chico* dramas were short plays, often with musical scores, which presented a sentimental view of the life of the lower classes. These plays lent themselves to a focus on local color and were therefore popular throughout Latin America, especially in Argentina where, by 1914, they took on their own distinctive form as *sainete orillero* and dominated the commercial theatre market. The best-known writer of this form was Alberto Vacarezza (1888–1939).

The naturalist plays were full length and far less sentimental. Florencio Sánchez (1875–1910), born in Uruguay but working mostly in Argentina, became the most highly regarded naturalist dramatist in Latin America during this period. He wrote more than twenty full-length plays. His best-known works, including *My Son the Lawyer* (1904), *Down the Gully* (1905), and *The Tigress* (1907), examine the conflict between the old rural system, which was rapidly being destroyed by accelerating immigration, and urbanization, with its resultant poverty and degradation of the human spirit. He was surrounded by a host of lesser writers in Buenos Aires.

Around the time of the First World War, theatres were started by immigrant communities, unions, and social welfare organizations. Out of the experiences of these people came *grotesco criollo*, a form that blended the short comic *sainete orillero* with the lack of sentimentality found in the plays of the naturalists. Armando Discépolo (1887–1971) is credited with initiating this form with *Mateo* (1923), in which he looks at the destroyed dreams of an immigrant community where the dominant social order ceases to function.

El Teatro del Pueblo (The People's Theatre), founded by Leónidas Barletta in 1925, soon became the leading independent theatre of the time, producing such plays as *Saverio the Cruel* (1936), *The Creator of Ghosts* (1936), and *The Desert Island* (1938), all experiments in expressionism by the famous novelist Roberto Arlt (1900–1942). Independent theatres also introduced the country to the works of Cocteau, Pirandello, and O'Neill. Eventually over 50 such theatres were created in Argentina, and many similar companies could be found all over Latin America. As the Depression came to South America during the early 1930s, governments began to subsidize some theatres, and Argentina's Teatro de la Comedia (1936), which became the Teatro Municipal de Buenos Aires in 1943, was an early model for the effective partnership of government and the arts in Latin America.

The development of a national theatre in Brazil was hampered by its continued dedication to French cultural inspiration. This was epitomized by the Amazon Theatre at Manaus, the provincial capital of Amazonia. There, 900 miles into the Amazon jungle, a spectacular French opera house was built by wealthy local rubber plantation owners in 1896. To underscore its French inspiration, the ceiling of the auditorium was painted to represent a vision of the heavens being viewed from beneath the Eiffel tower. The theatre had 250 seats at orchestra level and 450 seats distributed among its 90 boxes, arranged in three tiers. Many of the best touring shows of the time were brought to this frontier mecca until the rubber boom ended in the early 1920s, but it did nothing to encourage the development of an indigenous theatre. (Nonetheless, the Amazon Theatre became a national treasure in 1965.) Because of this strong French influence, reviews (*revistas*) were enormously popular. They contained considerable political satire until the Vargas dictatorship began censoring them in 1937.

Although in other areas of the arts Brazilians were in the forefront of experimentation with expressionism, futurism, surrealism, and other antirealist forms, such experiments had little impact on the nation's theatre. Independent theatres like the Teatro de Brinquedo, founded by Álvaro Moreyra in the early 1920s, and the Colméia (1922) struggled on without much immediate effect. Oswald de Andrade's (1890–1954) *King of the Candle* was perhaps the most highly regarded modernist script of its day, but it was not performed even by the independent groups. *May God Recompense You* (1932) by Joracy Camargo (1898–1973), by contrast, was the most successful Brazilian play of the period. It evoked a strongly leftist examination of bourgeois values that was extremely popular throughout South America at this time, but it was in all other respects a very traditional thesis play. Pedro Bloch (1914–2004) was equally conventional though heavily influenced by Pirandello. His plays were performed on Broadway in the early 1950s and some became the basis for early soap operas on Brazilian television.

It was not until 1940, with the establishment of Os Comediantes, that nonrealistic techniques of staging, design, and dramaturgy began to meet with some success. When the Polish director Zbigniew Ziembinski joined the company in 1941, he was able to bring first-hand experience with German expressionism to the Brazilian stage. His production of *The Wedding Gown* (1943) by Nelson Rodrigues (1912–1980), now considered Brazil's greatest dramatist, is generally said to mark the beginning of modern Brazilian theatre.

The development of theatre in Mexico was delayed by the revolution of 1910, which was followed by a succession of reformist governments. Although the worst of the turmoil was over by 1920, there was no real stability until the election of Lázaro Cárdenas in 1934.

The Teatro National in Mexico City was a perfect symbol of this arrested development. In 1900 it was torn down as part of a major urban renewal project. Rebuilding began in 1905, but political unrest delayed its completion until 1934 and it was not to house a resident national theatre company until 1974. The venerable Teatro Principal was renovated in 1900 but by the late 1920s was reduced to being open only on weekends, and when it was destroyed by fire in 1931 it was not rebuilt. Several smaller theatres were constructed both in the capital and in the provinces before the revolution, including the state-of-the-art Teatro-Circo Xicoténcarl (1912), which was the only one to open during the revolutionary years. But the most noticeable trend in the first half of the twentieth century was for theatres to be converted into cinemas, as was happening worldwide.

Zarzuela and short comedies dominated the commercial theatres in Mexico as they did elsewhere. Naturalistic plays were the most successful form of legitimate drama and plays like *The Revenge of the Soil* (1904) highlighted the grievances of the lower classes which lay at the heart of the coming revolution.

A number of companies set themselves the task of reforming Mexican theatre during this time. As early as 1923, the well-known actor-manager María Tereza Montoya (1898–1974) secured a municipal subsidy to stage a season of Mexican plays. In 1925 seven Mexican dramatists known as the *Grupo de los Siete Autores* dedicated themselves to writing plays inspired by the European *avant-garde*. Most of the plays of this group were produced by Comedia Mexicana, founded by playwright Amalia González Caballero de Castillo Ledón (1898–1986) in 1922 (though it did not become a significant producing organization for several years.) Its production of *Father Merchant* (1929), by Carlos Díaz Dufoo (1861–1941), was its greatest success, becoming the first Mexican play to achieve a run of 100 performances.

The two most important figures involved in Mexican theatre in this period were Xavier Villaurrutia (1903–1950) and Rodolfo Usigli (1905–1979). Both had studied at Yale with George Pierce Baker. Villaurrutia returned to write plays that focused on the *avant-garde's* concern with the subconscious mind and complex human relationships. He co-founded the experimental Teatro de Ulises, with Salvador Novo (1904–1974) in 1928 and when it closed in 1932 joined the Teatro de Orientación, for which he wrote his most successful plays. Villaurrutia was the most experimental antirealist of his generation but he also began a vogue for adaptations of Greek classics with plays like *The Ivy* (1941), an adaptation of Euripides' *Hippolytus*.

Usigli was less experimental but more aggressively independent as a writer-director. He was concerned with the social problems that he believed arose out of the nation's lack of confidence, a lack he blamed on Mexico's colonial past. He saw the subjugation of women as an especially egregious consequence of that past and believed it led to a kind of sexual hypocrisy that was the focus of much of his sardonic wit. His play, *The Gesticulator* (sometimes called *The Imposter*, written in 1937 but not produced until 1947), deals with a second-rate history professor who pretends to be an important revolutionary leader long presumed dead. It is an indictment of the inability of people to live life without playing a role but was interpreted by many of his contemporaries as a criticism of the revolution and was therefore banned shortly after it opened. Today it is considered one of the most important of modern Mexican plays. Another of his plays to be produced in 1947, *The Crown of Shadows* (1943), is also considered to be a classic of Mexican theatre. In it, he examines the theme of history's influence on the present by looking at the downfall of the Emperor Maximilian. He founded the Teatro de Medianoche in 1940, with the declared purpose of operating without a subsidy, but the experiment failed after one season. Usigli was also an important drama critic, an influential university professor, a diplomat, and the author of several important histories of theatre in Mexico.

Another dominant figure of the 1930s was Julio Bracho, who formed a series of experimental theatres and managed not only to secure one of the first state subsidies for such an organization but also to tour the provinces with the first experimental company to be seen there. In the 1940s the major figure was Seki Santo (1905–1966), a young Japanese director who had studied with Stanislavski and worked with Meyerhold for five years before immigrating to Mexico in 1939. He founded the Teatro de la Reforma (1948) dedicated to "theatre of the people for the people," which inspired a number of imitators. Santo inspired and helped to train many of those who would lead Mexican theatre in the second half of the century.

The theatres in other Latin American countries generally followed similar patterns of development to those outlined here, though many of them progressed more slowly and were still focused on naturalism and light comedy well into the 1950s.

LOOKING AT THEATRE HISTORY

Following World War I, the American stage began to show the influence of Europe. American scene designers transformed the kinds of setting that had been typical on the New York stage. The results came to be labeled the "new stagecraft," although essentially it was new only in America, since for the most part it was merely an adaptation of scenic practices that had long dominated European stages. In writing about the transformation, Kenneth Macgowan noted:

> No art was so thoroughly conventionalized as was scenery-making when the new stagecraft began its reforms. The flat scenery and those large color cut-outs that ornamented the Christmas extravaganzas were all

a flimsy pretense of reality [as were the landscapes and paneled rooms]. . . . It was against all of these unreal and unbeautiful conventionalisms that the new stagecraft "made war."

Kennneth Macgowan, "The New Stagecraft in America," *Century Magazine* 87 (Jan. 1914), 416–21.

Perhaps the most controversial American production of the 1920s was Arthur Hopkins' presentation in 1921 of *Macbeth*, starring Lionel Barrymore with settings by Robert Edmond Jones. (See Fig. 19.7.) Even though the new stagecraft had been welcomed by many critics, Jones's symbolic setting offended many, and their disparaging (even insulting) reviews frightened many contemporary designers, with the result that most Broadway designers subsequently seldom deviated from a style best described as modified realism. Kenneth Macgowan described Jones's vision of *Macbeth*:

> [Jones] saw the dominant element of Macbeth as the abnormal influence of the power symbolized. . . in the witches. He tried to visualize the superhuman nature of these mystic forces in gigantic masks appearing high in the air above the blasted heath. Through the rest of the play, he placed upon the stage very simple and abstract forms to carry the mood induced by the supernatural influences which seize and dominate the characters constantly throughout Macbeth.
>
> Kenneth Macgowan, *Theatre of Tomorrow.* New York, 1921.

Eugene O'Neill quickly became the American playwright most admired at home and abroad. His adoption of several styles ranging through realism, expressionism, symbolism, and other modes marked him as a writer constantly experimenting. Among his plays, *Mourning Becomes Electra*, a play heavily influenced by Aeschylus' *Oresteia*, was one of the most ambitious. In his review, Hiram Motherwell wrote:

> to write three good acts which hang together is at least ten times as difficult as to write one. To write fourteen is a hundred times as difficult. . . . O'Neill has here proved himself the foremost playwright of our generation. . . . O'Neill has acknowledged that he sought in this play to render in terms intelligible to moderns the Greek "sense of fate." . . . The conflict of compulsions which O'Neill presents is not political, or even ethical. It is psychological. It is genuinely modern. O'Neill owes little to the Greek tragedy save the outline of his story. . . . The play pretty much sums up all that we moderns know about the deepest springs of human behavior.
>
> Hiram Motherwell, *Theatre Guild Magazine* (December 1931), 15–17.

One of the ways of studying theatre history is through the theories of art that lie behind practice. Perhaps for no period is this more helpful than the twentieth century, which has seen artistic movements come and go with bewildering rapidity. The proliferation was especially evident between 1910 and 1925, and many movements of that time introduced ideas and techniques that were to resurface in the 1960s. Because they are often based on unfamiliar premises, modern artistic movements have frequently seemed merely perverse, bizarre, or incomprehensible to those unaware of their goals. If we are to understand artistic movements, therefore, we must explore the theoretical premises that underlie them. Only then will we see why they depict human experience as they do and why the techniques they employ are consistent with their intent. Understanding may not cause us to admire the artistic products, but it will prevent us from reaching uninformed judgments. It will also help us understand the forces that have given rise to the extreme variety in modern theatre, where "newness" often seems an artistic principle and major goal.

Immediately following World War I, the movement with the greatest impact on theatre was expressionism. An excellent overview of the movement can be gained from John Willett's *Expressionism* (New York, 1970), but little of the theory has been translated into English. Here are some excerpts from a statement written by Yvan Goll in 1918 about his vision of a new "superdrama":

> [Expressionism will depict] man's battle against everything that is thinglike and animallike around and within him. . . . The writer must recognize that there are realms quite different from that of the five senses. . . . His first task will be to destroy all external form. . . . Man and objects will be stripped as clean as possible and looked at through a magnifying glass for greater effect. . . . The theatre must not restrict itself to "real" life; it will become "superreal" when it learns what lies behind things. Pure realism was the worst mistake ever made in literature. . . . Art, if it wishes to educate, improve, or be effective in any way, must destroy everyday man . . . to make him become once more the child he once was. The easier way to do this is through the grotesque. . . . Consequently, the new theatre must use technological means that are equivalent to the ancient mask . . . the phonograph to distort the voice, masks . . . which typify through . . . physical distortions [equivalent to] the inner distortions of the plot. . . . We are searching for the Superdrama.
>
> Yvan Goll, Preface to *The Immortal Ones* (Cologne, 1920).

The most influential theoreticians of the theatre between the two world wars were Bertolt Brecht and Antonin Artaud. They were united in their dislike for conventional, realistic theatre, but divided in their conceptions of the ideal theatre. Brecht's theories took shape over many years. (His theoretical writings have been collected in John Willett's *Brecht on Theatre.*) Perhaps the most systematic statement of his views is found in "A Short Organum for the Theatre." In it, Brecht states his dislike for the traditional theatre which lulls the spectator into a belief that social conditions are fixed, and he proposes to replace it with one which distances ("alienates") the audience from the stage events in such a way as to make it judge them critically:

42. . . . *A representation that alienates is one which allows us to recognize its subject, but at the same time makes it seem unfamiliar . . .*

43. . . . *The new alienations are only designed to free socially-conditioned phenomena from that stamp of familiarity which protects them from our grasp today.*

47. *In order to produce A-effects the actor has to discard whatever means he has learnt of getting the audience to identify itself with the characters which he plays. . .*

48. *At no moment must he go so far as to be wholly transformed into the character played. . . . He has just to show the character*

74. *So let us invite all the sister arts of the drama, not in order to create an "integrated work of art" in which they all offer themselves up and are lost, but so together with the drama they may further the common task in their different ways; and their relations with one another consist in this: that they lead to mutual alienation.*

"A Short Organum for the Theatre," *Brecht on Theatre,* trans. by John Willett (New York: Hill and Wang, 1964), 179–205.

Brecht later sought to clarify his position on alienation in acting with this note:

The contradiction between acting (demonstration) and experience (empathy) often leads the uninstructed to suppose that only one or the other can be manifest in the work of the actor (as if the Short Organum concentrated entirely on acting and the old tradition entirely on experience). In reality it is a matter of two mutually hostile processes which fuse in the actor's work. . . . His particular effectiveness comes from the tussle and tension of the two opposites, and also from their depth.

"Appendices to the Short Organum," *Brecht on Theatre,* 276–281.

Artaud's major essays on theatre were collected in *The Theatre and Its Double* (1938). Here are some excerpts from one of the essays, "Theatre of Cruelty, First Manifesto":

The theatre will never find itself again . . . except by furnishing the spectator with the truthful precipitates of dreams, in which his taste for crime, his erotic obsessions, his savagery, his chimeras, his utopian sense of life and matter, even his cannibalism, pour out, on a level not counterfeit and illusory, but interior. . . .

Every spectacle will contain . . . cries, groans, apparitions, surprises, theatricalities of all kinds, costumes taken from certain ritual models; resplendent lighting, incantational beauty of voices, . . . physical rhythm of movements whose crescendo and decrescendo will accord exactly with the pulsation of movements familiar to everyone. . . .

We abolish the stage and the auditorium and replace them by a single site, without partition or barrier of any kind. . . . A direct communication will be reestablished between the spectator and the spectacle, . . . from the fact that the spectator placed in the middle of the action, is engulfed and physically affected by it.

There will not be any set. . . .

We shall not act a written play, but we shall make attempts at direct staging, around themes, facts, or known works. . . .

Without an element of cruelty at the root of every spectacle, the theatre is not possible. In our present state of degeneration it is through the skin that metaphysics must be made to re-enter our minds. . . .

Antonin Artaud, *The Theatre and Its Double,* trans. M. C. Richards (New York: Grove Press, 1958).

20

Continental European and Latin American Theatre in the Mid Twentieth Century

World War II was the most extensive war ever fought in terms of people killed, property destroyed, and the number of countries involved. It made use of the most deadly weapons yet devised, including bombers, ballistic missiles, and atomic bombs. The causes of the war were numerous, including problems left unsolved by World War I, the rise of totalitarian governments with their denial of civil liberties and, in some instances, programs of genocide, and the territorial ambitions of such countries as Germany, Italy, and Japan. The German extermination camps are one of the great blots on human history. At the end of the war Europe was divided into sectors, with the east dominated by the Soviet Union and the west by the United States. There followed a "cold war" as the two nations sought to maintain or extend their influence. As a result, during the 1950s the world seemed under the threat of an atomic holocaust capable of ending life on earth. It was an age of anxiety and stress. A major stabilizing force was the United Nations, which provided a forum for debate and international cooperation, but it was often ineffective, since a few major powers had the right to veto its decisions.

Latin American countries, for the most part, sided with the Allies during World War II. Many, like Brazil, Mexico, and Peru, declared their allegiances quite early, while others, like Argentina, maintained a pro-Axis "neutrality" for several years before joining the Allied cause in 1945. Following the war these countries continued to struggle with the interrelated problems of political and economic instability. This instability often made them battlegrounds for the competing political models of communism, democracy, and totalitarianism, and thus became important parts of the Cold War strategies of the two super powers.

INTERNATIONAL DEVELOPMENTS

At the end of World War II, international cooperation was sought in every aspect of life. The formation of the United Nations was followed by many other organizations designed to promote international understanding. The International Theatre Institute (ITI) was founded in 1947 under the auspices of the United Nations Educational, Scientific, and Cultural Organization (UNESCO), which provided it with a yearly subsidy. From 1950 until 1968 the ITI published *World Theatre,* a periodical designed to disseminate information. The ITI also held frequent international meetings, and after 1954 sponsored an annual festival, the Théâtre des Nations. Other organizations also promoted the exchange of ideas. Among these were the International

Organization of Architects, Scenographers, and Theatre Technicians; the International Association of Theatre Critics; and the International Federation for Theatre Research.

International cooperation also encouraged the development of the theatre throughout the world. Consequently, theatres were established in parts of the world that formerly had few or none. In geographical scope, the theatre became more extensive after 1945 than at any time in the past.

FRENCH THEATRE AND DRAMA, 1940–1968

During World War II, the theatre in Paris was relatively prosperous after France capitulated to Germany. Productions were numerous and well attended, although with the exceptions of those by Dullin, Baty, Barsacq, and the Comédie Française, few were outstanding. The end of the war brought many stresses, as production costs rose and films and television drained away audiences. The postwar government, attempting to play a more decisive role than its predecessors, took steps to aid the theatre. In 1946 the Ministry of Arts and Letters began to subsidize productions of selected new plays and new companies; an annual competition was also inaugurated among the new troupes for the best production and direction. Furthermore, the state theatres were reorganized. The Opéra and Opéra-Comique were placed under a single management, and the Comédie Française and Odéon were merged, the Odéon being called the Salle Luxembourg and the main house the Salle Richelieu. At first, the Salle Luxembourg was restricted to new or recent plays, but this scheme proved impractical and both branches came to present similar repertories. When Pierre Dux, Administrator of the Comédie Française from 1944 to 1947, instituted new regulations designed to reduce his actors' film appearances and other outside commitments, many of the leading *sociétaires,* including Jean-Louis Barrault, Madeleine Renaud, Marie Bell, and Aimé Clairond, resigned. As a result, the troupe

FIG. 20.1
Europe after World War II.

lost much of its strength, and, although it slowly rebuilt under the administrations of Pierre-Aimé Touchard (between 1947 and 1953) and Pierre Descaves (between 1953 and 1959), its prestige suffered seriously.

The government also encouraged decentralization of the theatre, which by 1945 was restricted primarily to Paris. Consequently, in 1947 subsidized regional dramatic centers began to be established. The first, the Dramatic Center of the East, was based at Strasbourg, and a second was opened almost immediately at St. Etienne; in 1949, Le Grenier, a troupe which had been performing since 1945, was designated the Dramatic Center for Toulouse, and in the same year a fourth center was established at Rennes. Other centers were inaugurated at Aix-en-Provence (1952), Tourcoing (1960), and Bourges (1963). By the late 1960s the number of Dramatic Centers had grown to twelve. In addition to performing in its home theatre, each Center typically toured towns in its region or developed schemes to bring audiences to its theatre from outlying areas. Furthermore, both national and local authorities aided the many dramatic festivals founded after 1945, most notably at Avignon (beginning in 1947) and Aix-en-Provence (beginning in 1948). By the 1960s more than fifty festivals were being held annually.

The major leaders in the postwar years were Barrault and Vilar. Jean-Louis Barrault (1910–1994), after studying with Dullin and working with Artaud and the mime artist Etienne Decroux, had attained an enviable reputation as an actor in both theatre and film before the war began. In 1940 he became a *sociétaire* at the Comédie Française, where in 1943 his production of Claudel's *The Satin Slipper* popularized what came to be called "total theatre." Claudel's play, written between 1919 and 1924, had previously been considered unplayable because of its length and complexity, for the events span a century and occur in Spain, Italy, Africa, America, and at sea. A drama of love and salvation, *The Satin Slipper* was shaped by Barrault into a powerful theatrical experience that influenced other directors for many years. Although Barrault was later to refine his ideas, in 1943 he had already formulated his basic outlook. He declared that the text of a play is like an iceberg, since only about one-eighth is visible; it is the director's task to complete the playwright's text by revealing the hidden portions through the imaginative use of all the theatre's resources. Barrault sought a synthesis of elements from both Copeau's and Artaud's approaches.

In 1946, after resigning from the Comédie Française, Barrault (with Madeleine Renaud, whom he had married in 1940) formed the Compagnie

FIG. 20.2
Barrault's production of Claudel's *Christophe Colombe* at the Théâtre Marigny, 1953. Courtesy Agence de Presse Bernand.

Madeleine Renaud-Jean-Louis Barrault. With such major actors as André Brunot, Edwige Feuillère, and Pierre Brasseur, Barrault produced about forty plays ranging from the *Oresteia* to contemporary *avant-garde* works before he gave up his Théâtre Marigny in 1956.

Jean Vilar (1912–1971), a fellow student of Barrault at Dullin's school, was much slower in achieving recognition, and had worked in a number of companies before being employed to organize the festival at Avignon in 1947. His work there and his own performances in Paris (most notably as Pirandello's Henry IV in Barsacq's production) led in 1951 to his appointment as director of the Théâtre National Populaire (TNP), then on the verge of collapse. Although not immediately successful, by 1954 the TNP was one of the most popular troupes in France. Vilar's productions always placed major emphasis upon the actor, reinforced by costume and lighting, and he usually restricted scenery to platforms or a few set pieces. Vilar was the first producer to achieve wide popularity with the approach advocated by the Cartel (whose following had always been limited). Although the TNP's principal home was at the Palais de Chaillot in Paris, it also played at the Avignon Festival and toured throughout France. It soon commanded greater popular support than any of the other state troupes, all of which played almost exclusively in Paris.

In addition to founding several new dramatic centers, the Gaullist regime also promoted municipal cultural centers (*maisons de la culture*) and supplied 50 percent of the funds to finance them. The first of the cultural centers was opened in 1962; eventually there were about twenty, including those in the suburbs of Paris.

FIG. 20.3

Vilar's production of Marivaux's *Triumph of Love* at the Théâtre Nationale Populaire, 1956. Setting by Leon Gischia. Courtesy Agence de Presse Bernand.

Malraux also reorganized the state theatres. He removed the Odéon from the control of the Comédie Française, renamed it the Théâtre de France, and installed Barrault's company in it. Similarly, the Théâtre National Populaire was elevated to a rank equal to that of the other state theatres.

Many changes in the postwar theatre were intimately connected with experiments in dramaturgy, notably those of the absurdists. This movement did not come to the fore until the 1950s, however, and much of the major writing of the postwar period was to come from dramatists well known before 1940. Among these, the most prolific was Jean Anouilh, with such works as *Invitation to the Chateau* (1947), *Waltz of the Toreadors* (1952), *The Lark* (1953), *Becket* (1960), *Dear Antoine* (1970), and *The Pants* (1978). In these plays Anouilh continued to explore the problem of maintaining integrity in a world based upon compromises. Other prewar dramatists who made important contributions after 1945 include Marcel Achard, with *Patate* (1957) and *Eugene the Mysterious* (1964); and Armand Salacrou, with *Nights of Wrath* (1946) and *Boulevard Durand* (1960).

Among the most respected of the new dramatists was Henry de Montherlant (1896–1972), whose novels had won a wide following before the war.

Although he had written a few minor plays, Montherlant's first produced work was *The Dead Queen* (1942), directed by Barrault at the Comédie Française. Its success led Montherlant to write *The Master of Santiago* (1948), *Port-Royal* (1954), *The Cardinal of Spain* (1960), and *The Civil War* (1965). *The Master of Santiago* is often considered Montherlant's most characteristic work because of its simple external action, complex psychology, and elevated style. The motif of sacrifice and the harsh rejection of all mediocrity runs through it. In all of Montherlant's work, the interest resides as much in the intellectual positions taken up by the characters as in their psychological traits and actions.

Postwar French drama exerted its greatest influence through existentialist and absurdist plays. Following the war, existentialism as a philosophical outlook attracted considerable attention, especially through the essays and plays of Jean-Paul Sartre (1905–1980), a philosopher and novelist who turned to drama in 1943 with *The Flies,* and went on to write *No Exit* (1944), *Dirty Hands* (1948), *The Devil and the Good Lord* (1951), and *The Condemned of Altona* (1959). All illustrate Sartre's existentialist views. Denying the existence of God, fixed standards of conduct, and verifiable moral codes, Sartre argued that human beings are "condemned to be free." Thus, people must choose their own values and live by them, for "man is only what he does. Man becomes what he chooses to be." Sartre's plays show characters faced with choices which require them to reassess their outlooks, forge their own standards, and then live by them uncompromisingly. In the uncertainty that followed the war, Sartre attracted a wide following, for he cast doubt upon the conformism that had made possible the Nazi atrocities. Sartre also believed that it is necessary for people to be politically "engaged," even though the choices open to them are seldom ideal. In *Dirty Hands* he argues that to participate in political action invariably means that one's hands will get dirty, but that refusing to become politically engaged merely means that others will make the choices that determine events.

The work of Albert Camus (1913–1960) was to be of comparable importance. Before turning to drama, Camus had been a theatre worker in his native Algeria, a journalist, and the editor of a clandestine newspaper during the German occupation of France. His dramatic output was small: *Cross-Purposes* (1944), *Caligula* (performed 1945), *State of Siege* (1948), *The Just Assassins* (1949), and a few adaptations. His influence on the theatre came in part from his essay, "The Myth of Sisyphus" (1943), in which his discussion of the "absurd" was to supply the name for the absurdist movement. In this essay,

Camus argues that the human condition is absurd because of the gap between people's hopes and the irrational universe into which they are born. For Camus, the only remedy lies in each individual's search for a set of standards (admittedly without any objective basis) that will allow her or him to bring order out of this chaos. Although Camus denied being an existentialist, his conclusions were similar to those of Sartre.

Camus and Sartre differed most in their ideas about "engagement," for Camus rejected the conclusion advocated by Sartre in *Dirty Hands* and denied the validity of choosing between two immoral positions. Their difference on this point led to a prolonged and bitter debate. Between them, nevertheless, they supplied the philosophical basis for the absurdist movement which began to emerge in the early 1950s.

Although Sartre and Camus rejected rationalistic views of the universe, their plays were cast in traditional dramatic form. Since they began with the assumption that the world is irrational and then went on to create order out of chaos, their plays had dramatic actions that developed linearly through cause and effect. On the other hand, the absurdists, while for the most part accepting Sartre's philosophical outlook, tended to concentrate upon the irrationality of human experience without suggesting any path beyond. By employing a succession of episodes unified merely by theme or mood instead of a cause-to-effect arrangement, they arrived at a structure paralleling the chaos which was their usual dramatic subject. The sense of absurdity was heightened by the juxtaposition of incongruous events producing seriocomic and ironic effects. Because they viewed language as the major rationalistic tool, the absurdists often demonstrated its inadequacy and subordinated it to nonverbal devices. Of the absurdists, four—Beckett, Ionesco, Genet, and Adamov—were to be most important.

Samuel Beckett (1906–1989) was the first of the absurdists to win international fame—with *Waiting for Godot* which in 1953 brought absurdism its first popular attention both in France and elsewhere. Irish by birth, Beckett first went to Paris in the 1920s and settled there permanently in 1938. He began writing around 1930 but did not turn to drama until after World War II. His plays include *Endgame* (1957), *Krapp's Last Tape* (1958), *Happy Days* (1961), *Play* (1963), *Come and Go* (1966), *Not I* (1973), *That Time* (1976), and several other short pieces. In many ways, Beckett seems the characteristic dramatist of the 1950s, a decade made anxious by the threat of atomic holocaust. In fact, Beckett's characters often seem to have been set down in a world already ravaged by some disaster which threatens human survival. Beckett is

FIG. 20.4

Original production of Beckett's *Waiting for Godot,* Théâtre de Babylone, Paris, 1953. Directed by Roger Blin, seated at left. Courtesy Pic, Paris.

not so much concerned with people as social and political creatures as with the human condition in a metaphysical sense. His spiritual derelicts are usually isolated in time and space; they torment and console themselves and others, raise questions which cannot be answered, and struggle on in a world that seems to be disintegrating around them.

Eugène Ionesco (1909–1994), a Roumanian by birth, labeled his first work, *The Bald Soprano* (1949), an "anti-play" to indicate a rebellion against conventional drama. The early works, which include *The Lesson* (1950) and *The Chairs* (1952), attracted little attention at first, but steadily grew in reputation after 1953, when Anouilh published an article praising *Victims of Duty.* These early plays, as well as *Amedée* (1954) and *The New Tenant* (1957), are mainly negative, for they concentrate upon the clichés of language and thought and the irrationality of materialist values. Later works, such as *The Killer* (1959), *Rhinoceros* (1960), *Exit the King* (1962), *Hunger and Thirst* (1966), *Macbett* (1972), and *The Man with the Suitcases* (1975), took a somewhat more positive view by showing protagonists who hold out against conformity, although they cannot offer any rational explanation for their actions.

FIG. 20.5

Genet's *The Screens,* Théâtre de France, 1966. Directed by Roger Blin. Madeleine Renaud is at center. Courtesy Pic, Paris.

Unlike Beckett, Ionesco is concerned primarily with social relationships, typically those of middle-class characters in family situations. Two themes run through most of his work: the deadening nature of materialistic, bourgeois society, and the loneliness and isolation of the individual. Perhaps ultimately his vision of the human condition differs little from Beckett's, but it is conceived in more domestic terms. All of his plays seek to discredit clichés, ideologies, and materialism. His characters tend to be unthinking automatons oblivious of their own mechanical behavior, just as material objects tend to proliferate and take over the space that should be occupied by people. Ionesco is especially antipathetic to the notion that drama should be didactic. To him truth means the absence of commitment, for commitment involves a fatal step toward conformity.

Jean Genet (1910–1986) spent much of his life in prison, a background that figures prominently in much of his writing. His first plays, *The Maids* (presented by Jouvet in 1947) and *Deathwatch* (produced by Herrand in 1949), were at first unsuccessful, and his reputation was to be made with *The Balcony*

(1956), *The Blacks* (1959), and *The Screens* (1961, not produced in France until 1966). Genet's characters rebel against organized society and suggest that deviation is essential if human beings are to achieve integrity. The plays also imply that nothing has meaning without its opposite—law and crime, religion and sin, love and hate—and therefore that deviant behavior is as valuable as the accepted virtues. Genet, viewing all systems of value as entirely arbitrary, transforms life into a series of ceremonies and rituals which give an air of stability and importance to otherwise nonsensical behavior.

Arthur Adamov (1908–1971), born in Russia and educated in Switzerland, was attracted early to surrealism, a movement that influenced most absurdist drama. Turning to playwriting in 1947, Adamov's first work was produced in 1950. The early plays, for example *The Invasion* (1950), *Parody* (1952), and *All Against All* (1953), show a seriocomically cruel world of moral destructiveness and personal anxieties in which the characters are condemned to eternal failure by their inability to communicate with each other. Time and place are usually indefinite, as in

FIG. 20.6

Arrabal's *The Automobile Graveyard* at the Théâtre des Arts, Paris, 1967. Directed by Victor Garcia. Courtesy Agence de Presse Bernand, Paris.

dreams. Adamov's later plays became progressively more socially oriented, especially after 1956, when he denounced his earlier work and adopted a Brechtian form. This new outlook was reflected in *Paolo Paoli* (1957), a commentary upon the materialism and hypocrisy which preceded World War I, and *Spring '71* (1960), which idealizes the men who created the Paris Commune in 1871. Adamov's late plays, staged by Roger Planchon's company, are indicative of the decline of interest in absurdism around 1960 and increased concern for plays of social action. Many critics now consider that Adamov's conversion marked a major turning point in postwar French theatre.

As a label, absurdism was popularized by Martin Esslin's *The Theatre of the Absurd* (1961) but, since it was never a conscious movement, it is difficult to specify those authors who should be considered among its ranks. Absurdism did not encompass all of the experimental dramatists of the time, of whom there were many in France. Among those who probably should not be labeled absurdists, some of the best were Jacques Audiberti (1899–1965), whose *Quoat-Quoat* (1946), *The Black Feast* (1948), and *The Sentry-Box* (1965) stress the power of evil and sex over human affairs; and Jean Tardieu (1903–1995), who concentrated upon one-act "chamber" plays, such as *The Information Window* (1955) and *The ABC of Our Life* (1959), treating human enslavement to social conventions.

After 1960, the best known of the *avant-garde* dramatists was Fernando Arrabal (1932–) who, born in Spain, moved to Paris in 1955. His early plays, such as *Fando and Lis* (1958), emphasize a childish,

thoughtless cruelty couched in a form similar to that used by the absurdists. Around 1962 Arrabal became interested in what he called *théâtre panique*, "a ceremony—partly sacrilegious, partly sacred, erotic and mystic, a putting to death and exaltation of life, part Don Quixote and part Alice in Wonderland." Among his later works are *Solemn Communion* (1966), *The Architect and the Emperor of Assyria* (1967), *And They Handcuffed the Flowers* (1970), and *Young Barbarians Today* (1975). Of these, the second is perhaps most characteristic. It includes only two characters, who enact a series of ritualized human situations: master and slave, judge and criminal, mother and child, male and female, sadist and masochist, and so on. Eventually one decides that he must be punished and asks the other to kill and eat him. When this is done, they seem somehow to merge. But now a new figure appears, apparently beginning the whole cycle over again. Through such plays, Arrabal not only challenged all values, he ferreted out the hidden corners of the human psyche. Following the death of Franco, Arrabal spent much of his time in Spain, where he continued to write plays, among them *The Mad Laughter of the Lillputians* and *Orangutan Opening.*

Most of the *avant-garde* drama was first produced in small, out-of-the-way theatres by adventurous directors. Many of them were heavily influenced by Artaud and later were France's most respected directors. Of these, perhaps the most important was Roger Blin (1907–1984), a disciple of Artaud, who, after working with Dullin and Barrault, became closely associated with the absurdist movement around 1949. He is especially noted for his staging of plays by Beckett and Genet. Other important directors include André Reybaz (1922–), who introduced Audiberti, Ghelderode, and Ionesco to Parisian audiences and worked with a number of *avant-garde* theatres before becoming director of the Dramatic Center at Tourcoing in 1960; Georges Vitaly (1917–), who worked with Reybaz before founding the Théâtre LaBruyère in 1953; and Jean-Marie Serreau (1915–1973), a pupil of Dullin, who directed the first productions of Adamov's plays before opening the Théâtre de Babylone with Blin in 1952 and going on to direct at many other theatres. Beginning as members of the *avant-garde,* most of these directors were later to work regularly with such established troupes as the Comédie Française, the Théâtre de France, and various Dramatic Centers.

After 1960, several French playwrights treated political and socioeconomic themes. Aimé Cesaire (1913–), a black writer born in Martinique, in *The Tragedy of King Christophe* (1963), *A Season in the Congo* (1966), and *A Tempest* (1969), was especially

FIG. 20.7

Planchon's production of Adamov's adaptation of Gogol's *Dead Souls,* 1960. Setting by René Allio. Théâtre de la Cité, Villeurbanne. Courtesy Pic, Paris.

concerned with the problems of postcolonialism. These plays, all directed by Serreau, made a deep impression on French audiences. Gabriel Cousin (1918–) wrote in the Brechtian vein, although with a Christian rather than a Marxist slant. In such plays as *Ordinary Love* (1958) and *Cycle of the Crab* (1969), he dealt with major world problems, such as hunger, racism, and nuclear threat, but always from the viewpoint of working-class characters. Armand Gatti (1924–) also wrote a variation of Brechtian drama in which he advocated a humanitarian socialism and expressed hope for the exploited people of the world. Among these plays were *The Imaginary Life of the Scavenger August Geai* (1956), *A Single Man* (1966), and *V as in Vietnam* (1967). Beginning in the late 1960s, Gatti worked directly with ordinary people in writing plays, as in *The Lion, Its Cage and Its Wings* (1975), a series of six programs in which immigrant workers expressed their views of France.

Among the directors who came to the fore in the early 1960s, the most important was Roger Planchon (1931–), after 1957 head of the Théâtre de la Cité in Villeurbanne, an industrial suburb of Lyons, where he was successful in attracting the working-class audience he sought. In his productions, Planchon borrowed many techniques from film (since he considered this medium most familiar to his unsophisticated theatregoers) and from Brecht. He made liberal use of projections (captions, commentaries, and pictures) and

often utilized turntables to show the action from different angles, as in the cinema. He presented plays by Molière, Marivaux, Shakespeare, Kleist, Marlowe, Racine, Brecht, and other major writers, but he usually gave them working-class interpretations. Consequently, his productions were often controversial. But their liveliness, richness, clarity, and novelty won Planchon one of the largest followings in France. Planchon was to be even more important after 1968.

SOVIET THEATRE AND DRAMA, 1940–1968

During the war years the Russian theatre was devoted primarily to building morale. Since governmental strictures were considerably relaxed, many thought that the end of the war would bring still greater freedom. Instead, restrictions even more severe than those of the 1930s were imposed in 1946, and in 1948 all subsidies, except those granted to a few favored theatres, were stopped. The loss of governmental financial support was a severe blow, since 450 of Russia's 950 theatres had been destroyed during the war. By 1953 only about 250 were left.

Artistic restrictions made socialist realism the only acceptable style and the Moscow Art Theatre's methods standard. Political control was strengthened in 1949 when party-appointed administrative directors were placed in complete charge of each theatre. Most Western plays were removed from the repertory, and new Russian works were expected to uphold government policy. Konstantin Simonov's *Alien Shadow* (1949) and Nikolai Pogodin's *The Missouri Waltz* (1950) are typical of the numerous anti-American plays of the period. Other postwar dramas, such as Vsevelod Vishnevsky's *1919—The Unforgettable Year* (1949) and A. Stein's *Prologue* (1952), glorify Stalin's role in the development of Communism.

Following Stalin's death in 1953, especially after Khrushchev's denunciation of Stalin in 1956, there was a relaxation of the former strictures. Censorship in the sense of prior judgment was no longer practiced, although many pressures were still exerted on drama, most notably through the governing boards of theatres. Realism remained the dominant style and didacticism the dominant aim, but neither was systematically enforced and both declined in popularity. In new plays, individual concerns were treated more frequently, as in Pogodin's *Sonnet of Petrarch* (1957), about a middle-aged married man's affair with a young girl, while the theme of vindication from unjust charges, typified by Alexander Volodin's (1919–2001) *Factory Girl* (1957), became common. The conflict between generations, exemplified

FIG. 20.8
Pogodin's *Sonnet of Petrarch* at the Mayakovsky Theatre, Moscow, 1957. From Komissarzkevsky, *Moscow Theatres.*

in Victor Rozov's (1913–) *The Unequal Struggle* (1960), also became a popular subject. By 1960 anti-American plays had largely disappeared from the repertory, while many previously banned Russian plays became acceptable. The penchant for reshaping classics to bring out propagandistic themes also had lessened.

One result of relaxed strictures was the presentation of many foreign plays for the first time in the USSR. For example, in 1960 Brecht's works were introduced into the repertory, and soon plays by Miller, Osborne, Williams, and others were being performed with some frequency. On the other hand, few absurdist dramas were produced, being considered too "formalistic."

The changes brought a loss of prestige for the Moscow Art Theatre, although it continued to be the most favored company in terms of subsidies, salaries, and other government standards. Nevertheless, by the 1960s the Moscow Art Theatre was looked upon by the public as something of a museum. As the MAT declined in prestige, others rose. Some of the changes can be attributed to the abandonment in 1956 of the fixed pay scales, ranks, and prohibitions against changing companies which had hampered actors since the 1930s. Other changes can be attributed to shifts in taste. Of the older theatres, the Vakhtangov, under the direction of Reuben Simonov, became the most popular, for Vakhtangov's methods provided the most acceptable alternative to socialist realism. The Theatre of Satire, under Valentin Pluchek, also grew in esteem after it created a sensation in 1954 with productions of Mayakovsky's *The Bedbug* and *The Bathhouse* in a style not unlike

Meyerhold's. At the Mayakovsky Theatre (formerly the Theatre of the Revolution), Nikolai Okhlopkov returned to his prewar experimentation with performer-audience relationships. In the late 1950s he restaged Pogodin's *Aristocrats,* with the audience surrounding the playing area as in his prewar productions. The most famous of Okhlopkov's postwar productions was probably *Hamlet* (1954), in which the compartmentalized setting created a prison-like world from which Hamlet wishes to escape. Two other prewar directors, Yuri Zavadsky at the Mossoviet Theatre and Alexei Popov at the Central Theatre of the Soviet Army, also linked the prewar and postwar theatres.

In Leningrad, the Pushkin Theatre occupied a prewar position comparable to that of the Moscow Art Theatre in Moscow and during the 1950s its prestige suffered similarly. The most admired theatre in Leningrad was the Gorky, after 1956 under the direction of Georgi Tovstogonov (1915–1989), noted for giving classics contemporary significance. Using realistic set pieces, Tovstogonov often dispensed with walls, ceilings, and similar details, and employed such cinematic techniques as moving the action forward on platforms for "close-up" effects.

The most innovative postwar company was Moscow's Sovremennik (Contemporary) Theatre, founded in 1957, the first new company to be authorized in Russia since the 1930s. Under the leadership of Oleg Yefremov (1927–2000), the Contemporary drew most of its personnel and methods

FIG. 20.9
Okhlopkov's production of *Hamlet* at the Mayakovsky Theatre, Moscow, 1954.

from the Moscow Art Theatre or its training school. The principal departures of the new company lay in its concentration on plays (such as those by Brecht, Osborne, Shatrov, and Rozov) thought to be relevant to present-day life and in its use of simplified settings rather than the elaborate mountings typical at the MAT. By the late 1960s, the Russian theatre had moved away from the restrictions and standards imposed during the Stalinist era. But pressure to conform to party needs was still evident, and the government continued to make its presence felt when deviations became more than it wished to countenance.

THEATRE AND DRAMA IN CZECHOSLOVAKIA, 1940–1968

Following World War II, most of Eastern Europe came under the domination of Russia. As a result, theatre in these countries was subjected to restrictions similar to those imposed in the USSR. Following the break with Stalinism in 1956, however, strictures were considerably relaxed and experimentation flourished, especially in Czechoslovakia.

Czechoslovakia made its greatest international impact in the field of technology and design and above all through the work of Josef Svoboda (1920–2002). Although he began his career around 1945, Svoboda

FIG. 20.10

Svoboda's setting for *Their Day* by Josef Topol at the National Theatre, Prague, 1959. This was Svoboda's first attempt to apply Laterna Magika techniques to theatrical design. Photo copyrighted by Jaromir Svoboda.

was unable to demonstrate his great versatility until the late 1950s when socialist realism was no longer the standard mode. Much of his work was an extension of experimentation begun with multimedia in the 1930s by E. F. Burian (1904–1959) and Miroslav Kouril (1911–1984). It was also heavily indebted to the Prague Institute of Scenography, founded in 1957 and headed by Kouril, for its staff and facilities did much of the experimentation.

The turning point in Svoboda's career came in 1958 when he began collaborating with the director Alfred Radok on two projects—Polyekran and Laterna Magika, both using a number of screens on which still and moving pictures were projected. Laterna Magika also integrated live actors into the performance. Both of these forms were shown at the Brussels World's Fair in 1958 and elicited enormous excitement. In 1959 Svoboda began to carry over many of the technical devices into his stage work. Subsequently, he experimented continuously with means to create a completely flexible stage which could change from scene to scene as the needs of the action changed. In addition to screens and projections, he also developed platforms and steps that could move vertically, horizontally, and laterally to alter rapidly the spatial relationships and size of the acting area. He also explored the potentials for stage use of such materials as mirrors, plastic, and various kinds of netting, and used most of these as surfaces on which to project images (or in some instances to reflect the action as seen from above, behind, or at an angle). He designed settings in almost every style and after 1960 was among the best known and most influential designers in the world. Svoboda's work did much to call attention to the high quality of the Czech theatre as a whole. In the 1960s there were about fifty-six companies in Czechoslovakia, but those best known abroad (aside from the Prague National Theatre) were a group of small theatres in Prague, most of which came into existence after 1962 when the government created the State Theatre Studio to assist experimental companies. Of these, three were especially outstanding. The Theatre Behind the Gate, founded in 1965 by Otomar Krejca, shared its 435-seat theatre with the Laterna Magika, for both of which Svoboda was principal designer. It was noted for its imaginative staging and thoughtful interpretation of Czech and foreign plays. The Cinoherni (Actors' Club), founded in 1965 and headed by Jaroslav Vostry, performed in a theatre seating 220. Its primary emphasis was on ensemble acting (probably the best in Czechoslovakia) and a wide-ranging repertory drawn from world drama. The Theatre on the Balustrade, founded in 1958 and headed from 1962 until 1969 by Jan Grossman, seated about 200. This company was the primary home of absurdist drama in Czechoslovakia and had as its resident playwright Václav Havel (1936–), usually considered the leading contemporary Czech dramatist. His bitingly satirical treatments of bureaucracy, *The Garden Party* (1963), *The Memorandum* (1965), and *The Conspirators* (1974) came to be known and admired throughout the world. During later years, when he was imprisoned or refused productions, he continued to write. Among his later plays are *Largo Desolato* (1984) and *Temptation* (1985).

In 1968 the vitality of Czech theatre was severely curtailed following the invasion by Warsaw Pact troops sent to end the liberalization that had been underway in Czechoslovakia. Many theatre directors were removed from their posts and many plays were forbidden publication or production. Václav Havel was subsequently imprisoned several times for his continued resistance to government violations of human rights. These repressive measures were to continue until 1989, when within a few weeks' time not only were the restrictions removed but Havel was also named president of Czechoslovakia.

GERMAN THEATRE AND DRAMA, 1940–1968

When Germany surrendered to the Allies in 1945, all theatres were closed for a time but soon began to reopen under the surveillance of occupation forces. After 1945, the German theatre recovered rapidly and by the 1960s was one of the most stable in the world. Although Germany was divided into East and West after 1945, the theatre in the two areas shared many common characteristics. In both, the system of state-supported resident companies was reinstated. By the 1960s, there were 175 professional theatres in West Germany, of which 120 were government-owned, and in East Germany there were about 135 theatres, all state-owned. Almost every city had a dramatic company and many had an opera and ballet troupe of good quality. Typically, all of the subsidized troupes in a single city were under one manager (or *Intendant*), appointed by the city or state, and shared physical facilities and a staff of directors and designers. In large cities, such as Berlin, there were multiple facilities, each with its own Intendant and company. A *dramaturg* (with a sizable staff) worked with each company on its choice of plays and other artistic matters.

Although more than a hundred theatre buildings were destroyed during the war, a phenomenal rebuilding program after 1950 replaced most of them.

FIG. 20.11
Wieland Wagner's production of *Tannhäuser*, Bayreuth, 1954. Note the absence of three-dimensional scenery and the dependence on light and projections. From *Décor de Théâtre dans le Monde depuis 1935*.

In the new buildings, sight lines were considerably improved, boxes were eliminated, and the number of balconies reduced. The prewar emphasis upon complex stage machinery continued. For example, the Schiller Theater, opened in West Berlin in 1951, had a revolving stage, elevators, and rolling platform stages. Most of the theatres were of the conventional proscenium-arch type. A few small theatres intended as second houses were more flexible, but there was little experimentation with audience-performer spatial relationships.

In addition to permanent resident troupes, festivals were of considerable importance in postwar Germany. The most famous was still the Bayreuth Festival, revived in 1951 under the direction of Wieland Wagner (1917–1966) until his death and then under his brother Wolfgang Wagner (1919–). After the war, Wagner's operas were performed for the first time at Bayreuth with simple scenic investiture and atmospheric lighting, much like that advocated by Appia, instead of the historical realism that had been used since Wagner's time. Bitterly opposed by traditionalists, the new methods won wholehearted approval from others.

In Austria, the pattern of postwar reconstruction paralleled that in Germany. By the 1960s there were thirty-six theatres in Austria, twenty of which were located in Vienna. Four of these were state theatres, the Staatsoper and the Volksoper for opera, the Burgtheater and the Akademietheater for drama, while the Theater-in-der-Josefstadt and the Volkstheater were subsidized by the city of Vienna. The festival at Salzburg, reopened in 1946, also resumed its position as one of the finest in the world.

Among postwar German directors, perhaps the most important were Kortner, Gründgens, and Hilpert. Fritz Kortner (1892–1970) was considered the leading expressionist actor of the 1920s. After spending the Nazi years in exile, he returned to Germany in 1949, working primarily in Berlin and Munich. His total dedication, long rehearsal periods, and detailed attention to the emotional lives of characters made him perhaps the most influential director of the postwar period. Gustav Gründgens (1899–1963), Intendant of the Berlin National Theater under the Nazis and Hitler's favorite actor, known especially for his portrayal of Mephistopheles, served after the war as Intendant in Düsseldorf and later in Hamburg, coming to be seen as the primary preserver of German theatrical tradition. Heinz Hilpert (1890–1967), a leading actor who served as Intendant of the Deutsches Theater under the Nazis, worked primarily in Göttingen after the war. He was noted especially for his Shakespearean productions

and for directing the premieres of Zuckmayer's postwar dramas. Both Gründgens and Hilpert justified their cooperation with the Nazis as a desire to preserve German culture in a time of barbarism. In 1951, Erwin Piscator returned to Germany and directed for numerous companies before being named Intendant of the Freie Volksbühne in West Berlin in 1962. He was especially instrumental in popularizing the documentary drama that emerged in the 1960s. Other major directors in Germany included Harry Buchwitz, Hans Schalla, Boleslag Barlow, Rudolf Sellner, Wolfgang Langhoff, Wolfgang Heinz, and Walter Felsenstein.

Of all German companies the most famous was the Berliner Ensemble, located in East Berlin and devoted primarily to the plays of Brecht. After Brecht returned to Europe in 1947, his plays rapidly found their way into the repertories of most German troupes and his theory was soon known throughout the world. His fame was confirmed through the work of the Berliner Ensemble. Opened in 1949 with *Mother Courage,* the Berliner Ensemble for a time shared the Deutsches Theater with another troupe. In 1954 it was given the Theater-am-Schiffbauerdamm, the house in which Brecht's *Threepenny Opera* was first produced in 1928. With its appearances in Paris in 1954 and 1955, the Berliner Ensemble became internationally famous and thereafter was considered one of the world's finest troupes. After Brecht's death in 1956, the company continued under the direction of Helene Weigel (1900–1971), Brecht's wife, who had been its official director from the beginning. Brecht's methods were also retained by the company's principal directors.

Upon returning to Germany, Brecht reestablished associations with several persons with whom he had collaborated before 1933: Erich Engel (1891–1966), who had directed the original production of *Threepenny Opera* in 1928, staged many of the Berliner Ensemble's plays; major German actors, among them Therese Giehse (1898–1975), Lionel Steckel (1901–1971), and Ernst Busch (1900–1980), appeared in Berliner productions; and Teo Otto (1904–1968) and Caspar Neher (1897–1962), Germany's most influential designers, did a number of productions for Brecht. Along with Karl von Appen, the Berliner's principal designer after 1954, Otto and Neher moved postwar German stage design toward the frank manipulation of stage means. Through a few architectural elements, set pieces, projections, and lighting, they achieved settings both functional and beautiful.

Brecht also trained a number of directors who were to play a significant role in German theatre. Benno Besson (1922–) worked at the Berliner

FIG. 20.12
Gustav Gründgens's production of Goethe's *Faust* at the Neue Schauspielhaus, Hamburg. At left, Will Quadflieg as Faust; at right, Gründgens as Mephisto. Courtesy Theatersammlung, Universitat Hamburg.

Ensemble from 1949 until 1958, then at the Deutsches Theater until he became Intendant of the Volksbühne in 1969; he came to be considered one of East Germany's most important directors. Manfred Wekwerth (1929–), with the Ensemble after 1951, was one of the company's mainstays after Brecht's death and eventually became its head. Peter Palitzsch (1918–2004) and Egon Monk (1927–), after working with the Ensemble, emigrated to West Germany, where they were highly influential directors.

Much of the Berliner Ensemble's achievement stemmed from its long and careful rehearsals, sometimes extending over several months. When each production was ready, a *Modellbuch* containing 600 to 800 action photographs was made. The published *Modellbücher* have influenced many producers who have never seen the company perform. The Berliner Ensemble demonstrated the validity of Brecht's theories, while the humanitarian and social emphases of his plays suggested an alternative to the absurdists (who concentrated on personal anxieties).

If Germany and Austria rebuilt one of the best systems of subsidized theatres in the world, they were less successful in developing significant new dramatists, for until the late 1950s the major German dramatist was Brecht, all of whose major works were written before 1946. Zuckmayer also returned to Germany. His *The Devil's General* (1946) introduced the theme that was to dominate German drama until the 1960s—public guilt and responsibility, especially under the Nazis. Wolfgang Borchert (1921–1947) won fame with one play, *The Man Outside* (1947), about a returning soldier trying to adjust to civilian life, but died before he could fulfill the promise shown by that work. Fritz Hochwalder (1911–1986) found a wide audience at home with *The Holy Experiment* (1943), *The Fugitive* (1945), and *The Public Prosecutor* (1949), all of which pose questions of individual responsibility and public guilt, but he never won a following outside of German-speaking territories.

The major drama in German during the 1950s was written by two Swiss playwrights, Frisch and Duerrenmatt, both of whom were encouraged by Kurt Hirschfeld (1902–1964) and Oskar Walterlin (1895–1961) of the Zurich Schauspielhaus, one of the best in Europe during the Nazi regime because so many refugees settled in Switzerland. Max Frisch (1911–1991) was trained as an architect but turned to writing in 1944. His reputation rests primarily upon *The Chinese Wall* (1946), *Biedermann and the Firebugs* (1958), and *Andorra* (1961), all of which treat questions of guilt. In each play the past is reviewed and the characters construct elaborate rationalizations for their actions; none is really willing to accept

FIG. 20.13
Brecht's production of his *The Caucasian Chalk Circle* at the Berliner Ensemble, 1954. Setting by Karl von Appen. From *Décor de Théâtre dans le Monde depuis 1935.*

responsibility. Although it is clear that Frisch longs for a world of integrity, he seems to suggest that it is unattainable because human beings do not learn from their mistakes. Through techniques influenced

FIG. 20.14
Duerrenmatt's *The Physicists* at the Kammerspiele, Munich, 1962. Directed by Hans Schweikart. Courtesy *World Theatre.*

by Wilder, Strindberg, Brecht, and others, he embodied his search and disillusionment in symbolic and nightmarish fantasy.

Friedrich Duerrenmatt (1921–1990) began writing plays in 1947. Of his many works, the most successful were *The Visit* (1956), *The Physicists* (1962), and *Play Strindberg* (1969). Like Frisch, Duerrenmatt was concerned with moral questions, which he suggested will not be solved satisfactorily because people are so readily corrupted by promises of power or wealth. Duerrenmatt was much more detached than Frisch. He emphasized the grotesqueness of the human condition, which he expressed through a rather dark comedy. Although concerned with moral dilemmas, he showed the human instinct for good corrupted either by power and greed or by chance. He avoided bitterness by standing at a distance and viewing events sardonically.

Because the majority of significant postwar German drama dealt with questions of guilt related to larger political and social issues, it differed considerably in tone from the French absurdist drama, which attracted few German exponents. Germany's major plays in the 1960s took the form of "documentary drama" or the "theatre of fact" in which actual events, often quite recent, were used to explore the by-then characteristic concern for guilt and responsibility in public affairs and morality. The best-known writers of the form were Hochhuth, Weiss, and Kipphardt, although all wrote other types of plays as well.

Rolf Hochhuth (1931–) came to prominence with *The Deputy* (1963), which seeks to place much of the blame for the extermination of Jews on Pope Pius XII's refusal to take a decisive stand against Hitler's policies. This accusation made the play controversial wherever it was performed, and in many countries it was forbidden. *The Soldiers* (1967) also aroused considerable consternation because of its suggestion that Winston Churchill conspired in the death of General Sikorski, president of the Polish government in exile, because Sikorski endangered the Anglo-Russian alliance. In the late 1960s Hochhuth seemed to tire of factual material. After writing a number of less provocative plays, Hochhuth returned to controversy with *Wessies in Weimar: Scenes from an Occupied Land* (1993) concerning the murder of an official whose job it is to sell off businesses previously owned by the East German state; the play implies that the murder was justified considering what was being done to a defenseless population.

Peter Weiss (1916–1982) worked as a graphic artist, filmmaker, and journalist before winning fame as a playwright. Although he began writing in the 1940s, his first play was not produced until 1962. His international reputation dates from 1964 with the production of *The Persecution and Assassination of Jean-Paul Marat as Performed by the Inmates of the Asylum of Charenton Under the Direction of the Marquis de Sade* (usually shortened to *Marat/Sade*). Set in 1808 in the asylum at Charenton where the Marquis de Sade is confined, it shows the presentation of a play written by de Sade for performance by the inmates before a fashionable audience from nearby Paris. The play that de Sade has written is Brechtian in form, and is intended by Weiss to provoke thought about political and social justice. The asylum serves as a metaphor for the world, and the play's ending (in which the inmates get out of hand) suggests what happens when the sensual and anarchistic outlook of a de Sade is given full rein. Peter Brook's production of *Marat/Sade* (seen first in London and then in New York) was to be one of the most influential of the decade, combining as it did devices of the "theatre of cruelty" with Brechtian social and political arguments embedded within the Artaudian swirl of visual and aural effects.

Marat/Sade is only partially factual, but in his next play, *The Investigation* (1965), Weiss passed over fully into documentary drama. Set in a courtroom, *The Investigation* utilizes dialogue taken from the official

FIG. 20.15

Weiss's *Marat/Sade*. Premiere production; Schiller Theater, Berlin, 1964. Directed by Konrad Swinarski; designed by Peter Weiss. Photography by Heinz Köster.

hearings into the extermination camp at Auschwitz. Weiss' subsequent documentary plays include *The Song of the Lusitanian Bogey* (1967), about the suppression of native Africans by the Portuguese in Angola, and *A Discourse on the Previous History and Development of the Long War of Liberation in Vietnam as an Example of the Necessity for the Armed Fight of the Suppressed Against Their Suppressors as Well as the Attempt of the United States of America to Destroy the Foundations of the Revolution* (1968).

Like Hochhuth, Weiss in the late 1960s began to retreat from documentary drama, although his work continued to be based on historical sources. *Trotsky in Exile* (1970) uses material from Trotsky's life to stimulate thought about his ideas and to raise questions about our own political perspectives. *Hölderlin* (1971) is based on the life of the nineteenth-century German poet who spent much of his time locked away from the world.

Heinar Kipphardt (1922–1982) first won international renown with *In the Case of J. Robert Oppenheimer* (1964), all the dialogue for which is excerpted from the United States Senate's hearings into the loyalty of Oppenheimer after he resisted development of the hydrogen bomb. Kipphardt's primary concern, however, is with the conflict between a scientist's responsibility to his country and his duty to humanity at large.

Other playwrights continued the earlier concern with collective guilt. Among the most important of these writers was Martin Walser (1927–) in such plays as *Oak and Angora* (1962) and *The Black Swan* (1964). The latter contrasts the younger generation, who seem overly sensitive about the Nazi period, with the older generation, who lead seemingly placid lives despite their own involvement in Naziism. Most of Walser's subsequent plays, such as *The Battle of the Bedroom* (1967) and *Children's Game* (1971) treated more private subjects. But in *The Pig Play—Scenes from the Sixteenth Century* (1975) and *In Goethe's Hand* (1982), he made historical events reflect the political fears and lack of certainty among today's workers and intellectuals.

Tankred Dorst (1925–) was representative of German playwrights concerned with political subjects. His early plays were in the absurdist vein. A representative play, *Freedom for Clemens* (1961), shows how an imprisoned man gradually realizes that freedom is an internal state independent of external circumstances. Dorst's later plays are more straightforward. More recent plays include *Herr Paul* (1994), about the inability to change, and *The Shadow Line* (1995) about the decline of tolerance and enlightenment as seen through the powerlessness of intellectuals.

THEATRE AND DRAMA IN ITALY, 1940–1968

After World War II the position of the Italian playwright remained as difficult as it had been a century earlier, for there was still a conflict between the demand for realism (which required the use of some regional dialect) and for universality (which required a more literary speech). Consequently, playwrights normally wrote with one specific region in mind. Occasionally a dramatist was able to attract a national following, but only a few achieved international stature in the postwar years. Ugo Betti (1892–1953) began writing plays in 1927, but his reputation rests primarily upon his late works, *Corruption in the Palace of Justice* (1948), *The Queen and the Rebels* (1951), and *The Burnt Flower Bed* (1953). All of Betti's plays are concerned with crises of conscience, especially among those who have gained influence through questionable means. His preoccupation with guilt and power struck a responsive chord in the postwar consciousness.

Eduardo de Filippo (1900–1984) began writing around 1930. Although set in Naples and written in the Neapolitan dialect, his plays achieve universality because they show characters struggling to survive in the face of poverty, disease, and strained family relationships. They mingle the serious, comic, and pathetic with closely observed local detail. Among his best works are *Naples' Millionares* (1945), *Filumena* (1946), *Saturday, Sunday, and Monday* (1959), and *The Boss* (1960). De Fillipo, also a fine

FIG. 20.16
Giorgio Strehler's production of Goldoni's *Servant of Two Masters* at the Piccolo Teatro, Milan. Setting by Ezi Frigerio. From *Scene Design Throughout the World Since 1950*.

FIG. 20.17
Vittorio Gassman in his own production of Alfieri's *Oreste*, 1957. Setting by Gianni Polidori. Courtesy *World Theatre*.

the Teatro Stabile founded in Turin in 1955 and headed by Gianfranco de Bosio (1924–). By the 1960s there were ten of these resident companies in Italy. These companies, in which most of the leading actors were veterans of Strehler's theatre, toured throughout Italy.

Two Italian directors won international fame in the postwar years. Luchino Visconti (1906–1976) was one of the originators of the neorealism that gave Italian film much of its renown during the 1950s; and he brought the same stylistic quality to his stage productions. His best-known work was done in opera, especially in a series of productions starring Maria Callas. Franco Zeffirelli (1923–) began his career as a designer for Visconti, perhaps the greatest influence on his work. He turned to directing in 1953, at first primarily in opera, and by 1958 was being invited to direct abroad. He built a reputation for bringing classics down to earth (his productions of *Romeo and Juliet* and *Hamlet* were especially well received). In most of his productions (which he also designed), Zeffirelli used neorealistic settings and business, an approach which led on the one hand to accusations that he swamped the text with visual details and on the other to praise for bringing a sense of concreteness to works that all too often remain inaccessible to audiences.

actor, worked for many years with his brother, Peppino de Filippo (1903–1980), one of Italy's most popular performers.

In production, touring companies continued to dominate, but a few permanent resident companies were founded. The most important of the resident troupes was the Piccolo Teatro, established in Milan in 1947 by Giorgio Strehler (1921–1997) and Paolo Grassi (1919–1981). Given a rent-free theatre by the city of Milan and later the first dramatic company in Italy to receive a governmental subsidy, the Piccolo Teatro was a self-contained organization with a permanent troupe of twenty to thirty actors and a training school. Strehler directed about three-fourths of the plays (the majority by Goldoni, Brecht, and Shakespeare) but invited well-known foreign directors to stage others. He leaned heavily toward Brechtian techniques, as did his designers, Luciano Damiani (1923–) and Ezio Frigerio (1930–). Partially because of its foreign tours, the Piccolo Teatro came to be considered not only Italy's finest troupe but one of the best in the world. Permanent theatres were also established elsewhere in Italy. Perhaps the best of these were the Teatro Stabile in Genoa, founded in 1952 and headed by Luigi Squarzina (1922–), and

THEATRE AND DRAMA IN LATIN AMERICA, 1940–1968

Commercial theaters after the war reestablished the traditions of providing a well-produced classical repertory and hosting touring shows from Europe. The independent, experimental theatres, meanwhile, continued to grow, building new theatres, reclaiming those that had been taken over by cinema, and converting found spaces to theatrical uses. By 1950 Argentina, Brazil, and Mexico, and to a lesser extent Chile, Cuba, Puerto Rico, and Uruguay, had developed distinctive experimental theatres that were serving as training grounds for young artists throughout South America. Acting styles were generally based on some version of the Stanislavsky system, taught by those who had trained at the Moscow Art Theatre (like Hedy Crilla and Galina Tolmacheva in Argentina, or Seki Sano in Mexico), or by those who had trained with Stanislavsky's former students in Europe or had worked with the Actors Studio in the United States. Production methods were increasingly influenced by Brecht's ideas on epic theatre, however, while playwrights took their inspiration from Lorca, Miller, O'Neill, Pirandello, Tennessee Williams, and the absurdists. The proliferation of international festivals that grew up during the 1950s ensured that new ideas and approaches were shared throughout Latin America.

The Bridge (1949) by author-director Carlos Gorostiza (1920–) marked a turning point in Argentinean theatre when it became the first "independent theatre" play to receive a commercial run. This was a complex play in which the first and fifth acts duplicate the action of the second and fourth in order to show the same events from different points of view. Gorostiza continued to be influential in Argentine theatre well into the 1980s, with over twenty plays, including *Bread of Madness* (1958), *The Neighbors* (1966), *Beloved Brothers* (1978), and *Papi* (1984). Other successful authors of this period included Samuel Eichelbaum (1894–1967), who had written important dramas in the 1920s, the best of which was probably *The Bad Thirst* (1920), about hereditary sexual impulses like those explored by Ibsen and Wedekind. He returned to playwriting with *A 1900s Dandy* (1940) and *Divorce Nuptial* (1941) and remained a dominant figure in Argentine theatre until his last play, *Underground* (1966). Uruguayan playwright Conrado Nalé Roxlo (1898–1971) wrote the lyrical *The Mermaid's Tale* (1941), while Juan Oscar Ponferrada (1907–1990) wrote the *Devil's Carnival* (1943) and Bernardo Canal Feijó (1893–1971) wrote *The Tales of Juan* (1954), two plays that revived an interest in folklore.

After Juan Perón was deposed in 1955 Argentina experienced a period that, although it was politically unstable, was relatively liberal when it came to the treatment of theatre. Professional theatres outside Buenos Aires expanded, especially in the province of Córdoba where a number of theatres were built and subsidized by the government. Independent theatres, too, spread to the provinces, though their major concentration was always in the capital. Groups El Galpó, from Uruguay, attracted Argentine playwrights for collaborative projects that inspired many imitators in Buenos Aires.

Agustín Cuzzani (1924–1990) was an advocate for individual liberty and lampooned the pettiness of state bureaucracy in plays like *The Center Forward Died at Dawn* (1955) and *Sempronio* (1958). *Stories to be Told* (1957), developed by Osvaldo Dragún (1929–1999) with the Teatro Popular Fray Mocho, achieved international recognition for its expressionistic treatment of the exploitation of the individual in the interest of economic survival (the issue that had caused Dragún disillusionment with Perón's government). This play was first performed at the Independent Theatre Festival in Mar del Plata, one of a growing number of influential provincial festivals of the period. Dragún's other 1957 play, *Those at Table*

10, was the most performed play of its day, and he continued as a successful writer into the 1980s. Andrés Lizárraga (1919–1982) led the epic theatre movement with his three-part revisionist history of the 1810 War of Independence, *Trilogy about May* (1960).

In response to the political turmoil of the 1950s, the "new realists" came to the forefront. These writers, including Roberto Cossa (1934–) and Ricardo Halac (1935–), wrote about the frustrations of the young who were growing increasingly cynical in a culture that seemed incapable of solving its political problems. Plinio Marcos (1935–), on the other hand, wrote about the degradation of life in the slums. When General Ongania took control of the government in 1966, repressive policies were put in place and the theatre struggled to find a way to respond.

Brazil's Teatro Brasileiro de Comédia (TBC) was the most highly regarded of the independent theatres in that country until it closed in 1964. It was primarily noted for its European repertory and its imported Italian directors, who brought the highest artistic standards to its productions. On the occasions when TBC produced plays by Brazilian authors like Jorge Andrade (1922–1984), Dias Gomes (1922–1999), and Gianfrancesco Guarnieri (1934–), however, its reputation ensured that those authors received international attention. Nelson Rodrigues, meanwhile, continued to be a major force, adding such plays as *The Kiss on the Asphalt* (1961) and *All Nudity Shall Be Punished* (1965) to his work of the 1940s.

The far more radical Teatro de Arena was founded by José Renato in São Paulo in 1953. This was a politically committed company dedicated to finding an authentic Brazilian theatre. Augusto Boal (1930–), after studying in the United States, joined this company as a director in 1956, and his early play, *Lean Husband, Boring Wife,* was produced there in 1957, as was his most important political protest play, *Revolution in South America* (1960). Boal teamed up with Guarnieri in 1962 to produce a famous series of open-stage productions that combined epic theatre techniques with Brazilian folk theatre and music to tell stories of important figures from Brazil's past, drawing parallels with events in the present. After the military coup of 1964, Boal's outspoken Marxism began to get him into trouble, and following the crackdown of 1968 he was imprisoned. Boal was released and went into exile in Argentina when the Teatro de Arena was closed in 1971. While in exile, he developed his concepts of *teatro jornal,* a production approach reminiscent of the "Living Newspaper" productions of the Federal Theatre Project in the United States in the 1930s, and *teatro invisível,* a highly controversial technique in which performances are presented in a public space for an audience that is not aware that what they are seeing is staged. While in exile Boal also dedicated himself to writing books explaining his approach, the most popular of which, *Theatre of the Oppressed* (1975), brought him international recognition. His later books, *Rainbow of Desire* (1994) and *Legislative Theatre* (1998), represent his later rethinking of the uses of theatre in society.

Numerous other theatres were inspired by the radicalism of the Teatro de Arena, and among the most important of those was the Teatro Oficina, directed by José Celso Martinez Corrêa and known for its commitment to street theatre. In 1967 Teatro Oficina gave the first performance of Andrade's 1929 masterpiece, *King of the Candle,* which was hailed as one of the most innovative productions in Brazilian theatre history. The Teatro Oficina, like so many other theatres of the time, was closed (1973) by the political repression of the 1970s. When the American Living Theatre arrived in Brazil in 1970, they discovered just how effective a government could be at repressing dissent as they, too, were arrested and expelled.

The poorer northern sections of Brazil saw little theatre but inspired writers like Ariano Suassuna (1927–) to write *The Rogue's Trial* (sometimes called *The Ceremony of the Compassionate,* 1956), an adaptation of the traditional *auto* which incorporated aspects of mysticism and local humor to depict human beings as the puppets in God's puppet show. It became one of the most produced shows in Brazil and won international recognition.

Theatre in Mexico expanded rapidly in the 1950s, and much of the more experimental work being done was supported by the government through both the Instituto Nacional de Bellas Artes (INBA, founded 1947) and the Universidad Nacional Autónoma de México (UNAM, the National University), which ran its own professional theatre. The dramatic activity they funded encouraged a building boom, and between 1953 and 1958 no fewer than twenty-two new theatres were constructed in Mexico City, including the Teatro del Granero, the country's first theatre in the round. In 1960 the government committed itself to making theatre accessible to everyone and through the Instituto Mexicano del Seguro had forty theatres built across the country. It also established a touring system under the direction of José Solé (1934–) and José Ignacio Retes (1918–2004), who provided a wide-ranging repertory of plays for this circuit. In 1977 this forty-theatre circuit was designated the Teatro de la Nación.

Under the continuing influence of Rodolfo Usigli, a new generation of playwrights came into prominence in Mexico. The first of the new playwrights was José Revueltas (1914–1976), whose play *The Quadrant of Loneliness* (1950) was an evocation of the psychologically devastating effects of the massive overcrowding already overtaking Mexico City—a theme later taken up by Sergio Magaña (1924–) in *The Signs of the Zodiac* (1951), the first major success of his long career. Mexico's most versatile and widely known dramatist, Emilio Carballido (1925–), began his career in 1950 with *Rosalba and the Llaveros,* a comedy in which the world of a conservative provincial family is turned upside down by a visit from their city cousin. His many other plays range from the existential *Medusa* (1958) to the satiric *The Watchmaker of Córdoba* (1960) to the hauntingly desolate *I Too Speak of the Rose* (1966). Carballido's later plays, like *Rose of Two Aromas* (1992), lacked the innovative energy of his earlier dramas.

Luisa Josefina Hernández (1928–), whose early work dealt with the frustrations of provincial life, especially for Mexico's women, went on to write plays that challenged the existing political and social system. Her plays include *The Royal Guest* (1957), a study of incest; *Popol Vuh* (1966), based on the sacred book of the Maya; and *The Festival of the Mulatto's* (1979), her most nonrealistic piece. She was given Usigli's chair in theatre at the National University when he entered diplomatic service.

Héctor Mendoza (1932–) was a successful playwright when he joined a group of artists that included the actor-playwright Juan José Arreola (1918–2001), whose play *Everybody's Time* (1963) dealt with the crash of an airplane into the Empire State Building, and the poet Octavio Paz to create the Poesia en Voz Alta (Poetry Out Loud) series. From 1956 to 1963, this was the most experimental theatre venture in Mexico and made Mendoza the most highly regarded director since Seki Sano. Many of the most important directors of the next generation began their careers under Mendoza's tutelage. Among the many successful Mexican playwrights who began their careers in the years between World War II and 1968 were Carlos Solórzano (1922–), a writer of expressionistic plays; Elena Garro (1920–1998), a surrealist; Hugo Argüelles (1932–2003), one of the first to be linked to the concept of "magic realism"; and Oscar Villegas (1943–), whose works were early examples of what was to become known as postmodernism. Felipe Santander (1934–) had only moderate success in this period, but his later musical review, *The Extension Agent* (1978), was the most popular play of that decade.

The Mexican theatre of this period challenged a great many established norms but rarely made the kind of attacks on the national government that were so common in other parts of Latin America. This may be because the government was so supportive of theatre or may only explain the government's willingness to support it. In 1968, however, Mexican students joined the protest movements that had been sweeping the United States, France, and other nations. On October 2 they were fired on by the military, leaving over 300 dead and hundreds more injured. The relationship between the government and the theatre was never the same thereafter.

By the 1960s, then, the theatre had fully recovered from the destruction of the war years. For the most part, however, it had continued along lines that had been established earlier, although there were a few notable exceptions, especially in France and England. But during the 1960s, new tensions and outlooks gathered strength, and by 1968 the theatre was entering a period of enormous controversy and, in most countries, a period of enormous vitality. Repressive governments, political unrest, and economic crisis in many of the Latin American countries through the 1970s and 1980s, however, delayed any vibrant revival of theatre there until the 1990s.

LOOKING AT THEATRE HISTORY

In studying theatre history we need to be concerned about the "ideological climate" of an age. Is it a period in which there is strong agreement or sharp division? If so, about what? What is being defended or attacked? What is so taken for granted that it need not be questioned or discussed? What is privileged and what marginalized? What heirarchies of power (church/state, rank/class, male/female, nature/culture, individual/society, and so on) are evident? In no period is there total agreement on values and goals, but in most there is a discernible dominant ideology that is used to provide cohesiveness and a measure of stability. In others, there is sufficient disagreement to produce disarray. Whatever the case, the theatre reflects the ideological stances and tensions of its time.

After World War II, conflicts among ideologies were especially evident: capitalism/communism; equal rights/privilege established by custom or law; individual right/law and order; developed world/ third world; and so on. Immediately following World War II, a crisis in belief, attributable in large part to the Nazi extermination camps and the threat of world destruction from atomic warfare, fueled interest in existentialism and absurdism. This crisis in belief was perhaps most clearly defined by Albert Camus:

A world that can be explained even with bad reasons is a familiar world. But, on the other hand, in a universe suddenly divested of illusions and lights, man feels an alien, a stranger. His exile is without remedy since he is deprived of the memory of a lost home or the hope of a promised land. This divorce between man and his life . . . is properly the feeling of absurdity. . . . I said that the world is absurd, but I was too hasty. This world in itself is not reasonable, that is all that can be said. But what is absurd is the confrontation of this irrational and wild longing for clarity whose call echoes in the human heart. . . . The absurd is born of this confrontation between the human need and the unreasonable silence of the world.

Albert Camus, "The Myth of Sisyphus," *The Myth of Sisyphus and Other Essays*, trans. Justin O'Brien (New York: Alfred A. Knopf, 1967), 6ff.

It was Martin Esslin who in 1961 first invented a label, "theatre of the absurd," for plays that seemed to stem from the position set forth by Camus:

The hallmark of [the theatre of the absurd] is its sense that certitudes and unshakable basic assumptions of former ages have been swept away, that they have been tested and found wanting, that they have been discredited as cheap and somewhat childish illusions. . . .
This sense of metaphysical anguish at the absurdity of the human condition is, broadly speaking the theme of the plays of Beckett, Adamov, Ionesco, Genet, and the other writers in this book. But it is not merely the

subject-matter that defines what is here called the Theatre of the Absurd. . . . [That theatre also] strives to express its sense of the senselessness of the human condition and the inadequacy of the rational approach by the open abandonment of rational devices and discursive thought. . . . [It seeks] to achieve a unity between its basic assumptions and the form in which they are expressed.

Martin Esslin, *The Theatre of the Absurd,* revised and updated edition (Woodstock, N.Y.: The Overlook Press, 1973), 4–6.

Eugène Ionesco was not only one of the most successful but also one of the most argumentative of absurdist playwrights, often taking issue with the directors of his plays and with critics. (Many of his comments are collected in *Notes and Counter Notes.*) Here are some reactions motivated by the American production of *Rhinoceros* in 1961:

Some critics blame me for denouncing evil without saying what good is . . . but it is so easy to rely on a system of thought that is more or less mechanical. . . . An unworkable solution one has found for oneself is infinitely more valuable than a ready-made ideology that stops men from thinking. . . .

One of the great critics of New York complains that, after destroying one conformism, I put nothing else in its place, leaving him and the audience in a vacuum. That is exactly what I wanted to do. A free man should pull himself out of vacuity on his own, by his own efforts and not by the efforts of other people.

Notes and Counter Notes, Writings on the Theatre, trans. Donald Watson (New York: Grove Press, 1964), 207–211.

By the 1960s, all the technological means of the space age were being adapted to theatrical purposes, barriers between the arts were being broken down, and multimedia events of all sorts were flourishing. Josef Svoboda is probably the best known of those who sought to extend the theatre's range of expression through technological devices. Here are some excerpts from his statements about the production of Luigi Nonno's opera *Intoleranza* (produced in Boston in 1965):

Instead of film I used television techniques in such a way as to project a TV image onto many screens placed on the stage. . . . We were able to transmit parallel actions that were performed in adjoining studios, in fact in studios as far as three miles from the stage. All these studios were joined with each other by audio and visual monitors, so that the actors could see the conductor in relation to themselves, the actors in the studio could see what was being played on the stage, and . . . the actors on the stage see what was played in the studios. In this way, the conductor was absolute master of the rhythm of the performance. . .

Jarka Burian, *The Scenography of Josef Svoboda* (Middletown, Conn.: Wesleyan University Press, 1971), 103.

21
English-Language Theatre in the Mid Twentieth Century

With the coming of the war in 1939, the English theatre was soon at a virtual standstill. At the height of the German blitz, only one theatre remained open in London. The Old Vic company retreated to the provinces, Donald Wolfit (1902–1968) organized lunchtime programs, and a few others attempted to keep the theatre alive, but for the most part English theatrical life was almost completely disrupted.

Every attempt was made to return to normal immediately following the war, but the economies of Europe had been devastated and it seemed that everything in England was in need of rebuilding. The English theatre did little more than try to pick up where it had left off before the war. But by the mid-1950s, frustration and cynicism were setting in, especially among the young, and a new generation of playwrights, directors, actors, and designers stepped in to express this frustration, setting in motion a dynamic reinvigoration of theatre.

In the United States, Canada, Australia, and New Zealand, theatre suffered less interruption during the war, but with many theatre artists involved in the war effort and rationing limiting the resources available, it could do little more than maintain the status quo. At war's end the economies of these countries recovered more quickly than did those of the European nations, and this made it easier for theatre artists to return to what they had done before the war and gave them

less motivation to change. The Cold War with its ever-present threat of nuclear annihilation, McCarthyism and the civil rights movement in the United States, the Korean War, and the Vietnam War were among the many troubling events that caused profound uncertainties about the directions in which the governments of these countries were going. By the late 1950s the theatre had begun to reflect those uncertainties.

ENGLISH THEATRE AND DRAMA, 1940–1968

Following World War II, the English commercial theatre was largely innocuous. The leading dramatist was Terence Rattigan (1911–1977), who began to write plays in 1933, achieved his first popular success with *French Without Tears* (1936), and after the war turned to more serious subjects in *The Winslow Boy* (1946), *The Browning Version* (1948), *Separate Tables* (1955), and *Ross* (1960). Although Rattigan created compelling situations and interesting characters, the "drawing room" atmosphere of his plays perpetuated familiar traditions.

The commercial theatre also took poetic drama under its wing for a time during the 1950s, after E. Martin Browne generated considerable enthusiasm with his productions at the Mercury Theatre. With

A Phoenix Too Frequent (1946), Browne called attention to Christopher Fry (1907–2005), and this led John Gielgud to produce *The Lady's Not for Burning* (1949), which established Fry's reputation and revived interest in poetic drama. Fry went on to write *Venus Observed* (1949), *The Dark Is Light Enough* (1954), *A Yard of Sun* (1970), and several adaptations. T. S. Eliot also returned to playwriting with *The Cocktail Party* (1949), which enjoyed considerable popular success following its production at the Edinburgh Festival. He went on to write *The Confidential Clerk* (1953) and *The Elder Statesman* (1958). All of these plays by Eliot were modernized and adapted versions of ancient Greek dramas. By 1955 interest in poetic drama was on the wane.

After the war, the Old Vic company was the most respected in England. It returned to London in 1944, having spent the war years in the provinces. At first it played in the New Theatre, for its own building had been partially destroyed by bombing. At this time, the management passed from Tyrone Guthrie to Laurence Olivier, Ralph Richardson, and John Burrell, who presented a series of brilliant productions (among them *Oedipus Rex, Richard III, Love for Love,* and *Peer Gynt*) that made the Old Vic one of the most admired companies in the world. In 1946 the Old Vic also established a theatre school under the direction of Michel Saint-Denis, assisted by George Devine and Glen Byam Shaw, who utilized principles drawn primarily from Copeau. Closely allied with this school was a company—the Young Vic, under the direction of George Devine—that performed for young audiences. After 1946 the Old Vic also had a second branch in Bristol.

FIG. 21.2

Zeffirelli's production of *Romeo and Juliet* at the Old Vic, 1960. From *Scene Design Throughout the World Since 1950.*

Unfortunately, after 1948 the Old Vic began to decline, as Olivier and Richardson began to devote increasing amounts of time to outside commitments. In 1949 the management passed to Hugh Hunt (1911–1993), who had served as director of the Bristol Old Vic since its formation. The return of the company to the repaired Old Vic Theatre in 1950 created considerable conflicts between the school and the Young Vic troupe, and in 1952 both of the latter were dissolved. Hunt resigned and made his way to Australia to run the Elizabethan Theatre Trust, leaving Michael Benthall (1919–1974) in charge of the Old Vic, which he ran from 1953 to 1958. The company was still good though relatively young (the leading players were John Neville, Barbara Jefford, and Paul Rogers). But the days of greatness were over, although they were recaptured briefly in 1960 with Franco Zeffirelli's brawling, lusty production of *Romeo and Juliet.* In 1963 the Old Vic company was dissolved and its building became the first home of the National Theatre.

As the Old Vic declined, the Stratford Festival Company gained in prestige, largely because of several reforms made by Barry Jackson, head of the theatre between 1946 and 1948. Under Jackson's management, the company became a self-contained producing organization with its own technical staff providing costumes and scenery; storage space was added and the stage was remodeled. Jackson also gained control over the entire festival so that its activities could be coordinated, and he enlivened the troupe by the addition of such vital young directors and actors as Peter Brook (1925–) and Paul Scofield

FIG. 21.1

T. S. Eliot's *The Cocktail Party,* premiere production, 1949. At center, Rex Harrison as Harcourt-Reilly. Photo by Anthony Buckley.

(1922–). Between 1948 and 1956 the management was assumed by Anthony Quayle (1913–1989), who was joined in 1953 by Glen Byam Shaw. Such outstanding actors as Gielgud, Olivier, Redgrave, and Peggy Ashcroft appeared often, and in 1951 the number of productions given annually was reduced to permit more careful preparation. For the first time, London's critics attended the performances regularly and soon Stratford was being elevated in their reviews above the Old Vic. During the 1950s, novel interpretations also came to be accepted as the norm rather than as aberrations.

Festivals—such as those at Edinburgh, Chichester, Malvern, Glyndebourne, Canterbury, and Aldeburgh—also added considerably to the vitality of the English theatre during the 1950s. Nevertheless, by 1956 the English theatre seemed to many observers to be living on its past reputation. Then, quite unexpectedly, a "renaissance" occurred. The change can be attributed to two producing organizations, the English Stage Company and the Theatre Workshop, and to the dramatists with whom they worked.

The English Stage Company, founded in 1956, was placed under the artistic management of George Devine (1910–1966), who began his career as an actor in 1932, taught at Michel Saint-Denis's London Theatre Studio from 1936 to 1939, and directed the Young Vic Company after the war. Playing at the Royal Court Theatre, once the home of Granville Barker's troupe, the English Stage Company intended to emphasize new English plays and foreign works not yet seen in England. Failing to uncover a backlog of unproduced English dramas, Devine placed a notice in *The Stage,* which induced John Osborne (1929–1994) to submit *Look Back in Anger.* The production of Osborne's play in 1956 is usually considered the turning point in postwar British theatre.

Osborne's break with the past is not to be found in his dramaturgy (*Look Back in Anger* is straightforwardly realistic), but in his attack upon class distinctions and upon the complacency and inertia of all classes. Its protagonist, Jimmy Porter, seems to have no positive solution to suggest for the long list of moral, social, and political betrayals he denounces. Although essentially negative in tone, the play caught the contemporary rebellious mood so well that Jimmy came to represent an entire generation of "angry young men." Osborne's next play, *The Entertainer* (1957), has as its protagonist a disintegrating music hall performer (originally played by Laurence Olivier). Here England's progressive decline in vigor and values is symbolized in three generations of the Rice family of entertainers. Olivier's great critical success as Archie Rice rejuvenated his career and forged a bridge between the old and new theatres.

FIG. 21.3

Osborne's *Look Back in Anger* at the Royal Court Theatre, 1956. The actors are Kenneth Haigh, Alan Bates, and Mary Ure. Directed by Tony Richardson. Photo by Houston Rogers.

Thereafter, major established actors appeared increasingly in the new dramas.

Osborne's work after 1960 was very uneven in quality. Among his successful plays were *Luther* (1961), a psychological study of the religious reformer, and *Inadmissible Evidence* (1965), a moving evocation of the wasted life of an outwardly successful, middle-aged lawyer. Although Osborne's later works from *A Patriot for Me* (1965) to *Déjàvu* (1992) met with little success, he is still considered one of the most important of postwar dramatists.

Next to Osborne, the Royal Court's most important dramatist of the early years was probably John Arden (1930–), author of *Live Like Pigs* (1958), *Sergeant Musgrave's Dance* (1959), *The Happy Haven* (1960), *Armstrong's Last Goodnight* (1964), and several other plays. Arden's work was both praised highly and said to be confused. Because he treated contemporary problems but did not seem to take sides, audiences found it difficult to decide what he intended. But practically all of the plays pursued the same themes—the conflict between order and anarchy, between conformity and freedom, between those who wish to impose some pattern or principle and those who resist such efforts.

The Theatre Workshop was founded in 1945 by a group of young people dissatisfied with the commercial theatre on both artistic and social grounds. Joan Littlewood (1914–2005) soon became its leader. Having few financial resources, the company toured England and the continent before settling in 1953 in a London suburb, Stratford East, a working-class district.

Two playwrights, Behan and Delaney, were especially associated with the Theatre Workshop. Brendan Behan's (1923–1965) first play, *The Quare Fellow,* written in 1945, was presented by the Theatre Workshop in 1956. A mixture of the comic and serious, it shows a cross-section of prison life on the eve of a prisoner's execution. Similarly, *The Hostage* (1958) is built around varying attitudes toward the impending death of an I.R.A. agent and the hostage who is to be killed in reprisal. Many diversions (song, dances, and character vignettes) enliven the play. Shelagh Delaney's (1939–) *A Taste of Honey* (1958) is the story of a young girl and her slatternly mother set against a closely observed background. The belief that Littlewood had a strong hand in reshaping the plays of both Behan and Delaney is supported in part by the failure of both to produce significant drama except with the Workshop.

The Theatre Workshop was also noted for its production style, perhaps best exemplified in *Oh, What a Lovely War!* (1963), a biting satire on the First World War. As the director of more than 150 of its productions, Littlewood was responsible for establishing the company's approach. She drew heavily on Brechtian and music hall conventions, but also on Stanislavsky, especially by emphasizing "through lines" of action and improvisation. Her ultimate aim was to create a theatre to which the working classes would go with the same regularity and enthusiasm as to fun palaces or penny arcades.

FIG. 21.4

Joan Littlewood's production of *Oh, What a Lovely War!* at the Theatre Workshop, 1963. Design by John Bury. Photo courtesy *The Report.*

Within a framework of conventions borrowed from popular entertainments, she sought to imbed some lasting message or significant content.

Several of the Theatre Workshop's successful productions were moved to commercial theatres, and this practice so weakened the company that Littlewood eventually resigned. Subsequently, she returned occasionally to direct productions for the Workshop, although it was no longer the vital force that it unquestionably was during the years between 1955 and the early 1960s.

Arnold Wesker (1932–), perhaps England's most socially conscious playwright of the late 1950s, is best known for his trilogy—*Chicken Soup with Barley* (1958), *Roots* (1959), and *I'm Talking about Jerusalem* (1960)—which trace the declining sense of purpose in the socialist movement and seek to show that workers have settled for too little and have chosen the wrong paths in seeking to remedy ills. In *The Kitchen* (1958) Wesker explores working-class conditions through the microcosm of a kitchen in a large restaurant, and in *Chips with Everything* (1962) he uses an air force camp to show that enlisted men are exploited and systematically deprived of all that is best in entertainment, art, and living conditions.

In 1962 Wesker became the leader of a working-class art movement called Center 42 (named from the 1961 Trades Union Congress resolution number 42, which called for popularization of the arts among workers). With Center 42 Wesker intended to supply plays and music of high quality for festivals throughout the country, but after a brief burst of energy it confined its activities to the Roundhouse, a converted railroad building in north London. In 1971 Center 42 was disbanded. The few plays Wesker wrote after 1962 met with little success.

Another popular dramatist, Peter Shaffer (1926–), also began his career during the 1950s. Shaffer wrote quite diverse plays, ranging through the realistic *Five Finger Exercise* (1958) to such absurdist comedies as *The Private Ear* and *The Public Eye* (1962) and *Black Comedy* (1965). He is most admired, however, for *The Royal Hunt of the Sun* (1964), a story about the Spanish conquest of Peru which Shaffer has described as "an attempt to define the concept of God"; *Equus* (1973), a psychological study of a boy who has blinded several horses and of the psychiatrist who treats him; and *Amadeus* (1979), which shows the destruction of the naive and clumsy genius, Mozart, by his mediocre, urbane, and jealous rival Salieri. Of his later plays only *Lettice and Lovage* (1988) was viewed as significant.

Robert Bolt (1924–1995), came to public attention with *The Flowering Cherry* (1957), a quasi-Chekhovian study of self-deception and failure, and later wrote *Vivat, Vivat Regina* (1970), treating the story of Elizabeth I and Mary of Scotland. But he is best known for *A Man for All Seasons* (1960) an often revived play based on the life and martyrdom of Sir Thomas More.

The playwright who achieved the greatest international reputation was Harold Pinter (1930–), who, after beginning his career as an actor, turned to playwriting in 1957 with *The Room.* Thereafter he wrote regularly for the theatre, television, and films. His stage works include *The Dumb Waiter* (1957), *The Birthday Party* (1958), *The Caretaker* (1960), *The Homecoming* (1965), *Old Times* (1970), *No Man's Land* (1975), *Betrayal* (1978), *A Kind of Alaska* (1982), *Moonlight* (1993), and numerous others. Although there is much variety among them, almost all of Pinter's plays have in common a few characteristics: everyday situations that gradually take on an air of mystery or menace; unexplained, unrevealed, or ambiguous motivations or background information; and authentic, seemingly natural though carefully wrought dialogue. With Pinter silence is an integral part of language, which he treats as a stratagem used by characters to cover their psychological nakedness. Thus, "unspoken subtext" is often as important as dialogue. In Pinter's plays everything may at first seem amusing or pleasantly ambiguous, but gradually the tone changes to anxiety, pathos, or fear as the characters confront some predicament and seek to defend themselves against some unknown, often undefined danger from outside or within the room in which the action occurs. As a dramatist, Pinter falls somewhere between Beckett and Chekhov. Like Beckett, he isolates characters and lets them wrestle with their anxieties in an unverifiable universe; like Chekhov, he creates a realistic texture of background and dialogue in which surface act and speech are merely evasions or disguises of deeper conflicts and uncertainties.

Much of the English theatre's postwar accomplishment was made possible by a change in attitude toward subsidies. Until World War II, no direct governmental aid had ever been given the arts. Then, in 1940, the Council for the Encouragement of Music and the Arts (CEMA) was given £50,000 to assist in wartime work. In 1946 CEMA became the Arts Council, an independent organization financed by government funds. It never had much money (in the 1960s it had only about one million dollars annually for drama), but it used it to encourage organizations that seemed capable of providing leadership. In 1948 Parliament also authorized local governments to allot a percentage of their revenues to support the arts. As a result, several municipalities began to provide subsidies for local resident

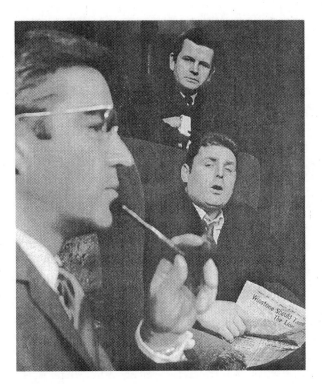

FIG. 21.5

Pinter's *The Homecoming* at the Royal Shakespeare Company, 1965. Michael Craig as Teddy, Terence Rigby (seated) as Joey, and Ian Holm as Lenny. Directed by Peter Hall. Courtesy Royal Shakespeare Company.

companies, of which by the 1960s there were more than fifty in Great Britain, most performing a mixed repertory of classics and recent works. Among the best of these were the companies in Bristol, Birmingham, Manchester, Nottingham, Coventry, and Glasgow.

After 1960, two companies, in addition to the English Stage Company, were especially important in English theatrical life: the Royal Shakespeare Company and the National Theatre. In 1961 the Shakespeare Memorial Theatre was given a new charter and a new title, the Royal Shakespeare Company (RSC). Its new status owed most to Peter Hall (1930–) who, after beginning his directing career in 1955, had worked at Stratford since 1957 and had been named head of its company in 1960. Upon assuming the new post, Hall at once set out to overcome one of the troupe's principal problems: the inability to hold a company together and build an ensemble because the season at Stratford lasted only about six months each year. To remedy this situation, Hall took a lease on the Aldwych Theatre in London and transformed the organization into a year-round operation. Thereafter, the company divided its efforts between Stratford and London. Hall also broadened

FIG. 21.6
Peter Shaffer's *Royal Hunt of the Sun* at the National Theatre, London, 1964. Courtesy National Theatre, London.

produced a series of programs under the overall title, "Theatre of Cruelty." Out of this season came Brook's production of Weiss' *Marat/Sade,* one of the most influential productions of the decade and the one that did most to draw attention to Artaud's theories. By the mid-1960s the RSC was London's major *avant-garde* troupe, noted both for its innovative techniques and for its wide-ranging repertory, with plays by Hochhuth, Pinter, and numerous continental and British dramatists of the past and present. The Aldwych also became the home of the World Theatre Season, an arrangement under which each spring from 1964 to 1975 major companies from throughout the world came to London for limited engagements.

Under Hall, the RSC's most characteristic productions used a simplified realism that owed much to Brecht. Verse was spoken in a measured downbeat. The visual style owed much to John Bury (1925–2000), Hall's principal designer after 1963. Bury avoided decorative and illustrative scenery; rather, his settings were functional skeletal structures. Costumes and props usually looked long-used. The high point of Hall's work was probably the cycle of Shakespeare's history plays, which he presented in 1963–1964 under the overall title *The War of the Roses.*

Of the directors associated with the RSC, Peter Brook (1925–) was the most influential. He began directing while still in his teens and first worked at

the repertory to include plays other than those by Shakespeare so that actors would have diversified experience.

By 1962 the RSC's activities had been so enlarged that Peter Brook and Michel Saint-Denis were added to the management. The RSC also began an experimental program, and in 1963–1964 Peter Brook, in collaboration with Charles Marowitz,

FIG. 21.7
Henry VI, one part of the cycle, *The War of the Roses,* 1964. Directed by Peter Hall; designed by John Bury. From the Tom Holte Theatre Photographic Collection. Courtesy the Shakespeare Birthplace Trust, Stratford-upon-Avon.

Stratford in 1946. During the 1950s he built an enviable reputation with productions starring such actors as Olivier, Paul Scofield, and the Lunts, and with plays by such authors as Shakespeare, Fry, Anouilh, Eliot, Duerrenmatt, and Genet. But he is now best known for a series of productions after 1960, including *King Lear* (1962), *Marat/Sade* (1964), *A Midsummer Night's Dream* (1970), and *Mahabharata* (1985). As a director, Brook was not so much an innovator as an eclectic who transformed borrowings from many sources into his own vital expression. For example, for *A Midsummer Night's Dream* he borrowed from Meyerhold, *commedia dell'arte,* circus, and radical theatre groups of the 1960s, but the results were uniquely his own. For this production, Brook sought to divest the play of its romantic aura of fairies and haunted woodlands and to make it more immediately relevant to his time. He interpreted the script as an exploration of love, and consequently he used the same pair of actors as Theseus and Hippolyta and Oberon and Titania, and treated the enchanted scenes as lessons on love for the betrothed royal couple. The stage was enclosed on three sides by white, unadorned walls broken only by two nearly invisible doors at the rear. The forest was suggested by loosely coiled metal springs attached to fishing rods. The flying was accomplished with trapezes lowered and raised to varying heights within the setting. Most of the performers wore a kind of coverall, but there was a sprinkling of *commedia dell'arte,* circus, and other costumes. Despite all these distinctive features, the text was given its full poetic value. Such novel and imaginative approaches made Brook one of the most effective and respected directors of the age.

Beginning in the 1960s the RSC had a powerful rival in the National Theatre. England was one of the last European countries to establish a national theatre, though it had long contemplated such a move. Parliamentary approval for the company was given in the late 1940s but it was not implemented until 1963, when the Old Vic company was dissolved and its building assigned to the new troupe. Laurence Olivier was named director and Kenneth Tynan (1927–1980) literary advisor. The National Theatre rapidly built a reputation for excellence through its extremely eclectic choice of plays and production styles. It sought to assemble for each production the team best suited to that script. Consequently, it utilized numerous English and foreign directors (among them Brook, George Devine, Jonathan Miller, Franco Zeffirelli, Ingmar Bergman, and Victor Garcia) and designers (among them Motley, Sean Kenny, Josef Svoboda, and René Allio). It also from time to time staged seasons of experimental plays. It was often said that the National Theatre was an

FIG. 21.8

Peter Brook's production of *A Midsummer Night's Dream,* 1970. Oberon and Puck (on trapezes) watch Titania and Bottom. Design by Sally Jacobs. Courtesy Royal Shakespeare Company.

actors' theatre, whereas the RSC was a director's theatre, and the English Stage Company a playwrights' theatre.

THEATRE AND DRAMA IN THE UNITED STATES, 1940–1968

After World War II the most influential figures in U.S. theatre were probably the director Elia Kazan and the designer Jo Mielziner, for through their joint work on such plays as Williams' *A Streetcar Named Desire* (1947) and Miller's *Death of a Salesman* (1949) they established the approach to production that was to remain dominant into the 1960s. Under Mielziner's influence, stage settings eliminated nonessential features, thereby creating a "theatricalized realism." On the other hand, acting moved increasingly toward a psychological truth

FIG. 21.9
The National Theatre's production of Strindberg's
The Dance of Death, 1967. The actors are Geraldine
McEwan, Robert Stephens, and Laurence Olivier.
Photograph by Zoë Dominic.

rooted in the characters' inner motivations. It was an extension of the Group Theatre's approach as taught at the Actors Studio.

Founded in 1947 by Robert Lewis (1909–1997), Elia Kazan, and Cheryl Crawford, the Actors Studio was designed to permit selected actors to work and develop by applying the Stanislavsky method, with special emphasis on intention and action. But in 1948 Lewis resigned and Lee Strasberg became the dominant force and shifted the emphasis to emotion memory and exploration of the actor's psyche as the key to truth in acting. Marlon Brando (1924–2004), with his characterization of the inarticulate and uneducated Stanley Kowalski of *A Streetcar Named Desire,* came to epitomize in the popular mind the Actors Studio ideal. In 1956 the Studio added a program designed to assist playwrights, and in 1960 a workshop for directors. By the 1960s, however, the influence of the Actors Studio had begun to decline as interest turned toward nonrealistic and period drama, for which the Studio's approach came to seem too limited. Nevertheless, it remained a powerful force.

After the war, the theatre was seriously threatened by the rapid development of television. In 1948 there were only 48 stations, but by 1958 there were 512 and over 50 million television sets. The new medium's free entertainment came at just the time when production costs in the theatre were rapidly increas-

ing. Between 1944 and 1960 the price of tickets doubled, and the costs of mounting a show increased at a still faster rate. Under these circumstances, Broadway producers tended to seek vehicles with broad appeal, and to avoid both plays and production styles that might offend or confuse spectators. Nevertheless, the Broadway theatre continued the decline that had begun before the war. It reached a low point in the season of 1949–1950, when only fifty-nine new productions were mounted, but then slowly climbed to about seventy, a number that could not be greatly increased because of the relatively small number of available theatres (about thirty in the 1950s).

In the late 1940s the reduction of U.S. theatre to a small number of Broadway productions served to motivate several attempts to diversify. One of the most important results was the off-Broadway movement. By playing in out-of-the-way theatres or improvised auditoriums, production costs could be cut considerably, and works which would not appeal to a mass audience could be played for smaller groups. The off-Broadway movement can properly be traced back to the little theatres of the World War I era. The little theatre movement had declined markedly during the 1930s but began to revive during World War II. In 1943 the city of New York acquired the Mecca Temple on 55th Street and converted it into the City Center, where opera, musical comedy, ballet, and drama were played for limited engagements at moderate prices. Under the general direction of Jean Dalrymple (1910–1998), the City Center was to build enviable ballet and opera troupes that would be transferred to Lincoln Center in 1966. Another significant effort came in 1946–1947 when Eva Le Gallienne, Margaret Webster (1905–1972), and Cheryl Crawford established the American Repertory Company (modeled on Le Gallienne's earlier Civic Repertory Company), which performed a season of six plays before being forced by financial difficulties to close.

The more typical off-Broadway groups, however, were begun by relatively unknown directors. A major upturn in prestige came in 1952, when the Circle in the Square presented to high critical praise Williams' *Summer and Smoke,* a failure on Broadway. Soon off-Broadway was viewed as a workable alternative to Broadway's commercialism. By 1955–1956, there were more than ninety off-Broadway groups, and they, rather than Broadway companies, gave the first performances in New York of works by such authors as Brecht, Ionesco, and Genet.

Of the off-Broadway groups, two—Circle in the Square and the Phoenix Theatre—were of special importance during the 1950s. The Circle in the Square was opened in 1951 by José Quintero

FIG. 21.10

Tennessee Williams' *A Streetcar Named Desire*. At center, Jessica Tandy as Blanche; second from right, Marlon Brando as Stanley. Directed by Elia Kazan; setting by Jo Mielziner. Courtesy Graphic House, Inc.

(1924–1999) and Theodore Mann (1924–). In this former nightclub, the actor–audience relationship was entirely flexible, although spectators normally were seated around three sides of a rectangular acting area. Here such performers as Geraldine Page, Jason Robards, Jr., George C. Scott, and Coleen Dewhurst came to prominence. After his triumph with O'Neill's *The Iceman Cometh* in 1956, Quintero was asked to direct the Broadway production of *Long Day's Journey into Night*. Its cumulative record made the Circle in the Square one of the most respected of off-Broadway theatres.

The Phoenix Theatre was inaugurated in 1953 by Norris Houghton (1909–2001) and T. Edward Hambleton (1911–2005) in an out-of-the-way but fully equipped conventional theatre. It presented a diverse program of plays by such authors as Aristophanes, Shakespeare, Turgenev, Ibsen, Shaw, Pirandello, Ionesco, and Montherlant. It also attempted to use a different director for each play and frequently included well-known actors among its casts. Beginning in the late 1950s, the Phoenix employed a permanent acting company, which under the direction of Stuart Vaughan presented a series of plays each season. This arrangement lasted until the early 1960s, when Houghton and Hambleton formed a liaison with the Association of Producing Artists and thereafter became primarily presenters of that company's offerings.

For the most part, off-Broadway theatres in the 1950s were little concerned with experimentation in staging except in their use of arena and thrust stages. They were most interested in repertory, seeking to present a more challenging drama than that favored by Broadway.

During the 1960s the New York theatre continued to be enlivened by off-Broadway. Of the many off-Broadway groups, probably the most influential was the Living Theatre, founded in 1946 by Judith Malina (1926–) and Julian Beck (1925–1985). Originally interested in poetic drama and nonrealistic production techniques, during the 1950s they came under the influence of both Artaud and Brecht. A major turning point in their work came in 1959 with their production of Jack Gelber's *The Connection*, a drama in which the audience supposedly is being allowed to watch the making of a documentary film about dope addicts. The overall effect was that of a naturalistic slice of life. The production won awards in New York and subsequently at the Théâtre des Nations in Paris. Another important production was Kenneth Brown's *The Brig* (1963), which re-creates the repetitive and senseless routine of a day in a Marine prison. In 1964 the company went abroad after losing its theatre for failure to pay taxes. By the late 1960s it would be one of the world's most controversial companies.

The off-Broadway theatre was beginning to undergo many of the same economic pressures felt by Broadway by 1960, and consequently it began to be less adventurous than in earlier years. As it declined,

FIG. 21.11
Jo Mielziner's setting for Arthur Miller's *Death of a Salesman*. Photograph by Peter A. Juley & Son. Courtesy Mr. Mielziner.

it was supplemented by off-off-Broadway. It is usual to date off-off-Broadway from 1958 when Joe Cino began to use his Café Cino as an art center. By 1961 plays were a regular part of his offerings, and others had begun to take up the idea. Soon plays were being presented wherever space could be found. Most of the participants were unpaid and budgets were infinitesimal, but by 1965 some 400 plays by more than 200 playwrights had been seen off-off-Broadway.

The most influential of the off-off-Broadway producers of the 1960s was Ellen Stewart (1919–), who began to present plays in a basement room in 1961. After trouble with fire inspectors, she created the La MaMa Experimental Theatre Club (ostensibly a private organization and therefore exempt from many regulations governing public performances). By 1969–1970 La MaMa alone produced more plays than were seen on Broadway that season. In 1969 the La MaMa organization acquired its own building with two theatres, and in 1974 it quadrupled its space through the acquisition of an annex.

Beginning in 1964, Stewart also took productions abroad, where her freewheeling experiments attracted such favorable attention that she was invited to found branches in several countries. Thus the La MaMa organization came to be known

throughout the world. Stewart considered La MaMa to be a playwright's theatre intended to nourish talent. Her tolerance of innovation meant that many La MaMa plays were amateurish, but it also meant that many talented writers were given a hearing they might otherwise have been denied. Nevertheless, La MaMa illustrates well two basic characteristics of off-off-Broadway in the 1960s—the determined pursuit of novelty and the lack of standards by which to judge it.

Other important off-off-Broadway groups of the 1960s included the Judson Poets' Theatre, founded in 1961 by Al Carmines and especially important for promoting small-scale musicals, many of them written by Carmines and Cuban-born playwright Maria Irene Fornes (1930–); the American Place Theatre, founded in 1964 by Wynn Handman to rejuvenate the American theatre by encouraging outstanding authors to write plays, and later housed in one of the mid-Manhattan skyscrapers which, owing to tax incentives, included theatres; and Theatre Genesis, established in 1964 by Ralph Cook and housed in St. Mark's in the Bowery.

Another attempt to diversify New York's theatre was Lincoln Center for the Performing Arts (with facilities for opera, ballet, concerts, and plays). In anticipation of the Center's completion, a repertory

FIG. 21.12

O'Neill's *The Iceman Cometh* at Circle in the Square, 1956. Directed by José Quintero. Photograph by Jerry Dantzic.

company was formed in 1963 under the direction of Elia Kazan and Robert Whitehead (1916–2002). Expectations were high, since at that time Kazan was considered the finest director in America and since he was promised new plays by Arthur Miller (*After the Fall* and *Incident at Vichy*) and S. N. Behrman (*But for Whom, Charlie*). The results were so disappointing that after one season Kazan and Whitehead resigned. They were replaced by Herbert Blau (1926–) and Jules Irving (1924–1979), who had been outstandingly successful at the Actors' Workshop in San Francisco. In 1965 the company moved into its newly completed home (the Vivian Beaumont Theatre, designed by Eero Saarinen and Jo Mielziner) at Lincoln Center. But Blau and Irving soon ran into difficulties, and in 1967 Blau resigned. Thereafter Irving continued slowly to build a company, but eventually the artistic and financial problems became so great that in 1973 he resigned.

For a time New York also had a second repertory company, the Association of Producing Artists (APA). Founded in 1960 by Ellis Rabb (1930–1998), the APA formed a liaison in 1964 with the Phoenix Theatre, which thereafter served as its producer. Its repertory was eclectic, ranging through works by Shaw, Chekhov, Pirandello, Shakespeare, Ionesco, and others. The company was sometimes accused of being too conservative because it only produced already proven works, but for a time it provided the most impressive cross-section of drama to be seen in the United States. The APA won high critical praise but because of financial difficulties disbanded in 1970.

After the war there were also attempts to decentralize the theatre. One leader in this area was the American National Theatre and Academy (ANTA), which had been chartered by Congress in 1935 to stimulate the rejuvenation of the theatre outside of New York and to form an academy to train personnel. Owing to lack of funds, little was accomplished, although ANTA became the principal American center for collecting and exchanging information about the theatre. After the war, the attempt to found regional theatres was given its first important impetus by Margo Jones (1913–1955), who successfully established an arena theatre in Dallas in 1947. Other pioneering groups include the Alley Theatre, founded in Houston in 1947 by Nina Vance (1914–1980); the Arena Stage, opened in Washington in 1949 by Edward Mangum (1914–2001) and Zelda Fichandler (1924–); and the Actors' Workshop, begun in 1952 in San Francisco by Jules Irving and Herbert Blau. At first, most of the groups struggled along with semiprofessional personnel while gradually building audiences.

The 1960s saw the greatest expansion of the U.S. theatre outside of New York since the nineteenth century. The first important impetus came in 1959 when the Ford Foundation made sizable grants to a number of small companies that had gained footholds in cities scattered throughout the country. The financial boost permitted such groups as the Alley Theatre, the Arena Stage, and the Actors' Workshop to become fully professional and relatively stable. The movement toward resident companies was further strengthened when Tyrone Guthrie announced his intention of founding a theatre in Minneapolis. When this theatre was opened in 1963 the favorable publicity motivated other cities to seek similar companies. By 1966 more actors were being employed by the roughly thirty-five regional theatres than were employed in New York. These troupes resembled European subsidized theatres in presenting a repertory of classics and recent successes and in relying little on new plays. To aid cooperation and communication among these not-for-profit theatres, the Theatre Communications Group (TCG) was established in 1961.

Summer festivals also added diversity. The success of the Shakespeare Festivals at Ashland, Oregon (1935), and San Diego (1949) inspired Joseph Papp to establish the New York Shakespeare Festival in 1954. Beginning in 1957 it gave free performances each summer in Central Park where the municipally owned Delacorte Theatre (seating 2263) was inaugurated in 1962. This was followed by the American Shakespeare Festival, Stratford, Connecticut (1955), the Colorado Shakespeare Festival, Boulder (1958), Utah Shakespeare Festival, Cedar City (1961), the Great Lakes Shakespeare Festival, Lakewood, Ohio (1962), the New Jersey Shakespeare Festival (1963), and many more. Summer theatres, most of them in resort areas, also steadily increased in numbers. Additionally, by the early 1960s approximately 1500 colleges and universities were offering theatre courses and productions.

For a time after the war, the United States seemed to be rich in playwrights. Its stature increased considerably with the return of O'Neill's plays to the repertory following the success of *The Iceman Cometh* in 1956. *A Long Day's Journey into Night* (written 1939–1941 and first produced 1957) was one of the most impressive plays of the 1950s; subsequently other previously unproduced works by O'Neill were performed to critical acclaim. Although he declined in power, Maxwell Anderson also continued to write. Among his postwar plays, *Joan of Lorraine* (1946) and *Anne of the Thousand Days* (1948) were especially

popular. Clifford Odets regained some of his former strength with *The Country Girl* (1950) and *The Flowering Peach* (1954); William Saroyan returned with *The Cave Dwellers* (1957), Lillian Hellman with *The Autumn Garden* (1951) and *Toys in the Attic* (1960), S. N. Behrman with *The Cold Wind and the Warm* (1959) and *But for Whom, Charlie* (1962), and Thornton Wilder with *The Matchmaker* (1954).

The most outstanding new writers were Williams and Miller. Tennessee Williams (1911–1983) achieved his first success in 1945 with *The Glass Menagerie* and rapidly consolidated it with *A Streetcar Named Desire* (1947), *Cat on a Hot Tin Roof* (1955), *Sweet Bird of Youth* (1959), and *Night of the Iguana* (1961). But by the late 1950s Williams was being accused of repeating himself and thereafter his critical stature declined, although he continued to write up until his death. His later work includes *The Milk Train Doesn't Stop Here Anymore* (1962), *Slapstick Tragedy* (1966), *This Is [an Entertainment]* (1976), and *Vieux Carré* (1978).

Williams's strength lay in his ability to create interesting characters caught in critical or violent situations as they seek to recover a past or create a future more satisfying than the vulgar and materialistic present. As the dramatic action progresses, the protagonist is usually forced to abandon his/her illusions, often after physical or moral degradation at the hands of callous or vicious characters. Williams's sensational situations often obscured his concern for the survival of love and beauty in a materialistic world. To achieve his effects, Williams used theatrical means imaginatively, manipulating them, sometimes quite obviously, to focus attention on the inner truth of character and situation. No American playwright commanded so wide an audience as did Williams between 1945 and 1960.

Arthur Miller (1915–2005) achieved his first success with *All My Sons* (1947), an Ibsenesque play about a manufacturer of airplane engines who has put profit above the safety of wartime pilots. Miller's reputation now rests primarily upon *Death of a Salesman* (1949), *The Crucible* (1953), and *A View from the Bridge* (1955). That reputation declined somewhat with *After the Fall* (1964) and *Incident at Vichy* (1964), but rose again with *The Price* (1968). His later works, among which have been *The Creation of the World and Other Business* (1973), *The Archbishop's Ceiling* (1986), *The Ride Down Mount Morgan* (1991), *The Last Yankee* (1993), and *Broken Glass* (1994) have not met with the critical acclaim of his early plays. Through most of Miller's plays run the same ideas. His characters stray because of overly narrow (often materialistic) values and find peace in some more meaningful understanding of themselves and of their

FIG. 21.13

The Guthrie Theatre, Minneapolis. Note the thrust stage and steeply banked seating. Tyrone Guthrie's production of Chekhov's *The Three Sisters,* 1963. Courtesy the Guthrie Theatre.

roles in society. Miller is often called a "social" dramatist, but his interests have always been moral, for in his plays, though society may encourage false values, it remains the individual's responsibility to sort out the true from the false. Miller clearly implies that it is possible to maintain one's integrity within the framework of society. Of Miller's work, *Death of a Salesman* is usually considered most significant, perhaps because it dramatizes so successfully the conflict in the American consciousness between the desire for material success and the desire for adventure and happiness.

Few other new playwrights lived up to their initial promise. William Inge (1913–1973) gained a considerable following with such works as *Come Back, Little Sheba* (1950), *Picnic* (1953), *Bus Stop* (1955), and *The Dark at the Top of the Stairs* (1957), but his work now seems essentially a more naive version of Williams's. Other popular dramatists of the time include Robert Anderson (1917–), with *Tea and Sympathy* (1953) and *You Know I Can't Hear You When the Water's Running* (1966); and Paddy Chayefsky (1923–1981) with *The Tenth Man* (1959) and *Gideon* (1961).

After 1960 production costs continued to soar with the result that Broadway ticket prices became ever higher. The need to attract large audiences led New York's producers to restrict their offerings primarily to musicals, comedies, and plays that had proven popular elsewhere. Broadway gradually gave up the out-of-town tryout and increasingly imported productions from America's resident theatres or from London. Thus, it lost its significance as a presenter of new plays while remaining the primary center of the American commercial theatre.

The most successful playwright on Broadway after 1960 was Neil Simon (1927–), who after a somewhat tentative beginning with *Come Blow Your Horn*

(1961) turned out a string of hits, among them *Barefoot in the Park* (1963), *The Odd Couple* (1965), *The Last of the Red Hot Lovers* (1970), *The Sunshine Boys* (1972), *Chapter Two* (1979), *Biloxi Blues* (1984), *Broadway Bound* (1986), *Lost in Yonkers* (1991), *Laughter on the 23d Floor* (1993), and *Proposals* (1997), all combining zany humor, eccentric characters, and hints of pain and desperation beneath the comic surface.

The most prestigious American playwright of the 1960s was Edward Albee (1928–), whose first four plays, all short, were produced off-Broadway in 1960–1961. These early works, especially *The Sand-box* (1959) and *The American Dream* (1960), were thought to ally Albee with the absurdists, but with *Who's Afraid of Virginia Woolf?* (1962), his first full-length play and first Broadway success, he demonstrated an affinity to Williams and Strindberg through his exploration of tortured psychological relationships. In this play, the façades of the characters are gradually stripped away during the course of an all-night drinking bout, revealing people who create hells for each other through their inability to accept weaknesses. Most of Albee's subsequent work has been concerned with values. *Tiny Alice* (1964), a puzzling parable, seems to suggest that human beings reconcile themselves to their lot by constructing unverifiable systems to explain why they have been martyred by life; *A Delicate Balance* (1966) shows several characters seeking to escape anxieties; and *Seascape* (1974) suggests that human beings have lost their vitality and that the future belongs to other creatures (here two amphibians who crawl out of the water onto the beach) as they discover love and consideration. In these complex plays, Albee became increasingly abstract and for a time he fell from favor but would regain much of his following in the 1990s.

In the early 1960s Arthur Kopit (1937–) was often ranked with Albee. He first came to prominence in 1960 with *Oh, Dad, Poor Dad, Mama's Hung You in the Closet and I'm Feeling So Sad,* a parodistic work reminiscent of Tennessee Williams's more bizarre creations but using absurdist conventions. In it, Mme Rosepettle, whose household includes piranhas, Venus's-flytraps, and the stuffed body of her dead husband, tries to protect her son from life's harsh realities only to have him break free from her domination. Kopit had little further success until *Indians* (1968), in which he used Buffalo Bill's Wild West Show as a framework for suggesting how the betrayal of Native Americans has been transformed into entertainment, thus permitting us to ignore the reality. It is a variation on the by-now familiar theme of the American dream gone awry.

FIG. 21.14

Albee's *A Delicate Balance* as performed by the Royal Shakespeare Company, 1967. Courtesy Royal Shakespeare Company.

The period between 1940 and 1968 was something like a golden age of musical comedy. The pattern was established by Richard Rodgers and Oscar Hammerstein with *Oklahoma* (1943), *Carousel* (1945), *South Pacific* (1949), and *The King and I* (1951). It was followed, with many variations, by Alan Jay Lerner and Frederick Loewe with *Brigadoon* (1947), *My Fair Lady* (1956), and *Camelot* (1960); Frank Loesser with *Guys and Dolls* (1950) and *Most Happy Fella* (1956); Leonard Bernstein with *Candide* (1956) and *West Side Story* (1957); Jule Styne with *Funny Girl* (1964); Jerry Bock with *Fiddler on the Roof* (1964); Jerry Herman with *Hello, Dolly!* (1964) and *Mame* (1966); and John Kander with *Cabaret* (1966) and *Zorba* (1968). All were large-cast, multiple-set productions with lavish (often athletic) dance sequences, tuneful songs, and easily understood plots.

CANADIAN THEATRE TO 1968

In the years following the war, all the elements that would lead to the modern Canadian theatre were put into place, including the reestablishing of professional theatres, large-scale government support for the arts, the establishing of summer festivals and year-round regional theatres, and the advent of the alternative (often called the alternate) theatre movement.

While amateur theatres remained important, many, like the New Play Society (NPS, 1946–1971), were making the transition to becoming fully professional. Established by Dora Mayor Moore (1888–1979), one of the most important figures in Canadian theatre, NPS succeeded when many others failed, largely because of the success of its musical review, *Spring Thaw.* From 1948 until NPS

FIG. 21.15

Leonard Bernstein's *Candide,* directed by Harold Prince. For this production, designers Eugene and Franne Lee altered the interior of a Broadway theatre to integrate the performance-audience spaces. Photo by Martha Swope Photography, Inc.

disbanded, *Spring Thaw* brought in much-needed revenues and provided an early showcase for many of the most talented theatre artists in Toronto. But the real influence of the New Play Society came through its theatre school (established in 1950) where many leading actors and directors of the modern Canadian theatre got their start in the days before the National Theatre School opened in Montreal in 1960.

In contrast to NPS, Vancouver's influential Everyman Theatre (1946–1953), founded by Sydney Risk (1908–1985), was professional from the start, as was Montreal's Théâtre du Rideau Vert, founded in 1948 by Yvette Brind'amour (1918–1992). The latter was the first of the important French-speaking professional companies which, until the late 1950s, outnumbered the English-language theatres in Canada. By far the most influential of those French-speaking companies, however, was Le Théâtre du Nouveau Monde (Theatre of the New World) founded in 1951 by Jean Gascon (1921–1988) and Jean-Louis Roux (1923–). The success of its European tours in the 1950s made it the best known Canadian theatre outside of North America. Gascon went on to become the first Executive Director of the National Theatre School (1960–1967), with Michel

Saint-Denis as Artistic Director, and the first Canadian Artistic Director of the Stratford Festival (1967–1974).

Government funding for theatre, led by the Saskatchewan Arts Board of 1948, became a major influence on modern Canadian theatre during these years. A Royal Commission on National Development in the Arts, Letters and Sciences, known as the Massey-Lévesque Commission, was established in 1949 to determine what the country needed to do in order to establish a cultural identity. The commission made a series of recommendations in 1951 that led to the formation of the Canadian Council/ Conseil des Arts du Canada in 1957. One of the commission's most significant findings was that theatrical development in Canada was being hampered by a lack of theatre facilities. Few theatres had been built since the turn of the century, while many old theatres had been converted to cinemas. The Canadian Council immediately encouraged government funding for the building of new multipurpose theatres. When these multipurpose theatres proved unsatisfactory, the Council began to promote arts centers with multiple venues, best exemplified by the National Arts Center (1969) in Ottawa, which included an opera house, a thrust stage, and a studio theatre. By the mid-1970s, the Canadian Council was also promoting the restoration of many older theatres. But perhaps the commision's most important finding was that professional theatres need government subsidy. The Council began by providing such funding for three companies in 1957. By the end of the century, despite over a decade of low-growth budgets, it would be providing subsidies to nearly 250 theatres with awards equaling from 10 to 40 percent of their budgets.

Summer festival and year-round regional theatres were soon established, offering a repertory of classical and contemporary European and U.S. plays. Such a repertory was thought both to acknowledge Canada's cultural heritage and to establish its place among modern nations. New Canadian plays were encouraged by such companies, but they were expected to fit into an international repertory. Toronto's Jupiter Theatre (1951–1954) tried to sustain a more experimental repertory but soon failed. The Crest Theatre (1953–1966) lasted longer with a mix of new Canadian plays, experimental plays, and plays from the standard repertory, but it was always in financial difficulties.

The Stratford Festival, established by Tom Patterson at Stratford, Ontario, in 1953, was immediately successful with a standard repertory almost completely dedicated to Shakespeare for its classical component. Tyrone Guthrie was hired as artistic director for the 2262-seat Greek-style auditorium that was set up within a large tent (the permanent theatre was erected in 1956). Designer Tanya Moiseiwitsch (1914–2003) created a permanent stage that was to be a modern expression of the essential elements of the stages used in Shakespeare's day. This was the first thrust stage in Canada, and it became the prototype for the highly successful Chichester Festival Theatre in England (1962) and the equally successful Guthrie Theatre in Minneapolis (1963). But while this theatre has long been the most internationally respected theatre in Canada, it has also been a target of criticism by Canadian nationalists. They see little value for Canada's national aspirations in the Festival's repertory and in its approach to production. The highly regarded Shaw Festival (founded 1962) in Niagara-on-the-Lake, is dedicated to European drama written in Shaw's lifetime but has attracted less criticism. The Charlottetown Festival (founded in 1965) is admired for its commitment to original Canadian musicals.

John Hirsch (1930–1989) and Tom Hendry (1929–) were co-founders of the Manitoba Theatre Center in 1958, which was created from the merger of two amateur theatre companies. Together they coordinated a highly successful standard repertory of classical plays interspersed with contemporary plays, predominantly light comedies. They also developed an effective touring program for taking plays into area schools. This was the first professional regional theatre in Canada, and it served as a model for the twelve others that would join it by 1984.

By 1959, Toronto's Workshop Theatre (TWT, 1959–1989) had started mounting a challenge to everything the festivals and regional theatres would come to represent. Founded by George Luscomb (1926–1999) and modeled after Joan Littlewood's Workshop Theatre in London, TWT was the first of what would, in the 1970s, become known as an alternative theatre. Alternative theatres, like the earlier independent theatres, set themselves against the existing theatre establishment. But the alternative theatres were opposed to the European and U.S. text-based, director-focused theatre that the independent theatres had championed and that both the festival theatres and the regional theatres came to embody. Those who led the alternative theatre movement argued that regional theatres had no real identity because all of them performed the standard repertory. Such a repertory might be part of Canada's cultural heritage, they conceded, but it was a colonial heritage and therefore should not be the foundation of a modern cultural identity for the nation. Alternative theatres rejected the standard repertory and championed community-based performance pieces. They also insisted on a return to theatre that was actor-focused, and therefore they emphasized collective creation. The Theatre Passe Muraille (theatre beyond walls), founded in 1968 by Jim Garrard (1939–), rapidly became Canada's premier alternative theatre, embodying much of what the movement stood for in its dedication to new Canadian plays (it would eventually produce over 300), to community-based theatre, and to collective creation. The most influential of the French-Canadian alternative theatres (le jeune théâtre) was the Grand Cirque Ordinaire (1969–1978), whose focus on nonverbal "sociopoetic" theatre became the inspiration for some of the most innovative Canadian theatre of the 1980s and 1990s. When the Festival of Underground Theatre was held in Toronto in 1970, it established the legitimacy of the alternative theatre movement, which then became the dominant force in Canadian theatre.

Numerous playwrights had come to prominence in the 1950s and 1960s. John Coulter (1888–1990) continued the trend of dramatizing stories from Canadian history with his epic-style play, *Riel* (1949), about the leader of a nineteenth-century Canadian rebellion against the British. Robertson Davis (1913–1995) wrote plays poking fun at the lack of culture among his fellow Canadians, beginning with *Fortune My Foe* (1948). Félix Leclerc (1914–1988) wrote a series of comedies on life in Québec starting with *Ring the Morning Bells* (1954). But it was the dramatists of the 1960s who received the greater international recognition. These include Françoise Loranger (1913–1995), whose first play, *A house . . . one day* (1965) focused on the breakdown of the middle-class family, and whose second play, *Five More Minutes* (1967), was the first major drama to address feminist issues. George Ryga's (1932–1987) *The Ecstasy of Rita Joe* (1967) took on the issue of racism in a story about a Native American woman's struggle to comprehend white urban society. Finally, John Herbert (1926–2001), founder of the influential Garret Theatre Studio (1965– 1970), became internationally known for *Fortune in Men's Eyes* (1967), a play dealing with homophobia in the prison system.

The alternative theatres that would come to prominence after 1968 would be inspired first by Canadian determination to establish an identity separate from England—a determination most clearly represented by the introduction of the maple leaf flag in 1963—and second by a determination to establish an identity separate from that of the United States, a determination made more urgent by the desire of Canadians to distance themselves from the Vietnam War.

AUSTRALIA AND NEW ZEALAND THEATRE TO 1968

Though Australia and New Zealand had active little theatres that produced a number of plays by local dramatists, theatre remained dominated by vaudeville, reviews, and a commercial theatre largely imported from England and the United States. With the introduction of television in 1956, even the vaudeville houses and review theatres began to close. The best actors and writers continued to turn to radio drama or seek careers abroad.

In 1943 the Australian Council for Music and the Arts was created to promote the arts in the schools. In 1947 Tyrone Guthrie was asked to consider the feasibility of creating a National Theatre for Australia. When he reported that such a project would be premature, he set off a nationalistic debate on Australia's postcolonial identity. Tours by the Old Vic Company in 1948 and by the Stratford Memorial Theatre (featuring several expatriate Australian actors) in 1949 and 1952 were inspirations, but they were also forceful reminders of how much needed to be done if theatre in Australia or New Zealand was to achieve world-class standards.

The first steps to improve the situation in Australia were taken in 1954 with the formation of the Australian Elizabethan Theatre Trust. Though it was named in honor of Queen Elizabeth II's visit to Australia and headed by a British director, Hugh Hunt, it was charged with the task of making theatre as vital a force in Australia as it had been in the London of Shakespeare's day. The Trust immediately leased the abandoned 1500-seat Majestic (1917) and renamed it the Elizabethan Theatre. It got off to a rather inauspicious start by mounting two plays by the English playwright Terrence Rattigan, with casts dominated by English actors. The nationalists were outraged, but these productions did establish the quality of performance the Trust was aspiring to. Australia's greatest expatriate actress, Judith Anderson (1898–1992), was lured back to Sydney by the Trust in 1955 to star in a production of *Medea*—with a remarkable cast of Australian actors including the young Zoë Caldwell (1934–) as a member of the chorus. The Trust also sponsored a tour of *Summer of the Seventeenth Doll* (1955) by Ray Lawler (1921–), which rapidly became Australia's best-known and most loved play. Over time the Trust supported important productions of a large number of plays by Australian authors. In 1958 the Trust established its first playwriting award, adopted the Young Elizabethan Players (founded 1955), founded the National Institute of Dramatic Art on the campus of University of New South Wales, and began to identify and support the most promising semiprofessional companies in each of the six states. In 1958–1959 they formed the Elizabethan Trust Opera (which became the autonomous Australian Opera in 1969), the Australian Ballet, and the Trust Players (1959–1962). The Trust also assisted in the establishment of the Marionette Theatre of Australia (1965–1988) and in 1967 funded the Elizabethan Trust Orchestra, divided into Sydney and Melbourne ensembles. Thus, by the time the Australian Council for the Arts was established in 1968 (it became the Australian Council in 1974), the Trust had achieved its primary objectives. In trying to avoid duplicating the system of subsidizing theatre companies which the Australian Council began to undertake in 1968, however, the Trust lost its focus and ran into trouble with a series of poor investments in commercial productions. By 1991 it was bankrupt and after reorganization became little more than a friends-of-the-arts organization for Sydney.

The Trust had promoted Shakespeare as a vital component of any English-language theatre, and this inspired the University of Western Australia at Perth to build the New Fortune Theatre quadrangle in 1964. This was the first attempt to build a space that followed the dimensions provided in the contract for London's original Fortune Playhouse of 1600. It was not a reconstruction but an attempt to recreate the fundamental spatial relationships of the Elizabethan playhouses. The New Fortune did not stop with the stage, however; it also recreated the auditorium. The theatre was instrumental in moving Australian thinking about theatre away from naturalism. Dorothy Hewett (1923–2002), one of Australia's more successful playwrights of the 1970s and 1980s, got her start in this theatre before she scored her first real success with *The Chapel Perilous* (1971). In the meantime the university built the 600-seat Octagon Theatre (1969), the most successful of the numerous thrust stages it inspired throughout Australia.

But by the time the New Fortune was built, Australia's first alternative theatre was already underway. The Emerald Hill Theatre in South Melbourne (1961–1966), co-founded by one of Melbourne's most successful directors, Wal Cherry (1932–1986), and actor-director George Whaley, was committed to an *avant-garde* repertory and high standards of production. But it never really found an audience and closed after five years. By this time Australia was caught up in the controversies that surrounded its participation in the Vietnam War, and a more politicized theatre was coming to the forefront. La MaMa, established by Betty Burstall in 1967, was, like its namesake in New York, a resource center for anyone who could persuade Burstall that they had a project worth doing in Melbourne. For the first three years the resources of La MaMa included a resident acting company, and in the first two years La MaMa staged or provided space for productions of twenty-five plays by Australian authors, many of them plays of protest.

In New Zealand, little theatre groups from the Unity Theatre, Wellington (1944–1978), to the Globe Theatre, Dunedin (1961–), were still the only outlet for plays by local authors. The Community Arts Service Theatre at Auckland (1947–1962) provided the only equivalent to a regional theatre as it performed a standard repertory of classics and modern European plays throughout the North Island, but it showed no interest in the work of local writers. The most significant attempt to start a National Theatre in New Zealand came with the formation of New Zealand Players in Wellington in 1953. Founded by Richard and Edith Campion, who had received their training at the Old Vic, this company performed an excellent repertory with high production standards, but they were unable to attract a subsidy and finally closed in 1960. After the Queen Elizabeth II Arts Council of New Zealand was established in 1964, subsidies became available for the first time and a number of professional and semiprofessional theatres were established. Of these the most important were the fully professional Mercury Theatre, founded at Auckland by Anthony Richardson (1926–1982), who trained many of New Zealand's most influential theatre artists (it closed in 1992); and the semiprofessional Downstage Theatre, Wellington (1964–), which did more than any other theatre to promote works by New Zealanders.

LOOKING AT THEATRE HISTORY

During the 1950s, dissatisfactions were not expressed solely through absurdist drama. In England, the most powerful impact was made by the "angry young men" who expressed themselves in relatively traditional dramatic forms. Although it is now usual to suggest that Osborne's *Look Back in Anger* was recognized immediately as a turning point in English drama, most reviewers of the time voiced serious reservations about it. Here are some excerpts from one of the most negative reviews:

We should be very frank about this. If more plays like tonight's Look Back in Anger are produced, the

"Writer's Theatre" at the Royal Court must surely sink. I look back in anger upon a night misconceived and mis-spent. . . . The principal character is self-pitying, uncouth, cheaply vulgar. . . .

J. C. Trewin in *The Birmingham Post*, 8 May 1956.

Fortunately, others were more perceptive:

Of course, Look Back in Anger is not a perfect play. But it is a most exciting one, abounding with life and vitality and the life it deals with is life as it is lived at this very moment—not a common enough subject in the English theatre. . . . Don't miss this play. If you are young, it will speak to you. If you are middle-aged, it will tell you what the young are feeling. . . .

T. C. Worsley in *The New Statesman.*

Between 1945 and 1960, the dominant production style in the United States was exemplified in the combined work of Elia Kazan (as director) and Jo Mielziner (as designer). Here, in his review of Tennessee Williams's *Cat on a Hot Tin Roof* (1955), Eric Bentley gives a good description of their work:

Jo Mielziner's setting consists of a square and sloping platform with one of its corners, not one of its sides, jutting towards the audience. A corner of a ceiling is above, pointing upstage. On the platform are minimum furnishings for a bed-sitting room. Around the room, steps and space suggest the out of doors. The whole stage is swathed in everchanging light and shade. . . .

Such is the world of Elia Kazan, as we know it from his work on plays by more authors than one. The general scheme is that not only of Streetcar *but also of* Salesman: *an exterior that is also a view of an interior—but, more important, a view of man's exterior*

that is also a view of his interior, the habitat of his body and the country of his memories and dreams. A theatre historian would probably call this world a combination of naturalism and expressionism. . . .

It is one of the distinctive creations of American theatre. . . . With the means of the new American theatre (school of Lee Strasberg and Harold Clurman) it does reach the cherished end of the older theatre (true grandeur of performance) at a time when the older theatre itself . . . is failing to do so. . . .

I do not think the reason for this resides in the formality itself. The effectiveness of this grandeur results . . . from the interaction between formality in the setting, lighting, and grouping and an opposite quality . . . in the individual performances. The externals of the physical production belong . . . to the old theatre, but the acting is internal, "Stanislavskyite." Within the formal setting, from the fixed positions in which they are made to stand, the actors live their roles with that vigilant, concentrated, uninterrupted nervous intensity which Mr. Kazan always manages to give. . . .

The New Republic, April 4, 1955.

22
The Theatre of Africa

Africa is now thought to be the place from which the very first humans originated. It is an enormously large land mass with a great diversity of geography, climate, politics, and languages (more than 800 local languages are spoken on the continent). African cultures along the northern coast have interacted with European and Middle Eastern cultures for millennia, while those along Africa's eastern coast have a long history of trading relations with countries of the Middle East and India. The cultures of central and western Africa were less well known outside the continent, and geographical isolation, along with the lack of a common language or any written languages, limited how much these central and western cultures knew even about each other. Europeans began to establish small colonies in parts of west Africa in the sixteenth century and south Africa in the seventeenth. But the major period of colonization came after 1885 when the leaders of Europe divided the continent into spheres of influence. By 1900 European countries were in control of all but Liberia and Ethiopia. The colonies were reorganized during World War I and again during World War II. By the mid 1960s, most had won their independence.

After gaining independence many of the new states had to contend with colonial borders that had been set by European treaties which took little notice of geography and no notice of ethnic identities or language groupings. To manage this problem, most resorted to adopting the same control systems that had existed under colonial rule, including the use of a European language as the official language of the new state. (Only Tanzania adopted an African language, Swahili, as its official language, while most North African countries returned to using Arabic.) These "neocolonial" governments became the focus of much animosity as various groups sought to create territorial boundaries that better fit the realities of traditional African relationships among various communities. The resulting civil wars have led to a seemingly continuous redrawing of the map of Africa.

SOME BASIC ISSUES AND PROBLEMS

The majority of African cultures did not develop a written language. They maintained their historic records orally through the tradition of the *griot,* a storyteller who committed to memory and passed on to successors a record of the community. Colonial powers were dismissive of these histories and such long narratives were difficult to pass on fully in the areas plagued by civil wars following independence. So by the time the importance of these oral histories was recognized and techniques were developed

FIG. 22.1
Map of Africa today.

for using them effectively, many had already been lost. As a result, establishing the history of pre-colonial Africa below the Sahara poses a constant challenge for historians, though a great deal of progress has been made in recent years.

The slave trade went on much longer in Africa than it did elsewhere in the world. While only a small part of the total trading economy, the slave trade probably had a greater influence on the spread of African performance traditions, both on the continent and beyond, than other forms of commerce had as those sold into slavery often took their local performance traditions with them. But the achievements of those who are classed as slaves are rarely documented or even acknowledged. As a result, little is written, for example, about the cultural influences east Africans had on the Islamic states during the long history of the slave trade between these two areas. Similarly, the cultural influences that west Africans had on the Americas as a result of the large numbers of people who were transported as slaves, have only recently begun to be examined. Such studies have shown the ways in which Africans had a significant impact on the art and music of other cultures (to say nothing of food production and numerous other activities). They have also pointed to potentially important new insights into African performance traditions as they existed before the major period of European colonization. But there is still a great deal more research to be done in this area.

Another problem in discussing African performance is the complexity of performance elements. In indigenous forms, words are often the least important element. Other "languages," especially those of drumming and dance, communicate more to many African audiences than words do. To these can be added visual imagery, symbolism, gesture, mask, and costume, all of which may convey specific meaning and resonance difficult to describe or explain. The dancing, music, and song have a communal character, and audiences respond by clapping in rhythm, singing refrains, repeating phrases, or making comments. Frequently songs and anecdotes are incorporated that seemingly have little to do with narrative structure and are not documented on the rare occasion when scripts are produced. Perhaps most importantly, indigenous performance is so embedded in its specific culture that outsiders may be baffled by what is transparently clear to insiders. Under colonialism, even native-born scholars were sometime turned into outsiders by the education system.

Each colonial power, faced with multiple language and ethnic groups within a single administrative territory, made its own European language the official language of that territory. The most common colonial languages were English and French, and in many areas one of these was the only language that local groups shared. Local languages were converted into written form, often by missionaries who wished to translate the Bible, and when Western-style schools were established this made it possible to teach in both the local and the colonial language at the lower grade levels. At the upper levels, however, education was most commonly conducted in the official European language. The curriculum was European and included the classics of European drama which students performed on European-style proscenium-arch stages. Many advanced students were also sent to universities in Europe. Those Africans who aspired to be writers usually chose a colonial language because it was the only way to reach a significant audience either within Africa or abroad, since local-language audiences were so limited. As a consequence, when African countries gained their independence after sixty years or more of colonial rule, their leaders, like the members of their upper classes, were nearly always European educated. Therefore, institutions like national theatres were established on European models. But the use of local languages and indigenous performance modes also gained in popularity, often serving as a protest against colonialist and neocolonialist values and practices. Writing (or improvising) in African languages and using African performance traditions was encouraged by those who wished to establish an independent African identity. Increasingly it was argued that the use of African languages was essential for the "decolonization of African minds." The result has been a blending of European-inspired forms of theatre with the great variety of indigenous forms of performance, which has created a vigorous and dynamic spectrum of theatre in contemporary Africa. Only a small portion of Africa's rich theatre history can be covered here, and only from a few representative countries, but this should be sufficient to give a clear indication of the vitality of theatre across the African continent.

NIGERIA

Nigeria is Africa's most populous and densely populated country. It includes some 250 different ethnic groups. The first Europeans, the Portuguese, arrived in 1472. The British began occupying Nigerian territory in 1861 and continued encroachment thereafter, but did not unify all of present-day Nigeria until 1914. Nigeria became fully independent in 1960.

Nigeria was the site of several kingdoms prior to the coming of the Europeans. One of these was centered around Ifa, a sacred Yoruba city, in the thirteenth century, and another in Benin in the fifteenth century. Both produced ceremonial art objects that are now valued internationally. Since public performance was the usual medium of expression and communication in indigenous Nigerian cultures, one kind of performance or another went on throughout the year's cycle. The Ijo of southern Nigeria, for example, had sagas that required several days to perform by storytellers accompanied by musicians, while the audience was expected to participate by repeating phrases or joining in "call and response." Dance theatre and puppetry were popular everywhere.

One of the major festivals among the Yoruba of Nigeria is the *egungen,* which can be traced back at least to the fourteenth century, when it was already fully established. *Egungen* refers to ancestors and establishes a spiritual link between the living and the dead, the present and the past. The festival was performed annually at the beginning of the planting season. On the night before the festival, in an all-night ceremony, sacrifices were offered and petitions for blessing and prosperity were addressed to the dead in the sacred *egungen* grove. On the day of the festival, the masked and costumed *egungen,* along with priests and other members of the cult, emerged from the sacred grove dancing to the accompaniment of drummers and made their way toward the house of the chief. The masqueraders continued until a "carrier" appeared whose function it was to gather up the accumulated evil of the community and carry it away in a canoe. *Egungen* masqueraders may also dance at funerals and on other occasions. Joel Adedeji has traced the development of Alarinjo theatre out of *egungen* masquerades in the seventeenth century. Alarinjo theatre, with its masked actors, was performed at the court of the Oyo Yoruba kingdom, and a guild system developed to make sure that the secrets and skills of the art did not pass to others. There were separate guilds for musicians, carvers of masks, and actors. During the first part of the nineteenth century, internecine warfare led to the breakup of the kingdom and the guilds. Alarinjo theatre was then performed by professional traveling companies. The performances of the traveling groups took the form of a variety show, mainly improvised and therefore capable of endless change. They also depended much on audience participation. Some remnants of Alarinjo theatre survive to the present day, especially in Yoruba opera.

In the late nineteenth and early twentieth centuries Christian churches presented dramatized Bible stories and religious plays but much of the entertainment presented for colonial audiences was patterned after English music halls. It was partially from these that the most popular contemporary theatrical form, Yoruba opera (now usually called Yoruba traveling theatre), emerged, although Alarinjo was also an influence. Yoruba opera was first developed by Hubert Ogunde (1916–1990), who had participated in *egungen* masquerades and an Alarinjo-type company. He wrote his first piece, *The Garden of Eden and the Throne of God,* in 1944, and staged it to benefit his church. In 1945, his *Strike and*

FIG. 22.2

Masked dancers at an Owuru Festival in Nigeria. Originally seven performers were used in the dance, but the number has dwindled to two. Photo courtesy Phil Peek.

Hunger, concerning the plight of workers, turned to more political concerns, and in 1946 he established a professional company (the first in modern Nigeria) with which he toured thereafter wherever there were concentrations of Yoruba-speaking populations, even outside of Nigeria. By 1947, the form of his work had taken shape: an opening glee (or rousing musical number), followed by a topical and satirical story with dialogue, songs, and dances, ending with another glee. Although the emphasis was upon entertainment, there was always a clear moral message. After independence, Ogunde sought through such plays as *Yoruba Awake* (1964) to encourage national unity. Between 1944 and 1972, Ogunde created and performed some thirty-eight different operas. Many of his anticolonial pieces were censored or forbidden and at one time he was imprisoned. Ogunde worked hard to remain in touch with popular feelings and grievances, and his plays always concerned problems or issues of current interest. His company was tremendously popular. In the 1980s, Ogunde further enhanced his status by making and appearing in films. So many others came to emulate Ogunde that by 1981 there were some 120 companies with about 3600 full-time employees. To serve their needs, Ogunde founded the Association of Theatre Practitioners of Nigeria.

Another important figure in Yoruba opera was Duro Ladipo (1931–1978), who found his inspiration in Yoruba oral tradition, music, myth, and masquerade, perhaps influenced by Alarinjo theatre. Unlike most Yoruba opera companies, Ladipo used traditional Yoruba musical forms and instruments.

His first opera, *The Ghost Catcher* (1962), opened his Mbari-Mbayo Center, which he founded to train performers and visual artists. His most famous opera, *The King Did Not Hang* (1964), concerning the Yoruba god of lightning, was performed with great success on international tours by the Duro Ladipo Theatre. Overall, his operas are usually considered to be literarily superior to those of his contemporaries, and in 1969 *The King Did Not Hang* became the first Yoruba opera to be published. Ladipo was also an accomplished musician and visual artist. In addition to operas, Ladipo also wrote *Eda,* an adaptation of *Everyman.*

Yoruba traveling theatre has proven to be a very adaptable form. It may use traditional music, dance, and myth, or it may incorporate the latest styles in music and comment on the latest fads in behavior. It may use a variety of playing spaces, most of them simple so they can be prepared quickly. The costumes are colorful. The language is Yoruba (and sometimes pidgin English) and is mostly sung; there is constant musical accompaniment, either of drumming or various instruments or of singing. The songs are rehearsed but the dialogue is mostly improvised. There is always strong interaction with the audience. Yoruba opera has increasingly appeared on television and in films and videos, so much so that live performance is seriously threatened except within universities.

English-language plays also came to play a significant role in Nigeria's theatrical life. The Glover Memorial Hall, which served the needs of Europeans and certain black elite clubs, opened in Lagos in 1899. Such theatres were intended to promote European culture. In 1904, D. A Oloyede's *King Elejigbo and Princess Abeje of Kotangora* was the first play written by a Nigerian to be presented there (under the auspices of a church-sponsored drama group). Church and government schools usually had assembly halls with raised stages and proscenium arches, and Nigerian students who attended those schools were taught that this was the appropriate arrangement for theatrical presentations. School productions of plays by such authors as Shakespeare and Molière were encouraged. After World War II, the British Broadcasting Corporation also beamed European radio dramas into Nigeria. This was how most of Nigeria's future playwrights were educated. Thus, English-language playwriting, which began to flourish around the time of independence in 1960, reflected a tension between European and indigenous forms.

The best-known Nigerian playwright is Wole Soyinka (1934–), son of an Anglican priest but familiar with the *egungen* masquerades and other traditional performance. He attended university in both

FIG. 22.3

Wole Soyinka's *The Beatification of Area Boy* as performed at the West Yorkshire Playhouse, Leeds, England, in 1995. Photo by Eckhard Breitinger. Courtesy Mr. Breitinger.

Nigeria and England, and then worked at London's Royal Court Theatre in 1959–1960 when that company was at its peak as a promoter of new plays. He returned to Nigeria in 1960 and founded the 1960 Masks, a company that presented his first major play, *A Dance of the Forests* (1960), for the celebration of independence. It was also a warning about the future. In it, tribes assemble for a great feast and petition the gods for well-being, but instead the gods send two accusers who suggest that a dreadful future can be avoided only by sacrifice and self-knowledge, a frequent idea in Soyinka's plays. Soyinka also wrote light-hearted plays, among them *The Trials of Brother Jero* (1964), a satire on a religious huckster, and *The Lion and the Jewel* (1964), about a teacher who, in rebellion against tradition, refuses to pay a bride price for the woman he wishes to marry and loses her to the village chief—an obvious commentary on the tension between tradition and change. Other plays include *Kongi's Harvest* (1967), a satire on power seekers who lose sight of the people's need in their search for dominance; and *Madmen and Specialists* (1970), a bitter play written after Soyinka had been detained by government authorities for two years, showing the healer having been turned into a killer, although at the end his sister is taught another art of healing by the earth mothers. After his release from detention, Soyinka went into exile until 1976, during which time his *The Bacchae of Euripides* (1973) was presented at England's National Theatre, and during which he wrote *Death and the King's Horseman* (1975), concerning an episode in Nigeria's colonial past. After he returned to Nigeria, he produced his *Opera Wonyosi* (1977), an adaptation of Brecht's *Threepenny Opera,* treating an African tyrant and those who benefit from cooperating with him. *A Play of Giants* (1985) parodies some of Africa's worst modern tyrants, among them Idi Amin, Jean-Bedel Bokassa, Francisco Macias Nguema, and Joseph Mobutu, and attacks Western powers for sitting idly by.

In his plays, Soyinka draws on the symbolism, masks, and imagery of his Yoruba heritage. He also shows the potential for Yoruba traditions to recall the people to their responsibilities in the face of those who all too often are concerned only with power and wealth. In 1986, Soyinka won the Nobel Prize for Literature, the first African to be so honored. Under the military rule of General Sani Abacha after 1993, Soyinka was condemned as an enemy of the state but managed to escape from the country. In 1997 he was convicted in absentia of treason but continued his criticism of the military regime. His *Beatification of Area Boy* (1994) is a satire on life under Abacha seen through the vendors and homeless who pass their days in a Lagos square. After Abacha was removed as ruler, Soyinka returned to Nigeria in 1998. Since then he has written only one drama, *Document of Identity* (1999), a play for radio. Soyinka now devotes most of his time to human rights.

John Pepper Clark-Bekederemo (1936–) won international recognition with plays that reflect Ijo life and folktales. His *Song of a Goat* (1964), first produced by Soyinka's company, tells the story of a man whose wife betrays him with his brother, whom he kills. He then walks into the sea; his wife subsequently dies in childbirth. A chorus creates an atmosphere resembling that of Greek tragedy. *Masquerade* (1964) has as its main character Tufa, the now grown-up son born at the end of *Song of a Goat*. When his past is revealed, his father-in-law insists that his daughter leave Tufa, and when she refuses, he kills her; Tufa revenges her death before he himself is killed. *The Raft* (1964) shows four men adrift on a raft in the Niger delta, each of whom tells his own

FIG. 22.4

A scene from John Pepper Clark-Bekederemo's *The Raft,* directed by Martin Banham, University of Leeds Workshop Theatre. Courtesy Mr. Banham; photo by Trevor Faulkner.

story. In *Ozidi* (1966) the title character, helped by the magic of his grandmother, avenges the death of his father and the humiliation of his brother. It is an encapsulation of a major Ijo saga. In one version of this saga a storyteller took all the roles, usually to musical accompaniment. In another version, it involved the entire community and used music, dance, and mime. The performance of the saga required several years to prepare and about seven full days to perform. It was long one of Nigeria's major traditional forms. Clark-Bekederemo, however, had great

FIG. 22.5
Femi Osofisan's *Nkrumah ni . . . Africa ni*. The scene shows Nkrumah celebrating his birthday in exile. Photo courtesy Eckhard Breitinger.

difficulty finding anyone who could still recall the saga in its entirety, but he transcribed what could be recalled and published it in 1977. During much of his playwriting career, Clark-Bekederemo was a professor of English at the University of Lagos. He resigned this position in the early 1980s and founded a professional theatre devoted to African plays in English.

Ola Rotimi (1936–), after studying at Yale University, returned to Nigeria and founded the Ori Olokun Acting Company in 1968. Its first production was of Rotimi's *The Gods Are Not to Blame* (1968), an adaptation of Sophocles' *Oedipus Rex* into a Yoruba background. This remains one of Rotimi's best-known works. Rotimi later turned to Nigerian history in *Kurunmi* (1969), concerning the struggle for the Oyo crown of the Ijaiye people; a highly theatrical piece making extensive use of singers, musicians, dancers, and a chorus, its noble title character and his people are ultimately destroyed.

Femi Osofisan (1946–) is the best known of a new generation of playwrights who have been critical of their predecessors for being too little concerned with issues of class and socioeconomic structures. These new writers have attracted a wide following among students and others who feel that Nigerian economic and power structures need to be revolutionized to make them more equitable for the masses. Osofisan's *No More the Wasted Breed* (1982) and *Another Raft* (1989) are direct critiques of plays by Soyinka and Clark-Bekederemo. His best known play is *The Chattering and the Song* (1976) which concerns the underground Farmers Movement. In it, the rehearsal of a play, about a nineteenth century rebel, serves metaphorically as a rehearsal for revolution which promises equity and sharing.

Another playwright in the vein was Ken Saro-Wiwa (1941–1995), who wrote *The Transistor Radio,* but was best known for a television series, *Basi and Company*. His political activism got him executed in spite of protest from around the world.

Among the greatest influences on contemporary Nigerian theatre and performance are the government and the universities. Around 1970, after the end of a brutal civil war (a direct result of colonial inclusion of antagonistic ethnic groups within the same country), Nigeria became a federation of states, almost all of which established a state arts council, a university, and a television channel. By 1985 there were twenty-three universities, of which eight offered graduate training in theatre and performance. Several of these also supported theatre companies, many of which traveled with productions. All of the states gave support for preserving traditional performance, and several universities encouraged and documented traditional performance. Some established centers to promote theatre for development, which work with communities to develop plays and performance designed to raise consciousness about local problems or national issues and to seek solutions for them. Although financial support for all these endeavors declined somewhat in the 1980s with the downturn in the price of oil, one of Nigeria's major sources of wealth, the national commitment to theatre and performance remained firm.

GHANA

Like other African countries, Ghana has many languages, the principal ones being Akan, Dagbani, Fanti, Ewe, Ga, Hausa, and Moshi. English is the official language. When the Portuguese visited Ghana, first around 1450, they found so much gold that thereafter it was referred to by Europeans as the Gold Coast. Later it figured prominently in the slave trade. In 1874, England made part of it a British colony and in 1901 extended control over the remainder. In 1957, when Britain granted the Gold Coast and British Togoland (previously a German protectorate) their independence, the two territories combined to create present-day Ghana; it was the first black African colony to become independent.

Also like other African countries, Ghana has a rich heritage of indigenous performance, especially dance-drama, storytelling, and ceremonies. Most of the traditional forms incorporate music, dancing, masks, and costumes, and some include short dramatic scenes. All of them are community based and emphasize the importance of community over individuality. Several, including the storytelling tradition of *Anansesem* (spider stories), have exerted considerable influence on contemporary drama.

One major type of theatre—the Concert Party—parallels Yoruba opera and may have influenced it. The Concert Party is sometimes traced from the work of Mr. Yalley, the headmaster of an elementary school who began in 1918 to give concerts (a mixture of jokes, singing, and dancing for which he wore various disguises, including minstrel makeup) for Empire Day celebrations. But it is Ishmael (Bob) Johnson, a pupil of Yalley's, who is credited with giving the Concert Party its distinctive form by intermingling elements from many sources, including Yalley's performances, American black vaudeville, silent films, and spider storytelling conventions. In 1930, Johnson created the first of his "trios," *The Two Bobs and Their Carolina Girl* (consisting of Johnson, J. "Bob" Ansah, and C. B. Hutton). As developed by Johnson, the Concert Party began with an opening section which included a musical number sung and danced by the trio; a ragtime song by one of the Bobs; and a joking duet between the two Bobs. This was followed by a comic play about one hour in length. The plays, parts of which were always improvised and always used music and dance, were sometimes given in English, sometimes in a local language, and sometimes in pidgin English. In addition to being entertaining, most Concert Parties dealt with contemporary topics and sought to provoke their audiences to think about them. By 1960, when Johnson formed the Musicians' Union of Ghana, there were about twenty-eight trios but the number has declined in recent years. The Concert Party was the first fully professional theatre in Ghana. It was also a popular form in the neighboring Republic of Togo. Written drama did not begin to flourish, however, until after independence in 1957.

Two of Ghana's major playwrights—Sutherland and Aidoo—were women. Efua Sutherland (1924–1996) was the most important figure in Ghanaian theatre after independence. Associated with President Nkrumah until his overthrow in 1966, she

FIG. 22.6

A joint performance by the National Dance Company of Ghana and Abibigromma (the Resident Theatre Company of the School of Performing Arts, University of Ghana, Legon) during a residency at the University of Texas. Both companies are now part of the National Theatre of Ghana. Photo by Robert Pandya. Courtesy Performing Arts Center, University of Texas at Austin.

sought to create a theatre that would embody the social ideals of the state. She founded an open-air theater, the Ghana Drama Studio, in Accra in 1957, and helped to establish the School of Music and Drama at the University of Ghana in Lagon, where she encouraged research about traditional performance. She also sought to strengthen the storytelling tradition through the establishment of the *Kodzidan* (Story House) in Ekumfi-Atwia and by organizing its space to fit the storytelling tradition rather than using the colonialist proscenium-arch structure. She helped to encourage children's theatre through some of her own plays, such as *Vulture! Vulture!* and *Tahinta*. She was also a major director.

Ama Ata Aidoo (1942–) is noted for two plays. *The Dilemma of a Ghost* (1964) concerns a man who returns from America with a black American wife, and the tensions this creates within the man's family, who have deep-rooted prejudices about slave ancestry. It includes a chorus, who expresses fear of outsiders, whispers rumors, and spreads gossip. It is noted for being told from a woman's point of view and for its concern with male-female relationships. *Anowa* (1970) is set in the nineteenth century and concerns the conflict that develops between husband and wife after the husband decides, over the wife's objections, to buy slaves. The husband becomes impotent, which the wife believes is connected with slave ownership. Eventually, both husband and wife commit suicide. Once again, Aidoo is concerned with the lack of positive male-female communication, and she uses a chorus in a way that reminds the audience that the implications of the action reach beyond the particular situation. Aidoo worked with Sutherland's Drama Studio and was later the Minister of Education. She has spent many years living abroad.

Joe C. de Graft (1924–1978) was another of Ghana's major writers. His *Sons and Daughters* (1964) concerns a self-made African who seeks to force his youngest son and daughter to follow the path of their older siblings into professions other than art and dance, which the younger ones have chosen. A strong commentary on contemporary values and education, this play was very popular throughout English-speaking Africa. In *Through a Film Darkly* (1966), an educated young African man rejects his black fiancée to go away with a white English woman, only later to be rejected by her (she considers him merely an anthropological specimen). When he returns home, now bitterly antiwhite, he is confronted by his former fiancée who feels disgraced; she then commits suicide, as the young man subsequently does. This play, which treats both black-white relationships and the demand that newly educated Africans play roles in multiple cultures, was also popular throughout Africa.

Another influential playwright is Mohammed Ben-Abdallah (1944–). Among the best-known of his later plays are *The Trial of Mallam Ilya* (which makes extensive use of puppets) and *The Land of a Million Magicians* (1991), an adaptation of Brecht's *The Good Woman of Setzuan*. He has held a variety of government posts, including head of the National Commission on Culture and played a prominent role in the building of the National Theatre along European lines, which includes facilities both for a professional dance company and a professional theatre company, Abibigromma, the only professional companies (other than Concert Parties) in Ghana.

As in Nigeria, the theatre was greatly assisted in Ghana by universities and government programs. Although there is still little fully professional theatre in Ghana, aside from the Concert Party and the new national theatre, performance in its various guises is pervasive and dynamic. There has also been increasing emphasis upon festivals.

SIERRA LEONE

Sierra Leone became a British colony in 1896 and was granted its independence in 1961. Its population is composed of fourteen main groups. The Mende is the largest, with the Temne next in size. Creoles (descendants of returned enslaved Africans) make up only about 1 percent of the population, but their language, Krio, is the most widely spoken. English is the official language.

Storytelling is especially important among the Mende. There are two major types, historical and fictional. The historical, called *Ngawovei*, are spoken documents which preserve the past. They may be narrated, chanted, or sung, but are presented without any attempt at dramatization. The goal is historical fidelity. The fictional stories, *Domei*, are usually the creations of the storytellers, although they draw on an accumulated body of tales which each storyteller can borrow or alter. Storytelling is most popular in the time after the harvest season has ended. A performance usually takes place in the evening, and may last until well after midnight. Most storytellers are amateurs, but there are a few accomplished professionals who move from one village to another. Though the narrative may provide a framework, other elements tend to dominate. The storyteller may begin with a song, riddle, or joke that establishes the theme of the story. There are many digressions, some caused by voiced skepticism from the audience. The performance usually occurs in a large open space, typically a circle, and the narrator may move about so as to include all the audience. He also takes on the role of various characters. Songs are numerous and contribute to mood. Dance may also be used but is less important. Costume is usually minimal. The audience is fully involved. The musician and singing chorus are drawn from the audience, but any spectator is free to join in, and the audience almost always provides rhythmic hand-clapping. Sometimes the storyteller assigns roles to audience members. Consequently, the entire performance has the air of spontaneous improvisation.

Freetown, the capital of Sierra Leone, has a number of small theatre groups, most associated with the University of Sierra Leone, the National Theatre League, or schools. Among the most successful of its playwrights has been Thomas Decker who campaigned for many years for a theatre using Krio, the language of some 60 percent of the population. His work came to fruition after the success of his translation of *Julius Caesar* in 1964 and subsequently *As You Like It*. Juliana John furthered the process by writing original works in Krio. This trend was accelerated through the work of Yulisa Amadu Maddy (1936–), one of Africa's most radical dramatists, concerned with exposing the hypocrisy of those in positions of power, especially when religion figures in the deceptions. All of his plays deal with problems of the masses and demand social reform. Maddy left

Sierra Leone to become Director of the Zambian National Dance Troupe and then spent a few years in Europe working as a director and writing novels. Upon returning to Sierra Leone, he produced *Big Berrin* (1976), which in Krio, the language of the play, means "big death." The title apparently refers to the living death of the urban poor as seen in their plight and thwarted dreams. A highly theatrical play with much stylized music (including a chorus) and mime, it suggests the ritual of a funeral. Maddy was subsequently imprisoned, illustrating the dilemma of the African dramatist who wishes to use the theatre in the cause of social reform, and has lived abroad since his release in the late 1970s.

Krio theatre is very popular, especially with urban audiences. Much of it is based in storytelling, mime, music, and dance, and depends especially on a narrator and chorus. Performances can be found in the streets, bars, and other public places. Most productions originate in Freetown, the capital, but many tour to other areas. In recent years, a devastating civil war has greatly reduced theatrical activity.

KENYA

Kenya, located in East Africa, is quite different from the tropical West African countries. Much of it is dry, bush-covered plains, but there are fertile strips along the coast and in the southwestern part (where about 80 percent of the population lives). There are about forty indigenous groups. The British first arrived in 1887, and by 1903 the entire area was under British control. Britain urged Europeans to settle in Kenya, and many did, establishing large plantations, farms, or businesses. The goal was to create a European-style country. The refusal of the settler population to share or yield control explains why, unlike most of Britain's other colonies, independence was gained only after several years of terrorist activity and warfare by the Mau Mau. Independence was won in 1963. A large proportion of the settlers remained, and much of the wealth and power continued under their domination even after the government was in the hands of Africans. The official language of Kenya is Swahili, but English is used for many official proceedings.

Prior to independence, much of the theatre activity in Kenya was of the English community theatre type or was performed by English touring companies. In 1952, the colonial government established in Nairobi a national theatre, which primarily served the settler population and those Africans who had allied themselves with colonial power. After independence, it continued along the same lines, and

not until 1968 was an African, Seth Adagala, named head of the theatre, although this did little to change the theatre's program. He established the National Theatre Drama School, which supplied the National Theatre with a trained company that performed in Nairobi and toured widely.

Only the schools and universities encouraged black students to participate in theatre. Under the colonial government, a Drama Festival brought schools together in competition with productions of set plays from the curriculum (at first, always European and judged by Europeans). As African plays began to be published after independence, they gradually began to be included in the festivals. The University of Nairobi also expanded its theatre and drama program beyond the European canon and performance modes. It encouraged explorations of indigenous forms and experiments in new modes of writing and performance. African plays from other countries were also studied and produced. These influences combined to provoke nationalistic concerns and to produce a number of Kenyan playwrights of importance.

The first full-length play by an East African, *The Black Hermit* (1962), was written by Ngugi wa Thiong'o (1938–). It deals with an educated African who must decide whether to return to his tribe or to follow other paths.

In 1976 Ngugi reluctantly agreed to assist a local group in creating the Kamiriithu Community Educational and Culture Centre at Limuru as an integrated rural development program, using theatre to raise consciousness, stimulate thought, and provoke action. This project is significant in being the first

FIG. 22.7

Scene from *Afadhali Mchawi (Better Than the Witch)*, a performance created and directed by Graham Hyslop in Nairobi, Kenya in 1964. From the private collection of Louis A. Mbughuni. Courtesy Mr. Mbughuni.

Theatre for Development program that was initiated by a community rather than being imposed by university students or other outsiders. At Kamiriithu, the project was the conception of the community, and it was community members who persuaded Ngugi to join them. They built an open-air theatre entirely with volunteer labor. The Kenyan government suppressed the play after seven weeks, detained Ngugi wa Thiong'o for a year, and fired Ngugi wa Mirii from his university appointment. After his release, Ngugi wa Thiong'o returned to work at the Centre, where in 1982 he was denied permission to perform his *Mother Sing to Me,* concerning resistance to colonial oppression by various Kenyan peoples (the play used multiple African languages and included some eighty songs from eight Kenyan ethnic groups). The government closed the Centre and razed the theatre. Nevertheless, the work of the Centre came to be seen throughout Africa as a model for a true people's theatre. Ngugi wa Thiong'o went into exile and, after working for a time in Zimbabwe, has taught at New York University. He also published *Decolonizing the Mind* (1986) and *Moving the Center* (1993), important critiques of colonialism and neocolonialism.

The Kamiriithu experience gave rise to a populist political (sometimes radical) theatre movement in Kenya. The Tamaduni Players in Nairobi, for example, developed their own plays about street life and performed *The Trial of Dedan Kimathi* in Swahili. Other theatres were founded in townships and working-class suburbs. In 1986 these groups held a four-day festival in Nairobi. Nevertheless, the government kept a close watch, using laws that required every theatre group to register and each script to be read and approved prior to production. The large gap between the privileged and the masses, which Ngugi had brought to consciousness, increasingly became the basis for theatrical works.

Kenyan theatre is caught in a confrontation between the neocolonialist theatre favored by the government and theatre (often harassed by the government) which depicts the marginalization and repression of the common people. In the 1990s, a professional theatre began to emerge with the formation of such companies as Sarakasi Ltd. and the Miujiza Players that also demonstrated a greater concern for Kenyan issues.

UGANDA

Uganda has a rich heritage of indigenous performance (ritual initiations, celebrations, storytelling, etc.) in which dance and music are essential for observing major community occasions and creating communal emotional experiences. Uganda's royal courts retained groups of musicians and dancers for such performances. It became a British protectorate in the late nineteenth century and was granted independence in 1962. It uses English as its official language.

Makerere University, long the only university in East Africa, played a major role in the development of modern theatre in Uganda. Its dramatic society mounted the first production of *The Black Hermit* by Ngugi wa Thiong'o in 1962. In 1971 the university developed a department of music, dance, and drama, which offered undergraduate and graduate programs, along with productions. After independence, the taste for theatre became nationwide, and both local and traveling companies proliferated. In 1965, Makerere University started its Free Traveling Theatre, and soon most theatre groups felt the need to tour. This attempt to take theatre to the people was at least in part a rejection of elitist colonial theatre. A national theatre was built in 1959, and in 1963 it added a drama school. Nevertheless, most companies are amateur, although the Ugandan theatre has been fully Africanized. (Many socialist artists in Africa consider professional theatre to be a legacy of colonial capitalism best avoided.) During the repressive regimes of Obote and Amin between 1966 and 1978, many prominent theatre people were killed or exiled, but the theatre recovered rapidly after 1986 under Yoweri Museveni as semi-professional and amateur groups flourished. The best work was done in musical satire and dance drama (perhaps because it did not pose a language problem). One of the countries most devastated by AIDS, Uganda has made considerable use of theatre in its campaigns against it.

Uganda has produced some important playwrights, among them Serumaga, Ruganda, and Rugyendo. Robert Serumaga (1939–1982), after graduating from Trinity College, Dublin, and gaining some theatre experience in England, returned to Uganda in 1966 and founded the semi-professional Theatre Limited in 1968. This theatre later participated in international festivals in Manila, Belgrade, and elsewhere. Serumaga subsequently headed the Abafumi Players which, owing to political upheavals, later settled in Nairobi. Serumaga was concerned with finding a form for an authentic African theatre, and consequently in his plays he used music, song, imagery, and dance to enhance or replace words. One of his earliest works, *Renga Moi* (1972), which he toured widely, is focused around a chief who must defend his village and way of life. Serumaga extended his use of indigenous techniques in *A Play* (1967), *The Elephants* (1970), and *Majangwa*

FIG. 22.8

Robert Serumaga's *Majangwa* as performed by the Pride Theatre, Kampala, Uganda. Photograph by Eckhard Breitinger. Courtesy Mr. Breitinger.

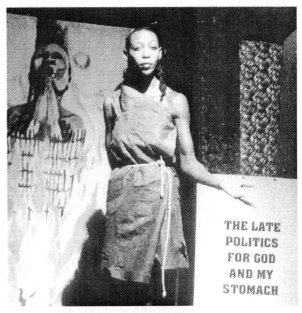

FIG. 22.9

A woman pleads for religious tolerance in Alex Mukulu's *The Wounds of Africa*. Photo by Eckhard Breitinger. Courtesy Mr. Breitinger.

(1971), but later moved into dance drama. The best known of his plays is *The Elephants,* which concerns characters in an East African university who manipulate each other to maintain their own self-esteem; the play implies that they may be elephants on the outside but are no more than mice on the inside.

John Ruganda (1941–), unlike most of his contemporaries, wrote in the realistic mode. His major plays include *The Burdens* (1972), *Black Mamba and Covenant with Death* (1973), *Music without Tears* (1982), *Echoes of Silence* (1987), and *The Floods* (1988). *The Burdens,* which brought Ruganda to prominence, deals with a disgraced politician now living in poverty with his wife and children, and drowning his disappointment in drink and adultery; the wife seeks to help him recover his dignity and position, but his drive is gone and ultimately she is driven to kill him. *The Floods,* apparently commenting on the regime of Idi Amin, explores the psychology behind such brutality. Ruganda later taught at the University of Nairobi in Kenya.

Similarly, Mukotani Rugyendo worked outside of Uganda (as an editor in Tanzania). His plays, including *The Barbed Wire, The Contest,* and *And the Storm Gathers* (all published 1977), argue the need for a socialist African state. Of these, *The Barbed Wire* is typical in showing how a rich man tries to acquire the communal land of a peasant community for his own gain. *The Contest* makes use of storytelling traditions in the contest for a wife between two heroes (one representing capitalism, the other socialism). The drummer is the master of ceremonies, and the audience is the final arbiter.

FIG. 22.10

A Theatre for Development AIDS play, *Mutabani,* played by Nthuuha Cramactors in Bundibuyo, Uganda. Photo by Eckhard Breitinger. Courtesy Mr. Breitinger.

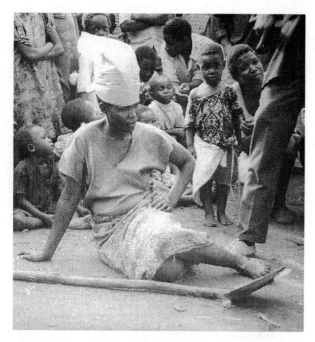

FIG. 22.11
Street theatre in Kampala, Uganda, 1994. Photo by
Eckhard Breitinger. Courtesy Mr. Breitinger.

The Royal Court Theatre in London has worked
with theatres in Uganda since 1994 in seeking to
develop new playwrights. Six Ugandan writers and
directors have attended the International Residency
program in London, and in 1996 a series of play development workshops led to a National Playwriting
Network based at the National Theatre in Kampala.
Its members meet throughout the year and at intervals present a festival of new plays. The most successful of the new writers is Charles Mulekwa, whose
play *A Time of Fire* was produced by the Birmingham Repertory Company in 1999. He has also been
commissioned to write a play for the Royal Court.

TANZANIA

Tanzania encompasses some 120 ethnic groups. It
was a German protectorate from the late nineteenth
century until after World War I, when it was ceded
to the British. As Tanganyika, it achieved independence in 1961, and was united with Zanzibar (another British protectorate granted independence in
1963) in 1964 to become Tanzania. Its official language is Swahili.

As do other African countries, Tanzania has a rich
heritage of traditional performance modes, including initiation rites, celebration dances related to such
events as weddings, harvests, and other social events,

storytelling, and recitations. Also as in other African
countries, colonial powers sought to discourage these
native expressions until the late 1940s. This change
in policy led to the rapid proliferation of dance
groups. Colonial schools introduced European-style
theatre in the 1920s and in the late 1950s inaugurated competitions among the schools.

Many changes came with the Arusha Declaration
in 1967, a blueprint for socialism which discouraged
production of foreign plays and encouraged writing
in Swahili. Almost all of Tanzania's major playwrights
emerged after 1967. Most supported the call to socialism, but after 1978 many also expressed disillusionment over corruption among the ruling elite.
One of the most important of these playwrights was
Ebrahim Hussein (1943–), whose plays include
Kinjeketile (1970), *The One Who Got What She De-
served* (1970), *The Dock in the Village* (1976), and
Wedding (1980). *Kenjeketile* is sometimes considered
to be one of Africa's finest plays. It deals with the
Maji Maji uprising in Tanganyika against German
oppressors in 1904. Kenjekitile, seen as the agent of
the god Hongo, heals the divisions among the Tan-
ganyikans by convincing them that the holy water
he anoints them with makes them invincible but,
while this gives them united strength, it also makes
them walk fearlessly into hails of German gunfire and
so lose the battle their common effort might have
won. The play raises consciousness about the necessity of united struggle against oppression as well as
the need to act in accordance with reason.

Traditional dance changed after 1967 to accommodate the call of socialism. Its popularity gave rise

FIG. 22.12
Scene from *Mafuta (Oil)*, devised and performed by the
Paukwa Theatre Group at the University of Dar es
Salaam, Tanzania. Photo courtesy Paukwa Theatre
Group.

to some thirty dance companies in the capital, Dar es Salaam. A new performance type, *Ngonjera,* was created after 1967, consisting of recitations of poetry enriched by the use of costumes, props, movement, and gesture. Performed especially at national festivals and on other official occasions, it became one of the most popular of theatrical forms, especially in the schools. Among the common people, the most popular form was *Vichekesho,* composed of improvised sketches, music, and dance. The universities involved themselves in trying to discover appropriate forms for Tanzanian theatre through study and experimentation with indigenous performance, as well as with contemporary domestic and foreign practices.

After the 1970s, concern for "theatre for development" became increasingly important in Tanzania. Workshops and long-term projects were conducted in villages by faculty connected with universities. Leading figures in this work were Penina Muhando Mlama (1948–) and Amandina Lihamba. Their theatre for development projects differed from those elsewhere in Africa in stressing the use of indigenous performance techniques rather than spoken drama. Mlama was also a playwright especially concerned with women's rights in such works as *My Respect* (1974), *I Divorce You* (1976), and *Mother the Main Pillar* (1982), but she largely abandoned writing her own plays when she began her theatre for development work. She has also been head of the Department of Art, Music, and Theatre at the University of Dar es Salaam.

Tanzanian dramatists have published many plays, but since they are written in Swahili and since few have been translated into European languages, they remain little known outside of Africa.

SENEGAL

During its precolonial history, Senegal was included within a number of successive African empires from the eighth century C.E. onward. Europeans began to establish stations there as early as the fifteenth century, and it eventually became a French colony. All of Senegal was under French rule by 1895, when it became the headquarters of the French West African Federation, which included several colonies. It gained full independence in 1960. Senegal has many language groups, but French is the official language.

As with other colonial powers, the French sought to discourage indigenous performance and ritual, but with little success, since those performances were based in religious beliefs about the origin of the world, human relationships to the gods, and the necessity of maintaining continuity between the dead and the living.

Perhaps the greatest influence on the development of theatre in French was the William Ponty School, a teacher-training college established in Senegal in 1930 to educate teachers from all over French West Africa. Between 1933 and 1948, stories from the various cultural groups of West Africa were dramatized and presented as end-of-the-year projects. The spoken part, rather stiff and elementary, was in French, while the sung text was in an African language. The play was further filled out with African songs and dances. In making these dramatizations, the French never forgot their "civilizing" mission, for though African life, customs, and history were included in the plays, the perspective was French. Teachers were encouraged to perform the Ponty plays in their schools or to evolve their own plays according to the Ponty formula when they returned to their countries. Students were also encouraged to tour West African colonies with these plays during the holidays. In 1937 a troupe was sent by the school to the International Exhibition in Paris, where it performed two plays to considerable acclaim.

In 1948, the colonial school systems were overhauled and emphasis shifted from the Ponty school to the French Cultural Centers established in all the French African colonies. In these centers between 1951 and 1958, a drama competition was held each year, and the winning group in each colony was sent to a competition among colonies. Almost all of the plays produced in the French colonies during these years were first mounted for this contest. After independence, which came to most colonies around 1960, the former French colonies adopted a comparable scheme for their Youth Festivals, held annually or biannually. Each country was divided into regions, within which a competition was held, and the winning production was sent on to the national festival. Out of these festivals, some individual participants were selected for specialized theatrical training, often in France or some other European country.

The first theatre to be built in Dakar, the capital of Senegal, was opened in 1954. Perhaps the most successful play staged there was a dramatization of a work by Birago Diop, *Sarzan* (1955), based in the story-telling tradition. Following independence, Senegal in 1965 established the Daniel Sorano National Theatre. Its first director was Maurice Sonar Senghor (1927–), nephew of the Senagalese president. The Daniel Sorano Theatre also included a Theatre Arts Department charged with training theatrical personnel. In 1966, Senegal hosted the First Festival of Negro Arts (later called The World

Festival of African Arts and Culture, FESTAC), and in 1969 it won first prize at the First Panafrican Cultural Festival held in Algiers. Productions from the Daniel Sorano Theatre also toured in France as well as in Africa and won prizes in Lagos (1977), Lyon (1979), and Carthage (1987 and 1995). Despite this record, state support for its national theatre drastically decreased during the 1980s, cutting in half the size of the company and leading to the closing of its training school for six years.

After independence, theatre training in all of French-speaking Africa was enhanced by the French government's ongoing interest in its former colonies. Partially out of the desire to ensure the continued importance of French language and culture in Africa, France, through its Ministry of Cooperation, sent companies to Africa to set a standard for performance. This program was supplemented by another under which France sent major practitioners to give workshops to enhance skills. In addition, it sponsored a few African directors each year to attend festivals at Avignon and elsewhere in France. Among the more far-reaching of its efforts, France after 1966 organized and sponsored through its state radio network an Inter-African Radio Theatre annual competition in playwriting open to all French-speaking Africans. Five prizes were awarded each year, the fifth being chosen by listeners. After 1978, a company from the author's country was commissioned to produce the grand prize-winning play and take it on tour to neighboring countries. Archival recordings of the plays were made and the five prize-winning plays each year were published.

It should also be noted that Senegal was the center in Africa of *négritude,* a concept set forth in the 1930s and promoted especially after 1945. Negritude involved a sense of the common inheritance and destiny of French-educated black intellectuals in Africa and the Caribbean. It advocated revolt against colonialist values, and glorified the African past and the beauty and harmony of traditional African society, which was seen as being founded on black emotion and intuition as opposed to white reason and logic. Its main African exponent was L.-S. Senghor, the first president of Senegal. Its influence was considerable in several African countries.

SOUTH AFRICA

The Republic of South Africa occupies the southern tip of Africa. Most of the population is concentrated in the eastern half, which has fertile farmland, whereas the western half is primarily grassland or desert.

The history of theatre in South Africa is bound up in the complexities of its colonial and recent past. Because of its strategic location and resources, South Africa began early to be coveted by Europeans. Beginning around 1652 the Netherlands encouraged Dutch immigrants to settle there. Around 1814 the British seized part of the territory and soon encouraged English settlement. Not wishing to live under British rule, the Dutch settlers (the Boers, now called Afrikaners) moved inland and established their own states. During all this, the indigenous peoples were seeking to defend their territory, and for approximately 100 years, beginning in the 1770s, there was frequent fighting. It was during this time that the Zulu king, Shaka, was killed (1828). By the 1880s, most of the native people were confined to territories not unlike Native American reservations in the United States.

The discovery of diamonds (1867), and later gold (1886), in Boer territory, began a struggle with the British which by 1902, after two wars, left Britain in possession of the entire territory. Reconciliation between the English and the Afrikaners led in 1910 to the formation of the Union of South Africa. The Union won independence from Britain in 1931 but remained a member of the British Commonwealth until 1961, when it became the Republic of South Africa. The latter change came largely in response to international controversy over South Africa's policy of "apartheid," a system that had gradually evolved to separate whites and nonwhites, especially after the 1920s, but had intensified after 1950 when a law requiring separate white and nonwhite residential areas was passed. As a result of this law, much of the black population was moved to impoverished townships, isolated but near enough to cities or industrial facilities to allow blacks to work as ill-paid laborers. Separate homelands, always the least desirable land, were set up for blacks, who were considered to be citizens of those homelands. All black men had to carry "passes," a provision that made it possible to control black movement and employment, and when black men left the homelands to work elsewhere, they were not allowed to bring their families, thus disrupting family life. For blacks, South Africa became a police state. Two other groups, coloreds (mixed race) and Asians (primarily Indians), also lived under separate government-established sets of restrictions, though not as severe as those that governed blacks.

Separate black schools provided minimal training, and protests over education led in 1976 to black student riots, beginning in Soweto and spreading throughout the country. This was one of the crucial events in South African history and a major boost for the Black Consciousness movement. The African National Congress (ANC), beginning in the 1950s, was the chief internal oppositional force to apartheid, but owing to government suppression and the detainment of ANC leaders, not until 1990 did the government finally agree to start dismantling apartheid after international boycotts made a change in policy inevitable. In 1994 the country's first democratic elections brought the selection of Nelson Mandela, a black lawyer who had been imprisoned for many years for his opposition to apartheid, as president. In 1995, South Africa rejoined the British Commonwealth. The process of reforming civil and economic rights for the native Africans is still under way.

As in other African countries, indigenous performances were numerous and of long standing before the arrival of Europeans. Men who had left their homelands to work in urban areas brought with them elements of their traditional practices and, in intermingling with men from still other areas, they developed mixtures of traditional and modern ceremony and dance to create new types of indigenous performance. As protest against white domination increased, traditional practices frequently were invoked as models for contemporary black performance modes and many plays sought to recover indigenous history and culture.

The first performance of a European play in South Africa came in the 1780s, and after 1801, when the African Theatre was founded in Cape Town, theatrical performances were available occasionally through visiting companies from England and elsewhere. During the last part of the nineteenth century, the discovery of diamonds and gold brought an influx of new immigrants, whose presence, especially in urban areas, motivated the building of theatres based on European models in which European plays could be performed.

English settlers could draw on a long tradition of plays in their own language, so there was little incentive for them to write new plays. Their attention was focused more on providing facilities and making arrangements for the foreign companies who found it profitable to tour South Africa. I. W. Schlesinger's African Theatres, founded in 1913, was a major builder of theatres and manager of tours until about 1930. But there was no tradition of writing plays in Afrikaans, a language that had evolved out of Dutch (with influence from English and several other languages). After about 1880 Afrikaners became especially concerned to establish the validity of their language and culture, and they placed high priority on creating a literature of their own and seeking international acceptance of it. The first

Afrikaans play, *Magrita Prinslo* by S. J. du Toit (1847–1911), was produced in 1897. It antedated any South African play in English.

Unlike the English-speaking South Africans, Afrikaners also had to create their own productions. In 1907, the first Afrikaans theatre group, the Afrikaans-Hollandse Toneelvereniging, was founded, and plays of emerging Afrikaner dramatists were toured by amateur groups through the mostly rural areas where the majority of Afrikaners lived. The Afrikaners were to remain essentially rural and conservative, distinguishing themselves from the English, who were primarily urban and liberal. Afrikaans theatre expanded through a growing network of essentially amateur companies and organizations. The first professional Afrikaans company was established by Paul de Groot in 1925 when Afrikaans and English were the official languages of South Africa.

Touring companies from England declined in number in the 1930s, but a mixture of professional and amateur South African companies remained. The work of amateur theatres received greater recognition and was better coordinated after the formation of the Federation of Amateur Theatrical Societies of South Africa in 1938. This was followed in 1947 by the first state-funded agency intended to assist professional theatres, the National Theatre Organization. This organization did much to encourage both Afrikaans and English professional theatre for white audiences between 1947 and 1963.

Around 1960, South African theatre began to enter a new phase, precipitated in large part by internal and external conflict over apartheid. Withdrawal from the British Commonwealth and the formation of the Republic of South Africa were in large part motivated by this conflict, and international censure began to increase consciousness and protest about apartheid at home. In 1963, foreign playwrights refused to allow their plays to be staged in South Africa, and in 1966 British Equity forbade its members to act in segregated theatres (mixed audiences were forbidden by South African law between 1966 and 1977). These decisions deprived South African theatres of a large proportion of their repertory and virtually eliminated English touring companies, thereby creating an increased market for both South African plays and performers. In 1963, the National Theatre Organization was replaced by Performing Arts Councils, one for each of the provinces that made up South Africa, and support for the theatre was channeled through them. Because of constraints imposed by the government, these councils had to be conservative in what they supported, and thus they did little to encourage innovative drama at a time when the need for change was being felt. They did eventually build impressive theatres, and offered training and experience to theatre practitioners.

The people best served by the councils were Afrikaans, who tended not to oppose government policies, and it was during the 1960s and 1970s that some of the best Afrikaans playwrights were active. Pieter-Dirk Uys (1945–) has alternated writing plays and writing and performing in cabarets and revues. He has appeared thousands of times both at home and abroad as his satirical drag character Evita Bezuidenhout, an Afrikaans grand dame (often called "the most famous white woman in South Africa"), who prior to the abandonment of apartheid helped to reveal its ridiculousness and who after 1994 interviewed numerous prominent government officials on television (thereby helping South Africans understand figures who under apartheid had been demonized by the white government). He is one of the best known and most popular performers in South Africa. His plays include *Paradise Is Closing Down* (1977), *Beyond the Rubicon* (1986), and *Just Like Home* (1988). In recent years he has performed one-person shows primarily seeking to make young people and politicians more aware of the dangers of AIDS. The best known of these shows is *Foreign AIDS* (2001).

Because of government restrictions, many white English-language and virtually all black playwrights worked outside the subsidized theatre. Black interest in theatre, other than traditional performance, can be traced back to at least the 1920s. In 1927, G. B. Sinxo's *Debeza's Baboons* became the first play in the Xhosa language to be performed. The first drama in English by a black person to be published, H. I. E. Dhlomo's (1903–1956) *The Girl Who Killed to Save: Nongquase the Liberator* (1935), concerns a Xhosa seer whose prophecies led to mass killing of cattle in the late nineteenth century. Dhlomo interpreted the discrediting of the seer as a triumph for Christianity. Dhlomo had already founded the Bantu Dramatic Society in 1933 with the goal of developing black African drama, although the society also performed European drama.

Other far-reaching work came by way of another path. In 1927, Esau Mthethwa founded the first company of black actors, the Lucky Stars, with which he performed for audiences using the Zulu language. Although the material came from Zulu daily life and included a great deal of song and dance, the goal seems to have been to teach lessons through satire and humor. This company performed throughout the country until 1936. The next major development in black performance came around 1952, when Alf Herbert, a Johannesburg promoter, began to assemble and tour popular entertainments called African

FIG. 22.13

Shakespeare's *Othello* as performed at the Market Theatre, Johannesburg. Directed by Janet Suzman. The actors are Joanna Weinberg, Richard Haines, and John Kani. Photograph by Ruphin Coldyzer. Courtesy Market Theatre.

Jazz and Variety. The Union of South African Artists (usually called Union Artists), formed in 1953 to protect the rights of black artists, developed Herbert's idea further and in 1959 created and staged the musical, *King Kong*, based on the life of the heavyweight boxing champion, Ezekial Dhlamini. This was the first example of what came to be called the "township musical," a fusion of urban working-class culture, popular forms of entertainment, jazz, and other forms of township music. Using the money made from *King Kong*, the Union Artists founded the African Music and Drama Association and sponsored a theatre workshop and drama school in Johannesburg. In 1961, they opened a theatre, the Rehearsal Room, where a large number of persons, both black and white, who would later play significant roles in South African theatre (including Athol Fugard and Gibson Kente) worked together.

After the law forbidding mixed casts and mixed audiences was passed in 1965, Gibson Kente (1932–) broke away from the Union Artists and in 1967 formed his own township company. Township theatre was commercial. It was created and performed in the townships and reflected township life. Music and dance were the essential ingredients; the dialogue was largely improvised by the performers. Since there were no township theatre buildings, these pieces were staged in a variety of spaces, usually for no more than one night in the same location. Casts were large and, consequently, pay was low. Kente's company continued throughout the 1980s to be the most popular in South Africa.

In the 1970s, black political theatre grew out of the Black Consciousness movement, which had originated in the universities. Not being able to act politically, this movement chose theatre as a means of uniting blacks, reminding them of their history and lost culture, and building resistance. Out of this movement came the People's Experimental Theatre (PET), founded in 1973. The members of PET and several other companies associated with Black Consciousness were detained in 1975 but, despite this setback, their cause was greatly enhanced in 1976 when students in Soweto rebelled against the educational system. In seeking to put down the demonstrations, soldiers fired on and killed a large number of students. Demonstrations quickly spread to other parts of the country. Thereafter, no one could be unaware of Black Consciousness. The influence of the militant Pan Africanist Congress, whose slogan was "One settler, one bullet," also grew.

Because of raised consciousness and unhappiness over government policies, the most vital theatre in South Africa in the 1970s was a committed theatre, whether white or black, which explored new ways of working and new modes of performance. In many instances blacks and whites worked together. The major alternative theatres were the Space Theatre, opened in Cape Town by Brian Astbury, Yvonne Bryceland, and Athol Fugard in 1972, and the Market Theatre in Johannesburg which came into being in 1976 when The Company, under Mannie Manim and Barney Simon, took over a converted fruit market. Playwrights who had their first productions at the Space include Athol Fugard, John Kani, and Winston Ntshona's *Sizwe Bansi Is Dead, Statements after an Arrest under the Immorality Act,* and *The Island;* and works by other major South African playwrights, among them Pieter-Dirk Uys's *Pity about People, Selle ou Storie,* and *God's Forgotten;* Geraldine Aron's (1941–) *Bar and Ger;* and Fatima Dike's (1948–) *The Sacrifice of Kreli* and *The First South African.* (Dike was the first black South African woman to have a play published. She has been commissioned by the Robben Island Museum to write a play about the political activists, including Nelson Mandela, who were imprisoned on Robben Island.) The Market Theatre's long roll of important plays includes works by Fugard, Uys, and such black writers as Matsemela Manaka, Maishe Maponya, and Zakes Mda. Other alternative theatres included The Glass Theatre in Cape Town; The Junction Avenue Theatre Company, the Box Theatre, and the Nunnery Theatre in Johannesburg; the Window Theatre in East London; the Serpent Players in Port Elizabeth; and several churches, institutes, and universities. Most of these were run by whites, but they included black performers and writers, and most used subterfuges to get around the prohibition against mixed casts and audiences prior to the removal of this restriction in 1977.

Between 1971 and 1973, the white playwright Athol Fugard and the black actors Winston Ntshona and John Kani, experimenting with collective creation, produced *Sizwe Bansi Is Dead* and *The Island.* The former play, concerning obtaining a "pass" by taking on a dead man's identity, was very successful not only in Africa but also in the United States and elsewhere. Barney Simon (1934–1995) who had worked with Joan Littlewood in London, was involved at the Market Theatre with several plays growing out of group collaboration. One of these, *Woza Albert!* (1980), originated with Mbongeni Ngema (1955–) and Percy Mtwa who, while performing in a Gibson Kente production, began work on a play about what would happen if Jesus were to come back to South Africa, including questions about what blacks would think about him and how the white government would react. Eventually Simon became the director and joint author of this

FIG. 22.14

Woza Albert! by Mbongeni Ngema, Percy Mtwa, and Barney Simon. The performers are Ngema and Mtwa. Courtesy Market Theatre, Johannesburg.

FIG. 22.15

Starbrites as directed by Barney Simon at the Market Theatre. Photo by Ruphin Coldyzer. Courtesy Market Theatre, Johannesburg.

work, one of the most popular plays ever to come out of Africa. It later toured the United States and elsewhere and won the Edinburgh Festival Fringe First Prize and some twenty other awards. It was performed by the two black actor-authors, who shifted rapidly among multiple roles, using a few props and costumes pieces on a sparsely furnished stage. To play white characters, they placed half a pink squash ball over their noses.

Both Ngema and Mtwa went on to create other pieces. Mtwa's *Bopha!* (1985) looks at apartheid through its effect on a black family. It sets an activist son against his policeman father, whose job it is to enforce the laws of apartheid. Eventually the policeman realizes that he has become an enemy of his own people and quits his job. Like other black plays, this one makes use of storytelling narration, music, dance, humor, and anger. It was made into a film in 1993. In 1982, Ngema founded a theatre group, Committed Artists, out of which came a number of international successes. His *Asinamali* (1985) is set in a South African jail, where five male characters recount, through words, song, dance, satire, humor, and outrage, what has led to their imprisonment. Each has come a different route—murder, unemployment, mistaken identity, violation of the Immorality Act, political activism—all resulting from apartheid. The title—"we have no money"—is the cry against rent increases of township demonstrators, whose leader, Msizi Dube, was killed by police but whose death led to the formation of a group dedicated to ending racial inequality. Ngema had even greater success, including international tours, with *Sarafina* (1986), which emphasizes the importance of women in the Soweto

uprising, especially that of Sarafina who emerges as the most committed activist, and the female schoolteacher, who teaches her students the history of blacks that is not in the history books. It was eventually made into a Hollywood movie. The money made on these musicals allowed Ngema to provide employment to increased numbers of theatrical personnel and to offer them training. *Township Fever* (1990), a fusion of township musical with serious drama and dance, was based on a transport strike in 1987 during which several strikers were charged with murdering "scab" workers.

Matsemala Manaka (1955–), founder of the Soyikwa Theatre Group, began writing with *The Horn* (1977) and won international attention with *Egoli—The City of God* (1979), which toured Europe and was voted Play of the Year in London. It deals with the destruction of a family caused by the labor system under which men must leave their homelands to find work. Despite its grim story, it ends on a note of promise as workers declare their freedom. In 1983, two of his one-act plays, *Imbumba* (1979) and *Pula* (1982), won first prize in the Edinburgh Festival's fringe. *Children of Asazi* (1984) is set against the government's order to remove people from the Alexandra township in Johannesburg and focuses on a young activist caught between personal ties and his need to protest the government's action. Songs and the music of a jazz saxophonist play key roles in the performance. Manaka worked primarily in the townships, although he occasionally presented work at the Market Theatre.

Most black playwrights concentrated on contemporary problems, but occasionally dealt with their historical and cultural heritage. Perhaps the best of such plays was *uNosilimela* (1973) by Credo Mutwa

FIG. 22.16

Bopha! by Percy Mtwa and Cast. Photo by Ruphin Coudyzer. Courtesy Market Theatre, Johannesburg.

(1921–), developed in part in collaboration with Workshop '71. It was subsequently presented in Soweto and elsewhere. The staging demands made it so difficult to move from one venue to another that the production, though still popular, closed in 1975. The play draws on the history, legends, aspirations, and various indigenous performance traditions of the Bantus in its narrative, ritualistic, satirical, and allegorical sequences as the title character seeks to discover who she is, ultimately becoming the proud inheritor of African history and culture. It suggests the need for blacks to give up imitating foreign cultures and return to their own.

By far the best known among South Africa's white playwrights is Athol Fugard (1932–), often mistakenly considered by those outside the country to be South Africa's only playwright of note. Fugard began his playwriting career with *No-good Friday* (1959), written and staged while working with the Union Artists in Johannesburg between 1958 and 1961; *The Blood Knot* (1961), which shows two brothers struggling to maintain their relationship in the face of racial laws that threaten to separate them, was the first production of the Rehearsal Room there. After a few years of theatrical experience in Europe, Fugard settled in Port Elizabeth, where he wrote a series of plays about the effects of South Africa's laws and social attitudes on working-class characters. These include *Hello and Goodbye* (1965), *People Are Living There* (1968), and *Boesman and Lena* (1969). Between 1971 and 1973, as indicated earlier, he developed plays in collaboration with John Kani and Winston Ntshona. Subsequently, Fugard returned to writing alone. *Master Harold and the Boys* (1982) is a play often considered to be autobiographical about a white boy's friendship with a black worker who serves as a surrogate father and how, through attitudes learned from apartheid, the boy destroys that relationship. *My Children, My Africa* (1989) is set in a school where a rivalry for achievement between a black boy and a white girl develops toward friendship but is interrupted by a boycott in which the boy feels compelled to participate and which leads to the death by a mob of the black teacher who has attempted to bring them together. In *Playland* (1992), two men—one black, one white—with violent pasts meet in an amusement park (playland) and in the course of the action confront each other, their pasts, and themselves. It suggests a microcosm of South Africa in which an exorcism of white-black experience and guilt is played out, a theme he takes up again in *Sorrows and Rejoicings* (2001). In recent years, Fugard has been attacked by some of his countrymen for his stance as a passive observer, who depicted but did little to change life in South Africa.

Among South Africa's other white playwrights. Paul Slabolepszy (1948–) is among the most prolific and popular. He is especially noted for his multilingual and comic representations of ordinary characters which do not address directly but suggest a great deal about African politics. His many plays include *Saturday Night at the Palace* (1981), *Making Like America* (1986), and *Victoria Almost Falls* (1993). Anthony Akerman (1949–) began writing plays while in exile, but returned to South Africa in 1992. His plays, which include *A Man out of the Country* (1985), *A World Elsewhere* (1987), and *First Loves* (1993), reflect the conflict in what it means to be South African. Another major playwright is Reza de Wet, who writes both in Afrikaans and English and in 1994 won the Herzog Prize, the highest honor in Afrikaans literature. Wet's experimental pieces use various theatrical metaphors to deal with sexual and psychological taboos. Her plays, which have been especially popular with younger audiences, include a trilogy, *Trits,* and *A Worm in the Bud.*

Since the late 1980s, South African theatre was caught up in uncertainty and transition. In 1987 the performing arts councils changed their rules to permit blacks to serve on their boards of directors. They also decided to create outreach programs. By 1990, much of what had been thought of as alternative theatre in the 1960s and 1970s had entered the mainstream. Among developments of the 1980s was the emergence of a workers theatre under the sponsorship of trade unions. In these performances, workers presented plays intended to educate other workers about the hidden structures that control their professions. Theatre was also used in the fight against AIDS, among the most effective programs being "Puppets against AIDS," a project of the African Research and Educational Puppetry Program, which performed skits while a narrator described the action and supplied information. Johannesburg's Handspring Puppet Company, founded in 1981 by Adrian Kohler and Basil Jones, is the most internationally famous puppet theatre in South Africa. Kohler and Jones write the plays and manipulate the puppets in full view of the audience, as in Bunraku. They often work with William Kentridge, one of South Africa's best-known painters, printmakers, and filmmakers. Their joint productions have toured widely.

Changes were also felt in the universities. The drama department at the University of Zululand began shifting its curriculum away from Western forms to indigenous South African forms and popular theatre. Its classes increasingly focused on workshops and playmaking. Other universities also reexamined their programs and sought to adapt to new conditions. Almost everywhere the question of language was raised (under the new government there are eleven official languages, although English dominates), and dance became increasingly important. That South African theatre today is vigorous is attested by the annual Grahamstown Festival to which productions are brought from all over the country. Founded in 1970 and formerly primarily a festival of white theatre, since the late 1980s the number of black entries has increased each year. In the late 1990s, approximately 500 theatre events were being seen annually in the festival's main and fringe venues. The primary issue being discussed and dramatized was how to define and realize a just society and a genuinely South African theatre.

NORTH AFRICA

Some aspects of North African history are discussed in chapter one. As has been indicated, ancient Egyptian ritual-drama is among the oldest performance modes of which we have knowledge. Subsequently, those portions of North Africa that bordered the Mediterranean became parts of the Hellenistic, Roman, and Byzantine worlds and participated in the theatre of those times. In the seventh and eighth centuries C.E., all of northern Africa was conquered by Moslems, and Arabic gradually became the official language and Islam the official religion. Since that religion was antipathetic to it, theatre was of little importance. Storytelling, sometimes with enactment of portions, was common from the ninth century onward, and shadow puppetry, imported from Persia or Turkey, was long the most popular form of theatrical entertainment.

Egypt has played the largest role in North Africa's theatre. During much of the nineteenth and early twentieth centuries, Egypt was under English domination or occupation. During the nineteenth century theatrical companies began to appear. The first Western-style production dates from 1870. In this and subsequent productions, singing and dancing were the primary attractions, with story of secondary concern. Men played all the roles.

Theatre in Egypt has flourished primarily in the twentieth century. The most important troupe in the early years was that of Jurj Abyad, established in 1910 with the encouragement of the minister of education. It performed entirely in Arabic, presenting comedy and tragedy and both European and Arabic works. Egypt's first important playwright was Ahmad Shauqi (1868–1931), author of six historical plays and one comedy. His serious plays include *The Fall of Cleopatra* and *Qambiz (Cambyses)*, retellings of stories that had been dramatized in Elizabethan England

and whose views of their subjects Shauqi sought to amend. Of still greater importance was Tawfiq al-Hakim (1898–1987), sometimes called the father of modern Egyptian drama, who wrote some eighty plays which deal with philosophical and religious issues, and explore such social questions as the position of women and the search for happiness in a world of war, poverty, and disease. Among his early dramas, one of the most important (in part because it was the opening production in 1935 of the newly formed Egyptian National Theatre Troupe) was *The Sleepers in the Cave*, based on a parable from the Quran. Others of his plays include *The Sultan Who Could Not Make Up His Mind* (1960), *The Tree Climbers* (1962), *Fate of the Cockroach* (1966), and *The Donkey Market* (1975). Al-Hakim's plays were intended primarily to be read. In contrast, Ashad Rushdy wrote with the stage in mind. Surprisingly, Rushdy largely escaped censorship despite the social and political criticism contained in his plays, some of the best-known of which are *The Butterfly* (1959) and *Egypt My Love* (1967).

After 1967, the theatre in Egypt began to decline because of poor economic conditions, the increase in Islamic fundamentalism, and the introduction of television. Egypt's role as the primary source of drama in the Arab world metamorphosed into that of primary source of Arabic television programs and films. Since the early 1990s, Egypt has hosted the Cairo International Festival of Experimental Theatre, financed by the government. In twelve days each September, more than fifty companies from the Middle East, Europe, Australia, North and South America, Japan, and elsewhere present plays. There are also symposia and wide-ranging discussions of theatre.

Other North African countries—Morocco, Algeria, and Tunisia—were long dominated by France. Algeria was annexed as a province of France in 1830 and became an independent country again only in 1962. After independence, Algeria established a conservatory (under the direction of Bachtarzi Mahiedine) to train actors, and a National Theatre (under the direction of Mustapha Kateb). Both of these men were interested in developing a theatre that could serve all the people. The best-known of all Algerian dramatists is Kateb Yacine (1929–), whose *The Encircled Corpse* (1958), a strong attack on French colonialism, aroused so much hostility in France (produced there in the midst of the Algerian war for independence) that performances had to be moved to Brussels. A second play, *The Ancestors Redouble Their Ferocity*, created almost as great a furor. His *Mohamed, Take Your Suitcase*, concerning Algerian immigrants in France, achieved considerable success, especially among French immigrant audiences. In recent years, theatre in Algeria has encountered increased opposition from Islamic fundamentalism.

Both Morocco and Tunisia regained independence in 1956, and both have since established national theatres, although neither has produced playwrights or directors of more than local significance. In Tunisia, Izz al-Din al-Madani (1938–) and in Morocco Tayyib al Siddiqui (1938–) have both sought to create a specifically Arab form of drama.

In addition to the countries discussed above, there are many others which have not been covered. All deserve attention, but few have played a major role in documented African theatre.

LOOKING AT THEATRE HISTORY

In studying African theatre, most of us soon become aware of its "otherness"—its unlikeness to the traditions with which we are most familiar. In studying Western theatre, we are in a position to examine it from an "insider's" point of view, for we are looking at our own inherited or created traditions and conventions, many of them so familiar that we have ceased to be conscious of them. When most of us see or hear the words *play, theatre,* or *performer,* we almost automatically form images based on experience with Western theatre. When we turn to African theatre, we may at first be inclined to impose on it Western assumptions and associations, thereby seriously misperceiving it. Although Westerners are unlikely ever to be able to experience African theatre from the "inside"—that is, as someone does who has grown up within African traditions—they can improve their perceptions by ceasing to consider Western notions of theatre as "normative," "commonsensical," or "valid," as opposed to the "aberrational," "exotic," or "flawed" notions of cultures with which they are unfamiliar. Although theatre can always be better understood by viewing it within its cultural context, this is especially true of African modes that have existed since precolonial times, few of which fit easily into Western concepts of "theatre" and most of which were integrated into the life of the society rather than being discrete "events." In societies that did not have a written language, performance had ramifications larger than those usually associated with theatre in Western culture.

It is difficult for non-Africans to gain an understanding of indigenous African performance as a total experience because those who write about it often take it out of its cultural context or tend to divide it into its components, each of which is studied in isolation from the rest, a practice which disrupts the totality forged by the several "languages" of performance as they work off each other, often improvisationally. Additionally, those who write about performance have a tendency to ignore much of the improvisation, repetition, and elaboration in order to present an orderly account:

> . . . while [African] performers often specialize in certain performance genres—drumming, dancing, singing—these activities rarely happen in isolation. Meanwhile, as drummers, dancers, singers, and others are communicating and negotiating with each other in the process of performance, scholars isolate them from each other in their representations by focusing on one genre to the exclusion of others. . . .
> . . . Performance is then reduced to a linear, unidimensional structure organized sequentially and normatized—not by performers—but by social scientific procedures.

Margaret Thomson Drewal, "The State of Research on Performance in Africa," *Africa Studies Review,* 34, 3 (Dec. 1991) 16.

Colonial authorities tried to forbid or control indigenous performance, in part because they considered it pagan and in part because they feared its potential for subversion. They were seldom fully successful in their attempts:

> Since public performance is the usual medium adopted by the arts in indigenous African as in other societies, it was not difficult to find one kind or another going on throughout the year's cycle. Drama, dance, poetry, storytelling, music, and the creation of sculpture lent themselves readily to performance, which naturally exploited contemporary religious and social realities. . . .

*the Christians raided ancestral shrines and forbade
African converts to participate in their cultural
association's activities, or even play their musical
instruments. . . . To . . . pronounce their practices evil
or barbaric was the best way to stamp out the art forms
and politics engendered by them.*

*. . . The reaction of the indigenous theater to
colonial efforts to gag it was similar in many African
countries. The Igbo in Nigeria created new plays
featuring British colonial officers—administrators, police,
missionaries—and their families as characters to replace
the banned traditional characters.*

J. Indu Amankulor, "English-Language Drama and
Theater," *A History of Twentieth-Century African
Literatures,* ed. by Oyekan Owomoyela (Lincoln:
University of Nebraska Press, 1993), 139–40.

Among the major issues in contemporary African
theatre has been the intended audience. For whom
is theatre being done? This questioning leads inevitably to language. In what language should the
dramatist write? Ngugi wa Thiong'o poses the issue
clearly:

*The moment you write in English you assume a
readership who can speak and read English, and in this
case it can only mean the educated African élite or the
foreigners who speak the language. This means that you
are precluding in terms of class the peasantry, or the
workers in Africa who do not read or understand these
foreign languages.*

Ngugi wa Thiong'o, Interview, *Kunapipi,* 1 (1981).
Quoted in Ingrid Björkman, *"Mother Sing For Me":
People's Theatre in Kenya* (London: Zed Books,
1989), 3.

23

Continental European and Latin American Theatre in the Late Twentieth Century

By 1968 enormous stresses had developed in almost every country. Protests moved away from the nonviolent tactics favored by civil rights advocates to confrontations. Such patterns of protest and violence were symptomatic of deep-seated doubts about the validity of long-accepted conventions of behavior and traditional values and about the ability of social institutions to deal effectively with changing needs. Individuals and groups began to elevate their own ideals above existing laws, to assert their obligation to live by their own standards, and to demand the alteration or destruction of anything contrary to their views. The result was a fragmented society lacking agreement about both goals and means.

The theatre could not remain aloof from the stresses of the time. It was caught in a struggle between those who wished to maintain tradition and those who championed innovation and change. This conflict provoked much controversy over the nature and function of theatre. The old conception of art as detached contemplation (or as the pursuit of some superior beauty and order) was challenged by those who wished to use it to provoke thought and action about pressing social and political issues.

Throughout the 1960s, prosperity gave the theatre considerable economic stability, for it was possible to gain financial support both for traditional and innovative work. The old and the new coexisted,

sometimes in uneasy alliance, but often in radical opposition. By the 1980s, however, conservatism, both political and economic, reasserted itself and the exuberance of earlier years faded. By the end of the decade, as the Soviet empire collapsed and ethnic conflicts increased, uncertainty was once more apparent.

SOVIET AND RUSSIAN THEATRE TO 1990

The turn away from Stalinism that began in 1956 was sporadic thereafter. But the policies of *glasnost* introduced by Mikhail Gorbachev in the 1980s were to bring profound changes that would ultimately lead to the breakup of the Soviet Union. Still, from 1968 until the time of that breakup in the late 1980s, Soviet theatre enjoyed a popularity probably unsurpassed anywhere in the world. Moscow's approximately 30 theatres were usually filled each night. Soviet government statistics indicated that attendance in the late 1980s was high throughout the Soviet Union, with some 110 million people attending more than 600 professional theatres, including over 60 for children and youth.

During the 1960s, growing dissatisfaction with socialist realism led to a revival of interest in Meyerhold, Tairov, and Vakhtangov. Exhibitions were devoted to their productions; a complete edition of Meyerhold's writings was finally published; and in 1974 the centenary of Meyerhold's birth was celebrated with performances, articles, conferences, and commemorative stamps. But Vakhtangov's methods were the most widely adopted as they provided the most readily acceptable alternative to socialist realism.

The Moscow Art Theatre continued to command the greatest official prestige after 1968, and its actors the highest salaries of any theatre in the USSR. By 1973 its programs had become so extensive and its company so large that a new and lavish theatre was built to augment its facilities. In 1987 the complexities of the organization (exacerbated by operating in two separate theatres located in different parts of Moscow) led to the division of the company into two parts, one headed by Oleg Yefremov, the other by Tatyana Doronina. Rivalries among the two divisions considerably tarnished the company's public image.

The Contemporary (Sovremennik) Theatre, meanwhile, continued to gain in prestige, especially after 1970 when one of its founders, Oleg Yefremov (1927–2000), was named head of the Moscow Art Theatre. Oleg Tabakov (1935–) became director of the Contemporary, and in 1974 it too was given a new theatre (a remodeled cinema with rehearsal rooms and workshops) to augment its facilities. Tabakov left two years later to pursue an independent career. He established his own highly regarded Tabakov Studio Theatre, became director of the Moscow Art Theatre's Studio-School, and also created the American

Studio of the Moscow Art Theatre. The Contemporary Theatre, meanwhile, under the direction of Galina Volchek, had expanded its activities to include touring and visited the United States in 1996 and 1998.

The most controversial and experimental theatre was the Moscow Theatre of Drama and Comedy (usually called the Taganka after the suburb in which it was located). Headed after 1964 by Yuri Lyubimov (1917–), it made liberal use of dynamic movement, dance, mime, masks, puppets, and projections, and reshaped scripts or adapted novels from a critical perspective. Its tendency to produce works considered to be on the edge of permissibility and its "formalistic" production techniques (influenced by Meyerhold, Vakhtangov, and Brecht) kept the Taganka highly visible and controversial. A number of its productions were censored or forbidden, but it was especially popular with young audiences. At the Congress of the All-Union Society of Theatre Workers in 1970, the Taganka was the only company singled out for censure. Nevertheless, in 1977 it was permitted to make a foreign tour, and thereafter Lyubimov was occasionally permitted to direct in Western Europe. While in the West, he harshly condemned Soviet opposition to his work, and in 1984, while abroad, he was removed from his post at the Taganka and stripped of his citizenship. Subsequently, he directed throughout Europe and the United States, staging a number of highly acclaimed productions, most notably adaptations of Dostoyevsky's

FIG. 23.1
Yuri Lyubimov's production of Albert Camus' adaptation of Dostoyevsky's *The Possessed*, 1985. Design by Lazaridis Stefanos. Photo by Agence de Presse Bernand, Paris.

Crime and Punishment and *The Possessed*, the latter for the Théâtre de l'Europe in 1985. Lyubimov was succeeded at the Taganka in 1984 by another of Russia's controversial directors, Anatoly Efros (1925–1987), several of whose productions at other theatres had been withdrawn from the repertory or censored.

Other innovative directors included Vasilyev, Sturua, and Dodin. Anatoly Vasilyev (1942–) began directing in the 1960s and came to international attention in the 1980s when his productions of Viktor Slavkin's *Cerceau* and Pirandello's *Six Characters in Search of an Author* played at various international festivals. *Cerceau*, which treats a reunion of old acquaintances in an isolated country house, was developed through improvisational techniques reminiscent of Grotowski's. Pirandello's mingling of life and art in *Six Characters* was mirrored in Vasileyev's intermingling of audience and performers and frequent switching of roles among the actors.

Robert Sturua (1938–), working at the Rustaveli Theatre in Tbilisi, gained international recognition in the 1980s, especially with his productions of Shakespeare's *Richard III* and *King Lear*, both of which were given political interpretations. In *Richard III*, Richmond followed Richard everywhere, taking notes and observing, apparently to ready himself to take over the role of ruler. In *King Lear*, the action occurred in a police state which seemed literally to disintegrate around the characters. He continued his productions of Shakespeare with *Macbeth* in 1996, which shows love giving way to desire for power.

Playwriting also underwent several ups and downs after 1968, for although strictures were relaxed, prior to the late 1980s the price for overstepping the bounds could be severe. Vasili Aksyonov (1932–), for example, had won considerable success with such plays as *Always for Sale* (1966), a commentary on popular culture using song, dance, masks, and film to depict a conformist society, and *Your Murderer* (1977), which drew on absurdist techniques reminiscent of Ionesco's *Rhinoceros* and its protagonist who refuses to go along with the crowd. But because of his involvement with a banned book, Aksyonov was forced to emigrate to the United States in 1980. Other writers—such as Chingiz Aitmatov (1928–) and Kaltai Mukhamedzhanov (1928–) in *The Ascent of Mount Fuji* (1973) and G. Baklanov in *Fasten Your Seat Belts* (1975)—though they treated the problem of maintaining integrity in the face of authoritarian demands for conformity, stopped short of criticizing the Soviet system. A greater number of dramatists continued to write traditional dramas. Among the most successful playwrights were Aleksandr Vampilov (1937–1972), whose *Last Summer in Chulimsk* (1972)

FIG. 23.2
Askyonov's *Always for Sale* at the Contemporary Theatre, Moscow. Directed by Oleg Yefremov.

presents a gallery of characters in a Siberian village but concentrates on a young girl who, rejected by a visitor, is condemned to a life of disappointment; Mikhail Roshchin (1933–), whose extremely popular *Valentin and Valentina* (1971) treats young lovers caught in a generational conflict; and Aleksei Arbuzov (1908–1986), one of the most popular and prolific of Russian dramatists. Arbuzov began writing plays in the 1930s but was especially successful after 1968 with such plays as *Old Fashioned Comedy* (1976, produced on Broadway in 1978 as *Do You Turn Somersaults?*), which treats awakening love between two older people, and *Remembrances* (1981), about the pull between family loyalty and extramarital temptations.

Two of Russia's most admired playwrights were Radzinsky and Petrushevskaya. Edvard Radzinsky (1936–) first gained popularity with *104 Pages about Love* (1964), a work that helped to establish a trend toward plays about personal lives. Originally directed by Anatoly Efros, it was subsequently performed in more than 120 theatres before being made into a ballet and a film. His later work, especially his trilogy composed of *Conversations with Socrates* (1978), *Lunin* (1981), and *Theatre in the Time of Nero and Seneca* (1981), uses historical subjects to stir up thought about oppressive authority and its inability to enslave the human spirit. Ludmilla Petrushevskaya (1938–) won considerable fame with short, realistic, seemingly plotless plays filled with wry humor. Two of the most popular were *Cinzano* (1975) and *Smirnova's Birthday* (1975), a pair of related plays, one about men and the other about women, in which the characters discuss life as each group simultaneously but in separate locations consumes the Cinzano they bought with the money that was supposed to cover the expenses of a funeral. Other notable playwrights included Maria Arbotova, Sergei Kokovkin, Alexander Galin, and Olga Mukhina.

THEATRE IN POLAND AND CZECHOSLOVAKIA TO 1990

Like the rest of Eastern Europe, Poland came under Soviet domination following World War II, but it was the first to ease restraints after 1956. In 1968, when Poland's participation in the invasion of Czechoslovakia led to protests at home, new strictures were imposed. These restrictions gradually eased, but in 1982 fear of the Solidarity movement led the government to impose martial law. In 1989, after democratic reform ousted the Communists, almost all restraints were removed. Thus, the degree of government control varied drastically after 1945.

For several years after 1956 the dominant dramatic mode was absurdism, although it took a more satirical and didactic turn than in France. The vogue was initiated with the plays of Stanislaw Ignacy Witkiewicz (1885–1939), a previously neglected surrealist writer of the interwar years, whose theoretical work, *Pure Form in the Theatre* (1920), along with such plays as *The Water Hen* (1921), *The Madman and the Nun* (1923), and *The Mother* (1924), won increasing acceptance. The plays of Beckett were also popular and helped to establish the taste for absurdist drama.

Soon several new dramatists appeared, of whom the most important were Rósewicz and Mrozek. Tadeusz Rósewicz (1921–), already famous as a poet, began writing plays in 1960. His *The Card Index* (1960) and *He Left Home* (1964) did much to establish the pattern that would be followed by subsequent writers, with whom the most common theme was the search for a lost order even as the concept of absolutes was rejected. He continued to explore this theme in such plays as *The Laocoon Group* (1974), *White Marriage* (1975), and *The Trap* (1982).

Although within Poland Rósewicz was perhaps the most respected of contemporary dramatists, abroad he was overshadowed by Slawomir Mrozek (1932–), whose plays depended rather heavily on caricature. For example, *The Police* (1958), one of Mrozek's numerous short plays, shows how the secret police, having been so successful that they are in danger of being abolished, order one of their own men to become an enemy agent so they may survive. Mrozek also wrote full-length plays, of which the best known is *Tango* (1964), one of the most popular of all new plays in Europe during the late 1960s. *Tango* is a parable about the decay of values, which

has become so complete that only brute force is truly effective; consequently those who are most willing to exercise power, ruthlessly and without regard for humanistic principles, become the rulers. Mrozek continued this vein in *A Happy Event* (1971), in which he depicts left-wing anarchist youth in the form of a grown-up baby who tyrannizes his parents, blows up their house, and ends up helpless in the ruins; and in *The Emigrés* (1974), a two-character play which suggests that the left-wing intellectual and the worker depend on each other to give their lives significance. His later plays include *The Ambassador* (1981) and *Alpha* (1984). *Love in the Crimea* (1994) is a satirical history of Russia in the twentieth century. Using Chekhov-like characters and situations, its first act takes place in 1910 (Czarist Russia), the second in 1928 (Communist Russia), and the third in the 1990s (marketplace Russia). Mrozek, who left Poland in 1963, returned after spending his exile in France and Mexico.

Among later dramatists, Janusz Glowacki (1938–) was one of the most popular. He first began to write plays in the late 1970s. Because of his sympathy with the Solidarity movement, Glowacki came under increasing attack in the 1980s, and eventually fled to the United States. The best known of his early plays is *Cinders* (1979), which focuses on a girls' reformatory production of Cinderella and its leading actress, who chooses suicide rather than submit to the repressive circumstances in which she finds herself. The best known of the later plays, written after Glowacki arrived in the United States, are *Hunting Cockroaches* (1985), which shows a Polish emigré couple trying to adjust to their new environment and a new set of problems, and *Antigone in New York* (1993), in which emigrés bury a body in New York's Tompkins Square Park.

Internationally, Poland was perhaps best known for its innovative directors rather than for its dramatists. By far the best known was Jerzy Grotowski (1933–1999), who founded the Theatre of 13 Rows in Opole in 1959, which became the Polish Laboratory Theatre when they moved to Wroclaw (Breslau) in 1965. Grotowski gained an international reputation when his company began to tour and he began working with foreign troupes and lecturing widely on his methods. The collection of essays by and about him published under the title *Towards a Poor Theatre* (1968) became one of the most influential works of the period.

Ironically, Grotowski began to alter his interests just as he won international acceptance. Thus, the first phase of his work ended around 1970. During this phase, Grotowski began with the premise that the theatre has borrowed too heavily from other media, especially film and television, and thus has violated its own essence, which he sought to recover by eliminating everything except its two essential elements: the actor and the audience. He called his approach "poor theatre" (in contrast with technologically "rich" theatre) since it avoided all machinery and minimized all spectacle not created by the actor. His performers were not allowed to use makeup or change costume to indicate a change in role or within a character; all music had to be produced by the actors themselves; he used no scenery in the traditional sense, although a few functional properties might be rearranged or used in various ways as the action demanded; he abandoned the proscenium-arch stage in favor of a large room which could be rearranged for each production. In this way, actors were thrown back on their own resources.

During this period, actor training was the focus of Grotowski's concerns. His system required actors to gain absolute control over themselves physically, vocally, and psychically, so that during performances they might transform themselves as demanded by the production. Grotowski wanted his actors to arouse a sense of wonder because of their ability to exceed what the spectators can envision ever being able to do.

FIG. 23.3
Grotowski's production of *The Constant Prince*, adapted from Calderón's play. For this production, the space was arranged so that the spectators looked down on the acting space much as in a medical operating theatre; Grotowski suggested that in this performance symbolic "psychic surgery" took place. Photo by Agence de Presse Bernand, Paris.

In this early phase, Grotowski looked upon the theatre as a secular ritual to which spectator-witnesses were admitted. He believed that the audience is the other essential ingredient of a performance and that it must be put in a position to play its role unselfconsciously. (He argued that attempts to involve the audience directly in the action only make it self-conscious.) Therefore, for each production he decided how the audience should respond psychologically and then arranged the space to create the appropriate psychic distance.

In preparing a production, Grotowski searched in a script to find archetypal patterns that have universal meaning for audiences today. Much of the script might be abandoned and the remainder rearranged. The ultimate aim was to make the actors and the audience confront themselves in something analogous to a religious experience. Among his most highly regarded productions from this period were *Akropolis* (first done in 1962), *The Constant Prince* (first done in 1965), and *Apocalypsis cum Figuris* (first done in 1968), all of which were restaged several times.

By 1970 Grotowski had come to believe that his group had reached the end of its search for technical mastery, and he decided to create no new productions. He realized that, while his actors had been able to eliminate the blocks that stood in their way as performers, they had not broken down the blocks that stood between performer and audience. He then set out to eliminate "the idea of theatre," in the sense of an actor playing for an audience, and to find a way of incorporating spectators into "a meeting, not a confrontation; a communion, where we can be totally ourselves." Consequently, he sought to develop means for leading participants back into the elemental connections between people and their bodies, the natural world, and each other.

The first major revelation of the new work came during the summer of 1975 when approximately 500 people from all over the world attended a "research university" organized by Grotowski at Wroclaw under the sponsorship of the Théâtres des Nations, which that year was held in Warsaw. The group included students, teachers, and journalists, as well as several famous directors—among them Peter Brook, Jean-Louis Barrault, Luca Ronconi, and Joseph Chaikin. Some of the activities involved groups going into the woods for 24 hours during which they were led through ritualized myths and archetypal experiences involving fire, air, earth, water, eating, dancing, playing, planting, and bathing. Through this process, participants were expected to rediscover the roots of the theatre in pure ritualized experience, as well as to discover their own true being.

After 1975, Grotowski began studying the diverse ritual performances of Japan, India, Haiti, Mexico, Africa, and elsewhere, and used these experiences to enhance the work he had done earlier. He labeled this new phase the Theatre of Sources, and in 1983 he became head of an institute at the University of California, Irvine, devoted to continuing this research with a renewed concern for physical, vocal, psychological, and performance discipline. (In 1984 the Polish Laboratory Theatre was disbanded.) In 1985, a center to assist his work was established in Pontadera, Italy, and subsequently Grotowski spent most of his time there. Although Grotowski's work went through several phases after 1960, it is the work done before 1970 which continues to be of greatest interest.

Next to Grotowski, the best known of Poland's directors was Tadeusz Kantor (1915–1990). Originally an artist and designer, he founded his own company, Cricot 2, in 1955. It was Kantor who in 1956 reintroduced Witkiewicz's plays and initiated the interest in absurdist drama. Little known outside of Poland until after 1970, he subsequently appeared at major theatre festivals throughout the world. One

FIG. 23.4

Tadeuz Kantor's *Wielopole, Wielopole* with the Cricot 2 Company. Photograph by Carol Rosegg.

of Kantor's best known productions was *The Dead Class* (1975), set in a school room where the characters, elderly corpse-like people, confront their younger selves, represented by effigies; the role of the teacher was played by Kantor, who remained on stage throughout, conducting the actors, music, and overall pacing. *Wielopole, Wielopole* (1980) evokes the suffering of the Polish people at the time of World War I, caught between the church and the army and subjected to mass murder and personal loss. In *I Shall Never Return* (1988), Kantor himself was the central character in a kind of summing up of his career with fragments from and allusions to many of his productions.

In Czechoslovakia, the Soviet invasion in 1968 dealt a sharp blow to that country's theatre. Beginning in 1969 censorship was reimposed. In that year Grossman and Havel were removed from their posts at the Balustrade, Havel's plays were banned, and the Cinoherni was forced to change many of its policies. In 1971 Krejca was removed as director at the Gate and in 1972, reportedly because the actors remained loyal to him, the Gate was disbanded; in 1976 Krejca was permitted to leave the country for a permanent post in West Germany. The Prague Institute of Scenography was also closed. In 1977 Havel and several other writers were put on trial, and Havel was sent to prison, the first of six times. A number of writers and other theatre artists left the country. Perhaps because of his great international reputation, Svoboda was able to continue his work with little hindrance. With the fall of the Soviet Union, Czechoslovakia moved rapidly toward liberalization.

GERMAN THEATRE TO 1990

By the mid-1960s, German playwrights seem to have tired of preoccupation with guilt and were moving away from the postwar apolitical stance toward a leftist analysis of contemporary social problems. Many of the new dramas were related to the folk-play tradition through their choice of characters from everyday life, their use of dialects and colloquial speech (as opposed to the high German which had long been a standard on the German stage), and their concern for neo-naturalistic situations. They also were influenced by Odon von Horvath (1901–1938), whose plays such as *Tales of the Vienna Woods* (1930) and *Kasimir and Karoline* (1931), depicting the terror and repression that lies beneath the familiar and banal, had been banned in Germany since the 1930s but were revived in the 1960s to great acclaim.

Perhaps the most successful writer in this tradition was Franz Xaver Kroetz (1946–), whose most characteristic plays use the speech and behavior patterns of his native Bavaria to depict the brutalization of the proletariat. The best examples of this work are *Dairy Farm* (1972) and its sequel *Ghost Train* (1972), which develop the relationship of two misfits—an older farm worker and the mentally retarded adolescent daughter of the farm's owner. Many of the details are naturalistic, moving through rape, attempted abortion, and child murder, although the emphasis is upon the societal conditions which underlie the actions rather than on sensational events. By arousing consciousness, he hoped to stimulate his viewers to take steps to change their situation. Kroetz was among the most controversial and popular of contemporary German-language dramatists. He also frequently directed productions.

Somewhat related to Kroetz's work was that of Martin Sperr (1944–), especially in his trilogy treating successively peasant life, small town life, and city life: *Hunting Scenes from Lower Bavaria* (1966), *Tales of Landshut* (1967), and *Munich Freedom* (1971). All depict human beings as selfish, corruptible, and cruel.

Botho Strauss (1944–) worked as a dramaturg for Peter Stein, Germany's most admired director, before beginning his playwriting career in 1971. His first success came with *Three Acts of Recognition* (1976), in which he questioned the relationship between life and art. In *Big and Little* (1978), perhaps his best-known work, the characters, isolated in cell-like cubicles, seek unsuccessfully to make contact with others, although the very search seems a delusion. Among his later plays, one of the best was *Visitor* (1989) which, using rehearsal as a metaphor for role-playing, suggests that we live in the world like visitors at a play, denying the necessity for dealing with the problems that are presented to us. Thomas Bernhard (1931–1989), an Austrian writer, turned to playwriting in 1970 with *A Feast for Boris.* His subsequent dramas include *Minetti* (1976) and *Arrived* (1982). His plays use clichés, mechanical behavior, irony, and parody to comment on human behavior. Bernhard's pervasive misanthropy often led to protests against his plays, as it did with his final work, *Heroes' Square* (1989), in which he accused Austria of still being anti-Semitic and falling apart under an alliance of political parties and the Catholic Church.

Peter Handke (1942–) followed a different tack than most of his contemporaries, being concerned above all with language as ideology and manipulator of behavior. He began his playwriting career in 1966 with a group of short "speech plays" in which he abandoned plot, character, and environment. In one of these, *Offending the Audience,* four unnamed and undifferentiated speakers make, attack, and reformulate statements about theatregoing and the nature of theatrical illusion.

FIG. 23.5

Kroetz's *Dying Farmer* at the Deutsches Schauspielhaus, Hamburg, 1985. Design by Wilfried Minks. Photograph by Roswitha Hecke.

One of Handke's best-known works is *Kaspar* (1968), in which a young man who has been brought up in total isolation (and therefore without speech) is gradually reduced to conformity and schizophrenia by making him accept behavioral codes. In these and other plays, *My Foot My Tutor* (1969), *The Ride Across Lake Constance* (1971), *The Unreasonable Are Dying Out* (1974), *Slow Homecoming* (1982), and *The Hour in Which We Knew Nothing of Each Other* (1992), Handke is preoccupied with the way human beings are reduced to or enact conformity.

The only East German playwright to achieve international fame was Heinar Müller (1929–1995), who began writing plays in 1956 with *The Scab,* a work about factory quotas written in the socialist realism mode. Later he turned to historical subjects, as in *Philoktetes* (1966), to provide a perspective on the present. Beginning in the late 1970s, his plays became increasingly indirect and allusive as in *Hamletmachine* (1977), a short work, most of it without designated characters or dialogue, using *Hamlet* as a reference point for a critique of the intellectual's position in the contemporary world. He subsequently wrote a trilogy of works similar to *Hamletmachine* but based in the Medea myth, and a number of other similar short pieces, among them *Description of a Picture* (1985), which he labeled "explosions of memory." His final play, *Germania 3* was

FIG. 23.6

Botho Strauss's *Big and Little* at the Schaubühne am Halleschen Ufer, West Berlin, 1978. Directed by Peter Stein; design by Karl-Ernst Herrmann. Photo by Ruth Walz.

about Hitler, Stalin, the failure of East Germany, and other aspects of twentieth-century German history. In the 1990s, Müller's plays were among the most frequently produced throughout Germany. He also turned to directing in Berlin, Bayreuth, and elsewhere, and at the time of his death was director of the Berliner Ensemble.

After 1968 Brecht's plays continued to grow in popularity, and by the 1970s had surpassed even those of Shakespeare in numbers of annual performances in Germany. Brecht's works and theory were also significant in the leftward trend that dominated German production until the 1980s. Brecht's own company, however, had to deal with a number of problems. By the time of Helene Weigel's death in 1971, the Berliner Ensemble was considered by many to have become a museum. When Ruth Berghaus (1927–1996) was named director, she attempted to revitalize the company through highly experimental productions of such plays as Wedekind's *Spring's Awakening* and Strindberg's *Miss Julie*. Her efforts met with considerable opposition, being damned by many critics as "self-indulgent formalism." In 1977 she was replaced by Manfred Wekwerth (1929–), who had worked closely with Brecht. Under Wekwerth, the company regained much of it former vitality. In 1993 it was privatized, although it continued to receive some $16 million in subsidy. A five-person management—composed of Peter Palitzsch, Peter Zadek, Matthias Langhoff, Fritz Marquardt, and Heinar Müller—was installed in 1992. Brecht's heirs, having been removed from positions of power, for a time denied the theatre permission to present any of Brecht's plays. The Berliner Ensemble was left to seek a new artistic vi-

sion from a group of directors who had little in common, and the management arrangement soon disintegrated. By 1994 only Müller was left.

The Festival Theatre at Bayreuth also underwent significant changes during the 1970s. In 1973 the Wagner family relinquished much of its control over the festival and archival materials when the Richard Wagner Foundation was formed. This foundation was created to maintain, but not run, the festival; it provided that a member of the Wagner family was to direct future festivals "if no better qualified applicants come forward." In 1976 the one-hundredth anniversary of the festival was celebrated with great fanfare and controversy over the innovative staging of the *Ring* by the French director, Patrice Chereau, who interpreted this cycle as a commentary on the Industrial Revolution and capitalism. These productions came to seem conservative alongside those of Harry Kupfer in 1988, in which the gods resembled gangsters in a nightmarish technological world nearing its end.

Another festival, the Berlin Theatertreffen, inaugurated in 1963, helped to give focus to the current state of German-language theatre. Each year ten productions, presumably the most significant, innovative, or provocative in Germany, Austria, or Switzerland, were invited to the festival. The choices, often controversial, provided a fair measure of theatrical trends in German-language theatre.

The stresses of the late 1960s also led to the formation of free theatres, cooperatives (which linked a number of small companies), and lunchtime theatres. They seem also to have stimulated interests in children's theatre. Formerly, most theatres had per-

FIG. 23.7

Handke's *Kaspar* at the Chelsea Theatre Center, Brooklyn, 1973. Directed by Carl Weber; video by Video Free America. Photograph Amnon Nomis. Courtesy Chelsea Theatre Center.

formed one children's play each year (usually at Christmas and most often based on a fairy tale). During the 1970s, some companies were formed to play exclusively for children and youth. Of these, the best known was Grips in West Berlin. Like several other troupes, Grips abandoned fairy tales for material related directly to the children's own lives. This approach, usually referred to as "emancipatory theatre," aimed to free its audience from "false ideologies" and traditional repressions. A number of theatres also catered exclusively to adolescents. In 1976 the Alliance for Children's and Young People's Theatre was formed to help the companies deal with common problems and concerns. An annual festival of theatres for young audiences was also established.

Another significant controversy developed over managerial practices. Perhaps the greatest source of unhappiness was the almost unlimited decision-making power of the government-appointed theatre managers (Intendanten). The dissatisfaction came to a head in 1969 when in several cities actors interrupted performances to discuss the social realities reflected by their status in the theatre. Such crises were resolved in various ways. Cologne appointed a triumvirate of directors, each with a group of performers; Wuppertal turned to a six-person directorate under a supervisor; Frankfurt and Kiel attempted a participatory directorate in which every member of the company was involved; and in West Berlin a commune (in which Peter Stein was the most prominent figure) was established. Nevertheless, most companies continued under the old system, although many of the more conservative Intendants were replaced by less conservative directors. Many of the new organizational schemes were soon found too cumbersome and were abandoned or altered.

Among the important directors after 1968, some of the most innovative and influential were Heyme, Palitzsch, and Zadek. Hansgünther Heyme (1935–), once an assistant to Piscator, was named head of the Cologne company in 1968. In 1969 his production of Schiller's *Wallenstein* became one of the most influential productions of the time. Heyme reduced Schiller's trilogy to a single play and reshaped the text so as to illuminate the ideological forces that Schiller had glossed over. Later Heyme headed theatres in Essen and Bremen and was director of the Ruhr Festival. Among his later productions, one of the most memorable was Gaston Salvatore's *King Congo* (1991), set in 1884 when a Congress of European rulers divided up Africa. Peter Palitzsch (1918–2004), Brecht's chief dramaturg, defected to West Germany in 1961 when the Berlin Wall was erected. In the West, his staging of Brecht's plays were extremely influential and motivated a number of young directors to experiment with and elaborate on Brechtian techniques. Peter Zadek (1926–), though born in Germany, grew up in England and worked there until 1958. He directed many English plays and was often said to have infused an English influence into German staging. He headed the theatres in Bremen (1964–1967), Bochum (1972–1975), and, after a period of freelancing, Hamburg. Zadek often incorporated music hall and revue elements into his productions, and his innovative (sometimes seemingly perverse) interpretations of plays made him a figure of constant controversy and admiration.

By far the most respected director after 1968 was Peter Stein (1937–), eight of whose first twelve productions were included in the Berlin Theatertreffen. His staging of Goethe's *Tasso* at Bremen in 1969 was considered a watershed production. Goethe's play, a revered classic which had long been staged with loving respect, was radically altered by Stein to clarify the ideology underlying the play; ultimately the production became a critique of Goethe's failure to face the realities of his situation (and of theatre artists today) who, in accepting state subsidies and public patronage, place themselves in much the

FIG. 23.8

Peter Stein's production of Ibsen's *Peer Gynt* at the Schaubühne am Halleschen Ufer, West Berlin, 1971. Design by Karl-Ernst Herrmann; Werner Rehm in the role of Peer. The scene shows Begriffenfeldt's asylum under the Sphinx. Photo by Ruth Walz.

same kind of subordination as Tasso with his noble patrons in the Renaissance. When Stein and several of his actors insisted on reading political statements to the audience at intermission, they were fired. They then formed a theatre collective and eventually settled in West Berlin's Schaubühne. This collective, which included some of West Germany's most talented actors—among them Bruno Ganz, Edith Clever, Jutta Lampe, and Michael König—was soon considered the best company in the nation.

During the 1970s, Stein's interpretational approach came to dominate German directing. The entire company was involved in exhaustive explorations of the historical and ideological contexts of the plays and their authors. Scripts were reshaped to explore the ideological relationships obscured by the text's form and to clarify those relationships by revealing their contradictions and the determinants that had shaped them. In other words, a production became simultaneously a performance of a script and a critique of that script's ideological limitations, as well as an indication of its pertinence today. Productions also increasingly treated the theatre (rather than some fictional locale) as the scene of the action and the stage as a place where reality is to be examined rather than presented. Thus, Stein's and many other German theatres in the 1970s and 1980s were essentially dialectical.

In 1981 Stein's company moved to the Schaubühne am Lehniner Platz theatre complex. Departing from the proscenium-arch mode that had dominated postwar German theatre architecture, it is a long, open space which can, by activating metal walls, be divided into three separate performance spaces. Its 76 floor sections can be raised, lowered, or tilted to create almost any configuration, both for staging and seating.

During the 1980s, the German theatre retreated from its leftist biases and ideological critiques, and many directors, among them Stein, turned to "text-true" productions. Stein's 1984 staging of Chekhov's *The Three Sisters,* astonishingly realistic and meticulously true to the text, became the company's most popular production. In 1985 Stein resigned as director of the Schaubühne, although he returned to direct regularly. He began to stage opera, earning especially high praise for his work with the Welsh National Opera. In 1988, Jurgen Grosch, an East German who had emigrated to the West, was named director of the Schaubühne.

During the 1980s, Jürgen Flimm (1941–) emerged as a major director who staged plays from the past in ways that commented on the human condition today. For example, his *Uncle Vanya* made no attempt to evoke Russia but concentrated instead on time as the destroyer of hopes and illusions. This interpretation was made concrete by Erich Wonder's set with a back wall in which a narrow opening moved slowly but continuously—three centimeters per second—to reveal views beyond the neutral room in which the action occurred. Similarly Flimm's production of *Platonov* suggested that we cannot begin a new life because we do not know what to do with the one we have. As head of the Thalia Theater in Hamburg, Flimm made it one of the most adventurous companies in Germany. It became noted especially for producing a number of Robert Wilson's pieces.

One of Germany's best-known artists is Pina Bausch (1940–), creator of the Wuppertal Dance Theater. Trained in dance, she transformed her ballet company into one that broke down the barriers between dance and spoken or musical theatre by combining movement, speech, singing, spectacle, and other elements into nonlinear, nonliterary performances that expressed anxieties, obsessions, conflicts, and hopes ranging through the everyday and comic to the epic and terrifying. Since the 1980s hers has been one of the most honored theatre companies in the world and has served as a model for those who wish to break down the barriers among the arts and create a nontraditional theatre.

THEATRE AND DRAMA IN ITALY TO 1990

After 1968, Giorgio Strehler continued to be Italy's most respected director. When the Piccolo Teatro failed to get the new building it had been seeking and was not named a national theatre as had seemed likely, Strehler resigned as its head in 1968. The company continued under the direction of Paolo Grassi (with Strehler as occasional guest director) until 1972 when Grassi was named head of the LaScala opera company. Meantime, Strehler founded the Gruppo Teatro e Azione, the first professional theatre cooperative in Italy. All of this company's productions were successful, with Brecht's *Saint Joan of the Stockyards* (staged in 1970) being especially outstanding. In 1972, Strehler resumed the directorship of the Piccolo Teatro, which he retained until 1992.

In 1983 Strehler also became director of the Théâtre de l'Europe, which he founded with the cooperation of the French government as a company in which outstanding theatres from all over Europe would participate. The primary home of the Théâtre de l'Europe was the Odéon in Paris, but its membership included major companies in Barcelona, Berlin, Budapest, Düsseldorf, Stockholm, Milan, Paris, and elsewhere. Strehler inaugurated the Théâtre de l'Europe with his production of Shakespeare's *The Tempest* (subsequently seen at the Olympic Arts Festival in Los Angeles in 1984 and elsewhere). Strehler treated *The Tempest* as a play about the theatre with Prospero as director-magician who calls up the characters and events. At the end, Prospero, now in the auditorium, breaks his staff and the stage collapses; he asks the public to release him, as he is releasing them, from the world of illusion so they can return to the real world with the perceptions they have gained in the theatre. This production was one of the most praised of its time. Strehler contributed several other productions to the Théâtre de l'Europe, among them works by such dramatists as Lessing, Corneille, and Strindberg.

Other innovative directors include Fo, Ronconi, and Bene. Dario Fo (1926–) began to write and perform in the late 1940s, first in radio and subsequently in theatre. With his wife, Franca Rame (1929–), he later formed a company which produced satirical topical plays, most of them by Fo, who was also the principal actor. Following the major political upheavals of 1968, Fo adopted a more radical stance and sought to attract a working-class audience with agit-prop plays satirizing capitalism, the Italian Communist party, the Italian state, the church, and other enemies of the idiosyncratic communism he championed. His satire was so wideranging that he offended every political faction. Nevertheless, by the late 1970s Fo had become so popular that he was invited to present some of his plays on Italian state television. He also came to be increasingly in demand internationally both as playwright and performer.

FIG. 23.9

Dario Fo's *Accidental Death of an Anarchist* as produced at the Arena Stage, Washington, 1984. Directed by Douglas C. Wager; scenic design by Karl Eigsti; costumes by Marjorie Slainman; lighting by Allen Lee Hughes. Photo by Joan Marcus.

Among Fo's most popular plays are *Mistero Buffo* (1969), which combines elements from medieval religious drama, mime, and contemporary life (and makes extensive use of his own made-up language, *grammelot,* rendered intelligible by Fo's expressive pantomime), and *We're All in the Same Boat—But That Man Over There, Isn't He the Boss* (1971), based on Italian political events between 1911 and 1923, when Mussolini came to power. In England and America, Fo's *Can't Pay? Won't Pay* (1974), in which housewives rebel against economic exploitation, and *Accidental Death of an Anarchist* (1970), concerning a man's attempt to discredit the police's version of how a political rebel died while in custody, were especially popular. Fo also wrote a number of feminist plays with Franca Rame under the collective title, *Female Parts* (1981). All of Fo's productions were bitingly satirical and theatrically imaginative,

making use of devices drawn from practically all forms of popular entertainment. Fo has been one of the few modern Italian playwrights to attract an international audience.

Luca Ronconi (1933–) was an actor before turning to directing in 1963. He developed a distinctive, highly theatrical style in productions of Renaissance English dramas, but he first gained international prominence in 1968 with his production of *Orlando Furioso,* seen first at the Spoleto Festival and later in Belgrade, Milan, Paris, New York, and elsewhere. The text was adapted by Edoardo Sanguineti from Lodovico Ariosto's sixteenth-century epic poem, an enormously long work about chivalric adventures involving mythical creatures, enchanted castles, sorcerers, and other fanciful beings. Rather than performing the episodes in strict sequence, two or more progressed simultaneously in different parts of the theatrical space, since Ronconi believed that this achieved the same effect of disorder and fantasy induced by reading the poem. About fifty wheeled wagons were used in a large open space, which was

FIG. 23.10

Ronconi's *Orlando Furioso,* first performed at the Festival of Two Worlds, Spoleto, 1969. Note the wheeled wagons on which the performers stand surrounded by the audience. Photography by Pic, Paris.

also occupied by the audience, who moved about choosing what to watch.

Ronconi's subsequent productions are less known but several were equally imaginative. For the Spoleto Festival in 1982, Ronconi adapted Ibsen's *Ghosts* for presentation in the crypt of a church which had been converted into a glass-covered conservatory encompassing both acting and audience space. Expressionistic and slow-moving, the four-hour production treated the characters, all dressed in black and gray, as literal ghosts.

The actor-director-dramatist Carmelo Bene (1937–) was among the major *avant-garde* figures of Italy after 1968. He was especially noted for deconstructing well-known plays (among them *Hamlet, Romeo and Juliet,* and *Edward II*) to reveal those themes and ideas he found most significant. His *Othello* reduced Shakespeare's cast to eight, all dressed in white and all atop a giant bed, to explore jealousy and the pattern of dominance and male bonding in the play.

Beginning in the 1970s, a number of Italian companies rejected traditional dramatic texts in favor of electronic media, surrealistic visual imagery, pantomime, and music. Among the more popular of these companies were La Gaia Scienza, Falso Movimento, Krypton, and Trademark.

Italy was less fortunate in writers than directors. Virtually no contemporary playwright other than Fo won international acceptance, although a number were well known within Italy. Among these were Franco Brusato, Guiseppe Patroni Griffi, Luigi Squarzina, and Umberto Marino.

THEATRE IN FRANCE TO 1990

In May 1968 an uprising of students and workers virtually paralyzed France and prompted President De-Gaulle to retire in 1969. These events also motivated a reevaluation of the role of theatre in French life and resulted in a number of changes. In the early 1970s, the government reorganized the national theatre system. In 1968, Barrault had resigned as head of the Théâtre de France, and, since the troupe was under contract to him, the Odéon was left without a troupe. The Odéon was assigned to the Comédie Française, which used it primarily as a home for new and *avant-garde* works or for visiting companies. (In 1983, it became the home of the Théâtre de l'Europe.) In 1975, the rules governing the Comédie Française were revised to increase the number of *sociétaires* (there are now thirty-four), to reduce the length of contracts from twenty to ten years, and to grant greater freedom for actors to perform elsewhere. All of these

changes were intended to make the Comédie more attractive to major actors. The company's theatre was also extensively remodeled in preparation for the celebration of the troupe's three-hundredth anniversary in 1980 (and refurbished again in 1994).

As a part of its reorganization of the national theatre system, the government for the first time designated some companies other than those in central Paris as national theatres. Those raised to this status were the Théâtre National de Strasbourg (a former dramatic center); the Théâtre de l'Est Parisien (located in a working-class suburb of Paris); and Planchon's troupe in Villeurbanne, which was assigned the title Théâtre National Populaire. (The Parisian-based troupe that had held that title was renamed the Théâtre National de Chaillot.)

For a time the program of decentralization also continued. By 1975 there were some fifteen Maisons de la Culture, eighteen Centres Dramatiques, and about two dozen other provincial companies, all competing for subsidies. But, because many subsidized companies, both in Paris and in the provinces, had been sympathetic to the demonstrators in 1968 and had permitted their theatres to be used as forums for debate, the government treated many companies with suspicion. Throughout the 1970s subsidies tended to be small for those companies that supported left-wing causes. Inflation also resulted in subsidies being eaten up by administrative costs and building maintenance. Some provincial groups virtually gave up producing their own productions and depended on touring groups, a practice which the French called "garaging."

During the 1970s the government was often accused of being interested primarily in institutionalizing culture. Many critics also charged that the crisis of 1968 had arisen because the government had lost touch with the common people, a charge also leveled against many theatres. Some established directors tried to respond. Upon leaving the Théâtre de France, Jean-Louis Barrault conceived and directed *Rabelais* (1968), a three-hour adaptation of material drawn from Rabelais's writings and intended as a timely commentary on repression and revolution. Drawing liberally on practically all recent trends in staging, the production was originally presented in a sports arena in Paris before being seen in London, New York, and elsewhere. In 1970 Barrault attempted to duplicate this success with a project based on Jarry's life and writings, *Jarry sur la Butte,* but the results were disappointing. In 1971 Barrault became director of the Théâtre des Nations, an international festival which until 1976 was always held in Paris. (Thereafter it was held in a different country each year, and featured productions from various countries, workshops, lectures, and discussions designed to provoke thought and to encourage understanding and innovation.) Barrault also continued his own company, which after 1974 performed at the Théâtre D'Orsay and subsequently at the Théâtre Rond-Point.

Roger Planchon (1931–) was among those most interested in reshaping the French theatre. Long considered Brecht's major champion in France, he continued, after assuming the directorship of the Théâtre National Populaire in 1972, to seek ways of making his productions accessible to the working class. He wrote a number of plays, among them *The Black Pig* (1972) and *Gilles de Rais* (1976), all of which begin with actual historical events of a violent nature and then search for adequate explanations. His staging of these works mingled Brechtian and Artaudian devices to create rich stage imagery designed to surprise audiences with unexpected reflections of its own world. Despite the great power of Planchon's productions, he was never able to attract the large working-class audience he sought, a situation he declared inevitable until society itself changes.

In 1972, Planchon chose Patrice Chereau (1944–) to be co-director of the TNP. Chereau, an advocate of popular theatre who had established a company in one of Paris' communist-dominated suburbs,

FIG. 23.11

Planchon's production of Michel Vinaver's *Overboard* at the Théâtre Nationale Populaire, 1974. Photo by Agence de Presse Bernand, Paris.

believed, as Planchon did, that although one should not compromise standards in order to appeal to the working class, one should seek to make theatre available and understandable to the masses. At the TNP he directed Marlowe's *Massacre in Paris,* Ibsen's *Peer Gynt,* and Dorst's *Toller* to considerable acclaim but attracted greatest international attention in 1976 when he staged Wagner's Ring cycle at Bayreuth so as to link it with a debasement of values stemming from the Industrial Revolution. From 1982 to 1990 he was director of the Théâtre des Amandiers in Nanterre, a working-class suburb of Paris, where in 1984 he created a sensation with his staging of Genet's *The Screens* as a reflection of the racial tensions created in France by the influx of African workers. Almost all of Chereau's major productions were done in collaboration with one designer, Richard Peduzzi. After leaving Nanterre, Chereau devoted much of his efforts to directing opera but he returns to the theatre often.

Another approach to reaching a broader audience involved creating plays dealing with the experiences of the theatre's own audience. Among the groups to follow this path was the Théâtre Populaire de Lorraine (under the direction of Jacques Kraemer), which after 1968 gave up the practice it had followed since 1963 of presenting a repertory composed primarily of the classics. After 1968, it created works about Lorraine, especially the iron and steel industry which dominates that area. It offended most of the leaders of the region, but it built strong support among the audiences it most sought.

One of the most innovative groups was the Grand Magic Circus, headed by Jerome Savary (1942–), who argued that if the theatre's failure had resulted from attempts to make the working classes accept "high" culture, the remedy must lie in using "low" culture to alter accepted art forms. His company began to attract wide favorable attention in 1970 with the collectively created *Zartan,* about "Tarzan's deprived brother" and described by Savary as the "marvelous story of colonialism from the Middle Ages to the present." The company, performing on beaches, in hospitals, parks, and other comparable spaces, won a considerable following with productions that had the zest of children's theatre, circus, and carnivals created by extensive exchanges between audience and performers, improvisations, acrobatic feats, satirical thrusts, and stunning effects of all sorts. Savary stated his dislike of Grotowski and the Living Theatre (both of which he labeled "cerebral") and sought to appeal to all types of audiences in a very direct manner. In 1989, his success in making theatre accessible to the general public was recognized with his appointment as director of the Théâtre National de Chaillot, where

FIG. 23.12
Patrice Chereau's production of Genet's *The Screens*, 1984. Design by Richard Peduzzi. Théâtre des Amandiers, Nanterre. Photo by Agence de Presse Bernand, Paris.

he was noted for the extravagant visual spectacle and frenetic energy of his productions.

The most significant of the post-1968 companies was the Théâtre du Soleil, formed in 1964 with Ariane Mnouchkine (1940–) as its driving force. The company first gained recognition in 1967 with Wesker's *The Kitchen*. During the uprisings of 1968, it performed this production in factories where it received overwhelmingly favorable response from the workers. It decided then to become a theatre collective in which all members would receive the same salary. Its first major success came in 1970 with *1789*, about the beginnings of the French Revolution and suggesting that the Revolution was subverted by those more concerned about property than justice. Staged on platforms surrounding a standing audience (which was treated as the mob), it was highly praised and extremely successful. First performed in Milan, *1789* was subsequently presented in France at the Cartoucherie (an abandoned cartridge factory) in the Parisian suburb of Vincennes, which was thereafter the company's home. Despite its great critical reputation, the company was so destitute that between 1973 and 1975 most of its members had to go on unemployment (a practice still common with the company when it is not performing). In the early

1980s, Mnouchkine reorganized the company and mounted a series of Shakespearean productions—*Richard II*, both parts of *Henry IV*, and *Twelfth Night*—all incorporating liberal borrowings from Kabuki or Sanskrit conventions. When performed at the Olympics Art Festival in Los Angeles in 1984, these were the most highly praised of all the offerings. Among the theatre's most successful productions was *Les Atrides*, composed of Euripides' *Iphigenia at Aulis* and Aeschylus' trilogy *The Oresteia*. It was mounted over a period of two years (1990–1992) and was performed in France, Italy, Germany, England, Canada, and the United States. Drawing on Asian forms, most clearly Kathakali, its integration of dance, music, spectacle, and gripping drama was a major achievement. By the 1990s, the Théâtre du Soleil was one of the most respected companies in the world. With actors from twenty-one countries, it was also one of the most multicultural.

The Avignon Festival also played an important role in French theatre after 1968. As early as 1966 it had begun to increase its playing spaces, and eventually included about twelve official spaces and countless "fringe" spaces. Consequently, Avignon became increasingly diverse, accommodating major French groups, companies from various French-speaking areas of the world, numerous alternative theatres, and major artists and companies from foreign countries. Thus, it came to provide a representative cross-section of theatre work in France and elsewhere, offering about

FIG. 23.13
The chorus in Ariane Mnouchkine's production of Euripides' *Iphigenia at Aulis* with the Théâtre du Soleil in 1990. It was the first play in a tetralogy of plays, the remainder of which was made up of Aeschylus' *The Oresteia*. The four plays were presented under the overall title, *Les Atrides* (The House of Atreus). Photo © Martine Frank-Magnum. Courtesy Magnum Photos, Inc.

50 official events and about 500 fringe events during a one-month period. By the 1990s, under the direction of Bernard Faivre d'Arcier, it was the premier cultural event for French-language theatre in the world.

Important new directors came to the fore after 1980. Among the most important of these was Jean-Pierre Vincent (1942–) who, as director of the Théâtre National de Strasbourg from 1975 to 1983, converted it into one of the most influential theatres in France because of his work with new playwrights and use of innovative working methods.

Another important director was Antoine Vitez (1930–1990), director of the Théâtre National de Chaillot from 1981 until 1988, when he became director of the Comédie Française. His most notable productions were radical reinterpretations of plays by Racine, Molière, Hugo, and Claudel. In his productions, he worked closely with his designer, Yannis Kokkos, and his actors to break down and reshape realistic conventions. Settings were usually composed of a few elements that could be moved about by the actors; pieces treated in the script as scenery, such as sailing ships on which the characters were supposedly located, were sometimes models which could be picked up and moved about by the actors; strong lateral lighting often divided the stage into planes of action; the actors shifted from naturalistic to non-realistic conventions, emphasizing discontinuities. Vitez did not seek to impose unity but rather to let the audience be aware of the complexities, contradictions, and multiple possibilities for interpretation. Upon his death, he was succeeded at the Comédie Française by Jacques Lassalle (1936–), who brought in a number of foreign directors and emphasized new plays. Accused of having subverted the company's cultural role, Lassalle was replaced in 1993 by Jean-Pierre Miquel (1940–), who adopted a more conservative approach. The Comédie Française also managed the much smaller Théâtre du Vieux Colombier (once Jacques Copeau's theatre). In the late 1990s, the two houses together were presenting more than twenty productions each year.

Although few French playwrights who came to the fore after 1968 were able to win an international following, several achieved high critical standing at home. Perhaps the most important of these were Grumberg and Vinaver. Jean-Paul Grumberg (1939–) began to write for the stage in the mid-1960s but did not achieve success until 1971 with *Amorphe d'Ottenburg,* a parable about the Nazis. One of his best-known works is *Dreyfus* (1974), set in a Jewish ghetto in a Polish town around 1930 where amateurs, while rehearsing a play about the Dreyfus affair, explore the phenomenon of anti-Semitism. It won the

FIG. 23.14

Antoine Vitez's production of Hugo's *Hernani* at the Théâtre National de Chaillot, Paris, 1985. Design by Yannis Kokkos. Photo by Agence de Presse Bernand, Paris.

critics award as the best play of the 1974–1975 season. *Comings and Goings at the Expo* (1975) takes place at the time of the Universal Exposition in 1900 and points up the banality of the forces that would lead to World War I. Much of it is set against the music of a *café concert.*

Michel Vinaver (1926–), though he wrote some plays in the 1950s, did not come to prominence until 1973 with Planchon's production of *Overboard.* This play is far more complex than Planchon's version might suggest. Its primary concern is with how American marketing strategies have altered European business, but through numerous discontinuous and seemingly unrelated plot strands, it ultimately suggests the interconnectedness of everything that makes up a society, including how the corporate world displaces the world of myth and personal integrity. Vinaver's subsequent plays, including *Bending Over Backwards* (1980) and *The Usual* (1983), include no punctuation and almost no stage directions, thus remaining open to multiple interpretations since both what the characters are doing or what is meant by what is said remain ambiguous. Other significant playwrights include Bernard-Marie Koltès (1948–1989), Hélène Cixous, Olivier Py, and Xavier Durringer.

Under the leadership of Jack Lang, Minister of Culture during the 1980s and early 1990s, France continued to increase its support for the arts. In 1992,

FIG. 23.15
Jean-Paul Grumberg's *Comings and Goings at the Expo*, Théâtre de l'Oédon, Paris, 1975. Directed by Jean-Pierre Vincent. Design by Yannis Kokkos. Photo by Agence de Presse Bernand, Paris.

it appropriated $2.3 billion for cultural projects, and subsequently government officials pledged to devote 1 percent (about $3 billion) of the national budget to cultural projects. The allocation of support to theatre was about $500 million annually.

LATIN AMERICAN THEATRE TO 1990

Brazilian theatre did not begin to recover from the political oppression that followed the crackdown of 1968 until a new regime came to power in 1979. During those difficult years dramatists who wanted their plays produced avoided social commentary or at least disguised it behind a mask of humor as in *Miss Margarida's Way* (*Apareceu a Margarida,* 1973) by Roberto de Athayde (1949–). Groups like "Asdrubal Brought His Trombone" Theatre (Asdrubal Trouse Seu Trombone, 1974), meanwhile, resorted to irreverent productions of classic plays. With the lifting of restrictions in 1979, plays that had been

banned in the 1960s and 1970s were quickly brought to the stage with *Break the Heart* or *Heart Stopping* (*Rasga Coração,* 1974), by Luis Vianna Filho (1936–1974), as perhaps the most important of this rather large group that included plays of feminist writers Leilah Assunção (1943–) and Consuelo Castro (1947–). But it was the Center for Theatrical Investigation (Centro de Pesquisa Teatral), established in 1978 under the direction of José Antunes Filho (1929–), that set the tone for the new direction Brazilian theatre was about to take. Antunes Filho's production of *Macunaíma* (1979), which told the story of a Native American's journey from his idyllic home in the forests to the degenerate city and back again, made eclectic use of nudity, spectacular athleticism, and highly evocative visual elements to create scenes of remarkable beauty. Brazilian theatre became dominated by a style of theatre of images not unlike that being developed in Canada. Directors who trained under Antunes Filho, like Bia Lessa (1952–), best known for her production of *Orlando* (1992), and Ulysses Cruz (1952–), best known as the founder of the Flying Bull Theatre (O Boi Voador, 1985), took the lead in this new theatre. But Gerald Thomas (1954–) may best exemplify its tendencies. He is acclaimed as an imaginative director who, along with Daniela Thomas (1959–), his usual scene designer, creates remarkable visual images. But he is equally well regarded as an adapter of works by Kafka and author of such plays as *Flash and Crash* (1992). Because of adaptations and director-written scripts, few Brazilian playwrights have been able to achieve real success in recent years, and among those who have, problems getting their works translated have made them little known outside Brazil.

In Argentina, political turmoil and economic instability worked against major new developments after 1968. Throughout the 1970s and into the 1980s a great deal of experimentation of all kinds was carried out, but it seems to have had no definable direction beyond reflecting the disorientation felt generally within the society. When companies like the Open Theatre (Teatro Abierto, 1981) showed signs of becoming too political, their theatres were mysteriously burned down, sometimes on several occasions. But after Argentina's disastrous war with Great Britain over the Falklands in 1982, a less-repressive government came to power. Except for a burst of plays from noted dramatist Osvoldo Dragün (1929–) and Carlos Gorostiza (1920–), however, this did not lead to a release of pent-up theatrical energies like that seen after liberalization in Brazil. The new government favored decentralizing theatre to take the focus off of Buenos Aires, and while Argentina continues to have a very active theatre community, it no longer exerts the influence it had in Latin America prior to 1968.

In Mexico, the forty theatres that were linked into the National Theatre touring circuit in 1977 continued to provide a high-quality standard repertory of classical and modern European plays supplemented with the best work of Latin American writers and, from time to time, new plays by local playwrights like Oscar Liebra (1944–1990). The National Theatre company, however, was disbanded in 1982, and after that most of the actual theatres were increasingly used for musical reviews and, in the case of the largest theatres, as touring houses for the large-scale American or British musicals being staged in the commercial theatres by producers like Manolo Fábregas (1921–1996) and Silvia Pinal (1931–).

The *avant-garde* theatre faded in the 1980s, but director Héctor Mendoza (1938–) continued to do innovative work with his updatings of classical texts, while Juan José Gurrola (1935–) highlighted elements of the text that might otherwise have gone unnoticed in his productions. The truly experimental work, however, was being done at festivals starting with the Garden Day (*Jornadas Alarconianas*) festivals and the Mexico City Festival, both established in 1989. These festivals attracted companies from around the world.

LOOKING AT THEATRE HISTORY

Perhaps not surprisingly, a major goal in the 1960s was to create a new, superior unity by eliminating those things standing in the way of a more truthful vision. Thus, several theatre theorists and practitioners sought to arrive at the essence of theatre by identifying and eliminating accretions that divert us from its fundamental nature. These attempts are probably best articulated in Grotowski's concept of the "poor theatre":

> By gradually eliminating whatever proved superfluous, we found that theatre can exist without make-up, without autonomic costume and scenography, without a separate performance area (stage), without lighting and sound effects, etc. It cannot exist without the actor-spectator relationship of perceptual, direct, "live" communion . . . . when rigorously tested in practice it undermines most of our usual ideas about theatre. It challenges the notion of theatre as a synthesis of disparate creative disciplines . . . This "synthetic theatre" is the contemporary theatre, which we readily call the "Rich Theatre"—rich in flaws.

Jerzy Grotowski, *Towards a Poor Theatre* (New York: Simon and Schuster, 1968), 19.

Contemporary theatre has seen considerable borrowing and adaptation of conventions from other cultures. About this transculturalism or interculturalism, Carl Weber writes:

> Whenever a society's stage was ripe for a change because its traditional performance codes had become obsolete, i.e., no longer responded to a perceived social reality, experimentation with ideas and forms lifted from other cultures was conducted. Emerging new modes of performance were frequently evolved from a transculturation of foreign structures and ideas . . . . The growing number of international festivals is breaking down the barriers between the world's theatre cultures. An international community is emerging where those who make and those who consume theatre become increasingly familiar with the multitude of forms and issues presented on the stages of all nations. Foreign performance modes are welcomed not in spite of but because of their Otherness.

"AC/TC Currents of Theatrical Exchange," *Interculturalism and Performance*, eds. Bonnie Marranca and Gautam Dasgupta (New York: PAJ Publications, 1991), 36.

24

English-Language Theatre in the Late Twentieth Century

The stresses that affected theatre throughout Europe were felt perhaps even more strongly in the English-speaking countries, especially the United States, where they were focused around the Vietnam War and the struggle for civil rights and equality. The success of the North Vietnamese in the Tet offensive against South Vietnam in early 1968, the assassination of Martin Luther King in April, and the assassination of Robert F. Kennedy in June all served to radicalize those in both the peace and the civil rights movements. By August all of this energy exploded in the riots surrounding the Democratic convention in Chicago. In November, the United States elected the conservative Richard M. Nixon as president.

Among the avant-garde of the English-language theatre, the concern for aesthetic values was largely replaced by the demand that theatre serve as a weapon in exposing and fighting outmoded values and practices both political and civil. The focus increasingly centered around issues of gender, race, and class. For a time the avant-garde had an impact even on the mainstream commercial theatres. But the expected radical change in government and social organizations that so many had anticipated failed to occur. A general disillusionment was strengthened by the Watergate scandal of the early 1970s in the United States, followed by the near collapse of the

British economy in 1976, the "Winter of Discontent" strikes in England (1978–1979), and the Iranian hostage crisis faced by the United States (1979–1981). Powerfully conservative governments were elected in both countries in the early 1980s. The commercial English-language theatres reflected this trend first toward disillusionment and then toward conservatism, while avant-garde groups became increasingly focused on serving specific audiences of like-minded people.

BRITISH THEATRE TO 1990

After George Devine's retirement in 1965, the new managers (William Gaskill, Lindsay Anderson, and Anthony Page) of the English Stage Company (ESC) wished to produce Bond's *Saved* and Osborne's *A Patriot for Me*. When denied licenses, they reconstituted the ESC as a private club open only to members, a practice that had long been used to gain exemption from censorship. Nevertheless, the Lord Chamberlain brought and won a suit against the ESC. The resulting controversy became so heated that in 1968 Parliament abolished the censorship laws that had existed since 1737. Suddenly, it was possible to address topics and show behavior that had long been forbidden and playwrights and theatre

FIG. 24.1

Edward Bond's *Saved* as produced by the English Stage Company at the Royal Court Theatre, London. Photo by John Haynes.

companies immediately began to test the limits of this new-found freedom.

The change in law gave impetus to small "fringe" groups comparable to American off-off-Broadway companies. They performed almost anywhere an audience could be assembled, at any time including lunchtime or late at night, as well as the more traditional hours. They exhibited great flexibility in approach, great freedom in the subjects they addressed, and great ingenuity in attracting audiences that had previously ignored the theatre. Among the fringe groups, some of the most effective were Interaction, the People Show, the Portable Theatre, Soho Poly, Joint Stock, Bubble Theatre, Monstrous Regiment, 7:84 Theatre Company, and the Tricycle Theatre, the only one which still remains an important company in London. Fringe theatres brought much needed vitality and variety to the theatre.

Ironically, the English Stage Company's focus on new plays was made less significant by the success of the fringe companies its efforts had made possible. In 1980, the management of the ESC passed to Max Stafford-Clark, who sought various means of stemming the company's decline. He added a Young Writers' Festival devoted to the plays of teenaged dramatists, arranged exchanges of productions with Joseph Papp's Public Theatre in New York, and formed an alliance with the Joint Stock Company (presenting plays, such as those by Caryl Churchill, that had been developed by that fringe group). Nevertheless, its activities steadily eroded during the 1980s, going from sixteen productions a year in the

early 1980s to four in 1989, when the Theatre Upstairs had to be closed.

In 1968, the Royal Shakespeare Company (RSC) also entered a period of change when Peter Hall, Peter Brook, and Michel Saint-Denis resigned as its directors. Trevor Nunn (1940–), a young director with little managerial experience, succeeded them. Working closely with the designer Christopher Morley (until 1974), Nunn moved the company away from the Brechtian Neorealism that Hall had favored. Morley's minimalist settings often resembled large empty boxes, but they served to focus attention on the acting which was far more flamboyant and stylized than under Hall. This approach also characterized Brook's *Midsummer Night's Dream* in 1970, a production which toured extensively to enormous critical acclaim and did much to relieve the company's financial stresses. In 1974, the RSC opened a small theatre, The Other Place, in Stratford, and in 1977 a similar space, The Warehouse, in London, both devoted to new plays and experimental productions. In 1978, Terry Hands (1941–), who had been directing for the company for several years, was named joint artistic director with Nunn. During the late 1970s, the company gained added acclaim with its monumental productions of *Nicholas Nickleby* (an eight-hour adaptation of Charles Dickens's novel), *The Greeks* (an adaptation of ten Greek plays), and a cycle of Shakespeare's history plays.

In 1982, the RSC moved into its long-awaited new home in London, the Barbican, with its two playing spaces. The Pit, a flexible space which replaced the Warehouse, seated approximately 200. The large Barbican theatre held 1166. Its stage was 73 feet wide by 48 feet deep with a 30-foot-high opening. Above the stage, 109 feet of flyspace permitted the storage of scenery at two levels to facilitate the presentation of the rotating repertory. In 1986, the company opened a new theatre in Stratford, the Swan, a 400-seat open-stage facility intended primarily for non-Shakespearean plays written between 1570 and 1750. During the 1980s, the RSC also produced several musicals, among them *Les Miserables,* and this, along with Nunn's involvement in outside activities, provoked considerable criticism of his management. He resigned in 1987 and Terry Hands became sole artistic director. Hands left the post in 1991, and was succeeded by Adrian Noble (1951–), long one of RSC's major directors.

Those who had headed the RSC before 1968 continued their careers elsewhere. Michel Saint-Denis spent his remaining years (he died in 1971) with the actor-training programs at the Juilliard School in New York and the National Theatre School of Canada, thereby extending a tradition

FIG. 24.2
The Royal Shakespeare Company's production of
Nicholas Nickleby, adapted from Charles Dickens's novel
by David Edgar. Directed by Trevor Nunn and John Caird
(1980). Photo by Martha Swope.

1985 in an abandoned quarry as a part of the Avignon Festival. Using a cast from sixteen countries (among them Ryszard Cieslak, formerly the principal actor in Grotowski's company), and elaborate costumes, music, and dance, it offered nine hours of spectacular and absorbing drama. Subsequently it was performed in many European and American cities and was shown on television. Through his various productions, Brook probably did more than any other director to examine the nature of theatre and cross-cultural performance conventions.

After leaving the RSC, Peter Hall served as director of the Royal Covent Garden Opera Company before being appointed to succeed Laurence Olivier as head of the National Theatre in 1973. (Olivier's service to the theatre was recognized in 1970 when he became the first English actor to be elevated to the nobility.) In addition to administering a complex organization and directing several plays, Hall had to cope with numerous problems related to the company's new home. Scheduled to open in 1974, the building was not ready until 1976, by which time its cost had escalated to some $32 million. When completed, it housed three performance spaces: the 890-seat Lyttleton proscenium theatre; the 1160-seat Olivier open-stage theatre with a revolving stage 40 feet in diameter divided into two parts that could be lowered to workshops 45 feet below; and the 400-seat Cottesloe laboratory theatre. There were more than 100 dressing rooms, several stage-sized rehearsal

reaching back to Copeau. Peter Brook, after staging *A Midsummer Night's Dream* for the RSC in 1970, became director of the International Center for Theatre Research in 1971. Based in Paris, the Center included actors from all over the world. There Brook sought to discover means for transcending the barriers created by differing languages and cultures. The Center gave its first performance, *Orghast,* in 1971 at the Persepolis Festival in Iran; this production had a mixed reception, in part because it used an entirely invented language in an attempt to transcend any specific language. Subsequently, the company traveled in Africa, worked with the National Theatre of the Deaf and El Teatro Campesino in America, with aborigines in Australia, and with groups in many other parts of the world in an attempt to understand various communicative processes.

In Paris, Brook's company created a number of its own works as well as performing such well-known classics as *The Cherry Orchard.* It made its greatest impact with adaptations done in collaboration with the writer Jean-Claude Carrière, especially the *Mahabharata,* the Indian epic on which he and Brook started working in 1976. It was first performed in

FIG. 24.3
Peter Brook's production of Jean-Claude Carrière's
adaptation of the Sanskrit epic, *Mahabharata.* First
performed at the Avignon Festival, 1985. Design by Chloe
Oblensky. Photo by Agence de Presse Bernand, Paris.

FIG. 24.4
National Theatre, London. Auditorium and stage of the Olivier Theatre. Courtesy National Theatre. Photograph by Reg Wilson.

rooms, and numerous workshops. But the high costs aroused considerable hostility, especially among fringe groups who argued that many small companies could have been supported with this money. This hostility increased when in 1975–1976 it was noted that one-quarter of the Arts Council's drama budget went to the National Theatre. Hall found himself besieged, and after 1976 much of his energy was spent in promoting the "national" role of his theatre. After 1980 productions were sent on tour in Britain for an average of twenty weeks annually. Nevertheless, the privileged status of the National continued to make it a ready target for criticism.

The stated goal of the National was to present a diverse repertory of classic, new, and neglected plays selected from the whole of world drama. Among the National's directors, some of the most important were Peter Wood, Peter Gill, Richard Eyre, Bill Bryden, Michael Bogdanov, and David Hare. Its large and constantly changing acting company included from time to time Maggie Smith, Joan Plowright, Irene Worth, Fiona Shaw, Ian McKellan, Michael Gambon, Anthony Hopkins, Alan Bates, and Albert Finney. By the mid-1980s, Hall, like Nunn at the RSC, came under heavy criticism for his outside activities and he too resigned in 1988. Leadership then passed to Richard Eyre (1943–), who had worked in both the fringe and regional theatres before coming to the National in 1981. In 1988, to honor the twenty-fifth anniversary since its founding at the Old Vic, the

company received a new name: the Royal National Theatre. By that time it had presented more than 300 productions and was acknowledged to be one of the world's major theatrical companies.

Outside of London, local resident companies continued to play an important role, and during the 1970s they were joined by numerous provincial fringe companies, many of which toured. Additional diversity was provided by festivals, especially the Edinburgh Festival, which steadily increased its number of offerings to become the largest and most diverse festival in Europe.

Many of those who had begun their playwrighting careers earlier continued to be productive after 1968, among them John Osborne, Peter Shaffer, and Harold Pinter. Of the new playwrights, perhaps the most controversial was Edward Bond (1935–), who achieved overnight notoriety in 1965 with a private performance by the ESC of *Saved,* in which a baby is stoned to death in its carriage by its father and his roustabout friends. Selfishness, callousness, and violence continued to be preoccupations in Bond's later works which include *Lear* (1971), *Bingo* (1973), *The Fool* (1975), *The Woman* (1978), and a trilogy presented under the collective title, *War Plays* (1985). Bond was denounced by many critics as sensational, decadent, and overly preoccupied with violence, but ultimately his plays were based on moral (even self-righteous) concerns about a world in which the lack of love and compassion breeds a callousness that accepts the horrible as normal.

David Storey (1933–) began his career as a novelist and turned to playwriting in 1967 with *The Restoration of Arnold Middleton.* His subsequent plays include *The Contractor* (1970), *Home* (1970), *The Changing Room* (1971), and *Stages* (1992). Storey is concerned above all with various kinds of alienation: class from class, person from person, person from self, the reality from the ideal, and so on. These various forms of alienation are perhaps most fully developed in *Home,* set in an asylum where the four main characters, through seemingly random dialogue, point up the ironic implications about alienation contained in the multiple meanings of the play's title. Storey also often gave focus to his concerns through detailed physical activity. In *The Contractor* a group of working men put up a tent for a wedding in the first act and take it down in the last act; during this process a cross-section of attitudes and relationships are demonstrated by workmen and their employers.

Tom Stoppard (1937–) came to prominence in 1967 with *Rosencrantz and Guildenstern Are Dead,* a play reminiscent of Beckett's works, in which Stoppard makes protagonists of two attendant lords from *Hamlet* who sense that important events are going on

FIG. 24.5
Peter Hall's production of Shakespeare's *Coriolanus* at the National Theatre, 1984. Designed by John Bury. Ian McKellen down center as Coriolanus and behind him Irene Worth as Volumnia. Photo by John Haynes.

around them but are killed without understanding anything about the events of which they have been a part. Stoppard continued this highly theatrical exploration of the nature of reality in such plays as *The Real Inspector Hound* (1968), *Jumpers* (1972), *Travesties* (1974), *The Real Thing* (1982), and *Hapgood* (1988). His plays are noted for their brilliant use of language and his ability to clearly and cleverly explain complex philosophical or scientific ideas.

David Hare (1947–) began his career with Portable Theatre, a fringe group. Among his plays are *Slag* (1969), *Teeth'n'Smiles* (1975), *Plenty* (1978), and *A Map of the World* (1983). Most of these plays develop the same basic themes: how the desire to gain and maintain power and wealth undermine and destroy personal integrity, shared values, and concern for the common good. The early plays tend to focus on working-class characters, whereas the later plays focus on intellectuals.

Hare often collaborated with Howard Brenton (1942–). Their best known joint work is *Pravda*

FIG. 24.6
David Storey's *The Contractor* at the Royal Court Theatre, London, 1970. Directed by Lindsay Anderson. Photo by Tom Murray.

FIG. 24.7

Tom Stoppard's *The Real Thing* (1982) as directed by Mike Nichols at the Plymouth Theatre, New York, 1984. Setting by Tony Walton, costumes by Anthea Sylbert, lighting by Tharon Musser. The performers are Glenn Close and Jeremy Irons. Photo by Martha Swope.

(1985), in which a newspaper tycoon gains almost unchallenged control over public information. Brenton also wrote a number of controversial plays on his own, including *The Churchill Play* (1974) and *Romans in Britain* (1980). The latter, which drew parallels between the Roman occupation of England and the British presence in Ireland, was especially controversial, in part because of its treatment of violence as humorous but also because a play so critical of the British government was performed at the National Theatre. Brenton reemerged as a leading playwright in 2006 when the Royal National Theatre staged his *Paul*, a play dealing with the early formation of Christianity, and Shakespeare's Globe commissioned his *In Extremis*, about the legendary love between the medieval scholar Peter Abelard and his student, Heloise.

Caryl Churchill (1938–) wrote many of her plays for the Joint Stock Company and the ESC. Like Hare and Brenton, her plays were primarily about power, powerlessness, and exploitation, but with a strong feminist perspective. She first gained wide recognition with *Cloud 9* (1979), which with great humor (and cross-gender casting) explores how stereotyping social forces determine gender roles. *Top Girls* (1982) contrasts famous women of the past (who recall the prices they had to pay for asserting themselves in a man's world) and a group of contemporary women (still caught in the rat race of a male-dominated society). *Fen* (1983) treats female farmworkers in East Anglia seeking to cope with low wages and impossible lives, while *Mad Forest* (1990)

explores life in Romania before and after the fall of dictatorship in that country.

Alan Ayckbourn (1939–) has long been one of England's most popular and prolific playwrights (in 1975, he had five plays running in the West End). Nearly all his plays are developed at the Stephen Joseph Theatre in Scarborough, where he has served as artistic director since 1970. His numerous plays include *How the Other Half Loves* (1970), *The Norman Conquests* (1973), *A Chorus of Disapproval* (1985), and *A Small Family Business* (1987). Ayckbourn is known for his wit, his innovative manipulation of space and time, and for the sense of desperation that underlies even his most farcical works.

Michael Frayn (1933–) had his first success with the comedy *Alphabetical Order* (1975) but it was *Noises Off* (1982) that first brought him international fame. He wrote a number of other successful plays in the 1980s and became a highly regarded translator of Chekhov.

One of the best English-language playwrights is Irish. Brian Friel (1929–) first came to prominence

FIG. 24.8

Caryl Churchill's *Cloud 9* at the Royal Court Theatre, London, 1979. Photo by John Holmes.

with *Philadelphia, Here I Come* (1964), concerning a young man's attempt to emigrate to America and the complications it creates. Numerous plays followed, among the most successful of which were *Translations* (1981), which parallels a British map-making unit who are changing Gaelic to English names in 1833 and the British military presence in Northern Ireland in the 1970s and 1980s; and *Dancing at Lughnasa* (1990), in which an adult man recalls his childhood with his mother and aunts for whom dancing ultimately becomes a means of release from their narrow existence.

THEATRE IN THE UNITED STATES AFTER 1968

In many ways, 1968 was a watershed in U.S. theatre. In that year nudity and obscenity were introduced on Broadway in the musical *Hair!* In 1969, *Che!* brought explicit sexual acts on stage, and later that year *Oh, Calcutta* included a large number of scenes performed entirely in the nude. Although protests against obedience to authority, unquestioning patriotism, and accepted codes of behavior and dress had been increasing since the late 1950s, the introduction of nudity and obscenity seemed to accelerate these trends, and by 1970 almost all previously accepted standards were under attack.

Hair! (written by Galt McDermot, Gerome Ragni, and James Rado) was also significant for popularizing a new type of musical. Almost all of its elements were derived from the youth-oriented culture of the day: its antiestablishment stance, lifestyle, and dress; its highly amplified rock music; and its dance forms. Eventually it was performed throughout the world and almost everywhere became a focal point for those wishing to throw off behavioral restraints.

Stephen Sondheim (1930–) was by far the most successful and experimental writer of musicals after 1968. His *Company* (1970) had no chorus, instead using the principal performers in song-and-dance sequences; *Pacific Overtures* (1976) drew on conventions of the Japanese theatre; *Sweeney Todd* (1979) approached opera in its use of music throughout; *Sunday in the Park with George* (1984) explored artistic creation; and *Into the Woods* (1987) exposed the darker side of fairy tales. All Sondheim's works offered ironic views of human behavior and social values and avoided the happy endings of earlier musicals; most were organized around a concept rather than a story.

Some of the most popular musicals after 1968— *Jesus Christ, Superstar; Evita; Cats; Phantom of the Opera;* and *Sunset Boulevard*—were by the English composer Andrew Lloyd Webber (1948–), while

FIG. 24.9

Hair! as produced on Broadway in 1968. Directed by Tom O'Horgan. Photo by Martha Swope.

others—*Les Miserables* and *Miss Saigon*—were by the French team Alain Boublil and Claude-Michel Schönberg, challenging the conviction that musicals were primarily an American form.

FIG. 24.10

Stephen Sondheim's *Sweeney Todd,* 1979. Directed by Harold Prince. The actors are Angela Lansbury and Len Cariou. Photo by Martha Swope.

The year 1968 was also significant because it saw the return of the Living Theatre to the United States. Between 1964 and 1968 the company had toured throughout Europe, becoming increasingly committed to anarchy and revolution and serving as a magnet for disaffected and radical groups. Its major productions after 1964 were works of its own creation: *Mysteries and Smaller Pieces, Frankenstein,* and *Paradise Now,* all advocating freedom from restraints. Its best-known production was *Paradise Now* (1968), in part because it coincided with and mirrored the great unrest then evident in Europe and America. The action of the piece was divided into eight parts designed to increase the audience's political perceptions and to move ever nearer the present; at the end the audience was urged to move into the streets to continue the revolution. All barriers between actors and spectators were eliminated and both roamed the stage and auditorium indiscriminately. The performers were intensely aggressive, confronting spectators, and seeking to overcome, through insults and obscenities, all opposition. The overall effect was that of an inflammatory political meeting.

When the Living Theatre returned to the United States in 1968 it toured throughout the country and everywhere aroused bitter controversy and debate over the nature of theatre and the role of art in society. In 1984, when it presented a repertory of four works in New York, U.S. critics found its work amateurish and lacking in significant content. After Beck's death in 1985, Malina continued the company, although on a much reduced scale.

FIG. 24.11

The Living Theatre's *Paradise Now.* From the film *Paradise Now: The Living Theatre in Amerika* by Marty Topp; produced by Universal Mutant; Ira Cohen, producer. Courtesy Mark Hall Amitin.

Despite its later decline in popularity, the Living Theatre's significance during the 1960s and 1970s cannot be denied. For a time the disaffected almost everywhere echoed its attitudes and practices: denigration of any text that could not be transformed into an argument for anarchy or social change; downgrading language in favor of Artaudian techniques; athleticism in performance; insistence on confronting and overriding audiences; evangelical tone; and freewheeling lifestyle. Its work influenced not only theatre, but also the development of rock concerts in the 1970s, which in turn influenced theatre artists in the 1990s.

The theatre groups most closely related to the Living Theatre were the so-called radical companies. Of these, the most important were The San Francisco Mime Troupe, the Bread and Puppet Theatre, the Free Southern Theatre, and El Teatro Campesino. The San Francisco Mime Troupe was founded in 1959 by R. G. Davis to perform silent plays, but after 1966 it turned to agit-prop spoken plays about current issues which it performed in a broad caricature style. The Bread and Puppet Theatre was founded in 1961 by Peter Schumann. Using puppets of varying sizes (some over twenty feet tall), live actors, and stories based on myths, the Bible, and well-known tales, it sought to promote love, charity, and humility and to denounce the evils of materialism and deception. The Free Southern Theatre, founded in 1963 by Gilbert Moses and John O'Neal, was an extension of the civil rights movement. It sought to raise the consciousness of Southern African Americans. El Teatro Campesino, founded in 1965 by Luis Valdez to dramatize the plight of agricultural workers in California, subsequently devoted itself to plays designed to encourage Mexican-Americans to take pride in their heritage. After 1968 there were also a number of "guerrilla" theatre groups that seized on a gathering or occasion to present unscheduled, brief, pithy, attention-getting skits as a means of arousing interest in some issue. As the mood of the country changed in the late 1970s, guerrilla theatre declined.

In New York, the off-off-Broadway groups were those most concerned with innovation. One of the most important, the Open Theatre, was founded in 1963 by Peter Feldman and Joseph Chaikin (1935–2003), an actor with the Living Theatre who chose not to go into exile with that company. The Open Theatre was more nearly a workshop than a producing organization, and showed its work publicly only at irregular intervals. It was concerned especially with exploiting those aspects of the theatre that distinguish it from films and television—the sense of direct human contact and its constantly changing components. It drew heavily on "role playing" and "games" theories of human behavior, especially as

FIG: 24.12

The Bread and Puppet Theatre's *Domestic Resurrection Circus,* as performed in Vermont, 1974. Photo by Craig Hamilton.

they relate to "transformation" (that is, the idea that reality constantly shifts as people take on and discard roles in relation to the changing context). Actors performed in a large open space and moved freely out of one role into another in a series of transformations.

The relationship between the Open Theatre and its playwrights was close. Typically, the writer supplied an outline, scenes, situations, or motifs; working from this base, the actors explored the possibilities through improvisations, metaphorical associations, and other techniques; the playwright then selected and sharpened those results that seemed most effective. Some of these experiments came to nothing, but other yielded outstanding results, especially in collaboration with Terry and Van Itallie. Megan Terry (1932–) was probably best known for *Viet Rock* (1966), a play about the horrors of war in Vietnam. She also used transformational techniques in works not written for the Open Theatre, most notably in *Approaching Simone* (1970), which traces the life of the French philosopher and mystic Simone Weil. Jean-Claude Van Itallie's (1936–) best-known work is *The Serpent* (1969), which mingles material from the Bible with more recent events, such as the assassinations of John F. Kennedy and Martin Luther King, Jr., and suggests that the serpent is that impulse within people that makes them break the limits set on them, whereas God is an idea invented by people to set limits on themselves.

In 1970 the Open Theatre was reconstituted as a collective and thereafter performed primarily for university and prison audiences. It was dissolved in 1973. Chaikin subsequently worked as a director and actor until a stroke in 1984 forced him to cease, although he was able to return to limited performing and directing beginning in the late 1980s.

The La MaMa organization continued to play a major role in off-off-Broadway after 1968. In addition to assisting new playwrights, it hosted other companies, American and foreign (including Growtowski and Kantor), and developed its own ensembles, some of which specialized in plays of interest to particular ethnic groups (Puerto Rican, African American, Native American, and others).

There were a number of other significant off-off-Broadway companies. The Circle Repertory Company (founded in 1969 with Marshall Mason as artistic director) emphasized the development of new plays by its own closeknit working group, of which the best-known member was Lanford Wilson. In 1986, Mason was succeeded by Tanya Berezin as artistic director. The company eventually declared bankruptcy and ceased to exist in 1997. The Manhattan Theatre Club (under the direction of Lynne

FIG. 24.13

New York Shakespeare Festival production of Shakespeare's *King John,* 1967, in the Delacorte Theatre in Central Park. Photo by George E. Joseph.

Meadow) also developed playwrights through readings and productions in its three theatres, becoming one of the most successful of the off-Broadway companies. But of all the off-Broadway groups, the New York Shakespeare Festival was the most important. It was the creation of Joseph Papp (1921–1991), who in 1954 founded the New York Shakespeare Festival, which each summer after 1957 gave performances free of charge in Central Park, where the

municipally owned Delacorte Theatre was inaugurated in 1962 to accommodate it. In 1967 Papp persuaded the City of New York to acquire the Astor Library and lease it to him for a token fee. He converted it into the Public Theatre with five auditoriums. It opened with *Hair!* (which after its initial run was restaged on Broadway to become one of the greatest hits of the decade). Subsequently, Papp ran an increasingly complex program and supplied

Broadway with several hits, among them *Chorus Line*. By the time Papp died in 1991, he had presented more than 400 works.

Broadway continued to be the heart of the commercial theatre in the United States, and acceptance there continued to be the mark of success. In the 1920s, Broadway had 80 theatres and presented about 218 productions each year. About 150 of these were new plays; only about 45 were new musicals. By 1990, Broadway had 35 theatres and presented just over 30 productions each year. New plays accounted for only about one-third of the total.

Much of the vitality of U.S. theatre after 1968 came from the nonprofit theatres, most of them located outside of New York. By the 1990s there were more than 250, and among them they were mounting more than 3000 productions each year. They varied considerably in size, facilities, total program, and quality, but they offered live performances throughout the United States.

Of these companies, only a few can be mentioned. The Yale Repertory Theatre, established in 1966 by Robert Brustein (1927–) and after 1978 headed by Lloyd Richards (1919–2006), owed its distinction in part to its close association with the Yale Drama School, then the most influential U.S. theatre training program. Richards established a special working relationship with the South African playwright Athol Fugard and gave the premiere performances of some of his plays, including *Master Harold and the Boys* (1982) and *The Road to Mecca* (1984). Subsequently, he established a similar relationship with August Wilson. In addition, Richards served as artistic director of the Eugene O'Neill Theatre Center, which each summer hosts the National Playwrights Conference, where writers are assisted in developing their plays. In 1992, Richards was succeeded at the Yale Repertory and Drama School by Stan Wojewodski, Jr.

Brustein established the American Repertory Theatre at Harvard University in 1979, which quickly became famous for its adventurous repertory staged by some of the most innovative directors in America, including Andrei Serban, Liviu Ciulei, JoAnne Akalaitis, Ron Daniels, and Robert Wilson. It achieved international stature through its appearances at numerous festivals at home and abroad.

The Actors Theatre of Louisville, under the direction of Jon Jory (1938–), played a significant role in developing new playwrights through its annual festival (beginning in 1976–1977) of new plays and its annual "Classics in Context," which included productions, symposia, and films related to a particular period or writer. The Guthrie Theatre in Minneapolis, a leading regional company since its formation in 1963, was especially innovative after

FIG. 24.14
Yale Repertory Theatre's production of August Wilson's *Ma Rainey's Black Bottom*. Directed by Lloyd Richards. The actress is Theresa Merritt. Photo by George G. Slade. Courtesy Yale Repertory Theatre.

1981 under the direction of Liviu Ciulei (1923–), a Romanian director noted for his provocative interpretations of standard works and under his successors, Garland Wright (1946–1998) and Joe Dowling (1948–). Other outstanding regional companies included the Arena Stage in Washington under the direction of Zelda Fichandler (1924–) and the Mark Taper Forum in Los Angeles under the direction of Gordon Davidson (1933–).

Beginning in the 1980s, Chicago, Los Angeles, and Seattle became increasingly important theatre centers. In 1979 Chicago had twenty-two companies, but by 1990 the number had grown to 110, although not all were fully professional. Among these, perhaps the best known was the Steppenwolf Theatre (established in 1976) which included among its members Gary Sinise, John Malkovich, Laurie Metcalf, and Glenne Headley, all of whom went on to stardom in New York and Hollywood. The Goodman Theatre (founded in 1925) gained national recognition through its work after 1978 under Gregory Mosher, especially the U.S. premieres of such plays as David Mamet's *Glengarry Glen Ross* and David Rabe's *Hurlyburly* and with Mosher's appointment in 1985 to head the Lincoln Center company. Mosher was succeeded at the Goodman Theatre by Robert Falls (1954–). The major companies of Los Angeles and the southern California area, in addition to the Mark Taper Forum, included the South Coast Repertory Company, the LaJolla Playhouse, and San Diego's Old Globe Theatre. Seattle's companies included A Contemporary Theatre, Intiman Theatre Company, and the Seattle Repertory Theatre.

The regional theatres derived much of their support from federal, state, and municipal agencies, but increasingly depended on grants from foundations and corporations. Government support of the arts began in 1965 when federal legislation established the National Endowment for the Arts as an agency to make grants of appropriated funds to groups or projects for artistic merit or for potential growth in excellence and service. The federal government also encouraged each state to establish an arts council, and consequently most states now have an official body charged with assisting and encouraging the arts. Many of these groups provide at least some financial support to theatres. In addition, some regional councils linked member states in an effort to coordinate plans for promoting the arts, and within states numerous communities formed arts councils to deal with local concerns and needs. Despite these advances, few theatre groups had any assurance of continuing financial assistance (unlike European companies) and consequently they seldom could make long-range plans.

FIG. 24.15

Beckett's *Endgame* as directed by JoAnne Akalaitis at the American Repertory Theatre, Cambridge. Changes made in the setting and casting from those demanded in the script brought objections from Beckett. Photo by Richard Feldman.

After 1968, a number of new and significant dramatists appeared. One of the most respected is Sam Shepard (1943–), who began his playwriting career in 1964 in the off-off-Broadway theatre. His extremely large output includes *Mad Dog Blues* (1971), *The Tooth of Crime* (1972), *Curse of the Starving Class* (1976), *Buried Child* (1978), *True West* (1980), *Fool for Love* (1982), and *A Lie of the Mind* (1985). Although there is much variety in his work, a number of themes recur: attempts to escape or deny the past; the cowboy and the West as basic American myths; the family as a battle zone; and characters caught between empty dreams and insubstantial reality.

Lanford Wilson (1937–) wrote numerous works, among them *Balm in Gilead* (1965), *Hot L Baltimore* (1973), *Talley's Folly* (1979), *The Fifth of July* (1980), and *Burn This* (1987). The story line of the plays is minimal; the focus is on character relationships and the eventual revelation of hidden feelings, hopes, and disappointments.

David Rabe (1940–) wrote most of his early plays in response to the war in Vietnam. *The Basic Training of Pavlo Hummel* (1971) shows the gradual dehumanization of a naive and patriotic young soldier, while *Sticks and Bones* (1971) concerns a veteran blinded in Vietnam and the effect of his return home on his family. *Streamers* (1976), which takes place just as the Vietnam War is beginning, derives much of its power from the veteran soldiers who in recalling the Korean conflict make us recognize the price exacted by all wars. Rabe's later play, *Hurlyburly* (1984), treats characters in Hollywood who seemingly are unaware of the casual cruelties they practice on each other to keep ahead in the Hollywood game; its sequel, *Those the River Keeps* (1993) explores how the chaos of contemporary life drives people apart.

David Mamet (1947–), who began his career in Chicago, has written primarily about the debasement and distortion of human beings by the materialistic goals of American society. Most of his characters are preoccupied with power or money, which they pursue through the manipulation of others. Reiterative speech (often scatological) reveals characters trapped by stereotyped attitudes and insubstantial values. Among Mamet's plays, some of the best known are *American Buffalo* (1977), *Glengarry Glen Ross* (1983), and *Speed-the-Plow* (1988). Like Shepard, Mamet has increasingly turned to film work.

Terrence McNally (1939–) had his first play produced in 1964 and wrote steadily for the theatre thereafter. It was not until the late 1980s that he became truly successful with *Frankie and Johnny at the Claire de Lune* (1987) and *The Lisbon Traviata* (1989). His plays deal primarily with the gaps between people and the importance of trying to bridge them.

FIG. 24.16

Liviu Ciulei's production of Shakespeare's *The Tempest* at the Guthrie Theatre, Minneapolis, 1981. In this production, the stage was surrounded by a trough of blood in which floated artifacts representative of Western civilization. Photo by Bruce Goldstein. Courtesy Guthrie Theatre.

Other male playwrights deserving mention include John Guare, A. R. Gurney, Richard Nelson, Jon Robin Baitz, Donald Margulies, Robert Schenkkan, Horton Foote, and John Patrick Shanley.

After 1968 female playwrights achieved greatly increased acceptance. Among the best known of these were Norman, Fornès, Henley, and Wasserstein. Marsha Norman (1947–), who wrote primarily about existential dilemmas, first gained recognition with *Getting Out* (1977), dealing with a woman leaving prison; the protagonist is represented by two personae, before and after prison, to show how she remakes her life. Norman's most successful play, *'night Mother,* the Pulitzer Prize winner of 1983, concerns a woman who prepares for and ultimately commits suicide. She also wrote the book for the musicals *The Secret Garden* (1991) and *Red Shoes* (1993). Marìa Irene Fornés (1930–), a versatile and prolific Cuban-born writer, was best known in the 1960s for the small-scale musicals she wrote with Al Carmines. After virtually giv-

ing up writing for a time, she returned with such works as *Fefu and Her Friends* (1977), which reunites eight women on a weekend retreat, where they look back over their lives and seek to understand themselves within a patriarchal society, and *The Conduct of Life* (1985), set in Latin America, which draws parallels between the subjugation of women and political subjugation. Beth Henley (1952–) wrote about complex and bizarre relationships in small Southern towns. Among her plays, which include *The Miss Firecracker Contest* (1984), *The Lucky Spot* (1986), and *Abundance* (1990), the best known is *Crimes of the Heart* (1977, the Pulitzer Prize winner of 1980), in which three sisters, faced with the death of their grandfather and charges of attempted murder, eventually recognize the ways in which they have short-changed themselves. Wendy Wasserstein (1950–2006) made her first impact with *Uncommon Women and Others* (1977), a collage about the struggles of young college women, but her reputation rests primarily on

FIG. 24.17
Sam Shephard's *True West* with John Malkovich (left) and Gary Sinise. Directed by Gary Sinise. Photo by Martha Swope.

The Heidi Chronicles (1988, the Pulitzer Prize play of 1989), in which the action, ranging over some twenty years, traces the protagonist's awakening feminist consciousness and her eventual sense of betrayal.

Another positive development was the reemergence of a strong African American theatre. It began in 1963 with the Free Southern Theatre and received additional impetus in 1965 when LeRoi Jones and others founded the Black Arts Repertoire Theatre School in New York, although this organization soon came to an end. Other organizations sprang up throughout the country, and by the late 1960s there were more than forty groups. Three were of special importance. Spirit House was founded in 1966 by LeRoi Jones, who breaking with the past, took the name Imamu Baraka, then changed it to Amiri Baraka and returned to his home in Newark, where he wrote and produced plays denouncing whites and promoting a wholly black society. The New Lafayette Theatre, founded in 1967 by Robert Macbeth, served as a cultural center for Harlem. It also served as a clearinghouse for African American groups throughout the country through an information service and through *Black Theatre Magazine*. Unfortunately, dissension within the company brought its dissolution in 1973. The Negro Ensemble Company

FIG. 24.18
David Rabe's *Streamers*. Directed by Mike Nichols. Photo by Martha Swope.

FIG. 24.19

The Negro Ensemble Company's production of Joseph Walker's *The River Niger*, 1972. Photo by Bert Andrews.

(NEC), founded in New York in 1968 and directed by Douglas Turner Ward, produced a wide range of plays meaningful to African Americans but not necessarily written by African Americans. The longest lasting of the three groups, the NEC was by the mid-1990s only sporadically active. Other African American companies were formed throughout the United States. In 1988, the inaugural National Black Arts Festival was held to celebrate the artistic achievements of African Americans. It was followed in 1989 by the first National Black Theatre Festival with attendance by representatives of nearly 200 African American theatre groups (professional and nonprofessional) from throughout the United States. These organizations have continued to meet biannually to witness performances and to discuss common issues.

Lorraine Hansberry (1930–1965) won recognition with *A Raisin in the Sun* (1959), a compassionate drama about a hardworking black family in Chicago whose dreams are shattered but whose values mature in the process. Before her untimely death, Hansberry completed only one other play, *The Sign in Sidney Brustein's Window* (1964), concerning a naive idealist who is too busy to recognize the problems within his own family. Some of Hansberry's uncompleted works were later assembled and staged by her husband, Robert Nemiroff. Amiri Baraka (LeRoi Jones, Imamu Baraka, 1934–) in such early plays as *The Toilet* (1964) and *Dutchman* (1964) treated black-white relationships as confrontational and violent, but his contempt for misguided blacks and whites was well-balanced. After 1965, he depicted all whites as devils incarnate. One of the best of these plays, *Slave Ship* (1969), traces the black experience from Africa to the present in America, and shows the unremitting and sadistic treatment of blacks by whites. Baraka eventually abandoned his black nationalism in favor of revolutionary socialism, and his late plays show this shift. *Boy and Tarzan Appear in a Clearing* (1983), for example, shows the leaders of present-day black Africa as greedy and corrupt, and suggests the need to overcome this behavior, learned from white colonists. Ed Bullins (1935–) was resident dramatist and associate director of the New Lafayette Theatre and editor of *Black Theatre Magazine*. All of Bullins' plays, among them *Clara's Old Man* (1965), *The Electronic Nigger* (1968), *The Pig Pen* (1970), *The Taking of Miss Janie* (1975), *Daddy* (1977), and *Boy x Man* (1997), are united by his concern for pride in blackness and contempt for blacks who seek to deny their blackness.

Two of the most effective African American playwrights are Wilson and Wolfe. August Wilson (1945–2006) won his first success with *Ma Rainey's Black Bottom* (1984), about the humiliations, small victories, and defeats of African American musicians working for exploitative whites in Chicago in the 1920s. Wilson announced his intention of writing a play about the African American experience in each decade of the twentieth century. Of these, the most praised have been *Fences* (1985), winner of the Pulitzer Prize in 1987, and *The Piano Lesson* (1988), the 1990 Pulitzer Prize winner. *Fences* is set in Pittsburgh in the 1950s just before the civil rights movement gained force. It explores the psychological and economic wounds inflicted on an African American family by social and employment barriers. *The Piano Lesson* takes up the decade of the 1930s and the conflict that arises when a family's cultural heritage (represented by an heirloom piano) is thrown into conflict with their economic future (represented by land the family has worked since slave days). Others of his plays include *Joe Turner's Come and Gone* (1986) and *Two Trains Running* (1990). Wilson's plays, unlike those of several earlier African American dramatists, do not exploit themes of rage about whites but concentrate on African American identity and quests for fulfillment and dignity. George C. Wolfe gained wide recognition with *The Colored Museum* (1986), a sometimes satirical and always insightful commentary on African American life and art, and *Jelly's Last Jam* (1991) which told the story of the famous jazz musician, Jelly Roll Morton. Wolfe became best known as a Broadway director. Other African American playwrights include Charles Fuller, Ntozake Shange, Adrienne Kennedy, Alice Childress, Leslie

Lee, Lonne Elder III, Joseph Walker, Charles Gordone, Richard Wesley, Ron Milner, Philip Hayes Dean, and Vinette Carroll.

Other ethnic and minority groups also won increased acceptance. The first Asian American dramatist to gain national prominence was David Henry Hwang (1957–), who intermingled Asian and Western theatrical conventions. He began his playwriting career in 1979 and had his first major success with *M. Butterfly* (1988), about a French diplomat who declared that he did not know that the Beijing Opera star he had lived with for twenty years was a man. Hwang uses this story to suggest that the West has always looked upon the East as a submissive female accepting domination by the macho West. Other works by Hwang include *F.O.B.* (1980), *Face Value* (1992), *Golden Child* (1996), and a number of collaborations with the composer Philip Glass. Asian American theatre was nourished by such groups as the East-West Players founded in Los Angeles in 1965; the Northwest Asian American Theatre, founded in Seattle in 1973; the Asian American Theatre Company, founded in San Francisco in 1973; and the Pan Asian Repertory Theatre founded in New York in 1977.

After 1968, Hispanic American theatres also gained strength. A 1985 survey found 101 groups: 29 Chicano, 24 Cuban, 28 Puerto Rican, and 20 with a variety of allegiances. Some performed only in Spanish, some only in English, and some were bilingual. Some of the best known groups were INTAR, Repertorio Espagnol, and the Puerto Rican Traveling Theatre, all in New York, and El Teatro Campesino and the Bilingual Foundation of the Arts in California. An international festival of Chicano and Latino theatre was held beginning in 1970, at first annually and then biannually, under the auspices of TENAZ (Teatros Nacionales de Aztlan), the oldest artistic organization of the Chicano and Latino theatre community.

Along with Maria Irene Fornes, the best-known Hispanic American playwright was Luis Valdez (1940–), who, after his work in support of the United Farm Workers Union, turned to writing plays about Aztec myth and Mexican-American life. His *Zoot Suit* (1978), concerning a notorious murder trial of Mexican-Americans in Los Angeles during World War II, was also made into a movie. His folk musical, *Corridos* (1983), is a series of vignettes based on traditional songs. Each year, Valdez's company presents *La Pastorela,* his adaptation of the shepherds' visit to the newborn Christ. Milcha Sanchez-Scott is best known for *Roosters* (1987), a play of family relationships built around the metaphor of cockfighting. Other plays by Sanchez-Scott are *Dog Lady, Latina,* and *El Dorado.* Cherríe Moraga offers a Latina

lesbian perspective on relationships in such plays as *Giving Up the Ghost* and *La Ofrenda*. Other Hispanic American playwrights include Estela Portillo Trambley, Omar Torres, Miguel Piñero, José Rivera, Nilo Cruz, and Eduardo Machado.

Native American theatre groups have been few in number. The first all-Native American repertory company, the Native American Theatre Ensemble, was founded by Hanay Geiogamah (1945–) in 1972. With the support of La MaMa it presented plays based on myths and contemporary life with the aim of building pride in the Native American heritage. Geiogamah's own plays include *Body Indian* (1972) and *49* (1982). Spiderwoman Theatre, founded in 1975 by three Native American sisters, took their group's name from the Hopi goddess of creation. Its productions, which are multimedia interweavings of narrative, include *Lysistrata Numbah* and *Sun, Moon, and Feather.*

Gay and lesbian theatre also made considerable impact. One of its best known exponents was Charles Ludlam (1943–1987), head of the Ridiculous Theatrical Company after 1967 and author of several plays, among them *Bluebeard* (1970), *Camille* (1973), and *The Mystery of Irma Vep* (1984), which parodied familiar genres and the absurdities of life and art. Ludlam also acted in the plays, often playing several roles, many of them female. After Ludlam's death, the company was continued by Everett Quinton. Harvey Fierstein (1954–) won mainstream acceptance with *Torch Song Trilogy* on Broadway in 1981 and with the book of the musical *La Cage aux Folles* (1983).

Lesbian plays failed to make their way into the mainstream, but were numerous. Jane Chambers' *Last Summer at Bluefish Cove* (1980) and Holly Hughes' *The Well of Horniness* (1985) were among the best known. Several theatres, scattered throughout the country, were devoted to producing gay or lesbian drama.

Much that happened in the theatre after 1968 reflected a cluster of ideas and practices that came to be called "postmodernism"—an imprecise label, but one that suggests a significant break with "modernism." Under modernism a variety of styles had flourished, but within any one, the artist usually sought unity by adhering consistently to the set of conventions associated with that mode. If there were disparate elements, they were ultimately harmonized into a unified whole. Postmodernists, on the other hand, were undisturbed by lack of consistency or continuity. They allowed disparities to exist without seeking to mask them, and they juxtaposed styles and moods that previously would have been considered incompatible or inconsistent. They collapsed categories which under modernism had been treated as distinct; boundaries were breached between the sexes, the arts, cultures, dramatic forms, and performance styles.

Postmodern art was often reflexive, calling attention to the fact that it was being made and how it was being made. It might include overt references to other works. It tended to value popular and high culture equally and to intermingle them. This led to distinctions between a "work" (the physical document written by the author) and a "text" (what individual readers find when they interrogate a script), and to the idea that the author has no more right than anyone else in the text, since no one (including the author) can dictate how a work can be interpreted. In effect, audiences became partial authors of the text they perceive. This idea, along with the principle of no closure of meaning, provided justification, if any were needed, for directors to depart drastically from dramatists' instructions. Sometimes, it was argued, works (especially classics) have become so enshrined within accepted interpretations that we can see them afresh only upon being subjected to a radically different (even "blasphemous") interpretation.

Such interminglings were foreshadowed in "happenings," which themselves harked back to concepts and conventions introduced by the futurists, dadaists, and surrealists. One key figure was Allan Kaprow (1927–), a painter and art historian, who in the 1950s became interested in "environments" (that is, the extension of the concept of art to include the entire setting in which it is exhibited or in which it occurs); believing that all those who attend an exhibit become a part of the total experience, he began to give the spectators things to do. In 1959 he published an outline for an artistic event that he labeled a "happening" because he considered the term to be neutral. Later that year he gave the first public showing of such an event—*18 Happenings in 6 Parts.* For it, the gallery was divided into three compartments; different activities went on in each but simultaneously, and images were projected onto a variety of surfaces while music and sound effects provided a background. All those who attended became a part of the event as they carried out instructions given them when they entered.

Many of these ideas were carried over into *environmental theatre,* a term popularized by Richard Schechner (1934–), editor of *TDR (The Drama Review).* In 1968 Schechner published six "axioms" designed to clarify environmental theatre.

1. Events may be placed on a continuum with "Pure/Art" at one end and "Impure/Life" at the other, extending from traditional theatre at one pole through environmental theatre to happenings and ending with public events and demonstrations at the other pole. Environmental theatre is located somewhere between traditional theatre and happenings.

2. In environmental theatre "all the space is used for performance; all the space is used for the audience." Spectators are both "scene-makers" and "scene-watchers," for, as in a street scene from daily life, those who watch are part of the total picture, even when they consider themselves to be mere spectators.

3. "The event can take place either in a totally transformed space or in a 'found' space." Space may be converted into an "environment," or accepted as an environment that the production will be adapted to.

4. "Focus is flexible and variable."

5. "All production elements speak their own language" rather than being mere supports for words.

6. "A text need be neither the starting point nor the goal of a production. There may be no text at all."

Thus the site of a performance is made an integral part of the whole, encompassing both actors and spectators so they may interact as an entity.

FIG. 24.20
The Performance Group's *Commune,* 1970. Photo by Elizabeth Le Compte.

In 1968 Schechner formed his own company, the Performance Group. Its theatre was a converted garage with towers and platforms scattered about, all of which could be used by both actors and spectators. The company's first production was *Dionysus in 69*, a reworking of Euripides' *The Bacchae* into a series of rituals, most of them relating to sexuality, freedom, or repression. Overall, the production became a plea for greater freedom coupled with a warning against blindly throwing off restraints. Subsequently, the group presented Sam Shepard's *The Tooth of Crime* (1973), a play about rivalries in the pop music world treated in terms of gangsterism; and, in 1975, Brecht's *Mother Courage*. In 1980 Schechner left the company.

The performance space was then taken over by The Wooster Group, which since 1975 had existed as a unit within Schechner's company. Under its artistic director, Elizabeth LeCompte (1944–), it developed its own pieces, several of them based on the autobiographical recollections of Spalding Gray (1941–2004), one of its principal members. It won high critical praise and international recognition through appearances at festivals abroad. It also applied deconstructionist techniques more fully than any other U.S. company, especially in *Route 1 & 9* (1981) and *L.S.D.* (1983). In the former, portions of *Our Town* were juxtaposed with a blackface vaudeville routine and a pornographic film, thereby showing what is marginalized or ignored in Wilder's idyllic picture of America: ethnic groups, sex, and the industrial wastelands through which run the highways referred to in the piece's title. Somewhat similarly, *L.S.D.* borrowed portions of Miller's *The Crucible* and used them reflexively to illuminate parallels between colonial witchcraft and present-day witch-hunts as they relate to induced visions and violations of accepted behavior. Because of Miller's violent opposition to the use of passages from his play, the piece was never performed as planned.

The Wooster Group's conflict with Miller, along with another at the American Repertory Theatre, where Samuel Beckett threatened legal action when JoAnne Akalaitis set Beckett's *Endgame* in an abandoned subway station, aroused heated debate over long-simmering issues about the rights of authors to have their works performed as they had been written versus the rights of directors to interpret scripts however they thought most effective. The debate brought to the fore many issues (still unresolved) central to postmodernism.

Similar controversy was evoked by virtually every production directed by Andrei Serban (1943–), a Romanian director who came to the United States in 1969, although he worked with scripts whose authors were no longer alive. In such productions as *The Cherry Orchard* at Lincoln Center in 1977, Handel's *Alcina* at the New York City Opera in 1983, *Uncle Vanya* at La MaMa in 1983, *King Stag* for the American Repertory Theatre in 1984, and *Figaro* on Broadway in 1985, Serban used iconoclastic visual imagery to create contemporary resonances and at the same time comment on the dramatic situations, characters, and ideas in ways intended to break through received ideas about the plays so they might be seen afresh.

Peter Sellars (1957–) worked in comparable ways. His Handel's *Orlando* at the American Repertory Theatre transformed the adventurers of Handel's opera into astronauts; his *Mikado* at the Chicago Lyric Opera was set in the boardroom of a contemporary Japanese corporation; his production of Shakespeare's *Pericles* used a jive-talking black performer as narrator; and his production of Sophocles' *Ajax* used a deaf actor in the leading role. In the late 1980s, he turned his attention primarily to opera, especially operas by Mozart. In 1993 his production of Aeschylus's *The Persians,* staged for the Los Angeles Festival and subsequently seen in Paris and Berlin, included a dancing messenger telling of a battle that takes place during the Gulf War, Sudanese music, and a ghost who spoke in sign language.

Lee Breuer (1937–) worked with the Actors' Workshop in San Francisco, studied Grotowski's theatre and the Berliner Ensemble, and directed Beckett's *Play* in Paris before joining with several others to create Mabou Mines, of which he was artistic director (1970–1976), when it became a "theatre collaborative"—nine people who worked both within and outside the group. By 1990, Mabou Mines had presented some thirty-eight works and had performed widely in America, Europe, Asia, and Australia. Although it performed some works by others (especially Beckett), it generated most of its pieces within the company. Those written by Breuer were often partially autobiographical, relying heavily on verbal-visual puns, esoteric references, and electronic devices. His *Prelude to Death in Venice* (1979), which he stated he had written to help him understand his own clinging to youth, interwove a puppet as alter ego and recorded voices that metamorphosed from mother to girlfriend, from father to agent; quotations from Thomas Mann's novel and images from Dracula films. These seemingly disjointed elements were ultimately related through associations with the Oedipal impulse, youth, aging, and death. His *Gospel at Colonus* (1984) blended Sophocles' *Oedipus at Colonus* (which Breuer thought reflected the Greek ecstatic impulse) with the gospel service of a black church in today's America. Another member of

FIG. 24.21
The Wooster Group's *L.S.D.* Photo by Nancy Campbell.

Mabou Mines, JoAnne Akalaitis, was also well known for experimental pieces and as a director, especially of *Endgame* for the American Repertory Theatre in 1984 and of Genet's *The Screens* for the Guthrie Theatre in 1989. Although Mabou Mines continues, it had by the early 1990s lost some of its best-known members and its work no longer aroused the interest it once had.

Many aspects of postmodernism came together in the pieces of Robert Wilson (1942–), among them *Deafman Glance* (1971), *The Life and Times of Joseph Stalin* (1972), *A Letter to Queen Victoria* (1974), *Death, Destruction and Detroit* (1979), and *CIVIL warS* (1983–1984). In these pieces, Wilson borrowed eclectically from several media, cultures, and historical periods and juxtaposed seemingly unrelated images in ways reminiscent of surrealism. Movement often created a hypnotic effect through its slow pace (crossing the stage might take an hour). Most of the pieces were very long—from four to twelve hours, and one continued for seven days and nights. He usually began with some striking image or perception, which he then allowed to expand through a chain of associations. According to Wilson, there is in his pieces nothing to understand, only things to experience. Spectators are left to construct their own interpretation from the evocative, indeterminate, discontinuous, time-warped images and sounds.

While continuing to create his own pieces, Wilson began to stage works by others or to collaborate with others both in Europe and America. In his staging of Euripides' *Alcestis,* at the American Repertory Theatre in 1986, he intermingled the original text with Heiner Müller's *Description of a Picture* (used as a prologue), a Japanese kyogen play (which parodied many of *Alcestis's* themes) set to music by Laurie Anderson, and a number of laser projections. Despite the seeming incongruities of these varied elements, all were linked by the theme of death and rebirth. Others of Wilson's staging of classics include Wagner's *Parsifal*, Ibsen's *When We Dead Awaken*, Gertrude Stein's *Doctor Faustus Lights the Lights*, Büchner's *Danton's Death*, and Debussy's *Pélléas and Melisande*. His collaborative works include *Einstein on the Beach* (1976) with Philip Glass, and *The Black Rider* (1989), an adaptation of von Weber's opera *Der Freischutz,* with Tom Waits and William S. Burroughs. Wilson always has several projects underway at the same time, many of them not due for completion until several years in the future. Because Wilson's productions are so expensive to mount, he has worked most often in the subsidized theatres of Europe, where he is generally considered one of the most significant artists of his time. Probably no other artist so fully embodied the postmodern vision.

FIG. 24.22
Robert Wilson's *CIVIL warS*. A segment presented at the American Repertory Theatre, Cambridge. Photo by Richard Feldman.

Many postmodern and *avant-garde* productions, both American and foreign, are presented at the Brooklyn Academy of Music (BAM), which since 1982 has mounted annually the Next Wave Festival. It offers in brief engagements productions by contemporary artists and companies that probably would not otherwise have been seen in New York, among them the Théâtre du Soleil, Pina Bausch's dance-theatre company, several productions by Robert Wilson, Peter Brook, Lee Breuer, Peter Sellars, and many less well known artists on the "cutting edge."

During the 1980s, performance art and the type of theatre presented by the Wooster Group, Mabou Mines, and Wilson began to intersect. In the 1970s, performance art, a successor to happenings, was usually brief, minimally rehearsed, and given one time only. Because most champions of performance art thought pieces should avoid impersonation and emphasize personal, near-improvisatory elements, they saw themselves in opposition to theatre. But in the 1980s performance art and theatre began to overlap, creating what was often called "interarts" or "new theatre," labels that could cover a wide spectrum of performers and performance modes. Some of its best known practitioners were solo performers. Spalding Gray, after leaving the Wooster Group in 1979, presented over fifteen autobiographical monologues,

among the most successful of which were *Swimming to Cambodia, Monster in a Box, Gray's Anatomy,* and *It's a Slippery Slope.* Eric Bogosian (1953–), in his monologues *Drinking in America* (1986) and *Sex, Drugs & Rock and Roll* (1987), created multiple male characters addicted to profanity and power. Other significant practitioners of this new theatre were Meredith Monk, Laurie Anderson, John Kelly, and Ping Chong.

CANADIAN THEATRE TO 1990

Just as a national identity came into focus for Canada in the 1960s, a radical separatist movement arose in French-speaking Quebec Province, giving that identity a dual focus. When the referendum on independence for Quebec failed in 1980, Canada was also entering an economic recession. The combination of these two events seems to have inspired theatre artists to move beyond the exploration of Canada's national identity in order to examine race, gender, and ethnicity as foundations for personal identity.

The 1970s were best known for the collective creations of the alternative theatres like *The Farm Show* (1972) by Theatre Passe Muraille, *Not Working, She's Got Too Much to Do* (1975) by Théâtre des Cuisines, and *They Club Seals, Don't They* (1978) by Newfoundland's Mummers Theatre. They also included highly ritualistic, dream-like imagistic productions such as *The Purple Room of the Archbishop* (1978), created by L'Eskabel Théâtre.

The experimental work of troupes like L'Eskabel was carried into the 1980s by such groups as Carbon 14, Omnibus, Primus, and Théâtre Repére (where Robert Lepage began his career). These theatres developed a highly visual style that became known internationally as Theatre of Images. Other innovations came from groups like Necessary Angel (1978), whose production of *Tamara* (1980) by John Krizanc became an international phenomenon. This production asked audience members to select one of nine characters to follow as the story progressed into a variety of locations.

The 1980s opened with the Edmonton Fringe Festival, which marked another turning point in Canadian theatre. Modeled after the fringe festival started in Edinburgh, Scotland, in 1947, the Edmonton festival inspired so many imitators that Canada now has the largest concentration of fringe festivals in the world.

The explosion of small theatres dedicated to new Canadian plays that started with the alternative theatres in the 1970s and expanded further with the fringe theatres of the 1980s brought with it a determination to promote those works both nationally and internationally. In 1971 the Playwright Circle was established. It sought to win an agreement that all theatres receiving government subsidy would dedicate at least 50 percent of each season to Canadian plays. No regional theatre would agree to this, but many of the smaller theatres did. This organization, which became the Playwrights Union of Canada in 1984, provides a catalogue and Web site featuring over 2000 works by Canadian dramatists. The Association Québécoise des Auteurs Dramatiques (founded in 1965) provides a similar service for over 3000 plays by French-Canadian dramatists.

Of the hundreds of dramatists represented by these organizations, several have won both national and international acclaim. Among those are Michel Tremblay (1942–), who had his first major success with *The Sister-in-law* (1968), a play set in a working-class neighborhood of Montreal, written in "street French." Tremblay has had a long list of successful plays, including *Like Death Warmed Over* (1970), *Hello There, Hello* (1975), *Albertine in Five Times* (1984), and *For the Pleasure of Seeing Her Again* (1998). David French (1939–) provided a romanticized view of life in Newfoundland in a series of plays starting with *Leaving Home* (1972) and running through *That Summer* (2000). He is best known, however, for *Jitters*

(1980), in which the rehearsal of a Canadian play becomes a forum for critiquing the pervasive influence of U.S. culture in Canada. Canada's most successful dramatist has been George F. Walker (1947–), who began playwriting in 1970. Walker's plays have been heavily influenced by the nonlinear rhythms of electronic media. *Gossip* (1977) was the first of his plays to be commercially successful, and it has been followed by a long list of others, including *Criminals in Love* (1984), *Escape from Happiness* (1992), and *Heaven* (2000). Judith Thompson has become known for her complex and highly emotional dramas from *The Crackwalker* (1981) to *Sled* (1995).

THEATRE IN AUSTRALIA AND NEW ZEALAND TO 1990

In the years after 1968, the six state theatres of Australia became the mainstay for the standard repertory. While these theatres were not the primary venue for new Australian work, they did begin to have foreign plays translated by Australian writers rather than depending on existing English translations. Australia also took a major step in attracting the attention of the world to its commitment to the arts by building the Sydney Opera House, with its trademark sail-like design, in 1973. Since that time, major arts complexes have been opened in Adelaide (1973), Melbourne (1984), and Brisbane (1985). J. C. Williamson Ltd. rebuilt Her Majesty's theatre in 1973, but by 1976, after over a century of dominance, the venerable company was bankrupt. Harry M. Miller (1934–) took over as the premier producer in the country, having already brought *The Boys in the Band* (1968), *Hair!* (1969), and *Jesus Christ Superstar* (1972) to Australian audiences, but his empire was short lived as he was convicted of fraudulent misappropriation of funds in 1978. British producer Cameron Mackintosh soon filled the void by bringing his productions of *Cats* (1981), *Les Misérables* (1985), and *Miss Saigon* (1995) to Australia. But Sydney did not have adequate theatres to house such productions, and this prompted developer David Marriner to buy up a number of old theatres and cinemas and have them lavishly renovated. Across the nation old theatres were torn down or renovated and new ones built, not just to house the state theatres, but to provide modern innovative spaces for a growing number of alternative theatres that were thriving under the new system of Australian Council funding.

Melbourne's La MaMa Theatre continued to produce up to forty plays a year in the 1970s and 1980s, but it no longer had a resident company. In 1970 the La MaMa company decided to strike out on its own. Its members moved into the old Pram Factory and changed their name to the Australian Performing Group (APG). APG was known for its political activism and its collective productions such as *Betty Can Jump* (1972) and its most successful effort, *The Hills Family Show* (1975). But it is remembered now for its championing of Australian playwrights. Its resident playwright was Jack Hibberd (1940–) who was best known for his audience participation dramas like *Dimboola* (1969), in which the audience is treated like guests at a wedding. Though he continued to write such plays through *Liquid Amber* (1982), he has been one of Australia's most versatile dramatists. Among the most successful of the other dramatists were John Romeril (1945–), who wrote the highly political *The Floating World* (1974) about trade relations with Japan, and David Williamson (1942–), who has become Australia's most popular and most internationally known dramatist since his first success with *The Removalist* (1971), a play about abusive policemen which went on to a successful run in London in 1973. Seven of his plays have been widely produced outside Australia, including *The Club* (1977), about the tensions within a sports team as old loyalties give way to commercialism, which went on to play on Broadway in 1978, and *Money and Friends* (1992), which had a successful run in Los Angeles. Despite its success APG closed in 1980, but not before two of its members had gone on to found the equally influential Playbox Theatre Center in 1976.

Rex Cramphorn (1941–1991), one of Australia's most successful directors, created the Performance Syndicate in Sydney in 1969. The Syndicate's unique contributions to Australian theatre were its introduction of performance techniques from Asia and, after Cramphorn went to study with Grotowski in 1972, its introduction of the concepts of "poor theatre" to Australia's theatre artists. Just as the Performance Syndicate was getting underway, *The Legend of King O'Malley* (1970), a political satiric review by Michael Boddy (1934–) and Bob Ellis (1942–), became the most successful alternative theatre piece in the country. Its director, John Bell (1940–), was inspired by this success to establish the Nimrod Street Theatre (1970). The Nimrod quickly became the most innovative and influential alternative theatre in Australia, inspiring the formation of a number of other troupes, including the Black Theatre Group (founded by Betty Fisher), Griffin Theatre Company, the Sydney Theatre Company, and Company B. The Nimrod became famous for *Hamlet on Ice* (1972), but it also produced work by many of Australia's best playwrights. Peter Kenna (1930–1987), who had his first success when the Trust Players produced his *The*

Slaughter of St Teresa's Day in 1959, gave the Nimrod one of its best successes with *A Hard God* (1973). Alex Buzo (1944–), whose play *Norm and Ahmed* (1968) was at the heart of the battle over censorship, had already had *Rooted* (1969) produced in the United States when Nimrod did his play *Tom* (1972). But most of the Nimrod writers, like the prolific Alma De Groen (1941–) and the equally prolific Louis Nowra (1950–), were early in their careers. The Nimrod eventually became too successful to maintain its alternative theatre identity, lost its focus, and closed in 1987. Bell, however, went on to form the Bell Shakespeare Company in 1990.

Through the 1980s, fringe theatres in Australia, like those in many other countries, became less interested in nationalistic politics and more interested in issues of race, ethnicity, and gender. The Woman's Theatre Group of Melbourne (1974–1976) had already stimulated interest in women writers and directors. The Gay Theatre Company of Sydney and the In the Pink company at Melbourne promoted gay and lesbian writers. Companies like The Deck Chair Theatre Company at Perth, along with Doppio Teatro and the Gilgul Theatre at Adelaide, produce plays for ethnic communities. Perth's Black Swan Theatre, founded in 1991 under director Andrew Rose, is the country's first multiethnic theatre and works to develop aboriginal actors, directors, and writers. But it is at Australia's four major international arts festivals—at Perth, Sydney, Melbourne (all annual), and Adelaide (biennial)—along with Sydney's Gay and Lesbian Mardi Gras, that most such work is seen.

By the end of the 1980s, directors like Jim Sharman (1945–) and Gale Edwards (1955–) had become international successes without having to leave Australia. Playwrights and actors who in earlier years would have left the country to find a career, were now finding success and staying home. This was also the time when aboriginal theatre, led by the playwright-activist Jack Davis (1917–2000), came into its own.

In New Zealand, Downstage received a new theatre space in 1974 and continued to be one of the strongest producers of new plays in the country. It had passed up the opportunity to produce a play by Roger Hall (1939–) called *Glide Time* (1976), however. That civil service comedy was produced by a Wellington actor's cooperative called Circa, and the play went on to be the most successful in New Zealand's history. Hall's second play, *Middle Aged Spread* (1978), became an award-winning comedy in London's West End, and Hall continues to be New Zealand's most prolific and most highly regarded dramatist. Meanwhile, the government funding that had started in 1964 had led to the creation of nine semi-professional theatres which formed themselves into the Association of Community Theatres (ACT). Of those, the Court Theatre at Christchurch was the first to become known for its adventurous repertory. Among its most successful productions were *Foreskin's Lament* (1980) by Greg McGee (1950–), a play which uses a rugby team as a symbol of New Zealand's post-colonial struggle to find its place in the world; Michelanne Forster's *Daughters of Heaven* (1991) about a murder involving lesbian schoolgirls; and the "songplays" of its co-founder Mervyn Thompson (1936–1992). Other important members of the community theatre group were Centerpoint Theatre at Palmerstone North, the Fortune at Dunedin, Bats at Wellington, and the Auckland Theatre Company. Declining government subsidies reduced ACT membership to five active theatres by 1986; by 1994 there would be only three.

As in other countries, fringe theatres have developed to replace the independent theatres. Taki Rua was founded in Wellington in 1983 to promote Maori performance, which has had a profound influence on New Zealand's theatre. They have pro-

duced works by Maori writers Harry Dansey (1920–1979), Rori Hapipi (1935–), and John Broughton (1947–) among others. Pacific Theatre, founded at Auckland by Justine (1961–) and Paul Simei-Barton (1958–), focuses on plays that express the immigrant experience of Pacific Islanders. While there have been no theatres specifically dedicated to gay or lesbian plays, the socialist lesbian playwright Renée (1929–) has seen a large number of her plays produced, as has feminist dramatist, Lorae Parry (1953–). Vincent O'Sullivan has been New Zealand's most postmodern dramatist with plays like *Shuriken* (1983), which incorporates expressionism with music hall and Noh drama and inserts of newsreel footage.

Throughout the English-speaking world, if there is any trend to be seen, it is for the politically activist theatres of the late 1960s to grow disillusioned during the 1970s and then to find a focus on issues of race, gender, and ethnicity by the 1990s. In major centers like Broadway and London's West End, musicals and comedies continued to dominate and the serious plays produced there only occasionally addressed political or socially sensitive issues.

LOOKING AT THEATRE HISTORY

Challenging the dominant culture was a hallmark of the 1960s. In this, the Living Theatre played a leading role. Its challenge reached a climax in *Paradise Now* (1968), described by the company as "a vertical ascent toward Permanent Revolution." The production's most notorious feature, direct confrontation with audiences, was little understood, for in actuality the audience was cast as obstacles to successful revolution. Here is a passage from the printed version of the work:

> The Confrontations are an attempt to define and thereby understand the characteristics of the stumbling block at each [phase], and of the form of action that can overcome it. Thus at the beginning the stumbling block is The Culture which is overcome by Aesthetic Assault; and at the end the stumbling block is Stasis which is overcome by Impetus. The Confrontations are guides to the relationship between the actor and the public at each

> stage of the trip. The Resistance to the Revolutionary Change is treated as the obstacle. The energy form designed is an appropriate strategy for the actor to use to transform the obstacle.

> Paradise Now, Collective Creation of the Living Theatre, written down by Judith Malina and Julian Beck (New York: Vintage Books, 1971), 11–12.

By the mid-1970s, much that had been intended as an attack on the dominant ideology had been absorbed into it. Hilton Kramer interpreted this absorption as a rejection of the attack, although it might equally well be seen as an absorption of both old and new into an altered dominant mode:

> The appetite for assaults on the audience and on the medium, has clearly diminished. . . .
> Does this mean that the innovations of the 60s have disappeared without trace? Not at all, but where they

survive . . . they have been . . . co-opted by the establishment, and put to eminently more benign use.

"A Yearning for 'Normalcy'—The Current Backlash in the Arts," *The New York Times*, May 23, 1976, sec. 2, 1, 25.

That Kramer's perception was not entirely adequate is suggested by Elinor Fuch's observations on postmodernism:

These characteristics—the collapse of traditional boundaries, an absorption with the theatre's own artifacts and techniques and styles—are the best reason we have for calling such theatre postmodern. . . . Some such perception of the inversion and breakdown of historical cultural values in the past two decades has bred the sense of "postness" that has invaded virtually every human enterprise in Western society. We are post-industrial, post-capitalist, post-humanist, post-apocalyptic, even post-cognitive.

"The Death of Character," *Theatre Communications*, 5 (March 1983), 2.

25
Contemporary Theatre

By the late 1980s, several world events suggested new directions that would affect the development of theatre in the coming years. Among the most important of these was the collapse of the Soviet Union and the destruction of the Berlin Wall in 1989, both of which helped to mark the end of the Cold War that had dominated European and American policies since the end of World War II. In Czechoslovakia dissident groups rose up against the Communist regime and installed a multiparty government in 1989, and in 1990 Communist dominance of Poland came to an end when Solidarity leader Lech Walesa was elected president. Also in 1990 the United States became involved in the Gulf War, which seriously affected worldwide relations with the Middle East. These and other indications of change would be reflected in theatre in the following years. In Asia, India experienced rapid economic growth in the 1990s as it was able to use its extensive education system to take advantage of the technology boom. The economic reforms China had initiated in 1978, also began to fully take hold and accelerate, especially after 1994. Japan's economy, which had stagnated in the 1980s and early 1990s, began to expand again by the end of the century. Economic prosperity allowed more attention to be paid to the arts, and in China brought with it a degree of liberalization that had not been seen for decades.

The terrorist attack on the Pentagon and New York's World Trade Center on September 11, 2001 has been the defining moment so far in the twenty-first century. This has caused tensions between the Western nations and Islamic fundamentalists that have had profound implications for international relations, while the preoccupation with security in many countries has triggered debates over civil liberties.

THEATRE IN ASIA

Present-day India has many successful dramatists, although relatively few are known outside of India. Even within India fame is difficult to achieve because most dramatists write in one of the regional languages. (India has 17 major languages and some 22,000 dialects.) Some of the best-known contemporary Indian playwrights are Adya Rangacharya (1904–1985), Badal Sircar (1925–), Vijay Tendulkar (1928–), Girish Karnad (1938–), Utpal Dutt (1939–), Mahesh Elkunchwar (1939–), and Mahesh Dattani (1958–).

There is much interest in contemporary plays. In Mombai (formerly Bombay), the Prithvi Theatre has held sixteen festivals since its founding in 1978 to showcase modern drama, both Indian and international. Such interest is not confined to Bombay. In

2000–2001, a six-month-long festival of German plays was staged in fourteen cities. The performing arts are also taught and promoted by the National Academy of Music, Dance, and Drama, founded in 1953 and located in New Delhi. It works in cooperation with its counterparts in the various states and with voluntary organizations throughout India.

The Indian theatre today is extremely diverse, ranging from productions of Sanskrit plays, dance dramas, and folk dramas to modern realistic works. The influence of India on other countries, nevertheless, continues to derive primarily from its classical forms.

Western-style drama made considerable headway in China after the empire was replaced by a republic in 1912. At first this form was called "new drama" or "modern drama," but since the late 1920s it has most often been labeled "spoken drama" to distinguish it from the essentially operatic mode of traditional forms. Originally many spoken dramas were translations or adaptations of foreign works, especially those by Shakespeare, Chekhov, Shaw, Galsworthy, and Ibsen. Native authors also attempted the new style, but the first to win wide critical and commercial success was Cao Yu (1910–1996), usually considered the finest Chinese dramatist of the twentieth century. His works, such as *Thunderstorm* (1933), *Sunrise* (1935), and *The Bridge* (1945), deal with contemporary social problems, especially the conflict between old and new standards.

After the Communists assumed control over the mainland in 1949, Beijing Opera underwent a number of changes. A committee was set up to revise plays to conform to Communist doctrine, and some plays were removed from the repertory. Many new Beijing Operas on contemporary themes were written, some use of scenery was permitted for their performances, and the orchestra was removed from the stage, though it was also enlarged and allowed to use some Western musical instruments. The Cultural Revolution of 1966 led to the suppression of Beijing Opera and most traditional theatre forms, and for a time all professional theatre ceased except for the performance of a few "model" plays. Professional theatre made a gradual comeback, and when the Cultural Revolution was rejected many traditional forms were revived. By 1980 there were 2072 traditional theatre companies, and of the more than 2500 productions performed nationwide in 1980, more than 2200 were of traditional plays and only 176 of spoken drama. By 1990 more than 360 forms of traditional theatre, scattered throughout China, were being performed. As the theatre revived, spectators were forbidden to smoke, but refreshments were usually still available in the auditorium. In many theatres, noisy verbal response was replaced by applause and even in Beijing Opera the voices of performers began to be electronically amplified. Today the greatest challenge to the traditional forms of Chinese theatre has come from the decline in attendance, especially in the cities where the availability of television and movies has altered tastes and theatre-going habits.

The most popular of all Chinese dramas after 1949 was *The White-Haired Girl* (1945), by Hi Jingchi (or Ho Ching-chih) and Ding Yi (or Ting Yi), which in its original form borrowed heavily from Western operatic conventions. It was subsequently transformed into a spoken drama, a Beijing Opera, several regional types, and a ballet (which during the Cultural Revolution was treated as a model work). It tells the story of a girl who, sold into slavery and raped by her master, flees to the mountains where she is mistaken for a goddess because her hair has turned white; she eventually joins the Communist rebels and with their help achieves an honored place in society. This ideologically based story is typical of many others. After the end of the Cultural Revolution, much greater freedom in theatrical subjects and conventions was permitted, but this trend was halted by the crackdown following the student "democracy movement" in 1989. Recently, restrictions have begun to lessen again.

Although little known outside of China, a number of playwrights have achieved recognition within China since 1949. Among these, some of the most prominent are Wu Han, Zong Fuxian, Cui Dezhi, Bai Hua, Sha Yexin, Gao Xingjian, Ma Zhongjun, Lao She, and Sun Huizhu. Two directors, Meng Jinghui and Lin Zhaohua, have been the major supporters of spoken drama. The China Theatrical School is the primary trainer of actors.

China has begun to build major theatrical complexes similar to those in the West. In Shanghai, the major theatrical center of the nation, the new Grand Theatre, which includes a main auditorium seating 1800 and two smaller halls (seating 600 and 200), is one of Asia's largest and most advanced theatrical structures. In the large auditorium, the main stage, rear stage, and two side stages can be rotated, raised, or lowered; its orchestra pit accommodates 120 musicians. Other Chinese cities, among them Shenzhen and Nanking, are also building opera houses. The new National Theatre Complex in Beijing is an egg-shaped building, 430 feet long and 135 feet high, which includes an opera house, concert hall, and two theatres. It is reported to have cost over 360 million dollars and is representative of the commitment China has made to its professional theatre traditions.

After the end of Japan's isolation and the fall of the shogunate in the late nineteenth century, many of the earlier restrictions on the theatre were removed. Women were allowed to appear on the stage, and entrepreneurs were allowed to open new theatres. The major novelty, however, was the introduction of Western-style drama and theatrical conventions. The earliest productions in this mode came in the 1880s, but *shimpa* (as this movement was called) reached its peak between 1904 and 1909, and then declined. Since World War II there have been attempts to revive *shimpa*. These plays have typically been sentimental, romantic, or melodramatic.

Still another offspring of the Western movement is *shingeki* (or new theatre). It began from two sources. First, in 1906, Tsubouchi Shoyo (1859–1935), a professor of English at Waseda University in Tokyo, founded the Literary Arts Society to train young amateur actors in Western theatre and to stage plays by Shakespeare, Ibsen, Shaw, Chekhov, Strindberg, and others. Tsubouchi also established a theatre museum at Waseda University which has become a major center for theatre research. Second, in 1909, Osanai Kaoru and the Kabuki actor Ichikawa Sadanji established the Free Theatre to retrain professional theatre artists to perform Western drama. At first committed to realism and to the Stanislavsky method, *shingeki* has in recent decades become eclectic in outlook and experimental in approach.

Japan's best known post-World War II dramatists were Kobo Abe (1924–1993) and Yukio Mishima (1925–1970). An admirer of Brecht, Abe wrote a number of protest plays, among them *Slave Hunting* (1955), a denunciation of postwar traffic in the remains of the war dead. Others of his best known plays include *Friends* (1967), *The Green Stocking* (1974), and *Image Hunting* (1978). Mishima, an admirer of Japanese tradition, wrote about forty plays, including several Noh and Kabuki dramas. Among his *shingeki* works, perhaps the best known are *The Nest of the White Ant* (1955), about the hollow lives of Japanese emigrés in Brazil, and *Madame de Sade*, a play about the wife of the Marquis de Sade that achieved considerable popularity in Europe and America.

Contemporary dramatists include Juro Kara (1940–), author of *Virgin Mask* and *John Silver;* Seiichi Yashiro, author of *They Vanished at Dawn, Hokusai Sketchbooks,* and *Bewitching;* Minoru Betsuyaku (1937–), author of *The Elephant, The Move,* and *Buried Scenery;* Masakazu Yamazaki, author of *Zeami, The Boat Is a Sailboat,* and *Hideyoshi and Ricky;* Oriza Hirata, author of *Tokyo Notes, Citizens of Seoul,* and *Citizens of Seoul 1919;* and Ryo Iwamatsu, author of *Tea and a Lecture, Romance Is Banned,* and *Futon and Daruma.* Unlike the plays of the 1980s, which tended toward apocalyptic spectacles, plays since the 1990s have become more naturalistic and analytic. They are often referred to as "quiet theatre" to distinguish them from the raw energy of plays that dominated the 1980s.

Among contemporary Japanese directors, by far the best known is Tadashi Suzuki (1939–), who began his work in the student theatre at Waseda University and eventually established his own theatre, the Suzuki Company of Toga. Suzuki developed a highly disciplined acting mode which synthesized martial arts, Kabuki, and Noh techniques. He also sought to build a bridge between Japanese and Western theatre; his most famous productions are adaptations of Greek myths, among them *The Trojan Women, The Bacchae,* and *Clytemnestra,* all of which were performed in the West to great acclaim. Many U.S. schools came to offer training in the Suzuki method, described in Suzuki's *The Way of Acting.* To Suzuki's theatre center in Togamura groups of professional actors came annually from many countries for training and to perform theatrical productions of international interest. In 1993, in collaboration with Anne Bogart, he established the Saratoga (New York) International Theatre Institute.

Yukio Ninagawa (1935–) is another internationally known director, especially noted for his productions of Western classics, among them *Peer Gynt, Macbeth,* and *A Midsummer Night's Dream,* although he has also directed many contemporary Japanese plays. He has received important artistic awards both in Japan and Britain (including an honorary doctorate from Edinburgh University).

Perhaps Japan's best-known cultural export is the *avant-garde* dance form, Butoh, which sets out to assault the senses. A theatre of protest, it uses full body paint (usually white), near or complete nudity, shaved heads, and grotesque costumes. Sankai Juku was the best known of the early Butoh companies, but the number has greatly increased and they now perform throughout the world.

Since 1989, Japan has built more than two dozen performance halls. Most are devoted to specialized uses, including opera, concerts, dance, and Western-style theatre. Contemporary forms of entertainment are now considerably more popular with audiences than are Noh, Bunraku, and Kabuki, although the traditional forms still command respect in Japan and are of special interest in Europe and America, where knowledge of Japanese contemporary theatre is slight.

THEATRE IN RUSSIA

The collapse of communism, the breakup of the Soviet Union, and the removal of censorship around 1990 raised hopes that the arts would blossom, but many of these hopes were dashed by economic problems. When state subsidies that had supported most theatres were reduced by about three-fourths (or in many instances stopped altogether) and inflation diminished the purchasing power of what was left, most companies struggled just to remain active. A large number of theatre artists emigrated, and many well-known companies toured internationally in an attempt to earn foreign currency. Several prominent Russian directors and theatre companies entered into exchange programs with European and American theatres and universities. After ten years of decline, the Russian theatre began to recover. Outside of St. Petersburg and Moscow, there are now 400 to 600 theatres, many of which receive government subsidies; about 100 theatres in Moscow are subsidized by the city government. The Cultural Ministry of Russia announced that it would increase its budget by 25 percent to $350 million in 2002. That same year, the Russian theatre experienced one of it greatest tragedies when terrorists took the audience of Moscow's Nord-Ost theatre hostage. All 41 terrorists and 114 audience members were killed when a narcotic gas was used by the military in an attempt to end the crisis.

In the 1990s, Moscow used festivals to increase interest in its theatrical life. One of the most important of these was the Chekhov Festival, founded in 1992 and held every two years with participation from several countries. The annual Golden Mask Festival (founded in 1995) honors the top achievements in drama, musical theatre, dance, and puppetry by theatres from throughout Russia. The Third National Theatre Olympics was held in Moscow in 2001. (The first was held in Greece in 1995, the second in Japan in 1999.) It included 150 productions from 35 countries presented over a period of 70 days. Among the participants were Robert Wilson, Tadashi Suzuki, Declan Donellan, and many other foreign and Russian directors.

The management of several companies changed during the 1990s. Oleg Yefremov (1927–2000), who had headed the Moscow Art Theatre for thirty years, died in 2000 and was succeeded by Oleg Tabakov (1935–). Tabakov had been a founder of the Sovremennik Theatre, was head of the Moscow Theatre-Studio (which had been granted official status in 1987), and was the creator of more than 760 roles. Anatoly Smeliansky succeeded Tabakov as director of the Theatre-Studio.

The Taganka Theatre underwent several changes in management. Following Anatoly Efros' death in 1987, Nikolai Gubenko (1941–) was named head of the Taganka. The changed status of this company was perhaps most clearly indicated when in 1989 Gubenko

was named Minister of Culture, the first professional artist to hold that position since the 1920s. With the breakup of the Soviet Union, he lost that post and returned to the Taganka. After Gorbachev proclaimed the policy of *glasnost,* Lyubimov's citizenship was restored, and he returned to the Taganka. Among his most successful productions there were *Boris Godunov* (1993) and *Medea* (1995). Eventually Gubenko (who had been one of Lyubimov's staunchest supporters) became alienated from Lyubimov, and the animosity that developed led to the theatre's being divided into two rival companies, much as the Moscow Art Theatre had been earlier. One of Lyubimov's most successful productions was a circus-like *Marat/Sade* performed in Prague in 2000.

During the 1990s, new plays were not highly valued in Russia. This situation led to the establishment of the Playwright and Director Center and the Debut Center, which have developed a cooperative relationship with the Royal Court Theatre in London. A few playwrights, however, champion innovation in playwriting, among them Maxim Kurochkin (1970–), whose *Kitchen* (2001) was commissioned, directed, and starred in by Oleg Menshikov, Russia's top stage and screen actor. This very popular play interweaves contemporary life with the German Nibelung saga, social satire, and bitter irony. Another of Kurochkin's plays, *Steel Will,* concerning the invention of a new Slavic mythology, won an award in 1998 for innovative writing.

Among the leading directors of Russia, in addition to those already mentioned, are Victor Fomenko, Galina Volchek, Kama Ginkas, Henrietta Yanovskaya, Valery Fokin, and Lev Dodin. Fomenko (1932–) has rejected large-scale theatre. His *Innocent*

FIG. 25.1

Vakhtangov Theatre production of *Innocent as Charged* (1993), Victor Fomenko adaptation of a play by Ostrovsky. Photo of the New York tour by Stephanie Berger © 2001.

FIG. 25.2

Maly Theatre Production of *Brothers and Sisters* (1985). Seven-hour dramatization of Fedor Abramov's novel directed by Lev Dobin. Photo of the New York tour by Stephanie Berger © 2001.

between the end of World War II and 1949; in it the characters' initial optimism gradually gives way to disillusionment. It has been performed in more than fourteen countries and won the Europe Theatre Prize in 2000 (previous winners were Peter Brook, Giorgio Strehler, and Robert Wilson). Other productions by Dodin include *Stars in the Morning Sky* (1988) about prostitutes and others rounded up before the 1980 Moscow Olympics, *Gaudeamus* (1991) concerning humiliations and violence among army conscripts, and *Chevengur* (2000), a dramatization of an anti-utopian novel by Andrei Platonov, for which Dodin won a Golden Mask award.

By the early twenty-first century, Russian theatre had begun to recover from the setbacks it had endured during the 1990s, but it still had many obstacles to overcome. After the dissolution of the Soviet Union, theatre achieved considerably more freedom but paid for it through economic hardships.

as Charged (a reworking of a play by Ostrovsky) concerning a long-lost child, opened in Moscow in 1993; it began a vogue for plays written for small spaces with action on a more-human scale. Some critics praised it as the end of ideological drama. Formerly with the Vakhtangov Theatre, he now heads his own Fomenko Studio. Galina Volchek, one of the founders of the Sovremennik, long considered one of Moscow's leading theatres, is now its director. This theatre has also won much praise abroad, including in New York, to which she brought productions of plays by Chekhov in 1996 and 1997. Kama Ginkas (1941–) is noted for his small, intense, and highly personal productions. His *The Room of Laughter* was named the best production at the Gold Mask Festival in 2000. He is married to Yanovskaya, artistic director of the Young Spectators Theatre in Moscow since 1987, considered one of the top five directors in Russia. Her productions have been seen at several European festivals. Valery Fokin (1946–) gained wide recognition after 1994 for his *A Hotel Room in the Town of NN*, written to be performed in a completely enclosed setting; it won several awards (including a Golden Mask) and has toured in seven countries. He is also the founder of the Meyerhold Arts Center, one of the few companies to have a new theatre built especially for it, signaling the renewed acceptance of Meyerhold.

Lev Dodin (1944–) began his professional career in 1967 and became artistic director of the Maly Drama Theatre in St. Petersburg in 1983. He gained national and international recognition with his seven-hour dramatization of Fedor Abramov's novel *Brothers and Sisters* (1985), about life on a collective farm

THEATRE IN POLAND AND THE CZECH REPUBLIC

As in Russia, the triumph of Poland's Solidarity movement in 1989 led to greater freedom in society but worsened the economic situation. In seeking to cope with these problems, the government discontinued subsidies to all but eight theatres, leaving many struggling to survive. This struggle continued through the 1990s.

The triumph of Solidarity also permitted playwrights and other theatrical personnel to return to Poland. Slawomir Mrozek returned to a strong welcome of his plays, as did Janusz Glowacki, whose *The Fourth Sister* (referring ironically to Chekhov's play) was a mixture of the grotesque and the realistic in a tale about sisters in today's Moscow who long to escape that world. The work of Witold Gombrowicz (1904–1969) also gained renewed popularity after his novel *Ferdydurke* was adapted for the stage and presented in Lublin in 1998. This play, in an English translation by Allen Kuharski, has been performed in several American cities since 2000.

Perhaps the major event was the death of Jerzy Grotowski in 1999. He had labeled the final phase of his work, which was concerned with the transformation of the individual, "art as vehicle." These explorations took place primarily at the Fondazione Pontadera Teatro in Italy, supported by the Italian government and administered by Thomas Richards. Disciples came there in an attempt to understand Grotowski's concept of "Action"—how an actor creates precise movements with the body as a way to communicate character, story, and the actor's intentions. Beginning in 1996 a separate research center called the Workcenter of Jerzy Grotowski and Thomas Richards was opened to participants from around the world. The work done there was based in part on Stanislavsky's theories of physical actions. Grotowski's work at Pontedera continues under the guidance of Richards.

In Czechoslovakia in 1989 the overwhelming desire for democratic reform brought an end to the Communist regime. Vaclav Havel, only recently released from prison, became the country's president, and censorship was discontinued. Unfortunately, depressed economic conditions led to a severe reduction in subsidies for theatres, while attendance declined. Many theatres had to reduce personnel by 30 to 40 percent.

Under the new government, theatres rushed to produce Havel's plays, as well as those of other dissident writers. Many of the small theatres that had been so active prior to 1968 were reestablished, and their former directors, such as Otomar Krejca and Jan Grossman, were returned to their posts. A sense of political inequity among the regions of the nation soon led to the division of Czechoslavkia into two new states, the Czech Republic (with Havel as president) and Slovakia.

In 1992 the Alfred Radok Awards were established in the Czech Republic to honor the outstanding Czech production of each calendar year. During the first decade of the awards, three directors stood out: Hana Buresova, Jan Antonin Pitinsky, and Petr Lebl. Hana Buresova (1959–) worked in various theatres before joining the Labyrint in 1992. She first won the Radok Award for her production of Grabbe's *Don Juan and Faust,* a play usually considered unstageable. It remained in the repertory for several years. She also staged an adaptation of *The Barber of Seville,* using *commedia* elements and frank theatricality. She went on to direct *Murder in the Cathedral* and several Czech plays. J. A. Pitinsky (1956–) won consecutive Radok awards in 1995 and 1996 and a third in 2000. He is probably best known for an adaptation of Thomas Mann's *The Magic Mountain* in 1997.

Petr Lebl (1965–1999) became head of the Theatre on the Balustrade upon Jan Grossman's death in 1993. He established his reputation with a radical adaptation of Genet's *The Maids* in 1993 and a controversial production of Chekhov's *The Seagull* in 1994. He followed these with *The Inspector General* (1995), *Cabaret* (1995), and Chekhov's *Ivanov* (1997) and *Uncle Vanya* (1999); during the run of the last of these he committed suicide. His death puzzled and saddened many, for he was considered by most critics to be the best Czech director of his time.

The Alfred Radok Awards also include an annual prize for the best new unproduced script. A New Wave Festival in 2000 featured new Czech work, and the Theatre on the Balustrade initiated monthly readings of new, unproduced Czech plays. Foreign plays dominated the Czech stage in the 1990s because, some have speculated, the loss of strong political opposition provided no focus for dissent. For whatever reason, native playwriting did not flourish. Havel largely gave up playwriting, and no one took his place. Among contemporary playwrights, Arnost Goldflam and Jan Kraus are perhaps the best known.

The Prague Quadrenniel, at which designers, technicians, and theatre architects from around the world exhibit their work and discuss issues that affect their profession, continues to be the preeminent gathering in its field. It also acknowledges the strong role that Czech designers and technicians have played (and continue to play) both nationally and internationally.

THEATRE IN GERMANY

The destruction of the Berlin Wall and the reunification of East and West Germany brought new opportunities, but also posed new challenges because the financial cost of reunification was so great. East and West Berlin, for example, had duplicate arts institutions, and how to maintain, merge, or abandon some has remained a major problem. In 1999 Berlin was subsidizing 100 cultural institutions despite serious doubt that all were needed. In Germany, there is little federal subsidy of the arts. Rather, each of Germany's sixteen states establishes its own arts budget, which is supplemented by municipal budgets. Though after 1989 subsidies decreased and left some theatres stranded, Germany's support for the arts was still among the highest in the world, about $1.9 billion per year, although governments were hardpressed to continue their past commitments. In 2001 Germany had some 150 publicly owned theatres (plus about 280 private theatres).

Some well-established theatres underwent major changes. Despite strong objections, Berlin's Schiller Theater was closed, and in 1993 the Berliner Ensemble was privatized, although it continued to receive $16 million in subsidies. A five-person management—composed of Peter Palitzsch, Peter Zadek, Matthias Langhoff, Fritz Marquardt, and Heinar Müller—was installed. Brecht's heirs, having been removed from positions of power, for a time denied the theatre permission to present any of Brecht's plays. The managerial arrangement soon collapsed. By 1994 only Müller was left and after he died in 1995 the theatre was adrift for a time. Celebrations in 1998 of the centennial of Brecht's birth revived much of his former prestige, and the Berliner Ensemble's reputation recovered considerably after 1999 when Claus Peymann, who since 1986 had headed Vienna's Burgtheater (considered by many the best German-language theatre), assumed direction of the company.

Within Germany, the Schaubühne in Berlin, founded in 1970 by Peter Stein and a group of actors, was considered to be Berlin's most important company. When Stein left the company in 1985, he was succeeded by Luc Bondy, then Jurgen Grosch from 1988 to 1992 and Andrea Breth from 1992 to 1998. Problems within the company led to its dissolution in 1999. It was reconstituted in 2000 by Thomas Ostermeier and Jens Hilje, who invited Sasha Waltz, head of one of the most respected Tanztheaters in Germany, to join them as a full partner. They are struggling to revive the reputation of the theatre.

After leaving the Schaubühne, Stein directed in Italy and France, and from 1992 to 1997 was supervisor of dramatic performances at the Salzburg Festival, one of the richest and most prestigious in Europe. Its director from 1989 to 2001, Gerard Mortier (1943–), however, did not like Stein's monumental stagings and replaced him with Frank Baumbauer, artistic director of the Deutsches Schauspielhaus in Hamburg. During Mortier's tenure as head of the Salzburg Festival, many of the world's most famous directors—Robert Wilson, Patrice Chereau, Luc Bondy, Christoph Marthaler, Robert Lepage, and Peter Sellars—staged productions there. Peter Ruzicka became director of the festival in 2002. Mortier ran the Ruhr Triennale festival (2002–2004), using fourteen remodeled spaces in abandoned factories before taking over as artistic director of the Paris National Opera.

Other important festivals include the Berlin Theatertreffen, which each year hosts the ten best German-language productions of that season; the Bonn Biennale, inaugurated in 1992 with a focus on new plays from throughout Europe; and the Vienna Festival, which since World War II has hosted not only German-language productions, but also others from Eastern Europe, Russia, and elsewhere. The Bayreuth Festival continued to be one of the best known in the world, but for several years has been bogged down in controversy over who will succeed Wolfgang Wagner (1919–) as director.

Stein directed the two parts of Goethe's *Faust* after leaving Salzburg. The finished work, produced in 2000, took fifteen hours to perform. This was the first time the play had ever been presented in its

FIG. 25.3

Peter Stein's fifteen-hour production of the full text of Goethe's *Faust,* Hannover, Germany. Photo courtesy of Ruth Walz Fotografin © 2000.

entirety (with no cuts and faithfully following the script and its stage directions). While the production was admired by many, Stein was denounced by others for betraying the "director's theatre" he had helped to establish at the beginning of his career.

Germany has a number of well-known and admired directors. In the early 1990s, Thomas Langhoff at the Deutsches Theater in Berlin and Dieter Dorn at the Kammerspiele in Munich staged productions that rivaled those at the Burgtheater in Vienna. Frank Baumbauer (1946–), after serving as director of the Bavarian State Theater in Munich and the Basel (Switzerland) Schauspielhaüs, became director of the Schauspielhaüs in Hamburg in 1993. This theatre was named Germany's best three times by critics before Baumbauer left to become head of the theatre section of the Salzburg Festival.

Frank Castorf (1952–), as director of the Berlin Volksbühne after 1992, became known for his irreverent treatment of texts and his unusual casting. Often called a "text destroyer" because of his anarchic, antirealistic, and grotesque mountings of scripts, he was especially popular with young audiences. Christoph Marthaler (1952–) also valued production over text, although he is best known for composing his own theatre pieces. He became head of Schauspiel Zurich in 2000. Einar Schleef (1945–), known for his antiliterary, antirealist productions, was especially interested in choral performances, as seen in his production of Elfriede Jelinek's *Sports Play* at the Burgtheater in 1998. Other important directors include Leander Haussmann, Matthias Hartmann, and Klaus Bachler.

FIG. 25.4

Christoph Marthaler's 2000 revival of *The Beautiful Prospect* (1926) by the influential Hungarian playwright Ödön von Horváth (1901–1938), at the Schauspielhaus, Zürich. Photo courtesy of Ruth Walz Fotografin ©.

Perhaps the best known of contemporary German-language playwrights is Elfriede Jelinek (1947–). Her *Illness, or Modern Women* (1987) contrasts the blood men have spilled in battle with the blood women shed as part of their nature. Many of her plays have been very controversial. *The Farewell* (2000) was an attack on Jorg Haider, the right-wing leader of Austria, mixed with passages from the *Oresteia*. It used thirteen identically dressed actors who served as a chorus, much as in her 1998 *Sports Play*. Other of her plays include *Service Area, or Cosi fan Tutte* (1994), *Stechen, Stab und Stangl* (1997), and *Him Nothing but Him* (sometimes called *He Not as Himself,* 1998). In 2004, Jelinek won the Nobel Prize for Literature. Other recent playwrights include Theresia Walser (1968–) with *King Kong's Daughters* (1999), David

FIG. 25.5

Elfriede Jelinek's play *Him Nothing but Him* (1998). Photo courtesy of Ruth Walz Fotografin ©.

Gieselmann with *Herr Kolpert* (2001), Marius von Mayenburg (1973–), and Moritz Rinke (1967–).

THEATRE IN ITALY

Giorgio Strehler continued to play a major role in Italy. In 1989 he relinquished the directorship of the Théâtre de l'Europe in Paris to Lluís Pasqual (1951–), head of Madrid's Teatro Maria Guerrero, and returned to the Teatro Piccolo in Milan, where he was involved in a project based on Goethe's *Faust* (in collaboration with Josef Svoboda). Called *Faust Fragments,* the first part opened in 1989 and was followed by three more parts, each three hours long. Strehler himself played the role of Faust in what he called "contaminations," with some scenes fully staged and others read by actors standing behind lecterns. In 1992–1993 Strehler turned his attention to productions honoring the two-hundredth anniversary of Goldoni's death, as did almost all of Italy's professional companies, and in 1995 he staged a much-praised production of Pirandello's *Mountain Giants.* Strehler was also successful in getting new facilities for his company. The Teatro Studio, seating 423, was opened in 1986. A large theatre (begun in 1979) was finally completed in the 1990s after an expenditure of $66 million. By the time he died in 1997, Strehler had directed more than 250 productions.

Following Strehler's death, Luca Ronconi (1933–) was appointed director of the Piccolo Teatro. Ronconi had been highly praised for his adaptation of Ibsen's *Peer Gynt* under the title *Toward Peer Gynt* and for O'Neill's *Mourning Becomes Electra,* both staged at the Teatro di Roma, which Ronconi had made second only to Strehler's company since joining it in 1994. He was noted for both the artistic impact and the gigantic cost of his productions. Upon taking his post at the Piccolo Teatro, he staged Hugo's *Ruy Blas* in 1997 and an adaptation of *The Brothers Karamazov* done in three parts, each four hours long.

Mario Martone (1959–), a Neapolitan director, succeeded Ronconi at the Teatro di Roma. There he oversaw the conversion of a former industrial complex into a theatre center, the first phase of which opened in 1999. One of its most striking offerings was a monumental production of Wagner's *Parsifal,* which used several different spaces in the complex simultaneously.

In 1998 Italy's cultural minister, Walter Veltroni, persuaded Parliament to enact the first national legislation concerning theatre in Italy. It recognized spoken drama as a fundamental aspect of national culture and acknowledged the state's responsibility for sustaining and promoting it. Much of that responsibility was assigned to regional and local authorities, but it recognized two theatres—the Piccolo Teatro in Milan and the Teatro di Roma—as national theatres. According to the legislation, each region will be expected to maintain at least one central theatre, which must produce at least four productions each year and host touring groups.

Dario Fo continued to be recognized as Italy's major playwright and director, especially after he was awarded the Nobel Prize for Literature in 1997. His recent plays include *Johan Padan and the Discovery of the Americas* (1995), *Sex? Thanks, Just for the Hell of It* (1995), *The Devil with Boobs* (1997), and *Coppia Aperta, quasi Spalancate* (2001), a satire on marriage. Fo, in his more than seventy plays, has continued to be primarily concerned with the corruption of power and the inept bureaucracy of state and church. In 2001, to celebrate the fiftieth anniversary of the writing and performing career of Fo and his wife, Franca Rame, the Italian Cultural Institute in New York sponsored a Fo festival which divided its performances among several northeastern cities in the United States.

THEATRE IN FRANCE

Festivals flourished in France, especially after 1990. Among the more than fifty, the one held in Avignon, under the direction of Bernard Faivre d'Arcier since 1992, has continued to be the most prestigious. In 2001 it mounted its fifty-fifth season, presenting more than fifty works in some thirty spaces over a one-month period. Long considered a major showcase of French culture, the festival began to feature theatre from other cultures beginning in 1994. Japan was the first to be welcomed, followed by Russia, Taiwan, Korea, Latin America, and Eastern Europe, although French-language companies remained the primary focus. Fringe performances at the Avignon Festival Off, administered by Alain Leonard, have grown steadily, since no would-be participants are turned away. Typically, it now attracts more than 550 productions each year.

The Festival d'Automne in Paris has grown considerably both in size and reputation since 1990. Begun in 1972, it originally lasted four weeks. Now it begins in late September and continues for three months. This festival seeks to present the best contemporary creations from beyond France and often commissions productions. It has been especially interested in American artists, inviting Robert Wilson, Richard Foreman, Laurie Anderson, Merce Cunningham, the Wooster Group, and many others to participate. It was the co-sponsor, with New York's Lincoln Center, of the production of *The Peony Pavilion,* which created international outrage when cultural authorities in Shanghai sought to forbid its performance in the West. Although the festival has a small budget, it has been very successful in persuading other Parisian arts groups to stage or sponsor experimental works.

France has about 400 theatres that receive some subsidy from the government. There are 5 national theatres, 43 dramatic centers (10 of them regional), and 63 theatres classified as National Stages, all subsidized by the Ministry of Culture. Taken all together, these theatres serve every region in France. In the mid-1990s, government officials pledged to devote 1 percent (about $3 billion) of the national budget to cultural projects. Though that goal has yet to be realized, France does allocate about $500 million to theatre annually,

The Comédie Française remained the primary national theatre. When Antoine Vitez, its administrator, died in 1990, he was succeeded by Jacques Lasalle (1937–), who employed a number of foreign directors and increased the number of recent plays in the repertory. Accused of having subverted the company's role of preserving French culture, Lasalle was replaced in 1993 by Jean-Pierre Miquel (1940–), who returned to a more conservative approach. In 1998 the Comédie Française, for the first time in its existence, staged a play by a living foreign dramatist— Tom Stoppard's *Arcadia.* In 2001 Miquel was succeeded by Marcel Bozonnet, former director of the Conservatoire National Superieur d'Art Dramartique, France's most prestigious theatre training school. The Comédie Française also manages the much smaller Théâtre du Vieux Colombier (once Jacques Copeau's theatre). By 2000 the two houses were presenting more than twenty productions each year.

The company with the greatest international reputation continued to be the Théâtre du Soleil, headed by Ariane Mnouchkine. Her first major production in the 1990s was *Les Atrides,* composed of Euripides' *Iphigenia at Aulis* and Aeschylus' trilogy *The Oresteia.* It was mounted over a period of two years (1990–1992) and was performed in France, Italy, Germany, England, Canada, and the United States. Drawing on Asian forms, most clearly Kathakali, its integration of dance, music, spectacle, and gripping drama was a major achievement. In 1994 the company staged Hélène Cixous' *The Forsworn City, or the Awakening of the Furies,* concerning the French government's allowing the use of blood it knew to be contaminated with HIV. Mnouchkine's 1995 production of Molière's *Tartuffe* was given an Algerian flavor with overtones of the restrictions demanded by Muslim fundamentalists. *Drums on the Dike* (1999), written by Cixous, concerns characters in an unspecified Asian country who live under the threat of a flood that will destroy half of the kingdom. Which half is to be spared—the district of artists or the district of factories? Mnouchkine's actors were given travel grants to observe theatre in Vietnam, Taiwan, Japan, and Indonesia. In the production, some scenes used conventions borrowed from Vietnamese water puppets, but for the most part actors played puppets based on Japanese Bunraku and were manipulated by other actors playing their handlers. In the final scene, the flood annihilates all life. Then the puppet master wades through the water, retrieves small, inanimate puppets, and lines them up to dry on the edge of the stage. This highly praised production, after its debut in France, was seen in Canada, Australia, and Korea, and was scheduled to be seen elsewhere.

Next to Mnouchkine, Oliver Py (1966–) is perhaps France's most admired director. After starting his own theatre at the age of nineteen with a government grant, he first came to prominence in 1995 with *La Servante,* made up of five pieces dealing with spreading an angel's message, staged continuously over twenty-four hours. As the play ended, its epilogue dovetailed into the play's prologue, ready to start all over again. His *Face of Orpheus* (1997) was four hours long, during which a young masked man is dismembered alive and the pieces of his body auctioned. At the end, when the mask is removed, the auctioneer discovers that the young man is his son. In 1998 Py was named director of the Centre Dramatique National in Orleans. He wrote and directed *Requiem for Srebrnica,* in 1999, a series of journalistic pieces about the war in Bosnia. Other important French directors include Daniel Mesguich, Stephane Braunschweig, Stanislas Nordey, Georges Lavaudant, Jerome Savary, and Jorge Lavelli.

Few recent French playwrights have won wide recognition. Yasmin Reza (1959–) is probably the best known, and she was at first only grudgingly admired in France because she wrote for the Boulevard theatres. She drew wide attention, however, when *Art* (1994) was produced in more than thirty countries and won major awards in London and New York. This was followed by productions of *The Unexpected Man* (1995), later translated and produced in England by the Royal Shakespeare Company; *Conversations after a Burial* (written in 1987 but best known through a revival by the Almeida Theatre in London); and *Life × 3* (2000), which was premiered almost simultaneously in Paris, Vienna, Athens, and London. All of her plays use small casts and take place in very restricted spaces. The gradual and subtle unveiling of unacknowledged feelings that characterizes her plays has won her a wide and enthusiastic audience.

THEATRE IN BRITAIN

Several theatres in England were beneficiaries of the National Lottery Fund, a percentage of whose receipts was allotted to the Arts Council of England beginning in 1995. One beneficiary, the Royal Court Theatre, after a $43 million renovation, reopened in 2000 with a season that included sixteen world premieres. Since 1992 the Royal Court has enlarged its influence by working with theatres in several countries in programs designed to encourage new playwrights. These cooperative endeavors have extended to France, Germany, Israel, Palestine, Romania, Bulgaria, Russia, Spain, Uganda, and the United States. The programs include residencies by playwrights, a new-writers festival, partnerships with specific theatres, and co-productions of single newly commissioned plays.

Another beneficiary of lottery funding is Shakespeare's Globe Theatre—a reconstruction of the first Globe Playhouse of 1599—created by American actor-director Sam Wanamaker (1919–1993). The Globe received $18.5 million from the lottery fund in 1995 and was able to open for its first season in 1997. The theatre is an open-air structure with three levels of galleries seating 1000 people, surrounding a yard where 600 to 700 people stand around a large platform stage. It has no facilities for modern stage lighting or scenery. Under the artistic direction of actor–manager Mark Rylance (1960–), the company mixed "original practices" productions (in which they explore the production methods of the period in which the play was written), with modern and postmodern stagings of plays by Shakespeare, his contemporaries, and modern authors commissioned to write for the Globe. It has also hosted Shakespearean productions from Brazil, Cuba, India, Japan, and South Africa. The theatre has attracted a large following with consistently high rates of tickets sales. Several of its productions have earned considerable critical acclaim, including the all-male, original practices productions of *Twelfth Night* (2002) and *Measure for Measure* (2005), both of which toured the United States, its postmodern *The Golden Ass* (2002), and its all-female *Taming of the Shrew* (2003). Dominic Dromgoole (1964–) who had worked with Peter Hall at the Old Vic and built his reputation as the director of the Oxford Stage Company, replaced Rylance as artistic director in 2006.

Covent Garden also benefited from the National Lottery. It reopened in 1999 after a $360 million redevelopment. The only part of the 1858 structure that was not torn down and rebuilt was the auditorium. The building now includes a new studio theatre, additional rehearsal and dressing rooms, and expanded backstage facilities. In 2001 Tony Hall became director of the company, succeeding Michael Kaiser, who returned to the United States to head the Kennedy Center. In 1999 the Sadler's Wells Theatre also reopened after extensive renovation partially funded by the lottery.

Concern about the decline of regional theatres in Britain led the Arts Council to commission a report covering fifty theatres. "Roles and Functions of the English Regional Producing Theatres," completed in 2000, concluded that all of the theatres were underfunded, with the result that they were concentrating on "safe" plays and avoiding innovation. It concluded that not only was more funding needed, but also more risk-taking.

A few companies within London achieved enviable reputations and were often considered models for other independent companies. The Almeida Theatre, under the joint direction of Jonathan Kent and Ian McDiarmid beginning in 1990, mounted an average of five plays a year to high critical praise. Among their most successful productions were Racine's *Britannicus* and *Phaedra* (1998) with Diana Rigg and Toby Stephens; *Medea,* for which Rigg won a Tony; *Hamlet,* for which Ralph Fiennes won a Tony; *Richard II* and *Coriolanus* (2000) with Fiennes playing the title role in each; and an adaptation of Frank Wedekind's Lulu plays (2001). Many of the Almeida's productions also played in the United States. Michael Attenborough succeeded Kent and McDairmid as artistic director in 2002 and the Almeida was able to return to its refurbished theatre in 2003. It has continued to be one of England's most award-winning companies.

The Théâtre de Complicité was founded in 1983 as a collective, but Simon McBurney has dominated this experimental physical theatre company, which combines movement, design, and text to create a multilayered expressiveness. Among its highly praised productions, some of the best were *Street of Crocodiles* (1992), a depiction of provincial Polish life in the early twentieth century; *The Three Lives of Luci Cabrol* (1994); Ionesco's *The Chairs* (1997); *Mnemonic* (1999), which intermingles a story about the discovery of a 5000-year-old body on a glacier in the Alps with another about a couple in the twenty-first century; and *The Noise of Time* (2000), a contemplation of Shostakovich which involved the Emerson String Quartet, four actors, and multimedia.

Cheek by Jowl was founded by Declan Donellan (1953–) and Nick Ormerod (1951–) in 1981. Among its many highly praised productions were *Measure for Measure* (1994) and *As You Like It* (1995), with an all-male cast, including Adrian Lester, who won special acclaim as Rosalind. Donellan and Ormerod have also staged a number of plays for the National Theatre and other companies. They sought to make theatre accessible through performances of classic plays using the simplest of means. Beginning in 1985, their productions were nominated for major awards each year. As a permanent company, Cheek by Jowl was abandoned in 1998, although Donellan and Ormerod have continued to work together

FIG. 25.6
The Almeida Theatre production of *Celebration* (2000), by Harold Pinter. Photo of the New York tour by Stephanie Berger © 2001.

FIG. 25.7

Théâtre de Complicité 1998 revival of *Street of Crocodiles: A Dance of the Mind* (1992), based on the autobiographical works of Bruno Schulz (1892–1942), the influential Polish-Jewish writer slain by a Gestapo officer. Photo of the New York tour by Stephanie Berger © 1998.

on such productions as Tony Kushner's *Homebody/Kabul* (2001).

England's two major companies continued to be the Royal National Theatre and the Royal Shakespeare Company. In 1988 leadership of the National Theatre (Royal was added to its title in 1988 to mark its twenty-fifth anniversary) passed to Richard Eyre (1943–), who had worked both in the fringe and regional theatres before coming to the National in 1981. As director of the company, Eyre sought to keep it vital by making room for more experimental productions and by bringing in young directors, among them Deborah Warner, Sam Mendes, Katie Mitchell, Phyllida Lloyd, and Stephen Daldry, all among England's most successful directors during the 1990s. In 1997, like the Royal Court, the National underwent extensive renovations, financed by proceeds from the National Lottery. In 1997 Eyre was succeeded by Trevor Nunn. In seeking to convince the public that the company was national in more than name, Nunn imported some regional theatre productions and toured some of its own to other English cities and in spite of continual criticism was able to increase the size, if not the diversity of the audiences. In 2003 Nicholas Hytner (1956–) took over. He has combined an adventurous and highly successful repertory intended to appeal to a diverse audience with a system of low-priced tickets provided by corporate sponsors to significantly expand the audience base of the National.

Adrian Noble (1951–), long one of the Royal Shakespeare Company's major directors, became its head in 1990. In 1997 he significantly shortened the RCS's seasons at the Barbican Theatre in London to allow the company to tour England during the summer months. (The Barbican has replaced the RSC summer season with the Barbican International Theatre Event or BITE.) In 2001 Noble announced that the RSC would cease to play at the Barbican at the end of the 2001–2002 season and that the company would undertake its first major restructuring in forty years. Instead of hiring actors on long-term contracts which often required them to split their time between Stratford-on-Avon and London, he proposed to use short-term contracts; create several small companies that would premiere plays in different cities throughout the year; and expand the company's work abroad. The RSC also expects to renovate its headquarters in Stratford-on-Avon including tearing down its Festival Theatre (1932) and replacing it with a new one. (The Arts Council has authorized $71 million in matching funds for this undertaking.) During the 2000–2001 season the RSC presented, in chronological order, eight of Shakespeare's history plays about England in the fifteenth century. Noble's proposal to tear down the old Festival Theatre met with considerable opposition, and in 2003 he stepped down as artistic director and was replaced by associate director, Michael Boyed (1955–). Boyed has proposed to preserve the shell of the Festival Theatre and to renovate the interior into a polygonal structure with galleries. For the 2006 season the RSC invited companies from around the world to join in staging the entire Shakespeare cannon.

After he resigned as director of the National Theatre in 1988, Peter Hall founded his own company designed to bridge the gap between the British and American theatres and to move productions between London and New York. His first two offerings—Tennessee Williams' *Orpheus Descending* with Vanessa Redgrave, and Shakespeare's *The Merchant of Venice* with Dustin Hoffman—played in both cities, but the exchange then stopped. In 1997 Hall's company settled into the Old Vic, where it performed a repertory of classic plays that included *Waiting for Godot, The Seagull, The Provok'd Wife, King Lear,* and others. When the Old Vic was put on the market in 1998, Hall's company moved to a series of theatres in the West End. In 2000 Hall returned to directing in both London and New York, and in 2001 he rejoined the RSC for a specially developed production of *Tantalus* at the Denver Arts Center. In 2004 Hall also became artistic director of the unfinished Rose of Kingston Theatre just outside London, a theatre

FIG. 25.8
Shakespeare's Globe Theatre 1998 production of
Merchant of Venice, with Mark Rylance as Bassanio and
Norbert Kentrup as Shylock. Courtesy of Shakespeare's
Globe, London. Photo by John Tramper © 1998.

modeled after the sixteenth-century theatre which
stood across the road form Shakespeare's Globe.

For a time after Hall's company left it, the future
of the historic Old Vic Theatre seemed in jeopardy.
But in 1998 it was sold to the Old Vic Theatre Trust
2000, which has booked a series of successful transfer productions into the building. They have also
mounted a number of London premiers including
Matthew Bourne's *Car Man* (2000) which combined
the music of the opera *Carmen* with a story adapted
from *The Postman Always Rings Twice*. Bourne first
achieved popular acclaim with his all-male *Swan Lake*
(1998), noted for breaking down the boundaries between dance and theatre. The Oscar-winning American actor Kevin Spacey (1959–) was appointed
actor-manager of the Old Vic in 2004 and launched
a series of well-received productions, including
Richard II (2005), in which he played the title role.

Peter Brook continued his work with the International Center for Theatre Research in Paris. In
1992, on the hundredth anniversary of Maeterlinck's
Pelléas and Mélisande, Brook presented a reworking
of Debussy's operatic setting of the play, *Impressions
of Pelléas,* in which the action, a combination of myth
and hothouse passion, swirled around two grand pi-
anos in a stripped-down nineteenth-century drawing room. Later works included *The Man Who* (1994)
based on Oliver Sachs's case studies of the deranged,
and *Who's There?* (1995), a work which looks at how

a play is transformed into a performance by viewing
rehearsals of *Hamlet* through the eyes of some of the
most important theatrical visionaries of the twentieth century: Stanislavsky, Meyerhold, Craig, Brecht,
and Artaud. His own adaptation of *Hamlet, The
Tragedy of Hamlet* starring Adrian Lester, opened in
Paris in 1999, and then toured several European and
Asian countries as well as several cities in the United
States in 2001. In 2005 he directed *Tierno Bokar,*
based on the life of a West African Sufi of the 1930s,
and a touring production of *The Grand Inquisitor*
adapted from Dostoyevsky.

Several of England's established playwrights continued to be active after 1990. Harold Pinter, in addition to writing new plays such as *Moonlight* (1993),
Ashes to Ashes (1996), and *Celebration* (2000), was
honored with a festival devoted to his works in New
York in 2001 and was awarded the Nobel Prize for
Literature in 2005. Tom Stoppard continued to be
praised for such complex plays as *Arcadia* (1993)
which envisions the story around an obscure event
in the life of Lord Byron; *The Invention of Love*
(1997), dealing with the great classical scholar A. E.
Houseman; the three-part *The Coast of Utopia* (2002)
about a group of expatriate Russians caught up in
the European Revolution of the mid-nineteenth
century; and *Rock 'n' Roll* (2006) which looks at
Czechoslovakia's "Velvet Revolution."

Caryl Churchill's *The Skriker* (1994) intermingles
the natural and supernatural as a "shape changer" leads
other characters into the dark world of the unconscious. Her *Blue Heart* (1997) is made up of two short
plays, "Heart's Desire" and "Blue Kettle"; in the second of which, the use of conventional language is
gradually lost until only the words *blue* and *kettle* are
left. *Far Away* (2000) is an end-of-the-world vision
in which human response to suffering is deadened.
Churchill usually works with Max Stafford-Clark, director of Out of Joint, a company he founded in 1993
after the Joint Stock Company was abandoned. David
Hare remained prolific with *Skylight* (1995), *Amy's
View* (1997), *Via Dolorosa* (1998), and *My New Zinc
Bed* (2000). In 2005 he wrote *Stuff Happens,* one of
the most political of the plays concerning the invasion of Iraq by the United States in the aftermath of
the 9/11 attacks. Michael Frayn won critical praise
and major awards with *Copenhagen* (1998), about
Werner Heisenberg's (father of Germany's nuclear
program) visit to Niels Bohr (a Danish physicist who
had been Heisenberg's mentor) during the Second
World War. This was followed by a popular comedy,
Alarms and Excursions (1999), about characters who
become victims of their electronic devices, and a return to serious drama with *Democracy* (2003) concerning a German political scandal of the 1970s.

FIG. 25.9

Copenhagen (1998), by Michael Frayn. Photo of the New York production by Joan Marcus © 1999.

Alan Ayckbourn continued his success with plays that cleverly manipulate time, space, and misunderstandings. *Communicating Doors* (1994) moves from 1978 to 1998 to 2018 in an effort to alter history; *Comic Potential* (1998) has as its focus a robotic actor; and *The Things We Do for Love* (1999) suggests that despite desperate efforts, few people find the love they hope for. *House* and *Garden* (1999) are two plays written to be staged simultaneously on two separate stages using the same actors. He has continued these explorations with such plays as *Virtual Reality* (2000), a trilogy of plays called *Damsels in Distress* (2001), and *Private Fears in Public Places* and *Improbable Fiction* (2005).

Among England's young playwrights, Sarah Kane (1971–1999) attracted the most attention, perhaps because she committed suicide just as she was being critically recognized. Her first important play was *Blasted* (1995), which in the beginning shows an abusive sexual relationship between a middle-aged journalist and a young female family friend, but widens out to include various atrocities. Eventually the man is raped; his eyes are sucked out; and he tries to eat a dead baby. Many audience members were outraged. *Phaedra's Love* (1996) is based on Seneca's version of Phaedra and Hippolytus. *Crave* (1998) is made up of poetic exchanges without stage directions among four characters who are identified only by letters of the alphabet. *4.48 Psychosis* (staged in 2000) refers to 4:48 A.M., the darkest hour, and concerns suicidal despair.

In 1999 *The Color of Justice* by Richard Norton-Taylor became one of England's most popular plays. Composed primarily of excerpts from a hearing into an apparent racially motivated murder that was largely ignored by the police, it was performed originally in the fringe Tricycle Theatre, but response to the play led to its transfer to a large West End theatre.

Other recent playwrights include Patrick Marber with *Closer* (1997); Mark Ravenhill with *Shopping and Fucking* (1996), *Some Explicit Polaroids* (1998), and *Mother Clap's Molly House* (2001), about male prostitution in the eighteenth century and the present; David Grieg, whose *Victoria* concerns three women who try to escape economic bonds in 1936, 1974, and 1996; and Joe Penhall with *Blue/Orange,* about race and class in a power struggle between two psychiatrists and a black patient.

Although the English musical seemed to lose its strong appeal, Andrew Lloyd Webber was able to use $145 million of the profits from his earlier works to acquire ten of London's leading theatres and variety halls in 2000. Cameron Mackintosh also secured ownership of seven theatres, and SFX Entertainment, the organization that dominates touring in the United States, bought twenty-three theatres scattered throughout England. Lloyd Webber argued that a dangerous situation is created when theatres are not owned by theatre professionals. Neither he nor Mackintosh gave up producing musicals, but they were unable to duplicate their successes of the past.

Despite the disruption of a terrorist attack on its subway and bus systems in July, London theatres posted one of their best years in 2005 with total attendance of over 12 million people and total sales of over 375 million British pounds. The surprise of the year was that while attendance at musicals was up 4.9%, according to the Society of London Theatres, the attendance at plays was up 5.1%.

THEATRE IN IRELAND

As Ireland became a major European computer center, its new prosperity encouraged the growth of theatre. The Abbey theatre celebrated its centenary in 2004, amidst a financial crisis that pitted its board against its artistic director, Ben Barne, who resigned the following year. Under managing director Fiach MacConghail, who joined the Abbey in 2005, the large deficit was paid by a grant from the Irish government and the Abbey began preparations for the move to its new location in the Dublin Docklands area. The Gate, Dublin's second most important theatre, devoted so much attention to filming all of Samuel Beckett's plays under the overall supervision of its director, Michael Colgan, that many thought it had entered a state of serious decline; responding to these accusations, the company has made an effort to restore its former reputation. Other important theatres in Ireland include Rough Magic, which staged a festival of international new plays in 2000; and the Druid Theatre in Galway, directed by Garry Hynes, who has won considerable international attention, especially for her productions of Martin McDonagh's plays. (She won the Tony Award for best director for her production of McDonagh's *The Beauty Queen of Leenane* in 1998, making her the first woman to win that award.)

As elsewhere, there are many festivals in Ireland. The Gate used a festival in 1991 to do all of Beckett's plays. There have also been festivals devoted to the works of William Butler Yeats, Brian Freil, John Millington Synge, and Oscar Wilde. The Galway Arts Festival takes place in July, the Limerick festival in January, the Dublin Fringe in September, the Dublin Theatre Festival in October, and the Queens Festival in Belfast in November.

Ireland is known above all for its playwrights. Martin McDonagh (1970–) had his first production in 1996 at the Druid Theatre. His grotesque and ironic stories of life in rural Ireland soon attracted a

FIG. 25.10

Lonesome West (1999) by Martin McDonagh. Photo of the New York tour by Joan Marcus © 1999.

wide audience. They include *The Cripple of Inishman* (presented by the National Theatre in London), *The Beauty Queen of Lenane, A Skull in Connemara,* and the *Lonesome West* (all presented first by the Druid Theatre), and *The Lieutenant of Inishmore* (2001), written for the Royal Shakespeare Company.

Conor McPherson (1971–) is a prolific playwright, many of whose plays are made up of alternating monologues. His dramas include *This Lime Tree Bower* (1996), which shows three men discussing sex and robbery and ending in public nudity; *The Weir,* in which four men and a woman exchange stories in a pub; *The Good Thief* in which an underworld Dublin man roughs up people for a living; and *Dublin Carol,* three short scenes about a man estranged from his family at Christmas.

Other recent playwrights include Mark O'Rowe (1970–) with *Howie the Rookie* (1999), two interrelated monologues about two nights that lead to savage deaths; Sebastian Barry (1955–) with *The Steward of Christendom,* set in a mental home, where the last police chief before Ireland's independence relives and tries to justify his opposition to the Irish rebels; Marie Jones (1951–), whose *Stones in His Pockets* (1999), about the impact of a film company on an Irish village, became an international favorite as two actors portray numerous characters; and Marina Carr (1964–), considered to be Ireland's leading female writer, with *On Rafferty Hill* (2000), in which a young woman is raped on stage by her father.

THEATRE IN CANADA

While the social and political activism of the works of Brazil's Augusto Boal were the inspiration for a great many of Canada's fringe groups of the 1980s, the corporal mime training of the French master, Jacques Lecoq (1921–), as adapted by Richard Pochinko (1946–1989), has inspired a major movement in "physical theatre" in the 1990s. The aim of this movement has been the retheatricalization of theatre and, for many companies, the depoliticizing of it. This movement has been energized by three of Canada's most successful exports of the 1990s: Robert Lepage (1957–), and the Cirque du Soléil (Circus of the Sun).

Lepage has become an international celebrity for highly imagistic works inspired by his early experience with rock concerts that were given a story line in the 1970s and 1980s. Along with his controversial adaptations of Shakespeare, Lepage has received considerable acclaim for productions of *Vinci* (1986), *Polygraph* (1988), *The Seven Streams of the River Ota* (1996), *Zulu Time* (1999), *The Far Side of the Moon*

(2000), and *The Andersen Project* (2006). Through his work Lepage has been increasingly concerned with finding a middle ground between theatre and film. The Cirque du Soléil (founded in 1984) produces circuses without animals in which highly unusual and visually stunning acts are organized around an impressionistic story line. Their work has been seen as a demonstration of the potential of postmodern performance techniques in the theatre. Starting with *Cirque Réinvente* (1987), the group began to tour outside Canada. The company now has four shows in residence at Las Vegas hotels—*Mystére* (1993), *"O"* (1998), *Zumanity* (2003), and *KÁ* (2004)—and is scheduled to add a fifth concerning the 1960s rock group, The Beatles, in 2006. *La Nouba* (1998) is in residence at Disney World while up to four shows tour, including their most recent show, *Varekai*.

Tremblay and Walker have continued to be among Canada's most visible dramatists, but the search for a national cultural identity undertaken by the alternative theatres in the 1970s led to the development of fringe theatres that looked for a cultural identity independent of nationalism in the 1980s. In the 1990s those fringe theatres brought attention to a number of dramatists, many of whom wrote on racial, ethnic, or gender themes, including Ron Chambers, Marty Chan, Brad Fraser, Tomson Highway, M. J. Kang, Stewart Lemoine, Daniel MacIvor, Clem Martini, Rick Miller, Andrew Moodie, and a long list of others.

Canada's two major theatre production companies, Mirvish Productions and Livent, have probably had the greatest impact on Canadian theatre in recent years, however. The father-and-son team of Ed Mirvish (1914–) and David Mirvish (1947–) have produced everything from Royal Shakespeare Company productions to the latest fringe theatre successes. But they are best known for producing already successful mega-musicals from *Les Miserables* and *Miss Saigon* to *The Lion King, Rent,* and *Mamma Mia*. Since buying the Royal Alexandra Theatre (1907) in Toronto in 1962, they have built the spectacular Princess of Wales Theatre (1993), the first privately built theatre in Canada in eight-five years, and acquired the Canon theatre (formerly the Pantages) in 2001. Mirvish Productions continues to be the most active production company in Toronto, producing *The Lord of the Rings* in 2006, the most expensive musical in Canadian history. (Ed Mirvish bought the Old Vic in London in 1982, painstakingly restored it, and ran it successfully until selling it in 1998.) Livent, run by Garth Drabinsky (1948–) from 1992 to 1998, generated a long list of awards and even greater profits from a series of musical revivals and adaptations from *Kiss of the Spider Woman* (1993) to

FIG. 25.11

Jonathan Larson's *Rent* (1996). Photo of the New York tour by Joan Marcus © 1996.

Show Boat (1994), *Barrymore* (1997), *Fosse* (1998), and *Ragtime* (1999). Drabinsky also undertook the renovations of historically important theatres from the Apollo (New York), to the Oriental (Chicago), to the Pantages (Toronto) before he was indicted in the United States for securities fraud in 1999.

The success of these commercial producers has brought significant attention to the Canadian theatre, and Toronto is now said to be the third largest English-language theatre market in the world. But these productions have also taken Canadian theatre back to a focus on a colonial repertory, drained away audiences and resources from the smaller theatres, and caused many political figures to argue that the theatre in Canada is no longer in need of government subsidies.

THEATRE IN THE UNITED STATES

After 1990, one of the most controversial issues involved subsidization of the arts, which since the

1960s had played a major role in the impressive increase in theatres throughout the United States. The National Endowment for the Arts (NEA) has always been the focus of this controversy as the appropriateness of the government's subsidizing any of the arts, especially if standards of decency were not adopted and enforced, has always been questioned. Despite its critics, the NEA had commanded considerable support and had received small annual increases in appropriations through 1992, when federal budgetary support reached its high point of $175.9 million, about 70 cents per capita. Tolerance of the NEA both inside and outside of Congress began to erode in 1990, however, when Four performance artists, Tim Miller, John Fleck, Holly Hughes, and Karen Finley (collectively called the NEA Four), all noted for works that openly and frankly treated sex, gender, and power, were awarded NEA grants in a category reserved for individual artists. An intense and ongoing controversy followed over whether the government should be allowed to spend citizens' tax dollars to subsidize art considered by many to be indecent and counter to community standards. A law designed to ensure that grants would not be approved if they did not take into account "general standards of decency and respect for the diverse beliefs and values of the American public" was quickly passed by Congress and though it was challenged in court, it was eventually upheld by the Supreme Court in 1998. The Court left unsettled the issue of who was to define "general standards of decency" or decide when these standards had been violated. The grants to the four artists were retracted, and the NEA's grants to individuals program was terminated. Congressional controversy over the NEA continued, and its budget was reduced substantially, reaching only about $98 million in 2000. Although many expect that the NEA's budget will increase, the future of the agency and the amount of government support it can expect remain uncertain. Some of the retrenchment was offset by state, municipal, foundation, and corporate financial support, but the combined support remains slight in comparison with that given the arts in many European countries.

Almost 350 not-for-profit theatres in the United States are affiliated with the Theatre Communications Group (TCG). In spite of declining federal support, many of them are more solidly established and in 2000 more were at least breaking even financially than ever before. A significant number have either built new facilities or substantially increased their existing facilities and programs. The League of Chicago Theatres has nearly 150 members. In 1999 the Chicago Shakespeare Theatre, directed by Barbara Gaines, opened its new theatre on Navy Pier, while

Chicago's famed Goodman Theatre, under the direction of Robert Falls, opened a new complex in 2001, both built with substantial assistance from the City of Chicago. Anchored by the Kennedy Center, Arena Stage, and the Shakespeare Theatre, the Washington, D.C.-area now has nearly 100 professional theatre companies. Arena Stage, under the direction of Molly Smith, celebrated its fiftieth year by beginning renovations that will double the size of its building. The Shakespeare Theatre, directed by Michael Kahn, will open its second theatre in 2007. The Olney Theatre, The Round House Theatre, and The Studio Theatre also opened new buildings there since 2000. The Guthrie Theatre in Minneapolis, directed by Joe Dowling, opened a new three-theatre complex in 2006. A complex with four theatres is part of the plan of the restoration of the World Trade Center site in New York. Numerous university campuses across the country have also opened or announced their intention to build multi-million-dollar performing arts centers. While this is just a representative sample of the range of projects being undertaken, they are an indicator of the overall health of the theatre market.

The large number of resident companies scattered throughout the United States offered opportunities for directors to work with many different theatres, most of which employ visiting directors for at least some of their productions. In 2000 the Denver Theatre Center produced *Tantalus*, a ten-and-a-half-hour production based on Greek myths, written by John Barton (of the Royal Shakespeare Company) and directed by Peter Hall. Among the American directors, Daniel Sullivan (1940–) is much in demand. After serving as director of the Seattle Repertory Company for 18 years, he became well known for directing plays that were developed through a series of regional theatre productions before they opened in New York. He directed most of Wendy Wasserstein's plays as well as *Dinner with Friends* by Donald Marguiles (the Pulitzer Prize-winning play of 2000), *Proof* by David Auburn (the Pulitzer Prize-winning play in 2001), and numerous important revivals including O'Neill's *Moon for the Misbegotten* and Shaw's *Major Barbara*.

Robert Wilson continues to be one of America's best-known directors, though most of his work was still done in Europe until recently. After 1990, he averaged eight to twelve premieres throughout the world each year at almost every major festival and opera house in Europe. Many of these productions were of well-known works, such as Büchner's *Danton's Death* (1993), Bela Bartók's *Bluebeard's Castle* (1995), Strindberg's *A Dream Play* at Stockholm's Stadtsteater in 1998, and Brecht's *Flight over the Ocean*

FIG. 25.12

Peter Hall's production of John Barton's ten-hour Trojan War epic *Tantalus* (2001), at the Denver Center of the Performing Arts. Greg Hicks (as Priam, black costume) with the Chorus. Photo by P. Switzer © 2001.

at the Berliner Ensemble in honor of the hundredth anniversary of Brecht's birth, in 1998. Some of his original works after 1990 include *Alice* (1992), an adaptation of *Alice in Wonderland,* with Tom Waits and Paul Schmidt, and *Time Rocker* (1996), a collaboration with Darryl Pinckney and Lou Reed based on H. G. Wells's *Time Machine.* His *White Raven* (2001), developed with composer Philip Glass, and *I La Galigo* (2005), a work inspired by *Sureq Galigo,*

FIG. 25.13

Wendy Wasserstein's *The Sisters Rosenweig.* The actors are Madeline Kahn, Jane Alexander, and Frances McDormand. Photo by Martha Swope © 1993.

the sacred epic poem of the Bugis people of Indonesia, were both performed at Lincoln Center Festivals. Wilson has established a school called the Watermill Center on Long Island, where he now develops many of his productions.

Julie Taymor (1952–) became internationally known with her production of *The Lion King,* for which she became the first woman to win a Tony Award for directing a musical in 1998. Building on an extremely varied background that included studying mime in Paris and living in Indonesia, she brings a wide range of theatre practice from various countries to her work, perhaps most notably the puppetry of Bali. Working with various companies in New York and elsewhere, Taymor won sufficient recognition that the MacArthur Foundation rewarded her with a "genius" award in 1991. In New York she directed several of Shakespeare's plays, including *The Tempest* and *Titus Andronicus* (later made into a film) for the Theatre for a New Audience, and in resident companies she designed costumes and masks for several productions, perhaps most notably for Andrei Serban's *King Stag* at the American Repertory Theatre. She was highly praised for *Juan Darién* (the dramatization of a Uruguayan story) at Lincoln Center, but her major triumph came with the production of *The Lion King* on Broadway (which she directed and for which she designed costumes and masks) for the Disney Corporation. In 2000 she directed and designed *The Green Bird* on Broadway, a production she had worked on elsewhere for many years. Her multiple talents have placed her in the forefront of American theatre artists.

Anne Bogart (1951–) is one of America's most controversial directors. She sometimes surrounds a script with a "play within a play" framework that forces audiences to see the play in a new light, as in *South Pacific,* which she set in a clinic for emotionally disturbed war veterans. For a time, she created plays that examined American entertainment forms, as in *American Vaudeville* (1993) and *Marathon Dancing* (1994). She directed frequently for the American Repertory Theatre and for one season was director of the Trinity Repertory Theatre in Providence, but her approach proved incompatible with that company. In 1993 she co-founded with Tadashi Suzuki, the Japanese director and acting theorist, the Saratoga International Theatre Institute (SITI), where acting workshops and symposia are held, and where Bogart develops productions in collaboration with her students. Whenever she directs at other theatres, she insists that at least some members of her SITI company be employed, since they are familiar with her working methods. She

FIG. 25.14

Ghost Sonata by August Strindberg, directed by Ingmar Bergman (1918–). Since the 1950s Bergman has been one of Sweden's most highly acclaimed stage directors. He was better known in Europe as a filmmaker than a stage director until his tax exile in Germany from 1976 to 1985, when he did a series of notable productions. He is now especially admired as an interpreter of Strindberg's plays. Photo of the New York tour by Stephanie Berger © 2001.

has directed several of Charles L. Mee's and Naomi Iizuka's plays.

Bogart is also noted for her rejection of the Stanislavsky system of actor training in favor of Viewpoints, many of whose features are adapted from postmodern dance and focus on formal elements such as movement and space. Instead of emphasizing one method, Viewpoints seeks to create new theatrical languages by borrowing from a variety of sources. It favors "sampling"—juggling many dramatic techniques and combining them with almost any aspect of contemporary culture. Bogart has argued that since we live in a fragmented world, acting itself needs to be fragmented.

As in other countries, one of the most notable developments in the United States after 1990 was the proliferation of festivals. The bringing together of companies (often from places widely separated geographically and culturally) came to seem in its variety more attractive than long-run, stand-alone productions. Festivals offer opportunities to see in rapid succession and in a concentrated period of time events that, were they to be seen on their home ground, might require extensive and expensive travel. With festivals, productions were brought to the spectator and demanded prompt decisions to attend before the opportunity vanished. Such festivals have had a long tradition as places where theatre artists can share new ideas and where audiences can be exposed to a wide range of approaches to performance. There is a growing concern that the sheer number of festivals, however, might be encouraging a lack of diversity as theatre artists develop a festival style that focuses on visual images.

Festivals became so numerous in the United States after 1990 that only a few can be named. Each summer Lincoln Center hosts a festival of theatre, dance, and music that presents outstanding companies from across the world. Some of its productions have included *The Peony Pavilion* (from China, performed for the first time ever in its entirety), Vietnamese water puppets, the opera *White Raven* by Philip Glass and Robert Wilson (which had been commissioned by the Portuguese government to commemorate its fifteenth-century explorers), a two-week festival devoted to the plays of Harold Pinter, and numerous other events from throughout the world. In 2001 the New York International Fringe Festival (founded in 1997) offered 180 productions in twenty performance spaces utilizing 2000 artists from twelve countries.

FIG. 25.15

Julie Taymor's production of *Green Bird* on Broadway (2000). Photo by Joan Marcus © 2000.

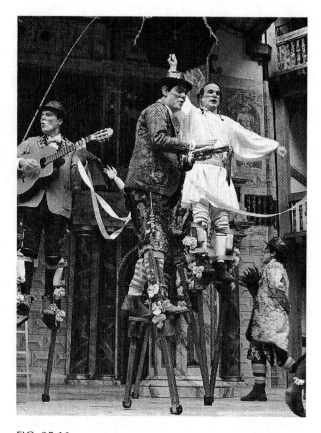

FIG. 25.16

Brazil's Grupo Galpão is one of many that tours to
international festivals each year. This production of
Romeu & Julieta, in a translation by Onestaldo de
Pennafort, has been one of their great successes.
Courtesy of Shakespeare's Globe, London. Photo of the
London tour by Sheila Burnett © 2000.

The Asian Performing Arts Festival held in New
York in 2001 included companies from Indonesia,
Thailand, Vietnam, Japan, and elsewhere. The Hen-
son International Festival of Puppet Theatre (founded
in 1991 and held every two years) attracted twenty-
six companies in its tenth-anniversary year. The International Hispanic Theatre Festival held in New
York in 2001 included productions from Mexico,
Brazil, Bolivia, Ecuador, and elsewhere. The National Black Theatre Festival celebrated its twelfth
anniversary in Winston-Salem in 2001 with more
than 100 performances over six days. In 2000 the
Magic Theatre in San Francisco staged a week-long
Playwrights in Danger Festival featuring plays by authors who have risked their lives to write about
things they believe in; it included plays from Nigeria, Singapore, Egypt, Algeria, and Argentina. By
far the greatest number of festivals (too numerous to
count) are devoted to Shakespeare.

Despite the appeal of festivals, Broadway remained for many the measure of acceptance, even
though by the mid-1990s only about 10 percent
of the productions it offered originated there. The
rest came from London or non-Broadway theatres,
or were revivals. The cost of mounting a production on Broadway increased between 350 and 400
percent between 1967 and 1997. Ticket prices increased at a slower rate, but by 1997 some musicals were charging $75 for tickets, and by 2001 the
price had increased to $100 or more. In the 1990s,
Broadway's thirty-five theatres presented an average of about thirty productions each year (compared to fifty or sixty in the 1970s). Few of these
were of spoken drama. In the late 1980s and 1990s,
Broadway was most hospitable to the English musicals of Andrew Lloyd Webber, and in 1996 *Cats*
became the longest running production in Broadway's history with 7485 performances and earnings
of more than $400 million. The popularity of new
imported musicals seemed to decline during the
1990s, although *Miss Saigon* did not close until
2000 after some 4100 performances. Many of the
musicals that replaced imports were revivals, such
as *Carousel, Cabaret,* and *Kiss Me Kate.* Through the
early 1990s, Stephen Sondheim continued to be
the most popular American composer of musicals,
but his output dropped off considerably thereafter.
Probably the most popular American musical of
the late 1990s was Jonathan Larson's *Rent* (1996),
partly based on Puccini's *La Bohême,* but transposed
and updated to New York's Lower East Side (sadly,
the author died shortly before the show opened).
In the late 1990s, many musicals—among them
Contact, Swing, Fosse, Tap Dogs, Riverdance, and
Stomp—were more nearly dance entertainments
than traditional musicals. After 2000 popular musicals—such as *The Full Monty* (with book by Terrence McNally, music and lyrics by David Yazbek)
and *The Producers* (book, music, and lyrics by Mel
Brooks)—returned to the story-based form, but
they also marked a new trend—adapting popular
movies for the stage. Harold Prince, America's most
successful director of musicals, devoted his energies
to rejuvenating the American musical by helping
writers develop their works at his Prince Music
Theatre in Philadelphia.

The image of Broadway was brightened by the
42d Street Development Project (a city-and state-
sponsored plan approved in 1984), which transformed an area of urban blight into something
resembling the showplace that Broadway had been
early in the twentieth century. Using this plan, several decrepit theatres in the Times Square area were
reclaimed. The Livent Corporation remodeled and

linked two theatres to create the Ford Center for the Performing Arts; the New Victory Theatre (opened in 1995) was devoted to limited runs of productions from throughout the world intended for young audiences. The Selden Theatre was transformed into the American Airlines Theatre and became home to the Roundabout Theatre, the second-largest nonprofit company in America. The Disney Corporation took over the renovated New Amsterdam Theatre (formerly the Ziegfeld Theatre) as home for *The Lion King*. A new ten-story building, the 42nd Street Studios, housing fourteen rehearsal studios, the offices of several nonprofit arts organizations, and a 200-seat theatre, was opened in 1999. The project also included a hotel, restaurants, shops, a wax museum, and movie theatres. As in London, 2005 was a record-breaking year on Broadway both in terms of attendance and overall revenue.

This rejuvenation encouraged similar changes in the neighboring Theatre Row, made up of off-Broadway and off-off-Broadway theatres. The best known of these theatres, Playwrights Horizons, devoted to developing new plays, razed its building in 2001 to make way for a new $24 million, five-story complex. Five other new theatres were also built, one with 199 seats and four with 99 seats; in addition, a 499-seat house, to be used for productions on their way to Broadway. The distinctions between Broadway, off-Broadway, and off-off-Broadway theatres are primarily contractual. According to Actors Equity standards, Broadway theatres have a seating capacity of 500 or more; off-Broadway theatres seat 100 to 499; and off-off-Broadway 99 or fewer. Most of the spoken dramas produced in New York appear in off-Broadway or off-off-Broadway theatres. It is difficult to specify how many there are (there were more than 400 not-for-profit theatres in New York in 2001). Some of the best known of these—including ones that pioneered off-Broadway—went bankrupt in the 1990s. Among these were Circle in the Square (1951–1997), the most important off-Broadway house in the 1950s and the one usually associated with the revival of interest in Eugene O'Neill's plays; the Circle Repertory Theatre (1969–1996), supporter of new plays and playwrights, perhaps most notably Lanford Wilson; and the Ridiculous Theatrical Company (1967–1999), founded by Robert Ludlum, who wrote, directed, and acted in most of the gender-bending productions the theatre was known for.

Other established off-Broadway theatres continued to be leaders. Perhaps the most important of these was the Public Theatre (New York Shakespeare Festival), which was headed for thirty-seven years by Joseph Papp before he turned over the artistic direction to JoAnne Akalaitis (1937–) shortly before his death in 1991. The choice of a director noted primarily for her postmodern productions with the *avant-garde* collective Mabou Mines and a few resident theatres came as a surprise, since it seemed to place the Public Theatre on a path quite different from the one Papp had cultivated. Unfavorable response to her productions led to her replacement in 1993 by George C. Wolfe (1955–), who was much more successful, especially in attracting a youthful and diversified audience. Wolfe's success as head of the company, as a director, and as a playwright made him one of the most influential figures in the New York theatre, but by 2001 the most powerful members of the theatre's board of directors had resigned in protest over Wolfe's financial management. Wolfe stepped down in 2004, turning the Public Theatre over to Oskar Eustis (1958–) the former artistic director of Trinity Repertory in Providence, Rhode Island, where he was best known for developing new plays.

The La MaMa organization also continued to be active, offering a crowded season of plays in New York each year, and since 1990 running the La MaMa Umbria International, a cultural center and artists' residence in Italy. Other important off-Broadway and off-off-Broadway theatres included the Manhattan Theatre Club, under the direction of Lynne Meadow, noted for its productions of new plays; the Drama Department; the Pearl Theatre Company; the Atlantic Theatre Company; Target Margin; Tectonic Theatre Company; the New York Theatre Workshop; and many others.

The *avant-garde* continued to flourish in New York. The Wooster Group, in keeping with its past practice, borrowed portions of well-known plays, reconfigured their structure, and combined them with other materials, as in *Brace Up!* its 1991 reimagining of Chekhov's *Three Sisters*, which made considerable use of video cameras and interaction among live actors and video images; it also borrowed the Stage Manager from *Our Town* who interviewed characters from Chekhov's play. In 1999 the Wooster Group presented *House/Lights* at the Festival d'Automne in Paris; it is working on a piece based on Phaedra and another project drawing on William Faulkner's novel, *As I Lay Dying*. Richard Foreman continued to write and produce plays at his Ontological-Hysteric Theatre. *Zomboid!* (2006), which is billed as a "film/performance project," marked his fifteenth straight production in his own theatre space at St. Mark's Church in New York, which was acquired in 1992. In addition to local *avant-garde* companies, numerous U.S. and foreign troupes were presented each year by the Brooklyn Academy of Music in its Next Wave Festivals, which sought to keep Americans abreast of the best and most provocative recent work being done elsewhere.

In the 1990s *avant-garde* theatre took on new shapes as it melded with other art forms. "Theatre" was used less often than earlier to describe these new works, which instead were more often associated with performance art (or just performance) than with traditional theatre. One of the principal homes of this type of performance was P.S. 122 (an abandoned public school building in the East Village). Originally it merely rented space to various groups, but it later became a producing organization as well. By 2000 it had presented more than 5000 artists and had commissioned a large number of new plays and dance works. By then it was presenting more than 150 productions each year (10 to 20 of which it had commissioned). The emphasis was always on the new and provocative, and productions were aimed primarily at an audience in their mid-twenties to mid-thirties.

In addition to the blending of art forms, dramatic forms themselves underwent considerable change. Monologues and narrative became dominant devices in many plays, and subject matter was often autobiographical or biographical. Many plays were performed by a single actor or a very small cast. Most required little scenery and few props or costumes, but lighting effects (and sometimes multimedia) were occasionally complex. Among their attractions for producers were the limited resources required to mount them. Some of the better known of these works are Anna Deveare Smith's (1951–) *Fires in the Mirror* and *Twilight: Los Angeles* about issues of race and class as revealed in neighborhood riots; John Leguizamo's (1964–) semi-autobiographical sketches of Latino life, *Mambo Mouth, Freak,* and *Sexaholix;* Eve Ensler's *The Vagina Monologues,* and Danny Hoch's *Jails, Hospitals & Hip-Hop* and *Till the Break of Dawn.*

The 1990s saw a rapid expansion of experimentation with computer technologies and the ways in which they can be used to enhance live performance. George Coates' Performance Works in San Francisco was in the forefront of this experimentation with productions such as *Desert Music* (1992), *Nowhere NowHere* (1994), and *Crazy Wisdom* (2001). In all of these, computer-generated images interacted with live actors on stage. The expense of such work has forced Performance Works to limit its experimentation, but several university theatres have continued to work along these lines. Computer controls have long since changed the way lights, sound, and sets are designed in the theatre, but more recent innovations have focused on the ways in which computer sensors and motion detectors can allow actors to interact with set pieces, props, lights, sound, computer-generated images, and real-time animations. Productions have also made use of the Internet to allow actors on different continents to perform in the same play at the same time. In such productions the audience sees live actors interacting with video projections of actors from other locations, all performing their roles as if they were on the same stage. Complete plays have been produced on the World Wide Web using a wide variety of approaches, and the proliferation of Web-cam monitoring of public spaces has inspired a new form of guerilla theatre in which actors produce short plays in view of these cameras after notifying potential audience members to watch for their performance on the relevant World Wide Web site. Just as the introduction of film at the turn of the twentieth century caused artists to undertake a reevaluation of what makes theatre a distinctive art form, computer technology has encouraged a similar reevaluation at the turn of the twenty-first century.

Gaining renown as a playwright became much rarer for Americans after 1990, perhaps because success on Broadway had always been the major indicator of acceptance. David Mamet remains the most recognized contemporary American dramatist, in part because his work in films gained him much prominence. He wrote the controversial play *Oleanna* (1992), *Cryptogram* (1994), and *The Old Neighborhood* (1995) before turning to farce with *Boston Marriage* (1999) and *Romance* (2005). Terrence McNally also continued to achieve and maintain a high level of success with such plays as *Lips Together, Teeth Apart* (1991), *Love! Valor! Compassion!* (1994), and *Master Class* (1995), as well as the books for the musicals *Kiss of the Spider Woman* (1993), *Ragtime* (1998), *The Full Monty* (2000), and *Chita Rivera* (2005). His *Corpus Christi* (1997), a retelling of the life of Christ, was the focus of significant protests wherever it was played.

August Wilson was also internationally regarded as one of America's great playwrights until his death in 2005. His later plays included *Seven Guitars* (1995) and *King Hedlley II* (2000), the latter about the constricted lives of black characters in Pittsburgh during the 1980s. Aside from his plays, Wilson made his greatest impact with an impassioned speech in 1996 to the Theatre Communication Group national conference concerning the lack of financial support for African American professional theatres, which he declared essential if African Americans were to explore their own culture and history in a context not dominated by white society.

FIG. 25.17

Final scene of Tony Kushner's *Angels in America: Millennium Approaches* directed by George C. Wolfe. The actors are Stephen Spinella and Ellen McLaughlin. Photo by Joan Marcus © 1993.

Edward Albee, after years of neglect, returned to prominence after his *Three Tall Women* won the Pulitzer Prize in 1994. His more recent plays include *The Play about the Baby* (1996), *The Goat, or, Who is Sylvia?* (2000) and *Occupant* (2001) and an update of his first play, *The Zoo Story* (1959) under the title *Peter & Jerry* (2005).

Among new playwrights, Tony Kushner (1956–) was the most praised American dramatist of the 1990s, almost entirely for *Angels in America: A Gay Fantasia on National Themes* (1991–1993), presented in two parts: *Millennium Approaches* and *Perestroika*. This epic play, which required more than six hours to perform, was not only about the AIDS crisis in the 1980s but also about the moral crisis in the United States as concern for self leads to rejection of the needs of others, even loved ones. But the possibility of change is also suggested by the titles of the two parts. Others of Kushner's plays include *Slavs* (1994) and *Hydriotaphia* (written as a one-act play in 1987; rewritten in three acts in 1997). *Homebody/Kabul* (2001), another epic play, concerns Islam and a daughter's search for her missing mother in both London and Afghanistan.

Suzan-Lori Parks (1963–) has become one of the best known dramatists of the 2000s. Her second play, *Imperceptible Mutabilities in the Third Kingdom* (1989) won an Obie award and was followed by *Death of the Last Black Man in the Whole Entire World* (1990), *The America Play* (1994), *Venus* (1998), *In the Blood* (2000, based on *The Scarlet Letter*), and *Topdog/Underdog* (2001) which won the Pulitzer Prize for Drama in 2002. Most of her plays have been discontinuous, postmodern ruminations on the black experience in American society. *Topdog/Underdog,* more linear and naturalistic than her earlier plays, depicts a world of hustlers and victims. It concerns two brothers, Lincoln (who now impersonates Abraham Lincoln in a side show) and Booth (who seeks to master three-card monte, at which Lincoln formerly excelled), and the struggle for dominance between the two.

Another playwright whose recognition greatly increased during the 1990s was Charles L. Mee (1939–), a magazine editor and historian before turning to playwriting. His first play to have a major production in New York was *The Imperialists at the Club Cave Canem* (1988), one of a series of political plays that questions U.S. foreign policy. He later turned to Greek plays; after deconstructing them, he used their themes as foundations for contemporary plays, transformed into the language and people of America today. His *Orestes* is set on the White House lawn following the Gulf War and seeks to explore American society's malfunctions. *Big Love* was inspired by Aeschylus's *The Suppliants,* and *True Love* is based on Euripides' *Hippolytus* and Racine's *Phèdre. First Love* is about an elderly couple who fall in love for the first time. These three plays were presented in New York in 2001 and were sometimes spoken of as a trilogy. *Bobrauschenbergamerica,* meant to emulate the style of Rauschenberg's assemblages as well as to comment on the evolution of culture in the twentieth century, was first performed at the Actors Theatre of Louisville's Humana Festival in 2001.

Paula Vogel (1951–) began writing plays in the 1980s with such works as *And Baby Makes Seven* (1984). Her best known plays are *Baltimore Waltz* (1992), a tribute to her brother who died of AIDS, and the Pulitzer Prize winning *How I Learned to Drive* (1997), in which the protagonist tells how as a teenager she was seduced by her uncle (who is treated sympathetically). Others of her plays include

Desdemona: A Play about a Handkerchief; Hot 'n' Throbbing (1994), and *The Mineola Twins* (1996). All of these plays have a strong feminist point of view. Other significant American playwrights included David Auburn (who won the 2001 Pulitzer Prize for *Proof*), Neil LaBute, Kenneth Lonergan, Lynn Nottage, and John Patrick Shanley.

The American theatre continued to achieve considerable diversity in the 1990s. In addition to those already mentioned in earlier chapters, Latino writers proliferated. Migdalia Cruz's *Miriam's Flowers* concerns a boy killed in an accident who watches over his family, and Edwin Sanchez's *Unmerciful Good Fortune* is about a woman arrested as a serial killer because of information she has as a clairvoyant. Among the best-known Latino writers were Jose Rivera (1955–) and Eduardo Machado (1950–). Rivera completed *Marisol* (1992), an apocalyptic fantasy, when he was a writer in residence at the Royal Court Theatre in London; he followed with *References to Salvador Dali Makes Me Hot,* a story that juxtaposes the literal and the surreal, and *Giants Have Us in Their Books* in which a runaway tiger is blamed for the sexual chill that has settled over New York. Machado was greatly influenced by Maria Irene Fornes, with whom he worked closely. He is especially noted for his *Floating Islands* trilogy (*The Modern Ladies of Guanabocoa, Fabiola,* and *Broken Eggs*). The first of these plays is set in Cuba in the 1920s and 1930s, the second in Cuba in the 1950s and 1960s, and the third in California in 1979. They trace the fortunes of a formerly wealthy family that

FIG. 25.19

Proof, by David Auburn, the Pulitzer Prize winning play in 2001 directed by Daniel Sullivan. Actors Johanna Day and Mary-Louise Parker are on stage. Photo of the New York production by Joan Marcus © 2000.

attempts to adjust to new conditions in Cuba and the United States. *Havana Is Waiting* (first performed at the Humana Festival in 2001 under the title *When the Sea Drowns in Sand*) is a semi-autobiographical play about a Cuban American who returns to his original homeland for the first time since he was eight years old.

Similarly, new Asian American playwrights gained critical acceptance after 1990. Han Ong (1967–), with *The L.A. Plays* (1993), *Middle Finger* (2000), and *Watcher* (2001), became in 1997 the youngest artist and the first Filipino American to be given a MacArthur Foundation "genius" grant. Jessica Hagedorn (1950–) won critical praise for the adaptation of her novel *Dogeaters* (1998), about life in Manila under Ferdinand Marcos's presidency. Naomi Iizuka (1965–), born in Japan, lived in several countries but received much of her schooling in the United States, including law school at Yale University, before she turned to theatre. Her plays include *Carthage* (1993), which transfers the story of Dido and Aeneas to the rough streets of Los Angeles; *Tattoo Girl* (1994), about a young female trumpet player seeking meaning in her life; *Skin* (1995), which blends Büchner's *Woyzeck* with the lives of contemporary rootless Californians; *Polaroid Stories* (1997), about homeless young people (first produced at the Humana Festival); and *36 Views* (2001), which examines authenticity in art and human relationships. Her plays are free-form, but combine great emotional intensity and lyricism with cutting humor and a concern for the rougher aspects of life.

FIG. 25.18

How I Learned to Drive (1997), Pulitzer Prize-winning play by Paula Vogel. Courtesy of Center Stage, Baltimore, Maryland. Melissa Leo and Dennis Parlato are on stage. Photo by Richard Anderson © 1998.

LOOKING AT THEATRE HISTORY

Contemporary practitioners have sought in various ways to sharpen the audience's perceptions about both the theatre and the world in which we live. Some have offered ironic critiques of social, religious, and political institutions. Others have sought to reach us by drawing on theatrical traditions from other cultures. Still others have forced us to see, as if new, plays that had become so familiar that we no longer were moved by them. Some have sought to forge a new theatre by imaginative integration of existing forms with new technology. These and other practices are indications of the vitality of the theatre that challenges us to consider both the accomplishments of the present and the potential of the future.

Long one of Italy's favorite playwrights, Dario Fo's reputation was solidified after 1997 when he won the Nobel Prize for Literature. He is said to be the most frequently translated living writer, his plays having been performed in thirty languages. The Vatican pronounced one version of Fo's *Mistero Buffo* (it is altered each time it is performed) "the most blasphemous show in the history of television." About his work, Fo has said:

> I have tried to make it clear to young people that a writer should be linked to his times and that the writer who is linked to his times should put his hands into the awful things of life. You have to plunge into the muck. . . . There is no such thing as living comedy unless it has its roots in things that are tragic.

Dario Fo, comments at Barnard College, September 2000.

Ariane Mnouchkine is often said to be France's most accomplished director. Her productions, created through work with a collective, take shape over several months. About the foundations of her work, Mnouchkine has said:

> [Working with a collective] is very important. I always said that . . . when I would not be able to do it anymore like that I would stop. . . . I'm like a midwife. I help to give birth. . . . Our sources, our tools at Théâtre du Soleil are traditions. . . . Our inspiration comes from traditional theatres, real traditional theatres. . . . My love for Asia and for Asian theatre has determined much of my work. My theatrical parents are India, Japan, and China.

In Contact with the Gods? Directors Talk Theatre. Edited by Maria M. Delgado and Paul Heritage. Manchester:

University of Manchester Press, 1996. From an interview conducted by Delgado in 1995.

Peter Brook believes that many audiences attend productions of classics with preconceived notions of what they will see based upon their knowledge of the play and past productions. To undermine this tendency, Brook has altered many well-known plays and operas, including *Carmen, Pelléas and Melisande,* and most recently *Hamlet* (retitled *The Tragedy of Hamlet*). Here is Brook's response to a suggestion that audiences are shocked by his cutting and rearrangement of Shakespeare's text.

> I would say that is good news if it's a shock. That's part of the aim. The reason for doing Hamlet is for people to receive it as a new experience. The first thing was to break the disastrous habit that exists with a play like Hamlet—the fact that people come to the play humming the tune, as they say on Broadway, before they enter the theatre. . . . The first thing I had to do was cut through the enormous superstructure of prejudices and do away with the various conceptions of Hamlet. If this production broke through expectations, that is already good news.

Margaret Croyden, "A Certain Path; an Exclusive Conversation with Peter Brook," *American Theatre* (May/June 2001), p. 18.

The Canadian writer-actor-director Robert Lepage is in the forefront of those seeking to expand the theatre's ability to communicate on several levels. He calls *Zulu Time,* on which he began working in 1999, a techno-cabaret. About it, he has said:

> We were wondering how to connect poetics and dramaturgical ideas and heartfelt emotions with the new tools we have around. Technology comes in with a new vocabulary, and we're still stuttering, trying to figure out exactly how to use it.
>
> [In Zulu Time] We're working with letters of the alphabet, so the show has 26 scenes. Each letter refers to the international radio transmission code that aviators use. . . . Zulu Time is the military's universal clock. . . . The show reflects this idea, that the notion of time and space have been unified.

From an interview with Robert Lepage by Don Shewey. *The New York Times,* September 16, 2001.

INDEX